W9-DEF-080

IMPORTANT

HERE IS YOUR REGISTRATION CODE TO ACCESS MCGRAW-HILL PREMIUM CONTENT AND MCGRAW-HILL ONLINE RESOURCES

For key premium online resources you need THIS CODE to gain access. Once the code is entered, you will be able to use the web resources for the length of your course.

Access is provided only if you have purchased a new book.

If the registration code is missing from this book, the registration screen on our website, and within your WebCT or Blackboard course will tell you how to obtain your new code. Your registration code can be used only once to establish access. It is not transferable.

To gain access to these online resources

1. **USE** your web browser to go to: **http://www.mhhe.com/hld6e**

2. **CLICK** on "First Time User"

3. **ENTER** the Registration Code printed on the tear-off bookmark on the right

4. After you have entered your registration code, click on "Register"

5. **FOLLOW** the instructions to setup your personal UserID and Password

6. **WRITE** your UserID and Password down for future reference. Keep it in a safe place.

If your course is using WebCT or Blackboard, you'll be able to use this code to access the McGraw-Hill content within your instructor's online course.

To gain access to the McGraw-Hill content in your instructor's WebCT or Blackboard course simply log into the course with the user ID and Password provided by your instructor. Enter the registration code exactly as it appears to the right when prompted by the system. You will only need to use this code the first time you click on McGraw-Hill content.

These instructions are specifically for student access. Instructors are not required to register via the above instructions.

The McGraw-Hill Companies

McGraw-Hill Irwin

Thank you, and welcome to your McGraw-Hill Online Resources.

ISBN 0-07-313495-3 AUTHOR: HODGETTS
TITLE: INTERNATIONAL MANAGEMENT, 6/E

3J8H-XYEW-3DC6-TTCF-XM7A

REGISTRATION CODE
REGISTRATION CODE

The McGraw-Hill Companies

McGraw-Hill Irwin

International Management

Culture, Strategy, and Behavior

Sixth Edition

Richard M. Hodgetts
Florida International University

Fred Luthans
University of Nebraska

Jonathan P. Doh
Villanova University

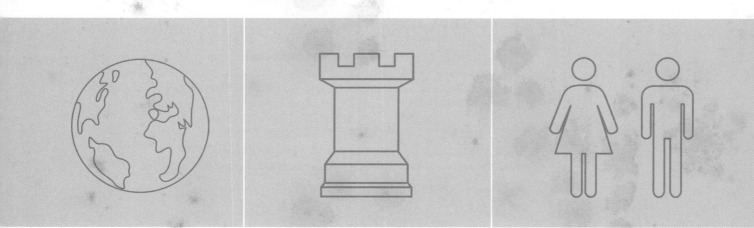

McGraw-Hill
Irwin

Boston   Burr Ridge, IL   Dubuque, IA   Madison, WI   New York   San Francisco   St. Louis
Bangkok   Bogotá   Caracas   Kuala Lumpur   Lisbon   London   Madrid   Mexico City
Milan   Montreal   New Delhi   Santiago   Seoul   Singapore   Sydney   Taipei   Toronto

McGraw-Hill
Irwin

INTERNATIONAL MANAGEMENT: CULTURE, STRATEGY, AND BEHAVIOR

Published by McGraw-Hill/Irwin, a business unit of The McGraw-Hill Companies, Inc., 1221 Avenue of the Americas, New York, NY, 10020. Copyright © 2006, 2003, 2000, 1997, 1994, 1991 by The McGraw-Hill Companies, Inc. All rights reserved. No part of this publication may be reproduced or distributed in any form or by any means, or stored in a database or retrieval system, without the prior written consent of The McGraw-Hill Companies, Inc., including, but not limited to, in any network or other electronic storage or transmission, or broadcast for distance learning.

Some ancillaries, including electronic and print components, may not be available to customers outside the United States.

This book is printed on acid-free paper.

4 5 6 7 8 9 0 VNH/VNH 0 9 8 7

ISBN-13: 978-0-07-296108-9

ISBN-10: 0-07-296108-2

Editorial director: *John E. Biernat*
Sponsoring editor: *Ryan Blankenship*
Editorial assistant: *Allison J. Clelland*
Senior marketing manager: *Lisa Nicks*
Lead producer, Media technology: *Victoria Bryant*
Project manager: *Laura Griffin*
Production supervisor: *Gina Hangos*
Lead designer: *Pam Verros*
Photo research coordinator: *Lori Kramer*
Media project manager: *Betty Hadala*
Supplement producer: *Gina F. DiMartino*
Developer, Media technology: *Brian Nacik*
Cover photographs: *©Straiss/Curtis/Masterfile, ©Martin Barraud/GettyImages, ©Zoran Milich/Masterfile*
Typeface: *10/12 Times Roman*
Compositor: *The GTS Companies, York/PA Campus*
Printer: *Von Hoffmann Corporation*

Library of Congress Cataloging-in-Publication Data

Hodgetts, Richard M.
 International management: culture, strategy, and behavior / Richard M. Hodgetts, Fred Luthans, Jonathan Doh.—6th ed.
  p. cm.
 Includes bibliographical references and index.
 ISBN 0-07-296108-2 (alk. paper)
 1. International business enterprises—Management. 2. International business enterprises—Management—Case studies. I. Luthans, Fred. II. Doh, Jonathan P. III. Title.
HD62.4.H63 2006
658′.049—dc22

2004057945

www.mhhe.com

Preface

The environment for international management has taken some unprecedented twists and turns over the past few years. The global reverberations from 9/11, the preemptive war in Iraq, increasing criticism of "exporting jobs" and "rightsizing" to meet global competition, to name but a few, present a challenging set of circumstances for current and aspiring international managers. While globalization and economic integration continue unabated, growing pressures regarding the distribution of the benefits of economic development have raised serious questions about the responsibilities of countries and corporations to the global "common good." At the same time, corporate scandals in the United States, Europe, Japan, and many developing countries have raised awareness of the importance of well-functioning governance systems and broader regulatory oversight of management practices at home and abroad. These developments have generated calls for new ethical values and practices that consider the social and environmental responsibilities essential not only to "do the right thing" but also to attain competitive advantage in the global economy.

These largely unanticipated developments underscore and reinforce the importance of understanding different cultures, national systems, and corporate management practices around the world. Now, more than ever, all students must recognize that they will have the qualifier "international" in front of whatever their chosen career field. The world is now interconnected not only geographically but also electronically and psychologically; it is hard to imagine any business or nonbusiness organization that is not directly affected by globalization. The challenge in today's uncertain geopolitical and economic environment is to learn and effectively practice international management. Nothing can be taken for granted, and international managers no longer have the luxury of burying their inadequacies and mistakes in a robust world economy. Those with the knowledge and skills to apply the contents of this text on international management will be taking a huge step toward gaining a competitive advantage over those who do not have such a perspective. They will be in a strong position to gain a broad understanding and to take specific steps for implementation of effective managing across cultures.

In the sixth edition of *International Management*, we have taken care to retain the effective foundation gained from research and practice over the past decades. At the same time, we have fully incorporated important new and emerging developments that have changed what international managers are currently facing and likely to face in the coming years. Of special importance is that students of international management understand what will be expected of them from the range of stakeholders with whom they interact.

With the passing of the legendary Richard Hodgetts, our co-author and friend, we dedicate this new edition to his memory. We also enthusiastically welcome a new author to the team, Jonathan Doh from Villanova University. An active researcher, teacher, consultant, and practitioner, Jonathan brings considerable experience, energy, and passion in the areas of international strategy, emerging markets and institutions, corporate social responsibility, and a deep understanding of globalization and its implications for international management (see more on Jonathan in "About the Authors").

Although we have extensive new material in this edition, as described below, we nevertheless have streamlined the text to make it even more user-friendly, reducing the number of chapters from 17 to 15, and condensing or repositioning material so that the most essential elements of each chapter are even clearer and more accessible. (For current adopters, we've provided a brief "map" on page xxix that shows the relationship between the 15 chapters of the sixth edition and the 17 that appeared in the fifth.) We continue to take a balanced approach in the sixth edition of *International Management: Culture, Strategy, and Behavior.* Whereas other texts stress culture, strategy, or behavior, we feel that our emphasis on all three and the resulting synergy has been a primary reason why the previous editions have been the market-leading international management text. Specifically, this edition has the following chapter distribution: environment (3 chapters), culture (4 chapters), strategy (4 chapters), and organizational behavior/human resource management (4 chapters). Because international management is such a dramatically changing field, all the chapters have been updated and improved. In most chapters there are 20 or 30 new references (and thus new real-world examples and research results). As always, we emphasize a balance of research and application.

In particular for the sixth edition, we have incorporated important new content in the areas of globalization/antiglobalization, global corporate responsibility, strategy for emerging markets, international entrepreneurship and new ventures, offshoring and outsourcing, managing alliances and joint ventures, and other important developments in the international management field. We have added emphasis throughout on global ethics and corporate responsibility, recent corporate governance scandals, the importance of global leadership, and the implications of these phenomena for today's and tomorrow's international managers. This new content is not just from popular periodicals; we've incorporated the latest research on international management, including research on the rise of emerging markets, international new ventures, and findings of the comprehensive GLOBE study on cross-cultural leadership.

Another exciting dimension of this edition is the addition of all new chapter-opening articles from *BusinessWeek*. These are very recent, relevant, short news stories to grab readers' interest and attention. A transition paragraph leads readers into the chapter topic. At the end of each chapter, there is a pedagogical feature titled "The World of *BusinessWeek*— Revisited." Here we pose several discussion questions based on the opening news article. Answering them requires readers to draw from the chapter material. Suggested answers to these discussion questions appear in the Instructor's Manual, where we also provide some multiple choice and true–false questions that draw directly from the story for instructors who want to include this material in their tests.

Another end-of-chapter feature is the "Internet Exercise." The purpose of each exercise is to encourage students to use the Internet to find information from the Web sites of prominent MNCs to answer relevant questions about the chapter topic. An end-of-book feature is a series of skill-building and experiential exercises for aspiring international managers. These in-class exercises represent the various parts of the text (culture, strategy, and behavior) and provide hands-on experience.

The use of cases is featured and enhanced in this edition. The two short end-of-chapter cases have been updated. These cases—"In the International Spotlight" and "You Be the International Management Consultant"—can be read and discussed in class. "Integrative Cases" positioned at the end of each part provide opportunities for reading and analysis outside of class. Review questions provided for each case are intended to facilitate lively and productive written analysis or in-class discussion. Our "Brief Integrative Cases" typically explore a specific situation or challenge facing an individual or team. Our longer and more detailed "In-Depth Integrative Cases" provide a broader discussion of the challenges facing a company. These two formats—new to this edition—allow maximum flexibility so that instructors can use the cases in a tailored and customized fashion. Accompanying each in-depth case is a short exercise that can be used in class to reinforce both the substantive topic and students' skills in negotiation, presentation, and analysis. About half of the "Integrative Cases" are new to this edition. Several new cases were developed specifically (and exclusively) for this book, including cases on Wal-Mart, HP–Compaq, BP, AirAsia, and Chiquita. (Of course, instructors also have access to McGraw-Hill's extensive Primis case database, which includes thousands of cases from major sources such as Harvard Business School, Ivey, Darden, and NACRA case databases.) In addition to the popular skill-building exercises, we've included two new in-class simulations as an end-of-book feature.

Along with the new or updated "International Management in Action" boxed application examples within each chapter and other pedagogical features at the end of each chapter (i.e., "Key Terms," "Review and Discussion Questions," "The World of *Business-Week*—Revisited," and "Internet Exercise"), the end-of-part brief and in-depth cases, and the end-of-book skill-building exercises and simulations provide the complete package for relating text material to the real world of international management. To help instructors teach international management, this text is accompanied by a revised and expanded Instructor's Resource Manual and Test Bank. This edition includes entirely new and high-caliber PowerPoint presentation slides for each chapter and a set of videos complementing many of the key concepts and examples from the text.

International Management is generally recognized to be the first "mainline" text of its kind. Strategy casebooks and specialized books in organizational behavior, human resources, and, of course, international business, finance, marketing, and economics preceded it, but there were no international management texts before this one, and it remains the market leader. We have had sustainability because of the effort and care put into the revisions. We hope you agree that the sixth edition continues the tradition and remains the best "world-class" text for the study of international management.

We would like to acknowledge those who have helped to make this book a reality. Special thanks go to our growing number of colleagues throughout the world who have given us many ideas and inspired us to think internationally. Closer to home, Luthans would like to give special recognition to two international management scholars. First is Henry H. Albers, former Chair of the Management Department at the University of Nebraska and former Dean at the University of Petroleum and Minerals, Saudi Arabia, to whom previous editions of this book were dedicated. He had a significant influence on my early career and stimulated me to research and write in the field of management and, most importantly, to think globally. More recently, I would like to acknowledge the influence of Sang M. Lee, currently Chair of the Management Department at Nebraska and President of the Pan Pacific Business Association. He is a true "Global-Academic," and I appreciate his stimulation, advice, and support. Also, for this new edition we would like to thank Erik Holt for his research assistance and Lawrence Beer for contributing the "Roots of Globalization" insert.

In addition, we would like to acknowledge the help that we received from the many reviewers from around the globe, whose feedback guided us in preparing the sixth edition of the text. These include Alan N. Miller, University of Nevada, Las Vegas; Lawrence A. Beer, Arizona State University; Lauryn Migenes, University of Central Florida; Constance Campbell, Georgia Southern University; Timothy Wilkinson, University of Akron; Scott Kenneth Campbell, Georgia College & State University; Janet S. Adams, Kennesaw State University; William Newburry, Rutgers Business School; Dr. Dharma deSilva, Center for International Business Advancement (CIBA); Christine Lentz, Rider University. Our thanks, too, to the reviewers of previous editions of the text: Yohannan T. Abraham, Southwest Missouri State University; Kibok Baik, James Madison University; R. B. Barton, Murray State University; Mauritz Blonder, Hofstra University; Gunther S. Boroschek, University of Massachusetts–Boston; Charles M. Byles, Virginia Commonwealth University; Helen Deresky, SUNY Plattsburgh; Val Finnigan, Leeds Metropolitan University; David M. Flynn, Hofstra University; Robert T. Green, University of Texas at Austin; Jean M. Hanebury, Salisbury State University; Richard C. Hoffman, Salisbury State University; Johan Hough, University of South Africa; Mohd Nazari Ismail, University of Malaya; Robert Kuhne, Hofstra University; Robert C. Maddox, University of Tennessee; Douglas M. McCabe, Georgetown University; Jeanne M. McNett, Assumption College; Ray Montagno, Ball State University; Rebecca J. Morris, University of Nebraska–Omaha; Ernst W. Neuland, University of Pretoria; Yongsun Paik, Loyola Marymount University; Richard B. Peterson, University of Washington; Suzanne J. Peterson, University of Nebraska–Lincoln; Joseph A. Petrick, Wright State University; Richard David Ramsey, Southeastern Louisiana University; Mansour Sharif-Zadeh, California State Polytechnic University, Pomona; Jane H. Standford, Texas A&M–Kingsville University; Dale V. Steinmann, San Franscisco State University; Randall Stross, San Jose State University; George Sutija, Florida International University; David Turnipseed, Georgia Southern

College; Katheryn H. Ward, Chicago State University; Aimee Wheaton, Regis College; Marion M. White, James Madison University; Corinne Young, University of Tampa; and Anatoly Zhuplev, Loyola Marymount University.

Finally, thanks to the team at McGraw-Hill who worked on this book: John Biernat, Editorial Director; Ryan Blankenship, Sponsoring Editor; Lindsay Harmon and Allison Clelland, Editorial Assistants; Lisa Nicks, Marketing Manager; Laura Griffin, Project Manager; Gina Hangos, Production Supervisor; Betty Hadala, Media Project Manager; Gina DiMartino, Supplement Producer; Victoria Bryant, Media Producer; Lori Kramer, Photo Research Coordinator; and Pam Verros, Designer. Last but by no means least, we greatly appreciate the love and support provided by our families.

Fred Luthans and Jonathan P. Doh

HODGETTS LUTHANS DOH

The sixth edition of

International Management: Culture, Strategy, and Behavior is still setting the standard. Current authors Fred Luthans and Jonathan P. Doh have taken care to retain the effective foundation gained from research and practice over the past decades. At the same time, they have fully incorporated important new and emerging developments that have changed what international managers are currently facing and likely to face in the coming years.

✕

NEW *streamlined structure and content.* This allows for greater flexibility and adaptability for courses of different lengths and formats.

NEW *sections on globalization/antiglobalization, global corporate responsibility, strategy for emerging markets, international entrepreneurship and new ventures, offshoring and outsourcing.* These important emerging issues in International Management are reshaping the business environment and forcing companies to adjust their strategies and operations.

ENHANCED *coverage of the challenges and opportunities of alliances and joint ventures.* Alliances and joint ventures and other cooperative arrangements are on the rise; this treatment explores their arrangements from a *managerial* perspective.

ADDED *emphasis on global ethics and corporate responsibility, recent corporate governance scandals, and implications for global managers.* The AACSB Ethics Task Force has recommended an infusion of ethics and social responsibility throughout business curricula; the challenges associated with ethics, social responsibility, and governance in the international managerial environment are some of the most important subjects in business education today.

STILL SETTING THE STANDARD. . .

LATEST RESEARCH *on International Management, including research on the rise of emerging markets, international new ventures, and findings of the GLOBE study on cross-cultural leadership.* Research in International Management has uncovered new insights related to these cutting-edge topics: we incorporate and integrate this research within established and new frameworks.

ALL NEW *BusinessWeek chapter opening cases emphasizing current issues in International Management.* These include articles on offshoring and outsourcing, and cases on BMW, Heineken, Parmalat, GE, and others.

FRESH *brief and in-depth integrative cases at the end of each part.* This format provides short cases to be used for in-class discussion and longer cases to serve as the basis for assignments, analyses, and presentations. All cases include custom review questions; each in-depth case also includes a short in-class exercise.

SPECIALLY DESIGNED *cases developed specifically for this book.* The cases emphasize corporate responsibility, strategy in emerging markets, global leadership, and international entrepreneurship. These cases include: *Wal-Mart's Japan Strategy*, *The HP–Compaq Merger and Its Global Implications*, *Lord John Brown and BP's Global Shift, Can the Budget Airline Model Work in Asia? The Story of AirAsia*, and *Chiquita's Global Turnaround*.

COMPREHENSIVE *management/negotiation simulations, including " 'Frankenfoods' or Rice Bowl for the World: The U.S-EU Dispute over Trade in Genetically Modified Organisms."* Experiential exercises are one of the most effective tools in management education. The addition of these exercises provides students with real-world applied practices in International Management.

About the Authors

FRED LUTHANS is the George Holmes Distinguished Professor of Management at the University of Nebraska–Lincoln. He is also a senior research scientist with Gallup Inc. He received his BA, MBA, and PhD from the University of Iowa, where he received the Distinguished Alumni Award in 2002. While serving as an officer in the U.S. Army from 1965–1967, he taught leadership at the U.S. Military Academy at West Point. He has been a visiting scholar at a number of colleges and universities and has lectured in most European and Pacific Rim countries. He has taught international management as a visiting faculty member at the universities of Bangkok, Hawaii, Henley in England, Norwegian Management School, Monash in Australia, Macau, Chemnitz in the former East Germany, and Tirana in Albania. A past president of the Academy of Management, in 1997 he received the Academy's Distinguished Educator Award. In 2000 he became an inaugural member of the Academy's Hall of Fame for being one of the "Top Five" all-time published authors in the prestigious Academy journals. Currently, he is co-editor-in-chief of the *Journal of World Business,* editor of *Organizational Dynamics,* co-editor of *Journal of Leadership and Organization Studies,* and the author of numerous books. His book *Organizational Behavior* (Irwin/McGraw-Hill) is now in its 10th edition. He is one of very few management scholars who is a Fellow of the Academy of Management, the Decision Sciences Institute, and the Pan Pacific Business Association, and he has been a member of the Executive Committee for the Pan Pacific Conference since its beginning 20 years ago. This committee helps to organize the annual meeting held in Pacific Rim countries. He has been involved with some of the first empirical studies on motivation and behavioral management techniques and the analysis of managerial activities in Russia; these articles have been published in the *Academy of Management Journal, Journal of International Business Studies, Journal of World Business,* and *European Management Journal.* Since the very beginning of the transition to a market economy after the fall of communism in Eastern Europe, he has been actively involved in management education programs sponsored by the U.S. Agency for International Development in Albania and Macedonia, and in U.S. Information Agency programs involving the Central Asian countries of Kazakhstan, Kyrgyzstan, and Tajikistan. Professor Luthans's most recent international research involves the relationship between psychological variables and attitudes and performance of managers and entrepreneurs across cultures. He is applying his positive approach to organization behavior (POB) and authentic leadership to effective global management.

JONATHAN P. DOH is Assistant Professor of Management in the College of Commerce and Finance at Villanova University, where he serves as founding Director of the Center for Responsible Leadership and Governance. He holds a PhD in strategic and international management from George Washington University, an MA from the Rockefeller College of Public Affairs and Policy at SUNY–Albany, and a BA from SUNY–Plattsburgh, where he was a 2002/2003 distinguished visiting alumnus. A Senior Associate at the Center for Strategic and International Studies in Washington, D.C., Doh also serves on the Executive Faculty of the Graduate School of Business Administration, Zurich, Switzerland. In 2003, he was a visiting professor at the University of Auckland, New Zealand. Previously, he was on the faculty of American University and Georgetown University, where he taught international business and global strategy. From 1990 to 1995, he served as an international economist and senior trade official with the U.S. Department of Commerce. He was Director for Trade Policy in the Office of Canada during implementation of the U.S.–Canada Free Trade Agreement, and Director of the NAFTA Affairs Division during approval and implementation of NAFTA. He is a frequent speaker to business and foreign affairs groups and has participated in lecture tours sponsored by the U.S. State Department and U.S. Information Agency in Germany, Mexico, Hong Kong, and Canada. His research and teaching interests include international corporate strategy, international business–government relations, the telecommunications and electric power industries, and global corporate citizenship and social responsibility. Recent articles appear in the leading international business (IB) journals (*Journal of International Business Studies, Management International Review, Journal of World Business*), in the journals of the Academy of Management (*Academy of Management Review, Academy of Management Executive, Academy of Management Learning and Education, Academy of Management Best Paper Proceedings*), as well as in numerous other management and IB journals, including *California Management Review, International Business Review, Journal of Management Studies, Journal of Business Ethics,* and *Long Range Planning.* His volume *Globalization and NGOs: Transforming Business, Governments, and Society,* co-edited with Hildy Teegen, was published by Praeger in 2003. The *Handbook on Responsible Leadership and Governance in Global Business*, co-edited with Stephen Stumpf, will be published by Edward Elgar in 2005. He serves on the editorial boards of the *Academy of Management Learning and Education,* the *Journal of International Business Studies,* the *Journal of Management Studies,* and the *Journal of Leadership and Organizational Studies.* In addition to his teaching and research, Doh has served as a consultant to Motorola Corporation, to Asea Brown Boveri, and to the Government of Thailand, and he has conducted executive management courses for public and private organizations, including Deutsche Bank Asia. He has been a consulting adviser to the Global Energy Group of Deloitte Touche Tohmatsu International.

Brief Contents

Part One   **Environmental Foundation**

  1   Globalization and Worldwide Developments   2

  2   The Political, Legal, and Technological Environment   34

  3   Ethics and Social Responsibility   54

      Colgate's Distasteful Toothpaste   77

      Advertising or Free Speech? The Case of Nike and Human Rights   80

      Pharmaceutical Companies, Intellectual Property, and the Global AIDS Epidemic   82

Part Two   **The Role of Culture**

  4   The Meanings and Dimensions of Culture   92

  5   Managing Across Cultures   124

  6   Organizational Cultures and Diversity   152

  7   Cross-Cultural Communication and Negotiation   178

      Cross-Cultural Conflicts in the Corning–Vitro Joint Venture   211

      Integrating National and Organizational Cultures: Chemical Bank's Mergers in Europe   213

      Euro Disneyland   216

      Wal-Mart's Japan Strategy   226

Part Three   **International Strategic Management**

  8   Strategy Formulation and Implementation   234

  9   Entry Strategies and Organizational Structures   260

  10   Managing Political Risk, Government Relations, and Alliances   292

  11   Management Decision and Control   316

      KNP, N.V.   345

      Can Reliance Compete?   350

      The HP–Compaq Merger and Its Global Implications   352

      Can the Budget Airline Model Succeed in Asia? The Story of AirAsia   358

Organizational Behavior and Human Resource Management

Part Four

12   Motivation Across Cultures   366

13   Leadership Across Cultures   396

14   Human Resource Selection and Development Across Cultures   430

15   Labor Relations and Industrial Democracy   476

     A Copy Shop Goes Global   509

     The Road to Hell   512

     Lord John Browne and BP's Global Shift   515

     Chiquita's Global Turnaround   521

Skill-Building and Experiential Exercises

Personal Skill-Building Exercises   530

     1. The Culture Quiz   530

     2. Using *Gung Ho* to Understand Cultural Differences   535

     3. "When in Bogotá . . ."   537

     4. The International Cola Alliances   540

     5. Who to Hire?   544

In-Class Simulations   547

     1. "Frankenfoods" or Rice Bowl for the World: The U.S.–EU
         Dispute over Trade in Genetically Modified Organisms   547

     2. Cross-Cultural Conflicts in the Corning–Vitro Joint Venture   553

References   557
Endnotes   561
Glossary   582
Name and Organization Index   588
Subject Index   599

Contents

Part One   **Environmental Foundation**

1   Globalization and Worldwide Developments   **2**

Objectives of the Chapter   2

The World of *BusinessWeek:* Software   2

Introduction   6

Globalization and Internationalization   7

   Globalization, Antiglobalization, and Global Pressures   7

   Global and Regional Integration   9

   Trends in International Investment and Trade   12

Economic Performance and Issues of the Major Regions   15

   North America   15

   South America   18

   Europe   19

   Asia   23

   Other Developing and Emerging Countries   27

The World of *BusinessWeek*—Revisited   29

Summary of Key Points   30

Key Terms   30

Review and Discussion Questions   31

Answers to the In-Chapter Quiz   31

Internet Exercise: Franchise Opportunities at McDonald's   31

In the International Spotlight: India   32

You Be the International Management Consultant:
Here Comes the Competition   33

2   The Political, Legal, and Technological Environment   **34**

Objectives of the Chapter   34

The World of *BusinessWeek*: The Milk Just Keeps on Spilling   34

Political Environment   36

   China   37

   Europe   38

   Russia   39

   Central and Eastern Europe   40

   The Middle East   41

Legal and Regulatory Environment   42

    Basic Principles of International Law   42

    Examples of Legal and Regulatory Issues   43

    Regulation of Trade and Investment   45

Technological Environment and Global Shifts in Production   46

    E-Business   47

    Telecommunications   48

    Technology, Outsourcing, and Offshoring   48

The World of *BusinessWeek*—Revisited   50

Summary of Key Points   51

Key Terms   51

Review and Discussion Questions   51

Internet Exercise: Hitachi Goes Worldwide   51

In the International Spotlight: Vietnam   52

You Be the International Management Consultant: A Chinese Venture   53

3   Ethics and Social Responsibility   54

Objectives of the Chapter   54

**The World of *BusinessWeek*: Poor Nations
Can't Live by Markets Alone**   54

Ethics and Social Responsibility Around the World   56

    Ethical Problems and Concerns in Japan   57

    Ethical Problems and Concerns in Europe   59

    The Status of Women Managers in Europe   60

    Ethical Problems and Concerns in China   62

Corporate Social Responsibility   65

    The Rise of Civil Society and NGOs   66

    Response to Social Obligations   66

    Corporate Governance   68

    Corruption and the Foreign Corrupt Practices Act Revisited   68

    International Assistance   71

The World of *BusinessWeek*—Revisited   72

Summary of Key Points   73

Key Terms   73

Review and Discussion Questions   73

Internet Exercise: Social Responsibility at Johnson & Johnson and HP   74

In the International Spotlight: Saudi Arabia   75

You Be the International Management Consultant: It Sounds a Little Fishy   76

Brief Integrative Case 1: Colgate's Distasteful Toothpaste   77

Brief Integrative Case 2: Advertising or Free Speech? The Case of Nike and Human Rights 80

In-Depth Integrative Case 1: Pharmaceutical Companies, Intellectual Property, and the Global AIDS Epidemic 82

Part Two   The Role of Culture

4   The Meanings and Dimensions of Culture   92
Objectives of the Chapter   92
The World of *BusinessWeek:* Will Coke's Water Meet Its Waterloo?   92
The Nature of Culture   93
Cultural Diversity   94
Values in Culture   97
Hofstede's Cultural Dimensions   101
Power Distance   102
Uncertainty Avoidance   102
Individualism   102
Masculinity   103
Integrating the Dimensions   105
Attitudinal Dimensions of Culture   107
Work Value and Attitude Similarities   107
Country Clusters   108
Trompenaars's Cultural Dimensions   109
Universalism vs. Particularism   110
Individualism vs. Communitarianism   112
Neutral vs. Emotional   113
Specific vs. Diffuse   113
Achievement vs. Ascription   114
Time   114
The Environment   115
Cultural Patterns or Clusters   116
Integrating Culture and Management: The GLOBE Project   117
Culture and Management   118
GLOBE's Cultural Dimensions   118
GLOBE Country Analysis   119

The World of *BusinessWeek*—Revisited   119
Summary of Key Points   120
Key Terms   120
Review and Discussion Questions   121
Internet Exercise: BMW Goes National and International   121

In the International Spotlight: Taiwan 122

You Be the International Management Consultant:
A Jumping-Off Place 123

5 Managing Across Cultures 124

Objectives of the Chapter 124

The World of *BusinessWeek:* Waking Up Heineken 124

The Strategy for Managing Across Cultures 128

Strategic Predispositions 128

Meeting the Challenge 129

Cross-Cultural Differences and Similarities 133

Parochialism and Simplification 133

Similarities Across Cultures 135

Many Differences Across Cultures 135

Cultural Differences in Selected Countries and Regions 140

Doing Business in China 140

Doing Business in Russia 142

Doing Business in India 144

Doing Business in France 145

Doing Business in Arab Countries 146

The World of *BusinessWeek*—Revisited 148

Summary of Key Points 148

Key Terms 149

Review and Discussion Questions 149

Internet Exercise: Sony's Approach 149

In the International Spotlight: Mexico 150

You Be the International Management Consultant: Beijing, Here We Come! 151

6 Organizational Cultures and Diversity 152

Objectives of the Chapter 152

The World of *BusinessWeek:* A Tale of Two Auto Mergers 152

The Nature of Organizational Culture 154

Definition and Characteristics 154

Interaction Between National and Organizational Cultures 155

Organizational Cultures in MNCs 159

Family Culture 161

Eiffel Tower Culture 161

Guided Missile Culture 162

Incubator Culture 163

Managing Multiculturalism and Diversity 165

Phases of Multicultural Development 165

Types of Multiculturalism 167

Potential Problems Associated with Diversity   169

Advantages of Diversity   170

Building Multicultural Team Effectiveness   171

The World of *BusinessWeek*—Revisited   173

Summary of Key Points   174

Key Terms   174

Review and Discussion Questions   175

Internet Exercise: Hewlett-Packard's International Focus   175

In the International Spotlight: Japan   176

**You Be the International Management Consultant:
A Good-Faith Effort Is Needed**   177

7   Cross-Cultural Communication and Negotiation   178

Objectives of the Chapter   178

The World of *BusinessWeek*: A New World for Microsoft?   178

The Overall Communication Process   180

Verbal Communication Styles   181

Interpretation of Communications   183

Communication Flows   184

Downward Communication   184

Upward Communication   186

Communication Barriers   187

Language Barriers   187

Cultural Barriers   189

Perceptual Barriers   190

The Impact of Culture   192

Nonverbal Communication   193

Achieving Communication Effectiveness   196

Improve Feedback Systems   196

Provide Language Training   197

Provide Cultural Training   197

Increase Flexibility and Cooperation   197

Managing Cross-Cultural Negotiations   199

The Negotiation Process   200

Cultural Differences Affecting Negotiations   201

Negotiation Tactics   202

Bargaining Behaviors   204

The World of *BusinessWeek*—Revisited   207

Summary of Key Points   207

Key Terms   207

Review and Discussion Questions   208

Internet Exercise: Working Effectively at Toyota   208

In the International Spotlight: China   209

You Be the International Management Consultant: Foreign or Domestic?   210

Brief Integrative Case 1: Cross-Cultural Conflicts in the
Corning–Vitro Joint Venture   211

Brief Integrative Case 2: Integrating National and Organizational Cultures:
Chemical Bank's Mergers in Europe   213

In-Depth Integrative Case 1: Euro Disneyland   216

In-Depth Integrative Case 2: Wal-Mart's Japan Strategy   226

International Strategic Management   Part Three

8   Strategy Formulation and Implementation   234

Objectives of the Chapter   234

The World of *BusinessWeek:* Ford Learns the
Lessons of Luxury   234

Strategic Management   236

   The Growing Need for Strategic Management   237

   Benefits of Strategic Planning   238

   Approaches to Formulating and Implementing Strategy   238

   Global vs. Regional Strategies   242

The Basic Steps in Formulating Strategy   244

   Environmental Scanning   245

   Internal Resource Analysis   246

   Goal Setting for Strategy Formulation   246

Strategy Implementation   247

   Location Considerations for Implementation   248

   The Role of the Functional Areas in Implementation   250

Specialized Strategies   252

   Strategies for Emerging Markets   252

   Entrepreneurial Strategy and New Ventures   254

The World of *BusinessWeek*—Revisited   255

Summary of Key Points   256

Key Terms   256

Review and Discussion Questions   256

Internet Exercise: Dropping In on Dell Computer   257

In the International Spotlight: Poland   258

You Be the International Management Consultant: Go East,
Young People, Go East   259

9   Entry Strategies and Organizational Structures   260

Objectives of the Chapter   260

The World of *BusinessWeek:* Intel Inside—Russia, That Is   260

Entry Strategies and Ownership Structures   261

Wholly Owned Subsidiary   262

Mergers and Acquisitions   263

Alliances and Joint Ventures   263

Licensing   265

Franchising   266

Export/Import   266

The Organizational Challenge   268

Basic Organizational Structures   269

Initial Division Structure   270

International Division Structure   270

Global Structural Arrangements   271

Transnational Network Structures   276

Nontraditional Organizational Arrangements   277

Organizational Arrangements from Mergers and Acquisitions   278

*Organizational Arrangements from Joint
Ventures and Strategic Alliances*   278

Organizational Arrangements from Keiretsus   278

The Emergence of the Electronic Network Form of Organization   280

Organizing for Product Integration   281

The Changing Role of Information Technology in Organizing   282

Organizational Characteristics of MNCs   283

Formalization   283

Specialization   285

Centralization   286

Putting Organizational Characteristics in Perspective   286

The World of *BusinessWeek*—Revisited   288

Summary of Key Points   288

Key Terms   289

Review and Discussion Questions   289

Internet Exercise: Organizing for Effectiveness   289

In the International Spotlight: Australia   290

**You Be the International Management Consultant:
Getting In on the Ground Floor   291**

**10   Managing Political Risk, Government Relations,
and Alliances   292**

Objectives of the Chapter   292

The World of *BusinessWeek:* Oil Shortage?   292

The Nature and Analysis of Political Risk   **295**

Macro and Micro Analysis of Political Risk   *297*

Analyzing the Expropriation Risk   *300*

The Role of Operational Profitability in Risk Analysis   *301*

Managing Political Risk and Government Relations   **302**

Developing a Comprehensive Framework or Quantitative Analysis   *302*

Formulating and Implementing Responses to Political Risk: Corporate Political Strategies   *304*

Managing Alliances   **308**

The Alliance Challenge   *309*

The Role of Host Governments in Alliances   *310*

Examples of Challenges and Opportunities in Alliance Management   *310*

The World of *BusinessWeek*—Revisited   **312**

Summary of Key Points   **312**

Key Terms   **312**

Review and Discussion Questions   **313**

Internet Exercise: Motorola in China   **313**

In the International Spotlight: Peru   **314**

You Be the International Management Consultant: Going to Gdansk   **315**

11   Management Decision and Control   **316**

Objectives of the Chapter   **316**

The World of *BusinessWeek*: BMW   **316**

Decision and Control Linkages   **319**

Decision-Making Process and Challenges   **320**

Comparative Examples of Decision Making   *321*

Factors Affecting Decision-Making Authority   *322*

Total Quality Management Decisions   *324*

Decisions for Attacking the Competition   *326*

The Controlling Process   **328**

Types of Control   *329*

Approaches to Control   *331*

Control Techniques   **335**

Financial Performance   *335*

Quality Performance   *336*

Personnel Performance   *338*

The World of *BusinessWeek*—Revisited   **341**

Summary of Key Points   **341**

Key Terms   **342**

Review and Discussion Questions   **342**

Internet Exercises: Looking at the Best   **342**

In the International Spotlight: Spain   343
You Be the International Management Consultant: Expansion Plans   344

Brief Integrative Case 1: KNP, N.V.   345

Brief Integrative Case 2: Can Reliance Compete?   350

In-Depth Integrative Case 1: The HP–Compaq Merger and
Its Global Implications   352

In-Depth Integrative Case 2: Can the Budget Airline Model
Succeed in Asia? The Story of AirAsia   358

Part Four

Organizational Behavior and Human Resource Management

12   **Motivation Across Cultures**   366
Objectives of the Chapter   366
The World of *BusinessWeek:* GE Breaks the Mold to Spur Innovation   366
The Nature of Motivation   368
      The Universalist Assumption   369
      The Assumption of Content and Process   370
The Hierarchy-of-Needs Theory   370
      The Maslow Theory   371
      International Findings on Maslow's Theory   371
The Two-Factor Theory of Motivation   375
      The Herzberg Theory   375
      International Findings on Herzberg's Theory   377
Achievement Motivation Theory   380
      The Background of Achievement Motivation Theory   380
      International Findings on Achievement Motivation Theory   380
Select Process Theories   382
      Equity Theory   382
      Goal-Setting Theory   383
      Expectancy Theory   384
Motivation Applied: Job Design, Work Centrality, and Rewards   384
      Job Design   384
      Sociotechnical Job Designs   386
      Work Centrality   386
      Reward Systems   390
      Incentives and Culture   390

The World of *BusinessWeek*—Revisited   391
Summary of Key Points   392

Key Terms 393

Review and Discussion Questions 393

Internet Exercise: Motivating Potential Employees 393

In the International Spotlight: Singapore 394

You Be the International Management Consultant: Motivation Is the Key 395

13 Leadership Across Cultures 396

Objectives of the Chapter 396

The World of *BusinessWeek:* Richard Branson's Next
Big Adventure 396

Foundation for Leadership 398

Philosophical Background: Theories X, Y, and Z 399

Leadership Behaviors and Styles 400

Leadership in the International Context 404

Attitudes of European Managers Toward Leadership Practices 404

Japanese Leadership Approaches 407

Differences Between Japanese and U.S. Leadership Styles 408

Similarities Between Japanese and U.S. Leadership Styles 409

Leadership in China 411

Leadership in the Middle East 412

Leadership Approaches in Developing Countries 414

Recent Findings and Insights About Leadership 415

Transformational, Transactional, and Charismatic Leadership 415

Qualities for Successful Leaders 417

Culture Clusters and Leader Effectiveness 419

Leader Behavior, Leader Effectiveness, and Leading Teams 419

Cross-Cultural Leadership: Insights from the GLOBE Study 421

Ethically Responsible Global Leadership 423

Entrepreneurial Leadership and Mindset 424

The World of *BusinessWeek*—Revisited 425

Summary of Key Points 425

Key Terms 426

Review and Discussion Questions 426

Internet Exercise: Taking a Closer Look 427

In the International Spotlight: Germany 428

You Be the International Management Consultant: An Offer from Down Under 429

14 Human Resource Selection and Development Across Cultures 430

Objectives of the Chapter 430

The World of *BusinessWeek:* Look Who's Going Offshore 430

The Importance of International Human Resources 432

Sources of Human Resources 433

Home-Country Nationals 433

Host-Country Nationals 434

Third-Country Nationals 435

Inpatriates 436

Subcontracting and Outsourcing 437

Selection Criteria for International Assignments 438

General Criteria 438

Adaptability to Cultural Change 439

Physical and Emotional Health 440

Age, Experience, and Education 440

Language Training 441

Motivation for a Foreign Assignment 441

Spouses and Dependents or Work–Family Issues 442

Leadership Ability 443

Other Considerations 444

International Human Resource Selection Procedures 444

Testing and Interviewing Procedures 444

The Adjustment Process 445

Compensation 446

Common Elements of Compensation Packages 446

Tailoring the Package 450

Individual and Host-Country Viewpoints 451

Candidate Motivations 451

Host-Country Desires 451

Repatriation of Expatriates 453

Reasons for Returning 453

Readjustment Problems 453

Transition Strategies 455

Training in International Management 456

The Impact of Overall Management Philosophy on Training 458

The Impact of Different Learning Styles on Training and Development 459

Reasons for Training 460

Types of Training Programs 463

Standardized vs. Tailor-Made 464

Cultural Assimilators 467

Other Approaches 468

Global Leadership Development 468

The World of *BusinessWeek*—Revisited 470

Summary of Key Points 471

Key Terms 472

Review and Discussion Questions 472

Internet Exercise: Going International with Coke 473

In the International Spotlight: Russia 474

You Be the International Management Consultant:
A Selection Decision 475

15 Labor Relations and Industrial Democracy 476

Objectives of the Chapter 476

The World of *BusinessWeek*: Labor's Savvy Charge on China Trade 476

Labor Relations in the International Arena 478

The U.S. Approach to Labor Relations 478

Labor Relations in Other Countries 479

How Industrial Conflict Is Handled Around the World 483

International Structure of Unions 485

Intergovernmental Organizations 485

Transnational Union Affiliations 486

Extensions of Domestic Contracts 486

Industrial Democracy 487

Common Forms of Industrial Democracy 487

Industrial Democracy in Selected Countries 487

Strategic Management of International Labor Relations 492

The Philosophical Backdrop 492

Labor Costs 493

New Labor Force Trends and Pressures 494

Organizing International Industrial Relations 499

A Final Word 500

Joint Partnering 500

Continued Research and Learning 501

The World of *BusinessWeek*—Revisited 504

Summary of Key Points 504

Key Terms 505

Review and Discussion Questions 505

Internet Exercise: Challenges of a New World Auto Industry 506

In the International Spotlight: Brazil 507

You Be the International Management Consultant: They're Back 508

Brief Integrative Case 1: A Copy Shop Goes Global 509

Brief Integrative Case 2: The Road to Hell 512

In-Depth Integrative Case 1: Lord John Browne and BP's Global Shift 515

In-Depth Integrative Case 2: Chiquita's Global Turnaround 521

Skill-Building and Experiential Exercises

Personal Skill-Building Exercises   530
   1. The Culture Quiz   530
   2. Using *Gung Ho* to Understand Cultural Differences   535
   3. "When in Bogotá . . ."   537
   4. The International Cola Alliances   540
   5. Who to Hire?   544

In-Class Simulations   547
   1. "Frankenfoods" or Rice Bowl for the World: The U.S.–EU
      Dispute over Trade in Genetically Modified Organisms   547
   2. Cross-Cultural Conflicts in the Corning–Vitro Joint Venture   553

References   557
Endnotes   561
Glossary   582
Name and Organization Index   588
Subject Index   599

Content Map

Hodgetts, Luthans, 5th edition

Hodgetts, Luthans, Doh, 6th edition

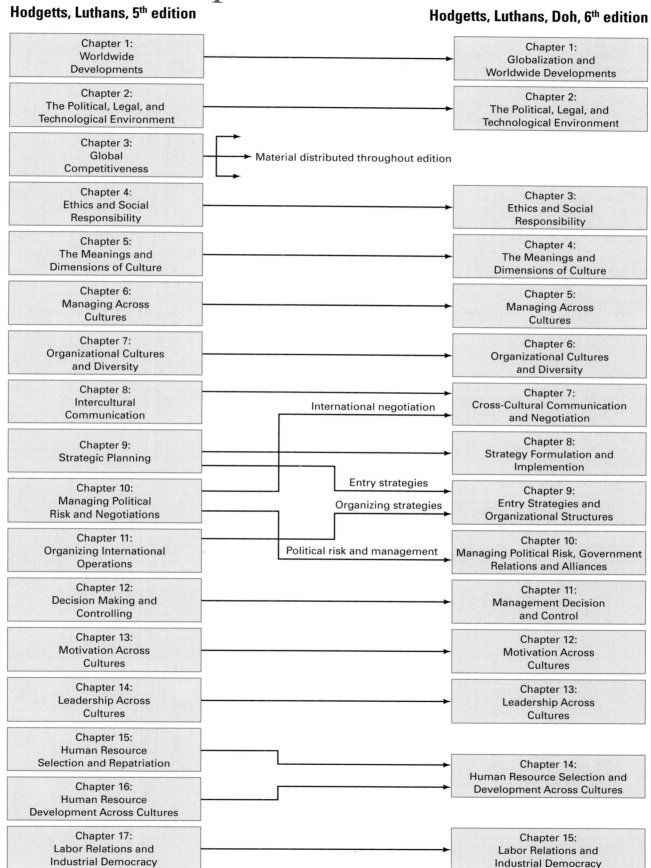

Chapter 1:
Worldwide
Developments

Chapter 1:
Globalization and
Worldwide Developments

Chapter 2:
The Political, Legal, and
Technological Environment

Chapter 2:
The Political, Legal, and
Technological Environment

Chapter 3:
Global
Competitiveness

Material distributed throughout edition

Chapter 4:
Ethics and Social
Responsibility

Chapter 3:
Ethics and Social
Responsibility

Chapter 5:
The Meanings and
Dimensions of Culture

Chapter 4:
The Meanings and
Dimensions of Culture

Chapter 6:
Managing Across
Cultures

Chapter 5:
Managing Across
Cultures

Chapter 7:
Organizational Cultures
and Diversity

Chapter 6:
Organizational Cultures
and Diversity

Chapter 8:
Intercultural
Communication

International negotiation

Chapter 7:
Cross-Cultural Communication
and Negotiation

Chapter 9:
Strategic Planning

Chapter 8:
Strategy Formulation and
Implemention

Chapter 10:
Managing Political
Risk and Negotiations

Entry strategies

Organizing strategies

Chapter 9:
Entry Strategies and
Organizational Structures

Chapter 11:
Organizing International
Operations

Political risk and management

Chapter 10:
Managing Political Risk, Government
Relations and Alliances

Chapter 12:
Decision Making and
Controlling

Chapter 11:
Management Decision
and Control

Chapter 13:
Motivation Across
Cultures

Chapter 12:
Motivation Across
Cultures

Chapter 14:
Leadership Across
Cultures

Chapter 13:
Leadership Across
Cultures

Chapter 15:
Human Resource
Selection and Repatriation

Chapter 14:
Human Resource Selection and
Development Across Cultures

Chapter 16:
Human Resource
Development Across Cultures

Chapter 17:
Labor Relations and
Industrial Democracy

Chapter 15:
Labor Relations and
Industrial Democracy

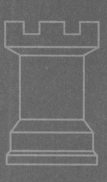

PART ONE

ENVIRONMENTAL FOUNDATION

Chapter 1

GLOBALIZATION AND WORLDWIDE DEVELOPMENTS

The global economy has arrived. In the United States, dramatically increasing numbers of not only large corporations but medium and small firms are going international, and a growing percentage of overall revenue is coming from overseas markets. The same is true throughout Europe, Asia, and the rest of the world. In addition, globalization is presenting challenges for governments, corporations, and communities around the world. As a result, international management, the process of applying management concepts and techniques in a multinational environment, is rapidly gaining importance.

Although there has been considerable historical evolution, the overriding focus of this opening chapter is to examine the process of globalization and developments of the last few years. The end of the cold war and the onset of the Information Age have created a new world and true global competition. These developments both create and influence the opportunities, challenges, and problems that managers in the international arena will face during the years ahead. Since the environment facing international management is so all-encompassing, this chapter is mostly concerned with the economic dimensions and the next chapter is focused more on the political, legal, and technological dimensions. The specific objectives of this chapter are:

1. **ASSESS** the implications of globalization for countries, industries, firms, and communities.

2. **REVIEW** current trends in international investment and trade.

3. **EXAMINE** the present economic status in the major regions of the global community.

4. **ANALYZE** some of the major developments and issues in the various regions of the world.

The World of *BusinessWeek*

BusinessWeek

Software

Will Outsourcing Hurt America's Supremacy?

The once dazzling career prospects for U.S. software programmers are now in doubt. Just look at global giants, from IBM and Electronic Data Systems to Lehman Brothers and Merrill Lynch. They're rushing to hire tech workers offshore while liquidating thousands of jobs in America. In the past three years, offshore programming jobs have nearly tripled, from 27,000 to an estimated 80,000, according to Forrester Research Inc. and Gartner Inc. figures that by year-end, 1 of every 10 jobs in U.S. tech companies will move to emerging markets. U.S. software developers "are competing with everyone else in the world who has a PC," says Robert R. Bishop, chief executive of computer maker Silicon Graphics Inc.

For many of America's 3 million software programmers, it's paradise lost. Just a few years back, they held the keys to the Information Age. Their profession not only lavished many with stock options and six-figure salaries but also gave them the means to start companies that could change the world—the next Microsoft, Netscape, or Google. Now, these veterans of Silicon Valley and Boston's Route 128 exchange heart-rending job-loss stories on Web sites such as **yourjobisgoingtoindia.com**. Suddenly, the programmers share the fate of millions of industrial workers, in textiles, autos, and steel, whose jobs have marched to Mexico and China.

"Leap of Faith"

This exodus throws the future of America's tech economy into question. For decades, the U.S. has been the world's

Software programming is the iconic job of the Information Age, but not all programmers are created equal. Here's the breakdown of software jobs and their prospects:

1 ARCHITECTS A few thousand tech visionaries sketch out entire systems to handle complex jobs. Adam Bosworth, for example, is the chief architect at BEA Systems.

PAY $150,000 to $250,000.

OUTLOOK Outsourcing is a nonissue.

2 RESEARCHERS They're key to innovation, which is crucial for the U.S. But there are only about 25,000 in the country, many in academia, where tenure trumps pay.

PAY $50,000 in academia to $195,000 in private sector.

OUTLOOK Prospects should brighten somewhat with the economy, but these jobs can move offshore, too.

3 CONSULTANTS Business-savvy consultants advise corporations about their technology needs, help them install new software, and create new applications from scratch.

PAY $72,000 to $200,000.

OUTLOOK Still bright for Americans. U.S. customers want face time with consultants.

4 PROJECT MANAGERS Crucial cogs in global software factories. They coordinate the work of teams in different countries and time zones and provide dependable products on schedule.

PAY $96,000 to $130,000.

OUTLOOK Good managers can write their own tickets. Pay has jumped 14.3% in the past two years.

5 BUSINESS ANALYSTS Go-betweens. About 100,000 analysts figure out what a business needs and turn it into a spec sheet for programmers. It's a key role now since the company and its programmers are often apart.

PAY $52,000 to $90,000.

OUTLOOK A relatively safe haven for programmers—if they have communications skills and a grip on business.

6 BASIC PROGRAMMERS The foot soldiers in the information economy, they write the code for applications and update and test them. Numbering about 1 million, they are one-third of all U.S. software engineers and programmers.

PAY Has tumbled 15% since 2002. Now $52,000 to $81,000.

OUTLOOK Watch out. Many of these jobs can be done anywhere. Forrester predicts 18% of them will be offshore within six years.

Source: Forrester Research, Foote Partners, Kennedy Information Inc., *BusinessWeek*.

technology leader—thanks in large part to its dominance of software, now a $200 billion-a-year U.S. industry. Sure, foreigners have made their share of the machines. But the U.S. has held on to control of much of the innovative brainwork and reaped rich dividends, from Microsoft to the entrepreneurial hotbed of Silicon Valley. The question now is whether the U.S. can continue to lead the industry as programming spreads around the globe from India to Bulgaria. Politicians are jumping on the issue in the election season. And it will probably rage on for years, affecting everything from global trade to elementary-school math and science curriculums.

Countering the doomsayers, optimists from San Jose, Calif., to Bangalore see the offshore wave as a godsend, the latest productivity miracle of the Internet. Companies that manage it well—no easy task—can build virtual workforces spread around the world, not only soaking up low-cost talent but also tapping the biggest brains on earth to collaborate on complex projects. Marc Andreessen, Netscape Communications Corp.'s co-founder and now chairman of Opsware Inc., a Sunnyvale (Calif.) startup, sees this reshuffling of brainpower leading to bold new applications and sparking growth in other industries, from bioengineering to energy. This could mean a wealth of good new jobs, even more than U.S. companies could fill. "It requires a leap of

faith," Andreessen admits. But "in 500 years of Western history, there has always been something new. Always always always always always."

This time, though, there's no guarantee that the next earth-shaking innovations will pop up in America. India, for example, has high-speed Internet, a world-class university, and a venture-capital industry that's starting to take shape in Bombay. What's more, the country is luring back entrepreneurs and technologists who lived in Silicon Valley during the bubble years. Many came home to India after the crash and now are sowing the seeds of California's startup culture throughout the subcontinent. What's to stop them from mixing the same magic that Andreessen conjured a decade ago when he co-founded Netscape? It's clear that in a networked world, U.S. leadership in innovation will find itself under siege.

The fallout from this painful process could be toxic. One danger is that high-tech horror stories—the pink slips and falling wages—will scare the coming generation of American math whizzes away from software careers, starving the tech economy of brainpower. While the number of students in computer-science programs is holding steady—for now—the elite schools have seen applications fall by as much as 30% in two years. If that trend continues, the U.S.

3

The Software Vitality Drain

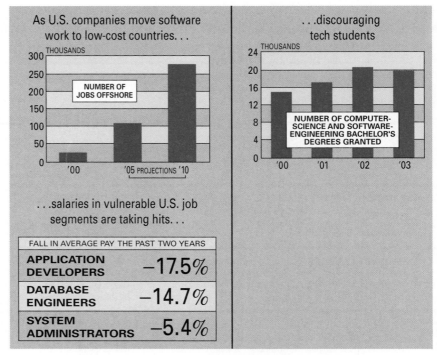

As U.S. companies move software work to low-cost countries. . .

NUMBER OF JOBS OFFSHORE

THOUSANDS

'00   '05 PROJECTIONS '10

. . .salaries in vulnerable U.S. job segments are taking hits. . .

FALL IN AVERAGE PAY THE PAST TWO YEARS	
APPLICATION DEVELOPERS	−17.5%
DATABASE ENGINEERS	−14.7%
SYSTEM ADMINISTRATORS	−5.4%

. . .discouraging tech students

THOUSANDS

NUMBER OF COMPUTER-SCIENCE AND SOFTWARE-ENGINEERING BACHELOR'S DEGREES GRANTED

'00   '01   '02   '03

Sources: Forrester Research Inc.; Computer Research Assn., based on undergraduates in PhD-granting universities; Foote Partners, *BusinessWeek.*

will be relying more than ever on foreign-born graduates for software innovation. And as more foreigners decide to start careers and companies back in their home countries, the U.S. could find itself lacking a vital resource. Microsoft CEO Steven A. Ballmer says the shortfall of U.S. tech students worries him more than any other issue. "The U.S. is No. 3 now in the world and falling behind quickly No. 1 [India] and No. 2 [China] in terms of computer-science graduates," he said in late 2003 at a forum in New York.

Fear in the industry is palpable. Some of it recalls the scares of years past: OPEC buying up the world in the '70s and Japan Inc. taking charge a decade later. The lesson from those episodes is to resist quick fixes and trust in the long-term adaptability of the U.S. economy. Job-protection laws, for example, may be tempting. But they could hobble American companies in the global market-place. Flexibility is precisely what has allowed the U.S. tech industry to adapt to competition from overseas. In 1985, under pressure from Japanese rivals, Intel Corp. exited the memory-chip business to concentrate all its resources in microprocessors. The result: Intel stands unrivaled in the business today.

While the departure of programming jobs is a major concern, it's not a national crisis yet. Unemployment in the industry is 7%. So far, the less-creative software jobs are the ones being moved offshore: bug-fixing, updating antiquated code, and routine programming tasks that require many hands. And some software companies are demonstrating

that they can compete against lower-cost rivals with improved programming methods, more automation, and innovative business models.

For the rest of the decade, the U.S. will probably maintain a strong hold on its software leadership, even as competition grows. The vast U.S. economy remains the richest market for software and the best laboratory for new ideas. The country's universities are packed with global all-stars. And the U.S. capital markets remain second to none. But time is running short for Americans to address this looming challenge. John Parkinson, chief technologist at Cap Gemini Ernst & Young, estimates that U.S. companies, students, and universities have five years to come up with responses to global shifts. "Scenarios start to look wild and wacky after 2010," he says. And within a decade, "the new consumer base in India and China will be moving the world."

People Skills

To thrive in that wacky world, programmers must undergo the career equivalent of an extreme makeover. Traditionally, the profession has attracted brainy introverts who are content to code away in isolation. With so much of that work going overseas, though, the most successful American programmers will be those who master people skills. The industry is hungry for liaisons between customers and basic programmers and for managers who can run teams of programmers scattered around the world. While pay for basic application development has plummeted 17.5% in the past two years, according to Foote Partners, a consultant in New Canaan, Conn., U.S. project managers have seen their pay rise an average of 14.3% since 2002.

Finding those high-status jobs won't be easy. Last summer, 34-year-old Hal Reed was so hungry for a programming job that he answered an ad in the *Boston Globe* for contract work at cMarket, a Cambridge, Mass., startup. The pay was $45,000—barely more than an outsourcing company charges for Indian labor. But he took it. Fortunately for him, he was able to convince his new boss quickly that he was much more than a programmer. He could lead a team. Within weeks, his boss nearly doubled Reed's pay and made him the chief software architect. "He had great strategic thinking skills," says Jon Carson, cMarket's chief executive. "You can't outsource that."

Ultrafast Track

Where the prospects for U.S. tech grads seem to narrow as they peer into the future, graduates overseas are looking down an eight-lane highway, especially those positioned on India's ultrafast track. The country pins high hopes on the 3,000 students in the six Institutes of Technology. Their alumni are stars locally and worldwide—including Yogen Dalal, a top venture capitalist at Mayfield, and Desh Deshpande, founder of Sycamore Networks and Cascade Communications. The challenge for upcoming graduates is to move beyond the achievements of Dalal and Deshpande, who notched their successes for U.S. companies, and to make their mark with new Indian companies.

That means bypassing the bread-and-butter service giants, such as Tata, Infosys, and Wipro, that dominate the Indian stage. To get their hands on exciting research and more creative programming, students are banking mostly on U.S. companies in India, including Intel, Texas Instruments, and Veritas. In addition, the search giant Google Inc. and the Web portal Yahoo! are setting up research and development centers in India this year.

Opportunities are also opening up in the venture capital arena. While venture-capital investing didn't exist in India until a few years ago, the industry is starting to take root. In 2003, India's 85 venture-capital firms invested about $162 million in tech companies, according to estimates from the India trade group National Association of Soft-

ware & Services Cos. That's up from zero in 1998. Still, it's miles short of the financial support available to U.S. programmers. The 700 U.S. venture firms poured $9.2 billion into tech startups last year, according to market researcher VentureOne.

Multicultural Edge

Diversity is another advantage the U.S. has over India. Take a stroll through the leafy ITT campus in Bombay, and practically everyone is Indian. The scene at Carnegie Mellon in Pittsburgh, by contrast, feels like the U.N. Classmates joke in Asian and European languages, and a strong smell of microwaved curry floats in the air. This atmosphere extends to American tech companies. With their diverse workforces, American companies can field teams that speak Mandarin, Hindi, French, Russian—you name it. As global software projects take shape, with development ceaselessly following the path of daylight around the globe, multicultural teams have a big edge. Who better than U.S.-based workers to stitch together these projects and manage them? "These people can act as bridges to the global economy," says Amar Gupta, a technology professor at Massachusetts Institute of Technology's Sloan School of Management.

The question is whether the technology industry can respond quickly enough to a revolution that's racing ahead on Internet time. While U.S. companies strive to maintain their positions as leaders in the tech industry, countries like India are setting out to build their own Silicon Valleys.

While the leader is looking cautiously over his shoulder, the challenger is chugging single-mindedly ahead. No matter which way they may zig or zag, both of them are prepared to encounter rough competition from every corner of the globe. There's no such thing as a safe distance in software anymore.

By Stephen Baker and Manjeet Kripalani
With Robert D. Hof and Jim Kerstetter in San Mateo, Calif.

Source: **From "The Software: Programming Jobs Are Heading Overseas . . .," by Stephen Baker and Manjeet Kripalani, *BusinessWeek,* March 1, 2004, pp. 84–91. Reprinted with permission.**

This opening story illustrates a growing dichotomy in the globalization of business. Since the turn of the century, U.S. software firms have been increasingly reliant on cheaper labor and production sources in many developing countries. In the late 1990s, a high demand for these nascent skills fueled a surge of demand for software programmers in the U.S. market. Many skilled immigrants from India and elsewhere filled this demand. More recently, however, advances in global communications and technology have allowed firms to move many programming jobs to other countries, causing dislocation in the United States but greater economic opportunity abroad. As trade barriers continue to fall and technological advances accelerate, the "offshoring" trend will continue as companies strive for operational efficiencies by outsourcing production and labor. In order to adapt to globalization and changing conditions, as noted in the article, countries like the United States and India will have to create a flexible framework to effectively respond to the increasing mobility of capital, jobs, and knowledge. In this chapter, we will examine the globalization phenomenon, the current state of the business environment around the world, and how globalization and the many trade agreements that have recently been implemented are changing the way business is conducted in many countries and regions worldwide. As you read this chapter, keep in mind that globalization is moving at a rapid pace and that all nations, including the United States, as well as individual companies and their managers, are going to have to keep a tight pulse on the current environment if they hope to be competitive in the years ahead.

■ Introduction

international management
Process of applying management concepts and techniques in a multinational environment and adapting management practices to different economic, political, and cultural environments.

MNC
A firm having operations in more than one country, international sales, and a nationality mix of managers and owners.

International management is the process of applying management concepts and techniques in a multinational environment and adapting management practices to different economic, political, and cultural environments. Today more firms than ever are earning some of their revenue from international operations. Many of these companies are multinational corporations (MNCs, for short). An **MNC** is a firm that has operations in more than one country, international sales, and a nationality mix of managers and owners. Table 1–1 shows the top ten global ranked MNCs by market value, sales, profits, and share-price gain. One example is British Petroleum (BP), which has acquired a number of rivals, including Amoco, making it one of the largest integrated oil and gas producers in the world. BP recently finalized its $8.1 billion deal with Russian oil producer TNK, one of the large energy firms created in the wake of the Soviet collapse a decade before. After two years of problematic negotiations, the deal marked the first time a Western oil company had been successful in acquiring a major equity stake in a Russian oil firm.[1] Another is Dell Computer, which now has three manufacturing plants in Ireland, passing Intel as the country's largest foreign employer.[2] A third is the Solectron Corporation of Milpitas, California, known worldwide for its high-quality manufacturing processes, which bought

Table 1–1
The Top 10 Global MNCs Ranked by Market Value, Sales, Profits, and Share-Price Gain, 2003

Market Value Billions of U.S. Dollars		Sales Billions of U.S. Dollars		Profits Billions of U.S. Dollars		Share-Price Gain	
1 General Electric	$328.11	1 Wal-Mart Stores	$258.68	1 ExxonMobil	$20.96	1 Mizuho Financial	636%
2 Microsoft	284.43	2 BP	232.57	2 Citigroup	17.85	2 Research in Motion	550
3 ExxonMobil	283.61	3 ExxonMobil	222.88	3 General Electric	15.00	3 UFJ Holdings	420
4 Pfizer	269.66	4 Royal Dutch/Shell	201.93	4 HSBC Holdings	11.65	4 SK	383
5 Wal-Mart Stores	241.19	5 General Motors	183.24	5 Royal Dutch/Shell	11.41	5 Rakuten	381
6 Citigroup	239.43	6 DaimlerChrysler	166.61	6 Vodafone Group	11.36	6 Sumitomo Mitsui Fin.	331
7 BP	193.05	7 Ford Motor	164.20	7 Bank of America	10.81	7 Elan	311
8 AIG	191.18	8 Toyota Motor	156.48	8 Toyota Motor	10.51	8 Bharti Tele-Ventures	276
9 Intel	184.66	9 Mitsubishi	137.32	9 Microsoft	9.99	9 Yahoo! Japan	241
10 Royal Dutch/Shell	174.83	10 General Electric	134.19	10 BP	9.54	10 Mitsui Trust Hldgs.	229

Data: Morgan Stanley Capital International, Standard & Poor's Compustat
Source: http://images.businessweek.com/mz/04/30/0430_62intbg1_a.gif

a Japanese-based auto electronics plant from the Sony Corporation.[3] A fourth is IBM, whose Global Services division, which recently acquired PriceWaterhouseCoopers' consulting arm, is helping the company provide quality service to clients in more countries than any industry rival.[4] A fifth is General Electric, which has operations in every major market worldwide, including Russia and China, where its businesses run the gamut from medical-imaging equipment to plastics to insurance.[5] And in the automobile industry, every major manufacturer has multinational operations. Over the last decade in Latin America alone, Ford built a car plant in Brazil, Volkswagen retooled its Mexican facilities to launch the new Beetle, and DaimlerChrysler built a new plant to produce engines in Brazil.[6] General Motors has not only been actively investing in Latin America, but is making pickup trucks and sport utility vehicles in China and Buicks in Shanghai and recently agreed to spend $99 million on a joint venture with Russian automaker Avtovaz to sell cars in emerging markets worldwide. GM has also paid $125 million to buy the remaining 50 percent of Saab, laid out $2.4 billion for a 20 percent stake in Fiat, $1.3 billion for 20 percent of Fuji Heavy Industries, and $653 million to double its 10 percent position in Suzuki Motor.[7]

These companies are not alone. In recent years such well-known American MNCs as Avon Products, Chevron, Citicorp, Coca-Cola, Colgate Palmolive, Du Pont, Exxon-Mobil, Eastman Kodak, Gillette, Hewlett-Packard, McDonald's, Motorola, Ralston Purina, Texaco, the 3M Company, and Xerox have all earned more annual revenue in the international arena than they have stateside. In addition, MNCs from emerging economies such as India, Brazil, and China are providing formidable competition to their North American, European, and Japanese counterparts. Reliance Industries, India's largest employer, whose sales equal 3.5 percent of the country's gross domestic product, more than the combined global sales of India's outsourcing companies, is now competing with leading MNCs around the world in the energy, telecommunications, textiles, and financial services industries.[8] Reliance has been termed the "General Electric of India" for its broad-based portfolio of companies and its global ambitions.[9] As a result, increasingly firms are finding that they must develop international management expertise. Managers from today's MNCs must learn to work effectively with those from many different countries. Moreover, as this decade unfolds, more and more small and medium-sized businesses will find that they are being affected by the trend toward internationalization. Many of these companies will be doing business abroad, and those who do not will find themselves doing business with MNCs operating locally. In either event, these growing businesses will need to be concerned with international management if only to improve their ability to interact and work well with MNCs that they are supplying or that are supplying them on a local basis.

■ Globalization and Internationalization

International business is not a new phenomenon; however, the volume of international trade has increased dramatically over the last decade. Today, every nation and an increasing number of companies buy and sell goods in the international marketplace. A number of developments around the world have helped to fuel this activity.

Globalization, Antiglobalization, and Global Pressures

Globalization can be defined as the process of social, political, economic, cultural, and technological integration among countries around the world. Evidence of globalization can be seen in increased levels of trade, capital flows, and migration. Globalization has been facilitated by technological advances in transnational communications, transport, and travel. In recent years, globalization has accelerated, creating both opportunities and challenges to global business.

globalization
The process of social, political, economic, cultural, and technological integration among countries around the world.

Tracing the Roots of Modern Globalization

Globalization is often presented as a new phenomenon associated with the post–World War II period. In fact, globalization is not new. Rather, its roots extend back to ancient times. Globalization emerged from long-standing patterns of transcontinental trade that developed over many centuries. The act of barter is the forerunner of modern international trade. During different periods of time, nearly every civilization contributed to the expansion of trade.

Middle Eastern Intercontinental Trade

In ancient Egypt, the King's Highway or Royal Road stretched across the Sinai into Jordan and Syria and into the Euphrates valley. These early merchants practiced their trade following one of the earliest codes of commercial integrity: *Do not move the scales, do not change the weights, and do not diminish parts of the bushel. . . .* Land bridges later extended to the Phoenicians, the first middlemen of global trade. Over 2,000 years ago, traders in silk and other rare valued goods moved east out of the Nile basin to Baghdad and Kashmir and linked the ancient empires of China, India, Persia, and Rome. At its height, the Silk Road extended over 4,000 miles, providing a transcontinental conduit for the dissemination of art, religion, technology, ideas, and culture. Commercial caravans crossing land routes in Arabian areas were forced to pay tribute—a forerunner of custom duties—to those who controlled such territories. In his youth, the Prophet Muhammad traveled with traders, and prior to his religious enlightenment the founder of Islam himself was a trader. Accordingly, the Qur'an instructs followers to respect private property, business agreements, and trade.

Trans-Saharan Cross-Continental Trade

Early tribes inhabiting the triad cities of Mauritania, in ancient West Africa below the Sahara, embraced caravan trade with the Berbers of North Africa. Gold from the sub-Saharan area was exchanged for something even more prized—salt, a precious substance needed for retaining body moisture, preserving meat, and flavoring food. Single caravans of nearly 2,500 camels, stretching five miles, earned their reputation as ships of the desert as they ferried gold powder, slaves, ivory, animal hides, and ostrich feathers to the northeast, returning with salt, wool, gunpowder, porcelain pottery, silk, dates, millet, wheat, and barley from the East.

China as an Ancient Global Trading Initiator

In 1421, a fleet of over 3,750 vessels set sail from China to cultivate trade around the world for the emperor. The voyage reflected the emperor's desire to collect tribute in exchange for trading privileges with China and China's protection. The Chinese, like modern-day multinationals, sought to extend their economic reach while recognizing principles of economic equity and fair trade. In the course of their global trading, the Chinese introduced uniform container measurements to enable merchants to transact business using common weight and dimension measurement systems. Like the early Egyptians and later the Romans, they used coinage as an intermediary form of value exchange or specie, thus eliminating complicated barter transactions.

European Trade Imperative

The concept of the alphabet came to the Greeks via trade with the Phoenicians. During the time of Alexander the Great, transcontinental trade was extended into Afghanistan and India. With the rise of the Roman Empire, global trade routes stretched from the Middle East through central Europe, Gaul, and across the English Channel. In 1215 King John of England signed the Magna Carta, which stressed the importance of cross-border trade. By the time of Marco Polo's writing of *The Description of the World,* at the end of the thirteenth century, the Silk Road from China to the city-states of Italy was a well-traveled commercial highway. His tales, which chronicled journeys with his merchant uncles, gave Europeans a taste for the exotic, further stimulating the consumer appetite that propelled trade and globalization. Around 1340 Francisco Balducci Pegolotti, a Florentine mercantile agent, authored *Practica Della Mercatura* ("Practice of Marketing"), the first widely distributed reference on international business and a precursor to today's textbooks. The search for trading routes contributed to the Age of Discovery and encouraged Christopher Columbus to sail west in 1492.

Globalization in U.S. History

The Declaration of Independence, which set out grievances against the English crown upon which a new nation was founded, cites the desire to "establish Commerce" as a chief rationale for establishing an independent state. The king of England is admonished "For cutting off our trade with all parts of the world," providing one of the earliest antiprotectionist free-trade statements from the New World.

Globalization, begun as trade between and across territorial borders in ancient times, was historically and is even today the key driver of world economic development. The first paths in the creation of civilization were taken in the footsteps of trade. In fact the word meaning "footsteps" in the old Anglo-Saxon language is *trada,* from which the modern English word *trade* is derived. Contemporary globalization is a new branch of a very old tree whose roots were planted in antiquity.

On the plus side, global trade and investment continue to grow, bringing wealth, jobs, and technology to many regions around the world. According to the World Trade Organization (WTO), merchandise exports rose by 16 percent to $7.3 trillion and commercial services exports by 12 percent to $1.8 trillion in 2003.[10] For both merchandise and services trade, this was the strongest annual increase in nominal terms since 1995.[11] On the other hand, as the pace of global integration quickens, so have the cries against globalization and the emergence of new concerns over mounting global pressures.[12] These pressures can be seen in protests at the meetings of the WTO, International Monetary Fund (IMF), and other global bodies, and in the growing calls by developing countries to make the global trading system more responsive to their economic and social needs. Nongovernmental organizations (NGOs) have become more active in expressing concerns about the potential shortcomings of economic globalization.[13]

Proponents believe that the benefits of globalization are evident in lower prices, greater availability of goods, better jobs, and access to technology. Critics of globalization point to the high number of jobs moving abroad, increasingly characterized by the **offshoring** of business services jobs to lower-wage countries. They also point to growing trade deficits and slow wage growth as examples of how globalization is damaging the economy. Moreover, critics argue that when production moves to countries to take advantage of lower labor costs or less regulated environments, this creates a "race to the bottom" in which companies and countries place downward pressure on wages and working conditions.[14] Proponents respond that job losses are a natural consequence of economic and technological change, and that offshore outsourcing actually improves the competitiveness of American companies and increases the size of the overall economic pie.[15]

offshoring
The migration of service jobs to low-wage nations.

Globalization has raised particular concerns over environmental and social impacts. According to antiglobalization activists, if corporations are free to locate anywhere in the world, the world's poorest countries will relax, or simply eliminate, environmental standards and social services in order to attract first-world investment and the jobs and wealth that come with it. Proponents of globalization contend that even within the developing world, it is protectionist policies, not trade and investment liberalization, that result in environmental and social damage. They believe globalization will force higher-polluting countries such as China and Russia into an integrated global community that takes responsible measures to protect the environment. However, given the significant changes required in many developing nations to support globalization, such as better infrastructure, greater educational opportunities, and other improvements, most supporters concede that there may be some short-term detrimental impacts. Over the long term, globalization supporters believe industrialization will create wealth that will enable new industries to employ more modern, environmentally friendly technology.

These contending perspectives are unlikely to be resolved anytime soon. Instead, a vigorous debate among countries, MNCs, and civil society will likely continue and will affect the context in which firms do business internationally. Business firms operating around the world must be sensitive to different perspectives on the costs and benefits of globalization and adapt and adjust their strategies and approaches to these differences.

Global and Regional Integration

Although the status of and issues facing major regions of the global economy are given detailed attention in the last part of this chapter, several important developments have had a direct impact on internationalization and should be noted here. Obviously, the horrific consequences of terrorism and its threat around the world have made a permanent mark on how and where international business is conducted. However, some of the more routine but still important developments have been:

1. Over the past half-century, succeeding rounds of global trade negotiations have resulted in dramatically reduced tariff and nontariff barriers among countries. These efforts reached their crest in 1994 with the conclusion of the

World Trade Organization (WTO)
The global organization of countries that oversees rules and regulations for international trade and investment.

Uruguay Round of multilateral trade negotiations under the General Agreement on Tariffs and Trade (GATT) and the creation of the **World Trade Organization (WTO)** to oversee the conduct of trade around the world. The WTO is the global organization of countries that oversees rules and regulations for international trade and investment, including agriculture, intellectual property, services, competition, and subsidies. Recently, however, the momentum of global trade agreements has slowed.[16] In December 1999, trade ministers from around the world met in Seattle to launch a new round of global trade talks. In what later became known as the "Battle in Seattle," protesters disrupted the meeting and developing countries who felt their views were being left out of the discussion succeeded in ending the discussions early and postponing a new round of trade talks.[17] Two years later, in November 2001, the members of the WTO met again and successfully launched a new round of negotiations at Doha, Qatar, to be known as the **"Development Round,"** reflecting the recognition by members that trade agreements needed to explicitly consider the needs of and impact on developing countries.[18] However, after a lack of consensus among WTO members regarding agricultural subsidies and the issues of competition and government procurement, progress slowed. At a meeting in Cancún in September 2003, a group of 20-plus developing nations led by Brazil and India united to press developed countries such as the United States, the EU, and Japan to reduce barriers to agricultural imports.[19] Failure to reach agreement resulted in another setback, and although there have been attempts to restart the negotiations, they have remained stalled.

North American Free Trade Agreement (NAFTA)
A free-trade agreement between the United States, Canada, and Mexico that has removed most barriers to trade and investment.

2. Partly as a result of the slow progress in multilateral trade negotiations, the United States and many other countries have pursued bilateral and regional trade agreements. The United States, Canada, and Mexico make up the **North American Free Trade Agreement (NAFTA),** which in essence has removed all barriers to trade among these countries and created a huge North American market. A number of economic developments have occurred because of this agreement, and all are designed to promote commerce in the region. Some of the more important include (1) the elimination of tariffs as well as import and export quotas; (2) the opening of government procurement markets to companies in the other two nations; (3) an increase in the opportunity to make investments in each other's country; (4) an increase in the ease of travel between countries; and (5) the removal of restrictions on agricultural products, auto parts, and energy goods. Many of these provisions will take place gradually. For example, in the case of Mexico, quotas on Mexican products in the textile and apparel sectors were phased out over time, and customs duties on all textile and products were eliminated over ten years.[20] Negotiations between NAFTA members and many Latin American countries, such as Chile, have concluded and others are ongoing. Moreover, other regional and tactical trade agreements including the U.S.–Singapore Free Trade Agreement, concluded in May 2003, and the U.S.–Central American Free Trade Agreement **(CAFTA),** concluded in May 2004, were negotiated in the same spirit as NAFTA.[21] In addition, the 34 democratically elected governments of the Western Hemisphere are also working toward an agreement that would create the world's largest free-trade region by January 2005 as part of the **Free Trade Agreement of the Americas (FTAA).**[22] These negotiations, however, like those under the WTO, have stalled due to differences between developing countries, like Brazil, and developed nations, like the United States. Agreements like NAFTA and CAFTA not only reduce barriers to trade but also require additional domestic legal and business reforms in developing nations to protect property rights. Most of these agreements now include supplemental commitments on labor and the environment to encourage countries to upgrade their working

Free Trade Agreement of the Americas (FTAA)
A proposed free trade agreement among the 34 democratically-governed countries of the Western Hemisphere.

conditions and environmental protections, although some critics believe the agreements do not go far enough in ensuring worker rights and environmental standards.

3. The European Union (EU) has made significant progress over the past decade in becoming a unified market. In 2003 this group consisted of 15 nations: Austria, Belgium, Denmark, Finland, France, Germany, Great Britain, Greece, Holland, Ireland, Italy, Luxembourg, Portugal, Spain, and Sweden. In May 2004, 10 additional countries joined the EU: Cyprus, the Czech Republic, Estonia, Hungary, Latvia, Lithuania, Malta, Poland, Slovakia, and Slovenia.[23] Not only have most trade barriers between the members been removed, but a subset of European countries have adopted a unified currency called the "euro."[24] As a result, it is now possible for customers to compare prices between most countries, and business firms can lower their costs by conducting business in one, uniform currency. With access to the entire pan-European market, large MNCs can now achieve the operational scale and scope necessary to reduce costs and increase efficiencies. Even though long-standing cultural differences remain, the EU is better integrated as a single market than NAFTA, CAFTA, or the allied Asian countries. With many additional countries poised to join the EU, the resulting pan-European market will be one that no major MNC can afford to ignore.

4. Although Japan has experienced economic problems for about 10 years, it continues to be the primary economic force in the Pacific Rim. Japan recently has invested relatively more in its own backyard of Asia than in any other part of the world. Japanese MNCs want to take advantage of the underdeveloped and huge Asian markets. At the same time, China is proving to be a major economic force (some experts forecast that China eventually will be the biggest economy in the world). Although all of the economies in Asia are now feeling the impact of the economic uncertainty of the post–9/11 era, the Four Tigers (Hong Kong, Taiwan, South Korea, and Singapore) have been doing relatively well, and the Southeast Asia countries of Malaysia, Thailand, Indonesia, and even Vietnam are bouncing back to become major export-driven economies. As in other parts of the world, an economic bloc called ASEAN (Association of Southeast Asian Nations), made up of Indonesia, Malaysia, the Philippines, Singapore, Brunei, Thailand, and in recent years Cambodia, Myanmar, and Vietnam, promotes exports to other countries.

5. Central and Eastern Europe, Russia, and the other republics of the former Soviet Union currently are still trying to make the transition to market economies. Although the Czech Republic, Slovenia, Poland, and Hungary have accelerated this process through their accession to the EU, others (the Balkan countries, Russia, and the other republics of the former Soviet Union) still have a long way to go. However, all are a target for MNCs looking for expansion opportunities. For example, after the fall of the Berlin Wall in 1989, Coca-Cola quickly began to sever its relations with most of the state-run bottling companies in the former communist-bloc countries. The soft drink giant began investing heavily to import its own manufacturing, distribution, and marketing techniques. To date, Coca-Cola has pumped billions into Central and Eastern Europe—and this investment is beginning to pay off. Its business in Central and Eastern Europe has been expanding at twice the rate of its other foreign operations.

6. Economic activity in Latin America continues to be volatile. Despite the continuing political and economic setbacks these countries periodically experience, economic and export growth continues in Brazil, Chile, and Mexico. Additionally, while outside MNCs continually target this geographic area, there also is a great deal of cross-border investment between Latin American countries. Regional trade agreements are helping in this cross-border process,

including NAFTA, which ties the Mexican economy more closely to the United States than to Latin America. The pending CAFTA agreement between the United States and Central American countries presents new opportunities for bolstering trade, investment, services, and working conditions in the region. Within South America there is Mercosur, a common market created by Argentina, Brazil, Paraguay, and Uruguay, and the Andean Common Market, a subregional free-trade compact that is designed to promote economic and social integration and cooperation between Bolivia, Colombia, Ecuador, Peru, and Venezuela.

7. There also is recent economic progress among other less developed nations. A good example is India, which for years has had a love–hate relationship with multinational businesses. The Indian government has been known for its slow-moving bureaucracy, and this has been a major stumbling block in attracting foreign capital. In recent years, however, there has been a dramatic turnaround in government policy, and a growing number of multinationals recently have been attracted to India. Much of this spurt has resulted from the Indian government's willingness to reduce the bureaucratic red tape that accompanies the necessary approvals to move forward with investments. In addition, business service jobs such as programmers and call-center operators are creating many new opportunities for Indians.

Those are specific, geographic examples of emerging internationalism. Equally important to this new climate of globalization, however, are recent developments in both international investment and trade.

Trends in International Investment and Trade

Approximately 80 percent of all international investments come from developed countries. For example, foreign direct investment (FDI), the term used to indicate the amount invested in property, plant, and equipment in another country, in the United States stood at almost $1.3 trillion by the end of 2002, while U.S. FDI abroad was approximately $1.5 trillion. The largest investors in the United States in recent years have been Great Britain, Japan, the Netherlands, Germany, and Canada. Conversely, the major stake for U.S. investors has been the EU, followed by Canada and then Japan. Tables 1–2 and 1–3 provide additional information on FDI in the United States and by U.S. investors.

As nations become more affluent, they begin looking for countries with economic growth potential where they can invest funds. Over the last two decades, for example, Japanese MNCs have invested not only in their Asian neighbors but in both the United States and the EU. European MNCs, meanwhile, have made large financial commitments in Japan, and more recently in China, because they see Asia as having continued growth potential. American multinationals have followed a similar approach in regard both to Europe and to Asia.

In addition to these types of investments, international trade increased substantially over the last two decades. For example, in 1983 the United States exported slightly over $200 billion of goods and services and imported $269 billion of goods and services. By the end of 2003, U.S. exports were in the range of $1.3 trillion annually, and imports were close to $1.8 trillion.

EU trade also increased sharply. This is particularly true for exports and imports between EU members, both of which are now in excess of $2 trillion annually.[25] Japan, despite its ongoing economic problems, has also seen continual increases in its annual exports and imports.[26]

When international trade statistics for all countries are examined, what is particularly interesting about these data is that the *percentage* of world trade that is accounted for by the three major trading blocs—the United States, the EU, and Japan—has remained

Table 1–2
Foreign Direct Investment in the United States, 2002–2003 (in millions of dollars)

	2002	2003
All countries	1,340,011	1,378,001
Canada	96,437	105,255
Europe	982,062	1,000,532
(select countries)		
United Kingdom	218,175	230,374
Germany	139,620	148,774
France	141,400	143,341
South and Central America	19,198	20,636
(select countries)		
Mexico	7,483	6,680
Brazil	997	663
Other Western Hemisphere	50,167	48,921
(select countries)		
Bermuda	8,088	5,914
Netherland Antilles	4,014	4,048
UK islands, Caribbean	28,260	28,949
Africa	2,298	2,187
Middle East	7,456	7,931
(select countries)		
Israel	3,699	3,834
Kuwait	986	1,155
Asia and Pacific	183,392	192,539
(select countries)		
Japan	150,499	159,258
Australia	23,136	24,652
Taiwan	2,569	2,708
Singapore	650	−162
Hong Kong	1,879	1,981

Source: Bureau of Economic Analysis, U.S. Department of Commerce, 2004, http://www.bea.doc.gov/bea/di/fdipos/fdipos-03.htm.

fairly consistent. Over the last two decades this group's share of world exports and imports has remained in the range of 55–59 percent. Simply stated, this triad accounts for most of the world's international trade, and the United States is the major economic power among the three. As seen in Table 1–4, the United States sells over $813 billion of goods and services to its top 10 trading partners and, in turn, buys over $470 billion of goods and services from them. One area of recent concern in the United States is trade with China. In 2003, the United States imported $124 billion in goods from China but exported only about $28.4 billion, creating tensions in the U.S.–China trading relationship. These tensions have resulted in a call by some U.S. government officials that China allow its currency to float in order to reduce the perceived price advantage of keeping the yuan at an artificially low value.[27]

Finally, it is important to note that foreign investment and trade do not rely exclusively on MNCs exporting or setting up operations locally. In some cases, it is far easier to buy a domestic firm. Beer companies, for example, are finding that customers like local products, so rather than trying to sell them an imported beer, the MNC will invest in or buy a local brewery. Moreover, the name of the local company may remain the same, so that many local residents are unaware that the firm has changed hands. To illustrate this point,

Table 1–3
Foreign Direct Investment by the United States Abroad, 2002–2003 (in millions of dollars)

	2002	2003
All countries	1,601,414	1,788,911
Canada	170,169	192,409
Europe	848,599	963,087
(select countries)		
United Kingdom	239,219	272,640
Germany	67,404	80,163
France	42,999	47,914
South and Central America	131,973	141,449
(select countries)		
Mexico	55,724	61,526
Brazil	27,615	29,915
Other Western Hemisphere	152,597	162,574
(select countries)		
Bermuda	80,048	84,609
UK islands, Caribbean	49,806	54,507
Africa	16,290	18,960
Middle East	14,671	16,942
(select countries)		
Israel	5,632	6,208
Saudi Arabia	3,823	4,217
Asia and Pacific	267,125	292,490
(selected countries)		
Japan	65,939	73,435
Australia	34,409	40,985
Taiwan	7,608	10,961
Singapore	52,449	57,589
Hong Kong	41,571	44,323
China	10,499	11,877

Source: Bureau of Economic Analysis, U.S. Department of Commerce, 2004, http://www.bea.doc.gov/bea/di/usdpos/pos_03.htm.

Table 1–4
Top 10 Trading Partners of the United States, 2003 (in millions of dollars)

Rank	Importing Country	U.S. Exports	Rank	Exporting Country	U.S. Imports
1	Canada	169,924	1	Canada	221,595
2	Mexico	97,412	2	China	152,436
3	Japan	52,004	3	Mexico	138,060
4	United Kingdom	33,828	4	Japan	118,037
5	Germany	28,832	5	Germany	68,113
6	China	28,368	6	United Kingdom	42,795
7	South Korea	24,073	7	South Korea	37,229
8	Netherlands	20,695	8	Taiwan	31,599
9	Taiwan	17,448	9	France	29,219
10	France	17,053	10	Ireland	25,747

Note: Exports are "free along side" (f.a.s.) basis; imports are customs basis.
Source: Office of Trade and Economic Analysis, U.S. Department of Commerce, 2004, http://www.bea.doc.gov/bea/di1.htm.

answer the following questions about well-known products sold in the United States; then check your answers at the end of the chapter:

1. Where is the parent company of Braun household appliances (electric shavers, coffee makers, etc.) located?
   a. Switzerland   *b.* Germany   *c.* the United States   *d.* Japan

2. The BIC pen company is
   a. Japanese   *b.* British   *c.* U.S.-based   *d.* French

3. The company that owns Häagen-Dazs ice cream is in
   a. Germany   *b.* the U.S.   *c.* Sweden   *d.* Japan

4. RCA television sets are produced by a company based in
   a. France   *b.* the United States   *c.* Malaysia   *d.* Taiwan

5. The firm that owns Green Giant vegetables is
   a. U.S.-based   *b.* Canadian   *c.* British   *d.* Italian

6. The owners of Godiva chocolate are
   a. U.S.-based   *b.* Swiss   *c.* Dutch   *d.* Swedish

7. The company that produces Vaseline is
   a. French   *b.* Anglo-Dutch   *c.* German   *d.* U.S.-based

8. Wrangler jeans are made by a company that is
   a. Japanese   *b.* Taiwanese   *c.* British   *d.* U.S.-based

9. The company that owns Holiday Inn is headquartered in
   a. Saudi Arabia   *b.* France   *c.* the United States   *d.* Britain

10. Tropicana orange juice is owned by a company that is headquartered in
    a. Mexico   *b.* Canada   *c.* the United States   *d.* Japan

This quiz helps to illustrate how transnational today's MNCs have become. This trend is not restricted to firms in North America, Europe, or Asia. An emerging global community is becoming increasingly interdependent economically. Although there may be a true, totally integrated global market in the near future, at present *regionalization,* as represented by North America, Europe, Asia, and the less developed countries, is most descriptive of the world economy.

■ Economic Performance and Issues of the Major Regions

International investment and trade are more likely to occur between nations in close geographic proximity; for example, in North America, Mexico, and Canada are two of the United States' largest trading partners. However, there also is a growing trend toward expanding these horizons and doing business with nations thousands of miles away. For example, Japan is a major trading partner of the United States, and China does more business with the United States than with most other nations. The following sections examine trends that are occurring in each major region of the world and the impact of these developments on international management.

North America

As noted earlier, North America constitutes one of the three largest trading blocs in the world. The combined purchasing power of the United States, Canada, and Mexico is close to $12 trillion. Even though there will be more integration both globally and regionally, effective international management still requires knowledge of individual countries.

United States   U.S. MNCs have holdings throughout the world. In Europe, General Motors and Ford command dominant market positions, and they are finally beginning to make inroads in Asia as well. U.S. MNCs also do extremely well in the European computer market and are a major force in this industry throughout the Pacific Rim. Telecommunications is another high-tech area where the United States has a large international market share. U.S. firms compete with each other in the international arena as well. For example, AT&T now finds itself getting international competition from the U.S. "Baby Bells" (the regional firms that used to be part of AT&T). These firms are becoming more interested in expanding their market coverage and meeting the growing worldwide demand for higher-quality telephone services.

U.S. consumer-goods companies also are finding overseas markets to be very attractive. For example, Coca-Cola has a soft drink plant and distribution operation in Moscow and has a huge presence throughout Eastern Europe. Toys "R" Us has expanded in Germany and Japan, and it is gaining market share in both locales. U.S. airline companies, such as Delta, United, and American, also are expanding into Europe.

At the same time, foreign MNCs are finding the United States to be a lucrative market for expansion. BMW has set up operations in South Carolina, and Mercedes produces a lower-priced car ($25,000 range) in Alabama designed to help it gain U.S. market share. Other examples of outside investment in the United States include SmithKline Beecham PLC of Britain, which paid almost $3 billion to acquire the over-the-counter drug business of Sterling Winthrop Inc., an Eastman Kodak unit. Hoechst AG of Germany paid over $7 billion for Marion Merrell Dow Inc., a Dow Chemical subsidiary. France Telecom and Deutsche Telecom combined to pay over $4 billion for a 20 percent stake in the Sprint Corporation.

Even though Japanese firms are going to Asia more than in the past, they now are turning to the United States to find suppliers who can help increase the quality of their products while keeping down costs. For example, Toyota, Isuzu, and Suzuki all are buying antilock brake systems from General Motors. IBM is selling computers to Mitsubishi Electric, and Sun Microsystems Inc. is selling workstations to Japanese firms. Understanding these developments in the United States contributes to the field of international management.

Canada   Canada is the United States' largest trading partner, a position it has held for many years. The United States also has considerable foreign direct investment in Canada, more than in any other country except the United Kingdom. This helps to explain why most of the largest foreign-owned companies in Canada are totally or heavily U.S.-owned.

The legal and business environment in Canada is similar to that in the United States, and this similarity helps to promote trade between the two countries. Geography, language, and culture also help, as does NAFTA, which will assist Canadian firms in becoming more competitive worldwide. They will have to be able to go head-to-head with their U.S. and Mexican competitors as trade barriers are removed. This should result in greater efficiency and market prowess on the part of the Canadian firms, which must compete successfully or go out of business.

In recent years, Canadian firms have begun investing heavily in the United States. For example, Canadian Pacific has purchased the Delaware & Hudson Railway, and Bombardier Inc. has bought the Learjet Corporation of Wichita, Kansas. Meanwhile, Bronfman Inc., best known for its Canadian whiskeys, sold its large stake in Du Pont for $1.4 billion (less than market value) to buy 80 percent of MCA (now called Universal) and purchased Polygram, the largest music company in the world.[28] Canadian firms also do business in many other countries, including Mexico, Great Britain, Germany, and Japan, where they find ready markets for Canada's vast natural resources, including lumber, natural gas, crude petroleum, and agriproducts.

At the same time, Canada is becoming a target for increased international investment, especially by firms from the United States. American, Delta, and Northwest airlines all have expanded their Canadian routes. DaimlerChrysler, Ford, and General Motors all have plants in Canada, and so do other major U.S. MNCs, including IBM, Kodak, and Xerox. Again, a major reason for this outside investment is to tap Canada's vast natural resources, which offer a potential bonanza to enterprising firms. Another reason is the growing population and increasing purchasing power of the country. Still another is the chance to take advantage of the opportunities provided under the NAFTA provisions.

Mexico   By the early 1990s, Mexico had recovered from its economic problems of the previous decade and had become the strongest economy in Latin America. In 1994, Mexico became part of NAFTA, and it appeared to be on the verge of becoming the major economic power in Latin America. The country's economic optimism proved to be short-lived, however. By late 1994, the value of the peso collapsed, and the economy took a nosedive. By early 1995, the United States, the International Monetary Fund, and the Bank for International Settlements were teaming up to create a $50 billion assistance package. At the same time, the government of Mexico was instituting a number of important economic changes, which included cutting the federal budget (thus holding down the country's spiraling deficit), instituting wage and price controls to limit growing inflation, and privatizing more state-held businesses to raise money and stimulate economic growth. These moves helped to bring the Mexican economy back on its course, and the loans were paid back before they were due.

In 2000 the 71-year hold of the Institutional Revolutionary Party on the presidency of the country came to an end, and many investors believe that the administration of Vicente Fox has been especially pro-business. Economic growth in 2001 was in the range of 3 percent but fell to 1 percent in 2002.[29] The country is now producing almost 2 million light vehicles annually.[30] In addition, Mexico now has a highly competitive textile industry and has replaced China as the major exporter of garments to the United States.[31] However, like the United States and other countries of the world, Mexico's economy faces an uncertain future.

In the meantime, Mexico has built a very strong **maquiladora** industry. Long before NAFTA, this was an arrangement by the Mexican government that permitted foreign manufacturers to send materials to their Mexican-based plants, process or assemble the products, and then ship them back out of Mexico with only the value added being taxed. Ford Motor, for example, took advantage of this opportunity and annually exports engines from its Chihuahua plant to the United States. General Motors assembles car radios in its Matamoros plant for shipment north. Hundreds of other large firms have followed suit, taking advantage of the low-cost but quality-conscious Mexican workforce.

U.S. labor unions argue that this arrangement has cost many jobs in the United States, but the U.S. Department of Labor reports that maquiladora operations actually support jobs by helping U.S. firms maintain their international competitiveness. For example, Packard Electric has noted that without maquiladora operations, it would have closed its Warren, Ohio, plant and moved everything to Southeast Asia.

Because of NAFTA, Mexican businesses are finding themselves able to take advantage of the U.S. market by replacing goods that were previously purchased from Asia. Mexican firms are now able to produce products at highly competitive prices thanks to lower-cost labor and proximity to the American market. Location has helped hold down transportation costs and allows for fast delivery. As a result, Hewlett-Packard has increased imports of copier products from Mexican manufacturers, and IBM is pushing its Asian suppliers to set up joint ventures in Mexico, so that its own costs and inventories can be reduced.[32] Overseas auto producers are also turning their attention to this market location opportunity. Volkswagen, Nissan, and DaimlerChrysler have production facilities in Mexico. As a result, when coupled with the American auto firms that have operations there, almost 1 million cars and trucks for the U.S. market are now being made in Mexico.[33]

The government of Mexico has also been active in negotiating trade agreements with more than a dozen individual countries and many economic regions, such as the

maquiladora
A **maquiladora** is a factory, the majority of which are located in Mexican border towns, that imports materials and equipment on a duty- and tariff-free basis for assembly or manufacturing.

EU.[34] Mexican firms are also expanding their worldwide operations. A retail group controlled by billionaire Carlos Slim Helu bought CompUSA, the largest chain of personal computer stores in the United States.[35] Grupo Industrial Bimbo SA, a large food company that provides all of the buns for McDonald's units in Mexico, Peru, Colombia, and Venezuela, has built a factory in the Czech Republic to manufacture candy for the local market.[36] Mexican firms, taking advantage of a new arrangement that the government has negotiated with the EU, can now export goods into the European community without having to pay a tariff. So Volkswagen of Mexico can export cars to the EU and save the 7 percent duty it used to pay as long as the Mexican content of the cars is in the prescribed 45–60 percent range.[37]

Today Mexican companies employ approximately 70,000 workers in more than two dozen countries and generate almost $8 billion in revenues.[38] In addition, the country's trade with both the EU and Asia is on the rise, which is important to Mexico because it wants to reduce its overreliance on the U.S. market.

South America

Over the years, countries in South America have had difficult economic problems. They have accumulated heavy foreign debt obligations and experienced severe inflation. Although most have tried to implement economic reforms reducing their debt, the last few years have again seen a downturn in the economy.[39]

Brazil is a case in point. From 1992 to 1995, the country's GDP rose by 5 percent annually, and inflation, which was running as high as 50 percent in some months, dropped to 5 percent by mid-1998. In 2002, however, GDP slowed to 1.5 percent and inflation crept back up to 8.3 percent. Still, Brazil continues to attract outside investors, partly drawn to opportunities created by Brazil's privatization of telecommunications and other infrastructure sectors.[40] (See "International Management in Action: Telecommunications Privatization in Brazil.") Examples include Compaq Computer, which opened a factory capable of producing 400,000 personal computers annually. Anheuser-Busch spent $105 million on a brewery to market Budweiser to Brazilians, and General Electric constructed $9 billion worth of coal-fired power electricity plants in the southern part of the country. At the same time, many other well-known companies have set up operations in Brazil, including Arby's, J.C. Penney, Kentucky Fried Chicken, McDonald's, and Wal-Mart.[41] All of this international business activity should spell success. However, by the turn of the century, Brazil was experiencing difficulties in the volatile world economy and its future remains uncertain.

Chile has been an economic success story in South America. Annual average growth of GDP over the last five years was higher than that for any other country in South America except Argentina.[42] In addition, Chile's export volume increased dramatically and the amount of foreign direct investment was on the rise. However, in the last couple of years the economy has weakened, GDP growth has fallen below 3 percent, and its future is uncertain.

Argentina, one of the strongest economies overall with abundant natural resources, a highly literate population, an export-oriented agricultural sector, and a diversified industrial base, has suffered recurring economic problems of inflation, external debt, capital flight, and budget deficits. Growth in 2000 was a negative 0.8 percent as both domestic and foreign investors remained skeptical of the government's ability to pay debts and maintain the peso's fixed exchange rate with the U.S. dollar. The economic situation worsened in 2001 with high inflation, massive withdrawals from the banks, and a further decline in consumer and investor confidence.[43] Government efforts to achieve a "zero deficit," to stabilize the banking system, and to restore economic growth proved unsuccessful in the face of the mounting economic pressures. The peso's peg to the dollar was abandoned in January 2002, and the peso was floated in February. Subsequently, the peso's value plunged and inflation accelerated, but by mid-2002 the economy had stabilized. Led by record exports, the economy began to recover in 2003 with output up 5.5 percent, falling unemployment, and inflation receding to 4.2 percent at year-end.[44]

Despite the ups and downs, a major development in South America is the growth of intercountry trade, spurred on by the progress toward free market policies. For example, beginning in 1995, 90 percent of trade among Mercosur members was duty-free. At the same time, South American countries are increasingly looking to do business with the United States.[45] In fact, a survey of businesspeople from Argentina, Brazil, Chile, Colombia, and Venezuela found that the U.S. market, on average, was more important for them than any other. Some of these countries, however, also are looking outside of the Americas for growth opportunities. Mercosur continues talks with the EU to create free trade between the two blocs, and Chile has joined the Asia-Pacific Economic Cooperation group.[46] These developments help to illustrate the economic dynamism of South America and, especially in light of Asia's recent economic problems, explain why so many multinationals are interested in doing business within this part of the world.

Europe

Although often in the past overshadowed because of Asia's spectacular growth, major economic developments have occurred in Europe over the past decade. One interesting development has been the privatization of traditionally nationalized industries. Another has been the full emergence of the EU as an operational economic union, and yet another the close economic linkages established between the EU and newly emerging Central and Eastern European countries. Including the former communist bloc, today Greater Europe is a trading area of about 550 million mostly middle-class consumers in at least 25 countries.

The EU The ultimate objective of the EU is to eliminate all trade barriers among member countries (like between the states in the United States). This economic community eventually will have common custom duties as well as unified industrial and commercial policies regarding countries outside the union. Another goal that has finally largely become a reality is a single currency and a regional central bank.

Such developments will allow companies based in EU nations that are able to manufacture high-quality, low-cost goods to ship them anywhere within the EU without paying duties or being subjected to quotas. This helps to explain why many North American and Pacific Rim firms have established operations in Europe; however, all these outside firms are finding their success tempered by the necessity to address local cultural differences.

As a result of differing local tastes, EU-based firms follow the international strategy adage "Plan globally, act locally." Although this strategy also applies to other parts of the world and will be covered in subsequent chapters, it must be given special consideration if unity in Europe is to become a reality. For example, EU appliance makers will add a self-cleaning option to ovens for the French market but leave this option out of units for the German market, where food generally is cooked at lower temperatures. Another interesting strategy is to draw heavily on a network of factories in the EU that can produce both components and finished goods. For example, the Philips television factory in Brugge, Belgium, uses tubes that are supplied from a factory in Germany, transistors that come from France, plastics that are produced in Italy, and electronic components that come from another factory in Belgium.

The most common way that foreign MNCs have gained a foothold in the EU is by using two strategy approaches: acquisitions and alliances. Also, cooperative research and development (R&D) programs are becoming increasingly common as firms team up to share expenses. Siemens and Philips have used this approach to develop computer chips, and IBM has a number of agreements with European firms for developing advanced computer technology. EU-based firms also are able to obtain financial assistance through the **European Research Cooperation Agency (Eureka),** which funds projects in the fields of energy, medical technology, biotechnology, communications, information technology, transportation, new materials, robotics, production automation, lasers, and the environment.

European Research Cooperation Agency (Eureka)
An EU agency that funds projects in a number of fields with the objective of making Europe more productive and competitive in the world market.

Telecommunications Privatization in Brazil

http://www.v-brazil.com/business/phone-privatization.html

Privatization has become the most widely used and most effective way to carry out reform in the telecommunications industry, liberating firms from the constraints imposed by the almost universal requirement that they operate as government-owned or highly regulated monopolies. The structure, organization, financial underpinnings, and operational environment of telecommunications firms have all been transformed. Many telecommunications companies have been allowed, for the first time in history, to become innovative, privately owned enterprises competing, sometimes fiercely, with one another both locally and, in some cases, globally. Brazil is an excellent example of a developing nation that has adopted mass privatization of the telecommunications industry.

On July 29, 1998, the Brazilian government privatized the state-owned telecommunications sector, Telebras, for a total sale price of R$22.057 million or approximately US$19 billion. This included the sale of Brazil's single long-distance telecommunication provider, Embratel, which was purchased by a consortium led by MCI for $2.28 billion through its fully owned Brazilian subsidiary, Startel. In conjunction with Brazil's Telecommunications Act of 1997, which established the regulatory conditions for competition, this privatization has resulted in sweeping changes to Brazil's telecom environment. There is now competition in each of eight geographic regions and in the long-distance market, resulting in lower telecommunication prices for Brazilian consumers. Privatization should also help speed up the Internet adoption rates since local firms might be forced to bundle services (at a lower cost) in order to compete with global players. Cyber cafés are now common in major cities such as Rio de Janerio and São Paulo. Privatization has also created opportunities for U.S. and European telecommunications companies that have entered this burgeoning market.

Since Brazil's deregulation was put into effect in 1997, the market for telecommunications has risen along with the growth of the nation's infrastructure. One of the largest emerging countries with potential for a sustainable growth, Brazil has the biggest and most modern industrial park in Latin America. With continued assistance from Anatel, Brazil's regulatory agency similar to the FCC in the United States, Brazil's telecommunications market has been transformed from a monopoly to an open and competitive global market.

The objective of Eureka is to make Europe more productive and competitive in the world market. In the years ahead, the EU will continue to be a major focal point for international investment. U.S. firms in particular have been buying businesses in the EU, joining in strategic alliances with EU firms, and exporting into the European market.

The challenge for the future of the EU is to absorb its eastern neighbors, the former communist-bloc countries. This could result in a giant, single European market. In fact, a unified Europe could become the largest economic market in terms of purchasing power in the world. Such a development is not lost on Asian and U.S. firms, which are working to gain a stronger foothold in Eastern European countries as well as the existing EU. In recent years, foreign governments have been very active in helping to stimulate and develop the market economies of Central and Eastern Europe to enhance their economic growth as well as world peace.

Central and Eastern Europe In December 1989, the Berlin Wall came down, and 2 years later, on December 8, 1991, the Soviet Union ceased to exist. Each of the individual republics that made up the U.S.S.R. in turn declared its independence. The Russian Republic has the most population, territory, and influence, but others, such as Ukraine, also are industrialized and potentially can be important in the global economy. Of the ideas promoted by former Soviet president Mikhail Gorbachev, *glasnost* (openness) has been achieved, but *perestroika* (economic and political restructuring) is still having major problems. A brief overview of the historical developments in Russia is shown in Table 1–5. Of most importance to the study of international management are the Russian economic reforms, the dismantling of Russian price controls (allowing supply and demand to determine prices), and privatization (converting the old communist-style public enterprises to private ownership).

Table 1–5
The Three Eras of the Soviet Union

Traditional Russian Society (Pre-1917)	Red Executive Managers (1917–1987)	Market-Oriented (1987–present)
Centralization of authority and responsibility	Centralized leadership	Sharing of power with numerous stakeholders in state enterprises
Collective action	Communist domination	Responsibility for private enterprise success
Dual ethical standards (honesty in personal relationships, deception in business relationships)	Party service	
	Rise of collective enterprises	Effective delegation of responsibility to employees
Feelings ranging from helplessness (only a religious savior will deliver people from their plight) to bravado (belief in one's ability to outsmart others)	Dual ethical standards (honesty in personal conduct with employees, dishonesty in business dealings)	Use of informal influence to obtain favors
	Use of informal influence to obtain favors	Bipolar extremes of cynicism in problem solving
	Feelings of helplessness due to producing inferior products and bravado in operating some of the world's largest organizations	Use of overpromising to both clients and business partners
		A high degree of achievement motivation regarding quality service and products but social contempt for success

Source: Adapted from Sheila Puffer, "Understanding the Bear: A Portrait of Russian Business Leaders," *Academy of Management Executive,* February 1994, pp. 41–61. Copyright 1994 by Academy of Management. Reproduced with permission of Academy of Management via Copyright Clearance Center.

Clearly, Russia still has tremendous problems. In fact, by the turn of the century, once-mighty Russia's economy was not nearly as strong as the economies of its once-dominated neighbors, the Czech Republic, Hungary, and Poland. Even with rapid economic progress, closing the gap with their Western European neighbors will take many more years.

One of the ways that Russia is attempting to get its economy going is by removing many administered prices and subsidies and letting free-market forces take over. The problem with this strategy is that it results in very high inflation (demand is much greater than supply). Hyperinflation is very hard on the people, and for political expediency, this slows down price reforms. In 2002, inflation remained high at 15 percent, placing mounting pressure on fixed-wage earners and consumers.[47]

On the positive side, many efforts are under way to help stimulate the Russian economy. Russia has been given membership in the International Monetary Fund (IMF), which has pledged development loans to help the country make the transition to a free-market economy, and also put together a loan package to help keep the economy from collapsing.[48] In addition, the Group of Seven (the United States, Germany, France, England, Canada, Japan, and Italy) has pledged billions for humanitarian and other types of assistance. So, while the Russian economy likely will have a number of years of painfully slow economic recovery and many current problems, most economic experts predict that if the Russians can hold things together politically and maintain social order, things should get better in the long run.

Besides freeing up prices, the other major development that is needed for Russia to transform into a market economy is privatization. Russian enterprises no longer are fully subsidized, and they no longer can automatically sell all their output to the state. Enterprises are increasingly becoming more self-sustaining and are operating in more of a market-based environment. Privatization has taken a number of different forms, including turning a large number of state-run businesses over to the workers and managers, letting them set up a board of directors and run the operation. In addition, an increasing number of public enterprises issued stock, and both employees and outside investors purchased ownership. Shareholders not only get equity but also a vote in how the company is run.

Although these economic reforms are being implemented slowly, there are significant problems in Russia associated with growing crime of all kinds as well as political uncertainty. Many foreign investors feel that the risk is still too high.[49] Russia is such a large market, however, and has so much potential for the future, that many MNCs feel they must get involved. For example, Alcatel, the giant French telecommunications company, has a $2.8 billion contract to supply advanced digital telephone equipment switches. McDonald's opened a restaurant in Moscow in the early 1990's and now operates more than 50 restaurants throughout the country. Overall, however, Russia still has a long way to go in becoming like its Western neighbors. The *Economist* Intelligence Unit (EIU) has reported that Russia was one of the least successful countries in Central and Eastern Europe in making the transition to a market economy, and it also was ranked as one of the most politically risky countries in the world.[50]

Former communist countries that have become most visible in the international arena include the Czech Republic, Hungary, and Poland. All three initially were battered by inflation, unemployment, and slow economic growth during their transition efforts. Yet all three made significant progress, and they have been successful in attracting Western capital. Although recently they have been experiencing economic problems as will be discussed in the next chapter, they have been able to attract outside investors, including (1) Volkswagen taking a $6.6 billion stake in the Skoda Auto Works; (2) Japan's Fravalex purchasing the glass manufacturer Sklo-Union Teplice for $1 billion; (3) Linde of Germany investing $106 million in Technoplyn, a natural gas company; (4) US West and Bell Atlantic entering into an $80 million telecommunications joint venture with the Czech government to produce telephone switches; (5) Swedish furniture maker Ikea investing $60 million in a furniture production plant in Trnava; and (6) Siemens of Germany investing $35 million for an interest in Electromagnetica, a medical equipment company, and $15 million in Tesla Karin, a telecommunications firm. There also has been a movement toward teaching Western-style business courses, as well as MBA programs in all the Central European countries.

In Hungary, state-owned hotels have been privatized, and Western firms, attracted by the low cost of highly skilled, professional labor, have been entering into joint ventures with local companies. MNCs also have been making direct investments, as in the case of General Electric's purchase of Tungsram, the giant Hungarian electric company. Another example is Britain's Telfos Holdings, which paid $19 million for 51 percent of Ganz, a Hungarian locomotive and rolling stock manufacturer. Still others include Suzuki's investment of $110 million in a partnership arrangement to produce cars with local manufacturer Autokonzern, Ford Motor's construction of a new $80 million car component plant, and Italy's Ilwa $25 million purchase of the Salgotarjau Iron Works.

Poland had a head start on the other former communist-bloc countries. General political elections were held in June 1989, and the first noncommunist government was established well before the fall of the Berlin Wall. In 1990, the Communist Polish United Workers Party dissolved, and Lech Walesa was elected president. Earlier than its neighbors, Poland instituted radical economic reforms (characterized as "shock therapy"). Although the relatively swift transition to a market economy has been very difficult for the Polish people, with very high inflation initially, continuing unemployment, and the decline of public services, Poland's economy has done relatively well. However, political instability and risk, large external debts, a still-deteriorating infrastructure, and only modest education levels have led to continuing economic problems.

Although Russia, the Czech Republic, Hungary, and Poland are the largest and receive the most media coverage, other former communist countries also are struggling to right their economic ships. A small but particularly interesting example is Albania. Ruled ruthlessly by the Stalinist-style dictator Enver Hoxha for over four decades following World War II, Albania was the last, but most devastated, Eastern European country to abandon communism and institute radical economic reforms. At the beginning of the 1990s, Albania started from zero. Industrial output initially fell over 60 percent, and inflation reached 40 percent monthly. Today, Albania still struggles but is slowly making progress.[51]

The key for Albania and the other Eastern European countries is to maintain the social order, establish the rule of law, rebuild the collapsed infrastructure, and get factories and other value-added, job-producing firms up and running. Foreign investment must be forthcoming for these countries to join the global economy. A key challenge for Albania and the other "have-not" Eastern European countries will be to make themselves less risky and more attractive for international business.

Asia

Despite the severe economic downturn starting in 1997, Asia in general has bounced back and promises to continue being one of the major players in the world economy.[52] Because there are far too many nations to allow for comprehensive coverage here, the following provides insights into the economic status and international management challenges of selected Asian countries.

Japan During the 1970s and 1980s, Japan's economic success had been without precedent. The country had a huge positive trade balance, the yen was strong, and in manufacturing and consumer goods the Japanese became recognized as a world leader.

Analysts ascribe Japan's phenomenal success to a number of factors. Some areas that have received a lot of attention are the Japanese cultural values supporting a strong work ethic and group/team effort, consensus decision making, the motivational effects of guaranteed lifetime employment, and the overall commitment that Japanese workers have to their organizations. However, as seen in "International Management in Action: Separating Myths from Reality," at least some of these assumptions about the Japanese workforce have turned out to be more myth than reality and some of the former strengths have become weaknesses in the new economy. For example, consensus decision making turns out to be too time-consuming in the speed-based new economy.

Some of the early success of the Japanese economy can be attributed to the **Ministry of International Trade and Industry (MITI).** This is a governmental agency that identifies and ranks national commercial pursuits and guides the distribution of national resources to meet these goals. In recent years, MITI has given primary attention to the so-called ABCD industries: automation, biotechnology, computers, and data processing.

Another major reason for Japanese success was the use of **keiretsus.** This Japanese term stands for the large, vertically integrated corporations whose holdings provide much of the assistance needed in providing goods and services to end users. Being able to draw from the resources of the other parts of the keiretsu, a Japanese MNC often can get things done more quickly and profitably than its international competitors.

Over the years, Japanese multinationals have invested billions of dollars abroad. In both the United States and the EU, Japanese auto firms have built new assembly plants. Japanese MNCs have made controversial acquisitions as well, including such well-known U.S. landmarks as Rockefeller Center, the Pebble Beach golf course, and Columbia Pictures. Beginning in the 1990s, however, there was a marked slowdown in overseas investment, and Japan's international holdings declined. This decline was mostly attributable to the slowing of the Japanese economy; however, poor management decisions also played an important role. For example, in the case of Rockefeller Center, Mitsubishi found that it was unable to generate sufficient revenue to pay the huge interest on its mortgage. As a result, it sought protection under American bankruptcy laws, causing a furor among the investors who held the mortgage and demanded the company dip into its corporate coffers and make the payments.[53]

In the past few years, the Japanese economy appears to have begun pulling out of a decade-long recession.[54] The government has had great difficulty correcting the situation. During the 1980s many major Japanese banks made large loans to local businesses. Some of these loans were backed up with real estate, while others were based on projected revenues. In the early 1990s when the Japanese real estate market collapsed, these loans were no longer fully collateralized and the borrowers, in most cases, could not afford to pay the

Ministry of International Trade and Industry (MITI)
A Japanese government agency that identifies and ranks national commercial pursuits and guides the distribution of national resources to meet these goals.

keiretsu
An organizational arrangement in Japan in which a large group of vertically integrated companies bound together by cross-ownership, interlocking directorates, and social ties provide goods and services to end users.

One objective of multicultural research is to learn more about the customs, cultures, and work habits of people in other countries. After all, a business can hardly expect to capture an overseas market without knowledge of the types of goods and services the people there want to buy. Equally important is the need to know the management styles that will be effective in running a foreign operation. Sometimes this information can be quite surprising. For example, recent analysis of Japanese management styles and techniques reveals that much of what Americans "know" about the Japanese may not always be true. Here are some examples that provide food for thought about Japanese management:

1. Many people believe that the Japanese are hardworking by nature. However, recent research shows that there is little difference in productivity among workers in Japanese plants throughout the world. Moreover, many of the differences that do exist are a result of factors such as subcontracting, vendors, and labor regulation. In addition, research among workers at Japanese municipal offices and the national railways shows that many of these workers are not industrious at all.

2. Most Japanese do not have lifelong employment. In fact, about the one-third that did in the past no longer have this security in recent years of the economic downturn. In addition, because of compulsory retirement, many workers must leave their jobs between the ages of 55 and 60. If they do not have a good retirement program or have not saved enough for their later years,

they may have to get another job at a greatly reduced salary.

3. Many Japanese managers are not participative managers; they tend to be autocratic. One study found that almost half of all Japanese executives indicated that they autocratically set annual goals for their division; in contrast, only 32 percent of U.S. managers follow this practice.

4. Young Japanese college graduates entering the workforce express a desire to stay with their firm for a lifetime and say they are willing to work hard to get ahead. After only a few years on the job, however, these attitudes change, and only about one-third feel this way. In short, company loyalty among many Japanese may not be as high as commonly believed.

5. Most Japanese do not work long hours because they enjoy work. The most common reason is that their family needs the money for living expenses. A second common reason is that the boss works long hours, and the staff are afraid to leave the office until the manager does. As a result, many employees end up staying at the office until late in the evening.

These examples show the importance of studying international management and learning via systematic analysis and firsthand information how managers in other countries really do behave toward their employees and their work. Such analysis is critical in separating international management myths from reality.

debt. At the same time, the economy began slowing and many businesses found that with reduced profits they could not meet their loan obligations to the banks. By the turn of the century the situation was so bad that most of the major banks had billions of dollars in uncollectible loans on their books and lacked the financial resources to make additional loans that could help turn around the economy.[55] At the same time the government began insisting that the banks write off their bad loans and straighten out their portfolios. Coupled with these problems, international competition increased and small and medium-sized Japanese firms found themselves scurrying to stay afloat as corporate bankruptcies reached record levels.[56] Yet despite these setbacks, Japan remains a formidable international competitor (the second largest economy behind the United States) and is well poised in all three major economic regions: the Pacific Rim, North America, and Europe.

Japan also has been the target of foreign investment. Automakers such as BMW and Mercedes annually dominate foreign auto sales in the Japanese market. Meanwhile, Ford and General Motors, among others, are working on building market share in the Japanese auto market. IBM, Coca-Cola, Dow, McDonald's, and Toys "R" Us also do well in Japan, collectively accounting for annual sales of over $150 billion. Moreover, the future likely will see even greater progress. Other MNCs, particularly those from the EU and newly industrialized Pacific Rim countries, are targeting the Japanese market as well. Given that Japan relies heavily on exporting to sustain its economic growth, the years ahead should prove to be interesting as international managers from around the world continue to compete against down but not out Japan Inc.

China During the 1980s, China's average annual real economic growth was about 10 percent. From 1990 to 1995 GDP maintained this spectacular rate of growth, and in 2000, despite a severe economic downturn in the late nineties by its Asian neighbors, the awakened giant China reported an annual GDP growth of 8 percent.[57] This continuing growth in tough times shows that its economy is healthy and growing stronger. In 2002, GDP growth was 8 percent, and in 2003, it was 9.1 percent, meeting China's forecasts and providing needed jobs for the continual influx of workers from the countryside. Indeed, some analysts became concerned in late 2003 and 2004 that China's growth was unsustainable after it reported 9.7 percent GDP growth in the first quarter of 2004.[58]

Despite being caught up in the economic problems facing all of Asia, China continues to attract foreign investment.[59] Among others, Motorola has put $120 million into facilities producing semiconductors and mobile phones, General Motors has a $100 million investment in a truck assembly plant, and Procter & Gamble has invested $10 million in a joint-venture factory to produce laundry and personal care products. Additionally, the country's exports remain high, with the United States, Japan, and the EU importing billions of dollars of goods from China every year.[60]

At the same time, however, China remains a major political risk for investors.[61] The one country, two systems (communism and capitalism) is a delicate balance to maintain, and foreign businesses are often caught in the middle. Most MNCs find it very difficult to do business in and with China and many have yet to make a profit. Many of them have also found that product pirating is still common, and while the government has promised to prosecute companies that engage in this illegal and unethical practice, much remains to be done about it. Perhaps even more disconcerting for MNCs is that contractual agreements often prove to be worthless.[62] For example, McDonald's received a long-run lease on property in Beijing and built a large restaurant there; since then the government has told the company that it must move because the entire area is to be razed and turned into a huge office and retail complex. This is not an isolated incident. Outside chemical producers have found themselves facing $10,000-per-product "registration fees," and U.S. law firms operating in Shanghai were forced to close until the government granted them new licenses. German and Japanese banks have found that collecting loans from the government can be extremely difficult as well. In addition, some securities firms have learned that Chinese clients sometimes refuse to pay for trades that turn out to be losers, and there is no government protection for such actions. Simply put, China remains a complicated and high-risk venture. Even so, MNCs know that China with its 1.3 billion people will be a major world market and that they must have a presence there.

The Four Tigers In addition to Japan and China, there are four other widely recognized economic powerhouses in Asia. Note that the traditionally used term "newly industrialized countries" (NICs) is not used because they are not really new anymore. South Korea, Hong Kong, Singapore, and Taiwan have arrived as major economic powers and are now commonly referred to as the "Four Tigers." The GDP of all four had grown rapidly up until the problems starting in the Southeast Asian countries of Thailand, Indonesia, and Malaysia in 1997 began to affect them also.

In South Korea, the major conglomerates, called **chaebols,** include such internationally known firms as Samsung, Daewoo, Hyundai, and the LG Group. Many key managers in these huge firms have attended universities in the West, where in addition to their academic programs, they learned the culture, customs, and language. Now they are able to use this information to help formulate competitive international strategies for their firms. This will be very helpful for South Korea, which among the Four Tigers was hardest hit by the 1997 Southeast Asian economic crisis. Its GDP declined in the late 1990s, and the value of

chaebols
Very large, family-held Korean conglomerates that have considerable political and economic power.

its currency dropped almost 50 percent against the dollar.[63] This led the government to announce plans for investigating the ethical and even illegal practices of the chaebols, privatizing a wide range of industries, and withdrawing some of the restrictions on overall foreign ownership.[64] Since then things have started improving. By 2002, GDP growth had recovered to 6.3 percent, inflation remained low, and new company formations reached an all-time high.[65]

Bordering southeast China and now part of the PRC (People's Republic of China), Hong Kong has been the headquarters for some of the most successful multinational operations in Asia. Hong Kong has had some economic problems like its neighbors but has bounced back. Although it can rely heavily on southeast China for manufacturing, there is still uncertainty about the future and the role that the Chinese government intends to play in local governance.[66] Although the transition has gone smoothly so far, there is the risk that the business climate could radically change. However, the former British colony should continue to play a strong international role in the Pacific Rim.

Singapore is a major success story. It has been hurt least by the economic downturn because of its solid foundation. A major problem Singapore now faces is how to continue expanding this economic foundation in the face of increasing international competition. To date, however, Singapore has emerged as an urban planner's ideal model and the leader and financial center of Southeast Asia. As shown in Table 1–6, Singapore continues to be near the top of the list of the world's most competitive nations.

The fourth Tiger, Taiwan, has progressed from a labor-intensive economy to one that is dominated by more technologically sophisticated industries, including banking, electricity generation, petroleum refining, and computers. Although its economy has also been hit by the downturn in Asia, like the other Tigers it has bounced back and remains a major economic power in the Pacific Rim. China considers Taiwan to be a breakaway province, and this not only continues to be a real threat to geopolitics but also contributes to risk in doing business there. However, Taiwan's government continues to work out its relationship with the mainland to at least maintain the status quo.

Each of the Four Tigers has been the target of foreign MNCs. For example, IBM and Hewlett-Packard, determined to build their local shares of the computer market, have invested in laboratories and factories within these countries. Motorola has followed the same strategy in enlarging its telecommunications market. Other major MNCs in "Tiger Country" range from the Japanese (Matsushita, Nissan, and Sharp) to the Europeans

Table 1–6
The World's Most Competitive Nations, 2004 Ranking

Country	Rank
United States	1
Singapore	2
Canada	3
Australia	4
Iceland	5
Hong Kong	6
Denmark	7
Finland	8
Luxembourg	9
Ireland	10

Source: World Competitive Scoreboard, 2004.

(Volkswagen, Philips, and Nestlé). As a result, the amount of trade and investment occurring between the Four Tigers and the rest of the world continues to expand.

Southeast Asian Countries   Besides Singapore, other countries of Southeast Asia also should be recognized. Although not yet having the economic prowess of the Four Tigers and suffering economic problems starting in 1997, Thailand, Malaysia, Indonesia (sometimes called the "Baby Tigers"), and now Vietnam[67] have economically developed along the lines of the Four Tigers. All have a relatively large population base and inexpensive labor; unlike the Four Tigers, they do have considerable natural resources. These countries were also known to have social stability, but in the aftermath of the economic crisis there has been considerable turmoil in this part of the world, especially in the fourth largest populated country in the world, Indonesia. Nevertheless, as Japan and the Four Tigers have begun to level off and mature, these export-driven Southeast Asian countries remain attractive to outside investors. MNCs from Japan, the Four Tigers, North America, and the EU all want to have a presence in these countries.

Other Developing and Emerging Countries

In contrast to the fully developed countries of North America, Europe, and Asia are the less developed countries (LDCs) around the world. An LDC typically is characterized by two or more of the following: low GDP, slow (or negative) GDP growth per capita, high unemployment, high international debt, a large population, and a workforce that is either unskilled or semiskilled. In some cases, such as in the Middle East, there also is considerable government intervention in economic affairs. Emerging markets are developing economies that exhibit sustained economic reform and growth. Table 1–7 ranks 24 emerging markets by several key indicators. Although complete coverage of all LDCs and emerging economies is beyond the scope of this chapter, the following focuses on representative countries and regions.

India   With a population of about 1 billion and growing, India has traditionally had more than its share of political and economic problems. Per capita GDP remains low, but the recent trend of locating software and other higher value-added services has helped to bolster a large middle- and upper-class market for goods and services. Although India's economic growth does not compare with that of countries such as China, there has been a steady growth in recent years. The government continues its attempt to attract investors and further stimulate economic growth.

For a number of reasons, India is attractive to multinationals, and especially to U.S. and British firms. Many Indian people speak English and are very well educated and are known for advanced information technology expertise. Also, the Indian government is providing funds for economic development. For example, India is expanding its telecommunication systems and increasing the number of phone lines fivefold, a market that AT&T is vigorously pursuing. Many frustrations remain in doing business in India (see "In the International Spotlight" at the end of this chapter), but there is little question that the country will receive increased attention in the years ahead.

Middle East and Central Asia   Israel, the Arab countries, Iran, Turkey, and the Central Asian countries of the former Soviet Union are considered by the World Bank to be LDCs. Because of their oil, however, some people would consider these countries to be economically rich. Recently, this region has been in the world news because of the aftermath of the September 11, 2001, terrorism attack on the United States. However, these countries continue to try to balance the geopolitical, religious forces with economic viability. For example, Israel has been hard hit by inflation, and although the GDP per capita in 2002 was $19,500, there are balance-of-payment problems. Economic problems continue to plague all the countries in the region. Despite the tragedies and economic problems, the Middle East countries continue to be active in the international business arena, and students of

Table 1–7
Market Potential Indicators Ranking for Emerging Markets, 2003

Countries	Market Size	Market Growth	Market Intensity	Market Consumption Capacity	Commercial Infrastructure	Economic Freedom	Market Receptivity	Country Risk
Hong Kong	21	13	1	18	1	2	2	2
Singapore	24	19	9	—	2	7	1	13
South Korea	6	16	4	3	3	9	9	1
Israel	22	9	3	6	5	6	4	4
China	1	8	24	8	15	24	18	12
Hungary	23	17	7	1	6	4	8	3
Czech Republic	10	18	16	2	4	3	5	5
Poland	10	10	2	4	7	8	14	15
India	2	12	20	10	13	16	23	14
Mexico	5	3	6	17	14	11	6	10
Chile	18	5	10	20	8	1	11	8
Thailand	16	7	21	11	17	10	7	11
Malaysia	17	1	23	16	16	21	3	6
Turkey	9	2	13	9	11	19	13	21
Russia	3	21	22	15	8	22	15	7
Indonesia	7	6	15	7	23	18	12	23
Brazil	4	11	19	21	12	14	22	20
Peru	20	15	11	12	22	12	21	9
Egypt	13	4	5	5	24	23	20	16
Philippines	12	20	14	14	21	13	10	17
South Africa	8	14	17	22	19	4	16	18
Venezuela	14	23	12	13	20	19	17	22
Argentina	11	24	8	—	10	15	24	24
Colombia	15	22	18	19	18	17	19	19

Source: GlobalEdge.

international management should have a working knowledge of these countries' customs, culture, and management practices.

The Arab and Central Asian countries rely almost exclusively on oil production. The price of oil greatly fluctuates, and the Organization of Petroleum Exporting Countries (OPEC) has trouble holding together its cartel. In recent years the price has been relatively high, and world demand is likely to keep it there.

Most industrial nations rely, at least to some degree, on imported oil, and Arab countries have invested billions of dollars in U.S. property and businesses. Many people around the world, including those in the West, work for Arab employers. For example, the bankrupt United Press International was purchased by the Middle East Broadcasting Centre, a London-based MNC owned by the Saudis.

Africa   Even though they have considerable natural resources, on the whole African nations remain very poor and undeveloped, and international trade is not a major source of income. Although African countries do business with developed countries, it is on a limited scale. One major problem of doing business in the African continent is the overwhelming diversity of about 750 million people divided into 3,000 tribes that speak 1,000 languages and dialects. Also, there is political instability in many countries with the associated risks, especially as far as direct foreign investment is concerned.

In recent years, Africa, especially sub-Saharan Africa, has had a number of severe problems. In addition to tragic tribal wars, there has been the spread of terrible diseases such as AIDS and Ebola. In 2002–2003, the WTO agreed to relax intellectual property rights (IPR) rules to allow for greater and less costly access by African countries to antiviral AIDS medications (see the In-Depth Integrative Case at the end of Part I). While globalization has opened up new markets for developed countries, developing nations in Africa lack the institutions, infrastructure, and economic capacity to take full advantage of these opportunities.[68] Other big problems include poverty, starvation, illiteracy, corruption, social breakdown, vanishing resources, overcrowded cities, drought, and homeless refugees. There is still hope in the future for Africa despite this bleak situation, however, because African countries remain virtually untapped. Not only are there considerable natural resources, but the diversity can also be used to advantage. For example, many African people are familiar with the European cultures and languages of the former colonial powers (e.g., English, French, Dutch, and Portuguese), which can serve them well in international business. Also, the spirit of these emerging countries has not been broken. There are continuing efforts to stimulate economic growth.[69] Examples of what can be done include Togo, which has sold off many of its state-owned operations and leased a steel-rolling mill to a U.S. investor, and Guinea, which has sold off some of its state-owned enterprises and cut its civil service force by 30 percent. A special case is South Africa, where apartheid, the former white government's policies of racial segregation and oppression, has been dismantled and the healing process is progressing. Long-jailed former black president Nelson Mandela is recognized as a world leader. These significant developments have led to an increasing number of the world's MNCs returning to South Africa; however, there continue to be both social and economic problems that, despite Mandela's and his successors' best efforts, signal uncertain times for the years ahead. One major initiative is the country's Black Economic Empowerment (BEE) program, designed to reintegrate the disenfranchised majority into business and economic life.

The World of *BusinessWeek*—Revisited

Having read this chapter, you should now be more cognizant of the impacts of globalization and worldwide economic developments on international management. Although controversial, globalization appears unstoppable. The creation of free-trade agreements worldwide has helped to trigger economic gains in many developing nations. The consolidation and expansion of the EU will continue to open up borders and make it easier and more cost-effective for exporters from less developed countries to do business there. In Asia, formerly closed economies such as India and China have opened up, and other emerging Asian countries such as South Korea, Singapore, Malaysia, and Thailand have begun to bounce back from the economic crises of the late 1990s. Continued efforts to privatize, deregulate, and liberalize many industries will increase consumer choice and lower prices as competition increases. At the same time, however, continued concerns over the negative spillovers from globalization will remain and may even grow in the coming years. In particular, concerns over offshoring of jobs from developed to developing countries has created insecurity in developed countries while generating economic opportunities in emerging economies.

In light of these developments, answer the following questions: (1) What are some of the pros and cons of globalization and free trade? (2) How does offshoring affect developed and developing countries differently? (3) Which regions of the world are most likely to benefit from globalization and integration in the years to come, and which may experience dislocations?

SUMMARY OF KEY POINTS

1. Globalization—the process of increased integration among countries—continues at an accelerated pace, creating opportunities and challenges for the global economy and international management.

2. International trade and investment have been increasing dramatically over the years. Major multinational corporations (MNCs) have holdings throughout the world, from North America to Europe to the Pacific Rim to Africa. Some of these holdings are a result of direct investment; others are partnership arrangements with local firms. Small firms also are finding that they must seek out international markets to survive in the future. The internationalization of nearly all business has arrived.

3. International economic activity is most pronounced in the triad of North America, Europe, and the Pacific Rim. In North America, the United States, Canada, and Mexico have the North American Free Trade Agreement (NAFTA), which is turning the region into one giant market. In South America, there is an increasing amount of intercountry trade, sparked by Mercosur and the Andean Pact nations. Additionally, trade agreements such as the Central American Free Trade Agreement (CAFTA) and others are linking countries of the Western Hemisphere together, perhaps culminating in a Free Trade Agreement of the Americas (FTAA).

4. In Europe, the 15 original countries of the European Union (EU) as of 2003 form a major economic power, and the former communist countries to the east are seeking membership in the EU. The Central European countries of the Czech Republic, Poland, and Hungary already are becoming trading partners, and if Russia and the other Eastern European countries make progress in their transformation efforts, then Greater Europe will be an even more formidable market in the future.

5. Although having economic problems and uncertainty like the rest of the world, Asia is another major regional power, as shown not only by Japan but also the economies of China and the Four Tigers (Singapore, South Korea, Hong Kong, and Taiwan). Other areas of the world, including India, the Middle East and Central Asia, and Africa, continue to have complex problems but still hold economic promise for the future. Emerging markets in all regions present both opportunities and challenges for international managers.

KEY TERMS

chaebols, *25*
European Research Corporation Agency (Eureka), *19*
Free Trade Agreement of the Americas (FTAA), *10*
globalization, *7*

international management, *6*
keiretsu, *23*
maquiladora, *17*
Ministry of International Trade and Industry (MITI), *23*
MNC, *6*

North American Free Trade Agreement (NAFTA), *10*
offshoring, *9*
World Trade Organization (WTO), *9*

REVIEW AND DISCUSSION QUESTIONS

1. How has globalization affected different world regions? What are some of the benefits and costs of globalization for different sectors of society (companies, workers, communities)?

2. How do NAFTA and CAFTA affect the economies of the Americas? What importance do these economic pacts have for international managers in Europe and Asia?

3. How has the formation of the EU created new opportunities for member countries? Of what importance are these opportunities to international managers in other geographic regions such as North America or Asia?

4. Why are Russia and Eastern Europe of interest to international managers? Identify and describe some reasons for such interest.

5. Many MNCs have secured a foothold in Asia, and many more are looking to develop business relations there. Why does this region of the world hold such interest for international management? Identify and describe some reasons for such interest.

6. Why would MNCs be interested in South America, India, the Middle East and Central Asia, and Africa, the LDCs of the world? Would MNCs be better off focusing their efforts on more industrialized regions? Explain.

ANSWERS TO THE IN-CHAPTER QUIZ

1. **c.** Gillette, a U.S.-based MNC, owns the Braun company.
2. **d.** Bic SA is a French company.
3. **b.** The British MNC Grand Metropolitan PLC recently sold Häagen-Dazs to The Pillsbury Company of the United States.
4. **a.** Thomson SA of France produces RCA televisions.
5. **a.** Britain's Grand Metropolitan PLC also sold the Green Giant product line to The Pillsbury Company of the United States.
6. **a.** Godiva chocolate is owned by Campbell Soup, an American firm.

7. **b.** Vaseline is manufactured by the Anglo-Dutch MNC Unilever PLC.
8. **d.** Wrangler jeans are made by the VF Corporation based in the United States.
9. **d.** Holiday Inn is owned by Britain's Bass PLC, recently renamed Six Continents.
10. **c.** Tropicana orange juice was purchased by U.S.-based PepsiCo.

INTERNET EXERCISE: FRANCHISE OPPORTUNITIES AT McDONALD'S

One of the best-known franchise operations in the world is McDonald's; and in recent years the company has been working to expand its international presence. Why? Because the U.S. market is becoming saturated and the major growth opportunities lie in the international arena. Visit the McDonald's Web site **www.mcdonalds.com** and find out what is going on in the company. Begin by perusing the latest annual report and see how well the company is doing both domestically and internationally. Then turn to the franchise information that is provided and find out how much it would cost to set up a franchise in the following countries: Belgium, Brazil, South Korea, Mexico, Slovenia, and Turkey. Which seems the most attractive

international investment? In addition to this group, in what other countries is the firm seeking franchisees? Would any of these seem particularly attractive to you as investor? Which ones? Why?

Then, based on this assignment and the chapter material, answer these last three questions: (1) Will the fact the euro has become the standard currency in the EU help or hinder a new McDonald's franchisee in Europe? (2) If there are exciting worldwide opportunities, why does McDonald's not exploit these itself instead of looking for franchisees? (3) What is the logic in McDonald's expansion strategy?

India

India is located in southern Asia, with the Bay of Bengal on the east and the Arabian Sea on the west. One-sixth of the world's population (approximately 1 billion people) lives within the country's 1.27 million square miles. Though Hindi is the dominant language in terms of number of speakers (it is the mother tongue to over 40 percent of Indians), India is essentially a multilingual nation with more than 10 other languages spoken by 20 million people or more. These include Telugu, Tamil, Marathi, and Bengali. Most states are divided along linguistic lines, with that language accepted as the "official" language in different states (one each). English serves as the national language among the educated Indians. Higher education in science and engineering is in English. The Indian economy derives only a quarter of its output from agriculture, with services contributing almost 55 percent. However, more than 70 percent of Indians are directly or indirectly dependent on agriculture. Three quarters of Indians live in over 600,000 villages. Many of these communities lack infrastructure such as roads, power, and telecommunications. Hence, India's rural population presents a huge untapped potential for many marketers. The country operates as a democratic republic, and for the most part, one party has dominated the government since independence in 1947. At that time, India was born of the partition of the former British Indian empire into the new countries of India and Pakistan. This division has been a source of many problems through the years. For example, much to the dismay of the world community, both countries had nuclear tests in a cold war atmosphere. Also, many millions of Indians still live at the lowest level of subsistence, and the per capita income is very low. India's misaligned central and local public finances have contributed to an overall fiscal deficit of more than 10 percent of GDP.

In the past, doing business in India has been quite difficult. For example, it took PepsiCo three years just to set up a soft drink concentrate factory, and Gillette, the U.S. razor blade company, had to wait eight years for its application to enter the market to be accepted. Additionally, many MNCs have complained that there are too many barriers to effective operations. In the mid-1970s, the country changed its rules and required that foreign partners hold no more than 40 percent ownership in any business. As a result, some MNCs left India.

In recent years, the government has been relaxing its bureaucratic rules, particularly those relating to foreign investments. From 1981 to 1991, total foreign direct investment in India increased by $250 million, and between 1991 and 1993, it jumped by an additional $2.5 billion. In 2000, foreign direct investment exceeded $3 billion and is projected to grow by 7 percent in 2004. Most of this investment has come from the United States and nonresident Indians. One reason for this change in the nation's policies toward business is that the government realizes many MNCs are making a critical choice: India or China? Any monies not invested in India may be lost to China forever. Additionally, it can be seen that foreign investments are having a very positive effect on the Indian economy. After the first big year of new investments (1991), India's annual GDP jumped to over 4 percent. In 2003, GDP increased by more than 8 percent.

With the disbandment of the "License Raj," a socialist-inspired system that made government permits mandatory for almost every aspect of business, the climate for foreign investment has improved markedly. Coca-Cola was able to get permission for a 100-percent-owned unit in India in eight weeks, and Motorola received clearance in two days to add a new product line—and did all of this via fax. Other companies that have reported rapid progress include DaimlerChrysler, Procter & Gamble, and Whirlpool. At the same time, however, not everything is roses. Many MNCs are still reporting problems.

Nevertheless, the Indian government's new approach is helping a great deal. In addition, there are other attractions that entice MNCs to India. These include (1) a large number of highly educated people, especially in critically short-supply areas such as medicine, engineering, and computer science; (2) widespread use of English, long accepted as the international language of business; and (3) low wages and salaries, which often are 10 to 30 percent of those in the world's economic superpowers. While these factors will continue to have a positive impact, the growing debate over jobs outsourced from the United States could dampen some of the impressive growth prospect for India. In addition, the election upset of May 2004, in which the opposition National Congress Party defeated the ruling BJP Party, suggests Indians are concerned about attention to social needs, not just economic growth.

www.ib-net.com

Questions

1. What is the climate for doing business in India? Is it supportive of foreign investment?

2. How important is a highly educated human resource pool for MNCs wanting to invest in India? Is it more important for some businesses than for others?

3. Given the low per capita income of the country, why would you still argue for India to be an excellent place to do business in the coming years?

Here Comes the Competition

The Wadson Company is a management research firm headquartered in New Jersey. The company was recently hired by a large conglomerate with a wide range of products, ranging from toys to electronics and financial services. This conglomerate wants Wadson to help identify an acquisition target. The conglomerate is willing to spend up to $2.5 billion to buy a major company anywhere in the world.

One of the things the research firm did was to identify the amount of foreign direct investment in the United States by overseas companies. The research group also compiled a list of major acquisitions by non-U.S. companies. It gathered these data to show the conglomerate the types of industries and companies that are currently attractive to the international buyers. "If we know what outside firms are buying," the head of the research firm noted, "this can help us identify similar overseas businesses that may also have strong growth potential. In this way, we will not confine our list of recommendations to U.S. firms only." In terms of direct foreign investment by industry, the researchers found that the greatest investment was being made in manufacturing (almost $100 billion). Then, in descending order, came wholesale trade, petroleum, real estate, and insurance.

On the basis of this information, the conglomerate has decided to purchase a European firm. "The best acquisitions in the United States have already been picked," the president told the board of directors. "However, I'm convinced that there are highly profitable enterprises in Europe that are ripe for the taking. I'd particularly like to focus my attention on France and Germany." The board gave the president its full support, and the research firm will begin focusing on potential European targets within the next 30 days.

Questions

1. Is Europe likely to be a good area for direct investment during the years ahead?

2. Why is so much foreign money being invested in U.S. manufacturing? Based on your conclusions, what advice would be in order for the conglomerate?

3. If the conglomerate currently does not do business in Europe, what types of problems is it likely to face?

Chapter 2

THE POLITICAL, LEGAL, AND TECHNOLOGICAL ENVIRONMENT

The environment that international managers face is changing rapidly. The past is proving to be a poor indicator of what will happen in the future. Changes are not only more common now but also more significant than ever before, and these dramatic forces of change are creating new challenges. Although there are many dimensions in this new environment, most relevant to international management would be the economic environment that was covered in the last chapter and the cultural environment covered in the chapters of Part 2. Also important are the political, legal and regulatory, and technological dimensions of the environment. The objective of this chapter is to examine how the political, legal and regulatory, and technological environments have changed in recent years. Some major trends in each that will help dictate the world in which international managers will compete also are presented. The specific objectives of this chapter are:

1. **EXAMINE** some of the major changes that are currently taking place in the political environment of China, Europe, Russia, and Central and Eastern Europe.

2. **PRESENT** an overview of the legal and regulatory environment in which MNCs operate worldwide.

3. **REVIEW** key technological developments as well as their impact on MNCs now and in the future.

The World of *BusinessWeek*

BusinessWeek

The Milk Just Keeps On Spilling

Why Did Many Big Banks Keep Floating Parmalat's Debt?

The prisoners have been talking. And talking. From his cell at Milan's gloomy 18th century San Vittore prison, Calisto Tanzi has admitted to magistrates that he cooked the books for more than a decade—and skimmed off at least $640 million from his publicly traded dairy company, Parmalat, to plug losses at family businesses. Parmalat's ex-chief financial officer Fausto Tonna has provided some fifty hours of testimony detailing how he and Tanzi pulled off the biggest fraud in European financial history. Both were arrested in December along with seven other Parma executives, accountants, and advisers on suspicion of false accounting, fraud, and market-rigging after the globe-spanning dairy company went belly-up.

You've heard many of the details: The $13 billion in missing assets that no one can account for. The $5 billion Bank of America account that didn't exist—and the forged letter on BofA stationery that allegedly fooled auditors into thinking it did. The bewildering constellation of offshore subsidiaries. The faked invoices for hundreds of millions in bogus sales. The $640 million of Parmalat funds gone missing in the Cayman Islands investment fund. The family travel business, Parmatour, run by daughter Francesca, that received a mysterious series of cash infusions. More revelations surface every day.

But there's a parallel tale to this Italian family saga. It's a story of globalization gone wrong. Evidence is emerging that many investment bankers in Italy, Germany, and London harbored doubts about Parmalat's numbers for years,

Once Italian regulators started asking questions, it didn't take long for the web of fraud to unravel

JAN.-FEB., 2003
Reports circulate among bankers about Parmalat's balance sheet and high level of debt.

MARCH, 2003
Italian stock market authority Consob requests an explanation for the company's high cash reserves given the elevated level of debt.

AUG. 6, 2003
Consob demands to see audit work for 2002 done by Deloitte Touche and Grant Thornton. The firms provide documents by Sept. 23.

OCT. 31, 2003
Deloitte admits it does not have sufficient information to certify first-half accounts.

NOV. 11, 2003
Company publishes Deloitte's Oct. 31 report, revealing a $640 million Parmalat investment in a Cayman Islands fund called Epicurum.

DEC. 8, 2003
Parmalat fails to repay a $192 million bond issue that comes due, setting off trading panic.

DEC. 9, 2003
Tanzi and son Stefano admit to executives from private equity fund Blackstone that Parmalat's financial accounts are inaccurate.

DEC. 15, 2003
Tanzi resigns and is replaced by turnaround specialist Enrico Bondi.

DEC. 17, 2003
Bank of America declares an alleged $5 billion Parmalat account does not exist and that a letter confirming the funds to the auditor was forged.

DEC. 22-24, 2003
Parmalat shares suspended from trading. Italian officials declare Parmalat bankrupt.

Data: *BusinessWeek*, OECO, Hoover's.

Source: www.businessweek.com/magazine/content/04_04/b3867075_mz054.htm

suspicious of its superheated growth. They also wondered why an Italian dairy company needed to raise so much debt if it had billions in cash. Other banks, meanwhile, liked what they saw: a fast-growing company in an easy-to-understand business, with books audited by one of the Big Four—all good reasons to court Parmalat for its steady business in stock and bond offerings.

Beyond Crony Capitalism

Did Parmalat's banks, then, deliberately ignore the warning signs? Or were they, too, taken in by the colossal fraud, as most of them vigorously claim? One thing is clear: The global clout of the top banks helped spread the mayhem among investors from London to Alaska. Some $1.5 billion in Parmalat bonds were sold to U.S. investors alone, mainly through private placements. Bankers, accountants, legal advisers—even some members of Calisto Tanzi's family—all claim they had no idea what was going on. "What's appalling is that the mistakes were made by many banks all over the world. This goes beyond crony capitalism in Italy. Parmalat was a totally international affair," says Valter Lazzari, professor of banking and finance at Bocconi University in Milan.

The next bombshells from the Parmalat affair, therefore, are likely to concern the bankers, accountants, and other financial advisers who worked with the company over nearly two decades. A U.S.-based class action filed Jan. 5 on behalf of Parmalat investors targets Citigroup, Deloitte Touche Tohmatsu, and Grant Thornton International, in addition to Parmalat management. The charges range from assisting in manipulative financial transactions to participation in the falsification of audit-confirmation documents. Citigroup and Deloitte firmly deny wrongdoing, insisting they were victims of the fraud: "We believe [the suit] is baseless and without

merit," says a Citigroup spokesman. Deloitte points out that it alerted investors to problems late in 2003. A Grant Thornton International spokesperson says the firm feels it is not liable, and that its former Italian partnership should bear responsibility if there was misdoing.

The pressure on the banks, though, keeps growing. Italian magistrates raided the Milan offices of Deutsche Bank. They are also questioning officials at Bank of America and Citigroup in Italy, as well as the top execs at Italy's largest banks. Prosecutors suspect some outsiders from banks, law firms, and accounting companies were involved in the fraud. Those close to the investigation say the Parmalat dragnet could also ensnare members of Italy's financial establishment. "Everyone is running for cover," says one banker.

Several bankers told *BusinessWeek* they suspected trouble at Parmalat years before its fall. "Things have been strange [there] since the mid-1980s," says one senior investment banker, who steered clear of all business with the company. "It smelled bad." As the fast-growing dairy group returned time and again to the markets—issuing some $8 billion in bonds between 1993 and 2003—analysts, investment bankers, and fund managers all began questioning Parmalat's hunger for debt despite its seeming mountain of cash.

Tonna's standard reply: The company was on an acquisition spree and needed cash—and the liquid funds were earning good returns. By early 2003, equity analysts were becoming increasingly dubious. "The actual size of Parmalat's net financial debt is, in our view, much higher than the $2.3 billion reported by the company," said an analyst at Auerbach Grayson & Co. on Jan. 24, 2003, putting the figure at $4.5 billion. A research report sent to investors by Merrill Lynch & Co. as well as internal reports by Lehman Brothers Inc. and Goldman, Sachs & Co. also raised questions. "If a company like Parma is very, very well managed, it earns about 6% to 7% operating margins. Parmalat was reporting 12%," says one Milan banker.

Reassuring Reports

Some banks issued reassuring research reports until a month before the collapse. An October equity report by Deutsche Bank rated Parmalat's shares a buy, noting strong cash flow, which warranted a higher premium. Citibank issued an optimistic bulletin on the company in November. That was shortly before Parmalat failed to meet a $184 million payment to bondholders and admitted, under pressure from Deloitte, that it could not liquidate some $640 million the dairy company said it held in a Cayman Islands fund named Epicurum. Financial markets panicked, and CEO Tanzi appointed turnaround specialist Enrico Bondi as adviser. But when Bondi suggested liquidating a $5 billion Bank of America account to pay debts, "the rabbit popped out of the hat," in the words of one banker: The bank account was fictitious.

Long before that day of reckoning, Parmalat had a spectacular run, tapping regularly into global markets after it went public in 1990. Between 1990 and 2003, Parmalat raised a total of about $8 billion in debt globally. Bank of America arranged $743 million in debt sales between 1997 and 2002. Chase Manhattan, Bank of Boston, and Merrill Lynch together sold $290 million of debt. The cash injections fueled frenetic growth, including 17 acquisitions in 1993 alone, boosting revenues from $800 million in 1990 to $9.7 billion.

Hiding a Pile of Losses

Tanzi and Tonna admitted to investigating magistrates that they falsified accounts to hide growing losses from their

Latin American businesses and keep raising money. Tanzi found international investment banks willing to help until nearly the end. Deutsche Bank purchased a significant amount of Parmalat's shares just one month prior to the revelation from Bank of America. The sell-off came two days after BofA, when asked by Grant Thornton to verify the $5 billion Parmalat claimed it held at the bank, told the auditors, and then the Securities & Exchange Commission, that no such account existed. Deutsche Bank officials insist the purchase was made on behalf of another client and decline to comment further, except to say they are cooperating with Italian investigators. On Jan. 13, Standard & Poor's said it relied on documents from Deutsche Bank when it retained Parmalat's rating at BBB−, investment grade, only one notch above junk, prior to the September bond issue.

Private-equity firms did sense impending disaster. In a last-minute maneuver, Tanzi and his son Stefano met in Italy with executives of New York private-equity specialist Blackstone Group on Dec. 9 about a possible buyout. During the course of discussions, they confirmed that $12.8 billion was missing from the company's balance sheet, according to a lawsuit filed by the SEC. Blackstone managers refused to work with Parmalat unless it publicly restated its books, and decided to steer clear. Thousands of investors wish they had done the same.

By Gail Edmondson in Parma, with David Fairlamb in Frankfurt, Nanette Byrnes in New York, and bureau reports.

Source: **From "The Milk Just Keeps on Spilling: Why Did Many Big Banks Keep Floating Parmalat's Debt?" by Gail Edmondson,** *BusinessWeek,* **January 26, 2004, pp. 24, 54. Reprinted with permission.**

The opening case provides an excellent example of some of the problems associated with globalization within the context of political, legal, and technological environments. Clouded by long-standing relationships and their commitment to growth, Parmalat's stakeholders—shareholders, government officials, and others—appeared to turn a blind eye to the firm's suspicious financial management practices. Given its global scope, Parmalat's collapse has had an adverse impact in both world consumer and financial markets, especially the U.S. bond market. In an era of accelerating integration and technological advancement, political and legal developments in one region of the world can have profound impacts in many others. MNCs must therefore be sensitive to the changing political, legal, and technological landscape in which they operate.

■ Political Environment

The domestic and international political environment has a major impact on MNCs. As government policies change, MNCs must adjust their strategies and practices to accommodate the new perspectives and actual requirements. Moreover, in a growing number of geographic regions and countries, governments appear to be less stable; therefore, these areas carry more risk than they have in the past. The assessment of political risk will be given specific attention in Chapter 10, but the following examines political developments in selected areas and countries that are particularly relevant to today's international management. While some convergence among political systems is evident, significant differences across countries and regions remain.

China

China is an emerging economic power that cannot be ignored by international business. The Chinese political environment, however, is very complex and risky because of the government's desire to balance national, immediate needs with the challenge of a free market economy and globalization. Since joining the WTO in December 2001, China has made trade liberalization a top priority. For example, at the present time the Chinese government is trying to sustain its economic growth. If growth is slower than 7 percent, the economy will likely not be able to generate enough jobs to take in the more than 10 million Chinese that enter the workforce each year, as well as the millions being laid off by restructured state enterprises. In the past, economic growth was not a problem. In 1992, for example, the country's GDP increased by 14 percent. This rate continued to decline throughout the 1990s, but recently high growth rates have resumed, with GDP growth reaching 9.1 percent in 2003.[1]

In order to ensure that the economy does not fall into the economic malaise that has been sweeping the rest of Asia, the Chinese government has stepped up efforts to encourage foreign investment. Yet, by 2003–2004 there were indications that the country's economic strength was showing signs of fatigue. For example, foreign investment is slowing because cash-starved Asian companies can no longer afford to build in China; and Chinese exporters are seeing overseas business customers shift to less expensive factories in Thailand and Malaysia. At the same time, local unemployment is starting to rise and bad loans are piling up in the state-owned banks.

While the Chinese government has made strides toward a free-market economy, bureaucratic structures still protect many local and state-owned firms from competition. In response, the government has begun giving approval to projects that had been bogged down in bureaucratic red tape and announced a series of steps to open up the economy.[2] Some of these include (1) speeding up a program to convert state enterprises, which still account for a significant amount of industrial output, into corporations owned by shareholders; (2) dramatically expanding the size of capital markets by authorizing hundreds of new stock listings annually in Shanghai and Shenzhen; (3) allowing government bodies to sell off most of the country's 305,000 state enterprises and letting those that could not be sold go bankrupt; (4) accelerating worker retraining, building low-cost housing, and creating other social services to relieve burdens on state enterprises and care for millions of workers who would lose their jobs; and (5) reducing tariffs to 10 percent.[3]

Despite these developments, MNCs face a host of major obstacles when doing business with and in China. For example, government regulations severely hamper multinational activity and favor domestic companies.[4] Additionally, it is difficult to find qualified people, and when a multinational does and then invests money in training these individuals, it is common to find them leaving for jobs with other companies.[5] Yet the biggest problem may well be that the government does not know what it wants from multinational investors, and this is what accounts for the mixed signals and changes in direction that it continually sends. Those who have studied China's economic transition over the past decade have noted that this transition is unusual in that it is planned by a state that maintains an active involvement of governmental institutions in business affairs. This approach is so different from anything that MNCs have previously encountered that the experiences of these firms in other emerging economies is often insufficient to provide them the guidelines and insights that they need to do business in China. In fact, the researchers found, the peculiarities of China's system not only generate uncertainties for MNCs, but the nature of the transition challenges the capabilities of current international business theory.[6]

Typical of the problems faced by multinationals in China is an example provided by Qualcomm Corporation. The firm had wanted to sell China narrowband CDMA (code division multiple access) technology. However, Qualcomm was unsuccessful in convincing the government that it could build enough products locally and this doomed its plans for CDMA production in China, a technology that is in use in the United States and a few other countries. Instead, China's current network, the world's largest mobile network with over 40 million subscribers, will use primarily the GSM technology that is popular in Europe.[7] This was a big blow to Qualcomm, but the company is not alone. China's WTO accession agreement allows it to continue to restrict investment in telecom projects to minority shares, effectively giving the government the green light in mandating that foreign investors partner with Chinese companies.[8] Most MNCs have found that doing business in China is both challenging and frustrating. Here is a recent report of auto firms trying to do business in China:

> The auto companies are especially instructive, because they are some of the highest-profile foreign investors in China. Like most multinationals lured by China's fabled masses, auto companies have wrung their hands in frustration over the strict central control of business deals, the unpredictable unwritten rules and the lack of a functioning legal system. Peugeot, which had an early venture, gave up. DaimlerChrysler has threatened to leave. Profits are nonexistent, except for the biggest players; about 100 companies, including scores of inefficient domestic makers, compete.[9]

Yet the auto firms remain because of the huge market there. In 1990 approximately 58,000 cars were made and sold in China. By 2005, this total was projected to be 25 million. The government allows only a small number of imports, so local production is important, and companies like General Motors, Ford, DaimlerChrysler, Mercedes, Toyota, and other major manufacturers are determined to stay the course. For the time being, however, largely due to the political environment, China remains an elusive, uncertain prize for most MNCs.

Europe

Far away from Chinese politics, the political situation in Europe also continues to change. Although privatization and economic liberalization continue to reinforce EU-wide political and economic integration, leaders in major countries, as well as the EU itself, are finding it difficult to firmly establish a foothold of power. As a result, international managers must remain alert as to how political changes may impact their business.

For example, in France, the 12-year reign of the Socialists under François Mitterrand ended in mid-1995. Mitterrand was replaced by Jacques Chirac, a more conservative Gaullist, and this heralded a host of political changes impacting on doing business in France. The same kind of changes are occurring in the other major European countries. In Germany, Helmut Kohl was re-elected in late 1994 but soon was having troubles. Three months into his new term, he was forced to consider forming a coalition with the opposition Social Democrats, who already controlled the upper house of Parliament. More recently, Gerhard Schröder, subsequent to his 1998 election as chancellor succeeding Kohl, faced a similar situation involving the Green Party. In Great Britain, political change has been even more pronounced. The Labor Party swept into power in 1997 with a strong majority. Since then, under the leadership of Tony Blair, Britain's economy continued to improve, and the government moved more into the middle of the political continuum as seen by one of its programs designed to reduce the welfare roles by offering work incentives to the unemployed.[10] This strategy is a strong reversal of earlier Labor Party philosophy and shows that the winds of political change can alter very quickly. Blair's support of the Iraq War, however, has severely weakened his position, and the future of Labor rule in the U.K. is uncertain.[11] In Spain, voters ousted the ruling party of conservative Prime Minister Jose Maria Aznar in early 2004, apparently in part out of opposition to Aznar's troop commitments in Iraq and close relationship with the United States.[12] More broadly, with the exception of the U.K., most European countries opposed U.S.-led intervention in Iraq, and these sentiments may sometimes spill over into business relationships and dealings.

That the nations of Western Europe, with the exception of Norway and Switzerland, now are part of the EU only adds to the complexity of the political environment. MNCs cannot avoid political risks even when doing business with individual countries because of what the EU may dictate. It is important to realize that there are vast cultural differences, as will be pointed out in Chapter 5, but also that the fate of the EU members is interdependent. Now, what happens to one can often influence the others. A good example is provided by France and Germany. Today, Franco-German relations are the cornerstone of a united Europe. The two are tied closely together in a number of ways. For example, each is the other's major trading partner; each has a vested interest in the other doing well. MNCs doing business in either country find that they must focus on developments in both nations, as well as in the EU at large. Simply put, Europe is no longer a series of fragmented countries; it is a giant and expanding interwoven region in which international management must be aware of what is happening politically not only in the immediate area of operations but also throughout the continent.[13]

Russia

Along with China, Russia presents one of the most extreme examples of how the political environment impacts on international management. Boris Yeltsin governed Russia throughout the 1990s, and when he resigned in 2000 and turned the reins over to Vladimir Putin, the economy was in shambles. Neglect, corruption, and confusing changes in economic policy had taken their toll.[14] The country's infrastructure was literally falling apart. Electricity was regularly cut off throughout the country, gas pipelines sprang leaks on a daily basis, industrial accidents were commonplace, toxic waste seeped from industrial plants into drinking water supplies, and almost half of the country's freight and passenger railroad cars needed to be replaced. Worse yet, the little funds that were available to begin rebuilding the infrastructure were in the hands of inefficient managers.[15] By one estimate, it would take at least $100 billion to minimally rebuild Russia's infrastructure, a sum that is four times the country's current annual budget.

What makes the international business situation even worse is that infrastructure reform such as in the legal, financial, and trade sectors is a political quagmire. For example, President Putin approved an ambitious plan of reform to spur growth by improving conditions for investment and by deregulating the giant Soviet-era enterprises such as the United Energy Systems, the giant electric company, and the Railways Ministry. However, many people are concerned that this will result in higher prices, and they have appealed to top Kremlin officials who have stalled these types of reforms. At the same time, machinery and equipment are breaking down all over the country because there are no funds to pay for repairs, many trains no longer operate, and most roads are pitted with potholes. Highly educated individuals such as scientists and engineers who work in the atomic energy sector, are so poorly paid that many of them are looking for other jobs.

Despite continued economic reforms, the outlook for Russia is still uncertain. President Putin's recent crackdowns on independent media outlets critical of his administration have raised concerns about political and economic freedom.[16] Real GDP growth in 2002 was 4.3 percent, but this was down from 6 percent growth in 2000.[17] Moreover, monthly inflation that stood at almost 40 percent in August 1998 had fallen to around 15 percent by mid-2002.[18] In addition, Putin's administration has gotten a tax reform bill enacted that both simplifies the tax code and slashes tax rates. Under the new law, individuals pay a flat tax of 13 percent on income, and business payroll taxes have been cut. This is good news for the country's middle class that has weathered the economic crisis of 1998 and is looking for a stable economy. Many of these people are entrepreneurs who own their own shops, restaurants, hotels, bakeries, and computer software firms or are managers of large Russian enterprises or multinational firms. In this country of 145 million, there are around 30 million people in the middle, and this group accounts for 30 percent of the country's $1.4 trillion gross domestic product.[19] So there is a large, productive group of people in Russia that can also be a market for outside MNC goods and services.

The challenge for the Russian government is to keep the economy on an even keel while attracting more foreign investment. One of the big problems is corruption. The European Bank for Reconstruction and Development reports that almost a third of firms

---

Table 2–1
Key Elements of Russia's WTO Accession Deal with the EU

Tariffs

Russia will not exceed an average tariff level of 7.6% for industrial goods, 11% for fishery products, and 13% for agricultural goods.

Tariff rate quotas for fresh and frozen meat and poultry will be around €600 million ($720 million) per year.

Energy

Russian gas prices to domestic industrial users will gradually be increased.

Russia's state gas corporation, Gazprom, will retain its export monopoly. Export duties on gas will be capped at 30%.

Airlines

Russia will revamp the charges currently applied to EU airlines flying over Siberia to make them cost-based and nondiscriminatory.

Banking

Russia will maintain a ban on foreign banks opening branches.

Under existing rules, foreign banks are allowed to open only wholly or partly owned subsidiaries.

Services

Russia has committed to cross-border provision and commercial establishment of certain services.

Sectors include telecoms, transport, financial services, postal, construction, distribution, environmental, news agency, and tourism.

Source: Reuters.

---

doing business in Russia indicate that they are required to give bribes in order to do business and that these monies add more than 4 percent to the overall cost of doing business there.[20] As more MNCs invest in Russia, these unethical practices will face increasing scrutiny.[21] To date, many multinationals feel that the risk is too great. Still, most view Russia as they do China; it is too large and potentially lucrative a market to ignore. This is why General Motors recently struck a deal to manufacture cars in Russia. GM has partnered with Avtovaz, the country's largest domestic carmaker, to produce sport utility vehicles under the Chevrolet brand name. GM joins others, including BMW, Fiat, Ford, and Renault, that currently have Russian operations. There is a big demand for cars. Only 12 percent of Russians now own an auto, compared to 25 percent of the population of Poland. However, most Russians cannot afford to pay much for an auto. Analysts estimate that no more than 30,000 people can buy a car that costs $10,000 or more. On the other hand, if the economy continues to improve, these auto firms, like other foreign investors, will find that their decision to invest was a wise one. A lot of what happens, however, will be determined by the political environment.[22] One positive development occurred in May 2004 when Russia and the EU agreed on terms for Russia's entry into the WTO, a significant step in Russia's long-standing efforts to join the group (see Table 2–1).[23]

Central and Eastern Europe

Besides Russia, the political situation in the rest of the postcommunist countries in Central and Eastern Europe is also in a state of flux. As of May 2004, many of these countries, including Poland, Hungary, and the Czech Republic, had joined the EU.[24] These nations have undergone tremendous economic reforms in preparation for joining the EU. However, many problems remain as these countries merge with the existing EU structure and work to make the transition from a centrally planned to a market economy. A good example is Poland.

In late 1997 Polish voters replaced a government of former communists and brought in a coalition of trade unionists, nationalists, and free marketers. Since then, the government's plan to streamline the economy and get the country moving has been fraught with problems.

By the end of 2002, the unemployment rate stood at 18 percent, and there were high unemployment pockets in the agriculture and industrial sectors. In addition, the Russian crisis and an economic slowdown in the EU had dampened Polish exports; however, inflation had fallen to about 2 percent in 2002, and as the EU economies begin to improve, things will continue to get better.

Hungary, one of the strongest economies in Central Europe, had annual GDP increases of over 5 percent in both 2000 and 2001, with GDP growth of 3.3 percent in 2002. Unemployment was below 7 percent, and consumer price inflation, which was as high as 30 percent in 1995, is now in the range of 6 percent. The government is trying to maintain a positive investment image, which will be important given that foreign investors have put more money per capita into Hungary than anywhere else in postcommunist Europe and they want to see results. The future success of Hungary will depend heavily on the ability of the government to maintain this economic momentum in the face of accession to the EU.[25]

The Czech Republic in its transition privatized very quickly, gambling that private owners could reorganize and manage firms more effectively than the state. The government also allowed Czech citizens to bid for shares in newly privatized firms—and for a time the country was pointed to as one of the success stories in Central Europe. However, in the late 1990s the country went into a recession, its trade deficit ballooned, and there was negative economic growth of almost 3 percent. Since then things have started to turn around. By late 2002 the economy was growing at an annual rate of almost 4 percent, supported by growing exports to EU members. While high current accounts deficits stemming from high demand for imports persist, private economic activity remained strong throughout 2003.[26]

The governments of the Balkan countries (e.g., Bulgaria, Romania, and Albania) and, with the possible exception of the Baltic states (Estonia, Latvia, and Lithuania), the republics of the former Soviet Union still face severe problems. The governments of these former communist countries all went at the necessary economic reforms (freeing up prices, privatization, elimination of subsidies, and building the needed financial and legal systems and supporting infrastructure) at a much slower pace than Poland, Hungary, or the Czech Republic. Now, they are paying the price with generally depressed economies and lack of foreign investment. Conversely, the Baltic states—Estonia, Latvia, and Lithuania—have been successful in streamlining reforms.

The Middle East

Conducting business in the Middle East is, in many ways, similar to operating a business in the Western world. A thorough knowledge of the regulations governing business activities, the legal environment, tax regimes, accepted accounting methods, business structures, import/export regulations, manpower and labor regulations, restrictions on foreign capital, investment incentives, and the presence of exchange controls is necessary to succeed in the region. The Arab countries have been a generally positive place to do business, for many of these nations are seeking modern technology and most have the financial ability to pay for quality services. Worldwide fallout from the war on terrorism, the Afghanistan and Iraq wars, and the ongoing Israel-Arab conflicts, however, have raised tensions in the Middle East considerably, making the business environment there risky and potentially dangerous.

It is impossible to establish meaningful business relationships in the Middle East without some understanding and knowledge of Islam. Today, for a fifth of the world's population (about 1 billion followers) who are Muslim, Islam is both a religion and a way of life. For Muslims, Islam provides a framework of life and society. It is a simple, personal, religion of peace, mercy, and forgiveness. In recent years, radical Islamic fundamentalist groups preaching anti-Western rhetoric have taken up aggression against the United States and its global allies. Most notable are the September 11, 2001 attacks on the United States and the March 2004 train bombing in Madrid, Spain. As a result, many nations, including Iraq, Iran, and Syria, have become targets of antiterrorism movements, making conducting business for Westerners both difficult and risky.[27] In June 2004, the U.S. State Department released a warning recommending that U.S. citizens in Saudi Arabia on nonessential business leave the country.[28]

■ Legal and Regulatory Environment

One reason why today's international environment is so confusing and challenging for MNCs is that they face many different laws and regulations in their global business operations. These factors affect the way businesses are developed and managed within host nations, so special consideration must be paid to the subtle differences in the legal codes from one country to another. Adhering to disparate legal frameworks sometimes prevents large MNCs from capitalizing on manufacturing economies of scale and scope within these regions. In addition, the sheer complexity and magnitude requires special attention. This, in turn, results in slower time to market and greater costs. MNCs must take time to carefully evaluate the legal framework in each market in which they do business before launching products or services in those markets.

There are four foundations on which laws are based around the world. Briefly summarized, these are:

Islamic law
Law that is derived from interpretation of the Qur'an and the teachings of the Prophet Muhammad and is found in most Islamic countries.

socialist law
Law that comes from the Marxist socialist system and continues to influence regulations in countries formerly associated with the Soviet Union as well as China.

common law
Law that derives from English law and is the foundation of legislation in the United States, Canada, and England, among other nations.

civil or code law
Law that is derived from Roman law and is found in the non-Islamic and nonsocialist countries.

principle of sovereignty
An international principle of law which holds that governments have the right to rule themselves as they see fit.

nationality principle
A jurisdictional principle of international law which holds that every country has jurisdiction over its citizens no matter where they are located.

territoriality principle
A jurisdictional principle of international law which holds that every nation has the right of jurisdiction within its legal territory.

1. **Islamic law.** This is law derived from interpretation of the Qur'an and the teachings of the Prophet Muhammad. It is found in most Islamic countries in the Middle East and Central Asia.

2. **Socialist law.** This law comes from the Marxist socialist system and continues to influence regulations in former communist countries, especially those from the former Soviet Union, as well as present-day China, Vietnam, North Korea, and Cuba. Since socialist law requires most property to be owned by the state or state-owned enterprises, MNCs have traditionally shied away from these countries.

3. **Common law.** This comes from English law, and it is the foundation of the legal system in the United States, Canada, England, Australia, New Zealand, and other nations.

4. **Civil or code law.** This law is derived from Roman law and is found in the non-Islamic and nonsocialist countries such as France, some countries in Latin America, and even Louisiana in the United States.

With these broad statements serving as points of departure, the following sections discuss basic principles and examples of the international legal environment facing MNCs today.

Basic Principles of International Law

When compared with domestic law, international law is less coherent because its sources embody not only the laws of individual countries concerned with any dispute but also treaties (universal, multilateral, or bilateral) and conventions (such as the Geneva Convention on Human Rights or the Vienna Convention of Diplomatic Security). In addition, international law contains unwritten understandings that arise from repeated interactions among nations. Conforming to all the different rules and regulations can create a major problem for MNCs. Fortunately, much of what they need to know can be subsumed under several broad and related principles that govern the conduct of international law.

Sovereignty and Sovereign Immunity   The **principle of sovereignty** holds that governments have the right to rule themselves as they see fit. In turn, this implies that one country's court system cannot be used to rectify injustices or impose penalties on another unless that country agrees. So, while U.S. laws require equality in the workplace for all employees, U.S. citizens who take a job in Japan cannot sue their Japanese employer under the provisions of U.S. law for failure to provide equal opportunity for them.

International Jurisdiction   International law provides for three types of jurisdictional principles. The first is the **nationality principle,** which holds that every country has jurisdiction (authority or power) over its citizens no matter where they are located. Therefore, a U.S. manager who violates the American Foreign Corrupt Practices Act while traveling abroad can be found guilty in the United States. The second is the **territoriality principle,** which holds that every nation has the right of jurisdiction within its legal territory. Therefore, a German firm that sells a defective product in England can be sued under English law even though the company is headquartered outside of England. The third is the **protective principle,** which holds that every country has jurisdiction over behavior that adversely affects its national security, even if that conduct occurred outside the country. Therefore, a French firm that sells secret U.S. government blueprints for a satellite system can be subjected to U.S. laws.

Doctrine of Comity   The **doctrine of comity** holds that there must be mutual respect for the laws, institutions, and government of other countries in the matter of jurisdiction over their own citizens. Although this doctrine is not part of international law, it is part of international custom and tradition.

Act of State Doctrine   Under the **act of state doctrine,** all acts of other governments are considered to be valid by U.S. courts, even if such acts are inappropriate in the United States. As a result, for example, foreign governments have the right to set limits on the repatriation of MNC profits and to forbid companies from sending more than this amount out of the host country.

Treatment and Rights of Aliens   Countries have the legal right to refuse admission of foreign citizens and to impose special restrictions on their conduct, right of travel, where they can stay, and what business they may conduct. Nations also can deport aliens. For example, the United States has the right to limit the travel of foreign scientists coming into the United States to attend a scientific convention and can insist they remain within five miles of the hotel. After the horrific events of 9/11, the U.S. government began greater enforcement of laws related to illegal aliens. In addition, closer scrutiny of visitors and temporary workers, including expatriate workers from India and elsewhere who have migrated to the United States for high-tech positions, may result in worker shortages.[29]

Forum for Hearing and Settling Disputes   This is a principle of U.S. justice as it applies to international law. At their discretion, U.S. courts can dismiss cases brought before them by foreigners; however, they are bound to examine issues such as where the plaintiffs are located, where the evidence must be gathered, and where property to be used in restitution is located. One of the best examples of this principle is the Union Carbide pesticide plant disaster in Bhopal, India. Over 2,000 people were killed and thousands left permanently injured when a toxic gas enveloped 40 square kilometers around the plant. The New York Court of Appeals sent the case back to India for resolution.

Examples of Legal and Regulatory Issues

The principles described above help to form the international legal and regulatory framework within which MNCs must operate. The following examines some examples of specific laws and situations that can have a direct impact on international business.

Foreign Corrupt Practices Act   During the special prosecutor's investigation of the Watergate scandal in the early 1970s, a number of questionable payments made by U.S. corporations to public officials abroad were uncovered. These bribes became the focal point of investigations by the U.S. Internal Revenue Service, Securities and Exchange Commission (SEC), and Justice Department. This concern over bribes in the international arena eventually culminated in the 1977 passage of the **Foreign Corrupt Practices Act (FCPA),** which makes it illegal to influence foreign officials through personal payment or political contributions. The objectives of the FCPA were to stop U.S. MNCs from initiating or perpetuating corruption in foreign governments and to upgrade the image of both the United States and its businesses abroad.

Critics of the FCPA feared the loss of sales to foreign competitors, especially in those countries where bribery is an accepted way of doing business. Nevertheless, the U.S. government pushed ahead and attempted to enforce the act. Some of the countries that were named in early bribery cases under the law included Algeria, Kuwait, Saudi Arabia, and Turkey. The U.S. State Department tried to convince the SEC and Justice Department not

protective principle
A jurisdictional principle of international law which holds that every country has jurisdiction over behavior that adversely affects its national security, even if the conduct occurred outside that country.

doctrine of comity
A jurisdictional principle of international law which holds that there must be mutual respect for the laws, institutions, and government of other countries in the matter of jurisdiction over their own citizens.

act of state doctrine
A jurisdictional principle of international law which holds that all acts of other governments are considered to be valid by U.S. courts, even if such acts are illegal or inappropriate under U.S. law.

Foreign Corrupt Practices Act (FCPA)
Made into U.S. law in 1977 because of concerns over bribes in the international business arena, this act makes it illegal to influence foreign officials through personal payment or political contributions.

to reveal countries or foreign officials who were involved in its investigations for fear of creating internal political problems for U.S. allies. Although this political sensitivity was justified, for the most part, several interesting developments occurred: (1) MNCs found that they could live within the guidelines set down by the FCPA; and (2) many foreign governments actually applauded these investigations under the FCPA, because it helped them to crack down on corruption in their own country.

One analysis reported that since passage of the FCPA, U.S. exports to "bribe prone" countries actually increased.[30] Investigations reveal that once bribes were removed as a key competitive tool, more MNCs were willing to do business in that country. This proved to be true even in the Middle East, where many U.S. MNCs always assumed that bribes were required to ensure contracts. There is evidence showing that this is no longer true in most cases, and where it is true those companies that engage in bribery face a strengthened FCPA that now allows the courts to both fine and imprison guilty parties.[31]

Bureaucratization   Very restrictive foreign bureaucracies are one of the biggest problems facing MNCs. This is particularly true when bureaucratic government controls are inefficient and not corrected. A good example is Japan, whose political parties feel more beholden to their local interests than to those in the rest of the country. As a result, it is extremely difficult to reorganize the Japanese bureaucracy and streamline the ways things are done, because so many politicians are more interested in the well-being of their own districts than in the long-run well-being of the nation as a whole. In turn, parochial actions create problems for MNCs trying to do business there. The administration of Prime Minister Junichiro Koizumi of Japan is helping reduce some of this bureaucracy.[32] Certainly the long-running recessionary economy of the country is leading to reforms in the nation's antiquated banking system, opening up the Japanese market to more competition.[33]

Japanese businesses are also becoming more aware of the fact that they are dependent on the world market for many goods and services, and that when bureaucratic red tape drives up the costs of these purchases, local consumers pay the price. These businesses are also beginning to realize that government bureaucracy can create a false sense of security and leave them unprepared to face the harsh competitive realities of the international marketplace.

A good example was provided during the mid-1990s when the value of the yen rose sharply and resulted in a decline in international sales by local businesses. Foreign purchasers were unwilling to buy Japanese products that cost 30–40 percent more than they did just a few years earlier. At the same time, foreign firms exporting goods into the Japanese market found that they could easily compete because their prices were lower than those of Japanese producers whose costs were pegged to the high-value yen. As a result, Chrysler cut the price of its Jeep Cherokee by 10 percent and sales rose; and American computer manufacturers such as Compaq and IBM, largely on the basis of price, were able to double their share of the Japanese market. Since this time the yen has declined in market value and local businesses have been able to recapture some lost market share. However, local firms still face greater international competition than ever before.

Additionally, Japan now faces new problems. One of these is that the cost of doing business in Japan is often higher than in other Asian countries. As a result, there has been a recent trend by MNCs toward buying from these less expensive sources. In an effort to deal with this new challenge, the Japanese will have to continue to cut bureaucratic red tape and open their markets to foreign competition. The accompanying "International Management in Action: The United States Goes to the Mat" shows the pressure that has been put on Japan to open its markets. Only in this way in the long run will the Japanese drive down their own costs of doing business and remain competitive against world-class organizations.

Privatization   Another example of the changing international regulatory environment is the current move toward privatization by an increasing number of countries. The German government, for example, has sped up privatization and deregulation of its telecommunications market. This has opened a host of opportunities for MNCs looking to create joint ventures with local German firms. Additionally, the French government is putting some of its businesses on the sale block. Meanwhile, in China the government has ordered the

The United States Goes to the Mat

For a number of years, the United States has demanded that Japan open its markets and provide the same access that Japanese MNCs are accorded. One of the strategies used by the U.S. government has been to negotiate purchasing targets. For example, in the case of automobiles, the Japanese government several years ago agreed to buy a specific amount of U.S.-made auto parts. This strategy now seems to be a thing of the past, however. Japanese negotiators believe it was a mistake and say they will hold fast in future negotiations.

For their part, U.S. administrations have pushed hard to level the playing field for trading with Japan. In the past, the United States threatened to impose a major import tax on luxury Japanese cars coming into America. Some observers noted, however, that the U.S. government immediately tempered its hard line with a willingness to set an early date for talks with the Japanese about the trade impasse. The administration countered that this concession was quite minor and used simply to meet a condition set forth by the World Trade Organization (WTO). According to WTO rules, in the absence of a mutual agreement on a date to meet, the parties are required to get together before new sanctions are instituted. This does not mean that there will be a settlement, however, only that the two parties will discuss their differences.

One major roadblock to an early resolution of U.S. demands is that EU countries want to be included in these negotiations. They argue that any arrangement between the United States and Japan will result in their being denied market access. After all, if the Japanese agree to buy $6 billion of U.S.-made auto parts, this is market share that cannot be captured by EU MNCs. The EU wants Japan to open its markets to all countries and let each compete on the level playing field.

How far will Japan go in giving concessions? How determined is the United States to wrestle additional agreements from the Japanese? These questions are yet unanswered. One thing is certain, however: Japan is a major world market, and its citizens have enormous purchasing power. Therefore, all nations will continue efforts to break down trade walls and get into the lucrative Japanese market. For example, General Motors sells its Saturn line in Japan through a network of stand-alone dealerships. The cost of distributing and retailing vehicles in Japan is extremely high, but GM feels that the strong market there is worth this risk. Additionally, GM has been selling Saturns in Taiwan and believes this experience has helped reduce the risk in the Japanese market.

The steps being taken by the U.S. government and some of the major MNCs, such as GM, are important in opening up the Japanese market. Much needs to be done, however, and the U.S. government believes that success in this area will require it to "go to the mat" with Japan. The outcome promises to be not only interesting, but vital to the success of world trade.

military to close or sell off between 10,000 and 20,000 companies that earn an estimated $9.5 billion annually. Known collectively as PLA Inc., the Chinese Army's business interests stretch from Hong Kong to the United States and include five-star hotels, paging services to golf courses, and Baskin-Robbins ice cream franchises. When the government cut the military budget during the early 1990s, it allowed the Army to make up this shortfall by earning commercial revenue. However, now the government has decided that the Army must get out of this end of the business and let the free market take over.[34] As described in Chapter 1's "International Management in Action: Telecommunications Privatization in Brazil," many developing countries are privatizing their telecommunications monopolies to provide greater competition and access to service.

Regulation of Trade and Investment

The regulation of international trade and investment is another area in which individual countries use their legal and regulatory policies to affect the international management environment. The rapid increase in trade and investment has raised concerns among countries that others are not engaging in fair trade, based on the fundamental principles of international trade as specified in the WTO and other trade and investment agreements. Specifically, international trade rules require countries to provide "national treatment," which means that they will not discriminate against others in their trade relations. Unfortunately, many countries engage in government support (subsidies) and other types of practices that distort trade. For example, many developing countries require that foreign MNCs take on local partners in order to do business. Others mandate that MNCs employ a certain percentage of local workers or produce a specific amount in their country. These practices are not limited to developing countries. Japan, the United States, and many European countries use standards, "buy local" regulations, and other policies to protect domestic industries and restrict trade. It should be noted, however, that the general trend has been to reduce trade and investment barriers among all countries.

In response to real or perceived unfair trading practices and to concerns over large and increasing trade deficits, the United States and other countries undertake investigations of unfair trading practices, some of which result in retaliatory tariffs. In the United States, there has been particular concern about trade with China, partly resulting from the fact that the Chinese economy is not fully market-based. In 2003, the United States imported $152.4 billion in goods from China but exported only $28.4 billion, resulting in a massive bilateral trade deficit of $124 billion. In response to trade deficits and concerns about the condition of domestic industry, the United States initiated a series of actions in 2002 and 2003 in which tariffs were placed on steel imports.[35] Although these sanctions were partially lifted in 2004, the United States and other countries will continue to use trade regulations when they perceive unfair trading practices around the world.

■ Technological Environment and Global Shifts in Production

The technological environment is changing at lightning speed. For example, while semiconductor firms are now working to develop new memory chips for personal computers,[36] other high-tech firms are trying to create technologies that will replace the PC with even better computing architecture.[37] At the same time, computers, telephones, televisions, and wireless forms of communication have merged to create multimedia products and to allow users anywhere in the world to communicate with each other. Today the number of people who use cellular phones is greater than ever, and in countries such as Finland, Norway, and Sweden over half the population are cellular subscribers.[38] In addition, a growing number of people have access to the Internet, allowing them to obtain information from literally millions of sources. In the United States more than three-quarters of those 12 years of age or older go online regularly.[39] In addition to Internet access, other specific ways in which technology will affect international management in the next decade include:

1. Rapid advances in biotechnology that are built on the precise manipulation of organisms, which will revolutionize the fields of agriculture, medicine, and industry.

2. The emergence of nanotechnology, in which nanomachines will possess the ability to remake the whole physical universe.

3. Satellites that will play a role in learning. For example, communication firms will place tiny satellites into low orbit, thus making it possible for millions of people, even in remote or sparsely populated regions such as Siberia, the Chinese desert, and the African interior, to send and receive voice, data, and digitized images through handheld telephones.

4. Automatic translation telephones, which will allow people to communicate naturally in their own language with anyone in the world who has access to a telephone.

5. Artificial intelligence and embedded learning technology, which will allow thinking that formerly was felt to be only the domain of humans to occur in machines.

6. Silicon chips containing up to 100 million transistors, allowing computing power that now rests only in the hands of supercomputer users to be available on every desktop.

7. Supercomputers that are capable of 1 trillion calculations per second, which will allow advances such as simulations of the human body for testing new drugs and computers that respond easily to spoken commands.[40]

The development and subsequent use of these technologies have greatly benefited the mostly developed countries in which they were first deployed. However, the most positive effects should be seen in developing countries where inefficiencies in labor and production impede growth. Although all of these technological innovations will affect international management, specific technologies will have especially pronounced effects in transforming economies and business practices. The following discussion highlights some specific dimensions of the technological environment currently facing international management.

E-Business

As the Internet becomes increasingly common, it is having a dramatic effect on international commerce. For example, millions of Americans have purchased books from Amazon.com and the company has now expanded its operations around the world. So have a host of other electronic retailers (e-tailers) who are discovering that their home-grown retailing expertise can be easily transferred and adapted for the international market.[41] Dell Computer has been offering B2C (electronic business-to-consumer) goods and services in Europe for a number of years, and the automakers are now beginning to move in this direction. Most automotive firms sell custom cars online.[42] Other firms are looking to use e-business to improve their current operations. For example, Deutsche Bank has overhauled its entire retail network with the goal of winning affluent customers across the continent.[43] Yet the most popular form of e-business is for business-to-business or B2B dealings such as placing orders and interacting with suppliers worldwide. Recent estimates of B2B global transactions in 2004 put the figure in excess of $2.3 trillion.[44] Business-to-consumer (B2C) transactions will not be as large, but this is an area where many MNCs are trying to improve their operations. In 2000 B2C transactions in the United States were around $25 billion and are forecasted to reach over $140 billion by 2004. In Europe B2C transactions in 2000 were over $2.75 billion and are forecasted by some analysts to increase to over $165 billion in the next five years.

The area of e-business that will most affect global customers is e-retailing and financial services. For example, customers can now use their keyboard to pay by credit card, although security remains a problem. However, the day is fast approaching when electronic cash (e-cash) will be common. This scenario already occurs in a number of forms. A good example is prepaid smart cards, which are being used mostly for telephone calls and public transportation. An individual can purchase one of these cards and use it in lieu of cash. This idea is blending into the Internet, allowing individuals to buy and sell merchandise and transfer funds electronically. The result will be global digital cash, which will take advantage of existing worldwide markets that allow buying and selling on a 24-hour basis.

This technological development also will have a major impact on financial institutions. After all, who will need the local corner ATM when they can tap into their funds through the Internet? Similarly, companies will not have to wait for their money from buyers, thus eliminating (or at least substantially reducing) bad debts while increasing their working capital. Therefore, if General Electric shipped $12 million of merchandise to Wal-Mart in Hong Kong with payment due on delivery, the typical 7- to 10-day waiting period between payment and collection of international transactions would, for all intents and purposes, be eliminated.[45]

Of course, e-cash will create many problems, and it will take some time for these to be resolved. For example, if a Mexican firm pays for its merchandise in pesos, there must be some system for converting these pesos into U.S. dollars. At present, such transactions are handled through regulated foreign exchange markets. In the near future, these transactions likely will be denominated in a single, conventional currency and exchanged at conventional market rates. It is equally likely, however, that the entire system of transactions eventually will become seamless and require no processing through foreign exchange markets. One expert explained it this way:

> Ideally, the ultimate e-cash will be a currency without a country (or a currency of all countries), infinitely exchangeable without the expense and inconvenience of conversion between local denominations. It may constitute itself as a wholly new currency with its own denomination— the "cyber dollar," perhaps. Or, it may continue to fix itself by reference to a traditional currency, in which case the American dollar would seem to be the likeliest possibility. Either way, it is hard to imagine that the existence of an international, easy-to-use, cheap-to-process, hard-to-tax electronic money will not then force freer convertibility on traditional currencies.[46]

Telecommunications

The most obvious dimension of the technological environment facing international management today is telecommunications. To begin with, it no longer is necessary to hardwire a city to provide residents with telephone service. This can be done wirelessly, thus allowing people to use cellular phones, pagers, and other telecommunications services. As a result, a form of technologic leapfrogging is occurring, in which regions of the world are moving from a situation where phones were unavailable to one where cellular is available everywhere, including rural areas, because the infrastructure needed to support this development can be installed both quickly and relatively inexpensively. In addition, technology is merging the telephone and the computer. As a result, in Europe and Asia growing numbers of people are now accessing the Web through their cell phones. While this development has not attracted a large market in the United States, over 125 million Asians and 50 million Europeans now use this service.[47] Over the next decade, the merging of the Internet and wireless technology will radically change the ways people communicate.[48] Wireless technology is also proving to be a boon for less developed countries such as in South America and Eastern Europe where customers once waited years to get a telephone installed.

One reason for this rapid increase in telecommunications services is many countries' belief that without an efficient communications system their economic growth may stall. Additionally, governments are accepting the belief that the only way to attract foreign investment and know-how in telecommunications is to give up control to private industry. As a result, while most telecommunications operations in the Asia-Pacific region were state-run a decade ago, a growing number are now in private hands. Singapore Telecommunications, Pakistan Telecom, Thailand's Telecom Asia, Korea Telecom, and Globe Telecom in the Philippines all have been privatized, and MNCs have helped in this process by providing investment funds. Today, NYNEX holds a stake in Telecom Asia; Bell Atlantic and Ameritech each own 25 percent of Telecom New Zealand; and Bell South has an ownership position in Australia's Optus. At the same time, Australia's Telestra is moving into Vietnam, Japan's NTT is investing in Thailand, and Korea Telecom is in the Philippines and Indonesia.

Many governments are reluctant to allow so much private and foreign ownership of such a vital industry; however, they also are aware that foreign investors will go elsewhere if the deal is not satisfactory. The Hong Kong office of Salomon Brothers, a U.S. investment bank, estimates that to meet the expanding demand for telecommunication service in Asia, companies will need to considerably increase the investment, most of which will have to come from overseas. MNCs are unwilling to put up this much money unless they are assured of operating control and a sufficiently high return on their investment.

A good example occurred in China, where the government announced that foreign investors who were interested in building and operating power plants would have their annual rate of return (ROI) capped at 12 percent. Investors immediately began looking for more lucrative opportunities in other power-hungry Asian nations, and now China has increased the ROI cap to continue attracting deals. China presently is facing a similar backlash from telecommunications firms as well, which are only allowed to provide advice and to supply and manufacture telecommunication equipment for the Chinese market and are banned from the potentially more lucrative business of owning or operating these services.

Unlike China, however, other developing countries are eager to attract telecommunication firms and offer liberal terms. Cable & Wireless of Great Britain has opened an office in Hanoi. In Hong Kong, while the local telephone monopoly will not lose its grip on international services until 2006, its monopoly on local services has ended, and private groups are competing to provide service.

Technology, Outsourcing, and Offshoring

In international management, technology also impacts the number of employees who are needed to carry out operations effectively. As MNCs use advanced technology to help them communicate, produce, and deliver their goods and services internationally, they face a new challenge: how technology will affect the nature and number of their employees. Some informed observers note that technology already has eliminated much, and in the future will eliminate even more of the work now being done by middle management and white-collar staff. Mounting cost pressures resulting from increased globalization of competition and profit expectations exerted by investors have placed pressure on MNCs to outsource or offshore production to take advantage of lower labor and other costs.[49] In the past century, machines replaced millions of manual laborers, but those who worked with their minds were able to thrive and survive. During the past three decades in particular, blue-collar, smokestack industries such as steel and autos have been downsized by technology, and the result has been a permanent restructuring of the number of employees needed to run factories efficiently. In the 1990s, the same thing happened in the white-collar service industries (insurance, banks, and even government). Most recently, the same has occurred with the dot-com bubble bursting and hundreds of thousands of jobs being lost, probably forever.

Some experts predict that in the future technology has the potential to largely displace employees in all industries, from those doing low-skilled jobs to those holding positions traditionally reserved for human thinking. For example, voice recognition is helping to replace telephone operators; the demand for postal workers has been reduced severely by address-reading devices; and cash-dispensing machines can do 10 times more transactions in a day than bank tellers, so tellers can be reduced in number or even eliminated entirely in the future. Also, expert (sometimes called "smart") systems can eliminate human thinking completely. For example, American Express has an expert system that performs the credit analysis formerly done by college-graduate financial analysts. In the medical field, expert systems can diagnose some illnesses as well as doctors can, and robots capable of performing certain operations are starting to be used.

Emerging information technology also makes work more portable. As a result, MNCs have been able to move certain production activities overseas to capitalize on cheap labor resources. This is especially true for work that can be easily contracted with overseas locations. For example, low-paid workers in India and Asian countries now are being given subcontracted work such as labor-intensive software development and code-writing jobs. A restructuring of the nature of work and of employment is resulting from such information technology; Figure 2–1 identifies some winners and losers in the workforce in recent years.

The new technological environment has both positives and negatives for MNCs and societies as a whole. On the positive side, the cost of doing business worldwide should decline thanks to the opportunities that technology offers in substituting lower-cost machines for higher-priced labor. Over time, productivity should go up, and prices should go down. On the negative side, many employees will find either their jobs eliminated or their wages and salaries reduced because they have been replaced by machines and their skills are no longer in high demand. This job loss from technology can be especially devastating in developing countries. However, it doesn't have to be this way. A case in point is South Africa's showcase for automotive productivity, the Delta Motor Corporation's Opel Corsa plant in Port Elizabeth. To provide as many jobs as possible, this world-class operation automated only 23 percent compared to more than 85 percent of European and North American auto assembly.[50] Also, some industries can add jobs. For example, in the computer and information technology industry, even with its ups and downs, the negative has been offset by the positive. For example, over the last decade, employment in the U.S. computer software industry has increased. In less developed countries such as India, a high-tech boom in recent years has created jobs and opportunities for a growing number of people.[51] Additionally, even though developed countries such as Japan and the United States are most affected by technological displacement of workers, both nations still lead the world in creating new jobs and shifting their traditional industrial structure toward a high-tech, knowledge-based economy.

The precise impact that the advanced technological environment will have on international management over the next decade is difficult to forecast. One thing is certain,

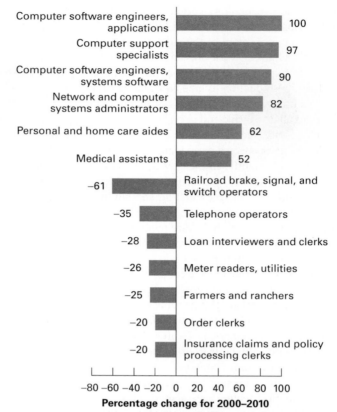

Figure 2–1

Winners and Losers in Selected Occupations: Percentage Change Forecasts for 2000–2010

Computer software engineers, applications — 100
Computer support specialists — 97
Computer software engineers, systems software — 90
Network and computer systems administrators — 82
Personal and home care aides — 62
Medical assistants — 52
−61 — Railroad brake, signal, and switch operators
−35 — Telephone operators
−28 — Loan interviewers and clerks
−26 — Meter readers, utilities
−25 — Farmers and ranchers
−20 — Order clerks
−20 — Insurance claims and policy processing clerks

−80 −60 −40 −20 0 20 40 60 80 100

Percentage change for 2000–2010

Source: U.S. Bureau of Labor Statistics, http://www.bls.gov/emp/empfastestind.pdf.

however; there is no turning back the technological clock. MNCs and nations alike must evaluate the impact of these changes carefully and realize that their economic performance is closely tied to keeping up with, or ahead of, rapidly advancing technology.

The World of *BusinessWeek*—Revisited

As the *BusinessWeek* article at the beginning of this chapter illustrates, the forces of globalization are drastically altering political, legal, and technological environments worldwide. Because of Parmalat's vast global footprint, the scandals at Parmalat reverberated across the globe, adversely affecting both institutional and individual investors in the United States, Europe, and Asia. Now more than ever, international managers need to be aware of how differing political, legal, and technological environments are affecting their business and how globalization, security concerns, and other developments influence these environments. Changes in political, legal, and environmental conditions open up new business opportunities and close some old ones.

In light of the information you have learned from reading this chapter, you should have a good understanding of these environments and some of the ways in which they will affect companies doing businesses abroad. Drawing on this knowledge, answer the following questions: (1) How will changes in the political and legal environment in Europe affect U.S. MNCs conducting business there? (2) How might rules governing corruption prevent scandals such as Parmalat's? (3) How does technology result in greater integration and dependencies among economies, political systems, and financial markets?

SUMMARY OF KEY POINTS

1. Today's political environment presents a myriad of challenges for MNCs. China is going through a transition as the old guard passes from the scene. The political situation in Europe also continues to change. Russia is facing political and economic problems and social upheaval, and the rest of Central and Eastern Europe has had varying degrees of success with their newfound freedom and continue to struggle with their past.

2. The current legal and regulatory environment is both complex and confusing. There are many different laws and regulations to which MNCs doing business internationally must conform, and each nation is unique. Also, MNCs must abide by the laws of their own country. For example, U.S. MNCs must obey the rules set down by the Foreign Corrupt Practices Act. MNCs doing business in Japan and the EU face a wide range of bureaucratic rules and regulations that often are both time-wasting and inefficient. Privatization and regulation of trade also affect the legal and regulatory environment in specific countries.

3. The technological environment is changing quickly and is having a major impact on international business. This will continue in the future. For example, money transfers and exchange are changing dramatically. Also, areas such as telecommunications offer developing countries new opportunities to leapfrog into the 21st century. New markets are being created for high-tech MNCs that are eager to provide telecommunications service. Technological developments also impact both the nature and the structure of employment, shifting the industrial structure toward a more high-tech, knowledge-based economy. MNCs that understand and take advantage of this high-tech environment should prosper, but they also must keep up, or ahead, to survive.

KEY TERMS

act of state doctrine, *43*

civil or code law, *42*

common law, *42*

doctrine of comity, *43*

Foreign Corrupt Practices Act (FCPA), *43*

Islamic law, *42*

nationality principle, *42*

principle of sovereignty, *42*

protective principle, *43*

socialist law, *42*

territoriality principle, *42*

REVIEW AND DISCUSSION QUESTIONS

1. In what way does the political environment around the world create challenges for MNCs? Would these challenges be less for those operating in the EU than for those in Russia or China? Why or why not?

2. How do the following legal principles impact on MNC operations: the principle of sovereignty, the nationality principle, the territoriality principle, the protective principle, and principle of comity?

3. How could the national and local government bureaucracy in Japan impede the operations of a U.S. MNC doing business there? What are some Japanese laws or regulations that would reduce the MNC's effectiveness?

4. Why are developing countries interested in privatizing their telecommunications industries? What opportunities does this privatization have for telecommunication MNCs?

INTERNET EXERCISE: HITACHI GOES WORLDWIDE

Hitachi products are well known in the United States, as well as in Europe and Asia. However, in an effort to continue maintaining its international momentum, the Japanese MNC is continuing to push forward into new markets while also developing new products. Visit the MNC at its Web site **www.hitachi.com** and examine some of the latest developments that are taking place. Begin by reviewing the firm's current activities in Asia, specifically Hong Kong and Singapore. Then look at how it is doing business in North America. Finally, read about its European operations. All of these are available at this Web site. Then answer these three questions: (1) What kinds of products does the firm offer? What are its primary areas of emphasis? (2) In what types of environments does it operate? Is Hitachi primarily interested in developed markets or is it also pushing into newly emerging markets? (3) Based on what it has been doing over the last 2–3 years, what do you think Hitachi's future strategy will be in competing in the environment of international business during the first decade of the new millennium?

Vietnam

Located in Southeast Asia, the Socialist Republic of Vietnam is bordered to the north by the People's Republic of China, to the west by Laos and Cambodia, and to the east and south by the South China Sea. The country is a mere 127,000 square miles but has a population of almost 80 million. The language is Vietnamese and the principal religion Buddhism, although there are a number of small minorities, including Confucian, Christian (mainly Catholic), Caodist, Daoist, and Hoa Hao. In recent years, the country's economy has been up and down, but average per capita income still is in the hundreds of dollars as the peasants remain very poor.

One of the reasons that Vietnam has lagged behind its fast-developing neighbors in Southeast Asia, such as Thailand and Malaysia, is its isolation from the industrial West, and the United States in particular, because of the Vietnam War. From the mid-1970s, the country had close relations with the U.S.S.R., but the collapse of communism there forced the still-communist Vietnamese government to work on establishing stronger economic ties with other countries. The nation recently has worked out many of its problems with China, and today, the Chinese have become a useful economic ally. Vietnam would most like to establish a vigorous trade relationship with the United States, however. Efforts toward this end began over a decade ago, but because of lack of information concerning the many U.S. soldiers still unaccounted for after the war, it was not until 1993 that the United States permitted U.S. companies to take part in ventures in Vietnam that were financed by international aid agencies. Then, in 1994, the U.S. trade embargo was lifted, and a growing number of American firms began doing business in Vietnam.

Caterpillar began supplying equipment for a $2 billion highway project. Mobil teamed with three Japanese partners to begin drilling offshore. Exxon, Amoco, Conoco, Unocal, and Arco negotiated production-sharing contracts with Petro Vietnam. General Electric opened a trade office and developed plans to use electric products throughout the country. AT&T began working to provide long-distance service both in and out of the country. Coca-Cola began bottling operations. Within the first 12 months, 70 U.S. companies obtained licenses to do business in Vietnam. Besides the United States, the largest investors have been Singapore, Taiwan, Japan, South Korea, and Hong Kong, which collectively have put over $22 billion into the country.

Over the past couple of years, Vietnamese authorities have acted swiftly to implement the structural reforms needed to modernize the national economy and to produce more competitive exports for sale in the global economy. In July 2000 the United States and Vietnam signed a bilateral trade agreement that opens up trade and foreign investment in Vietnam and gives Vietnamese exporters access to the vast U.S. market. The treaty, which entered into force near the end of 2001, is also expected to increase foreign direct investment from the United States over the next decade. This, in turn, should help stimulate direct investment from other pro-trade societies around the world. As in China, many U.S. firms have found doing business in Vietnam frustrating because of the numerous and ever-changing bureaucratic rules enacted by the communist government officials, but if relations between the two countries continue on their present course, more and more opportunities should open up for American multinationals.

Questions

1. In what way does the political environment in Vietnam pose both an opportunity and a threat for American MNCs seeking to do business there?

2. Why are U.S. multinationals so interested in going into Vietnam? How much potential does the country offer? Conversely, how much benefit can Vietnam derive from a business relationship with U.S. MNCs?

3. Will there be any opportunities in Vietnam for high-tech American firms? Why or why not?

A Chinese Venture

The Darby Company is a medium-size communications technology company headquartered on the west coast of the United States. Among other things, Darby holds a patent on a mobile telephone that can operate effectively within a five-mile radius. The phone does not contain state-of-the-art technology, but it can be produced extremely cheaply. As a result, the Chinese government has expressed interest in manufacturing and selling this phone throughout their country.

Preliminary discussions with the Chinese government reveal that some major terms of the agreement that it would like include: (1) Darby will enter into a joint venture with a local Chinese firm to manufacture the phones to Darby's specifications; (2) these phones will be sold throughout China at a 100 percent markup, and Darby will receive 10 percent of the profits; (3) Darby will invest $35 million in building the manufacturing facility, and these costs will be recovered over a 5-year period; and (4) the government in Beijing will guarantee that at least 100,000 phones are sold every year, or it will purchase the difference.

The Darby management is not sure whether this is a good deal. In particular, Darby executives have heard all sorts of horror stories regarding agreements that the Chinese government has made and then broken. The company also is concerned that once its technology is understood, the Chinese will walk away from the agreement and start making these phones on their own. Because the technology is not state-of-the-art, the real benefit is in the low production costs, and the technological knowledge is more difficult to protect.

For its part, the Chinese government has promised to sign a written contract with Darby, and it has agreed that any disputes regarding enforcement of this contract can be brought, by either side, to the World Court at the Hague for resolution. Should this course of action be taken, each side would be responsible for its own legal fees, but the Chinese have promised to accept the decision of the Court as binding.

Darby has 30 days to decide whether to sign the contract with the Chinese. After this time, the Chinese intend to pursue negotiations with a large telecommunications firm in Europe and try cutting a deal with them. Darby is more attractive to the Chinese, however, because of the low cost of producing its telephone. In any event, the Chinese are determined to begin mass-producing cellular phones in their country. "Our future is tied to high-tech communication," the Chinese minister of finance recently told Darby's president. "That is why we are so anxious to do business with your company; you have quality phones at low cost." Darby management is flattered by these kind words but still not sure if this is the type of business deal in which it wants to get involved.

Questions

1. How important is the political environment in China for the Darby Company? Explain.

2. If a disagreement arises between the two joint-venture partners and the government of China reneges on its promises, how well protected is Darby's position? Explain.

3. Are the economic and technological environments in China favorable for Darby? Why or why not?

Chapter 3

ETHICS AND SOCIAL RESPONSIBILITY

The current concern that all businesses and the general public have for ethical behavior and social responsibility is not restricted to the domestic situation. In this era of a global economy, MNCs must be concerned with how they carry out their business and their social role in host countries. This chapter examines business ethics and social responsibility in the international arena, and it looks at some of the critical social issues that will be confronting MNCs in the years ahead. The discussion includes ethical decision making in various countries, regulation of foreign investment, and current responses to social responsibility by today's multinationals. The specific objectives of this chapter are:

1. **Examine** some of the major ethical issues and problems confronting MNCs in selected countries.

2. **Discuss** some of the pressures on and action being taken by selected industrialized countries and companies to be more socially responsive to world problems.

3. **Explain** some of the initiatives to bring greater accountability to corporate conduct and limit the impacts of corruption around the world.

The World of *BusinessWeek*

BusinessWeek

Poor Nations Can't Live by Markets Alone

The '90s Boom and Free-Market Reforms Adopted by Developing Countries Haven't Done Enough to Improve Their Lot, Says a U.N. Study

Today, the 1990s are remembered as a decade of enormous progress for market economics. From Eastern Europe to Latin America to Africa, governments lowered trade barriers, privatized industries, and took World Bank and International Monetary Fund advice more seriously on reining in public spending.

So is the developing world better for it? Not really, says a new report by the U.N. Development Programme. If you set aside countries like China and India, which both achieved great strides in reducing poverty but also have advantages due to their size, the bulk of developing nations were no better off in the 1990s than they were in previous decades, says the UNDP's 2003 Human Development Report.

In fact, the study concludes, the '90s were on balance a step backward for poor nations. In the '80s, the report notes, every nation but four saw a rise in living standards over the decade as measured by the UNDP's Human Development Index, which includes everything from infant mortality to education levels. In contrast, 21 of 129 developing nations saw living standards drop in the '90s, according to the UNDP. Life expectancy, which historically has steadily grown longer, dropped in 34 nations.

Punctured Myth

Most surprising, 54 countries saw per-capita income decline—a dramatic reversal from the '80s. The trend was most pronounced in sub-Saharan Africa. Half of national economies in Latin America and the Caribbean also declined, as well as Eastern European and Central Asian states such as Moldova, Tajikistan, the Russian Federation, and Ukraine.

What's remarkable is that this deterioration coincided with the so-called Washington Consensus, a set of free-market policies pushed by the IMF, World Bank, and the U.S. government under Presidents George H. W. Bush and Bill Clinton. "The 1990s punctured the myth that if you followed the Washington Consensus, growth would follow as surely as light follows night," says UNDP Administrator Mark Malloch Brown.

So what exactly is the UNDP advocating—a march back toward socialism? Hardly. The report's point isn't that it was wrong for countries to open their markets to trade, promote the private sector, and adopt fiscal prudence. Indeed, considering how many developing nations still clung to growth-strangling socialist or protectionist policies in the '80s, "the Washington Consensus had its time and place," says Malloch Brown.

Steep Hurdles

The problem was that macro policies were overemphasized as a panacea for the Third World's ills, he argues. The World Bank and IMF downplayed the importance of more down-to-earth measures needed to spur sustainable development and reduce poverty, such as investments in health care, education, roads, and clean water.

The World Bank and IMF put such a high priority on budgetary prudence that in many cases they actually told impoverished nations to reduce such basic infrastructure spending. "After more than a decade of economic reform," he says, "we found that new policies and institutions alone—while critical—are not enough."

The hurdles that the world's poorest nations must clear are too steep to overcome with just marketplace magic, the UNDP argues. Given their high population growth and uneven income distribution, most nations in sub-Saharan Africa would need to generate annual economic growth of at least 6% before poverty levels would markedly decline. That would require heavy investment by local entrepreneurs

and foreigners. But it's virtually impossible for nations like Burkina Faso or Chad to lure that level of investment without massive infusions of foreign aid.

Clobbered by Commodities

Size and geographical location also have an impact on the ability to foster growth. For example, countries with access to the sea can ship exports to foreign markets. Meanwhile, even though landlocked Bolivia and Uganda embraced World Bank–prescribed policies, "neither have reaped the returns that were expected," says Malloch Brown.

Similarly, big nations like China, India, and Brazil, all with provinces and states wealthier than others in their countries, saw growth as dynamic development spread from richer coastal regions into the more backward, often heavily populated areas in the interior.

Dependence on exports of a single commodity can also set economies back in harsh ways. Unable to compete in manufacturing, many poor countries still rely heavily on oil, coffee, copper, timber, or other mining and agricultural goods for most of their foreign exchange. But prices for most of these commodities have dropped sharply over the past decade as global production rose.

Uganda, for example, has had a hard time maintaining growth despite economic reforms because it still relies heavily on exports of coffee, whose price has plunged in recent years because of oversupply. Even in agricultural goods where African nations are competitive, high trade barriers or subsidies for domestic farmers in the U.S., Europe, and Japan also make it difficult to export.

Other factors at work in holding developing nations back:

- **Contagious diseases.** More than 10 million people die of preventable illnesses such as tuberculosis, malaria, and respiratory infections every year. More than 90% of 42 million people living with AIDS are in developing nations. In some nations, 40% of the adult population have AIDS. And infection rates are rising. Little wonder that labor productivity in Africa is abysmal, and foreign investment in manufacturing is minimal.

- **Adverse environmental conditions.** Some of the poorest nations in Africa and Central Asia are plagued with terrible conditions for agriculture. An estimated 1.7 billion people live in nations with fresh-water shortages, while soil degradation affects 1 billion people living in arid lands. Many of these countries cannot grow enough food to feed themselves, much less export.

- **Social inequity.** Countries with the most persistently high poverty rates also tend to have the biggest gaps between the richest 20% of the population and the poorest 20%. Low education levels (just 57% of children in sub-Saharan Africa are enrolled in primary school), discrimination against women, lack of access to credit, and low levels of property ownership for common people are among the factors that foster inequitable income distribution. So even though some poor nations post economic growth, the gains often don't trickle down to the masses.

Case in point: Bolivia. This South American nation grew by 3.5% annually during the '90s. But with its huge income gap, it would have to expand by at least 6% a year to reduce poverty.

The bottom line of the UNDP report is that before the world's poorest nations can begin to escape their poverty traps, they need much more than better economic policies. They also need huge infusions of resources. And since foreign investment isn't coming, for now it will have to come through foreign aid by rich nations.

It's unlikely the 2003 Human Development Report will spark a massive increase in foreign aid from rich countries, which have grown deaf to such pleas. But at the very least, it could prompt Western governments and donor agencies to craft more realistic and sophisticated strategies for helping the world's poorest nations.

By Pete Engardio in New York

Source: From "Poor Nations Can't Live by Markets Alone," by Pete Engardio, *BusinessWeek,* July 16, 2003. Reprinted with permission.

The news article that opens this chapter presents the interesting challenge of how to make globalization and international business beneficial to poor nations as well as rich. It also points up an ethical dilemma for MNCs doing business in developing countries. Should MNCs feel a sense of responsibility for improving welfare in the nations and regions where they do business, or is it the job of governments to help promote equitable economic growth worldwide? Historically, governments in developed countries have imposed tariff and nontariff barriers against imports from developing countries, especially on certain commodities such as sugar, corn, and wheat. These restrictions limited export opportunities for developing countries, which, in turn, have impeded economic growth. Now, more than ever, the trade policies of rich nations will have a substantial impact on the economic status of developing nations.

Regardless of these conditions, MNCs are under increasing pressure to adopt a more socially responsible approach to doing business and to adhere to specific ethical codes in their business dealings. The recent scandals at Enron, Parmalat, and many other corporations have provided added impetus for MNCs to solidify their ethical commitments. However, enforcing a single ethical code becomes complicated by the very multinational character of MNCs. Each country or region has its own cultural standards and values, which must be considered individually. As this chapter will illustrate, increasing demands for corporations to be more ethical and socially responsible in their business dealings present challenges for MNCs. As a result, it is extremely important for international managers to understand the role and impact of ethics and corporate social responsibility as they do business across the globe.

■ Ethics and Social Responsibility Around the World

The ethical behavior of business and the broader social responsibilities of corporations have become major issues in the United States and all countries around the world. Ethical scandals and questionable business practices have received considerable media attention and aroused the public's concern about ethics in international business and attention to the social impact of business operations.

Ethics is the study of morality and standards of conduct. In recent years a growing number of MNCs have formulated codes of ethics to guide their behavior and ensure that their operations conform to these standards worldwide. Part of the corporate credo of Johnson & Johnson, the giant MNC, reads as follows:

> We are responsible to our employees, the men and women who work with us throughout the world. Everyone must be considered as an individual. We must respect their dignity and recognize their merit. They must have a sense of security in their jobs. Compensation must be fair and adequate, and working conditions clean, orderly and safe. We must be mindful of ways to help our employees fulfill their family responsibilities. Employees must feel free to make suggestions and complaints. There must be equal opportunity for employment, development and advancement for those qualified. We must provide competent management, and their actions must be just and ethical.
>
> We are responsible to the communities in which we will live and work and to the world community as well. We must be good citizens—support good works and charities and bear our fair share of taxes. We must encourage civic improvements and better health and education. We must maintain in good order the property we are privileged to use, protecting the environment and natural resources.[1]

Ethics is important in the study of international management, because ethical behavior in one country sometimes is viewed as unethical behavior in other countries. Considerable attention has been given in the management literature to ethical problems in the United States; not so well known are the ethical issues in other parts of the world.[2] The following sections examine some of the ethical problems that occur in international business in selected countries.

Recent corporate scandals at Arthur Andersen, Enron, Parmalat, Ahold, Worldcom, Qwest, and Tyco have reinforced the vital role of ethics in the conduct of business. In each of these cases, the failure to adhere to strong ethical standards had damaging effects on workers, investors, and managers. As a result, these firms have suffered irreparable damage that has affected all stakeholders. Today, firms doing business in the United States must be cognizant of new ethical laws and standards such as the Sarbanes-Oxley Act (SOA). Passed in 2002, the act requires the CEO and CFO of a company to approve and declare accurate all financial statements provided to the SEC for publication. At its core, SOA compliance hinges on managing all of an organization's unstructured content related to financial controls and making that content appropriately accessible across and outside the organization for audit and verification. New auditing and board rules were put in place to help ensure the transparency of all disclosures. MNCs looking to do business in the United States must comply with these changes. Ethical norms and guidelines change from one country to the next so MNCs, to some extent, must rely on their local teams to execute under local rules. Compliance with these new guidelines can be a financial burden for some firms, especially as they coordinate reporting for dispersed global subsidiaries. The cost of noncompliance, however, is undoubtedly higher, so MNCs are working hard to implement these rules throughout their global operations.

ethics
The study of morality and standards of conduct

Ethical Problems and Concerns in Japan

In both internal and external business relations, Japan, like the United States, has had more than its share of ethical problems in recent years. Some of the most devastating and widely publicized have occurred in both the political and the business arenas.

Political and Business Scandals   Japan not only has struggled economically but also has been rocked by a number of political scandals. In one recent case, a Japanese cabinet member was forced to resign after admitting that he had received $1.8 million for advisory work from the Mitsubishi Trust and Banking Corporation and had also accepted $800,000 from a condominium developer.[3] A few days later the chief cabinet secretary, the second highest ranking job after the prime minister, acknowledged that he had accepted a political donation of $68,000 from two people, an amount far in excess of the $12,000 limit.[4] In another case, the finance director for the Japanese Public Highway Corporation was accused of accepting lavish entertainment from a stock brokerage firm. Tokyo prosecutors charged the official with being influenced by this largesse and, in turn, selecting the brokerage as the chief underwriter of $800 million worth of bonds issued by the Highway Corporation.[5] As a result of the investigation, more than 30 executives of Japanese financial institutions were arrested. Additionally, four officials of the Finance Ministry and one from the Bank of Japan were taken into custody on charges of having accepted bribes in the form of entertainment. However, very little happened as a result of these actions except that the chief prosecutor in Tokyo was transferred to a remote coastal city and the investigation came to a halt.[6]

Another scandal that has rocked Japan has been the failure of its banking system to take corrective action and help out the country's drawn-out recession. This problem seems to have been caused by both the government and business. The government failed to institute strong procedures designed to prevent the banks from taking large, dangerous risks, and the banks failed to adjust their loan policies, write off bad loans, and accept the responsibility for their errors. As a result, the total amount of uncollectible loans by major Japanese banks was greater than their total equity. Simply put, many of them were technically bankrupt![7]

Japanese business firms have also come under scrutiny for unethical and illegal practices. Mitsubishi Motors, for example, has admitted that it systematically concealed customer complaints in Japan for more than 20 years and some top managers knew about the cover-up.[8] The company failed to inform car owners about possible auto defects and did not file this information with the government. One of the ways Mitsubishi did this was by maintaining two sets of records of customer complaints: those to be reported to the authorities and those to be hidden.[9] The police launched an investigation into allegations that the firm was criminally negligent in covering up these defects,[10] and the company began a massive recall of over 600,000 vehicles in Japan and another 200,000 in overseas markets.

In another instance, Nissan Motors was charged with encouraging employees to mislead government inspectors. In a manual distributed to employees, the company told the workers to "put away secret materials" when government officials held surprise inspections and to switch their computer screens to the one designed for inspection.[11] In its defense, the firm responded by saying that these instructions were meant to apply only to materials that had not been completed and approved by a supervisor.

Hostile Work Environment Issues   Japanese firms have also been facing charges of sexual harassment in the workplace, an issue on which more and more Japanese women are fighting back. Several years ago, a Japanese woman won a judgment of $12,500 from her company. This was the first lawsuit ever filed in Japan charging sexual harassment, and it set off a wave of concern. Within 48 hours of the verdict, the government had issued 10,000 copies of a booklet on sexual harassment, and all were quickly snapped up.

Despite a heightened sensitivity in recent years, sexual harassment remains a major social issue in Japan. A good example is provided by a Japanese saleswoman for a large bank who was visiting clients with a male deputy branch manager. This manager made improper advances toward her, but when she reported the incident the only thing the company did was to give her a new work partner. Soon afterward the branch manager approached the woman and told her that her previous partner had been having work problems and he would like the two of them to again become job partners. The woman refused, quit her job, and filed a sexual harassment lawsuit against the firm.

One of the major reasons why sexual harassment remains a problem in Japan is that traditionally many male managers regard female employees as mere assistants and, following a stereotype, feel that women employees will soon marry and leave the firm. So women are often not given the opportunity for promotion and are not considered for management positions. Additionally, sexual harassment is a new concept to many Japanese managers. One labor economist recently tried to put the issue into perspective by noting that most Japanese managers do not consider it a moral issue or think about why it happens or of improving the work environment. In fact, while many Japanese know that there are sexual harassment lawsuits filed in the United States, they fail to grasp why it is such an important issue for Americans. One analyst recently conveyed this idea by noting that in Japan, "There is no specific law against sexual harassment, so those suing must use general civil law. Suits can take years in the courts, and awards are typically only a few thousand dollars. And victory can be difficult."[12]

Equal Opportunity Issues There are a number of equal opportunity issues that Japanese firms face. One of the most prominent is the refusal to hire women or promote them into management positions. Many women who are in the last year of their college program, for example, find that company interviewers are interested in hiring them only for secretarial or other dead-end jobs. They quickly learn that there is a two-track recruiting process in many Japanese firms: one for men and one for women. Labor market experts say that the business rationale for excluding women from professional jobs is the belief that they will quit to get married after only a few years. One college graduate who applied to almost 50 firms and got just three job offers summed up her experience by saying, "What I've learned is that if a company has a choice between a man and a woman, they will choose the man, even if he is of lesser ability."[13]

This type of thinking has also created problems for Japanese firms doing business overseas. For example, a few years ago the U.S. Equal Employment Opportunity Commission filed a lawsuit against Mitsubishi charging the firm with sexual harassment of more than 300 women. The company eventually settled the case, agreeing, among other things, to donate $100,000 to women's causes as well as to make substantial cash payments to some of the women who had brought lawsuits of their own.[14] In yet another lawsuit, Honda of America Manufacturing Inc. agreed to give 370 African Americans and women a total of $6 million in back pay to resolve a federal discrimination complaint.

Social Responsibility Implication from Lobbying Another area of ethical concern has been the Japanese lobbying effort in the United States.[15] Japan, more than other countries, spends millions of dollars every year for lobbying in Washington. For this money, Japanese firms have been able to hire very savvy, effective lobbyists. Is it ethical for Japanese firms to hire bankrolled, well-connected, talented lobbyists to argue their case in Washington? Is it ethical for former U.S. cabinet officers and elected officials to become lobbyists for Japan? Certainly, these activities are legal. Many Americans feel that the interests of the United States and Japan are not the same when it comes to business dealings, however, and that Americans are being shortchanged in the process. To the extent that these feelings persist, Japanese lobbying will continue to be an area of ethical concern during the years ahead.

Ethical Problems and Concerns in Europe

Ethical behavior in European countries is an important area of interest in international management, because in some respects, these countries differ sharply from Japan and the United States. Although ethical issues are a concern throughout the world and in all European countries, France and Germany seem to get most of the attention in the literature.

One study surveyed 124 U.S., 72 French, and 70 German managers.[16] Each was asked to respond to a series of five vignettes that examined ethical situations related to coercion and control, conflict of interest, the physical environment, paternalism, and personal integrity. In most cases, the U.S. managers' responses were quite different from those of their European counterparts. The following is an example of one of the vignettes:

Rollfast Bicycle Company has been barred from entering the market in a large Asian country by collusive efforts of the local bicycle manufacturers. Rollfast could expect to net 5 million dollars per year from sales if it could penetrate the market. Last week a businessman from the country contacted the management of Rollfast and stated that he could smooth the way for the company to sell in his country for a price of $500,000.[17]

The executives from the three countries were asked how they would respond to the request for payment. The Americans were opposed to paying the money; 39 percent of them said that a bribe was unethical or illegal under the Foreign Corrupt Practices Act. Only 12 percent of the French managers felt that way, and none of the Germans agreed. However, 55 percent of the French and 29 percent of the Germans said that paying the money was not unethical but merely the price to be paid for doing business.

In each of the other four vignettes, the managers were given situations that presented them with a variety of ethical dilemmas such as conflicts of interest or questionable behaviors. Summing up the responses of managers to all five scenarios, the researchers concluded:

> If one were to generalize, the U.S. managers were noticeably more concerned with ethical and legal questions. Their French and German counterparts appeared to worry more about maintaining a successful business posture. To be sure, there was some overlapping of responses; however, the differences remained.[18]

This cross-national research on ethical behavior shows that MNCs must be aware that the ethical practices of their home country may be quite different from those of countries where they do business. A number of reasons account for these differences, including culture, personal values, incentives, and the obvious legal restrictions.

The Status of Women Managers in Europe

Because most European countries have experienced only limited population growth in recent years, integration of women into the workforce has become a critical goal. As in the United States and Japan, however, women in Europe have encountered equal opportunity problems and a "glass ceiling" in the managerial ranks. After spending extended periods in the workforce, women have found it extremely difficult to break through to executive-level positions. The following discussion examines the current status of women managers in three of the largest European nations: France, Germany, and Great Britain.

France The proportion of French women in the labor force from 1900 until 1970 remained at about 35 percent. Since then, however, more than 2.5 million women have entered the workforce, compared with less than 300,000 men. This trend would seem to indicate that women now should be gaining a greater foothold in the managerial ranks—and to a degree this is true. Over the last 40 years, the number of women who are managers has increased almost twice as fast as the number of managerial positions has increased. The greatest gains have been in product promotion and sales, import-export, sales administration, real estate, urban planning and architecture, socioeconomic studies, and chemistry.

Although French women are making strides in the management ranks, they still are underrepresented in corporate management. Women still are far behind men in the ranks of corporate management and in the traditional functions of manufacturing and sales. A number of reasons are given for this underrepresentation. One is that promotion into top management depends on more than diplomas, abilities, and ambitions. As in the United States and Japan, women in France face many obstacles when trying to break the glass ceiling. As one analysis of women managers in France notes:

> Being a manager includes having to work long hours, travel, make difficult decisions, motivate people, and achieve high objectives—most often with limited resources and strong business competitors. For women managers, it also often means fighting within their own company to establish a reputation as a leader—since women are rarely spontaneously seen as leaders, avoiding or responding appropriately to sexist criticisms, motivating employees to accept and execute their decisions, and sometimes hiding their family problems. Women frequently have more difficulty than men getting access to information necessary to make wise career decisions. Although it is important for women to understand the organization's career criteria, few companies in France provide such information through either equal opportunity managers or assertiveness courses.[19]

From a legal standpoint, French law guarantees equal treatment and equal professional opportunities. Enforcement of these guarantees is fairly weak, however, and organizations that could be valuable to women usually are uninvolved. For example, unions have generally resisted taking on women's issues, and there are no organizations in France comparable to the National Organization for Women in the United States that could promote equal opportunity issues. Even French associations of women managers are limited in their efforts and, for the most part, focus primarily on social networking. So, while some French companies have promoted women into higher-level positions and have affirmative action programs in place, these firms unfortunately still are the exception rather than the rule. As one analyst recently put it, "Companies' needs for the best possible managers will favor highly qualified women; but to succeed, these women will most likely have to accept even more difficult working conditions."[20]

Germany Before unification, about half of working-age women in West Germany and almost all of those in East Germany were in the workforce. In both West and East, however, women held few top management positions. Studies of large West German firms found that fewer than 10 percent of top managers and only a slightly higher percentage of managers at the next level were women, and only a handful were members of managing boards of public companies. In East Germany, one-third of all management positions were held by women, but these primarily were low-level jobs. With the unification of Germany, the status of women in management does not look any more promising. One reason is that professional qualifications appear to relate inversely to hierarchical position. Antal and Krebsbach-Gnath explained this seeming paradox as follows:

> The higher the position, the less significance the organization attaches to . . . "objective" criteria. The factors that receive more weight in promotion decisions for senior management positions are both less objective and more often based on traditional male career patterns. In effect, therefore, they discriminate against women. Among the factors listed in one study for promotion into upper-level management were professional competence, effectiveness, professional experience, length of experience, time with the company, commitment to the job, and professional and regional mobility. To the extent that "objective" factors and qualifications, such as education and training that women can consciously acquire, play a lesser role in decision making, other sociopsychological and systemic factors assume increasing importance and create less easily surmountable barriers to career development for women.[21]

Unlike some other countries, Germany has introduced laws that mandate equal opportunity and the creation of equal opportunity positions throughout the public sector. Today, all German states must ensure that their legislation provides for equal treatment of men and women in the workplace. But use of quotas is unacceptable, and this makes the legislation difficult to enforce. Additionally, those individuals who are designated as equal opportunity officers typically have difficulty carrying out their tasks, because they often lack the needed authority to enforce their decisions.

In the private sector, there has been some progress toward increasing the number of women in upper-level management positions through the introduction of voluntary equal opportunity programs. Some German firms also have nominated individuals or groups and assigned them the responsibility of ensuring equal opportunity for all personnel. Another, and more recent, development is the inclusion of company-level, work-family agreements between employers and workers' representatives regarding parental leave and return plans. These plans allow employees to take a longer parental leave than is granted by law, and to attract these employees back, these plans guarantee an equivalent job on returning from the extended leave.

Some analysts believe that Germany's growing need for competent managers likely will increase the number of women in management and the opportunity for them to achieve higher-level positions. On the other side, critics argue this is wishful thinking and that what is needed is stronger legislation. Still others contend that until there is a fundamental change in the way that male managers view the role and status of women, nothing significant will happen. These arguments all point to one conclusion: Opportunities for women managers in Germany remain limited and do not seem likely to improve significantly in the near future.

Great Britain   By the turn of the century, approximately 13 million women were in the British workforce, which was about 45 percent of the country's total workforce. The number of women in management and related occupations has been steadily increasing over the last two decades. Once again, however, as in other countries, women in Great Britain are not well represented at the highest levels of organizations.

Most women managers in Britain are employed in retail distribution, hotel and catering, banking, finance, medical and other health services, and food, drink, and tobacco. Almost all of these managers are at the lowest levels, and they have a long way to go if they hope to reach the top. Legislation designed to prevent discrimination in the workplace is proving to be of limited value; however, a number of steps are being taken to help British women attain equal opportunity in employment.

In recent years, British women have been setting up their own associations, such as the Women's Engineering Society, to develop sources for networking and to increase their political lobbying power. There also is a national association, known as The 300 Group, that campaigns for women seeking election to Parliament. In addition, women have become very active in joining management and professional associations, such as the Hotel, Catering and Institutional Management Association, the Institute of Personnel Management, and the Institute of Health Service Management. Women now constitute 50 percent or more of the membership in these professional associations.

At the same time, a growing number of British companies are proactively trying to recruit and promote women into the management ranks. They are introducing career development programs specifically for women and are prepared to take whatever steps are necessary to ensure that outstanding women remain with the company. For example, the National Westminster Bank allows women managers to leave for up to five years to raise their children and then return to a management position at their previous level. Firms also are designing strategies to ensure that equal opportunities are, in fact, being implemented. Chief executives and directors of leading companies formed a group known as Opportunity 2000. One of the group's goals is to provide a wide range of assistance to women who are interested in business careers; in particular, the focus is on helping firms to demonstrate a commitment to these goals, change their old ways of doing business, communicate their desires to potential women managers, and make the necessary financial and time commitments that are needed to ensure success.

At the same time discrimination lawsuits are becoming more commonplace in the U.K. In 1994 approximately 4,500 sex and race discrimination lawsuits were filed with Employment Tribunals in England and Wales. In 2002 this number was in excess of 9,500, an increase of over 110 percent.[22] In one lawsuit, a woman working as an investment banker at Deutsche Bank's London office and earning over $400,000 annually resigned and sued the company for sex discrimination. She won her case before a tribunal and received an out-of-court settlement of over $1.4 million. Most settlements involve much smaller sums and, unlike the United States, in the U.K. there are limits for compensation from legal actions. Nevertheless, with the large increase in the number of lawsuits, many British companies are realizing that they need to take action to ensure that they are not sued. Among large firms one of the most popular approaches is that taken by the British branch of UBS A.G. of Switzerland. The company has created a new position, global head of diversity, and it is this person's job to ensure that all employees are treated fairly. Meanwhile, the legal system in the U.K. continues to change, making it easier to sue for bias, raising the amounts that can be awarded, shifting the burden of proof from claimants to defendants, and allowing third parties such as the British Equal Opportunity Commission to sue on behalf of individuals. Given the changing legal and social environment, a growing number of firms are starting to adopt a much more proactive stance regarding discrimination.

Ethical Problems and Concerns in China

Along with the tremendous opportunities offered in China, MNCs doing business there face a variety of ethical problems. After the violent, June 1989 crackdown on student protesters in Beijing's Tiananmen Square, many MNCs questioned whether any business should be conducted in China until more freedom and human rights were restored.

Despite continuing ethical issues such as piracy of intellectual property and human rights violations such as the use of prisoner and child labor, most MNCs still feel there are too many opportunities in China to be ignored. One of these is low-cost labor. Workers in China are not well paid, and to meet the demand for output, they often are forced to work 12 hours a day, 7 days a week. In some cases, children are used for this work and are paid very little, usually only one-half of the already very low adult's wages. The government also has been using prison labor to produce goods for the export market. In addition, with China now totally open to the outside world, there has been a rush to get rich under the market reforms and this has been accompanied by a dramatic increase in crime and illegal business activities.

These developments have led to friction between the U.S. Congress and China. A closer look at the existing piracy, counterfeiting, and industrial spying problems illustrates some of the major ethical challenges facing MNCs in China.

Piracy, Counterfeiting, and Industrial Spying Problems   In recent years the U.S. government has been taking a hard line on Chinese piracy of intellectual property (e.g., patents, copyrights, and trademarks) and demanding that China crack down on those who are copying illegally. The music business is a good example. The International Federation of Phonographic Industries estimates that music piracy in China cost the industry close to $1 billion since 1998.[23] China's system is more opaque, which means that it lacks transparency and does less to enforce rules against piracy and other unethical practices, than any other country in the world. Commenting on this, one analyst recently noted:

> China's legal system is riddled with loopholes. In much of the world, counterfeiting refers to the unauthorized production and sale of exact copies of genuine goods, down to the trademarks, and there is a growing trend to enact comprehensive anticounterfeiting criminal laws. But in China there isn't even a clear definition of counterfeiting. An old trademark law utilizes vague terms like "large" and "relatively large" to determine whether cases rise to a criminal level. In 1993, China issued more specific regulations (*i.e.,* suggesting the prosecution of thrice-captured offenders), but a criminal-code amendment in 1997 [left] enforcement officials scratching their heads as to whether the . . . regs still apply.[24]

A new trademark law passed at the end of 2001, and the law's implementing regulations, which followed in September 2002, help brand owners far more than any Chinese regulation has ever done to tackle copyright infringement.[25] Not only in music but in film, software, and most popular consumer products of all kinds, pirating is rampant. For example, within a week of the U.S. release of the film *Dr. Seuss: How the Grinch Stole Christmas,* videodisc copies were selling on China streets for about $1.20 each,[26] and Hollywood hits such as *Gladiator* could be purchased on DVD for $2 soon after they were first shown in American theatres.[27] In an effort to deal with this problem, the U.S. government has been putting pressure on the Chinese government to close down factories that produce pirated films, and there has been some progress.

In addition to taking direct action against pirating, the Chinese government has been offering rewards to those who provide information leading to the closing of an illegal operation.[28] However, the problem is not easily resolved.[29] For example, Macau near Hong Kong is a nucleus of Asia's fake CD-ROM manufacturing, but law enforcement personnel give it wide latitude because of the personal danger they face in trying to enforce piracy laws there.[30] "International Management in Action: Get Tough . . . or Else" gives some more specific examples of the huge pirating problem in China.

In addition to piracy and counterfeiting problems, Chinese-backed industry spying on outside MNCs has increased dramatically. According to a survey, 1,300 major U.S. MNCs now see China as their major foreign economic-espionage threat. Some examples include:

- Amgen discovered that a Chinese spy had infiltrated its organization and was trying to steal a vial of cell cultures for Epogen, now a $1.5 billion-a-year anemia drug.

Get Tough . . . or Else

A growing number of multinationals are very concerned about doing business in China. For example, within hours of the time their goods are on the street, many find that counterfeiters are already working on developing their own version of the product—and in many cases, these clones look just like the original. Today, there are fake cans of Coca-Cola, fake McDonald's hamburger restaurants, fake versions of the Jeeps that Chrysler manufactures with a joint-venture partner in Beijing, and fake Gillette razor blades.

Personal care product companies such as Henkl of Germany and Procter & Gamble of the United States estimate that about a quarter of the goods bearing their names in China are fake. Nike says that its potential annual losses in China resulting from counterfeit operations are about the size of its legitimate business in the United States. And pharmaceutical firms find that their drugs are often copied and distributed under their own name. Pfizer began selling Viagra in China in July 2000. By the end of the year, three local producers had introduced ripped-off versions of the pill and within the next 90 days another 30 companies had done so.

Even more disconcerting is that when counterfeiters are caught, the Chinese government often does very little about it. The Gillette Razor Blade Company is a good example of this. The Huaxing Razor Blade Factory was producing Gillette look-alike blades and packaging them in the same blue package as that used by Gillette. After Chinese authorities raided the factory, they fined the company $3,500 and told management that it was illegal to produce counterfeit blades and they were to stop. Five months later, when it became evident that the company was still manufacturing the blades, there was a second raid, followed by a fine of $3,300. At that time, the manager was asked why he not only kept producing the blades but also used the same packaging as before. He remarked that he did not want to throw away packaging that had already been printed. "We didn't want to waste it," he said.

Will such a "slap on the wrist" type of enforcement stop the counterfeiting? This is unlikely, because the fines are small compared with the revenues being generated. The Chinese government also does not seem to be very interested in taking sterner measures. In fact, in some cases when MNCs have complained that counterfeiters have gone back to their old ways, inspectors have refused to take any additional action, arguing that "we already addressed that issue and we are now moving on to other matters." Such an attitude worries MNCs, because they feel there is no protection for their intellectual properties. A lawyer who has represented several U.S. companies in trademark disputes in China put it this way:

In most countries, if you have 10 pirates, you can go after one, expect seven to stop, and then figure out how to get the remaining two. But in China, when you go after one the other nine see exactly what you're doing. Not only do they keep pirating, but you invite 10 more to join in.

Unless the government of China takes more stringent steps to do something about pirating and counterfeiting, MNCs likely will take action of their own. One of the most commonly mentioned steps is to demand that Chinese exports to the United States be limited and that levies be assessed on these goods to offset the loss of revenues being sustained by the U.S. MNCs. In the final analysis, it appears that China will have to get tough on pirates and counterfeiters . . . or else.

- A Chinese spy in Hong Kong was recently caught using sophisticated telecommunications software to secretly listen in on sensitive phone conversations between American executives.
- A Chinese engineer at a Boulder, Colorado, software company allegedly stole proprietary source code and peddled it to a Chinese company. As a result, the U.S. company went out of business.[31]

A related problem is joint ventures in which Chinese partners break the agreement and walk off with patents or capital or simply start an operation that is in direct competition with the venture. Kimberly-Clark is a good example.

Its plant in Handan, which is 97% owned by [Kimberly-Clark], produces around $10 million annually of feminine-care pads. Located in the northeastern province of Hebei, it is one of 12 company factories in China. The operation seemed to be running smoothly until last spring, when plant officials noticed a nearby factory was making a similar product. Worse, the Americans discovered that the head of the rival operation was Li Hongzhi, who was picked by Kimberly-Clark's Chinese partner, Xingha Factory Co., to be the manager of the joint venture. Li was "stealing" and "diverting materials" such as spare parts and pulp from the venture to the new factory, alleged . . . Kimberly-Clark's vice-president for corporate communications.[32]

Kimberly-Clark went to the U.S. Embassy to complain and eventually the situation was satisfactorily resolved. The same was not true for Chicago-based Borg-Warner Automotive Inc. Soon after this company signed a joint-venture agreement, the firm realized that its Chinese partner had no intention of making the deal work. In fact, the partner intended to set up a rival operation. So Borg-Warner filed a request with the requisite Chinese agency to end the joint venture, pointing out that its partner had not fulfilled its obligation to provide utilities such as water and electricity and the company was therefore unable to accept the factory site that had been given to it. The Chinese regulatory agency rejected Borg-Warner's request, and in the interim the Chinese partner filed a lawsuit against Borg-Warner for rejecting the plant site. In the judgment that ensued, a Chinese court awarded all of the joint-venture assets of $2.2 million, 60 percent of which came from Borg-Warner, to the Chinese partner. By the time the American MNC found out about the judgment, it was too late to appeal the decision at the local level.

The examples discussed here are representative of the many that are coming out of China and the rest of the world. And they all reinforce the same point: Doing international business can be very risky, and even joint ventures with in-country partners do not ensure that an MNC will be protected from the adverse effects of unethical and illegal actions.[33]

■ Corporate Social Responsibility

In addition to expectations that they adhere to specific ethical codes and principles, corporations are under increasing pressure to contribute to the societies and communities in which they operate, and to adopt more socially responsible business practices in their entire range of operations. **Corporate social responsibility (CSR)** can be defined as the actions of a firm to benefit society beyond the requirements of the law and the direct interests of the firm.[34] Pressure for greater attention to CSR has emanated from a range of stakeholders, including civil society (the broad societal interests in a given region or country) and from **nongovernmental organizations (NGOs).** These groups have urged MNCs to be more responsive to the range of social needs in developing countries, including addressing concerns about working conditions in factories or service centers and attending to the environmental impacts of their activities.[35] As a result of recent ethics scandals and concerns about the lack of corporate responsibility, according to World Economic Forum's Gallup International Poll released in November 2002, leaders of NGOs are the most trusted of the eight leadership categories tested, while leaders of MNCs and leaders of the USA were the least trusted (see Figure 3–1).[36]

corporate social responsibility (CSR) The actions of a firm to benefit society beyond the requirements of the law and the direct interests of the firm.

nongovernmental organizations (NGOs) Private, not-for-profit organizations that seek to serve society's interests by focusing on social, political, and economic issues such as poverty, social justice, education, health, and the environment.

Figure 3–1

Trust in Leaders: Percentage Saying "A Lot" and "Some Trust"

NGO leaders	56
Leaders at the U.N.	42
Spiritual/religious leaders	41
Leaders of Western Europe	36
Managers of the global economy	36
Managers of the national economy	35
Executives of MNCs	33
Leaders of the U.S.A.	27

0 10 20 30 40 50 60

Average Across All 15 Countries Surveyed

Source: From *Voice of the People Survey, 2002.* Reprinted with permission of Gallup International.

British Petroleum, Johnson & Johnson, and many other MNCs take their CSR commitment seriously. These firms have integrated their response to CSR pressures into their core business strategies and operating principles around the world (see the section "Responses to Social Obligations" and the Internet exercise later in this chapter).

The Rise of Civil Society and NGOs

The emergence of organized civil society and NGOs has dramatically altered the business environment globally and the role of MNCs within it. Although social movements have been part of the political and economic landscape for centuries, the emergence of NGO activism in the United States during the modern era can be traced to mid-1984, when a range of NGOs, including church and community groups, human rights organizations, and other anti-apartheid activists, built strong networks and pressed U.S. cities and states to divest their public pension funds of companies doing business in South Africa. This effort, combined with domestic unrest, international governmental pressures, and capital flight, posed a direct, sustained, and ultimately successful challenge to the white minority rule, resulting in the collapse of apartheid.

Since then, NGOs generally have grown in number, power, and influence. Large, global NGOs such as Save the Children, Oxfam, CARE, World Wildlife Fund, and Conservation International are active in all parts of the world. Their force has been felt in a range of major public policy debates, and NGO activism has been responsible for major changes in corporate behavior and governance. Some observers now regard NGOs as a counterweight to business and global capitalism. NGO criticisms have been especially sharp in relation to the activities of MNCs such as Nike, Levi's, Chiquita, and others whose sourcing practices in developing countries have been alleged to exploit low-wage workers, take advantage of lax environmental and workplace standards, and otherwise contribute to social and economic problems. More recently, business process offshoring firms have been implicated as well. Two recent examples illustrate the complex and increasingly important impact of NGOs on MNCs.

In January 2004, Citigroup announced it would no longer finance certain projects in emerging markets identified by the Rainforest Action Network (RAN) as damaging to the environment. This announcement came after several years of aggressive pressure and lobbying by RAN, including full-page advertising in daily newspapers showing barren landscapes and blackened trees, lobbying by film and television personalities urging consumers to cut up their credit cards, blockades of Citigroup branches, and campaigns involving schoolchildren who sent cards to Citigroup's chairman, Sanford Weil, asking him to stop contributing to the extinction of endangered species.[37] After heavy lobbying from NGOs, in August 2003, the U.S. pharmaceutical industry dropped its opposition to relaxation of intellectual property provisions under the WTO to make generic, low-cost antiviral drugs available to developing countries facing epidemics or other health emergencies[38] (see the In-Depth Integrated Case at the end of Part 1).

Many NGOs recognize that MNCs can have positive impacts on the countries in which they do business, often adhering to higher standards of social and environmental responsibility than local firms. In fact, MNCs may be in a position to transfer "best practices" in social or environmental actions from their home to host countries' markets. In some instances, MNCs and NGOs collaborate on social and environmental projects and in so doing contribute both to the well-being of communities and to the reputation of the MNC. The emergence of NGOs that seek to promote ethical and socially responsible business practices is beginning to generate substantial changes in corporate management, strategy, and governance.

Response to Social Obligations

MNCs are increasingly engaged in a range of responses to growing pressure to contribute positively to the social and environmental progress of the communities in which they do business. One mechanism is agreements and codes of conduct in which MNCs commit to maintain certain standards in their domestic and global operations. These agreements, which include the U.N. Global Compact (see Table 3–1), the Global Reporting Initiative, the social accountability "SA8000" standards, and the ISO 14000 environmental quality standards, provide some assurances that when MNCs do business around the world, they will maintain a minimum level of social and environmental standards in the workplaces and communities in which they are doing business.[39] These codes help offset the real or perceived concern that companies move jobs to get around higher labor or environmental standards in their home markets. They may also contribute to the raising of standards in the developing world by "exporting" higher standards to local firms in those countries.

Individual companies have also taken steps to develop strong ethical principles and integrate social responsibility into their business operations, often with the help of NGOs.[40] In the case of pharmaceutical companies and access to AIDS medications, a number of companies initiated or expanded alliances with those very NGOs that had opposed the companies over the issue of relaxation of rules pertaining to intellectual property rights (IPR). Once an agreement was reached, these NGOs, such as Doctors Without Borders and Oxfam, helped the companies deliver drugs to the target populations and to restore the companies' legitimacy, which had been damaged as a result of their initial opposition to modification of the IPR rules.

Hewlett-Packard has initiated a series of "i-communities" in economically deprived areas such as the town of Kuppam in the state of Andhra Pradesh, India. These communities use public/private/NGO partnerships to enhance economic development through technology. NGOs promote the projects and enlist community support. HP is able to use the projects to build markets, test products, and expand global marketing knowledge.[41] The experience provides HP with valuable knowledge of how to identify and negotiate with rural customers, which positions it to improve its ability to do business in rural markets of India and other countries in the future. In addition, HP has

---

Table 3–1
Principles of the Global Compact

Human Rights

Principle 1: Support and respect the protection of international human rights within their sphere of influence.

Principle 2: Make sure their own corporations are not complicit in human rights abuses.

Labor

Principle 3: Freedom of association and the effective recognition of the right to collective bargaining.

Principle 4: The elimination of all forms of forced and compulsory labor.

Principle 5: The effective abolition of child labor.

Principle 6: The elimination of discrimination with respect to employment and occupation.

Environment

Principle 7: Support a precautionary approach to environmental challenges.

Principle 8: Undertake initiatives to promote greater environmental responsibility.

Principle 9: Encourage the development and diffusion of environmentally friendly technologies.

Anti-Corruption

Principle 10: Business should work against all forms of corruption, including extortion and bribery.

Source: The U.N. Global Compact,
http://www.unglobalcompact.org/gc/unweb.nsf/content/thenine.htm.

received positive reputation effects in development circles. Mattel's board independently contracts with the International Center for Corporate Accountability, an NGO, to provide unscheduled on-site audits of its factories and its first- and second-tier suppliers to determine compliance with the company's Global Manufacturing Principles. Motorola is engaged in efforts to certify literally thousands of suppliers for meeting its global corporate responsibility standards. In some instances, it has accepted suppliers' standards as meeting or exceeding those of Motorola itself.

Hence, companies are very actively trying both to respond to pressure to be more socially responsible and to develop proactive strategies to demonstrate their commitment to social and environmental progress around the world, especially in developing countries.[42]

Corporate Governance

The global ethical and governance scandals have placed corporations under intense scrutiny regarding their oversight and accountability. Corporate governance is increasingly high on the agenda for directors, investors, and governments alike in the wake of financial collapses and corporate scandals in recent years. These collapses and scandals have not been limited to a single country, or even a single continent, but have been a global phenomenon. **Corporate governance** can be defined as the system by which business corporations are directed and controlled.[43] The corporate governance structure specifies the distribution of rights and responsibilities among different participants in the corporation—such as the board, managers, shareholders, and other stakeholders—and spells out the rules and procedures for making decisions on corporate affairs. By doing this, it also provides the structure through which the company objectives are set, and the means of attaining those objectives and monitoring performance.

Governance rules and regulations differ among countries and regions around the world. For example, the U.K. and U.S. systems have been termed "outsider" systems because of dispersed ownership of corporate equity among a large number of outside investors. Historically, although institutional investor ownership is predominant, institutions generally do not hold large shares in any given company; hence they have limited direct control.[44] In contrast, in an insider system, such as in many continental European countries, ownership tends to be much more concentrated, with shares often being owned by holding companies, families, or banks. In addition, differences in legal systems, as described in Chapter 2, also affect shareholders' and other stakeholders' rights and, in turn, the responsiveness and accountability of corporate managers to these constituencies. Notwithstanding recent scandals, in general, North American and European systems are considered comparatively responsive to shareholders and other stakeholders. In regions with less well developed legal and institutional protections and poor property rights, such as some countries in Asia, Latin America, and Africa, forms of "crony capitalism" may emerge in which weak corporate governance and government interference can lead to poor performance, risky financing patterns, and macroeconomic crises.

Corporate governance will undoubtedly remain high on the agenda of governments, investors, NGOs, and corporations in the coming years, as pressure for accountability and responsiveness continues to increase.

Corruption and the Foreign Corrupt Practices Act Revisited

As noted in Chapter 2, government corruption is a pervasive element in the international business environment. Recently publicized scandals in Russia, China, Pakistan, Lesotho, South Africa, Costa Rica, Egypt, and elsewhere underscore the extent of corruption globally, especially in the developing world. Recently, however, a number of initiatives have been taken by governments and companies to begin to stem the tide of corruption.[45]

The Foreign Corrupt Practices Act (FCPA) makes it illegal for U.S. companies and their managers to attempt to influence foreign officials through personal payments or

corporate governance
The system by which business corporations are directed and controlled.

political contributions. Prior to passage of the FCPA, some American multinationals had engaged in this practice, but realizing that their stockholders were unlikely to approve of these tactics, the firms typically disguised the payments as entertainment expenses, consulting fees, and so on. The FCPA not only prohibits these activities but the U.S. Internal Revenue Service continually audits the books of MNCs. Those firms that take deductions for such illegal activities are subject to high financial penalties, and individuals who are involved can even end up going to prison.

Strict enforcement of the FCPA has been applauded by many people. At the same time some critics wonder if such a strong social responsibility stance has not hurt the competitive ability of American MNCs. On the positive side, many U.S. multinationals have now increased the amount of business in countries where they used to pay bribes. Additionally, many institutional investors in the United States have made it clear that they will not buy stock in companies that engage in unethical practices and will sell their holdings if they hold stock in such firms. Given that these institutions have hundreds of billions of dollars invested, senior-level management must be responsive to their needs.

Looking at the effect of the FCPA on U.S. multinationals, it appears that the law has had far more of a positive effect than a negative one. In fact, some observers wonder if companies did not overstate the importance of such covert activities. And given the growth of American MNCs in recent years, it seems fair to conclude that bribes are not a basic part of business in many countries, for when multinationals stopped this activity, they were still able to sell in that particular market.

On the other hand, this does not mean that bribery and corruption is a thing of the past. Figure 3–2 gives the latest corruption index of countries around the world. Notice that the U.S. ranks 18th by this independent analysis. However, a report issued by the U.S. Commerce Department contends that since 1994, foreign companies have used bribes to edge out U.S. MNCs on a large number of international business deals. The report describes a case of bribery involving the contract for a power-generating plant in Central Europe as follows:

> A European company was awarded the multimillion-dollar contract even though the Central European government's own review board had recommended the contract be awarded to a U.S. firm. The report says there was clear evidence that a power-company official had been given a cash bribe by the European company that won the contract. The company used the same practice to win other contracts in Eastern and Central Europe, according to the report.[46]

These experiences reveal that bribery continues to be a problem for U.S. MNCs. At the same time, to comply with the provisions of the FCPA, U.S. firms must be careful not to follow suit and resort to bribery themselves. In particular, changes in the law make FCPA violators subject to Federal Sentencing Guidelines. As a result, when two Lockheed Corporation executives were found guilty of paying a $1 million bribe to a member of the Egyptian parliament in order to secure the sale of aircraft to the Egyptian military, one of the executives was sentenced to probation and fined $20,000 and the other, who initially fled prosecution, was fined $125,000 and sentenced to 18 months in prison.[47]

Another development that promises to give teeth to "anti-bribing" is the recent formal agreement by a host of industrialized nations that have agreed to outlaw the practice of bribing foreign government officials. The treaty, signed in Paris by 29 nations that belong to the Organization for Economic Cooperation and Development, marked a victory for the United States, which outlawed foreign bribery two decades previously but had not been able to persuade other countries to follow its lead. As a result, American firms had long complained that they lost billions of dollars in contracts each year to rivals that bribed their way to success.[48]

This treaty does not outlaw most payments to political party leaders. In fact, the treaty provisions are much narrower than U.S. negotiators wanted, and there undoubtedly will be ongoing pressure from the American government to expand the scope and coverage of the agreement. For the moment, however, it is a step in the direction of a more ethical

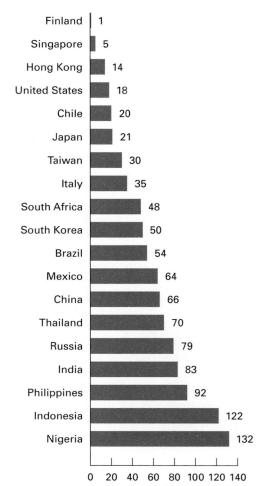

Figure 3–2

Corruption Index: Ranking of Least Corrupt to Most

Source: Adapted from Transparency International, October 7, 2003, http://www.transparency.org/pressrelease_ archive/2003/2003.10.07.epi.en.html.

level playing field in global business. Additionally, in summing up the impact and value of the treaty, one observer noted that:

> For their part, business executives say the treaty . . . reflects growing support for anti-bribery initiatives among corporations in Europe and Japan that have openly opposed the idea. Some of Europe's leading industrial corporations, including a few that have been embroiled in recent allegations of bribery, have spoken out in favor of tougher measures and on the increasingly corrosive effect of corruption.[49]

In addition to the 29 members of the OECD, a number of developing countries, including Argentina, Brazil, Bulgaria, Chile, and the Slovak Republic, have signed on to the OECD agreement. Latin American countries have established the Organization of American States (OAS) Inter-American Convention Against Corruption, which entered into force in March 1997, and more than 25 Western Hemisphere countries are signatories to the convention, including Argentina, Brazil, Chile, Mexico, and the United States. As a way to prevent the shifting of corrupt practices to suppliers and intermediaries, the Transparent Agents Against Contracting Entities (TRACE) standard was developed after a review of the practices of 34 companies. It applies to business intermediaries, including sales agents, consultants, suppliers, distributors, resellers, subcontractors, franchisees, and joint-venture partners, so that final producers, distributors, and customers can be confident that no party within a supply chain participated in corruption.

Both governments and companies have made important steps in their efforts to stem the spread of corruption, but much more needs to be done in order to reduce and eventually eliminate the impact of corruption on companies and the broader societies in which they operate.[50]

International Assistance

In addition to government and corporate-sponsored ethics and social responsibility practices, governments and corporations are increasingly collaborating to provide assistance to communities and locales around the world through global partnerships. This assistance is particularly important for those parts of the world that have not fully benefited from globalization and economic integration, such as described in the opening case. Using a cost-benefit analysis of where investments would have the greatest impact, a recent study identified the top priorities around the world for development assistance. The results of this analysis are presented in Table 3–2. Controlling and preventing AIDS, fighting malnutrition, reducing subsidies and trade restrictions, and controlling malaria are shown to be the best investments. Governments, international institutions, and corporations are involved in several ongoing efforts to address some of these problems.[51]

At the United Nations Millennium Summit in September 2000, world leaders placed development at the heart of the global agenda by adopting the Millennium Development Goals (see Table 3–3). The eight Millennium Development Goals constitute an ambitious agenda to significantly improve the human condition by 2015. The goals set clear targets for reducing poverty, hunger, disease, illiteracy, environmental degradation, and discrimination against women.[52] For each goal, a set of targets and indicators have been defined and are used to track the progress in meeting the goals.

A more specific initiative is the Global Fund to Fight AIDS, Tuberculosis and Malaria, which was established in 2001. By July 2003, more than $2 billion had been paid

Table 3–2
Copenhagen Consensus Development Priorities

Project rating		Challenge	Opportunity
Very good	1	Diseases	Control of HIV/AIDS
	2	Malnutrition	Providing micro nutrients
	3	Subsidies and trade	Trade liberalization
	4	Diseases	Control of malaria
Good	5	Malnutrition	Development of new agricultural technologies
	6	Sanitation and water	Small-scale water technology for livelihoods
	7	Sanitation and water	Community-managed water supply and sanitation
	8	Sanitation and water	Research on water productivity in food production
	9	Government	Lowering the cost of starting a new business
Fair	10	Migration	Lowering barriers to migration for skilled workers
	11	Malnutrition	Improving infant and child nutrition
	12	Malnutrition	Reducing the prevalence of low birth weight
	13	Diseases	Scaled-up basic health services
Bad	14	Migration	Guest-worker programs for the unskilled
	15	Climate	"Optimal" carbon tax
	16	Climate	The Kyoto protocol
	17	Climate	Value-at-risk carbon tax

Source: Copenhagen Consensus
Note: Some of the proposals were not ranked

Table 3–3
The U.N. Millennium Development Goals

Goal 1: Eradicate extreme poverty and hunger.

Goal 2: Achieve universal primary education.

Goal 3: Promote gender equality and empower women.

Goal 4: Reduce child mortality.

Goal 5: Improve maternal health.

Goal 6: Combat HIV/AIDS, malaria, and other diseases.

Goal 7: Ensure environmental sustainability.

Goal 8: Develop a Global Partnership for Development.

Source: www.unmillenniumproject.org.

---

in by developed countries to the Global Fund. In addition to leading country donors that included the United States, the EU, individual European countries, and Japan, the Gates Foundation contributed $100 million, and other corporations are being solicited for contributions. In April 2002, the Global Fund made its first awards to programs in over 40 countries, totaling $616 million.[53]

Through these and other efforts, MNCs, governments, and international organizations are providing a range of resources to communities around the world to assist them as they respond to the challenges of globalization and development. International managers will increasingly be called upon to support and contribute to these initiatives.

The World of *BusinessWeek*—Revisited

The *BusinessWeek* article that opens this chapter discusses concerns over the rising economic disparity between developed and developing nations despite the growing trend toward global free trade. In particular, there are concerns that corporations and governments are not doing enough to meet their social obligations in the developing world. In this chapter we focused on ethics and social responsibility in global business activities, including the role of governments, MNCs, and NGOs in advancing greater ethical and socially responsible behavior.

In addition, global ethical and governance scandals have rocked the financial markets and implicated dozens of individual companies. New corporate ethics guidelines passed in the United States have forced many MNCs to take a look at their own internal ethical practices and make changes accordingly. Lawmakers in Europe and Asia have also made adjustments in rules over corporate financial disclosure. The continuing trend toward globalization and free trade appears to be encouraging development of a set of global ethical, social responsibility, and anticorruption standards. This may actually help firms cut compliance costs as they realize the economies of having common global frameworks. The old message "This is how we've always done business" will have to give way to a new standard of ethical conduct.

Having read the chapter, answer the following questions: (1) Do governments and companies in developed countries have an ethical responsibility to contribute to economic growth and social development in developing countries? (2) Are governments, companies, or NGOs best equipped to provide this assistance? (3) Do corporations have a responsibility to use their "best" ethics and social responsibility practices when they do business in other countries, even if those countries' practices are different?

SUMMARY OF KEY POINTS

1. Ethics is the study of morality and standards of conduct. It is important in the study of international management because ethical behavior often varies from one country to another. For example, in recent years in Japan, political and business scandals and apparent cases of avoiding minority hiring have drawn attention to the need for another look at ethical and socially responsible behavior. Japan's lobbying efforts in Washington also have been questioned from an ethical standpoint.

2. Research in France and Germany reveals that European and U.S. MNCs seem to have different standards of ethics that result in different types of decisions and business practices. For example, U.S. MNCs do not believe in bribing businesspeople or politicians to gain favors, but some studies find that more respondents in samples of both German and French managers were not as concerned with bribes as being unethical and instead felt payoffs were merely a cost of doing business. In the area of equal opportunity for women, the Europeans have goals for fully integrating women into the workforce and even EU legislation to ensure equal pay and equal treatment in employment. However, like U.S. women,

European women are still being deprived of equal opportunities and are underrepresented in the managerial ranks, although some progress is being made in European firms.

3. Ethics also is a problem in countries such as China. Since the violent crackdown at Tiananmen Square and continued ethical and human rights violations, many MNCs have questioned whether they should do business with the Chinese. Too often those that found the low labor cost attractive overlooked the fact that the Chinese factory employees work long hours for very low pay and some of these workers are underage or are prisoners. These types of exploitive practices have ethical implications.

4. During the years ahead, multinationals likely will become more concerned about being socially responsible. NGOs are forcing the issue. Countries are passing laws to regulate ethical practices and governance rules for MNCs. MNCs are being more proactive (often because they realize it makes good business sense) in making social contributions in the regions in which they operate, and in developing codes of conduct to govern ethics and social responsibility.

KEY TERMS

corporate governance, *68*
corporate social responsibility (CSR), *65*

ethics, *57*
nongovernmental organizations (NGOs), *65*

REVIEW AND DISCUSSION QUESTIONS

1. What lessons can U.S. multinationals learn from the political and bribery scandals in Japan that can be of value to them in doing business in this country? Discuss two.

2. In recent years, some prominent spokespeople have argued that those who work for the U.S. government in trade negotiations should be prohibited for a period of five years from accepting jobs as lobbyists for foreign firms. Is this a good idea? Why or why not?

3. How do ethical practices differ in the United States and in European countries such as France and

Germany? What implications does your answer have for U.S. multinationals operating in Europe?

4. Why are many MNCs reluctant to produce or sell their goods in China? What role can the Chinese government play in helping to resolve this problem?

5. Why are MNCs getting involved in corporate social responsibility? Are they displaying a sense of social responsibility, or is this merely a matter of good business? Defend your answer.

INTERNET EXERCISE: SOCIAL RESPONSIBILITY AT JOHNSON & JOHNSON AND HP

In this chapter, the social responsibility actions of companies such as Johnson & Johnson and Hewlett-Packard (HP) were discussed.

At Johnson & Johnson, social responsibility flows from the company's credo. Go to the J&J Web site, **www.jnj.com**, to the sections "Our Credo" and "Social Responsibility." Then answer these questions: (1) Which stakeholders are most important to J&J and why? (2) How does J&J ensure that all of its many operating companies adhere to the credo? (3) What are the main areas of social responsibility activities for J&J, and how do they relate to the credo?

At Hewlett-Packard, "global citizenship" means engaging in public/private partnerships and demonstrating model behavior and activities in governance, environmental policy and practices, community engagement models, and "e-inclusion initiatives." Go to the HP Web site, **www.hp.com**, to the sections on "global citizenship" and "e-inclusion." Then answer these questions: (1) What does it mean to be a "global citizen" at HP? (2) How does HP measure and evaluate its success in global citizenship? (3) What is "e-inclusion" and what are some specific examples of projects that advance HP's "e-inclusion" goals?

Saudi Arabia

Saudi Arabia is a large Middle Eastern country covering 865,000 square miles. Part of its east coast rests on the Persian Gulf, and much of the west coast rests along the Red Sea. One of the countries on its borders is Iraq. After Iraq's military takeover of Kuwait in August 1990, Iraq threatened to invade Saudi Arabia. This, of course, did not happen, and Saudi Arabia was not an Iraqi target during the U.S. led war in Iraq during 2003–2004. However, accusations stemming from rumors of terrorist financing activities have made Saudi Arabia a focus in the global war on terrorism, and Saudi Arabia itself was the target of terrorist attacks in 2003–2004.

There are approximately 22 million people in Saudi Arabia, and the per capita income is around $11,500. This apparent prosperity is misleading because most Saudis are poor farmers and herders who tend their camels, goats, and sheep. In recent years, however, more and more have moved to the cities and have jobs connected to the oil industry. Nearly all are Arab Muslims. The country has the two holiest cities of Islam: Mecca and Medina. The country depends almost exclusively on the sale of oil (it is the largest exporter of oil in the world) and has no public debt. The government is a monarchy, and the king makes all important decisions but is advised by ministers and other government officials. Royal and ministerial decrees account for most of the promulgated legislation. There are no political parties.

Recently, Robert Auger, the executive vice president of Skyblue, a commercial aircraft manufacturing firm based in Kansas City, had a visit with a Saudi minister. The Saudi official explained to Auger that the government planned to purchase 10 aircraft over the next two years. A number of competitive firms were bidding for the job. The minister went on to explain that despite the competitiveness of the situation, several members of the royal family were impressed with Auger's company. The firm's reputation for high-quality performance aircraft and state-of-the-art technology gave it the inside track. A number of people are involved in the decision, however, and in the minister's words, "Anything can happen when a committee decision is being made."

The Saudi official went on to explain that some people who would be involved in the decision had recently suffered large losses in some stock market speculations on the London Stock Exchange. "One relative of the King, who will be a key person in the decision regarding the purchase of the aircraft, I have heard, lost over $200,000 last week alone. Some of the competitive firms have decided to put together a pool of money to help ease his burden. Three of them have given me $100,000 each. If you were to do the same, I know that it would put you on a par with them, and I believe it would be in your best interests when the decision is made." Auger was stunned by the suggestion and told the minister that he would check with his people and get back with the minister as soon as possible.

As soon as he got back to his temporary office, Auger sent a coded message to headquarters asking management what he should do. He expects to have an answer within the next 48 hours. In the interim, he has had a call from the minister's office, but Auger's secretary told the caller that Auger had been called away from the office and would not be returning for at least two days. The individual said he would place the call again at the beginning of this coming week. In the interim, Auger has talked to a Saudi friend whom he had known back in the United States and who was currently an insider in the Saudi government. Over dinner, Auger hinted at what he had been told by the minister. The friend seemed somewhat puzzled about what Auger was saying and indicated that he had heard nothing about any stock market losses by the royal family or pool of money being put together for certain members of the decision-making committee. He asked Auger, "Are you sure you got the story straight, or as you Americans say, is someone pulling your leg?"

Questions

1. What are some current issues facing Saudi Arabia? What is the climate for doing business in Saudi Arabia today?

2. Is it legal for Auger's firm to make a payment of $100,000 to help ensure this contract?

3. Do you think other firms are making these payments, or is Auger's firm being singled out? What conclusion can you draw from your answer?

4. What would you recommend that Skyblue do?

It Sounds a Little Fishy

For the past two years, the Chicago-based Brattle Company has been thinking about going international. Two months ago, Brattle entered into negotiations with a large company based in Paris to buy one of its branches in Lyon, France. This would give Brattle a foreign subsidiary. Final arrangements on the deal should be completed within a month, although a few developments have occurred that concern the CEO of Brattle, Angela Scherer.

The most serious concern resulted from a conversation that Scherer had with one of the Lyon firm's largest customers. This customer had been introduced to Scherer during a dinner that the Paris headquarters gave in her honor last month. After the dinner, Scherer struck up a conversation with the customer to assure him that when Brattle took over the Lyon operation, they would provide the same high-quality service as their predecessor. The customer seemed interested in Scherer's comments and then said, "Will I also continue to receive $10,000 monthly for directing my business to you?" Scherer was floored; she did not know what to say. Finally she stammered, "That's something I think you and I will have to talk about further." With that, the two shook hands and the customer left. Scherer has not been back in touch with the customer since the dinner and is unsure of what to do next.

The other matter that has Scherer somewhat upset is a phone call from the head of the Lyon operation last week. This manager explained that his firm was very active in local affairs and donated approximately $5,000 a month to charitable organizations and philanthropic activities. Scherer is impressed with the firm's social involvement but wonders whether Brattle will be expected to assume these obligations. She then told her chief financial officer, "We're buying this subsidiary as an investment and we are willing to continue employing all the local people and paying their benefits. However, I wonder if we're going to have any profits from this operation after we get done with all the side payments for nonoperating matters. We have to cut back a lot of extraneous expenses. For example, I think we have to cut back much of the contribution to the local community, at least for the first couple of years. Also, I can't find any evidence of payment of this said $10,000 a month to that large customer. I wonder if we're being sold a bill of goods, or have they been paying him under the table? In any event, I think we need to look into this situation more closely before we make a final decision on whether to buy this operation."

Questions

1. If Scherer finds out that the French company has been paying its largest customer $10,000 a month, should Brattle back out of the deal? If Brattle goes ahead with the deal, should it continue to make these payments?

2. If Scherer finds out that the customer has been making up the story and no such payments were actually made, what should she do? What if this best customer says he will take his business elsewhere?

3. If Brattle buys the French subsidiary, should Scherer continue to give $5,000 monthly to the local community? Defend your answer.

Colgate's Distasteful Toothpaste

Colgate is a well-known consumer products company based in New York. Its present products are in the areas of household and personal care, which include laundry detergents such as Ajax and Fab, health care products manufactured for home health care, and specialty products such as Hill pet food. The household products segment represents approximately 75 percent of company revenues, while the specialty segment accounts for less than 7 percent. Colgate's value has been set in excess of $5.6 billion. Through both recessionary and recovery periods in the United States, Colgate has always been advocated by investment analysts as a good long-term stock.

Colgate's domestic market share has been lagging for several years. In the 1970s, when diversification seemed to be the tool to hedge against risk and sustain profits, Colgate bought companies in various industries, including kosher hot dogs, tennis and golf equipment, and jewelry. However, such extreme diversification diverted the company's attention away from its key moneymaking products: soap, laundry detergents, toothpaste, and other household products. The product diversification strategy ended in 1984 when Reuben Mark became CEO. At the young age of 45, he ordered the sale of parts of the organization that deviated too far from Colgate's core competency of personal and household products. He followed consultant Tom Peters's prescription for excellence: "Stick to the knitting."

Colgate's International Presence

Colgate traditionally has had a strong presence overseas. The company has operations in Australia, Latin America, Canada, France, and Germany. International sales presently represent one-half of Colgate's total revenue. In the past, Colgate always made a detailed analysis of each international market for demand. For instance, its entry into South America required an analysis of the type of product that would be most successful based on the dental hygiene needs of South American consumers. Because of this commitment to local cultural differences, the company has the number-one brand of toothpaste worldwide, Total.

To gain a strong share of the Asian market without having to build its own production plant, Colgate bought a 50 percent partnership in the Hawley and Hazel group in August 1985 for $50 million. One stipulation of this agreement was that Colgate had no management prerogatives: Hawley and Hazel maintained the right to make the major decisions in the organization. This partnership turned out to be very lucrative for Colgate, with double-digit millions in annual sales.

Enter the Distasteful Toothpaste

Hawley and Hazel is a chemical products company based in Hong Kong. The company was formed in the early part of the twentieth century, and its only product of note, believe it or not, was called "Darkie" toothpaste. Over the years, this had been one of the popular brands in Asia and had a dominant presence in markets such as Taiwan, Hong Kong, Singapore, Malaysia, and Thailand.

"Darkie" toothpaste goes back to the 1920s. The founder of this product, on a visit to the United States, loved Al Jolson, then a very popular black-faced entertainer (i.e., a white person with black makeup on his face). The founder decided to re-create the spirit of this character in the form of a trademark logo for his toothpaste because of the character's big smile and white teeth. When the founder returned to Asia, he copyrighted the name "Darkie" to go along with the logo. Since the 1920s, there has been strong brand loyalty among Asians for this product. One housewife in Taipei whose family used the product for years remarked, "The toothpaste featuring a Black man with a toothy smile is an excellent advertisement."

The Backlash Against Colgate

"Darkie" toothpaste had been sold in Asia for about 65 years. After Colgate became partners with Hawley and Hazel and its distasteful product, however, there was a wave of dissatisfaction with the logo and name from U.S. minorities and civil rights groups. There really has been no definite source on how this issue was passed to U.S. action groups and the media; however, a book entitled *Soap Opera: The Inside Story of Procter and Gamble* places responsibility in the hands of Procter & Gamble in an effort to tarnish Colgate's image and lower its market share.

The Americans' irate response to "Darkie" was a surprise to the Hawley and Hazel group. The product had always been successful in their Asian markets, and there had been no complaints. In fact, the success of "Darkie" had led the firm to market a new product in Japan called "Mouth Jazz," which had a similar logo. A spokesperson for Hawley and Hazel remarked, "There had been no problem before, you can tell by the market share that it is quite well received in Asia."

ICCR, the Interfaith Center on Corporate Responsibility, started the fight against Colgate about 10 years ago when it received a package of "Darkie" toothpaste from a consumer in Thailand. ICCR is composed of institutional investors that influence corporations through stock ownership. At the time the movement against Colgate's racially offensive product started, three members of ICCR already owned a small amount of stock in the company, and they filed a shareholder petition against Colgate requesting a change in the logo and name.

In a letter to Colgate, the ICCR executive director summarized the position against the distasteful toothpaste as follows:

> "Darkie" toothpaste is a 60-year-old product sold widely in Hong Kong, Malaysia, Taiwan and other places in the Far East. Its packaging includes a top-hatted and gleaming-toothed smiling likeness of Al Jolson under the words "Darkie" toothpaste. As you know, the term "Darkie" is deeply offensive. We would hope that in this new association with the Hawley and Hazel Chemical Company, that immediate action will be taken to stop this product's name so that a U.S. company will not be associated with promoting racial stereotypes in the Third World.

In response to this letter, R. G. S. Anderson, Colgate's director of corporate development, replied, "No plans exist or are being contemplated that would extend marketing and sales efforts for the product in Colgate subsidiaries elsewhere or beyond this Far East area." Anderson then went on to explain that Darkie's founder was imitating Al Jolson and that in the Chinese view, imitation was the "highest form of flattery." The ICCR then informed Colgate that if the logo was not changed, the organization would create a media frenzy and help various civil rights action groups in a possible boycott.

Because Colgate still refused to remove the logo, ICCR did form a coalition with civil rights groups such as the NAACP and the National Urban League to start protest campaigns. The protest took many forms, including lobbying at the state and local levels. At one point, after heavy lobbying by the ICCR, the House of Representatives in Pennsylvania passed a resolution urging Colgate to change the name and logo. Similar resolutions had been proposed in the U.S. Congress.

The pressures at home placed Colgate in a difficult position, especially as it had no management rights in its agreement with Hawley and Hazel. In the Asian market, neither Colgate nor Hawley and Hazel had any knowledge of consumer dissatisfaction because of racial offensiveness, despite the fact that the local Chinese name for "Darkie" (pronounced *hak ye nga goh*) can be translated as "Black Man Toothpaste." The logo seemed to enhance brand loyalty. One Asian customer stated, "I buy it because of the Black man's white teeth."

The demographics of the Asian market may help to explain the product's apparent acceptance. There are a relatively small number of Africans, Indians, Pakistanis, and Bangladeshis in the region; therefore, the number of people who might be offended by the logo is low. Also, some people of color did not seem disturbed by the name. For example, when asked about the implications of "Darkie" toothpaste, the secretary of the Indian Chamber of Commerce noted, "It doesn't offend me, and I'm sort of dark-skinned."

Initially, Colgate had no intentions of forcing Hawley and Hazel to change the product. R. G. S. Anderson issued another formal statement to the ICCR as follows: "Our position . . . would be different if the product were sold in the United States or in any Western English-speaking country; which, as I have stated several times, will not happen." Hawley and Hazel concurred with the stance. The alliance was very fearful of a loss of market share and did not believe that the complaints were issues relevant to Pacific Rim countries. A spokesperson for the alliance referred to the protest campaign as "a U.S. issue." The trade-off for revamping a successful product was deemed to be too risky and costly.

Colgate's Change of Heart

The issue did not go away. As U.S. leaders in Congress began to learn about this very offensive logo and name, the pressure on Colgate mounted. Interestingly, however, the value of Colgate's stock increased throughout this period of controversy. Wall Street seemed oblivious to the charges against Colgate, and this was another reason why Colgate took no action. Colgate management believed that an issue about overseas products should not have a negative effect on the company's domestic image. However, pressures continued from groups such as the Congressional Black Caucus, a strong political force. Colgate finally began to waver, but because of its agreement with Hawley and Hazel, it felt helpless. As one Colgate executive remarked, "One hates to let exogenous things drive your business, but you sometimes have to be aware of them."

Colgate CEO Reuben Mark eventually became very distressed over the situation. He was adamantly against racism of any kind and had taken actions to exhibit his beliefs. For instance, he and his wife had received recognition for their involvement in a special program for disadvantaged teenagers. He commented publicly about the situation as follows: "It's just offensive. The morally right thing dictates that we must change. What we have to do is find a way to change that is least damaging to the economic interests of our partners." He also publicly stated that Colgate had been trying to change the package since 1985, when it bought into the partnership.

Colgate's Plan of Action to Repair the Damage

The protest campaign initiated by ICCR and carried further by others definitely caused Colgate's image to be tarnished badly in the eyes not only of African Americans but of all Americans. To get action, some members of the Congressional Black Caucus (including Rep. John Conyers, D-Mich.) even bypassed Colgate and tried to negotiate directly with Hawley and Hazel. To try to repair the damage, two years after ICCR's initial inquiry, Colgate, in cooperation with Hawley and Hazel, finally developed a plan to change the product. In a letter to ICCR, CEO Mark stated, "I and Colgate share your concern that the caricature of a minstrel in black-face on the package and the name 'Darkie' itself could be considered racially offensive." Colgate and Hawley and Hazel then proposed some specific changes for the name and logo. Names considered included Darlie, Darbie, Hawley, and Dakkie. The logo options included a dark, nondescript silhouette and a well-dressed black man. The alliances decided to test-market the options among their Asian consumers; however, they refused to change the Chinese name ("Black Man Toothpaste"), which is more used by their customers.

They decided that changes would be implemented over the course of a year to maintain brand loyalty and avoid advertising confusion with their customers. There was the risk that loyal customers would not know if the modified name/logo was still the same toothpaste that had proven itself through the years. Altogether, the process would take approximately three years, test marketing included. Colgate also decided to pay for the entire change process, abandoning their initial suggestion that the change be paid for by Hawley and Hazel.

Colgate and Hawley and Hazel then made a worldwide apology to all insulted groups. Although Hawley and Hazel was slow to agree with the plan, a spokesperson emphasized that racial stereotyping was against its policy. It also helped that Hawley and Hazel would pay no money to make the needed changes. They felt that the product was too strong to change quickly; thus, three years was not too long to implement the new logo and name fully into all Asian markets. Further, they insisted that as part of the marketing campaign, the product advertising use the following statement in Chinese, "Only the English name is being changed. Black Man Toothpaste is still Black Man Toothpaste."

Response Worldwide

Colgate and Hawley and Hazel still suffer from the effects of their racially offensive product. In 1992, while dealing with its own civil rights issues, the Chinese government placed a ban on Darlie toothpaste because of the product's violation of China's trademark laws. Although the English name change was implemented across all markets, the retained Chinese name and logo still were deemed derogatory by the Chinese, and the government banned the product. Also, Eric Molobi, an African National Congress representative, was outraged at the toothpaste's logo on a recent visit to the Pacific Rim. When asked if Darlie toothpaste would be marketed in his country, the South African representative replied, "If this company found itself in South Africa it would not be used. There would be a permanent boycott."

Today, the name of Colgate cannot be found anywhere on the packaging of what is now called Darlie toothpaste. In a strategic move, Colgate has distanced itself completely away from the controversial product. In the Thailand and Indonesia health-products markets, Colgate even competes against Darlie toothpaste with its own brand.

Questions for Review

1. Identify the major strategic and ethical issues faced by Colgate in its partnership with Hawley and Hazel.

2. What do you think Colgate should have done to handle the situation?

3. Is it possible for Colgate and Hawley and Hazel to change the toothpaste's advertising without sacrificing consumer brand loyalty? Is that a possible reason for Colgate's not responding quickly to domestic complaints?

4. In the end, was a "no management rights" clause good for Colgate? What could have happened during the negotiations process to get around this problem?

Source: This case was prepared by Professor Alisa L. Mosley, Jackson State University, as the basis for class discussion. It is not intended to illustrate either effective or ineffective managerial capability or administrative responsibility.

Advertising or Free Speech?

The Case of Nike and Human Rights

Nike Inc., the global leader in the production and marketing of sports and athletic merchandise including shoes, clothing, and equipment, has enjoyed unparalleled worldwide growth for many years. Consumers around the world recognize Nike's brand name and logo. As a supplier to and sponsor of professional sports figures and organizations, and as a large advertiser to the general public, Nike is widely known. It was a pioneer in offshore manufacturing, establishing company-owned assembly plants and engaging third-party contractors in developing countries.

In 1990, *Life* magazine published a photo of a 12-year-old Pakistani boy stitching a Nike embossed soccer ball. The photo caption noted that the job took a whole day and the child was paid US$.60 for his effort. Up until this time, the general public was neither aware of the wide use of foreign labor nor familiar with the working arrangements and treatment of laborers in developing countries. Since 1990, Nike has become a poster child for the questionable unethical use of offshore workers in poorer regions of the world. This label has continued to plague the corporation as many global human interest and labor rights organizations have monitored and often condemned Nike for its labor practices around the world.

Nike executives have been frequent targets at public events, especially at universities where students have pressed administrators and athletic directors to ban products that have been made under "sweatshop" conditions. Indeed, at the University of Oregon, a major gift from Phil Knight, Nike's CEO, was held up in part because of student criticism and activism against Nike on campus.

In 2003 the company employed 86 compliance officers (up from just 3 in 1996) to monitor its plant operations and working conditions and ensure compliance with its published corporate code of conduct. Even so, the stigma of past practices—whether perceived or real—remains emblazoned on its image and brand name. Nike finds itself constantly defending its activities, striving to shake this reputation and perception.

In 2002 an individual sued Nike, alleging that the company knowingly made false and misleading statements in its denial of direct participation in abusive labor conditions abroad. Through corporate news releases, full-page ads in major newspapers, and letters to editors, Nike defended its conduct and sought to show that allegations of misconduct were unwarranted. The action by the plaintiff, a local citizen, was predicated on a California state law prohibiting unlawful business practices. He alleged that Nike's public statements were motivated by marketing and public relations issues and were simply false. According to the allegation, Nike's statements misled the public and thus violated the California statute. Nike countered by claiming its statements fell under and within the protection of the First Amendment, which protects free speech. The state court concluded that a firm's public statements about its operations have the effect of persuading consumers to buy its products and therefore are, in effect, advertising. Therefore, the suit could be adjudicated on the basis of whether Nike's pronouncements were false and misleading. The court stated that promoting a company's reputation was equivalent to sales solicitation, a practice clearly within the purview of state law. The majority of justices summarized their decision by declaring, "because messages in question were directed by a commercial speaker to a commercial audience, and because they made representations of fact about the speaker's own business operations for the purpose of promoting sales of its products, we conclude that these messages are commercial speech for purposes of applying state laws barring false and misleading commercial messages" (*Kasty v. Nike Inc.*, 2002). The conclusion reached by the court was that statements by a business enterprise to promote its reputation must, like advertising, be factual representations and that companies have a clear duty to speak truthfully about such issues.

If that judgment is sustained, it could create a minefield for multinational firms. It would effectively elevate statements on human rights treatment by companies to the level of corporate marketing and advertising. Under these conditions, it might be difficult for MNCs to defend themselves against allegations of human rights abuses. In fact, action such as the issuance and dissemination of a written company code of conduct or statements in which a firm pledges to honor commitments to principles constructed to foster good corporate practices, such as the U.N. Global Compact, could fall into the category of advertising declarations. Although *Kasty v. Nike* was settled by the parties before it was reviewed under appeal, the issues that it raised remain to be addressed by global companies.

Questions for Review

1. What ethical issues faced by MNCs in their treatment of foreign workers could bring allegations of misconduct in their operations?

2. Would the use of third-party independent contractors insulate MNCs from being attacked? Would that practice offer MNCs a good defensive shield against charges of abuse of "their employees"?

3. Do you think that statements by companies that describe good social and moral conduct in the treatment of their workers are part of the image those companies create and therefore are part of their advertising message? Do consumers judge companies and base their buying decision on their perceptions of corporate behavior and values? Is the historic "made in" question (e.g., "Made in the USA") now being replaced by a "made by" inquiry (e.g., "Made *by* Company X" or "Made *for* Company X by Company Y")?

4. Given the principles noted in the case, how can companies comment on their positive actions to promote human rights so that consumers will think well of them? Would you propose that a company (a) do nothing, (b) construct a corporate code of ethics, or (c) align itself with some of the universal covenants or compacts prepared by international agencies?

Source: © McGraw-Hill Irwin. This case was prepared by Lawrence A. Beer, the W.P. Carey School of Business at Arizona State University, as the basis for class discussion. It is not intended to illustrate either effective or ineffective managerial capability or administrative responsibility.

Pharmaceutical Companies, Intellectual Property, and the Global AIDS Epidemic

In August 2003, after heavy lobbying from nongovernmental organizations (NGOs) such as Doctors Without Borders, the U.S pharmaceutical industry finally dropped its opposition to relaxation of the intellectual property rights (IPR) provisions under World Trade Organization (WTO) regulations to make generic, low-cost antiviral drugs available to developing countries like South Africa facing epidemics or other health emergencies.[1] Although this announcement appeared to end a three-year dispute between multinational pharmaceutical companies, governments, and NGOs over the most appropriate and effective response to viral pandemics in the developing world, the specific procedures for determining what constitutes a health emergency had yet to be worked out. Nonetheless, the day after the agreement was announced, the government of Brazil said it would publish a decree authorizing imports of generic versions of patented AIDS drugs that the country said it could no longer afford to buy from multinational pharmaceutical companies. Although the tentative WTO agreement would appear to allow such production under limited circumstances, former U.S. trade official Jon Huenemann remarked, "They're playing with fire . . . The sensitivities of this are obvious and we're right on the edge here."[2]

Although developed and developing country governments, NGOs, large pharmaceutical companies, and their generic competitors all had a hand in this agreement, it was unclear how it would be implemented and whether action would be swift enough to stem the HIV/AIDS epidemic ravaging South Africa and many other countries.

The AIDS Epidemic and Potential Treatment

In 2003, HIV/AIDS was the number-one cause of death among young adults aged 15–19 around the world. According to the World Health Organization, in 2003 there were approximately 40 million people living with AIDS, with 5 million newly infected, and 3 millions deaths (see Table 1). Since 1980, AIDS has killed more than 25 million people. HIV is especially deadly because it often remains dormant in an infected person for years without showing symptoms and is transmitted to others often without the knowledge of either person. HIV leads to AIDS when the virus attacks the immune system and cripples it, making the person vulnerable to diseases.[3]

The health of a nation's population is closely correlated with its economic wealth. Poor countries lack resources for

Table 1 Regional HIV/AIDS Statistics, 2003

	Adults and Children Living with HIV/AIDS	Adults and Children Newly Infected with HIV	Adult Prevalence Rate [%]*	Adult and Child Deaths Due to AIDS
Sub-Saharan Africa	25.0–28.2 million	3.0–3.4 million	7.5–8.5	2.2–2.4 million
North Africa and Middle East	470 000–730 000	43 000–67 000	0.2–0.4	35 000–50 000
South and South-East Asia	4.6–8.2 million	610 000–1.1 million	0.4–0.8	330 000–590 000
East Asia and Pacific	700 000–1.3 million	150 000–270 000	0.1–0.1	32 000–58 000
Latin America	1.3–1.9 million	120 000–180 000	0.5–0.7	49 000–70 000
Caribbean	350 000–590 000	45 000–80 000	1.9–3.1	30 000–50 000
Eastern Europe and Central Asia	1.2–1.8 million	180 000–280 000	0.5–0.9	23 000–37 000
Western Europe	520 000–680 000	30 000–40 000	0.3–0.3	2 600–3 400
North America	790 000–1.2 million	36 000–54 000	0.5–0.7	12 000–18 000
Australia and New Zealand	12 000–18 000	700–1 000	0.1–0.1	<100
TOTAL	40 million	5 million	1.1%	3 million
	[34–46 million]	[4.2–5.8 million]	[0.9–1.3]	[2.5–3.5 million]

*The proportion of adults [15 to 49 years of age] living with HIV/AIDS in 2003, using 2003 population numbers. The ranges around the estimates in this table define the boundaries within which the actual numbers lie, based on the best available information. These ranges are more precise than those of previous years, and work is under way to increase even further the precision of the estimates that will be published mid-2004.

Source: World Health Organization.

Table 2   **Prices (in $) of Daily Dosage of ARV, April 2000**

Drug	U.S.A.	Côte d'Ivoire	Uganda	Brazil	Thailand
Zidovudine	10.12	2.43	4.34	1.08	1.74
Didanosine	7.25	3.48	5.26	2.04	2.73
Stavudine	9.07	4.10	6.19	0.56	0.84
Indinavir	14.93	9.07	12.79	10.32	NA
Saquinavir	6.5	4.82	7.37	6.24	NA
Efavirenz	13.13	6.41	NA	6.96	NA

Source: UNAIDS, *2000 Report on the Global HIV/AIDS Epidemic.*

health care generally, and for vaccination in particular. They are unable to provide sanitation and to buy drugs for those who cannot afford them. They also have lower levels of education, and therefore people are less aware of measures needed to prevent the spread of disease.[4] There is no cure or vaccine for AIDS. Therefore, public health experts place a high priority on prevention. However, only a small percentage of the funds targeted to prevent AIDS was deployed in developing countries.

Drugs help combat AIDS by prolonging the lives of those infected and by slowing the spread of the disease. These drugs significantly reduce deaths in developed countries. Treatment, however, is very expensive. As with most medicines, manufacturers hold patents for drugs, thereby limiting competition from generic products and allowing firms to price well above manufacturing costs in order to recoup R&D investment and make a fair profit.

In 2000–2001, a year's supply of a "cocktail" of antiretroviral (ARV) drugs used to fight AIDS cost between $10,000 and $12,000 in developed countries, putting it beyond the reach of those in most developing countries, where per capita income is a fraction of this cost (see Tables 2 and 3).[5] This discrepancy provokes strong reactions. Dr. James Orbinski, president of Doctors Without Borders (Médecins Sans Frontières), an international humanitarian nongovernmental organization (NGO) that won the 1999 Nobel Peace Prize, lamented, "The poor have no consumer power, so the market has failed them. I'm tired of the logic that says: 'He who can't pay dies.'"[6]

AIDS in Southern Africa

In sub-Saharan Africa, approximately 26 million people are living with AIDS. Of the 3 million AIDS deaths globally in 2003, approximately two-thirds or 2.2 million were in sub-Saharan Africa (see Table 1).[7] The disease took a heavy toll on women and children. By the end of 2003, more than 2 million children were infected in the region and a disproportionate percentage of infected adults were women.

Most HIV transmission among southern Africans occurred through sexual activity rather than blood transfusion or use of infected needles. As a result of historic and economic factors, there are large numbers of single migrant male communities in southern Africa. These communities, many of whom served the mining industry, are at great risk of AIDS transmission. Mark Lurie of South Africa's Medical Research Council explained: "The migratory labour system is highly conducive to the spread of HIV. You take large numbers of rural men, put them 4 kilometres underground and give them easy access to alcohol and commercial sex workers (prostitutes)—then, every once in a while you send these workers back to the rural areas."[8]

There is great stigma attached to AIDS in southern Africa. On International AIDS Day in 1998, Gugu Dlamini, a South African AIDS activist, declared on television that she was HIV-positive and was subsequently stoned to death for having shamed her community. Dr. Peter Piot, head of UNAIDS (the AIDS program of the United Nations), pointed out the tragic irony in the situation: Some of those who murdered Dlamini probably had AIDS but didn't know it—25 percent of her community was infected.[9]

In the nation of South Africa, one out of every nine residents has HIV/AIDS. The disease had slashed South African life expectancy from 66 years to below 50, a level not seen since the late 1950s. Large pharmaceutical companies and the U.S. government resisted calls to relax intellectual property laws that were thought to limit the provision of low-cost AIDS treatments. South African

Table 3   **Estimated Number of People in 2002 Who Needed "Triple Therapy" AIDS Treatment, Compared with the Number Who Received Treatment (in thousands)**

	In Need of Treatment	Received Treatment
Latin America and the Caribbean	370	196
North Africa and Middle East	7	3
Eastern Europe and Central Asia	80	7
Asia Pacific	1,000	43
Sub-Saharan Africa	**4,100**	**50**

Source: UNAIDS, *2002 Report on the Global HIV/AIDS Epidemic.*

Table 4   **2003 Global Pharmaceutical Sales by Region**

World Audited Market	2003 Sales ($bn)	% Global Sales ($)	% Growth (constant $)
North America	229.5	49%	+11%
European Union	115.4	25	8
Rest of Europe	14.3	3	14
Japan	52.4	11	3
Asia, Africa, and Australasia	37.3	8	12
Latin America	17.4	4	6
Total	$466.3bn	100%	+9%

Source: IMS World Review (2004).

president Thabo Mbeki himself had been accused of engaging in "denial" as he had disputed established wisdom regarding the source of and treatment for AIDS. Meanwhile, South Africans continued to die from the disease, and the South African economy also suffered direct and indirect costs from the disease's ravaging effects.[10]

The Global Pharmaceutical Industry, R&D, and Drug Pricing

Most of the global $466 billion of pharmaceutical sales in 2003 were in the developed countries of North America, Japan, and Western Europe (see Table 4). Leading pharmaceutical companies were large and profitable (see Table 5), although all of them have come under pressure from a range of factors—most notably, calls for lower health care costs in most major industrialized countries. Drug discovery was a long, expensive, and uncertain process. In recent years, the annual R&D expenditures of the members of the Pharmaceutical Research and Manufacturers of America (an industry association of American pharmaceutical and biotechnology companies) have been more than $30 billion. The development of a new drug, starting with laboratory research and culminating in FDA approval, was estimated to take 10 to 15 years and cost around $800 million on average. Only 30 percent of drugs marketed were reported to earn revenues that matched average R&D costs.[11]

Government funding of basic scientific research contributes significantly to fundamental knowledge that was useful in drug discovery. However, governments usually did not get involved in funding the process of commercialization, which was left to the pharmaceutical industry. Critics berated the U.S. government for failing to recover part of the profits from successful drugs that had benefited from basic research funded by the government, and a recent book on this subject alleges that taxpayers foot the bill for most drug discoveries, not pharmaceutical companies.[12]

Like most for-profit firms, pharmaceutical companies pursue opportunities with high profit potential. A spokesman for Aventis, a French-German pharmaceutical company, said, "We can't deny that we try to focus on top markets—cardiovascular, metabolism, anti-infection, etc. But we're an industry in a competitive environment—we have a

commitment to deliver performance for shareholders."[13] The industry tended to focus on diseases prevalent in its major markets. Drug patents enable companies to charge prices several times the variable manufacturing costs and generate hefty margins that helped recover R&D costs and deliver profits. Drugs tend to be relatively price insensitive during the period of patent protection.

Prices vary considerably across markets, as illustrated by the price of fluconazole, an antifungal agent as well as a cure for cryptococcal meningitis, which attacked 9 percent of people with AIDS and killed them within a month. Pfizer's sales of the drug were reported to be approximately $1 billion a year. According to a study by Doctors Without Borders, wholesale prices for fluconazole averaged $10 per pill and ranged from $3.60 in Thailand to $27 in Guatemala. Pfizer claimed the range was narrower ($6). Prices were considerably lower in countries that did not uphold foreign patents for pharmaceuticals. In India, Bangladesh, and Thailand it was sold by generic manufacturers for prices ranging from 30 to 70 cents.[14] (Some of the countries that didn't recognize patents for pharmaceuticals did have laws for patent protection of other products.)

The pharmaceutical industry was criticized for spending large sums on sales, marketing, and lobbying. Pfizer's spokesman, Brian McGlynn, countered, "yes, we spend a lot of money on advertising and marketing. But we don't sell soda pop. It's an enormous transfer of knowledge from our lab scientists to doctors, through those sales reps."[15]

Table 5   **2001 Financials for Selected Pharmaceutical Companies ($b)**

	Merck	Pfizer	GlaxoSmithKline
Country	U.S.	U.S.	U.K.
Revenue	47.7	32.3	29.7
COGS	29.0	5.0	6.9
SG&A	6.2	11.3	12.2
R&D	2.5	4.8	3.8
Net income	7.3	7.8	4.4

Source: Sushil Vachani, "South Africa and the AIDS Epidemic, Vilkapala 29, no.1 (January–March 2004), pp. 104; and company annual reports.

Companies also spent heavily on lobbying governments on issues such as a proposed U.S. government–managed prescription drugs plan for the elderly, which could create pressure to cap drug prices, and on strengthening and enforcing intellectual property protections.

WTO and Intellectual Property Rights[16]

Intellectual property rights (IPR) grant investors rights for original creations. The goal of IPR protection is to stimulate creativity and innovation. In general, copyrights are protected for literary and artistic works extending 70 years after the author's death. Trademarks can be protected indefinitely if they continue to be distinctive. Inventions, industrial designs, and trade secrets are protected through patents for a finite period, usually 20 years. The overall objective is to protect the fruits of investment made in developing new technology so as to provide incentives and funding for R&D. Intellectual property rights, such as patents, prevent people from using inventors' creations without permission. Internationally, the United States and other countries have argued that given appropriate protection, technology transfer would be facilitated between countries by means of foreign direct investment and licensing.

The WTO's Agreement on Trade-Related Aspects of Intellectual Property Rights (TRIPS), which was agreed to under the Uruguay Round of the GATT (1986–1994), attempted to bring conformity among different nations' protection of IPR. TRIPS covered five basic areas (see Exhibit 1). Patent protection extended a minimum of 20 years. Governments could deny patent protection on certain grounds (e.g., public order or morality) or for certain classes of inventions (e.g., surgical methods, plants, and so on). If the patent holder abused the rights granted by the patent (e.g., by refusing to supply the product to the market), the government could, under prescribed conditions, issue compulsory licenses that allowed competitors to produce the product.[17]

In a medical emergency a country could resort to two actions: compulsory licensing, with which it could have generic products manufactured while paying a royalty to the patent holder, and parallel importing, which meant importing legally produced copies of a product that was cheaper in a foreign country than in the importing country. However, the WTO guidelines did not define a medical emergency. Developing countries' view of what constituted a medical emergency was substantially different from that held by drug companies and the U.S. government.

In 1996, in part as a response to international pressures, Brazil passed a law recognizing patents. This law specified that products commercialized anywhere before May 15, 1997, would forever remain unpatented in Brazil. The Brazilian government encouraged local companies to produce unlicensed copies of several AIDS drugs, which it bought from them to distribute to its patients free of charge in a policy of universal access. This benefited many of the

Exhibit 1   **Broad Areas Covered by the WTO Agreement on Trade-Related Aspects of Intellectual Property Rights (TRIPS)**

1. Basic principles
   a. National treatment. Equal treatment of foreign and domestic nationals.
   b. Most-favored-nation treatment. Equal treatment of nationals of all WTO members.
   c. Technological progress. Intellectual property rights had to strike a balance between technological innovation and technology transfer. The objective was to enhance economic and social welfare by making both producers and users benefit.
2. How to provide adequate protection.
3. Enforcement.
4. Dispute settlement.
5. Special transitional arrangements. WTO agreements took effect January 1, 1995. Developed countries were given one year to bring their laws and practices in line with TRIPS. Developing countries were given 5 years and least developed countries 11 years.

Source: WTO, http://www.wto.org/english/tratop_e/trips_e/trips_e.htm.

approximately 85,000 AIDS patients.[18] AIDS deaths were halved between 1996 and 1999. Between 1996 and 2000, local production, together with bulk imports, reduced annual treatment costs by 80 percent for double therapy (a cocktail of two AIDS drugs, both nucleosides) and by about 35 percent for triple therapies (two nucleosides and a protease inhibitor or non-nucleoside).[19]

For drugs that had valid patents in Brazil, the government attempted to negotiate lower prices. When negotiations between Merck and the Brazilian government over prices of the drug Stocrin stalled, the government threatened to license the drug compulsorily under the provisions of Brazilian law. When Merck learned a copy was being developed in a government lab, it threatened to file a lawsuit. The U.S. government filed a complaint with the WTO, but Brazil refused to budge.[20] President Fernando Cardoso defended the practice, suggesting that this approach was not one of commercial interest, but rather a moral issue that could not be solved by the market alone. The pharmaceutical industry association's position on intellectual property rights was summarized as follows:

> Strong intellectual property protection is the key to scientific, technological and economic progress. Such protection is the *sine qua non* of a vibrant and innovative pharmaceutical industry—and thus to patients—in the United States and around the world. Without such protection, far fewer drugs would be developed, fewer generic copies would be manufactured, and the flow of medicines to the public would be greatly slowed—to the detriment of patients, public health, and economic development throughout the world.[21]

Pharmaceutical companies were worried about more than losing contributions from sales of a drug faced with a knockoff in a specific country. They feared a domino effect—compulsory licensing spreading across developing countries and sharply hurting profits in multiple markets. Even more alarming was the prospect that prices in developed countries might sink either because of a gray market in generics or because of pressure to cap prices as information on the significant price differential between countries became widely available and developed-country consumers clamored for lower prices.

Drug Pricing in Developing Countries: Government, Industry, and NGO Perspectives[22]

Dr. Christopher Ouma, who cared for AIDS patients in a Kenyan public hospital, pointed out that half his patients couldn't pay the $2.60 daily bed charge. He usually didn't tell patients' families about the existence of drugs to treat AIDS. "This is where the doctor's role goes from caregiver to undertaker," he added. "You talk to them about the cheapest method of burial. Telling them about the drugs is always kind of a cruel joke."[23]

Drug companies had been reluctant to provide AIDS drugs to developing countries at prices much lower than those charged in developed countries. They expressed concern that distributing drugs in unregulated and unreliable environments could risk creating new strains of drug-resistant HIV. In 1997, South Africa passed a law to permit compulsory licensing of essential drugs. Pharmaceutical companies including Bristol-Myers Squibb and Merck sued the South African government in an attempt to delay implementation of the law.

The Clinton administration lobbied the South African government to reverse its decision. Members of Congress sympathetic to drug companies drafted a requirement that the State Department report on the administration's efforts to stop South Africa before the country could receive American aid. The State Department reported in February 1999 that "all relevant agencies of the U.S. government . . . have been engaged in an assiduous, concerted campaign to persuade the government of South Africa to withdraw or modify" the relevant parts of the law. U.S. Trade Representative Charlene Barshefsky placed South Africa on the "301 watch list," which puts a nation on notice that U.S. trade sanctions will be imposed if it doesn't change its policies.[24]

The *Washington Post* reported, "Critics have accused U.S. trade policy of placing the profits of drug companies above public health, moving to block poor countries from manufacturing the drugs themselves, despite international laws that permit countries to do so when facing a public health emergency."[25] The British newspaper *Guardian* referred to the U.S. government's actions as "trade terrorism" and called for efforts to "defend developing countries against U.S. aggression."[26] The World Bank official who oversaw the Bank's African health investments and its annual $800 million drug procurement said the drug-price structure "shows an increasing disconnect with the needs of the majority of the people in the world." The Bank was "comfortable" with the practices permitted under the WTO's TRIPS provisions for health emergencies, compulsory licensing, and parallel importing.[27]

As the U.S. government began to exert pressure on developing countries, AIDS activists and NGOs, such as Doctors Without Borders, Act-Up, Health Action International, and the Consumer Project on Technology, swung into action. They targeted the public appearances of Vice President Al Gore during his presidential campaign. In September 1999, the administration backed off from the threats of placing trade sanctions against South Africa. The administration informed the South African government it would not object to issuance of compulsory licenses for essential drugs provided this was done within WTO guidelines.

In December 1999, President Bill Clinton told members of the WTO that the U.S. government would show "flexibility" and allow countries to obtain cheaper drugs during health emergencies on a case-by-case basis.[28] NGOs immediately called on the U.S. government to end trade pressure on poor countries in health care industry disputes.[29] Over the following year, the U.S. government declared it would not block compulsory licenses in the rest of sub-Saharan Africa and Thailand, and elsewhere on a selected basis.

In the summer of 2000, at the 13th International AIDS Conference in Durban, South Africa, Boehringer Ingelheim, a German pharmaceutical company, offered to make its AIDS drug, viramune, available for free. Bristol-Myers Squibb, Merck, and Glaxo Wellcome made similar offers. NGOs and developing governments, however, criticized the companies for making the announcements without consulting and working with the concerned governments, and for placing restrictions on distribution.[30] Doctors Without Borders suggested the industry focus on "concrete action" rather than publicity.

Jack Watters, Pfizer's medical director for Africa, defended the conditions of the company's pilot free-drug program in South Africa: "We want to evaluate how much impact the program has on survival." The company was also concerned about corruption and diversion of supplies. He added, "There's no guarantee that the drug will find its way to the people who need it most."[31]

NGO activists continued to press the U.S. government, the WTO, and the pharmaceutical industry to make it easier for developing countries to produce or import generics. Robert Weissman, co-director of Essential Action, a Washington NGO, said, "There's a global health crisis of historic proportions, and there's an existing set of treatments that allow people to live indefinitely with the disease. But instead of trying to deliver medicine to the sick, we are worrying about the intellectual rights of the pharmaceutical companies." He added, "The overriding point is that, no matter what kind of charity companies dole out, countries should have the right to make generic drugs."[32] Some felt that if the pharmaceutical industry really wanted to make its products available it should drop its lawsuit against the South African government.

In spring 2001, three U.S. pharmaceutical companies—Merck, Bristol-Myers Squibb, and Abbott—announced they would sell HIV drugs to developing countries at cost. GlaxoSmithKline offered 90 percent discounts.[33] Merck planned to use the United Nations Human Development Index and offer the lowest prices to countries that received "low" rankings or had an AIDS infection rate of 1 percent or higher. It offered Brazil, which didn't fall in that category, prices about 75 percent higher. Still, this was a steep discount compared to U.S. prices. Merck would sell efavirenz in Brazil for $920 per year per patient (compared to $4,700 in the United States) and Crixivan for $1,029 ($6,000 in the United States).[34] In October 2002, Merck announced further cuts in the price for Stocrin from the (already reduced) price of $1.37 per patient per day to $0.95 per patient per day in the poorest, hardest-hit countries. The price for middle-development countries with less than 1 percent HIV prevalence will be $2.10 per patient per day, down from $2.52.

On September 5, 2002, GlaxoSmithKline announced a price cut for antiretroviral drugs and malaria drugs for poor countries. This was on top of previous price cuts. The British company said it would cut the prices of its HIV/AIDS drugs by as much as 33 percent and the prices of its antimalarial drugs by as much as 38 percent in developing countries. The cheaper drugs could help health workers fight two of the deadliest diseases that afflict the developing world. Under the new pricing plan, GlaxoSmithKline said it would supply its AIDS and antimalarial drugs at not-for-profit prices to the public sector, non-governmental organizations, aid agencies, the United Nations, and the Global Fund to Fight AIDS, Tuberculosis and Malaria. To prevent cut-price drugs from being reimported into the West, Glaxo said it would seek regulatory approval to provide special packaging for the cut-price drugs.

Indian generic manufacturers, such as Cipla, offered among the lowest prices in the world. Over the years Cipla has developed a range of pharmaceuticals. It began exporting in 1946 when it sold a hypertension drug to an American company. In 1985 the U.S. FDA approved Cipla's bulk drug manufacturing facilities. By 2001 Cipla exported drugs worth $100 million. This included sales to leading generic-drug manufacturers in the United States and Europe. Cipla's net income in 2001–2002 was $48 million on sales of $292 million. Its manufacturing facilities had been approved by the WHO and regulatory authorities in the United States, Germany, and the U.K. Its major export markets were the Americas (41%), Europe (24%), and the Middle East and Africa (12% each). In late 2001 Cipla

agreed to supply a three-drug antiretroviral combination to Nigeria for $350 per person per year.[35] The Nigerian government initiated a $4 million pilot program covering 10,000 adults and 5,000 children in which it planned to charge patients $120 per year and cover the remaining cost from government funds.[36]

In March 2002 the WHO released its first list of companies that are regarded as manufacturers of safe AIDS drugs. In compiling the list, the WHO had asked manufacturers to apply to be listed and then inspected the facilities of any company that was legally operating in its own country irrespective of whether it was a patent holder or not. The head of UNAIDS, Dr. Peter Piot, hoped the list would pave the way for patients to "gain greater access to affordable HIV medicines of good quality." Of the 41 drugs listed, 26 were sold by multinationals and 10 by Cipla.

In October 2002, the Global Fund announced that it would encourage developing countries to buy cheap generic drugs instead of expensive branded ones. Anxious to maximize the impact on its limited resources, the Fund announced it would impose three conditions on recipient nations: that they purchase the cheapest drugs, that they only buy drugs of guaranteed quality, and that they comply with international laws and their own laws. It was unclear, however, how this last provision squared with the WTO TRIPS agreement.

The Global Fund

In April 2001, while addressing an African summit in Nigeria, U.N. Secretary General Kofi Annan proposed creation of a global fund to combat AIDS. He stressed the need to ratchet up spending on fighting AIDS in developing countries from the current $1 billion level to $7–10 billion. He noted that pharmaceutical companies were beginning to accept that "generic medication can be produced where it can save lives." The previous week pharmaceutical companies had dropped their lawsuit against the South African government over patent laws.[37]

The proposal attracted significant support from world leaders. In May 2001, President George W. Bush announced $200 million in seed money for the fund. The following month, addressing delegates from 180 nations at a U.N. conference, U.S. Secretary of State Colin Powell declared, "No war on the face of the world is more destructive than the AIDS pandemic. I was a soldier. I know of no enemy in war more insidious or vicious than AIDS, an enemy that poses a clear and present danger to the world." He added, "We hope this seed money will generate billions more from donors all over the world, and more will come from the United States as we learn where our support can be most effective."

The Global Fund, set up as an independent corporation, was broadened to address not just AIDS but tuberculosis and malaria as well. By July 2003, more than

Table 6 **Leading Donors (Paid to Date) to the Global Fund, July 2004**

Country	$m
U.S.A.	623
EU	401
France	304
Japan	230
Italy	215
U.K.	173
Gates Foundation	100

Source: theglobalfundatm.org.

$2 billion had been paid in by developed countries (see Table 6). In addition to leading country donors that included the United States, the EU, individual European countries, and Japan, the Gates Foundation contributed $100 million. In April 2002, the Global Fund made its first awards, totaling $616 million, to programs in 40 countries. Slightly more than half was designated for Africa. Experts predicted that the Fund's success hinged on how effective it proved to be as a "hard-nosed judge of its grantees' performance."

In October 2003, the Fund announced it would slow the pace of its awards to one round per year because it had fallen short of its fund-raising goals and was concerned about running out of money. The Fund announced it had received pledges through 2008 of about $5.2 billion, well short of its $8–$10 billion goal.[38] The decision came as the Fund announced $623 million in grants to 71 disease prevention and treatment programs in about 50 countries. This round of grants, the third, was substantially smaller than the $884 million awarded in January 2003. In June 2003, it was announced that Jack Valenti, longtime lobbyist for the motion picture industry, would assume the presidency of a group set up to raise money for the fund.

Pressure Mounts

In June 2002, two weeks before the 14th International AIDS Conference in Barcelona, the WTO council responsible for intellectual property extended until 2016 the transition period during which least-developed countries (LDCs) did not have to provide patent protection for pharmaceuticals.[39]

Previously they'd been expected to comply by 2006. (See Exhibit 2 for a list of least-developed countries.)

The July 2002 International AIDS Conference in Barcelona ended with cautious optimism. The delegates from 194 countries felt that perhaps the success in containing AIDS in developed countries could be replicated in developing countries given the right effort. Right at the end of the conference, Joep Lange, president of the International AIDS Society, said, "If we can get Coca-Cola and cold beer to every remote corner of Africa, it should not be impossible to do the same with drugs." The conference wasn't without protests. Activists tore down the European Union exhibition stand, demanding larger contributions to the Global Fund. They heckled U.S. Health Secretary Tommy Thompson, demanding the United States do more to improve health systems in developing countries.

The World Health Organization estimated that given the public health infrastructure in developing countries, the maximum that could be spent productively each year by 2005 was about $9 billion. This assumed $4.8 billion for prevention and $4.2 billion for treatment. It was estimated that the amount currently devoted to prevention was $1.2 billion. With a commitment of $4.8 billion per year to prevention, 29 million infections could probably be avoided by 2010.

Several challenges remained. Drug prices had fallen significantly, but they weren't low enough for everyone. The large pharmaceutical companies were selling antiretroviral combinations for about $1,200 per person per year in some developing countries, and the lowest generic prices out of India were $209. Health economists estimated that prices needed to fall as low as $30–$40 per person per year for drugs to reach the poorest recipients. Such low prices were unlikely to materialize anytime soon. NGOs, such as Doctors Without Borders, were expected to push for optimizing use of scarce funds by deploying Global Fund allocations for purchase of generics only. Tough decisions needed to be made about the allocation of resources between AIDS and other diseases, and between prevention and treatment of AIDS.

In September 2003, a report was released by the United States saying that despite recent increases in spending to fight AIDS in Africa, the funding of such efforts by 2005 was projected to be about half of what would be needed by then. The report, "Accelerating Action Against AIDS in Africa," noted that a few areas in Africa have made significant strides

Exhibit 2 **Countries Classified as Least-Developed by WTO**

Angola	Djibouti	Maldives	Sierra Leone
Bangladesh	Gambia	Mali	Solomon Islands
Benin	Guinea	Mauritania	Tanzania
Burkina Faso	Guinea Bissau	Mozambique	Togo
Burundi	Haiti	Myanmar	Uganda
Central African Republic	Lesotho	Niger	Zambia
Chad	Madagascar	Rwanda	
Congo	Malawi	Senegal	

against the epidemic, providing evidence that the challenge, though daunting, is not insurmountable.[40]

Nonetheless, there continued to be concern over the South Africa government's lack of aggressive action to combat the disease. Fortunately, South Africa had a better developed infrastructure and health care delivery system than many other African nations. However, the funds deployed for fighting AIDS were modest. The allocation for AIDS education was $13 million for five years. The amount for conventional AIDS programs was raised to $100 million under pressure.[41] At a more macro level the proportion of the South African budget earmarked for health had trended down gradually from 11.2 percent in 1999–2000 to 11.0 percent in 2001–2002 while that for defense had risen from 5.4 to 6.4 percent. Critics questioned the wisdom of levying the 14 percent value-added tax on drugs, which was on top of import duties.[42]

The actions and statements of officials did not go as far as critics wanted. Activists were frustrated with government efforts to control incidence of AIDS in newborn babies, 70,000 of whom were born with HIV in 2000. Risk of transmission from an infected mother to her baby could be cut 50 percent with medication. The government had accepted free drugs from Boehringer Ingelheim for a pilot program covering 10 percent of the population. In December 2001 the Treatment Action Campaign, an NGO led by activists associated with the country's liberation struggle, sued and obtained a court verdict directing the government to offer the program nationally. The government remained reluctant to make the treatment universally available and planned to appeal.

In early August 2003, the South African government reversed its policy on AIDS and signed the Global Fund to produce the first generic AIDS drug in South Africa. Aspen Pharmacare, a South African firm, announced it would be the initial provider of generic treatments. Backed by many activist groups, including the influential Treatment Action Campaign, revisions to the $41 million deal detailed an operational plan to make the drugs available by the end of September 2003. South African president Thabo Mbeki finally agreed to the long-standing proposal after a recent World Bank report predicted "a complete economic collapse" within four generations if the government didn't act swiftly.

The WTO Agreement and Its Aftermath

In August 2003, the United States and other WTO members announced that they had finalized a solution to streamline the supply of disease-fighting medications to poor countries. As part of the compromise deal, the United States agreed to language that would allow compulsory licensing only for "genuine health reasons" and not for commercial advantage. The August 2003 accord in which the United States and other WTO members agreed to a solution to streamline the supply of disease-fighting medications to poor countries appeared to prompt action.

On December 10, 2003, Britain's GlaxoSmithKline and Germany's Boehringer Ingelheim agreed to expand the licensing of their patented AIDS drugs to three generic manufacturers in South Africa and other African countries as part of an out-of-court settlement with South Africa's Treatment Action Campaign. In return, the South African Competition Commission, a government body that monitors free-market practices, agreed to drop a yearlong probe into whether the companies had overcharged for their AIDS drugs. Glaxo and Boehringer Ingelheim already have existing agreements with a fourth generic manufacturer, South Africa's Aspen Pharmacare. Under the settlement pact in South Africa, Glaxo also agreed to cap royalty fees at no more than 5 percent of net sales and to extend the generic licenses to the private and public sectors. It said it would allow the generic licensees to export AIDS drugs manufactured in South Africa to 47 sub-Saharan African countries. The Competition Commission said it had not asked for a fine or administrative penalty against Glaxo, which is the world's largest maker of AIDS medicines.[43]

Shareholder activists have also begun to put pressure on companies to provide more comprehensive reporting about their potential to support efforts to fight AIDS. In March 2004, a consortium of religious investors forwarded shareholder resolutions at four top drug makers, asking the companies to assess how much charity work they are doing for HIV and AIDS in developing countries and to estimate how much the epidemic could affect their businesses. The Interfaith Center on Corporate Responsibility (ICCR) wants the shareholders of Pfizer, Bristol-Myers Squibb, Merck, and Abbott to consider their proposals. The ICCR and the roughly 30 religious groups it is working with are requesting that the companies offer shareholders a report of their conclusions six months after the annual meetings. Although the boards of directors at Pfizer, Merck, and Abbott said they opposed the measure, Coca-Cola's board recently said it supports a similar shareholder proposal to assess the business risks associated with the HIV/AIDS epidemic.[44]

In October 2003, former president Bill Clinton announced a landmark program that attacks two of the toughest obstacles to treating AIDS in the developing world: high drug prices and low-quality health infrastructures. The Clinton Foundation HIV/AIDS Initiative reached a deal with four generic-drug companies, including one in South Africa, to slash the price of antiretroviral AIDS medicine. Engineered by longtime Clinton adviser Ira Magaziner, the agreement will cut the price of a commonly used triple-drug regimen by almost a third, to about 38 cents a day per patient from an already cut-rate generic price of about 55 cents. The lowest available price for the same regimen using patented versions of the drugs in developing nations is $1.54. For a key drug, nevirapine, the price will be cut by almost half.[45] In April 2004, Clinton's foundation announced that these special drug prices were being extended from the initial 16 countries in the Caribbean and Africa to any country supported by UNICEF, the World Bank and the U.N.-administered Global Fund to Fight AIDS, Tuberculosis and Malaria. "With these agreements, we are one step closer to making sure future generations can live without the scourge of AIDS," Clinton said in a statement released by his U.S.-based foundation.

Under the Clinton Foundation agreement, five generic-drug manufacturers—Pharmacare Holdings of South Africa and the Indian companies Cipla, Hetero Drugs, Ranbaxy Laboratories, and Matrix Laboratories—provide basic HIV treatment for as little as $140 per person per year, one-third to one-half of the lowest price available elsewhere. Diagnostic tests are supplied by five different companies and include machines, training, chemicals, and maintenance at a price that is up to 80 percent cheaper than the normal market price. "This new partnership works to break down some of the barriers—such as price, supply and demand—that are impeding access to lifesaving AIDS medicines and diagnostics in developing countries," said UNICEF Executive Director Carol Bellamy.[46]

Questions for Review

1. Do pharmaceutical companies have a responsibility to distribute drugs for free or at low cost in developing countries? What are the main arguments for and against such an approach?

2. What are the principal arguments of pharmaceutical companies that oppose making exceptions to IPR laws for developing countries? What are the arguments by NGOs and others for relaxing IPR laws?

3. What impact would you expect South Africa's decision to levy duties on drug imports from Western nations to have on the international distribution of drugs to South Africa?

4. In June 2002, the WTO extended the transition period during which least-developed countries (LDCs) had to provide patent protection for pharmaceuticals. In your opinion, is this an appropriate change in policy or a dangerous precedent? What could be some of the negative ramifications of this resolution? What about the effects for other industries?

5. Given the initiatives announced by global development and aid organizations and among pharmaceutical companies themselves, was it necessary to relax IPR rules in order to ensure that adequate supplies of AIDS medications would be available for distribution in the developing world?

6. What role do MNCs have in providing funding or other assistance to international organizations such as the Global Fund?

Exercise

Although the WTO has now agreed to relax intellectual property rules in order to facilitate the production and distribution of inexpensive generic antivirals, the conditions under which this provision allows for production or importation of generics ("genuine health reasons") are unclear. The WTO is to hold a hearing for interested parties to provide input about how these rules should be implemented. Your group represents the interests of one of the key stakeholders (see table) and will be responsible for arguing that stakeholder's position.

Team	Stakeholder
1	The WTO
2	Doctors Without Borders (NGO)
3	CIPLA (Indian generic manufacturer)
4	GlaxoSmithKline (representing pharma companies)
5	Government of Brazil (representing developing countries)
6	The Clinton Foundation HIV/AIDS Initiatives

Discuss with your group the major points to make to advance your perspectives. Come prepared to make a 5-minute presentation summarizing how you would like the WTO to implement the new rules. The WTO group should ask questions during the hearing. It should then take 10 minutes to deliberate and come up with a proposed plan incorporating the interests of all of the stakeholders.

Source: © McGraw-Hill Irwin. This case was prepared by Jonathan Doh and Erik Holt of Villanova University as the basis for class discussion. It is not intended to illustrate either effective or ineffective managerial capability or administrative responsibility. The authors thank Sushil Vachani for comments, suggestions, and input.

PART TWO

THE ROLE
OF CULTURE

Chapter 4

THE MEANINGS AND DIMENSIONS OF CULTURE

OBJECTIVES OF THE CHAPTER

A major challenge of doing business internationally is to adapt effectively to different cultures. Such adaptation requires an understanding of cultural diversity, perceptions, stereotypes, and values. In recent years, a great deal of research has been conducted on cultural dimensions and attitudes, and the findings have proved useful in providing integrative profiles of international cultures. However, a word of caution must be given when discussing these country profiles. It must be remembered that stereotypes and overgeneralizations should be avoided; there are always individual differences and even subcultures within every country.

This chapter examines the meaning of culture as it applies to international management, reviews some of the value differences and similarities of various national groups, studies important dimensions of culture and their impact on behavior, and examines attitudinal dimensions and country clusters. The specific objectives of this chapter are:

1. **DEFINE** the term *culture,* and discuss some of the comparative ways of differentiating cultures.

2. **DESCRIBE** the concept of cultural values, and relate some of the international differences, similarities, and changes occurring in terms of both work and managerial values.

3. **IDENTIFY** the major dimensions of culture relevant to work settings, and discuss their effect on behavior in an international environment.

4. **DISCUSS** the value of country cluster analysis and relational orientations in developing effective international management practices.

The World of *BusinessWeek*

BusinessWeek

Will Coke's Water Meet Its Waterloo?

Dasani's European Invasion Faces Resistance from Nestlé and Danone Brands

Talk about carrying coals to Newcastle. Coca-Cola Co. is heading into Europe, where finicky consumers choose from the world's best-known spring waters, with Dasani, the bottled water Coke successfully launched in its home market five years ago. While Dasani now ranks No. 2 in the U.S. behind PepsiCo Inc.'s Aquafina, challenging honored brands on their home turf could prove a far tougher battle. Dasani hit the British market in February and promptly suffered a major public-relations disaster. And Continental rivals are gearing up to fight Coke off when Dasani arrives on their side of the Channel later this spring.

You can't blame Coke for trying. Bottled water is a growing part of the company's product mix, and the British market is exploding as health-conscious consumers shift away from carbonated beverages. Water sales in Britain have nearly tripled since 1998, to an estimated $1.9 billion last year, according to Mintel International Group Ltd., a London market research firm.

But Dasani has had a rocky start among Britons. Days after Coke introduced it, the company was forced to defend Dasani's source: It's purified tap water. Pricing Dasani near the top of the market made matters worse: Only Perrier and Vittel cost more. Critics had a field day. "Tap water," ran one headline in *The Guardian,* "it's the real thing."

So far, Coke executives are taking the negative publicity in stride. Vinay Kapoor, Coke's director of new beverages

Coke's Dasani costs more than bottled mineral water		
Highland Spring	**Evian**	**Dasani**
$5.07* Mineral water from Scotland	$5.79* French mineral water	$6.25* Purified tap water

*Price of a pack of six 1.5-liter
bottles in Britain   Data: Tesco.com

Source: www.businessweek.com/magazine/content/
04_13/b3876089_mz054.htm

for Europe, blames the backlash on confusion about Dasani, which undergoes complex purification processes, including a filtering technique called reverse osmosis that NASA uses to make water for the space station. Dasani also contains added minerals such as magnesium sulfate, which give it a distinctive flavor. Kapoor is counting on a marketing blitz to reverse Dasani's image. In late March, Coke will spend $14 million on TV, print, and radio ads in Britain. "We're going to face a degree of clarification," Kapoor concedes.

French Challenge

That's for sure. But as Coke goes into France and Germany, it faces more than a PR glitch. Coke will supply these markets from springs in Belgium and Germany, and it will spend $9 million on a print and TV campaign in France. But the challenges are many—especially in France.

For one thing, France's per-capita consumption of bottled water already tops 140 liters a year, according to Mintel. For another, growth is at the lower end of the market, while Dasani will be in the middle. Finally, there are two European giants to contend with: Nestlé, which produces Perrier and

Aquarel, and Groupe Danone, which brings Evian and Volvic forth from the ground. Between them the two companies control half the French market. "In France, the market is completely saturated," says Cedric Boehm, an analyst at Morgan Stanley in London. "It has been very difficult to establish new brands."

Nestlé seems especially intent on keeping things that way. It even has a strategy-planning task force code-named Nicola—which translates loosely as "no cola." Nestlé executives are particularly confident about Aquarel, a mid-range water that is likely to be Dasani's closest competitor.

Coke remains unfazed. Its worldwide bottled water sales have grown more than 50% in each of the last three years. In 2003, that growth helped Coke's total revenues rise 8%, to $21 billion. Coke is counting on aggressive marketing and its distribution network to put Dasani on Europe's map. But the water wars won't be won easily.

By Laura Cohn in London, with Carol Matlack in Paris and Dean Foust in Atlanta

Source: Reprinted from "Will Coke's Water Meet Its Waterloo?" March 29, 2004, online edition of *BusinessWeek* by special permission. Copyright © 2004 by The McGraw-Hill Companies, Inc. www.businessweek.com

The opening news article provides an illustration of how important it is for MNCs to be responsive to differences in culture if they are to be successful. In their introduction of Dasani water in Europe, Coke executives did not take into consideration the cultural preferences of European consumers of bottled water. Although Coke clarified its product and message, it will have a difficult time recovering and expanding the Dasani brand in Europe after such a miscalculation. Through a better understanding of the importance of cultural norms on buying behavior, Coke might have realized that its U.S. bottled water product could not succeed in Europe without some modifications. MNCs that understand the cultures in which they do business will be better equipped to meet the needs of local consumers and to successfully manage their global operations.

■ The Nature of Culture

The word *culture* comes from the Latin *cultura*, which is related to cult or worship. In its broadest sense, the term refers to the result of human interaction.[1] For the purposes of the study of international management, **culture** is acquired knowledge that people use to

culture
Acquired knowledge that people use to interpret experience and generate social behavior. This knowledge forms values, creates attitudes, and influences behavior.

interpret experience and generate social behavior.[2] This knowledge forms values, creates attitudes, and influences behavior. Most scholars of culture would agree on the following characteristics of culture:

1. *Learned.*   Culture is not inherited or biologically based; it is acquired by learning and experience.

2. *Shared.*   People as members of a group, organization, or society share culture; it is not specific to single individuals.

3. *Transgenerational.*   Culture is cumulative, passed down from one generation to the next.

4. *Symbolic.*   Culture is based on the human capacity to symbolize or use one thing to represent another.

5. *Patterned.*   Culture has structure and is integrated; a change in one part will bring changes in another.

6. *Adaptive.*   Culture is based on the human capacity to change or adapt, as opposed to the more genetically driven adaptive process of animals.[3]

Because different cultures exist in the world, an understanding of the impact of culture on behavior is critical to the study of international management.[4] If international managers do not know something about the cultures of the countries they deal with, the results can be quite disastrous. For example, a partner in one of New York's leading private banking firms tells the following story:

> I traveled nine thousand miles to meet a client and arrived with my foot in my mouth. Determined to do things right, I'd memorized the names of the key men I was to see in Singapore. No easy job, inasmuch as the names all came in threes. So, of course, I couldn't resist showing off that I'd done my homework. I began by addressing top man Lo Win Hao with plenty of well-placed Mr. Hao's—sprinkled the rest of my remarks with a Mr. Chee this and a Mr. Woon that. Great show. Until a note was passed to me from one man I'd met before, in New York. Bad news. "Too friendly too soon, Mr. Long," it said. Where diffidence is next to godliness, there I was, calling a room of VIPs, in effect, Mr. Ed and Mr. Charlie. I'd remembered everybody's name—but forgot that in Chinese the surname comes *first* and the given name *last*.[5]

Cultural Diversity

There are many ways of examining cultural differences and their impact on international management. Culture can affect technology transfer, managerial attitudes, managerial ideology, and even business–government relations. Perhaps most important, culture affects how people think and behave. Table 4–1, for example, compares the most important cultural values of the United States, Japan, and Arab countries. A close look at this table shows a great deal of difference among these three cultures. Culture affects a host of business-related activities, even including the common handshake. Here are some contrasting examples:

Culture	Type of Handshake
United States	Firm
Asian	Gentle (shaking hands is unfamiliar and uncomfortable for some; the exception is the Korean, who usually has a firm handshake)
British	Soft
French	Light and quick (not offered to superiors); repeated on arrival and departure
German	Brusk and firm; repeated on arrival and departure
Latin American	Moderate grasp; repeated frequently
Middle Eastern	Gentle; repeated frequently[6]

Table 4–1
Priorities of Cultural Values: United States, Japan, and Arab Countries

United States	Japan	Arab Countries
1. Freedom	1. Belonging	1. Family security
2. Independence	2. Group harmony	2. Family harmony
3. Self-reliance	3. Collectiveness	3. Parental guidance
4. Equality	4. Age/seniority	4. Age
5. Individualism	5. Group consensus	5. Authority
6. Competition	6. Cooperation	6. Compromise
7. Efficiency	7. Quality	7. Devotion
8. Time	8. Patience	8. Patience
9. Directness	9. Indirectness	9. Indirectness
10. Openness	10. Go-between	10. Hospitality

Note: "1" represents the most important cultural value, "10" the least.

Source: Adapted from information found in F. Elashmawi and Philip R. Harris, *Multicultural Management* (Houston: Gulf Publishing, 1993), p. 63.

In overall terms, the cultural impact on international management is reflected by these basic beliefs and behaviors. Here are some specific examples where the culture of a society can directly affect management approaches:

- *Centralized vs. decentralized decision making.* In some societies, top managers make all important organizational decisions. In others, these decisions are diffused throughout the enterprise, and middle- and lower-level managers actively participate in, and make, key decisions.

- *Safety vs. risk.* In some societies, organizational decision makers are risk-averse and have great difficulty with conditions of uncertainty. In others, risk taking is encouraged, and decision making under uncertainty is common.

- *Individual vs. group rewards.* In some countries, personnel who do outstanding work are given individual rewards in the form of bonuses and commissions. In others, cultural norms require group rewards, and individual rewards are frowned on.

- *Informal vs. formal procedures.* In some societies, much is accomplished through informal means. In others, formal procedures are set forth and followed rigidly.

- *High vs. low organizational loyalty.* In some societies, people identify very strongly with their organization or employer. In others, people identify with their occupational group, such as engineer or mechanic.

- *Cooperation vs. competition.* Some societies encourage cooperation between their people. Others encourage competition between their people.

- *Short-term vs. long-term horizons.* Some cultures focus most heavily on short-term horizons, such as short-range goals of profit and efficiency. Others are more interested in long-range goals, such as market share and technologic development.

- *Stability vs. innovation.* The culture of some countries encourages stability and resistance to change. The culture of others puts high value on innovation and change.

These cultural differences influence the way that international management should be conducted. "International Management in Action: Business Customs in Japan" provides some examples from a country where many international managers are unfamiliar with day-to-day business protocol.

Business Customs in Japan

When doing business in Japan, foreign businesspeople should follow certain customs if they wish to be as effective as possible. Experts have put together the following guidelines:

1. Always try to arrange for a formal introduction to any person or company with which you want to do business. These introductions should come from someone whose position is at least as high as that of the person whom you want to meet or from someone who has done a favor for this person. Let the host pick the subjects to discuss. One topic to be avoided is World War II.

2. If in doubt, bring a translator along with you. For example, the head of Osaka's $7 billion international airport project tells the story of a U.S. construction company president who became indignant when he discovered that the Japanese project head could not speak English. By the same token, you should not bring along your lawyer, because this implies a lack of trust.

3. Try for a thorough personalization of all business relationships. The Japanese trust those with whom they socialize and come to know more than they do those who simply are looking to do business. Accept afterhours invitations. However, a rollicking night out on the town will

not necessarily lead to signing the contract to your advantage the next morning.

4. Do not deliver bad news in front of others, and if possible, have your second-in-command handle this chore. Never cause Japanese managers to lose face by putting them in a position of having to admit failure or say they do not know something that they should know professionally.

5. How business is done is often as important as the results. Concern for tradition, for example, is sometimes more important than concern for profit. Do not appeal solely to logic, because in Japan, emotional considerations often are more important than facts.

6. The Japanese often express themselves in a vague and ambiguous manner, in contrast to the specific language typically used in the United States. A Japanese who is too specific runs the risk of being viewed as rudely displaying superior knowledge. The Japanese avoid independent or individual action, and they prefer to make decisions based on group discussions and past precedent. The Japanese do not say no in public, which is why foreign businesspeople often take away the wrong impression.

Another way of depicting cultural diversity is through concentric circles. Figure 4–1 provides an example. The outer ring consists of the explicit artifacts and products of the culture. This level is observable and consists of such things as language, food, buildings, and art. The middle ring contains the norms and values of the society. These can be both formal and informal, and they are designed to help people understand how they should behave. The inner circle contains the basic, implicit assumptions that govern behavior. By understanding these assumptions, members of a culture are able to organize themselves in a way that helps them increase the effectiveness of their problem-solving processes and interact well with each other. In explaining the nature of the inner circle, Trompenaars and Hampden-Turner have noted that:

> The best way to test if something is a basic assumption is when the [situation] provokes confusion or irritation. You might, for example, observe that some Japanese bow deeper than others. . . . If you ask why they do it the answer might be that they don't know but that the other person does it too (norm) or that they want to show respect for authority (value). A typical Dutch question that might follow is: "Why do you respect authority?" The most likely Japanese reaction would be either puzzlement or a smile (which might be hiding their irritation). When you question basic assumptions you are asking questions that have never been asked before. It might lead others to deeper insights, but it also might provoke annoyance. Try in the USA or the Netherlands to raise the question of why people are equal and you will see what we mean.[7]

A supplemental way of understanding cultural differences is to compare culture as a normal distribution, as in Figure 4–2, and then to examine it in terms of stereotyping, as in

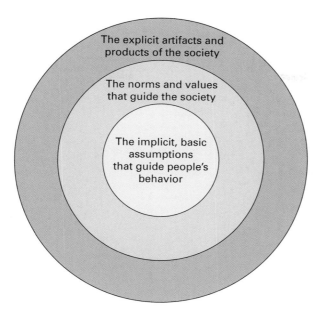

Figure 4–1

A Model of Culture

Figure 4–3. French culture and American culture, for example, have quite different norms and values. So the normal distribution curves for the two cultures have only limited overlap. However, when one looks at the tail ends of the two curves, it is possible to identify stereotypical views held by members of one culture about the other. The stereotypes are often exaggerated and used by members of one culture in describing the other, thus helping reinforce the differences between the two while reducing the likelihood of achieving cooperation and communication. This is one reason why an understanding of national culture is so important in the study of international management.

Values in Culture

A major dimension in the study of culture is values. **Values** are basic convictions that people have regarding what is right and wrong, good and bad, important and unimportant. These values are learned from the culture in which the individual is reared, and they help

values
Basic convictions that people have regarding what is right and wrong, good and bad, important and unimportant.

Figure 4–2

Comparing Cultures as Overlapping Normal Distributions

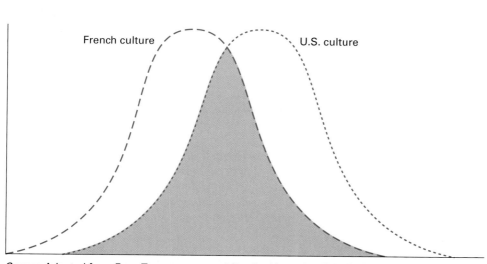

Source: Adapted from Fons Trompenaars and Charles Hampden-Turner, *Riding the Waves of Culture: Understanding Diversity in Global Business,* 2nd ed. (New York: McGraw-Hill, 1998), p. 25.

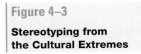

Figure 4–3

**Stereotyping from
the Cultural Extremes**

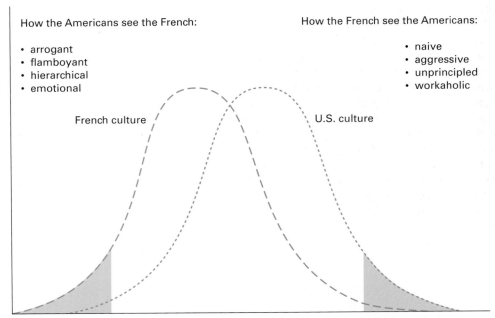

How the Americans see the French:

- arrogant
- flamboyant
- hierarchical
- emotional

French culture

How the French see the Americans:

- naive
- aggressive
- unprincipled
- workaholic

U.S. culture

Source: Adapted from Fons Trompenaars and Charles Hampden-Turner, *Riding the Waves of Culture: Understanding Diversity in Global Business,* 2nd ed. (New York: McGraw-Hill, 1998), p. 23.

to direct the person's behavior. Differences in cultural values often result in varying management practices. Table 4–2 provides an example. Note that U.S. values can result in one set of business responses and that alternative values can bring about different responses.

Value Differences and Similarities Across Cultures   Personal values have been the focus of numerous intercultural studies. In general, the findings show both differences and similarities between the work values and managerial values of different cultural groups. For example, one study found differences in work values between Western-oriented and tribal-oriented black employees in South Africa.[8] The Western-oriented group accepted most of the tenets of the Protestant work ethic, but the tribal-oriented group did not. The results were explained in terms of the differences of the cultural backgrounds of the two groups.

Differences in work values also have been found to reflect culture and industrialization. Researchers gave a personal-values questionnaire (PVQ) to over 2,000 managers in five countries: Australia ($n = 281$), India ($n = 485$), Japan ($n = 301$), South Korea ($n = 161$), and the United States ($n = 833$).[9] The PVQ consisted of 66 concepts related to business goals, personal goals, ideas associated with people and groups of people, and ideas about general topics. Ideologic and philosophic concepts were included to represent major value systems of all groups. The results showed some significant differences between the managers in each group. U.S. managers placed high value on the tactful acquisition of influence and on regard for others. Japanese managers placed high value on deference to superiors, on company commitment, and on the cautious use of aggressiveness and control. Korean managers placed high value on personal forcefulness and aggressiveness and low value on recognition of others. Indian managers put high value on the nonaggressive pursuit of objectives. Australian managers placed major importance on values reflecting a low-key approach to management and a high concern for others.[10] In short, value systems across national boundaries often are different.

At the same time, value similarities exist between cultures. In fact, research shows that managers from different countries often have similar personal values that relate to success.

Table 4–2
U.S. Values and Possible Alternatives

U.S. Cultural Values	Alternative Values	Examples of Management Function Affected
Individuals can influence the future (when there is a will there is a way).	Life follows a preordained course, and human action is determined by the will of God.	Planning and scheduling
Individuals should be realistic in their aspirations.	Ideals are to be pursued regardless of what is "reasonable."	Goal setting and career development.
We must work hard to accomplish our objectives (Puritan ethic).	Hard work is not the only prerequisite for success. Wisdom, luck, and time also are required.	Motivation and reward system.
A primary obligation of an employee is to the organization.	Individual employees have a primary obligation to their family and friends.	Loyalty, commitment, and motivation.
Employees can be removed if they do not perform well.	The removal of an employee from a position involves a great loss of prestige and will rarely be done.	Promotion.
Company information should be available to anyone who needs it within the organization.	Withholding information to gain or maintain power is acceptable.	Organization, communication, and managerial style.
Competition stimulates high performance.	Competition leads to imbalances and disharmony.	Career development and marketing.
What works is important.	Symbols and the process are more important than the end point.	Communication, planning, and quality control.

Source: Adapted from information found in Philip R. Harris and Robert T. Moran, *Managing Cultural Differences* (Houston: Gulf Publishing, 1991), pp. 79–80.

England and Lee examined the managerial values of a diverse sample of U.S. ($n = 878$), Japanese ($n = 312$), Australian ($n = 301$), and Indian managers ($n = 500$). They found that:

1. There is a reasonably strong relationship between the level of success achieved by managers and their personal values.

2. It is evident that value patterns predict managerial success and could be used in selection and placement decisions.

3. Although there are country differences in the relationships between values and success, findings across the four countries are quite similar.

4. The general pattern indicates that more successful managers appear to favor pragmatic, dynamic, achievement-oriented values, while less successful managers prefer more static and passive values. More successful managers favor an achievement orientation and prefer an active role in interaction with other individuals who are instrumental to achieving the managers' organizational goals. Less successful managers have values associated with a static and protected environment in which they take relatively passive roles.[11]

"International Management in Action: Common Personal Values" discusses these findings in more depth.

Values in Transition   Do values change over time? George England found that personal value systems are relatively stable and do not change rapidly.[12] However, changes are taking place in managerial values as a result of both culture and technology. A good example is the Japanese. Reichel and Flynn examined the effects of the U.S. environment on the cultural values of Japanese managers working for Japanese firms in the United States. In

Common Personal Values

One of the most interesting findings about successful managers around the world is that while they come from different cultures, many have similar personal values. Of course, there are large differences in values within each national group. For example, some managers are very pragmatic and judge ideas in terms of whether they will work; others are highly ethical-moral and view ideas in terms of right or wrong; still others have a "feeling" orientation and judge ideas in terms of whether they are pleasant. Some managers have a very small set of values; others have a large set. Some have values that are related heavily to organization life; others include a wide range of personal values; others have highly group-oriented values. There are many different value patterns; however, overall value profiles have been found within successful managers in each group. Here are some of the most significant:

U.S. managers
- Highly pragmatic
- High achievement and competence orientation
- Emphasis on profit maximization, organizational efficiency, and high productivity

Japanese managers
- Highly pragmatic
- Strong emphasis on size and growth
- High value on competence and achievement

Korean managers
- Highly pragmatic
- Highly individualistic
- Strong achievement and competence orientation

Australian managers
- High moral orientation
- High humanistic orientation
- Low value on achievement, success, competition, and risk

Indian managers
- High moral orientation
- Highly individualistic
- Strong focus on organization compliance and competence

The findings listed here show important similarities and differences. Most of the profiles are similar in nature; however, note that successful Indian and Australian managers have values that are distinctly different. In short, although values of successful managers within countries often are similar, there are intercountry differences. This is why the successful managerial value systems of one country often are not ideal in another country.

particular, they focused attention on such key organizational values as lifetime employment, formal authority, group orientation, seniority, and paternalism. Here is what they found:

1. Lifetime employment is widely accepted in Japanese culture, but the stateside Japanese managers did not believe that unconditional tenure in one organization was of major importance. They did believe, however, that job security was important.

2. Formal authority, obedience, and conformance to hierarchic position are very important in Japan, but the stateside managers did not perceive obedience and conformity to be very important and rejected the idea that one should not question a superior. However, they did support the concept of formal authority.

3. Group orientation, cooperation, conformity, and compromise are important organizational values in Japan. The stateside managers supported these values but also believed it was important to be an individual, thus maintaining a balance between a group and a personal orientation.

4. In Japan, organizational personnel often are rewarded based on seniority, not merit. Support for this value was directly influenced by the length of time the Japanese managers had been in the United States. The longer they had been there, the lower their support for this value.

5. Paternalism, often measured by a manager's involvement in both personal and off-the-job problems of subordinates, is very important in Japan. Stateside Japanese managers disagreed, and this resistance was positively associated with the number of years they had been in the United States.[13]

Other researchers have found supporting evidence that Japanese values are changing—and not just among managers outside the country. One study examined value systems among three groups of managers in Japan: (1) a group of Japanese managers who had graduated from the Japanese Institute for International Studies and Training at least 10 years previously; (2) a group of Japanese management trainees who currently were enrolled in the Institute; and (3) a group of U.S. MBA students who were taking MBA courses at the Institute.[14] The results showed that the Japanese managers were greatly concerned with job security, whereas the U.S. MBA students valued achievement. The Japanese managers put great importance on group success; the U.S. MBA students highly valued personal success. Although there were some exceptions, the two groups had contrasting values. The profiles of the Japanese students, meanwhile, fell between these two extremes. Two-thirds of responses were in this middle range. The researchers therefore concluded that "the data seem to indicate a significant difference in values between Japanese respondents who have already attained responsible managerial positions in their organization and the Japanese management trainees, who have held lower positions and been employed less long with their present company or government agency."[15]

Recently there is increasing evidence that individualism in Japan is on the rise. The country's long economic slump has convinced many Japanese that they cannot rely on the large corporations or the government to ensure their future. They have to do it for themselves. As a result, today a growing number of Japanese are starting to embrace what is being called the "era of personal responsibility." Instead of denouncing individualism as a threat to society, they are proposing it as a necessary solution to many of the country's economic ills. A vice-chairman of the nation's largest business lobby summed up this thinking at the opening of a recent conference on economic change when he said, "By establishing personal responsibility, we must return dynamism to the economy and revitalize society."[16] This thinking is supported by Lee and Peterson's research which reveals that a culture with a strong entrepreneurial orientation is important to global competitiveness, especially in the small business sector of an economy. So this current trend may well be helpful to the Japanese economy in helping it meet foreign competition at home.[17]

■ Hofstede's Cultural Dimensions

Some researchers have attempted to provide a composite picture of culture by examining its subparts, or dimensions. In particular, Dutch researcher Geert Hofstede found there are four dimensions of culture that help to explain how and why people from various cultures behave as they do.[18] His initial data were gathered from two questionnaire surveys with over 116,000 respondents from over 70 different countries around the world—making it the largest organizationally based study ever conducted. The individuals in these studies all worked in the local subsidiaries of IBM. As a result, Hofstede's research has been criticized because of its focus on just one company; however, he has countered this criticism. Hofstede is well aware of

> the amazement of some people about how employees of a very specific corporation like IBM can serve as a sample for discovering something about the culture of their countries at large. "We know IBMers," they say, "they are very special people, always in a white shirt and tie, and not at all representative of our country." The people who say this are quite right. IBMers do not form representative samples from national populations. . . . However, samples for cross-national comparison need not be representative, as long as they are functionally equivalent. IBM employees are a narrow sample, but very well matched. Employees of multinational companies in general and of IBM in particular form attractive sources of information for comparing national traits, because they are so similar in respects other than nationality: their employers . . . , their kind of work, and—for matched occupations—their level of education. The only thing that can account for systematic and consistent differences between national groups *within* such a homogenous multinational population is nationality itself. The national environment in which people were brought up *before* they joined this employer. Comparing IBM subsidiaries therefore shows national culture differences with unusual clarity.[19]

Hofstede's massive study continues to be a focal point for additional research. The four now-well-known dimensions that Hofstede examined were (1) power distance, (2) uncertainty avoidance, (3) individualism, and (4) masculinity.

Power Distance

Power distance is "the extent to which less powerful members of institutions and organizations accept that power is distributed unequally."[20] Countries in which people blindly obey the orders of their superiors have high power distance. In many societies, lower-level employees tend to follow orders as a matter of procedure. In societies with high power distance, however, strict obedience is found even at the upper levels; examples include Mexico, South Korea, and India. For example, a senior Indian executive with a PhD from a prestigious U.S. university related the following story:

> What is most important for me and my department is not what I do or achieve for the company, but whether the [owner's] favor is bestowed on me. . . . This I have achieved by saying "yes" to everything [the owner] says or does. . . . To contradict him is to look for another job. . . . I left my freedom of thought in Boston.[21]

The effect of this dimension can be measured in a number of ways. For example, organizations in low-power-distance countries generally will be decentralized and have flatter organization structures. These organizations also will have a smaller proportion of supervisory personnel, and the lower strata of the workforce often will consist of highly qualified people. By contrast, organizations in high-power-distance countries will tend to be centralized and have tall organization structures. Organizations in high-power-distance countries will have a large proportion of supervisory personnel, and the people at the lower levels of the structure often will have low job qualifications. This latter structure encourages and promotes inequality between people at different levels.[22]

Uncertainty Avoidance

Uncertainty avoidance is "the extent to which people feel threatened by ambiguous situations, and have created beliefs and institutions that try to avoid these."[23] Countries populated with people who do not like uncertainty tend to have a high need for security and a strong belief in experts and their knowledge; examples include Germany, Japan, and Spain. Cultures with low uncertainty avoidance have people who are more willing to accept that risks are associated with the unknown, that life must go on in spite of this. Examples here include Denmark and Great Britain.

The effect of this dimension can be measured in a number of ways. Countries with high-uncertainty-avoidance cultures have a great deal of structuring of organizational activities, more written rules, less risk taking by managers, lower labor turnover, and less ambitious employees.

Low-uncertainty-avoidance societies have organization settings with less structuring of activities, fewer written rules, more risk taking by managers, higher labor turnover, and more ambitious employees. The organization encourages personnel to use their own initiative and assume responsibility for their actions.

Individualism

Individualism is the tendency of people to look after themselves and their immediate family only.[24] Hofstede measured this cultural difference on a bipolar continuum with individualism at one end and collectivism at the other. **Collectivism** is the tendency of people to belong to groups or collectives and to look after each other in exchange for loyalty.[25]

Like the effects of the other cultural dimensions, the effects of individualism and collectivism can be measured in a number of different ways.[26] Hofstede found that

Table 4–3
Countries and Regions Used in Hofstede's Research

ARA	Arab countries (Egypt, Lebanon, Libya, Kuwait, Iraq, Saudi Arabia, U.A.E.)	JPN	Japan
		KOR	South Korea
ARG	Argentina	MAL	Malaysia
AUL	Australia	MEX	Mexico
AUT	Austria	NET	Netherlands
BEL	Belgium	NOR	Norway
BRA	Brazil	NZL	New Zealand
CAN	Canada	PAK	Pakistan
CHL	Chile	PAN	Panama
COL	Colombia	PER	Peru
COS	Costa Rica	PHI	Philippines
DEN	Denmark	POR	Portugal
EAF	East Africa (Kenya, Ethiopia, Zambia)	SAF	South Africa
EQA	Equador	SAL	Salvador
FIN	Finland	SIN	Singapore
FRA	France	SPA	Spain
GBR	Great Britain	SWE	Sweden
GER	Germany	SWI	Switzerland
GRE	Greece	TAI	Taiwan
GUA	Guatemala	THA	Thailand
HOK	Hong Kong	TUR	Turkey
IDO	Indonesia	URU	Uruguay
IND	India	USA	United States
IRA	Iran	VEN	Venezuela
IRE	Ireland	WAF	West Africa (Nigeria, Ghana, Sierra Leone)
ISR	Israel		
ITA	Italy	YUG	Yugoslavia
JAM	Jamaica		

Source: Adapted from Geert Hofstede, *Cultures and Organizations: Software of the Mind* (London: McGraw-Hill U.K., Ltd., 1991), p. 55. Used with permission.

wealthy countries have higher individualism scores and poorer countries higher collectivism scores (see Table 4–3 for the country abbreviations used in Figure 4–4 and subsequent figures). Note that in Figure 4–4, the United States, Canada, Australia, Denmark, and Sweden, among others, have high individualism and high GNP. Conversely, Indonesia, Pakistan, and a number of South American countries have low individualism (high collectivism) and low GNP. Countries with high individualism also tend to have greater support for the Protestant work ethic, greater individual initiative, and promotions based on market value. Countries with low individualism tend to have less support for the Protestant work ethic, less individual initiative, and promotions based on seniority.

Masculinity

Masculinity is defined by Hofstede as "a situation in which the dominant values in society are success, money, and things."[27] Hofstede measured this dimension on a continuum ranging from masculinity to femininity. Contrary to some stereotypes and connotations, **femininity** is the term used by Hofstede to describe "a situation in which the dominant values in society are caring for others and the quality of life."[28] Countries with a high masculinity index, such as

masculinity
A cultural characteristic in which the dominant values in society are success, money, and things.

femininity
A cultural characteristic in which the dominant values in society are caring for others and the quality of life.

Figure 4–4

Individualism Index vs. Per Capita GNP

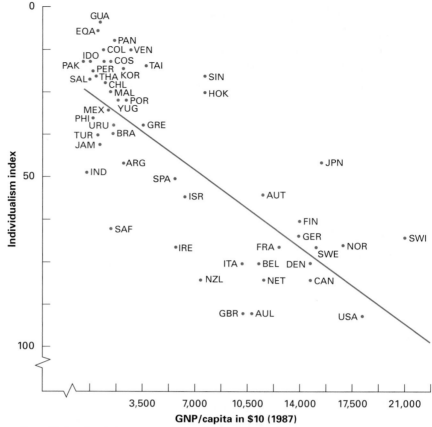

Source: Geert Hofstede, *Cultures and Organizations: Software of the Mind* (London: McGraw-Hill U.K., Ltd., 1991), p. 75. Used with permission.

the Germanic countries, place great importance on earnings, recognition, advancement, and challenge. Individuals are encouraged to be independent decision makers, and achievement is defined in terms of recognition and wealth. The workplace is often characterized by high job stress, and many managers believe that their employees dislike work and must be kept under some degree of control.

Countries with a low masculinity index (Hofstede's femininity dimension), such as Norway, tend to place great importance on cooperation, a friendly atmosphere, and employment security. Individuals are encouraged to be group decision makers, and achievement is defined in terms of layman contacts and the living environment. The workplace tends to be characterized by low stress, and managers give their employees more credit for being responsible and allow them more freedom.

Cultures with a high masculinity index, such as the Japanese, tend to favor large-scale enterprises, and economic growth is seen as more important than conservation of the environment. The school system is geared toward encouraging high performance. Young men expect to have careers, and those who do not often view themselves as failures. Fewer women hold higher-level jobs, and these individuals often find it necessary to be assertive. There is high job stress in the workplace, and industrial conflict is common.

Cultures with a low masculinity index (high femininity) tend to favor small-scale enterprises, and they place great importance on conservation of the environment. The school system is designed to teach social adaptation. Some young men and women want careers; others do not. Many women hold higher-level jobs, and they do not find it necessary to be assertive. Less job stress is found in the workplace, and there is not much industrial conflict.

Integrating the Dimensions

A description of the four dimensions of culture is useful in helping to explain the differences between various countries, and Hofstede's research has extended beyond this focus and shown how countries can be described in terms of pairs of dimensions. Figure 4–5, which incorporates power distance and individualism, provides an example.

In Figure 4–5, the United States is located in the lower left-hand quadrant. Americans have very high individualism and relatively low power distance. They prefer to do things for themselves and are not upset when others have more power than they do. In fact, Americans are taught to believe that everyone is equal, so they are not overly impressed by individuals with important titles or jobs. Australians, Canadians, British, Dutch, and New Zealanders have the same basic values. Conversely, many of the underdeveloped or newly industrialized countries, such as Colombia, Hong Kong, Portugal, and Singapore, are characterized by large power distance and low individualism. These nations tend to be collectivist in their approach.

Figure 4–6 plots the uncertainty-avoidance index for the 53 countries against the power-distance index. Once again, there are clusters of countries. Many of the Anglo nations tend to be in the upper left-hand quadrant, which is characterized by small power distance and weak uncertainty avoidance (they do not try to avoid uncertainty). These countries tend to be moderately unconcerned with power distance, and they are able to accept conditions of uncertainty. In contrast, many Latin countries (in both Europe and the Western Hemisphere), Mediterranean countries, and Asian nations (e.g., Japan and Korea) are characterized by high power distance and strong uncertainty avoidance. Most other Asian countries are characterized by large power distance and weak uncertainty avoidance.

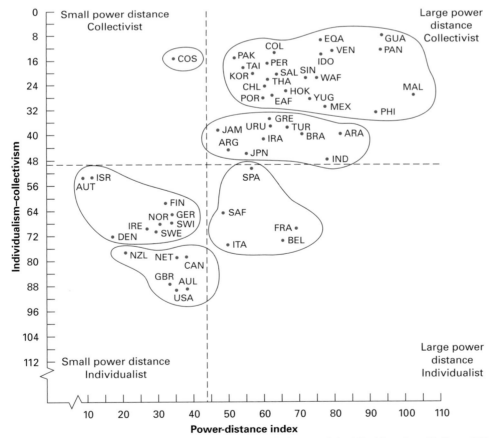

Figure 4–5

A Power-Distance and Individualism–Collectivism Plot

Source: Geert Hofstede, *Cultures and Organizations: Software of the Mind* (London: McGraw-Hill U.K., Ltd., 1991), p. 54. Used with permission.

Figure 4–6

A Power-Distance and Uncertainty-Avoidance Plot

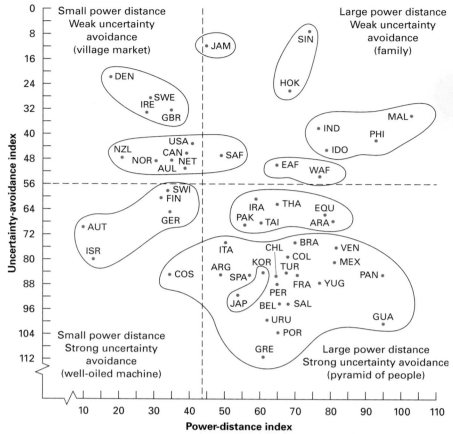

Source: Geert Hofstede, *Cultures and Organizations: Software of the Mind* (London: McGraw-Hill U.K., Ltd., 1991), p. 141. Used with permission.

Figure 4–7 plots the position of 53 countries in terms of uncertainty avoidance and masculinity–femininity. The most masculine country is Japan, followed by the Germanic countries (Austria, Switzerland, Germany) and Latin countries (Venezuela, Mexico, Italy). Many countries in the Anglo cluster, including Ireland, Australia, Great Britain, and the United States, have moderate degrees of masculinity. So do some of the former colonies of Anglo nations, including India, South Africa, and the Philippines. The Northern European cluster (Denmark, Sweden, Norway, the Netherlands) has low masculinity, indicating that these countries place high value on factors such as quality of life, preservation of the environment, and the importance of relationships with people over money.

The integration of these cultural factors into two-dimensional plots helps to illustrate the complexity of understanding culture's effect on behavior. A number of dimensions are at work, and sometimes they do not all move in the anticipated direction. For example, at first glance, a nation with high power distance would appear to be low in individualism, and vice versa, and Hofstede found exactly that (see Figure 4–5). However, low uncertainty avoidance does not always go hand in hand with high masculinity, even though those who are willing to live with uncertainty will want rewards such as money and power and accord low value to the quality of work life and caring for others (see Figure 4–7). Simply put, empirical evidence on the impact of cultural dimensions may differ from commonly held beliefs or stereotypes. Research-based data are needed to determine the full impact of differing cultures. However, some interesting attempts have been made to classify countries in uniform clusters on variables such as attitudes and to deal with cultures on a more structured basis. These efforts are described in the next section.

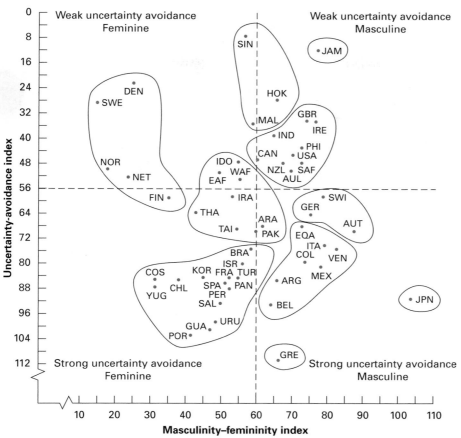

Figure 4–7

A Masculinity–Femininity and Uncertainty-Avoidance Plot

Source: Geert Hofstede, *Cultures and Organizations: Software of the Mind* (London: McGraw-Hill U.K., Ltd., 1991), p. 123. Used with permission.

■ Attitudinal Dimensions of Culture

For well over two decades, researchers have attempted to cluster countries into similar cultural groupings for the purpose of studying similarities and differences. Such research also helps us to learn the reasons for cultural differences and how they can be transcended. Much of the initial research in this area examined similarities among countries based on employee work values and attitudes.

Work Value and Attitude Similarities

Drawing on his extensive data, Hofstede was able to use the four cultural dimensions discussed in the last section to compile a series of country clusters, as shown in Figures 4–5, 4–6, and 4–7. His work was only preliminary, but it served as a point of departure for other multicultural research, which revealed many similarities in both work values and attitudes among certain countries. For example, early research by Ronen and Kraut reported that "countries could be clustered into more or less homogeneous groups based on intercorrelations of standard scores obtained for each country from scales measuring leadership, role descriptions, and motivation."[29] These researchers then attempted to cluster the countries by use of the mathematic technique of nonparametric multivariate analysis, known as **smallest space analysis (SSA).** Simply put, this approach maps the relationships of various culture dimensions among the countries by showing the distance between each. By looking at the resulting two-dimensional map, one can see those countries that are similar to each other and those that are not.

smallest space analysis (SSA)
A nonparametric multivariate analysis. This mathematic tool maps the relationship among countries by showing the distance between each. By looking at this two-dimensional map, it is possible to see those countries that are similar to each other and those that are not.

Drawing on the work of many earlier researchers as well as that of 4,000 technical employees in 15 countries, Ronen and Kraut were able to construct SSA maps of various countries, including the United States, France, India, Sweden, and Japan. These maps showed five country clusters: (1) Anglo-American (United States, United Kingdom, Australia); (2) Nordic (Norway, Finland, Denmark); (3) South American (Venezuela, Mexico, Chile); (4) Latin European (France and Belgium); and (5) Germanic (Germany, Austria, and Switzerland). Commenting on the overall value of their research, Ronen and Kraut concluded:

> An important aspect of this study is the potential for practical application by multinational organizations. For example, knowledge of relative similarities among countries can guide the smooth placement of international assignees and the establishment of compatible regional units, and predict the ease of implementing various policies and practices across national boundaries.[30]

Since Ronen and Kraut, additional multicultural studies have been conducted, and the number of countries and clusters has increased. These country clusters are particularly important in providing an overall picture of international cultures.[31]

Country Clusters

To date, perhaps the most integrative analysis of all available findings has been provided by Ronen and Shenkar.[32] After conducting a thorough review of the literature, they found that eight major cluster studies had been conducted over the previous 15 years. These studies examined variables in four categories: (1) the importance of work goals; (2) need deficiency, fulfillment, and job satisfaction; (3) managerial and organizational variables; and (4) work role and interpersonal orientation. Each of the eight country cluster studies had produced different results. Some had focused only on one part of the world, such as the Far East or the Middle East; others had been more international in focus but arrived at different cluster groupings. Based on careful analysis of these research efforts, Ronen and Shenkar identified eight country clusters and four countries that are independent and do not fit into any of the clusters (see Figure 4–8).

Each country in Figure 4–8 that has been placed in a cluster is culturally similar to the others in that cluster. In addition, the closer a country is to the center of the overall circle, the greater its per capita gross national product (GNP). Those countries with similar GNPs will not necessarily have intercluster similarity, but to the extent that GNP influences values and culture, these countries will have converging cultural values.

Not everyone agrees with the synthesis presented in Figure 4–8. Some researchers place India and Israel in the Anglo culture because of the strong Anglo ties of these countries. Others combine the Nordic and Germanic clusters into one. Still others believe that some of the Latin European countries, such as Italy, Portugal, and Spain, are culturally much closer to those of the South American culture and cluster them there. Nevertheless, Figure 4–8 does provide a useful model and point of departure for examining international culture. The concept of country clusters is useful to those studying multinational management as well. Ronen and Shenkar note:

> As multinational companies increase their direct investment overseas, especially in less developed and consequently less studied areas, they will require more information concerning their local employees in order to implement effective types of interactions between the organization and the host country. The knowledge acquired thus far can help one to understand better the work values and attitudes of employees throughout the world. American theories work very well for Western nations. Are they equally applicable in non-Western countries? Clearly, more cluster research is called for, including research in countries from all parts of the globe.[33]

Empirical evidence shows that international managers share a common international culture, so there may well be much more convergence than previously has been believed.

Figure 4–8

A Synthesis of Country Clusters

Source: Simcha Ronen and Oded Shenkar, "Clustering Countries on Attitudinal Dimensions: A Review and Synthesis," *Academy of Management Journal,* September, 1985, p. 449. Copyright 1985 by Academy of Management. Reproduced with permission of Academy of Management via Copyright Clearance Center.

There also may be much more recent adaptation to the local culture by national firms than many outside observers realize. In short, although recognizing cultural diversity still is vital, convergence and flexibility in the international arena are gaining momentum.

■ Trompenaars's Cultural Dimensions

Both the Hofstede cultural dimensions and the Ronen and Shenkar country clusters are widely recognized and accepted in the study of international management. A more recent description of how cultures differ, by another Dutch researcher, Fons Trompenaars, is receiving increasing attention as well. Trompenaars' research was conducted over a 10-year period and published in 1994.[34] He administered research questionnaires to over 15,000 managers from 28 countries and received usable responses from at least 500 in each nation; the 23 countries in his research are presented in Table 4–4. Building heavily on value orientations and the relational orientations of well-known sociologist Talcott Parsons,[35] Trompenaars derived five relationship orientations that address the ways in which people deal with each other; these can be considered to be cultural dimensions that are analogous to Hofstede's dimensions. Trompenaars also looked at attitudes toward both time and the environment, and the result of his research is a wealth of information helping to explain how cultures differ and offering practical ways in which MNCs can do business in various countries. The following discussion examines each of the five relationship orientations as well as attitudes toward time and the environment.[36]

Table 4–4	
Trompenaars's Country Abbreviations	
Abbreviation	**Country**
ARG	Argentina
AUS	Austria
BEL	Belgium
BRZ	Brazil
CHI	China
CIS	Former Soviet Union
CZH	Former Czechoslovakia
FRA	France
GER	Germany (excluding former East Germany)
HK	Hong Kong
IDO	Indonesia
ITA	Italy
JPN	Japan
MEX	Mexico
NL	Netherlands
SIN	Singapore
SPA	Spain
SWE	Sweden
SWI	Switzerland
THA	Thailand
UK	United Kingdom
USA	United States
VEN	Venezuela

Universalism vs. Particularism

universalism
The belief that ideas and practices can be applied everywhere in the world without modification.

particularism
The belief that circumstances dictate how ideas and practices should be applied and something cannot be done the same everywhere.

Universalism is the belief that ideas and practices can be applied everywhere without modification. **Particularism** is the belief that circumstances dictate how ideas and practices should be applied. In cultures with high universalism, the focus is more on formal rules than on relationships, business contracts are adhered to very closely, and people believe that "a deal is a deal." In cultures with high particularism, the focus is more on relationships and trust than on formal rules. In a particularist culture, legal contracts often are modified, and as people get to know each other better, they often change the way in which deals are executed. In his early research, Trompenaars found that in countries such as the United States, Australia, Germany, Sweden, and the United Kingdom, there was high universalism, while countries such as Venezuela, the former Soviet Union, Indonesia, and China were high on particularism. Figure 4–9 shows the continuum.

In follow-up research, Trompenaars and Hampden-Turner uncovered additional insights regarding national orientations on this universalism–particularism continuum. They did this by presenting the respondents with a dilemma and asking them to make a decision. Here is one of these dilemmas along with the national scores of the respondents:[37]

> You are riding in a car driven by a close friend. He hits a pedestrian. You know he was going at least 35 miles per hour in an area of the city where the maximum allowed speed is 20 miles per hour. There are no witnesses. His lawyer says that if you testify under oath that he was driving 20 miles per hour it may save him from serious consequences. What right has your friend to expect you to protect him?

> (*a*) My friend has a definite right as a friend to expect me to testify to the lower figure.

> (*b*) He has some right as a friend to expect me to testify to the lower figure.

> (*c*) He has no right as a friend to expect me to testify to the lower figure.

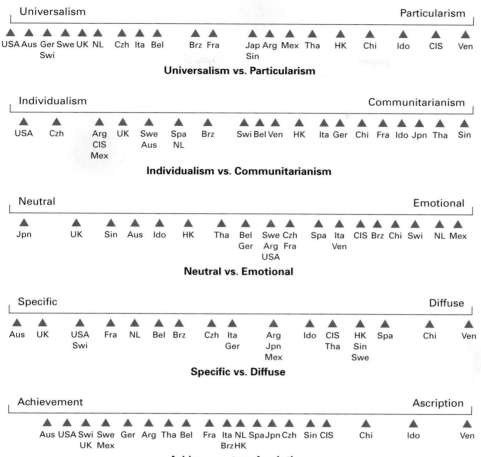

Figure 4–9

Trompenaars's Relationship Orientations on Cultural Dimensions

Source: Adapted from information found in Fons Trompenaars, *Riding the Waves of Culture* (New York: Irwin, 1994), and Charles M. Hampden-Turner and Fons Trompenaars, "A World Turned Upside Down: Doing Business in Asia," in *Managing Across Cultures: Issues and Perspectives,* ed. Pat Joynt and Malcolm Warner (London: International Thomson Business Press, 1996), pp. 275–305.

With a high score indicating strong universalism (choice *c*) and a low score indicating strong particularism (choice *a*), here is how the different nations scored:

Universalism (no right)

Canada	96
United States	95
Germany	90
United Kingdom	90
Netherlands	88
France	68
Japan	67
Singapore	67
Thailand	63
Hong Kong	56

Particularism (some or definite right)

China	48
South Korea	26

As noted earlier, respondents from universalism cultures (e.g., North America and Western Europe) felt that the rules applied regardless of the situation, while respondents from particularism cultures were much more willing to bend the rules and help their friend.

Based on these types of findings, Trompenaars recommends that when individuals from particularist cultures do business in a universalist culture, they should be prepared for rational, professional arguments and a "let's get down to business" attitude. Conversely, when individuals from universalist cultures do business in a particularist environment, they should be prepared for personal meandering or irrelevancies that seem to go nowhere and should not regard personal, get-to know-you attitudes as mere small talk.

Individualism vs. Communitarianism

communitarianism
Refers to people regarding themselves as part of a group.

Individualism and communitarianism are key dimensions in Hofstede's earlier research. Although Trompenaars derived these two relationships differently than Hofstede, they still have the same basic meaning, although in his more recent work Trompenaars has used the word *communitarianism* rather than *collectivism*. For him, individualism refers to people regarding themselves as individuals, while **communitarianism** refers to people regarding themselves as part of a group. As shown in Figure 4–9, the United States, former Czechoslovakia, Argentina, the former Soviet Union (CIS), and Mexico have high individualism. These findings of Trompenaars are particularly interesting, because they differ somewhat from those of Hofstede, as reported in Figure 4–5. Although the definitions are not exactly the same, the fact that there are differences (e.g., Mexico and Argentina are collectivistic in Hofstede's findings but individualistic in Trompenaars's research) points out that cultural values may be changing (i.e., Hofstede's findings may be dated). For example, with Mexico now part of NAFTA and the global economy, this country may have moved from dominant collectivistic or communitarianistic cultural values to more individualist values. Trompenaars also found that the former communist countries of Czechoslovakia and the Soviet Union now appear to be quite individualistic, which of course is contrary to assumptions and conventional wisdom about the former communist bloc. In other words, Trompenaars points out the complex, dynamic nature of culture and the danger of overgeneralization.

In his most recent research, and again using the technique of presenting respondents with a dilemma and asking them to make a decision, Trompenaars posed the following situation. If you were to be promoted, which of the two following issues would you emphasize most: (a) the new group of people with whom you will be working or (b) the greater responsibility of the work you are undertaking and the higher income you will be earning? The following reports the latest scores associated with the individualism of option *b*—greater responsibility and more money.[38]

Individualism (emphasis on larger responsibilities and more income)

Canada	77
Thailand	71
United Kingdom	69
United States	67
Netherlands	64
France	61
Japan	61
China	54
Singapore	50
Hong Kong	47

Communitarianism (emphasis on the new group of people)

Malaysia	38
Korea	32

These findings are somewhat different from those presented in Figure 4–9 and show that cultural changes may be occurring more rapidly than many people realize. For example, the latest findings show Thailand very high on individualism (possibly indicating an increasing entrepreneurial spirit/cultural value) whereas the Thais were found to be low on individualism a few years before, as shown in Figure 4–9. At the same time, it is important to remember that there are major differences between people in high-individualism societies and those in high-communitarianism societies. The former stress personal and individual matters; the latter value group-related issues. Negotiations in cultures with high individualism typically are made on the spot by a representative, people ideally achieve things alone, and they assume a great deal of personal responsibility. In cultures with high communitarianism, decisions typically are referred to committees, people ideally achieve things in groups, and they jointly assume responsibility.

Trompenaars recommends that when people from cultures with high individualism deal with those from communitarianism cultures, they should have patience for the time taken to consent and to consult, and they should aim to build lasting relationships. When people from cultures with high communitarianism deal with those from individualist cultures, they should be prepared to make quick decisions and commit their organization to these decisions. Also, communitarianistics dealing with individualists should realize that the reason they are dealing with only one negotiator (as opposed to a group) is that this person is respected by his or her organization and has its authority and esteem.

Neutral vs. Emotional

A **neutral culture** is one in which emotions are held in check. As seen in Figure 4–9, both Japan and the United Kingdom are high-neutral cultures. People in these countries try not to show their feelings; they act stoically and maintain their composure. An **emotional culture** is one in which emotions are openly and naturally expressed. People in emotional cultures often smile a great deal, talk loudly when they are excited, and greet each other with a great deal of enthusiasm. Mexico, the Netherlands, and Switzerland are examples of high emotional cultures.

Trompenaars recommends that when individuals from emotional cultures do business in neutral cultures, they should put as much as they can on paper and submit it to the other side. They should realize that lack of emotion does not mean disinterest or boredom, but rather that people from neutral cultures do not like to show their hand. Conversely, when those from neutral cultures do business in emotional cultures, they should not be put off stride when the other side creates scenes or grows animated and boisterous, and they should try to respond warmly to the emotional affections of the other group.

neutral culture
A culture in which emotions are held in check.

emotional culture
A culture in which emotions are expressed openly and naturally.

Specific vs. Diffuse

A **specific culture** is one in which individuals have a large public space they readily let others enter and share and a small private space they guard closely and share with only close friends and associates. A **diffuse culture** is one in which public space and private space are similar in size and individuals guard their public space carefully, because entry into public space affords entry into private space as well. As shown in Figure 4–9, Austria, the United Kingdom, the United States, and Switzerland all are specific cultures, while Venezuela, China, and Spain are diffuse cultures. In specific cultures, people often are invited into a person's open, public space; individuals in these cultures often are open and extroverted; and there is a strong separation of work and private life. In diffuse cultures, people are not quickly invited into a person's open, public space, because once they are in, there is easy entry into the private space as well. Individuals in these cultures often appear to be indirect and introverted, and work and private life often are closely linked.

An example of these specific and diffuse cultural dimensions is provided by the United States and Germany. A U.S. professor, such as Robert Smith, PhD, generally would be called "Dr. Smith" by students when at his U.S. university. When shopping, however, he

specific culture
A culture in which individuals have a large public space they readily share with others and a small private space they guard closely and share with only close friends and associates.

diffuse culture
A culture in which public space and private space are similar in size and individuals guard their public space carefully, because entry into public space affords entry into private space as well.

might be referred to by the store clerk as "Bob," and he might even ask the clerk's advice regarding some of his intended purchases. When golfing, Bob might just be one of the guys, even to a golf partner who happens to be a graduate student in his department. The reason for these changes in status is that, with the specific U.S. cultural values, people have large public spaces and often conduct themselves differently depending on their public role. At the same time, however, Bob has private space that is off-limits to the students who must call him "Doctor Smith" in class. In high-diffuse cultures, on the other hand, a person's public life and private life often are similar. Therefore, in Germany, Herr Professor Doktor Schmidt would be referred to that way at the university, local market, and bowling alley—and even his wife might address him formally in public. A great deal of formality is maintained, often giving the impression that Germans are stuffy or aloof.

Trompenaars recommends that when those from specific cultures do business in diffuse cultures, they should respect a person's title, age, and background connections, and they should not get impatient when people are being indirect or circuitous. Conversely, when individuals from diffuse cultures do business in specific cultures, they should try to get to the point and be efficient, learn to structure meetings with the judicious use of agendas, and not use their titles or acknowledge achievements or skills that are irrelevant to the issues being discussed.

Achievement vs. Ascription

achievement culture
A culture in which people are accorded status based on how well they perform their functions.

ascription culture
A culture in which status is attributed based on who or what a person is.

An **achievement culture** is one in which people are accorded status based on how well they perform their functions. An **ascription culture** is one in which status is attributed based on who or what a person is. Achievement cultures give high status to high achievers, such as the company's number-one salesperson or the medical researcher who has found a cure for a rare form of bone cancer. Ascription cultures accord status based on age, gender, or social connections. For example, in an ascription culture, a person who has been with the company for 40 years may be listened to carefully because of the respect that others have for the individual's age and longevity with the firm, and an individual who has friends in high places may be afforded status because of whom she knows. As shown in Figure 4–9, Austria, the United States, Switzerland, and the United Kingdom are achievement cultures, while Venezuela, Indonesia, and China are ascription cultures.

Trompenaars recommends that when individuals from achievement cultures do business in ascription cultures, they should make sure that their group has older, senior, and formal position-holders who can impress the other side, and they should respect the status and influence of their counterparts in the other group. Conversely, he recommends that when individuals from ascription cultures do business in achievement cultures, they should make sure that their group has sufficient data, technical advisers, and knowledgeable people to convince the other group that they are proficient, and they should respect the knowledge and information of their counterparts on the other team.

Time

Aside from the five relationship orientations, another major cultural difference is the way in which people deal with the concept of time. Trompenaars has identified two different approaches: sequential and synchronous. In cultures where *sequential* approaches are prevalent, people tend to do only one activity at a time, keep appointments strictly, and show a strong preference for following plans as they are laid out and not deviating from them. In cultures where *synchronous* approaches are common, people tend to do more than one activity at a time, appointments are approximate and may be changed at a moment's notice, and schedules generally are subordinate to relationships. People in synchronous-time cultures often will stop what they are doing to meet and greet individuals coming into their office.

A good contrast is provided by the United States, Mexico, and France. In the United States, people tend to be guided by sequential-time orientation and thus set a schedule and stick to it. Mexicans operate under more of a synchronous-time orientation and thus tend to be much more flexible, often building slack into their schedules to allow for interruptions. The French are similar to the Mexicans and, when making plans, often determine the objectives they want to accomplish but leave open the timing and other factors that are beyond their control; this way, they can adjust and modify their approach as they go along. As Trompenaars noted, "For the French and Mexicans, what was important was that they get to the end, not the particular path or sequence by which that end was reached."[39]

Another interesting time-related contrast is the degree to which cultures are past or present oriented as opposed to future-oriented. In countries such as the United States, Italy, and Germany, the future is more important than the past or the present. In countries such as Venezuela, Indonesia, and Spain, the present is most important. In France and Belgium, all three time periods are of approximately equal importance. Because different emphases are given to different time periods, adjusting to these cultural differences can create challenges.

Trompenaars recommends that when doing business with future-oriented cultures, effective international managers should emphasize the opportunities and limitless scope that any agreement can have, agree to specific deadlines for getting things done, and be aware of the core competence or continuity that the other party intends to carry with it into the future. When doing business with past- or present-oriented cultures, he recommends that managers emphasize the history and tradition of the culture, find out whether internal relationships will sanction the types of changes that need to be made, and agree to future meetings in principle but fix no deadlines for completions.

The Environment

Trompenaars also examined the ways in which people deal with their environment. Specific attention should be given to whether they believe in controlling outcomes (inner-directed) or letting things take their own course (outer-directed). One of the things he asked managers to do was choose between the following statements:

1. What happens to me is my own doing.
2. Sometimes I feel that I do not have enough control over the directions my life is taking.

Managers who believe in controlling their own environment would opt for the first choice; those who believe that they are controlled by their environment and cannot do much about it would opt for the second.

Here is an example by country of the sample respondents who believe that what happens to them is their own doing:[40]

United States	89%
Switzerland	84%
Australia	81%
Belgium	76%
Indonesia	73%
Hong Kong	69%
Greece	63%
Singapore	58%
Japan	56%
China	35%

In the United States, managers feel strongly that they are masters of their own fate. This helps to account for their dominant attitude (sometimes bordering on aggressiveness) toward the environment and discomfort when things seem to get out of control. Many Asian cultures do not share these views. They believe that things move in waves or natural shifts and one must "go with the flow," so a flexible attitude, characterized by a willingness to compromise and maintain harmony with nature, is important.

Trompenaars recommends that when dealing with those from cultures that believe in dominating the environment, it is important to play hardball, test the resilience of the opponent, win some objectives, and always lose from time to time. For example, representatives of the U.S. government have repeatedly urged Japanese automobile companies to purchase more component parts from U.S. suppliers to partially offset the large volume of U.S. imports of finished autos from Japan. Instead of enacting trade barriers, the United States was asking for a quid pro quo. When dealing with those from cultures that believe in letting things take their natural course, it is important to be persistent and polite, maintain good relationships with the other party, and try to win together and lose apart.

Cultural Patterns or Clusters

Like Hofstede's and the earlier work of Ronen and Shenkar, Trompenaars's research lends itself to cultural patterns or clusters. Table 4–5 relates his findings to the five relational orientations, categorized into the same types of clusters that Ronen and Shenkar used (see Figure 4–8).

Table 4–5
Cultural Groups Based on Trompenaars's Research

	Anglo Cluster	
Relationship	United States	United Kingdom
Individualism Communitarianism	X	X
Specific relationship Diffuse relationship	X	X
Universalism Particularism	X	X
Neutral relationship Emotional relationship	X	X
Achievement Ascription	X	X

	Asian Cluster				
Relationship	Japan	China	Indonesia	Hong Kong	Singapore
Individualism Communitarianism	X	X	X	X	X
Specific relationship Diffuse relationship	X	X	X	X	X
Universalism Particularism	X	X	X	X	X
Neutral relationship Emotional relationship	X	X	X	X	X
Achievement Ascription	X	X	X	X	X

	Latin American Cluster			
Relationship	Argentina	Mexico	Venezuela	Brazil
Individualism Communitarianism	X	X	X	X
Specific relationship Diffuse relationship	X	X	X	X
Universalism Particularism	X	X	X	X
Neutral relationship Emotional relationship	X	X	X	X
Achievement Ascription	X	X	X	X

(continued)

Table 4–5 *(continued)*
Cultural Groups Based on Trompenaars's Research

Relationship	Latin European Cluster			
	France	Belgium	Spain	Italy
Individualism			X	
Communitarianism	X	X		X
Specific relationship	X	X		
Diffuse relationship			X	X
Universalism	X	X		X
Particularism			X	
Neutral relationship			X	
Emotional relationship	X	X		X
Achievement			X	
Ascription	X	X		X

Relationship	Germanic Cluster			
	Austria	Germany	Switzerland	Czechoslovakia
Individualism	X			
Communitarianism		X	X	X
Specific relationship	X		X	X
Diffuse relationship		X		
Universalism	X	X	X	X
Particularism				
Neutral relationship	X			X
Emotional relationship		X	X	
Achievement	X	X		X
Ascription			X	

Source: Adapted from information in Fons Trompenaars, *Riding the Waves of Culture* (New York: Irwin, 1994).

There is a great deal of similarity between the Trompenaars and the Ronen and Shenkar clusters. Both the United States and United Kingdom profiles are the same, except for the neutral (U.K.) and emotional (U.S.) dimension. So are those in most of the Asian countries, including Japan, which was left out of the Ronen and Shenkar clusters and labeled an independent. Brazil, which also was left out of the Ronen and Shenkar clusters, continues to be sufficiently different from other members of the Latin American group in the Trompenaars-derived Table 4–5. In other words, Brazil still appears to be independent. Additionally, while France and Belgium, in the Latin European Trompenaars group, have identical profiles, Spain is significantly different from both of them as well as from Italy. This shows that earlier cluster groups, such as that of Ronen and Shenkar, may need to be revised in light of more recent data.

Overall, Table 4–5 shows that a case can be made for cultural similarities between clusters of countries. With only small differences, Trompenaars's research helps to support and, more important, to extend the work of Hofstede as well as Ronen and Shenkar. Such research provides a useful point of departure for recognizing cultural differences, and it provides guidelines for doing business effectively around the world.

■ Integrating Culture and Management: The GLOBE Project

The **GLOBE** (Global Leadership and Organizational Behavior Effectiveness) research program reflects an additional approach to measuring cultural differences. The GLOBE project extends and integrates previous analyses of cultural attributes and variables. At the heart of the project is the study and evaluation of nine different cultural attributes using middle managers from 825 organizations in 62 countries.[41] A team of 170 scholars worked

GLOBE (Global Leadership and Organizational Behavior Effectiveness)
A multi-country study and evaluation of cultural attributes and leadership behaviors among more than 17,000 managers from 825 organizations in 62 countries.

together to survey over 17,000 managers in three industries: financial services, food processing, and telecommunications. When developing the measures and implementing the studies, they also used archival measures of country economic prosperity and of the physical and psychological well-being of the cultures studied. Countries were selected so that every major geographic location in the world was represented. Additional countries, including those with unique types of political and economic systems, were selected to create a complete and comprehensive database upon which to build the analyses.[42]

The GLOBE study is interesting because its nine constructs were defined, conceptualized, and operationalized by a multicultural team of researchers. In addition, the data in each country were collected by investigators who were either natives of the cultures studied or had extensive knowledge and experience in those cultures.

Culture and Management

GLOBE researchers adhere to the belief that certain attributes that distinguish one culture from others can be used to predict the most suitable, effective, and acceptable organizational and leader practices within that culture. In addition, they contend that societal culture has a direct impact on organizational culture and that leader acceptance stems from tying leader attributes and behaviors to subordinate norms.[43]

The GLOBE project set out to answer many fundamental questions about cultural variables shaping leadership and organizational processes. The meta-goal of GLOBE is to develop an empirically based theory to describe, understand, and predict the impact of specific cultural variables on leadership and organizational processes and the effectiveness of these processes. Specific objectives include answering these fundamental questions:[44]

- Are there leader behaviors, attributes, and organizational practices that are universally accepted and effective across cultures?
- Are there leader behaviors, attributes, and organizational practices that are accepted and effective in only some cultures?
- How do attributes of societal and organizational cultures affect the kinds of leader behaviors and organizational practices that are accepted and effective?
- What is the effect of violating cultural norms that are relevant to leadership and organizational practices?
- What is the relative standing of each of the cultures studied on each of the nine core dimensions of culture?
- Can the universal and culture-specific aspects of leader behaviors, attributes, and organizational practices be explained in terms of an underlying theory that accounts for systematic differences across cultures?

GLOBE's Cultural Dimensions

The GLOBE project identified nine cultural dimensions:[45]

1. *Uncertainty avoidance* is defined as the extent to which members of an organization or society strive to avoid uncertainty by reliance on social norms, rituals, and bureaucratic practices to alleviate the unpredictability of future events.
2. *Power distance* is defined as the degree to which members of an organization or society expect and agree that power should be unequally shared.
3. *Collectivism I: societal collectivism* refers to the degree to which organizational and societal institutional practices encourage and reward collective distribution of resources and collective action.
4. *Collectivism II: in-group collectivism* refers to the degree to which individuals express pride, loyalty, and cohesiveness in their organizations or families.
5. *Gender egalitarianism* is defined as the extent to which an organization or a society minimizes gender role differences and gender discrimination.

Table 4–6
GLOBE Cultural Variable Results

Variable	Highest Ranking	Medium Ranking	Lowest Ranking
Assertiveness	Spain, U.S.	Egypt, Ireland	Sweden, New Zealand
Future Orientation	Denmark, Canada	Slovenia, Egypt	Russia, Argentina
Gender Differentiation	South Korea, Egypt	Italy, Brazil	Sweden, Denmark
Uncertainty avoidance	Austria, Denmark	Israel, U.S.	Russia, Hungary
Power distance	Russia, Spain	England, France	Denmark, Netherlands
Collectivism/Societal	Denmark, Singapore	Hong Kong, U.S.	Greece, Hungary
In-group collectivism	Egypt, China	England, France	Denmark, Netherlands
Performance orientation	U.S., Taiwan	Sweden, Israel	Russia, Argentina
Humane orientation	Indonesia, Egypt	Hong Kong, Sweden	Germany, Spain

6. *Assertiveness* is defined as the degree to which individuals in organizations or societies are assertive, confrontational, and aggressive in social relationships.

7. *Future orientation* is defined as the degree to which individuals in organizations or societies engage in future-oriented behaviors such as planning, investing in the future, and delaying gratification.

8. *Performance orientation* refers to the extent to which an organization or society encourages and rewards group members for performance improvement and excellence.

9. *Humane orientation* is defined as the degree to which individuals in organizations or societies encourage and reward individuals for being fair, altruistic, friendly, generous, caring, and kind to others.

The first six dimensions have their origins in Hofstede's cultural dimensions. The collectivism I dimension measures societal emphasis on collectivism; low scores reflect individualistic emphasis, and high scores reflect collectivistic emphasis by means of laws, social programs, or institutional practices. The collectivism II scale measures in-group (family or organization) collectivism such as pride in and loyalty to family or organization and family or organizational cohesiveness. In lieu of Hofstede's masculinity dimension, the GLOBE researchers developed the two dimensions they labeled "gender egalitarianism" and "assertiveness." Likewise, the future orientation, performance orientation, and humane orientation measures have their origin in past research.[46] These measures are therefore integrative and combine a number of insights from previous studies.

GLOBE Country Analysis

The initial results of the GLOBE analysis are presented in Table 4–6. The GLOBE analyses correspond generally with those of Hofstede and Trompenaars, although with some variations resulting from the variable definitions and methodology.

We will explore additional implications of the GLOBE findings as they relate to managerial leadership in Chapter 13.

The World of *BusinessWeek*—Revisited

The article that opens this chapter illustrates the importance of MNCs gaining an understanding of the culture of the countries in which they do business. With proper market research, Coca-Cola might have realized that Dasani did not contain the ingredients preferred by European bottled-water consumers. Now, Coke must spend time and money to change the brand image with no guaranteed results. Having read this chapter, you should understand the impact culture has on the actions of MNCs, including general management practices and relations with employees and customers, and on maintaining overall reputation.

Based on your reading of the article and on Hofstede's and Trompenaars's cultural dimensions, answer the following questions: (1) In what way could understanding of European values and preferences be useful to Coke? (2) How might collectivist tendencies influence the eating and drinking preferences of Europeans? (3) If a particular food or beverage product is popular in the United States, would it necessarily be popular in Europe? Why or why not?

SUMMARY OF KEY POINTS

1. Culture is acquired knowledge that people use to interpret experience and generate social behavior. Culture also has the characteristics of being learned, shared, transgenerational, symbolic, patterned, and adaptive. There are many dimensions of cultural diversity, including centralized vs. decentralized decision making, safety vs. risk, individual vs. group rewards, informal vs. formal procedures, high vs. low organizational loyalty, cooperation vs. competition, short-term vs. long-term horizons, and stability vs. innovation.

2. Values are basic convictions that people have regarding what is right and wrong, good and bad, important and unimportant. Research shows that there are both differences and similarities between the work values and managerial values of different cultural groups. Work values often reflect culture and industrialization, and managerial values are highly related to success. Research shows that values tend to change over time and often reflect age and experience.

3. Hofstede has identified and researched four major dimensions of culture: power distance, uncertainty avoidance, individualism, and masculinity. Each will affect a country's political and social system. The integration of these factors into two-dimensional figures can illustrate the complexity of culture's effect on behavior.

4. In recent years, researchers have attempted to cluster countries into similar cultural groupings to study similarities and differences. Through use of smallest space analysis, they have constructed two-dimensional maps that illustrate the similarities in work values and attitudes between countries. These syntheses, one of which is provided in Figure 4–8, help us to understand intercultural similarities.

5. Research by Trompenaars has examined five relationship orientations: universalism–particularism, individualism–communitarianism, affective–neutral, specific–diffuse, and achievement–ascription. Trompenaars also looked at attitudes toward time and toward the environment. The result is a wealth of information helping to explain how cultures differ as well as practical ways in which MNCs can do business effectively in these environments. In particular, his findings update those of Hofstede while at the same time help to support the previous work by both Hofstede and Ronen and Shenkar on clustering countries.

6. Recent research undertaken by the GLOBE project has attempted to extend and integrate cultural attributes and variables as they relate to managerial leadership and practice. These analyses confirm much of the Hofstede and Trompenaars research, with greater emphasis on differences in managerial leadership styles.

KEY TERMS

achievement culture, *114*

ascription culture, *114*

collectivism, *102*

communitarianism, *112*

culture, *93*

diffuse culture, *113*

emotional culture, *113*

femininity, *103*

GLOBE, *117*

individualism, *102*

masculinity, *103*

neutral culture, *113*

particularism, *110*

power distance, *102*

smallest space analysis (SSA), *107*

specific culture, *113*

uncertainty avoidance, *102*

universalism, *110*

values, *97*

REVIEW AND DISCUSSION QUESTIONS

1. What is meant by the term *culture*? In what way can measuring attitudes about the following help to differentiate between cultures: centralized or decentralized decision making, safety or risk, individual or group rewards, high or low organizational loyalty, cooperation or competition? Use these attitudes to compare the United States, Germany, and Japan. Based on your comparisons, what conclusions can you draw regarding the impact of culture on behavior?

2. What is meant by the term *value*? Are cultural values the same worldwide, or are there marked differences? Are these values changing over time, or are they fairly constant? How does your answer relate to the role of values in a culture?

3. What are the four dimensions of culture studied by Geert Hofstede? Identify and describe each. What is the cultural profile of the United States? Of Asian countries? Of Latin American countries? Of Latin European countries? Based on your comparisons of these four profiles, what conclusions can you draw

regarding cultural challenges facing individuals in one group when they interact with individuals in one of the other groups?

4. Of what value is Figure 4–8 on country clusters to the study of international management? Offer at least three advantages or benefits of the figure.

5. As people engage in more international travel and become more familiar with other countries, will cultural differences decline as a roadblock to international understanding, or will they continue to be a major barrier? Defend your answer.

6. What are the characteristics of each of the following pairs of cultural characteristics derived from Trompenaars's research: universalism vs. particularism, neutral vs. emotional, specific vs. diffuse, achievement vs. ascription? Compare and contrast each pair.

7. In what way is time a cultural factor? In what way is the need to control the environment a cultural factor? Give an example for each.

INTERNET EXERCISE: BMW GOES NATIONAL AND INTERNATIONAL

BMW is an internationally known auto firm. However, in recent years the company has been finding that its success in Europe does not necessarily translate into the American market, the largest, richest target for overseas sales. Visit the BMW site at **www.bmw.com** and look at what the big automaker is doing in both Europe and the United States. Compare and contrast the similarities and differences in

these markets. Then answer these three questions: (1) How do you think cultural differences affect the way the firm operates in Europe and in the United States? (2) In what way is culture a factor in auto sales? (3) Is it possible for a car company to transcend national culture and produce a global automobile that is accepted by people in every culture? Why or why not?

Taiwan

Taiwan is an island located 100 miles off the southeast coast of the China mainland. Taiwan is only 13,900 square miles, and with a population of approximately 23 million, it has one of the highest population densities in the world. In 1949, the communists under Mao Zedong defeated the Nationalists under Chiang Kai-shek and the latter government moved to Taiwan, where it established dominance. The People's Republic of China still considers Taiwan to be a breakaway province, and tensions between the two flare up frequently.

The government of Taiwan was totally controlled by the Nationalists until 1996 when the first democratic election was held. In 2000 the Democratic Progressive Party candidate, Chen Shui-bian, was elected president for a four-year term, although the Nationalist Party continued to hold over 50 percent of the seats in the country's parliament, the Legislative Yuan. He was reelected by a narrow margin in March 2004 after an apparent assassination attempt appeared to bolster his position.

The country's gross domestic product is approximately $406 billion and per capita GDP is around $18,000. In the late 1990s many Asian economies slowed down sharply, caught in a vicious economic crisis. Japan, South Korea, Indonesia, Thailand, and Malaysia all saw their GDP growth decline, and some of them, especially Japan, are still running budget deficits as high as 10 percent of GDP. Taiwan, on the other hand, had steady GDP growth in the range of 6 percent throughout this period. In particular, the country's economy has been managed carefully through a combination of tight exchange controls, low foreign debt, conservative fiscal policies, and relatively austere and transparent banking.

Taiwan is one of the 15 largest trading powers in the world, and one of the strongest sectors of its economy is information technology. The value of computer-related products produced in Taiwan is over $35 billion annually. Taiwanese manufacturers build two-thirds of the motherboards and keyboards sold worldwide, in addition to 60 percent of the monitors and almost 40 percent of the notebook PCs. A number of major high-tech firms have set up operations on the island, including Sun Microsystems, Microsoft, and Intel. All three realized that costs here are lower than in most other places and the quality of the workforce would allow them to produce state-of-the-art products. Other firms, including locally based manufacturers, also followed this strategy. As a result, by the mid-1990s Taiwan had leapfrogged South Korea in the production of PCs. Some of this success was a result of Taiwanese firms entering into a series of private-label contracts with U.S. importers.

By the late 1990s Taiwan-based chipmakers were investing billions of dollars annually in semiconductor fabrication plants. By 2002 annual investment in research, development, and new capacity was in excess of $17 billion. The world is so dependent on Taiwan for computer-related equipment that when a devastating earthquake hit the island in September 1999, the global informational technology (IT) market shuddered and the price of PC chips immediately rose sharply. Although the IT companies emerged relatively unscathed, the incident served to underscore the importance of Taiwan's semiconductor, electronic components, and PC industry. During the first decade of the millennium Taiwan's importance in these areas is likely to grow.
www.asiapages.com

Questions

1. What are some current issues facing Taiwan? What is the climate for doing business in Taiwan today?

2. In terms of cultural dimensions, is Taiwan much different from the United States? (Use Figure 4–7 in your answer.) Why or why not?

3. In what way might culture be a stumbling block for firms seeking to set up businesses in Taiwan?

4. How are the three high-tech firms in this case managing to sidestep or overcome cultural barriers?

A Jumping-Off Place

A successful, medium-sized U.S. manufacturing firm in Ohio has decided to open a plant near Madrid, Spain. The company was attracted to this location for three reasons. First, the firm's current licensing agreement with a German firm is scheduled to come to an end within six months, and the U.S. manufacturer feels that it can do a better job of building and selling heavy machinery in the EU than the German firm. Second, the U.S. manufacturer invested almost $300 million in R&D over the last three years. The result is a host of new patents and other technological breakthroughs that now make this company a worldwide leader in the production of specialized heavy equipment. Third, labor costs in Spain are lower than in most other EU countries, and the company feels that this will prove extremely helpful in its efforts to capture market share in Greater Europe.

Because this is the manufacturer's first direct venture into the EU, it has decided to take on a Spanish partner. The latter will provide much of the on-site support, such as local contracts, personnel hiring, legal assistance, and governmental negotiations. In turn, the U.S. manufacturer will provide the capital for renovating the manufacturing plant, the R&D technology, and the technical training.

If the venture works out as planned, the partners will expand operations into Italy and use this location as a jumping-off point for tapping the Central and Eastern European markets. Additionally, because the cultures of Spain and Italy are similar, the U.S. manufacturer feels that staying within the Latin European cultural cluster can be synergistic. Plans for later in the decade call for establishing operations in northern France, which will serve as a jumping-off point for both Northern Europe and other major EU countries, such as Germany, the Netherlands, and Belgium. However, the company first wants to establish a foothold in Spain and get this operation working successfully; then it will look into expansion plans.

Questions

1. In what way will the culture of Spain be different from that of the United States? In answering this question, refer to Figures 4–5, 4–6, 4–7, and 4–8.

2. If the company expands operations into Italy, will its experience in Spain be valuable, or will the culture be so different that the manufacturer will have to begin anew in determining how to address cultural challenges and opportunities? Explain.

3. If the firm expands into France, will its previous experiences in Spain and Italy be valuable in helping the company address cultural challenges? Be complete in your answer.

Chapter 5

MANAGING ACROSS CULTURES

Traditionally, both scholars and practitioners assumed the universality of management. There was a tendency to take the management concepts and techniques that worked at home into other countries and cultures. It is now clear, from both practice and cross-cultural research, that this universality assumption, at least across cultures, does not hold up. Although there is a tendency in a borderless economy to promote a universalist approach, there is enough evidence from Nancy Adler and other cross-cultural researchers to conclude that the universalist assumption that may have held for U.S. organizations and employees is not generally true in other cultures.[1]

The overriding purpose of this chapter is to examine how MNCs can and should manage across cultures. This chapter puts into practice Chapter 4 on the meaning and dimensions of culture and serves as a foundation and point of departure for Chapters 8 and 9 on strategic management. The first part of this chapter addresses the traditional tendency to attempt to replicate successful home-country operations overseas without addressing cultural differences. Next, attention is given to cross-cultural challenges, focusing on how differences can impact multinational management strategies. Finally, the cultures in specific countries and geographic regions are examined. The specific objectives of this chapter are:

1. **EXAMINE** the strategic dispositions that characterize responses to different cultures.

2. **DISCUSS** cross-cultural differences and similarities.

3. **REVIEW** cultural differences in select countries and regions, and note some of the important strategic guidelines for doing business in each.

The World of *BusinessWeek*

BusinessWeek

Waking Up Heineken

Earnings are Flat. Its Stock Is in a Slump. Beer Drinking Is Down, Too. Can the Dutch Brewer Keep Growth Flowing?

History stares Heineken boss Anthony Ruys in the face every morning when he shows up for work. The Dutch brewer's chief executive sits in a dark-paneled office surrounded by stern portraits of three generations of Heineken ancestors. The corporate offices in Amsterdam extend from the building that once served as the family manse. And if Ruys were ever to forget that he was the guardian of a company that traces its roots back more than 400 years, he would have to reckon with his main shareholder: Charlene de Carvalho-Heineken, a descendant of the company's founder. "There's a long tradition," says Ruys with typical Dutch understatement.

Starched white collars are no longer the order of the day at 21 Tweede Weteringplantsoen, but Heineken headquarters is still a pretty buttoned-down place. True, the vending machines in the corridors are stocked with—what else?—Heineken. But they're programmed not to dispense the brew until after 4 p.m. "Not much has changed" since Charlene's father, Alfred H. "Freddy" Heineken, ran the company, says Ruys, a 56-year-old former Unilever executive who was elevated to the top job 10 years after joining the company, a relatively short tenure by Heineken standards. Freddy, a legendary bon vivant with a hard nose for business, passed away last year. And while no one from Ruys on down would dare dishonor his memory by claiming that anything as radical as a revolution is in the making at Heineken, there's an unmistakable whiff of change in the air.

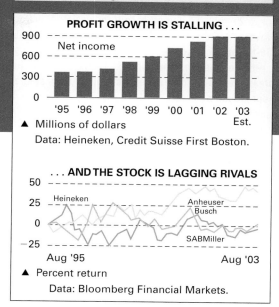

PROFIT GROWTH IS STALLING . . .

Net income

'95 '96 '97 '98 '99 '00 '01 '02 '03
Est.

▲ Millions of dollars

Data: Heineken, Credit Suisse First Boston.

. . . AND THE STOCK IS LAGGING RIVALS

Heineken

Anheuser-Busch

SABMiller

Aug '95   Aug '03

▲ Percent return

Data: Bloomberg Financial Markets.

It's about time, too. The world's No. 3 brewer, with $11 billion a year in sales, can no longer take for granted the strengths that have made its squat green bottle the envy of the business. Budweiser may have crowned itself the "King of Beers," but it only reigns in the U.S. Heineken, recognized everywhere from Houston to Hong Kong, is the closest thing there is to a global beer brand. That's an achievement none of the world's top brewers, from No. 1 Anheuser-Busch to No. 2 SABMiller and No. 4 Interbrew, have been able to match.

Trouble is, the $367 billion world beer market is changing. Beer consumption is declining in the U.S. and Europe, the source of two-thirds of Heineken's profits, thanks to tougher drunk-driving laws and a growing appreciation for wine. At the same time, the beer marketplace is becoming ever more crowded, thanks to a flood of new brands, from low-carbohydrate brews to imports from Italy and the Czech Republic. But the numbers of players are shrinking. Heineken, one of the first European brewers to realize the value of cross-border deals, now risks falling behind more aggressive rivals. To overcome these challenges, Ruys is pushing Heineken to break out of its play-it-safe corporate culture. Freddy had a knack for marketing, but he was financially conservative and in later years held Heineken back, even as SABMiller and Interbrew grew through big-ticket acquisitions. Heineken's future success will depend on preserving Freddy's spirit—while meeting challenges that Freddy never anticipated.

Ruys is already making his mark. He shelled out more than $3 billion last year for a dozen acquisitions. The biggest target, BBAG, a family-owned company based in Linz, Austria, was one of the first brewers to go east after the collapse of the Soviet bloc. Once the $2.1 billion deal closes later this year, Heineken will be the biggest beermaker in seven countries in Eastern Europe. Advertising and packaging are becoming more daring, in a bid to capture the sought-after twentysomething segment. Witness the recent debut of Heineken's silver-and-green aluminum "bottle," which sells at trendy clubs in Europe and the U.S. for three times the price of Heineken on tap. "Our strategy is right, but we can be sharper after so many years of success," says Ruys.

That success is no longer guaranteed. The convergence of a weak global economy, an unusually rainy summer in the U.S., and SARS, which emptied watering holes

across Asia, will break a six-year streak of double-digit profit growth. Then there's the strong euro, which is crimping earnings from the U.S., a market that accounts for more than a quarter of all profits. Analysts now estimate the company will just barely match its net profit last year of $900 million on sales of $11.6 billion. But even in the face of all these obstacles, the Dutch brewer has managed to defend its global market share of 7%. "The brand Heineken is as healthy as it has ever been," concedes Joseph J. Fisch Jr., who imports rival Dutch lager Grolsch into the U.S.

Others are not so sure. Some worry the company could face years of flat sales. "We are nervous that what some commentators see as a one-off blip could be rather fundamental," says Ian Shackleton, a London-based analyst for Credit Suisse First Boston, which rates Heineken "underperform." Over the past 12 months, Heineken's share price has declined 10%, to just under $37.

Top management in Amsterdam is not quite panicked, but there's definitely a sense of urgency seeping into the ranks. Heineken's boss is resorting to tough tactics to stir the troops out of their complacency. A video produced for staff viewing only features a young Italian man saying: "I hate beer." The message: Heineken needs to win over consumers who haven't yet developed a strong loyalty to a particular beverage. That's why Ruys and his top lieutenants have been travelling to places like Madrid and Shanghai to down a cold one with groups of randomly selected young people.

It's a tough balancing act—reaching out to younger customers without alienating the middle-aged beer drinkers who are Heineken's core customers. "Heineken seems to be an obsolete brand to me," says Véronique dos Santos, a 29-year-old human-resources assistant in Paris who favors Mexican import Corona or Desperados, a tequila-flavored concoction. "It's in danger of becoming a tired, reliable, but unexciting brand," warns John A. Quelch, a professor at Harvard Business School who has studied the beer industry.

Lucky for Heineken, it owns Desperados. The brand is produced by French brewer Fischer, which Heineken acquired in 1996. Such niche labels are a small, but profitable avenue for growth. Paulaner, a wheat beer Heineken picked up in Bavaria, is finding a market in the U.S. And in one of globalization's ironies, Amstel Bright, a light-tasting lager brewed in the Dutch colony of Curaçao, is being exported to the Netherlands, Amstel's birthplace.

Ruys & Co. aren't stopping there. To spice up the image of its namesake brand, Heineken is giving marketing a makeover. It has arranged tie-ins with big-budget youth films, such as *The Matrix: Reloaded,* and sponsored events such as a sweepstakes where winners got to attend a Heineken house party in Jamaica. Yet management has been careful not to stray into the testosterone-soaked territory that is the domain of rivals like Adolph Coors Co. One new commercial features blond triplets and an exploding keg—a spoof aimed at the Coors twins. The strategy has started to pay off in the U.S., where the average age of the Heineken drinker has descended from about 40 in the mid-1990s to the early 30s today. Ruys's goal is to push that down into the high-20s in coming years.

Heineken's not exactly the only company trying to score with twentysomethings. Today's beer drinkers are awash in a sea of choices. Consider the $67 billion U.S. market, probably the most keenly contested of them all. There, Heineken beer and its sister brand, Amstel Light, which together have about 22% of the import market, are under attack from an ever-growing constellation of imports and malt-based drinks such as Smirnoff Ice and Sky Blue. Americans developed a taste for thirst-quenching Corona while vacationing on Mexican beaches, helping the brand overtake Heineken in the late 1990s to become the top import in the U.S.

Meanwhile, SABMiller, the product of last year's merger of South African Breweries and Milwaukee-based Miller, is pushing its Czech-brewed Pilsner Urquell, while Brussels-based Interbrew is making inroads with Stella Artois. Even Anheuser-Busch, which commands an eye-popping 52% of the domestic market, is playing the import game: Anheuser World Select, which debuted earlier this year, is fashioned from imported hops and comes in a green bottle suspiciously similar to Heineken's. There's a reason the premium market is getting so crowded: Beer consumption in the U.S. has declined 1% since 2000, amid tighter drunk-driving laws. But at the same time, imports have grown 16% as consumers choose quality over quantity.

The U.S. is just one battleground. The beer industry is in the midst of a furious wave of consolidation. The business is more fragmented than most: The top four brewing companies control less than a third of the global market.

Heineken's World	

The Dutch brewer operates in 170 countries, and its portfolio includes dozens of lesser known local brands. Below is a sampling:

Netherlands	Heineken, Amstel, Kylian, Lingen's Blond, Murphy's Irish Red
U.S.	Heineken, Amstel Light, Paulaner (wheat beer), Moretti
China	Tiger, Reeb*
Singapore	Heineken, Tiger
France	Heineken, Amstel, Buckler (nonalcoholic), Desperados (tequila-flavored beer)
Germany	Paulaner, Kulmbacher, Thurn und Taxis
Italy	Heineken, Amstel, Birra Moretti
Poland	Heineken, Zywiec
Kazakhstan	Tian Shan, Amstel
Panama	Soberana, Panama
Egypt	Fayrouz (nonalcoholic)
Israel	Maccabee, Gold Star*
Nigeria	Amstel Malta, Maltina

*Minority Interest.   Data: Heineken.

By comparison, the top four spirits makers control half the world market. But that's changing as big brewers scramble to acquire strong local brands and the distribution networks that go with them. "The era of global brands is coming," says Alan Clark, Budapest-based managing director of SABMiller Europe, which snapped up Italy's Peroni in May.

Heineken has a head start there. It ranked second only to Budweiser in a global brand survey jointly undertaken by *BusinessWeek* and Interbrand earlier this year. Heineken "is recognized everywhere," says Kevin Baker, director of alcoholic beverages at British market researcher Canadean Ltd. How recognized? One U.S. wholesaler recently asked a group of marketing students to identify an assortment of beer bottles that had been stripped of their labels. Only one incited instant recognition: the stubby green Heineken container.

No company can afford to pin its entire fortune on a single product, however. That's why Ruys has spent the last year adding new labels to Heineken's shelf, pouncing on brewers in places like Panama, Egypt, and Kazakhstan. In Egypt, Ruys bought a majority stake in Al Ahram Beverages Co. and hopes to use the Cairo-based brewer's fruit-flavored, nonalcoholic malts as an avenue into other Muslim countries.

Now Heineken plans to take a breather, according to company execs. "We are interested in growing, but not at any price," says Ruys. Heineken has dropped out of the bidding for German brewer Brau und Brunnen, whose stable of national brands is likely to fetch a hefty premium over the company's $430 million stock market value.

Tightfisted Freddy would probably have balked at paying so rich a price. But these days it's his only child and heir, Charlene, 49, and her husband, former Olympic skier Michel de Carvalho, who call the shots. As Heineken's controlling shareholder, the London resident and mother of five retains a say over a broad range of business decisions, from new packaging to acquisitions, though she is nowhere as involved in the day-to-day running of the company as her father was. "Must-have strategic acquisitions will always be looked at," says Michel de Carvalho, 59, a member of Heineken's supervisory board and Vice-Chairman of Investment Banking at Citigroup in London. (De Carvalho traditionally speaks for the family.) Proof of that is Heineken's decision to cough up $2.1 billion for BBAG. Deutsche Bank figures that Heineken won't recover the cost of capital—the deal is being financed with a mix of cash and loans—until 2007 at the earliest.

Publicly, the Heineken heiress has vowed to keep the company independent. Last year, addressing shareholders of Heineken Holding, the separately traded company that controls just over 50% of the operating entity Heineken NV, she said: "We are a part of [Heineken's] past, its present, and its future." However, industry insiders speculate that Freddy's daughter might be willing to sell the family jewels if the price was right. A hostile takeover would be all but impossible under Heineken's current ownership structure. "Our mission is to hand a healthy company to the next generation," says de Carvalho, who rules out any sale of the company.

Despite last year's changing of the guard, the past remains very much present at Heineken. It's all about evolution—not revolution. The company's advertising remains refreshingly offbeat, a nod to Freddy's wry sense of humor. One commercial in the U.S. showed a young man plunging his arm deep into a barrel filled with ice and bottled beer. He gropes around fruitlessly until his whole body begins to shiver. Finally, he hauls out a Heineken. Popping it open, he joins a group of friends—who are gripping Heinekens and shivering. "They've done a very good job of not being snooty—using accessible jokes and imagery," says Bob Garfield, ad critic of trade weekly *Advertising Age*.

The Dutch brewer is stepping up marketing to Hispanics, who account for one-quarter of U.S. sales. A new Spanish-language spot shows a group of men playing dominoes. They pause for a moment as one of them demonstrates how to pour a glass of beer without stirring up too much foam. "Heineken is for professionals—in beer," says a voice-over. "We want to bring over the values of the brand in a different way," says Frans van der Minne, president and CEO of Heineken USA Inc. Heineken may move a little slower than its competitors, but no one questions its staying power. "It takes a long time to build a brand. People today are not prepared to put that time in," says Sir Frank Lowe, founder of London-based Lowe & Partners Worldwide, which handled Heineken advertising in Britain and the U.S. until a conflict emerged with another client, Interbrew. Heineken, he says, "has the will and patience to stick it out." Looks like the slow pour could still win in the end.

By Jack Ewing in Amsterdam, with Gerry Khermouch in New York and Jennifer Picard in Paris.

The news story that opens this chapter highlights the importance of management across cultures. Heineken's earnings have been flat as per capita consumption of beer in the United States and Europe has declined. In addition, new brands have been popping up everywhere and rivals have been spending substantial sums on promotion. To compete globally, Heineken must draw on its strength as a global company with global brands, yet adjust and adapt its management and message to different cultures. In particular, it must consider how best to execute programs at the local level, a challenge for all MNCs. To remain viable in the coming years, MNCs must continue to have a plan for managing across cultures.

■ The Strategy for Managing Across Cultures

As MNCs become more transnational, their strategies must address the cultural similarities and differences in their varied markets.[2] A good example is provided by Renault, the French auto giant. For years Renault manufactured a narrow product line that it sold primarily in France. Because of this limited geographic market and the fact that its cars continued to have quality-related problems, the company's performance was at best mediocre. Several years ago, however, Renault made a number of strategic decisions that dramatically changed the way it did business. Among other things, it bought controlling stakes in Nissan Motor of Japan, Samsung of South Korea, and Dacia, the Romanian automaker. The company also built a $1 billion factory in Brazil to produce its successful Megane sedan and acquired an idle factory near Moscow to manufacture Renaults for the eastern European market.

Today, Renault is a multinational automaker with operations on four continents. The challenge the company now faces is to make all of these operations profitable. This will not be easy. Nissan's annual losses have been running in triple-digit millions in recent years, and Samsung has to be brought back from bankruptcy. Meanwhile Dacia is operating in one of Europe's most dismal economies. Fortunately, Renault is grossing over $40 billion annually from its own businesses, so it has the necessary funds to implement turnaround strategies for these acquisitions. Now it needs to straighten out its international operations and get everything working in harmony.[3] One of the recent steps it has taken to do this is the decision to meld its own sales organizations with those of Nissan in Europe, thus creating one well-integrated, efficient sales force on the continent. Another step has been to start producing Nissan models in the Brazilian plant so that it can expand its South American offerings by more efficiently using current facilities. One of the company's long-run goals is by 2010 to have 10 common platforms, or underbodies, that will allow it to build Renaults and Nissans everywhere, while maintaining the look, feel, and identity of their separate brands.[4] At the same time the firm is working to improve its effectiveness in dealing with governments, unions, and employees, as well as to understand the cultural differences in customer preferences in Europe, Asia, and the Americas.

Strategic Predispositions

Most MNCs have a cultural strategic predisposition toward doing things in a particular way. This orientation or predisposition helps to determine the specific steps the MNC will follow. Four distinct predispositions have been identified: ethnocentric, polycentric, regiocentric, and geocentric.

A company with an **ethnocentric predisposition** allows the values and interests of the parent company to guide strategic decisions. Firms with a **polycentric predisposition** make strategic decisions tailored to suit the cultures of the countries where the MNC operates. A **regiocentric predisposition** leads a firm to try to blend its own interests with those of its subsidiaries on a regional basis. A company with a **geocentric predisposition** tries to integrate a global systems approach to decision making. Table 5–1 provides details of each of these orientations.

If an MNC relies on one of these profiles over an extended time, the approach may become institutionalized and greatly influence strategic planning. By the same token, a

ethnocentric predisposition
A nationalistic philosophy of management whereby the values and interests of the parent company guide strategic decisions.

polycentric predisposition
A philosophy of management whereby strategic decisions are tailored to suit the cultures of the countries where the MNC operates.

regiocentric predisposition
A philosophy of management whereby the firm tries to blend its own interests with those of its subsidiaries on a regional basis.

geocentric predisposition
A philosophy of management whereby the company tries to integrate a global systems approach to decision making.

Table 5–1
Orientation of an MNC Under Different Profiles

	Orientation of the Firm			
	Ethnocentric	**Polycentric**	**Regiocentric**	**Geocentric**
Mission	Profitability (viability)	Public acceptance (legitimacy)	Both profitability and public acceptance (viability and legitimacy)	Same as regiocentric
Governance	Top-down	Bottom-up (each subsidiary decides on local objectives)	Mutually negotiated between region and its subsidiaries	Mutually negotiated at all levels of the corporation
Strategy	Global integration	National responsiveness	Regional integration and national responsiveness	Global integration and national responsiveness
Structure	Hierarchical product divisions	Hierarchical area divisions, with autonomous national units	Product and regional organization tied through a matrix	A network of organizations (including some stakeholders and competitor organizations)
Culture	Home country	Host country	Regional	Global
Technology	Mass production	Batch production	Flexible manufacturing	Flexible manufacturing
Marketing	Product development determined primarily by the needs of home country customers	Local product development based on local needs	Standardize within region, but not across regions	Global product, with local variations
Finance	Repatriation of profits to home country	Retention of profits in host country	Redistribution within region	Redistribution globally
Personnel practices	People of home country developed for key positions everywhere in the world	People of local nationality developed for key positions in their own country	Regional people developed for key positions anywhere in the region	Best people everywhere in the world developed for key positions everywhere in the world

Source: Adapted from Balaji S. Chakravarthy and Howard V. Perlmutter, "Strategic Planning for a Global Business," *Columbia Journal of World Business,* Summer 1985, pp. 5–6. Copyright 1985, Columbia Journal of World Business. Used with permission from Elsevier.

---

predisposition toward any of these profiles can provide problems for a firm if it is out of step with the economic or political environment. For example, a firm with an ethnocentric predisposition may find it difficult to implement a geocentric strategy, because it is unaccustomed to using global integration. Commonly, successful MNCs use a mix of these predispositions based on the demands of the current environment described in the chapters in Part 1.

Meeting the Challenge

Despite the need for and tendency of MNCs to address regional differentiation issues, many MNCs are committed to a **globalization imperative,** which is a belief that one worldwide approach to doing business is the key to both efficiency and effectiveness. One study, involving extensive examination of 115 medium and large MNCs and 103 affiliated subsidiaries in the United States, Canada, France, Germany, Japan, and the United Kingdom, found an overwhelming preponderance to use the same strategies abroad as at home.[5]

Despite these tendencies to use home strategies, effective MNCs are continuing their efforts to address local needs. A number of factors are helping to facilitate this need to develop unique strategies for different cultures, including:

1. The diversity of worldwide industry standards such as those in broadcasting, where television sets must be manufactured on a country-by-country basis.

globalization imperative
A belief that one worldwide approach to doing business is the key to both efficiency and effectiveness.

2. A continual demand by local customers for differentiated products, as in the case of consumer goods that must meet local tastes.

3. The importance of being an insider, as in the case of customers who prefer to "buy local."

4. The difficulty of managing global organizations, as in the case of some local subsidiaries that want more decentralization and others that want less.

5. The need to allow subsidiaries to use their own abilities and talents and not be restrained by headquarters, as in the case of local units that know how to customize products for their market and generate high returns on investment with limited production output.

By responding to the cultural needs of local operations and customers, MNCs find that regional strategies can be used effectively in capturing and maintaining worldwide market niches. One of the best examples is Warner-Lambert, which has manufacturing facilities in Belgium, France, Germany, Italy, Ireland, Spain, and the United Kingdom. Each plant is specialized and produces a small number of products for the entire European market; in this way, each can focus on tailoring products for the unique demands of the various markets.

The globalization vs. national responsiveness challenge is even more acute when marketing cosmetics and other products that vary greatly in consumer use. For example, marketers sell toothpaste as a cosmetic product in Spain and Greece but as a cavity-fighter in the Netherlands and United States. Soap manufacturers market their product as a cosmetic item in Spain but as a functional commodity in Germany. Moreover, the way in which the marketing message is delivered also is important. For example:

- Germans want advertising that is factual and rational; they fear being manipulated by "the hidden persuader." The typical German spot features the standard family of two parents, two children, and grandmother.

- The French avoid reasoning or logic. Their advertising is predominantly emotional, dramatic, and symbolic. Spots are viewed as cultural events—art for the sake of money—and are reviewed as if they were literature or films.

- The British value laughter above all else. The typical broad, self-deprecating British commercial amuses by mocking both the advertiser and consumer.[6]

Meanwhile, in China, McDonald's has worked hard to befriend young children and make them feel special. One way is by recording their names and birth dates in a special list called "The Book of Little Honorary Guests" and then sending them cards and urging them to drop by their local McDonald's.

> The burger joints are all run by locals. And far from accepting the same McDonald's that Americans do, Asian consumers gradually twist McDonald's to their own purposes. Rather than being fast, efficient take-out joints, many McDonald's restaurants are more akin to Seattle coffee houses—places to hang out for the young. In several places, McDonald's has gone so native that many of its customers do not realize it is American. In China, one of its appeals is the fact that its menu is so limited; there is no danger of losing face because the table next door orders a more expensive dish. As [one observer] concludes, people come for the experience, not the product; and they make sure that it is their experience—not one foisted upon them by an American juggernaut.[7]

In some cases, however, both the product and the marketing message are similar worldwide. This is particularly true for high-end products, where the lifestyles and expectations of the market niche are similar regardless of the country. Heineken beer, Hennessey brandy, Porsche cars, and the *Financial Times* all appeal to consumer niches that are fairly homogeneous regardless of geographic locale. The same is true at the lower end of the market for goods that are impulse purchases, novel products, or fast foods, such as Coca-Cola's

Ten Key Factors for MNC Success

Why are some international firms successful while others are not? Some of the main reasons are that successful multinational firms take a worldwide view of operations, support their overseas activities, pay close attention to political winds, and use local nationals whenever possible. These are the overall findings of a report that looked into the development of customized executive education programs. Specifically, there are 10 factors or guidelines that successful global firms seem to employ. Successful global competitors:

1. See themselves as multinational enterprises and are led by a management team that is comfortable in the world arena.

2. Develop integrated and innovative strategies that make it difficult and costly for other firms to compete.

3. Aggressively and effectively implement their worldwide strategy and back it with large investments.

4. Understand that technologic innovation no longer is confined to the United States and develop systems for tapping technologic innovation abroad.

5. Operate as if the world is one large market rather than a series of individual, small markets.

6. Have organization structures that are designed to handle their unique problems and challenges and thus provide them the greatest efficiency.

7. Develop a system that keeps them informed about political changes around the world and the implications of these changes on the firm.

8. Have management teams that are international in composition and thus better able to respond to the various demands of their respective markets.

9. Allow their outside directors to play an active role in the operation of the enterprise.

10. Are well managed and tend to follow such important guidelines as sticking close to the customer, having lean organization structures, and encouraging autonomy and entrepreneurial activity among the personnel.

soft drinks, Levi's jeans, pop music, and ice-cream bars. In most cases, however, it is necessary to modify products as well as the market approach for the regional or local market. One analysis noted that the more marketers understand about the way in which a particular culture tends to view emotion, enjoyment, friendship, humor, rules, status, and other culturally based behaviors, the more control they have over creating marketing messages that will be interpreted in the desired way.

Figure 5–1 provides an example of the role that culture should play in advertising by recapping the five relationship orientations identified through Trompenaars's research (see Chapter 4). Figure 5–1 shows how value can be added to the marketing approach by carefully tailoring the advertising message to the particular culture. For example, advertising in the United States should target individual achievement, be expressive and direct, and appeal to U.S. values of success through personal hard work. On the other hand, the focus in China and other Asian countries should be much more indirect and subtle, emphasizing group references, shared responsibility, and interpersonal trust.

The need to adjust global strategies for regional markets presents three major challenges for most MNCs. First, the MNC must stay abreast of local market conditions and sidestep the temptation to assume that all markets are basically the same. Second, the MNC must know the strengths and weaknesses of its subsidiaries so that it can provide these units with the assistance needed in addressing local demands. Third, the multinational must give the subsidiary more autonomy so that it can respond to changes in local demands. "International Management in Action: Ten Key Factors for MNC Success" provides additional insights into the ways that successful MNCs address these challenges.

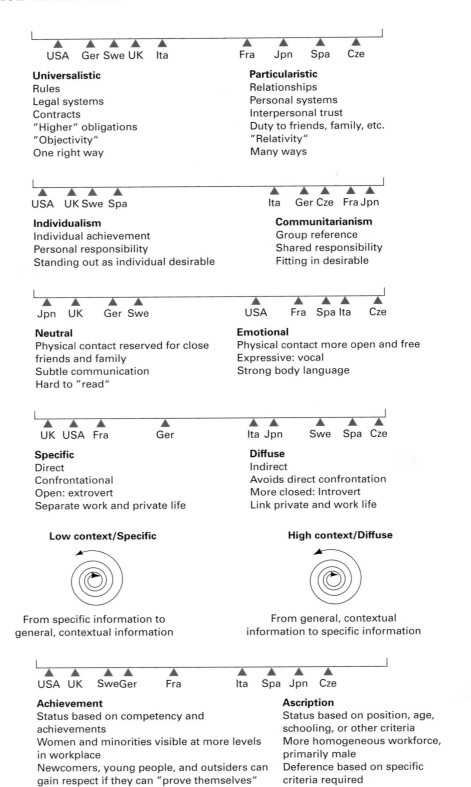

Source: Lisa Hoecklin, *Managing Cultural Differences: Strategies for Competitive Advantage* (Workingham, England: Addison-Wesley, 1995), p. 107, which is drawn from information found in Fons Trompenaars, *Riding the Waves of Culture: Understanding Diversity in Global Business* (New York: Irwin, 1994).

■ Cross-Cultural Differences and Similarities

As shown in Chapter 4, cultures can be similar or quite different across countries. The challenge for MNCs is to recognize and effectively manage the similarities and differences. For instance, the way in which MNCs manage their home businesses often should be different from the way they manage their overseas operations.[8] After recognizing the danger for MNCs of drifting toward parochialism and simplification because of cultural differences, the discussion in this section shifts to some examples of cultural similarities and differences and how to effectively manage across cultures by a contingency approach.

Parochialism and Simplification

Parochialism is the tendency to view the world through one's own eyes and perspectives. This can be a difficult problem for many international managers, who often come from advanced economies and believe that their state-of-the-art knowledge is more than adequate to handle the challenges of doing business in less developed countries. In addition, many of these managers have a parochial point of view fostered by their background.[9] A good example is provided by Randall and Coakley, who studied the impact of culture on successful partnerships in the former Soviet Union. Initially after the breakup of the Soviet Union, the republics called themselves the Commonwealth of Independent States (CIS). Randall and Coakley found that while outside MNC managers typically entered into partnerships with CIS enterprises with a view toward making them efficient and profitable, the CIS managers often brought a different set of priorities to the table.

parochialism
The tendency to view the world through one's own eyes and perspectives.

Commenting on their research, Randall and Coakley noted that the way CIS managers do business is sharply different from that of their American counterparts. In particular, there is an inconsistency between CIS cultural norms, their past training, and their work experiences, and the emerging economic structure and way in which they must do business if they hope to succeed in the international arena. This led the researchers to conclude:

> As behavioral change continues to lag behind structural change, it becomes imperative to understand that this inconsistency between what economic demands and cultural norms require manifests problems and complexities far beyond mere structural change. In short, the implications of the different perspectives on technology, labor, and production . . . for potential partnerships between U.S. and CIS companies need to be fully grasped by all parties entering into any form of relationship.[10]

Simplification is the process of exhibiting the same orientation toward different cultural groups. For example, the way in which a U.S. manager interacts with a British manager is the same way in which he or she behaves when doing business with an Asian executive. Moreover, this orientation reflects one's basic culture. Table 5–2 provides an example, showing several widely agreed-on, basic cultural orientations and the range of variations for each. Asterisks indicate the dominant U.S. orientation. Quite obviously, U.S. cultural values are not the same as those of managers from other cultures; as a result, a U.S. manager's attempt to simplify things can result in erroneous behavior. Here is an example of a member of the purchasing department of a large European oil company who was negotiating an order with a Korean supplier:

simplification
The process of exhibiting the same orientation toward different culture groups.

> At the first meeting, the Korean partner offered a silver pen to the European manager. The latter, however, politely refused the present for fear of being bribed (even though he knew about the Korean custom of giving presents). Much to our manager's surprise, the second meeting began with the offer of a stereo system. Again the manager refused, his fear of being bribed probably heightened. When he gazed at a piece of Korean china on the third meeting, he finally realized what was going on. His refusal had not been taken to mean: "let's get on with business right away," but rather: "If you want to get into business with me, you had better come up with something bigger."[11]

Understanding the culture in which they do business can make international managers more effective.[12] Unfortunately, when placed in a culture with which they are unfamiliar, most international managers are not culturally knowledgeable, so they often

Table 5–2 Six Basic Cultural Variations	
Orientations	**Range of Variations**
What is the nature of people?	Good (changeable/unchangeable)
	A mixture of good and evil*
	Evil (changeable/unchangeable)
What is the person's relationship to nature?	Dominant*
	In harmony with nature
	Subjugation
What is the person's relationship to other people?	Lineal (hierarchic)
	Collateral (collectivist)
	Individualist*
What is the modality of human activity?	Doing*
	Being and becoming
	Being
What is the temporal focus of human activity?	Future*
	Present
	Past
What is the conception of space?	Private*
	Mixed
	Public

Note: *Indicates the dominant U.S. orientation.
Source: Adapted from the work of Florence Rockwood Kluckhohn and Fred L. Stodtbeck.

misinterpret what is happening. This is particularly true when the environment is markedly different from the one in which they live. Consider, for example, the difference between the cultures in Japan and the United States. Japan has what could be called a high-context culture, which possesses characteristics such as:

1. Relationships between people are relatively long lasting, and individuals feel deep personal involvement with each other.
2. Communication often is implicit, and individuals are taught from an early age to interpret these messages accurately.
3. People in authority are personally responsible for the actions of their subordinates, and this places a premium on loyalty to both superiors and subordinates.
4. Agreements tend to be spoken rather than written.
5. Insiders and outsiders are easily distinguishable, and outsiders typically do not gain entrance to the inner group.

These Japanese cultural characteristics are markedly different from those of low-context cultures such as the United States, which possess the following characteristics:

1. Relationships between individuals are relatively short in duration, and in general, deep personal involvement with others is not valued greatly.
2. Messages are explicit, and individuals are taught from a very early age to say exactly what they mean.
3. Authority is diffused throughout the bureaucratic system, and personal responsibility is hard to pin down.
4. Agreements tend to be in writing rather than spoken.
5. Insiders and outsiders are not readily distinguished, and the latter are encouraged to join the inner circle.[13]

These differences help to explain why Japanese managers in the United States often have trouble managing local operations, and vice versa.[14] At the same time, it is important to realize that while there are cultural differences, there also are similarities. Therefore, in managing across cultures, not everything is totally different. Some approaches that work at home also work well in other cultural settings.

Similarities Across Cultures

When internationalization began to take off in the 1970s, many companies quickly admitted that it would not be possible to do business in the same way in every corner of the globe. There was a secret hope, however, that many of the procedures and strategies that worked so well at home could be adopted overseas without modification. This has proved to be a false hope. At the same time, some similarities across cultures have been uncovered by researchers. For example, a co-author of this text (Luthans) and his associates studied through direct observation a sample of managers ($n = 66$) in the largest textile factory in Russia to determine their activities.[15] Like U.S. managers studied earlier, Russian managers carried out traditional management, communication, human resources, and networking activities. The study also found that, as in the United States, the relative attention given to the networking activity increased the Russian managers' opportunities for promotion, and that communication activity was a significant predictor of effective performance in both Russia and the United States.[16]

Besides the similarities of managerial activities, another study at the same Russian factory tested whether organizational behavior modification (O.B. Mod.) interventions that led to performance improvements in U.S. organizations would do so in Russia.[17] As with the applications of O.B. Mod. in the United States, Russian supervisors were trained to administer social rewards (attention and recognition) and positive feedback when they observed workers engaging in behaviors that contributed to the production of quality fabric. In addition, Russian supervisors were taught to give corrective feedback for behaviors that reduced product quality. The researchers found that this O.B. Mod. approach, which had worked so well in the United States, produced positive results in the Russian factory. They concluded that "the class of interventions associated with organizational behavior modification are likely to be useful in meeting the challenges faced by Russian workers and managers are given initial support by the results of this study."[18]

In another cross-cultural study, this time using a large Korean sample (1,192 employees in 27 large Korean firms), Luthans and colleagues analyzed whether demographic and situational factors identified in the U.S.-based literature had the same antecedent influence on the commitment of Korean employees.[19] As in the U.S. studies, Korean employees' position in the hierarchy, tenure in their current position, and age all related to organizational commitment. Other similarities with U.S. firms included: (1) as organizational size increased, commitment declined; (2) as structure became more employee focused, commitment increased; and (3) the more positive the perceptions of organizational climate, the greater the employee commitment. The following conclusion was drawn:

> This study provides beginning evidence that popular constructs in the U.S. management and organizational behavior literature should not be automatically dismissed as culture bound. Whereas some organizational behavior concepts and techniques do indeed seem to be culture specific . . . a growing body of literature is demonstrating the ability to cross-culturally validate other concepts and techniques, such as behavior management. . . . This study contributed to this cross-cultural evidence for the antecedents to organizational commitment. The antecedents for Korean employees' organizational commitment were found to be similar to their American counterparts.[20]

Many Differences Across Cultures

Despite similarities between cultures in some studies, far more differences than similarities have been found. In particular, MNCs are discovering that they must carefully investigate and understand the culture where they intend to do business and modify their approaches appropriately.

Sometimes these cultures are quite different from the United States—as well as from each other! One human resource management (HRM) example has been offered by Trompenaars, who examined the ways in which personnel in international subsidiaries were appraised by their managers. The head office had established the criteria to be used in these evaluations but left the prioritization of the criteria to the national operating company. As a result, the outcome of the evaluations could be quite different from country to country because what was regarded as the most important criterion in one subsidiary might be ranked much lower on the evaluation list of another subsidiary. In the case of Shell Oil, for example, Trompenaars found that the firm was using a HAIRL system of appraisal. The five criteria in this acronym stood for (a) Helicopter—the capacity to take a broad view from above; (b) Analysis—the ability to evaluate situations logically and completely; (c) Imagination—the ability to be creative and think outside the box; (d) Reality—the ability to use information realistically; and (e) Leadership—the ability to effectively galvanize and inspire personnel. When Shell's operating companies in four countries were asked to prioritize from top to bottom these five criteria, the results were as follows:

Netherlands	France	Germany	Britain
Reality	Imagination	Leadership	Helicopter
Analysis	Analysis	Analysis	Imagination
Helicopter	Leadership	Reality	Reality
Leadership	Helicopter	Imagination	Analysis
Imagination	Reality	Helicopter	Leadership

Quite obviously, personnel in different operating companies were being evaluated differently. In fact, no two of the operating companies in the four countries had the same criterion at the top of their lists. Moreover, the criterion at the top of the list for operating companies in the Netherlands—reality—was at the bottom of the list for those in France; and the one at the top of the list in French operating companies—imagination—was at the bottom of the list of the Dutch firms. Similarly, the German operating companies put leadership at the top of the list and helicopter at the bottom, while the British companies did the opposite! In fact, the whole list for the Germans is in the exact reverse order of the British list.[21]

Other HRM differences can be found in areas such as wages, compensation, pay equity, and maternity leave. Here are some representative examples.

1. The concept of an hourly wage plays a minor role in Mexico. Labor law requires that employees receive full pay 365 days a year.

2. In Austria and Brazil, employees with one year of service are automatically given 30 days of paid vacation.

3. Some jurisdictions in Canada have legislated pay equity—known in the United States as comparable worth—between male- and female-intensive jobs.

4. In Japan, compensation levels are determined by using the objective factors of age, length of service, and educational background rather than skill, ability, and performance. Performance does not count until after an employee reaches age 45.

5. In the United Kingdom, employees are allowed up to 40 weeks of maternity leave, and employers must provide a government-mandated amount of pay for 18 of those weeks.

6. In 87 percent of large Swedish companies, the head of human resources is on the board of directors.[22]

These HRM practices certainly are quite different from those in the United States, and U.S. MNCs need to modify their approaches when they go into these countries if they hope to be successful. Compensation plans in particular provide an interesting area of contrast across different cultures.

Table 5–3
Cultural Clusters in the Pacific Rim, EU, and United States

	Power Distance	Individualism	Masculinity	Uncertainty Avoidance
Pacific Rim				
Hong Kong, Malaysia, Philippines, Singapore	+	−	+	−
Japan	+	−	+	+
South Korea, Taiwan	+	−	−	+
EU and United States				
France, Spain	+	+	−	+
Italy, Belgium	+	+	+	+
Portugal	+	−	−	+
Greece	+	−	+	+
Denmark, Netherlands	−	+	+	−
Germany	−	+	+	+
Great Britain, Ireland, United States	−	+	+	−

Note: + indicates high or strong; − indicates low or weak.

Source: Based on research by Hofstede and presented in Richard M. Hodgetts and Fred Luthans, "U.S. Multinationals' Compensation Strategies for Local Management: Cross-Cultural Implications," *Compensation and Benefits Review,* March–April 1993, p. 47. Copyright © 1993 by Sage Publications, Inc. Reprinted by permission of Sage Publications, Inc.

Drawing on the work of Hofstede (see Chapter 4), it is possible to link cultural clusters and compensation strategies. Table 5–3 shows a host of different cultural groupings, including some in Asia, the EU, and Anglo countries. Each cluster requires a different approach to formulating an effective compensation strategy, and after analyzing each such cluster, we suggest that:

1. In Pacific Rim countries, incentive plans should be group based. In high-masculinity cultures (Japan, Hong Kong, Malaysia, the Philippines, Singapore), high salaries should be paid to senior-level managers.

2. In EU nations such as France, Spain, Italy, and Belgium, compensation strategies should be similar. In the latter two nations, however, significantly higher salaries should be paid to local senior-level managers because of the high masculinity index. In Portugal and Greece, both of which have a low individualism index, profit-sharing plans would be more effective than individual incentive plans, while in Denmark, the Netherlands, and Germany, personal-incentive plans would be highly useful because of the high individualism in these cultures.

3. In Great Britain, Ireland, and the United States, managers value their individualism and are motivated by the opportunity for earnings, recognition, advancement, and challenge. Compensation plans should reflect these needs.[23]

Additionally, some MNCs have found that compensation plans that are very attractive to their local workforce have no value for members of their international workforce.[24] For example, when the Gillette Company decided to offer stock to its 33,000 employees worldwide, the firm discovered that its plan was not global in terms of worker interest.[25] Other companies have had similar experiences. Some of the reasons are provided in Table 5–4; others include low employee disposable income and a feeling that stocks are risky investments. Simply put, workers in other cultures often do not have the same view of compensation plans as U.S. workers do. This is why many MNCs now are developing their own contingency-based compensation strategies that are geared toward meeting the needs of the local workers.

Table 5–4
Problems with U.S. Employee Stock Plans in Select Countries

Country	Reasons for Lack of Success
Belgium	Problematic. Some stock plans conflict with a government-imposed wage freeze.
Brazil	Impossible. Foreign-exchange controls prohibit out-of-country stock investment; phantom stock plans are a headache.
Britain	Easy. But sometimes labor unions can get in the way.
Eastern Europe	Forget it. Even if you get government permission, chances are you talked to the wrong bureaucrat.
Germany	Can I get that in deutsche marks? U.S. plans suffer when the dollar is weak.
Israel	Difficult. Exchange controls forced National Semiconductor to a third-party system, but the plan has only scant participation.
Luxembourg	Tax haven. Great place to set up a trust to administer stock plans.
Mexico	May regret it. Labor laws can force a one-time stock grant into an annual event.
Netherlands	No thanks. Employees may like the stock options, but they will not appreciate a hefty tax bill up front.
Philippines	Time-consuming. Requires government approval and lots of worker education.

Source: Adapted from information found in Tara Parker-Pope, "Culture Clash," *Wall Street Journal,* April 12, 1995, p. R7.

Figure 5–2 shows how specific HRM areas can be analyzed contingently on a country-by-country basis. Take, for example, the information on Japan. When it is contrasted with U.S. approaches, a significant number of differences are found. Recruitment and selection in Japanese firms often are designed to help identify those individuals who will do the best job over the long run. In the United States, people often are hired based on what they can do for the firm in the short run, because many of them eventually will quit or be downsized. Similarly, the Japanese use a great deal of cross-training, while the Americans tend to favor specialized training. The Japanese use group performance appraisal and reward people as a group; at least traditionally, Americans use manager–subordinate performance appraisal and reward people as individuals. In Japan, unions are regarded as partners; in the United States, management and unions view each other in a much more adversarial way. Only in the area of job design, where the Japanese use a great deal of participative management and autonomous work teams, are the Americans beginning to employ a similar approach. The same types of differences can be seen in the matrix of Figure 5–2 among Japan, Germany, Mexico, and China.

These differences should not be interpreted to mean that one set of HRM practices is superior to another. In fact, recent research from Japan and Europe shows these firms often have a higher incidence of personnel-related problems than U.S. companies. For example, one study found that Japanese MNCs ($n = 34$) and European MNCs ($n = 23$) had more problems than U.S. MNCs ($n = 24$) in areas such as (1) home-country personnel who possessed sufficient international management skills; (2) home-country personnel who wanted to work abroad; (3) difficulty in attracting high-caliber local nationals; and (4) high turnover of local employees. Additionally, when compared with Japanese MNCs, U.S. multinationals had less friction and better communication between their home-country expatriates and local employees, and there were fewer complaints by local employees regarding their ability to advance in the company.[26]

Figure 5–2 clearly indicates the importance of MNCs using a contingency approach to HRM across cultures. Not only are there different HRM practices in different cultures, but there also are different practices within the same cultures. For instance, one study involving 249 U.S. affiliates of foreign-based MNCs found that in general, affiliate HRM

| Figure 5–2 | A Partially Completed Contingency Matrix for International Human Resource Management |

	Japan	Germany	Mexico	China
Recruitment and selection	• Prepare for long process • Ensure that your firm is "here to stay" • Develop trusting relationship with recruit	• Obtain skilled labor from government subsidized apprenticeship program	• Use expatriates sparingly • Recruit Mexican nationals at U.S. colleges	• Recent public policy shifts encourage use of sophisticated selection procedures
Training	• Make substantial investment in training • Use general training and cross-training • Training is everyone's responsibility	• Reorganize and utilize apprenticeship programs • Be aware of government regulations on training	• Use bilingual trainers	• Careful observations of existing training programs • Utilize team training
Compensation	• Use recognition and praise as motivator • Avoid pay for performance	• Note high labor costs for manufacturing	• Consider all aspects of labor cost	• Use technical training as reward • Recognize egalitarian values • Use "more work more pay" with caution
Labor relations	• Treat unions as partners • Allow time for negotiations	• Be prepared for high wages and short work week • Expect high productivity from unionized workers	• Understand changing Mexican labor law • Prepare for increasing unionization of labor	• Tap large pool of labor cities • Lax labor laws may become more stringent
Job design	• Include participation • Incorporate group goal setting • Use autonomous work teams • Use uniform, formal approaches • Encourage co-worker input • Empower teams to make decision	• Utilize works councils to enhance worker participation	• Approach participation cautiously	• Determine employee's motives before implementing participation

Source: Fred Luthans, Paul A. Marsnik, and Kyle W. Luthans, "A Contingency Matrix Approach to IHRM," *Human Resource Management Journal* 36, no. 2 (1997). Copyright © 1997 John Wiley & Sons, Inc. This material is used by permission of John Wiley & Sons, Inc.

practices closely follow local practices when dealing with the rank and file but even more closely approximate parent-company practices when dealing with upper-level management.[27] In other words, this study found that a hybrid approach to HRM was being used by these MNCs.

Aside from the different approaches used in different countries, it is becoming clear that common assumptions and conventional wisdom about HRM practices in certain countries no longer are valid. For example, for many years, it has been assumed that Japanese employees do not leave their jobs for work with other firms, that they are loyal to their first employer, and that it would be virtually impossible for MNCs operating in Japan to recruit talent from Japanese firms. Recent evidence, however, reveals that job-hopping among Japanese employees is increasingly common. One report concluded:

> While American workers, both the laid-off and the survivors, grapple with cutbacks, one in three Japanese workers willingly walks away from his job within the first 10 years of his career, according to the Japanese Institute of Labor, a private research organization. And many more are thinking about it. More than half of salaried Japanese workers say they would switch jobs or start their own business if a favorable opportunity arose, according to a survey by the Recruit Research Corporation.[28]

These findings clearly illustrate one important point: Managing across cultures requires careful understanding of the local environment, because common assumptions and stereotypes may not be valid. Cultural differences must be addressed, and this is why cross-cultural research will continue to be critical in helping firms learn how to manage across cultures.[29]

■ Cultural Differences in Selected Countries and Regions

Chapter 4 introduced the concept of country clusters, which is the idea that certain regions of the world have similar cultures. For example, the way that Americans do business in the United States is very similar to the way that British do business in England. Even in this Anglo culture, however, there are pronounced differences, and in other clusters, such as in Asia, these differences become even more pronounced. "International Management in Action: Managing in Hong Kong" depicts such differences. Chapter 1 examined some important worldwide developments, and the next sections focus on cultural highlights and differences in selected countries and regions that provide the necessary understanding and perspective for effective management across cultures.

Doing Business in China

The People's Republic of China (PRC or China, for short) has had a long tradition of isolation. In 1979, Deng Xiaoping opened his country to the world. Although his bloody 1989 put-down of protesters in Tiananmen Square was a definite setback for progress, China is rapidly trying to close the gap between itself and economically advanced nations and to establish itself as a power in the world economy. As noted in Chapter 1, China is actively trading in world markets, is a member of the WTO, and is a major trading partner of the United States. Despite this global presence, many U.S. and European multinationals still find that doing business in the PRC can be a long, grueling process.[30] Very few outside firms have yet to make a profit in China. One primary reason is that Western-based MNCs do not appreciate the important role and impact of Chinese culture.

Experienced travelers report that the primary criterion for doing business in China is technical competence. For example, in the case of MNCs selling machinery, the Chinese want to know exactly how the machine works, what its capabilities are, and how repairs and maintenance must be handled. Sellers must be prepared to answer these questions in precise detail. This is why successful multinationals send only seasoned engineers and technical people to the PRC. They know that the questions to be answered will require both knowledge and experience, and young, fresh-out-of-school engineers will not be able to answer them.

A major cultural difference between the PRC and many Western countries is the issue of time. The Chinese tend to be punctual, so it is important that those who do business with them arrive on time. During meetings, such as those held when negotiating a contract, the Chinese may ask many questions and nod their assent at the answers. This nodding usually means that they understand or are being polite; it seldom means that they like what they are hearing and want to enter into a contract. For this reason, when dealing with the Chinese, one must keep in mind that patience is critically important. The Chinese will make a decision in their own good

Managing across cultures has long been recognized as a potential problem for multinationals. To help expatriates who are posted overseas deal with a new culture, many MNCs offer special training and coaching. Often, however, little is done to change expatriates' basic cultural values or specific managerial behaviors. Simply put, this traditional approach could be called the *practical school of management thought,* which holds that effective managerial behavior is universal and a good manager in the United States also will be effective in Hong Kong or any other location around the world. In recent years, it generally has been recognized that such an approach no longer is sufficient, and there is growing support for what is called the *cross-cultural school of management thought,* which holds that effective managerial behavior is a function of the specific culture. As Black and Porter pointed out, successful managerial action in Los Angeles may not be effective in Hong Kong.

Black and Porter investigated the validity of these two schools of thought by surveying U.S. managers working in Hong Kong, U.S. managers working in the United States, and Hong Kong managers working in Hong Kong. Their findings revealed some interesting differences. The U.S. managers in Hong Kong exhibited managerial behaviors similar to those of their counterparts back in the United States; however, Hong Kong managers had managerial behaviors different from either

group of U.S. managers. Commenting on these results, the researchers noted:

This study . . . points to some important practical implications. It suggests that American firms and the practical school of thought may be mistaken in the assumption that a good manager in Los Angeles will necessarily do fine in Hong Kong or some other foreign country. It may be that because firms do not include in their selection criteria individual characteristics such as cognitive flexibility, cultural flexibility, degree of ethnocentricity, etc., they end up sending a number of individuals on international assignments who have a tendency to keep the same set of managerial behaviors they used in the U.S. and not adjust or adapt to the local norms and practices. Including the measurement of these characteristics in the selection process, as well as providing cross-cultural training before departure, may be a means of obtaining more effective adaptation of managerial behaviors and more effective performance in overseas assignments.

Certainly the study shows that simplistic assumptions about culture are erroneous and that what works in one country will not necessarily produce the desired results in another. If MNCs are going to manage effectively throughout the world, they are going to have to give more attention to training their people about intercultural differences.

time, and it is common for outside businesspeople to make several trips to China before a deal is finally concluded. Moreover, not only are there numerous meetings, sometimes these are unilaterally canceled at the last minute and rescheduled. This often tries the patience of outsiders and is inconvenient in terms of rearranging travel plans and other problems.

Another important dimension of Chinese culture is **guanxi,** which means "good connections."[31] In turn, these connections can result in such things as lower costs for doing business.[32] Yet guanxi goes beyond just lower costs. Yi and Ellis surveyed Hong Kong ($n = 68$) and PRC Chinese ($n = 30$) managers and found that both groups agreed that guanxi networking offered a number of potential benefits, including increased business, higher sales revenue, more sources of information, greater prospecting opportunities, and the facilitation of future transactions.[33] In practice, guanxi resembles nepotism, where individuals in authority make decisions on the basis of family ties or social connections rather than objective indices. Tung has reported that:

guanxi
In China, it means "good connections."

> In a survey of 2,000 Chinese from Shanghai and its surrounding rural community, 92% of the respondents confirmed that *guanxi* played a significant role in their daily lives. Furthermore, the younger generation tended to place greater emphasis on *guanxi.* In fact, *guanxi* has become more widespread in the recent past. . . . Most business practitioners who have experience in doing business with East Asians will readily agree that in order to succeed in these countries "who you know is more important than what you know." In other words, having connections with the appropriate individuals and authorities is often more crucial than having the right product and/or price.[34]

Additionally, outsiders doing business in China must be aware that Chinese people will typically argue that they have the guanxi to get a job done, when in reality they may or may not have the necessary connections.

In China, it is important to be a good listener. This may mean having to listen to the same stories about the great progress that has been made by the PRC over the past decade. The Chinese are very proud of their economic accomplishments and want to share these feelings with outsiders.

When dealing with the Chinese, one must realize they are a collective society in which people pride themselves on being members of a group. This is in sharp contrast to the situation in the United States and other Western countries, where individualism is highly prized. For this reason, one must never single out a Chinese and praise him or her for a particular quality, such as intelligence or kindness, because doing so may embarrass the individual in the presence of his or her peers. It is equally important to avoid using self-centered conversation, such as excessive use of the word "I," because it appears that the speaker is trying to single him- or herself out for special consideration.

The Chinese also are much less animated than Westerners. They avoid open displays of affection, do not slap each other on the back, and are more reticent, retiring, and reserved than North or South Americans. They do not appreciate loud, boisterous behavior, and when speaking to each other, they maintain a greater physical distance than is typical in the West.

Cultural highlights that affect doing business in China can be summarized and put into some specific guidelines as follows:

1. The Chinese place values and principles above money and expediency.[35]

2. Business meetings typically start with pleasantries such as tea and general conversation about the guest's trip to the country, local accommodations, and family. In most cases, the host already has been briefed on the background of the visitor.

3. When a meeting is ready to begin, the Chinese host will give the appropriate indication. Similarly, when the meeting is over, the host will indicate that it is time for the guest to leave.

4. Once the Chinese decide who and what is best, they tend to stick with these decisions. Therefore, they may be slow in formulating a plan of action, but once they get started, they make fairly good progress.

5. In negotiations, reciprocity is important. If the Chinese give concessions, they expect some in return. Additionally, it is common to find them slowing down negotiations to take advantage of Westerners desiring to conclude arrangements as quickly as possible. The objective of this tactic is to extract further concessions. Another common ploy used by the Chinese is to pressure the other party during final arrangements by suggesting that this counterpart has broken the spirit of friendship in which the business relationship originally was established. Again, through this ploy, the Chinese are trying to gain additional concessions.

6. Because negotiating can involve a loss of face, it is common to find Chinese carrying out the whole process through intermediaries. This allows them to convey their ideas without fear of embarrassment.[36]

7. During negotiations, it is important not to show excessive emotion of any kind. Anger or frustration, for example, is viewed as antisocial and unseemly.

8. Negotiations should be viewed with a long-term perspective. Those who will do best are the ones who realize they are investing in a long-term relationship.[37]

Doing Business in Russia

As pointed out in Chapter 1, the Russian economy has experienced severe problems,[38] and the risks of doing business there cannot be overstated.[39] At the same time, however, by following certain guidelines, MNCs can begin to tap the potential opportunities. Here are some suggestions for being successful in Russia:

1. Build personal relationships with partners. Business laws and contracts do not mean as much in Russia as they do in the West. When there are contract disputes, there is little protection for the aggrieved party because of the time and effort needed to legally enforce the agreement. Detailed contracts can be hammered out later on; in the beginning, all that counts is friendship.

2. Use local consultants. Because the rules of business have changed so much in recent years, it pays to have a local Russian consultant working with the company. Russian expatriates often are not up-to-date on what is going on and, quite often, are not trusted by local businesspeople who have stayed in the country. So the consultant should be someone who has been in Russia all the time and understands the local business climate.

3. Consider business ethics. Ethical behavior in the United States is not always the same as in Russia. For example, it is traditional in Russia to give gifts to those with whom one wants to transact business, an approach that is often regarded as bribery in the United States.

4. Be patient. In order to get something done in Russia, it often takes months of waiting. Those who are in a hurry to make a quick deal are often sorely disappointed.

5. Stress exclusivity. Russians like exclusive arrangements and often negotiate with just one firm at a time. This is in contrast to Western businesspeople who often "shop" their deals and may negotiate with a half dozen firms at the same time before settling on one.

6. Remember that personal relations are important. Russians like to do business face-to-face. So when they receive letters or faxes, they often put them on their desk but do not respond to them. They are waiting for the businessperson to contact them and set up a personal meeting.

7. Keep financial information personal. When Westerners enter into business dealings with partners, it is common for them to share financial information with these individuals and to expect the same from the latter. However, Russians wait until they know their partner well enough to feel comfortable before sharing financial data. Once trust is established, then this information is provided.

8. Research the company. In dealing effectively with Russian partners, it is helpful to get information about this company, its management hierarchy, and how it typically does business. This information helps ensure the chances for good relations because it gives the Western partner a basis for establishing a meaningful relationship.

9. Stress mutual gain. The Western idea of "win–win" in negotiations also works well in Russia. Potential partners want to know what they stand to gain from entering into the venture.

10. Clarify terminology. For-profit business deals are new in Russia, so the language of business is just getting transplanted there. As a result, it is important to double-check and make sure that the other party clearly understands the proposal, knows what is expected and when, and is agreeable to the deal.[40]

11. Be careful about compromising or settling things too quickly, because this is often seen as a sign of weakness. During the Soviet Union days, everything was complex and so Russians are suspicious of anything that is conceded easily. If agreements are not reached after a while, a preferred tactic on their part is to display patience and then wait it out. However, they will abandon this approach if the other side shows great patience because they will realize that their negotiating tactic is useless.

12. Written contracts are not as binding to Russians as they are to Westerners. Like Asians, Russians view contracts as binding only if they continue to be mutually beneficial. One of the best ways of dealing with this is to be able to continually show them the benefits associated with sticking to the deal.[41]

Those 12 steps can be critical to the success of a business venture in Russia. They require careful consideration of cultural factors, and it often takes a lot longer than initially anticipated. However, the benefits may be worth the wait. And when everything is completed, there is a final cultural tradition that should be observed: Fix and reinforce the final agreements with a nice dinner together and an invitation to the Russians to visit your country and see your facilities.[42]

Doing Business in India

In recent years, India has begun to attract the attention of large MNCs. Unsaturated consumer markets, coupled with cheap labor and production locations, have helped make India a desirable market for global firms.[43] The government continues to play an important role in this process, although recently many of the bureaucratic restrictions have been lifted as India works to attract foreign investment and raise its economic growth rate.[44] In addition, although most Indian businesspeople speak English, many of their values and beliefs are markedly different from those in the West. Thus, understanding Indian culture is critical to successfully doing business in India.

Shaking hands with male business associates is almost always an acceptable practice. U.S. businesspeople in India are considered equals, however, and the universal method of greeting an equal is to press one's palms together in front of the chest and say *namaste,* which means "greetings to you." Therefore, if a handshake appears to be improper, it always is safe to use *namaste.*

Western food typically is available in all good hotels. Most Indians do not drink alcoholic beverages, however, and many are vegetarians or eat chicken but not beef. Therefore, when foreign businesspeople entertain in India, the menu often is quite different from that back home. Moreover, when a local businessperson invites an expatriate for dinner at home, it is not necessary to bring a gift, although it is acceptable to do so. The host's wife and children usually will provide help from the kitchen to ensure that the guest is well treated, but they will not be at the table. If they are, it is common to wait until everyone has been seated and the host begins to eat or asks everyone to begin. During the meal, the host will ask the guest to have more food. This is done to ensure that the person does not go away hungry; however, once one has eaten enough, it is acceptable to politely refuse more food.

For Western businesspeople in India, shirt, trousers, tie, and suit are proper attire. In the southern part of India, where the climate is very hot, a light suit is preferable. In the north during the winter, a light sweater and jacket are a good choice. Indian businesspeople, on the other hand, often will wear local dress. In many cases, this includes a *dhoti,* which is a single piece of white cloth (about five yards long and three feet wide) that is passed around the waist up to half its length and then the other half is drawn between the legs and tucked at the waist. Long shirts are worn on the upper part of the body. In some locales, such as Punjab, Sikhs will wear turbans, and well-to-do Hindus sometimes will wear long coats like the Rajahs. This coat, known as a *sherwani,* is the dress recognized by the government for official and ceremonial wear. Foreign businesspeople are not expected to dress like locals, and in fact, many Indian businesspeople will dress like Europeans. Therefore, it is unnecessary to adopt local dress codes.

When doing business in India, one will find a number of other customs useful to know, such as:

1. It is important to be on time for meetings.
2. Personal questions should not be asked unless the other individual is a friend or close associate.
3. Titles are important, so people who are doctors or professors should be addressed accordingly.
4. Public displays of affection are considered to be inappropriate, so one should refrain from backslapping or touching others.

5. Beckoning is done with the palm turned down; pointing often is done with the chin.

6. When eating or accepting things, use the right hand because the left is considered to be unclean.

7. The *namaste* gesture can be used to greet people; it also is used to convey other messages, including a signal that one has had enough food.

8. Bargaining for goods and services is common; this contrasts with Western traditions, where bargaining might be considered rude or abrasive.[45]

Finally, it is important to remember that Indians are very tolerant of outsiders and understand that many are unfamiliar with local customs and procedures. Therefore, there is no need to make a phony attempt to conform to Indian cultural traditions. Making an effort to be polite and courteous is sufficient.[46]

Doing Business in France

Many in the United States believe that it is more difficult to get along with the French than with other Europeans. This feeling probably reflects the French culture, which is markedly different from that in the United States. In France, one's social class is very important, and these classes include the aristocracy, the upper bourgeoisie, the upper-middle bourgeoisie, the middle, the lower-middle, and the lower. Social interactions are affected by class stereotypes, and during their lifetime, most French people do not encounter much change in social status. Unlike an American, who through hard work and success can move from the lowest economic strata to the highest, a successful French person might, at best, climb one or two rungs of the social ladder. Additionally, the French are very status conscious, and they like to provide signs of their status, such as knowledge of literature and the arts; a well-designed, tastefully decorated house; and a high level of education.

The French also tend to be friendly, humorous, and sardonic (sarcastic), in contrast to Americans, for example, who seldom are sardonic. The French may admire or be fascinated with people who disagree with them; in contrast, Americans are more attracted to those who agree with them. As a result, the French are accustomed to conflict and during negotiations accept that some positions are irreconcilable and must be accepted as such. Americans, on the other hand, believe that conflicts can be resolved and that if both parties make an extra effort and have a spirit of compromise, there will be no irreconcilable differences. Moreover, the French often determine a person's trustworthiness based on their firsthand evaluation of the individual's character. This is in marked contrast to Americans, who tend to evaluate a person's trustworthiness based on past achievements and other people's evaluations of this person.

In the workplace, many French people are not motivated by competition or the desire to emulate fellow workers. They often are accused of not having as intense a work ethic as, for example, Americans or Asians. Many French workers frown on overtime, and statistics show that on average, they have the longest vacations in the world (4 to 5 weeks annually). On the other hand, few would disagree that they work extremely hard in their regularly scheduled time and have a reputation for high productivity. Part of this reputation results from the French tradition of craftsmanship. Part of it also is accounted for by a large percentage of the workforce being employed in small, independent businesses, where there is widespread respect for a job well done.

Most French organizations tend to be highly centralized and have rigid structures. As a result, it usually takes longer to carry out decisions. Because this arrangement is quite different from the more decentralized, flattened organizations in the United States, both middle- and lower-level U.S. expatriate managers who work in French subsidiaries often find bureaucratic red tape a source of considerable frustration. There also are marked differences at the upper levels of management. In French companies, top managers have far more authority than their U.S. counterparts, and they are less accountable for their actions. While top-level U.S. executives must continually defend their decision to the CEO or board of directors, French executives are challenged only if the company has poor performance. As a result, those who have studied French management find that they take a more auto-cratic approach.[47]

In countries such as the United States, a great deal of motivation is derived from pro-fessional accomplishment. Americans realize there is limited job and social security in their country, so it is up to them to work hard and ensure their future. The French do not have the same view. While they admire Americans' industriousness and devotion to work, they believe that quality of life is what really matters. As a result, they attach a great deal of importance to leisure time, and many are unwilling to sacrifice the enjoyment of life for dedication to work.

The values and beliefs discussed here help to explain why French culture is so dif-ferent from that in other countries. Some of the sharp contrasts with the United States, for example, provide insights regarding the difficulties of doing business in France. Additional cultural characteristics, such as the following, also help to explain the difficulties that out-siders may encounter in France:

1. When shaking hands with a French person, use a quick shake with some pres-sure in the grip. A firm, pumping handshake, which is so common in the United States, is considered to be uncultured.

2. It is extremely important to be on time for meetings and social occasions. Being "fashionably late" is frowned on.

3. During a meal, it is acceptable to engage in pleasant conversation, but personal questions and the subject of money are never brought up.

4. Great importance is placed on neatness and taste. Therefore, visiting business-people should try very hard to be cultured and sophisticated.[48]

5. The French tend to be suspicious of early friendliness in the discussion and dislike first names, taking off jackets, or disclosure of personal or family details.

6. In negotiations the French try to find out what all of the other side's aims and demands are at the beginning, but they reveal their own hand only late in the negotiations.

7. The French do not like being rushed into making a decision, and they rarely make important decisions inside the meeting. In fact, the person who is ultimately responsible for making the decision is often not present.

8. The French tend to be very precise and logical in their approach to things, and will often not make concessions in negotiations unless their logic has been defeated. If a deadlock results, unlike Americans, who will try to break the impasse by suggesting a series of compromises by both sides, the French tend to remain firm and simply restate their position.[49]

Doing Business in Arab Countries

The intense media attention given to the Iraq War, terrorist actions, and continuing conflicts in the Middle East have pointed out that Arab cultures are distinctly different from Anglo cultures.[50] Americans often find it extremely hard to do business in Arab countries, and a number of Arab cultural characteristics can be cited for this difficulty.

One is the Arab view of time. In the United States, it is common to use the cliché "Time is money." In Arab countries, a favorite expression is *Bukra insha Allah,* which means "Tomorrow if God wills," an expression that explains the Arabs' fatalistic approach to time. Arabs believe that Allah controls time, in contrast to Westerners, who believe that they control their own time. As a result, if Arabs commit themselves to a date in the future and fail to show up, they feel no guilt or concern because they believe they have no control over time in the first place.

A word of caution on overgeneralizing is needed here and in all of the examples used throughout this chapter's discussion of cultural characteristics. There are many Arabs who are very particular about promises and appointments. There are also many Arabs who are very proactive and not fatalistic. The point is that there are always exceptions and stereotyping in cross-cultural dealings is unwarranted.

Another Arab cultural belief that generally holds is that destiny depends more on the will of a supreme being than on the behavior of individuals. A higher power dictates the outcome of important events, so individual action is of little consequence. This thinking affects not only Arabs' aspirations but also their motivation. Also of importance is that the status of Arabs largely is determined by family position and social contact and connections, not necessarily by their own accomplishments. This view helps to explain why some Middle Easterners take great satisfaction in appearing to be helpless. In fact, helplessness can be used as a source of power, for in this area of the world, the strong are resented and the weak compensated. Here is an example:

> In one Arab country, several public administrators of equal rank would take turns meeting in each other's offices for their weekly conferences, and the host would serve as chairman. After several months, one of these men had a mild heart attack. Upon his recovery, it was decided to hold the meetings only in his office, in order not to inconvenience him. From then on, the man who had the heart attack became the permanent chairman of the conference. This individual appeared more helpless than the others, and his helplessness enabled him to increase his power.[51]

This approach is quite different from that in the United States, where the strong tend to be compensated and rewarded. If a person were ill, such as in this example, the individual would be relieved of this responsibility until he or she had regained full health. In the interim, the rest of the group would go on without the sick person, and he or she may lose power.

Another important cultural contrast between Arabs and Americans is that of emotion and logic. Arabs often act based on emotion; in contrast, those in an Anglo culture are taught to act on logic. Many Arabs live in unstable environments where things change constantly, so they do not develop trusting relationships with others. Americans, on the other hand, live in a much more predictable environment and develop trusting relationships with others.

Arabs also make wide use of elaborate and ritualized forms of greetings and leave-takings. A businessperson may wait past the assigned meeting time before being admitted to an Arab's office. Once there, the individual may find a host of others present; this situation is unlike the typical one-on-one meetings that are so common in the United States. Moreover, during the meeting, there may be continuous interruptions, visitors may arrive and begin talking to the host, and messengers may come in and go out on a regular basis. The businessperson is expected to take all this activity as perfectly normal and remain composed and ready to continue discussions as soon as the host is prepared to do so.

Business meetings typically conclude with an offer of coffee or tea. This is a sign that the meeting is over and that future meetings, if there are to be any, should now be arranged.

Unlike the case in many other countries, titles are not in general use on the Arabian Peninsula, except in the case of royal families, ministers, and high-level military officers. Additionally, initial meetings typically are used to get to know the other party. Business-related discussions may not occur until the third or fourth meeting. Also, in contrast to the common perception among many Western businesspeople who have never been to an Arab country, it is not necessary to bring the other party a gift. If this is done, however, it should be a modest gift. A good example is a novelty or souvenir item from the visitor's home country.

Arabs attach a great deal of importance to status and rank. When meeting with them, one should pay deference to the senior person first. It also is important never to criticize or berate anyone publicly. This causes the individual to lose face, and the same is true for the person who makes these comments. Mutual respect is required at all times.

Other useful guidelines for doing business in Arab cultures include:

1. It is important never to display feelings of superiority, because this makes the other party feel inferior. No matter how well someone does something, the individual should let the action speak for itself and not brag or put on a show of self-importance.

2. One should not take credit for joint efforts. A great deal of what is accomplished is a result of group work, and to indicate that one accomplished something alone is a mistake.

3. Much of what gets done is a result of going through administrative channels in the country. It often is difficult to sidestep a lot of this red tape, and efforts to do so can be regarded as disrespect for legal and governmental institutions.

4. Connections are extremely important in conducting business. Well-connected businesspeople can get things done much faster than their counterparts who do not know the ins and outs of the system.

5. Patience is critical to the success of business transactions. This time consideration should be built into all negotiations, thus preventing one from giving away too much in an effort to reach a quick settlement.

6. Important decisions usually are made in person, not by correspondence or telephone. This is why an MNC's personal presence often is a prerequisite for success in the Arab world. Additionally, while there may be many people who provide input on the final decision, the ultimate power rests with the person at the top, and this individual will rely heavily on personal impressions, trust, and rapport.[52]

The World of *BusinessWeek*—Revisited

As the *BusinessWeek* article at the beginning of the chapter indicates, doing business in different cultures presents MNCs with a variety of challenges. In the case of Heineken, its core customers are in North America and Europe, two regions that possess many disparate cultures. As a result, Heineken faces a host of potential problems if it does not treat each region—and even country—individually. In addition, growth markets in other regions feature cultures even farther removed from Heineken's home markets. Further, the competitive environment is getting more intense and firms that do not tailor products and services to local tastes will face challenges. This makes effective management across cultures all the more imperative.

Now that you have read this chapter, you should have a good understanding of the importance and difficulties of managing across cultures. Using this knowledge as a platform, answer the following questions: (1) How does Heineken's history and tradition help or harm its efforts to become a global brewing powerhouse? (2) How would you characterize Heineken's approach to international management in terms of the four basic predispositions? (3) What are some of the cultural differences Heineken will have to manage as it expands in North America, Europe, and around the world?

SUMMARY OF KEY POINTS

1. One major problem facing MNCs is that they sometimes attempt to manage across cultures in ways similar to those of their home country. MNC dispositions toward managing across cultures can be characterized as (1) ethnocentric, (2) polycentric, (3) regiocentric, and (4) geocentric. These different approaches shape how companies adapt and adjust to cultural pressures around the world.

2. One major challenge when dealing with cross-cultural problems is that of overcoming parochialism

and simplification. Parochialism is the tendency to view the world through one's own eyes and perspectives. Simplification is the process of exhibiting the same orientation toward different cultural groups. Another problem is that of doing things the same way in foreign markets as they are done in domestic markets. Research shows that in some cases, this approach can be effective; however, effective cross-cultural management more commonly requires approaches different than those used at home. One area where this is particularly evident is human resource management. Recruitment, selection, training, and compensation often are carried out in different ways in different

countries, and what works in the United States may have limited value in other countries and geographic regions.

3. Doing business in various parts of the world requires the recognition and understanding of cultural differences. Some of these differences revolve around the importance the society assigns to time, status, control of decision making, personal accomplishment, and work itself. These types of cultural differences help to explain why effective managers in China or Russia often are quite different from those in France, and why a successful style in the United States will not be ideal in Arab countries.

KEY TERMS

ethnocentric predisposition, *128*
geocentric predisposition, *128*
globalization imperative, *129*

guanxi, *141*
parochialism, *133*
polycentric predisposition, *128*

regiocentric predisposition, *128*
simplification, *133*

REVIEW AND DISCUSSION QUESTIONS

1. Define the four basic predispositions MNCs have toward their international operations.

2. If a locally based manufacturing firm with sales of $350 million decided to enter the EU market by setting up operations in France, which orientation would be the most effective: ethnocentric, polycentric, regiocentric, or geocentric? Why? Explain your choice.

3. In what way are parochialism and simplification barriers to effective cross-cultural management? In each case, give an example.

4. Many MNCs would like to do business overseas in the same way that they do business domestically. Do research findings show that any approaches that work

well in the United States also work well in other cultures? If so, identify and describe two.

5. In most cases, local managerial approaches must be modified for doing business overseas. What are three specific examples that support this statement? Be complete in your answer.

6. What are some categories of cultural differences that help make one country or region of the world different from another? In each case, describe the value or norm and explain how it would result in different behavior in two or more countries? If you like, use the countries discussed in this chapter as your point of reference.

INTERNET EXERCISE: SONY'S APPROACH

Sony is a multinational corporation that sells a wide variety of goods in the international marketplace. These range from electronics to online games to music—and the Japanese MNC is even in the entertainment business (Sony Pictures Entertainment), producing offerings for both the big screen as well as for television. Visit the MNC's web site at **www.sony.com** and read about some of the latest developments in which the company is engaged. Pay close attention to its new offerings in the areas of electronics, television shows, movies, music, and on-line games. Then answer these three questions: (1) What type

of cultural challenges does Sony face when it attempts to market its products worldwide? Is demand universal for all of these offerings or is there a "national responsiveness/ globalization" challenge, as discussed in the chapter, that must be addressed? (2) Investigate the Sony credit card that the company is now offering online. Is this a product that will have worldwide appeal, or is it more likely to be restricted to more economically advanced countries? (3) In managing its far-flung enterprise, what are two cultural challenges that the company is likely to face and what will it need to do to respond to these?

Mexico

Located directly south of the United States, Mexico covers an area of 756,000 square miles. It is the third-largest country in Latin America and the thirteenth-largest in the world. The most recent estimates place the population at around 107 million, and this number is increasing at a rate of about 1.4 percent annually. As a result, today Mexico is one of the "youngest" countries in the world. Approximately 55 percent of the population is under the age of 20, while a mere 4 percent is 65 years of age or older.

Today, even though the economy is uncertain as in the rest of the world, Mexico has made itself attractive for foreign investment. Trade agreements with the United States and Canada (NAFTA), the EU, Japan, and dozens of Latin American countries have begun to fully integrate the Mexican economy into the global trading system. Multinationals in a wide variety of industries, from computers to electronics and from pharmaceuticals to manufacturing, have invested billions of dollars in the country. Telefonica, the giant Spanish telecommunications firm, is putting together a wireless network across Latin America, and Mexico is one of the countries that it has targeted for investment. Meanwhile, manufacturers not only from the United States but also from Asia to Europe have helped sustain Mexico's booming maquiladora assembly industry. By the turn of the century over 1.2 million people were employed in this industry including 600,000 in the two border states of Baja California and Chihuahua.

Thomson SA, the French consumer electronics firm, has three plants in the border states that make export TVs and digital decoder boxes. And like a growing number of MNCs located in Mexico, the firm is now moving away from importing parts and materials from outside and producing everything within the country. One reason for this move is that under the terms of the North American Free Trade Agreement only parts and materials originating in one of the three NAFTA trading partners are now allowed to enter the processing zones duty-free. Anything originating outside these three countries is subject to tariffs of as much as 25 percent. So the French MNC Thomson is building a picture-tube factory in Baja California so that it will no longer have to import dutiable tubes from Italy. In many cases, imported items from the European Union, however, are allowed to enter duty-free because in 1999 Mexico signed a free-trade agreement with the EU. As a result, a host of firms, including Philips Electronics and Siemens, poured large amounts of investment into the country. At the same time Mexico also has begun negotiating another free-trade pact with the four Nordic countries, raising the likelihood that firms such as Nokia, Ericsson, and Saab-Scania will also invest heavily in the country.

While many European MNCs are now investing in Mexico, the United States still remains the largest investor. Over 60 percent of all outside investment is by U.S. firms. Asian companies, in particular Japanese MNCs, also have large holdings in the country, although these firms have been scaling back in recent years because of the import duties and the fact that Mexican labor costs are beginning to rise, thus making it more cost-effective to produce some types of goods in Asia and export them to North America. The largest investments in Mexico are in the industrial sector (around 60 percent of the total) and services (around 30 percent).

One of the major benefits of locating in Mexico is the highly skilled labor force that can be hired at fairly low wages when compared with those paid elsewhere, especially in the United States. Additionally, manufacturing firms that have located there report high productivity growth rates and quality performance. A study by the Massachusetts Institute of Technology on auto assembly plants in Canada, the United States, and Mexico reported that Mexican plants performed well. Another by J. D. Power and Associates noted that Ford Motor's Hermisillo plant was the best in all of North America. Computer and electronic firms are also finding Mexico to be an excellent choice for new expansion plants.

www.mexicool.com

Questions

1. Why would multinationals be interested in setting up operations in Mexico? Give two reasons.

2. Would cultural differences be a major stumbling block for U.S. MNCs doing business in Mexico? For European firms? For Japanese firms? Explain your answer.

3. Why might MNCs be interested in studying the organizational culture in Mexican firms before deciding whether to locate there? Explain your logic.

Beijing, Here We Come!

A large toy company located in Canada is considering a business arrangement with the government of China (PRC). Although company representatives have not yet visited the PRC, the president of the firm recently met with their representatives in Ottawa and discussed the business proposition. The Canadian CEO learned that the PRC government would be quite happy to study the proposal, and the company's plan would be given a final decision within 90 days of receipt. The toy company now is putting together a detailed proposal and scheduling an on-site visit.

The Canadian firm would like to have the mainland Chinese manufacture a wide variety of toys for sale in Asia as well as in Europe and North America. Production of these toys requires a large amount of labor time, and because the PRC is reputed to have one of the largest and least expensive workforces in the world, the company believes that it can maximize profit by having the work done there. For the past five years, the company has had its toys produced in Taiwan. Costs there have been escalating recently, however, and because 45 percent of the production expense goes for labor, the company is convinced that it will soon be priced out of the market if it does not find another source.

The company president and three officers plan on going to Beijing next month to talk with government officials. They would like to sign a five-year agreement with a price that will not increase by more than 2 percent annually. Production operations then will be turned over to the mainland Chinese, who will have a free hand in manufacturing the goods.

The contract with the Taiwanese firm runs out in 90 days. The company already has contacted this firm, and the latter understands that its Canadian partner plans to terminate the arrangement. One major problem is that if it cannot find another supplier soon, it will have to go back to the Taiwanese firm for at least two more years. The contract stipulates that the agreement can be extended for another 24 months if the Canadian firm makes such a request; however, this must be done within 30 days of expiration of the contract. This is not an alternative that appeals to the Canadians, but they feel they will have to take it if they cannot reach an agreement with the mainland Chinese.

Questions

1. What is the likelihood that the Canadians will be able to reach an agreement with the mainland Chinese and not have to go back to their Taiwanese supplier? Explain.

2. Are the Canadians making a strategically wise decision in letting the Chinese from the PRC handle all the manufacturing, or should they insist on getting more actively involved in the production process? Defend your answer.

3. What specific cultural suggestions would you make to the Canadians regarding how to do business with the mainland Chinese?

Chapter 6

ORGANIZATIONAL CULTURES AND DIVERSITY

OBJECTIVES OF THE CHAPTER

The previous two chapters focused on national cultures. The overriding objective of this chapter is to examine the interaction of national culture (diversity) and organizational cultures and to discuss ways in which MNCs can manage the often inherent conflicts between national and organizational cultures. Many times, the cultural values and resulting behaviors that are common in a particular country are not the same as those needed for a successful MNC; therefore MNCs must learn to deal with this diversity/ challenge. Although the field of international management has long recognized the impact of national cultures, only recently has attention been given to the importance of managing organizational cultures and diversity. This chapter first examines common organizational cultures that exist in MNCs, then presents and analyzes ways in which multiculturalism and diversity are being addressed by the best, world-class multinationals. The specific objectives of this chapter are:

1. **DEFINE** exactly what is meant by *organizational culture,* and discuss the interaction of national and MNC cultures.

2. **IDENTIFY** the four most common categories of organizational culture that have been found through research, and discuss the characteristics of each.

3. **PROVIDE** an overview of the nature and degree of multiculturalism and diversity in today's MNCs.

4. **DISCUSS** common guidelines and principles that are used in building multicultural effectiveness at the team and the organizational levels.

The World of *BusinessWeek*

BusinessWeek

A Tale of Two Auto Mergers

Nissan is Thriving, While Mitsubishi Can't Get Out of the Ditch. What Happened Is a Case Study in How to Make Turnarounds Work in Japan

Not long ago, Mitsubishi Motors CEO Rolf Eckrodt and Nissan Motors CEO Carlos Ghosn were seen as the kind of managers who could bring radical change to Japan Inc. Their jobs: to fix Mitsubishi and Nissan, midsize car companies with faded brands, awesome debt loads, and uncertain futures. Today, Nissan is one of the hottest carmakers on the planet, increasingly admired for its quality and design. Mitsubishi, left in the lurch by controlling investor DaimlerChrysler, may be on its way to the minor leagues.

The contrast was underscored on April 26, when Ghosn reported record profits for Nissan, while Eckrodt stepped down at Mitsubishi, which is expected to report a $660 million loss.

One failed. One triumphed. How come? The answer is a case study in corporate Japan's tendency to avoid unpleasant truths and shun radical solutions—and a lesson in how important it is for outsiders to confront that tendency. It's something DaimlerChrysler Chairman Jürgen E. Schrempp and his team never figured out. Even more galling is the fact that Daimler actually took a close look at Nissan but was scared off by its $19 billion debt load. Mitsubishi seemed a safer bet.

Fast Moves

What undid Mitsubishi was that very safety factor: the carmaker's strong partners inside the mighty Mitsubishi *keiretsu*. Although Mitsubishi Motors was spun off as an independent company in 1970, Daimler execs figured the deep-pocketed group, which included Bank of Tokyo–Mitsubishi, would help supply needed talent and capital. Instead, having such allies created a false sense of complacency.

In contrast, Nissan and its suppliers belonged to a far weaker *keiretsu* that couldn't afford to rescue anyone. "We were a collapsing company" when France's Renault took a controlling interest in 1999, recalls Ghosn. With Nissan plants running at a money-losing 51% of capacity, Ghosn acted quickly, shuttering five of them, reducing the workforce by 23,000, and shifting production of more models to the U.S.; Nissan reported a $6.2 billion loss in 2000 but quickly returned to profitability. It now boasts the industry's best margins and bold new models such as the Titan pickup.

And Eckrodt? He was capable of the telling gesture. When he arrived in early 2001, after Daimler forked over $2.4 billion to acquire a 37% stake in Mitsubishi, one of his first acts was to give top executives fist-size chunks of the Berlin Wall, each emblazoned with the words "Leave no stone unturned."

No Bad News

Few at Mitsubishi would take that message to heart. By the end of 2003, Eckrodt had slashed Mitsubishi supplier costs by 15%, cut the workforce by 16%, doubled research and development spending from 2000 levels, and hired top-flight designers. Yet analysts say the Germans didn't push hard enough—and should have taken full control of the company to overcome the resistance to change. Many investors wanted Eckrodt to close at least one assembly plant in Japan and another in Australia, phase out money-losing models at home, shift production of its Pajero sport-utility vehicle to China, and crack down on quality problems.

Eckrodt could never break other parts of the Mitsubishi culture. This was a company whose managers were so reluctant to relay bad news to higher-ups that they squelched complaints about quality defects for decades to avoid costly product recalls. Many Daimler critics also say its culture contributed to the failed turnaround: The push was always on for results, and few wanted to alert Stuttgart to major problems. Later, to help U.S. sales, Mitsubishi resorted to an ultragenerous financing campaign—no money down and no payments for a year. The result was almost half a billion in bad loans.

In a parting statement, Eckrodt said Mitsubishi's future was bright. The Germans, however, are wondering what hit them. "It's an absolute disaster," a Daimler exec says of the company's $2 billion investment in Mitsubishi. "We can't sell it. It's worth nothing." Mitsubishi's *keiretsu* will probably bail it out, but it will remain a diminished force. The moral of the story: Turnarounds work in Japan—but only if they're ruthless enough.

By Brian Bremner with Gail Edmondson in Frankfurt

Source: Reprinted from "A Tale of Two Auto Mergers," May 10, 2004, online edition of *BusinessWeek* by special permission. Copyright © 2004 by the McGraw-Hill Companies, Inc. www.businessweek.com

The opening news article speaks to challenges presented by the integration of two companies with different organizational cultures and traditions. Daimler had considered acquiring or taking an interest in Nissan but was scared off by its debt load, feeling Mitsubishi had greater potential. However, management did not consider the differences in culture between the two companies and the dependencies between Mitsubishi and its keiretsu partners. Middle management at Mitsubishi was very hesitant to report any bad news up the chain of command, especially in production and quality, two critical areas for success in automotive production. Unfortunately, this lack of communication continued, and Daimler's new brand performed poorly from the outset. Nissan, on the other hand, had a weaker keiretsu, and this independence forced the company to perform well on its own. As a result, when France's Renault took over, it was able to effect immediate change.

Conflicting organizational cultures often present a mix of intangible elements that can have concrete and detrimental effects on companies. To make improvements, Daimler must attempt to instill a different culture at Mitsubishi without disrupting the flow of everyday business. In this chapter we will explore the nature and characteristics of organizational culture as it relates to doing business in today's global context. In addition, strategies and guidelines for establishing a strong organizational culture in the presence of diversity will be presented.

■ The Nature of Organizational Culture

The chapters in Part 1 provided the background on the external environment, and the chapters so far in this part have been concerned with the external culture. Regardless of whether this environment or cultural context impacts on the MNC, when individuals join an MNC, not only do they bring their national culture, which greatly affects their learned beliefs, attitudes, values, and behaviors, with them, but at the same time they enter into an organizational culture. Employees of MNCs are expected to "fit in." For example, at PepsiCo, personnel are expected to be cheerful, positive, enthusiastic, and have committed optimism; at Ford, they are expected to show self-confidence, assertiveness, and machismo.[1] Regardless of the external environment or their national culture, managers and employees must understand and follow their organization's culture to be successful. In this section, after first defining organizational culture, we analyze the interaction of national and organizational cultures. An understanding of this interaction has become recognized as vital to effective international management.

Definition and Characteristics

organizational culture
Shared values and beliefs that enable members to understand their roles and the norms of the organization.

Organizational culture has been defined in several different ways. In its most basic form, organizational culture can be defined as the shared values and beliefs that enable members to understand their roles and the norms of the organization. A more detailed definition is offered by organizational cultural theorist Edgar Schein, who defines it as a pattern of shared basic assumptions that the group learned as it solved its problems of external adaptation and internal integration, and that has worked well enough to be considered valid and, therefore, to be taught to new members as the correct way to perceive, think, and feel in relation to those problems.[2]

Regardless of how the term is defined, a number of important characteristics are associated with an organization's culture. These have been summarized as:

1. Observed behavioral regularities, as typified by common language, terminology, and rituals.
2. Norms, as reflected by things such as the amount of work to be done and the degree of cooperation between management and employees.
3. Dominant values that the organization advocates and expects participants to share, such as high product and service quality, low absenteeism, and high efficiency.
4. A philosophy that is set forth in the MNC's beliefs regarding how employees and customers should be treated.
5. Rules that dictate the do's and don'ts of employee behavior relating to areas such as productivity, customer relations, and intergroup cooperation.
6. Organizational climate, or the overall atmosphere of the enterprise as reflected by the way that participants interact with each other, conduct themselves with customers, and feel about the way they are treated by higher-level management.[3]

This list is not intended to be all-inclusive, but it does help to illustrate the nature of organizational culture.[4] The major problem is that sometimes an MNC's organizational culture in one country's facility differs sharply from organizational cultures in other countries. For example, managers who do well in England may be ineffective in Germany, despite the fact that they work for the same MNC. In addition, the cultures of the English and German subsidiaries may differ sharply from those of the home U.S. location. Effectively dealing with this multiculturalism within the various locations of an MNC is a major challenge for international management.

A good example is provided by the German MNC Hoechst AG, the very large chemical company that employs more people on the other side of the Atlantic than in Germany. As its chairman has noted, "We are not merely a German company with foreign interests. One could almost say we are a nonnational company." And because of the high labor costs in Germany, the firm has been expanding its operations to lower-cost regions. It has also been selling some of its German operations while purchasing businesses in other countries. In the process, Hoechst has also made its top management less German. For example, a Brazilian and an American are members of the firm's nine-member board. The company is also trying to change its culture through new performance-based pay programs. However, getting people to buy into the new culture has proven a challenge.

In some cases companies have deliberately maintained two different business cultures because they do not want one culture influencing the other. A good example is J.C. Penney, the giant department store chain. A couple of years ago, the well-known retailer bought control of Renner, a Brazilian retail chain with 20 stores. Rather than impose its own culture on the chain, however, Penney's management took a back seat. Recognizing Renner's reputation for value and service among its middle-class customers, Penney let the Brazilian managers continue to run the stores while it provided assistance in the form of backroom operations, merchandise presentation, logistics, branding, and expansion funds. In a country where fashion is constantly evolving, Renner is able to keep up with the market by changing fashion lines seven to eight times a year. The company also provides rapid checkout service, credit cards to individuals who earn as little as $150 a month, and interest-free installment plans that allow people to pay as little as $5 a month toward their purchases. Thanks to Penney's infusion of capital, in the first two years Renner opened 30 more stores and sales jumped from $150 million to over $300 million.

Interaction Between National and Organizational Cultures

There is a widely held belief that organizational culture tends to moderate or erase the impact of national culture. The logic of such conventional wisdom is that if a U.S. MNC set up operations in, say, France, it would not be long before the French employees began to "think like Americans." In fact, evidence is accumulating that just the opposite may be true. Hofstede's research found that the national cultural values of employees have a significant impact on their organizational performance, and that the cultural values employees bring to the workplace with them are not easily changed by the organization. So, for example, while some French employees would have a higher power distance than Swedes and some a lower power distance, chances are "that if a company hired locals in Paris, they would, on the whole, be less likely to challenge hierarchical power than would the same number of locals hired in Stockholm."[5]

Andre Laurent's research supports Hofstede's conclusions.[6] He found that cultural differences actually are more pronounced among foreign employees working within the same multinational organization than among personnel working for firms in their native lands. Nancy Adler summarized these research findings as follows:

> When they work for a multinational corporation, it appears that Germans become more German, Americans become more American, Swedes become more Swedish, and so on. Surprised by these results, Laurent replicated the research in two other multinational corporations, each with subsidiaries in the same nine Western European countries and the United States. Similar to the first company, corporate culture did not reduce or eliminate national differences in the second and third corporations. Far from reducing national differences, organization culture maintains and enhances them.[7]

There often are substantial differences between the organizational cultures of different subsidiaries, and of course, this can cause coordination problems. For example, when the Upjohn Company of Kalamazoo, Michigan, merged with Pharmacia AB of Sweden, which also has operations in Italy, the Americans failed to realize some of the cultural differences between themselves and their new European partners. As was reported in the *Wall Street Journal,* "Swedes take off the entire month of July for vacation, virtually en masse, and Italians take off August. Everyone in *Europe* knows, that is, but apparently hardly anyone in Kalamazoo, Mich., does."[8] As a result, a linkup that was supposed to give a quick boost to the two companies, solving problems such as aging product lines and pressure from giant competitors, never got off the ground. Things had to be rescheduled, and both partners ended up having to meet and talk about their cultural differences, so that each side better understood the "do's and don'ts" of doing business with the other.

When the two firms first got together, they never expected these types of problems. Upjohn, with household names such as Rogaine and Motrin, had no likely breakthroughs in its product pipeline, so it was happy to merge with Pharmacia. The latter had developed a solid roster of allergy medicines, human-growth hormone, and other drugs, but its distribution in the United States was weak and its product line was aging. So a merger seemed ideal for both firms. The big question was how to bring the two companies together. Given that Pharmacia had recently acquired an Italian firm, there was a proposal by the European group that there be three major centers—Kalamazoo, Stockholm, and Milan—as well as a new headquarters in London. However, this arrangement had a number of built-in

---

Table 6–1
Dimensions of Corporate Culture

Motivation

Activities	Outputs
To be consistent and precise. To strive for accuracy and attention to detail. To refine and perfect. Get it right.	To be pioneers. To pursue clear aims and objectives. To innovate and progress. Go for it.

Relationship

Job	Person
To put the demands of the job before the needs of the individual.	To put the needs of the individual before the needs of the job.

Identity

Corporate	Professional
To identify with and uphold the expectations of the employing organizations.	To pursue the aims and ideals of each professional practice.

Communication

Open	Closed
To stimulate and encourage a full and free exchange of information and opinion.	To monitor and control the exchange and accessibility of information and opinion.

Control

Tight	Loose
To comply with clear and definite systems and procedures.	To work flexibly and adaptively according to the needs of the situation.

Conduct

Conventional	Pragmatic
To put the expertise and standards of the employing organization first. To do what we know is right.	To put the demands and expectations of customers first. To do what they ask.

Source: Reported in Lisa Hoecklin, *Managing Cultural Differences: Strategies for Competitive Advantage* (Workingham, England: Addison-Wesley, 1995), p. 146.

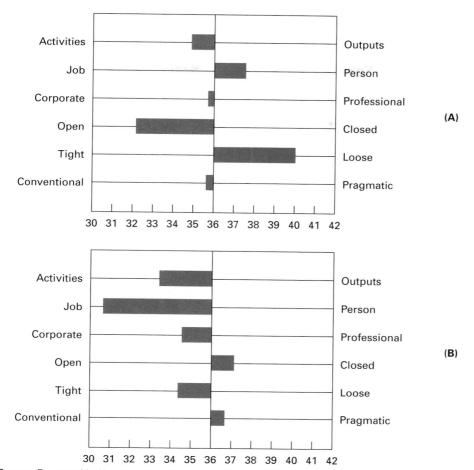

Figure 6–1

Europeans' Perception of the Cultural Dimensions of U.S. Operations (A) and European Operations (B) of the Same MNC

Source: Reported in Lisa Hoecklin, *Managing Cultural Differences: Strategies for Competitive Advantage* (Workingham, England: Addison-Wesley, 1995), pp. 147–148.

problems. For one, the executives in Italy and Sweden were accustomed to reporting to local bosses. Second, the people in London did not know a great deal about how to coordinate operations in Sweden and Italy. American cultural values added even more problems in that at Upjohn workers were tested for drug and alcohol abuse, but in Italy waiters pour wine freely every afternoon in the company dining room and Pharmacia's boardrooms were stocked with humidors for executives who liked to light a cigar during long meetings. Quite obviously, there were cultural differences that had to be resolved by the companies. In the end, Pharmacia & Upjohn said they would meld the different cultures and attitudes and get on with their growth plans. However, one thing is certain: The different cultures of the merged firms created a major challenge.

In examining and addressing the differences between organizational cultures, Hofstede provided the early database of a set of proprietary cultural-analysis techniques and programs known as DOCSA (Diagnosing Organizational Culture for Strategic Application). This approach identifies the dimensions of organizational culture summarized in Table 6–1. It was found that when cultural comparisons were made between different subsidiaries of an MNC, different cultures often existed in each one. Such cultural differences within an MNC could reduce the ability of units to work well together. An example is provided in Figure 6–1, which shows the cultural dimensions of a California-based MNC and its European subsidiary as perceived by the Europeans. A close comparison of these perceptions reveals some startling differences.

The Europeans viewed the culture in the U.S. facilities as only slightly activities oriented (see Table 6–1 for a description of these dimensions), but they saw their own European operations much more heavily activities oriented. The U.S. operation was viewed as moderately people oriented, but their own relationships were viewed as very job oriented. The Americans were seen as having a slight identification with their own organization, while the Europeans had a much stronger identification. The Americans were perceived as being very open in their communications; the Europeans saw themselves as moderately closed. The Americans were viewed as preferring very loose control, while the Europeans felt they preferred somewhat tight control. The Americans were seen as somewhat conventional in their conduct, while the Europeans saw themselves as somewhat pragmatic. If these perceptions are accurate, then it obviously would be necessary for both groups to discuss their cultural differences and carefully coordinate their activities to work well together.

This analysis is relevant to multinational alliances. It shows that even though an alliance may exist, the partners will bring different organizational cultures with them. Lessem and Neubauer, who have portrayed Europe as offering four distinct ways of dealing with multiculturalism (based on the United Kingdom, French, German, and Italian characteristics), provide an example, and Table 6–2 briefly describes each of these sets of cultural characteristics. A close examination of the differences highlights how difficult it can be to do business with two or more of these groups, because each group perceives things differently from the others. Another example is the way in which negotiations occur between groups; here are some contrasts between French and Spanish negotiators:[9]

French	Spanish
Look for a meeting of minds.	Look for a meeting of people.
Intellectual competence is very important.	Social competence is very important.
Persuasion through carefully prepared and skilled rhetoric is employed.	Persuasion through emotional appeal is employed.
Strong emphasis is given to a logical presentation of one's position coupled with well-reasoned, detailed solutions.	Socialization always precedes negotiations, which are characterized by an exchange of grand ideas and general principles.
A contract is viewed as a well-reasoned transaction.	A contract is viewed as a long-lasting relationship.
Trust emerges slowly and is based on the evaluation of perceived status and intellect.	Trust is developed on the basis of frequent and warm interpersonal contact and transaction.

Table 6–2
European Management Characteristics

	Characteristic			
Dimension	Western (United Kingdom)	Northern (France)	Eastern (Germany)	Southern (Italy)
Corporate	Commercial	Administrative	Industrial	Familial
Management attributes				
Behavior	Experiential	Professional	Developmental	Convivial
Attitude	Sensation	Thought	Intuition	Feeling
Institutional models				
Function	Salesmanship	Control	Production	Personnel
Structure	Transaction	Hierarchy	System	Network
Societal ideas				
Economics	Free market	Dirigiste	Social market	Communal
Philosophy	Pragmatic	Rational	Holistic	Humanistic
Cultural images				
Art	Theatre	Architecture	Music	Dance
Culture	(Anglo-Saxon)	(Gallic)	(Germanic)	(Latin)

Source: Reported in Lisa Hoecklin, *Managing Cultural Differences: Strategies for Competitive Advantage* (Workingham, England: Addison-Wesley, 1995), p. 149.

McDonald's Tackles Eating Habits in Brazil

People in Brazil like to buy American goods. This is one reason why McDonald's, with perhaps the strongest organizational culture representing American values, is rapidly expanding its investment in this country. Over the last three years the firm has spent almost $500 million to nearly double the number of restaurants in Brazil. At the same time, sales growth has been slow, and when the inflation rate is factored into the investment equation, McDonald's is not taking home a great deal of profit. Nor have things been helped along by the fact that the firm has had to discount its prices in order to increase demand. This Brazilian experience by McDonald's is an example where organizational culture, no matter how strong, is affected by national culture.

A challenge is how to get more Brazilians to eat at their local McDonald's. Over the last 36 months the company's Brazilian revenues have more than doubled to about $800 million. However, much of this demand has come from upper- and middle-class customers. As the company begins to further penetrate the market, it will have to begin making inroads among those consumers for whom a milkshake and a hamburger seem exotic. An accompanying challenge is that of changing the culture and getting people to eat breakfast at a local unit. In Brazil people have breakfast at home, thus making it next to impossible to market offerings such as Egg McMuffins. And even getting people to come to the unit for lunch can be difficult. Most workers are accustomed to going home for lunch—and then taking a nap.

The company is currently facing a big gamble that the economy will remain sufficiently strong and it can change the eating habits of millions of people and get them to come to Mickey D's on a regular basis. Unfortunately, some of this may be wishful thinking. As one observer recently noted:

Especially in the lower-income areas, McDonald's finds that old habits die hard. Just a couple of blocks from a McDonald's in a working-class Rio neighborhood, delivery man Manoel Ribeiro stands at the counter of a typical Brazilian greasy spoon feasting on a baked ham-and-cheese wrap and a boiled egg—a meal that costs half the $2.80 or so that he would pay for a Big Mac. "I work too hard for my money to experiment on American food," he says, between bites. His attitude isn't uncommon in a country where per-capita income runs about $3,500 a year. (Gibson and Moffett)

The challenge for McDonald's is going to be to keep its prices low and to convince a growing number of people that a Big Mac and a milkshake can be a meal for everybody—not just for North Americans. The firm also hopes that by lowering its prices, it will be able to break down some of these cultural barriers. Recent research, however, shows that even with these lower prices, annual sales have been flat in dollar terms. Moreover, while the company continues to open more and more new stores, current unit owners believe that this strategy is simply drawing business away from them. As one of them explained it, "There is a definite limit as to how much fast food in this market is ready to consume now" (Gibson and Moffett). Obviously Mickey D, regardless of its strong organizational culture, has work cut out for it to penetrate the Brazilian market.

Such comparisons also help to explain why it can be difficult for an MNC to break into foreign markets where there is only local competition. "International Management in Action: McDonald's Tackles Eating Habits in Brazil" provides an illustration. When dealing with these challenges, MNCs must work hard to understand the varying nature of the organizational cultures in their worldwide network and to both moderate and adapt their operations in a way that accommodates these individual units. Similarly, at the end of Part 2, the Brief Integrative Case on the Chase-Chemical merger in Europe demonstrates the sensitivities and challenges when simultaneously integrating different national and organizational cultures. A large part of this process calls for carefully understanding the nature of the various organizational cultures, and the next section examines the different types in detail.

■ Organizational Cultures in MNCs

Organizational cultures of MNCs are shaped by a number of factors, including the cultural preferences of the leaders and employees. In the international arena, some MNCs have subsidiaries that, except for the company logo and reporting procedures, would not be easily recognizable as belonging to the same multinational.[10]

Given that many recent international expansions are a result of mergers or acquisition, the integration of these organizational cultures is a critical concern in international management. Numeroff and Abrahams have suggested that there are four steps that are critical in this process: (1) The two groups have to establish the purpose, goal, and focus of their merger. (2) Then they have to develop mechanisms to identify the most important organizational structures and management roles. (3) They have to determine who has authority over the resources needed for getting things done. (4) They have to identify the expectations of all involved parties and facilitate communication between both departments and individuals in the structure.

> Companies all over the world are finding out firsthand that there is more to an international merger or acquisition than just sharing resources and capturing greater market share. Differences in workplace cultures sometimes temporarily overshadow the overall goal of long-term success of the newly formed entity. With the proper management framework and execution, successful integration of cultures is not only possible, but the most preferable paradigm in which to operate. It is the role of the sponsors and managers to keep sight of the necessity to create, maintain, and support the notion of a united front. It is only when this assimilation has occurred that an international merger or acquisition can truly be labeled a success.[11]

In addition, there are three aspects of organizational functioning that seem to be especially important in determining MNC organizational culture: (1) the general relationship between the employees and their organization; (2) the hierarchical system of authority that defines the roles of managers and subordinates; and (3) the general views that employees hold about the MNC's purpose, destiny, goals, and their places in them.[12] When examining these dimensions of organizational culture, Trompenaars suggested the use of two continua. One distinguishes between equity and hierarchy; the other examines orientation to the person and the task. Along these continua, which are shown in Figure 6–2, he identifies and describes four different types of organizational cultures: family, Eiffel Tower, guided missile, and incubator.[13]

In practice, of course, organizational cultures do not fit neatly into any of these four, but the groupings can be useful in helping to examine the bases of how individuals relate to each other, think, learn, change, are motivated, and resolve conflict. The following discussion examines each of these cultural types.

Figure 6–2

Organizational Cultures

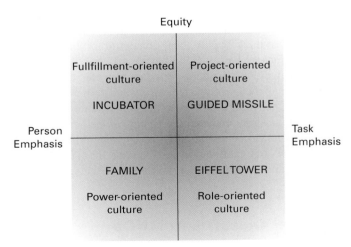

Source: Adapted from Fons Trompenaars, *Riding the Waves of Culture: Understanding Diversity in Global Business* (Burr Ridge, IL: Irwin, 1994), p. 154.

Family Culture

Family culture is characterized by a strong emphasis on hierarchy and orientation to the person. The result is a family-type environment that is power-oriented and headed by a leader who is regarded as a caring parent and one who knows what is best for the personnel. Trompenaars found that this organizational culture is common in countries such as Turkey, Pakistan, Venezuela, China, Hong Kong, and Singapore.[14]

In this culture, personnel not only respect the individuals who are in charge but look to them for both guidance and approval as well. In turn, management assumes a paternal relationship with personnel, looks after employees, and tries to ensure that they are treated well and have continued employment. Family culture also is characterized by traditions, customs, and associations that bind together the personnel and make it difficult for outsiders to become members. When it works well, family culture can catalyze and multiply the energies of the personnel and appeal to their deepest feelings and aspirations. When it works poorly, members of the organization end up supporting a leader who is ineffective and drains their energies and loyalties.

This type of culture is foreign to most managers in the United States, who believe in valuing people based on their abilities and achievements, not on their age or position in the hierarchy. As a result, many managers in U.S.-based MNCs fail to understand why senior-level managers in overseas subsidiaries might appoint a relative to a high-level, sensitive position even though that individual might not appear to be the best qualified for the job. They fail to realize that family ties are so strong that the appointed relative would never do anything to embarrass or let down the family member who made the appointment. Here is an example:

> A Dutch delegation was shocked and surprised when the Brazilian owner of a large manufacturing company introduced his relatively junior accountant as the key coordinator of a $15 million joint venture. The Dutch were puzzled as to why a recently qualified accountant had been given such weighty responsibilities, including the receipt of their own money. The Brazilians pointed out that the young man was the best possible choice among 1,200 employees since he was the nephew of the owner. Who could be more trustworthy than that? Instead of complaining, the Dutch should consider themselves lucky that he was available.[15]

family culture
A culture that is characterized by a strong emphasis on hierarchy and orientation to the person.

Eiffel Tower Culture

Eiffel Tower culture is characterized by strong emphasis on hierarchy and orientation to the task. Under this organizational culture, jobs are well defined, employees know what they are supposed to do, and everything is coordinated from the top. As a result, this culture—like the Eiffel Tower itself—is steep, narrow at the top, and broad at the base.

Unlike family culture, where the leader is revered and considered to be the source of all power, the person holding the top position in the Eiffel Tower culture could be replaced at any time, and this would have no effect on the work that organization members are doing or on the organization's reasons for existence. In this culture, relationships are specific, and status remains with the job. Therefore, if the boss of an Eiffel Tower subsidiary were playing golf with a subordinate, the subordinate would not feel any pressure to let the boss win. In addition, these managers seldom create off-the-job relationships with their people, because they believe this could affect their rational judgment. In fact, this culture operates very much like a formal hierarchy—impersonal and efficient.

> Each role at each level of the hierarchy is described, rated for its difficulty, complexity, and responsibility, and has a salary attached to it. There then follows a search for a person to fill it. In considering applicants for the role, the personnel department will treat everyone equally and neutrally, match the person's skills and aptitudes with the job requirements, and award the job to the best fit between role and person. The same procedure is followed in evaluations and promotions.[16]

Eiffel Tower culture
A culture that is characterized by strong emphasis on hierarchy and orientation to the task.

Eiffel Tower culture most commonly is found in Northwest European countries. Examples include Denmark, Germany, and the Netherlands. The way that people in this culture learn and change differs sharply from that in the family culture. Learning involves the accumulation of skills necessary to fit a role, and organizations will use qualifications in deciding how to schedule, deploy, and reshuffle personnel to meet their needs. The organization also will employ such rational procedures as assessment centers, appraisal systems, training and development programs, and job rotation in managing its human resources. All these procedures help to ensure that a formal hierarchic or bureaucracy-like approach works well. When changes need to be made, however, the Eiffel Tower culture often is ill-equipped to handle things. Manuals must be rewritten, procedures changed, job descriptions altered, promotions reconsidered, and qualifications reassessed.

Because the Eiffel Tower culture does not rely on values that are similar to those in most U.S. MNCs, U.S. expatriate managers often have difficulty initiating change in this culture. As Trompenaars notes:

> An American manager responsible for initiating change in a German company described to me the difficulties he had in making progress, although the German managers had discussed the new strategy in depth and made significant contributions to its formulation. Through informal channels, he had eventually discovered that his mistake was not having formalized the changes to structure or job descriptions. In the absence of a new organization chart, this Eiffel Tower company was unable to change.[17]

Guided Missile Culture

guided missile culture
A culture that is characterized by strong emphasis on equality in the workplace and orientation to the task.

Guided missile culture is characterized by strong emphasis on equality in the workplace and orientation to the task. This organizational culture is oriented to work, which typically is undertaken by teams or project groups. Unlike the Eiffel Tower culture, where job assignments are fixed and limited, personnel in the guided missile culture do whatever it takes to get the job done. This culture gets its name from high-tech organizations such as the National Aeronautics and Space Administration (NASA), which pioneered the use of project groups working on space probes that resembled guided missiles. In these large project teams, more than a hundred different types of engineers often were responsible for building, say, a lunar landing module. The team member whose contribution would be crucial at any given time in the project typically could not be known in advance. Therefore, all types of engineers had to work in close harmony and cooperate with everyone on the team.

To be successful, the best form of synthesis must be used in the course of working on the project. For example, in a guided missile project, formal hierarchical considerations are given low priority, and individual expertise is of greatest importance. Additionally, all team members are equal (or at least potentially equal), because their relative contributions to the project are not yet known. All teams treat each other with respect, because they may need the other for assistance. This egalitarian and task-driven organizational culture fits well with the national cultures of the United States and United Kingdom, which helps to explain why high-tech MNCs commonly locate their operations in these countries.

Unlike family and Eiffel Tower cultures, change in guided missile culture comes quickly. Goals are accomplished, and teams are reconfigured and assigned new objectives. People move from group to group, and loyalties to one's profession and project often are greater than loyalties to the organization itself.

Trompenaars found that the motivation of those in guided missile cultures tends to be more intrinsic than just concern for money and benefits. Team members become enthusiastic about, and identify with, the struggle toward attaining their goal. For example, a project team that is designing and building a new computer for the Asian market may be highly motivated to create a machine that is at the leading edge of technology, user-friendly, and likely to sweep the market. Everything else is secondary to this overriding objective. Thus, both intragroup and intergroup conflicts are minimized and petty problems between team members set aside; everyone is so committed to the project's main goal that no one has time for petty disagreements. As Trompenaars notes:

> This culture tends to be individualistic since it allows for a wide variety of differently specialized persons to work with each other on a temporary basis. The scenery of faces keeps changing. Only the pursuit of chosen lines of personal development is constant. The team is a vehicle for the shared enthusiasm of its members, but is itself disposable and will be discarded when the project ends. Members are garrulous, idiosyncratic, and intelligent, but their mutuality is a means, not an end. It is a way of enjoying the journey. They do not need to know each other intimately, and may avoid doing so. Management by objectives is the language spoken, and people are paid for performance.[18]

Incubator Culture

Incubator culture is the fourth major type of organizational culture that Trompenaars identified, and it is characterized by strong emphasis on equality and personal orientation. This culture is based heavily on the existential idea that organizations per se are secondary to the fulfillment of the individuals within them. This culture is based on the premise that the role of organizations is to serve as incubators for the self-expression and self-fulfillment of their members; as a result, this culture often has little formal structure. Participants in an incubator culture are there primarily to perform roles such as confirming, criticizing, developing, finding resources for, or helping to complete the development of an innovative product or service. These cultures often are found among start-up firms in Silicon Valley, California, or Silicon Glen, Scotland. These incubator-type organizations typically are entrepreneurial and often founded and made up by a creative team who left larger, Eiffel Tower–type employers. They want to be part of an organization where their creative talents will not be stifled.

Incubator cultures often create environments where participants thrive on an intense, emotional commitment to the nature of the work. For example, the group may be in the process of gene splitting that could lead to radical medical breakthroughs and extend life. Often, personnel in such cultures are overworked, and the enterprise typically is underfunded. As breakthroughs occur and the company gains stability, however, it starts moving down the road toward commercialization and profit. In turn, this engenders the need to hire more people and develop formalized procedures for ensuring the smooth flow of operations. In this process of growth and maturity, the unique characteristics of the incubator culture begin to wane and disappear, and the culture is replaced by one of the other types (family, Eiffel Tower, or guided missile).

As noted, change in the incubator culture often is fast and spontaneous. All participants are working toward the same objective. Because there may not yet be a customer who is using the final output, however, the problem itself often is open to redefinition, and the solution typically is generic, aimed at a universe of applications. Meanwhile, motivation of the personnel remains highly intrinsic and intense, and it is common to find employees working 70 hours a week—and loving it. The participants are more concerned with the unfolding creative process than they are in gathering power or ensuring personal monetary gain. In sharp contrast to the family culture, leadership in this incubator culture is achieved, not gained by position.

The four organizational cultures described by Trompenaars are "pure" types and seldom exist in practice. Rather the types are mixed and, as shown in Table 6–3, overlaid with one of the four major types of culture dominating the corporate scene. Recently, Trompenaars and his associates have created a questionnaire designed to identify national patterns of corporate culture as shown in Figure 6–3.

incubator culture
A culture that is characterized by strong emphasis on equality and orientation to the person.

Table 6–3
Summary Characteristics of the Four Corporate Cultures

Characteristic	Corporate Culture			
	Family	**Eiffel Tower**	**Guided Missile**	**Incubator**
Relationships between employees	Diffuse relationships to organic whole to which one is bonded	Specific role in mechanical system of required interaction	Specific tasks in cybernetic system targeted on shared objectives	Diffuse, spontaneous relationships growing out of shared creative process
Attitude toward authority	Status is ascribed to parent figures who are close and powerful	Status is ascribed to superior roles that are distant yet powerful	Status is achieved by project group members who contribute to targeted goal	Status is achieved by individuals exemplifying creativity and growth
Ways of thinking and learning	Intuitive, holistic, lateral and error-correcting	Logical, analytical, vertical, and rationally efficient	Problem centered, professional, practical, cross-disciplinary	Process oriented, creative, ad hoc, inspirational
Attitudes toward people	Family members	Human resources	Specialists and experts	Co-creators
Ways of changing	"Father" changes course	Change rules and procedures	Shift aim as target moves	Improvise and attune
Ways of motivating and rewarding	Intrinsic satisfaction in being loved and respected	Promotion to greater position, larger role	Pay or credit for performance and problems solved	Participation in the process of creating new realities
	Management by subjectives	Management by job description	Management by objectives	Management by enthusiasm
Criticism and conflict resolution	Turn other cheek, save other's face, do not lose power game	Criticism is accusation of irrationalism unless there are procedures to arbitrate conflicts	Constructive task-related only, then admit error and correct fast	Improve creative idea, not negate it

Source: Adapted from Fons Trompenaars and Charles Hampden-Turner, *Riding the Waves of Culture: Understanding Diversity in Global Business,* 2nd ed. (New York: McGraw-Hill, 1998), p. 183.

Figure 6–3

National Patterns of Corporate Culture

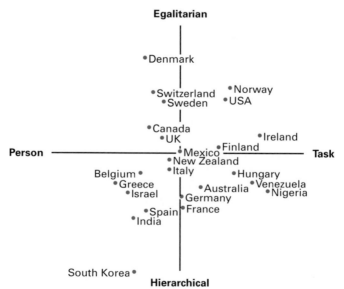

Source: Adapted from Fons Trompenaars and Charles Hampden-Turner, *Riding the Waves of Culture: Understanding Diversity in Global Business,* 2nd ed. (New York: McGraw-Hill, 1998), p. 184.

Matsushita Goes Global

In recent years, growing numbers of multinationals have begun to expand their operations, realizing that if they do not increase their worldwide presence now, they likely will be left behind in the near future. In turn, this has created a number of different challenges for these MNCs, including making a fit between their home organizational culture and the organizational cultures at local levels in the different countries where the MNC operates. Matsushita provides an excellent example of how to handle this challenge with its macro/micro approach. This huge, Japanese MNC has developed a number of guidelines that it uses in setting up and operating its more than 150 industrial units. At the same time, the company complements these macro guidelines with on-site micro techniques that help to create the most appropriate organizational culture in the subsidiary.

At the macro level, Matsushita employs six overall guidelines that are followed in all locales: (1) Be a good corporate citizen in every country, among other things, by respecting cultures, customs, and languages. (2) Give overseas operations the best manufacturing technology the company has available. (3) Keep the expatriate head count down, and groom local management to take over. (4) Let operating plants set their own rules, fine-tuning manufacturing processes to match the skills of the workers. (5) Create local research and development to tailor products to markets. (6) Encourage competition between overseas outposts and with plants back home.

Working within these macro guidelines, Matsushita then allows each local unit to create its own culture. The Malaysian operations are a good example. Since 1987, Matsushita has set up 13 new subsidiaries in Malaysia, and employment there has more than quadrupled, to approximately 25,000 people. Only 230 of these employees, however, are Japanese. From these Malaysian operations, Matsushita currently produces 1.3 million televisions and 1.8 million air conditioners annually, and 90 percent of these units are shipped overseas. To produce this output, local plants reflect Malaysia's cultural mosaic of Muslim Malays, ethnic Chinese, and Indians. To accommodate this diversity, Matsushita cafeterias offer Malaysian, Chinese, and Indian food, and to accommodate Muslim religious customs, Matsushita provides special prayer rooms at each plant and allows two prayer sessions per shift.

How well does this Malaysian workforce perform for the Japanese MNC? In the past, the Malaysian plants' slogan was "Let's catch up with Japan." Today, however, these plants frequently outperform their Japanese counterparts in both quality and efficiency. The comparison with Japan no longer is used. Additionally, Matsushita has found that the Malaysian culture is very flexible, and the locals are able to work well with almost any employer. Commenting on Malaysia's multiculturalism, Matsushita's managing director notes, "They are used to accommodating other cultures, and so they think of us Japanese as just another culture. That makes it much easier for us to manage them than some other nationalities" (Schlender).

Today, Matsushita faces a number of important challenges, including remaining profitable in a slow-growth, high-cost Japanese economy. Fortunately, this MNC is doing extremely well overseas, which is buying it time to get its house in order back home. A great amount of this success results from the MNC's ability to nurture and manage overseas organizational cultures (such as in Malaysia) that are both diverse and highly productive.

■ Managing Multiculturalism and Diversity

As the "International Management in Action" box on Matsushita indicates, success in the international arena often is greatly determined by an MNC's ability to manage both multiculturalism and diversity.[19] Both domestically and internationally, organizations find themselves leading workforces that have a variety of cultures (and subcultures) and consist of a largely diverse population of women, men, young and old people, blacks, whites, Latins, Asians, Arabs, Indians, and many others.

Phases of Multicultural Development

The effect of multiculturalism and diversity will vary depending on the stage of the firm in its international evolution. Table 6–4 depicts the characteristics of the major phases in this evolution. For example, Adler has noted that international cultural diversity has minimal impact on domestic organizations, although domestic multiculturalism has a highly significant impact. As firms begin exporting to foreign clients, however, and become what she calls "international corporations" (Phase II in Table 6–4), they must adapt their approach and

Table 6–4
The Evolution of International Corporations

Characteristics/ Activities	Phase I (Domestic Corporations)	Phase II (International Corporations)	Phase III (Multinational Corporations)	Phase IV (Global Corporations)
Primary orientation	Product/service	Market	Price	Strategy
Competitive strategy	Domestic	Multidomestic	Multinational	Global
Importance of world business	Marginal	Important	Extremely important	Dominant
Product/service	New, unique	More standardized	Completely standardized (commodity)	Mass-customized
	Product engineering emphasized	Process engineering emphasized	Engineering not emphasized	Product and process engineering
Technology	Proprietary	Shared	Widely shared	Instantly and extensively shared
R&D/sales	High	Decreasing	Very low	Very high
Profit margin	High	Decreasing	Very low	High, yet immediately decreasing
Competitors	None	Few	Many	Significant (few or many)
Market	Small, domestic	Large, multidomestic	Larger, multinational	Largest, global
Production location	Domestic	Domestic and primary markets	Multinational, least cost	Imports and exports
Exports	None	Growing, high potential	Large, saturated	Imports and exports
Structure	Functional divisions	Functional with international division	Multinational lines of business	Global alliances, hierarchy
	Centralized	Decentralized	Centralized	Coordinated, decentralized
Primary orientation	Product/service	Market	Price	Strategy
Strategy	Domestic	Multidomestic	Multinational	Global
Perspective	Ethnocentric	Polycentric/ regiocentric	Multinational	Global/multicentric
Cultural sensitivity	Marginally important	Very important	Somewhat important	Critically important
With whom	No one	Clients	Employees	Employees and clients
Level	No one	Workers and clients	Managers	Executives
Strategic assumption	"One way"/ one best way	"Many good ways," equifinality	"One least-cost way"	"Many good ways," simultaneously

Source: Nancy J. Adler, *International Dimensions of Organizational Behavior,* 2nd ed. (Boston: PWS-Kent Publishing, 1991), pp. 7–8. All text and images from *International Dimensions of Organizational Behavior* are used with the permission of the publisher. They may not be cut, pasted, altered, revised, modified, scanned, or adapted in any way without the prior written permission of the publisher, www.thomsonrights.com. Copyright © 1991 South-Western, a division of Thomson Learning, and its licensors. All rights reserved.

products to those of the local market. For these international firms, the impact of multiculturalism is highly significant. As companies become what she calls "multinational corporations" (Phase III), they often find that price tends to dominate all other considerations, and the direct impact of culture may lessen slightly. For those who continue this international evolution, however, and become full-blown "global corporations" (Phase IV), the impact of culture again becomes extremely important. Notes Adler:

> Global firms need an understanding of cultural dynamics to plan their strategy, to locate production facilities and suppliers worldwide, to design and market culturally appropriate products and services, as well as to manage cross-cultural interaction throughout the organization—from senior executive committees to the shop floor. As more firms today move

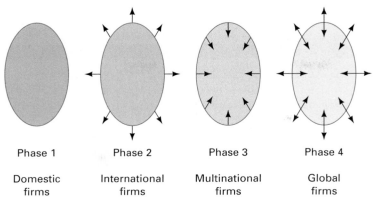

Figure 6–4

Location of International Cross-Cultural Interaction

Phase 1	Phase 2	Phase 3	Phase 4
Domestic firms	International firms	Multinational firms	Global firms

Source: Nancy J. Adler, *International Dimensions of Organizational Behavior,* 2nd ed. (Boston: PWS-Kent Publishing, 1991), p. 123. All text and images from *International Dimensions of Organizational Behavior* are used with the permission of the publisher. They may not be cut, pasted, altered, revised, modified, scanned, or adapted in any way without the prior written permission of the publisher, www.thomsonrights.com. Copyright © 1991 South-Western, a division of Thomson Learning, and its licensors. All rights reserved.

from domestic, international, and multinational organizations to operating as truly global organizations and alliances, the importance of cultural diversity increases markedly. What once was "nice to understand" becomes imperative for survival, let alone success.[20]

As shown in Figure 6–4, international cultural diversity traditionally affects neither the domestic firm's organizational culture nor its relationship with its customers or clients. These firms work domestically, and only domestic multiculturalism has a direct impact on their dynamics as well as on their relationship to the external environment.

Conversely, among international firms, which focus on exporting and producing abroad, cultural diversity has a strong impact on their external relationships with potential buyers and foreign employees. In particular, these firms rely heavily on expatriate managers to help manage operations; as a result, the diversity focus is from the inside out. This is the reverse of what happens in multinational firms, where there is less emphasis on managing cultural differences outside the firm and more on managing cultural diversity within the company. This is because multinational firms hire personnel from all over the world. Adler notes that these multinational firms need to develop cross-cultural management skills up the levels of the hierarchy. As shown in Figure 6–4, this results in a diversity focus that is primarily internal.

Global firms need both an internal and an external diversity focus (again see Figure 6–4). To be effective, everyone in the global organization needs to develop cross-cultural skills that allow them to work effectively with internal personnel as well as external customers, clients, and suppliers.

Types of Multiculturalism

For the international management arena, there are several ways of examining multiculturalism and diversity. One is to focus on the domestic multicultural and diverse workforce that operates in the MNC's home country. In addition to domestic multiculturalism, there is the diverse workforce in other geographic locales, and increasingly common are the mix of domestic and overseas personnel found in today's MNCs. The following discussion examines both domestic and group multiculturalism and the potential problems and strengths.

Domestic Multiculturalism   It is not necessary for today's organizations to do business in another country to encounter people with diverse cultural backgrounds. Culturally distinct populations can be found within organizations almost everywhere in the world. In Singapore, for example, there are four distinct cultural and linguistic groups: Chinese, Eurasian, Indian, and Malay. In Switzerland, there are four distinct ethnic communities:

Table 6–5
Perspectives of Older and Younger Generations in Small Chinese Family Businesses in Singapore

Older Generation	Younger Generation
Claim that they have more experiences.	Claim that they have more education.
Perceive that their role is to intervene for the workers and help them.	Perceive that their role is to hire competent workers and expect them to perform.
Believe that it is the boss's responsibility to solve problems.	Believe that it is the individual's responsibility to solve problems.
Stress that a boss has the obligation to take care of the workers.	Stress that workers have responsibility to perform the job well.
Emphasize that individuals should conform to the majority.	Emphasize that individuals should maximize their talents and potentials.
Believe that work cannot be divided clearly and like to be involved in everything.	Believe that a boss should mind his own work and leave the workers to do their jobs.
Perceive that work is more important than designation and organizational structure.	Perceive that designation and organizational structure are important in order to get the work done.
Believe that managers should help the workers to solve their problems.	Believe that managers should set objectives and achieve them.
Complain that the younger generation likes to use complicated management methods.	Complain that the old generation does things on an ad hoc basis.
Perceive that the younger generation likes to change and expects immediate results.	Perceive that the old generation is static and resistant to change.
Worry that the young generation is not experienced in running the business.	Frustrated that the old generation still holds on strongly to their power.
Emphasize that they have to take care of the old workers in the process of the company's growth.	Emphasize that they have to gain acceptance from their customers in order to enhance the firm's image as a modern company.
Emphasize that ethics are important in business.	Emphasize that strategy is important in business.
Anticipate that the young generation is going to have many difficulties if they adopt Western concepts of management.	Frustrated that the old generation does not let them test out their concepts of management.
Believe that one's ability is limited and one should be content with what one has.	Believe that there are a lot of opportunities for achievement and growth.

Source: Adapted from Jean Lee, "Culture and Management—A Study of Small Chinese Family Business in Singapore," *Journal of Small Business Management,* July 1996, p. 65.

French, German, Italian, and Romansch. In Belgium, there are two linguistic groups: French and Flemish. In the United States, millions of first-generation immigrants have brought both their languages and their cultures. In Los Angeles, for example, there are more Samoans than on the island of Samoa, more Israelis than in any other city outside Israel, and more first- and second-generation Mexicans than in any other city except Mexico City. In Miami, over one-half the population is Latin, and most residents speak Spanish fluently. More Puerto Ricans live in New York City than in Puerto Rico.

It is even possible to examine domestic multiculturalism within the same ethnic groups. For example, Lee, after conducting research in Singapore among small Chinese family businesses, found that the viewpoints of the old generation differ sharply from those of the younger generation. Table 6–5 provides specific contrasts between the old and young generations of Chinese.

In short, there is considerable multicultural diversity domestically in organizations throughout the world, and this trend will continue. For example, the U.S. civilian labor force of the next decade will change dramatically in ethnic composition. In particular, there will be a significantly lower percentage of white males in the workforce and a growing percentage of women, African Americans, Hispanics, and Asians.

Group Multiculturalism There are a number of ways that diverse groups can be categorized. Four of the most common include:

1. **Homogeneous groups,** in which members have similar backgrounds and generally perceive, interpret, and evaluate events in similar ways. An example would be a group of male German bankers who are forecasting the economic outlook for a foreign investment.

2. **Token groups,** in which all members but one have the same background. An example would be a group of Japanese retailers and a British attorney who are looking into the benefits and shortcomings of setting up operations in Bermuda.

3. **Bicultural groups,** in which two or more members represent each of two distinct cultures. An example would be a group of four Mexicans and four Canadians who have formed a team to investigate the possibility of investing in Russia.

4. **Multicultural groups,** in which there are individuals from three or more different ethnic backgrounds. An example is a group of three American, three German, three Uruguayan, and three Chinese managers who are looking into mining operations in Chile.

As the diversity of a group increases, the likelihood of all members perceiving things in the same way decreases sharply. Attitudes, perceptions, and communication in general may be a problem. On the other hand, there also are significant advantages associated with the effective use of multicultural, diverse groups. The following sections examine the potential problems and the advantages.

Potential Problems Associated with Diversity

Overall, diversity may cause a lack of cohesion that results in the unit's inability to take concerted action, be productive, and create a work environment that is conducive to both efficiency and effectiveness. These potential problems are rooted in people's attitudes.

An example of an attitudinal problem in a diverse group may be the mistrust of others. For example, many U.S. managers who work for Japanese operations in the United States complain that Japanese managers often huddle together and discuss matters in their native language. The U.S. managers wonder aloud why the Japanese do not speak English. What are they talking about that they do not want anyone else to hear? In fact, the Japanese often find it easier to communicate among themselves in their native language, and because no Americans are present, the Japanese managers ask why they should speak English. If there is no reason for anyone else to be privy to our conversation, why should we not opt for our own language? Nevertheless, such practices do tend to promote an attitude of mistrust.

Another potential problem may be perceptual. Unfortunately, when culturally diverse groups come together, they often bring preconceived stereotypes with them. In initial meetings, for example, engineers from economically advanced countries often are perceived as more knowledgeable than those from less advanced countries. In turn, this perception can result in status-related problems, because some of the group initially are regarded as more competent than others and likely are accorded status on this basis. As the diverse group works together, erroneous perceptions often are corrected, but this takes time. In one diverse group consisting of engineers from a major Japanese firm and a world-class U.S. firm, a Japanese engineer was assigned a technical task because of his stereotyped technical educational background. The group soon realized that this particular Japanese engineer was not capable of doing this job, however, because for the last four years, he had been responsible for coordinating routine quality and no longer was on the technologic cutting edge. His engineering degree from the University of Tokyo had resulted in the other members perceiving him as technically competent and able to carry out the task; this perception proved to be incorrect.

A related problem is inaccurate biases. For example, it is well known that Japanese companies depend on groups to make decisions. Entrepreneurial behavior, individualism,

Homogeneous group
A group in which members have similar backgrounds and generally perceive, interpret, and evaluate events in similar ways.

token group
A group in which all members but one have the same background, such as a group of Japanese retailers and a British attorney.

bicultural group
A group in which two or more members represent each of two distinct cultures, such as four Mexicans and four Taiwanese who have formed a team to investigate the possibility of investing in a venture.

multicultural group
A group in which there are individuals from three or more different ethnic backgrounds, such as three U.S., three German, three Uruguayan, and three Chinese managers who are looking into mining operations in South Africa.

and originality are typically downplayed.[21] However, in a growing number of Japanese firms this stereotype is proving to be incorrect.[22] Here is an example.

> Mr. Uchida, a 28-year-old executive in a small software company, dyes his hair brown, keeps a sleeping bag by his desk for late nights in the office and occasionally takes the day off to go windsurfing. "Sometimes I listen to soft music to soothe my feelings, and sometimes I listen to hard music to build my energy," said Mr. Uchida, who manages the technology-development division of the Rimnet Corporation, an Internet access provider. "It's important that we always keep in touch with our sensibilities when we want to generate ideas." The creative whiz kid, a business personality often prized by corporate America, has come to Japan Inc. Unlikely as it might seem in a country renowned for its deference to authority and its devotion to group solidarity, freethinkers like Mr. Uchida are popping up all over the workplace. Nonconformity is suddenly in.[23]

Still another potential problem with diverse groups is inaccurate communication, which could occur for a number of reasons. One is misunderstandings caused by words used by a speaker that are not clear to other members. For example, in a diverse group in which one of the authors was working, a British manager told her U.S. colleagues, "I will fax you this report in a fortnight." When the author asked the Americans when they would be getting the report, most of them believed it would be arriving in four days. They did not know that the common British word *fortnight* (14 nights) means two weeks.

Another contribution to miscommunication may be the way in which situations are interpreted. Many Japanese nod their heads when others talk, but this does not mean that they agree with what is being said. They merely are being polite and attentive. In many societies, it is impolite to say no, and if the listener believes that the other person wants a positive answer, the listener will say yes even though this is incorrect. As a result, many U.S. managers find out that promises made by individuals from other cultures cannot be taken at face value—and in many instances, the other individual assumes that the American realizes this!

Diversity also may lead to communication problems because of different perceptions of time. For example, many Japanese will not agree to a course of action on the spot. They will not act until they have discussed the matter with their own people, because they do not feel empowered to act alone. Many Latin managers refuse to be held to a strict timetable, because they do not have the same time-urgency that U.S. managers do. Here is another example, as described by a European manager:

> In attempting to plan a new project, a three-person team composed of managers from Britain, France, and Switzerland failed to reach agreement. To the others, the British representative appeared unable to accept any systematic approach; he wanted to discuss all potential problems before making a decision. The French and Swiss representatives agreed to examine everything before making a decision, but then disagreed on the sequence and scheduling of operations. The Swiss, being more pessimistic in their planning, allocated more time for each suboperation than did the French. As a result, although everybody agreed on its validity, we never started the project. If the project had been discussed by three Frenchmen, three Swiss, or three Britons, a decision, good or bad, would have been made. The project would not have been stalled for lack of agreement.[24]

Advantages of Diversity

While there are some potential problems to overcome when using culturally diverse groups in today's MNCs, there also are a host of benefits to be gained.[25] In particular, there is growing evidence that culturally diverse groups can enhance creativity, lead to better decisions, and result in more effective and productive performance.[26]

One main benefit of diversity is the generation of more and better ideas. Because group members come from a host of different cultures, they often are able to create a greater number of unique (and thus creative) solutions and recommendations. For example, a U.S. MNC recently was preparing to launch a new software package aimed at the mass consumer market. The company hoped to capitalize on the upcoming Christmas season with a strong advertising campaign in each of its international markets. A meeting of the sales managers from these markets in Spain, the Middle East, and Japan helped the company to revise and better target its marketing effort. The Spanish manager suggested that the company focus its campaign around the coming of the Magi (January 6) and not Christmas (December 25), because in Latin cultures, gifts typically are exchanged on the date that the Magi brought their gifts. The Middle East manager pointed out that most of his customers were not Christians, so a Christmas campaign would not have much meaning in his area. Instead, he suggested the company focus its sales campaign around the value of the software and how it could be useful to customers and not worry about getting the product shipped by early December. The Japanese manager concurred with his Middle East colleague but additionally suggested that some of the colors being proposed for the sales brochure be changed to better fit with Japanese culture. Thanks to these ideas, the sales campaign proved to be one of the most effective in the company's history.

A second major benefit is that culturally diverse groups can prevent **groupthink,** which is social conformity and pressures on individual members of a group to conform and reach consensus. When this occurs, group participants believe that their ideas and actions are correct and that those who disagree with them are either uninformed or deliberately trying to sabotage their efforts. Multicultural diverse groups often are able to avoid this problem, because the members do not think similarly or feel pressure to conform. As a result, they typically question each other, offer opinions and suggestions that are contrary to those held by others, and must be persuaded to change their minds. Therefore, unanimity is achieved only through a careful process of deliberation. Unlike homogeneous groups, where everyone can be "of one mind," diverse groups may be slower to reach a general consensus, but the decision may be more effective.

groupthink
Social conformity and pressures on individual members of a group to conform and reach consensus.

Building Multicultural Team Effectiveness

Multiculturally diverse teams have a great deal of potential to be either very effective or very ineffective.[27] As shown in Figure 6–5, Kovach reports that if cross-cultural groups are led properly, they can indeed be highly effective; unfortunately, she also found that if they are not managed properly, they can be highly ineffective. In other words, diverse groups are more powerful than single-culture groups. They can hurt the organization, but if managed effectively, they can be the best.[28] The following sections provide the conditions and guidelines for managing diverse groups in today's organizations effectively.

Understanding the Conditions for Effectiveness   Multicultural teams are most effective when they face tasks requiring innovativeness. They are far less effective when they are assigned to routine tasks. As Adler explains:

> Cultural diversity provides the biggest asset for teams with difficult, discretionary tasks requiring innovation. Diversity becomes less helpful when employees are working on simple tasks involving repetitive or routine procedures. Therefore, diversity generally becomes more

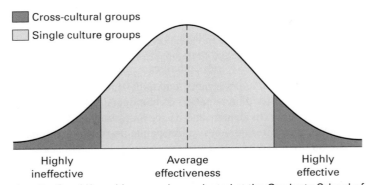

Highly ineffective   Average effectiveness   Highly effective

Cross-cultural groups
Single culture groups

Figure 6–5

Group Effectiveness and Culture

Source: Based on Dr. Carol Kovach's research, conducted at the Graduate School of Management, University of California at Los Angeles (UCLA), and reported in Nancy J. Adler, *International Dimensions of Organizational Behavior,* 2nd ed. (Boston: PWS-Kent Publishing, 1991), p. 135.

valuable during the planning and development of projects (the "work" stage) and less helpful during their implementation (the "action" stage). The more senior the team members, the more likely they are to be working on projects that can benefit from diversity. Diversity is therefore extremely valuable to senior executive teams, both within and across countries.[29]

To achieve the greatest amount of effectiveness from diverse teams, activities must be determined by the stage of team development (e.g., entry, working, and action). For example, in the entry stage, the focus should be on building trust and developing team cohesion. This can be a difficult task for diverse teams, whose members are accustomed to working in different ways. For example, Americans, Germans, and Swiss typically spend little time getting to know each other; they find out the nature of the task and set about pursuing it on their own without first building trust and cohesion. This contrasts sharply with individuals from Latin America, Southern Europe, and the Middle East, where team members spend a great deal of initial time getting to know each other. This contrast between task-oriented and relationship-oriented members of a diverse team may cause difficulty in creating cohesion. To counteract this problem, it is common in the entry stage of development to find experienced multicultural managers focusing attention on the team members' equivalent professional qualifications and status. Once this professional similarity and respect are established, the group can begin forming itself into a cohesive team.

In the work stage of development, attention may be directed more toward describing and analyzing the problem or task that has been assigned. This stage often is fairly easy for managers of multicultural teams, because they can draw on the diversity of the members in generating ideas. As noted earlier, diverse groups tend to be most effective when dealing with situations that require innovative approaches.

In the action stage, the focus shifts to decision making and implementation. This can be a difficult phase, because it often requires consensus building among the members. In achieving this objective, experienced managers work to help the diverse group recognize and facilitate the creation of ideas with which everyone can agree. In doing so, it is common to find strong emphasis on problem-solving techniques such as the nominal group technique (NGT), where the group members individually make contributions before group interaction and consensus is reached.

Using the Proper Guidelines   Besides some overall conditions, a number of specific guidelines for effectively managing culturally diverse groups have been identified. Here are some of the most useful:

1. Team members must be selected for their task-related abilities and not solely based on ethnicity. If the task is routine, homogeneous membership often is preferable; if the task is innovative, multicultural membership typically is best.

2. Team members must recognize and be prepared to deal with their differences. The goal is to facilitate a better understanding of cross-cultural differences and generate a higher level of performance and rapport. In doing so, members need to become aware of their own stereotypes, as well as those of the others, and use this information to better understand the real differences that exist between them. This can then serve as a basis for determining how each individual member can contribute to the overall effectiveness of the team.

3. Because members of diverse teams tend to have more difficulty agreeing on their purpose and task than members of homogeneous groups, the team leader must help the group to identify and define its overall goal. This goal is most useful when it requires members to cooperate and develop mutual respect in carrying out their tasks.

4. Members must have equal power so that everyone can participate in the process; cultural dominance always is counterproductive. As a result, managers of culturally diverse teams distribute power according to each person's ability to contribute to the task, not according to ethnicity.

5. It is important that all members have mutual respect for each other. This often is accomplished by managers choosing members of equal ability, making prior accomplishments and task-related skills known to the group, and minimizing early judgments based on ethnic stereotypes.

6. Because teams often have difficulty determining what is a good or a bad idea or decision, managers must give teams positive feedback on their process and output. This feedback helps the members to see themselves as a team, and it teaches them to value and celebrate their diversity, recognize contributions made by the individual members, and trust the collective judgment of the group.

These guidelines can be useful in helping leaders to manage culturally diverse teams effectively. World-class organizations use such an approach, and one good example is NUMMI (New United Motor Manufacturing), a joint venture between General Motors and Toyota that transformed an out-of-date GM plant in Fremont, California, into a world-class organization. This joint-venture partnership, formed over 20 years ago, continues to be a success story of how a culturally diverse workforce can produce state-of-the-art automobiles. The successful approach to culturally diverse work teams at NUMMI was built around four principles:

1. Both management and labor recognized that their futures were interdependent, thus committing them to a mutual vision.

2. Employees felt secure and trusted assurances that they would be treated fairly, thus enabling them to become contributors.

3. The production system formed interdependent relationships throughout the plant, thus helping to create a healthy work environment.

4. The production system was managed to transform the stress and conflict of everyday life into trust and mutual respect.[30]

In achieving success at NUMMI, Toyota sent trainers from Japan to work with its U.S. counterparts and teach the production system that would be used throughout the plant. During this period, both groups searched for points of agreement, establishing valuable relationships in the process. In addition, the Japanese taught the Americans some useful techniques for increasing productivity, including how to focus on streamlining operations, reduce waste, and blame mistakes on the situation or themselves (not on team members).

In overcoming multicultural differences at NUMMI, several changes were introduced— for example, (1) reserved dining rooms were eliminated, and all managers now eat in a communal cafeteria; (2) all reserved parking spaces were eliminated; and (3) GM's 80 job classifications were collapsed into only 3 to equalize work and rewards and ensure fairness. Commenting on the overall success of the joint venture, it was noted that

> Toyota managers resisted temptations to forge ahead with a pure version of the system. Both the Japanese and Americans learned as they went. By adopting a "go slow" attitude, the Japanese and Americans remained open to points of resistance as they arose and navigated around them. By tolerating ambiguity and by searching for consensus, Toyota managers established the beginnings of mutual respect and trust with the American workers and managers.[31]

NUMMI is only one example of the many successful multicultural workforces producing world-class goods and services. In each case, however, effective multinationals rely on the types of guidelines that have been highlighted in this discussion.

The World of *BusinessWeek*—Revisited

The *BusinessWeek* article at the beginning of this chapter presents an excellent example of the challenges facing executives who must manage in different organizational cultures. Having read this chapter, you should have a clearer understanding of how national culture might inhibit or enhance the effects of organizational culture. In the case of DaimlerChrysler and Mitsubishi, cultural norms within the two companies were quite different, and the differences were not squarely addressed until it was too late. The cultures of Renault and Nissan were also different, but managers found ways to overcome those differences for the common good of the firm.

When a firm from one country merges with a company from another country, both national and organizational cultures come into play. Each must be evaluated separately, and only then can an appropriate strategy for integrating cultures be developed. Given these facts, and drawing information from this chapter, answer these questions: (1) How might the organizational culture at a German firm differ from that of a Japanese one? (2) How would national cultural patterns at a French firm differ from those of a Japanese one? (3) What are two major organizational culture challenges faced by Daimler in managing Mitsubishi and by Renault in managing Nissan?

SUMMARY OF KEY POINTS

1. Organizational culture is a pattern of basic assumptions that are developed by a group as it learns to cope with its problems of external adaptation and internal integration and that are taught to new members as the correct way to perceive, think, and feel in relation to these problems. Some important characteristics of organizational culture include observed behavioral regularities, norms, dominant values, philosophy, rules, and organizational climate.

2. Organizational cultures are shaped by a number of factors. These include the general relationship between employees and their organization, the hierarchic system of authority that defines the roles of managers and subordinates, and the general views that employees hold about the organization's purpose, destiny, goals, and their place in the organization. When examining these differences, Trompenaars suggested the use of two continua: equity/hierarchy and person/task orientation, resulting in four basic types of organizational cultures: family, Eiffel Tower, guided missile, and incubator.

3. Family culture is characterized by strong emphasis on hierarchic authority and orientation to the person. Eiffel Tower culture is characterized by strong emphasis on hierarchy and orientation to the task. Guided missile culture is characterized by strong emphasis on equality in the workplace and

orientation to the task. Incubator culture is characterized by strong emphasis on equality and orientation to the person.

4. Success in the international arena often is heavily determined by a company's ability to manage multiculturalism and diversity. Firms progress through four phases in their international evolution: (1) domestic corporation, (2) international corporation, (3) multinational corporation, and (4) global corporation.

5. There are a number of ways to examine multiculturalism and diversity. One is by looking at the domestic multicultural and diverse workforce that operates in the MNC's home country. Another is by examining the variety of diverse groups that exist in MNCs, including homogeneous groups, token groups, bicultural groups, and multicultural groups. Several potential problems as well as advantages are associated with multicultural, diverse teams.

6. A number of guidelines have proved to be particularly effective in managing culturally diverse groups. These include careful selection of the members, identification of the group's goals, establishment of equal power and mutual respect among the participants, and delivering positive feedback on performance. A good example of how these guidelines have been used is the NUMMI joint venture created by General Motors and Toyota.

KEY TERMS

bicultural group, *169*

Eiffel Tower culture, *161*

family culture, *161*

groupthink, *171*

guided missile culture, *162*

homogeneous group, *168*

incubator culture, *163*

multicultural group, *169*

organizational culture, *154*

token group, *169*

REVIEW AND DISCUSSION QUESTIONS

1. Some researchers have found that when Germans work for a U.S. MNC, they become even more German, and when Americans work for a German MNC, they become even more American. Why would this knowledge be important to these MNCs?

2. When comparing the negotiating styles and strategies of French versus Spanish negotiators, a number of sharp contrasts are evident. What are three of these, and what could MNCs do to improve their position when negotiating with either group?

3. In which of the four types of organizational cultures—family, Eiffel Tower, guided missile, incubator—would most people in the United States feel comfortable? In which would most Japanese feel comfortable? Based on your answers, what conclusions could you draw regarding the importance of understanding organizational culture for international management?

4. Most MNCs need not enter foreign markets to face the challenge of dealing with multiculturalism. Do you agree or disagree with this statement? Explain your answer.

5. What are some potential problems that must be overcome when using multicultural, diverse teams in today's organizations? What are some recognized advantages? Identify and discuss two of each.

6. A number of guidelines can be valuable in helping MNCs to make diverse teams more effective. What are five of these? Additionally, what underlying principles guided NUMMI in its effective use of multicultural teams? Were the principles used by NUMMI similar to the general guidelines identified in this chapter, or were they significantly different? Explain your answer.

INTERNET EXERCISE: HEWLETT-PACKARD'S INTERNATIONAL FOCUS

Mention the name Hewlett-Packard, or HP for short, and people are likely to think of printers—an area where the MNC has managed to excel worldwide in recent years. However, HP has many other offerings besides printers and has rapidly expanded its product line into the international arena over the last decade. Visit its Web site at **www.hp.com** and review some of the latest developments. In particular, pay close attention to its product line and international expansion. Then choose three different countries where the firm is doing business: one from the Americas, one from Europe, and one from Southeast Asia or India. (The sites are all presented in the local language, so you might want to make India your choice because this site is in English.) Compare and contrast the product offerings and ways in which HP goes about marketing itself over the Web in these locations. What do you see as some of the major differences? Second, using Figure 6–2 and Table 6–3 as your guide, in what way are differences in organizational cultures internationally likely to present significant challenges to HP's efforts to create a smooth-running international enterprise? What would you see as two of the critical issues with which management will have to deal? Third, what are two steps that you think HP will have to take in order to build multicultural team effectiveness? What are two guidelines that can help them do this?

Japan

Japan is located in eastern Asia, and it comprises a curved chain of more than 3,000 islands. Four of these—Hokkaido, Honshu, Shikoku, and Kyushi—account for 89 percent of the country's land area. The population of Japan is approximately 128 million, with over 12 million people living in the nation's capital, Tokyo. According to the World Bank, the country's gross domestic product in 2003 was approximately $28,700 per capita. The country has been in the throes of an economic recession that has been going on for over 10 years. While economic conditions have been slowly improving, Japan's huge government debt, which is approaching 150 percent of GDP, and the aging of the population, are two long-run problems that must be addressed. On the positive side, Japan's economy surged in early 2004, with 5.6 percent GDP growth in the first quarter and a rise in industrial production of 3.3 percent.

An optimistic outlook is shared by two multinationals, one from the United States and the other from Germany. These two MNCs recently joined forces with a large Japanese MNC to create a new retailing chain throughout Japan. The joint venture will limit its merchandise selection to clothing and toys, which are two product areas where Japanese prices are relatively higher than those paid by consumers in other countries. The U.S. and German partners will design the clothing and toys, but they will be produced in Japan by local labor and sold there. The U.S. and German partners will contribute most of the capital needed for the venture, and they also will help design the production and distribution system as well as the retail store layout. The Japanese partner will be responsible for choosing the type of merchandise to be produced, managing or coordinating (for subcontractors) the production facilities, and handling the marketing.

To provide a managerial presence in Japan, the two foreign partners will share a new headquarters building with their local partner. Located approximately 60 miles outside of Tokyo, this building will house the senior-level management from all three MNCs as well as key finance, production, and marketing personnel. The plan is to have strategy and major decisions made at this headquarters, then disseminated to the production facilities and retail stores. The joint venture hopes to have six stores operating within 24 months, and 20 more within five years.
www.japanlink.com

Questions

1. What type of organizational culture is each of the three partners likely to have? (Use Figure 6–3 as a guide in answering this question.)

2. Which of the organizational cultures will be most different from that of the other two? Explain.

3. What types of problems might the culturally diverse top management team at headquarters create for the joint venture? Give some specific examples. How could these problems be overcome?

4. In terms of organizational culture, what is your estimate of success for this joint venture?

A Good-Faith Effort Is Needed

Excelsior Manufacturing is a medium-sized firm located in the northeastern part of the United States. Excelsior has long been known as a high-quality, world-class producer of precision tools. Recently, however, this MNC has been slowly losing market share in Europe because many EU companies are turning to other European firms to save on taxes and transportation costs. Realizing that it needed a European partner if it hoped to recapture this lost ground, Excelsior began looking to buy a firm that could provide it a strong foothold in this market. After a brief search, the MNC made contact with Quality Instrumentation, a Madrid-based firm that was founded five years ago and has been growing at 25 percent annually. Excelsior currently is discussing a buyout with Quality Instrumentation, and the Spanish firm appears to be interested in the arrangement as it will provide them with increased technology, a quality reputation, and more funding for European expansion.

Next week, owners of the two companies are scheduled to meet in Madrid to discuss purchase price and potential plans for integrating their overall operations. The biggest sticking point appears to be a concern for meshing the organizational cultures and the work values and habits of the two enterprises. Each is afraid that the other's way of doing business might impede overall progress and lead to wasted productivity and lost profit. To deal with this issue, the president of Excelsior has asked his management team to draft a plan that could serve as a guide in determining how both groups could coordinate their efforts.

On a personal level, the head of Excelsior believes that it will be important for the Spanish management team to understand that if the Spaniards sell the business, they must be prepared to let U.S. managers have final decision-making power on major issues, such as research and development efforts, expansion plans, and customer segmentation. At the same time, the Americans are concerned that their potential European partners will feel they are being told what to do and resist these efforts. "We're going to have to make them understand that we must work as a unified team," the president explained to his planning committee, "and create a culture that will support this idea. We may not know a lot about working with Spaniards and they may not understand a great deal about how Americans do things, but I believe that we can resolve these differences if we put forth a good-faith effort."

Questions

1. What do you think some of the main organizational culture differences between the two companies would be?

2. Why might the cultural diversity in the Spanish firm not be as great as that in the U.S. firm, and what potential problems could this create?

3. What would you recommend be done to effectively merge the two organizational cultures and ensure they cooperate harmoniously? Offer some specific recommendations.

Chapter 7

CROSS-CULTURAL COMMUNICATION AND NEGOTIATION

Communication takes on special importance in international management because of the difficulties in conveying meanings between parties from different cultures. The problems of misinterpretation and error are compounded in the international context. Chapter 7 examines how the communication process in general works, and it looks at the downward and upward communication flows that commonly are used in international communication. Then the chapter examines the major barriers to effective international communication and reviews ways of dealing with these communication problems. Finally, international negotiation is examined, with particular attention to how negotiation approaches and strategies must be adapted to different cultural environments. The specific objectives of this chapter are:

1. **DEFINE** the term *communication,* examine some examples of verbal communication styles, and explain the importance of message interpretation.

2. **ANALYZE** the common downward and upward communication flows used in international communication.

3. **EXAMINE** the language, perception, and culture of communication, and nonverbal barriers to effective international communications.

4. **PRESENT** the steps that can be taken to overcome international communication problems.

5. **DEVELOP** approaches to international negotiations that respond to differences in culture.

6. **REVIEW** different negotiating and bargaining behaviors that may improve negotiations and outcomes.

The World of *BusinessWeek*

BusinessWeek

A New World for Microsoft?

If the EU Ruling Against the Software Giant Is Upheld, It Could Force Changes in the Way Redmond Does Business

For 14 years, one regulator or another has chased after Microsoft—mostly unsuccessfully. In 1990, the Federal Trade Commission launched an investigation into a long list of allegedly predatory practices. The probe was dropped. In 1998, the Justice Dept. tried to prevent Microsoft from using its Windows monopoly to corner the emerging Web browser market. Microsoft fought back and got only a slap on the wrist. Now European regulators are taking their shot at restraining the software giant. Microsoft is fighting back again, but there's a reasonable chance that regulators will at last help rivals compete with Goliath on a more equal footing.

In its March 24 ruling, the European Union labeled Microsoft an abusive monopolist and issued a sweeping set of penalties. The company will have to offer computer makers in Europe two versions of its monopoly Windows operating system: one with Windows Media Player, which lets users watch videos and hear music, and one without. The EU also ruled that Microsoft must share technical information with rivals that will help their server software work better with Windows. And the commission slapped Microsoft with the biggest fine it has ever levied—$613 million. "We are simply ensuring that anyone who develops new software has a fair opportunity to compete in the marketplace," says Mario Monti, competition commissioner for the EU.

How the European Union's decision could hamper the software giant:

Bundling
Microsoft continually adds features to Windows. It's possible that competitors will use the ruling to prevent Microsoft from adding things and exercising its monopoly power to grab share in their markets. If Windows lacks jazzy new features, Microsoft's customers might not feel compelled to upgrade as often.

Information Sharing
Microsoft puts technology into its software for PCs, handhelds, and servers that smoothes interactions among them. The EU ruling forces Microsoft to disclose these "secret handshakes" among its products, which should allow server-software makers such as Sun Microsystems and IBM to compete more effectively.

Next-Generation Integration
Microsoft's next wave of desktop and server products, code-named Longhorn, is seen by rivals as a Pandora's Box of bundling. After the ruling, Microsoft may have to rethink the way it designs these products, weakening its ability to push into new markets and delaying Longhorn's arrival.

Target: Bundling

The ruling strikes at the heart of Microsoft's strategy. For more than a decade, it has bundled new features into Windows, giving customers reasons to upgrade—and often trouncing rivals in the process. But in finding that Microsoft has illegally leveraged the power of its Windows monopoly to destroy its competition, the EU is trying to do more than just punish Microsoft for past transgressions. If the ruling is upheld, it could seriously limit Microsoft's ability to add features to its software in the future. It also offers the potential of far faster relief for rivals who feel they've been wronged.

Although the ruling officially applies only to Europe, its impact is expected to be felt worldwide. "As far as the eye can see, Microsoft is going to be challenged by competitors and by governments anytime it wants to add something to Windows," says Michael A. Cusumano, a professor at Massachusetts Institute of Technology's Sloan School of Management.

Microsoft wasted no time dismissing the decision as overreaching on the part of Monti. "We believe that every company should be able to improve its products to meet the needs of consumers," says CEO Steven A. Ballmer. What's more, Ballmer calls the standards set by the 2002 settlement in the U.S. antitrust case "guiding principles." He says Microsoft doesn't plan to reconsider its future product design or bundling plans.

The company will appeal the ruling, and it plans to seek a stay of some, if not all, of the penalties. It argues that EU law only empowers the Commission to address "contractual tying," not the sort of technical bundling of products the company does. And it will argue that illegal tying exists only if it's inconsistent with commercial norms, which isn't the case here since every other operating system includes a media player.

Legal Hurdles

There isn't a lot of legal precedent, but to the extent it exists, it tends to favor Monti in the area of tying. For instance, in a 1994 case involving construction products maker Hilti Corp., the European Court of Justice—the highest court on the Continent—upheld a lower court ruling that the company could not force customers who bought its market-dominant nail guns to also buy nails. But in the area of interoperability, available legal precedent tends to favor Microsoft. In a 2002 case involving Intercontinental Marketing Services Health, the Court of First Instance held that dominant companies can refuse to license their intellectual property to rivals. That may give Microsoft grounds for objecting to rules that force it to share proprietary interface information with others.

For the time being, there are more questions than answers, but that uncertainty itself threatens to put Microsoft's software development strategy in doubt. For starters, Microsoft has to gin up a version of Windows without a media player within 90 days. Computer makers can decide if they want to buy Windows-lite and include digital media technology from a Microsoft rival, such as RealNetworks or Apple Computer. But since Microsoft can charge the same for both products, it's unlikely that the media-playerless version will appeal to PC makers. RealNetworks is considering offering computer makers that ship PCs with its media player exclusively the ability to offer free limited subscriptions for such products as its Rhapsody online music service.

The ruling could start to have more impact as soon as next year. That's when Microsoft is considering releasing an intermediate update of Windows that may include the ability to search the Web directly from the main Windows screen. That could put search rivals such as Google at a disadvantage since PCs don't ship with its service displayed in Windows. Google says it doesn't plan to try to block Microsoft in court, but the ruling may give Microsoft pause anyway.

Parole Officer

Those issues compound with Longhorn, the next major version of Windows, expected in 2006 or 2007. Microsoft

179

has talked about including everything from Internet search to speech-recognition software. If rivals complain to the EU, it might try to prevent some of the planned bundling. That could force Microsoft to rethink its design plans for Longhorn, which could delay the product. Microsoft, however, says it has reviewed Longhorn bundling plans with its developers and lawyers and believes they're legal.

Meanwhile, Microsoft's competitors can't wait to take advantage of Monti's ruling on sharing technical information. Right now, Microsoft's desktop and server software packages communicate with one another in a private language. "We have been excluded so far," says Matthew J. Szulik, CEO of Linux software distributor Red Hat. He hopes the ruling will give rivals what they need to smooth their interactions with Windows.

To make all this work, Monti is creating another precedent: a monitoring trustee. Much as federal Judge Harold H. Greene oversaw the breakup of AT&T a quarter-century ago, Monti will appoint a trustee to handle oversight of Microsoft's compliance. The idea is to keep up the pressure on Microsoft so it can't sidestep the penalties by bogging the Commission down in bureaucratic and technical wrangling.

Monopoly Power

While there's a long way to go in this case, it's fundamentally different from what Microsoft faced in the U.S. because EU regulators have more authority than their U.S. counterparts. They get to make an initial determination of liability and

propose a remedy without going to court. To forestall future anticompetitive behavior, they have the authority to quickly investigate and bring new charges against Microsoft if new complaints arise.

In addition, because the ruling contains findings about Microsoft's market dominance and tactics that rivals can use to build future cases, "new cases will be much easier because the law has already been decided," says New York University School of Law antitrust professor Eleanor M. Fox. That could put an end to the cycle that unnerves foes who land in Microsoft's crosshairs: endless legal skirmishes that delay rulings until long after Microsoft has used its monopoly power to pummel them in the marketplace.

It's still too early to say if the ruling will substantially alter Microsoft's conduct. Rivals were jubilant four years ago when U.S. District Judge Thomas Penfield Jackson ruled Microsoft a monopolist and ordered the company split in two. Microsoft managed to escape that fate, and it clearly expects to do the same here. But one thing's for certain: The Old World has imposed a new world order that could make Microsoft mighty uncomfortable.

By Jay Greene in Seattle, Andy Reinhardt in Brussels, and Mike France in New York

The opening news story provides an insightful illustration of the importance and challenges of cross-cultural communication and negotiation. Microsoft is one of the world's largest companies, and its technology has permeated every corner of the globe. Yet it continues to face challenges to its business practices, most notably a series of legal actions in the United States and Europe related to its relationships with suppliers and its "bundling" of services. Microsoft has had difficulty resolving these actions, and recent rulings by the EU demonstrate the challenges of effective communication and negotiations with different constituencies in differing country settings. To be successful, Microsoft must maintain trust and respect in the countries in which it does business. Some stakeholders (customers, suppliers, regulators) object to what they perceive as the company's overly aggressive strategy. This made it more difficult for Microsoft to enlist support in court. To turn things around, Microsoft must make a concerted effort, in each region it serves, to build positive relationships with the range of stakeholders with which it interacts. If the company can do this, its future looks bright.

■ The Overall Communication Process

communication
The process of transferring meanings from sender to receiver.

Communication is the process of transferring meanings from sender to receiver. On the surface, this appears to be a fairly straightforward process. On analysis, however, there are a great many problems in the international arena that can result in the failure to transfer meanings correctly.

Verbal Communication Styles

One way of examining the ways in which individuals convey information is by looking at their communication styles. In particular, as has been noted by Hall, context plays a key role in explaining many communication differences.[1] **Context** is information that surrounds a communication and helps convey the message. In high-context societies, such as Japan and many Arab countries, messages are often highly coded and implicit. As a result, the receiver's job is to interpret what the message means by correctly filtering through what is being said and the way in which the message is being conveyed. This approach is in sharp contrast to low-context societies such as the United States and Canada, where the message is explicit and the speaker says precisely what he or she means. These contextual factors must be considered when marketing messages are being developed in disparate societies. For example, promotions in Japan should be subtle and convey a sense of community (high context). Similar segments in the United States should be responsive to expectations for more explicit messages, a low-context environment. Figure 7–1 provides an international comparison of high-context/implicit and low-context/explicit societies. In addition, Table 7–1 presents some of the major characteristics of communication styles.

context
Information that surrounds a communication and helps to convey the message.

Indirect and Direct Styles In high-context cultures, messages are implicit and indirect. One reason is that those who are communicating—family, friends, co-workers, clients—tend to have both close personal relationships and large information networks. As a result, each knows a lot about others in the communication network; they do not have to rely on language alone to communicate. Voice intonation, timing, and facial expressions can all play roles in conveying information.

In low-context cultures, people often meet only to accomplish objectives. Since they do not know each other very well, they tend to be direct and focused in their communications.

A good example comparing these two kinds of culture—high context and low context—is the types of questions that are typically asked when someone is contacted and told to attend a meeting. In a high-context culture it is common for the person to ask, "Who will be at this meeting?" The individual wants to be prepared to interact correctly. In contrast, in a low-context culture the individual is likely to ask, "What is the meeting going to be about?" In the high-context society, the person focuses on the environment in which the meeting will take place. In the low-context society, the individual is most interested in the objectives that are to be accomplished at the meeting.

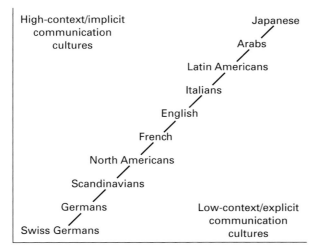

High-context/implicit communication cultures
Japanese
Arabs
Latin Americans
Italians
English
French
North Americans
Scandinavians
Germans
Swiss Germans
Low-context/explicit communication cultures

Figure 7–1

Explicit/Implicit Communication: An International Comparison

Source: Adapted from Martin Rosch, "Communications: Focal Point of Culture," *Management International Review* 27, no. 4 (1987), p. 60. Used with permission.

Table 7–1
Major Characteristics of Verbal Styles

Verbal Style	Major Variation	Interaction Focus and Content	Cultures in Which Characteristic Is Found
Indirect vs. direct	Indirect	Implicit messages	Collective, high context
	Direct	Explicit messages	Individualistic, low context
Succinct vs. elaborate	Elaborate	High quantity of talk	Moderate uncertainty avoidance, high context
	Exacting	Moderate amount of talk	Low uncertainty avoidance, low context
	Succinct	Low amount of talk	High uncertainty avoidance, high context
Contextual vs. personal	Contextual	Focus is on the speaker and role relationships	High power distance, collective, high context
	Personal	Focus is on the speaker and personal relationships	Low power distance, individualistic, low context
Affective vs. instrumental	Affective	Language is process oriented and receiver focused	Collective, high context
	Instrumental	Language is goal oriented and sender focused	Individualistic, low context

Elaborate and Succinct Styles There are three degrees of communication quantity—elaborate, exacting, and succinct. In high-context societies, the elaborate style is often very common. There is a great deal of talking, description includes much detail, and people often repeat themselves. This elaborate style is widely used in Arabic countries.

The exacting style is more common in nations such as England, Germany, and Sweden, to name three. This style focuses on precision and the use of the right amount of words to convey the message. If a person uses too many words, this is considered exaggeration; if the individual relies on too few, the result is an ambiguous message.

The succinct style is most common in Asia, where people tend to say few words and allow understatements, pauses, and silence to convey meaning. In particular, in unfamiliar situations, communicators are succinct in order to avoid risking a loss of face.

Researchers have found that the elaborating style is more popular in high-context cultures that have a moderate degree of uncertainty avoidance. The exacting style is more common in low-context, low-uncertainty-avoidance cultures. The succinct style is more common in high-context cultures with considerable uncertainty avoidance.

Contextual and Personal Styles A contextual style is one that focuses on the speaker and relationship of the parties. For example, in Asian cultures people use words that reflect the role and hierarchical relationship of those in the conversation. As a result, in an organizational setting, speakers will choose words that indicate their status relative to the status of the others. Commenting on this idea, Yoshimura and Anderson have noted that white-collar, middle-management employees in Japan, commonly known as salarymen, quickly learn how to communicate with others in the organization by understanding the context and reference group of the other party:

> A salaryman can hardly say a word to another person without implicitly defining the reference groups to which he thinks both of them belong. . . . [This is because] failing to use proper language is socially embarrassing, and the correct form of Japanese to use with someone else depends not only on the relationship between the two people, but also on the relationship

between their reference groups. Juniors defer to seniors in Japan, but even this relationship is complicated when the junior person works for a much more prestigious organization (for example, a government bureau) than the senior. [As a result, it is] likely that both will use the polite form to avoid social embarrassment.[2]

A personal style focuses on the speaker and the reduction of barriers between the parties. In the United States, for example, it is common to use first names and to address others informally and directly on an equal basis.

Researchers have found that the contextual style is often associated with high-power-distance, collective, high-context cultures. Examples include Japan, India, and Ghana. In contrast, the personal style is more popular in low-power-distance, individualistic, low-context cultures. Examples include the United States, Australia, and Canada.

Affective and Instrumental Styles The affective style is characterized by language that requires the listener to carefully note what is being said and to observe how the sender is presenting the message. Quite often the meaning that is being conveyed is nonverbal and requires the receiver to use his or her intuitive skills in deciphering what is being said. The part of the message that is being left out may be just as important as the part that is being included. In contrast, the instrumental style is goal oriented and focuses on the sender. The individual clearly lets the other party know what he or she wants the other party to know.

The affective style is common in collective, high-context cultures such as the Middle East, Latin America, and Asia. The instrumental style is more commonly found in individualistic, low-context cultures such as Switzerland, Denmark, and the United States.

Table 7–2 provides a brief description of the four verbal styles that are used in select countries. A close look at the table helps explain why managers in Japan can have great difficulty communicating with their counterparts in the United States and vice versa: The verbal styles are completely opposite.

Interpretation of Communications

The effectiveness of communication in the international context often is determined by how closely the sender and receiver have the same meaning for the same message.[3] If this meaning is different, effective communication will not occur. A good example is the U.S. firm that wanted to increase worker output among its Japanese personnel. This firm put an individual incentive plan into effect, whereby workers would be given extra pay based on their

---

Table 7–2
Verbal Styles Used in 10 Select Countries

Country	Indirect vs. Direct	Elaborate vs. Succinct	Contextual vs. Personal	Affective vs. Instrumental
Australia	Direct	Exacting	Personal	Instrumental
Canada	Direct	Exacting	Personal	Instrumental
Denmark	Direct	Exacting	Personal	Instrumental
Egypt	Indirect	Elaborate	Contextual	Affective
England	Direct	Exacting	Personal	Instrumental
Japan	Indirect	Succinct	Contextual	Affective
Korea	Indirect	Succinct	Contextual	Affective
Saudi Arabia	Indirect	Elaborate	Contextual	Affective
Sweden	Direct	Exacting	Personal	Instrumental
United States	Direct	Exacting	Personal	Instrumental

Source: Reported in Anne Marie Francesco and Barry Allen Gold, *International Organizational Behavior* (Upper Saddle River, NJ: Prentice-Hall, 1998), p. 60.

work output. The plan, which had worked well in the United States, was a total flop. The Japanese were accustomed to working in groups and to being rewarded as a group. In another case, a U.S. firm offered a bonus to anyone who would provide suggestions that resulted in increased productivity. The Japanese workers rejected this idea, because they felt that no one working alone is responsible for increased productivity. It is always a group effort. When the company changed the system and began rewarding group productivity, it was successful in gaining support for the program.

A related case occurs when both parties agree on the content of the message but one party believes it is necessary to persuade the other to accept the message. Here is an example:

> Motorola University recently prepared carefully for a presentation in China. After considerable thought, the presenters entitled it "Relationships do not retire." The gist of the presentation was that Motorola had come to China in order to stay and help the economy to create wealth. Relationships with Chinese suppliers, subcontractors and employees would constitute a permanent commitment to building Chinese economic infrastructure and earning hard currency through exports. The Chinese audience listened politely to this presentation but was quiet when invited to ask questions. Finally one manager put up his hand and said: "Can you tell us about pay for performance?"[4]

Quite obviously, the Motorola presenter believed that it was necessary to convince the audience that the company was in China for the long run. Those in attendance, however, had already accepted this idea and wanted to move on to other issues.

Still another example has been provided by Adler, who has pointed out that people doing business in a foreign culture often misinterpret the meaning of messages. As a result, they arrive at erroneous conclusions as in the following story of a Canadian doing business in the Middle East. The Canadian was surprised when his meeting with a high-ranking official was not held in a closed office and was constantly interrupted:

> Using the Canadian-based cultural assumptions that (a) important people have large private offices with secretaries to monitor the flow of people into the office, and (b) important business takes precedence over less important business and is therefore not interrupted, the Canadian interprets the . . . open office and constant interruptions to mean that the official is neither as high ranking nor as interested in conducting the business at hand as he had previously thought.[5]

■ Communication Flows

Communication flows in international organizations move both down and up. However, as Figure 7–2 humorously, but in many ways accurately, portrays, there are some unique differences in organizations around the world.

Downward Communication

downward
communication
The transmission of
information from superior
to subordinate.

Downward communication is the transmission of information from manager to subordinate. The primary purpose of the manager-initiated communication flow is to convey orders and information. Managers use this channel to let their people know what is to be done and how well they are doing. The channel facilitates the flow of information to those who need it for operational purposes.

In Asian countries, as noted earlier, downward communication is less direct than in the United States. Orders tend to be implicit in nature. Conversely, in some European countries, downward communication is not only direct but extends beyond business matters. For example, one early study surveyed 299 U.S. and French managers regarding the nature of downward communication and the managerial authority they perceived themselves as having. This study found that U.S. managers basically used downward communication for work-related matters. A follow-up study investigated matters that U.S. and French managers felt were within the purview of their authority.[6] The major differences involved work-related and nonwork-related activities: U.S. managers felt that it was within their authority

There are a number of different "organization charts" that have been constructed to depict international organizations. An epigram is a poem or line of verse that is witty or satirical in nature. The following organization designs are epigrams that show how communication occurs in different countries. In examining them, remember that each contains considerable exaggeration and humor, but also some degree of truth.

In America, everyone thinks he or she has a communication pipeline directly to the top.

America

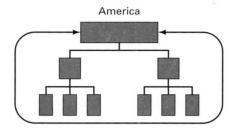

There are so many people in China that organizations are monolithic structures characterized by copious levels of bureaucracy. All information flows through channels.

China

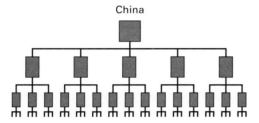

At the United Nations everyone is arranged in a circle so that no one is more powerful than anyone else. Those directly in front or behind are philosophically aligned, and those nearby form part of an international bloc.

United Nations

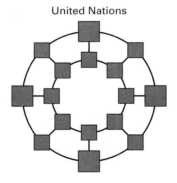

In France some people in the hierarchy are not linked to anyone, indicating how haphazard the structure can be.

France

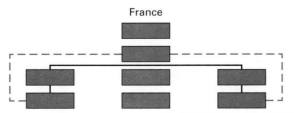

Figure 7–2

Communication Epigrams

Source: Adapted from Simcha Ronen, *Comparative and Multinational Management* (New York: Wiley, 1986), pp. 318–319. The epigrams in turn were derived from a variety of sources, including Robert M. Worchester of the U.K.-based Market and Opinion Research International (MORI), Ole Jacob Raad of Norway's PM Systems, and anonymous managers.

to communicate or attempt to influence their people's social behavior only if it occurred on the job or it directly affected their work. For example, U.S. managers felt that it was proper to look into matters such as how much an individual drinks at lunch, whether the person uses profanity in the workplace, and how active the individual is in recruiting others to join the company. The French managers were not as supportive of these activities. The researcher concluded that "the Americans find it as difficult [as] or more difficult than the French to accept the legitimacy of managerial authority in areas unrelated to work."[7]

Harris and Moran have noted that when communicating downward with non-native speakers, it is extremely important to use language that is easy to understand and allows the other person to ask questions. Here are 10 suggestions that apply not only for downward but for all types of communication:

1. Use the most common words with their most common meanings.
2. Select words that have few alternative meanings.
3. Strictly follow the basic rules of grammar—more so than would be the case with native speakers.
4. Speak with clear breaks between the words so that it is easier for the person to follow.
5. Avoid using words that are esoteric or culturally biased such as "he struck out" or "the whole idea is Mickey Mouse" because these clichés often have no meaning for the listener.
6. Avoid the use of slang.
7. Do not use words or expressions that require the other person to create a mental image such as "we were knee deep in the Big Muddy."
8. Mimic the cultural flavor of the non-native speaker's language, for example, by using more flowery communication with Spanish-speaking listeners than with Germans.
9. Continually paraphrase and repeat the basic ideas.
10. At the end, test how well the other person understands by asking the individual to paraphrase what has been said.[8]

Upward Communication

upward communication
The transfer of meaning from subordinate to superior.

Upward communication is the transfer of information from subordinate to superior. The primary purpose of this subordinate-initiated upward communication is to provide feedback, ask questions, or obtain assistance from higher-level management. In recent years, there has been a call for and a concerted effort to promote more upward communication in the United States. In other countries, such as in Japan, Hong Kong, and Singapore, upward communication has long been a fact of life. Managers in these countries have extensively used suggestion systems and quality circles to get employee input and always are available to listen to their people's concerns.

Here are some observations from the approach the Japanese firm Matsushita uses in dealing with employee suggestions:

> Matsushita views employee recommendations as instrumental to making improvements on the shop floor and in the marketplace. [It believes] that a great many little people, paying attention each day to how to improve their jobs, can accomplish more than a whole headquarters full of production engineers and planners.
>
> Praise and positive reinforcement are an important part of the Matsushita philosophy. . . . Approximately 90 percent of . . . suggestions receive rewards; most only a few dollars per month, but the message is reinforced constantly: "Think about your job; develop yourself and help us improve the company." The best suggestions receive company-wide recognition and can earn substantial monetary rewards. Each year, many special awards are also given, including presidential prizes and various divisional honors.[9]

Table 7–3
Matsushita's Philosophy

Basic Business Principles

To recognize our responsibilities as industrialists, to foster progress, to promote the general welfare of society, and to devote ourselves to the further development of world culture.

Employees Creed

Progress and development can be realized only through the combined efforts and cooperation of each member of the Company. Each of us, therefore, shall keep this idea constantly in mind as we devote ourselves to the continuous improvement of our Company.

The Seven Spiritual Values

1. National service through industry
2. Fairness
3. Harmony and cooperation
4. Struggle for betterment
5. Courtesy and humility
6. Adjustment and assimilation
7. Gratitude

Matsushita has used the same approach wherever it has established plants worldwide, and the strategy has proved very successful. The company has all its employees begin the day by reciting its basic principles, beliefs, and values, which are summarized in Table 7–3, to reinforce in all employees the reason for the company's existence and to provide a form of spiritual fabric to energize and sustain them. All employees see themselves as important members of a successful team, and they are willing to do whatever is necessary to ensure the success of the group.

Outside these Asian countries, upward communication is not as popular. For example, in South America, many managers believe that employees should follow orders and not ask a lot of questions. German managers also make much less use of this form of communication. In most cases, however, evidence shows that employees prefer to have downward communication at least supplemented by upward channels. Unfortunately, such upward communication does not always occur because of a number of communication barriers.

■ Communication Barriers

A number of common communication barriers are relevant to international management. The more important include language, culture, perception, and nonverbal communication.

Language Barriers

Knowledge of the home country's language (the language used at the headquarters of the MNC) is important for personnel placed in a foreign assignment. If managers do not understand the language that is used at headquarters, they likely will make a wide assortment of errors. Additionally, many MNCs now prescribe English as the common language for internal communication, so that managers can more easily convey information to their counterparts in other geographically dispersed locales.[10] Despite such progress, however, language training continues to lag in many areas, although in an increasing number of European countries, more and more young people are becoming multilingual.[11] Table 7–4 shows the percentage of European students who are studying English, French, or German.

Language education is a good beginning, but it is also important to realize that the ability to speak the language used at MNC headquarters is often not enough to ensure that the personnel are capable of doing the work. Stout recently noted that many MNCs worldwide

Table 7–4
Multilingualism in the EU Classroom

	Percentage of Pupils in General Secondary Education Learning English, French, or German as a Foreign Language, 1991–1992		
	English	French	German
Holland	96	65	53
Germany	93	23	—
Denmark	92	8	58
Spain	92	10	0.3
France	84	—	27
Belgium (Flemish)	68	98	22
Belgium (French)	58	1	6
Italy	61	33	3
Portugal	55	25	0.4
Britain	—	59	20
Ireland	—	69	24

Source: Eurostat (1995).

place a great deal of attention on the applicant's ability to speak English without considering if the person has other necessary skills such as the ability to interact well with others and the technical knowledge demanded by the job.[12] Additionally, in interviewing people for jobs, he has noted that many interviewers fail to take into account the applicant's culture. As a result, interviewers misinterpret behaviors such as quietness or shyness and use them to conclude that the applicant is not sufficiently confident or self-assured. Still another problem is that nonnative speakers may know the language but not be fully fluent, so they end up asking questions or making statements that convey the wrong message. After studying Japanese for only one year, Stout began interviewing candidates in their local language and made a number of mistakes. In one case, he reports, "a young woman admitted to having an adulterous affair—even though this was not even close to the topic I was inquiring about—because of my unskilled use of the language."[13]

More recently, written communication has been getting increased attention, because poor writing is proving to be a greater barrier than poor talking. For example, Hildebrandt has found that among U.S. subsidiaries studied in Germany, language was a major problem when subsidiaries were sending written communications to the home office. The process often involved elaborate procedures associated with translating and reworking the report. Typical steps included (1) holding a staff conference to determine what was to be included in the written message; (2) writing the initial draft in German; (3) rewriting the draft in German; (4) translating the material into English; (5) consulting with bilingual staff members regarding the translation; and (6) rewriting the English draft a series of additional times until the paper was judged to be acceptable for transmission. The German managers admitted that they felt uncomfortable with writing, because their command of written English was poor. As Hildebrandt noted:

> All German managers commanding oral English stated that their grammatical competence was not sufficiently honed to produce a written English report of top quality. Even when professional translators from outside the company rewrote the German into English, German middle managers were unable to verify whether the report captured the substantive intent or included editorial alterations.[14]

Problems associated with the translation of information from one language to another have been made even clearer by Schermerhorn, who conducted research among 153 Hong Kong Chinese bilinguals who were enrolled in an undergraduate management course at a major Hong Kong university. The students were given two scenarios written in either English or Chinese. One scenario involved a manager who was providing some form of personal support or praise for a subordinate. The research used the following procedures:

> [A] careful translation and back-translation method was followed to create the Chinese language versions of the research instruments. Two bilingual Hong Kong Chinese, both highly fluent in English and having expertise in the field of management, shared roles in the process. Each first translated one scenario and the evaluation questions into Chinese. Next they translated each other's Chinese versions back into English, and discussed and resolved translation differences in group consultation with the author. Finally, a Hong Kong professor read and interpreted the translations correctly as a final check of equivalency.[15]

The participants were asked to answer eight evaluation questions about these scenarios. A significant difference between the two sets of responses was found. Those who were queried in Chinese gave different answers from those who were queried in English. This led Schermerhorn to conclude that language plays a key role in conveying information between cultures, and that in cross-cultural management research, bilingual individuals should not be queried in their second language.

Cultural Barriers

Closely related to the language barriers are cultural barriers. For example, research by Sims and Guice compared 214 letters of inquiry written by native and nonnative speakers of English to test the assumption that cultural factors affect business communication. Among other things, the researchers found that nonnative speakers used exaggerated politeness, provided unnecessary professional and personal information, and made inappropriate requests of the other party. Commenting on the results and implications of their study, the researchers noted that their investigation

> indicates that the deviations from standard U.S. business communication practices were not specific to one or more nationalities. The deviations did not occur among specific nationalities but were spread throughout the sample of nonnative letters used for the study. Therefore, we can speculate that U.S. native speakers of English might have similar difficulties in international settings. In other words, a significant number of native speakers in the U.S. might deviate from the standard business communication practices of other cultures. Therefore, these native speakers need specific training in the business communication practices of the major cultures of the world so they can communicate successfully and acceptably with readers in those cultures.[16]

Research by Scott and Green has extended these findings, showing that even in English-speaking countries, there are different approaches to writing letters. In the United States, for example, it is common practice when constructing a bad-news letter to start out "with a pleasant, relevant, neutral, and transitional buffer statement; give the reasons for the unfavorable news before presenting the bad news; present the refusal in a positive manner; imply the bad news whenever possible; explain how the refusal is in the reader's best interest; and suggest positive alternatives that build goodwill."[17] In Great Britain, however, it is common to start out by referring to the situation, discussing the reasons for the bad news, conveying the bad news (often quite bluntly), and concluding with an apology or statement of regret (something that is frowned on by business-letter experts in the United States) designed to keep the reader's goodwill. Here is an example:

> Lord Hanson has asked me to reply to your letter and questionnaire of February 12 which we received today.
>
> As you may imagine, we receive numerous requests to complete questionnaires or to participate in a survey, and this poses problems for us. You will appreciate that the time it would take to complete these requests would represent a full-time job, so we decided some while ago to decline such requests unless there was some obvious benefit to Hanson PLC and our stockholders. As I am sure you will understand, our prime responsibility is to look after our stockholders' interests.
>
> I apologize that this will not have been the response that you were hoping for, but I wish you success with your research study.[18]

U.S. MNC managers would seldom, if ever, send that type of letter; it would be viewed as blunt and tactless. However, the indirect approach that Americans use would be viewed by their British counterparts as overly indirect and obviously insincere.

On the other hand, when compared to Asians, many American writers are far more blunt and direct. For example, Park, Dillon, and Mitchell reported that there are pronounced differences between the ways in which Americans and Asians write business letters of complaint. They compared the approach used by American managers for whom English is a first language, who wrote international business letters of complaint, with the approach of Korean managers for whom English is a second language, who wrote the same types of letters. They found that American writers used a direct organizational pattern and tended to state the main idea or problem first before sharing explanatory details that clearly related to the stated problem. In contrast, the standard Korean pattern was indirect and tended to delay the reader's discovery of the main point. This led the researchers to conclude that the U.S.-generated letter might be regarded as rude by Asian readers, while American readers might regard the letter from the Korean writer as vague, emotional, and accusatory.[19]

Perceptual Barriers

perception
A person's view of reality.

Perception is a person's view of reality. How people see reality can vary and will influence their judgment and decision making.[20] One example involves Japanese stockbrokers who perceived that the chances of improving their career would be better with U.S. firms, so they changed jobs. Another involves Hong Kong hoteliers who began buying U.S. properties because they had the perception that if they could offer the same top-quality hotel service as back home, they could dominate their U.S. markets. These are examples of how perceptions can play an important role in international management. Unfortunately, misperceptions also can become a barrier to effective communication. For example, when the Clinton administration decided to allow Taiwan president Lee Tenghui to visit the United States, the Chinese (PRC) government perceived this as a threatening gesture and took actions of its own. Besides conducting dangerous war games very near Taiwan's border as a warning to Taiwan not to become too bold in its quest for recognition as a sovereign nation, the PRC also snubbed U.S. car manufacturers and gave a much-coveted $1 billion contract to Mercedes-Benz of Germany.[21] The following sections provide examples of perception barriers in the international arena.

Advertising Messages   One way that perception can prove to be a problem in international management communication is evident when one person uses words that are misinterpreted by the other. Many firms have found to their dismay that a failure to understand home-country perceptions can result in disastrous advertising programs. Here are two examples:

> Ford . . . introduced a low cost truck, the "Fiera," into some Spanish-speaking countries. Unfortunately, the name meant "ugly old woman" in Spanish. Needless to say, this name did not encourage sales. Ford also experienced slow sales when it introduced a top-of-the-line automobile, the "Comet," in Mexico under the name "Caliente." The puzzling low sales were finally understood when Ford discovered that "caliente" is slang for a street walker.[22]

> One laundry detergent company certainly wishes now that it had contacted a few locals before it initiated its promotional campaign in the Middle East. All of the company's advertisements pictured soiled clothes on the left, its box of soap in the middle, and clean clothes on the right. But, because in that area of the world people tend to read from the right to the left, many potential customers interpreted the message to indicate the soap actually soiled the clothes.[23]

View of Others   Perception influences communication when it deals with how individuals "see" others. A good example is provided by the perception of foreigners who reside in the United States. Most Americans see themselves as extremely friendly, outgoing, and kind, and they believe that others also see them in this way. At the same time, many are not aware of what negative impressions they give to others. Another example is the way in

Doing It Right the First Time

Like other countries of the world, Japan has its own business customs and culture. And when someone fails to adhere to these traditions, the individual runs the risk of being perceived as ineffective or uncaring. The following addresses three areas that are important in being correctly perceived by one's Japanese counterparts.

Business Cards

The exchange of business cards is an integral part of Japanese business etiquette, and Japanese businesspeople exchange these cards when meeting someone for the first time. Additionally, those who are most likely to interface with non-Japanese are supplied with business cards printed in Japanese on one side and a foreign language, usually English, on the reverse side. This is aimed at enhancing recognition and pronunciation of Japanese names, which are often unfamiliar to foreign businesspeople. Conversely, it is advisable for foreign businesspeople to carry and exchange with their Japanese counterparts a similar type of card printed in Japanese and in their native language. These cards can often be obtained through business centers in major hotels.

When receiving a card, it is considered common courtesy to offer one in return. In fact, not returning a card might convey the impression that the manager is not committed to a meaningful business relationship in the future.

Business cards should be presented and received with both hands. When presenting one's card, the presenter's name should be facing the person who is receiving the card so the receiver can easily read it. When receiving a business card, it should be handled with care and if the receiver is sitting at a conference or other type of table, the card should be placed in front of the individual for the duration of the meeting. It is considered rude to put a prospective business partner's card in one's pocket before sitting down to discuss business matters.

Bowing

Although the handshake is increasingly common in Japan, bowing remains the most prevalent formal method of greeting, saying goodbye, expressing gratitude, or apologizing to another person. When meeting foreign businesspeople, however, Japanese will often use the handshake or a combination of both a handshake and a bow, even though there are different forms and styles of bowing, depending on the relationship of the parties involved. Foreign businesspeople are not expected to be familiar with these intricacies, and therefore a deep nod of the head or a slight bow will suffice in most cases. Many foreign businesspeople are unsure whether to use a handshake or to bow. In these situations, it is best to wait and see if one's Japanese counterpart offers a hand or prefers to bow and then to follow suit.

Attire

Most Japanese businessmen dress in conservative dark or navy blue suits, although slight variations in style and color have come to be accepted in recent years. As a general rule, what is acceptable business attire in virtually any industrialized country is usually regarded as good business attire in Japan as well. Although there is no need to conform precisely to the style of dress of the Japanese, good judgment should be exercised when selecting attire for a business meeting. If unsure about what constitutes appropriate attire for a particular situation, it is best to err on the conservative side.

---

which people act, or should act, when initially meeting others. "International Management in Action: Doing It Right the First Time" provides some insights regarding how to conduct oneself when doing business in Japan.

Another example of how the perceptions of others affect communication occurs in the way that some international managers perceive their subordinates. For example, a study examined the perceptions that German and U.S. managers had of the qualifications of their peers (those on the same level and status), managers, and subordinates in Europe and Latin America.[24] The findings showed that both the German and the U.S. respondents perceived their subordinates to be less qualified than their peers. However, although the Germans perceived their managers to have more managerial ability than their peers, the Americans felt that their South American peers in many instances had qualifications equal to or better than the qualifications of their own managers. Quite obviously, this perception will affect how U.S. expatriates communicate with their South American peers as well as how the expatriates communicate with their bosses.

Another study found that Western managers have more favorable attitudes toward women as managers than Asian or Saudi managers do.[25] This perception obviously affects the way these managers interact and communicate with their female counterparts. The same is true in the case of many Japanese managers, who, according to one survey, still regard women as superfluous to the effective running of their organizations and generally continue to not treat women as equals.[26]

The Impact of Culture

Besides language and perception, another major barrier to communication is culture, a topic that was given detailed attention in Chapter 4. Culture can affect communication in a number of ways, and one way is through the impact of cultural values.

Cultural Values　　One expert on Middle Eastern countries notes that people there do not relate to and communicate with each other in a loose, general way as do those in the United States. Relationships are more intense and binding in the Middle East, and a wide variety of work-related values influence what people in the Middle East will and will not do.

> In North American society, the generally professed prevalent pattern is one of nonclass-consciousness, as far as work is concerned. Students, for example, make extra pocket money by taking all sorts of part-time jobs—manual and otherwise—regardless of the socioeconomic stratum to which the individual belongs. The attitude is uninhibited. In the Middle East, the overruling obsession is how the money is made and via what kind of job.[27]

These types of values indirectly, and in many cases directly, affect communication between people from different cultures. For example, one would communicate differently with a "rich college student" from the United States than with one from Saudi Arabia. Similarly, when negotiating with managers from other cultures, knowing the way to handle the deal requires an understanding of cultural values.[28]

Another cultural value example is the way that people use time. In the United States, people believe that time is an asset and is not to be wasted. This is an idea that has limited meaning in some other cultures. Various values are reinforced and reflected in proverbs that Americans are taught from an early age. These proverbs help to guide people's behavior. Table 7–5 lists some examples.

Misinterpretation　　Cultural differences can cause misinterpretations both in how others see expatriate managers and in how the latter see themselves. For example, U.S. managers doing business in Austria often misinterpret the fact that local businesspeople always address them in formal terms. They may view this as meaning that they are not friends or are not liked, but in fact, this formalism is the way that Austrians always conduct

---

Table 7–5
U.S. Proverbs Representing Cultural Values

Proverb	Cultural Value
A penny saved is a penny earned	Thriftiness
Time is money	Time thriftiness
Don't cry over spilt milk	Practicality
Waste not, want not	Frugality
Early to bed, early to rise, makes one healthy, wealthy, and wise	Diligence; work ethic
A stitch in time saves nine	Timeliness of action
If at first you don't succeed, try, try again	Persistence; work ethic
Take care of today, and tomorrow will take care of itself	Preparation for future

Source: Drawn from Nancy J. Adler, *International Dimensions of Organizational Behavior,* 2nd ed. (Boston: PWS-Kent Publishing, 1991), pp. 79–80.

business. The informal, first-name approach used in the United States is not the style of the Austrians.

Culture even affects day-to-day activities of corporate communications.[29] For example, when sending messages to international clients, American managers have to keep in mind that there are many things that are uniquely American and overseas managers may not be aware of them. As an example, daylight savings time is known to all Americans, but many Asian managers have no idea what the term means. Similarly, it is common for American managers to address memos to their "international office" without realizing that the managers who work in this office regard the American location as the "international" one! Other suggestions that can be of value to American managers who are engaged in international communications include:

- Be careful not to use generalized statements about benefits, compensation, pay cycles, holidays, or policies in your worldwide communications. Work hours, vacation accrual, general business practices, and human resource issues vary widely from country to country.

- Since most of the world uses the metric system, be sure to include converted weights and measures in all internal and external communications.

- Keep in mind that even in English-speaking countries, words may have different meanings. Not everyone knows what is meant by "counterclockwise," or "quite good."

- Remember that letterhead and paper sizes differ worldwide. The 8½ by 11-inch page is a U.S. standard, but most countries use an A4 (8¼ × 11½-inch) size for their letterhead, with envelopes to match.

- Dollars are not unique to the United States. There are Australian, Bermudian, Canadian, Hong Kong, Taiwanese, and New Zealand dollars, among others. So when referring to American dollars, it is important to use "US$."

Many Americans also have difficulty interpreting the effect of national values on work behavior. For example, why do French and German workers drink alcoholic beverages at lunchtime? Why are many European workers unwilling to work the night shift? Why do overseas affiliates contribute to the support of the employees' work council or donate money to the support of kindergarten teachers in local schools? These types of actions are viewed by some people as wasteful, but those who know the culture of these countries realize that such actions promote the long-run good of the company. It is the outsider who is misinterpreting why these culturally specific actions are happening, and such misperceptions can become a barrier to effective communication.

Nonverbal Communication

Another major reason for perception problems is accounted for by **nonverbal communication,** which is the transfer of meaning through means such as body language and use of physical space. Table 7–6 summarizes a number of dimensions of nonverbal communication. The general categories that are especially important to communication in international management are kinesics, proxemics, chronemics, and chromatics.

Kinesics   **Kinesics** is the study of communication through body movement and facial expression. Primary areas of concern include eye contact, posture, and gestures. For example, when one communicates verbally with someone in the United States, it is good manners to look the other person in the eye. This area of communicating through the use of eye contact and gaze is known as **oculesics.** In some areas of the world oculesics is an important consideration because of what people should not do, such as stare at others or maintain continuous eye contact, because it is considered impolite to do these things.

Another area of kinesics is posture, which can also cause problems. For example, when Americans are engaged in prolonged negotiations or meetings, it is not uncommon

nonverbal communication
The transfer of meaning through means such as body language and the use of physical space.

kinesics
The study of communication through body movement and facial expressions.

oculesics
The area of communication that deals with conveying messages through the use of eye contact and gaze.

Table 7–6
Common Forms of Nonverbal Communication

1. Hand gestures, both intended and self-directed (autistic), such as the nervous rubbing of hands
2. Facial expressions, such as smiles, frowns, and yawns
3. Posture and stance
4. Clothing and hair styles (hair being more like clothes than like skin, both subject to the fashion of the day)
5. Interpersonal distance (proxemics)
6. Eye contact and direction of gaze, particularly in "listening behavior"
7. "Artifacts" and nonverbal symbols, such as lapel pins, walking sticks, and jewelry
8. Paralanguage (though often in language, just as often treated as part of nonverbal behavior—speech rate, pitch, inflections, volume)
9. Taste, including symbolism of food and the communication function of chatting over coffee or tea, and oral gratification such as smoking or gum chewing
10. Cosmetics: temporary—powder; permanent—tattoos
11. Time symbolism: what is too late or too early to telephone or visit a friend, or too long or too short to make a speech or stay for dinner
12. Timing and pauses within verbal behavior

Source: This information is found in J. C. Condon and F. S. Yousef, *An Introduction to Intercultural Communication* (Indianapolis, IN: Bobbs-Merrill, 1975), pp. 123–124.

---

for them to relax and put their feet up on a chair or desk, but this is insulting behavior in the Middle East. Here is an example from a classroom situation:

> In the midst of a discussion of a poem in the sophomore class of the English Department, the professor, who was British, took up the argument, started to explain the subtleties of the poem, and was carried away by the situation. He leaned back in his chair, put his feet up on the desk, and went on with the explanation. The class was furious. Before the end of the day, a demonstration by the University's full student body had taken place. Petitions were submitted to the deans of the various facilities. The next day, the situation even made the newspaper headlines. The consequences of the act, that was innocently done, might seem ridiculous, funny, baffling, incomprehensible, or even incredible to a stranger. Yet, to the native, the students' behavior was logical and in context. The students and their supporters were outraged because of the implications of the breach of the native behavioral pattern. In the Middle East, it is extremely insulting to have to sit facing two soles of the shoes of somebody.[30]

Gestures are also widely used and take many different forms. For example, Canadians shake hands, Japanese bow, Middle Easterners of the same sex kiss on the cheek. Communicating through the use of bodily contact is known as **haptics,** and it is a widely used form of nonverbal communication.

haptics
Communicating through the use of bodily contact.

Sometimes gestures present problems for expatriate managers because these behaviors have different meanings depending on the country. For example, in the United States, putting the thumb and index finger together to form an "O" is the sign for "okay." In Japan, this is the sign for money; in southern France, the gesture means "zero" or "worthless"; and in Brazil, it is regarded as a vulgar or obscene sign. In France and Belgium, snapping the fingers of both hands is considered vulgar; in Brazil, this gesture is used to indicate that something has been done for a long time. In Britain, the "V for victory" sign is given with the palm facing out; if the palm is facing in, this roughly means "shove it"; in non-British countries, the gesture means two of something and often is used when placing an order at a restaurant.[31] Gibson, Hodgetts, and Blackwell found that many foreign students attending school in the United States have trouble communicating because they are unable to interpret some of the most common nonverbal gestures.[32] A survey group of 44 Jamaican, Venezuelan, Colombian, Peruvian, Thai, Indian, and Japanese students at two major universities were given pictures of 20 universal cultural gestures, and each was asked to describe the nonverbal gestures illustrated. In 56 percent of the choices the respondents either gave an interpretation that was markedly different from that of Americans or reported that the nonverbal gesture had no meaning in their culture. These findings help to reinforce the need to teach expatriates about local nonverbal communication.

Proxemics   **Proxemics** is the study of the way that people use physical space to convey messages. For example, in the United States, there are four "distances" people use in communicating on a face-to-face basis (see Figure 7–3.) **Intimate distance** is used for very confidential communications. **Personal distance** is used for talking with family and close friends. **Social distance** is used to handle most business transactions. **Public distance** is used when calling across the room or giving a talk to a group.

One major problem for Americans communicating with people from the Middle East or South America is that the intimate or personal distance zones are violated. Americans often tend to be moving away in interpersonal communication with their Middle Eastern or Latin counterparts, while the latter are trying to physically close the gap. The American cannot understand why the other is standing so close; the latter cannot understand why the American is being so reserved and standing so far away. The result is a breakdown in communication.

Office layout is another good example of proxemics. In the United States, the more important the manager, the larger the office, and often a secretary screens visitors and keeps away those whom the manager does not wish to see. In Japan, most managers do not have large offices, and even if they do, they spend a great deal of time out of the office and with the employees. Thus, the Japanese have no trouble communicating directly with their superiors. A Japanese manager's staying in his office would be viewed as a sign of distrust or anger toward the group.

Another way that office proxemics can affect communication is that in many European companies, no wall separates the space allocated to the senior-level manager from that of the subordinates. Everyone works in the same large room. These working conditions often are disconcerting to Americans, who tend to prefer more privacy.

Chronemics   **Chronemics** refers to the way in which time is used in a culture. When examined in terms of extremes, there are two types of time schedules: monochronic and polychronic. A **monochronic time schedule** is one in which things are done in a linear fashion. A manager will address Issue A first and then move on to Issue B. In these societies, time schedules are very important and time is viewed as something that can be controlled and should be used wisely. In individualistic cultures such as the United States, Great Britain, Canada, and Australia, as well as many of the cultures in Northern Europe, managers adhere to monochronic time schedules.

This is in sharp contrast to **polychronic time schedules,** which are characterized by people tending to do several things at the same time and placing higher value on personal involvement than on getting things done on time. In these cultures, schedules are subordinated to personal relationships. Regions of the world where polychronic time schedules are common include Latin America and the Middle East.

proxemics
The study of the way people use physical space to convey messages.

intimate distance
Distance between people that is used for very confidential communications.

personal distance
In communicating, the physical distance used for talking with family and close friends.

social distance
In communicating, the distance used to handle most business transactions.

public distance
In communicating, the distance used when calling across the room or giving a talk to a group.

chronemics
The way in which time is used in a culture.

monochronic time schedule
A time schedule in which things are done in a linear fashion.

polychronic time schedule
A time schedule in which people tend to do several things at the same time and place higher value on personal involvement than on getting things done on time.

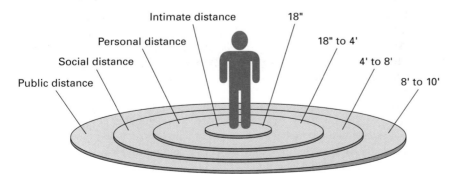

Figure 7–3

Personal Space Categories for Those in the United States

Intimate distance — 18"
Personal distance — 18" to 4'
Social distance — 4' to 8'
Public distance — 8' to 10'

Source: Adapted from Richard M. Hodgetts and Donald F. Kuratko, *Management,* 2nd ed. (San Diego, CA: Harcourt Brace Jovanovich, 1991), p. 384.

When doing business in countries that adhere to monochronic time schedules, it is important to be on time for meetings. Additionally, these meetings typically end at the appointed time so that participants can be on time for their next meeting. When doing business in countries that adhere to polychronic time schedules, it is common to find business meetings starting late and finishing late.

Chromatics Chromatics is the use of color to communicate messages. Every society uses chromatics, but colors that mean one thing in the United States may mean something entirely different in Asia. For example, in the United States it is common to wear black when one is in mourning, while in some locations in India people wear white when they are in mourning. In Hong Kong red is used to signify happiness or luck and traditional bridal dresses are red; in the United States it is common for the bride to wear white. In many Asian countries shampoos are dark in color because users want the soap to be the same color as their hair and believe that if it were a light color it would remove color from their hair. In the United States shampoos tend to be light in color because people see this as a sign of cleanliness and hygiene. In Chile a gift of yellow roses conveys the message "I don't like you," but in the United States the opposite message would be conveyed.

Knowing the importance of chromatics can be very helpful because, among other things, it can avoid embarrassing situations. A good example is the American manager in Peru who upon finishing a one-week visit to the Lima subsidiary decided to thank the assistant who was assigned to him. He sent her a dozen red roses. The lady understood the faux pas, but the American manager was somewhat embarrassed when his Peruvian counterpart smilingly told him, "It was really nice of you to buy her a present. However, red roses indicate a romantic interest!"

■ Achieving Communication Effectiveness

A number of steps can be taken to improve communication effectiveness in the international arena. These include improving feedback systems, providing language and cultural training, and increasing flexibility and cooperation.

Improve Feedback Systems

One of the most important ways of improving communication effectiveness in the international context is to open up feedback systems. Feedback is particularly important between parent companies and their affiliates. There are two basic types of feedback systems: personal (e.g., face-to-face meetings, telephone conversations, and personalized e-mail) and impersonal (e.g., reports, budgets, and plans). Both of these systems help affiliates to keep their home office aware of progress and, in turn, help the home office to monitor and control affiliate performance as well as set goals and standards.

At present, there seem to be varying degrees of feedback between the home offices of MNCs and their affiliates. For example, one study evaluated the communication feedback between subsidiaries and home offices of 63 MNCs headquartered in Europe, Japan, and North America.[33] A marked difference was found between the way that U.S. companies communicated with their subsidiaries and the way that European and Japanese firms did. Over one-half of the U.S. subsidiaries responded that they received monthly feedback from their reports, in contrast to less than 10 percent of the European and Japanese subsidiaries. In addition, the Americans were much more inclined to hold regular management meetings on a regional or worldwide basis. Seventy-five percent of the U.S. companies had annual meetings for their affiliate top managers, compared with less than 50 percent for the Europeans and Japanese. These findings may help to explain why many international subsidiaries and affiliates are not operating as efficiently as they should. The units may not have sufficient contact with the home office. They do not seem to be getting continuous assistance and feedback that are critical to effective communication.

Provide Language Training

Besides improving feedback systems, another way to make communication more effective in the international arena is through language training. Many host-country managers cannot communicate well with their counterparts at headquarters. Because English has become the international language of business, those who are not native speakers of English should learn the language well enough so that face-to-face and telephone conversations and e-mail are possible. If the language of the home office is not English, this other language also should be learned. As a U.S. manager working for a Japanese MNC recently told one of the authors, "The official international language of this company is English. However, whenever the home-office people show up, they tend to cluster together with their countrymen and speak Japanese. That's why I'm trying to learn Japanese. Let's face it. They say all you need to know is English, but if you want to really know what's going on, you have to talk *their* language."

Written communication also is extremely important in achieving effectiveness. As noted earlier, when reports, letters, and e-mail messages are translated from one language to another, preventing a loss of meaning is virtually impossible. Moreover, if the communications are not written properly, they may not be given the attention they deserve. The reader will allow poor grammar and syntax to influence his or her interpretation and subsequent actions. Moreover, if readers cannot communicate in the language of those who will be receiving their comments or questions about the report, their messages also must be translated and likely will lose further meaning. Therefore, the process can continue on and on, each party failing to achieve full communication with the other. Hildebrandt has described the problems in this two-way process when an employee in a foreign subsidiary writes a report and then sends it to his or her boss for forwarding to the home office:

> The general manager or vice president cannot be asked to be an editor. Yet they often send statements along, knowingly, which are poorly written, grammatically imperfect, or generally unclear. The time pressures do not permit otherwise. Predictably, questions are issued from the States to the subsidiary and the complicated bilingual process now goes in reverse, ultimately reaching the original . . . staff member, who receives the English questions retranslated.[34]

Language training would help to alleviate such complicated communication problems.

Provide Cultural Training

It is very difficult to communicate effectively with someone from another culture unless at least one party has some understanding of the other's culture.[35] Otherwise, communication likely will break down. This is particularly important for multinational companies that have operations throughout the world.[36] Although there always are important differences between countries, and even between subcultures of the same country, firms that operate in South America find that the cultures of these countries have certain commonalities. These common factors also apply to Spain and Portugal. Therefore, a basic understanding of Latin cultures can prove to be useful throughout a large region of the world. The same is true of Anglo cultures, where norms and values tend to be somewhat similar from one country to another. When a multinational has operations in South America, Europe, and Asia, however, multicultural training becomes necessary. "International Management in Action: Communicating in Europe" provides some specific examples of cultural differences.

As Chapter 4 pointed out, it is erroneous to generalize about an "international" culture, because the various nations and regions of the globe are so different. Training must be conducted on a regional or country-specific basis. Failure to do so can result in continuous communication breakdown.[37] Chapter 14 will give considerable attention to cultural training as part of selection for overseas assignments and human resource development.

Increase Flexibility and Cooperation

Effective international communications require increased flexibility and cooperation by all parties.[38] To improve understanding and cooperation, each party must be prepared to give

International Management in Action
Communicating in Europe

In Europe, many countries are within easy commuting distance of their neighbors, so an expatriate who does business in France on Monday may be in Germany on Tuesday, Great Britain on Wednesday, Italy on Thursday, and Spain on Friday. Each country has its own etiquette regarding how to greet others and conduct oneself during social and business meetings. The following sections examine some of the things that expatriate managers need to know to communicate effectively.

France

When one is meeting with businesspeople in France, promptness is expected, although tardiness of 5 to 10 minutes is not considered a major gaffe. The French prefer to shake hands when introduced, and it is correct to address them by title plus last name. When the meeting is over, a handshake again is proper manners.

French executives try to keep their personal and professional lives separate. As a result, most business entertaining is done at restaurants or clubs. When gifts are given to business associates, they should appeal to intellectual or aesthetic pursuits as opposed to being something that one's company produces for sale on the world market. In conversational discussions, topics such as politics and money should be avoided. Also, humor should be used carefully during business meetings.

Germany

German executives like to be greeted by their title, and one should never refer to someone on a first-name basis unless invited to do so. Business appointments should be made well in advance, and punctuality is important. Like the French, the Germans usually do not entertain clients at home, so an invitation to a German manager's home is a special privilege and always should be followed with a thank-you note. Additionally, as is the case in France, one should avoid using humor during business meetings.

Great Britain

In Britain, it is common to shake hands on the first meeting, and first names are always used in introductions.

Unlike the custom in France and Germany, it is common practice in Britain to arrive a little late for business and social occasions, and invitations to British homes are more likely than in some other European cultures. A typical gift for the host is flowers or chocolates.

During business meetings, suits and ties are common dress; however, striped ties should be avoided if they appear to be a copy of those worn by alumni of British universities and schools or by members of military or social clubs. Additionally, during social gatherings it is a good idea not to discuss politics, religion, or gossip about the monarchy unless the British person brings the topic up first.

Italy

In traditional companies, executives are referred to by title plus last name. It is common to shake hands when being introduced, and if the individual is a university graduate, the professional title *dottore* should be used.

Business appointments should be made well in advance, although punctuality is not essential. In most cases, business is done at the office, and when someone is invited to a restaurant, this invitation is usually done to socialize and not to continue business discussions. If an expatriate is invited to an Italian home, it is common to bring a gift for the host, such as a bottle of wine or a box of chocolates. During the dinner conversation, there is a wide variety of acceptable topics, including business, family matters, and soccer.

Spain

It is common to use first names when introducing or talking to people in Spain, and close friends typically greet each other with an embrace. Appointments should be made in advance, but punctuality is not essential.

If one is invited to the home of a Spanish executive, flowers or chocolates for the host are acceptable gifts. If the invitation includes dinner, any business discussions should be delayed until after coffee is served. During the social gathering, some topics that should be avoided include religion, family, and work. Additionally, humor rarely is used during formal occasions.

---

a little.[39] Take the case of International Computers Ltd., a mainframe computer firm that does a great deal of business in Japan. This firm urges its people to strive for successful collaboration in their international partnerships and ventures. At the heart of this process is effective communication. As put by Kenichi Ohmae:

> We must recognize and accept the inescapable subtleties and difficulties of intercompany relationships. This is the essential starting point. Then we must focus not on contractual or equity-related issues but on the quality of the people at the interface between organizations.

Table 7–7
Negotiation Styles from a Cross-Cultural Perspective

Element	United States	Japanese	Arabians	Mexicans
Group composition	Marketing oriented	Function oriented	Committee of specialists	Friendship oriented
Number involved	2–3	4–7	4–6	2–3
Space orientation	Confrontational; competitive	Display harmonious relationship	Status	Close, friendly
Establishing rapport	Short period; direct to task	Longer period; until harmony	Long period; until trusted	Longer period; discuss family
Exchange of information	Documented; step-by-step; multimedia	Extensive; concentrate on receiving side	Less emphasis on technology, more on relationship	Less emphasis on technology, more on relationship
Persuasion tools	Time pressure; loss of saving/making money	Maintain relationship referecnes; intergroup connections	Go-between; hospitality	Emphasis on family and on social concerns; goodwill measured in generations
Use of language	Open, direct, sense of urgency	Indirect, appreciative, cooperative	Flattery, emotional, religious	Respectful, gracious
First offer	Fair ±5 to 10%	±10 to 20%	±20 to 50%	Fair
Second offer	Add to package; sweeten the deal	−5%	−10%	Add an incentive
Final offer package	Total package	Makes no further concessions	−25%	Total
Decision-making process	Top management team	Collective	Team makes recommendation	Senior manager and secretary
Decision maker	Top management team	Middle line with team consensus	Senior manager	Senior manager
Risk taking	Calculated personal responsibility	Low group responsibility	Religion based	Personally responsible

Source: Lillian H. Chaney and Jeanette S. Martin, *Intercultural Business Communication*, 3rd ed. Copyright © 2004. Reprinted by permission of Pearson Education, Inc. Upper Saddle River, NJ.

Finally, we must understand that success requires frequent, rapport-building meetings by at least three organizational levels: top management, staff, and line management at the working level.[40]

Managing Cross-Cultural Negotiations

Closely related to communications but deserving special attention is managing negotiations.[41] **Negotiation** is the process of bargaining with one or more parties to arrive at a solution that is acceptable to all. Negotiation often follows assessing political risk and can be used as an approach to conflict management. If the risk is worth it, then the MNC must negotiate with the host country to secure the best possible arrangements. The MNC and the host country will discuss the investment the MNC is prepared to make in return for certain guarantees or concessions. The initial range of topics typically includes critical areas such as hiring practices, direct financial investment, taxes, and ownership control. Negotiation also is used in creating joint ventures with local firms and in getting the operation off the ground. After the firm is operating, additional areas of negotiation often include expansion of facilities, use of more local managers, additional imports or exports of materials and finished goods, and recapture of profits.

On a more macro level of international trade are the negotiations conducted between countries. The current balance-of-trade problem between the United States and

negotiation
Bargaining with one or more parties for the purpose of arriving at a solution acceptable to all.

China is one example. The massive debt problems of less developed countries and the opening of trade doors with Eastern European and newly emerging economies are other current examples.

The Negotiation Process

Several basic steps can be used to manage the negotiation process. Regardless of the issues or personalities of the parties involved, this process typically begins with planning.

Planning   Planning starts with the negotiators' identifying the objectives they would like to attain. Then they explore the possible options for reaching these objectives. Research shows that the greater the number of options, the greater are the chances for successful negotiations. While this appears to be an obvious statement, research also reveals that many negotiators do not alter their strategy when negotiating across cultures.[42] Next, consideration is given to areas of common ground between the parties. Other major areas include (1) the setting of limits on single-point objectives, such as deciding to pay no more than $10 million for the factory and $3 million for the land; (2) dividing issues into short- and long-term considerations and deciding how to handle each; and (3) determining the sequence in which to discuss the various issues.

Interpersonal Relationship Building   The second phase of the negotiation process involves getting to know the people on the other side. This "feeling out" period is characterized by the desire to identify those who are reasonable and those who are not. In contrast to negotiators in many other countries, those in the United States often give little attention to this phase; they want to get down to business immediately, which often is an ineffective approach. Adler notes:

> Effective negotiators must view luncheon, dinner, reception, ceremony, and tour invitations as times for interpersonal relationship building, and therefore as key to the negotiating process. When American negotiators, often frustrated by the seemingly endless formalities, ceremonies, and "small talk," ask how long they must wait before beginning to "do business," the answer is simple: wait until your opponents bring up business (and they will). Realize that the work of conducting a successful negotiation has already begun, even if business has yet to be mentioned.[43]

Exchanging Task-Related Information   In this part of the negotiation process, each group sets forth its position on the critical issues. These positions often will change later in the negotiations. At this point, the participants are trying to find out what the other party wants to attain and what it is willing to give up.

Persuasion   This step of negotiations is considered by many to be the most important. No side wants to give away more than it has to, but each knows that without giving some concessions, it is unlikely to reach a final agreement. The success of the persuasion step often depends on (1) how well the parties understand each other's position; (2) the ability of each to identify areas of similarity and differences; (3) the ability to create new options; and (4) the willingness to work toward a solution that allows all parties to walk away feeling they have achieved their objectives.

Agreement   The final phase of negotiations is the granting of concessions and hammering out a final agreement. Sometimes, this phase is carried out piecemeal, and concessions and agreements are made on issues one at a time. This is the way negotiators from the United States like to operate. As each issue is resolved, it is removed from the bargaining table, and interest is focused on the next. Asians and Russians, on the other hand, tend to negotiate a final agreement on everything, and few concessions are given until the end.

Simply put, to negotiate effectively in the international arena, it is necessary to understand how cultural differences between the parties affect the process.

Cultural Differences Affecting Negotiations

In negotiating effectively, it is important to have a sound understanding of the other side's culture. This includes consideration of areas such as communication patterns, time orientation, and social behaviors.[44] A number of useful steps can help in this process. One negotiation expert recommends the following:

1. Do not identify the counterpart's home culture too quickly. Common cues (e.g., name, physical appearance, language, accent, location) may be unreliable. The counterpart probably belongs to more than one culture.

2. Beware of the Western bias toward "doing." In Arab, Asian, and Latin groups, ways of being (e.g., comportment, smell), feeling, thinking, and talking can shape relationships more powerfully than doing.

3. Try to counteract the tendency to formulate simple, consistent, stable images.

4. Do not assume that all aspects of the culture are equally significant. In Japan, consulting all relevant parties to a decision is more important than presenting a gift.

5. Recognize that norms for interactions involving outsiders may differ from those for interactions between compatriots.

6. Do not overestimate your familiarity with your counterpart's culture. An American studying Japanese wrote New Year's wishes to Japanese contacts in basic Japanese characters but omitted one character. As a result, the message became "Dead man, congratulations."[45]

Other useful examples have been offered by Trompenaars and Hampden-Turner, who note that a society's culture often plays a major role in determining the effectiveness of a negotiating approach. This is particularly true when the negotiating groups come from decidedly different cultures such as an ascription society and an achievement society. As noted in Chapter 4, in an ascription society status is attributed based on birth, kinship, gender, age, and personal connections. In an achievement society, status is determined by accomplishments. As a result, each side's cultural perceptions can affect the outcome of the negotiation. Here is an example:

> sending whiz-kids to deal with people 10–20 years their senior often insults the ascriptive culture. The reaction may be: "Do these people think that they have reached our own level of experience in half the time? That a 30-year-old American is good enough to negotiate with a 50-year-old Greek or Italian?" Achievement cultures must understand that some ascriptive cultures, the Japanese especially, spend much on training and in-house education to ensure that older people actually are wiser for the years they have spent in the corporation and for the sheer number of subordinates briefing them. It insults an ascriptive culture to do anything which prevents the self-fulfilling nature of its beliefs. Older people are held to be important **so that** they will be nourished and sustained by others' respect. A stranger is expected to facilitate this scheme, not challenge it.[46]

U.S. negotiators have a style that often differs from that of negotiators in many other countries. Americans believe it is important to be factual and objective. In addition, they often make early concessions to show the other party that they are flexible and reasonable. Moreover, U.S. negotiators typically have authority to bind their party to an agreement, so if the right deal is struck, the matter can be resolved quickly. This is why deadlines are so important to Americans. They have come to do business, and they want to get things resolved immediately.

A comparative example would be the Arabs, who in contrast to Americans, with their logical approach, tend to use an emotional appeal in their negotiation style. They analyze things subjectively and treat deadlines as only general guidelines for wrapping up negotiations. They tend to open negotiations with an extreme initial position. However, the Arabs believe strongly in making concessions, do so throughout the bargaining process, and almost always reciprocate an opponent's concessions. They also seek to build a long-term relationship with their bargaining partners. For these reasons, Americans typically find it easier to negotiate with Arabs than with representatives from many other regions of the world.

Another interesting comparative example is provided by the Chinese. In initial negotiation meetings, it is common for Chinese negotiators to seek agreement on the general focus of the meetings. The hammering out of specific details is postponed for later get-togethers. By achieving agreement on the general framework within which the negotiations will be conducted, the Chinese seek to limit and focus the discussions. Many Westerners misunderstand what is happening during these initial meetings and believe the dialogue consists mostly of rhetoric and general conversation. They are wrong and quite often are surprised later on when the Chinese negotiators use the agreement on the framework and principles as a basis for getting agreement on goals—and then insist that all discussions on concrete arrangements be in accord with these agreed-upon goals. Simply put, what is viewed as general conversation by many Western negotiators is regarded by the Chinese as a formulation of the rules of the game that must be adhered to throughout the negotiations. So in negotiating with the Chinese, it is important to come prepared to ensure that one's own agenda, framework, and principles are accepted by both parties.

Before beginning any negotiations, negotiators should review the negotiating style of the other parties. (Table 7–7 on page 199 provides some insights regarding negotiation styles of the Americans, Japanese, Arabs, and Mexicans.) This review should help to answer certain questions: What can we expect the other side to say and do? How are they likely to respond to certain offers? When should the most important matters be introduced? How quickly should concessions be made, and what type of reciprocity should be expected? These types of questions help effectively prepare the negotiators. In addition, the team will work on formulating negotiation tactics. "International Management in Action: Negotiating with the Japanese," demonstrates such tactics, and the following discussion gets into some of the specifics.

Negotiation Tactics

A number of specific tactics are used in international negotiation. The following discussion examines some of the most common.

Location   Where should negotiations take place? If the matter is very important, most businesses will choose a neutral site. For example, U.S. firms negotiating with companies from the Far East will meet in Hawaii, South American companies negotiating with European firms will meet halfway, in New York City. A number of benefits derive from using a neutral site. One is that each party has limited access to its home office for receiving a great deal of negotiating information and advice and thus gaining an advantage on the other. A second is that the cost of staying at the site often is quite high, so both sides have an incentive to conclude their negotiations as quickly as possible. (Of course, if one side enjoys the facilities and would like to stay as long as possible, the negotiations could drag on.) A third is that most negotiators do not like to return home with nothing to show for their efforts, so they are motivated to reach some type of agreement.

Time Limits   Time limits are an important negotiation tactic when one party is under a time constraint. This is particularly true when this party has agreed to meet at the home site of the other party. For example, U.S. negotiators who go to London to discuss a joint venture with a British firm often will have a scheduled return flight. Once their hosts find out how long these individuals intend to stay, the British can plan their strategy accordingly. The "real" negotiations are unlikely to begin until close to the time that the Americans must

Negotiating with the Japanese

Some people believe that the most effective way of getting the Japanese to open up their markets to the United States is to use a form of strong-arm tactics, such as putting the country on a list of those to be targeted for retaliatory action. Others believe that this approach will not be effective, because the interests of the United States and Japan are intertwined and we would be hurting ourselves as much as them. Regardless of which group is right, one thing is certain: U.S. MNCs must learn how to negotiate more effectively with the Japanese. What can they do? Researchers have found that besides patience and a little table pounding, a number of important steps warrant consideration.

First, business firms need to prepare for their negotiations by learning more about Japanese culture and the "right" ways to conduct discussions. Those companies with experience in these matters report that the two best ways of doing this are to read books on Japanese business practices and social customs and to hire experts to train the negotiators. Other steps that are helpful include putting the team through simulated negotiations and hiring Japanese to assist in the negotiations.

Second, U.S. MNCs must learn patience and sincerity. Negotiations are a two-way street that require the mutual cooperation and efforts of both parties. The U.S. negotiators must understand that many times, Japanese negotiators do not have full authority to make on-the-spot decisions. Authority must be given by someone at the home office, and this failure to act quickly should not be interpreted as a lack of sincerity on the part of the Japanese negotiators.

Third, the MNC must have a unique good or service. So many things are offered for sale in Japan that unless the company has something that is truly different, persuading the other party to buy it is difficult.

Fourth, technical expertise often is viewed as a very important contribution, and this often helps to win concessions with the Japanese. The Japanese know that the Americans, for example, still dominate the world when it comes to certain types of technology and that Japan is unable to compete effectively in these areas. When such technical expertise is evident, it is very influential in persuading the Japanese to do business with the company.

These four criteria are critical to effective negotiations with the Japanese. MNCs that use them report more successful experiences than those who do not.

leave. The British know that their guests will be anxious to strike some type of deal before returning home, so the Americans are at a disadvantage.

Time limits can be used tactically even if the negotiators meet at a neutral site. For example, most Americans like to be home with their families for Thanksgiving, Christmas, and the New Year holiday. Negotiations held right before these dates put Americans at a disadvantage, because the other party knows when the Americans would like to leave.

Buyer–Seller Relations How should buyers and sellers act? As noted earlier, Americans believe in being objective and trading favors. When the negotiations are over, Americans walk away with what they have received from the other party, and they expect the other party to do the same. This is not the way negotiators in many other countries think, however.

The Japanese, for example, believe that the buyers should get most of what they want. On the other hand, they also believe that the seller should be taken care of through reciprocal favors. The buyer must ensure that the seller has not been "picked clean." For example, when many Japanese firms first started doing business with large U.S. firms, they were unaware of U.S. negotiating tactics. As a result, the Japanese thought the Americans were taking advantage of them, whereas the Americans believed they were driving a good, hard bargain.

The Brazilians are quite different from both the Americans and Japanese. Researchers have found that Brazilians do better when they are more deceptive and self-interested and their opponents more open and honest than they are.[47] Brazilians also tend to make fewer promises and commitments than their opponents, and they are much more prone to say no. However, Brazilians are more likely to make initial concessions. Overall, Brazilians are more like Americans than Japanese in that they try to maximize their advantage, but they are unlike Americans in that they do not feel obligated to be open and forthright in their approach. Whether they are buyer or seller, they want to come out on top.

Bargaining Behaviors

Closely related to the discussion of negotiation tactics are the different types of bargaining behaviors, including both verbal and nonverbal behaviors. Verbal behaviors are an important part of the negotiating process, because they can improve the final outcome. Research shows that the profits of the negotiators increase when they make high initial offers, ask a lot of questions, and do not make many verbal commitments until the end of the negotiating process. In short, verbal behaviors are critical to the success of negotiations.

Use of Extreme Behaviors Some negotiators begin by making extreme offers or requests. The Chinese and Arabs are examples. Some negotiators, however, begin with an initial position that is close to the one they are seeking. The Americans and Swedes are examples here.

Is one approach any more effective than the other? Research shows that extreme positions tend to produce better results. Some of the reasons relate to the fact that an extreme bargaining position (1) shows the other party that the bargainer will not be exploited; (2) extends the negotiation and gives the bargainer a better opportunity to gain information on the opponent; (3) allows more room for concessions; (4) modifies the opponent's beliefs about the bargainer's preferences; (5) shows the opponent that the bargainer is willing to play the game according to the usual norms; and (6) lets the bargainer gain more than would probably be possible if a less extreme initial position had been taken.

Although the use of extreme position bargaining is considered to be "un-American," many U.S. firms have used it successfully against foreign competitors. When Peter Ueberroth managed the Olympic Games in the United States in 1984, he turned a profit of well over $100 million—and that was without the participation of Soviet-bloc countries, which would have further increased the market potential of the games. In past Olympiads, sponsoring countries had lost hundreds of millions of dollars. How did Ueberroth do it? One way was by using extreme position bargaining. For example, the Olympic Committee felt that the Japanese should pay $10 million for the right to televise the games in the country, so when the Japanese offered $6 million for the rights, the Olympic Committee countered with $90 million. Eventually, the two sides agreed on $18.5 million. Through the effective use of extreme position bargaining, Ueberroth got the Japanese to pay over three times their original offer, an amount well in excess of the committee's budget.

Promises, Threats, and Other Behaviors Another approach to bargaining is the use of promises, threats, rewards, self-disclosures, and other behaviors that are designed to influence the other party. These behaviors often are greatly influenced by the culture. Graham conducted research using Japanese, U.S., and Brazilian businesspeople and found that they employed a variety of different behaviors during a buyer–seller negotiation simulation.[48] Table 7–8 presents the results.

The table shows that Americans and Japanese make greater use of promises than Brazilians. The Japanese also rely heavily on recommendations and commitment. The Brazilians use a discussion of rewards, commands, and self-disclosure more than Americans and Japanese. The Brazilians also say no a great deal more and make first offers that have higher-level profits than those of the others. Americans tend to operate between these two groups, although they do make less use of commands than either of their opponents and make first offers that have lower profit levels than their opponents'.

Nonverbal Behaviors Nonverbal behaviors also are very common during negotiations. These behaviors refer to what people do rather than what they say. Nonverbal behaviors sometimes are called the "silent language." Typical examples include silent periods, facial gazing, touching, and conversational overlaps. As seen in Table 7–9, the Japanese tend to use silent periods much more often than either Americans or Brazilians during negotiations. In fact, in this study, the Brazilians did not use them at all. The Brazilians did, however, make frequent use of other nonverbal behaviors. They employed facial gazing almost four

Table 7–8
Cross-Cultural Differences in Verbal Behavior of Japanese, U.S., and Brazilian Negotiators

Behavior and Definition	Number of Times Tactic Was Used in a Half-Hour Bargaining Session		
	Japanese	United States	Brazilian
Promise. A statement in which the source indicated an intention to provide the target with a reinforcing consequence which source anticipates target will evaluate as pleasant, positive, or rewarding.	7	8	3
Threat. Same as promise, except that the reinforcing consequences are thought to be noxious, unpleasant, or punishing.	4	4	2
Recommendation. A statement in which the source predicts that a pleasant environmental consequence will occur to the target. Its occurrence is not under the source's control.	7	4	5
Warning. Same as recommendation except that the consequences are thought to be unpleasant	2	1	1
Reward. A statement by the source that is thought to create pleasant consequences for the target.	1	2	2
Punishment. Same as reward, except that the consequences are thought to be unpleasant.	1	3	3
Positive normative appeal. A statement in which the source indicates that the target's past, present, or future behavior was or will be in conformity with social norms.	1	1	0
Negative normative appeal. Same as positive normative appeal, except that the target's behavior is in violation of social norms.	3	1	1
Commitment. A statement by the source to the effect that its future bids will not go below or above a certain level.	15	13	8
Self-disclosure. A statement in which the source reveals information about itself.	34	36	39
Question. A statement in which the source asks the target to reveal information about itself.	20	20	22
Command. A statement in which the source suggests that the target perform a certain behavior.	8	6	14
First offer. The profit level associated with each participant's first offer.	61.5	57.3	75.2
Initial concession. The differences in profit between the first and second offer.	6.5	7.1	9.4
Number of no's. Number of times the word "no" was used by bargainers per half-hour.	5.7	9.0	83.4

Source: Adapted from John L. Graham, "The Influence of Culture on the Process of Business Negotiations in an Exploratory Study," *Journal of International Business Studies,* Spring 1983, p. 88. Reproduced with permission of Palgrave Macmillan.

times more often than the Japanese and almost twice as often as the Americans. In addition, although the Americans and Japanese did not touch their opponents, the Brazilians made wide use of this nonverbal tactic. They also relied heavily on conversational overlaps, employing them more than twice as often as the Japanese and almost three times as often as Americans. Quite obviously, the Brazilians rely very heavily on nonverbal behaviors in their negotiating.

The important thing to remember is that in international negotiations, people use a wide variety of tactics, and the other side must be prepared to counter or find a way of dealing with them. The response will depend on the situation. Managers from different cultures will give different answers. Table 7–10 provides some examples of the types of characteristics needed in effective negotiators. To the extent that international managers have these characteristics, their success as negotiators should increase.

Table 7–9
Cross-Cultural Differences in Nonverbal Behavior of Japanese, U.S., and Brazilian Negotiators

Behavior and Definition	Number of Times Tactic Was Used in a Half-Hour Bargaining Session		
	Japanese	United States	Brazilian
Silent period. The number of conversational gaps of 10 seconds or more per 30 minutes.	5.5	3.5	0
Facial gazing. The number of minutes negotiators spend looking at their opponent's face per randomly selected 10-minute period.	1.3 minutes	3.3 minutes	5.2 minutes
Touching. Incidents of bargainers touching one another per half-hour (not including handshakes).	0	0	4.7
Conversational overlaps. The number of times (per 10 minutes) that both parties to the negotiation would talk at the same time.	12.6	10.3	28.6

Source: Adapted from John L. Graham, "The Influence of Culture on the Process of Business Negotiations in an Exploratory Study," *Journal of International Business Studies,* Spring 1983, p. 84. Reproduced with permission of Palgrave Macmillan.

Table 7–10
Culture-Specific Characteristics Needed by International Managers for Effective Negotiations

U.S. managers	Preparation and planning skill Ability to think under pressure Judgment and intelligence Verbal expressiveness Product knowledge Ability to perceive and exploit power Integrity
Japanese managers	Dedication to job Ability to perceive and exploit power Ability to win respect and confidence Integrity Listening skill Broad perspective Verbal expressiveness
Chinese managers (Taiwan)	Persistence and determination Ability to win respect and confidence Preparation and planning skill Product knowledge Interesting Judgment and intelligence
Brazilian managers	Preparation and planning skill Ability to think under pressure Judgment and intelligence Verbal expressiveness Product knowledge Ability to perceive and exploit power Competitiveness

Source: Adapted from Nancy J. Adler, *International Dimensions of Organizational Behavior,* 2nd ed. (Boston: PWS-Kent Publishing, 1991), p. 187, and from material provided by Professor John Graham, School of Business Administration, University of Southern California, 1983.

The World of *BusinessWeek*—Revisited

The *BusinessWeek* article that opens this chapter presents a summary of the legal challenges Microsoft faces in Europe. These challenges underscore the importance of effective communication and negotiation across cultures. The latest EU ruling against Microsoft might have been avoided if the company had been able to communicate its position and negotiate an outcome acceptable to the range of stakeholders. Effective two-way communication is an important process. Closer communication and interaction with customers, suppliers, partners, and regulators might have bolstered Microsoft's reputation and helped avoid these disputes.

A key to success in today's global economy is being able to communicate effectively within each country being served and to engage in effective negotiations across cultures. In linking the communication and negotiations concepts in this chapter with the challenges facing Microsoft, answer these questions: (1) In dealing with European consumers and regulators, what are two ways in which communication styles might prove to be a communication barrier? (2) How might Microsoft's aggressive approach to its management, marketing, and legal strategies create perception problems for the company? (3) How might Microsoft and other companies facing legal challenges better prepare and implement negotiation strategies as alternatives to legal proceedings?

SUMMARY OF KEY POINTS

1. Communication is the transfer of meaning from sender to receiver. The key to the effectiveness of communication is how accurately the receiver interprets the intended meaning.

2. Communicating in the international business context involves both downward and upward flows. Downward flows convey information from superior to subordinate; these flows vary considerably from country to country. For example, the downward system of organizational communication is much more prevalent in France than in Japan. Upward communication conveys information from subordinate to superior. In the United States and Japan, the upward system is more common than in South America or some European countries.

3. The international arena contains a number of communication barriers. Some of the most important are language, perception, culture, and nonverbal communication. Language, particularly in written communications, often loses considerable meaning during interpretation. Perception and culture can result in people's seeing and interpreting things differently, and as a result, communication can break down. Nonverbal communication such as body language, facial expressions, and use of physical space, time, and even color often varies from country to country and, if improper, often results in communication problems.

4. A number of steps can be taken to improve communication effectiveness. Some of the most important include improving feedback, providing language and cultural training, and encouraging flexibility and cooperation. These steps can be particularly helpful in overcoming communication barriers in the international context and can lead to more effective international management.

5. Negotiation is the process of bargaining with one or more parties to arrive at a solution that is acceptable to all. This process involves five basic steps: planning, interpersonal relationship building, exchanging task-related information, persuasion, and agreement. The way in which the process is carried out often will vary because of cultural differences.

6. There are a wide variety of tactics used in international negotiating. These include location, time limits, buyer–seller relations, verbal behaviors, and nonverbal behaviors.

KEY TERMS

chromatics, *196*

chronemics, *195*

communication, *180*

context, *181*

downward communication, *184*

haptics, *194*

intimate distance, *195*

kinesics, *193*

monochronic time schedule, *195*

negotiation, *199*

nonverbal communication, *193*

oculesics, *193*

perception, *190*

personal distance, *195*

polychronic time schedule, *195*

proxemics, *195*

public distance, *195*

social distance, *195*

upward communication, *186*

REVIEW AND DISCUSSION QUESTIONS

1. How does explicit communication differ from implicit communication? What is one culture that makes wide use of explicit communication? Implicit communication? Describe how one would go about conveying the following message in each of the two cultures you identified: "You are trying very hard, but you are still making too many mistakes."

2. One of the major reasons that foreign expatriates have difficulty doing business in the United States is that they do not understand American slang. A business executive recently gave the authors the following three examples of statements that had no direct meaning for her because she was unfamiliar with slang: "He was laughing like hell." "Don't worry; it's a piece of cake." "Let's throw these ideas up against the wall and see if any of them stick." Why did the foreign expat have trouble understanding these statements, and what could be said instead?

3. Yamamoto Iron & Steel is considering setting up a minimill outside Atlanta, Georgia. At present, the company is planning to send a group of executives to the area to talk with local and state officials regarding this plant. In what way might misperception be a barrier to effective communication between the representatives for both sides? Identify and discuss two examples.

4. Diaz Brothers is a winery in Barcelona. The company would like to expand operations to the United States and begin distributing its products in the Chicago area. If things work out well, the company then will expand to both coasts. In its business dealings in the Midwest, how might culture prove to be a communication barrier for the company's representatives from Barcelona? Identify and discuss two examples.

5. Why is nonverbal communication a barrier to effective communication? Would this barrier be greater for Yamamoto Iron & Steel (question 3) or Diaz Brothers (question 4)? Defend your answer.

6. For U.S companies going abroad for the first time, which form of nonverbal communication barrier would be the greatest, kinesics or proxemics? Why? Defend your answer.

7. If a company new to the international arena was negotiating an agreement with a potential partner in an overseas country, what basic steps should it be prepared to implement? Identify and describe them.

8. Wilsten Inc. has been approached by a Japanese firm that wants exclusive production and selling rights for one of Wilsten's new high-tech products. What does Wilsten need to know about Japanese bargaining behaviors to strike the best possible deal with this company? Identify and describe five.

INTERNET EXERCISE: WORKING EFFECTIVELY AT TOYOTA

In 2001 Toyota's Camry was the best-selling car in the United States and the firm's share of the American automobile market was solid. However, the company is not resting on its laurels. Toyota has expanded worldwide and is now doing business in scores of countries. Visit the firm's Web site and find out what it has been up to lately. The address is **www.toyota.com**. Then take a tour of the company's products and services including cars, air services, and sports vehicles. Next, go to the jobs section site and see what types of career opportunities there are at Toyota. Finally, find out what Toyota is doing in your particular locale. Then, drawing upon this information and the material you read in the chapter, answer these three questions: (1) What type of communication and negotiation challenges do you think you would face if you worked for Toyota and were in constant communication with home-office personnel in Japan? (2) What type of communication training do you think the firm would need to provide to you to ensure that you were effective in dealing with senior-level Japanese managers in the hierarchy? (3) Using Table 7–1 as your guide, what conclusions can you draw regarding communicating with the Japanese managers, and what guidelines would you offer to a non-Japanese employee who just entered the firm and is looking for advice and guidance regarding how to communicate and negotiate more effectively?

China

China, with more than 1.3 billion people, is the world's most populous country and has a rapidly growing economy. Economic development has proceeded unevenly. Urban coastal areas, particularly in the southeast, are experiencing more rapid economic development than other areas of the country. China has a mixed economy, with a combination of state-owned and private firms. A number of state-owned enterprises (SOEs) have undergone partial or full privatization in recent years. The Chinese government has encouraged foreign investment—in some sectors of the economy and subject to constraints—since the 1980s, defining several "special economic zones" in which foreign investors receive preferable tax, tariff, and investment treatment.

In March 2003, a long-expected transition in China's political leadership took place. Hu Jintao assumed the country's presidency as well as chairmanship of the ruling Communist Party. Wen Jinbao became the new premier. Former president Jiang Zemin retained the chairmanship of the Central Military Commission.

With China's entry into the World Trade Organization in November 2001, the Chinese government made a number of specific commitments to trade and investment liberalization that, if fully implemented, will substantially open the Chinese economy to foreign firms. In telecommunications, this will mean the lifting or sharp reduction of tariffs and foreign ownership limitations, but China will retain the right to limit foreign majority ownership of telecom firms. There are still lingering concerns about China's enforcement of intellectual property protection and its willingness to fully open access to its telecommunications market.

China's real GDP grew by 9.1 percent in 2003, an impressive performance given the SARS epidemic and the generally sluggish conditions in the global economy. This growth brought China's GDP to $1.41 trillion and, for the first time, boosted per capita GDP above $1,000. Indeed, there are concerns that China's economy may be growing too fast: The government is planning to hold economic growth to about 7 percent in 2004. Layoffs have been part of the restructuring of the SOEs, for many were severely overstaffed. The layoffs have created unemployment, which is a burden on the government budget as the government begins to provide social benefits that were previously the responsibility of the SOEs. The geographic concentration of privately owned industry in the urban centers along the coast also has created social strains. Today, China's investment laws seek to channel foreign investment into infrastructure building, industries involving advanced technologies, and high-value-added export-oriented products.

In June 2003, Bruce Claflin, CEO of struggling networking company 3Com Corp., caused quite a stir by announcing a joint alliance with China's Huawei Technologies—just weeks after Huawei had been sued on a range of intellectual property rights (IPR) violations by 3Com's Silicon Valley neighbor Cisco Systems. The suit claims that Huawei's products include some of Cisco's carefully guarded source code and that Huawei infringes on copyrights related to Cisco's computer commands.

According to Claflin, 3Com's negotiations with Huawei began in mid-2002, long before Cisco filed suit. Although he admits that the deal took some by surprise, Clafin insists that it was a "no brainer." "Let's face it, people have the perception of China as a low-tech, low-cost kind of place. But my first impression was that this was truly a great technology company. It blows your mind when everyone thinks China is all about exploiting low-cost labor."

Claflin believes that Cisco's argument of IPR infringement is more complicated than it sounds: "There are two courts they care about: the court of law and the court of public opinion. I bet there's not one company out there that doesn't somehow infringe on Cisco in some way." Cisco says it respects 3Com as a rival and is hopeful that 3Com's promise that products sold by the Huawei–3Com joint venture won't infringe on Cisco's patents will come to pass. Still, it's quite possible that Cisco will file suit against the joint venture, raising questions about IPR protections in China and the United States.
http://english.peopledaily.com.cn

Questions

1. Do you think China will continue to achieve record growth? What factors could hurt its prospects?
2. Today, because of an abundance of cheap labor, China is a hot destination for global corporate outsourcing. Do you think this will still be the case a decade from now? Why or why not?
3. What communication and negotiation challenges may have arisen in the three-way exchanges among Cisco, 3Com, and Huawei?
4. Can 3Com take any proactive measures to help limit the possibility of Cisco moving forward with litigation?

Foreign or Domestic?

Connie Hatley is a very successful businesswoman who has holdings in a wide variety of industries. Hatley recently was approached by one of the Big Three automakers and offered a multidealership arrangement. In return for investing $50 million in facilities, the auto manufacturer would be willing to give her five dealerships spread throughout the United States. These locations, for the most part, are in rural areas, but over the next decade, these locales likely will become much more populated. In addition, the company pointed out that a large percentage of new cars are purchased by individuals who prefer to buy in rural locations, because prices at these dealerships tend to be lower. Hatley has been seriously considering the offer, although she now has a competitive alternative.

A South Korean auto manufacturer has approached Hatley and offered her the same basic deal. Hatley indicated that she was wary of doing business with a foreign firm so far away, but the Korean manufacturer presented her with some interesting auto sales data: (1) Between 1981 and 2001, the South Korean share of the U.S. auto market went from 0 to over 3 percent. (2) South Korean automakers are capturing market share in the United States at a faster rate than any other competitor. (3) New technology is being incorporated into these Korean-built cars at an unprecedented rate, and the quality is among the highest in the industry. (4) Although the Big Three (GM, Ford, and Daimler-Chrysler) hold a large share of the U.S. auto market, their market share among those 45 years of age or younger is declining and being captured by foreign competitors. (5) The South Korean firm intends to increase its share of the U.S. market by 20 percent annually.

Hatley is very impressed with these data and forecasts. Recently, however, the Korean auto company's sales and market share have been declining; she is uneasy about having to deal with someone located halfway around the world. "If I don't receive scheduled deliveries, whom do I call?" she asked one of her vice presidents. "Also, we don't speak their language. If there is a major problem, how are we going to really communicate with each other? I like the proposal, and I'd take it if I were sure that we wouldn't have communication problems. However, $50 million is a lot of money to invest. If a mistake is made, I'm going to lose a fortune. They did experience some problems last year, and their sales were off that year. Of course, if the South Koreans are right in their long-range forecasts and I have no major problems dealing with them, my return on investment is going to be almost 50 percent higher than it will be with the U.S. manufacturer."

Questions

1. What specific types of communication problems might Hatley encounter in dealing with the South Koreans?
2. Can these communication problems be resolved, or are they insurmountable and will simply have to be tolerated?
3. Based on communication problems alone, should Hatley back away from the deal or proceed? Give your recommendation; then defend it.
4. What negotiation approaches might Hatley use if she wants to continue with the deal in order to increase her confidence that it will be successful?

Cross-Cultural Conflicts in the Corning–Vitro Joint Venture

Vitro is a Mexican glass manufacturer located in Monterrey, Mexico. Vitro's product line concentrates on drinkware but includes dozens of products, from automobile windshields to washing machines. Vitro has a long history of successful joint ventures and is globally oriented.

Corning Inc. is most famous for its oven-ready glassware; however, Corning has diversified into fiber optics, environmental products, and laboratory services. Like Vitro, Corning has a long history of successful joint ventures and globalization. Vitro and Corning share similar corporate cultures and customer-oriented philosophies.

After realizing such similarities and looking to capitalize on NAFTA by accessing the Mexican market, Corning Inc. entered into a joint venture with Vitro in the fall of 1992. The similarities in history, philosophy, culture, goals, and objectives of both companies would lead to the logical conclusion that this alliance should be an instant success. However, as Francisco Chevez, an analyst with Smith Barney Shearson in New York, said, "The cultures did not match . . . it was a marriage made in hell." As history reveals, Corning and Vitro dissolved the joint venture 25 months after the agreement. Both companies still have an interest in maintaining the relationship and continue to distribute each other's products.

A further look at the strategic history of Corning and the joint venture between Corning and Vitro will lead to a better understanding of the difficulties that are involved in creating and maintaining foreign alliances. A more in-depth investigation also will reveal the impact of culture on business transactions.

The Strategic History of Corning

Corning Inc. has been an innovative leader in foreign alliances for over 73 years. One of the company's first successes was an alliance with St. Gobain, a French glassmaker, to produce Pyrex cookware in Europe during the 1920s. Corning has formed approximately 50 ventures over the years. Only 9 have failed, which is a phenomenal number considering one recent study found that over one-half of foreign and national alliances do not succeed. Over the last five years, Corning's sales from joint ventures were over $3 billion, which contributed more than $500 million to its net income.

Corning enters into joint ventures for two primary reasons, which are best explained through examples of its past ventures. The first is to gain access to markets that it cannot penetrate quickly enough to obtain a competitive advantage. Corning currently has multiple ventures that exemplify market penetration. Samsung–Corning is an alliance in which Corning provided its distinctive competency of television tube production while Samsung provided expansion into the television market. Corning was able to achieve a strong market share in the Asian market, with sales in excess of $500 million.

The second reason is to bring its technology to market. For example, the strategic alliance of Corning with Mitsubishi led to the creation of Cometec Inc. Corning produces the ceramic substrates in automotive catalytic converters. The venture employs coating technology developed by Mitsubishi that extends Corning's business into stationary pollution control. Corning reports that the venture is quite successful.

Corning's CEO, James R. Houghton, summarizes the major criteria for deciding whether an equity venture is likely to succeed as follows:

1. You need a solid business opportunity.
2. The two partners should make comparable contributions to the new enterprise.
3. The new enterprise should have a well-defined scope and no major conflicts with either parent company.
4. The management of each parent firm should have the vision and confidence to support the venture through its inevitable rough spots.
5. An autonomous operating team should be formed.
6. Responsibility cannot be delegated.

Houghton also emphasizes that the most important dimension of a successful joint venture is trust between the partners.

Corning's track record indicates that it has been able to establish and run a large number of joint ventures successfully. What went wrong with the recent Vitro venture? Vitro and Corning seemed to have similar operating procedures, and Vitro's product line complemented Corning's consumer business. Therefore, how could a seemingly perfect alliance fail so miserably? Probing deeper into the Corning–Vitro joint venture reveals the important role that culture may play in international alliances.

Background on the Corning–Vitro Joint Venture

The Corning–Vitro venture seemed to be ideal. However, a strong Mexican peso, increased overseas competition, and strong cultural differences spelled trouble for the alliance. The economic problems are understandable, but the cultural differences should have been given more attention before the alliance was entered into.

Although both companies appeared so similar on the surface, they really were quite different. Cultural clashes erupted from the very beginning of the venture because of differing approaches to work. One example was in the marketing area. Vitro's sales approach was less aggressive than the Americans at Corning thought necessary; the slower, deliberate approach to sales in Mexico was a result of the previously highly controlled Mexican economy. Corning's more quick-action oriented and aggressive sales approach had developed from decades of competition.

Once in the venture, the Mexicans thought the Americans were too forward, and the Americans believed that their Mexican partners wasted time being too polite. The Americans perceived the Mexican characteristics to include an unwillingness to acknowledge problems and faults. With respect to speed, the Mexicans thought Corning moved too quickly, while the Americans thought Vitro moved too slowly.

Another obvious cultural difference was the conflicting styles and time allotment for decision making. Vitro is bureaucratic and hierarchical, and loyalty is to family members and patrons in the ranks of the company. Decisions often are left either to a member of the controlling family or to top executives, while middle-level managers seldom are asked to contribute their opinions, let alone to make important decisions. Mr. Loose (Corning's chief executive of the joint venture) observed, "If we were looking at a distribution decision, or a customer decision, we would have a group of people in a room, they would do an assessment, figure alternatives and make a decision, and I as chief executive would never know about it. My experience on the Mexican side is that someone in the organization would have a solution in mind, but then the decision had to be kicked up a few levels."

These examples indicate that culture was an especially sensitive issue between Corning and Vitro, and the alliance was not able to overcome these problems. Corning felt that the cross-cultural differences were depriving both companies of the flexibility to take the fast management action that is necessary in the dynamic business climate of both countries. Vitro basically agreed. Corning gave Vitro back its $130 million investment, and the joint venture was called off. The companies still recognize the opportunity to continue business with each other, however. They have changed their relationship into a mutual distribution of each other's products.

The Aftermath of the Breakup

Vitro and Corning each responded publicly to the dissolution of their alliance, and each indicated the strong differences in culture. Corning wanted to discuss the problems and learn from them, while Vitro was hesitant to criticize anyone, especially a visible U.S. partner like Corning. The Mexicans preferred to concentrate on continuation of the marketing arrangement between the companies. Houghton, the Corning CEO, openly spoke of the alliance as one that stopped making sense. He stated that cross-cultural differences inhibited the potential of the alliance. Corning's chief executive of the venture, Mr. Loose, openly acknowledged the different decision-making styles between the two cultures. Vitro executives were defensive and disappointed that Mr. Loose had expressed his views so frankly in public. "It is unfortunate that he made those comments," said an anonymous Vitro executive. The president of Vitro, Eduardo Martens, flatly denied that the cultural differences were any greater than in other alliances. In an interview with the *Harvard Business Review,* however, he admitted, "Business in Mexico is done on a consensus basis, very genteel and sometimes slow by U.S. standards."

Corning feels they learned a lesson in the failed Vitro alliance; both foreign and domestic alliances require additional skills and more management time. CEO Houghton says that alliances carry a lot of risk and misunderstandings, but they can be significantly beneficial to the operations of a company if they are done carefully and selectively. Corning continues to analyze why the cultural differences with Vitro were too strong to overcome.

Questions for Review

1. Identify and discuss Corning's strategic predisposition toward a joint venture with Vitro.

2. Cultural clashes among partners in joint ventures are not a new issue. Discuss why an MNC, and specifically Corning, would be interested in fully understanding the culture of a potential partner before deciding on an alliance.

3. If Corning and Vitro had decided to remain in the alliance, how could they have overcome their differences to make the partnership a success?

4. Discuss why both companies would continue to distribute each other's products after the joint venture failed. What impact might the public statements about the failure have on this relationship?

Source: This case was prepared by Professor Cara Okleshen of the University of Georgia as the basis for class discussion. It is not intended to illustrate either effective or ineffective managerial capability or administrative responsibility.

Integrating National and Organizational Cultures:
Chemical Bank's Mergers in Europe

On July 10, 1991, two major U.S. banks announced their intention to merge as equal partners, thus forming the second-largest bank in the country and one of the top ten in the world. Manufacturers Hanover Trust and Chemical Bank were long-standing competitors whose headquarters were directly opposite one another on New York's Park Avenue, and for both institutions the 1980s had been disastrous. Like many other banks at the time, they had major concentrations of problem loans to Latin America, commercial real estate ventures, and troubled energy companies, and both debt and equity investors were shunning their securities. The merger, creating the new Chemical Bank, was seen as a way to deal with these problems by generating expense savings of $1 billion while simultaneously raising new equity capital through a combination of a $1.5 billion stock offering and greater earnings power.

Merger Changes Strategy

Several months before the merger was announced, Herb Aspbury was named Group Executive for Europe for Manufacturers Hanover, and he relocated to London. Prior to this assignment, Aspbury had headed the company's North American Division, where he was responsible for wholesale banking activities in the United States and Canada. With the merger he became Senior Managing Director for the new bank, and the dynamics of his job changed dramatically. Although he was sent to Europe to "rationalize" the bank's presence in the region (i.e., cut costs), the merger became a positive event for shareholders and employees alike. There wasn't a great deal of overlap in Europe between the former competitors; instead, what Aspbury found was a complementary fit among the various businesses. The former Chemical Bank had concentrated its activities on its powerful foreign exchange and interest rate swaps businesses from its London dealing room; Manufacturers Hanover had been more active in raising debt capital through its London headquarters and its branches in Germany, Norway, France, Spain, Portugal, and Turkey.

A few skeptics questioned how the joining of two troubled banks might create a successful new bank, but from the start most media and securities analysts were positive about the combination. Their enthusiasm was based not only on the inherent logic of the deal from a cost standpoint, but also on the way in which management decisions were being made and communicated. For example, within days of the announcement, most senior positions were filled, thus preventing the natural infighting that occurs when uncertainty exists. It goes without saying that most lower-level employees didn't have the same degree of certainty, and the challenges that senior managers faced were abundant. In addition to keeping clients happy and revenue flowing, they had to build their new teams in a way that kept the best people from leaving, and they had to foster the idea that the new organization wasn't merely the sum of the parts. The organization would be a brand-new bank that everyone hoped would bear little resemblance to the troubled past.

National Cultural Challenges and Responses

Herb Aspbury and other international managers faced another level of complexity: the cross-border dimension. It was necessary not only to get former rivals to work together but also to deal with centuries-old cultural differences that could become major impediments to the business going forward. Whether the issue was the disdain that the proud Spanish team had for their colleagues in the U.K., or class distinctions remaining just below the surface in many countries, such issues had to be addressed quickly if the new Chemical Bank was to have a cohesive business throughout the region. Managing a business from New York with offices in Atlanta, Chicago, and Los Angeles was far different from managing a business from a place where the distances were shorter but the differences in language and history were more intense. Despite efforts by the European Union to create a unified market, most country managers at Chemical Bank and other major multinationals tended to focus inwardly and not think beyond their borders.

Fortunately the prospect of working for a successful new company helped managers overcome many of the obstacles in Europe. Focusing on common denominators rather than on differences was also important. Communication was a key element in this regard, and bimonthly meetings in London of the country managers became the norm. The meetings proved to be very effective for building personal relationships of mutual respect, thus overriding generations of cultural barriers. Another important factor was the reward system, which included a very generous bonus pool.

In the past, the tendency had been to build small kingdoms within countries and then use the local profit-and-loss statement as a lever for a good annual bonus. For some local managers and their teams, stature in the local community was even more important than money. Being seen as the president of Chemical Bank in Spain or in Portugal, for example, meant a great deal—but didn't necessarily benefit the European organization as a whole. Because management at the new Chemical Bank emphasized the P&L of the region as a whole, collaborative behavior became the goal and parochial attitudes were seen as an impediment.

To positively influence key staff members in the region, Aspbury invited 150 bankers from Chemical Europe to Marbella, Spain, for a four-day meeting. In addition to product seminars, business reviews, and exposure to top executives from New York, the sessions were designed to build relationships with colleagues throughout Europe so that greater cooperation would be fostered to enhance future business opportunities. It was also a chance to highlight the most successful deals of the previous year, particularly transactions involving two or more geographic teams (for example, a cross-border merger or a multicurrency debt origination on behalf of a United States client operating in several European countries). The message was that opening the borders to cooperative efforts was far more valuable to the bank and its employees than trying to be a local hero. A desirable outcome of the meetings in subsequent years was the fact that many people became close friends and looked forward to working across country borders.

Merger No. 2, Organizational Culture, and a New Strategy

By all measures the Chemical/Manufacturers Hanover merger was an enormous success around the world. Within six months of the completion of the deal, the new company was earning more in one month than its predecessors had earned in one quarter on a combined basis. The stock price rose from the high teens to the mid-fifties in two years, and the rating agencies upgraded the bank's long-term debt, thus reducing the cost of capital. Clients were also very happy, as evidenced by the new business Chemical was receiving at the expense of its competitors. Indeed, by late 1995, the company was in a position to acquire Chase Manhattan Corporation, a once proud bank struggling with problem loans and misguided expansion into overseas retail banking. Accordingly, after a summer of rumors, on August 28, 1995, Chase Manhattan and Chemical Bank announced plans to merge. Unlike the 1991 merger of equals, this was a takeover of Chase by Chemical, but because of the prominence of the Chase name around the world, Chemical Banking Corp. changed its name to Chase Manhattan Corp.

In theory an outright acquisition is easier because the acquirer can make decisions in an autocratic fashion and doesn't have to spend much time on consensus building. In practice it's not quite that simple. To extract maximum value from the purchase, it's important to select the best people and the best businesses from the combined entity. Complicating the integration of Chemical and Chase was a sense of shock and despair among older Chase employees, who felt betrayed by their management for selling the company to an "upstart."

For the second time in five years, Aspbury found himself with merger challenge in Europe, but one that was far more complex than the merger of Chemical Bank and Manufacturers Hanover. Chase had 5,000 employees in the region compared to 1,500 for Chemical, and Aspbury's responsibilities included all of Europe, Africa, and the Middle East, where Chase had offices and long-standing client relationships. Not only were there 150 people in Moscow, but offices in Greece, South Africa, and Uzbekistan were added to the equation. On the one hand, many people at Chase had never accepted the fact that their company was struggling and felt disenfranchised by the takeover. On the other hand, Chase had some outstanding bankers who welcomed the merger and quickly adapted to the new culture. Because Chase had been in the international arena for decades, many of its people had worked in New York and other major cities, had a broad vision of the world, and were accustomed to a global approach.

Once again the two major leadership challenges for Aspbury were team building and communication. Many Chase employees romanticized the past and still looked to the legendary David Rockefeller, who had retired as CEO in the early 1980s, to lead them forward. It soon became apparent that they would have difficulty adapting to the new organizational culture and would have to leave the bank. As the integration process moved forward, some Chase employees were actually convinced that the deal would die and the formal merger would never really happen. They too had to either accept reality or move on. The most talented people embraced the new opportunities the merger would afford and were ready to lead their best people.

As was the case in the 1991 merger, the market responded very positively to the announcement, and that reaction proved to be a powerful motivator. Because of the size of the new organization, Aspbury found that communication had to be both more frequent and more focused. The annual Marbella meetings had to be replaced, and more focus was needed on the "emerging markets" countries and products. Although the Moscow bankers might enjoy learning about investment-grade bonds and sophisticated derivative strategies, there was little opportunity to use these products in their market. Instead, they needed to know the bank's capabilities and risk tolerance in Eastern Europe and other developing economies, and they needed a crash course in capitalism. Many could spout capitalist terms, but very few really understood how free markets worked. Managing their expectations became a major challenge, for they were eager to exploit Chase's capabilities in their own markets. The bank, however, had to take a very cautious approach to the enormous risk in these new markets. Moving some of the best Russians, Poles, Hungarians, and Turks to London to work in specific industry and product groups gave them a much better overview of the organization and helped them understand the need to proceed cautiously in developing markets.

Leadership in Times of Change

It can be argued that nothing tests the management skills of a CEO like a merger. Not only must the business fit be there from the start (the so-called synergy), but the price has to be very realistic and the due diligence exacting. Unfortunately it's estimated that fewer than a third of all deals are successful in the end, as measured by financial results, market capitalization, and key management retention. Indeed, some mergers are "dead on arrival." All of the synergies in the world, however, can be destroyed by poor execution by various levels of management. Failing to take into account corporate cultural differences, to recognize the strengths and weaknesses of the various businesses and people, and to understand local cultures can be fatal. On the international side, the challenge is especially complex.

The interaction of organizational culture and national culture can create impediments to change and constrain managerial options. At the same time, a merger can reenergize organizations, break down barriers to change, and provide new opportunities. Balancing the interests of a range of stakeholders, dealing with people in an honest and straightforward fashion, and working with individuals to address some of the inevitable disruptions all go a long way toward increasing the likelihood of success in mergers involving different national and organizational cultures.

Questions for Review

1. What challenges do mergers create for managing national and organizational cultures?

2. How might the challenges associated with postmerger integration in Europe be affected by the fact that the parents of each company in both mergers were based in the United States?

3. What management skills are most important to making a cross-border merger successful? How might these skills differ from those needed during "routine" periods?

4. What specific steps were taken in the two mergers to try to align the interests of different parts of the organizations so that they were all working toward the overall good of the firm?

5. How might diversity among employees of different cultural backgrounds and with varying specialties and expertise actually strengthen an organization's culture after a merger?

Source: This case was prepared by Herbert F. Aspbury, retired Regional CEO for Europe, Africa, and the Middle East, Chase Manhattan Bank. It is provided as the basis for class discussion and is not intended to illustrate either effective or ineffective managerial capability or administrative responsibility.

Euro Disneyland

On January 18, 1993, Euro Disneyland chairperson Robert Fitzpatrick announced he would leave that post on April 12 to begin his own consulting company. Quitting his position exactly one year after the grand opening of Euro Disneyland, Fitzpatrick's resignation removed U.S. management from the helm of the French theme park and resort.

Fitzpatrick's position was taken by a Frenchman, Philippe Bourguignon, who had been Euro Disneyland's senior vice president for real estate. Bourguignon, 45 years old, faced a net loss of FFr 188 million for Euro Disneyland's fiscal year, which ended September 1992. Also, between April and September 1992, only 29 percent of the park's total visitors were French. Expectations were that closer to half of all visitors would be French.

It was hoped that the promotion of Philippe Bourguignon would have a public relations benefit for Euro Disneyland—a project that has been a publicist's nightmare from the beginning. One of the low points was at a news conference prior to the park's opening when protesters pelted Michael Eisner, CEO of the Walt Disney Company, with rotten eggs. Within the first year of operation, Disney had to compromise its "squeaky clean" image and lift the alcohol ban at the park. Wine is now served at all major restaurants.

Euro Disneyland, 49 percent owned by Walt Disney Company, Burbank, California, originally forecasted 11 million visitors in the first year of operation. In January 1993 it appeared attendance would be closer to 10 million. In response, management temporarily slashed prices at the park for local residents to FFr 150 ($27.27) from FFr 225 ($40.91) for adults, and to FFr 100 from FFr 150 for children in order to lure more French during the slow, wet winter months. The company also reduced prices at its restaurants and hotels, which registered occupancy rates of just 37 percent.

Bourguignon also faced other problems, such as the second phase of development at Euro Disneyland, which was expected to start in September 1993. It was unclear how the company planned to finance its FFr 8–10 billion cost. The company had steadily drained its cash reserves (FFr 1.9 billion in May 1993) while piling up debt (FFr 21 billion in May 1993). Euro Disneyland admitted that it and the Walt Disney Company were "exploring potential sources of financing for Euro Disneyland." The company was also talking to banks about restructuring its debts.

Despite the frustrations, Eisner was tirelessly upbeat about the project. "Instant hits are things that go away quickly, and things that grow slowly and are part of the culture are what we look for," he said. "What we created in France is the biggest private investment in a foreign country by an American company ever. And it's gonna pay off."

In the Beginning

Disney's story is the classic American rags-to-riches story, which started in a small Kansas City advertising office where Mickey was a real mouse prowling the unknown Walt Disney floor. Originally, Mickey was named Mortimer, until a dissenting Mrs. Disney stepped in. How close Mickey was to Walt Disney is evidenced by the fact that when filming, Disney himself dubbed the mouse's voice. Only in later films did Mickey get a different voice. Disney made many sacrifices to promote his hero-mascot, including selling his first car, a beloved Moon Cabriolet, and humiliating himself in front of Louis B. Mayer. "Get that mouse off the screen!" was the movie mogul's reported response to the cartoon character. Then, in 1955, Disney had the brainstorm of sending his movie characters out into the "real" world to mix with their fans and he battled skeptics to build the very first Disneyland in Anaheim, California.

When Disney died in 1966, the company went into virtual suspended animation. Their last big hit of that era was 1969's *The Love Bug,* about a Volkswagen named Herbie. Today, Disney executives trace the problem to a tyrannical CEO named E. Cardon Walker who ruled the company from 1976 to 1983, and to his successor, Ronald W. Miller. Walker was quick to ridicule underlings in public and impervious to any point of view but his own. He made decisions according to what he thought Walt would have done. Executives clinched arguments by quoting Walt like the Scriptures or Marx, and the company eventually supplied a little book of the founder's sayings. Making the wholesome family movies Walt would have wanted formed a key article of Walker's creed. For example, a poster advertising the unremarkable *Condorman* featured actress Barbara Carrera in a slit skirt. Walker had the slit painted over. With this as the context, studio producers ground out a thin stream of tired, formulaic movies that fewer and fewer customers would pay to see. In mid-1983, a similar low-horsepower approach to television production led to CBS's cancellation of the hour-long program *Walt Disney,* leaving the company without a regular network show for the first time in 29 years. Like a reclusive hermit, the company lost touch with the contemporary world.

Ron Miller's brief reign was by contrast a model of decentralization and delegation. Many attributed Miller's ascent to his marrying the boss's daughter rather than to any special gift. To shore Miller up, the board installed Raymond L. Watson, former head of the Irvine Co., as part-time chairperson. He quickly became full-time.

Miller sensed the studio needed rejuvenation and he managed to produce the hit film *Splash,* featuring an apparently (but not actually) bare-breasted mermaid, under the newly devised Touchstone label. However, the reluctance of freelance Hollywood talent to accommodate Disney's narrow range and stingy compensation often kept his sound instincts from bearing fruit. "Card [Cardon Walker] would listen but not hear," said a former executive. "Ron [Ron Miller] would listen but not act."

Too many box office bombs contributed to a steady erosion of profit. Profits of $135 million on revenues of $915 million in 1980 dwindled to $93 million on revenues of $1.3 billion in 1983. More alarmingly, revenues from the company's theme parks, about three-quarters of the company's total revenues, were showing signs of leveling off. Disney's stock slid from $84.375 a share to $48.75 between April 1983 and February 1984.

Through these years, Roy Disney Jr. simmered while he watched the downfall of the national institution that his uncle, Walt, and his father, Roy Disney Sr., had built. He had long argued that the company's constituent parts all work together to enhance each other. If movie and television production weren't revitalized, not only would that source of revenue disappear but the company and its activities would also grow dim in the public eye. At the same time the stream of new ideas and characters that kept people pouring into the parks and buying toys, books, and records would dry up. Now his dire predictions were coming true. His own personal shareholding had already dropped from $96 million to $54 million. Walker's treatment of Ron Miller as the shining heir apparent and Roy Disney as the idiot nephew helped drive Roy to quit as Disney vice president in 1977, and to set up Shamrock Holdings, a broadcasting and investment company.

In 1984, Roy teamed up with Stanley Gold, a tough-talking lawyer and a brilliant strategist. Gold saw that the falling stock price was bound to flush out a raider and afford Roy Disney a chance to restore the company's fortunes. They asked Frank Wells, vice chairperson of Warner Bros., if he would take a top job in the company in the event they offered it. Wells, a lawyer and a Rhodes scholar, said yes. With that, Roy knew that what he would hear in Disney's boardroom would limit his freedom to trade in its stock, so he quit the board on March 9, 1984. "I knew that would hang a 'For Sale' sign over the company," said Gold.

By resigning, Roy pushed over the first of a train of dominoes that ultimately led to the result he most desired. The company was raided, almost dismantled, greenmailed, raided again, and sued left and right. But it miraculously emerged with a skilled new top management with big plans for a bright future. Roy Disney proposed Michael Eisner as the CEO but the board came close to rejecting Eisner in favor of an older, more buttoned-down candidate. Gold stepped in and made an impassioned speech to the directors. "You see guys like Eisner as a little crazy . . . but every studio in this country has been run by crazies. What do you think Walt Disney was? The guy was off the goddamned wall. This is a creative institution. It needs to be run by crazies again."*

Meanwhile Eisner and Wells staged an all-out lobbying campaign, calling on every board member except two, who were abroad, to explain their views about the company's future. "What was most important," said Eisner, "was that they saw I did not come in a tutu, and that I was a serious person, and I understood a P&L, and I knew the investment analysts, and I read *Fortune.*"

In September 1984, Michael Eisner was appointed CEO and Frank Wells became president. Jeffrey Katzenberg, the 33-year-old, maniacal production chief followed Fisher from Paramount Pictures. He took over Disney's movie and television studios. "The key," said Eisner "is to start off with a great idea."

Disneyland in Anaheim, California

For a long time, Walt Disney had been concerned about the lack of family-type entertainment available for his two daughters. The amusement parks he saw around him were mostly filthy traveling carnivals. They were often unsafe and allowed unruly conduct on the premises. Disney envisioned a place where people from all over the world would be able to go for clean and safe fun. His dream came true on July 17, 1955, when the gates first opened at Disneyland in Anaheim, California.

Disneyland strives to generate the perfect fantasy. But magic does not simply happen. The place is a marvel of modern technology. Literally dozens of computers, huge banks of tape machines, film projectors, and electronic controls lie behind the walls, beneath the floors, and above the ceilings of dozens of rides and attractions. The philosophy is that "Disneyland is the world's biggest stage, and the audience is right here on the stage," said Dick Hollinger, chief industrial engineer at Disneyland. "It

Exhibit 1   How the Theme Parks Grew

1955	Disneyland
1966	Walt Disney's death
1971	Walt Disney World in Orlando
1982	Epcot Center
1983	Tokyo Disneyland
1992	Euro Disneyland

*Stephen Koepp, "Do You Believe in Magic?" *Time,* April 25, 1988, pp. 66–73.

takes a tremendous amount of work to keep the stage clean and working properly."

Cleanliness is a primary concern. Before the park opens at 8 a.m., the cleaning crew will have mopped and hosed and dried every sidewalk, every street, and every floor and counter. More than 350 of the park's 7,400 employees come on duty at 1 a.m., to begin the daily cleanup routine. The thousands of feet that walk through the park each day and chewing gum do not mix, and gum has always presented major cleanup problems. The park's janitors found long ago that fire hoses with 90 pounds of water pressure would not do the job. Now they use steam machines, razor scrapers, and mops towed by Cushman scooters to literally scour the streets and sidewalks daily.

It takes one person working a full eight-hour shift to polish the brass on the Fantasyland merry-go-round. The scrupulously manicured plantings throughout the park are treated with growth retarding hormones to keep the trees and bushes from spreading beyond their assigned spaces and destroying the carefully maintained five-eighths scale modeling that is utilized in the park. The maintenance supervisor of the Matterhorn bobsled ride personally walks every foot of track and inspects every link of tow chain every night, thus trusting his or her own eyes more than the $2 million in safety equipment that is built into the ride.

Eisner himself pays obsessive attention to detail. Walking through Disneyland one Sunday afternoon, he peered at the plastic leaves on the Swiss Family Robinson tree house noting that they periodically wear out and need to be replaced leaf by leaf at a cost of $500,000. As his family strolled through the park, he and his eldest son Breck stooped to pick up the rare piece of litter that the cleanup crew had somehow missed. This old-fashioned dedication has paid off. Since opening day in 1955, Disneyland has been a consistent money-maker.

Disney World in Orlando, Florida

By the time Eisner arrived, Disney World in Orlando was already on its way to becoming what it is today—the most popular vacation destination in the United States. But the company had neglected a rich niche in its business: hotels. Disney's three existing hotels, probably the most profitable in the United States, registered unheard-of occupancy rates of 92 percent to 96 percent versus 66 percent for the industry. Eisner promptly embarked on an ambitious $1 billion hotel expansion plan. Two major hotels, Disney's Grand Floridian Beach Resort and Disney's Caribbean Beach Resort, were opened during 1987–89. Disney's Yacht Club and Beach Resort along with the Dolphin and Swan Hotels, owned and operated by Tishman Realty & Construction, Metropolitan Life Insurance, and Aoki Corporation opened during 1989–90. Adding 3,400 hotel rooms and 250,000 square feet of convention space, this made it the largest convention center east of the Mississippi.

In October 1982, Disney made a new addition to the theme park—the Experimental Prototype Community of Tomorrow, or EPCOT Center. E. Cardon Walker, then president of the company, announced that EPCOT would be a "permanent showcase, industrial park, and experimental housing center." This new park consists of two large complexes: Future World, a series of pavilions designed to show the technological advances of the next 25 years, and World Showcase, a collection of foreign "villages."

Tokyo Disneyland

It was Tokyo's nastiest winter day in four years. Arctic winds and eight inches of snow lashed the city. Roads were clogged and trains slowed down. But the bad weather didn't keep 13,200 hardy souls from Tokyo Disneyland. Mikki Mausu, better known outside Japan as Mickey Mouse, had taken the country by storm.

Located on a fringe of reclaimed shoreline in Urayasu City on the outskirts of Tokyo, the park opened to the public on April 15, 1983. In less than one year, over 10 million people had passed through its gates, an attendance figure that has been bettered every single year. On August 13, 1983, 93,000 people helped set a one-day attendance record that easily eclipsed the old records established at the two parent U.S. parks. Four years later, records again toppled as the turnstiles clicked. The total this time: 111,500. By 1988, approximately 50 million people, or nearly half of Japan's population, had visited Tokyo Disneyland since its opening. The steady cash flow pushed revenues for fiscal year 1989 to $768 million, up 17 percent from 1988.

The 204-acre Tokyo Disneyland is owned and operated by Oriental Land under license from the Walt Disney Co. The 45-year contract gives Disney 10 percent of admissions and 5 percent of food and merchandise sales, plus licensing fees. Disney opted to take no equity in the project and put no money down for construction.

Exhibit 2   Investor's Snapshot: The Walt Disney Company (December 1989)

Sales (latest four quarters)	$4.6 billion
Change from year earlier	Up 33.6%
Net profit	$703.3 million
Change	Up 34.7%
Return on common stockholders' equity	23.4%
Five year average	20.3%
Stock price average (last 12 months)	$60.50–$136.25
Recent share price	$122.75
Price/Earnings Multiple	27
Total return to investors (12 months to 11/3/89)	90.6%

Source: Fortune, December 4, 1989.

"I never had the slightest doubt about the success of Disneyland in Japan," said Masatomo Takahashi, president of Oriental Land Company. Oriental Land was so confident of the success of Disney in Japan that it financed the park entirely with debt, borrowing ¥180 billion ($1.5 billion at February 1988 exchange rates). Takahashi added, "The debt means nothing to me," and with good reason. According to Fusahao Awata, who co-authored a book on Tokyo Disneyland: "The Japanese yearn for [American culture]."

Soon after Tokyo Disneyland opened in April 1983, five Shinto priests held a solemn dedication ceremony near Cinderella's castle. It is the only overtly Japanese ritual seen so far in this sprawling theme park. What visitors see is pure Americana. All signs are in English, with only small *katakana* (a phonetic Japanese alphabet) translations. Most of the food is American-style, and the attractions are cloned from Disney's U.S. parks. Disney also held firm on two fundamentals that strike the Japanese as strange—no alcohol is allowed and no food may be brought in from outside the park.

However, in Disney's enthusiasm to make Tokyo a brick-by-brick copy of Anaheim's Magic Kingdom, there were a few glitches. On opening day, the Tokyo park discovered that almost 100 public telephones were placed too high for Japanese guests to reach them comfortably. And many hungry customers found countertops above their reach at the park's snack stands.

"Everything we imported that worked in the United States works here," said Ronald D. Pogue, managing director of Walt Disney Attractions Japan Ltd. "American things like McDonald's hamburgers and Kentucky Fried Chicken are popular here with young people. We also wanted visitors from Japan and Southeast Asia to feel they were getting the real thing," said Toshiharu Akiba, a staff member of the Oriental Land publicity department.

Still, local sensibilities dictated a few changes. A Japanese restaurant was added to please older patrons. The Nautilus submarine is missing. More areas are covered to protect against rain and snow. Lines for attractions had to be redesigned so that people walking through the park did not cross in front of patrons waiting to ride an attraction. "It's very discourteous in Japan to have people cross in front of somebody else," explained James B. Cora, managing director of operations for the Tokyo project. The biggest differences between Japan and America have come in slogans and ad copy. Although English is often used, it's "Japanized" English—the sort that would have native speakers shaking their heads while the Japanese nod happily in recognition. "Let's Spring" was the motto for one of their highly successful ad campaigns.

Pogue, visiting frequently from his base in California, supervised seven resident American Disney managers who work side by side with Japanese counterparts from Oriental Land Co. to keep the park in tune with the Disney doctrine. American it may be, but Tokyo Disneyland appeals to such deep-seated Japanese passions as cleanliness, order, outstanding service, and technological wizardry. Japanese executives are impressed by Disney's detailed training manuals, which teach employees how to make visitors feel like VIPs. Most worth emulating, say the Japanese, is Disney's ability to make even the lowliest job seem glamorous. "They have changed the image of dirty work," said Hakuhodo Institute's Sekizawa.

Disney Company did encounter a few unique cultural problems when developing Tokyo Disneyland:

The problem: how to dispose of some 250 tons of trash that would be generated weekly by Tokyo Disneyland visitors?

The standard Disney solution: trash compactors.

The Japanese proposal: pigs to eat the trash and be slaughtered and sold at a profit.

James B. Cora and his team of some 150 operations experts did a little calculating and pointed out that it would take 100,000 pigs to do the job. And then there would be the smell . . .

The Japanese relented.

The Japanese were also uneasy about a rustic-looking Westernland, Tokyo's version of Frontierland. "The Japanese like everything fresh and new when they put it in," said Cora. "They kept painting the wood and we kept saying, 'No, it's got to look old.'" Finally the Disney crew took the Japanese to Anaheim to give them a firsthand look at the Old West.

Tokyo Disneyland opened just as the yen escalated in value against the dollar and the income level of the Japanese registered a phenomenal improvement. During this era of affluence, Tokyo Disneyland triggered an interest in leisure. Its great success spurred the construction of "leisurelands" throughout the country. This created an increase in the Japanese people's orientation toward leisure. But demographics are the real key to Tokyo Disneyland's success. Thirty million Japanese live within 30 miles of the park. There are three times more than the number of people in the same proximity to Anaheim's Disneyland. With the park proven such an unqualified hit, and nearing capacity, Oriental Land and Disney mapped out plans for a version of the Disney-MGM studio tour next door. This time, Disney talked about taking a 50 percent stake in the project.

Building Euro Disneyland

On March 24, 1987, Michael Eisner and Jacques Chirac, the French prime minister, signed a contract for the building of a Disney theme park at Marne-la-Vallee. Talks between Disney and the French government had dragged on for more than a year. At the signing, Robert Fitzpatrick, fluent in French, married to the former Sylvie Blondet, and the recipient of two awards from the French government, was introduced as the president of Euro Disneyland. He was expected to be a key player in wooing support from the

French establishment for the theme park. As one analyst put it, Disney selected him to set up the park because he is "more French than the French."

Disney had been courted extensively by Spain and France. The prime ministers of both countries ordered their governments to lend Disney a hand in its quest for a site. France set up a five-person team headed by Special Advisor to Foreign Trade and Tourism Minister Edith Cresson, and Spain's negotiators included Ignacio Vasallo, Director-General for the Promotion of Tourism. Disney pummeled both governments with requests for detailed information. "The only thing they haven't asked us for is the color of the tourists' eyes," moaned Vasallo.

The governments tried other enticements, too. Spain offered tax and labor incentives and possibly as much as 20,000 acres of land. The French package, although less generous, included spending of $53 million to improve highway access to the proposed site and perhaps speeding up a $75 million subway project. For a long time, all that smiling Disney officials would say was that Spain had better weather while France had a better population base.

Officials explained that they picked France over Spain because Marne-la-Vallee is advantageously close to one of the world's tourism capitals, while also being situated within a day's drive or train ride of some 30 million people in France, Belgium, England, and Germany. Another advantage mentioned was the availability of good transportation. A train line that serves as part of the Paris Metro subway system ran to Torcy, in the center of Marne-la-Vallee, and the French government promised to extend the line to the actual site of the park. The park would also be served by A-4, a modern highway that runs from Paris to the German border, as well as a freeway that runs to Charles de Gaulle airport.

Once a letter of intent had been signed, sensing that the French government was keen to not let the plan fail, Disney held out for one concession after another. For example, Disney negotiated for VAT (value-added tax) on ticket sales to be cut from a normal 18.6 percent to 7 percent. A quarter of the investment in building the park would come from subsidized loans. Additionally, any disputes arising from the contract would be settled not in French courts but by a special international panel of arbitrators. But Disney did have to agree to a clause in the contract which would require it to respect and utilize French culture in its themes.

The park was built on 4,460 acres of farmland in Marne-la-Vallee, a rural corner of France 20 miles east of Paris known mostly for sugar beets and Brie cheese. Opening was planned for early 1992 and planners hoped to attract some 10 million visitors a year. Approximately $2.5 billion was needed to build the park, making it the largest single foreign investment ever in France. A French "pivot" company was formed to build the park with starting capital of FFr 3 billion, split 60 percent French and 40 percent foreign, with Disney taking 16.67 percent. Euro Disneyland was expected to bring $600 million in foreign investment into France each year.

As soon as the contract had been signed, individuals and businesses began scurrying to somehow plug into the Mickey Mouse money machine—all were hoping to benefit from the American dream without leaving France. In fact, one Paris daily, *Liberation,* actually sprouted mouse ears over its front-page flag.

The $1.5 to $2 billion first phase investment would involve an amusement complex including hotels and restaurants, golf courses, and an aquatic park in addition to a European version of the Magic Kingdom. The second phase, scheduled to start after the gates opened in 1992, called for the construction of a community around the park, including a sports complex, technology park, conference center, theater, shopping mall, university campus, villas, and condominiums. No price tag had been put on the second phase, although it was expected to rival, if not surpass, the first phase investment. In November 1989, Fitzpatrick announced that the Disney–MGM Studios, Europe would also open at Euro Disneyland in 1996, resembling the enormously successful Disney–MGM Studios theme park at Disney World in Orlando. The new studios would greatly enhance the Walt Disney Company's strategy of increasing its production of live action and animated filmed entertainment in Europe for both the European and world markets.

"The phone's been ringing here ever since the announcement," said Marc Berthod of EpaMarne, the government body that oversees the Marne-la-Vallee region. "We've gotten calls from big companies as well as small—everything from hotel chains to language interpreters all asking for details on Euro Disneyland. And the individual mayors of the villages around here have been swamped with calls from people looking for jobs." he added.

Euro Disneyland was expected to generate up to 28,000 jobs, providing a measure of relief for an area that had suffered a 10 percent–plus unemployment rate for the previous year. It was also expected to light a fire under France's construction industry, which had been particularly hard hit by France's economic problems over the previous year. Moreover, Euro Disneyland was expected to attract many other investors to the depressed outskirts of Paris. International Business Machines (IBM) and Banque National de Paris were among those already building in the area. In addition one of the new buildings going up was a factory that would employ 400 outside workers to wash the 50 tons of laundry expected to be generated per day by Euro Disneyland's 14,000 employees.

The impact of Euro Disneyland was also felt in the real estate market. "Everyone who owns land around here is holding on to it for the time being, at least until they know what's going to happen," said Danny Theveno, a spokesman for the town of Villiers on the western edge of Marne-la-Vallee. Disney expected 11 million visitors in the first year. The break-even point was estimated to be between seven and eight million. One worry was that Euro Disneyland would cannibalize the flow of European visitors to Walt Disney

Exhibit 3   **Chronology of the Euro Disneyland Deal**

1984–85	Disney negotiates with Spain and France to create a European theme park
	Chooses France as the site
1987	Disney signs letter of intent with the French government
1988	Selects lead commercial bank lenders for the senior portion of the project
	Forms the Société en Nom Collectif (SNC)
	Begins planning for the equity offering of 51% of Euro Disneyland as required in the letter of intent
1989	European press and stock analysts visit Walt Disney World in Orlando
	Begin extensive news and television campaign
	Stock starts trading at 20–25 percent premium from the issue price

Source: Geraldine E. Willigan, "The Value-Adding CFO: An Interview with Disney's Gary Wilson," *Harvard Business Review,* January–February 1990, pp. 85–93.

World in Florida, but European travel agents said that their customers were still eagerly signing up for Florida, lured by the cheap dollar and the promise of sunshine.

Protests of Cultural Imperialism

Disney faced French communists and intellectuals who protested the building of Euro Disneyland. Ariane Mnouchkine, a theater director, described it as a "cultural Chernobyl." "I wish with all my heart that the rebels would set fire to Disneyland," thundered a French intellectual in the newspaper *La Figaro.* "Mickey Mouse," sniffed another, "is stifling individualism and transforming children into consumers." The theme park was damned as an example of American "neoprovincialism."

Farmers in the Marne-la-Vallee region posted protest signs along the roadside featuring a mean looking Mickey Mouse and touting sentiments such as "Disney go home," "Stop the massacre," and "Don't gnaw away our national wealth." Farmers were upset partly because under the terms of the contract, the French government would expropriate the necessary land and sell it without profit to the Euro Disneyland development company.

While local officials were sympathetic to the farmers' position, they were unwilling to let their predicament interfere with what some called "the deal of the century." "For many years these farmers have had the fortune to cultivate what is considered some of the richest land in France," said Berthod. "Now they'll have to find another occupation."

Also less than enchanted about the prospect of a magic kingdom rising among their midst was the communist dominated labor federation, the Confédération Générale du Travail (CGT). Despite the job-creating potential of Euro Disney, the CGT doubted its members would benefit. The union had been fighting hard to stop the passage of a bill which would give managers the right to establish flexible hours for their workers. Flexible hours were believed to be a prerequisite to the profitable operation of Euro Disneyland, especially considering seasonal variations.

However, Disney proved to be relatively immune to the anti-U.S. virus. In early 1985, one of the three state-owned

television networks signed a contract to broadcast two hours of dubbed Disney programming every Saturday evening. Soon after, *Disney Channel* became one of the top-rated programs in France.

In 1987, the company launched an aggressive community relations program to calm the fears of politicians, farmers, villagers, and even bankers that the project would bring traffic congestion, noise, pollution, and other problems to their countryside. Such a public relations program was a rarity in France, where businesses make little effort to establish good relations with local residents. Disney invited 400 local children to a birthday party for Mickey Mouse, sent Mickey to area hospitals, and hosted free trips to Disney World in Florida for dozens of local officials and children.

"They're experts at seduction, and they don't hide the fact that they're trying to seduce you," said Vincent Guardiola, an official with Banque Indosuez, one of the 17 banks wined and dined at Orlando and subsequently one of the venture's financial participants. "The French aren't used to this kind of public relations—it was unbelievable." Observers said that the goodwill efforts helped dissipate initial objections to the project.

Financial Structuring at Euro Disneyland

Eisner was so keen on Euro Disneyland that Disney kept a 49 percent stake in the project, while the remaining 51 percent of stock was distributed through the London, Paris, and Brussels stock exchanges. Half the stock under the offer was going to the French, 25 percent to the English, and the remainder distributed in the rest of the European community. The initial offer price of FFr 72 was considerably higher than the pathfinder prospectus estimate because the capacity of the park had been slightly extended. Scarcity of stock was likely to push up the price, which was expected to reach FFr 166 by opening day in 1992. This would give a compound return of 21 percent.

Walt Disney Company maintained management control of the company. The U.S. company put up $160 million of its own capital to fund the project, an investment which soared in value to $2.4 billion after the popular stock offering in Europe. French national and local authorities, by comparison, were providing about $800 million in low-interest loans and poured at least that much again into infrastructure.

Other sources of funding were the park's 12 corporate sponsors, and Disney would pay them back in kind. The "autopolis" ride, where kids ride cars, features coupes emblazoned with the "Hot Wheels" logo. Mattel Inc., sponsor of the ride, is grateful for the boost to one of its biggest toy lines.

The real payoff would begin once the park opened. The Walt Disney Company would receive 10 percent of admission fees and 5 percent of food and merchandise revenue, the same arrangement as in Japan. But in France, it would also receive management fees, incentive fees, and 49 percent of the profits.

A Saloman Brothers analyst estimated that the park would pull in three to four million more visitors than the 11 million the company expected in the first year. Other Wall Street analysts cautioned that stock prices of both Walt Disney Company and Euro Disney already contained all the Euro optimism they could absorb. "Europeans visit Disney World in Florida as part of an 'American experience,'" said Patrick P. Roper, marketing director of Alton Towers, a successful British theme park near Manchester. He doubted they would seek the suburbs of Paris as eagerly as America and predicted attendance would trail Disney projections.

The Layout of Euro Disneyland

Euro Disneyland is determinedly American in its theme. There was an alcohol ban in the park despite the attitude among the French that wine with a meal is a God-given right. Designers presented a plan for a Main Street USA based on scenes of America in the 1920s, because research indicated that Europeans loved the Prohibition era. Eisner decreed that images of gangsters and speak-easies were too negative. Though made more ornate and Victorian than Walt Disney's idealized Midwestern small town, Main Street remained Main Street. Steamships leave from Main Street through the Grand Canyon Diorama en route to Frontierland.

The familiar Disney Tomorrowland, with its dated images of the space age, was jettisoned entirely. It was replaced by a gleaming brass and wood complex called Discoverland, which was based on themes of Jules Verne and Leonardo da Vinci. Eisner ordered $8 or $10 million in extras to the "Visionarium" exhibit, a 360-degree movie about French culture which was required by the French in their original contract. French and English are the official languages at the park, and multilingual guides are available to help Dutch, German, Spanish, and Italian visitors.

With the American Wild West being so frequently captured on film, Europeans have their own idea of what life was like back then. Frontierland reinforces those images. A runway mine train takes guests through the canyons and mines of Gold Rush country. There is a paddle wheel steamboat reminiscent of Mark Twain, Indian explorer canoes, and a phantom manor from the Gold Rush days.

In Fantasyland, designers strived to avoid competing with the nearby European reality of actual medieval towns, cathedrals, and chateaux. While Disneyland's castle is based on Germany's Neuschwanstein and Disney World's is based on a Loire Valley chateau, Euro Disney's *Le Château de la Belle au Bois Dormant*, as the French insisted Sleeping Beauty be called, is more cartoon-like with stained glass windows built by English craftsmakers and depicting Disney characters. Fanciful trees grow inside as well as a beanstalk.

The park is criss-crossed with covered walkways. Eisner personally ordered the installation of 35 fireplaces in hotels and restaurants. "People walk around Disney World in Florida with humidity and temperatures in the 90s and they walk into an air-conditioned ride and say, 'This is the greatest,'" said Eisner. "When it's raining and miserable, I hope they will walk into one of these lobbies with the fireplace going and say the same thing."

Children all over Europe were primed to consume. Even one of the intellectuals who contributed to *Le Figaro*'s Disney-bashing broadsheet was forced to admit with resignation that his ten-year-old son "swears by Michael Jackson." At Euro Disneyland, under the name "Captain EO," Disney just so happened to have a Michael Jackson attraction awaiting him.

Food Service and Accommodations at Euro Disneyland

Disney expected to serve 15,000 to 17,000 meals per hour, excluding snacks. Menus and service systems were developed so that they varied both in style and price. There is a 400-seat buffeteria, 6 table service restaurants, 12 counter service units, 10 snack bars, 1 Discovery food court seating 850, 9 popcorn wagons, 15 ice-cream carts, 14 specialty food carts, and 2 employee cafeterias. Restaurants were, in fact, to be a showcase for American foods. The only exception to this is Fantasyland which re-creates European

Exhibit 4   The Euro Disneyland Resort

5,000 acres in size
30 attractions
12,000 employees
6 hotels (with 5,184 rooms)
10 theme restaurants
414 cabins
181 camping sites

Source: Roger Cohen, "Threat of Strikes in Euro Disney Debut," *New York Times,* April 10, 1992, p. 20.

fables. Here, food service will reflect the fable's country of origin: Pinocchio's facility having German food; Cinderella's, French; Bella Notte's, Italian; and so on.

Of course recipes were adapted for European tastes. Since many Europeans don't care much for very spicy food, Tex-Mex recipes were toned down. A special coffee blend had to be developed which would have universal appeal. Hot dog carts would reflect the regionalism of American tastes. There would be a ball park hot dog (mild, steamed, a mixture of beef and pork), a New York hot dog (all beef, and spicy), and a Chicago hot dog (Vienna-style, similar to bratwurst).

Euro Disneyland has six theme hotels which would offer nearly 5,200 rooms on opening day, a campground (444 rental trailers and 181 camping sites), and single family homes on the periphery of the 27-hole golf course.

Disney's Strict Appearance Code

Antoine Guervil stood at his post in front of the 1,000 room Cheyenne Hotel at Euro Disneyland, practicing his "Howdy!" When Guervil, a political refugee from Haiti, said the word, it sounded more like "Audi." Native French speakers have trouble with the aspirated "h" sound in words like "hay" and "Hank" and "Howdy." Guervil had been given the job of wearing a cowboy costume and booming a happy, welcoming Howdy to guests as they entered the Cheyenne, styled after a Western movie set.

"Audi," said Guervil, the strain of linguistic effort showing on his face. This was clearly a struggle. Unless things got better, it was not hard to imagine objections from Renault, the French car company that was one of the corporate sponsors of the park. Picture the rage of a French auto executive arriving with his or her family at the Renault-sponsored Euro Disneyland, only to hear the doorman of a Disney hotel advertising a German car.

Such were the problems Disney faced while hiring some 12,000 people to maintain and populate its Euro Disneyland theme park. A handbook of detailed rules on acceptable clothing, hairstyles, and jewelry, among other things, embroiled the company in a legal and cultural dispute. Critics asked how the brash Americans could be so insensitive to French culture, individualism, and privacy. Disney officials insisted that a ruling that barred them from imposing a squeaky-clean employment standard could threaten the image and long-term success of the park.

"For us, the appearance code has a real effect from a product identification standpoint," said Thor Degelmann, vice president for human resources for Euro Disneyland. "Without it we wouldn't be presenting the Disney product that people would be expecting."

The rules, spelled out in a video presentation and detailed in a guide handbook, went beyond height and weight standards. They required men's hair to be cut above the collar and ears with no beards or mustaches. Any tattoos must be covered. Women must keep their hair in one "natural color" with no frosting or streaking and they may make only limited use of make-up like mascara. False eyelashes, eyeliners, and eye pencil were completely off limits. Fingernails can't pass the end of the fingers. As for jewelry, women can wear only one earring in each ear, with the earring's diameter no more than three-quarters of an inch. Neither men nor women can wear more than one ring on each hand. Further, women were required to wear appropriate undergarments and only transparent panty hose, not black or anything with fancy designs. Though a daily bath was not specified in the rules, the applicant's video depicted a shower scene and informed applicants that they were expected to show up for work "fresh and clean each day." Similar rules are in force at Disney's three other theme parks in the United States and Japan.

In the United States, some labor unions representing Disney employees have occasionally protested the company's strict appearance code, but with little success. French labor unions began protesting when Disneyland opened its "casting center" and invited applicants to "play the role of [their lives]" and to take a "unique opportunity to marry work and magic." The CGT handed out leaflets in front of the center to warn applicants of the appearance code, which they believed represented "an attack on individual liberty." A more mainstream union, the Confédération Française Démocratique du Travail (CFDT) appealed to the Labor Ministry to halt Disney's violation of "human

Exhibit 5   **What Price Mickey?**

	Euro Disneyland	Disney World, Orlando
	Peak Season Hotel Rates	
4-person room	$97 to $345	$104–$455
	Campground Space	
	$48	$30–$49
	One-Day Pass	
Children	$26	$26
Adults	$40	$33

Source: BusinessWeek, March 30, 1992.

dignity." French law prohibits employers from restricting individual and collective liberties unless the restrictions can be justified by the nature of the task to be accomplished and are proportional to that end.

Degelmann, however, said that the company was "well aware of the cultural differences" between the United States and France and as a result had "toned down" the wording in the original American version of the guidebook. He pointed out that many companies, particularly airlines, maintained appearance codes just as strict. "We happened to put ours in writing," he added. In any case, he said that he knew of no one who had refused to take the job because of the rules and that no more than 5 percent of the people showing up for interviews had decided not to proceed after watching the video, which also detailed transportation and salary.

Fitzpatrick also defended the dress code, although he conceded that Disney might have been a little naive in presenting things so directly. He added, "Only in France is there still a communist party. There is not even one in Russia any more. The ironic thing is that I could fill the park with CGT requests for tickets."

Another big challenge lay in getting the mostly French "cast members," as Disney calls its employees, to break their ancient cultural aversions to smiling and being consistently polite to park guests. The individualistic French had to be molded into the squeaky-clean Disney image. Rival theme parks in the area, loosely modeled on the Disney system, had already encountered trouble keeping smiles on the faces of the staff, who sometimes took on the demeanor of subway ticket clerks.

The delicate matter of hiring French citizens as opposed to other nationals was examined in the more than two-year-long preagreement negotiations between the French government and Disney. The final agreement called for Disney to make a maximum effort to tap into the local labor market. At the same time, it was understood that for Euro Disneyland to work, its staff must mirror the multi-country make-up of its guests. "Casting centers" were set up in Paris, London, Amsterdam, and Frankfurt. "We are concentrating on the local labor market, but we are also looking for workers who are German, English, Italian, Spanish, or other nationalities and who have good communication skills, are outgoing, speak two European languages—French plus one other—and like being around people," said Degelmann.

Stephane Baudet, a 28-year-old trumpet player from Paris, refused to audition for a job in a Disney brass band when he learned he would have to cut his ponytail. "Some people will turn themselves into a pumpkin to work at Euro Disneyland." he said. "But not me."

Opening Day at Euro Disneyland

A few days before the grand opening of Euro Disneyland, hundreds of French visitors were invited to a pre-opening party. They gazed perplexed at what was placed before them. It was a heaping plate of spare ribs. The visitors were at the Buffalo Bill Wild West Show, a cavernous theater featuring a panoply of "Le Far West," including 20 imported buffaloes. And Disney deliberately didn't provide silverware. "There was a moment of consternation," recalls Fitzpatrick. "Then they just kind of said, 'The hell with it,' and dug in." There was one problem. The guests couldn't master the art of gnawing ribs and applauding at the same time. So Disney planned to provide more napkins and teach visitors to stamp with their feet.

On April 12, 1992, the opening day of Euro Disneyland, *France-Soir* enthusiastically predicted Disney dementia. "Mickey! It's madness," read its front-page headline, warning of chaos on the roads and suggesting that people may have to be turned away. A French government survey indicated that half a million might turn up with 90,000 cars trying to get in. French radio warned traffic to avoid the area.

By lunchtime on opening day, the Euro Disneyland car park was less than half full, suggesting an attendance of below 25,000, less than half the park's capacity and way below expectations. Many people may have heeded the advice to stay home or, more likely, were deterred by a one-day strike that cut the direct rail link to Euro Disneyland from the center of Paris. Queues for the main rides, such as Pirates of the Caribbean and Big Thunder Mountain railroad, were averaging around 15 minutes less than on an ordinary day at Disney World, Florida.

Disney executives put on a brave face, claiming that attendance was better than at first days for other Disney theme parks in Florida, California, and Japan. However, there was no disguising the fact that after spending thousands of dollars on the pre-opening celebrations, Euro Disney would have appreciated some impressively long traffic jams on the auto route.

Other Operating Problems

When the French government changed hands in 1986, work ground to a halt, as the negotiator appointed by the Conservative government threw out much of the ground work prepared by his Socialist predecessor. The legalistic approach taken by the Americans also bogged down talks, as it meant planning ahead for every conceivable contingency. At the same time, right-wing groups who saw the park as an invasion of "chewing-gum jobs" and U.S. pop-culture also fought hard for a greater "local cultural context."

On opening day, English visitors found the French reluctant to play the game of queuing. "The French seem to think that if God had meant them to queue, He wouldn't have given them elbows," they commented. Different cultures have different definitions of personal space, and Disney guests faced problems of people getting too close or pressing around those who left too much space between themselves and the person in front.

Disney placed its first ads for work bids in English, leaving smaller and medium-sized French firms feeling like foreigners in their own land. Eventually, Disney set up a data bank with information on over 20,000 French and European firms looking for work and the local Chamber of Commerce developed a video text information bank with Disney that small- and medium-sized companies through France and Europe would be able to tap into. "The work will come, but many local companies have got to learn that they don't simply have the right to a chunk of work without competing," said a Chamber official.

Efforts were made to ensure that sooner, rather than later, European nationals take over the day-to-day running of the park. Although there were only 23 U.S. expatriates among the employees, they controlled the show and held most of the top jobs. Each senior manager had the task of choosing his or her European successor.

Disney was also forced to bail out 40 subcontractors who were working for the Gabot-Eremco construction contracting group, which had been unable to honor all of its commitments. Some of the subcontractors said they faced bankruptcy if they were not paid for their work on Euro Disneyland. A Disney spokesperson said that the payments would be less than $20.3 million and the company had already paid Gabot-Eremco for work on the park. Gabot-Eremco and 15 other main contractors demanded $157 million in additional fees from Disney for work that they said was added to the project after the initial contracts were signed. Disney rejected the claim and sought government intervention. Disney said that under no circumstances would they pay Gabot-Eremco and accused its officers of incompetence.

As Bourguignon thought about these and other problems, the previous year's losses and the prospect of losses again in the current year, with their negative impact on the company's stock price, weighed heavily on his mind.

Questions for Review

1. Using Hofstede's four cultural dimensions as a point of reference, what are some of the main cultural differences between the United States and France?

2. In what way has Trompenaars's research helped explain cultural differences between the United States and France?

3. In managing its Euro Disneyland operations, what are three mistakes that the company made? Explain.

4. Based on its experience, what are three lessons the company should have learned about how to deal with diversity? Describe each.

Source: This case was prepared by Research Assistant Sonali Krishna under the direction of Professors J. Stewart Black and Hal B. Gregersen as the basis for class discussion. It is not intended to illustrate either effective or ineffective managerial capability or administrative responsibility. Reprinted by permission of the authors.

Wal-Mart's Japan Strategy

In March 2002, Wal-Mart first entered the Japanese market by acquiring a $46 million stake in Seiyu, the nation's fifth-largest supermarket retailer.[1] Another main player in the deal was Sumitomo Corp., a leading trading company in Japan. Sumitomo's solid business base and knowledge of the retail sector was viewed as helping Wal-Mart effectively enter and expand in this unique market. As part of the deal, Sumitomo increased its stake in Seiyu to 15.6 percent.

Although Seiyu's existing distribution channels gave Wal-Mart an established local partner, two years after the initial entry, its success was unclear. In September 2003, Seiyu forecast a loss of $83 million for the March–December period, blaming a poor economic environment and an unfavorable produce climate.[2] While Wal-Mart is confident of its decision, the two companies have a different approach to management strategy, operations, and marketing. Wal-Mart specializes in large-scale general merchandise stores, mainly in suburban areas. Seiyu had traditionally focused on profitable grocery stores in city-center locations. Over time, Wal-Mart is expected to move away from these locations and focus on opening new open-spaced outlets.

In addition to meeting its quantitative goals, Wal-Mart's ability to effectively relate to Seiyu's employees will be an integral piece of the mix. Japanese and Americans have many distinct sociocultural differences, and these variations must be understood and properly managed by those who will be overseeing Seiyu's operations. In the final analysis, Wal-Mart's lasting success will hinge on its ability to understand cultural nuances and properly convey its message to both Japanese consumers and employees alike.

Wal-Mart's International Expansion

Wal-Mart is one of the largest and most admired global companies (see Tables 1, 2, and 3). Relying on long-term opportunities outside of its domestic market to expand sales, Wal-Mart is slowly and steadily making its way in many international regions, especially Japan (see Tables 4 and 5). As of late 2003, if ranked separately, Wal-Mart's international division would have been number 33 on the Fortune 500 list. According to John Menzer, Wal-Mart's international division president and CEO, "our challenge is to rake up one-third of the company's sales, and take our global scale to the local level."[3] While Wal-Mart has been successful in making some inroads overseas, its success

has been far from universal. For example, in Mexico and the U.K., the company's efforts to offer the lowest price to customers backfired because of resistance from established retailers. In Mexico, three of the largest domestic retailers constructed a joint buying and operational alliance solely to compete with Wal-Mart.[4]

As Wal-Mart continues to expand its global operations, analysts are curious to see how the company is received and whether consumers' opinions in fragmented market settings are able to move past their desire for lower prices. So far, labor advocates and environmentalists have created headaches for the U.S behemoth, making start-up procedures both cumbersome and expensive.

Japan, home of the world's second-largest consumer market, has been aggressively targeted by Wal-Mart as a key piece in its international strategy. Historically, reaching Japan's fickle customer base has been quite a challenge. In Japan, consumers often equate bad quality with low prices. Not so in the United States. But Wal-Mart isn't naïve. It realizes that changing consumer perceptions won't be easy or cheap, especially in the wake of recent competitive moves intended to counter its entrance into the nation of the rising sun. Succeeding where many large corporations have failed before it means that Wal-Mart has to be able to capture a distinct place in the hearts and minds of the Japanese customer as, specifically, a retail destination that offers an abundance of quality goods at rock-bottom prices.

The timing seemed right for Wal-Mart's expansion to Japan. The Japanese economy had been in the midst of a prolonged recession but was showing some signs of recovery. The country seemed ready for a discount retailer who could provide lower-priced goods for cash-strapped consumers. In 2002, the nation's economy grew just 1.6 percent while household income dropped. During the quarter ending September 30, 2003, household income dropped 1.4 percent, and consumer spending flattened. With the country experiencing deflationary forces in the prices of consumer goods, Wal-Mart hoped it would begin to attract more and more bargain-hungry consumers.

Although real estate prices dropped substantially over the past couple of years, they are still relatively high. Rather than build massive supercenter-size stores, Japanese retailers often stick with smaller shops that are easier to open in densely populated urban areas. Through the Seiyu ownership, Wal-Mart has been able to avoid up-front building costs, giving itself a swift advantage over hobbled

Table 1 **Wal-Mart Balance Sheet as of December 31, 2003**

Wal-Mart Corporation Consolidated Balance Sheet (in millions)

	2003	2002	2001	2000
Assets				
Cash and equivalents	2,758	2,161	2,054	1,856
Accounts receivable	2,108	2,000	1,768	1,341
Inventories	24,891	22,614	21,442	19,793
Total current assets	30,483	27,878	26,555	24,356
PP & E (net)	48,700	42,556	37,617	32,839
Total assets	94,685	83,527	78,130	70,349
Liabilities and Shareholders Equity				
Accounts payable	17,140	15,617	15,092	13,105
Notes payable	4,538	2,257	4,234	1,964
Accrued liabilities	8,945	7,174	6,355	6,161
Total current liabilities	32,617	27,282	28,949	25,803
Long-term debt	16,607	15,687	12,501	13,672
Total liabilities	55,348	48,425	46,787	44,515
Shareholders equity	39,337	35,102	31,343	25,834
Total liabilities and shareholders equity	94,685	83,527	78,130	70,349

Source: Wal-Mart 2003 Annual Report.

Table 2 **Wal-Mart Income Statement, December 31, 2003**

Wal-Mart Income Statement (in millions, except per share amounts)

	2003	2002	2001	2000
Net revenue	244,524	217,799	191,329	165,013
Cost of sales	191,838	171,562	150,255	129,664
SG&A	41,043	36,173	31,550	27,040
Interest expense	925	1,186	1,195	841
Interest provisions	4,487	3,897	3,692	3,338
Net income	8,039	6,671	6,295	5,377
Basic EPS	$1.81	$1.49	$1.41	$1.21
Diluted EPS	$1.81	$1.49	$1.40	$1.20
Dividends per share	$0.30	$0.30	$0.28	$0.24

Source: Wal-Mart 2003 Annual Report.

Table 3 **The 10 Most Admired Global Companies**

Rank	Company	Country
1	**Wal-Mart Stores**	**U.S.**
2	General Electric	U.S.
3	Microsoft	U.S.
4	Johnson & Johnson	U.S.
5	Berkshire Hathaway	U.S.
6	Dell	U.S.
7	IBM	U.S.
8	Toyota Motor	Japan
9	Procter & Gamble	U.S.

Source: www.fortune.com.

Table 4   **Wal-Mart Time Line**

1962: First Wal-Mart opens in Rogers, Arkansas.

1968: Wal-Mart moves outside Arkansas with stores in Sikeston, Missouri, and Claremore, Oklahoma.

1969: Company incorporated as Wal-Mart Stores Inc.

1977: Wal-Mart makes first acquisition, 16 Mohr-Value stores in Michigan and Illinois.

1981: Wal-Mart makes second acquisition, 92 Kuhn's Big K stores.

1983: First Sam's Club opens in Midwest City, Oklahoma; U.S. Woolco stores acquired.

1985: Grand Central Stores acquired.

1988: David Glass named CEO of Wal-Mart Stores Inc.; first supercenter opens in Washington, Missouri; Supersaver units acquired.

1990: Wal-Mart becomes nation's number-one retailer; McLane Co. of Temple, Texas, acquired.

1991: Western Merchandisers Inc. of Amarillo, Texas, acquired; "Sam's American Choice" brand products introduced; Wal-Mart enters first international market with the opening of a unit in Mexico City.

1992: Sam Walton dies; S. Robson Walton named chairman of the board; Wal-Mart enters Puerto Rico.

1993: Wal-Mart International division formed with Bobby Martin as president; 91 Pace Warehouse clubs acquired.

1994: 122 Woolco stores in Canada acquired; three value clubs opens in Hong Kong.

1995: Wal-Mart enters its 50th state—Vermont; enters Argentina and Brazil.

1996: Wal-Mart enters China through a joint-venture agreement.

1997: Wal-Mart has first $100 billion year, with sales totaling $105 billion.

1998: Wal-Mart introduces Neighborhood Market concept in Arkansas; acquires 21 Wertkauf units in Germany; enters Korea.

1999: Wal-Mart acquires 74 Interspar units in Germany and ASDA Group PLC in the United Kingdom.

2000: H. Lee Scott named president and CEO.; Progressive Grocer names Wal-Mart its Retailer of the Year.

2002: Wal-Mart purchases a 34 percent interest in Japanese retailer Seiyu Ltd., with options to purchase up to 66.7 percent of the company.

2003: Wal-Mart sells McLane Co. subsidiary to Berkshire Hathaway Inc. *Fortune* magazine names Wal-Mart most-admired company.

Source: Walmart.com.

Table 5   **International Distribution Coverage as of December 31, 2003**
Wal-Mart Stores Inc. Global Distribution Coverage

Country	Number of Stores				
	1999	2000	2001	2002	2003
Argentina	13	11	12	12	11
Brazil	14	20	26	25	22
Korea	5	6	9	15	15
Canada	166	174	185	220	213
Mexico	458	496	452	625	552
Puerto Rico	15	15	16	21	52
China	6	11	16	31	26
Germany	95	95	95	92	94
United Kingdom	232	241	250	269	258

Source: Wal-Mart 2003 Annual Report.

Japanese retailers. Nevertheless, Wal-Mart's ultimate challenge will lie in its ability to convince Japanese consumers that its everyday low prices don't translate into poor product quality.

Retail Environment in Japan

Japan is the second-largest and one of the wealthiest economies in the world, with a GDP of $3.15 trillion and per capita GDP of about $25,000 (Exhibit 1). Japan's retail market has its own culture-specific quirks that are often difficult for outsiders to fully grasp. The sector has produced a few causalities in recent years, including the painful structuring of retailing bellwethers such as Mycal and Daiei.[5] With many of its global competitors struggling, Wal-Mart sensed an opportunity to strike in Japan. Concerned over past market-entry failures, Wal-Mart deliberated for over four years before purchasing a minority stake in Seiyu.[6] This sluggish pace has given many new and existing retailers adequate time to react to Wal-Mart's entrance. Archrival Carrefour, the world's second-largest retail chain, entered Japan about a month before Wal-Mart with its first store in Makuhari. Ostensibly, Carrefour's move was designed to steal market share from fledgling retail players before the U.S. retail giant had a chance to streamline with Seiyu. Big, traditional Japanese retail outlets have suffered from rising competition from newly emerging stores such as Uniglo leveraging low prices of imported goods. In addition, a decline in personal spending, in juxtaposition with a poor economic climate, has given discount retailers some traction with consumers who now need their money to work longer and harder.

There is bound to be some concern over Carrefour's preemptive entrance, but Wal-Mart is confident it has learned from past mistakes and knows that getting to market

Exhibit 1   Japan at a Glance, 2002

Area: 145,882 square miles

Location: East Asia

Population: 126.8 million (15% younger than 15; 67% between ages 15–65; 18% 65 and older)

Capital and largest city: Tokyo (population 34.8 million)

GDP: $3.15 trillion

GDP composition by sector: Agriculture 2%, Industry 35%, Services 63%

Per capita GDP: $24,900

GDP real growth rate: 1.3%

Labor force: 67.7 million

Unemployment: 4.7%

Inflation: −0.7%

Source: Racher Press Research.

faster doesn't necessarily equate to being better. For example, in Germany, where retail regulations and swift price competition are both fierce, Wal-Mart reacted before its inventory systems were in place, and the result was substantial operating losses.[7] While such a deliberate strategy might cost the firm some advantages, international head John Menzer believes the bit-by-bit approach is the way to go in Japan. "We've been criticized for going too slowly (in Japan). But we have to do it step-by-step. In three years, we'll be fully loaded."[8]

Japan's multilayered distribution networks have notoriously made selling merchandise more expensive for retailers. This is unfamiliar territory for Wal-Mart, which demands supplier accreditation before even considering the product line in the United States. Their ultimate goal is to eventually supersede the current network of suppliers and wholesalers. With a weak economy, suppliers may be convinced to sell direct in an attempt to produce incremental cash flows. Seiyu doesn't own a fleet of trucks or distribution warehouses, so Wal-Mart has been content with working with wholesalers during the short term. Typically, wholesalers' margins are between 7 and 20 percent, according to Jerry Black, managing director of global practices for Kurt Salmon and Associates, an Atlanta retail-consulting company. If Wal-Mart is eventually able to supersede the wholesaler segment, they will be in a much better position to distribute goods at a cheaper cost, which will enable them to pass along some of the price savings to customers. Changing the nature of the supply chain process in Japan will not be easy and is sure to be met with stiff resistance. According to Black, suppliers must decide whether they want to rock the boat by going to Wal-Mart directly.

A majority of the competition reacted swiftly as news of Wal-Mart's entrance began to surface. Aeon, a midsize retail player, began making adjustments as early as 2001. Along with remodeling existing stores and creating labor efficiencies, Aeon began a campaign to eliminate all middlemen from its supply chain.[9] Convincing suppliers to go direct has been quite a challenge, but Aeon has managed to get more than 20 existing partners to come on board and approximately 20 more are waiting in the wings. A survey by Goldman Sachs in 2003 found prices on Aeon's non-grocery items were approximately 9.4 percent below the local average, identical to discounts Wal-Mart has been offering through Seiyu stores.[10]

Ito-Yokado, Japan's leading supermarket retailer, has not reacted to Wal-Mart's entry in the same fashion. Ito is convinced that quality is what sells in Japan, and the firm has launched an aggressive marketing campaign entitled "Made in Japan" to convey its message. By labeling quality products with a traditional Japanese symbol, the rising sun, Ito-Yokado hopes to bring a sense of Japanese national pride to the surface. "Ito-Yokado isn't offering everyday low prices. It's offering higher quality," explains Yoshinobu Naito, an Ito-Yokado board member.[11] Ito has also balked at the idea of developing supercenters because it believes that land rates are still cost-prohibitive. Moreover, Ito has not reduced its staff as a means of cutting costs. It steadfastly believes that Japanese customers demand a quick entry and exit from its stores and eliminating staff would delay this process.

Entry Strategy: Too Slow or Just Right?

Wal-Mart has been very forthcoming about its entrance in Japan: slow and steady. Greg Penner, senior VP and CFO, Wal-Mart Japan, says Wal-Mart's stake in Seiyu will grow from its current 37 percent to 50 percent by December 2005 and to 67 percent by December 2007.[12] Drawing from its past international experiences in Germany and Mexico, and given the psychological dynamic of the Japanese consumer, Penner believes that the current strategy is the best way to avoid growing pains and mistakes made in Germany and Mexico.

In a land where department stores rule, Wal-Mart sees overwhelming potential. However, there is concern that such a deliberate pace will give the competition time to create barriers. Driving the strategy is the installation of Wal-Mart's Retail Link operation, a JIT inventory replenishment system shared between retailer and supplier, effectively eliminating the wholesaler and speeding up payables and receivables collections.[13] However, since getting burned in Germany and Mexico by cutting corners, Wal-Mart has been more than calculating in developing its infrastructure capabilities in Japan. According to Carl Steidtmann, chief economist at Deloitte Research, retail software will have to be translated into Japanese and Japanese suppliers and retailers will have to go through a transformation to adapt to Wal-Mart's technology-focused management systems.[14] Many analysts believe that a tight inventory management system is imperative if Wal-Mart is to become successful in Japan. Another obstacle to overcome is Japan's multilayered distribution system. While Wal-Mart is quick to bypass such networks within the United States, personal interaction when doing business is much more prevalent in Japan, making these distribution layers more difficult to supersede.

After a careful round of evaluations, Wal-Mart believed Seiyu was the partner best suited for its entry strategy. The logic was simple. By working through a local partner, Wal-Mart believed it could better wade through Japan's long and costly network of suppliers, which has long frustrated many other foreign investors. "Wal-Mart has to change the system from the inside out," said Seth Sulkin, president of Pacifica Malls K.K., which develops shopping centers in Japan. Since only the biggest Japanese retailers have leverage with manufacturers, partnering with an existing market leader should prove invaluable when attempting to negotiate direct deals. Moreover, Wal-Mart avoids having to build stores and can take advantage of Seiyu's well-recognized brand.

Starting in early 2000, Seiyu began divesting itself from failing formats and businesses and was able to develop some financial stability. With 414 stores and more than $9 billion in sales, a strong customer base, and heavy saturation in the Tokyo area, where real estate prices are exorbitant, Seiyu made a very attractive target. Furthermore, Seiyu's strength in food retailing gave Wal-Mart a natural extension for its supercenters, where food products are the most prominent. However, Seiyu is loaded with debt, with a debt-to-capital ratio more than twice the industry average. In the half year that ended in August 2003, Seiyu lost $77 million as sales slipped roughly 4 percent from the same period a year earlier. Wal-Mart has also pushed Seiyu to reduce the number of planned store closings from five to three because it believes it can make productivity gains in some of these existing outlets.

Penner strongly believes that over time Japanese customers will begin to see the value in Wal-Mart's unique selling proposition, one where low prices rule.[15] Wal-Mart hopes its "Every Day Low Prices" moniker will have a substantial impact given the troubled Japanese economy. So far that hasn't happened. Seiyu currently operates as high-low retailer; it offers special promotions to its customers depending on the day. For example, Seiyu stores run 100-yen specials on certain items on Tuesdays. This on-again, off-again promotional strategy is in sharp contrast with Wal-Mart's everyday deals. Executives believe it will take both time and effort to convince loyal Seiyu customers that rock-bottom prices are available every day. Eventually, Wal-Mart hopes customers will realize that the company doesn't offer lower-quality products at low prices but quality products close to the manufacturing cost of other retailers.

Labor and Human Resources Challenges

Labor costs have also been a problem. In response, Wal-Mart developed a five-year plan to reduce full-time employee hours by about 40 percent, partly through early retirement and an increase in part-time staff. Furthermore, Seiyu announced that it planned on cutting jobs by up to 40 percent, some 2,500 jobs, over a three-year period beginning in mid-2003.[16] The remaining employees will have to begin to learn to sell the Wal-Mart way.

To reinforce the importance of selling correctly, Wal-Mart is putting store managers through weeklong training sessions and has flown hundreds of Seiyu workers to company headquarters in Arkansas. "Japanese might think what we're doing is very tough, but they have to realize that this is the world standard," said Seiyu's CEO

Masao Kiuchi. Workers receive quite a bit of "cultural training" to teach them to be more outspoken, upbeat, and goal-oriented.

However, trainees have had a more difficult time with Wal-Mart's practice of continually praising co-workers. In a society where being humble is paramount, many workers have had difficulty accepting this type of praise. While achieving employee buy-in has been difficult at times, Jeff McAllister, Wal-Mart COO in Japan, is confident that their plan is working. "Once they understand what you want them to do, you get follow-through."[17] By computerizing all Seiyu's operations, remodeling dilapidated stores, and retraining staff, Wal-Mart will be in a better position to capitalize on the future.

The Wal-Mart Effect

In recent years, Japan's economy has been one of the poorest performers among developed nations, making the playing field well suited for Wal-Mart's deal-oriented businesses. Department store leaders Seibu, Mitsukoshi, and Takashimaya have all experienced flat growth over the last five years. Each has been able to generate over $1 billion in sales, but rates of return and margins remain low as supply-chain expenses creep upward. As a result, most retailers are burdened by high debt, resulting in higher department store prices. If Wal-Mart is able to construct supplier agreements in Japan similar to those in the United States, then it will have a huge advantage over its competitors in its ability to price low. Moreover, the Japanese market appears to be ready for value chains. A growing numbers of 100 yen stores, which are equivalent to dollar stores in the United States, are already popping up in major markets all over Japan.[18] Some retailers have seen this coming and are in the midst of a consolidation boom in an attempt to add both breadth and depth to fight Wal-Mart's size and strength. In June 2003, Seibu Department stores and Sogo Co. merged to form Millennium Retailing Inc., becoming one of Japan's largest department store groups.[19]

While these huge department stores are concerned about Wal-Mart's entrance, it doesn't appear to be keeping all of them up at night. Koji Nose, president of Mitsukoshi U.S.A., said recently, "Wal-Mart will have an effect, but not a big impact."[20] Wal-Mart's ability to find appropriate locations for its stores will have a material impact. Since the Japanese travel mostly by railroad instead of in cars, the firm is hoping to secure locations on edges of big cities where commuters shop. Most downtown cities in Japan are heavily saturated with retail shops, so finding alternative locations will be integral to getting top-of-mind awareness among consumers.

What's Next for Wal-Mart?

If Wal-Mart is able to duplicate what it has done in the United States, it may change the way consumer goods are sold and distributed in Japan. Cutting costs and streamlining its supply chain are two main priorities already in the works. Its partnerships with Seiyu and Sumitomo have already given Wal-Mart a large foothold in Japan's multi-dimensional distribution system.[21] If Wal-Mart is able to effectively skip the middleman, then it should be able to pass lower costs along to the customer. According to Bill Wertz, Wal-Mart's director of international corporate affairs, "We're reorganizing Seiyu in a style more consistent with Wal-Mart in the U.S."[22] Wal-Mart executives have been actively involved in the corporate transformation of Seiyu, but Seiyu's executives will continue to run the business. Retail Link is scheduled to be fully operational by 2004, giving executives little time to reorganize the entire operational structure.

In support of its international operations, Wal-Mart announced the opening of a Global Procurement (GP) USA Export Office in February 2003 at world headquarters in Arkansas. The GP USA Export Office will grant U.S. suppliers access to buyers in more than 17 countries and in so doing provide a service to those domestic suppliers who have been unable to navigate through restrictive import regulations in foreign countries. "We see the GP USA Export Office as a window to new markets," said Ken Easton, Wal-Mart's Senior VP of Global Procurement. "We want to sell American products globally, but we will also need to work with the U.S. government to break down barriers that we encounter."

Consistent with its policies in the United States, Wal-Mart has pushed Seiyu to increase the number of part-time employees by about 2,000 during the same three-year period. In the United States, Wal-Mart's human resource policies have been met with substantial backlash as employees complain that they are intentionally given fewer hours so that they do not qualify for full-time employee benefits, especially health care services. Union activity is also discouraged. How the Japanese worker will react to these policies is unknown, but they are sure to cause some controversy over the upcoming years.

With declining customer spending, price deflation, and economic recession expected to continue in the short term, Wal-Mart is confident it can make significant inroads under its low-price model. As Japanese customers become more value conscious, there arises a huge opportunity for discount retailers to capitalize on changing cultural conditions.

Questions for Review

1. Do you believe Wal-Mart can be successful by circumventing the current Japanese distribution system? What are some of the problems you foresee?

2. Do you agree with Wal-Mart's entry strategy? What are some of the inherent risks? Do you think that a faster market entry would be more effective?

3. In your opinion, what is the single most important thing Wal-Mart can do to ensure success in Japan? Explain.

4. Do you think Wal-Mart is doing enough cross-cultural training with its Seiyu employees? What are the greatest challenges Wal-Mart faces in relating to its Japanese employees?

Exercise

Pair up with a classmate. One of you will play the role of head of a retail distribution firm in Japan, while the other plays the role of a marketing strategist for Wal-Mart Inc. Debate and discuss the pros and cons of entering and participating in the Japanese distribution system and the difficulties that must be overcome.

Source: © McGraw-Hill Irwin. This case was prepared by Professor Jonathan Doh and Erik Holt of Villanova University as the basis for class discussion. It is not intended to illustrate either effective or ineffective managerial capability or administrative responsibility.

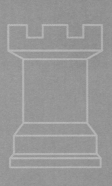

PART THREE

INTERNATIONAL
STRATEGIC
MANAGEMENT

STRATEGY FORMULATION AND IMPLEMENTATION

All major MNCs employ the formulation and implementation of strategies that results from a careful analysis of both external and internal environments. In this process, an MNC will identify the market environment for its goods and services and then evaluate its ability and competitive advantage to capture this market. The success of this strategic planning effort will largely depend on accurate forecasting of the external environment and a realistic appraisal of internal company strengths and weaknesses. In recent years, MNCs have relied on their strategic plans to help refocus their efforts by abandoning old domestic markets and entering new global markets. This strategic global planning process has been critical in their drive to gain market share, increase profitability, and in some cases, even survive.

Chapter 5 addressed overall management across cultures. This chapter focuses on strategic management in the international context, and the basic steps by which a strategic plan is formulated and implemented are examined. The specific objectives of this chapter are:

1. **DISCUSS** the meaning, needs, benefits, and approaches of the strategic planning process for today's MNCs.

2. **UNDERSTAND** the tension between pressures for global integration and national responsiveness and the four basic options for international strategies.

3. **IDENTIFY** the basic steps in strategic planning, including environmental scanning, internal resource analysis of the MNC's strengths and weaknesses, and goal formulation.

4. **DESCRIBE** how an MNC implements the strategic plan, such as how it chooses a site for overseas operations.

5. **REVIEW** the three major functions of marketing, production, and finance that are used in implementing a strategic plan.

6. **EXPLAIN** specialized strategies appropriate for emerging markets and international new ventures.

The World of *BusinessWeek*

BusinessWeek

Ford Learns the Lessons of Luxury

Its Deluxe Brands Have Made Strides, but Buyers Are a Demanding Lot

Mark Fields has the ebullience of a guy who's on a roll. Last year, Fields pulled off a nearly $1 billion profit swing at Ford Motor Co.'s collection of prestige auto brands. Thanks to a couple of hot new products—Jaguar's new flagship XJ sedans and Volvo's XC90 SUV—the Premier Automotive Group (PAG), which also includes Land Rover and Aston Martin, turned a 2002 operating loss of $897 million into a slim 2003 operating profit of $164 million and rang up a 17% gain in global sales. Thanks in large part to PAG, Fields's boss, Ford Chief Executive William C. Ford Jr., is now able to boast that he sells more luxury cars in the U.S. than anyone else.

But Fields, 43, isn't letting this go to his head. "A little success is fine," he quips, "as long as you don't inhale." And he has plenty of reason to be realistic. His boss is counting on him to squeeze a lot more out of Ford's luxury brands to make good on the CEO's turnaround plan. Yet since arriving two years ago from Ford's Mazda unit, Fields has had to undo mistakes made by his predecessors in the heady early days after Ford combined its luxury makes into PAG. In the process, Fields has learned a valuable lesson— that mass-market luxury is an oxymoron.

Fields had to change course from early plans to enrich revenues with big volume increases and to boost profits by sharing car chassis with some of Ford's more mundane mass-market models. Instead, he is leveraging car platforms within each luxury family and saving through common electronics and safety equipment. Now Fields will find it much tougher to meet PAG's mid-decade profit goal—to kick in one-third, or $2.3 billion, of Ford's promised $7 billion annual pretax profit. He still insists he can get there, and the expectation within Ford this year is that PAG will generate operating earnings of $550 million. Even with the changes Fields is making, says Standard & Poor's auto analyst Scott Sprinzen, "they still have pretty ambitious goals."

Fields had little choice but to rein in PAG. The unit was created in 1999 by former Ford CEO Jacques A. Nasser and Wolfgang Reitzle, the ex-BMW exec Nasser recruited to forge Ford's various European car-company acquisitions into a coherent, profitable unit. They wanted to create a money machine by pumping up sales volumes of PAG's high-profit cars while slashing costs by introducing economies of scale. Unfortunately, neither plan worked. Cranking out too many cars of an elite brand such as Jaguar damaged the exclusive image. That's why Fields ratcheted down PAG's unrealistic goal of boosting global sales by almost 50% in five years, to more than a million cars by 2006. Last year, PAG sold only 701,500 vehicles, and Fields no longer divulges sales targets.

PAG's initial platform-sharing plans also went awry. While sharing the basic structure of a car or truck can generate huge savings for most models, Ford discovered that it just won't wash in the luxury market. Most car buyers have no idea what a platform even is. But word quickly gets around when a new model shares its undercarriage with more plebeian cars. And it turns out that someone paying $40,000 for the luxury cachet of his first Jaguar cares a great deal that the car's guts are being shared with something that may cost only $20,000 or so.

Tarnished Image

PAG learned that lesson the hard way. Although Ford execs had debated for years the merits of sharing platforms in their luxury group, the results became clear when they tried it with the Jaguar X-Type sedan. Introduced in 2002, it offended Jag loyalists who knew from car reviews and press reports that the "Baby Jag" was based on the humble Ford Mondeo. That, plus initial quality woes, seriously tarnished the car's image and led to heavy discounting. Says Jim Bulin, head of Bulin Group, a Northville (Mich.) auto consultant: "This is a prostitution of something customers hold sacred."

Stylish Moves

Ford's Premier Automotive Group is taking these steps to boost earnings

Fewer Engines	Platform Sharing	Flexible Factories
Engines, while also costly, can be shared among luxury brands. Therefore, PAG plans to develop fewer engines and share them. Jaguar and **Land Rover** will go from a combined six engines to two. The same goes for technology such as navigation systems and safety innovations.	**Jaguar's** X-Type shares its chassis with the Ford Mondeo—a problem, since luxury owners often shun cars based on mass-market models. Eventually, each brand will develop one or two platforms of its own and rarely will share them with others.	Emulating **Volvo's** highly flexible Swedish plants, PAG wants some of its British factories to be able to build vastly different vehicles side by side. Jaguar's Halewood (England) plant is slated to add production of a Land Rover model by 2006.

Source: www.businessweek.com/magazine/ content/04_09/b3872120_mz 017. htm

---

Ford isn't alone in its platform-sharing dilemma. Audi is losing European sales as savvy consumers figure they can get a similar but cheaper car from Volkswagen. And much of the $4.3 billion General Motors Corp. invested recently in Cadillac went for building a plant, chassis, and engines that will be exclusive to Cadillac models. In Ford's case, the lesson is calculated in profits and prestige: In the U.S., where Jaguar X-type sales fell 19% last year, Ford has lopped $3,000 off the X-Type's $36,000 base price. The car had similar problems in Europe. A diesel version introduced there last fall has caught on, but industry insiders say Ford may phase out the car by decade's end.

Now, in most cases, each of PAG's divisions will have its own exclusive undercarriage. That is a costly choice, since a unique one costs $1 billion or more. "In general, in the auto industry, the Holy Grail is fewer [platforms]," Fields says. "But the customer's perception is what counts." Fields is pushing each PAG brand to derive as many vehicles as possible from each exclusive platform. Jaguar, for instance, may base its next S-Type on the new XJ's underpinnings instead of a Lincoln platform, as it does now. Land Rover, with an assortment of platforms, will take longer to consolidate. The six-figure Aston Martin will get its own chassis, instead of borrowing from Jaguar. Volvo, PAG's not-quite-luxury brand, will still share some platforms. Its entry-level S40 and S50 sedans share with Mazda and Ford of Europe, saving Volvo 10% to 20% on product-development costs, Fields says.

To ensure that the luxury brands' images are protected, Fields will look for other kinds of cost sharing that he believes customers won't detect—or won't mind. He is planning to share technology among PAG units, reasoning that few customers will care if a Jaguar and a Land Rover have identical navigation and sound systems, or even if they use state-of-the-art Volvo safety gear. The sharing also extends to costly engine development. Fields aims to reduce the number of engines at Jaguar and Land Rover from six to two. PAG divisions will also jointly develop a six-speed transmission.

Beyond that, PAG can choose unseen nuts-and-bolts items—brake pads, window-lift motors, or fasteners—from Ford's global parts bin to take advantage of bulk-purchase savings. PAG is also saving money by pooling the individual brands' resources for logistics, information technology, and other back-office expenses. Fields figures he can also cut costs—after a heavy initial investment—by bringing PAG's British factories up to snuff with greater quality and produc-

tivity, and by incorporating modern, flexible manufacturing equipment to allow side-by-side production of multiple models. Such moves would likely eliminate the need for one of Jag's three British plants. Ford executives decline to comment on that possibility.

Will all this save enough money to make up for abandoning platform sharing and settling for slower sales growth? Fields hasn't given up on the idea that building better Jags and Volvos can boost sales and profits substantially. For the sake of Bill Ford's turnaround plans and shareholders, he had better be right.

By Kathleen Kerwin in Detroit

Source: **Reprinted from "Ford Learns the Lessons of Luxury,"** *BusinessWeek,* **March 1, 2004, online edition, by special permission. Copyright © 2004 by the McGraw-Hill Companies, Inc. www.businessweek.com**

Strategic management—the formulation and implementation of a strategy—is a critical function in today's global business environment. As seen in the opening *BusinessWeek* story, Ford made tremendous gains in global sales during 2003. However, if the firm is to continue to meet its aggressive growth targets, it must have a strategy in place to effectively coordinate its worldwide efforts. In addition, Ford must incorporate the inevitability of changing customer preferences in disparate markets into its overall strategic plan. Although Ford has many opportunities to grow, it will need a comprehensive and integrated strategy to make them happen. This chapter will examine how multinational corporations use strategic management in their global operations. When formulated and implemented wisely, strategic management sets the course for a company's future. It should answer two simple questions, "Where are we going?" and "How are we going to get there?" Some strategies are consistent across markets while others must be adapted to regional situations, but in either case, a firm's global strategy should support decision making in all major operations. In Ford's case, an effective global strategy is imperative if the firm wishes to increase sales beyond its maturing home market.

As you read this chapter, think of yourself as a manager in a large auto firm. How might you go about developing a strategic plan to capture greater market share and expand the types of products you are selling?

■ Strategic Management

strategic management
The process of determining an organization's basic mission and long-term objectives, then implementing a plan of action for attaining these goals.

Strategic management is the process of determining an organization's basic mission and long-term objectives, and then implementing a plan of action for pursuing this mission and attaining these objectives. As companies go international, this strategic process takes on added dimensions. A good example is provided by Citibank, which opened offices in China in 1902 and continued to do business there until 1949, when the communists took power. However, in 1984 Citibank quietly returned, and over the last two decades the firm has been slowly increasing its presence in China.[1] The Chinese banking environment is closely regulated by the government, and Citibank's activities are currently restricted to making local currency loans to foreign multinationals and their joint-venture partners. As a result, the bank does only about 20 percent as much business here as it does in South Korea. However, China's admission into the World Trade Organization (WTO) is changing all of this. Under WTO provisions, elite local corporations such as the personal computer maker Legend, electronic goods manufacturer Konda, consumer appliance maker Haier, and telecom service provider China Telecom will all be able to turn to foreign banks for local currency loans. This will give Citibank a major opportunity to expand operations. Additionally, under WTO rules the bank is allowed to offer consumer financial services such as credit cards and home mortgages. Citibank believes that there is a large pent-up demand for credit cards, especially among businesspeople and yuppies who now carry around thick wads of currency to pay their bills and make purchases. Another opportunity Citibank sees is in the area of business-to-business (B2B) commerce. As more Chinese firms conduct commerce over the Internet, there will be an increase in Net-related financial services. Citibank has now hooked up with U.S.-based B2B site Commerce One to run its Net-based payment systems, and the bank believes that it can provide this same service for Chinese exporters.

Despite the huge potential market in China, however, Citibank is aware of the risks. In 1995 the firm was chosen as one of the first foreign banks to be issued a local-currency license. The bank felt certain that this was the opportunity it needed to break into the retail market, but this did not happen. In order to protect its domestic banks from competition, the government imposed a limit on the number of branches that foreign banks could open as well as to whom they could lend money and in what amounts. Quite simply, Citibank's opportunities were very limited. Will China being a member of the WTO change all of this? It might, but there are still a great many risks associated with doing business here. In particular, executives know that if foreign banks are given unrestricted access to China's retail customers, havoc could develop. It is estimated that Chinese customers have over $500 billion in savings. If these customers were to begin taking their money out of local banks and putting it into foreign ones, China's banks would be forced to stop lending to the country's state-owned enterprises (SOEs), most of which are losing money. In turn, these SOEs would go bankrupt and unemployment would skyrocket. The four major state-owned commercial banks currently control 70 percent of all financial assets in China, and approximately 30 percent of all their loans are uncollectible. So the Chinese government is unlikely to move quickly to open up the banking market. Nevertheless, Citibank sees China as a major market and is developing strategies to increase its presence there and ride out any financial storms. In order to do this, the bank will need a well-formulated strategic plan.

The Growing Need for Strategic Management

One of the primary reasons that MNCs such as Toyota or Citibank need strategic management is to keep track of their increasingly diversified operations in a continuously changing international environment. This need is particularly obvious when one considers the amount of foreign direct investment (FDI) that has occurred in recent years. Recent statistics reveal that FDI has grown three times faster than trade and four times faster than world gross domestic product (GDP).[2] These developments are resulting in a need to coordinate and integrate diverse operations with a unified and agreed-on focus. There are many examples of firms that are doing just this.

One is Ford Motor, which has reentered the market in Thailand and, despite a shrinking demand for automobiles there, is beginning to build a strong sales force and to garner market share. The firm's strategic plan here is based on offering the right combination of price and financing to a carefully identified market segment. In particular, Ford is working to keep down the monthly payments so that customers can afford a new vehicle. This is the same approach that Ford used in Mexico, where the currency crises of 1994 resulted in problems for many multinationals.

Another example of the growing need for strategic management is provided by Bertelsmann AG, the giant German book publisher that has entered the Chinese market.[3] Bertelsmann has created a giant book club that could dramatically change the way Chinese buy books. Since the late 1990s, this club has signed up over 1.5 million members, opened dozens of retail stores, and sold almost 10 million volumes. Moreover, Bertelsmann is now adding 2,000 new members every day, a growth rate that is easily sustainable given that approximately 180 million Chinese read books on a regular basis. The company's strategic plan calls for continual expansion well into the new millennium, driven by a wide assortment of books, low costs, and home delivery. In fact, things are going so well for Bertelsmann in China that the company has now sent salespeople to South Korea to lay the groundwork for a book club there and has plans for expanding to Japan, India, and Thailand.[4]

A third example of the growing need for strategic management is offered by the highly profitable GE Capital, which has been expanding rapidly in Europe. Since the mid-1980s the company has amassed assets in excess of $50 billion, much of this in the last several years. The firm began years ago by helping customers purchase General Electric products, but it has now expanded widely and provides diverse services ranging from equipment financing for middle-market firms, to consumer finance, to reinsurance. Relying on a well-coordinated strategic plan, the company sets targets for each of its stand-alone businesses. Overall, GE Capital looks for at least a 20 percent annual return on capital and strong growth. The approach flouts some time-honored traditions, as seen by the fact that each business handles its customers independently. So one customer can have multiple relationships with GE Capital.[5] And while this type of strategic planning approach may seem questionable to some, the company has been very successful using it. Revenues have been growing sharply, and annual earnings in recent years have been in excess of $5 billion.[6]

Benefits of Strategic Planning

Now that the needs for strategic planning have been explored, what are some of the benefits? Many MNCs are convinced that strategic planning is critical to their success, and these efforts are being conducted both at the home office and in the subsidiaries. For example, one study found that 70 percent of the 56 U.S. MNC subsidiaries in Asia and Latin America had comprehensive 5- to 10-year plans.[7] Others found that U.S., European, and Japanese subsidiaries in Brazil were heavily planning-driven[8] and that Australian manufacturing companies use planning systems that are very similar to those of U.S. manufacturing firms.[9]

Do these strategic planning efforts really pay off? To date, the evidence is mixed. Certainly, that the strategic plan helps an MNC to coordinate and monitor its far-flung operations must be viewed as a benefit. Similarly, that the plan helps an MNC to deal with political risk problems (see Chapter 10), competition, and currency instability cannot be downplayed.

Despite some obvious benefits, there is no definitive evidence that strategic planning in the international arena always results in higher profitability. Most studies that report favorable results were conducted at least a decade ago. Moreover, many of these findings are tempered with contingency-based recommendations. For example, one study found that when decisions were made mainly at the home office and close coordination between the subsidiary and home office was required, return on investment was negatively affected.[10] Simply put, the home office ends up interfering with the subsidiary, and profitability suffers.

Another study found that planning intensity (the degree to which a firm carries out strategic planning) is an important variable in determining performance.[11] Drawing on results from 22 German MNCs representing 71 percent of Germany's multinational enterprises, the study found that companies with only a few foreign affiliates performed best with medium planning intensity. Those firms with high planning intensity tended to exaggerate the emphasis, and profitability suffered. Companies that earned a high percentage of their total sales in overseas markets, however, did best with a high-intensity planning process and poorly with a low-intensity process. Therefore, although strategic planning usually seems to pay off, as with most other aspects of international management, the specifics of the situation will dictate the success of the process.

Approaches to Formulating and Implementing Strategy

Four common approaches to formulating and implementing strategy are (1) focusing on the economic imperative; (2) addressing the political imperative; (3) emphasizing the quality imperative; and (4) implementing an administrative coordination strategy.

Economic Imperative   MNCs that focus on the **economic imperative** employ a world-wide strategy based on cost leadership, differentiation, and segmentation. Many of these companies typically sell products for which a large portion of value is added in the up-stream activities of the industry's value chain. By the time the product is ready to be sold, much of its value has already been created through research and development, manufactur-ing, and distribution. Some of the industries in this group include automobiles, chemicals, heavy electrical systems, motorcycles, and steel. Because the product is basically homoge-neous and requires no alteration to fit the needs of the specific country, management uses a worldwide strategy that is consistent on a country-to-country basis.

> **economic imperative**
> A worldwide strategy based on cost leadership, differentiation, and segmentation.

The strategy also is used when the product is regarded as a generic good and there-fore does not have to be sold based on name brand or support service. A good example is the European PC market. Initially, this market was dominated by such well-known compa-nies as IBM, Apple, and Compaq. However, more recently, clone manufacturers have be-gun to gain market share. This is because the most influential reasons for buying a PC have changed. A few years ago, the main reasons were brand name, service, and support. Today, price has emerged as a major input into the purchasing decision. Customers now are much more computer literate, and they realize that many PCs offer identical quality performance. Therefore, it does not pay to purchase a high-priced name brand when a lower-priced clone will do the same things. As a result, the economic imperative dominates the strategic plans of computer manufacturers.

Another economic imperative concept that has gained prominence in recent years is global sourcing, which is proving very useful in formulating and implementing strategy.[12] A good example is provided by the way in which manufacturers are reaching into the sup-ply chain and shortening the buying circle. Li & Fung, Hong Kong's largest export trading company, is one of the world's leading innovators in the development of supply chain man-agement, and the company has managed to use its expertise to whittle costs to the bone. In-stead of buying fabric and yarn from one company and letting that firm work on keeping its costs as low as possible, Li & Fung gets actively involved in managing the entire process. How does it keep costs down for orders it receives from The Limited? The chairman of the company explained the firm's economic imperative strategy this way:

> We come in and look at the whole supply chain. We know The Limited is going to order 100,000 garments, but we don't know the style or the colors yet. The buyer will tell us that five weeks be-fore delivery. The trust between us and our supply network means that we can reserve undyed yarn from the yarn supplier. I can lock up capacity at the mills for the weaving and dying with the promise that they'll get an order of a specified size; five weeks before delivery, we will let them know what colors we want. Then I say the same thing to the factories, "I don't know the product specs yet, but I have organized the colors and the fabric and the trim for you, and they'll be delivered to you on this date and you'll have three weeks to produce so many garments."
>
> I've certainly made life harder for myself now. It would be easier to let the factories worry about securing their own fabric and trim. But then the order would take three months, not five weeks. So to shrink the delivery cycle, I go upstream to organize production. And the shorter production time lets the retailer hold off before having to commit to a fashion trend. It's all about flexibility, response time, small production runs, small minimum-order quantities, and the ability to shift direction as the trends move.[13]

Political Imperative   MNCs using the **political imperative** approach to strategic plan-ning are country-responsive; their approach is designed to protect local market niches. "International Management in Action: Point/Counterpoint" demonstrates this political imperative. The products sold by MNCs often have a large portion of their value added in the downstream activities of the value chain. Industries such as insurance and consumer packaged goods are examples—the success of the product or service generally depends heavily on marketing, sales, and service. Typically, these industries use a country-centered or multidomestic strategy.

> **political imperative**
> Strategic formulation and implementation utilizing strategies that are country-responsive and designed to protect local market niches.

A good example of a country-centered strategy is provided by Thums Up, a local drink that Coca-Cola bought from an Indian bottler in 1993. This drink was created back in the 1970s, shortly after Coca-Cola pulled up stakes and left India. In the ensuing two

A good example of the political imperative in action is the ongoing Kodak/Fuji dispute. Kodak has accused Fuji of blocking its growth in the Japanese market. Fuji has responded by arguing that Kodak has long held a monopoly-type position in the United States. This debate began when Kodak complained to the U.S. government and asked for help in further opening the door to the Japanese market. Kodak's argument included the following points:

1. Unlike film manufacturers in the United States, film manufacturers in Japan sell directly not to retailers or photofinishers but to distributors, and Fuji has close ties with the four dominant distributors. Fuji holds an equity position in two of them and gives all four both rebates and cash payments.

2. Fuji controls 430 Japanese wholesale photofinishing labs through ownership, loans, rebates, and other forms of operational support. Additionally, the Japanese government has helped to establish the system to impede Kodak.

3. Kodak has invested $750 million in Japan and garnered less than 10 percent of the market.

4. Fuji uses profits from the Japanese market to subsidize the dumping of its products in other countries, thus effectively reducing Kodak's worldwide market share.

5. The Japanese government has not vigorously enforced antimonopoly legislation, and this has helped Fuji to establish distribution dominance.

These charges are answered by Fuji, which contends that Kodak uses many tactics that prevent Fuji from gaining U.S. market share. These include:

1. Kodak gives U.S. retailers rebates and upfront payments that effectively exclude competitors. For example, Kodak offered Genovese Drug Stores of Glen Cove, New York, $40,000 plus rebates if the company would carry no branded film but Kodak, use only Kodak paper and processing chemicals, and give Kodak 80 percent of the chain's shelf-space allotment for film.

2. Kodak holds 70 percent of the U.S. wholesale photofinishing market through ownership and by giving discounts, advertising dollars, and other investments to land exclusive accounts.

3. Fuji has invested $2 billion in the United States and holds less than 11 percent of the market.

4. Kodak's worldwide operating profit margin over the last two decades is 13 percent, close to Fuji's 15.5 percent.

5. The U.S. government has not vigorously enforced consent decrees that were created to limit Kodak's U.S. marketing practices and ensure that Kodak did not gain an unfair advantage over competitors.

Will the U.S. government prevail in its efforts to help Kodak? Will Fuji be able to make further gains in the U.S. market? What role will political intervention play? These questions are yet to be answered. In the meantime, the two firms continue to compete—and cooperate. Together, they currently are developing a "smart film"—a new system that offers small cameras and film that can record information to improve the quality of processing. Whatever the outcome of their market-share argument, this strategic cooperative effort likely will continue.

decades the drink, which is similar in taste to Coke, made major inroads in the Indian market. But when Coca-Cola returned and bought the company, it decided to put Thums Up on the back burner and began pushing its own soft drink. However, local buyers were not interested. They continued to buy Thums Up and Coca-Cola finally relented. Today Thums Up is the firm's biggest seller and fastest growing brand in India, and the company spends more money on this soft drink than it does on any of its other product offerings, including Coke.[14] As one observer noted, "In India the 'Real Thing' for Coca-Cola is its Thums Up brand."

quality imperative
Strategic formulation and implementation utilizing strategies of total quality management to meet or exceed customers' expectations and continuously improve products or services.

Quality Imperative A **quality imperative** takes two interdependent paths: (1) a change in attitudes and a raising of expectation for service quality, and (2) the implementation of management practices that are designed to make quality improvement an ongoing process.[15] Commonly called "total quality management," or simply TQM, the approach takes a wide number of forms, including cross-training personnel to do the jobs of all members in their work group, process re-engineering designed to help identify and eliminate redundant tasks and wasteful effort, and reward systems designed to reinforce quality performance.

TQM covers the full gamut, from strategy formulation to implementation. TQM can be summarized as follows:

1. Quality is operationalized by meeting or exceeding customer expectations. Customers include not only the buyer or external user of the product or service but also the support personnel both inside and outside the organization who are associated with the good or service.

2. The quality strategy is formulated at the top management level and is diffused throughout the organization. From top executives to hourly employees, everyone operates under a TQM strategy of delivering quality products or services to internal and external customers.

3. TQM techniques range from traditional inspection and statistical quality control to cutting-edge human resource management techniques, such as self-managing teams and empowerment.[16]

Many MNCs make quality a major part of their overall strategy, because they have learned that this is the way to increase market share and profitability. For example, while the U.S. automakers have dramatically increased their overall quality in recent years to close the gap with Japanese auto quality, Japanese firms continue to have fewer safety recalls. Toyota and Honda continue to be ranked very high by American consumers, and Nissan's recent market performance shows that the firm is also a major competitor in this market.[17]

Another example of firms using quality as an integral part of their strategy is provided by Nortel, the Canadian telecom equipment manufacturer. A few years ago Nortel concluded that there would be a growing demand for optical networking technology to send and retrieve data. Investing heavily in research and development and acquiring companies with the technologies needed to complement these efforts, the company was able to create a reliable and affordable system just in time to meet a huge demand.

> Fiber-optic networks per se are nothing new. Major phone companies like AT&T, WorldCom, and Sprint have been installing fiber for years, mostly across long distances—spanning continents and crossing the ocean floors. . . . But in the past few years the rise of the Internet has created an explosion in data traffic and hence in the demand for bandwidth, or carrying capacity, by the world's telecom companies. Instead of just transporting phone conversations from Tupelo to Topeka, telecom networks are also being used to transmit e-mail, Web pages, and video to multiple locations all over the world. This vast quantity of information eats up enormous amounts of network capacity. So telecoms need to start lighting up all their fiber to handle the burgeoning load.[18]

Today, Nortel's high-quality system helps account for the fact that in 2001 the firm controlled over 40 percent of the global market for optical equipment. Its nearest competitor, Lucent, had a mere 15 percent share.

Simultaneously, a growing number of MNCs are finding that they must continually revise their strategies and make renewed commitment to the quality imperative because they are being bested by emerging market forces. Motorola, for example, found that its failure to anticipate the industry's switch to digital cell technology was a costly one.[19] In 1998 the company dominated the U.S. handset market and its StarTAC was popular worldwide. Five years later the firm's share of the $160 billion global market for handsets had shrunk from 22 percent to 10 percent and was continuing to fall, while Nokia, Ericsson, and Samsung in particular, with smaller, lighter, and more versatile offerings, were now the dominant players.[20] The lesson is clear: The quality imperative is neverending, and MNCs such as Motorola must meet this strategic challenge or pay the price.

Administrative Coordination   An **administrative coordination** approach to formulation and implementation is one in which the MNC makes strategic decisions based on the merits of the individual situation rather than using a predetermined economic or political strategy. A good example is provided by Wal-Mart, which has expanded rapidly into Latin America in recent years. While many of the ideas that worked well in the North American market served as the basis for operations in the Southern Hemisphere, the company soon

administrative coordination
Strategic formulation and implementation in which the MNC makes strategic decisions based on the merits of the individual situation rather than using a predetermined economically or politically driven strategy.

realized that it was doing business in a market where local tastes were different and competition was strong.

Wal-Mart is counting on its international operations to grow 25–30 percent annually, and Latin American operations are critical to this objective. For the moment, however, the company is reporting losses in Latin America, as it strives to adapt to the local markets. The firm is learning, for example, that the timely delivery of merchandise in places such as São Paulo, where there are continual traffic snarls and the company uses contract truckers for delivery, is often far from ideal. Another challenge is finding suppliers who can produce products to Wal-Mart's specification for easy-to-handle packaging and quality control. A third challenge is learning to adapt to the culture. For example, in Brazil, Wal-Mart brought in stock-handling equipment that did not work with standardized local pallets. It also installed a computerized bookkeeping system that failed to take into account Brazil's wildly complicated tax system.

Many large MNCs work to combine the economic, political, quality, and administrative approaches to strategic planning. For example, IBM relies on the economic imperative when it has strong market power (especially in less developed countries), the political and quality imperatives when the market requires a calculated response (European countries), and an administrative coordination strategy when rapid, flexible decision making is needed to close the sale. Of the four, however, the first three approaches are much more common because of the firm's desire to coordinate its strategy both regionally and globally.

Global vs. Regional Strategies

A fundamental tension in international strategic management is the question of when to pursue global or regional (or local) strategies. This is commonly referred to as the "globalization vs. national responsiveness conflict." As used here, **global integration** is the production and distribution of products and services of a homogeneous type and quality on a worldwide basis.[21] To a growing extent, the customers of MNCs have homogenized tastes, and this has helped to spread international consumerism. For example, throughout North America, the EU, and Japan, there has been a growing acceptance of standardized yet increasingly personally customized goods such as automobiles and computers. This goal of efficient economic performance through a globalization and mass customization strategy, however, has left MNCs open to the charge that they are overlooking the need to address national responsiveness through Internet and intranet technology.

National responsiveness is the need to understand the different consumer tastes in segmented regional markets and respond to different national standards and regulations imposed by autonomous governments and agencies.[22] For example, in designing and building cars, international manufacturers now carefully tailor their offerings in the American market. Toyota's "full-size" T100 pickup proved much too small to attract U.S. buyers. So the firm went back to the drawing board and created a full-size Tundra pickup that is powered by a V-8 engine and has a cabin designed to "accommodate a passenger wearing a 10-gallon cowboy hat." Honda has developed its new Model X SUV with more Americanized features, including enough interior room so that travelers can eat and sleep in the vehicle. Mitsubishi has abandoned its idea of making a global vehicle and has brought out its new Montero Sport sport-utility vehicle in the U.S. market with the features it learned that Americans want: more horsepower, more interior room, more comfort. Meanwhile, Nissan is doing what many foreign carmakers would have thought to be unthinkable just a few years ago. Today, U.S. engineers and product designers are now completely responsible for the development of most Nissan vehicles sold in North America. Among other things, they are asking children between the ages of 8 and 15, in focus-group sessions, for ideas on storage, cup holders, and other refinements that would make a full-size minivan more attractive to them.[23]

National responsiveness also relates to the need to adapt tools and techniques for managing the local workforce. Sometimes what works well in one country does not work in another, as seen by the following example:

> An American computer company introduced pay-for-performance in both the USA and the Middle East. It worked well in the USA and increased sales briefly in the Middle East before

global integration
The production and distribution of products and services of a homogeneous type and quality on a worldwide basis.

national responsiveness
The need to understand the different consumer tastes in segmented regional markets and respond to different national standards and regulations imposed by autonomous governments and agencies.

a serious slump occurred. Inquiries showed that indeed the winners among salesmen in the Middle East had done better, but the vast majority had done worse. The wish for their fellows to succeed had been seriously eroded by the contest. Overall morale and sales were down. Ill-will was contagious. When the bosses discovered that certain sales people were earning more than they did, high individual performances also ceased. But the principal reason for eventually abandoning the system was the discovery that customers were being loaded up with products they could not sell. As A tried to beat B to the bonus, the care of customers began to slip, with serious, if delayed, results.[24]

Global Integration vs. National Responsiveness Matrix
The issue of global integration vs. national responsiveness can be further analyzed conceptually via a two-dimensional matrix. Figure 8–1 provides an example.

The vertical axis in the figure measures the need for global integration. Movement up the axis results in a greater degree of economic integration. Global integration generates economies of scale (takes advantage of large size) and also capitalizes on further lowering unit costs (through experience curve benefits) as a firm moves into worldwide markets selling its products or services. These economies are captured through centralizing specific activities in the value-added chain. They also occur by reaping the benefits of increased coordination and control of geographically dispersed activities.

The horizontal axis measures the need for multinationals to respond to national responsiveness or differentiation. This suggests that MNCs must address local tastes and government regulations. The result may be a geographic dispersion of activities or a decentralization of coordination and control for individual MNCs.

Figure 8–1 depicts four basic situations in relation to the degrees of global integration vs. national responsiveness. Quadrants 1 and 4 are the simplest cases. In quadrant 1, the need for integration is high and for awareness of differentiation low. In terms of economies of scale, this situation leads to **global strategies** based on price competition. In

global strategy
Integrated strategy based primarily on price competition.

National responsiveness

	Low	High
High	1 — Global strategy	3 — Transnational strategy
Low	2 — International strategy	4 — Multi-domestic strategy

Global integration

Figure 8–1

Global Integration vs. National Responsiveness

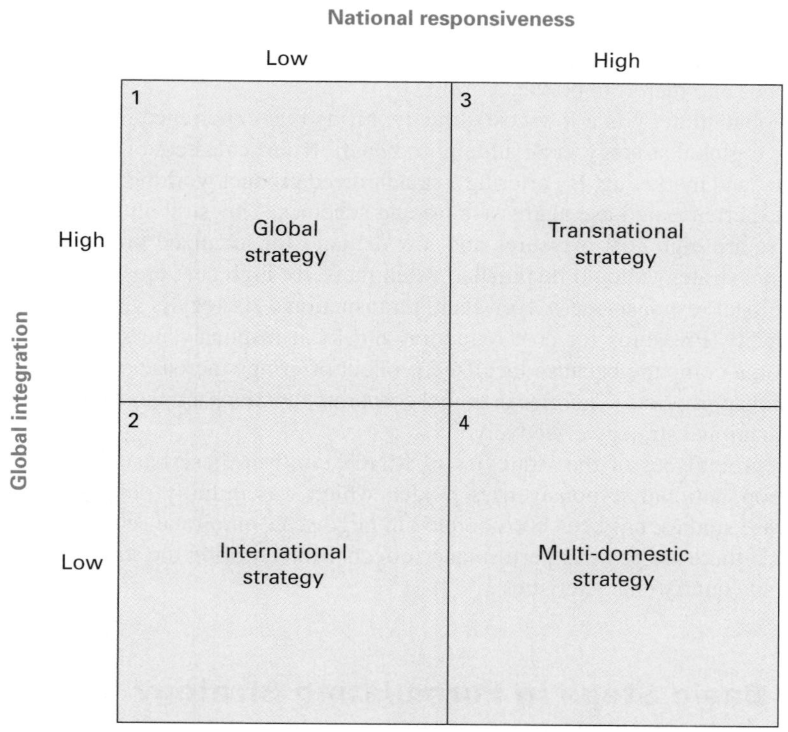

Source: Adapted from information in Christopher A. Bartlett and Sumantra Ghoshal, *Managing Across Borders: The Transnational Solution,* 2nd ed. (Boston: Harvard Business School Press, 1998).

this quadrant-1 type of environment, mergers and acquisitions often occur. The opposite situation is represented by quadrant 4, where the need for differentiation is high but the concern for integration low. This quadrant is referred to as **multi-domestic strategy.** In this case, niche companies adapt products to satisfy the high demands of differentiation and ignore economies of scale because integration is not very important.

multi-domestic strategy
Differentiated strategy emphasizing local adaptation.

Quadrants 2 and 3 reflect more complex environmental situations. Quadrant 2 incorporates those cases in which both the need for integration and awareness of differentiation are low. Both the potential to obtain economies of scale and the benefits of being sensitive to differentiation are of little value. Typical strategies in quadrant 2 are characterized by increased international standardization of products and services. This mixed approach is often referred to as **international strategy.** This situation can lead to lower needs for centralized quality control and centralized strategic decision making, while simultaneously eliminating requirements to adapt activities to individual countries.

international strategy
Mixed strategy combining low demand for integration and responsiveness.

In quadrant 3, the needs for integration and differentiation are high. There is a strong need for integration in production along with higher requirements for regional differentiation in marketing. MNCs trying to simultaneously achieve these objectives often refer to them as **transnational strategy.** Quadrant 3 is the most challenging quadrant and the one where successful MNCs seek to operate. The problem for many MNCs, however, is the cultural challenges associated with "localizing" a global focus.

transnational strategy
Integrated strategy emphasizing both global integration and local responsiveness.

Summary and Implications of Four Basic Strategies   MNCs can be characterized as using one of four basic international strategies: an international strategy, a multi-domestic strategy, a global strategy, and a transnational strategy. The appropriateness of each strategy depends on pressures for cost reduction and local responsiveness in each country served. Firms that pursue an international strategy have valuable core competencies that host-country competitors do not possess and face minimal pressures for local responsiveness and cost reductions. International firms such as McDonald's, Wal-Mart, and Microsoft have been successful using an international strategy. Organizations pursuing a multi-domestic strategy should do so when there is high pressure for local responsiveness and low pressures for cost reductions. Changing offerings on a localized level increases a firm's overall cost structure but increases the likelihood that its products and services will be responsive to local needs and therefore be successful.[25]

A global strategy is a low-cost strategy. Firms that experience high cost pressures should use a global strategy in an attempt to benefit from scale economies in production, distribution, and marketing. By offering a standardized product worldwide, firms can leverage their experience and use aggressive pricing schemes. This strategy makes most sense where there are high cost pressures and low demand for localized product offerings. A transnational strategy should be pursued when there are high cost pressures and high demands for local responsiveness. However, a transnational strategy is very difficult to pursue effectively. Pressures for cost reduction and local responsiveness put contradictory demands on a company because localized product offerings increase cost. Organizations that can find appropriate synergies in global corporate functions are the ones that can leverage a transnational strategy effectively.[26]

Recent analyses of the strategies of MNCs confirm these basic approaches. The globalization–national responsiveness model, which was initially developed from nine in-depth case studies, has been corroborated in large-scale empirical settings. Moreover, it appears as if there are positive performance effects from tailoring the strategy to particular industry and country characteristics.[27]

■ The Basic Steps in Formulating Strategy

The needs, benefits, approaches, and predispositions of strategic planning serve as a point of departure for the basic steps in formulating strategy. In international management, strategic planning can be broken into the following steps: (1) scanning the external environment for opportunities and threats; (2) conducting an internal resource analysis of company strengths and weaknesses; and (3) formulating goals in light of the external scanning and internal analysis. These steps are graphically summarized in Figure 8–2. The following sections discuss each step in detail.

Environmental Scanning

Environmental scanning attempts to provide management with accurate forecasts of trends that relate to external changes in geographic areas where the firm is currently doing business or considering setting up operations. These changes relate to the economy, competition, political stability, technology, and demographic consumer data.

> **environmental scanning**
> The process of providing management with accurate forecasts of trends related to external changes in geographic areas where the firm currently is doing business or is considering setting up operations.

Typically, the MNC will begin by conducting a forecast of macroeconomic and industry performance dealing with factors such as markets for specific products, per capita income of the population, and availability of labor and raw materials. A second common forecast will predict likely trends in monetary exchange rates, exchange controls, balance of payments, and inflation rates. A third is the forecast of the company's potential market share in a particular geographic area as well as that of the competitors. Other considerations include political stability, government pressure, nationalism, and related areas of political risk. These assessments are extremely important in determining the risk profile and profit potential of the region, which always is a major consideration when deciding where to set up international operations.

OpenTV Inc. provides an example of how this environmental scanning process works. The firm analyzed the environment in China and concluded that the market in Shanghai was ideal for its software. As a result, it signed a deal with Shanghai Cable Network to provide this company with "middle ware." When this software is installed in a subscriber's set-top box, it allows the user to interact with the television and do a number of different things—from shopping online to ordering a movie for viewing. Shanghai Cable has over 3 million customers, and one-third of them have broadband cable that lets them access the Internet and interact with television programs in what industry analysts say is one of the world's most advanced cable systems. If OpenTV's scan of the environment is correct, this business arrangement will help the firm become extremely profitable.[28] Another example of the effects of environmental scanning is Microsoft's purchase of 60 percent of Japan's second-largest cable firm, Titus Communication. After analyzing the environment, Microsoft concluded that there would be a shift to high-speed broadband services and it needed to have this technological capability in order to provide its customers with state-of-the-art services.[29] As a result, Microsoft made the decision to take an ownership position in Titus Communication.

Many other firms also have profited from astute environmental scanning. For example, Alcatel Alsthom of France made a series of clever acquisitions and alliances and now is the world's largest telephone equipment company. This has put Alcatel in an ideal position to garner market share in the rapidly growing telecommunications market.

Figure 8–2

Basic Elements of Strategic Planning for International Management

Internal Resource Analysis

When formulating strategy, some firms wait until they have completed their environmental scanning before conducting an internal resource analysis. Others perform these two steps simultaneously. Internal resource analysis helps the firm to evaluate its current managerial, technical, material, and financial strengths and weaknesses. This assessment then is used by the MNC to determine its ability to take advantage of international market opportunities. The primary thrust of this analysis is to match external opportunities (gained through the environmental scan) with internal capabilities (gained through the internal resource analysis).

key factor for success (KFS)
A factor necessary for a firm to effectively compete in a market niche.

An internal analysis identifies the key factors for success that will dictate how well the firm is likely to do. A **key factor for success (KFS)** is a factor that is necessary for a firm to compete effectively in a market niche. For example, a KFS for an international airline is price. An airline that discounts its prices will gain market share vis-à-vis competitors that do not. A second KFS for the airline is safety, and a third is quality of service in terms of on-time departures and arrivals, convenient schedules, and friendly, helpful personnel. In the automobile industry, quality of products has emerged as the number-one KFS in world markets. Japanese firms have been able to invade the U.S. auto market successfully because they have been able to prove that the quality of their cars is better than that of the average domestically built U.S. car. Toyota and Honda have had a quality edge over the competition in recent years in the eyes of U.S. car buyers. A second KFS is styling. The redesigned VW Beetle has been successful because customers like its looks.

The key question for the management of an MNC is: Do we have the people and resources that can help us to develop and sustain the necessary KFSs, or can we acquire them? If the answer is yes, the recommendation would be to proceed. If the answer is no, management would begin looking at other markets where it has, or can develop, the necessary KFSs.

Goal Setting for Strategy Formulation

In practice, goal formulation often precedes the first two steps of environmental scanning and internal resource analysis. As used here, however, the more specific goals for the strategic plan come out of external scanning and internal analysis. MNCs pursue a variety of such goals; Table 8–1 provides a list of the most common ones. These goals typically serve as an umbrella beneath which the subsidiaries and other international groups operate.

Profitability and marketing goals almost always dominate the strategic plans of today's MNCs. Profitability, as shown in Table 8–1, is so important because MNCs generally need higher profitability from their overseas operation than they do from their domestic operations. The reason is quite simple: Setting up overseas operations involves greater risk and effort. In addition, a firm that has done well domestically with a product or service usually has done so because the competition is minimal or ineffective. Firms with this advantage often find additional lucrative opportunities outside their borders. Moreover, the more successful a firm is domestically, the more difficult it is to increase market share without strong competitive response. International markets, however, offer an ideal alternative to the desire for increased growth and profitability.

Another reason that profitability and marketing top the list is that these tend to be more externally environmentally responsive, whereas production, finance, and personnel functions tend to be more internally controlled. Thus, for strategic planning, profitability and marketing goals are given higher importance and warrant closer attention. Ford's European operations offer an example. In recent years the automaker has been losing market share in the EU. In an effort to turn things around, the MNC scaled back production capacity and announced that it intends to push market share above 10 percent, reversing a trend that has seen its slice of the European auto pie drop from almost 12 percent in the 1980s to just over 6 percent recently.[30] In order to reach this objective, Ford closed plants, cut its European workforce, and transferred vehicle production to more efficient factories. After cutting costs, the company launched a proactive strategy to increase market share.[31] Ford in Europe has been working to create a fresh image by offering new models, designing a totally revised advertising campaign, and developing a revised dealership network.

Table 8–1
Areas for Formulation of MNC Goals

Profitability

Level of profits

Return on assets, investment, equity, sales

Yearly profit growth

Yearly earnings per share growth

Marketing

Total sales volume

Market share—worldwide, region, country

Growth in sales volume

Growth in market share

Integration of country markets for marketing efficiency and effectiveness

Operations

Ratio of foreign to domestic production volume

Economies of scale via international production integration

Quality and cost control

Introduction of cost-efficient production methods

Finance

Financing of foreign affiliates—retained earnings or local borrowing

Taxation—minimizing tax burden globally

Optimum capital structure

Foreign exchange management—minimizing losses from foreign fluctuations

Human Resources

Recruitment and selection

Development of managers with global orientation

Management development of host-country nationals

Compensation and benefits

However, these adjustments have been costly and contributed to poor financial performance. Ford recently announced that it expects its European unit to post a $1.2 billion loss for 2003. Whether Ford can go back to 12 percent of this market is questionable, but top management believes a goal of 10 percent is both realistic and necessary.

Once the strategic goals are set, the MNC will develop specific operational goals and controls, usually through a two-way process at the subsidiary or affiliate level. Home-office management will set certain parameters, and the overseas group will operate within these guidelines. For example, the MNC headquarters may require periodic financial reports, restrict on-site decisions to matters involving less than $100,000, and require that all client contracts be cleared through the home office. These guidelines are designed to ensure that the overseas group's activities support the goals in the strategic plan and that all units operate in a coordinated effort.

■ Strategy Implementation

Once formulated, the strategic plan next must be implemented. **Strategy implementation** provides goods and services in accord with a plan of action. Quite often, this plan will have an overall philosophy or series of guidelines that direct the process. In the case of Japanese electronic-manufacturing firms entering the U.S. market, Chang has found a common approach:

> To reduce the risk of failure, these firms are entering their core businesses and those in which they have stronger competitive advantages over local firms first. The learning from early entry enables firms to launch further entry into areas in which they have the next strongest competitive

strategy implementation
The process of providing goods and services in accord with a plan of action.

advantages. As learning accumulates, firms may overcome the disadvantages intrinsic to foreignness. Although primary learning takes place within firms through learning by doing, they may also learn from other firms through the transfer or diffusion of experience. This process is not automatic, however, and it may be enhanced by membership in a corporate network: in firms associated with either horizontal or vertical business, groups were more likely to initiate entries than independent firms. By learning from their own sequential entry experience as well as from other firms in corporated networks, firms build capabilities in foreign entry.[32]

International management must consider three general areas in strategy implementation. First, the MNC must decide where to locate operations. Second, the MNC must carry out entry and ownership strategies (discussed in Chapter 9). Finally, management must implement functional strategies in areas such as marketing, production, and finance.

Location Considerations for Implementation

In choosing a location, today's MNC has two primary considerations: the country and the specific locale within the chosen country. Quite often, the first choice is easier than the second, because there are many more alternatives from which to choose a specific locale.

The Country   Traditionally, MNCs have invested in highly industrialized countries, and research reveals that annual investments have been increasing substantially. In 1993, over $325 billion was spent on mergers and acquisitions worldwide. By 1997, the annual total had jumped to $1.6 trillion, although in the last few years activity dropped somewhat, to about $1.4 trillion annually.[33] Much of this investment, especially by American MNCs, has been in Europe, Canada, and Mexico.

In the case of Japan, multinational banks and investors from around the world have been looking for properties that are being jettisoned by Japanese banks that are trying to unload some of their distressed loans. The Japanese commercial property market collapsed starting in the mid-1990s, creating many opportunities for investors. One was U.S.-based MNC Bankers Trust, which bought a large plot of properties of a failed affiliate of Nippon Credit Bank Ltd. Bankers Trust paid $220 million for properties that had a face value of $2.2 billion.[34] Nonbanking MNCs are also actively engaged in mergers and acquisitions in Japan. Intuit Inc. of Menlo Park, California purchased a financial software specialist in Japan for $52 million in stock and spent $30 million for the Nihon Mikon Company, which sells small business accounting software. These purchases point to a new trend in Japan—the acquisition of small firms. However, many larger purchases have also been made, as seen in Table 8–2.

Foreign investors are also pouring into Mexico, although this investment activity has generated some political controversy in the United States.[35] One reason is that it is a gateway to the American and Canadian markets. A second reason is that Mexico is a very cost-effective place in which to manufacture goods. A third is that the declining value of the

Table 8–2
Representative MNC Acquisitions in Japan

Glaxo Wellcome	Purchased the remaining 50 percent of its Nippon Glaxo affiliate for $537 million.
Ford Motor	Picked up an additional 9 percent of Mazda, bringing its stake to 33.4 percent, for $430 million.
BASF	The German drugmaker purchased 51 percent of Hokuriku Seiyaku for $294 million.
Grande Group	The Singapore firm acquired 70 percent of Nakamichi for $286 million.
GE Capital	Bought 80 percent of Narubeni Car System, an auto-loan business, for $80 million.
Semi-Tech Group	The Hong Kong high-tech company put out $167 million for an additional 11 percent of Akai Electric.
Boehringer Ingelheim	The German firm acquired 9 percent of SS Pharmaceutical for $71 million.
Amersham International	The British drugmaker acquired 30 percent of Nihon Mediphysics for $76 million.

peso in the late 1990s hit many Mexican businesses hard and left them vulnerable to mergers and acquisitions—an opportunity not lost on many large multinationals.

> Britain's B.A.T. Industries PLC took control of Cigarrera La Moderna, Mexico's tobacco giant, in a $1.5 billion deal. A few days earlier, Philip Morris Cos. increased its stake in the second-largest tobacco company, Cigarros La Tabacalera Mexicana SA, to 50% from about 29% for $400 million. In June, Wal-Mart Stores Inc. announced plans to acquire control of Mexico's largest retailer, Cifra SA, in a deal valued at more than $1 billion. In July, Procter & Gamble Co. acquired a consumer-products concern, Loreto y Pena Pobre, for $170 million. Bell Atlantic Co. has acquired full control of its cellular-phone partner, Grupo Iusacell SA, with total investments of more than $1 billion. The list goes on and on and is expected to keep growing.[36]

MNCs often invest in advanced industrialized countries because they offer the largest markets for goods and services. In addition, the established country or geographic locale may have legal restrictions related to imports, encouraging a local presence. Japanese firms, for example, in complying with their voluntary export quotas of cars to the United States as well as responding to dissatisfaction in Washington regarding the continuing trade imbalance with the United States, have established U.S.-based assembly plants. In Europe, because of EU regulations for outsiders, most U.S. and Japanese MNCs have operations in at least one European country, thus ensuring access to the European community at large. In fact, the huge U.S. MNC ITT now operates in each of the original 12 EU countries.

Another consideration in choosing a country is the amount of government control. Traditionally, MNCs from around the world refused to do business in Eastern European countries with central planning economies. The recent relaxing of the trade rules and move toward free-market economies in the republics of the former Soviet Union and the other Eastern European nations, however, have encouraged MNCs to rethink their positions; more and more are making moves into this largely untapped part of the global market. The same is true in India, although the political climate can be volatile and MNCs must carefully weigh the risks of investing here.

Still another consideration in selecting a country is restrictions on foreign investment. Traditionally, countries such as China and India have required that control of the operation be in the hands of local partners. MNCs that are reluctant to accept such conditions will not establish operations there.

In addition to these considerations, MNCs will examine the specific benefits offered by host countries, including low tax rates, rent-free land and buildings, low-interest or no-interest loans, subsidized energy and transportation rates, and a well-developed infrastructure that provides many of the services found back home (good roads, communication systems, schools, health care, entertainment, and housing). These benefits will be weighed against any disincentives or performance requirements that must be met by the MNC, such as job-creation quotas, export minimums for generating foreign currency, limits on local market growth, labor regulations, wage and price controls, restrictions on profit repatriation, and controls on the transfer of technology. Commenting on the overall effect of these potential gains and losses, Garland and Farmer noted:

> These incentives and disincentives often make operations abroad less amenable to integration on a global basis; essentially they may alter a company's strategy for the region. They affect, for example, a firm's make-or-buy decision, intracorporate transfer policies (e.g., between subsidiaries or between headquarters and the subsidiaries), both horizontal and vertical sourcing arrangements, and so on. In effect, they weaken the MNC's mandate for global efficiency by encouraging the firm to suboptimize.[37]

Local Issues Once the MNC has decided the country in which to locate, the firm must choose the specific locale. A number of factors influence this choice. Common considerations include access to markets, proximity to competitors, availability of transportation and electric power, and desirability of the location for employees coming in from the outside.

One study found that in selecting U.S. sites, both German and Japanese firms place more importance on accessibility and desirability and less importance on financial considerations.[38] However, financial matters remain important: Many countries attempt to lure MNCs to specific locales by offering special financial packages.

Another common consideration is the nature of the workforce. MNCs prefer to locate near sources of available labor that can be readily trained to do the work. A complementary consideration that often is unspoken is the presence and strength of organized labor (Chapter 15 covers this topic in detail). Japanese firms in particular tend to avoid heavily unionized areas.

Still another consideration is the cost of doing business. Manufacturers often set up operations in rural areas, commonly called "green field locations," which are much less expensive and do not have the problems of urban areas. Conversely, banks often choose metropolitan areas, because they feel they must have a presence in the business district.

Some MNCs opt for locales where the cost of running a small enterprise is significantly lower than that of running a large one. In this way, they spread their risk, setting up many small locations throughout the world rather than one or two large ones. Manufacturing firms are a good example. Some production firms feel that the economies of scale associated with a large-scale plant are more than offset by potential problems that can result should economic or political difficulties develop in the country. These firms' strategy is to spread the risk by opting for a series of small plants throughout a wide geographic region.[39] This location strategy can also be beneficial for stockholders. Research has found that MNCs with a presence in developing countries have significantly higher market values than MNCs that operate only in countries that have advanced economies.[40]

The Role of the Functional Areas in Implementation

To implement strategies, MNCs must tap the primary functional areas of marketing, production, and finance. The following sections examine the roles of these functions in international strategy implementation.

Marketing   The implementation of strategy from a marketing perspective must be determined on a country-by-country basis. What works from the standpoint of marketing in one locale may not necessarily succeed in another. In addition, the specific steps of a marketing approach often are dictated by the overall strategic plan, which in turn is based heavily on market analysis.

German auto firms in Japan are a good example of using marketing analysis to meet customer needs. Over the past 15 years, the Germans have spent millions of dollars to build dealer, supplier, and service-support networks in Japan, in addition to adapting their cars to Japanese customers' tastes. Volkswagen Audi Nippon has built a $320-million import facility on a deepwater port. This operation, which includes an inspection center and parts warehouse, can process 100,000 cars a year. Mercedes and BMW both have introduced lower-priced cars to attract a larger market segment, and BMW now offers a flat-fee, three-year service contract on any new car, including parts. At the same time, German manufacturers work hard to offer first-class service in their dealerships. As a result, German automakers in recent years sell almost three times as many cars in Japan as their U.S. competitors do.

The Japanese also provide an excellent example of how the marketing process works. In many cases, Japanese firms have followed a strategy of first building up their market share at home and driving out imported goods. Then, the firms move into newly developed countries, honing their marketing skills as they go along. Finally, the firms move into fully developed countries, ready to compete with the best available. This pattern of implementing strategy has been used in marketing autos, cameras, consumer electronics, home appliances, petrochemicals, steel, and watches. For some products, however, such as computers, the Japanese have moved from their home market directly into fully developed countries and then on to the newly developing nations. Finally, the Japanese have gone directly to developed countries to market products in some cases, because the market in Japan was too small. Such products include color TVs, videotape recorders, and sewing machines. In general, once a firm agrees on the goods it wants to sell in the international marketplace, then the specific marketing strategy is implemented.

The implementation of marketing strategy in the international arena is built around the well-known "four Ps" of marketing: product, price, promotion, and place. As noted in the example of the Japanese, firms often develop and sell a product in local or peripheral markets before expanding to major overseas targets. If the product is designed specifically to meet an overseas demand, however, the process is more direct. Price largely is a function of market demand.[41] For example, the Japanese have found that the U.S. microcomputer market is price-sensitive; by introducing lower-priced clones, the Japanese have been able to make headway, especially in the portable laptop market. The last two Ps, promotion and place, are dictated by local conditions and often left in the hands of those running the subsidiary or affiliate. Local management may implement customer sales incentives, for example, or make arrangements with dealers and salespeople who are helping to move the product locally.

Production Although marketing usually dominates strategy implementation, the production function also plays a role. If a company is going to export goods to a foreign market, the production process traditionally has been handled through domestic operations. In recent years, however, MNCs have found that whether they are exporting or producing the goods locally in the host country, consideration of worldwide production is important. For example, goods may be produced in foreign countries for export to other nations. Sometimes, a plant will specialize in a particular product and export it to all the MNC's markets; other times, a plant will produce goods only for a specific locale, such as Western Europe or South America. Still other facilities will produce one or more components that are shipped to a larger network of assembly plants. That last option has been widely adopted by pharmaceutical firms and automakers such as Volkswagen and Honda.

As mentioned in the first part of the chapter, if the firm operates production plants in different countries but makes no attempt to integrate its overall operations, the company is known as a multi-domestic. A recent trend has been away from this scattered approach and toward global coordination of operations.

Finally, if the product is labor-intensive, as in the case of microcomputers, then the trend is to farm the product out to low-cost sites such as Mexico or Brazil, where the cost of labor is relatively low and the infrastructure (electric power, communications systems, transportation systems) is sufficient to support production. Sometimes, multiple sources of individual components are used; in other cases, one or two sources are sufficient. In any event, careful coordination of the production function is needed when implementing the strategy, and the result is a product that is truly global in nature.

Finance Use of the finance function to implement strategy normally is developed at the home office and carried out by the overseas affiliate or branch. When a firm went international in the past, the overseas operation commonly relied on the local area for funds, but the rise of global financing has ended this practice. MNCs have learned that transferring funds from one place in the world to another, or borrowing funds in the international money markets, often is less expensive than relying on local sources. Unfortunately, there are problems in these transfers.

Such a problem is representative of those faced by MNCs using the finance function to implement their strategies. One of an MNC's biggest recent headaches when implementing strategies in the financial dimension has been the revaluation of currencies. For example, in the late 1990s the U.S. dollar increased in value against the Japanese yen. American overseas subsidiaries that held yen found their profits (in terms of dollars) declining. The same was true for those subsidiaries that held Mexican pesos when that government devalued the currency several years ago. When this happens, a subsidiary's profit will decline. After its initial introduction in 1999, the euro declined against the U.S. dollar, but when the dollar subsequently came under pressure, the euro regained strength.

When dealing with the inherent risk of volatile monetary exchange rates, some MNCs have bought currency options that (for a price) guarantee convertibility at a specified rate. Others have developed countertrade strategies, whereby they receive products in exchange for currency. For example, PepsiCo received payment in vodka for its products sold in Russia. Countertrade continues to be a popular form of international business, especially in less developed countries and those with nonconvertible currencies.

■ Specialized Strategies

In addition to the basic steps in strategy formulation, the analysis of which strategies may be appropriate based on the globalization vs. national responsiveness framework, and the specific processes in strategy implementation, there are some circumstances that may require specialized strategies. Two that have received considerable attention in recent years are strategies for developing and emerging markets and strategies for international entrepreneurship and new ventures.

Strategies for Emerging Markets

Emerging economies have assumed an increasingly important role in the global economy and are predicted to compose more than half of global economic output by mid-century. Partly in response to this growth, MNCs are directing increasing attention to those markets. Foreign direct investment (FDI) flows into developing countries—one measure of increased integration and business activity between developed and emerging economies—grew from $23.7 billion in 1990 to $204.8 billion in 2001, a ninefold increase, helping to contribute to growth in the stock of FDI in developing countries from 5 percent to 20.5 percent of GDP over this same period.[42] In particular, the "big emerging markets"—Mexico, Brazil, Argentina, South Africa, Poland, Turkey, India, Indonesia, China, and South Korea—have captured the bulk of investment and business interest from MNCs and their managers.[43]

At the same time, emerging economies pose exceptional risks due to their political and economic volatility and their relatively underdeveloped institutional systems. These risks show up in corruption, failure to enforce contracts, red tape and bureaucratic costs, and general uncertainty in the legal and political environment.[44] MNCs must adjust their strategy to respond to these risks. For example, in these risky markets, it may be wise to engage in arm's-length or limited equity investments or to maintain greater control of operations by avoiding joint ventures or other shared ownership structures. In other circumstances, it may be wiser to collaborate with a local partner who can help buffer risks through its political connections.[45] Some of the factors relating to these conditions will be discussed in Chapters 9 and 10. However, two unique types of strategies for emerging markets deserve particular attention here.

First-Mover Strategies   Recent research has suggested that entry order into developing countries may be particularly important given the transitional nature of these markets. In general, in particular industries and economic environments, significant economies are associated with first-mover or early-entry positioning—being the first or one of the first to enter a market. These include capturing learning effects important for increasing market share, achieving scale economies that accrue from opportunities for capturing that greater share, and development of alliances with the most attractive (or in some cases the only) local partner. In emerging economies that are undergoing rapid changes such as privatization and market liberalization, there may be a narrow window of time within which these opportunities can be best exploited. In these conditions, first-mover strategies allow entrants to preempt competition, establish beachhead positions, and influence the evolving competitive environment in a manner conducive to their long-term interests and market position.

One study analyzed these benefits in the case of China, concluding that early entrants have reaped substantial rewards for their efforts, especially when collaborations with governments provided credible commitments that the deals struck in those early years of liberalization would not later be undone. First-mover advantages in some other transitional markets, such as Russia and Eastern Europe, are not so clear. Moreover, there may be substantial risks to premature entry—that is, entry before the basic legal, institutional, and political frameworks for doing business have been established.[46]

Privatization presents a particularly powerful case supporting the competitive effects of first-mover positioning. First movers who succeed in taking over newly privatized state-owned enterprises, such as telecom and energy firms, possess a significant advantage over later entrants, especially when market liberalization is delayed and the host government provides protection to the newly privatized incumbent firms. This was the case in 1998 when the Mexican government accepted a $1.757 billion bid for a minority (20.4 percent) but controlling interest in Telefonos de Mexico (Telmex) from an international consortium composed of Grupo Carso, Southwestern Bell, and France Cable et Radio, an affiliate of France Telecom. Although the Mexican market subsequently opened to competition, Telmex and its foreign partners (the first movers) maintained monopoly control over local networks and were able to bundle local and long-distance service, cross-market, and cross-subsidize, giving Telmex a strong advantage. Moreover, the Mexican government was responsive to providing the Telmex consortium protection and financial support for infrastructure investment, and it did so partly by charging new carriers to help Telmex pay for improvements needed for the long-distance network. In addition, Telmex was able to charge relatively high fees to connect to its network, and the long delay between the initial privatization and market opening allowed these advantages to persist.[47]

Strategies for the "Base of the Pyramid" Another area of increasing focus for MNCs is the 4 to 5 billion potential customers around the world who have heretofore been mostly ignored by international business, even within emerging economies, where most MNCs target only the wealthiest consumers. Although FDI in emerging economies has grown rapidly, most has been directed at the big emerging markets previously mentioned—China, India, and Brazil—and even there, most MNC emerging-market strategies have focused exclusively on the elite and emerging middle-class markets, ignoring the vast majority of people considered too poor to be viable customers.[48] Because of this focus, MNC strategies aimed at tailoring existing practices and products to better fit the needs of emerging-market customers have not succeeded in making products and services available to the mass markets in the developing world—the 4–5 billion people at the bottom of the economic pyramid who represent fully two-thirds of the world's population. Figure 8–3 shows the distribution of population and income around the world.

A group of researchers and companies have begun exploring the potentially untapped markets at the base of the pyramid (BOP). They have found that incremental adaptation of existing technologies and products is not effective at the BOP and that the BOP forces MNCs to fundamentally rethink their strategies.[49] Companies must consider smaller-scale strategies and build relationships with local governments, small entrepreneurs, and non-profits rather than depend on established partners such as central governments and large local companies. Building relationships directly and at the local level contributes to the reputation and fosters the trust necessary to overcome the lack of formal institutions such as intellectual property rights and the rule of law. The BOP may also be an ideal environment for incubating new, leapfrog technologies, including "disruptive" technologies that reduce environmental impacts and increase social benefit such as renewable energy and wireless telecom. Finally, business models forged successfully at the base of the pyramid have the potential to travel profitably to higher-income markets because adding cost and features to a low-cost model may be easier than removing cost and features from high-cost models.[50] This last finding has significant implications for the globalization–national responsiveness framework introduced at the beginning of the chapter and for the potential for MNCs to achieve a truly transnational strategy.

Figure 8–3

The World Population and Income Pyramid

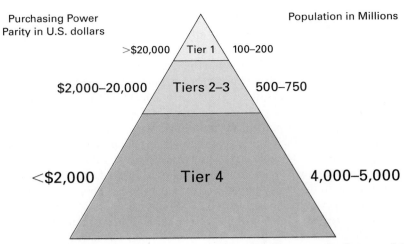

Purchasing Power Parity in U.S. dollars · Population in Millions

>$20,000 / Tier 1 / 100–200
$2,000–20,000 / Tiers 2–3 / 500–750
<$2,000 / Tier 4 / 4,000–5,000

Source: Adapted from C. K. Prahalad and Stuart L. Hart. "The Fortune at the Bottom of the Pyramid," *Strategy + Business,* Issue 26 (first quarter 2002), pp. 54–67.

Entrepreneurial Strategy and New Ventures

In addition to strategies that must be tailored for the particular needs and circumstances in emerging economies, another condition that calls for specialized strategies is the international management activities of entrepreneurial and new-venture firms. Most international management activities take place within the context of medium-large MNCs, but, increasingly, small and medium companies, often in the form of new ventures, are getting involved in international management. This has been made possible by advances in telecommunication and Internet technologies, and by greater efficiencies and lower costs in shipping, allowing firms that were previously limited to local or national markets to access international customers. These new access channels, however, suggest particular strategies that must be customized and tailored to the unique situations and resource limitations of small, entrepreneurial firms.[51]

International Entrepreneurship   International entrepreneurship has been defined as "a combination of innovative, proactive, and risk-seeking behavior that crosses national borders and is intended to create value in organizations."[52] The internationalization of the marketplace and the increasing number of entrepreneurial firms in the global economy have created new opportunities for small and new-venture firms to accelerate internationalization. This international entrepreneurial activity is being observed in even the smallest and newest organizations. Indeed, one study among 57 privately held Finnish electronics firms during the mid-1990s showed that firms that internationalize after they are established domestically must overcome a number of barriers to that international expansion, such as their domestic orientation, internal domestic political ties, and domestic decision-making inertia. In contrast, firms that internationalize earlier face fewer barriers to learning about the international environment.[53] Thus, the earlier in its existence that an innovative firm internationalizes, the faster it is likely to grow both overall and in foreign markets.

However, despite this new access, there remain limitations to international entrepreneurial activities. In another study, researchers show that deploying a technological learning advantage internationally is no simple process. They studied more than 300 private independent and corporate new ventures based in the United States. Building on past research about the advantages of large, established multinational enterprises, their results from 12 high-technology industries show that greater diversity of national environments is associated with increased technological learning opportunities even for new ventures, whose internationalization is usually thought to be limited.[54] In addition, the breadth, depth, and speed of technological learning from varied international environments is significantly enhanced by formal organizational efforts to integrate knowledge throughout a firm such as cross-functional teams and formal analysis of both successful and failed projects. Further, the research shows that venture performance (growth and return on equity) is improved by technological learning gained from international environments.

International New Ventures and "Born-Global" Firms   Another dimension of the growth of international entrepreneurial activities is the increasing incidence of international new ventures, or "born globals"—firms that engage in significant international activity a short time after being established. Building on an empirical study of small firms in Norway and France, researchers found that more than half of the exporting firms established there since 1990 could be classified as "born globals."[55] Examining the differences between newly established firms with high or low export involvement levels revealed that a decision maker's global orientation and market conditions are important factors.

Another study highlighted the critical role of innovative culture, as well as knowledge and capabilities, in this unique breed of international, entrepreneurial firm. An analysis of case studies and surveys revealed key strategies that engender international success among these innovative firms.[56] Successful born-global firms leverage a distinctive mix of orientations and strategies that allow them to succeed in diverse international markets. Firms whose possession of the foundational capabilities of international entrepreneurial orientation and international marketing orientation engender the development of a specific collection of organizational strategies. The most important business strategies employed by born-global firms are global technological competence, unique-products development, quality focus, and leveraging of foreign distributor competences.[57]

One clear example of a born-global firm is California-based Amazon.com. Like most U.S. Internet firms, Amazon.com has been able to diffuse its products and services on an international scale from the outset. Although differing levels of cultural similarities and technological sophistication impact Amazon's potential for success internationally, the Internet as a medium has removed certain entry barriers that have historically restricted quick market entry.[58] Ireland-based Resmed is another example of a successful company that was born global. In less than a decade, the company (a manufacturer of machines that relieve sleep disorders) has grown into a business that employs 220 people and turns over $66 million annually, of which 95 percent is generated overseas. North America is by far the company's largest market, accounting for 52 percent of sales, followed by Europe, which comprises 35 percent of sales.[59] Now more than ever, born global as a corporate strategy is becoming more attractive and less risky.

The World of *BusinessWeek*—Revisited

Looking back to the *BusinessWeek* article that opens this chapter, it is easy to see why Ford Motor Co. needs effective global strategic management. Ford must pursue a strategy that takes advantage of lower cost and standardization for its vehicles sold under the Ford brand, while protecting the image of the more exclusive brands such as Jaguar and Aston Martin, which are experiencing rapid growth in U.S. and European markets. In short, the company's global strategy must differentiate among the Ford brand and the brands of its higher-quality and image vehicles. At the same time, major competitors such as Toyota and GM are developing for their products and services global strategies that challenge Ford. The company that pursues the most appropriate strategy, within the context of its core competencies and the markets in which it does business, should be able to meet or outperform the competition.

Drawing on the need and benefits of strategic management, answer these questions: (1) Which imperative is likely to be relatively most important to MNCs in the coming decade: economic, political, or quality? (2) When MNCs scan the environment, what are two key areas for consideration that they must address? (3) How would you characterize Ford's strategy within the globalization–national responsiveness framework? (4) Should Ford consider pursuing first-mover strategies in the emerging markets in which it seeks to operate? Why or why not?

SUMMARY OF KEY POINTS

1. There is a growing need for strategic management among MNCs. Some of the primary reasons include: Foreign direct investment is increasing; planning is needed to coordinate and integrate increasingly diverse operations via an overall focus; and emerging international challenges require strategic planning.

2. A strategic plan can take on an economic focus, a political focus, a quality focus, an administrative coordination focus, or some variation of the four. The global integration–national responsiveness framework defines the four basic strategies employed by MNCs: international, global, multi-domestic, and transnational. Although transnational is often the preferred strategy, it is also the most difficult to implement.

3. Strategy formulation consists of several steps. First, the MNC carries out external environmental scanning to identify opportunities and threats. Next, the firm conducts an internal resource analysis of company strengths and weaknesses. Strategic goals then are formulated in light of the results of these external and internal analyses.

4. Strategy implementation is the process of providing goods and services in accord with the predetermined plan of action. This implementation typically involves such considerations as deciding where to locate operations, carrying out an entry and ownership strategy, and using functional strategies to implement the plan. Functional strategies focus on marketing, production, and finance.

5. Strategies for emerging markets and international entrepreneurship/new ventures may require specialized approaches targeted to these unique circumstances.

KEY TERMS

administrative coordination, *241*

economic imperative, *239*

environmental scanning, *245*

global integration, *242*

global strategy, *243*

international strategy, *244*

key factor for success (KFS), *246*

multi-domestic strategy, *244*

national responsiveness, *242*

political imperative, *239*

quality imperative, *240*

strategic management, *236*

strategy implementation, *247*

transnational strategy, *244*

REVIEW AND DISCUSSION QUESTIONS

1. Of the four imperatives discussed in this chapter—economic, political, quality, and administration—which would be most important to IBM in its efforts to make inroads in the Pacific Rim market? Would this emphasis be the same as that in the United States, or would IBM be giving primary attention to one of the other imperatives? Explain.

2. Define *global integration* as used in the context of strategic international management. In what way might globalization be a problem for a successful national organization that is intent on going international? In your answer, provide an example of the problem.

3. Some international management experts contend that globalization and national responsiveness are diametrically opposed forces, and that to accommodate one, a multinational must relax its efforts in the other. In what way is this an accurate statement? In what way is it incomplete or inaccurate?

4. When a large MNC such as Ford Motor sets strategic goals, what areas are targeted for consideration? Incorporate the information from Table 8–1 in your answer.

5. What particular conditions that MNCs face in emerging markets may require specialized strategies? What strategies might be most appropriate in response?

6. What conditions have allowed some firms to be born global? What are some examples of born global companies?

7. Mercedes changed its U.S. strategy by announcing that it is developing cars for the $30,000 to $45,000 price range (as well as its typical upper-end cars). What might have accounted for this change in strategy? In your answer, include a discussion of the implications from the standpoints of marketing, production, and finance.

INTERNET EXERCISE: DROPPING IN ON DELL COMPUTER

One of the largest computer firms in the world is Dell Computer. Dell does not sell its products in retail stores. In order to purchase a Dell computer, it is necessary to go to the firm's website, indicate the desired machine's configuration, and then arrange for the financing. Go to Dell's Web site at **www.dell.com** and examine some of the background on the firm and the computers it is now offering. Then answer these questions: How do you think international strategic management is reflected in what you see on the website? What major strategic planning steps would Dell need to carry out in order to remain a world leader in this direct-marketing niche? What potential threat, if it occurred, would prove most disastrous for Dell, and what could the company do to deal with the possibility of this negative development?

Poland

Poland is the sixth-largest country in Europe. It is bordered by Germany, the Czech Republic, and Slovakia in the west and south and by the former Soviet Union republics of Ukraine in the south, Belarus in the east, and Lithuania in the northeast. The northwest section of the country is located on the Baltic Sea. Named after the Polane, a Slavic tribe that lived more than a thousand years ago, Poland has beautiful countryside and rapidly growing cities. Rolling hills and rugged mountains rise in southern Poland.

There are approximately 39 million Poles, and GDP is around $227 billion. Poland's per capita GDP of $5,943 is about 40 percent of the EU average. Seventy percent of Poland's exports go to the EU. The Polish economy grew rapidly in the mid-1990s, but growth slowed considerably in recent years. Agriculture employs 26.3 percent of the workforce but contributes only 3.1 percent to GDP, reflecting relatively low productivity. Unlike the industrial sector, Poland's agricultural sector remained largely in private hands during the decades of communist rule. Most of the former state farms are now leased to farmer tenants. Lack of credit is hampering efforts to sell former state farmland. In preparation for accession into the EU, Poland began restructuring its agriculture sector. The EU is unwilling to subsidize the vast number of subsistence farms that do not produce for the market. The changes in agriculture are likely to strain Poland's social fabric, as family-based small farms are split up as the younger generation drifts toward the cities.

Throughout the 1990s the United States and other Western countries supported the growth of a free-enterprise economy by reducing Poland's foreign debt burden, providing economic aid, and lowering trade barriers. Poland graduated from USAID assistance in 2000. As a result of Poland's growth and investment-friendly climate, the country has received over $65 billion in direct foreign investment since 1990. However, the government continues to play a strong role in the economy, as seen in excessive red tape and the high level of politicization in many business decisions. Investors complain that state regulation is not transparent or predictable. The economy suffers from a lack of competition in many sectors, notably telecommunications. In early 2002, the government announced a new set of economic reforms designed in many ways to complete the process launched in 1990. The package acknowledges the need to improve Poland's investment climate, particularly the conditions for small and medium-sized enterprises, and better prepare the economy to compete as an EU member.

Despite continuing problems, the Poles have made some progress in establishing a viable economy. To take advantage of this economic situation, a medium-sized Canadian manufacturing firm has begun thinking about renovating a plant near Warsaw and building small power tools for the expanding Central and Eastern European market. The company's logic is fairly straightforward. There appears to be no competition in this niche, because there has been little demand for power tools in this area. As the postcommunist countries continue to struggle in their transition to a market economy, they will have to increase their productivity if they hope to compete with Western European nations. Small power tools are one of the products they will need to accomplish this goal.

A second reason for the Canadian firm's interest in setting up operations in Poland is that the price of labor is still relatively low. Other nearby countries have lower wage rates, but Warsaw, the company's specific choice, has a cadre of well-trained factory workers who could be recruited to this renovated factory. Product quality in the production of these tools is critical to success, so for this Canadian firm, Poland seems an ideal location.

In addition, Poland likely will continue receiving economic and moral support from Western Europe as well as Canada and the United States. Exporting from Poland to Western Europe or the United States therefore should be easier than from more developed countries. Moreover, the manufacturing firm is convinced that its proximity to Russia will open up that market as well. Transportation costs to Russia will be low vis-à-vis competitors, and the Russians currently are looking for ways to increase their own worker productivity.

Finally, there likely will be little competition for the next couple of years, because small power tools do not carry a very large markup and no other manufacturer is attempting to tap what the Canadian firm views as "an emerging market for the twenty-first century." However, a final decision on this matter is going to have to wait until the company has made a thorough evaluation of the market and the competitive nature of the industry.

www.poland.pl

Questions

1. What are some current issues facing Poland? What is the climate for doing business in Poland today?

2. Is the Canadian manufacturing firm using an economic, political, or quality imperative approach to strategy?

3. How should the firm carry out the environmental scanning process? Would the process be of any practical value?

4. What are two key factors for success that will be important if this project is to succeed?

Go East, Young People, Go East

Amanda Brendhart, Jose Gutierrez, and Rhoda Schreiber founded and are partners in a small electronics firm, Electronic Visions, that has developed and patented some state-of-the-art computer components. Visions has had moderate success selling these components to large U.S.-based computer manufacturers. The biggest problem is that in recent months, the computer market has begun to turn soft, and many of the manufacturers are offering substantial discounts to generate sales. Therefore, although Visions has found an increasing demand for its product, it now is grossing less money than it was several months ago.

To increase both sales and profit, the partners have decided to expand into Asia. Although this region is known for its low-cost computer production, the group believes that countries such as China, Malaysia, and Thailand soon will become more lucrative markets, because the U.S. government will make these countries open their doors to imports more fully. If trade barriers are removed, the partners are convinced that they can export the goods at very competitive prices. In addition, the partners intend to find a partner in each market so that they have someone to help with the marketing and financing of the product. Of course,

if the components can be produced more cheaply with local labor, the partnership is willing to forgo exporting and have everything produced locally.

At present, the group is trying to answer three questions. First, what is the best entry strategy to use in reaching the Asian markets? Second, what type of marketing strategy will be most effective? Third, if production must be coordinated between the United States and an overseas country, what is the best way to handle this? The partners believe that over the next two months, they will have a very good idea of what is going to happen regarding the opening of Asian markets. In the interim, they intend to work up a preliminary strategic plan that they can use to guide them.

Questions

1. What type of entry and ownership approach would you recommend? Defend your choice.
2. How could the partners use the four Ps of marketing to help implement strategy?
3. If production must be globally coordinated, will Visions have a major problem? Why or why not?

Chapter 9

ENTRY STRATEGIES AND ORGANIZATIONAL STRUCTURES

OBJECTIVES OF THE CHAPTER

The success of an international firm can be greatly affected by the overall structure and design of operations. There are a wide variety of organizational structures and designs from which to choose. Selecting the most appropriate structure depends on a number of factors, such as the desire of the home office for control over its foreign operations and the demands placed on the overseas unit by both the local market and the personnel who work there.

This chapter first presents and analyzes traditional organizational structures for effective international operations. Then it explores some of the new, nontraditional organizational arrangements stemming from mergers, joint ventures, and the Japanese concept of keiretsu. The specific objectives of this chapter are:

1. DESCRIBE how an MNC develops and implements entry strategies and ownership structures.

2. EXAMINE the major types of entry strategies and organizational structures used in handling international operations.

3. ANALYZE the advantages and disadvantages of each type of organizational structure, including the conditions that make one preferable to others.

4. DESCRIBE the recent, nontraditional organizational arrangements coming out of mergers, joint ventures, keiretsus, and other new designs including electronic networks and product development structures.

5. EXPLAIN how organizational characteristics such as formalization, specialization, and centralization influence how the organization is structured and functions.

The World of *BusinessWeek*

BusinessWeek

Intel Inside—Russia, That Is

Its Investment Arm Is Pouring Millions into the Tech Sector

Russia doesn't exactly spring to mind as the center of hot technology venture-capital plays. Despite a wealth of technical talent and a plentiful supply of unemployed engineers, the country hasn't succeeded in channeling much investment capital into tech startups. True, in the decade since the London-based European Bank for Reconstruction & Development (EBRD) began pumping money into 11 regional development funds across Russia, the EBRD and others have invested an estimated $450 million in business incubators and new companies. But that's about the same amount raised by U.S. startups every month in 2001, during the waning days of the economic boom. New venture-backed Russian tech companies number only in the dozens.

Yet there are signs that high-tech capital is finally trickling into Russia. The clearest signal came in mid-May, when Intel Capital, the $870 million investment arm of the world's largest chipmaker, opened a Moscow branch and poured $4 million into a fast-growing Russian technology company called ru-Net. It's the first of what parent Intel Corp. hopes will be a handful of deals that fund promising innovations and the growth of Russia's tech infrastructure. "We're investing not just to grow the market but also to identify technologies we can help bring out to the rest of the world," says Marie E. Trexler, Intel Capital's managing director for Central and Eastern Europe, who oversees the Moscow operation from London.

Other potential foreign and domestic investors will be closely watching Intel's experiment. Until now, says Charles Ryan, executive chairman of Moscow investment bank United Financial Group, most private equity in Russia has gone into oil, timber, and agriculture. "There is woefully little

Intel Capital sees big technology potential in Russia. Some areas where long-term investment gains are possible			
Materials Science	**Programming Prowess**	**Wireless Edge**	**Needy Infrastructure**
Breakthroughs in man-made crystals could lead to new semiconductor chips	Algorithms devised by Russian math whizzes could speed up everything from processors to software	Russia's strength in radio technology may help Intel's push into the communications business	A shortage of basic computing tools means a large market for off-the-shelf technology

Source: www.businessweek.com/magazine/content/03_25/b3838064_mz014.htm

investment in high tech," he says. The country's wealthy oligarchs shied away because Russia's laws didn't safeguard intellectual property.

Intel's arrival should assure local and foreign investors that "there's another investment option—in technology," says Jason Downes, ru-Net's general director. Albina Nikkonen, executive director of the St. Petersburg–based Russian Venture Capital Assn., agrees: "It's a very positive sign that a giant such as Intel has decided to finance our technologies." She hopes Intel will join her organization. That would be quite a coup: Intel Capital has poured more than $4 billion into 1,000 companies worldwide since it was established in the early 1990s and now ranks as the world's leading venture capitalist.

Trexler thinks the time is right for Russia because the country's legal system now offers adequate protection for minority investors. And tech is booming: Both Intel and Microsoft Corp. say Russia ranks among their fastest-growing markets. Market researcher IDC figures the country's information-technology sector should surge 12% this year—twice the predicted global rate—to $5.5 billion in sales. That helps explain Intel's interest. The chipmaker wants to find esoteric new technologies in areas such as materials science and software, but it also aims to promote its mainstay microprocessors. Ru-Net, for instance, runs a subsidiary known as TopS Business Integrator that will use

$10 million raised from Intel and other investors to expand its fast-growing PC and server-distribution business.

Intel Capital is not alone in attempting to exploit Russia's high-tech talent pool. A few European firms have also set up shop. One, Frankfurt-based Quadriga Capital, opened an office in St. Petersburg last summer, and it has already raised $30 million of a planned $120 million fund. Most venture-capital outfits are far smaller, though. One significant hurdle for all of them has been the difficulty in cashing out. Of the 76 companies funded by the EBRD since 1994, only eight have been sold to other investors. Lack of liquidity also has made floating shares on the Russian stock market difficult. But capital markets are slowly beginning to mature. Last year, Moscow-based RosBusinessConsulting staged Russia's first-ever technology initial public offering and raised $13 million. For budding entrepreneurs, increased investment inflow could be the first step in creating a silicon boom on the steppes of Russia.

By Andy Reinhardt in Paris, with Paul Starobin in Moscow

The opening news story on Intel describes a formidable challenge facing many multinationals. Intel's home markets are maturing and becoming increasingly competitive as globalization and free trade continue to gain steam. Intel's entry into Russia and other developing and transition economies presents many opportunities for growth, but Intel must integrate its entry and organizational strategies in order to achieve long-term success. Alliances and joint ventures are attractive, but they also expose firms to risk. In Russia, Intel decided to use one of its subsidiaries, Intel Capital, as its initial entry point. If successful, this approach should help solidify Intel's leadership position in the Russian market. In short, what form a company decides to take when entering a market and what type of organizational structure is chosen to support it will have a substantial impact on a firm's success.

■ Entry Strategies and Ownership Structures

There are a number of common entry strategies and ownership structures in international operations. Figure 9–1 reports some of the latest information regarding global expansion strategies in select world markets. Depending on the region of the world, some approaches

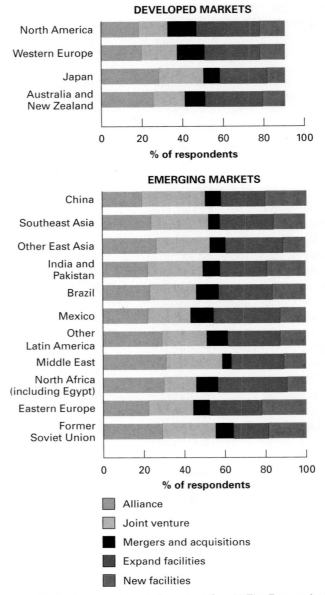

Figure 9–1

Preferred Strategies for Global Expansion

are more popular than others. For example, as shown, in Australia and New Zealand alliances and the expansion of facilities are common approaches, while in China joint ventures are widely used as its markets continue to open.[1] However, the most widely recognized are wholly owned subsidiaries, mergers and acquisitions, alliances and joint ventures, licensing agreements, franchising, and basic export and import operations. Depending on the situation, any one of these can be a very effective way to implement an MNC's strategy.

Wholly Owned Subsidiary

wholly owned subsidiary
An overseas operation that is totally owned and controlled by an MNC.

A **wholly owned subsidiary** is an overseas operation that is totally owned and controlled by an MNC. The primary reason for the use of fully owned subsidiaries is a desire by the MNC for total control and the belief that managerial efficiency will be better without outside partners. Host countries, however, often feel that the MNC is trying to gain economic control by setting up local operations but refusing to take in local partners. Some countries are concerned that the MNC will drive out local enterprises. In dealing with these concerns, many newly developing countries prohibit fully owned subsidiaries. A second drawback is that home-country unions sometimes oppose the creation of foreign subsidiaries, which they see as an attempt to "export jobs," particularly when the MNC exports goods to another country and then decides to set up manufacturing operations there. As a result, today many multinationals opt for a merger, alliance, or joint venture rather than a fully owned subsidiary.[2]

Mergers/Acquisitions

In recent years, a growing number of multinationals have acquired (fully or in part) their subsidiaries through **mergers/acquisitions.** One of the largest in terms of acquisition price was British Petroleum's (BP) purchase of Amoco for $48.2 billion.[3] A string of international acquisitions and mergers has made BP one of the largest and most profitable companies in the world.[4] Another example of a major merger/acquisition with mixed results was that of Daimler-Benz and Chrysler, now called DaimlerChrysler. In a deal valued at $39 billion, the German automaker effectively purchased Chrysler and, in the process, gained a lucrative North American market while opening the door in Europe for a Chrysler expansion. The strategic plan of the merged companies called for each to contribute a series of strengths toward making the firm a highly competitive operation. However, financial results since the merger have been less than spectacular.[5] DaimlerChrysler's net profit fell 91 percent, to $564 million, and it sold 210,800 fewer cars worldwide in 2003.[6] In addition, market share in Western Europe edged down 2.7 percent and remained flat in the United States. With worldwide auto sales down 6.5 percent in 2003 and marketing costs skyrocketing to 20 percent of revenues (due to sharp incentives increases), the short term looks bleak.[7] Although cross-border mergers and acquisitions remain a popular strategy for entering international markets, the challenges of postmerger integration are substantial.

merger/acquisition
The cross-border purchase or exchange of equity involving two or more companies.

Alliances and Joint Ventures

An **alliance** is any type of cooperative relationship among different firms. An international alliance is comprised of two or more firms from different countries. Some alliances are temporary; others are more permanent. A **joint venture (JV)** can be considered a specific type of alliance agreement under which two or more partners own or control a business. An international joint venture (IJV) is a JV comprised of two or more firms from different countries. Alliances and joint ventures can take a number of different forms, including cross-marketing arrangements, technology-sharing agreements, production-contracting deals, and equity agreements. In some instances, two parties may create a third, independent entity expressly for the purpose of developing a collaborative relationship outside their core companies. Alliances and joint ventures, like mergers and acquisitions, can pose substantial managerial challenges. We will discuss some of these at the end of the chapter and again in Chapter 10.

alliance
Any type of cooperative relationship among different firms.

international joint venture (IJV)
An agreement under which two or more partners from different countries own or control a business.

There are two types of alliances and joint ventures. The first type is the *nonequity venture,* which is characterized by one group's merely providing a service for another. The group providing the service typically is more active than the other. Examples include a consulting firm that is hired to provide analysis and evaluation and then make its recommendations to the other party, an engineering or construction firm that contracts to design or build a dam or series of apartment complexes in an undeveloped area of a partner's country, or a mining firm that has an agreement to extract a natural resource in the other party's country.

The second type is the *equity joint venture,* which involves a financial investment by the MNC in a business enterprise with a local partner. Many variations of this arrangement adjust the degree of control that each of the parties will have and the amount of money, technological expertise, and managerial expertise each will contribute.[8]

Most foreign firms are more interested in the amount of control they will have over the venture than in their share of the profits. Many local partners feel the same way, and this can result in problems. Nevertheless, alliances and joint ventures have become very popular in recent years because of the benefits they offer to both parties. Some of the most commonly cited advantages include:

1. *Improvement of efficiency.* The creation of an alliance or joint venture can help the partners achieve economies of scale and scope that would be difficult for one firm operating alone to accomplish. Additionally, the partners can spread the risks among themselves and profit from the synergies that arise from the complementarity of their resources.[9]

2. *Access to knowledge.* In alliances and joint ventures each partner has access to the knowledge and skills of the others. So one partner may bring financial and technological resources to the venture while another brings knowledge of the customer and market channels.

3. *Political factors.* A local partner can be very helpful in dealing with political risk factors such as a hostile government or restrictive legislation.

4. *Collusion or restriction in competition.* Alliances and joint ventures can help partners overcome the effects of local collusion or limits that are being put on foreign competition. By becoming part of an "insider" group, foreign partners manage to transcend these barriers.[10]

As noted above, alliance and joint-venture partners often complement each other and can thus reduce the risks associated with their undertaking. A good example is European truck manufacturing and auto component industries. Firms in both groups have found that the high cost of developing and building their products can be offset through joint ventures. In particular, some partners to these ventures have contributed financial assistance while others provide the distribution networks needed to move the product through channels. In March 2004, the joint venture between Alcatel and Fujitsu was awarded a $500 million contract to build a submarine cable network connecting Southeast Asia, the Middle East, and Western Europe.[11] Sharing risks, resources, and capabilities can often position two companies to gain more success together than alone.

Although much negotiation may be necessary before an alliance or joint-venture agreement is hammered out, the final result must be one that both sides can accept.[12] Many successful examples of such agreements have emerged in recent years. One of the most complex was the General Motors–Toyota agreement, which involved scores of groups and thousands of individuals. Other examples include General Motors' venture with the Polish government to build Opels in Poland, L. L. Bean's decision to sell clothing and equipment under a joint-venture agreement with two Japanese companies in Tokyo, Occidental Petroleum's joint venture in a northern China coal mining project, and Sony and America Online's joint venture for linking Sony's PlayStation 2 video game machine to the Internet.[13]

Alliances and joint ventures are proving to be particularly popular as a means for doing business in emerging-market economies. For example, in the early 1990s, foreigners signed more than 3,000 joint-venture agreements in Eastern Europe and the former republics of the Soviet Union, and interest remains high today. Careful analysis must be undertaken to ensure that the market for the desired goods and services is sufficiently large and that all parties understand their responsibilities, and that all are in agreement regarding the overall operation of the venture. If these problems can be resolved, the venture stands a good chance of success. "International Management in Action: Joint Venturing in Russia" illustrates some of the problems that need to be overcome for a joint venture to be successful. Some of the other suggestions that have been offered by researchers regarding participation in strategic alliances include:

1. Know your partners well before an alliance is formed.

2. Expect differences in alliance objectives among potential partners headquartered in different countries.

Joint venturing is becoming an increasingly popular strategy for setting up international operations. Russia is particularly interested in these arrangements because of the benefits they offer for attracting foreign capital and helping the country tap its natural resource wealth. However, investors are finding that joint venturing in Russia and the other republics of the former Soviet Union can be fraught with problems. For example, Chevron, which agreed to invest $10 billion over the next 25 years in developing the Tengiz oil field in Kazakhstan, found itself having to renegotiate the contract and drop its share of profits from 28 percent to under 20 percent. This became necessary because the original contract was negotiated with the Soviet Union under then President Mikhail Gorbachev; after the breakup, the new government was unwilling to abide by the previous terms. Renegotiation is not the only problem facing joint-venture investors in Russia. Others include the following:

1. Many Russian partners view a joint venture as an opportunity to travel abroad and gain access to foreign currency; the business itself often is given secondary consideration.

2. Finding a suitable partner, negotiating the deal, and registering the joint venture often take up to a year, mainly because the Russians are unaccustomed to some of the basic steps in putting together business deals.

3. Russian partners typically try to expand joint ventures into unrelated activities. Foreign investors are more prone to minimizing risk and not overextending operations by getting into new areas.

4. Russians do not like to declare profits, because a two-year tax holiday on profits starts from the moment the first profits are declared. Foreign partners are not influenced by this fact and often point out that because taxes must be paid in rubles, which have very little value, taxes are not a problem.

5. The government sometimes allows profits to be repatriated in the form of countertrade. However, much of what can be taken out of the country has limited value, because the government keeps control of those resources that are most salable in the world market.

These representative problems indicate why there is a growing reluctance on the part of some MNCs to enter into joint ventures in Russia. As one of them recently put it, "The country may well turn into an economic sink hole." As a result, many MNCs are very reluctant and are proceeding with caution.

3. Realize that having the desired resource profiles does not guarantee that they are complementary to your firm's resources.

4. Be sensitive to your alliance partner's needs.

5. After identifying the best partner, work on developing a relationship that is built on trust, an especially important variable in some cultures.[14]

Licensing

Another way to gain market entry, which may also be considered a form of alliance, is to acquire the right to a particular product by getting an exclusive license to make or sell the good in a particular geographic locale. A **license** is an agreement that allows one party to use an industrial property right in exchange for payment to the other party. In a typical arrangement, the party giving the license (the licensor) will allow the other (the licensee) to use a patent, a trademark, or proprietary information in exchange for a fee. The fee usually is based on sales, such as 1 percent of all revenues earned from an industrial motor sold in Asia. The licensor typically restricts licensee sales to a particular geographic locale and limits the time period covered by the arrangement. The firm in this example may have an exclusive right to sell this patented motor in Asia for the next five years. This allows the licensor to seek licensees for other major geographic locales, such as Europe, South America, and Australia.

Licensing is used under a number of common conditions. For example, the product typically is in the mature stage of the product life cycle, competition is strong, and profit

license
An agreement that allows one party to use an industrial property right in exchange for payment to the other party.

margins are declining. Under these conditions, the licensor is unlikely to want to spend money to enter foreign markets. However, if the company can find an MNC that is already there and willing to add the product to its own current offerings, both sides can benefit from the arrangement. A second common instance of licensing is evident when foreign governments require newly entering firms to make a substantial direct investment in the country. By licensing to a firm already there, the licensee avoids entry costs. A third common condition is that the licensor usually is a small firm that lacks financial and managerial resources. Finally, companies that spend a relatively large share of their revenues on research and development (R&D) are likely to be licensors, and those that spend very little on R&D are more likely to be licensees. In fact, some small R&D firms make a handsome profit every year by developing and licensing new products to large firms with diversified product lines.

Some licensors use their industrial property rights to develop and sell goods in certain areas of the world and license others to handle other geographic locales. This provides the licensor with a source of additional revenues, but the license usually is not good for much more than a decade. This is a major disadvantage of licensing. In particular, if the product is very good, the competition will develop improvement patents that allow it to sell similar goods or even new patents that make the current product obsolete. Nevertheless, for the period during which the agreement is in effect, a license can be a very low-cost way of gaining and exploiting foreign markets. Table 9–1 provides some comparisons between licensing and joint ventures and summarizes the major advantages and disadvantages of each.

Franchising

franchise
A business arrangement under which one party (the franchisor) allows another (the franchisee) to operate an enterprise using its trademark, logo, product line, and methods of operation in return for a fee.

Closely related to licensing is franchising. A **franchise** is a business arrangement under which one party (the franchisor) allows another (the franchisee) to operate an enterprise using its trademark, logo, product line, and methods of operation in return for a fee. Franchising is widely used in the fast-food and hotel/motel industries. The concept is very adaptable to the international arena, and with some minor adjustments for the local market, it can result in a highly profitable business. In fast foods, McDonald's, Burger King, and Kentucky Fried Chicken have used franchise arrangements to expand their markets from Paris to Tokyo and from Cairo to Caracas. In the hotel business, Holiday Inn, among others, has been very successful in gaining worldwide presence through the effective use of franchisees.

Franchise agreements typically require payment of a fee up front and then a percentage of the revenues. In return, the franchisor provides assistance and, in some instances, may require the purchase of goods or supplies to ensure the same quality of goods or services worldwide. Franchising can be beneficial to both groups: It provides the franchisor with a new stream of income and the franchisee with a time-proven concept and products or services that can be quickly brought to market.

Export/Import

As noted in the discussion in Chapter 8 on international entrepreneurship and new ventures, exporting and importing often are the only available choices for small and new firms wanting to go international.[15] These choices also provide an avenue for larger firms that want to begin their international expansion with a minimum of investment. The paperwork associated with documentation and foreign-currency exchange can be turned over to an export management company to handle, or the firm can handle things itself by creating its own export department. The firm can turn to major banks or other specialists who, for a fee, will provide a variety of services, including letters of credit, currency conversion, and related financial assistance.

A number of potential problems face firms that plan to export. For example, if a foreign distributor does not work out well, some countries have strict rules about dropping that

Table 9–1
Partial Comparison of Global Strategic Alliances

Strategy	Organization Design	Advantages	Disadvantages	Critical Success Factors	Strategic Human Resources Management
Licensing— manufacturing industries	Technologies	Early standardization of design Ability to capitalize on innovations Access to new technologies Ability to control pace of industry evolution	New competitors created Possible eventual exit from industry Possible dependence on licensee	Selection of licensee unlikely to become a competitor Enforcement of patents and licensing agreements	Technical knowledge Training of local managers on-site
Licensing— servicing and franchises	Geography	Fast market entry Low capital cost	Quality control Trademark protection	Partners compatible in philosophies/values Tight performance standards	Socialization of franchisees and licensees with core values
Joint ventures— specialization across partners	Function	Learning a partner's skills Economies of scale Quasivertical integration Faster learning	Excessive dependence on partner for skills Deterrent to internal investment	Tight and specific performance criteria Entering a venture as "student" rather than "teacher" to learn skills from partner Recognizing that collaboration is another form of competition to learn new skills	Management development and training Negotiation skills Managerial rotation
Joint venture— shared value-adding	Product or line of business	Strengths of both partners pooled Faster learning along value chain Fast upgrading of technologic skills	High switching costs Inability to limit partner's access to information	Decentralization and autonomy from corporate parents Long "courtship" period Harmonization of management styles	Team-building Acculturation Flexible skills for implicit communication

Source: David Lei and John W. Slocum Jr., "Global Strategic Alliances: Payoffs and Pitfalls," *Organizational Dynamics* 1, no. 1 (Winter 1991), p. 48. Copyright © 1991. Reprinted with permission from Elsevier.

distributor. So an MNC with a contractual agreement with a distributor could be stuck with that distributor. If the firm decides to get more actively involved, it may make direct investments in marketing facilities, such as warehouses, sales offices, and transportation equipment, without making a direct investment in manufacturing facilities overseas.

When importing goods, many MNCs make deals with overseas suppliers who can provide a wide assortment. It is common to find U.S. firms purchasing supplies and components from Korea, Taiwan, and Hong Kong. In Europe, there is so much trade between EU countries that the entire process seldom is regarded as "international" in focus by the MNCs that are involved.

Exporting and importing can provide easy access to overseas markets; however, the strategy usually is transitional in nature. If the firm continues to do international business, it will get more actively involved in terms of investment.

■ The Organization Challenge

A natural outgrowth of general international strategy formulation and implementation and specific decisions about how best to enter international markets is the question of how best to structure the organization for international operations. A number of MNCs have recently been rethinking their organizational approaches to international operations.

In recent years Motorola's share of the worldwide cellular market has been declining. In an effort to turn things around, the firm has been revamping its structure, replacing some of the top management team,[16] and committing itself to an increased presence in both Europe and Asia. For example, Motorola has built a $150 million plant in Flensburg, Germany. Even though the German labor costs are relatively high compared to labor costs in the United States as well as in other European locations, Motorola believes that it must be a major player in the growing European market, so it wants to have a local presence.[17]

Another example of worldwide reorganizing is provided by Coca-Cola, which now delegates a great deal of authority for operations to the local level. This move is designed to increase the ability of the worldwide divisions to respond to their local markets. As a result, decisions related to advertising, products, and packaging are handled by international division managers for their own geographic regions. As an example, in Turkey the regional division has introduced a new pear-flavored drink, while Coke's German operation launched a berry-flavored Fanta. This "local" approach was designed to help Coke improve its international reputation, although Coke's new management is rethinking some aspects of this approach in the face of increasing cost pressures.[18]

A third example of how firms are meeting international challenges through reorganization is provided by Li & Fung, Hong Kong's largest export trading company and an innovator in the development of supply chain management. The company has global suppliers worldwide who are responsible for providing the firm with a wide range of consumer goods ranging from toys to fashion accessories to luggage. In recent years Li & Fung reorganized and now manages its day-to-day operations through a group of product managers who are responsible for their individual areas. This new organizational arrangement emerged in a series of steps. In the late 1970s, the company was a regional sourcing agent. Big international buyers would come to Li & Fung for assistance in getting materials and products because the MNC was familiar with the producers throughout Asia and it knew the complex government regulations and how to successfully work through them. The MNC then moved into a more sophisticated stage in which it began developing the entire process for the buyer from concept to prototype to delivery of the goods. By the late 1980s, however, Hong Kong had become a very expensive place to manufacture products, and Li & Fung changed its approach and began organizing around a new concept called "dispersed manufacturing," which draws heavily on dissection of the value chain and coordinating the operations of many suppliers in different geographic locations. For example, when the MNC receives an order from a European retailer to produce a large number of dresses, it has to decide where to buy the yarn in the world market, which companies should get the orders to weave and dye the cloth, where supplemental purchases such as buttons and zippers should be made, and how final shipment must be made to the customer. Commenting on this overall process, the company president noted:

> This is a new type of value added, a truly global product that has never been seen before. The label may say "Made in Thailand," but it's not a Thai product. We dissect the manufacturing process and look for the best solution at each step. We're not asking which country can do the best job overall. Instead, we're pulling apart the value chain and optimizing each step—and we're doing it globally. Not only do the benefits outweigh the costs of logistics and transportation, but the higher value added also lets us charge more for our services. We deliver a sophisticated product and we deliver it fast. If you talk to the big global consumer products companies, they are all moving in this direction—toward being best on a global scale.[19]

■ Basic Organizational Structures

The preceding examples of Motorola, Coca-Cola, and Li & Fung show how MNCs are dramatically reorganizing their operations to compete more effectively in the international arena. As with other MNCs following this strategic route, a number of basic organization structures need to be considered. In many cases, the designs are similar to those used domestically; however, significant differences may arise depending on the nature and scope of the overseas businesses and the home office's approach to controlling the operation. Ideally, an overseas affiliate or subsidiary will be designed to respond to specific concerns, such as production technology or the need for specialized personnel. The overall goal, however, is to meet the needs of both the local market and the home-office strategy of globalization.

Figure 9–2 illustrates how the pressures for global integration and local responsiveness play out in a host of industries. As an MNC tries to balance these factors, an if–then contingency approach can be used. *If* the strategy needed to respond quickly to the local market changes, *then* there will be accompanying change in the organizational structure. Despite the need for such a flexible, fast-changing, contingency-based approach, most MNCs still slowly evolve through certain basic structural arrangements in international operations. The following sections examine these structures, beginning with initial, preinternational patterns.[20]

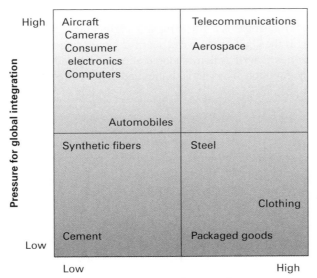

Figure 9–2

Organizational Consequences of Internationalization

Source: Adapted from Paul W. Beamish, J. Peter Killing, Donald J. LeCraw, and Harold Crookell, *International Management: Text and Cases* (Homewood, IL: Irwin, 1991), p. 99.

Initial Division Structure

Many firms make their initial entry into international markets by setting up a subsidiary or by exporting locally produced goods or services. A subsidiary is a common organizational arrangement for handling finance-related businesses or other operations that require an on-site presence from the start. In recent years, many service organization have begun exporting their expertise. Examples include architectural services, legal services, advertising, public relations, accounting, and management consulting. Research and development firms also fall into this category, exporting products that have been successfully developed and marketed locally.

An export arrangement is a common first choice among manufacturing firms, especially those with technologically advanced products. Because there is little, if any, competition, the firm can charge a premium price and handle sales through an export manager. If the company has a narrow product line, this export manager usually reports directly to the head of marketing, and international operations are coordinated by this department. If the firm has a broad product line and intends to export a number of different products into the international market, the export manager will head a separate department and often report directly to the president. These two arrangements work well as long as the company has little competition and is using international sales only to supplement domestic efforts.

If overseas sales continue to increase, local governments often exert pressure in these growing markets for setting up on-site manufacturing operations. A good example is the General Motors joint venture in China, where a large percentage of all parts are made locally. Additionally, many firms find themselves facing increased competition. Establishing foreign manufacturing subsidiaries can help the MNC to deal with both local government pressures and the competition. The overseas plants show the government that the firm wants to be a good local citizen. At the same time, these plants help the MNC greatly reduce transportation costs, thus making the product more competitive. This new structural arrangement often takes a form similar to that shown in Figure 9–3. Each foreign subsidiary is responsible for operations within its own geographic area, and the head of the subsidiary reports either to a senior executive who is coordinating international operations or directly to the home-office CEO.

International Division Structure

international division structure
A structural arrangement that handles all international operations out of a division created for this purpose.

If international operations continue to grow, subsidiaries commonly are grouped into an **international division structure,** which handles all international operations out of a division that is created for this purpose. This structural arrangement is useful as it takes a great deal of the burden off the chief executive officer for monitoring the operations of a series of overseas subsidiaries as well as domestic operations. The head of the international division coordinates and monitors overseas activities and reports directly to the chief executive

Figure 9–3

Use of Subsidiaries during the Early Stage of Internationalization

(Partial Organization Chart)

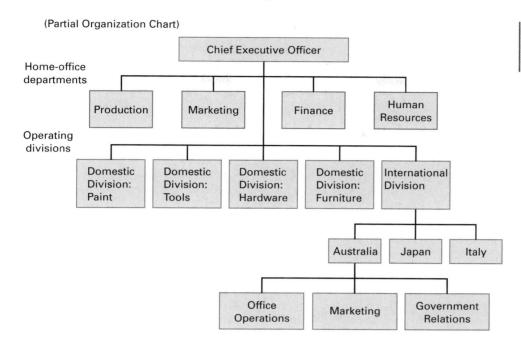

Figure 9–4

An International Division Structure

on these matters. Figure 9–4 provides an example. PepsiCo reorganized its international soft drink division into six such geographic business units covering 150 countries in which Pepsi does business. Each of these geographic units has self-sufficient operations and broad local authority.

Companies still in the developmental stages of international business involvement are most likely to adopt the international division structure. Others that use this structural arrangement include those with small international sales, limited geographic diversity, or few executives with international expertise.

A number of advantages are associated with use of an international division structure. The grouping of international activities under one senior executive ensures that the international focus receives top management attention. The structural arrangement allows the company to develop an overall, unified approach to international operations, and the arrangement helps the firm to develop a cadre of internationally experienced managers.

Use of this structure does have a number of drawbacks, however. The structure separates the domestic and international managers, which can result in two different camps with divergent objectives. Also, as the international operation grows larger, the home office may find it difficult to think and act strategically and to allocate resources on a global basis; thus, the international division is penalized. Finally, most research and development efforts are domestically oriented, so ideas for new products or processes in the international market often are given low priority.

Global Structural Arrangements

MNCs typically turn to global structural arrangements when they begin acquiring and allocating their resources based on international opportunities and threats. This international perspective signifies a major change in management strategy, and it is supported by the requisite changes in organization structure. It is important to remember that a structural framework is chosen only after the basic strategy is formulated, not vice versa. Global structures come in three common types: product, area, and functional.

Global Product Division   A **global product division** is a structural arrangement in which domestic divisions are given worldwide responsibility for product groups. Figure 9–5 provides an illustration. As shown, the manager who is in charge of product division C has

global product division
A structural arrangement in which domestic divisions are given worldwide responsibility for product groups.

Figure 9–5

A Global Product Division Structure

(Partial Organization Chart)

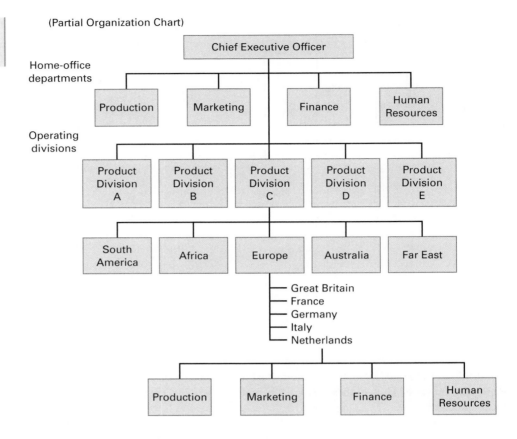

authority for this product line on a global basis. This manager also has internal functional support related to the product line. For example, all marketing, production, and finance activities associated with product division C are under the control of this manager.

The global product divisions operate as profit centers. The products generally are in the growth stage of the product life cycle, so they need to be promoted and marketed carefully. In doing so, global product division managers generally run the operation with considerable autonomy; they have the authority to make many important decisions. However, corporate headquarters usually will maintain control in terms of budgetary constraints, home-office approval for certain decisions, and mainly "bottom-line" (i.e., profit) results.

A global product structure provides a number of benefits. If the firm is very diverse (e.g., it produces products using a variety of technologies or has a wide variety of customers), the need to tailor the product to specific demands of the buyer becomes important. A global product arrangement can help to manage this diversity. Another benefit is the ability to cater to local needs. If many geographic areas must have the product modified to suit their particular desires (e.g., foods, toys, or electric shavers), a global product division structure can be extremely important. Still another benefit is that marketing, production, and finance can be coordinated on a product-by-product global basis. Firms also use a product division structure when a product has reached the maturity stage in the home country or in similar markets but is in the growth stage in others, such as less developed countries. An example might be color televisions or VCRs. These differing life cycles require close technologic and marketing coordination between the home and foreign market, which is best done by a product division approach. Other advantages of a global product division structure can be summarized as follows:

> It preserves product emphasis and promotes product planning on a global basis; it provides a direct line of communication from the customer to those in the organization who have product knowledge and expertise, thus enabling research and development to work on development of

products that serve the needs of the world customer; and it permits line and staff managers within the division to gain an expertise in the technical and marketing aspects of products assigned to them.[21]

Unfortunately, the approach also has some drawbacks. One is the necessity of duplicating facilities and staff personnel within each division. A second is that division managers may pursue currently attractive geographic prospects for their products and neglect other areas with better long-term potential. A third is that many division managers spend too much time trying to tap the local rather than the international market, because it is more convenient and they are more experienced in domestic operations.

Global Area Division   Instead of a global product division, some MNCs prefer to use a **global area division.** In this structure, illustrated in Figure 9–6, global operations are organized based on a geographic rather than a product orientation. This approach often signals a major change in company strategy, because now international operations are put on the same level as domestic operations. In other words, European or Asian operations are just as important to the company as North American operations. For example, when British Petroleum purchased Standard Oil of Ohio, the firm revised its overall structure and adopted a global area division structure. Under this arrangement, global division managers are responsible for all business operations in their designated geographic area. The chief executive officer and other members of top management are charged with formulating strategy that ensures that the global divisions all work in harmony.

A global area division structure most often is used by companies that are in mature businesses and have narrow product lines. These product lines often are differentiated based on geographic area. For example, the product has a strong demand in Europe but not in South America, or the type of product that is offered in France differs from that sold in England. In addition, the MNC usually seeks high economies of scale for production, marketing, and resource-purchase integration in that area. Thus, by manufacturing in this region rather than bringing the product in from somewhere else, the firm is able to reduce cost per unit and get the good to market at a very competitive price. Alcatel, the French telecommunications MNC, for example, set up its Asian headquarters in Shanghai, underscoring the company's confidence in China's booming telecommunications industry. The firm invested over $400 million in China and believes that this regional base will be critical in tapping a market where still less than 15 percent of the population have their own telephones.[22]

The geographic structure allows the division manager to cater to the tastes of the local market and make rapid decisions to accommodate environmental changes. A good

global area division
A structure under which global operations are organized on a geographic rather than a product basis.

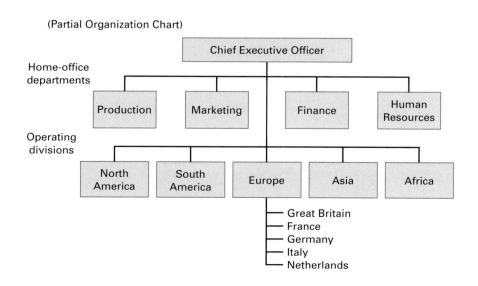

(Partial Organization Chart)

Figure 9–6

A Global Area Division Structure

example is food products. In the United States, soft drinks have less sugar than in South America, so the manufacturing process must be slightly different in these two locales. Similarly, in England, people prefer bland soups, but in France, the preference is for mildly spicy. In Turkey, Italy, Spain, and Portugal, people like dark, bitter coffee; in the United States, people prefer a milder, sweeter blend. In Europe, Canada, and the United States, people prefer less spicy food; in the Middle East and Asia, they like more heavily spiced food. A global area structure allows the geographic unit in a foods company to accommodate such local preferences.

The primary disadvantage of the global area division structure is the difficulty encountered in reconciling a product emphasis with a geographic orientation. For example, if a product is sold worldwide, a number of different divisions are responsible for sales. This lack of centralized management and control can result in increased costs and duplication of effort on a region-by-region basis. A second drawback is that new research and development efforts often are ignored by division groups because they are selling goods that have reached the maturity stage. Their focus is not on the latest technologically superior goods that will win in the market in the long run but on those that are proven winners and now are being marketed conveniently worldwide.

global functional division
A structure that organizes worldwide operations primarily based on function and secondarily on product.

Global Functional Division   A **global functional division** organizes worldwide operations based primarily on function and secondarily on product. This approach is not widely used other than by extractive companies, such as oil and mining firms. Figure 9–7 provides an example.

A number of important advantages are associated with the global functional division structure. These include (1) an emphasis on functional expertise, (2) tight centralized control, and (3) a relatively lean managerial staff. There also are some important disadvantages: (1) Coordination of manufacturing and marketing often is difficult. (2) Managing multiple product lines can be very challenging because of the separation of production and marketing into different departments. (3) Only the chief executive officer can be held accountable for the profits. As a result, the global functional process structure typically is favored only by firms that need tight, centralized coordination and control of integrated production processes and firms that are involved in transporting products and raw materials from one geographic area to another.

mixed organization structure
A structure that is a combination of a global product, area, or functional arrangement.

Mixed Organization Structures   Some companies find that neither a global product, an area, or a functional arrangement is satisfactory. They opt for a **mixed organization structure,** which combines all three into an MNC that supplements its primary structure with a secondary one and, perhaps, a tertiary one. For example, if a company uses a global

Figure 9–7

A Global Functional Structure

(Partial Organization Chart)

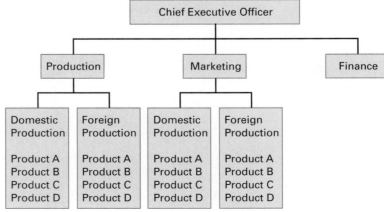

(Partial Organization Chart)

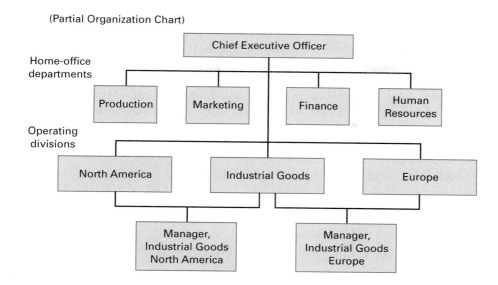

Figure 9–8

A Multinational Matrix Structure

area approach, committees of functional managers may provide assistance and support to the various geographic divisions. Conversely, if the firm uses a global functional approach, product committees may be responsible for coordinating transactions that cut across functional lines. In other cases, the organization will opt for a matrix structure that results in managers' having two or more bosses. Figure 9–8 illustrates this structure. In this arrangement, the MNC coordinates geographic and product lines through use of a matrix design.

In recent years, mixed organization structures have become increasingly popular. Sony's electronic businesses, including personal computers and cable-television set-top boxes, have been unified in one group. The company has also created a new division that will focus exclusively on the mobile phone business. In addition, the firm has created a management group called the "Global Hub" that will coordinate strategy across a host of Sony units including financial services, games, Internet services, and entertainment. Quite clearly, the company feels that it needs a mixed structure in order to juggle all of its worldwide holdings. Many other companies use a mixed structure, and one survey has found that more than one-third of the responding firms employ this organizational arrangement. The respondents reported the following:[23]

International operations organized into national subsidiaries with local coordination for production/services, marketing, human resources, etc.	11.8%
International division structure with senior management reporting to the president or CEO of the company.	14.7%
One or more regional headquarters used to coordinate production/services, marketing, and human resources among national operations.	20.6%
World-production or world-matrix structure used for coordination of international operations.	17.6%
Mixed forms of structure.	35.3%

Many advantages can be gleaned from a mixed organization structure. In particular, it allows the organization to create the specific type of design that best meets its needs. However, there are shortcomings associated with matrix structures. The most important is that as the matrix design's complexity increases, coordinating the personnel and getting everyone to work toward common goals often become difficult; too many groups go their own way. Thus, many MNCs have not opted for a matrix structure; they have found that simple, lean structures are the best design for them.

Transnational Network Structures

transnational network structure
A multinational structural arrangement that combines elements of function, product, and geographic designs, while relying on a network arrangement to link worldwide subsidiaries.

Besides matrix structures, another alternative international organizational design to recently emerge is the **transnational network structure.** This is designed to help MNCs take advantage of global economies of scale while also being responsive to local customer demands. The design combines elements of classic functional, product, and geographic structures, while relying on a network arrangement to link the various worldwide subsidiaries. At the center of the transnational network structure are nodes, which are units charged with coordinating product, functional, and geographic information. Different product line units and geographical area units have different structures depending on what is best for their particular operations. A good example of how the transnational network structure works is provided by N.V. Philips, which has operations in more than 60 countries and

| **Figure 9–9** | **The Network Structure of N.V. Philips** |

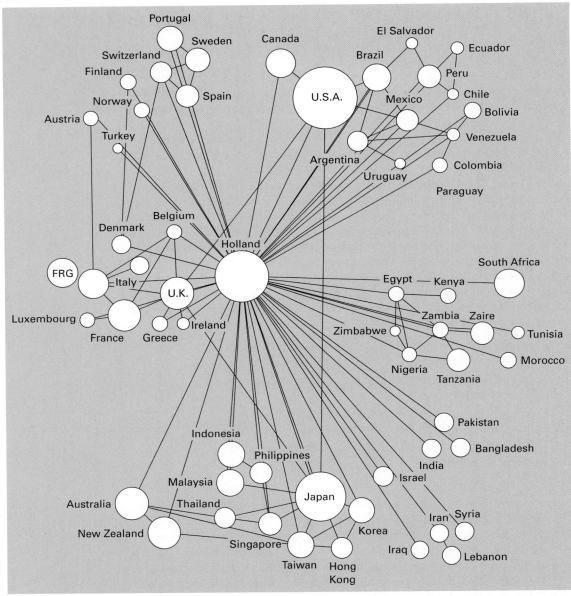

Source: See S. Ghoshal and C. A. Bartlett, "The Multinational Corporation as an Interorganizational Network," *Academy of Management Review,* October 1990, pp. 603–625.

Table 9–2
Control Mechanisms Used in Select Multinational Organization Structures

Type of Multinational Structure	Output Control	Bureaucratic Control	Decision-Making Control	Cultural Control
International division structure	Profit control	Have to follow company policies	Typically there is some centralization	Treated like all other divisions
Global area division	Use of profit centers	Some policies and procedures are necessary	Local units are given autonomy	Local subsidiary culture is often the most important
Global product division	Unit output for supply; sales volume for sales	Tight process controls are used to maintain product quality and consistency	Centralized at the product-division headquarters level	Possible for some companies, but not always necessary
Matrix structure	Profit responsibility is shared with product and geographic units	Not very important	Balanced between the global area and product units	Culture must support the shared decision making
Transnational network structure	Used for supplier units and for some independent profit centers	Not very important	Few decisions are centralized at headquarters; most are centralized in the key network nodes	Organization culture transcends national cultures, supports sharing and learning, and is the most important control mechanism

produces a diverse product line ranging from light bulbs to defense systems. In all, the company has eight product divisions with a varying number of subsidiaries in each—and the focus of these subsidiaries varies considerably. Some specialize in manufacturing, others in sales; some are closely controlled by headquarters, and others are highly autonomous.

The basic structural framework of the transnational network consists of three components: dispersed subunits, specialized operations, and interdependent relationships. *Dispersed subunits* are subsidiaries that are located anywhere in the world where they can benefit the organization. Some are designed to take advantage of low factor costs, while others are responsible for providing information on new technologies or consumer trends. *Specialized operations* are activities carried out by subunits that focus on particular product lines, research areas, and marketing areas, and are designed to tap specialized expertise or other resources in the company's worldwide subsidiaries. *Interdependent relationships* are used to share information and resources throughout the dispersed and specialized subunits.

The transnational network structure is difficult to draw in the form of an organization chart because it is complex and continually changing. However, Figure 9–9 on the previous page provides a view of N.V. Philips' network structure. These complex networks can be compared to some of the others that have been examined earlier in this chapter by looking at the ways in which the enterprise attempts to exercise control. Table 9–2 provides such a comparison.

■ Nontraditional Organizational Arrangements

In recent years, MNCs have increasingly expanded their operations in ways that differ from those used in the past. These include acquisitions, joint ventures, keiretsus, and strategic alliances. These organizational arrangements do not use traditional hierarchical structures and therefore cannot be shown graphically. The following sections describe how they work.

Organizational Arrangements from Mergers and Acquisitions

A recent development affecting the way that MNCs are organized is the increased use of mergers and acquisitions (M&As). In recent years, the annual value of worldwide M&As has reached as high as $6 trillion! One reason for this large figure is that a growing number of major MNCs are merging with, or being acquired by, other giant multinationals. In the past decade, for example, British Petroleum acquired Amoco for $48.2 billion, Daimler-Benz bought the Chrysler Corporation for $40.5 billion, while on a smaller scale Renault took over Samsung Motors for $350 million and the assumption of $200 million of Samsung debt.[24] In other cases, MNCs have taken an equity position but have not purchased the entire company. For example, Ford Motor owns 75 percent of Aston Martin Lagonda of Britain, 49 percent of Autolatina of Brazil, and 34 percent of Mazda of Japan; and DaimlerChrysler acquired one-third of Mitsubishi.[25]

In each of these examples, the purchasing MNCs fashioned a structural arrangement that attempts to promote synergy while encouraging local initiative by the acquired firm. The result is an organization design that draws on the more traditional structures that have been examined here but still has a unique structure specifically addressing the needs of the two firms.

Organizational Arrangements from Joint Ventures and Strategic Alliances

Other examples of recent organizational arrangements include joint-venture and strategic alliance agreements in which each party contributes to the undertaking and coordinates its efforts for the overall benefit of the venture.[26] These arrangements can take a variety of forms,[27] although the steps that are followed in creating and operating them often have a fair amount of similarity.[28] One good example of a joint venture is CALICA, which has two partners: Vulcan Materials, the leading firm in the U.S. aggregate materials market, and Grupo ICA of Mexico.[29] Working together, the two companies coordinate their activities in mining, shipping, distributing, and marketing gravel for use in highway and building construction. Another example is provided by Coca-Cola and Procter & Gamble (P&G). Coke has run behind Pepsi in snacks and noncarbonated drinks and recently considered buying Quaker Oats in order to strengthen itself in these areas. However, the $16 billion sales price was too high. So Coke entered into a joint venture with P&G.

These joint ventures require carefully formulated structures that allow each partner to contribute what it does best and to coordinate their efforts efficiently. In the case of Coke and P&G, this calls for clearly spelling out the responsibilities of all parties and identifying the authority that each will have for meeting specific targets.[30]

One of the main objectives in developing the structure for joint ventures is to help the partners address and effectively meld their different values, management styles, action orientation, and organization preferences. Figure 9–10 illustrates how Western and Asian firms differ in these four areas; the figure also is useful for illustrating the types of considerations that need to be addressed by MNCs from the same area of the world. Consider, for example, Matsushita Electric Industrial and Hitachi Ltd. The two agreed to join forces to develop new technology in three areas: smart cards, home network systems, and recyclable and energy-efficient consumer electronics.[31] The two firms will need to structure their organizational interface carefully to ensure effective interaction, coordination, and cooperation.

Organizational Arrangements from Keiretsus

Still another type of newly emerging organizational arrangement is the **keiretsu,** which is a large, often vertically integrated group of companies that cooperate and work closely with each other. A good example is the Mitsubishi Group, a keiretsu that consists of companies that are bound together not by authority relationships but rather by cross-ownership, long-term

keiretsu
In Japan, an organizational arrangement in which a large, often vertically integrated group of companies cooperate and work closely with each other to provide goods and services to end users; members may be bound together by cross-ownership, long-term business dealings, interlocking directorates, and social ties.

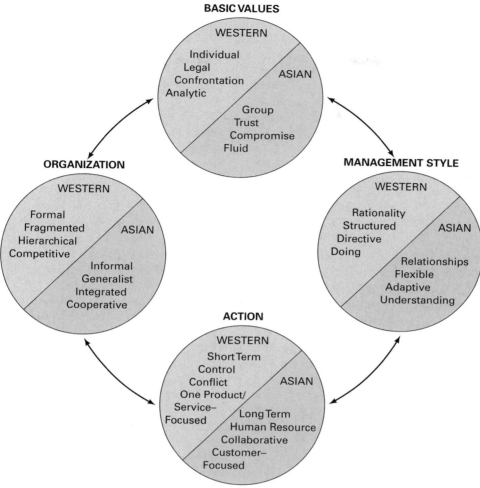

BASIC VALUES

WESTERN

Individual
Legal
Confrontation
Analytic

ASIAN

Group
Trust
Compromise
Fluid

ORGANIZATION

WESTERN

Formal
Fragmented
Hierarchical
Competitive

ASIAN

Informal
Generalist
Integrated
Cooperative

MANAGEMENT STYLE

WESTERN

Rationality
Structured
Directive
Doing

ASIAN

Relationships
Flexible
Adaptive
Understanding

ACTION

WESTERN

Short Term
Control
Conflict
One Product/
Service–
Focused

ASIAN

Long Term
Human Resource
Collaborative
Customer–
Focused

Source: From Frederic Swierczek and Georges Hirsch, "Joint Ventures in Asia and Multicultural Management," *European Management Journal,* June 1994, p. 203. Reprinted with permission of European Management Journal.

Figure 9–10

A Comparison of Asian and Western Management Features

business dealings, interlocking directorates, and social ties (many of the senior executives were college classmates). There are three flagship firms in the group: Mitsubishi Corporation, which is a trading company; Mitsubishi Bank, which finances the keiretsu's operations; and Mitsubishi Heavy Industries, which is a leading worldwide manufacturer. In addition, hundreds of other Mitsubishi-related companies contribute to the power of the keiretsu.

The Japanese are not the only ones using this organizational arrangement. Large U.S. MNCs are creating their own type of keiretsus. Ford Motor, for example, now focuses its attention only on automotive and financial services and has divested itself of most other businesses. In the process of reorganizing, Ford has created a giant, keiretsu-like arrangement that includes research and development (R&D), parts production, vehicle assembly, financial services, and marketing. For example, in R&D, Ford belongs to eight consortia that conduct research in areas such as improved engineering techniques, materials, and electric-car batteries. In parts production, Ford has equity stakes in Cummins (engines), Excel Industries (windows), and Decoma International (body parts, wheels), and it relies on these firms as major suppliers. In vehicle assembly, Ford has ownership interests in Europe, South America, and Asia and uses these arrangements to both manufacture and sell autos in these parts of the world. In financial services, Ford has seven wholly owned units that cover a wide gamut, from consumer credit to commercial lending.

Ford is not alone. Today, more and more U.S. firms are cooperating to improve their competitiveness and offset the impact of foreign keiretsus that have been rapidly moving across the continuum of business activity, from upstream R&D to downstream marketing. For example, in the area of research, there now are more than 250 R&D consortia in the United States that are sharing both costs and information.[32] In design and production, manufacturers and suppliers are becoming partners; for example, at John Deere, workers now team up with their counterparts at suppliers such as the McLaughlin Body Company to improve quality and cut costs. In the financing area, large companies such as Digital Equipment, IBM, and Novellus Systems are taking equity positions or lending money to their strategic suppliers to ensure high-quality parts and on-time delivery. In the marketing area, manufacturers and suppliers are selling and servicing each other's products. For example, Mazda buys vehicles from Ford for sale in the United States, and vice versa.

In fact, strategic partners and outsourcers are so important to the success of many MNCs that it is common to find them giving their partners direct access to their own computer systems. In this way, for example, an outsourcer can quickly determine the MNC's supply needs and adjust its own production schedule to meet these demands. This same type of close working B2B arrangement is used when providing services. For example, IBM works closely with the giant French MNC Thomson Multimedia SA, managing the firm's data centers, desktops, help desk, disaster recovery, and support services.[33]

Many companies are finding that M&As do not work out or they involve a considerable financial risk because of the high sales price. Joint ventures and strategic alliances are a good alternative. They provide MNCs with the opportunity to access a wide variety of competencies, thus reducing their own costs while ensuring that they have a reliable provider. Eircom, Ireland's dominant telecom provider, for example, has outsourced much of the support work associated with providing phone service, thus allowing the company to focus its primary attention on core telecommunications.[34] In addition, joint ventures and strategic alliances help promote cooperation between the participating organizations; and as the positive effects of these keiretsu-like arrangements continue to spread, more and more MNCs will be drawn to them.[35] The organizational arrangement that is used by many of these companies may be difficult to draw on paper, but it is proving to be very effective in practice.

The Emergence of the Electronic Network Form of Organization

Over the last few years there has been a major increase in the number of "electronic freelancers"—individuals who work on a project for a company, usually via the Internet, and move on to other employment when the assignment is done. In a way, these individuals represent a new type of electronic network organization, "temporary companies" that serve a particular, short-term purpose and then go on to other assignments. There are numerous examples.

> Consider the way many manufacturers are today pursuing radical outsourcing strategies, letting external agents perform more of their traditional activities. The U.S. computer-display division of the Finnish company Nokia, for example, chose to enter the U.S. display market with only five employees. Technical support, logistics, sales, and marketing were all subcontracted to specialists around the country. The fashion accessories company Topsy Tail, which has revenues of $80 million but only three employees, never even touches its products through the entire supply chain. It contracts with various injection-molding companies to manufacture its goods; uses design agencies to create its packaging; and distributes and sells its products through a network of independent fulfillment houses, distributors, and sales reps. Nokia's and Topsy Tail's highly decentralized operations bear more resemblance to the network model of organization than to the traditional industrial model.[36]

Many multinationals are beginning to rely increasingly on electronic freelancers (e-lancers, for short) to perform key tasks for them. In the case of General Motors, for example, outsourcers via computers work very closely with the company in providing both design and engineering assistance. The rise of the multinational university is yet another example. Growing numbers of academic institutions from Europe to North America are now offering both undergraduate and graduate courses, and in some cases full-fledged degree programs, via the Internet. In staffing these courses, the universities rely heavily on e-lancers with PhD degrees who are responsible for delivering the course online. In most cases, the university has little face-to-face contact with these e-lancers. Everything is done via computers.

These electronic network organizations are now becoming increasingly prominent. MNCs are realizing that the outsourcing function can be delivered online. Examples include design specifications, analytical computations, and consulting reports. So, in a way, this new structure is a version of the matrix design discussed earlier in the chapter. The major difference is that many of the people in the structure not only are temporary, contingent employees but never see each other and communicate exclusively in an electronic environment.

Organizing for Product Integration

Another recent organizing development is the emergence of designs that are tailored toward helping multinationals integrate product development into their worldwide operations. In the recent past, the use of cross-functional coordination was helpful in achieving this goal. However, MNCs have found that this arrangement results in people spending less time within their functions and thus becoming less knowledgeable regarding developments that are occurring in their specialized areas. A second shortcoming of the cross-functional approach is that it often leads to product teams becoming autonomous and thus failing to integrate their overall efforts with the organization at large.

Toyota created a structure that combines a highly formalized system with new structural innovations that ensure that projects are flexibly managed and, at the same time, able to benefit from the learning and experiences of other projects. In accomplishing this, Toyota employs six organizational mechanisms.

One of these is called mutual adjustment. In most companies this is achieved by assigning people to a specific project and having them meet face-to-face and work out a plan of action for designing the new product. At Toyota, however, design engineers are not assigned to specific projects; rather they remain in their functional area and they typically communicate through written messages. This approach ensures that all members remain dedicated to their primary functional area and that they communicate succinctly and directly with each—thus saving time.

A second mechanism employed by Toyota is the use of direct, technically skilled supervisors. In a typical arrangement, design engineers are led by individuals who are no longer doing engineering work; they are primarily responsible for seeing that others do this work. However, at Toyota supervisors remain highly skilled in the technical side of the work and are responsible for mentoring, training, and developing their engineers. So if anyone has a design-related problem, the supervisor is technically skilled and can provide this assistance.

A third mechanism is the use of integrative leadership. In typical product design structures, the manager in charge has full authority and relies on the engineering personnel to get the work done within time, cost, and quality parameters. At Toyota, however, these managers are responsible for coordinating the work of the functional specialists and serving less as a manager than as a lead designer on the entire project. In this way, they serve as the glue that binds together the whole process.

In typical design operations, engineers are hired from universities or from other companies where they have gained experience, and they remain in their engineering position indefinitely. At Toyota most of the technical training is provided in-house, and people are rotated within only one function such as body engineers who work on auto-body subsystems for most, if not all, of their careers. As a result, they are able to get more work done faster because they do not have to communicate and coordinate continually with their counterparts regarding what needs to be done. They are so familiar with their jobs that they know what needs to be done.

Another organizational difference is that in typical design work each new product calls for a new development process and there are complex forms and bureaucratic procedures for ensuring that everything is done correctly. At Toyota, standard milestones are created by the project leader, and simple forms and procedures are employed so that the work can be done simply and efficiently.

A final difference is that in many organizations design standards are obsolete and rigid. At Toyota, these standards are maintained by the people who are doing the work and are continually changed to meet new design demands.

The organizational approach used at Toyota is being carefully studied by other world-class auto manufacturers, who are coming to realize that the old way of organizing for product design is not sufficiently effective for dealing with the competitive challenges of the new millennium. In particular, a new organizational emphasis has to be placed on better blending the personnel and the work. Commenting on all of this, a group of experts who studied Toyota's approach wrote:

> the success of Toyota's system rides squarely on the shoulders of its people. Successful product development requires highly competent, highly skilled people with a lot of hands-on experience, deep technical knowledge, and an eye for the overall system. When we look at all the things that Toyota does well, we find two foundations for its product-development system: chief engineers using their expertise to gain leadership, and functional engineers using their expertise to reduce the amount of communication, supervision, trial and error, and confusion in the process. All the other coordinating mechanisms and practices serve to help highly skilled engineers do their job effectively. By contrast, many other companies seem to aspire to develop systems "designed by geniuses to be run by idiots." Toyota prefers to develop and rely on the skill of its personnel, and it shapes its product-development process around this central idea: people, not systems, design cars.[37]

The Changing Role of Information Technology in Organizing

Another major change that is taking place in the way multinationals organize themselves is related to the role of information technology (IT). After a slow start, Japanese firms are leading the way in redefining how IT will be used in the future. One of the major differences between IT in American multinationals and in their Japanese counterparts is that in Japan, IT is not seen as something special or different, but rather is viewed as being part of a fully integrated picture. In the process, Japanese firms carefully target how they are going to use information technology and try hard to neither overrate nor underrate its role and importance. A good contrast is provided by Seven-Eleven Japan and NSK, one of the world's leading bearings and auto component manufacturers.

In the case of Seven-Eleven Japan, the company has aggressively invested in IT and uses this system to monitor and meet customer needs. Japanese consumers place a high premium on product freshness. Many years ago the company began using its IT system to create a just-in-time arrangement that relies on multiple daily deliveries of products. Today, each store's fresh food changes over entirely three times a day, which allows managers to change their unit's physical layout throughout the day as the flow of customers shifts from housewives to students to working people. Moreover, the company's just-in-time system allows the stores to be extraordinarily responsive to consumers' shifting tastes. For example, if a particular kind of take-out lunch sells out by noon, extra stock can be in the store within an hour. Conversely, if it is raining, the IT system will remind cash register operators to put umbrellas on sale next to each register. This level of responsiveness is made possible by a sophisticated point-of-sale data-collection system and an electronic ordering system that links individual stores to a central distribution center.

In the case of NSK, the company uses a combination of highly integrated technology systems and low-tech systems. For example, for simulation and analysis in component

Table 9-3
Contrasting Approaches to Using Information Technology: Western and Japanese Views

Key Issue	How Western Firms Address the Matter	How Japanese Firms Address the Matter
How to decide the information systems needed by the business.	Develop an IT strategy that aligns with the company's business strategy.	Determine the basic way the firm competes, driven particularly by its operations goals, and use this to determine the IT investment.
How to determine if the investments in IT are worthwhile.	Adapt the capital budgeting process to manage and evaluate the IT investment.	Judge investments based on operational performance improvements.
When trying to improve a business process, how technology fits into management's thinking.	Assume that technology offers the smartest, cheapest way to improve performance.	Identify a performance goal and then select a technology that will help the firm achieve this goal in a way that supports the people doing the work.
How IT users and IT specialists should connect in the organization.	Teach specialists about business goals and develop technically adept, business-savvy chief information officers.	Encourage integration by rotating managers through the IT function and giving IT oversight to executives who oversee other functions.
How systems to improve organization performance can be designed.	Design the most technically elegant system possible and ask employees to adapt to it.	Design a system that makes use of the tacit and explicit knowledge that employees already possess.

Source: Adapted from M. Bensaou and Michael Earl, "The Right Mind-Set for Managing Information Technology," *Harvard Business Review,* September–October 1998, p. 121.

design, engineers rely on the firm's flexible-engineering information control system and an array of databases and expert systems. Quality engineers use handheld terminals to monitor quality data, which are automatically recorded from in-line sensors and inspection machines. Salespeople can search sophisticated databases and narrow the range of products that they will suggest to a customer. At the same time, NSK has a number of low-technology islands where the personnel use machinery and equipment that are over a decade old and rely on their own judgment in making decisions and processing information. By choosing the best mix of information technology, the company is able to maintain its competitiveness.[38]

Other contrasts between the ways in which IT issues are addressed by Western firms and Japanese companies are provided in Table 9–3. A close analysis of these contrasts shows that the integration of IT into the overall organizing process can have a dramatic effect on the performance of an organization.

■ Organizational Characteristics of MNCs

Although MNCs have similar organizational structures, they do not all operate in the same way. A variety of factors that help to explain the differences have been identified.[39] These include overall strategy, employee attitudes, and local conditions. Of particular significance to this discussion are the organizational characteristics of formalization, specialization, and centralization.

Formalization

Formalization is the use of defined structures and systems in decision making, communicating, and controlling. Some countries make greater use of formalization than others; in turn, this affects the day-to-day organizational functioning. One large research study of

formalization
The use of defined structures and systems in decision making, communicating, and controlling.

Korean firms found that, unlike employees in the United States, Korean workers perceive more positive work environments when expectations for their jobs are set forth more strictly and formally. In short, Koreans respond very favorably to formalization.[40] Korean firms tend to be quite formal, but this may not hold throughout Asia. For example, a study that investigated whether Japanese organizations are more formalized than U.S. organizations found that although Japanese firms tend to use more labor-intensive approaches to areas such as bookkeeping and office-related work than their U.S. counterparts, no statistical data support the contention that Japanese firms are more formalized.[41]

Another study of U.S. and Japanese firms in Taiwan divided formalization into two categories: objective and subjective.[42] Objective formalization was measured by things such as the number of different documents given to employees, organizational charts, information booklets, operating instructions, written job descriptions, procedure manuals, written policies, and work-flow schedules and programs. Subjective formalization was measured by the extent to which goals were vague and unspecified, use of informal controls, and use of culturally induced values in getting things done. The findings of this study are reported in Table 9–4.

Commenting on differences in the use of formalization, the researchers concluded that

> American and Japanese firms appear to have almost the same level of written goals or objectives for subordinates, written standards of performance appraisals, written schedules, programs, and work specifications, written duties, authority and accountability. However, managers in Japanese firms perceive less formalization than do managers in American firms. Less reliance on formal rules and structure in Japanese firms is also revealed by the emphasis on face-to-face or behavioral mode of control indicated by the ratio of foreign expatriates to total employees in subsidiaries.[43]

The study also found that U.S. MNCs tend to rely heavily on budgets, financial data, and other formalized tools in controlling their subsidiary operations. This contrasts with Japanese MNCs, in which wider use is made of face-to-face, informal controls. These findings reveal

Table 9–4
Organizational Characteristics of U.S. and Japanese Firms in Taiwan

Characteristics	U.S. Firms (*n* = 38)	Japanese Firms (*n* = 85)
Formalization (subjective)	3.54	3.47
Formalization (objective)	11.39	10.91
Horizontal specialization	12.89	10.02
Vertical specialization	7.04	7.75
Job routinization	2.25	2.86
Job autonomy	2.78	2.62
Foreign expatriates per 1,000 employees	4.2	16.6
Ratio of firms using quality circles (in percentages)	24	32

Note: The highest score for the subjective formalization index, job routinization index, and autonomy index is 6; the lowest score is 1. The highest score for the objective formalization index is 19; the lowest score is 0. The highest score for the horizontal specialization index is 16; the lowest score is 0. Ratios of foreign expatriates to total employees are calculated on the basis of firms with 50 or more employees.

Source: Adapted from Rhy-song Yeh and Tagi Sagafi-nejad, "Organizational Characteristics of American and Japanese Firms in Taiwan," *National Academy of Management Proceedings* (New Orleans, 1997), p. 113.

that although the outward structural design of overseas subsidiaries may appear to be similar, the internal functioning in characteristics such as formalization may be quite different.

In recent years, this formal/informal characteristic of organizations has become the focal point of increased attention.[44] One reason is that MNCs now realize there are two dimensions of formality/informality that must be considered: internal and external. Moreover, to a large degree, these formal/informal relationships require effective networking of a different type. As Yoshino and Rangan noted, there are

> two approaches that firms that must compete globally—and that includes most major firms— employ to achieve the layering of competitive advantages: (1) development of extensive *internal networks* of international subsidiaries in major national or regional markets and (2) forging *external networks* of strategic alliances with firms around the world. These approaches are not mutually exclusive, and increasingly firms are striving to build both types of networks.[45]

What is particularly interesting about these networking relationships is that each places a different set of demands on the MNC. In particular, external networking with joint-venture partners often involves ambiguous organizational mandates, less emphasis on systems and more on people, and ambiguous lines of authority. This is a marked difference from internal networking characteristics, where formality is much stronger than informality and the enterprise can rely on a shared vision, clear organizational mandates, and well-developed systems and lines of authority.[46] Table 9–5 summarizes the characteristics of these internal and external networks.

Specialization

As an organizational characteristic, **specialization** is the assigning of individuals to specific, well-defined tasks. Specialization in an international context can be classified into horizontal and vertical specialization.

Horizontal specialization assigns jobs so that individuals are given a particular function to perform, and people tend to stay within the confines of this area. Examples include jobs in areas such as customer service, sales, recruiting, training, purchasing, and marketing research. When there is a great deal of horizontal specialization, personnel will develop functional expertise in one particular area.

Vertical specialization assigns work to groups or departments where individuals are collectively responsible for performance. Vertical specialization also is characterized by distinct differences between levels in the hierarchy such that those higher up are accorded much more status than those farther down, and the overall structure usually is quite tall.

In the earlier, comparative study of 55 U.S. and 51 Japanese manufacturing plants, Japanese organizations had lower functional specialization of employees. Specifically,

specialization
An organizational characteristic that assigns individuals to specific, well-defined tasks.

horizontal specialization
The assignment of jobs so that individuals are given a particular function to perform and tend to stay within the confines of this area.

vertical specialization
The assignment of work to groups or departments where individuals are collectively responsible for performance.

Table 9–5
Internal vs. External Networks

Managerial Dimensions	Internal Network	External Network
Shared vision	Yes	No
Animating mindset	Cooperation	Cooperation and competition
Organizational mandates	Clear	Ambiguous
Organizational objective	Global optimization	Develop win-win approaches
Emphasis on systems	More	Less
Emphasis on people	Less	More
Lines of authority	Clear	Ambiguous at best

Source: Information drawn from Michael Yoshino and N. S. Rangan, *Strategic Alliances* (Boston: Harvard Business School Press, 1995), p. 203.

three-quarters of the functions listed were assigned to specialists in the U.S. plants, but less than one-third were assigned in the Japanese plants.[47] Later studies with regard to formalization have echoed this finding on specialization. As shown in Table 9–4, U.S. subsidiaries have more specialists than Japanese firms do.

By contrast, studies find that the Japanese rely more heavily on vertical specialization. They have taller organization structures in contrast to the flatter designs of their U.S. counterparts. Japanese departments and units also are more differentiated than departments and units in U.S. organizations. Vertical specialization can be measured by the amount of group activity as well, such as in quality circles. Table 9–4 shows that Japanese firms make much greater use of quality circles than the U.S. firms. Vertical specialization also can result in greater job routinization. Because one is collectively responsible for the work, strong emphasis is placed on everyone's doing the job in a predetermined way, refraining from improvising, and structuring the work so that everyone can do the job after a short training period. Again, Table 9–4 shows that the Japanese organizations make much wider use of job routinization than do U.S. organizations.

Centralization

centralization
A management system in which important decisions are made at the top.

decentralization
Pushing decision making down the line and getting the lower-level personnel involved.

Centralization is a management system in which important decisions are made at the top. In an international context, the value of centralization will vary according to the local environment and the goals of the organization. Many U.S. firms tend toward **decentralization,** pushing decision making down the line and getting the lower-level personnel involved. German MNCs centralize strategic headquarter-specific decisions independent of the host country and decentralize operative decisions in accordance with the local situation in the host country. "International Management in Action: Organizing in Germany" describes how relatively small German MNCs have been very successful with such a decentralization strategy. In some cases, large firms have also been very successful using a decentralized approach. Nokia, for example, has been described as "one of the least hierarchical big companies on earth, a place where it is often profoundly unclear who's in charge."[48] This hands-off approach promotes creativity, entrepreneurial effort, and personal responsibility. At the same time, however, in order to prevent operations from spinning out of control, the company exercises very tight financial discipline.

In contrast, researchers have found that Japanese organizations delegate less formal authority than their U.S. counterparts but permit greater involvement in decisions by employees lower in the hierarchy. At the same time, the Japanese manage to maintain strong control over their lower-level personnel by limiting the amount of authority given to the latter and carefully controlling and orchestrating worker involvement and participation in quality circles.[49] Other studies show similar findings.[50] When evaluating the presence of centralization by examining the amount of autonomy that Japanese give to their subordinates, one study concluded:

> In terms of job autonomy, employees in American firms have greater freedom to make their decisions and their own rules than in Japanese firms. . . . Results show that managers in American firms perceive a higher degree of delegation than do managers in Japanese firms. Also, managers in American firms feel a much higher level of participation in the coordinating with other units, . . . in influencing the company's policy related to their work, and in influencing the company's policy in areas not related to their work.[51]

The finding related to influence is explained in more detail in Table 9–6. U.S. managers in Taiwanese subsidiaries felt that they had greater influence than did their Japanese counterparts. Moreover, when statistically analyzed, these data proved to be significant.

Putting Organizational Characteristics in Perspective

MNCs tend to organize their international operations in a manner similar to that used at home. If the MNC tends to have high formalization, specialization, and centralization at its

Organizing in Germany

Like every other place in the world, Europe in general and Germany in particular have gone through economic ups and downs. German labor unions, the most powerful in Europe, were having to give ground, and major corporations were scaling back operations and reporting losses. At the same time, a number of medium- and small-sized German companies continued to be some of the most successful in the world. Part of this success resulted from their carefully designed decentralized organization structures, a result of company efforts to remain close to the customer. The goal of these German MNCs is to establish operations in overseas locales where they can provide on-site assistance to buyers. Moreover, these subsidiaries in most cases are wholly owned by the company and have centralized controls on profits.

A common practice among German MNCs is to overserve the market by providing more than is needed. For example, when the auto firm BMW entered Japan, its initial investment was several times higher than that required to run a small operation; however, its high visibility and commitment to the market helped to create customer awareness and build local prestige.

Another strategy is to leave expatriate managers in their positions for extended periods of time. In this way, they become familiar with the local culture and thus the market, and they are better able to respond to customer needs as well as problems. As a result, customers get to know the firm's personnel and are more willing to do repeat business with them.

Still another strategy the German MNCs use is to closely mesh the talents of the people with the needs of the customers. For example, there is considerable evidence that most customers value product quality, closeness to the customer, service, economy, helpful employees, technologic leadership, and innovativeness. The German firms will overperform in the area that is most important and thus further bond themselves to the customer.

A final strategy is to develop strong self-reliance so that when problems arise, they can be handled with in-house personnel. This practice is a result of German companies' believing strongly in specialization and concentration of effort. They tend to do their own research and to master production and service problems so that if there is a problem, they can resolve it without having to rely on outsiders.

How well do these German organizing efforts pay off? Many of these relatively small companies hold world market shares in the 70 to 90 percent range. These are companies that no one has ever heard about, such as Booder (fish-processing machines), Gehring (honing machines), Korber/Hauni (cigarette machines), Marklin & Cle (model railways), Stihl (chain saws), and Webasto (sunroofs for cars). Even so, every one of these companies is the market leader not only in Europe but also throughout the world, and in some cases its relative market strength is up to 10 times greater than that of the nearest competitor.

Table 9–6
Managers' Influence in U.S. and Japanese Firms in Taiwan

Managers' Work-Related Activity	U.S. Firm Average	Japanese Firm Average
Assigning work to subordinates	4.72	3.96
Disciplining subordinates	4.07	3.82
Controlling subordinates' work (quality and pace)	3.99	3.82
Controlling salary and promotion of subordinates	3.81	3.18
Hiring and placing subordinates	3.94	3.24
Setting the budget for own unit	3.45	3.16
Coordinating with other units	3.68	3.52
Influencing policy related to own work	3.22	2.85
Influencing policy not related to own work	2.29	1.94
Influencing superiors	3.02	3.00

Note: The highest score of means is 5 (very great influence); the lowest score is 1 (very little influence). The *T*-value for all scores is significant at the .01 level.

Source: Adapted from Rhy-song Yeh and Tagi Sagafi-nejad, "Organizational Characteristics of American and Japanese Firms in Taiwan," *National Academy of Management Proceedings* (New Orleans, 1987), p. 114.

home-based headquarters, these organizational characteristics probably will occur in the firm's international subsidiaries.[52] Japanese and U.S. firms are good examples. As the researchers of the comparative study in Taiwan concluded: "Almost 80 percent of Japanese firms and more than 80 percent of American firms in the sample have been operating in Taiwan for about ten years, but they maintain the traits of their distinct cultural origins even though they have been operating in the same (Taiwanese) environment for such a long time."[53]

These findings also reveal that many enterprises view their international operations as extensions of their domestic operations, thus disproving the widely held belief that convergence occurs between overseas operations and local customs. In other words, there is far less of an "international management melting pot" than many people realize. European countries are finding that as they attempt to unify and do business with each other, differing cultures (languages, religions, and values) are very difficult to overcome. A major challenge for the years ahead will be bringing subsidiary organizational characteristics more into line with local customs and cultures.

The World of *BusinessWeek*—Revisited

In this chapter, a number of different entry strategies and organizational arrangements are discussed. Some of these are fairly standard approaches used by MNCs; others represent hybrid or flexible arrangements. Increasingly, entry modes and organizational structures involve collaborative relationships in which control and oversight are shared. Having reviewed the range of options and Intel's challenges in Russia, answer the following questions: (1) What alternative entry modes should Intel consider for its Russia strategy? (2) Which organizational arrangements will be most useful as Intel expands its presence? (3) How can Intel protect its proprietary technology from partners or competitors?

SUMMARY OF KEY POINTS

1. MNCs pursue a range of entry strategies in their international operations. These include wholly owned subsidiaries, mergers and acquisitions, alliances and joint ventures, licensing and franchising, and exporting. In general, the more cooperative forms of entry (alliances, joint ventures, mergers, licensing) are on the rise.

2. A number of different organizational structures are used in international operations. Many MNCs begin by using an export manager or subsidiary to handle overseas business. As the operation grows or the company expands into more markets, the firm often will opt for an international division structure. Further growth may result in adoption of a global structural arrangement, such as a global production division, global area division structure, global functional division, or a mixture of these structures.

3. Although MNCs still use the various structural designs that can be drawn in a hierarchical manner, they recently have begun merging or acquiring other firms or parts of other firms, and the resulting organizational arrangements are quite different from those of the past. The same is true of the many joint ventures now taking place across the world. One change stems from the Japanese concept of keiretsu, which involves the vertical integration and cooperation of a group of companies. Although the Mitsubishi Group, with its 28 core member firms, is one of the best examples of this organizational arrangement, U.S. MNCs also are moving in this direction. Other examples of new MNC organizational arrangements include the emergence of electronic networks, new approaches to organizing for production development, and the more effective use of IT.

4. A variety of factors help to explain differences in the way that international firms operate. Three organizational characteristics that are of particular importance are formalization, specialization, and centralization. These characteristics often vary from country to country, so that Japanese firms will conduct operations differently from U.S. firms. When MNCs set up international subsidiaries, they often use the same organizational techniques they do at home without necessarily adjusting their approach to better match the local conditions.

KEY TERMS

alliance, *263*

centralization, *286*

decentralization, *286*

franchise, *266*

formalization, *283*

global area division, *273*

global functional division, *274*

global product division, *271*

horizontal specialization, *285*

international division structure, *270*

international joint venture, *263*

keiretsu, *278*

license, *265*

merger/acquisition, *263*

mixed organization structure, *274*

specialization, *285*

transnational network structure, *276*

vertical specialization, *285*

wholly owned subsidiary, *262*

REVIEW AND DISCUSSION QUESTIONS

1. One of the most common entry strategies for MNCs is the joint venture. Why are so many companies opting for this strategy? Would a fully owned subsidiary be a better choice?

2. A small manufacturing firm believes there is a market for handheld tools that are carefully crafted for local markets. After spending two months in Europe, the president of this firm believes that his company can create a popular line of these tools. What type of organization structure would be of most value to this firm in its initial efforts to go international?

3. If the company in question 2 finds a major market for its products in Europe and decides to expand into Asia, would you recommend any change in its organization structure? If yes, what would you suggest? If no, why not?

4. If this same company finds after three years of international effort that it is selling 50 percent of its output overseas, what type of organizational structure would you suggest for the future?

5. Why are keiretsus popular? What benefits do they offer? How can small international firms profit from these structures? Give an example.

6. In what way do formalization, specialization, and centralization have an impact on MNC organization structures? In your answer, use a well-known firm such as IBM or Ford to illustrate the effects of these three characteristics.

INTERNET EXERCISE: ORGANIZING FOR EFFECTIVENESS

Every MNC tries to drive down costs by getting its goods and services to the market in the most efficient way. A good example is auto firms such as Ford Motor and Volkswagen, which have worldwide operations. In recent years Ford has begun expanding into Europe and VW has begun setting up operations in Latin America. By building cars closer to the market, these companies hope to reduce their costs and be more responsive to local needs. At the same time this strategy requires a great deal of organization and coordination. Visit the websites of both firms and examine the scope of their operations. The address for Ford Motor is **www.ford.com** and for Volkswagen it is **www.vw.com**. Then, based on your findings, answer these questions: What type of organizational arrangement(s) do you see the two firms are using in coordinating their worldwide operations? Which of the two companies has the more modern arrangement? Do you think this increases that firm's efficiency or does it hamper the company's efforts to contain costs and be more competitive? Why?

Australia

Australia is the smallest continent but the sixth-largest country in the world. It lies between the Indian and Pacific oceans in the Southern Hemisphere and has a landmass of almost 3 million square miles (around 85 percent the size of the United States). Referred to as being "down under" because it lies entirely within the Southern Hemisphere, it is a dry, thinly populated land. The outback is famous for its bright sunshine, enormous numbers of sheep and cattle, and unusual wildlife, such as kangaroos, koalas, platypuses, and wombats. Over 19 million people live in this former British colony, and 20 million are projected within the next couple of years. Although many British customs are retained, Australians have developed their own unique way of life. One of the world's most developed countries, Australia operates under a democratic form of government somewhat similar to that of Great Britain. Gross domestic product is over $525 billion, with the largest economic sectors being services (71 percent), trade, and manufacturing.

A large financial-services MNC in the United States has been examining the demographic and economic data of Australia. This MNC has concluded that there will be increased demand for financial services in Australia during the next few years. As a result, the company is setting up an operation in the capital, Canberra, which is slightly inland from Sydney and Melbourne, the two largest cities.

This financial-services firm began in Chicago and now has offices in seven countries. Many of these foreign operations are closely controlled by the Chicago office. The overseas personnel are charged with carefully following instructions from headquarters and implementing centralized decisions. However, the Australian operation will be run differently. Because the country is so large and the population spread along the coast and to Perth in the west, and because of the "free spirit" cultural values of the Aussies, the home office feels compelled to give the manager of Australian operations full control over decision making.

This manager will have a small number of senior-level managers brought from the United States, but the rest of the personnel will be hired locally. The office will be given sales and profit goals, but specific implementation of strategy will be left to the manager and his or her key subordinates on site.

The home office believes that in addition to providing direct banking and credit card services, the Australian operation should seek to gain a strong foothold in insurance and investment services. As the country continues to grow economically, this sector of the industry should increase relatively fast. Moreover, few multinational firms are trying to tap this market in Australia, and those that are doing so are from British Commonwealth countries. The CEO believes that the experience of the people being sent to Australia (the U.S. expatriates) will be particularly helpful in developing this market. He recently noted, "We know that the needs of the Australian market are not as sophisticated or complex as those in the United States, but we also know that they are moving in the same direction as we are. So we intend to tap our experience and knowledge and use it to garner a commanding share of this expanding market." **www.csu.edu.au/australia**

Questions

1. What are some current issues facing Australia? What is the climate for doing business in Australia today?

2. What type of organizational structure arrangement is the MNC going to use in setting up its Australian operation?

3. Can this MNC benefit from any of the new organizational arrangements, such as a joint venture, the Japanese concept of keiretsu, or electronic networks?

4. Will this operation be basically centralized or decentralized?

Getting In on the Ground Floor

The EU currently is developing a strategy that will help member countries beat back the threat of U.S. and Asian competition and develop a strong technological base for new product development. European multinational firms currently are strong in a number of different areas. For example, Germany's Hoechst and BASF and Switzerland's Sandoz and Hoffman-LaRoche are major companies in chemicals and pharmaceutics. Philips of the Netherlands invented compact discs and is dominant in the television market. Many strong European-based MNCs could provide a solid base for the EU to defend itself from outside economic invasion.

Ruehter Laboratories, a high-tech R&D firm located in New Jersey, holds a number of important pharmaceutic patents and would like to expand its operation worldwide. The company is considering buying a small but highly profitable Dutch insulin-maker. "This acquisition will help us enter the European market by getting in on the ground floor," noted the president.

Although the Dutch firm is quite small, it has strong R&D prowess and likely will play a major role in biotechnology research during the years ahead. Ruehter has talked to the Dutch firm, and the two have arrived at a mutually acceptable selling price. While waiting for the lawyers to work out the final arrangements, Ruehter intends to reorganize its overall operations so that the home-office management can work more closely with its new Dutch subsidiary. There are two areas that Ruehter intends to address in its reorganization efforts: (1) how the subsidiary will be structurally integrated into the current organization; and (2) whether there can be any joint R&D efforts between the two groups.

Questions

1. What type of organization design would you recommend that Ruehter use?

2. If there were joint R&D efforts, would this be a problem?

Chapter 10

MANAGING POLITICAL RISK, GOVERNMENT RELATIONS, AND ALLIANCES

OBJECTIVES OF THE CHAPTER

Firms go international to become more competitive and profitable. Unfortunately, many risks accompany internationalization. One of the biggest emerges from the political situation of the countries in which the MNC does business. MNCs must be able to assess political risk and conduct skillful negotiations. An overview of the political environment in selected areas of the world has already been provided in Chapter 2. This chapter specifically examines what political risk is all about and how MNCs try to manage it. One major way is through effective evaluation and risk reduction. This process extends from risk identification and quantification to the formulation of appropriate responses, such as integration and protective and defensive techniques.

This chapter also describes the process for developing productive relationships with governments and for managing alliances with international partners, many of which are influenced by home- and host-government relations. The specific objectives of this chapter are:

1. **EXAMINE** how MNCs evaluate political risk.

2. **PRESENT** some common methods used for managing and reducing political risk.

3. **DISCUSS** strategies to mitigate political risk and develop productive relations with governments.

4. **DESCRIBE** challenges to and strategies for effectively managing alliances.

The World of *BusinessWeek*

BusinessWeek

Oil Shortage?

Saudi Arabia: There's Plenty in the Ground, but It Won't Be Easy to Get. The Kingdom May Need Major New Foreign Investors. Will It Dare Open Up?

Saudi officials like to fly visitors across the Empty Quarter, the forbidding desert that occupies the eastern portion of the kingdom, to visit the Shaybah oil field. Nestled amid stunning sand dunes like a ship in a vast ochre ocean, Shaybah is a source of national pride for the Saudis—akin to the Hoover Dam or the Apollo space missions for Americans. To outsiders, the message is: When it comes to oil, you can count on us. "We are the most reliable producer and supplier of crude in the whole world," says Mahmoud M. Abdul Baqi, exploration chief of Saudi Aramco, the giant state-owned company that produces most Saudi oil and gas and exerts powerful control over Saudi Arabia's economy.

But tours of Shaybah may no longer be enough to allay doubts about the shelf life of Saudi Arabia's oil fields and the reliability of its reserve estimates. Long-standing assumptions about Saudi oil are being questioned—with some observers wondering if Aramco is too resistant to needed outside investment. The doubts come at a time when the kingdom is coping with a domestic Islamist insurgency and a changing relationship with the U.S. The uncertainty is rattling the markets just as oil prices are pushing $40 a

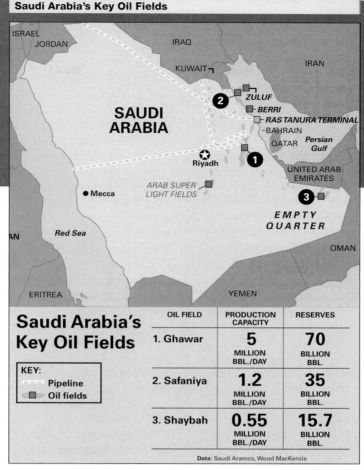

OIL FIELD	PRODUCTION CAPACITY	RESERVES
1. Ghawar	**5** MILLION BBL./DAY	**70** BILLION BBL.
2. Safaniya	**1.2** MILLION BBL./DAY	**35** BILLION BBL.
3. Shaybah	**0.55** MILLION BBL./DAY	**15.7** BILLION BBL.

Saudi Arabia's Key Oil Fields

KEY:
- Pipeline
- Oil fields

Data: Saudi Aramco, Wood MacKenzie

Source: www.businessweek.com/magazine/content/04_14/b3877009.htm

barrel and reserves of oil companies, especially those of Royal Dutch/Shell Group, are being revised downward.

Since it's widely assumed that Saudi Arabia controls about a quarter of the world's oil, any doubts about whether the kingdom has the goods go to the heart of the global economic system. Will the Saudis be able to raise production as demand rises and traditional oil sources elsewhere decline? "We cannot afford to be wrong about the ability of key exporters to meet growing oil demand to make up for disruptions in supply," says Robert E. Ebel, director of the energy program at the Center for Strategic & International Studies (CSIS), a Washington think tank. "Too much is at stake politically and financially."

"There Is No Plan B"

The most vocal skeptic is Matthew R. Simmons, chairman of Simmons & Co. International, a well-known Houston-based investment bank specializing in energy. He made headlines in February by telling a CSIS audience that the Saudi "miracle" of almost effortless, cheap production was nearing an end. Drawing on technical papers published by the Society of Petroleum Engineers and a February 2003

visit to Saudi oil fields, Simmons thinks the Ghawar Field, the world's largest, with production of 5 million bbl. per day, could be running dry. "The entire world assumes Saudi Arabia can carry everyone's energy needs on its back cheaply," says Simmons. "If this turns out not to work, there is no Plan B."

Simmons says the big problem is "no data" for the reserves of Saudi Arabia and other big Mideast producers. "No third-party inspector has examined the world's most important [energy] insurance policy for years." If the Saudis don't like the questions, he says, they should present "good, transparent data" to back up their claims. Simmons also suspects that most of the other big Saudi fields, including Abqaiq and Berri, could be past their peak. He speculates that the Saudis may soon have to develop fields once deemed marginal, boosting capital costs.

If Simmons is right, the Saudis could soon be in deep trouble. Their relations with the U.S. are already strained thanks to the participation of so many Saudis in the September 11 attacks. If it turns out they have much less oil than they claim, "the role of the kingdom would be completely devalued strategically," says Roger Diwan, a senior analyst at consultant PFC Energy in Washington.

293

With no alternative to oil in sight for decades, the U.S. and other consuming nations would increasingly need to look to other sources, such as Russia or Iraq.

Not surprisingly, the Saudis have reacted with shock and dismay to the skepticism. Some mutter darkly about conspiracies against their country. "What's the story? Why this sudden panic?" said Abdul Baqi in a meeting with *BusinessWeek* at Aramco's Dhahran headquarters in Saudi Arabia's Eastern Province.

Simmons' pronouncement is having one beneficial effect: The tight-lipped Saudis are opening up, to a degree. Three top Aramco reservoir engineers and geologists offered *BusinessWeek* a scenario as optimistic as Simmons' is gloomy. Even though it has been producing oil for decades, they say, Saudi Arabia has depleted only 28% of its proved reserves. Not only does it have 260 billion bbl. of proved reserves with a 90% probability of recovery, 100 billion more barrels of already discovered oil may be recoverable, especially as technology improves. "I think [Simmons' argument] is completely wrong—based on flawed statistics and very poor engineering analysis," says Nansen G. Saleri, a longtime Chevron veteran who is now Aramco's chief of reservoir management.

The Saudis conclude that the kingdom could easily ramp up to 10 million bbl. a day from its current 8.5 million and comfortably sustain that level through 2042. If demand is really strong, they insist, the kingdom could build up to 12 million bbl. a day by 2016 and hold that level out of existing reserves until 2033.

But while few in the industry doubt the Saudis have huge quantities of oil, experts warn that even the Saudis won't know their capabilities until an actual ramp-up. And the Saudis may face far greater challenges in developing their reserves and maintaining production than they would like to admit. "We think Saudi Arabia has huge reserves," says Fatih Birol, chief economist at International Energy Agency, a Paris-based intergovernmental group that monitors global energy supply. "We also recognize that these reserves may have geological surprises ranging from steep decline rates in some giant fields to water [problems]." In addition, if older fields elsewhere in the world run dry, Birol estimates that the Saudis would need to double current production capacity, to 20 million bbl. a day, by 2020.

The Saudis and some analysts are skeptical that demand will rise that much, even with behemoth China consuming as much as it can. One reason: Higher prices may curb the world's thirst. "Some of these long-term forecasts are way off the mark," says Saddad Husseini, who recently retired as Aramco's executive vice-president. "They show a minimal change in price and a huge increase in demand." But among outside analysts, there is lingering concern about whether the Saudis are moving fast enough to develop new sources of crude. "The issue is not whether there is enough oil but rather whether they have the willingness and the ability to develop it in a timely manner," says Edward L. Morse,

a former U.S. official for global energy policy and now a senior adviser at Hetco, a New York-based energy trader.

The numbers are huge. Doubling output would require much broader investment, perhaps $150 billion, Birol estimates. He worries that because Saudi Arabia and other big Mideast producers, such as Iran, are largely closed to foreign investment, there may be financing constraints. "If the reserves are closed to [foreign direct investment], they may not be able to find the necessary funds," he says.

For now, with oil prices high, Aramco doesn't seem to be having any problem making the case for its budget to the Saudi government. But economists in the kingdom think that in coming years, with a growing population and demand for more schools, hospitals, and other public services, Aramco could find its spending curtailed. Its executives shrug off such concerns.

Aramco executives also like to distinguish their organization from other national oil companies, arguing that Aramco retains the commercial ethos of its founding American partners—not the sometimes lax attitude common at most state-run organizations. Certainly, Aramco personnel are an elite among Saudi industry. Engineers display an American-style, can-do approach to their jobs. Onsite, at least, they wear Western clothes—not the cumbersome Saudi national uniform of white robes and checkered kaffiyehs. "I worked 18 years at Chevron, and I don't really see the difference," says Saleri. "In fact, as far as the ability to do things, we have tremendous empowerment."

Gingerly Pace

Yet Aramco is also different from an international oil company. It is managing gigantic fields with a long-term strategy rather than milking smaller ones for all they're worth, as majors often do. Shaybah is now producing about 550,000 bbl. a day—even though Aramco execs say that with close to 16 billion bbl. of reserves, the field could easily be milked for 1 million bbl. a day. An oil major, under pressure to maximize returns on capital, would likely be pumping at much nearer that level. But Aramco is proceeding at a gingerly pace, preferring to more fully understand Shaybah's reservoirs before pushing them harder, even though the field's high-quality crude brings a premium of a dollar or more per barrel over the heavier oil from other Saudi fields. "We drive slowly, not fast," says Saleri.

Aramco execs say they don't feel much urgency to add production capacity. They plan a hike of 1.4 million bbl. a day or so by 2009, but that might just make up for depletion in the years between. But Aramco execs may have another reason to downplay talk of a crisis: They don't want the government in Riyadh to invite oil majors in to develop the next generation of Saudi oil fields. Aramco isn't happy about the prospect of having foreign companies operating in the kingdom. They like having all of those reserves for themselves—and would probably balk at the hard-charging style of an Exxon Mobil Corp. or a BP PLC.

Partly because of Aramco's opposition, a four-year, high-profile effort led by Crown Prince Abdullah to attract global companies to explore for gas to power electricity, petro-chemical, and water projects worth tens of billions of dollars collapsed last year. It was replaced by much more modest wildcat exploration schemes. ExxonMobil and BP walked away, while Royal Dutch/Shell and Total agreed to an exploration deal. In March, several more global companies, including Russia's Lukoil, Spain's Repsol YPF, and Italy's ENI, signed gas-exploration deals.

One goal of the gas initiative, according to sources close to the project, was to break Aramco's domination of the Saudi oil-and-gas industry. But Crown Prince Abdullah and Foreign Minister Saud al Faisal underestimated the power of Aramco and Oil Minister Ali Naimi, a fierce advocate of the national company who was its first Saudi CEO. Naimi and his minions drove the majors crazy by restricting them

to exploration acreage they considered marginal. At the signing ceremony on March 7, Naimi hinted that it will be a long time before more foreign investors are let into the kingdom's oil-and-gas industry.

"It is necessary to slow down to know the results of this work," he said.

Still, Saudi Arabia is changing, and Naimi, who is 68, won't be in his job forever. Like the proverbial camel, international oil companies have their noses under the Saudi tent. As demand for oil rises, they hope they'll find a way in.

By Stanley Reed, with Stephanie Anderson Forest in Dallas

Source: Reprinted from "Oil Shortage?" *BusinessWeek,* April 5, 2004, online edition by special permission. Copyright © 2004 by the McGraw-Hill Companies, Inc. www.businessweek.com

The opening story illustrates the impact of political risk and the importance of solidifying strong government relations in the face of rapid globalization. Today, Saudi Arabia is one of the most valued countries in the world because of its dominance in global oil production, yet its political environment is uncertain. Actions taken by the Saudi government concerning oil create ripple effects throughout the world that are felt in gas prices and supply. As the article mentions, U.S. and Saudi relations have been strained since the terrorist attacks of September 11, 2001. While the Saudis claim to have more oil than they might indeed possess, the U.S. government and private companies must keep government relationships intact if they wish to continue to benefit from Saudi oil production. Furthermore, many MNCs, including airlines and energy companies, are heavily dependent on oil; any disruption of supply will have a devastating impact on these firms, as well as on consumers who will have to pay higher prices. MNCs must be able to evaluate and manage political risks on a global scale and contemplate the potential of alliances and other long-term cooperative relationships to help mitigate some of these risks. In this chapter, ways of evaluating political risks, managing government relations, and overseeing alliances will be explored.

■ The Nature and Analysis of Political Risk

Both domestic and international political developments have a major impact on MNCs' strategic plans. MNCs face hazards that originate directly from variation and unpredictability in political and governance systems. The state and its various institutions and agencies continue to pose a direct threat to multinational corporations through policy shifts in taxation or regulation, through outright or de facto expropriation, or by allowing the exploitation of assets by local firms. As government policies change, MNCs must adjust their strategies and practices to accommodate the new perspectives and actual requirements. Moreover, in a growing number of geographic regions and countries, governments appear to be less stable; therefore, these areas carry more risk than they did in the past. Applied to international management, **political risk** is the likelihood that a multinational corporation's foreign investment will be constrained by a host government's policies. Since the terrorist attacks of 9/11, political risk assessment has become vital to MNCs. Today, almost all countries are interested in sustaining investment from MNCs.[1]

political risk
The likelihood that a business's foreign investment will be constrained by a host government's policy.

Yet political risks persist, especially in the emerging economies of the world, which continue to struggle with political and institutional instability. The presence of policy and control mechanisms, coupled with traditional treatment of MNCs within these nations, allows firms to evaluate the inherent risk of doing business there. Examples of risk factors include freezing the movement of assets out of the host country, placing limits on the re-mittance of profits or capital, devaluing the currency, and refusing to abide by the con-tractual terms of agreements previously signed with the MNC. As rapid globalization continues, MNCs must be aware of the political risk factors present in doing business abroad and develop strategies to respond to them.

In the case of China, for example, the government was for several years very anxious to be admitted to the World Trade Organization (WTO). When this did not happen right away, China began making decisions that were in its own best short-run interests but cre-ated new political risks for MNCs doing business there. One analysis noted:

> A series of recent moves by Chinese authorities—price controls, currency restrictions, limits on sale of state-owned companies—seem to reflect a slowdown in the nation's effort to shift from a planned to a market economy. Whether such steps are justifiably cautious or simply timid, economists and business executives agree that they are likely to further deter trade and investment in the near future. Today, China's central bank announced new restrictions on for-eign exchange transactions, an attempt to control the flow of convertible currency out of the country. Officially described as a crackdown on illegal transactions, the moves will effectively make it more difficult for both domestic and international companies to move money in and out of China.[2]

These actions by the Chinese demonstrate restrictions on foreign investment in the telecommunications industry, one of the fastest growing industries in China and one that has attracted a great deal of attention from international investors.

Now that China has been admitted into the WTO, political risk still continues to be a major consideration for multinationals doing business there. As was brought out in Chapter 3, industrial piracy continues to be a big problem, and the Chinese government has yet to take effective action against it. For example, Procter & Gamble estimates that it loses $150 million in sales annually because of counterfeit brands, and DaimlerChrysler reports that fake brake disks, windshields, oil filters, and shock absorbers for Mercedes cars are being made and sold throughout the country. One reason for the reluctance of the Chinese government to take action may well be that state-owned factories are some of the biggest counterfeiters. Yamaha estimates that five of every six JYM 150-A motorcycles and ZY125 scooters bearing its name in China are fake; some state-owned factories turn out copies four months after Yamaha introduces a new model.[3] Another common complaint is the way rules and regulations are interpreted. A Mitsubishi factory manager, commenting on the fact that customs officials continually offer con-tradictory rulings, said, "One day one official will say I do not need to pay duty, the next day, a different official will say I have to."[4] Another growing concern is government censorship. All advertisements must be approved by censors who carefully screen ads to ensure that they are culturally and politically correct.[5] Multinationals are also concerned about the pressure that the Chinese government puts on businesses to do things a par-ticular way. MNCs in Hong Kong, now governed by the PRC, have reported meddling by Beijing.[6]

These types of actions by the Chinese increase the political risk of doing business in China. On the other side of the coin, however, Chinese MNCs must also assess the political risk inherent in doing business in the United States. The U.S. government has begun to review its trade policy with China. In particular, American trade officials claim that China has taken for granted its relationship with the United States and warn that if markets there are not opened for American goods there will be reciprocal action against Chinese firms that are selling in the United States.[7] Given the enormous trade deficit that the Americans have with China, this situation could end up creating major political risks for Chinese MNCs doing business in the politically stable but very risky United States.

Macro and Micro Analysis of Political Risk

Firms evaluate political risk in a number of ways. One is through **macro political risk analysis,** which reviews major political decisions that are likely to affect all business conducted in the country. For example, China's decision regarding restrictions on foreign-exchange transactions is a macro political risk because it affects all MNCs. **Micro political risk analysis** is directed toward government policies and actions that influence selected sectors of the economy or specific foreign businesses. China's government policies regarding investment in the telecommunications industry fall into the micro political risk category. Figure 10–1 reports the riskiness of investing in select countries. This risk rating is based on a series of criteria, including the nation's political structure, economic policies, and the state of the country's banking system. The following two sections examine both of these areas—macro and micro political risk—in more depth.

macro political risk analysis
Analysis that reviews major political decisions likely to affect all enterprises in the country.

micro political risk analysis
Analysis directed toward government policies and actions that influence selected sectors of the economy or specific foreign businesses in the country.

Macro Risk Issues and Examples   In recent years, macro risk analysis has become of increasing concern to MNCs because of the growing number of countries that are finding

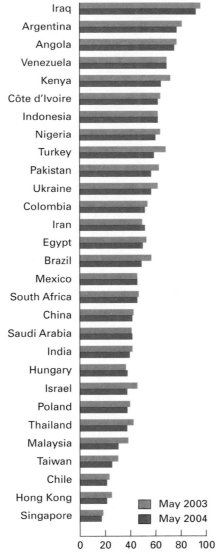

Figure 10–1

Country Risk

0 = minimum risk, 100 = maximum risk

their economies in trouble, as in Southeast Asia, or, even worse, that are unable to make the transition to a market-driven economy. A good example of the latter is Russia, which has been tightening controls on the flow of foreign currencies. This decision represents a change in direction from the free-market principles that Russia had been following in order to ensure that it continued to receive assistance from the International Monetary Fund.

Other examples of developments that fall within the realm of macro political risk are provided by India, a country whose legal system is stymied by a labyrinth of laws and bureaucratic red tape. In recent years, the Indian high courts have had a backlog of over 3 million cases. Moreover, approximately one-third of these cases have been winding their way through the legal system for more than five years. So while the government touts the fact that Indian law offers strong protection to foreign firms against counterfeiters, an MNC finding that it must rely on the Indian judicial system to enforce its proprietary rights is likely to be sadly disappointed. As a result, many MNCs accept this risk as a price of doing business in India and formulate strategies for managing the problem. A good example is provided by the Timken Company of Canton, Ohio, which makes bearings and alloy steel. When Timken found that the Indian market was rampant with fake Timken products, the MNC's initial reaction was to sue the counterfeiters. However, after realizing how long this would take, the MNC opted for a different strategy. Management switched the packaging of its products from cardboard boxes to heat-sealed plastic with eight-color printing and a hologram that could not be forged. Result: Within months the counterfeit market began drying up.

Timken is not alone, there are many counterfeit operations in India because the slow-moving judicial system encourages noncompliance. In fact, some counterfeiters have found that by filing countersuits they can tie up a case in court for years. For example, Ziff Davis Publishing, an American unit of Japan's Softbank Corporation, brought suit against a former Indian licensee for continuing to publish one of its computer magazines even though the license had expired. The defendant frivolously countersued, arguing that the magazine was generic and not proprietary. A similar brazen example hit Time Warner, owner of cable-television movie channel Home Box Office (HBO). This MNC won a temporary injunction preventing an Indian company from calling its movie channel Cable Box Office or CBO for short. So that firm changed its name to CVO standing for Cable Video Opera.

Many other newly emerging economies besides the big countries of China, Russia, and India also present macro political risks for MNCs. In Vietnam, for example, the communist government earned a bad name among foreign investors because of all the pitfalls they have to face. Until recently the Vietnamese government required all foreign investors to establish joint ventures with local partners. But even with this arrangement, getting things done proved to be extremely slow and difficult because of the numerous levels of bureaucracy to be dealt with. One international manager described his MNC's experience this way, "The negotiations would follow a serpentine path, with breakthroughs in one session often being erased in the next."[8] To date, macro political risks in Vietnam remain high and investors find themselves proceeding with caution.[9]

Another example of a macro consideration of political risk is an analysis of what would happen to a company's investment if opposition government leaders were to take control. In the 1970s U.S. companies in Iran failed to forecast the fall of the shah and rise of Khomeini. As a result, they lost their investment. Because of this Iranian experience, the situation in Iraq under militant dictator Saddam Hussein and the subsequent instability after his removal, and the terrorist attack on New York by ethnic Middle Easterners, many multinationals now are very reluctant to invest very heavily in most Middle Eastern countries. Recently, the government of Iran appeared to be interested in attracting foreign investment, but there is still a great deal of concern that this region is too politically explosive. Central, if not Eastern, Europe appears to be a better bet, as seen by the millions of dollars that MNCs have poured into transitionary postcommunist countries such as Hungary and Poland. This geographic region also is regarded as politically risky, however, as shown in the continuing conflict in the Balkans, the breakup of Czechoslovakia into the independent Czech Republic and Slovak Republic, the continuing problems in the former Soviet republics, and the political instability in the entire region. As a result, many multinationals have been tempering their expansion plans in these transitionary, still emerging economies.

Still another area of consideration in macro political risk is government corruption. Common examples include bribery and the use of government rules and regulations that require the inclusion of certain locals in lucrative business deals. In fact, one of the most commonly cited reasons for the severe economic problems in Indonesia in recent years is the corrupt practices of the government. Because the family of former president Suharto was involved in virtually every big business deal that took place under his regime, many loans and major projects were approved by banks and government agencies simply because these family members were part of the process. However, when these loans or projects ran into trouble, more money was poured in to shore up things—and no one dared to challenge these unsound decisions.

What are the most and the least corrupt nations in the world? Table 10–1 provides the results of a survey of 85 nations that ranked countries based on a wide variety of criteria.

Table 10–1
The 2003 Transparency International Corruption Perceptions Index

Country Rank	Country	Country Rank	Country
1	Finland	33	Estonia
2	Iceland		Uruguay
3	Denmark	35	Italy
	New Zealand		Kuwait
5	Singapore	37	Malaysia
6	Sweden		United Arab Emirates
7	Netherlands	39	Tunisia
8	Australia	40	Hungary
	Norway	41	Lithuania
	Switzerland		Namibia
11	Canada	43	Cuba
	Luxembourg		Jordan
	United Kingdom		Trinidad and Tobago
14	Austria	46	Belize
	Hong Kong	47	Saudi Arabia
16	Germany	48	Mauritius
17	Belgium	49	South Africa
18	Ireland	50	Costa Rica
	United States		Greece
20	Chile		South Korea
21	Israel	53	Belarus
	Japan	54	Brazil
23	France		Bulgaria
	Spain		Czech Republic
25	Portugal	57	Jamaica
26	Oman		Latvia
27	Bahrain	59	Colombia
	Cyprus		Croatia
29	Slovenia		El Salvador
30	Botswana		Peru
	Taiwan		Slovakia
32	Qatar		

Source: Transparency International, www.transparency.org; www.infoplease.com/
ipa/0/7/8/1/3/5/A0781359.html.

About half of the nations in the world were omitted from the survey because of the absence of reliable data. The United States ended up in 18th position. One reason for this apparently low ranking, in the view of analysts, is that the American press is very good at ferreting out stories about corruption, so practices in the United States that would go unnoticed in countries ranked ahead of the United States are widely publicized in local newspapers or reported on television and thus make the United States appear worse than it may be.

Micro Risk Issues and Examples   Micro risk issues often take forms such as industry regulation, taxes on specific types of business activity, and restrictive local laws. The essence of these micro risk issues is that some MNCs treated differently from others. A good example is the situation faced by MNCs importing steel into the U.S. market. In 1992 American steelmakers filed more than 80 complaints against 20 nations on a single day. They charged that foreign steelmakers were dumping their products in the U.S. market at artificially low prices. In 1998, the industry again demanded action against foreign producers who, in the first six months of that year, had doubled their imports into the American market. Domestic producers charged that steelmakers in Brazil, Japan, and Russia were dumping steel in the United States at unfairly low prices. What was even more troubling was that the American producers were in the process of negotiating with big auto and appliance makers for the steel that is sold under long-term contracts. Since steel prices had dropped sharply because of the alleged "dumping," the American firms were concerned that they would end up getting locked into contracts that offered very little, if any, profit. The American steelmakers were insisting that their government force foreign producers to raise their prices.[10] The George W. Bush administration did ultimately impose tariffs on steel, but these were, in part, subsequently rescinded. This experience underscores the uncertainty and volatility associated with micro political risks.

A related development is the impact of WTO and EU regulations on American MNCs. For example, the WTO recently ruled that the United States' 1916 Anti-Dumping Act violates global trade regulations and cannot be used by American firms to fend off imports.[11] Meanwhile on the European continent, the European Commission is investigating complaints by PepsiCo and other competitors that Coca-Cola has improperly attempted to shut down sales of its rivals.[12] The EU also examines all major mergers and acquisitions and has the authority to block such actions. For example, the EU refused to allow the General Electric (G.E.) and Honeywell merger, one of the best examples of globalization (the EU was able to stop the actions of perhaps the most powerful U.S. firm) as well as political risk (G.E. needed to better assess and manage the risk posed by the politicians and government bureaucrats in Brussels). Other examples include the EU's denying Volvo and Scania approval to merge and preventing Alcan Aluminum of Canada, Pechiney of France, and the Alusuisse Lonza Group of Switzerland, the world's three largest aluminum companies, from merging.[13] These regulatory actions are good examples of the types of micro risk issues that MNCs face from industry regulation.

Still another example of micro political risk is provided by countries in South America that face continued indebtedness and have introduced a variety of policies to promote exports and discourage imports. MNCs that feel they cannot abide by these policies will stay out; however, some that are looking for a location from which to produce and export goods will view these same government policies as very attractive. Table 10–2 lists criteria that MNCs could use to evaluate the degree of political risk.

Analyzing the Expropriation Risk

expropriation
The seizure of businesses by a host country with little, if any, compensation to the owners.

indigenization laws
Laws that require nationals to hold a majority interest in an operation.

Expropriation is the seizure of businesses with little, if any, compensation to the owners. Such seizures of foreign enterprises by developing countries were quite common in the old days. In addition, some takeovers were caused by **indigenization laws,** which required that nationals hold a majority interest in the operation. In the main, expropriation is more likely to occur in non-Western countries that are poor, relatively unstable, and suspicious of foreign multinationals.

Table 10–2
A Guide to Evaluation of Political Risk

External factors affecting subject country:
Prospects for foreign conflict
Relations with border countries
Regional instabilities
Alliances with major and regional powers
Sources of key raw materials
Major foreign markets
Policy toward United States
U.S. policy toward country
Internal groupings (points of power)

Government in power:
  Key agencies and officials
  Legislative entrenched bureaucracies
  Policies—economic, financial, social, labor, etc.
  Pending legislation
  Attitude toward private sector
  Power networks

Political parties (in and out of power):
  Policies
  Leading and emerging personalities
  Internal power struggles
  Sector and area strengths
  Future prospects for retaining or gaining power

Other important groups:
  Unions and labor movements
  Military, special groups within military
  Families
  Business and financial communities
  Intelligentsia
  Students
  Religious groups
  Media
  Regional and local governments
  Social and environmental activists
  Cultural, linguistic, and ethnic groups
  Separatist movements
  Foreign communities
  Potential competitors and customers

Internal factors:
Power struggles among elites
Ethnic confrontations
Regional struggles
Economic factors affecting stability (consumer inflation, price and
  wage controls, unemployment, supply shortages, taxation, etc.)
Anti-establishment movements
Factors affecting a specific project (custom-designed
  for each project)

Note: Information in the table is an abridged version of Probe's Political Agenda Worksheet, which may serve as a guide for corporate executives initiating their own political evaluations. Probe International is located in Stamford, CT.

Source: Benjamin Weinger, "What Executives Should Know About Political Risk," *Management Review,* January 1992, p. 20. Copyright © 1992 by American Management Association. Reproduced with permission of American Management Association via Copyright Clearance Center.

Some firms are more vulnerable to expropriation than others. Often, those at greatest risk are in extractive, agricultural, or infrastructural industries such as utilities and transportation, because of their importance to the country. In addition, large firms often are more likely targets than small firms, because more is to be gained by expropriating from large firms.

MNCs can take a wide variety of strategies to minimize their chances of expropriation. They can bring in local partners. They can limit the use of high technology so that if the firm is expropriated, the country cannot duplicate the technology. They also can acquire an affiliate that depends on the parent company for key areas of the operation, such as financing, research, and technology transfer, so that no practical value exists in seizing the affiliate.

The Role of Operational Profitability in Risk Analysis

Although expropriation is a major consideration, most MNCs are more directly concerned with operational profitability. Will they be able to make the desired return on investment? A number of government regulations can have a negative impact on their profitability. Requiring MNCs to use domestic suppliers instead of bringing in components or raw materials from other company-owned facilities or purchasing them more cheaply in the world market is one such regulation. Another is a restriction on the amount of profit that can be taken out of the country. A third is the wages and salaries that must be paid to the employees. Despite these difficulties, MNCs have become very interested in designing models and frameworks to understand and manage their political risk.

■ Managing Political Risk and Government Relations

For well over two decades, businesses have been looking for ways to manage their political risk. Quite often, the process begins with a detailed analysis of the various risks with which the MNC will be confronted, including development of a comprehensive framework that identifies the various risks and then assigns a quantitative risk or rating factor to them.

Developing a Comprehensive Framework or Quantitative Analysis

A comprehensive framework for managing political risk should consider all political risks and identify those that are most important. Schmidt has offered a three-dimensional framework that combines political risks, general investments, and special investments.[14] Figure 10–2 illustrates this framework, and the following sections examine each dimension in detail.

Political Risks Political risks can be broken down into three basic categories: transfer risks, operational risks, and ownership-control risks. **Transfer risks** stem from government policies that limit the transfer of capital, payments, production, people, and technology in or out of the country. Examples include tariffs on exports and imports as well as restrictions on exports, dividend remittance, and capital repatriation. **Operational risks** result from government policies and procedures that directly constrain the management and performance of local operations. Examples include price controls, financing restrictions, export commitments, taxes, and local sourcing requirements. **Ownership-control risks** are brought about by government policies or actions that inhibit ownership or control of local operations. Examples include foreign-ownership limitations, pressure for local participation, confiscation, expropriation, and abrogation of proprietary rights. For example, the Russian government canceled an agreement with the Exxon Corporation that would have allowed the firm to tap huge oil deposits in the country's far north. The Russian minister for natural resources cited "legal irregularities" as the reason for the decision. As a result, the $1.5 billion project came to a grinding halt. Commenting on the government's action, one Western investment banker in Russia said that "it raises the question of whether a deal is a deal in Russia, because Exxon is meticulous to

transfer risks
Government policies that limit the transfer of capital, payments, production, people, and technology in and out of the country.

operational risks
Government policies and procedures that directly constrain management and performance of local operations.

ownership-control risks
Government policies or actions that inhibit ownership or control of local operations.

Figure 10–2

A Three-Dimensional Framework for Assessing Political Risk

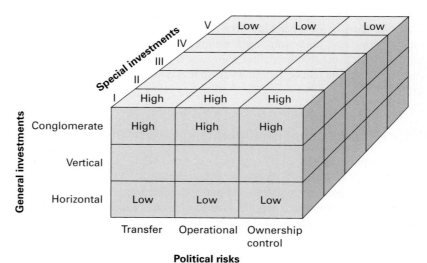

Source: David A. Schmidt, "Analyzing Political Risk," *Business Horizons,* July–August 1986, p. 50. Copyright 1986. Used with permission from Elsevier.

Sometimes It's All Politics

One of the biggest problems in doing business internationally is that yesterday's agreement with a government may be canceled or delayed by today's politicians who disagree with that earlier decision. Enron, the now bankrupt Houston-based U.S. energy consortium, discovered this when its power project in Dabhol, India, became the focal point of political interest. India's economic nationalists began accelerating a campaign to scrap a high-profile, U.S.-backed power project despite warnings of potential damage to the confidence of foreign investors in the country. These politicians wanted to abandon the $2.8 billion deal as well as all other power projects in the country that had been approved under the government's "fast track" provisions. The contract for the two-stage, 2,000+ megawatt plant was signed before the current politicians came to power in Maharashtra, the state where Dabhol is located.

What effect would this political move have on foreign investment in India? A number of foreign investors indicated that if the Enron project were canceled, they would review their investment plans for the country. A survey of international energy companies by the East-West Center in Hawaii found that of 13 Asian economies, India's investment climate ranked fifth from the bottom for power-sector investment. This seemed to have little effect on the politicians, who proceeded to cancel the project. Members of the political opposition, who supported the project, called it a mere political ploy designed to appeal to voters in the upcoming elections, and they urged foreign investors to sit tight and ride out the political storm. Many of these investors appeared to be apprehensive about taking such advice, and Enron announced plans for taking the case to international arbitration to reclaim the $300 million they had invested in the project—as well as $300 million in damages.

Eventually things were straightened out, but only for a while. More recently the Maharashtra State Electric Board defaulted on $64 million in unpaid power bills. The Board said that the company was charging too much for power and Enron served notice that it would terminate the power supply contract and pull out. As of fall 2002, following Enron's own collapse, the power purchase agreement was to be reworked, and the foreign investors—Enron's creditors, G.E., and Bechtel—were looking to divest their stakes in the venture, scrambling to recover whatever they could from the project.

The political climate in India is not unique. Russia also offers its share of jitters to investors. In particular, many joint ventures that were created during the Gorbachev era now are having problems. A good example is Moscow's Radisson-Slavjanskaya Hotel venture, in which American Business Centers of Irvine, California, owns a 40 percent stake. American Business Centers manages several floors of offices in the hotel, and now that the venture is making money, it appears that the Irvine firm's Russian partners and the Radisson hotel people are trying to oust them. The president of American Business Centers claims that his partners feel they do not need him any longer.

The dilemma faced by American Business Centers is becoming increasingly common in Russia. For example, the Seattle-based firm Radio Page entered into a joint venture with Moscow Public Telephone Network and another Russian company to offer paging services. Together, they built a system of telephone pagers in the Moscow region. Radio Page held a 51 percent stake. When annual revenues hit $5 million and the venture was on the verge of making $1 million, however, the agreement began to unravel. The Russian partners demanded control of the operation and even threatened to pull the critical radio frequencies if they did not get their way.

There is little that foreign joint-venture firms doing business in high-risk countries can do except try to negotiate with their partners. For instance, the political situation in Russia is so unstable that support from one government ministry may be offset by opposition from another, or, worse yet, the individuals supporting the foreign firm may be ousted from their jobs tomorrow. Economic considerations tend to be the main reason why firms seek international partners, but sometimes it seems that everything boils down to politics and the risks associated with dealing in this political environment.

a fault in following the letter of the law."[15] In any event, the decision provides a good example of ownership-control risks. Still another is provided in "International Management in Action: Sometimes It's All Politics."

General Nature of Investment   The general nature of investment examines whether the company is making a conglomerate, vertical, or horizontal investment (see Figure 10–2). In a **conglomerate investment,** the goods or services produced are not similar to those produced at home. These types of investments usually are rated as high risk, because foreign governments see them as providing fewer benefits to the country and greater benefits to the MNC than other investments. **Vertical investments** include the production of raw materials or intermediate goods that are to be processed into final products. These investments run

conglomerate investment
A type of high-risk investment in which goods or services produced are not similar to those produced at home.

vertical investment
The production of raw materials or intermediate goods that are to be processed into final products.

horizontal investment
An MNC investment in foreign operations to produce the same goods or services as those produced at home.

the risk of being taken over by the government because they are export oriented, and governments like a business that helps them to generate foreign capital. **Horizontal investments** involve the production of goods or services that are the same as those produced at home. These investments typically are made with an eye toward satisfying the host country's market demands. As a result, they are not very likely to be takeover targets.

Special Nature of Investment   The special nature of foreign direct investment relates to the sector of economic activity, technological sophistication, and pattern of ownership. There are three sectors of economic activity: (1) the primary sector, which consists of agriculture, forestry, and mineral exploration and extraction; (2) the industrial sector, consisting of manufacturing operations; and (3) the service sector, which includes transportation, finance, insurance, and related industries. Technological sophistication consists of science-based industry and non-science-based industry. The difference between them is that science-based industry requires the continuous introduction of new products or processes. Patterns of ownership relate to whether the business is wholly or partially owned.

The special nature of foreign direct investments can be categorized as one of five types (see Figure 10–2). Type I is the highest-risk venture; type V is the lowest-risk venture. This risk factor is assigned based on sector, technology, and ownership. Primary sector industries usually have the highest risk factor, service sector industries have the next highest, and industrial sector industries have the lowest. Firms with technology that is not available to the government should the firm be taken over have lower risk than those with technology that is easily acquired. Wholly owned subsidiaries have higher risk than partially owned subsidiaries.

Using a framework similar to that provided in Figure 10–2 helps MNCs to manage their political risks. A way to complement this framework approach is to give specific risk ratings to various criteria.

Quantifying the Variables in Managing Political Risk   Some MNCs attempt to manage political risk through a quantification process in which a range of variables are simultaneously analyzed to derive an overall rating of the degree of political risk in a given jurisdiction. This would allow an MNC, for example, to compare how risky a particular venture would be in Russia and in Argentina.

Factors that are typically quantified reflect the political and economic environment, domestic economic conditions, and external economic conditions. Each factor is given a minimum or maximum score, and the scores are tallied to provide an overall evaluation of the risk. Table 10–3 provides an example of a quantitative list of political risk criteria.

Formulating and Implementing Responses to Political Risk: Corporate Political Strategies

Once political risk has been analyzed by a framework, quantitative analysis, or both, the MNC then will attempt to manage the risk further through a carefully developed response. The MNC can also proactively improve its relationship with governments by means of preemptive political strategies to mitigate risk before it appears. Three related strategies should be considered: (1) relative bargaining power analysis; (2) integrative, protective, and defensive techniques; and (3) proactive political strategies.

Relative Bargaining Power Analysis   The theory behind relative bargaining power is quite simple. The MNC works to maintain a bargaining power position stronger than that of the host country. A good example arises when the MNC has proprietary technology that will be unavailable to the host country if the operation is expropriated or the firm is forced to abide by government decisions that are unacceptable to it. Over time, of course, this technology may become common, and the firm will lose its bargaining power. To prevent this from happening, however, the firm will work to develop new technology that again

Table 10–3
Criteria for Quantifying Political Risk

Major Area	Criteria	Scores Minimum	Maximum
Political and economic environment	1. Stability of the political system	3	14
	2. Imminent internal conflicts	0	14
	3. Threats to stability emanating from the outside world	0	12
	4. Degree of control of the economic system	5	9
	5. Reliability of the country as a trading partner	4	12
	6. Constitutional guarantees	2	12
	7. Effectiveness of public administration	3	12
	8. Labor relations and social peace	3	15
Domestic economic conditions	9. Size of population	4	8
	10. Per capita income	2	10
	11. Economic growth during previous 5 years	2	7
	12. Prospective growth during next 3 years	3	10
	13. Inflation during previous 2 years	2	10
	14. Accessibility of domestic capital market to foreigners	3	7
	15. Availability of high-quality local labor	2	8
	16. Possibility of giving employment to foreign nationals	2	8
	17. Availability of energy resources	2	14
	18. Legal requirements concerning environmental protection	4	8
	19. Traffic system and communication	2	14
External economic relations	20. Restrictions imposed on imports	2	10
	21. Restrictions imposed on exports	2	10
	22. Restrictions imposed on foreign investments in the country	3	9
	23. Freedom to set up or engage in partnerships	3	9
	24. Legal protection for brands and products	3	9
	25. Restrictions imposed on monetary transfers	2	8
	26. Reevaluations against the home market currency during previous 5 years	2	7
	27. Development of the balance of payments	2	9
	28. Drain on foreign funds through oil and other energy imports	3	14
	29. International financial standing	3	8
	30. Restrictions imposed on the exchange of local money into foreign currencies	2	8

Source: Adapted from E. Diehtl and H. G. Koglmayr, "Country Risk Ratings," *Management International Review* 26, no. 4 (1986), p. 6. Used with permission.

establishes the balance of power in its favor. As long as the host country stands to lose more than it will gain by taking action against the company, the firm has successfully minimized its political risk by establishing an effective bargaining position. Figure 10–3 provides an example. As long as the MNC's bargaining power remains at or above the diagonal line, the government will not intervene. At point E in the figure, however, this power declines, and the host country will begin to intervene.[16]

Integrative, Protective, and Defensive Techniques Another way that MNCs attempt to protect themselves from expropriation or minimize government interference in their operations is to use integration and the implementation of protective and defensive techniques. **Integrative techniques** are designed to help the overseas operation become part of the host country's infrastructure. The objective is to be perceived as "less foreign" and thus unlikely to be the target of government action. Some of the most integrative techniques include (1) developing good relations with the host government and other local political groups; (2) producing as much of the product locally as possible with the use of in-country suppliers and subcontractors, thus making it a "domestic" product; (3) creating joint

integrative techniques
Techniques that help the overseas operation become a part of the host country's infrastructure.

Figure 10–3

Relative Bargaining Power over Time

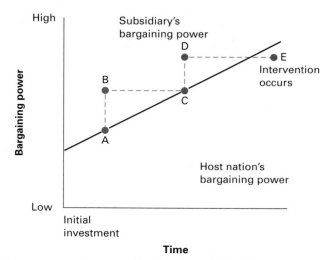

Source: Adapted from Thomas A. Pointer, "Political Risk: Managing Government Intervention," in *International Management: Text and Cases,* ed. Paul W. Beamish, J. Peter Killing, Donald J. LeCraw, and Harold Crookell (Homewood, IL: Irwin, 1991), p. 125.

ventures and hiring local people to manage and run the operation; (4) doing as much local research and development as possible; and (5) developing effective labor–management relations.

protective and defensive techniques
Techniques that discourage the host government from interfering in operations.

    Protective and defensive techniques are designed to discourage the host government from interfering in operations. In contrast to the integrative techniques, these actually encourage nonintegration of the enterprise in the local environment. Examples include (1) doing as little local manufacturing as possible and conducting all research and development outside the country; (2) limiting the responsibility of local personnel and hiring only those who are vital to the operation; (3) raising capital from local banks and the host government as well as outside sources; and (4) diversifying production of the product among a number of countries.

    When should a company use integrative techniques? Under what conditions should it employ protective and defensive techniques? Analysis reveals that this choice will be heavily influenced by characteristics such as the MNC's technology, management skills, and logistics and labor transmission. In all, four basic types of firms can be described using these characteristics.

    The first type consists of dynamic, high-technology MNCs that have unique knowledge that the host country would like. Computer companies are a good example. As seen in Figure 10–4, these firms do not rely very much on integrative techniques. They attempt to keep their distance from the host country and rely heavily on protective and defensive strategies.

    The second type consists of MNCs with low or stable technology. These MNCs make products that require little innovation or use relatively unsophisticated technology. Steel firms are an example. As seen in Figure 10–4, these firms typically use both high integration and high protective and defensive strategies, although they generally rely more on integration than the defensive approach.

    The third type consists of MNCs whose managers need to be highly skilled. For example, food production firms require advanced marketing and management skills to be competitive. These MNCs typically use a balanced approach of integration and protective and defensive techniques, but they are less concerned with either than low or stable technology firms are.

    The fourth type consists of MNCs characterized by highly labor-intensive products, high value in relation to weight or volume, and the need for a strong global marketing system for selling the product. Sewing machine companies are an example. Firms in this

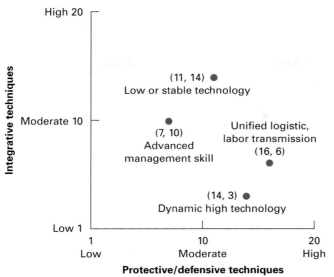

Source: Adapted from Ann Gregory, "Firm Characteristic and Political Risk Reduction in Overseas Ventures," *National Academy of Management Proceedings* (New York, 1982), p. 77.

category tend to rely more heavily on protective and defensive measures than any of the other three groups and to employ only moderate concern for integrative techniques (again, see Figure 10–4).

The strategic response that a firm takes in managing its political risk will be influenced by a variety of factors besides the firm's technology, management skills, logistics, and labor transmission. Others include the nature of the industry, local conditions in the host country, and philosophy of the management.

Proactive Political Strategies As mentioned at the beginning of the chapter, despite the general trend of developing countries seeking MNC investment, many developing-country governments continue to engage in practices that effectively overturn or renege on past deals.[17] In the last half of the 1990s, leaders of a number of countries in which autocratic or dictatorial governments controlled negotiations with foreign investors were toppled. The ousting of leaders in Peru, Indonesia, Malaysia, the Philippines, and Venezuela led to a backlash against incumbent foreign investors and forced many project leaders to withdraw or renegotiate the terms of their investments.[18] In Indonesia, President Suharto's 30 years of dictatorial and nepotistic government were totally discredited, and investors whose reputations were closely associated with his legacy face a challenging environment for preserving the economic viability of their presence. For example, the government of Indonesia reneged on its commitment to buy power from two projects sponsored by MidAmerica Energy Holdings, arguing that the projects, both of which were awarded on a sole-source contract basis under the Suharto regime, were overpriced and the government simply could not afford to pay.[19] Recently, Indonesia's minister of mines and energy, Purnamo Yusgiantora, said his government would fight in U.S. courts to release $130 million being held in a Bank of America escrow account after Karaha Bodas, a power developer, won an arbitration award in its dispute with the Indonesian government over cancellation of a geothermal plant that Karaha had agreed to build in collaboration with Indonesia's state electricity company.[20] The Bolivian government rescinded a 40-year contract with Aguas del Tunari—a consortium that included London-based International Water Ltd., Bechtel Enterprise Holdings, Italy's Montedison Energy Services, Spain's Abengoa Servicios Urbanos, and four of Bolivia's largest construction companies—to supply water to Cochabamba, Bolivia's third-largest city.

Often the challenges and complexity associated with governments' tendency to seek to renegotiate investment rules and contracts are worsened by the participation of both

proactive political strategies
Lobbying, campaign financing, advocacy, and other political interventions designed to shape and influence the political decisions prior to their impact on the firm.

national and subcentral governments in the project. In India, Brazil, and, increasingly, China, states and provinces wield significant power, and this has been a particular problem in the development and financing of power, water, and transport projects. The Linha Amarela project in Rio de Janeiro, an urban expressway that begins in the residential area of Rio and provides a direct link to the downtown area, was initially bid with an official traffic estimate of around 55,000 cars per day in 1993–1994. However, when construction was complete and the road opened for business in 1998, traffic exceeded that amount, reaching 80,000 vehicles per day in early 2001. When the new mayor of Rio, Cesar Maia, took office on January 1, 2001, he issued a number of decrees overturning policies of his predecessor. One of these decrees unilaterally dropped the toll by 20 percent, squeezing the foreign owner of the concession.

Because government policies can have a significant impact on business activities, and many governments face competing pressures from a range of stakeholders, corporations must adopt various proactive strategies both to affect government policy and to respond to competitors' efforts to influence that policy. Comprehensive strategies are especially important in unstable and transitional policy environments.[21] These strategies are designed, in part, to develop and maintain ongoing favorable relationships with government policy makers as a tool to mitigate risk before it becomes unmanageable. Broadly, strategies may include leveraging bilateral, regional, and international trade and investment agreements, drawing on bilateral and multilateral financial support, and using project finance structures to separate project exposure from overall firm risk. They also can include entering markets early in the privatization/liberalization cycle (the first-mover strategy discussed in Chapter 8), establishing a local presence and partnering with local firms, and pursuing preemptive stakeholder management strategies to secure relationships with all relevant actors.[22]

More specific proactive political strategies include formal lobbying, campaign financing, seeking advocacy through the embassy and consulates of the home country, and more formal public relations and public affairs activities such as grassroots campaigning and advertising.[23] Strategies must vary based on the particular political system (parliamentary vs. nonparliamentary), distribution of power (highly centralized vs. decentralized), and other variations in political systems.[24] Developing and maintaining ongoing relationships with political actors, including officials in power and in opposition parties, and with the range of stakeholders, including NGOs and others, can help to buffer host-government actions that may constrain or undermine MNC strategies and plans.[25] In the previous examples, had investors made low-level contacts with opposition groups, they may have aggravated existing relationships with government but secured some protections for the future. Knowing when—and how—to exercise such relationships is a difficult but necessary strategy.

■ Managing Alliances

Another dimension of management strategy related to political risk and government relations is managing relationships with alliance partners. Some partners may be current or former state-owned enterprises; others may be controlled or influenced by government agencies. For example, in China, most foreign investors have some sort of alliance or joint-venture relationships with Chinese state-owned enterprises. Motorola, one of the most active investors in China, has many alliances with state-owned enterprise, such as its joint venture with Nanjing Panda Electronics to produce a personal computer. The heart of the computer will be Motorola's Power PC chip, the major rival to Intel's Pentium.[26] Siemens AG chief executive Heinrich von Pierer recently announced a sweeping expansion of the company's business in China using its more than 45 joint ventures as the primary vehicle for expansion.[27] As mentioned in Chapter 9, alliances and joint ventures can significantly improve the success of MNC entry and operation in many international markets, especially emerging economies. Managing the relationships inherent in alliances, especially when governments are involved, can be especially challenging.

The Alliance Challenge

A rich and increasingly diverse recent literature has examined the motivations for collective action through international strategic alliances (ISAs). Researchers have begun to focus on specific explanations of ISA formation, the conditions that appear to lead to better or worse ISA performance and endurance, and the primary factors motivating firms to enter into such relationships.[28] Motivating factors include faster entry and payback, economies of scale and rationalization, complementary technologies and patents, and co-opting or blocking competition.[29]

In the strategic alliance literature, several researchers have argued that learning can be a powerful force in the initial motivations for, and ultimate success of, ISAs.[30] Some kinds of local knowledge cannot be internalized simply as a result of an MNC operating in a foreign market; acquisition of some kinds of local knowledge requires indigenous-firm experience through partnerships or alliances. Collaboration facilitates rapid market entry by allowing firms to share costs and risks, combine product and market complementarities, and reduce time-to-market.[31]

How an alliance relationship is developed is largely a function of interfirm negotiation. Alliances are an arena where both value-claiming activities (competitive, distributive negotiation) and value-creating activities (collaborative, integrative negotiation) take place. In order to lay claim to a larger share of the alliance pie, firms tend to seek an advantage over their partners. Firms do this by possessing superior resources or alternatives beyond the scope of the alliance. However, in order to create a "larger pie" through the combination of partner-firm resources and activities, firms must balance authority, allowing each firm to dictate certain activities within the alliance, and to commit to sharing and reciprocity where each partner firm plays some decision-making role. In these instances, alliance partners can create value through specialization gains or when the rationalization of redundant activities results in enhanced performance for the partners.[32]

A fundamental challenge of alliances, however, is managing operations with partners from different national cultures. Cultural difference may create uncertainties and misunderstandings in the relationship, which may lead to conflict and even dissolution of the venture. Indeed, an alliance may be viewed as a temporal structure designed to address a particular problem during a period in time; all alliances eventually outlast their purpose.

Differences in the cultural backgrounds of partners cause problems in alliances and international joint ventures (IJVs). One study tried to determine whether some differences are more disruptive than others. The researchers found that differences in uncertainty avoidance and in long-term orientation, in particular, cause problems. These differences have a negative impact on survival and decrease the likelihood that firms enter a foreign country through an alliance rather than a wholly owned subsidiary.[33] Apparently, these differences, which translate into differences in how partners perceive and adapt to opportunities and threats in their environment, are more difficult to resolve than differences along other cultural dimensions. Perhaps cultural differences in power distance, individualism, and masculinity are more easily resolved because they are mainly reflected in different attitudes toward the management of personnel—something firms can make explicit. In a study of Mexican firms with experience in alliances with U.S. counterparts, Mexican managers were found to view a balance of authority as a positive contributor to alliance performance, while authority advantage—even when to the benefit of the Mexican partner at the expense of the U.S. partner—was viewed as having a negative impact on performance.[34]

Successful management of alliances depends on situational conditions, management instruments, and performance criteria. Success factors may include partner selection, co-operation agreement, management structure, acculturation process, and knowledge management.[35] In particular, partner selection and task selection criteria have been identified as critical variables that influence alliance success or failure. Choosing the right partners, and defining the scope and limit to the alliance, appear to be the most important elements in determining if an alliance will succeed or fail.

One difficult but important aspect of successful alliance management is preparation for the likely eventual termination of the alliance.[36] Many firms are caught off guard when their partners are better prepared to deal with issues related to termination of the alliance than they are. After studying two dozen successful alliance "divorces," a group of researchers identified a number of legal and business issues that were critical to successful divorces. Legal issues include the conditions of termination, the disposition of assets and liabilities, dispute resolution, distributorship arrangements, protection of proprietary information and property, and rights over sales territories and obligations to customers. Business issues include the basic decision to exit, people-related issues, and relations with the host government.

The Role of Host Governments in Alliances

As previously mentioned, host governments are active in mandating that investors take on partners, and these mandates can pose managerial and operational challenges for MNCs. Many host governments require investors to share ownership of their subsidiaries with local partners—in some cases, state-owned or state-controlled partners. These mandates can include specific requirements that investors select local state-owned firms (China) or that investors form joint ventures to meet local regulatory requirements where restrictions or local-content rules apply (Central and Eastern Europe).[37]

Even when host governments do not require alliances or joint venture as a condition for entry, many MNCs find that having alliance or joint-venture partners is advantageous to their entry and expansion. This is especially so in highly regulated industries such as banking, telecommunications, and health care. In a study conducted of alliances among global telecommunications firms, firms were found to establish alliances with local partners primarily to gain market access and to contend with local regulations.[38] In another study, also of telecommunications projects in emerging markets, firms were found to take on local partners as a way to cope with emerging-markets environments characterized by arbitrary and unpredictable corruption.[39]

Even when alliances are dissolved, host governments can have a role. In particular, the host government of a partner may be unwilling to permit the alliance to terminate. It could object to the termination in an overt way, such as not permitting a foreign partner to sell its interest in the alliance.[40] There are also subtle ways to discourage a partner from leaving an alliance, such as blocking the repatriation of the foreign partner's investments in the alliance. It is also important to consider carefully the long-term effects of terminating an alliance on the ability of the company to do business in the same host country in the future.

In sum, host governments have a substantial role in the terms under which alliances are initially formed, the way in which they are managed, and even the terms of their dissolution. MNCs must be aware of these influences and use carefully crafted strategies to manage host-government involvement in their alliances.

Examples of Challenges and Opportunities in Alliance Management

Alliances and joint ventures are increasingly common modes of entry and operation in international business. A number of recent examples illustrate the challenges and opportunities associated with managing alliances.

A good example is provided by Ford Motor and Mazda. For a number of years the two have had a strategic alliance. Today, with guidance from its American partner, Mazda is trimming costs and introducing a host of popular new models in Asia. At the same time the company is beginning to gain ground in both North America and Europe. Part of this success is accounted for by Ford executives who reined in Mazda's freewheeling engineers and forced them to share auto platforms and to source more components overseas. Mazda also began following Ford's advice to use customer clinics, thus helping the company to develop low-priced, compact sport vehicles that are proving very popular in the Japanese market.

Over the next few years, Mazda intends to continue growing its market shares in North America and Europe. At the same time, the two firms are working closely together in Asia.

Starbucks Coffee International of Seattle, Washington, recently entered into a joint venture with the Beijing Mei Da Coffee Company to open coffee houses in China. Getting local consumers to switch from tea to coffee is likely to be a major challenge. However, for the moment, the joint venture is focusing on the training of local managers who will run the coffee shops. Recruits are sent to Tacoma, Washington, to learn how to make the various types of Starbucks coffee and to get a first-hand look at the company's culture. As one of the general managers for the Mei Da company put it, "People don't go to Starbucks for the coffee but for the experience. Focusing on the development of employees so that they can deliver that experience is our priority for now."[41] Part of Starbucks' strategy is also to show the new recruits that there are career and personal development opportunities in this new venture. This is an important area of emphasis for the firm because there is a major shortage of management personnel in China. As a result, many companies raid the management ranks of others, offering lucrative financial arrangements to those who are willing to change companies. One way that Starbucks is trying to deal with this is by encouraging the trainees to take responsibility, question the system, take risks, and make changes that will keep the customers coming back. Many foreign MNCs in China want the employees to do as they are told. Starbucks believes that its IJV emphasis on developing talent will give it an edge—and discourage people from leaving for higher financially attractive offers.

As these examples show, multinationals are and will be making a host of decisions related to IJVs. In Russia, the current trend is to renegotiate many of the old agreements and seek smaller deals that entail less bureaucratic red tape and are easier to bring to fruition. At the same time, the U.S. administration is trying to create a plan for providing assistance to the former Soviet republics, and this likely will generate increased interest in the use of IJVs.

Besides the former Soviet Union, other areas of the world previously closed to foreign investment are beginning to open up. One of these is Vietnam, which had a very auspicious beginning in the early 1990s when investors began flocking there. During this time period, Japan's Idemitsu Oil Development Company signed a deal with the Vietnamese government that gave the company the right to explore an offshore oil and gas field in the Gulf of Tonkin. A number of U.S. companies also targeted Vietnam for investment, and Citibank and Bank of America both were approved for branch status by the government. The bulk of their business was to be in wholesale banking and, in the case of Bank of America, advising the government on financing the rebuilding of the nation's weak power sector. Other firms that began giving serious consideration to Vietnam included AT&T, Coca-Cola, General Electric, ExxonMobil, and Ralston Purina, to name but five. As a result, by 1996 the country was attracting over $8 billion annually in foreign direct investment (FDI). Since then, however, FDI has dropped sharply.

In 2000, the Vietnam General Department of Statistics reported that annual FDI was in the range of a mere $300 million. Despite its promises, the bureaucratic communist government had not created an attractive environment. Ford Motor, for example, had spent over $100 million to build a factory near Hanoi, but because of pressure from its local rival, the Vietnam Motor Corporation, it had taken 16 months for Ford to get approval to sell its Laser sedan. By the end of 2000, the company had sold fewer than 1,000 vehicles, a far cry from the 14,000 that had been initially projected.[42] Many other firms reported similar experiences. At present, the Vietnamese government is trying to turn things around and promote investment and strategic alliances; and the latest trade agreement with the United States requires that the country open up its own markets in return for favorable treatment in the American market.[43] Among other things, the country's coffee production is skyrocketing and Vietnam currently exports over 20 percent of its coffee to the United States; so it is in the best interests of the country to open its markets. At the same time, a growing number of multinationals are reexamining Vietnam's potential and looking to create strategic alliances that will help them establish a foothold in one of the more promising emerging economies in Asia.[44]

The World of *BusinessWeek*—Revisited

A wide range of risks emanate from the political environment in which MNCs operate, and firms can employ an equally diverse set of strategies to mitigate those risks and improve their relations with governments. Some political risks, however, are more common and more critical than others. Less risk is associated with the outright expropriation of MNCs' assets today than ever before, but indirect expropriation in the form of governments reneging on former commitments is as problematic as ever. As we discussed in Chapter 2, the terrorist attacks of 9/11 caused MNCs to reconsider their policies and control mechanisms for political risk assessment. The management of both alliances and joint ventures is influenced by political risks, and each serves as a strategy to respond to those risks. The opening up of traditionally closed borders worldwide has amplified the need for MNCs to be aware of the political dangers of doing business in these areas and the role of alliances and joint ventures in responding to those dangers. The article that opens this chapter conveys the importance of mitigating risk by securing solid government relationships. Countries that are not in good standing with Saudi Arabia are especially likely to feel the adverse effects of a lack of supply in oil. Good political risk assessment and strong government relations are crucial to success in today's global environment.

After reading this chapter and considering the challenges associated with business in Saudi Arabia, answer the following questions: (1) What are two main concerns that MNCs should evaluate when doing business in Saudi Arabia? (2) How can MNCs protect themselves from government action? (3) What proactive political strategies might help protect MNCs from future changes in the political environment? (4) How might alliances and joint ventures reduce risk and help relationships with government actors and other stakeholders?

SUMMARY OF KEY POINTS

1. Political risk is the likelihood that the foreign investment of a business will be constrained by a host government's policies. In dealing with this risk, companies conduct both macro and micro political risk analyses. Specific consideration is given to changing host-government policies, expropriation, and operational profitability risk.

2. MNCs attempt to manage their political risk in two basic ways. One is by developing a comprehensive framework for identifying and describing these risks. This includes consideration of political, operational, and ownership-control risks. A second is by quantifying the variables that help constitute the risk.

3. Common risk management strategies are the use of relative bargaining power, integrative, protective, and defensive techniques, and proactive political strategies.

4. Effective alliance management includes careful selection of partners, defining the tasks and scope of the alliance, addressing cross-cultural differences, and responding to host-government requirements.

KEY TERMS

conglomerate investment, *303*

expropriation, *300*

horizontal investment, *304*

indigenization laws, *300*

integrative techniques, *305*

macro political risk analysis, *297*

micro political risk analysis, *297*

operational risks, *302*

ownership-control risks, *302*

political risk, *295*

proactive political strategies, *307*

protective and defensive
   techniques, *306*

transfer risks, *302*

vertical investment, *303*

REVIEW AND DISCUSSION QUESTIONS

1. What types of political risk would a company entering Russia face? Identify and describe three. What types of political risk would a company entering France face? Identify and describe three. How are these risks similar? How are they different?

2. Most firms attempt to quantify their political risk, although they do not assign specific weights to the respective criteria. Why is this approach so popular? Would the companies be better off assigning weights to each of the risks being assumed? Defend your answer.

3. If a high-tech firm wanted to set up operations in Iran, what steps might it take to ensure that the subsidiary would not be expropriated? Identify and describe three strategies that would be particularly helpful. How might proactive political strategies help protect firms from future changes in the political environment?

4. What are some of the challenges associated with managing alliances? How do host governments affect these?

INTERNET EXERCISE: MOTOROLA IN CHINA

Asia still offers great opportunities for multinational firms. However, given the slowdown that has occurred in this region in recent years, there are also great risks associated with doing business there. The large American-based MNC Motorola has determined that the opportunities are worth the risk and has staked a large claim in China and is determined to be a major player in the emerging Asian market. Visit Motorola's website at **www.motorola.com** and focus your attention on what this well-known MNC is now doing in Asia. Drawing from specific information obtained from the website, this chapter, and your reading of the current news, answer these questions: What political risks does Motorola face in Asia, particularly China? How can Motorola manage these risks? How can effective international negotiating skills be of value to the firm in reducing its political risk and increasing its competitive advantage in this area of the world?

Peru

Peru is located on the west coast of South America. It is the third-largest nation on the continent (only Brazil and Argentina have more area), and it covers almost 500,000 square miles (about 14 percent of the size of the United States). The land has enormous contrasts: a desert drier than the Sahara, the towering snow-capped Andes Mountains, sparkling grass-covered plateaus, and thick rain forests. Peru has approximately 27 million people, of whom about 20 percent live in Lima, the capital. More Indians (one-half of the population) live in Peru than in any other country in the Western Hemisphere. The ancestors of Peru's Indians are the famous Incas, who built a great empire. The rest of the population is mixed, and a small percentage is white.

The economy depends heavily on agriculture, fishing, mining, and services. GDP is approximately $139 billion and per capita income stood at around $5,000 in 2002. In recent years the economy has gained some relative strength, with GDP growth of more than 4 percent in 2003. In addition, the U.S. government recently began trade negotiations with Peru, Colombia, and Ecuador, perhaps leading to a formal trade agreement that would make permanent trade concessions under the earlier Andean Trade Preferences Act. In response, multinationals are now beginning to again consider investing in the country. One of these potential investors is a large New York bank that is considering a $25 million loan to the owner of a Peruvian fishing fleet. The owner wants to refurbish the fleet and add one more ship.

During the 1970s, the Peruvian government nationalized a number of industries and factories and began running them for the profit of the state. In most cases, these state-run ventures became disasters. In the late 1970s, the fishing fleet owner was given back his ships and allowed to operate his business as before. Since then, he has managed to remain profitable, but his ships are getting old and he needs an influx of capital to make repairs and add new technology. As he explained to the New York banker: "Fishing is

no longer just an art. There is a great deal of technology involved. And to keep costs low and be competitive on the world market, you have to have the latest equipment for both locating as well as catching and then loading and unloading the fish."

Having reviewed the fleet owner's operation, the large multinational bank believes that the loan is justified. The financial institution is concerned, however, that the Peruvian government might step in during the next couple of years and again take over the business. If this were to happen, it might take an additional decade for the loan to be repaid. If the government were to allow the fleet owner to operate the fleet the way he has over the last decade, the loan could be repaid within seven years.

Right now, the bank is deciding the specific terms of the agreement. Once these have been worked out, either a loan officer will fly down to Lima and close the deal or the owner will be asked to come to New York for the signing. Whichever approach is used, the bank realizes that final adjustments in the agreement will have to be made on the spot. Therefore, if the bank sends a representative to Lima, the individual will have to have the authority to commit the bank to specific terms. These final matters should be worked out within the next 10 days.
www.peru-explorer.com

Questions

1. What are some current issues facing Peru? What is the climate for doing business in Peru today?

2. What type of political risks does this fishing company need to evaluate? Identify and describe them.

3. What types of integrative and protective and defensive techniques can the bank use?

4. Would the bank be better off negotiating the loan in New York or in Lima? Why?

Going to Gdansk

When Poland made the necessary reforms to move toward a market economy, Andrzej Jaworski from Chicago, Illinois, began thinking this might be an excellent place to set up an overseas operation. Andrzej and his two brothers own a firm that produces specialized computer chips. The company has a series of patents that provide legal protection and allow it to dominate a small but growing segment of the computer market. Their sales estimates reached $147 million within three years, but they believe that this could rise to $200 million if they were to expand internationally. They have thought about setting up a plant in Belgium so that they could take advantage of the European market growth. They would prefer Poland, however, because their parents grew up there before leaving for the United States in 1948. "We feel that we know the Poles because we have grown up in a Polish household here in the Midwest," Andrzej explained to his banker. "We would like to see if the government would allow us to set up a small plant in Gdansk, train the necessary workers, and then export our product into the European Union."

One of the primary reasons that Andrzej believes that the Polish government would be agreeable to the plan is that not only is Poland moving to a market economy, but the country is still struggling with foreign debt, inflation, and outmoded technology. A state-of-the-art plant could help to reduce unemployment and provide an inflow of needed capital. However, the banker is concerned that because of the political risks and uncertainty in Central Europe in general and Poland in particular, the company may either lose its investment through government expropriation or find itself unable to get profits out of the country. Given that the company will have to invest approximately $20 million, the venture could seriously endanger the company's financial status.

Andrzej understands these risks but believes that with the help of an international management consultant, he can identify and minimize the problems. "I'm determined to push ahead," he told the banker, "and if there is a good chance of making this project a success, I'm going to Gdansk."

Questions

1. What are some of the political risks that Andrzej's firm will face if he decides to go ahead with this venture? Identify and describe two or three.

2. Using Figure 10–4, what strategy would you recommend that the firm use? Why?

3. In his negotiations with the Polish government, what suggestions or guidelines would you offer to Andrzej? Identify and describe two or three.

315

Chapter 11

MANAGEMENT DECISION AND CONTROL

OBJECTIVES OF THE CHAPTER

Although they are not directly related to internationalization, decision making and controlling are two management functions that play critical roles in international operations. In **decision making,** a manager chooses a course of action among alternatives. In **controlling,** the manager evaluates results in relation to plans or objectives and decides what action, if any, to take. How these functions are carried out is influenced by the international context. For example, the amount of decision-making authority given to subsidiaries is influenced by a number of international factors, such as the philosophy of the company and the amount of competition in the local environment. These factors may result in one international unit's having much more decision-making authority than another. Similarly, the tools and techniques that are used to control one subsidiary may differ from those used to control another.

This chapter examines the different decision-making and controlling management functions used by MNCs, notes some of the major factors that account for differences between these functions, and identifies the major challenges of the years ahead. The specific objectives of this chapter are:

1. **PROVIDE** comparative examples of decision making in different countries.

2. **PRESENT** some of the major factors affecting the degree of decision-making authority given to overseas units.

3. **COMPARE** and **CONTRAST** direct controls with indirect controls.

4. **DESCRIBE** some of the major differences in the ways that MNCs control operations.

5. **DISCUSS** some of the specific performance measures that are used to control international operations.

The World of *BusinessWeek*

BusinessWeek

BMW

Like Clockwork, BMW Is Rolling Out a New Model Every Three Months as It Guns for the Top Spot Among Premium Carmakers. But Will the Brand Suffer?

The lofty new modern art museum in Munich boasts a world-class collection of art, design, and architecture. But on May 19, the specially invited guests weren't there to gawk at the Picassos and Mirós. They were assembled to appraise the art Bavarians love best: The latest model from Bayerische Motoren Werke. More than 100 German car dealers crowded around the revamped 5 Series sedan, the heart of the BMW franchise. They gazed approvingly at the sleek surfaces and listened as engineers described the tight handling of the new steering and stability systems. Looming over the proceedings was a 10-meter high sculpture celebrating the beauty of auto design, created by none other than Christopher Bangle, the controversial American designer of BMW's new look and godfather of the latest 5.

Super-theatrical? Well, sure. But to the auto world, the latest Bimmer to hit the road is always a subject worthy of high drama. The Internet chat rooms of the global car-buff community have been buzzing about the fifth-generation 5 Series for months now. And they have a lot more to talk about than the latest rendition of BMW's biggest money-maker. The Munich company is rolling out a new or updated model nearly every three months through 2005 in a ramp-up more ambitious than anything the company has attempted before. "The [new] product initiative is critical to our future

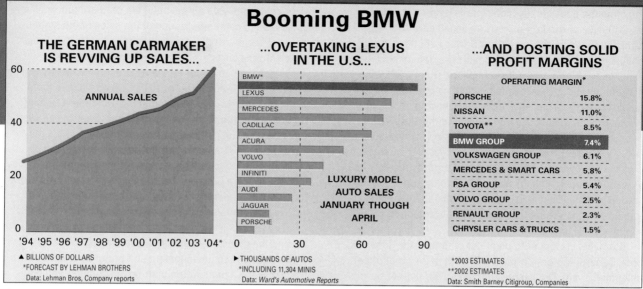

Booming BMW

THE GERMAN CARMAKER IS REVVING UP SALES...

ANNUAL SALES

▲ BILLIONS OF DOLLARS
*FORECAST BY LEHMAN BROTHERS
Data: Lehman Bros, Company reports

...OVERTAKING LEXUS IN THE U.S...

BMW*
LEXUS
MERCEDES
CADILLAC
ACURA
VOLVO
INFINITI
AUDI
JAGUAR
PORSCHE

LUXURY MODEL AUTO SALES JANUARY THOUGH APRIL

▶ THOUSANDS OF AUTOS
*INCLUDING 11,304 MINIS
Data: Ward's Automotive Reports

...AND POSTING SOLID PROFIT MARGINS

OPERATING MARGIN*	
PORSCHE	15.8%
NISSAN	11.0%
TOYOTA**	8.5%
BMW GROUP	7.4%
VOLKSWAGEN GROUP	6.1%
MERCEDES & SMART CARS	5.8%
PSA GROUP	5.4%
VOLVO GROUP	2.5%
RENAULT GROUP	2.3%
CHRYSLER CARS & TRUCKS	1.5%

*2003 ESTIMATES
**2002 ESTIMATES
Data: Smith Barney Citigroup, Companies

Source: www.businessweek.com/magazine/content/03_23/b3836005_mz044.htm

success," says BMW Chief Executive Helmut Panke. His goal: expand annual sales by 40% over the next five years, to 1.4 million cars, and beat out Mercedes-Benz as the No. 1 maker of premium cars in the world. "We won't give up, and we don't rest on our laurels," says the 56-year-old Panke. "We won't accept the position of No. 2."

Panke, a nuclear physicist by training who is passionate about cars, is pushing BMW into high gear. If the acceler-ated rollout works, BMW's new raft of models will power the carmaker to a new level of prominence and profitability in the global industry. But as factories ramp up production levels and juggle an increasingly complex variety of models, BMW will have to fight harder than ever to keep its margins and maintain the quality that underlies its success.

It all depends on how BMW's vaunted engineers and workers respond to the challenge. The expansion is well under way. In January, the company unveiled the new $377,760 Rolls-Royce Phantom, for which BMW is still build-ing an exclusive dealer network. The $37,760 Z4 roadster, which arrived in the U.S. at the end of 2002, hits European showrooms this spring, together with a diesel version of the Mini, the old British subcompact that under BMW's owner-ship is fast becoming a cult car. Next comes the 5 Series sedan, which goes to market in July. In the fall, the X3, a downsized sport-utility vehicle, makes its debut. At yearend, a revival of the high-performance 6 Series coupe hits the road, featuring some of BMW's most powerful engines.

In the fall of 2004, dealers will get their first deliveries of the new 1 Series subcompact that will go head-to-head with the Audi 3, the Mercedes A-Class, and the high-end versions of Volkswagen's Golf. Next year, BMW will intro-duce a 6 Series convertible and a station wagon version of the new 5 Series.

It's a high-speed shift from a carmaker that 10 years ago churned out just a handful of models—essentially the 3, 5, and 7 series. But remaking BMW became an imperative in the 1990s as the global auto market fragmented into hot new niches, and demand for luxury sedans—the company's core business—started to shrink as a percentage of total auto sales. "We can't make cars anymore that are three differently sized slices of the same sausage," says Panke.

But can Panke keep his highly tuned company on track as it accelerates? "The core strength of BMW will be chal-lenged," says Peter Soliman, vice-president at Booz Allen Hamilton Inc. in Düsseldorf. Management is being stretched to the limit, as BMW builds a new, $1.5 billion factory in Leipzig at breakneck pace. The Leipzig plant, slated for inauguration at the end of 2004, will employ 5,500 workers: the first 400 are already being trained in BMW's complex production methods.

Few expect a major product blunder from the company's highly esteemed Bavarian engineers. Even the top-of-the-line 7 Series sedan, which at first raised howls of criticism for a provocatively imposing trunk design and for its complicated electronic information system, has outsold its predecessor during its first full year on the market.

However, many are betting that BMW's vaunted profit margins will take a hit, at least in the short run. Although Panke vows earnings will be flat in 2003, analysts warn that they could slip by as much as 10%, as marketing costs peak this year on top of higher R&D spending. Panke's bet as-sumes turbocharged growth in the second half, prompted in part by the new 5 Series. The growing strength of the euro also poses a risk to BMW's dollar-denominated earnings. The company is hedged nearly 100% against its dollar risk this year and 60% for 2004—but only 30% for 2005.

317

The more pressing question: Can an ever-bigger BMW maintain the consistently high returns it once achieved with its exclusive portfolio? For starters, small cars such as the Mini, launched in 2001, and the 1 Series subcompact typically earn lower margins than do midsize sedans and luxury limousines. "Compared with volume producers, BMW's manufacturing costs are much higher, its product development process more costly, and its purchasing costs higher," warns Goldman, Sachs & Co. analyst Keith Hayes in a recent report. Chief Financial Officer Stefan Krause insists BMW will wring cost savings on the 1 Series to maintain its high margins. As for the Mini, he says profits are "way beyond our forecast," thanks to unexpectedly strong sales of loaded models. Buyers are snapping up options from navigation systems to sunroofs, ponying up as much as $35,000 for the cheeky little car.

But rivals are eager to point out other pitfalls. Robert A. Lutz, General Motors Corp. vice-chairman for product development, says Cadillac will not follow the path of German luxury brands in the march to obtain higher sales volumes: "After a couple of 1 Series, they'll have to bring in another brand on top to add prestige," he says. "The 1 Series will diminish the brand in the eyes of 7 Series buyers." Panke is adamant that future growth won't tarnish the BMW badge. "We are not competing with the mass market," he says.

BMW already may be showing some early signs of margin stress. Analysts warn the company has resorted to an aggressive leasing strategy to bolster sales in a weakening market in the U.S. and Europe, and to shore up aging models. That's standard industry practice, to be sure. But up to 75% of its luxury 7 Series sedans and 50% of the 5 Series are leased in the U.S. The company makes its profit by selling the car at the end of the lease to the leaseholder, a BMW dealer, or others.

But there's a risk. If the sale price of the leased cars doesn't match BMW's high residual value estimate, then the company could suffer a lower return on those cars than it has traditionally achieved. And while BMW enjoys some of the highest residual values in the industry, often running over 60% for a three-year-old car, it's unclear what will happen to values if an increasing number of leased cars hit the market down the road. Deutsche Bank recently calculated an implied incentive of around $4,300 in the 7 Series lease rates. "The bottom line from our analysis shows clearly that in the U.S., BMW is currently offering the most aggressive leasing terms," says Deutsche analyst Christian Breitsprecher in a recent report. Not so, says BMW's Krause—the leasing business is not being used to ratchet up subsidies on sales. For starters, he says, analysts' calculations use the original price for older models—models that don't apply to BMW's revamped lineup.

BMW is also redoubling efforts to keep costs down by sharing components across similar-sized cars, such as the 5 Series, the X5 and the 6 Series, as well as the 3 Series, the X3, and the 1 Series. The upcoming 1 Series will share about 60% of its components with the 3 Series. That will save costs, analysts agree, but if the cars are too similar, it could lead to a cannibalization of the sales of the higher-priced 3 Series. That's already happened at Volkswagen, which shares parts across a variety of brands.

As costs come under pressure, preserving quality will be critical. In the first quarter of 2003, BMW's Munich plant won the J.D. Power & Associates Inc. Gold Plant Quality Award. But in the premium car segment, blunders infuriate drivers more and get big headlines. BMW found out the hard way in 2001 when it introduced an innovative knob called the iDrive to control a slew of functions on the dashboard. Software problems with the iDrive left many owners fuming as their new, $69,000 sedans sat in the shop for weeks for software upgrades.

The real risk lies in the new models soon to hit streets around the globe. To speed the upcoming X3 to market, BMW outsourced development and production to Austria's Magna Steyr, a unit of Canadian-based supplier and engineering services giant Magna International Inc. Magna Steyr is dedicating an entire factory in Graz to making up to 150,000 X3s a year. Auto experts say the move could be an innovative alternative to building new plants, but warn that the strategy leaves BMW with only limited control over the final product.

Despite the risks, many are betting the Bavarian champion can deliver. BMW's factories are considered the most flexible and most productive in Germany; its suppliers are the industry's best; and the workforce among the industry's most talented.

BMW's obsession with performance and brand image helped the German auto maker close the yawning gap with Lexus in the U.S. in the 1990s. Munich headquarters read the message to improve quality and customer care loud and clear. BMW now offers a four-year warranty, including maintenance and service, in the price of the car, cutting out complaints that occasional technological glitches made the brand extremely expensive to maintain. "We took the pain out of owning a car," says Tom Purves, CEO of BMW North America.

Development teams that pore over everything from market feedback to new innovations are encouraged to engage in "friendly fighting" to decide the vital characteristics of a new BMW. The development of the new 5 Series shows the concept in action. As the team convened in 1998, marketers demanded more leg room in the back seat and more trunk space: Buyers of the old model had complained it was too small to hold several golf bags. The members of the engineering staff protested. Their goal was a car that accelerated faster and handled even more smoothly. Added weight and length were taboo for the gearheads.

In the end, both sides won. The muscular-looking 5 Series is not only taller, longer, and lighter than its predecessor, it's packed with new technologies that boost engine power, torque, handling, safety, and fuel efficiency. Drive the

231-horsepower 530i 5 Series around a set of sharp curves and it grips the road more like a sports car than a sedan, with its smooth engine effortlessly delivering top acceleration and tight control. One technological coup: a system called "active front steering," which reduces the effort needed to turn at slow speeds and makes the steering more sensitive and agile at high speeds. The powerful front end was designed to appear deep and short to give it a "low, hunkered look," that matches the increased performance, says designer Bangle. A smoother integration of the trunk and angular rear lights gives the rear a racy attitude.

BMW's brand image is tied tightly to such innovation. "BMW really captured the performance space in the market for themselves. They own it," says AutoPacific's Peterson. Sportiness and style made a convert of Debra J. Rosman, senior director of marketing for the NBA's Miami Heat. Rosman traded in her Lexus RX300 SUV for a BMW X5 with leather seats, wood trim, and an on-board computer. "BMW is hipper and cooler," says Rosman, whose monthly lease payments are well above the $450 she paid for the Lexus. Even rivals get the point. "I have to give BMW credit for consistency in their message," says Mike Wells, vice-president for marketing at Toyota's Lexus Div. The engine and styling variations offered by BMW are "clearly an advantage," he adds.

Of course, Lexus is not about to concede. Neither is Mercedes, whose elegant E-Class still outsells BMW's 5 Series worldwide. Mercedes' Stuttgart designers gave the 2002 remake of the E-Class a sportier line, shooting for the more dynamic brand image that BMW has played to advantage. Then there's Audi, which aims to make its cars even more fun than Bimmers, and a whole new generation of models at Cadillac. It's going to be a helluva race.

By Gail Edmondson in Munich, with Chris Palmeri in Los Angeles, Brian Grow in Atlanta, and Christine Tierney in Detroit

---

Source: **From "BMW,"** *BusinessWeek,* **(n.d), 2003, online edition. Copyright © 2003 by the McGraw-Hill Companies, Inc. www.businessweek.com. Reprinted with permission.**

The opening news story explains how BMW is expanding its product lines in an attempt to grow sales and achieve a higher level of profitability. This expansion strategy will have to be carefully managed in order to protect the solid image and reputation of the BMW brand and to avoid compromising quality. In the face of mounting global competition in the form of new offerings from Mercedes-Benz and Toyota's Lexus line, BMW must rely on its management control systems and decision processes to meet the needs of its worldwide operations. For example, decision-making norms in the U.K. will be carried out differently from those in Mexico. Likewise, operational controls such as management styles and employee performance requirements will vary from one country to another. To achieve its goal of expanding annual sales 40 percent by 2008, BMW must seamlessly integrate its strategy and implement it through decision-making and control systems that ensure high quality and performance.

■ Decision and Control Linkages

Decision making and **controlling** are two vital and often interlinked functions of international management. For example, in the mid-1990s Dell Computer's market share in Europe was a scant 2.5 percent and the company's troubles on the continent helped produce the firm's first-ever loss. Five years later Dell was one of the fastest-growing PC makers in Western Europe, taking market share from such major rivals as IBM. How did the company accomplish this feat? By fine-tuning its U.S. approach for success and installing new managers to make the right decisions and better control its German and French operations. For example, Dell's managers made the decision to continue focusing on direct selling to European consumers. Many critics claimed the U.S. approach would never work with Europeans. Yet this decision resulted in sales growth five times faster than that of the market. Now the challenge is to control this growth to maintain quality and profitability.

Another example is provided by Boeing and General Motors, two well-known MNCs that signed major deals with the Chinese government. Boeing agreed to sell the Chinese Civil Aviation Administration five 777-200 jetliners for approximately $685 million; and General Motors finalized a $1.3 billion joint venture with a Shanghai automotive company

decision making
The process of choosing a course of action among alternatives.

controlling
The process of evaluating results in relation to plans or objectives and deciding what action, if any, to take.

management decision and control
The choice of a course of action among alternatives and the evaluation of results of those choices in relation to plans or objectives.

to build Buick Century and Regal cars in China. The Boeing deal came after the giant aerospace MNC had been shut out of a number of contract bids in China and offers strong promise of even more business from the Chinese government. The GM deal is a 50/50 venture between the automotive MNC and the Shanghai Automotive Industry Corporation, a state-owned company. Both of these developments are viewed by the management decision makers of the respective American-based MNCs as opportunities to further open the China market and with proper controls increase their sales growth and profitability.[1]

Still another example is offered by Universal Studios Japan. In an effort to attract visitors to its Osaka location, this new theme park was specially built based on feedback from Japanese tourists at Universal parks in Orlando and Los Angeles. The company wanted to learn what these visitors liked and disliked and then use this information in its Osaka park. One theme clearly emerged: The Japanese wanted an authentic American experience but also expected the park to cater to their own cultural preferences. In the process, thousands of decisions were made regarding what to include and what to leave out. For example, seafood pizza and gumbo-style soup were put on the menu, but a fried-shrimp concoction with colored rice crackers was rejected. In a musical number based on the movie *Beetlejuice,* it was decided that the main character should talk in Japanese and his sidekicks would speak and sing in English. The decision to put in a restaurant called Shakin's, based on the 1906 San Francisco earthquake, was not a good idea because Osaka has had terrible earthquakes that killed thousands of people.

Other decisions were made to give the park a uniquely Japanese flavor. The nation's penchant for buying edible souvenirs inspired a 6,000-square-foot confection shop packed with Japanese sweets such as dinosaur-shaped bean cakes. Restrooms include Japanese-style squat toilets. Even the park layout caters to the tendency of Japanese crowds to flow clockwise in an orderly manner, contrary to more-chaotic U.S. crowds that steer right. And on the Jurassic Park water slide, millions of dollars were spent to widen the landing pond, redesign boat hulls, and install underwater wave-damping panels to reduce spray. Why? Many fastidious Japanese don't like to get wet, even on what's billed as one of the world's biggest water slides.[2]

Over the next few years, as Universal Studios Japan evaluates park revenues and feedback from visitors, it will be able to judge how well it is doing in giving customers an American experience in an environment that also addresses cultural considerations.

■ Decision-Making Process and Challenges

As indicated by the foregoing examples, a number of decision-making areas are receiving attention in international management. One of these is the locus of decision making. If decision making is centralized, most important decisions are made at the top; if decision making is decentralized, decisions are delegated to operating personnel. Another issue is how decision making is used to help the subsidiary respond to the economic and political demands of the country. Sometimes, these decisions are heavily economic in orientation and may concentrate on things such as return on investment for overseas operations. Other times, decisions are a result of cultural differences. For example, Ford Motor designed and built an inexpensive vehicle, the Ikon, for the Indian market. Engineers took apart the Ford Fiesta and totally rebuilt the car to address buyer needs. Some of the changes that were made included raising the amount of rear headroom to accommodate men in turbans, adjusting doors so that they opened wider in order to avoid catching the flowing saris of women, fitting intake valves to avoid auto flooding during the monsoon season, toughening shock absorbers to handle the pockmarked city streets, and adjusting the air-conditioning system to deal with the intense summer heat.[3] As a result of these decisions, the car is selling very well in India.

The way in which decision making is carried out will be influenced by a number of factors. Comparative examples offer one of the best ways to illustrate some of these differences.

Comparative Examples of Decision Making

Do decision-making philosophies and practices differ from country to country? Research shows that to some extent they do, although there also is evidence that many international operations, regardless of foreign or domestic ownership, use similar decision-making norms.

Most British organizations are highly decentralized. One major reason is that many upper-level managers do not understand the technical details of the business. Top-level managers depend heavily on middle managers to handle much of the decision making by decentralizing to their level.

The French use a different approach. One observer noted that many top French managers graduated from the Grandes Écoles and lack confidence in their middle managers.[4] As a result, decision making tends to be centralized.

In Germany, managers focus more on productivity and quality of goods and services than on managing subordinates. In addition, management education is highly technical, and a legal system called **codetermination** requires workers and their managers to discuss major decisions. As a result, German MNCs tend to be fairly centralized, autocratic, and hierarchical. Scandinavian countries also have codetermination, but the Swedes focus much more on quality of work life and the importance of the individual in the organization. As a result, decision making in Sweden is decentralized and participative.

codetermination
A legal system that requires workers and their managers to discuss major decisions.

The Japanese are somewhat different from the Europeans. They make heavy use of a decision-making process called **ringisei,** or decision making by consensus.

ringisei
A Japanese term that means "decision making by consensus."

> Under this system any changes in procedures and routines, tactics, and even strategies of a firm are organized by those directly concerned with those changes. The final decision is made at the top level after an elaborate examination of the proposal through successively higher levels in the management hierarchy, and results in acceptance or rejection of a decision only through consensus at every echelon of the management structure.[5]

Sometimes Japanese consensus decision making can be very time-consuming. However, in practice most Japanese managers know how to respond to "suggestions" from the top and to act accordingly—thus saving a great deal of time. Many outsiders misunderstand how Japanese managers make such decisions. In Japan, what should be done is called **tatemae;** what one really feels, which may be quite different, is **honne.** Because it is vital to do what others expect in a given context, situations arise that often strike Westerners as a game of charades. Nevertheless, it is very important in Japan to play out the situation according to what each person believes others expect to happen.

tatemae
A Japanese term that means "doing the right thing" according to the norm.

honne
A Japanese term that means "what one really wants to do."

To clarify this complicated but important Japanese decision-making process, here is a specific example offered by a Japanese scholar of a Mr. Seward, a Western employee of a Japanese firm:

> [Mr. Seward] joined a meeting as one of eight employees tasked with deciding where to go for a company trip. When the result of the vote was taken, it appeared that the group favored going to a place named Izu. At this point, one of the president's secretaries spoke up, saying, "The president wants to visit Suwa." In a tense atmosphere a second vote was taken, considering the president's opinion, and it turned out that the entire group, except Seward, voted for Suwa. Mr. Seward protested the procedure, insisting that, if members were forced to follow the president's opinion, there was no point in meeting and voting, but his objections were overridden and the company trip was set for Suwa.[6]

Many Westerners would ask why the president did not simply send out a memo announcing the destination of the meeting. The answer is that, for the president, having the meeting and taking a vote was *tatemae*—the right thing to do according to the normal procedure for reaching this kind of decision. At the same time, going to Suwa was *honne*—what the president wanted to do. Similarly, for the Japanese members of the committee, voting for Suwa was *tatemae* once the president's desires were made clear, while going to Izu was *honne,* what the employees really wanted to do. Obviously such culturally based subtleties make understanding whether decision making is centralized or decentralized across cultures very difficult.

MNCs based in the United States tend to use fairly centralized decision making in managing their overseas units. This approach provides the necessary control for developing a worldwide strategy, because it ensures that all units are operating according to the overall strategic plan.

As indicated by these examples, a number of decision-making approaches are used around the world. Most evidence, however, indicates that the overall trend is toward centralization. For example, in both delegation and decision-making authority of overseas subsidiaries, there is evidence of a fair degree of centralization in areas such as marketing policies, financial matters, use of expatriate personnel, and decisions on production capacity. The results of a comparative study are summarized as follows:

> The convergence in organizational practices in general, and decision making in particular, is taking place rapidly. This can be seen from the results of our recent study of United States, German, British, Japanese, and Swedish multinational companies. The results showed the United States management practices concerning decision making are the norms being followed by other nations. Other countries' practices correlated strongly with those of United States practices.[7]

A number of reasons help to account for this trend toward centralized decision making in international management areas. One is advanced information technology as well as the desire to increase economies of scale and to attain higher operational efficiency. Such centralized decision making, however, can stifle the creativity and flexibility needed by the subsidiary. In resolving this dilemma, effective MNCs try to manage each overseas operation on its own merits.

Factors Affecting Decision-Making Authority

A number of factors will influence international managers' conclusions about retaining or delegating decision making to a subsidiary. Table 11–1 lists some of the most important situational factors, and the following discussion looks at each in detail.

Company size influences decision making: Large organizations have a greater need for coordination and integration of operations. To ensure that all subsidiaries are effectively managed, the MNC will centralize the authority for a number of critical decisions. This

Table 11–1
Factors That Influence Centralization or Decentralization of Decision Making in Subsidiary Operations

Encourage Centralization	Encourage Decentralization
Large size	Small size
Large capital investment	Small capital investment
Relatively high importance to MNC	Relatively low importance to MNC
Highly competitive environment	Stable environment
Strong volume-to-unit-cost relationship	Weak volume-to-unit-cost relationship
High degree of technology	Moderate to low degree of technology
Strong importance attached to brand name, patent rights, etc.	Little importance attached to brand name, patent rights, etc.
Low level of product diversification	High level of product diversification
Homogeneous product lines	Heterogeneous product lines
Small geographic distance between home office and subsidiary	Large geographic distance between home office and subsidiary
High interdependence between the units	Low interdependence between the units
Fewer highly competent managers in host country	More highly competent managers in host country
Much experience in international business	Little experience in international business

centralization is designed to increase the overall efficiency of operations, and to the extent that centralization creates the desired uniformity and coordination, efficiency is increased.

The greater the MNC's capital investment, the more likely it is that decision making will be centralized. The home office wants to keep a tight rein on its investment and to ensure that everything is running smoothly. The subsidiary manager will be required to submit periodic reports, and on-site visits from home-office personnel are quite common.

The more important the overseas operation is to the MNC, the closer the MNC will control it. Home-office management will monitor performance carefully, and the subsidiary manager usually will not be allowed to make any major decisions without first clearing them with the MNC senior management. In fact, in managing important overseas operations, the home-office managers typically will appoint someone who they know will respond to their directives, and they will regard this individual as an extension of the central management staff.

In domestic situations, when competition increases, management will decentralize authority and give the local manager greater decision-making authority. This reduces the time that is needed for responding to competitive threats. In the international arena, however, sometimes the opposite approach is used. As competition increases and profit margins are driven down, home-office management often seeks to standardize product and marketing decisions to reduce cost and maintain profitability. More and more upper-level operating decisions are made by central management and merely implemented by the subsidiary, although in recent years there has been a trend toward decentralizing authority and letting those decisions be made at the local level.

If there is a strong volume-to-unit-cost relationship, firms that are able to produce large quantities will have lower cost per unit than those that produce smaller amounts. Under these conditions, home-office management typically will centralize decision making and assume authority over sourcing and marketing-related matters as well as overall strategy. This helps to ensure that the subsidiary's unit cost remains low.

The more sophisticated the level of technology, the greater is the degree of centralized decision making. The MNC will attempt to protect these resources by making technology-related decisions at the home office. This is particularly true for high-tech, research-intensive firms such as computer and pharmaceutic companies, which do not want their technology controlled at the local level.

If strong importance is attached to brand name, patent rights, and so forth, decision making likely will be centralized. The MNC will want to protect its rights by making these types of decisions in the home office.

The greater the amount of product and service diversification, the greater is the decentralization of the decision-making process, because the MNC typically will not have the staff or the resources for coordinating these diversified offerings on a worldwide basis. The home-office management will rely on the subsidiary management to handle this task. In addition, as the overseas unit becomes increasingly skilled in manufacturing and marketing products at the local level, the chance of the home management's recentralizing decision making becomes more remote.

If product and service lines are heterogeneous, differences often exist in the socio-economic, political, legal, and cultural environments in the various countries where the firm is operating. These differences typically result in the MNC's turning over operating control to the local subsidiaries. In addition, the greater the differences in the environment between the home country and the subsidiary, the more likely it is that the MNC will decentralize the decision-making process.

If the subsidiary and home office are far apart, decentralization is more likely than if the subsidiary is located near the home office. There is evidence that U.S. subsidiaries in North America are more closely controlled than those in South America and that those in the Far East are least controlled of all. The farther away the subsidiary, the more likely it is that the home office will give it increased autonomy.

The greater the degree of interdependence among the units, typically the greater is the centralization of decision making. The home office will want to coordinate and integrate the units into an effective system, usually from headquarters.

If the subsidiary has highly competent local managers, the chances for decentralization are increased, because the home office has more confidence in delegating to the local level and less to gain by making all the important decisions. Conversely, if the local managers are inexperienced or not highly effective, the MNC likely will centralize decision making and make many of the major decisions at headquarters.

If the firm has had a great deal of international experience, its operations likely will be more centralized. This finding is in accord with the research cited earlier, which shows a convergence toward more centralization by multinational firms.

In some areas of operation, MNCs tend to retain decision making at the top (centralization); other areas fall within the domain of subsidiary management (decentralization). It is most common to find finance, research and development, and strategic planning decisions being made at MNC headquarters, and the subsidiaries working within the parameters established by the home office. In addition, when the subsidiary is selling new products in growing markets, centralized decision making is more likely. As the product line matures and the subsidiary managers gain experience, however, the company will start to rely more on decentralized decision making. These decisions involve planning and budgeting systems, performance evaluations, assignment of managers to the subsidiary, and use of coordinating committees to mesh the operations of the subsidiary with the worldwide operations of the MNC. The right degree of centralized or decentralized decision making can be critical to the success of the MNC.

Total Quality Management Decisions

total quality management (TQM)
An organizational strategy and the accompanying techniques that result in the delivery of high-quality products or services to customers.

To achieve world-class competitiveness, MNCs are finding that a commitment to total quality management is critical. **Total quality management (TQM)** is an organizational strategy and accompanying techniques that result in delivery of high-quality products or services to customers.[8] The concept and techniques of TQM, which were introduced in Chapter 8 in relation to strategic planning, also are relevant to decision making and controlling.

One of the primary areas where TQM is having a big impact is in manufacturing. For example, in recent years, U.S. automakers have greatly improved the quality of their cars, but the Japanese have continuously improved quality and thus still have the lead. A number of TQM techniques have been successfully applied to improve the quality of manufactured goods. One is the use of concurrent engineering/interfunctional teams in which designers, engineers, production specialists, and customers work together to develop new products. This approach involves all the necessary parties and overcomes what used to be an all-too-common procedure: The design people would tell the manufacturing group what to produce, and the latter would send the finished product to retail stores for sale to the customer. Today, MNCs taking a TQM approach are customer-driven. They use TQM techniques to tailor their output to customer needs, and they require the same approach from their own suppliers.[9] IBM followed a similar approach in developing its AS/400 computer systems. Customer advisory councils were created to provide input, test the product, and suggest refinements. The result was one of the most successful product launches in the company's history.

empowerment
The process of giving individuals and teams the resources, information, and authority they need to develop ideas and effectively implement them.

A particularly critical issue is how much decision making to delegate to subordinates. TQM uses employee **empowerment.** Individuals and teams are encouraged to generate and implement ideas for improving quality and are given the decision-making authority and necessary resources and information to implement them. Many MNCs have had outstanding success with empowerment. For example, General Electric credits employee empowerment for cutting in half the time needed to change product-mix production of its dishwashers in response to market demand, and Kodak used the empowerment of its workers to increase productivity by teaching them how to inspect their own work, keep track of their own performance, and even fix their own machines.

Another TQM technique that MNCs are successfully employing to develop and maintain world-class competitiveness is rewards and recognition. These range from increases in pay and benefits to the use of merit pay, discretionary bonuses, pay-for-skills and knowledge plans, plaques, and public recognition. The important thing to realize is that the rewards and recognition approaches that work well in one country may be ineffective in another. For example, individual recognition in the United States may be appropriate and valued by workers, but in Japan, group rewards are more appropriate as Japanese do not like to be singled out for personal praise. Similarly, although putting a picture or plaque on the wall to honor an individual is common practice in the United States, these rewards are frowned on in Finland, for they remind the workers that their neighbors, the Russians, used this system to encourage people to increase output (but not necessarily quality) and now the Russian economy is in shambles.

Still another technique associated with TQM is the use of ongoing training to achieve continual improvement. This training takes a wide variety of forms, ranging from statistical quality control techniques to team meetings designed to generate ideas for streamlining operations and eliminating waste. In all cases, the objective is to apply what the Japanese call **kaizen,** or continuous improvement. By adopting a TQM perspective and applying the techniques discussed earlier, MNCs find that they can both develop and maintain a worldwide competitive edge. A good example is Zytec, the world-class, Minnesota-based manufacturer of power supplies. The customer base for Zytec ranges from the United States to Japan to Europe. One way in which the firm ensures that it maintains a total quality perspective is to continually identify client demands and then work to exceed these expectations. Another is to totally revise the company's philosophy and beliefs regarding what quality is all about and how it needs to be implemented. Table 11–2 provides some examples of the new thinking that is now emerging regarding quality.

kaizen
A Japanese term that means "continuous improvement."

Table 11–2
The Emergence of New Beliefs Regarding Quality

Old Myth	New Truth
Quality is the responsibility of the people in the Quality Control Department.	Quality is everyone's job.
Training is costly.	Training does not cost; it saves.
New quality programs have high initial costs.	The best quality programs do not have up-front costs.
Better quality will cost the company a lot of money.	As quality goes up, costs come down.
The measurement of data should be kept to a minimum.	An organization cannot have too much relevant data on hand.
It is human to make mistakes.	Perfection—total customer satisfaction—is a standard that should be vigorously pursued.
Some defects are major and should be addressed, but many are minor and can be ignored.	No defects are acceptable, regardless of whether they are major or minor.
Quality improvements are made in small, continuous steps.	In improving quality, both small and large improvements are necessary.
Quality improvement takes time.	Quality does not take time; it saves time.
Haste makes waste.	Thoughtful speed improves quality.
Quality programs are best oriented toward areas such as products and manufacturing.	Quality is important in all areas, including administration and service.
After a number of quality improvements, customers are no longer able to see additional improvements.	Customers are able to see all improvements, including those in price, delivery, and performance.
Good ideas can be found throughout the organization.	Good ideas can be found everywhere, including in the operations of competitors and organizations providing similar goods and services.
Suppliers need to be price competitive.	Suppliers need to be quality competitive.

Source: Reported in Richard M. Hodgetts, *Measures of Quality and High Performance* (New York: American Management Association, 1998), p. 14.

Indirectly related to TQM is ISO 9000: International Standards Organization (ISO) certification to ensure quality products and services. Areas that are examined by the ISO certification team include design (product or service specifications), process control (instruction for manufacturing or service functions), purchasing, service (e.g., instructions for conducting after-sales service), inspection and testing, and training. ISO 9000 certification is becoming a necessary prerequisite to doing business in the EU, but it also is increasingly used as a screening criterion for bidding on contracts or getting business in the United States and other parts of the world. For example, after a year of hard work, Foxboro Corporation, based in Massachusetts, obtained certification, and its business greatly increased.

Decisions for Attacking the Competition

Another series of key decisions relates to MNC actions that are designed to attack the competition and gain a foothold in world markets. "International Management in Action: Kodak Goes Digital, Making Film Obsolete" gives an example. Another is General Motors' decision to establish production operations on a worldwide basis and to be a major player throughout Asia, Australia, Europe, and South America, as well as in select areas of Africa. As a result of this decision, the company is now closing U.S. factories and building new assembly plants abroad. Between 1995 and 1999 GM opened a host of new facilities including a plant in Brazil that has an annual capacity of 120,000 units, as well as factories in Poland, India, Mexico, Thailand, and Shanghai, each of which has annual capacity of 100,000 units. By locating closer to the final customer and offering a well-designed and efficiently built car, the company has been able to increase its worldwide market share, thus more than offsetting the downturn it has encountered in the U.S. market, where overall share has dropped below 30 percent.

GM's expansion decisions, in many cases, have been designed to help it capture the lower end of the market with small, inexpensive cars. However, the company is also intent on appealing to the upper-level buyer as well, as seen by its decision to sell Cadillacs in Europe. This market is quite different from that in the United States. European buyers of luxury cars often settle for far less comfort and expect far more handling and performance. GM hopes to appeal to these buyers with many of the changes it introduced into the Cadillac Sevilles that it is selling in Europe. Differences between this car and the version marketed in the United States include (1) right-hand drive for the United Kingdom; (2) less interior clutter (e.g., unobtrusive cup holders); (3) simpler, more elegant interiors; (4) shorter overall length; (5) tighter suspension, wider wheel tracks, and better tires for high-speed driving; and (6) floor-mounted gearshift levers for automatic transmission.[10]

Will this decision result in greater sales for Cadillac in Europe? It is too early to tell, but the company's decision certainly does not have firms such as BMW or Mercedes concerned. The luxury-car market in Europe is highly competitive, and Europeans take pride in placing performance over comfort. Buyers like tight steering, rear-wheel drive, and smaller cars that provide greater gas mileage. Cadillac is not known for any of these. Nor does the car have a reputation for high-speed performance, something that people on the continent like, given that on European freeways it is common to find the traffic moving at 80–100 miles per hour.

Another example of decision making for attacking the competition is provided by BMW. While GM is trying to tap the upper market, BMW has made the decision to move down the line and gain small-car market share. The company is building small cars with a sales price in the range of $20,000. By sharing engines, gearboxes, and electrical systems from its other offerings, the firm intends to reduce its development and production costs and offer a reliable and competitively priced auto.[11] Other firms, including Mercedes and Audi, have done this and have not been particularly profitable, but BMW believes that it can succeed where they have not.

NEC offers a third example of how decision making is being used for attacking the competition. In 2001 the company held 8 percent of the world market for mobile transmitting infrastructure and was vying with major competitors such as Ericsson, Lucent, Nokia,

Kodak Goes Digital, Making Film Obsolete

Kodak has been attacking the competition in a number of ways. One has been to file a complaint with the U.S. government accusing its main competitor, Fuji, of blocking Kodak growth in the Japanese market and asking the administration to take steps to correct this situation. This is only a short-term strategy designed to increase the growth of Kodak film in one country, however. Of far more future importance are technological developments such as the emergence of inexpensive cameras that use digital technology, which will make film obsolete.

Under its current management, Kodak is in the throes of reorganizing and focusing its efforts on new growth areas while continuing to extract as much sales and profit as possible from its current product lines. For example, the firm recently created a digital imaging unit, thus gathering most of the firm's digital talent into one division. Before this, efforts at digital product development were spread through the divisions. At the same time, Kodak is working to reignite overall growth by focusing on the Asian market. The company believes that it can double its growth rate in photography, a tough challenge given that the world market is growing very slowly.

The real focus of Kodak's effort is in digital technology, however, and the company's strategy in this area finally appears to be getting into focus. Still, this digital thrust will not be easy, because of the difficulty both in generating research and development breakthroughs and in marketing the new products. Some of Kodak's earlier efforts were anything but spectacular. For example, the photo-CD, which is a compact disk that Kodak developed to store photographs for viewing on TV screens or PC monitors, flopped as a consumer product. Buyers balked at paying $500 for a player that plugs into a TV plus $20 per disk. Fortunately, the company did find a ready market among small businesses such as desktop publishers and real estate agents, which used the unit to display their offerings. The lesson is clear: Creating a new technologic product is not enough; it also is important to carefully identify the market where it can be sold successfully.

Kodak knows that the industry is going digital and the film business eventually will die out. Therefore, the company must be prepared to meet the future with new products such as the digital camera. In the interim, the firm also must push ahead in the film business and with new camera offerings such as its single-use, throwaway camera, which really is nothing more than an inexpensive cardboard-and-plastic box with a roll of film inside. Kodak extended this line to include telephoto, panoramic, portrait, and underwater versions of the camera. Most recently the company acquired Ofoto Inc., a leading online photography service. This acquisition is designed to facilitate the move into the online photography market and to help stimulate more rapid adoption of digital and online services by providing users with an easy way to store, share, and print pictures online. Management hopes that all these efforts will help Kodak to attack the competition successfully while continuing to develop and perfect digital products that will appeal to the masses.

and Nortel. Most of NEC's revenues come from its contracts with NTT, Japan's phone monopoly. However, the company is moving aggressively into the worldwide arena. Its prowess in fiber optics resulted in its winning a big AT&T network installation contract, and as the demand for fiber optics increases, NEC intends to exploit this strength.[12] The firm recently announced that it had developed a fiber-optic cable that is four times more powerful than that currently on the market. The company is also a world leader in manufacturing mobile handsets and the semiconductors used in mobiles and other devices. Its folding phones, for example, account for 40 percent of the Internet-capable handset market in Japan, and NEC is now looking to expand its international sales of these products.

Intel is another good example. The company has made a number of interesting decisions designed to stymie the competition. One is to bring out a new version of its Pentium chip at a much lower-than-expected price and cut the prices of its other chips, thus creating a strong demand for its products and forcing competitors to cut their prices. In a market where overall demand has been slowing, this strategy wreaks havoc on the competition. At the same time, however, lower prices mean that Intel must sell more products in order to increase revenues. One of the ways in which the firm is trying to do this is with an extension of its Xeon microprocessor family, which is aimed at more powerful desktop workstations and server systems than the firm has targeted in the past. Intel's server offerings generally were used in relatively lightweight machines such as those that serve up Web pages. This new push is designed to provide chips that are used in midsize servers such as those that run databases, as well as in some larger systems used in mission-critical tasks. These machines typically cost millions of dollars and run on dozens of microprocessors operating in parallel.[13] The company also teamed up with Hewlett-Packard to develop the Itanium chip, which offers greater speed because it can process 64 bits of data at a time rather than 32 bits. Working with HP, Intel is building servers for telecommunications and making three-in-one chips that have the ability to radically reduce the size of cell phones and hand-held computers.

■ The Controlling Process

As indicated earlier in this chapter, controlling involves evaluating results in relation to plans or objectives and deciding what action to take. An excellent illustration is Mitsubishi's purchase of 80 percent of Rockefeller Center in the late 1980s. The Japanese firm paid $1.4 billion for this choice piece of Manhattan real estate, and it looked like a very wise decision. Over the next six years, however, depressed rental prices and rising maintenance costs resulted in Mitsubishi sinking an additional $500 million into the project. Finally, in late 1995, the company decided it had had enough and announced that it was walking away from the investment. Mitsubishi passed ownership to Rockefeller Center Properties Inc., the publicly traded real-estate investment trust that held the mortgage on the Center. The cost of keeping the properties was too great for the Japanese firm, which decided to cut its losses and focus efforts on more lucrative opportunities elsewhere.

Another example is provided by Dana Corporation, the giant auto parts supply company, which in the last few years sold off some of its units, bought others, and refocused its business. Among the units that Dana sold were its clutch and transmission operation and heavy frame operations. In each case the company's control process indicated that the unit had low return on sales or investment, slow growth, operating losses, or eroding market share. At the same time, Dana purchased a piston rings and cylinder liners unit, a transmission unit, and a couple of axle units. Today this $9 billion company provides complete integrated systems engineering to auto manufacturers worldwide, and it is the largest independent supplier of fluid transfer, fluid power, and materials transfer components and systems in the vehicular and industrial markets.[14] The firm is also able to build complete modular chassis assemblies that fit right into trucks and cars.[15] Thanks to its control function and to effective decision making, Dana has been able to succeed in a highly competitive industry.

Another example of how the control process is being used by MNCs is in the personal computer (PC) business. Until about five years ago, PCs were built using the traditional model shown in Figure 11–1. Today the direct-sales model and the hybrid model are the most common (see Figure 11–1). PC firms are finding that they must keep on the cutting edge more than any other industry because of the relentless pace of technological change. This is where the control function becomes especially critical for success. For example, stringent controls keep the inventory in the system as small as possible. PCs are manufactured using a just-in-time approach (as in the case of a customer who orders the unit and has it made to specifications) or an almost just-in-time approach (as in the case of a retailer who orders 30 units and sells them all within a few weeks). Because technology in the PC industry changes so quickly, any units that are not sold in retail outlets within 60 days may be outdated and must be severely discounted and sold for whatever the market will bear. In turn, these costs are often assumed by the manufacturer. As a result, PC manufacturers are very much inclined to build to order or to ship in quantities that can be sold quickly. In this way the firm's control system helps to ensure that inventory moves through the system and profitability does not suffer.[16]

In many ways, the control function is conceptually and practically similar to decision making. Like decision making, the approaches used by multinationals in controlling their operations have long been an area of interest. Of particular concern has been how companies attempt to control their overseas operations to become integrated, coordinated units. Unfortunately, a number of control problems arise: (1) The objectives of the overseas operation and the corporation conflict. (2) The objectives of joint-venture partners and corporate

| Figure 11–1 | **Models of PC Manufacturing** |

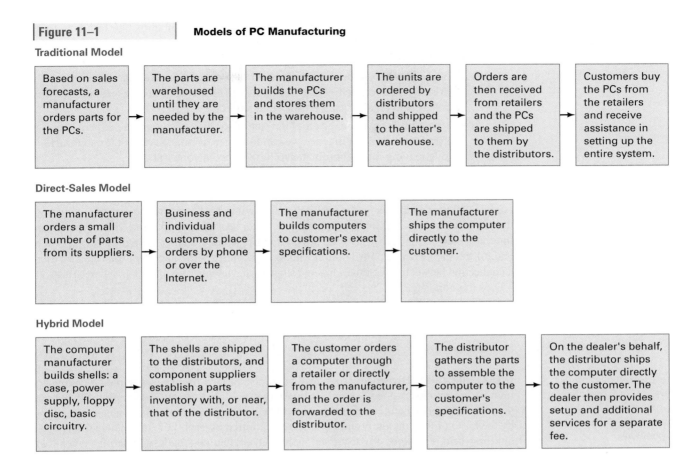

Traditional Model

Based on sales forecasts, a manufacturer orders parts for the PCs. → The parts are warehoused until they are needed by the manufacturer. → The manufacturer builds the PCs and stores them in the warehouse. → The units are ordered by distributors and shipped to the latter's warehouse. → Orders are then received from retailers and the PCs are shipped to them by the distributors. → Customers buy the PCs from the retailers and receive assistance in setting up the entire system.

Direct-Sales Model

The manufacturer orders a small number of parts from its suppliers. → Business and individual customers place orders by phone or over the Internet. → The manufacturer builds computers to customer's exact specifications. → The manufacturer ships the computer directly to the customer.

Hybrid Model

The computer manufacturer builds shells: a case, power supply, floppy disc, basic circuitry. → The shells are shipped to the distributors, and component suppliers establish a parts inventory with, or near, that of the distributor. → The customer orders a computer through a retailer or directly from the manufacturer, and the order is forwarded to the distributor. → The distributor gathers the parts to assemble the computer to the customer's specifications. → On the dealer's behalf, the distributor ships the computer directly to the customer. The dealer then provides setup and additional services for a separate fee.

management are not in accord. (3) Degrees of experience and competence in planning vary widely among managers running the various overseas units. (4) There are basic philosophic disagreements about the objectives and policies of international operations, largely because of cultural differences between home- and host-country managers. The following discussion examines the various types of control that are used in international operations and the approaches that are often employed in dealing with these types of problems.

Types of Control

There are two common, complementary ways of looking at how MNCs control operations. One way is by determining whether the enterprise chooses to use internal or external control in devising its overall strategy. The other is by looking at the ways in which the organization uses direct and indirect controls.

Internal and External Control   From an internal control standpoint, an MNC will focus on the things that it does best. At the same time, of course, management wants to ensure that there is a market for the goods and services that it is offering. So the company first needs to find out what the customers want and be prepared to respond appropriately. This requires an external control focus. Naturally, every MNC will give consideration to both internal and external perspectives of control. However, one is often given more attention than the other. In explaining this idea, Trompenaars and Hampden-Turner set forth four management views regarding how a control strategy should be devised and implemented:

1. No one dealing with customers is without a strategy of sorts. Our task is to find out which of these strategies work, which don't, and why. Devising our own strategy in the abstract and imposing it downwards only spreads confusion.

2. No one dealing with customers is without a strategy of sorts. Our task is to find out which of these strategies work and then create a master strategy from proven successful initiatives by encouraging and combining the best.

3. To be a leader is to be the chief deviser of strategy. Using all the experience, information, and intelligence we can mobilize, we need to devise an innovative strategy and then cascade it down the hierarchy.

4. To be a leader is to be the chief deviser of strategy. Using all the experience, information, and intelligence we can mobilize, we must create a broad thrust, while leaving it to subordinates to fit these to customer needs.

Trompenaars and Hampden-Turner ask managers to rank each of these four statements by placing a "1" next to the one they feel would most likely be used in their company, a "2" next to the second most likely, on down to a "4" next to the one that would be the last choice. This ranking helps managers better see whether they use an external or an internal control approach. Answer 1 focuses most strongly on an external-direct approach and rejects the internal control option. Answer 3 represents the opposite. Answer 2 affirms a connection between an external-directed strategy and an inner-directed one, whereas answer 4 does the opposite.[17]

Cultures differ in the control approach they use. For example, among U.S. multinationals it is common to find managers using an internal control approach. Among Asian firms an external control approach is more typical. Table 11–3 provides some contrasts between the two.

direct controls
The use of face-to-face or personal meetings for the purpose of monitoring operations.

Direct Controls   **Direct controls** involve the use of face-to-face or personal meetings to monitor operations. A good example is International Telephone and Telegraph (ITT), which holds monthly management meetings at its New York headquarters. These meetings are run by the CEO of the company, and reports are submitted by each ITT unit manager throughout the world. Problems are discussed, goals set, evaluations made, and actions taken that will help the unit to improve its effectiveness.

Table 11–3
The Impact of Internal and External-Oriented Cultures on the Control Process

Key Differences Between . . .

Internal Control	External Control
Often dominating attitude bordering on aggressiveness toward the environment.	Often flexible attitude, willing to compromise and keep the peace.
Conflict and resistance means that a person has convictions.	Harmony, responsiveness, and sensibility are encouraged.
The focus is on self, function, one's own group, and one's own organization.	The focus is on others such as customers, partners, and colleagues.
There is discomfort when the environment seems "out of control" or changeable.	There is comfort with waves, shifts, and cycles, which are regarded as "natural."

Tips for Doing Business with . . .

Internally Controlled (for externals)	Externally Controlled (for internals)
Playing "hardball" is legitimate to test the resilience of an opponent.	Softness, persistence, politeness, and long, long patience will get rewards.
It is most important to "win your objective."	It is most important to maintain one's relationships with others.
Win some, lose some.	Win together, lose apart.

Source: Adapted from Fons Trompenaars and Charles Hampden-Turner, *Riding the Waves of Culture: Understanding Diversity in Global Business,* 2nd ed. (New York: McGraw-Hill, 1998), pp. 160–161.

Another common form of direct control is visits by top executives to overseas affiliates or subsidiaries. During these visits, top managers can learn firsthand the problems and challenges facing the unit and offer assistance.

A third form is the staffing practices of MNCs. By determining whom to send overseas to run the unit, the corporation can directly control how the operation will be run. The company will want the manager to make operating decisions and handle day-to-day matters, but the individual also will know which decisions should be cleared with the home office. In fact, this approach to direct control sometimes results in a manager who is more responsive to central management than to the needs of the local unit.

A fourth form is the organizational structure itself. By designing a structure that makes the unit highly responsive to home-office requests and communications, the MNC ensures that all overseas operations are run in accord with central management's desires. This structure can be established through formal reporting relationships and chain of command (who reports to whom).

Indirect Controls **Indirect controls** involve the use of reports and other written forms of communication to control operations. One of the most common examples is the use of monthly operating reports that are sent to the home office. Other examples, which typically are used to supplement the operating report, include financial statements, such as balance sheets, income statements, cash budgets, and financial ratios, that provide insights into the unit's financial health. The home office will use these operating and financial data to evaluate how well things are going and make decisions regarding necessary changes. Three sets of financial statements usually are required from subsidiaries: (1) statements prepared to meet the national accounting standards and procedures prescribed by law and other professional organizations in the host country; (2) statements prepared to comply with the accounting principles and standards required by the home country; and (3) statements prepared to meet the financial consolidation requirements of the home country.

indirect controls
The use of reports and other written forms of communication to control operations.

Indirect controls are particularly important in international management because of the great expense associated with direct methods. Typically, MNCs will use indirect controls to monitor performance on a monthly basis, whereas direct controls are used semiannually or annually. This dual approach often provides the company with effective control of its operations at a price that also is cost-effective.

Approaches to Control

International managers can employ many different approaches to control. These approaches typically are dictated by the MNC's philosophy of control, the economic environment in which the overseas unit is operating, and the needs and desires of the managerial personnel who staff the unit. Working within control parameters, MNCs will structure their processes so that they are as efficient and effective as possible. Typically, the tools that are used will give the unit manager the autonomy needed to adapt to changes in the market as well as to attract competent local personnel. These tools will also provide for coordination of operations with the home office, so that the overseas unit is in harmony with the MNC's strategic plan.

Some control tools are universal. For example, all MNCs use financial tools in monitoring overseas units. This was true as long as three decades ago, when the following was reported:

> The cross-cultural homogeneity in financial control is in marked contrast to the heterogeneity exercised over the areas of international operations. American subsidiaries of Italian and Scandinavian firms are virtually independent operationally from their parents in functions pertaining to marketing, production, and research and development; whereas, the subsidiaries of German and British firms have limited freedom in these areas. Almost no autonomy on financial matters is given by any nationality to the subsidiaries.[18]

Some Major Differences MNCs control operations in many different ways, and these often vary considerably from country to country. For example, how British firms monitor their overseas operations often is different from how German or French firms do. Similarly, U.S. MNCs tend to have their own approach to controlling, and it differs from both European and Japanese approaches. When Horovitz examined the key characteristics of top management control in Great Britain, Germany, and France, he found that British controls had four common characteristics: (1) Financial records were sophisticated and heavily emphasized. (2) Top management tended to focus its attention on major problem areas and did not get involved in specific, detailed matters of control. (3) Control was used more for general guidance than for surveillance. (4) Operating units had a large amount of marketing autonomy.[19]

This model was in marked contrast to that of German managers, who employed very detailed control and focused attention on all variances large and small. These managers also placed heavy control on the production area and stressed operational efficiency. In achieving this centralized control, managers used a large central staff for measuring performance, analyzing variances, and compiling quantitative reports for senior executives. Overall, the control process in the German firms was used as a policing and surveillance instrument. French managers employed a control system that was closer to that of the Germans than to the British. Control was used more for surveillance than for guiding operations, and the process was centrally administered. Even so, the French system was less systematic and sophisticated.[20]

How do U.S. MNCs differ from their European counterparts? One comparative study found that a major difference is that U.S. firms tend to rely much more heavily on reports and other performance-related data. Americans make greater use of output control, and Europeans rely more heavily on behavioral control. Commenting on the differences between these two groups, the researcher noted: "This pattern appears to be quite robust and continues to exist even when a number of common factors that seem to influence control are taken into account."[21] Some specific findings from this study include:

1. Control in U.S. MNCs focuses more on the quantifiable, objective aspects of a foreign subsidiary, whereas control in European MNCs tends to be used to measure more qualitative aspects. The U.S. approach allows comparative analyses between other foreign operations as well as domestic units; the European measures are more flexible and allow control to be exercised on a unit-by-unit basis.

2. Control in U.S. MNCs requires more precise plans and budgets in generating suitable standards for comparison. Control in European MNCs requires a high level of companywide understanding and agreement regarding what constitutes appropriate behavior and how such behavior supports the goals of both the subsidiary and the parent firm.

3. Control in U.S. MNCs requires large central staffs and centralized information-processing capability. Control in European MNCs requires a larger cadre of capable expatriate mangers who are willing to spend long periods of time abroad. This control characteristic is reflected in the career approaches used in the various MNCs. Although U.S. multinationals do not encourage lengthy stays in foreign management positions, European MNCs often regard these positions as stepping-stones to higher offices.

4. Control in European MNCs requires more decentralization of operating decision than does control in U.S. MNCs.

5. Control in European MNCs favors short vertical spans or reporting channels from the foreign subsidiary to responsible positions in the parent.[22]

As noted in the discussion of decision making, these differences help to explain why many researchers have found European subsidiaries to be more decentralized than U.S. subsidiaries. Europeans rely on the managerial personnel they assign from headquarters to run the unit properly. Americans tend to hire a greater percentage of local management people and control operations through reports and other objective, performance-related data.

The difference results in Europeans' relying more on socioemotional control systems and Americans' opting for task-oriented, objective control systems.

Evaluating Approaches to Control   Is one control approach any better than the other? The answer is that each seems to work best for its respective group. Some studies predict that as MNCs increase in size, however, they likely will move toward the objective orientation of the U.S. MNCs. Commenting on the data gathered from large German and U.S. MNCs, the researchers concluded:

> Control mechanisms have to be harmonized with the main characteristics of management corporate structure to become an integrated part of the global organization concept and to meet situational needs. Trying to explain the differences in concepts of control, we have to consider that the companies of the U.S. sample were much larger and more diversified. . . . Accordingly, they use different corporate structures, combining operational units into larger units and integrating these through primarily centralized, indirect, and task-oriented control. . . . The German companies have not (yet) reached this size and complexity, so a behavioral model of control seems to be fitting.[23]

Approaches to control also differ between U.S. and Japanese firms. For example, one study surveyed the attitudes of a large sample of Japanese and U.S. controllers and line managers. Respondents were drawn from the 500 largest industrial firms in both countries. Some of the results are presented in Table 11–4.

One overall finding of the research was that Japanese controllers and managers prefer less participation in the control process than their U.S. counterparts do. In addition, the Japanese have longer-term planning horizons, view budgets as more of a communication device than a controlling tool, and prefer more slack in their budgets than the Americans. These results are extremely important in terms of adapting U.S. approaches to Japanese-owned subsidiaries. The study results suggest the following:

> U.S. managers who wish to design control systems for foreign divisions in Japan (or vice-versa) may wish to consider modifications to the typical domestic system, or they should at least be aware of the potential differences in responses to the system in the areas of budget development, evaluation against budgets, long-run/short-run orientation of budgets, the use of budget slack, and the use of analytic tools in developing inputs to the budget process to name a few.[24]

It is also important to understand why Japanese managers act as they do. Yoshimura and Anderson conducted a detailed analysis of white-collar middle managers in Japan in order to determine what foreign managers need to know about these "salarymen." One thing that the researchers found was that Japanese managers place human relationships ahead of economic efficiency. As a result, when Western managers try to penetrate Japanese markets by offering superior technology or lower price as their levers, they often find that these strategies do not work. If a Japanese company has had a satisfactory relationship with a supplier, the company may continue doing business with this firm even if it means accepting higher costs. Second, when dealing with a Japanese company, nothing is more important than a supplier's ability to meet this customer's expectations. When salarymen complain about non-Japanese companies and the products or service they provide, they usually contend that consistency is missing:

> They want their suppliers to understand customer expectations without being told explicitly, and they want assurance that even "unreasonable" expectations, such as midnight service, will be met. They don't want their relationship manager changed frequently because of turnover; a new contact may not understand their expectations immediately. Japanese overseas subsidiaries do business with their traditional suppliers because they want to maintain continuity in relationships, even if lower-cost local firms are available. The Japanese believe that, in the long run, if both parties contribute to the relationship in good faith, results will take care of themselves.[25]

Another thing that the researchers discovered is that sometimes performance results are not as high as they could be because of the fear of embarrassing others in the organization.

Table 11–4
Selected Beliefs Related to Planning and Control

| | Statement of Results—Average Responses | | | |
| | Japan | | United States | |
	Managers	Controllers	Managers	Controllers
To be useful in performance evaluation of managers, a budget must be revised continuously throughout the year.	3.07	3.14	2.70	2.48
It is important that budgets be very detailed.	3.38	3.31	2.93	2.97
It is appropriate to charge other activities when budgeted funds are used up.	3.01	2.91	1.96	1.52
Budgets should be developed from the bottom up rather than from the top down.	3.13	3.01	3.68	3.96
Budgets are useful in communicating the goal and planned activities of the company.	4.54	4.68	4.11	4.23
Budgets are useful in coordinating activities of various departments.	4.24	4.46	3.78	4.02
A manager who fails to attain the budgets should be replaced.	2.56	2.67	2.00	1.92
Top management should judge a manager's performance mainly on the basis of attaining budget profit.	3.25	3.38	2.27	2.07
It is important that executive compensation depend on a comparison of actual and budgeted performance.	3.18	3.18	3.55	3.56
It is important that managers who perform exceptionally well receive more money than other managers in similar positions.	3.84	3.92	4.28	4.14
It is important for a manager to have quantitative or analytic skills as opposed to people skills.	3.12	3.15	2.04	1.96
The best way to determine the value of capital projects is through the use of quantitative analysis.	3.61	3.80	3.23	3.37

Note: The response scale was as follows:

strongly disagree	1
disagree	2
neutral	3
agree	4
strongly agree	5

Source: Adapted from Lane Daley, James Jiambalvo, Gary L. Sundem, and Yasumasa Kondo, "Attitudes Toward Financial Control Systems in the United States and Japan," *Journal of International Business Studies,* Fall 1985, pp. 100–102.

For example, even though some decisions might result in higher returns on investment for the company, if these decisions put others in a bad light, they will not be made. This means that if a bank has two groups that are charged with buying and selling foreign currency and one of the groups concludes that the U.S. dollar is going to decline against the Japanese yen, it would be wise for this group to sell those dollars and buy yen. On the other hand, if there is another group in the bank that has a large position in dollars and will be unable to unload this currency very quickly, the first group might refuse to sell its dollars because this would end up making the group that held dollars look foolish and this is something that Japanese salarymen try very hard to avoid.

In fact, the avoidance of embarrassment—saving "face"—is one reason that many Japanese firms focus on long-term objectives rather than short-term ones. While their pronouncements seem to emphasize the long-term orientation of their company, in truth this approach is a way of deflecting embarrassment. After all, no one knows what will happen in the long run, so by pretending to be highly interested in 50-year goals, the management sidesteps any likelihood that its current performance will be criticized. After all, it can always argue that in the long run it will achieve high-level performance despite the fact that it is not doing very well at present. So in deciding which form of control to use, MNCs must determine whether they want a more bureaucratic or a more cultural control approach; and from the cultural perspective, it must be remembered that this control will vary across subsidiaries.

■ Control Techniques

A number of performance measures are used for control purposes. Three of the most common evaluate financial performance, quality performance, and personnel performance.

Financial Performance

Financial performance evaluation of a foreign subsidiary or affiliate usually is based on profit and return on investment. **Profit** is the amount remaining after all expenses are deducted from total revenues. **Return on investment (ROI)** is measured by dividing profit by assets; some firms use profit divided by owners' equity (returns on owners' investment, or ROOI) in referring to the return-on-investment performance measure. In any case, the most important part of the ROI calculation is profits, which often can be manipulated by management. Thus, the amount of profit directly relates to how well or how poorly a unit is judged to perform. For example, if an MNC has an operation in both country A and country B and taxes are lower in country A, the MNC may be able to benefit if the two units have occasion to do business with each other. This benefit can be accomplished by having the unit in country A charge higher prices than usual to the unit in country B, thus providing greater net profits to the MNC. Simply put, sometimes differences in tax rates can be used to maximize overall MNC profits. This same basic form of manipulation can be used in transferring money from one country to another, which can be explained as follows:

> Transfer prices are manipulated upward or downward depending on whether the parent company wishes to inject or remove cash into or from a subsidiary. Prices on imports by a subsidiary from a related subsidiary are raised if the multinational company wishes to move funds from the receiver to the seller, but they are lowered if the objective is to keep the funds in the importing subsidiary. . . . Multinational companies have been known to use transfer pricing for moving excess cash from subsidiaries located in countries with weak currencies to countries with strong currencies in order to protect the value of their current assets.[26]

The so-called bottom-line (i.e., profit) performance of subsidiaries also can be affected by a devaluation or revaluation of local currency. For example, if a country devalues its currency, then subsidiary export sales will increase, because the price of these goods will be lower for foreign buyers, whose currencies now have greater purchasing power. If the country revalues its currency, then export sales will decline because the price of goods for foreign buyers will rise, since their currencies now have less purchasing power in the subsidiary's country. Likewise, a devaluation of the currency will increase the cost of imported materials and supplies for the subsidiary, and a revaluation will decrease these costs because of the relative changes in the purchasing power of local currency. Because devaluation and revaluation of local currency are outside the control of the overseas unit, bottom-line performance sometimes will be a result of external conditions that do not accurately reflect how well the operation actually is being run.

Of course, not all bottom-line financial performance is a result of manipulation or external economic conditions. Sometimes other forces account for the problem. For example, one of Volkswagen's goals for a recent year was to earn a pretax 6.5 percent on revenues. The firm fell far short of this goal, earning only 3.5 percent before taxes. One reason for

profit
The amount remaining after all expenses are deducted from total revenues.

return on investment (ROI)
Return measured by dividing profit by assets.

this poor performance was that labor costs in Lower Saxony, where approximately half of its workforce is located, are very high. Workers here produce only 40 vehicles per employee annually in contrast to the VW plant in Navarra, Spain, which turns out 79 vehicles per employee per year. Why doesn't VW move work to lower-cost production sites? The major reason is that the state of Lower Saxony owns 19 percent of the company's voting stock, so the workers' jobs are protected.[27] Simply put, relying solely on financial results to evaluate performance can result in misleading conclusions.

Quality Performance

Just as quality has become a major focus in decision making, it also is a major dimension of the modern control process of MNCs. The term *quality control (QC)* has been around for a long time, and it is a major function of production and operations management. Besides the TQM techniques of concurrent engineering/interfunctional teams, employee empowerment, reward/recognition systems, and training, discussed earlier in this chapter in the context of decision making, another technique more directly associated with the control function is the use of quality circles, which have been popularized by the Japanese. A **quality control circle (QCC)** is a group of workers who meet on a regular basis to discuss ways of improving the quality of work. This approach has helped many MNCs to improve the quality of their goods and services dramatically.

quality control circle (QCC)
A group of workers who meet on a regular basis to discuss ways of improving the quality of work.

Why are Japanese-made goods of higher quality than the goods of many other countries? The answer cannot rest solely on technology, because many MNCs have the same or superior technology or the financial ability to purchase it. There must be other causal factors. "International Management in Action: How the Japanese Do Things Differently" gives some details about these factors. One study attempted to answer the question by examining the differences between Japanese and U.S. manufacturers of air conditioners.[28] In this analysis, many of the commonly cited reasons for superior Japanese quality were discovered to be inaccurate. One theory was that the Japanese focus their production processes on a relatively limited set of tasks and narrow product lines, but this was not so. Nor was support found for the commonly held belief that single sourcing provided Japanese firms with cost advantages over those using multiple sourcing; the firms studied regularly relied on a number of different suppliers. So, what were the reasons for the quality differences?

One reason was the focus on keeping the workplace clean and ensuring that all machinery and equipment were properly maintained. The Japanese firms were more careful in handling incoming parts and materials, work-in-process, and finished products than their U.S. counterparts. Japanese companies also employed equipment fixtures to a greater extent than did U.S. manufacturers in ensuring proper alignment of parts during final assembly.

The Japanese minimized worker error by assigning new employees to existing work teams or pairing them with supervisors. In this way, the new workers gained important experience under the watchful eye of someone who could correct their mistakes.

Another interesting finding was that the Japanese made effective use of QCCs. Quality targets were set, and responsibility for their attainment then fell on the circle while management provided support assistance. This was stated by the researcher as follows:

> In supporting the activities of their QCC's, the Japanese firms in this industry routinely collected extensive quality data. Information on defects was compiled daily, and analyzed for trends. Perhaps most important, the data were made easily accessible to line workers, often in the form of publicly posted charts. More detailed data were available to QCC's on request.[29]

This finding pointed out an important difference between Americans and Japanese. The Japanese pushed data on quality down to the operating employees in the quality circles, whereas Americans tended to aggregate the quality data into summary reports aimed at middle and upper management.

Another important difference is that the Japanese tend to build in early warning systems so that they know when something is going wrong. Incoming field data, for example, are reviewed immediately by the quality department, and problems are assigned to one of

How the Japanese Do Things Differently

Japanese firms do a number of things extremely well. One is to train their people carefully, a strategy that many successful U.S. firms also employ. Another is to try to remain on the technological cutting edge. A third, increasingly important because of its uniqueness to the Japanese, is to keep a keen focus on developing and bringing to market goods that are competitively priced.

In contrast to Western firms, many Japanese companies use a "target cost" approach. Like other multinational firms, Japanese companies begin the new product development process by conducting marketing research and examining the characteristics of the product to be produced. At this point, however, the Japanese take a different approach. The traditional approach used by MNCs around the world is next to go into designing, engineering, and supplier pricing, then to determine if the cost is sufficiently competitive to move ahead with manufacturing. Japanese manufacturers, in contrast, first determine the price that the consumer most likely will accept, and then they work with design, engineering, and supply people to ensure that the product can be produced at this price. The other major difference is that after most firms manufacture a product, they will engage in periodic cost reductions. The Japanese, however, use a kaizen approach, which fosters continuous cost-reduction efforts.

The critical difference between the two systems is that the Japanese get costs out of the product during the planning and design stage. Additionally, they look at profit in terms of product lines rather than just individual goods, so a consumer product that would be rejected for production by a U.S. or European firm because its projected profitability is too low may be accepted by a Japanese firm because the product will attract additional customers to other offerings in the line. A good example is Sony, which decided to build a smaller version of its compact personal stereo system and market it to older consumers. Sony knew that the profitability of the unit would not be as high as usual, but it went ahead because the product would provide another market niche for the firm and strengthen its reputation. Also, a side benefit is that once a product is out there, it may appeal to an unanticipated market. This was the case with Sony's compact personal stereo system. The unit caught on with young people, and Sony's sales were 50 percent greater than anticipated. Had Sony based its manufacturing decision solely on "stand-alone" profitability, the unit never would have been produced.

These approaches are not unique to Japanese firms. Foreign companies operating in Japan are catching on and using them as well. A good example is Coca-Cola Japan. Coke is the leading company in the Japanese soft drink market, which sees the introduction of more than 1,000 new products each year. Most offerings do not last very long, and a cost accountant might well argue that it is not worth the effort to produce them. However, Coca-Cola introduces one new product a month. Most of these sodas, soft drinks, and cold coffees survive less than 90 days, but Coke does not let the short-term bottom line dictate the decision. The firm goes beyond quick profitability and looks at the overall picture. Result: Coca-Cola continues to be the leading soft drink firm in Japan despite competition that often is more vigorous than that in the United States.

two categories: routine or emergency. Special efforts then are made to resolve the emergency problems as quickly as possible. High failure rates attributable to a single persistent problem are identified and handled much faster than they would be in U.S. firms.

Still another reason is that the Japanese work closely with their suppliers so that the latter's quality increases. In fact, research shows that among suppliers that have contracts with both American and Japanese auto plants in the United States, the Japanese plants get higher performance from their suppliers than do the Americans.[30] The Japanese are able to accomplish this because they work closely with their suppliers and help them develop lean manufacturing capabilities. Some of the steps that Japanese manufacturers take in doing this include (1) leveling their own production schedules in order to avoid big spikes in demand, thus allowing their suppliers to hold less inventory; (2) encouraging their suppliers to ship only what is needed by the assembly plant at a particular time, even if this means sending partially filled trucks; and (3) creating a disciplined system of delivery time windows during which all parts have to be received at the delivery plant. A close look at Table 11–5 shows that the 91 suppliers who were working for both Japanese and American auto firms performed more efficiently for their Japanese customers than for their American customers.

Management attitudes toward quality also were quite different. The Japanese philosophy: "Anything worth doing in the area of quality is worth overdoing." Workers are trained for all jobs on the line, even though they eventually are assigned to a single workstation. This method of "training overkill" ensures that everyone can perform every job perfectly and

Table 11–5
Performance of Suppliers When Serving U.S. and Japanese-Owned Auto Plants

Performance Indicators	Chrysler Suppliers ($n = 26$)	Ford Suppliers ($n = 42$)	GM Suppliers ($n = 23$)	Honda Suppliers ($n = 22$)	Nissan Suppliers ($n = 16$)	Toyota Suppliers ($n = 37$)
Inventory turnover	28.3	24.4	25.5	38.4	49.2	52.4
Work-in-process	3.0	3.9	7.2	4.0	3.8	3.0
Finished-goods storage time	4.8	5.4	6.6	5.3	4.9	3.2
Inventory on the truck	2.1	4.5	2.6	2.8	2.08	1.61
Inventory maintained at the customer's site	3.5	4.8	3.1	4.0	2.8	2.3
Percentage change in manufacturing costs compared to the previous year	0.69%	0.58%	0.74%	−0.9%	−0.7%	−1.3%
Percentage of late deliveries	4.4%	7.70%	3.04%	2.11%	1.08%	0.44%
Emergency shipping cost (per million sales dollars) in previous year	$1,235	$446	$616	$423	$379	$204

Source: Adapted from Jeffrey K. Liker and Yen-Chun Wu, "Japanese Automakers, U.S. Suppliers and Supply-Chain Superiority," *Sloan Management Review,* Fall 2000, p. 84.

results in two important outcomes: (1) If someone is moved to another job, he or she can handle the work without any additional assistance. (2) The workers realize that management puts an extremely high value on the need for quality. When questioned regarding whether their approach to quality resulted in spending more money than was necessary, the Japanese managers disagreed. They believed that quality improvement was technically possible and economically feasible. They did not accept the common U.S. strategy of building a product with quality that was "good enough."

These managers were speaking only for their own firms, however. Some evidence shows that, at least in the short run, an overfocus on quality may become economically unwise. Even so, firms must remember that quality goods and services lead in the long run to repeat business, which translates into profits and growth. From a control standpoint, however, the major issue is how to identify quality problems and resolve them as efficiently as possible. One approach that has gained acceptance in the United States is outlined by Genichi Taguchi, one of the foremost authorities on quality control. Taguchi's method is to dispense with highly sophisticated statistical methods unless more fundamental ways do not work. Figure 11–2 compares the use of the Taguchi method and the traditional method to identify the cause of defects in the paint on a minivan hood. The Taguchi approach to solving quality control problems is proving to be so effective that many MNCs are adopting it. They also are realizing that the belief that Japanese firms will correct quality control problems regardless of the cost is not true. As Taguchi puts it, "the more efficient approach is to identify the things that can be controlled at a reasonable cost in an organized manner, and simply ignore those too expensive to control."[31] To the extent that U.S. MNCs can do this, they will be able to compete on the basis of quality.

Personnel Performance

Besides financial techniques and the emphasis on quality, another key area of control is personnel performance evaluation. This type of evaluation can take a number of different

| Figure 11–2 | **Solving a Quality Problem: Taguchi Method vs. Traditional Method** |

Traditional Method Possible causes are studied one by one while holding the other factors constant.

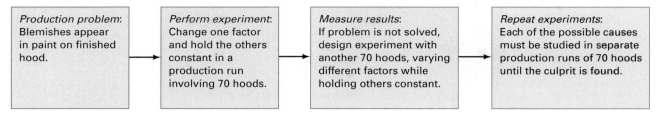

| *Production problem*: Blemishes appear in paint on finished hood. | → | *Perform experiment*: Change one factor and hold the others constant in a production run involving 70 hoods. | → | *Measure results*: If problem is not solved, design experiment with another 70 hoods, varying different factors while holding others constant. | → | *Repeat experiments*: Each of the possible causes must be studied in separate production runs of 70 hoods until the culprit is found. |

Taguchi Method Brainstorming and a few bold experiments seek to quickly find the problem.

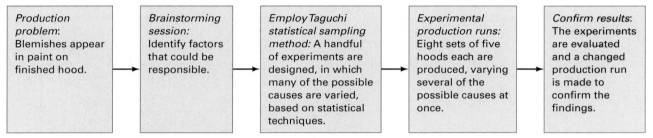

| *Production problem*: Blemishes appear in paint on finished hood. | → | *Brainstorming session*: Identify factors that could be responsible. | → | *Employ Taguchi statistical sampling method*: A handful of experiments are designed, in which many of the possible causes are varied, based on statistical techniques. | → | *Experimental production runs*: Eight sets of five hoods each are produced, varying several of the possible causes at once. | → | *Confirm results*: The experiments are evaluated and a changed production run is made to confirm the findings. |

Source: From information reported in John Holusha, "Improving Quality, the Japanese Way," *New York Times,* July 20, 1988, p. 35.

forms, although there is a great deal of agreement from firm to firm about the general criteria to be measured. Table 11–6 provides a list of the 50 most-admired global companies. What makes these MNCs so successful? Consultants at the Hay Group made an analysis of the best global firms and identified seven common themes:

1. Top managers at the most-admired companies take their mission statements seriously and expect everyone else to do the same.
2. Success attracts the best people—and the best people sustain success.
3. The top companies know precisely what they are looking for.
4. These firms see career development as an investment, not a chore.
5. Whenever possible, these companies promote from within.
6. Performance is rewarded.
7. The firms are genuinely interested in what their employees think, and they measure work satisfaction often and thoroughly.[32]

One of the most common approaches to personnel performance evaluation is the periodic appraisal of work performance. Although the objective is similar from country to country, how performance appraisals are done differs. For example, effective employee performance in one country is not always judged to be effective in another. Awareness of international differences is particularly important when expatriate managers evaluate local managers on the basis of home-country standards. A good example comes out of a survey that found Japanese managers in U.S.-based manufacturing firms gave higher evaluations to Japanese personnel than to Americans. The results led the researcher to conclude: "It seems that cultural differences and diversified approaches to management in MNCs of different nationalities will always create a situation where some bias in performance appraisal may exist."[33] Dealing with these biases is a big challenge facing MNCs.

Another important difference is how personnel performance control actually is conducted. A study that compared personnel control approaches used by Japanese managers in Japan with those employed by U.S. managers in the United States found marked differences.[34] For example, when Japanese work groups were successful because of the actions of a particular individual, the Japanese manager tended to give credit to the whole group. When the group was unsuccessful because of the actions of a particular individual, however,

Table 11–6
The 50 Most-Admired Global Companies, 2003

Rank	Company	Country
1	Wal-Mart Stores	U.S.
2	General Electric	U.S.
3	Microsoft	U.S.
4	Johnson & Johnson	U.S.
5	Berkshire Hathaway	U.S.
6	Dell	U.S.
7	IBM	U.S.
8	Toyota Motor	Japan
9	Procter & Gamble	U.S.
10	FedEx	U.S.
11	Coca-Cola	U.S.
12	Citigroup	U.S.
13	United Parcel Service	U.S.
14	Pfizer	U.S.
15	BMW	Germany
16	Sony	Japan
17	Intel	U.S.
18	Walt Disney	U.S.
19	Nokia	Finland
20	Home Depot	U.S.
21	Nestlé	Switzerland
22	PepsiCo	U.S.
23	Anheuser-Busch	U.S.
24	Honda Motor	Japan
25	Lowe's	U.S.
26	Target	U.S.
27	BP	Britain
28	Cisco Systems	U.S.
29	Colgate-Palmolive	U.S.
30	Merck	U.S.
31	American International Group	U.S.
32	Exxon Mobil	U.S.
33	Singapore Airlines	Singapore
34	Canon	Japan
35	L'Oréal	France
36	DuPont	U.S.
37	Costco Wholesale	U.S.
38	Royal Dutch/Shell Group	Britain/Netherlands
39	Verizon Communications	U.S.
40	Walgreen	U.S.
41	Caterpillar	U.S.
42	Northwestern Mutual	U.S.
43	Unilever	Britain/Netherlands
44	Eli Lilly	U.S.
45	Continental Airlines	U.S.
46	Gillette	U.S.
47	Vodafone	Britain
48	Bank of America	U.S.
49	Kellogg	U.S.
50	GlaxoSmithKline	Britain

the Japanese manager tended to perceive this one employee as responsible. In addition, the more unexpected the poor performance, the greater was the likelihood that the individual would be responsible. In contrast, individuals in the United States typically were given the credit when things went well and the blame when performance was poor.

Other differences relate to how rewards and monitoring of personnel performance are handled. Both U.S. and Japanese managers offered greater rewards and more freedom from close monitoring to individuals when they were associated with successful performance, no matter what the influence of the group on the performance. The Americans carried this tendency further than the Japanese in the case of rewards, however, including giving high rewards to a person who was a "lone wolf."[35]

A comparison of these two approaches to personnel evaluation shows that the Japanese tend to use a more social or group orientation, while the Americans are more individualistic. The researchers found that overall, however, the approaches were quite similar, and that the control of personnel performance by Japanese and U.S. managers is far more similar than different.

Such similarity also can be found in assessment centers used to evaluate employees. An **assessment center** is an evaluation tool that is used to identify individuals with the potential to be selected or promoted to higher-level positions. Used by large U.S. MNCs for many years, these centers also are employed around the world. A typical assessment center would involve simulation exercises such as these: (1) in-basket exercises that require managerial attention; (2) a committee exercise in which the candidates must work as a team in making decisions; (3) business decision exercises in which participants compete in the same market; (4) preparation of a business plan; and (5) a letter-writing exercise. These forms of evaluation are beginning to gain support, because they are more comprehensive than simple checklists or the use of a test or an interview and thus better able to identify those managers who are most likely to succeed when hired or promoted.

> **assessment center**
> An evaluation tool used to identify individuals with potential to be selected or promoted to higher-level positions.

The World of *BusinessWeek*—Revisited

This chapter focuses on two areas that are going to be critical to BMW's line extension strategy: management decision making and control systems. BMW is confident that expanding its offerings worldwide will help it compete against other luxury manufacturers in newly created niche segments. In the process, however, BMW is likely to face many challenges. Keeping a consistent brand message and maintaining its quality image are crucial to the company's long-term success. To preserve brand equity, BMW will need to pay special attention to how the brand is being managed locally as well as globally. As the company expands its production and offerings into more countries, the need for appropriate management controls and decision systems will become even more critical.

Having reviewed the opening case and the principal considerations in international management decision making and control, answer the following questions: (1) What kinds of direct control systems can BMW use to maintain product quality? (2) How might management styles in BMW's North American, Latin American, European, and Asian plants vary? (3) When the company measures quality performance, what two areas may need to be examined?

SUMMARY OF KEY POINTS

1. Decision making involves choosing from among alternatives. Some countries tend to use more centralized decision making than others, so that more decisions are made at the top of the MNC than are delegated to the subsidiaries and operating levels.

2. A number of factors help to influence whether decision making will be centralized or decentralized, including company size, amount of capital investment, relative importance of the overseas unit to the MNC, volume-to-unit-cost relationship, level of product diversification,

distance between the home office and the subsidiary, and the competence of managers in the host country.

3. There are a number of decision-making challenges with which MNCs currently are being confronted. These include total quality management (TQM) decisions and strategies for attacking the competition, among others.

4. Controlling involves evaluating results in relation to plans or objectives, then taking action to correct deviations. MNCs control their overseas operations in a number of ways. Most combine direct and indirect

controls. Some prefer heavily quantifiable methods, and others opt for more qualitative approaches. Some prefer decentralized approaches; others opt for greater centralization.

5. Three of the most common performance measures used to control subsidiaries are in the financial, quality, and personnel areas. Financial performance typically is measured by profit and return on investment. Quality performance often is controlled through quality circles. Personnel performance typically is judged through performance evaluation techniques.

KEY TERMS

assessment center, *341*
codetermination, *321*
controlling, *319*
decision making, *319*
direct controls, *330*
empowerment, *324*

honne, *321*
indirect controls, *331*
kaizen, *325*
management decision and control, *319*
profit, *335*
quality control circle (QCC), *336*

return on investment (ROI), *335*
ringisei, *321*
tatemae, *321*
total quality management (TQM), *324*

REVIEW AND DISCUSSION QUESTIONS

1. A British computer firm is acquiring a smaller competitor located in Frankfurt. What are two likely differences in the way these two firms carry out the decision-making process? How could these differences create a problem for the acquiring firm? Give an example in each case.

2. Would the British firm in question 1 find any differences between the way it typically controls operations and the way that its German acquisition carries out the control process?

3. How do U.S. and Japanese firms differ in the way they go about making decisions and controlling operations? How are the two similar? In each case, provide an example.

4. How are U.S. multinationals trying to introduce total quality management (TQM) into their operations? Give two examples. Would a U.S. MNC doing busi-

ness in Germany find it easier to introduce TQM concepts into German operations, or would there be more receptivity to them back in the United States? Why? What if the U.S. multinational were introducing these ideas into a Japanese subsidiary?

5. What are some common control approaches used by U.S. firms at home that may not work well in Europe? Identify and describe three. In your answer, be sure to explain how U.S. multinationals must change their approach in each case.

6. Why are Japanese firms likely to have trouble using their personnel performance evaluation techniques in the United States? Cite two reasons. What do these firms need to realize to make the necessary adjustments in their approach? Are these changes possible, or will the Japanese firms continue to have trouble?

INTERNET EXERCISES: LOOKING AT THE BEST

In Table 11–6, the 50 most-admired global companies are listed. Each of these companies uses decision making and controlling to help ensure its success in the world market. Visit two of these company sites: Sony and Nokia. The addresses are **http://www.sony.com** and **http://www.nokia.com**. Carefully examine what these firms are doing. For example, what markets are they targeting? What products and services are they offering?

What new markets are they entering? Then, after you are as familiar with their operations as possible, answer these two questions: (1) What types of factors may influence future management decision making in these two companies? (2) What types of control criteria would you expect these companies to use in evaluating their operations and determining how well they are doing?

Spain

Spain, which covers 195,000 square miles, is located on the Iberian Peninsula at the southwest corner of Europe; its southernmost tip is directly across from Morocco. The country has a population of approximately 40 million and a gross domestic product of about $850 billion ($21,200 per capita). Until the mid-1990s, Spain, known for its sunny climate, colorful bullfights, and storybook castles, was one of the most underdeveloped countries in Western Europe. Now, it is an industrialized country whose economy relies heavily on trade, manufacturing, and agriculture. Many of the old Spanish customs, such as taking a siesta (nap or rest) after lunch, are less common. Since 1978 the government has been a constitutional monarchy. The king is head of state and commander in chief of the armed forces, but legislative power rests in a bicameral parliament consisting of a congress of deputies and a senate.

Investors Limited, a partnership based in Hong Kong and headed by Stanley Wong, owns 17 medium and large hotels throughout Asia and a total of 9 others throughout the United Kingdom, France, and Germany. The group now plans on buying a large hotel in Madrid. This hotel was built at the turn of the 20th century but was completely refurbished in 1990 at a cost of $20 million. The current owners have decided that the return on investment, which has been averaging 5.2 percent annually, is too small to justify continuing the operation. They have offered the hotel to the Wong group for $60 million. One-half is payable immediately, and the rest would be paid in equal annual installments over five years.

Stanley Wong believes that this would be a good investment and has suggested to his partners that they accept the offer. "Europe is going to boom during the new millennium," he told them, "and Spain is going to be an excellent investment. This hotel is one of the finest in Madrid, and we are going to more than triple our investment by the end of the decade."

In the past, the partnership has handled all hotel investments in the same way. A handful of company-appointed managers are sent in to oversee general operations and monitor financial performance, and all other matters continue to be handled by those personnel who were with the hotel before acquisition. The investment group intends to handle the Madrid operation in the same way. "The most important thing," Stanley noted recently, "is that we keep control of key areas of performance such as costs and return on investment. If we do that and continue to offer the best possible service, we'll come out just fine."

www.sispain.org
www.red2000.com/spain/index.html

Questions

1. What are some current issues facing Spain? What is the climate for doing business in Spain today?

2. Do you think the Wong group, in running the hotel, should use centralized or decentralized decision making?

3. What types of direct controls might the Wong group use? What types of indirect control might be employed?

4. What are some likely differences between the control measures that the Wong group would use and those that typically are used in countries such as Spain?

Expansion Plans

Kranden & Associates is a very successful porcelain-manufacturing firm based in San Diego. The company has six world-renowned artists who design fine-crafted porcelain statues and plates that are widely regarded as collectibles. Each year, the company offers a limited edition of new statues and plates. Last year, the company made 30 new offerings. On average, 2,500 of each line are produced, and they usually are sold within six months. The company does not produce more than this number to avoid reducing the value of the line to collectors; however, the firm does believe that additional statues and plates could be sold in some areas of the world without affecting the price in North America. In particular, the firm is thinking about setting up production facilities in Rio de Janeiro, Brazil, and Paris, France.

The production process requires skilled personnel, but there are people in both Rio de Janeiro and Paris who can do this work. The basic methods can be taught to these people by trainers from the U.S. plant, because the production process will be identical.

The company intends to send three managers to each of its overseas units to handle setup operations and get the production process off the ground. This should take 12 to 18 months. Once this is done, one person will be left in charge, and the other two will return home.

The company believes that it will be able to sell just as much of the product line in Europe as it does in the United States. The South American market is estimated to be one-half that of the United States. Over the last five years, Kranden has had a return on investment of 55 percent. The company charges premium prices for its porcelain but still has strong demand for its products because of the high regard collectors and investors have for the Kranden line. The quality of its statues and plates is highly regarded, and the firm has won three national and two international awards for creativity and quality in design and production over the past 18 months. Over the last 10 years, the firm has won 17 such awards.

Questions

1. In managing its international operations, should the firm use centralized or decentralized decision making?

2. Would direct or indirect controls be preferable in managing these operations?

3. What kinds of performance measures should the company use in controlling these international operations?

Brief Integrative Case 1

KNP, N.V.

Koninklijke Nederlandse Paperfabrieken, N.V. (KNP), or Royal Dutch Papermills, produces and sells paper and board products to printing and packaging industries throughout the world. The firm originated in 1850 as a small papermill in Maastricht, the Netherlands. One of the firm's three papermaking mills operates in the city today. Another papermill is located across the Maas River in Belgium. The firm also produces packaging materials at various European locations and has investments in paper merchant operations in a number of countries.

The company's headquarters are in a modern office building in a newer section of the ancient and historic city of Maastricht. It is here that Wilmer Zetteler, the commercial director of KNP België, ponders the emerging international business strategy of KNP and the decisions that will be necessary to meet the challenges faced by the firm.

KNP and the World Paper Industry

The evolution of the papermaking industry and the emergence of the modern European economic system have shaped KNP. In the year following World War II, the relatively undamaged but depreciated plant at Maastricht produced only 10,000 tons of paper. By 1950, the firm was pioneering the production of coated paper. KNP was the first European producer of such papers to use technology obtained under a license from the Consolidated Paper Company in the United States. A companion plant that produces top-grade coated paper for brochures, art books, and catalogs is located at Nijmegen on the Waal River. Another mill at Meerssen, a town outside Maastricht, produces colored and watermarked paper.

The oil price shock of 1973 led the firm to reconsider its fundamental strategy and further specialize in the production of high-grade coated papers to gain prominence in international markets. The firm was already well known for this specialty, but managed to expand its position. A mill was constructed at Lanaken, across the Maas in Belgium, just north of the Albert Canal, to produce more lightweight coated paper. This paper is used for magazines, brochures, catalogs, and promotional material.

A separate packaging division of KNP has nine plants that produce various forms of carton board for the packaging industry and other industrial applications. These products include solid, folding, corrugated, and other board products for making boxes. In addition, the plants at Oude Pekela and Sappemeer produce a greyboard for jigsaw puzzles, books, and various types of deluxe packaging.

The plant at Oude Pekela in the Netherlands also produces solid board that is used in making boxes for shipping flowers, vegetables, fruits, and various exports. This board product is manufactured on machines similar to those that make paper, but the board machines at KNP use wastepaper rather than virgin pulp as a raw material in the manufacturing process. The firm owns and operates eight wastepaper collection firms that handle 250,000 tons of raw material a year. Some 30,000 tons of capacity were added in 1986 when two more firms were purchased.

A factory in the Dutch town of Eerbeek produces folding box board. The pharmaceutical and food industries use this product, which also is manufactured from wastepaper. Overall, KNP processes 500,000 tons of wastepaper a year.

KNP acquired in 1986 the German firm of Herzberger Papierfabrik Ludwig Osthushenrich GmbH and Co. KG, which manufactures boxes in four locations in western Germany. The Oberstot plant, gained in the Herzberger acquisition, also produces liner and corrugated board used in boxes and other packaging applications. The Herzberg and Oberau plants that were acquired also produce the corrugated materials used in box converting operations. These acquisitions increased the capacity of the packaging division of KNP by 60 percent.

In addition to the four German packaging plants, KNP owns box-making operations in the Netherlands, Italy, and Spain. Each is supplied with board stock manufactured by other divisions of the firm. KNP also has a joint venture with Buhrman-Tetterode, N.V., in operating a mill that can produce 350,000 tons of paper for the manufacture of corrugated board. With the addition of a fourth machine at the mill in 1986, this joint venture has become one of the principal suppliers of packaging paper of the European market.

KNP began a series of acquisitions of paper merchants beginning in the late 1970s. Each acquisition was a defensive strategy to prevent competitors from capturing existing channels of distribution of KNP products. KNP has paper merchant operations in Belgium, France, and the United Kingdom. The firm also owns a 35 percent interest in Proost en Brandt, one of the two largest paper merchants in the Netherlands, and a 51 percent share in Scaldia Papier B.V. in Nijmegen.

Exhibit 1 displays the group structure of KNP, while Exhibits 2 and 3 summarize the plant capacity of the principal divisions of the company. Exhibit 4 shows the location of facilities in the Netherlands.

Exhibit 1

KNP, N.V., Group and Divisional Organization

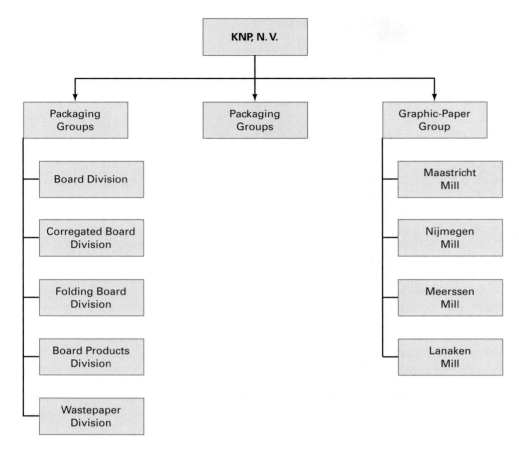

Exhibit 2

KNP, N.V., Plant Capacities of Packaging Group

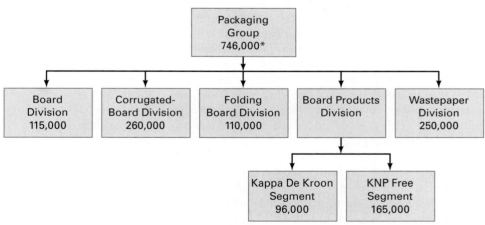

*Tons per annum

Internationalizing of the Firm

KNP's activity outside the Netherlands is not surprising. Like most Dutch manufacturers, the firm has always been an exporter and maintained an international perspective. The market for paper in the Netherlands is insufficient to support a plant. Europe is KNP's principal market. In 1986, 75 percent of its paper and 45 percent of its packaging materials were sold outside the Netherlands.

The modern manufacture of paper products depends on machines that produce large volumes. KNP has state-of-the-art technology that can produce such volumes.

The Netherlands has a population of 15 million, not nearly enough people to support a single modern paper manufacturing plant. On the other hand, the European Community has a population of about 275 million and a modern economy that can easily support a number of competing paper firms.

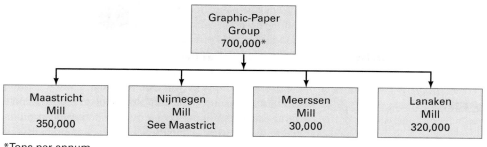

Exhibit 3

KNP, N.V., Plant Capacities of Graphic Paper Group

*Tons per annum

Exhibit 4

KNP Plant Locations

In most European countries, paper is traditionally marketed through paper merchants who distribute products to converters and printers. These merchants serve national or subnational markets.

Yet sometimes market development is not straightforward. When the demand for lightweight machine-coated paper emerged in the United States, KNP had a paper merchant on each coast for other products of the firm. But the lightweight coated product requires a more direct approach to the printing customer. KNP skirted traditional distributors and developed an exclusive relationship with the Wilcox-Walter-Furlong Paper Company, a paper merchant in Philadelphia that stocked KNP's product in the eastern United States. In the western United States, the firm marketed its product through the offices of MacMillan Bloedel, a firm with a 30 percent stock interest in KNP.

KNP's foreign activities can be divided into two segments and two stages. Part of the first stage has existed since the firm began exporting to adjacent nations in the early 19th century.

The second stage began with the development of the European Community, which was an important factor in the growth of KNP. The development of the company after World War II was typical of other manufacturers in Europe. Management knowledge and skill was necessary to seize the opportunity provided by the reconstruction of the European economy.

The European Community is designed to break down barriers that prevent economic activity. As the community emerged, paper firms and other businesses used skilled sales agents who were proficient in dealing with the new market. Firms succeeded in extending their markets by meeting the needs of each nation.

Language was not a barrier at KNP, where executives typically speak a number of European languages. Cultural differences also were not a factor.

Outside Europe, KNP initially exported specialized products to Africa and the Middle East. In the early 1980s, the company began exporting to Australia and the Far East and began testing markets in the United States and Canada. No special cultural and language barriers emerged, because of the company's previous experience in exporting to European nations.

KNP penetrated the United Kingdom market by working through a sales agent with contacts in the printing trades. Later, the company solidified its position in the United Kingdom by hiring an English paper merchant, Contract Papers Limited, to distribute its products. KNP now owns 45 percent interest in the company.

KNP today is one of Europe's largest exporters of coated paper and a leading producer of board. According to KNP's 1986 annual report, 31 percent of sales were in the Netherlands, 55 percent elsewhere in the European Community, and 14 percent elsewhere in the world.

Globalization of the Firm

KNP cannot be considered a fully globalized company because it does not manufacture products in the markets it serves. While the specialized paper products of KNP are global products, their manufacture does not fit the global integrated strategy as described by Yves Doz and other theorists of international business. Therefore, KNP would be best described as following a multi-focal international business strategy.

The paper industries of Europe and North America have different configurations. American firms tend to be more fully integrated vertically and horizontally with respect to the full range of forest products. European firms, with the exception of the Scandinavians, have little opportunity to buy extensive woodlands in their home countries. Because North American firms have woodlands and a large domestic market, it is difficult for European firms to become established in the market. The Swedes and Finns, on the other hand, have forest resources, but they are handicapped by poor markets for finished paper in their countries.

KNP has acquired foreign paper merchants with connections in various world markets. KNP owns Papetries Libert S.A. in Paris. The firm has a 51 percent holding in Saldiaa Papier, N.V., in Wilrijk, Belgium, and a 45 percent stake in Contract Papers (Holdings) Ltd. in London. In the Netherlands, KNP has a 35 percent interest in Proost en Brandt, N.V., in Amsterdam, and a 51 percent interest in Scaldia Papier B.V. in Nijmegen.

These acquisitions were made in 1978 and 1979 as a defensive move against competitors in the European Community. Competitors had begun acquiring paper merchants that sold KNP products and threatened to use them to promote their own products. Meanwhile, the paper merchants acquired by KNP continue to stock a full range of goods, including those produced by competitors.

No distinct figures are available on KNP's foreign revenues. Overall, distribution provided 2 percent of operating results, while the paper group provided 62.9 percent of operating revenues and 71.7 percent of operating results. The packaging group produced 29.2 percent of operating revenue and 26.3 percent of operating results. These figures ignore the influence of internal transfers, which made up 8.2 percent of the total operating activity of the firm.

Other Aspects of Globalization

In many respects, the creation of KNP België, N.V., in Lanaken is a prime example of the establishment of a greenfield manufacturing operation in a foreign country.

The Lanaken paper manufacturing operation was established at the point when the business strategy of the firm shifted toward the production of special grades of coated paper for the printing trades. This decision, just before the energy crisis in the early 1970s, enabled the firm to exploit those grades of specialty paper that had a higher value added in manufacture. The creation of the greenfield operation at Lanaken supported an offensive European niche strategy, while the acquisition of paper merchants in France, Belgium, and the United Kingdom was a defensive maneuver to prevent erosion of existing channels of distribution that supported the more extensive range of products produced by KNP.

The plant that was finally constructed at Lanaken had to be located somewhere in the heavy industrial triangle of northwest Europe to minimize transportation costs to key European markets. The Liege-Limburg-Aachen area is close to the heart of this triangle and has the necessary infrastructure for paper production. The nearby Albert Canal provides direct access to the facilities of the port of Antwerp and pulp shipments from worldwide sources.

The situation is somewhat different at the packaging materials operations of KNP in Germany, Italy, and Spain. Raw materials are shipped from KNP operations in the Netherlands and Germany. These locations are strategically situated to minimize transportation costs.

Future Globalization

A more important question is whether KNP would ever consider harvesting forest resources, given the limited opportunity to manufacture pulp in the Netherlands. In contrast, some American and Japanese firms have been enticed by less developed nations to develop and harvest forests so that they have sure sources of pulp. This is one example of globalization. Another example is shipping antiquated paper machines or converting equipment to less developed countries where labor and energy costs are lower.

Future Strategic Developments

The top management team at KNP is aware of these developments in the world paper industry. Zetteler will take these features into account as he helps plan KNP's future, as marketing and production strategies in the industry are already showing signs of change. For example, the firm in early 1987 started a 70,000-ton-capacity chemi-thermo-mechanical pulp line at the Lanaken mill. This is KNP's first integrated production operation that uses softwood drawn from the Ardennes, instead of the chemical pulp purchased in the international commodity markets. The firm is considering doubling this integrated capacity with a second pulp line in the next few years.

The emergence of KNP and other firms of integrated European producers of special papers would enhance competition in various world markets. The U.S. market has already been penetrated because of the declining value of the dollar and the superior quality of certain European paper products. Any firm that entered the U.S. market, however, would have to consider transportation costs and the advantages of U.S. producers that have forest resources.

Questions for Review

1. In formulating its strategy for the next decade, what are the first steps that KNP should undertake?

2. What type of organizational arrangement does the firm use currently? If it expanded operations into North America, what type of structure would you recommend it use? What other organizational changes would you recommend?

3. In controlling operations, on what types of performance should KNP be focusing its attention? If the firm were to expand operations into South America and Asia, how would this impact on the way it would need to control operations? Explain.

Source: This case was prepared by Alan Bauerschmidt, Professor of Management, University of South Carolina, and Daniel Sullivan, Professor of Management, Tulane University, as the basis for class discussion. It is not intended to illustrate either effective or ineffective managerial capability or administrative responsibility. Reprinted with permission of Alan D. Bauerschmidt.

Brief Integrative Case 2

Can Reliance Compete?

Recently, the Indian government did something unusual: It decided to reverse a policy that would have helped one of the nation's most formidable business empires. It's a curious tale. Early in the year, New Delhi had announced that, for a nominal fee, fixed-line phone operators would be allowed to offer limited mobile services without actually having to buy a mobile license. To foreign and local telecom outfits that had spent billions on such licenses, the announcement was a shock.

Industry execs soon figured out the biggest beneficiary of the policy would be Reliance Industries Ltd., a Bombay-based conglomerate with considerable political leverage. Time and again over the years, the government has altered regulations and policies in industries that Reliance has subsequently dominated. If the January telecom rule had prevailed, the group could have undercut its rivals on price, a key advantage in a business in which Reliance is only a peripheral player. The group denies exerting improper pressure on regulators and insists the change was meant to benefit consumers. And it has vowed to forge ahead anyway with its plans to offer cheap mobile service across India.

Still, the government's reversal must have been a wake-up call for a group that has been getting its way since a textile trader named Dhirubhai H. Ambani founded it in 1966. Over the years, Ambani and his sons, Anil, 42, and Mukesh, 44, have sold themselves to sympathetic officials as defenders of the Indian consumer—a gambit that has paid off handsomely. In the early 1990s, Reliance told New Delhi that the group could help reduce what the nation spends each year on refined oil imports if it built its own refinery. The government provided Reliance with incentives to build one in 1993—and India's purchases of refined oil supplies did indeed decline. In its telecom bid, Reliance promised to offer wireless calls for less than a quarter of the going rate.

"In the Past"

The Ambanis have come in for a fair amount of criticism, however. Their close ties with officialdom rankle rivals—though there is a long tradition of such relationships in India. Besides, insists the group's joint managing director, Anil Ambani, Reliance is a model corporate citizen. "Political linkages and controversy," he told *BusinessWeek* in March, "are all in the past. There is no substitute for performance." (Reliance subsequently refused to cooperate for this story.) Still, the Ambanis' putative power to shape a

> ### An Indian Giant: Reliance Industries
>
> **The Business** India's biggest private producer of textiles and refined oil products. Sales almost $13 billion. Stock has returned 27 percent on average over the past five years
>
> **The Family** Patriarch Dhirubhai Ambani founded the company in 1966. His sons, Anil and Mukesh, now run Reliance day-to-day.
>
> **The Future** The Ambanis want to dominate India's telecom industry by investing heavily in fiber-optics and offering cheap mobile service.
>
> **The Challenge** Taking on entrenched foreign telecom giants like AT&T, SingTel, and Hutchison.

nation's destiny has taken on almost mythic dimensions. When Reliance goes head-to-head with another company, the rival is almost invariably vanquished.

Yet the Ambanis also get high marks for their entrepreneurial grit and savvy use of capital markets. Nobody has built a major company in India as fast as this family. In less than 40 years, Reliance has grown so big that its production of oil products and petrochemicals accounts for 3 percent of India's GDP. The group is consistently profitable; last year, it earned $900 million on revenues of $12.9 billion, up 10 percent over 1999. Reliance is a favorite of Indian and overseas investors, while its creditors applaud its fiscal management.

What's not clear, however, is if Reliance knows how to compete against the world's best companies. It operates in a transitional India, where tariffs as high as 41 percent still protect some of its operations and tax breaks go straight to the bottom line. Many of its rivals are inefficient state companies. And Reliance's main market is its home market. Hence, Reliance faces a major test with its foray into telecom, where the likes of AT&T, Hutchison Whampoa, and Singapore Telecom already are active.

Reliance faces pressure on other fronts. Profit growth in its petrochemical business slowed last quarter amid slackening demand and expectations of a supply glut. In April, Raashid Alvi, a member of parliament, produced a 1,600-page report alleging that in 1993 Reliance diverted at least $230 million from its public oil company into private companies controlled by the Ambanis. They deny it.

Steady Earner

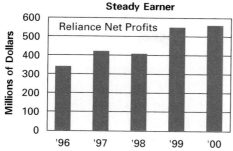

Data: Reliance Industries

In a sign that all may not be well, the group's share price has softened in recent weeks. And in May, Reliance postponed a listing of its subsidiary Reliance Petroleum Ltd. on the NYSE, saying it would instead divest 14 percent of its stake in the oil producer, worth $750 million, on the Luxembourg exchange, where listing rules are less stringent. "Reliance has always benchmarked itself globally," says R. Ravimohan, managing director of rating agency Credit Rating Information Services of India, which rates Reliance Industries as AAA. "But the real risk lies going forward—when it comes face-to-face with competition."

A few years ago, Reliance seemed untouchable—thanks mostly to its canny founder. A teacher's son who grew up in western Gujarat state, Dhirubhai Ambani burned to take on India's industrial dynasties, which had carved out monopolies with licenses bestowed on them by the state. In the early days, Ambani lacked the clout to extract the cheap government loans being doled out to better-connected businessmen. So in October 1977, he issued 2.8 million shares in Reliance Textile Industries, raising $1.8 million—one of the larger public issues in India at the time.

It was a turning point. Realizing that stock placements were the key to expansion, Ambani made sure investors were well-rewarded. And he still does: Over the past five years, Reliance investors have earned an average annual return of 27.5 percent. "At a time when other Indian companies were ripping off shareholders," says Ajay Sondhi, country head for UBS Warburg in Bombay, "Ambani figured out that if he made shareholders happy, they'd give him more money."

Ambani senior, 69, and his sons are today a formidable troika. The father remains the controlling patriarch and resident genius. He focuses on long-term plans, and his sons execute them. Stanford University–educated Mukesh is the quiet, clever strategist; even rivals admit he is a "world-class" businessman. Flamboyant Anil, a Wharton graduate,

is the group's public face. The brothers are often spied after midnight toiling in their office in Nariman Point, Bombay's financial district, not far from their palatial home.

Penny a Call

Much of their time is now taken with telecom. Reliance is spending $5 billion to build a 37,000-mile fiber-optic backbone through India and hopes to dominate domestic and global data and voice traffic. "We want to be a carrier's carrier," Anil says. He dismisses the recent controversy: "How can you contest the idea [that] a phone call will cost 75 percent less for ordinary Indians?"

Analysts say Reliance will find the telecom business hard going. For starters, its budget calling plan won't pay without government subsidies or artificially high long-distance rates. Other telecom players won't agree to that without demanding similar advantages. More important, Indians may not want to pay for such services as broadband and Internet data. And Reliance must do well against foreign rivals with deep pockets and local expertise.

Reliance insists it has done its homework and will pull in some $5 billion a year in revenues by decade's end in the Indian telecom market. Clearly, the company has staying power. It generates $1.4 billion in cash a year, which it's willing to spend to learn the business. "Reliance should be one of the leading players, given its finances and execution ability," says Sanjeev Prasad of Kotak Securities in Bombay.

It's testing time for Reliance. The giant started as the iconoclast of India's socialist economy, an upstart that mastered the system to break the back of India's industrial empires. Now, as India joins the global economy, Reliance wants to be there, too. To succeed, it will have to adopt new strategies. If Reliance pulls it off, the Ambanis may at last reap the one thing that has eluded them: universal respect.

By Manjeet Kripalani in Bombay

Questions for Review

1. What strategy have the Reliance owners used to gain favorable treatment from the Indian government? Do you think this is smart? What are the positives and the negatives?

2. Do you think Reliance can compete against outside MNCs who do business in India? Do you agree with analysts who say Reliance will find the telecom business hard going?

Source: From "Can Reliance Compete?" *BusinessWeek*, June 25, 2001, pp. 50–52. Copyright © 2001 by the McGraw-Hill Companies, Inc. Reprinted with permission.

The HP–Compaq Merger and Its Global Implications

Today's multinational corporations have the responsibility—and the imperative—to redefine their role on the world stage as they pursue business opportunities. . . . HP intends to be an exemplary corporate global citizen by engaging in unique public/private partnerships and modeling behavior and activities in our governance, environmental policy and practices, community engagement models, and our e-Inclusion initiatives to bridge the digital divide. Our technology, our people, and our legacy give us a unique vantage point and . . . capabilities to make lasting and meaningful contributions to the world.

Carly S. Fiorina, Chair and Chief Executive Officer of Hewlett-Packard[1]

Introduction

Two years after its multi-billion-dollar merger with Compaq Computer, Hewlett Packard's performance failed to appease Wall Street. Despite reporting profit for the third quarter of 2003, HP's numbers did not meet analysts' expectations. As a result, company shares slid more than 10 percent. HP was quick to blame weak sales, a sluggish overseas economy, and low prices of personal computers for its financial shortfall. An ominous quote from CEO Carly Fiorina summarized this position and future prospects: "We don't see a rapid upturn in information technology spending."[2] The analyst community was quick to criticize. Needham & Co analyst Charlie Wolf remarked, "It looks like the party is over. HP went through its restructuring and now they have to behave like an adult. It seems like they are so far incapable of doing so."[3] Soundview Technology Group's John B. Jones explained, "Carly Fiorina has lost credibility with Wall Street because she did not always acknowledge the company's weaknesses, preferring to put the brightest spin on results that have sometimes been uneven."[4]

In May 2003, shortly before the one-year anniversary of Hewlett's huge $19 billion merger with Compaq, two separate research firms reported that the combined HP–Compaq had lost the top spot in the worldwide personal computer marketplace to Dell. Although HP tried to play down the news, its impact was clear to industry observers: "Dell has clearly been the biggest beneficiary of this merger," said Forrester analyst Rob Enderle.[5]

On the upside, HP says it has scored some 200 global outsourcing deals since the merger closed, helping to make it a potential force in a field dominated by IBM and EDS. Although much work remains to be done in implementing the postmerger HP, the first year was relatively successful. However, it still may be too early to properly gauge its lasting impact. Critical to the firm's success is maintaining brand clarity overseas in the midst of a difficult reorganization process. Seamlessly integrating the two companies will be the major challenge for Fiorina and her management staff moving forward. Also of great concern is the health of the global technology sector. "When the merger happened, people thought the global market for technology couldn't get any worse, but in some ways it has," comments Yankee Group analyst Andrew Efstathiou.[6] As a result, it's important to consider the global tech spending slump when evaluating HP's first-year merged financials.

One dimension of the merger that did not receive substantial attention was the challenge of integrating HP's and Compaq's disparate global operations. More than any other of HP's many challenges, this one must be confronted if the new HP is to succeed. Tables 1 and 2 present combined HP financials for 2001–2003.

HP History

Hewlett Packard was founded in 1939 in a garage by two people, Bill Hewlett and David Packard, with $538 of working capital.[7] After a string of failures, their company's first successful product, an audio oscillator better than anything on the market, earned a U.S. patent and an order from Disney Studios for eight units to help produce the animated film *Fantasia*. On November 6, 1957, HP had its first public stock offering. Net revenues were $30 million with 1,778 employees and 373 products. In the 1960s, HP was listed on the New York and Pacific exchanges as "HWP" and had its first appearance on *Fortune* magazine's list of the 500 largest U.S. companies.

In 1967, HP started operations in Boeblingen, Germany, introducing a noninvasive fetal heart monitor that helped babies by detecting fetal distress during labor. In the 1970s, revenues increased to $365 million with over 16,000 employees. In the 1980s, revenues again increased to $6.5 billion with over 85,000 employees. In the late 1980s, the firm introduced the HP-85 and HP LaserJet printers. The latter is the company's most successful single product, now considered a standard for laser printing. In the 1990s, HP opened research facilities in Tokyo, Japan. Net revenues reached $13.2 billion with over 91,000 employees. Today

Table 1 HP Balance Sheet as of October 31, 2003

Hewlett-Packard Company and Subsidiaries Consolidated B/S
(in millions)

	2003	2002*	2001
Assets			
Cash and equivalents	14,118	11,192	4,197
Other current assets	8,454	6,940	5,094
Total current assets	40,996	36,075	21,305
PP&E (net)	6,482	6,924	4,397
Long-term investments and other assets	7,980	7,758	6,882
Total assets	74,708	70,710	32,584
Liabilities and Shareholders Equity			
Accounts payable	9.285	7,012	3,791
Notes payable	1,080	1,793	1,722
Other accrued liabilities	8,545	7,395	3,289
Total current liabilities	26,630	24,310	13,964
Long-term debt	6,494	6,035	3,729
Total liabilities	37,746	34,448	18,631
Shareholders equity	36,962	36,262	13,953
Total liabilities and shareholders equity	74,708	70,710	32,584

*Combined HP–Compaq data
Source: HP 2003 Annual Report.

Table 2 HP Income Statements, October 31, 2003

Hewlett-Packard Company and Subsidiaries I/S
(in millions, except per share amounts)

	2003	2002*	2001
Net revenue	73.061	56,588	45,226
Cost of revenues	70,165	57,600	43,787
Operating income	2,896	−1,012	1,439
Total interest expense/other income	−8	−40	−737
(Benefit from) provision for taxes	349	−129	78
Net income	2,593	−903	408
Basic EPS	0.83	−0.36	0.21
Diluted EPS	0.83	−0.36	0.21

*Combined HP–Compaq data
Source: HP 2003 Annual Report.

HP is a multinational company with 104 divisions, 123,000 employees worldwide, 19,000 products, and sales over $47 billion.

HP is a technology solutions provider to consumers, businesses, and institutions globally. The company's offerings span IT infrastructure, personal computing and access devices, global services, and imaging and printing for consumers, enterprises, and small and medium businesses.[8] HP remains a world leader in servers, printers, printer supplies, and PCs. However, swift competition from Dell, especially in servers and PCs, has upped the scales in the technology marketplace. Exhibit 1 presents a time line of HP's history and development.

Compaq History

Compaq Computer Corporation was founded in February 1982 by Rod Canion, Jim Harris, and Bill Murto. All three were senior managers at Texas Instruments who left and invested $1,000 each to form their own company. Sketched on a paper placemat in a Houston pie shop, the first product was a portable personal computer able to run all of the software being developed then for the IBM PC.[9]

Prior to the merger with HP, Compaq had begun to move away from Internet-related markets to concentrate on software and services in hopes of surviving a sagging PC business.[10] As part of the shift, Compaq unveiled a plan to

Exhibit 1   HP Time Line

1939: Hewlett-Packard Co. is born.

1957: Goes public and issues shares.

1966: HP Laboratories is established as the company's central research facility. HP manufactures its first computer, used for in-house testing.

1972: Branches into business computing with HP 300 mini-computer, which introduces the era of distributed data processing. Also, HP launches the first handheld scientific calculator, the HP 35.

1982: Introduces the HP 9000, the first desktop mainframe.

1984: Enters the printer business with its own line of inkjet and LaserJet printers.

1994: Collaborates with Intel to develop a common 64-bit microprocessor architecture.

1999: Hires Carly Fiorina, a former Lucent executive, as CEO.

2001: Announces plan to buy Compaq for $25 billion.

Exhibit 2   Compaq Time Line

1982: Compaq Computer Corp. is founded.

1983: Initial public offering raises $66 million.

1986: Pioneers 386-based desktop systems.

1989: Introduces its first notebook PC, the Compaq LTE, and its first server, the Compaq Systempro.

1991: Co-founder and chairman Rod Canion is ousted by the company board and replaced by Eckhard Pfeiffer.

1995: Acquires two networking product providers, Thomas-Conrad Corp. and NetWorth.

1997: Acquires Tandem Computer Inc., which focuses on high-end nonstop computing; also acquires remote access provider Microcom.

1998: Acquires Digital Equipment Corp.

1999: Pfeiffer quits; Compaq appoints former Oracle executive Michael Capellas as president and CEO.

2001: Compaq announces decision to shift its entire 64-bit series of AlphaServers to Intel's new Itanium processor by 2004.

quit making its own computer chips and instead rely solely on microprocessors made by chipmaker Intel Corp. In mid-2001, Compaq set up a solutions unit to focus on telecommunications, financial services, retail, and government/education with a goal of reaching health care, life sciences, media and entertainment, and manufacturing markets within six to nine months.

In July 2001, Compaq announced that it would cut 1,500 jobs because of sluggish sales. "It is now clear that the economic slowdown is spreading overseas, and we will therefore move more swiftly and go even deeper in our structural cost reduction programs," said Compaq chairman and CEO Michael Capellas in mid-2001.[11] The total job reduction in 2001 amounted to 8,500 positions, or 12 percent of the company's global workforce. According to Capellas, Compaq's revenue shortfall in 2001 was largely due to aggressive pricing and currency issues in Europe. Clearly, Compaq was affected more by conditions overseas than were many of its rivals, because of the breadth of its international operations. Moving forward, the outlook did not look promising. Businesses had little need to upgrade their existing machines for basic word processing, spreadsheets, and Internet access, and consumers were more interested in broadband access than in faster PCs. Exhibit 2 presents a time line of Compaq's history and development.

HP's International Operations

HP's computer products include eight manufacturing divisions in North America, Europe, and Asia, with sales and support in more than 110 countries.[12]

HP's global market strategy allows the company to expand in different countries in two distinct ways. First, HP allows practically anyone with Internet access to log on under the URL and order online. Sixty-five percent of all Internet sites are published exclusively in English. A visitor to HP's Web site, however, can select the country where he or she lives and read the pages in a language other than

English. Also available are software updates, technical support through e-mail, and 24/7 customer support for each country that HP serves.

THE NEW HP

The consolidated HP is organized into four business groups:[13]

- *Enterprise Systems Group:* Servers, storage, networking technology, and management software required to build infrastructure solutions.

- *HP Services:* Consulting and services to IT infrastructures.

- *Imaging and Printing Group:* Internet-savvy printers, digital imaging solutions, and digital publishing systems.

- *Personal Systems Group:* Personal computers, notebooks, handheld devices, personal storage, emerging Internet-access devices, and mobility technology.

Highly complementary products between HP and Compaq are scheduled to be phased out. HP thus believes that the new entity will be capable of delivering a superior product portfolio, one that would have been impossible without the merger. However, many challenges lie ahead.

Merger critics point out that Dell leapfrogged HP in the PC race during 2003. In addition, for the first couple of quarters after consummating the deal, HP saw its earnings suffer. In addition, 17,000 global employees were laid off as a result of the merger. Nevertheless, the news in 2003 looked a little brighter. HP managed to post a 50 percent increase in profits in the fourth quarter of 2002, though sales did not meet expectations. Even more important, the company landed some high-profile contracts for its international consulting and outsourcing services. In March 2003, it snagged a $243 million, five-year deal to provide help-desk and related services to Telecom Italia. In early April, it announced a tentative agreement to provide some $3 billion worth of global outsourcing services to consumer-goods maker Procter & Gamble over the next decade.

In the international government sector, HP won contracts with the state treasury of Slovakia, the employment agency ANPE in France, the Belgian Federal Portal, the Swedish government, the ministry of the interior in Bulgaria, and the European Parliament.[14] It captured more than 50 percent of the market in Spain for state-of-the-art hospital information systems. In sum, HP says it has scored some 200 outsourcing deals since the merger. "Services is one place where the merger has paid off already," according to Forrester analyst Rob Enderle. "Some of those bigger contracts, they would not have been able to get without having the Compaq consultants on board."[15]

However, in some areas, the merger results appear less transparent. The company's revenue slipped 9 percent from 2002, compared with the company's forecast that revenues would decline only 4.5 percent over the period. Although HP has done an admirable job of cutting operating expenses, it appears that they are still behind in growing their business. Jeff Clarke, HP's executive vice president of global operations, blames the revenue decline on the overall state of the technology industry, stating that the average for the tech sector was an 18 percent slump in revenue.[16] Because 25 percent of HP's revenues comes from consumer products such as PCs and printers, the firm is quite vulnerable to soft consumer spending worldwide.

According to the analyst community, a lack of worldwide integration has hampered attempts to create a unified HP. In some places, the company still divides evenly between Compaq and HP, even down to being able to find distinct groups of employees where integration was supposed to have occurred. In addition, the presence of the Compaq brand on a line of upgraded Presario computers, though it is not part of the corporate name, indicates that many integration issues are still to be solved.

Although much uncertainty remains, there have been many positives. In less than a year, HP was able to cut more than $3.1 billion worth of expenses. This figure was well beyond the $2.5 billion that Carly Fiorina predicted before the merger. Predictably, almost half of the savings came from cutting approximately 17,000 jobs between the two companies. Additional savings came from the elimination of duplicate operations. HP vice president of e-business Marius Haas, a former Compaq executive, told *E-Commerce Times* that integration in the online space is ahead of schedule.[17] Haas, who began working on the integration plan a full year before the deal went through, said his business unit was responsible for two of the four main objectives of the merger's first phase: the launching of the HP.com e-commerce site and the creation of an intranet for unified corporate communications.

Currently, 90 percent of HP's biggest customers are doing business electronically with the company—a key achievement in light of HP's desire to synergize its global operations. HP.com now attracts 1.2 million unique visitors daily and delivers 10.5 million page views, and the company's e-business marketing unit produces 3 million personalized newsletters that provide millions of dollars worth of sales leads each month.[18] Behind the scenes, other integration efforts have greatly reduced the number of different Web applications in use. Haas believes top-down management directives emphasizing that the integration plan was "sacred" helped accelerate the pace of change.[19]

HP and Developing Country Communities

In mid-2001, Carly Fiorina's proclamation that HP would be a company committed to global citizenship prompted the creation of an e-inclusion vision for HP. This vision was based on the premise that technology, in conjunction with communities, could help people learn, work, and thrive. The Internet has enabled firms to cross cultural boundaries by offering products and support on a global level. However, in some regions, technology infrastructure is not yet suitable enough to capitalize on the cost benefits of the Internet. Sponsored by HP, "i-communities" use public and private partnerships to boost economic development through technology while building markets, testing products, and honing the global savvy of HP leaders.[20]

Essentially, an "i-community" is a collaborative arrangement between the government and nonprofit or community-based organizations in a specific region to figure how information and communications technology can be used to accelerate sustainable economic development. Although there is a philanthropic component, HP has taken the time to closely link these projects with the company's overall global strategy. Keenly aware that its best growth opportunities depend on the infrastructure development of poorer nations, HP's international growth strategy focuses on the adoption of HP products in these regions. HP believes that it will reap both short- and long-term gains by helping these individual communities become self-sufficient in the digital age. Over the next couple of years, HP plans to aggressively target schools and train more teachers.[21] HP's ultimate goal is to have a sustainable project with limited corporate involvement. By doing so, HP believes that it will forge strong relationships with the communities that become actively involved and the outcome will be a trusted and more powerful brand image.

In the spring of 2004, HP's first commercial e-inclusion was ready for deployment.[22] The company had developed 12 products based on the needs of the communities in which it operates. This new project, based on experimentation in the Kuppam i-community in south India and Dikhotole Digital Village in Johannesburg, South Africa, will focus on delivering educational tools to the underprivileged. According to Maureen Conway, vice president of e-inclusion and emerging-market solutions at HP, "The focus of the work in India and in South Africa is to add to our business. So we are not going into this with philanthropic dollars, but with strategic business development dollars."[23]

Through these alliances, HP encourages local governments to begin expanding their technology infrastructure, hoping that the expansion will open new market opportunities for HP. Eventually, HP would like to have culturally relevant, sustainable solutions in each of the regions it serves. "Philanthropy, to be effective, has to be sustainable," explains CEO Carly Fiorina. "In the end, the most sustainable motivation there is, is enlightened self-interest."[24]

Problems and Challenges of Global Management

Of great concern to HP is how the merger will affect the totality of its international operations. Although overall revenues are down, HP executives have been quick to point out that lack of sales in the United States was offset by strong growth in HP's Asia-Pacific and European businesses. In the Asia-Pacific region, concerns over the breadth of Compaq's current operations in comparison with those of HP have raised doubts about the new entity's ability to seamlessly integrate the two companies' corporate cultures.

Before the merger, HP operated as a single Asia-Pacific entity, and Compaq's operations were split into three separate geographic locations—Australia/New Zealand, ASEAN/India, and China/Japan. Luckily, the corporate headquarters of both companies were located in Singapore, and that has helped expedite some of the consolidation issues. Because both firms owned a solid presence in the Asia-Pacific region, the merger reduced the competitive nature of the market, especially in the PC arena. Lillian Tay, an Asian hardware platform analyst, believes the merger doesn't have much "inherent business value." Even if she is

right, it's imperative that the merged companies effectively communicate their combined offering to the public, in order to capitalize on the solid growth present in the region.[25]

In February 2002, the Gartner Group surveyed 700 IT resellers across 11 countries in the Asia-Pacific region in order to gauge their opinion of the proposed merger (see Table 3). At the time of the survey, almost 60 percent believed the merger would be beneficial or make no difference, but it was clear that not all countries were thrilled by the idea of a unified HP–Compaq. HP must continue to develop and communicate a clearly defined channel strategy for each country. This, in turn, will help deliver an appropriate product mix in each region HP serves.

In the Philippines, HP has begun an initiative aimed at beefing up its presence all over the country. The company believes that through its "HP Stores" it can offer better direct service support to its customers. These stores are fully owned by HP, unlike most traditional computer hubs. Besides functioning as service centers, the stores serve as a product depot, making promotion and distribution easier in the region. Ultimately, these locations will be run by HP's reseller and distribution partners because HP does not sell directly to the customer. Successful implementation has already occurred in other countries, including Thailand (13 stores), Malaysia (10 stores), and Indonesia (11 stores). Eventually, HP would like to have 8 HP stores in the Philippines.[26]

In Europe, the merger resulted in a combined market share of 22 to 23 percent for personal computers but close to 47 percent for power servers and disk storage units.[27] Moving ahead, HP believes the merger will have a substantial impact on the European enterprise computing and consulting markets; it is hoping to become a one-stop shop destination for corporate customers. The European Commission approved the merger in early 2002 after competition experts found that it would not pose a detriment to Europe's IT sector. The commission agreed that HP would

Table 3   **Assessment of HP-Compaq Merger, Asia-Pacific Reseller Survey, 2002 (in percent)**

	Good	Bad	No Difference	No Comment
Asia-Pacific	38.4	21.4	18.3	21.9
Australia	23.6	20.0	34.5	21.9
China	67.3	32.7	0.0	0.0
Hong Kong	37.0	8.7	30.4	23.9
India	43.3	9.0	14.9	32.8
South Korea	36.4	36.4	20.5	6.7
Malaysia	46.8	12.8	10.6	29.8
New Zealand	29.8	31.9	17.0	21.3
Philippines	41.7	27.8	22.2	8.3
Singapore	29.3	17.1	12.2	41.4
Taiwan	28.6	11.4	14.3	45.7
Thailand	40.0	13.3	20.0	26.7

Source: Gartner (March 2002) as cited in "Asian Resellers Welcome HP/Compaq Merger," www.internetnews.com/ent-news/article.php/992921, March 18, 2002.

not be in a suitable position to raise prices, because of the lack of significant barriers to entry in this space.

If HP wants to continue to make inroads in Europe, it must be ready for swift competition from IBM, Dell, and Fujitsu-Siemens. In the U.K., Dell is already the top seller in the PC arena, with close to 20 percent of the market.[28] In Germany and France, Dell currently holds the fourth spot, but continues to make strides. Dell's success has been a function of its ability to penetrate the business and consumer markets of Europe. This is good news for HP because European consumers have begun to show a tendency to be less committed to buying through local retail channels and purchasing local brands.

The full impact of the HP–Compaq merger on HP's global strategy is still unclear. Integrating two large organizations is challenging enough in itself, but in an environment of fast-changing technology, fierce competition, and declining entry barriers, the challenge is formidable.

Questions for Review

1. Do you believe the new HP has communicated its combined offering effectively in its international markets? What else needs to be done?

2. What are some of the entry and organizational challenges that HP faces?

3. What will be the impact of the EU's single monetary union on HP in Europe? What are the pros? The cons?

4. Should HP move to a direct-selling model to battle Dell overseas? Why or why not?

5. What has HP done to respond to soft consumer spending worldwide? Do you believe the HP Stores will be effective in generating new business?

6. How much of an impact do you feel HP's i-communities will have on the company's future sales? Do you think this form of international corporate social responsibility will contribute to the bottom line? Explain.

7. In your opinion, what are the three best things Carly Fiorina has been able to accomplish by merging HP and Compaq?

Exercise

Divide into groups of two. One person will represent HP and the other person will represent Compaq. Debate and discuss the major issues surrounding the merging of two large corporate entities. Specifically, what are some of the integration challenges in Europe, given the political and economic environment?

Source: © McGraw-Hill Irwin. This case was prepared by Professor Jonathan Doh and Erik Holt of Villanova University as the basis for class discussion. It is not intended to illustrate either effective or ineffective managerial capability or administrative responsibility.

Can the Budget Airline Model Succeed in Asia?
The Story of AirAsia

Synopsis

In September 2001, Anthony Fernandes left his job as vice president and head of Warner Music's Southeast Asian operations, one of the most visible and prominent positions in Asia's music industry. He reportedly cashed in his stock options, took out a mortgage on his house, and lined up investors to take control of a struggling Malaysian airline with two jets and US$37 million in debt. Three days later, terrorists destroyed the World Trade Center.[1]

Within two years, AirAsia demonstrated that the low-fare model epitomized by Southwest and JetBlue in the United States, and by Ryanair and easyJet in Europe, has great potential in the Asian marketplace. In fact, AirAsia's success spawned numerous imitators and competitors. Yet questions remain as to whether the low-fare model can succeed and expand in Asia. Even if healthy market demand continues, it is unclear whether the influx of many new entrants will result in a shake-out such as has occurred in North America and Europe, compromising AirAsia's future in this increasingly competitive market.[2]

The Rise of Low-Fare Airlines in Asia

Following late on the global trend, low-fare airlines (LFAs) are rapidly emerging across Asia. In 2000, Skymark emerged in Japan, followed quickly by Air Do. Carriers modeled on leading American and European budget airlines also emerged in Thailand (PBAir and Air Andaman) and in Cambodia (Siem Reap Air). In late 2001, AirAsia was relaunched in Malaysia as a no-frills operation. In the Philippines, Cebu Pacific Airways, also expressly modeled on Southwest, has focused on restraining costs by selling online and operating out of secondary airports. India's first budget airline, Air Deccan, was launched in late August 2003.

LFAs have begun to make inroads into a number of Asian markets, but the long-term survival of these carriers depends on their ability to compete with Asia's traditional, full-service airlines. The prevailing sentiment among some of the Asian majors, expressed by the Asia Pacific Airlines Association in early 2003, is that "no-frill fliers are not a threat to Asian airlines."

Market Liberalization in the Asia-Pacific Region

Just a few years ago, most observers questioned whether Asia would ever emerge as a viable market for no-frills budget carriers similar to the United States' Southwest and Europe's Ryanair and easyJet. Recently, however, the environment changed dramatically. According to Peter Harbison of the Centre for Asia Pacific Aviation, a Sydney, Australia, consultancy, "The key ingredient is liberalization."[3]

Air transport liberalization in Asia began in the 1990s when Australia deregulated its domestic market. Virgin Blue was one of the few carriers that survived this initial battle with incumbents, and it has succeeded in establishing its position in the market. New Zealand was one of the first countries to privatize its national flag carrier and embrace airline liberalization. More recently, India and Japan have pursued deregulation of air transport in order to stimulate competition. Elsewhere in Asia, several countries have publicly embraced liberalization in the form of reciprocal access agreements: Singapore, Malaysia, Taiwan, South Korea, Brunei, and Pakistan all have open-skies air service agreements with the United States. In Taiwan and South Korea, liberalization measures in the late 1980s and early 1990s spawned the birth of carriers that are now major players in their countries' air service sectors, both domestic and international. In Thailand, the domestic market has undergone deregulation, and new private players are looking to expand. Indonesia has witnessed the emergence of a large number of new entrants, following government moves to allow more competition.

In India, Pakistan, Bangladesh, Nepal, the Philippines, and Malaysia, domestic markets underwent varying forms of deregulation in the early-to-mid-1990s, and today, despite some glitches, passengers generally experience much greater choice in domestic travel. The People's Republic of China has also been opening up its air transport market and system. Foreign investors are now permitted to enter joint ventures with, or buy stock of, domestic Chinese airlines. The first outside investment in China was George Soros's US$25 million acquisition of a 25 percent stake in Hainan Airlines in 1995. China Eastern and China Southern Airlines have also issued shares on international capital markets.[4] In Hong Kong, restrictions barring more than one locally based airline from operating on a particular route have been eased. These moves were long overdue in a region that has been resistant to change in the airline sector.

Low-Fare Airlines in Japan

Japan was the first Asian country to experience a real boom in both domestic and international travel in the 1960s.

Since then, Japan has retained the status of the largest air travel market among all Asia-Pacific countries as a result of the combination of its population size and a steadily growing disposable income. Japanese air travel growth rates increased rapidly until the late 1980s, when the market became more mature and reached a plateau in its growth pattern. The total Japanese travel market (both international and domestic) grew by only 6 percent from 1990 to 2000, which indicates that it was saturated with the product offered by the traditional full-service carriers.[5] Japan undertook comprehensive deregulation and liberalization in a range of sectors throughout the 1990s, partly as a strategy to jump-start its stagnant economy. One sector that was partly liberalized was air transport. Future growth in air transport could come from the introduction of the new business model represented by low-cost/low-fare carriers. Although the total supply of seats provided by the LFAs in the Japanese domestic market is still very small when compared to Japan Airlines (JAL) and All Nippon Airways (ANA), the two large traditional carriers, the potential for growth is significant as long as new entrants can successfully compete both with the full-service majors and with intermodal competition from high-speed rail.

Skymark, Japan's first real LFA, has pursued a business model similar to JetBlue or easyJet's differentiated LFA approach rather than the traditional Southwest or Ryanair no-frills, price leadership model. Skymark currently flies to four domestic points in Japan with B767 aircraft. It maintains high-frequency schedules on two of these (seven and three flights a day to Fukuoka and Kagoshima, respectively) and low-frequency schedules to the other two (twice a day to Aomori and Tokushima). The service is basic although all aircraft are equipped with a satellite TV entertainment system. Skymark's onboard product is further differentiated through offering business-class seats on flights to Fukuoka and Kagoshima. A special "Lady's Seat" with bigger seats and a selection of women's magazines is also offered on all domestic routes (10 seats are allocated for every flight). All of these additional features put Skymark closer to a hybrid LFA model. An advanced entertainment system draws parallels with the JetBlue onboard TV model, while the availability of business class and other special seats places Skymark in the same category as AirTran and Spirit in the United States.[6]

Another distinction from the classic LFA model is Skymark's charter operations from Tokyo to Seoul every weekend. The charter business is only secondary to Skymark, so it uses aircraft downtime to operate Korea charters at night or early in the morning, thereby maximizing total aircraft utilization. The distribution network includes all channels, such as direct reservation lines, Internet, and travel agents. The tickets for Korea charters can be purchased only through travel agents. Table 1 provides a comparison of the Skymark and AirAsia budget-air models.

Table 1 Comparison of Price and Features of AirAsia and Skymark

	AirAsia	Skymark
Price	Price leader: discounting up to 50% off the flat carrier fares	Price competitive: fares are 10–20% below the majors
Features	Basic: only economy cabin, pay for food and drinks, ticketless, no preassigned seating, no frequent flyer program	Original/customized: business-class cabin, special "Lady Seats," satellite TV, limited frequent flyer program through partnership with VISA and MasterCard
Quality	Acceptable: travel with a smile	Average: positioning as a high-end LFA
Availability	Selective: website, call center, preferred travel agents (60% of sales via Internet)	Selective: website, call center, H.I.S. group "parent" travel agencies (Internet sales limited)

Source: Authors' calculations.

Low-Fare Airlines in Malaysia

The emergence of the LFA model in Malaysia has been a result of deregulation and of the Malaysian government's desire to release Malaysian Airlines (MAS) from having to serve its perpetually money-losing domestic routes. Malaysia's geographical position provides natural conditions that encourage air travel, but only 6 percent of the adult population traveled by air in 2001.[7] This low figure indicates an underdeveloped aviation market that could be grown significantly through the introduction of low fares on domestic routes.

The policy of highly regulated domestic fares has been long maintained by the Malaysian government.[8] Such a policy created many headaches for the management of MAS, which "has reportedly been losing up to US$79 million annually" on its domestic routes.[9] The initial success of AirAsia may partly validate the Malaysian government's role in encouraging a LFA into its domestic market. However, the government-controlled MAS is starting to show concern about that same success. In the fall of 2002, MAS introduced discounted fares on limited seats on domestic routes. After its initial failure, AirAsia was transformed from a money-losing full-service airline into a low-cost, low-fare airline when a new group of investors, Tune Air Sdn Bhd, bought the shares and half the share of liabilities in the original airline in September 2001.[10]

How did Malaysians react to the introduction of this new business model in their country? The anecdotal evidence points out that they were as eager to embrace it as residents of the United States, U.K., and Ireland were when

Table 2 Fleet Comparisons Among Asia, North America, and Europe in 2001

Aircraft/Region	Asia	North America	Europe
Wide-body fleet	71%	15%	23%
Narrow-body fleet	29%	79%	77%

Source: AAPA, ATA, and AEA.

they were first given an opportunity to travel for a fraction of historical fares.[11] Conor McCarthy, AirAsia's operations director and a former director of operations for Ryanair, has specifically noted that the management of AirAsia has been encouraged by the similarities between the consumer market in Malaysia and in Ireland, Britain, and Germany when Ryanair first entered those markets.[12] Internet resources with consumer feedback about travel on Asian LFAs are fairly limited in comparison with similar North American or Western European travel-related Web sites. One traveler offered the following comment on an online discussion site after traveling on AirAsia in March 2003 from Kuala Lumpur to Penang: "It is good to see the no-frills model finally making headway in the Asia-Pacific region. No food, total scrum for the plane at the boarding announcement, crammed seats . . . but for the equivalent of around US$15, you can't complain. . . . Let's hope that the governments around the region put consumer interests ahead of protecting state-owned airlines."[13] Table 2 provides a comparison of the types of aircraft in use in major world regions.

The Rise of Air Asia

The emergence of Malaysian-based AirAsia resembles the story of Ryanair, the Irish low-cost carrier that has dramatically altered the passenger air transport landscape in Europe since the mid-1990s. Both carriers underwent a remarkable transformation from money-losing regional operators into profitable low-cost, low-fare airlines. AirAsia was initially launched in 1996 as a full-service regional airline offering slightly cheaper fares than its main competitor, Malaysian Airlines.[14] This business model failed because AirAsia could neither sufficiently stimulate the market nor attract enough passengers away from Malaysian Airlines to establish its own market niche.

Fernandes's Entrepreneurial Venture

Anthony Fernandes had a history of going his own way. Shipped off to boarding school in Britain to become a doctor like his father, Fernandes rebelled, earning an accounting degree and landing a job with the Virgin Group instead. Eventually he left Virgin for Warner Music, which sent him back to Malaysia in 1992. In 1997, he became vice president for the company's Southeast Asian operations. By 2001, however, he had tired of the politics at what had become AOL Time Warner and decided to start his own airline. This came as no surprise to those who knew him. Unlike many kids who aspired to becoming airline pilots, from an early age Fernandes had wanted to own his own airline.[15]

On a trip to Britain, he met Conor McCarthy, Ryanair's former director of group operations.[16] Fernandes had envisioned a low-cost airline competing on long-haul routes. McCarthy encouraged him to focus closer to home. In late 2001, AirAsia was up for sale. Founded in 1996 as Malaysia's second airline, AirAsia had been beset by problems from the beginning and failed to turn a profit. Fernandes enlisted leading low-cost-airline experts to restructure AirAsia's business model, and he persuaded McCarthy to join the executive team and become one of the investors.[17]

The investors announced an agreement on September 8, 2001, to buy AirAsia for a symbolic one ringgit (26 cents) and to assume 50 percent of net liabilities, or around 40 million ringgit.[18] The September 11 attacks resulted in lower costs for purchasing and leasing used airplanes. The new AirAsia was relaunched in January 2002 with three B737 aircraft as a low-fare, low-cost domestic airline. Its value proposition was described as "a Ryanair operational strategy, a Southwest people strategy, and an easyJet branding strategy."[19]

Fulfilling his boyhood dream, Tony Fernandes was running an airline company in which he had a personal stake of around 35 percent.

AirAsia's Strategy and Operations

AirAsia focuses on ensuring a very low cost structure as a cornerstone of its business strategy. It has been able to achieve a cost per average-seat-kilometer (ASK) of 2.5 cents, half that of Malaysia Airlines and Ryanair and a third that of easyJet.[20] The common fleet of B737-300s is leased at very competitive market rates due to the soft global market conditions for second-hand airplanes.

One important distinction of AirAsia's revenue model from the traditional LFAs comes from its active involvement in selling holiday packages marketed through its website and various tour operator partners. While enabling the carrier to reach more market segments with its product portfolio, this strategy must also add other costs usually associated with selling blocks of seats to the charter operators.[21]

Fernandes acknowledged that the timing of the AirAsia start-up in the aftermath of the tragic events of September 11, 2001, helped to ensure the lowest possible cost structure, with both leasing and operating aircraft costs sharply declining year over year. AirAsia today handles 11,000 passengers a day with a fleet of 18 planes, offering fares as low as $2.60 (Ryanair has fares between European cities for under one euro, about $1.25).[22] The revenue formula of

AirAsia mostly follows the traditional low-fare approach; only three different fare types are offered.[23] AirAsia's focus on Internet bookings and ticketless travel allows it to emphasize simplicity for the customer while securing low distribution costs. With the average fare being 40 to 60 percent lower than the fares of its full-service competitor, AirAsia has been able to achieve strong market stimulation in the domestic Malaysian air market.[24]

For example, the lowest fare for the trip from Kuala Lumpur to Penang on AirAsia starts from 39 ringgit. The same trip by bus would cost 40 ringgit and increase to 80 ringgit if traveling by car. The introduction of such super-competitive fares is starting to produce the same market growth effect that was achieved by the entry of Ryanair (in its low-fare form) into the U.K.–Ireland air travel market—travelers' switching from sea to air transportation. In the case of Malaysia, consumers are increasingly switching from bus to air travel. It is yet to be seen whether AirAsia successfully makes it through its initial start-up phase and reaches sustainable profitability. Starting with two planes bought from a Malaysian conglomerate in late 2001, the airline expected to have 30 aircraft by the end of 2004. This would be impressive growth but also raise concern because other LFAs faced their most serious challenges when they attempted to expand too fast.[25]

AirAsia expected to handle 3.2 million passengers in 2004, up from 2.1 million in 2003 and 1.1 million in 2002. The company quickly repaid its inherited debt and was profitable from the outset. Its profit margins (before interest, depreciation, amortization, and aircraft leasing costs) are around 35 percent, among the highest in the world, according to Michael McGhee, CSFB's airline analyst. For the half year ending June 30, 2004, AirAsia expected to make a profit of 42 million ringgit ($11 million), more than twice what it made in the entire previous year.[26]

Reaction to AirAsia's Success

The Malaysian government was supportive of AirAsia as long as it was taking over previously money-losing domestic routes and was serving as a benchmark for the restructuring of Malaysian Airlines. AirAsia's plans to enter into the traditionally profitable intra-regional markets to Thailand and other neighboring countries have met with less enthusiasm from the Malaysian government. The Malaysian regulatory authorities face the knotty problem of accommodating the growth plans of a new LFA at the cost of reducing the market value of government-owned Malaysian Airlines. Given the uncertainty about its ability to fly outside of Malaysia, AirAsia is proactively seeking creative ways to expand its market coverage by targeting cross-border markets in Singapore and Thailand.

The Malaysian towns serviced by AirAsia might attract residents of neighboring countries to try AirAsia when they travel to Kuala Lumpur if they can save half of the airfare by taking a simple car trip across the border. This possibility elicited a response from some of AirAsia's corporate neighbors, most notably Singapore Airlines (SIA), Asia's largest carrier by market capitalization. Singapore announced a low-fare subsidiary, and a former SIA deputy chairman, Lim Chin Beng, registered a company in June 2003, intending to operate as Singapore's third airline. Registered as "ValuAir," the airline seems likely to be a low-fare carrier—if it receives regulatory approval. Thai Airways International also announced its LFA as a joint venture with another company.[27] The indications are that AirAsia is causing competitive ripples that are likely to grow in scale and scope. See Table 3 on page 362.

The Future

Going International and Incumbent Competition

In January 2004, AirAsia started its first international service, from Kuala Lumpur to the Thai holiday island of Phuket. In February, it began flying from Johor Bahru across the border from Singapore. In 2005, it will start flying to Indonesia, a country with 235 million potential passengers. Expansion to India and China is reportedly also under discussion, two markets with a combined population of 2.3 billion.

At the same time, incumbents are striking back. In late 2003/early 2004, the number of budget airlines either flying or about to launch more than doubled from 7 to 15, most of them coming from spin-offs of traditional airlines. For example, Thai Airways announced an international carrier, Nok, and Singapore Airlines established its own budget airline with the founders of Ryanair. That airline, Tiger Airways, was scheduled to begin flying by the end of 2004. In April 2004, Australia's Qantas said that it was starting a new airline in Singapore. Qantas invested about 50 million Singapore dollars ($30 million) for a 49.9 percent stake in the new airline; Temasek Holdings, the powerful investment arm of the Singapore government, will own 19 percent; two local businessmen will hold the remainder. Although Temasek owns roughly 57 percent of Singapore Airlines, Temasek officials deny that its ownership in the two carriers represents a conflict of interest. "We think this new player will increase the pie," said Rachel Lin, a spokeswoman for Temasek. "Our interest is strictly for financial returns; we see both of them as potentially attractive investments." Moreover, as the government moves to defend its role as a hub for air travel by building an airport terminal designed to accommodate budget airlines, Singapore's founding prime minister and elder statesman, Lee Kuan Yew, recently warned Singapore Airlines that the government intended to protect Changi Airport's competitiveness, even at the flag carrier's expense.[28]

Some believe the incumbents in Asia—like those in the United States—face inherent disadvantages in their ability

Table 3   **AirAsia Fact Sheet**

Holding company	Tune Air Sdn Bhd
Operating company	AirAsia Sdn Bhd
Business description	Asia's first low-fare no-frills airline to introduce "ticketless" traveling, AirAsia will be unveiling more incentives in the future to encourage more air travel among Malaysians.
Head office	AirAsia Sdn Bhd Lot No N1 Level 4 Main Terminal Building Kuala Lumpur International Airport 64000 Sepang Selangor Darul Ehsan Malaysia
Established	December 12, 2001, Tune Air Sdn Bhd officially acquired 99.25 percent equity (51.68 million shares) of AirAsia from DRB-Hicom, making it the official holding company.
Chairman/director	YBhg Dato' Pahamin A. Rajab
Chief executive officer/director	Tony Fernandes
Director	Encik Kamarudin Meranun
Director	Encik Aziz Bakar
Employees	948
Customer base	2,200,000
Cities served	Alor Star, Kedah Bangkok, Thailand Johor Bahru, Johor Kota Kinabalu, Sabah Kota Bharu, Kelantan Kuala Terengganu, Terengganu Kuching, Sarawak Langkawi, Kedah Miri, Sarawak Penang Phuket, Thailand Sandakan, Sabah Sibu, Sarawak Tawau, Sabah Wilayah Persekutuan Kuala Lumpur Wilayah Persekutuan Labuan
Fleet	10 Boeing 737-300 aircraft, with an average age of 6 years
Available seats	148 seats
Weekly departures	**From/to KLIA, Kuala Lumpur:** 84 flights a week to Kuching 70 flights a week to Kota Kinabalu 56 flights a week to Penang 42 flights a week to Kota Bharu 28 flights a week to Miri, Langkawi, Kuala Terengganu, Johor Bahru and Alor Star 14 flights a week to Tawau, Labuan, Sandakan, Sibu and Phuket **From/to Senai Airport, Johor Bahru:** 28 flights a week to Kuching and Penang * 14 flights a week to Kota Kinabalu, Miri and Langkawi * 14 flights a week to Bangkok ** * starting from December 3, 2003 ** starting from February 2, 2004 (Daily flights are available to all destinations.)

Source: Company Web site.

to compete on cost and price because they do not have the cost discipline or the culture of budget start-ups. Thai Airways hired an advertising executive to run Nok, apparently with the intention of mimicking Tony Fernandes, but their choice appears to lack Fernandes's marketing and operational ability. Eric Kohn, who was number two at Deutsche BA, initially organized as a German-based low-price offshoot of British Airways, argues that established carriers are not set up to succeed in the low-cost space: "People at big airlines don't have accountability or a focus on costs. It is a lot easier to start an airline from scratch than to take a legacy airline and make a profit."[29]

"We feel pretty vindicated," Fernandes said in a telephone interview from his office at Kuala Lumpur International Airport. "A lot of people laughed at us at first."[30] Fernandes disputes analysts' warning that AirAsia is likely to run into more difficulties as it goes international. "I don't see why it makes any difference," he said. As for Asia's relative lack of bilateral agreements to allow new carriers to ferry passengers from country to country, Fernandes says competition for tourist revenue is pushing more countries to open up.

Fernandes says that relatively low landing fees in Asia make up for a scarcity of the cheaper satellite airports that low-cost carriers rely on in Europe and the United States. In September 2003, he set up a joint venture in Thailand, Thai AirAsia Aviation, which will fly not only to points in Thailand, but also to Cambodia and Vietnam. Despite liberalization, Fernandes decided to form a joint venture with Shin Corp., partly owned by the family of Thai prime minister Thaksin Shinawatra, in order to jump-start the process. The airline started flying in January 2004 with promotional fares as low as $2.50 from Bangkok to Phuket.[31]

The Low-Fare Future in Asia

Views on whether low-cost airlines will flourish in Asia vary. Three factors—regulation, population, and demographics—drive this calculus. Although the target consumer base for AirAsia is enormous—500 million people live within three hours of AirAsia's hubs in Kuala Lumpur and Bangkok, more than Western Europe's entire population—the failure of Asia's regulatory environment to keep pace and the uncertain demand for low-cost services create uncertainty.

Those who sell airplanes, airports, or advice tend to be of the opinion that low-cost carriers will redraw Asia's socioeconomic map, offering affordable international travel to millions and thereby fostering the integration of a region divided by water, politics, and poor infrastructure. However, some analysts who follow established carriers insist that the success of low-cost airlines depends on that map being redrawn. There are too few bilateral agreements that allow new, low-cost carriers to fly between countries, they say, and too few of the satellite airports that the airlines

need to keep costs low. Moreover, in a region where most people still earn less than $7 a day, not enough people are well enough off to support a budget airline industry, they contend. "The demographics don't support the low-cost carrier model in Asia," said Chin Y. Lim, an analyst at Morgan Stanley in Singapore.[32]

Others, however, see a large and growing market. They predict that low-cost carriers will tap pent-up demand among less affluent Asians who typically travel by bus and hardly expect attentive service. According to a survey by Axess Asia, a Bangkok-based aviation-and-hospitality consultancy, low fares are the deciding factor in decisions to go or stay home for budget-conscious travelers in Southeast Asia. "We're talking about a transformational shift in the way people travel in Asia," says James Reinnoldt, managing director of Axess Asia.[33] And although incomes are lower in Asia than in Europe, Timothy Ross, an analyst for UBS, says that the region's lower average incomes should boost rather than constrain demand for cheap fares. Moreover, the pattern in other regions suggests that once rules start to relax, growth follows. In the United States, budget carriers saw passenger numbers rise nearly 50 percent in the five years following deregulation, compared with 4 percent for traditional airlines. Low-cost carriers now have roughly a third of the market. In Australia, Virgin Blue took only three years to win a 30 percent market share.[34]

AirAsia already has assumed a populist flavor; its slogan is "Now everyone can fly." "We're bringing cheap travel to the masses," Fernandes says. With so many destinations being added to his route map, Fernandes said he had no doubt that AirAsia would find enough customers in the region's growing middle class. But just in case, AirAsia and its Thai affiliate are planning to fly to India and eventually to China.

The growth of low-fare carriers has great potential to spill over into the broader tourist and business travel economy: More air passengers generate higher demand for more hotel rooms. This connection is being seen in Australia, where Virgin Blue has taken nearly one-third of the domestic market from Qantas Airways. This has resulted in a sharp upturn in demand for economy hotels such as Accor. "In many cases, it's entirely new business that wouldn't have happened if it weren't for cheap air tickets," says Peter Hook, general manager for communications at Accor Asia Pacific.[35] In addition, low-fare carriers may offer options for Asian travelers to mix business with pleasure, as many North American and European business travelers do, by extending trips or bringing family members to accompany them. Ultimately, Fernandes pointed out, low-cost airlines in Asia have an advantage in that Asia has almost no interregional highways and no high-speed international rail. "There's a lot of sea in between," he said. "Air travel is the only way to develop interconnectivity in Asia."

But competition is growing. In addition to the many upstart carriers and joint ventures with majors, some significant players from outside the region are also making rumbles. After his success with Virgin Blue, Richard Branson expressed interest in investing in a low-fare operation specifically in Asia. David Bonderman, an airline financier who helped found Ireland's Ryanair, took a stake in Tiger Airways, Singapore Airlines' budget venture. So far, Hong Kong–based Cathay Pacific Airways is one of the few regional heavyweights to say it isn't likely to enter the fray.[36]

Maintaining the Entrepreneurial Spirit and Going Public

Tony Fernandes had entrepreneurial flair from the start, an approach that he maintains even as AirAsia grows and becomes more established. When he recently announced a joint venture, he made sure that he was photographed in front of the headquarters of Singapore Airlines, just to goad his rival. Like Richard Branson of Virgin, Fernandes has turned himself into his company's most effective marketing tool, sporting his trademark red baseball cap and boasting that he "loves a good party."[37] And like Virgin, AirAsia pushes the envelope in its advertising and marketing: "There's a new girl in town. She's twice the fun and half the price," reads AirAsia's latest advertising campaign. However, it is unclear whether this spirit could be maintained if AirAsia went public or was bought by a larger carrier.[38]

In February 2004, AirAsia announced that it had decided to defer its decision on a public listing until September to focus on domestic and regional expansion. AirAsia chief executive Tony Fernandes had told the *Financial Daily* that the company hoped to raise 760 million ringgit (US$200 million) from its initial public offering (IPO) but would make a final decision about whether to proceed later in the year. Although the IPO is important in order to help the carrier to cut costs and scale up services, Fernandes said that the main priority was to add new routes from AirAsia's two international hubs at Bangkok and Senai in Malaysia's southern Johor state. "We felt it is too fast for us to grow ourselves. For now, we want to focus on expansion plans in our Bangkok and Senai hubs," he said.[39]

Questions for Review

1. What opportunities exist in the Asia-Pacific region for the entrance of new low-fare airlines? How might demand for low-fare service differ in the Asia-Pacific region and in North America and Europe?

2. Do governments pose a significant obstacle to the expansion of low-fare airlines in Asia?

3. Compare AirAsia's strategy with the strategies of Southwest and Ryanair. How is it similar to and different from the strategies of those carriers?

4. Did Tony Fernandes weigh the range of political, economic, and operational risks when he took over AirAsia? What risks might he have overlooked?

5. How would you describe Tony Fernandes's entrepreneurial strategy?

6. How should AirAsia respond to the challenges posed by (*a*) new low-fare carriers entering the Asian marketplace and (*b*) low-fare strategies pursued by incumbent carriers?

7. How do you think the Asian passenger air transport marketplace will shake out? What lessons can be drawn from the North American and European experience?

Exercise

Anthony Fernandes and his team are preparing for an IPO and are presenting the case to underwriters and investors. Break into three groups representing these stakeholders (AirAsia, underwriters, and investors). The AirAsia group should make the case for an IPO to support expansion, describe the impact of this expansion on future earnings growth, and support this pitch with specific information about opportunities in the Asian market. The groups representing underwriters and investors should ask questions and seek clarification about the validity of the expansion plans, the potential impact of an IPO on the positions of existing investors and debt holders, and the overall market's receptivity to the IPO issue.

Source: This case was prepared by Professor Thomas Lawton of Imperial College London and Professor Jonathan Doh of Villanova University as the basis of class discussion. It is not intended to illustrate either effective or ineffective managerial capability or administrative responsibility. Reprinted with permission.

PART FOUR

ORGANIZATIONAL
BEHAVIOR AND
HUMAN RESOURCE
MANAGEMENT

Chapter 12

MOTIVATION ACROSS CULTURES

Motivation is closely related to the performance of human resources in modern organizations. When motivation is studied in the context of international management, it must be remembered that although the motivation process may be the same across cultures, what motivates people often is culturally based. What motivates employees in the United States may be only moderately effective in Japan, France, or Nigeria. Therefore, although motivation is the concept of choice for analyzing employee performance, an international context requires country-by-country, or at least regional, examination of differences in motivation.

This chapter examines motivation as a psychological process and explores how motivation can be used to understand and improve employee performance. It also identifies and describes internationally researched work-motivation theories and discusses their relevance for international human resource management. The specific objectives of this chapter are:

1. **DEFINE** *motivation,* and explain it as a psychological process.

2. **EXAMINE** the hierarchy-of-needs, two-factor, and achievement motivation theories, and assess their value to international human resource management.

3. **DISCUSS** how an understanding of employee satisfaction can be useful in human resource management throughout the world.

4. **EXAMINE** the value of process theories in motivating employees worldwide.

5. **RELATE** the importance of job design, work centrality, and rewards to understanding how to motivate employees in an international context.

The World of *BusinessWeek*

BusinessWeek

GE Breaks the Mold to Spur Innovation

Immelt Is Merging GE's Health Unit with Amersham—and Putting Its Chief in Charge

Despite its eclectic mix of businesses, General Electric Co. has long prided itself on an ability to beat all comers in one category: producing the best executives. So when GE completed its deal to buy Britain's Amersham PLC on April 8 for about $10.3 billion in stock, it seemed safe to assume that Chief Executive Jeffrey R. Immelt would send in his troops to whip the diagnostics-and-bioscience giant into shape. But instead, Immelt delivered the equivalent of a body blow to the GE culture. He took the honey-tongued Brit who headed Amersham, Sir William M. Castell, and put him in charge of what is a combined $14 billion GE Healthcare unit.

He's even making the guy a vice-chairman—a coveted title now limited to Robert C. Wright and Dennis D. Dammerman, a pair of "wise men" who have devoted their lives to GE. Moreover, the mammoth unit will be based outside the U.S.—less than an hour northwest of London, in the village of Chalfont St. Giles—another GE first.

Personalized Medicine

The point is not just to rattle the tree, as the Brits might say. Immelt is obsessed with rebuilding a culture of innovation within GE. Amersham's mission—to foster what Castell calls "personalized medicine" by bringing diagnosis and research down to the cellular level—sounds far bolder than building, say, a faster oven or a better lightbulb. And that's

GE is betting that Amersham's William Castell can keep the combined $14 billion GE Healthcare growing. But making an outsider CEO and a vice-chairman raises eyebrows.

Pros	Cons
Castell knows the complex world of molecular technology	He has limited background in operations that now make up 75% of the unit's sales
Keeps British science talent from feeling they're part of a huge U.S. industrial beast	He's not a product of the GE culture and may bristle at the system
He will let the CEO of the unit's preexisting operations continue running them	His elevation to vice-chairman may spark some grumbling among senior managers
His accent may be music to the ears of European regulators	Can he speak Six Sigma?

Source: www.businessweek.com/magazine/content/04-17/b3880109_mz017.htm

precisely the kind of pioneering technology Immelt thinks is needed to ensure that GE continues to be a powerhouse into the next century. Simply buying big companies and getting homegrown managers to squeeze out costs while ramping up sales isn't going to cut it, especially when you're already a $134 billion operation. Immelt wants more of the Wow! discoveries and Eureka! moments that spawn new paths of growth. Such breakthroughs have eluded GE in recent years. After essentially inventing such life-changing tools as light bulbs and X-ray machines, the Fairfield (Conn.) company has become better known for developing new iterations of existing equipment.

Immelt has already spent $100 million to overhaul the company's upstate New York research headquarters and invested heavily in overseas research and development. But he also needs more specialists—more people who understand what it takes to nurture creativity and passion in a particular field. Finding expert managers steeped in GE culture and its Six Sigma statistical dogma isn't a problem. "I know how to get the most out of a business," argues Immelt. What he wants is someone who can take the discipline of GE and meld it with the real firepower of Amersham. As Immelt puts it: "I want to know how to make two plus two equal seven."

That's the biggest reason for Castell's ascension. But there are also less lofty motivations for tweaking the GE management model. Castell's presence will help integrate the British operations, and having a unit based outside the U.S. with a foreign chief gives GE a more global image with customers. While Immelt insists that Castell never asked for such lofty titles or power within GE, insisting the "whole thing was in my head," according such prestige to an outsider was likely a sweetener to the deal. And some analysts note that European regulators, who have rejected GE deals in the past, no doubt smiled at the move.

Talent vs. Uniformity

The most important incentive was making sure the gem Immelt saw in Amersham didn't lose its luster with the acquisition. A critical task for GE was convincing European scientists that their culture would thrive in the belly of a beast renowned for its homogeneity and uniformity of style. These people—Amersham's primary assets—are moved more by the science of the human genome than the corporate bottom line. It's an issue GE also faces in absorbing and nurturing talent at places such as Universal Studios Inc., which became part of the GE clan in October after Vivendi Universal agreed to merge its entertainment assets with NBC, a deal that should be completed in a matter of weeks.

Still, there are risks to plucking a man whose business currently accounts for about a quarter of GE Healthcare's sales and making him head of the whole thing. One is Castell's lack of knowledge of the rest of the operations. More troubling, perhaps, is the message it sends to insiders who thought they must live and breathe GE to get to the top. "There is a rigorous management process where people work their whole lives to become senior officers," notes John G. Inch, an analyst at Merrill Lynch & Co. "Here, in one swoop, it's given to an outsider." Yet Inch supports the move, in part because Amersham has the potential for much faster growth than scanning machines and other parts of the healthcare subsidiary.

As it happens, Joseph M. Hogan, the manager who was running the unit before the Amersham deal got done, has agreed to stick around. Immelt notes that Hogan is now charged with running the GE Healthcare Technologies part of the unit. In essence, it's the same business he ran before, only now he has a new boss between him and the big chief. Immelt acknowledges that the move is a sacrifice for Hogan, whom he brought aboard 20 years ago, but notes that "sometimes I have to ask the indulgence of the people I hire." At 56, Immelt argues, Castell may only stay two to five years at the helm. Immelt is also moving to put him on the GE board, where he may remain longer.

Cutting-Edge

Hogan notes that the move signals "a cultural change within GE" toward "more risk around growth." And few areas sound more cutting-edge than individualized medicine. Amersham's technologies aim to predict disease before symptoms may even be present and then help doctors tailor therapies to a person's genetic profile. Its protein separation systems, for example, isolate the materials needed for biological drugs, while its imaging agents can highlight abnormal cells long before they're detected on traditional scanners. Given the enormous potential of such technology, Hogan says, the new management structure makes sense: "I truly believe it's the right thing to do."

Certainly, Castell wasn't initially champing at the bit to become Immelt's colleague. As he recalls, the two men had a series of chats in which "I repeatedly said I wasn't for sale, and he repeatedly said he wanted to continue discussions." Castell was more interested in acquiring others than being acquired. "We had a great vision of personalized medicine, and that vision was becoming a reality," he says. What he wanted was more scale.

Meanwhile, Immelt kept hammering him with offers through dozens of meetings and phone calls. That prompted the British executive to start approaching other companies to see if Amersham could perhaps stage a merger that would deliver the scale it needed to thrive without being absorbed into a larger company. But Immelt was on to that, too. He once tracked down Castell on his cell phone at 6:40 a.m. when the British executive was in California,

watching the surf before speaking to one such diagnostics company about a possible deal. "I said: 'Your intelligence is good. You're a cheeky bugger,'" recalls Castell. In July 2003, the GE chief flew over for lunch and said: "Come on, Bill. What do you think about price?" Finally, the chitchat turned into negotiation and, eventually, an agreement to pay a 45% premium on Amersham shares. Castell is pleased with the price, adding: "He couldn't have gotten it for less."

After 15 years of leading Amersham as an independent company, Castell certainly seems happy to be part of the GE family. But what really gets him excited is the science. On April 5, Amersham got 55,000 genes on one slide, three times more than previously possible. "We put the whole genome on one slide!" he boasts. That will open the door to testing for an array of genetic mutations and, down the road, discovering what diseases each individual is most at risk of developing. Such talk may require some translation on Wall Street, but it's music to Immelt's ears.

By Diane Brady in New York and
Kerry Capell in London

This opening news story illustrates the importance for MNCs to provide motivational incentives to their employees. GE's future success in Europe and around the world hinges on its ability to motivate executives and other employees. On the one hand, GE has a strong culture and set of values that have led to past success. On the other hand, GE's leadership recognizes that the company must push innovation. In addition to providing appropriate compensation, GE's management team must use effective strategies to motivate workers, gain trust, and emphasize the organization's reputation as a truly global company. In this chapter we will discuss the background, research, and implications of motivating international managers and others across cultures. Employees typically seek more than just fair compensation. They want to believe that they are making a difference. Effectively motivating across cultures can create competitive advantages that are difficult for competitors to match.

■ The Nature of Motivation

motivation
A psychological process through which unsatisfied wants or needs lead to drives that are aimed at goals or incentives.

Motivation is a psychological process through which unsatisfied wants or needs lead to drives that are aimed at goals or incentives. Figure 12–1 shows this motivation process. The three basic elements in the process are needs, drives, and goal attainment. A person with an unsatisfied need will undertake goal-directed behavior to satisfy the need. Motivation is an important topic in international human resource management, because many MNC managers assume they can motivate their overseas personnel with the same approaches that are used in the home country. Is this true, or do major differences require tailor-made, country-by-country motivation programs? As described in earlier chapters (especially Chapter 4),

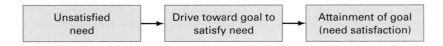

| Unsatisfied need | → | Drive toward goal to satisfy need | → | Attainment of goal (need satisfaction) |

Figure 12–1

The Basic Motivation Process

there obviously are some motivational differences caused by culture. The major question is: Are these differences highly significant, or can an overall theory of work motivation apply throughout the world? Considerable research on motivating human resources has looked at motivation in a large number of countries; however, before reviewing these findings, two generally agreed-on starting assumptions about work motivation in the international arena should be discussed.

The Universalist Assumption

The first assumption is that the motivation process is universal, that all people are motivated to pursue goals they value—what the work-motivation theorists call goals with "high valence" or "preference." The process is universal; however, culture influences the specific content and goals that are pursued. For example, one recent analysis suggests that the key incentive for many U.S. workers is money; for Japanese employees, it is respect and power; and for Latin American workers, it is an array of factors including family considerations, respect, job status, and a good personal life. Similarly, the primary interest of the U.S. worker is him- or herself; for the Japanese, it is group interest; and for the Latin American employee, it is the interest of the employer.[1] Simply put, motivation differs across cultures. Adler sums up the case against universality:

> Unfortunately, American as well as non-American managers have tended to treat American theories as the best or only way to understand motivation. They are neither. American motivation theories, although assumed to be universal, have failed to provide consistently useful explanations outside the United States. Managers must therefore guard against imposing domestic American theories on their multinational business practices.[2]

In the United States, personal and professional achievement is an important desire, and individual success through promotions and increased earnings may be an important goal. In China, however, group affiliation is an important need, and harmony is an important goal. Therefore, the ways to motivate U.S. employees are quite different from those used with Chinese workers. The motivational process is the same, but the needs and goals are not because of differences between the two cultures. This conclusion was supported in a study by Welsh, Luthans, and Sommer that examined the value of extrinsic rewards, behavioral management, and participative techniques among Russian factory workers. The first two motivational approaches worked well to increase worker performance, but the third did not. The researchers noted that

> this study provides at least beginning evidence that U.S.-based behavioral theories and techniques may be helpful in meeting the performance challenges facing human resources management in rapidly changing and different cultural environments. We found that two behavioral techniques—administering desirable extrinsic rewards to employees contingent upon improved performance, and providing social reinforcement and feedback for functional behaviors and corrective feedback for dysfunctional behaviors—significantly improved Russian factory workers' performance. By the same token, the study also points out the danger of making universalist assumptions about U.S.-based theories and techniques. In particular, the failure of the participative intervention does not indicate so much that this approach just won't work across cultures, as that historical and cultural values and norms need to be recognized and overcome for such a relatively sophisticated theory and technique to work effectively.[3]

At the same time, however, it is important to remember that as a growing number of countries begin moving toward free-market economies and as new opportunities for economic rewards emerge, the ways in which individuals in these nations are motivated will change. Commenting on the management of Chinese personnel, for example, Sergeant and Frenkel pointed out that new labor laws now allow both state enterprises and foreign-invested Chinese enterprises to set their own wage and salary levels. However, companies have to be careful about believing that they can simply go into the marketplace, pay high wages, and recruit highly motivated personnel. In particular, the researchers note that:

> Devising reward packages for Chinese employees has been difficult because of the range and complexity of nonwage benefits expected by workers as a legacy of the "iron rice bowl" tradition. However, health and accident insurance, pensions, unemployment and other benefits are increasingly being taken over by the state. There are two cultural impediments to introducing greater differentials in pay among workers of similar status: importance accorded to interpersonal harmony which would be disrupted by variations in earnings; and distrust of performance appraisals because in state enterprises evaluations are based on ideological principles and *guanxi* [connections].[4]

So some of what foreign MNCs would suspect about how to motivate Chinese employees is accurate, but not all. The same is true, for example, about Japanese employees. Many people believe that all Japanese firms guarantee lifetime employment and that this practice is motivational and results in a strong bond between employer and employee. In truth, much of this is a myth. Actually, less than 28 percent (and decreasing) of the workforce has any such guarantee, and in recent years a growing number of Japanese employees have been finding that their firms may do the best they can to ensure jobs for them but will not guarantee jobs if the company begins to face critical times. As in the West, when a Japanese firm has a crisis, people are often let go. This was clearly seen in recent years when the Japanese economy was stalled and the country's joblessness rate hit new highs.[5]

The Assumption of Content and Process

The second starting assumption is that work-motivation theories can be broken down into two general categories: content and process. **Content theories** explain work motivation in terms of *what* arouses, energizes, or initiates employee behavior. **Process theories** of work motivation explain *how* employee behavior is initiated, redirected, and halted.[6] Most research in international human resource management has been content oriented, because these theories examine motivation in more general terms and are more useful in creating a composite picture of employee motivation in a particular country or region. Process theories are more sophisticated and tend to focus on individual behavior in specific settings. Thus, they have less value to the study of employee motivation in international settings, although there has been some research in this area as well. By far the majority of research studies in the international arena have been content driven, but this chapter will examine research findings from both the content and the process theories.

The next section examines work motivation in an international setting by focusing on the three content theories that have received the greatest amount of attention: the hierarchy-of-needs theory, the two-factor motivation theory, and the achievement motivation theory. Then attention is focused on three process theories: equity theory, goal-setting theory, and expectancy theory. Each offers important insights regarding the motivation process of personnel in international settings.

content theories of motivation
Theories that explain work motivation in terms of what arouses, energizes, or initiates employee behavior.

process theories of motivation
Theories that explain work motivation by how employee behavior is initiated, redirected, and halted.

■ The Hierarchy-of-Needs Theory

The hierarchy-of-needs theory is based primarily on work by Abraham Maslow, a well-known humanistic psychologist now deceased.[7] Maslow's hierarchy of needs has received a great deal of attention in the U.S. management and organizational behavior field and from international management researchers, who have attempted to show its value in understanding employee motivation throughout the world.[8]

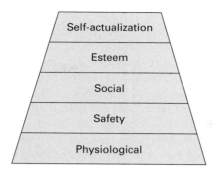

Figure 12–2

Maslow's Need Hierarchy

The Maslow Theory

Maslow postulated that everyone has five basic needs, which constitute a need hierarchy. In ascending order, beginning with the most basic need, they are physiological, safety, social, esteem, and self-actualization needs. Figure 12–2 illustrates this hierarchy.

Physiological needs are basic physical needs for water, food, clothing, and shelter. Maslow contended that an individual's drive to satisfy these physiological needs is greater than the drive to satisfy any other type of need. In the context of work motivation, these physiological needs often are satisfied through the wages and salaries paid by the organization.

Safety needs are desires for security, stability, and absence of pain. Organizations typically help personnel to satisfy these needs through safety programs and equipment and by providing security through medical insurance, unemployment and retirement plans, and similar benefits.

Social needs are needs to interact and affiliate with others and the need to feel wanted by others. This desire for "belongingness" often is satisfied on the job through social interaction within work groups in which people give and receive friendship. Social needs can be satisfied not only in formally assigned work groups but also in informal groups.

Esteem needs are needs for power and status. Individuals need to feel important and receive recognition from others. Promotions, awards, and feedback from the boss lead to feelings of self-confidence, prestige, and self-importance.

Self-actualization needs are desires to reach one's full potential, to become everything that one is capable of becoming as a human being. In an organization, an individual may achieve self-actualization not through promotion but instead by mastering his or her environment and setting and achieving goals.[9]

Maslow's theory rests on a number of basic assumptions. One is that lower-level needs must be satisfied before higher-level needs become motivators. A second is that a need that is satisfied no longer serves as a motivator. A third is that there are more ways to satisfy higher-level than there are ways to satisfy lower-level needs. Some of these assumptions came from Maslow's original work, some came from others' work, and some were modifications by Maslow himself. These assumptions have driven much of the international research on the theory.

International Findings on Maslow's Theory

Do people throughout the world have needs that are similar to those described in Maslow's need hierarchy? Research generally shows that they do. For example, in a classic study undertaken by Haire, Ghiselli, and Porter, a sample of 3,641 managers from 14 countries was surveyed. This study is quite dated but remains the most comprehensive and relevant one for showing different cultural impacts on employee motivation. Countries in this survey included the United States, Argentina, Belgium, Chile, Denmark, England, France, Germany, India, Italy, Japan, Norway, Spain, and Sweden.[10] With some minor modification, the researchers examined the need satisfaction and need importance of the four highest-level

physiological needs
Basic physical needs for water, food, clothing, and shelter.

safety needs
Desires for security, stability, and the absence of pain.

social needs
Desires to interact and affiliate with others and to feel wanted by others.

esteem needs
Needs for power and status.

self-actualization needs
Desires to reach one's full potential, to become everything one is capable of becoming as a human being.

needs in the Maslow hierarchy. Esteem needs were divided into two groups: esteem and autonomy. The former included needs for self-esteem and prestige; the latter, desires for authority and for opportunities for independent thought and action.

The results of the Haire group's study showed that all these needs were important to the respondents across cultures. It should be remembered, however, that the subjects in this huge international study were managers, not rank-and-file employees. Upper-level needs were of particular importance to these managers. The findings for select country clusters (Latin Europe, United States/United Kingdom, and Nordic Europe) show that autonomy and self-actualization were the *most important* needs for the respondents. Interestingly, these same managers reported that those were the needs with which they were *least satisfied,* which led Haire and his associates to conclude:

> It appears obvious, from an organizational point of view, that business firms, no matter what country, will have to be concerned with the satisfaction of these needs for their managers and executives. Both types of needs were regarded as relatively quite important by managers, but, at the present time at least, the degree to which they were fulfilled did not live up to their expectations.[11]

Since this classic study, other researchers have examined management groups from other countries. One follow-up study surveyed managers in eight East Asian countries and found that autonomy and self-actualization in most cases ranked high; however, the degree of satisfaction/dissatisfaction varied much more widely than that reported by Haire and his associates. Some East Asian managers apparently were quite dissatisfied with their ability to satisfy autonomy and self-actualization needs.

Both research studies indicate the value of examining motivation of human resources (in this case, managers) in country or geographic clusters. Each country or geographic region appears to have its own need-satisfaction profile. When using this information to motivate managers, MNCs would be wise to consider the individual country's or region's profile and adjust their approach accordingly.

Some researchers have suggested modifying Maslow's hierarchy by reranking the needs. Nevis believes that the Maslow hierarchy reflects a culture that is Western oriented and focused on the inner needs of individuals.[12] Obviously, not all cultures function in this way: Asian cultures emphasize the needs of society. Nevis suggested that a Chinese hierarchy of needs would have four levels, which from lowest to highest would be (1) belonging (social), (2) physiological, (3) safety, and (4) self-actualization in the service of society. If this is true, MNCs attempting to do business in China must consider this revised hierarchy and determine how they can modify their compensation and job-design programs to accommodate the requisite motivational needs. In any event, Nevis's idea is worth considering, because it forces the multinational firm to address work motivation based on those cultural factors that are unique to it.

The discussion so far indicates that even though the need-hierarchy concept is culturally specific, it offers a useful way to study and apply work motivation internationally. However, the well-known Dutch researcher Geert Hofstede and others have suggested that need-satisfaction profiles are *not* a very useful way of addressing motivation, because there often are so many different subcultures within any given country that it may be difficult or impossible to determine which culture variables are at work in any particular work setting. The Haire and follow-up studies dealt only with managers. Hofstede found that job categories are a more effective way of examining motivation. He reported a linkage between job types and levels and the need hierarchy. Based on survey results from over 60,000 people in more than 50 countries who were asked to rank a series of 19 work goals (see Tables 12–1 and 12–2), he found that:

- The top four goals ranked by professionals corresponded to "high" Maslow needs.
- The top four goals ranked by clerks corresponded to "middle" Maslow needs.
- The top four goals ranked by unskilled workers corresponded to "low" Maslow needs.
- Managers and technicians showed a mixed picture—having at least one goal in the "high" Maslow category.[13]

Table 12–1
Top-Ranking Goals for Professional Technical Personnel from a Large Variety of Countries

Rank	Goal	Questionnaire Wording
1	Training	Have training opportunities (to improve your present skills or learn new skills)
2	Challenge	Have challenging work to do—work from which you can get a personal sense of accomplishment
3	Autonomy	Have considerable freedom to adopt your own approach to the job
4	Up-to-dateness	Keep up-to-date with the technical developments relating to your job
5	Use of skills	Fully use your skills and abilities on the job
6	Advancement	Have an opportunity for advancement to higher-level job
7	Recognition	Get the recognition you deserve when you do a good job
8	Earnings	Have an opportunity for high earnings
9	Cooperation	Work with people who cooperate well with one another
10	Manager	Have a good working relationship with your manager
11	Personal time	Have a job which leaves you sufficient time for your personal or family life
12	Friendly department	Work in a congenial and friendly atmosphere
13	Company contribution	Have a job which allows you to make a real contribution to the success of your company
14	Efficient department	Work in a department which is run efficiently
15	Security	Have the security that you will be able to work for your company as long as you want to
16	Desirable area	Live in an area desirable to you and your family
17	Benefits	Have good fringe benefits
18	Physical conditions	Have good physical working conditions (good ventilation and lighting, adequate work space, etc.)
19	Successful company	Work in a company which is regarded in your country as successful

Source: Reprinted from Geert H. Hofstede, "The Colors of Collars," *Columbia Journal of World Business,* September 1972, p. 74. Copyright © 1972. Used with permission from Elsevier.

The tables from Hofstede's research show that self-actualization and esteem needs rank highest for professionals and managers, and that security, earnings, benefits, and physical working conditions are most important to low-level, unskilled workers. These findings illustrate that job categories and levels may have a dramatic effect on motivation and may well offset cultural considerations. As Hofstede noted, "There are greater differences between job categories than there are between countries when it comes to employee motivation."[14]

In deciding how to motivate human resources in different countries or help them to attain need satisfaction, researchers such as Hofstede recommend that MNCs focus most heavily on giving physical rewards to lower-level personnel and on creating for middle- and upper-level personnel a climate in which there is challenge, autonomy, the ability to use one's skills, and cooperation. Of course, this does not mean that executives are unmotivated by large compensation packages or that new employees are not looking for flexible compensation. As seen in "International Management in Action: Rethinking the Motivation Equation," compensation packages for personnel in Japan are beginning to change.

Overall, there seems to be little doubt that need-hierarchy theory is useful in helping to identify motivational factors for international human resource management. This theory

Table 12–2
The Four Most Important Goals Ranked by Occupational Group and Related to the Need Hierarchy

Goals Ranked in "Need Hierarchy"	Professionals (Research Laboratories)	Professionals (Branch Offices)	Managers	Technicians (Branch Offices)	Technicians (Manufacturing Plants)	Clerical Workers (Branch Offices)	Unskilled Workers (Manufacturing Plants)
High—Self-Actualization and Esteem Needs							
Challenge	1	2	1	3	3		
Training		1		1			
Autonomy	3	3	2				
Up-to-dateness	2	4		4			
Use of skills	4						
Middle—Social Needs							
Cooperation			3/4			1	
Manager			3/4		4	2	
Friendly department						3	
Efficient department						4	
Low—Security and Physiological Needs							
Security				2	1		2
Earnings					2		3
Benefits							4
Physical conditions							1

Source: Reprinted from Geert H. Hofstede, "The Colors of Collars," *Columbia Journal of World Business,* September 1972, p. 78. Copyright © 1972. Used with permission from Elsevier.

alone is not sufficient, however. Other content theories, such as the two-factor theory, add further understanding and effective practical application for motivating personnel.

■ The Two-Factor Theory of Motivation

The two-factor theory was formulated by well-known work-motivation theorist Frederick Herzberg and his colleagues. Like Maslow's theory, Herzberg's has been a focus of attention in international human resource management research over the years. This two-factor theory is closely linked to the need hierarchy.

The Herzberg Theory

The **two-factor theory of motivation** holds that two sets of factors influence job satisfaction: hygiene factors and motivators. The data from which the theory was developed were collected through a critical incident methodology that asked the respondents to answer two basic types of questions: (1) When did you feel particularly good about your job? (2) When did you feel exceptionally bad about your job? Responses to the first question generally related to job content and included factors such as achievement, recognition, responsibility, advancement, and the work itself. Herzberg called these job-content factors **motivators.** Responses to the second question related to job context and included factors such as salary, interpersonal relations, technical supervision, working conditions, and company policies and administration. Herzberg called these job-context variables **hygiene factors.** Table 12–3 lists both groups of factors. A close look at the two lists shows that the motivators are heavily psychological and relate to Maslow's upper-level needs and the hygiene factors are environmental in nature and relate more to Maslow's lower-level needs. Table 12–4 illustrates this linkage.

two-factor theory of motivation
A theory that identifies two sets of factors that influence job satisfaction: hygiene factors and motivators.

motivators
In the two-factor motivation theory, job-content factors such as achievement, recognition, responsibility, advancement, and the work itself.

hygiene factors
In the two-factor motivation theory, job-context variables such as salary, interpersonal relations, technical supervision, working conditions, and company policies and administration.

Table 12–3
Herzberg's Two-Factor Theory

Hygiene Factors	Motivators
Salary	Achievement
Technical supervision	Recognition
Company policies and administration	Responsibility
Interpersonal relations	Advancement
Working conditions	The work itself

Table 12–4
The Relationship Between Maslow's Need Hierarchy and Herzberg's Two-Factor Theory

Maslow's Need Hierarchy	Herzberg's Two-Factor Theory
Self-actualization	Motivators
	Achievement
	Recognition
	Responsibility
Esteem	Advancement
	The work itself
Social	Hygiene factors
	Salary
	Technical supervision
Safety	Company policies and administration
	Interpersonal relations
Physiological	Working conditions

Rethinking the Motivation Equation

For many years Japanese firms have used a traditional approach to motivating their personnel. Twice a year workers would be paid a bonus, and when they retired they would receive an additional lump-sum payment linked to their salary and length of time with the company. Additionally, the company would provide a package of perquisites for those who were going to be staying with the firm for their entire career. Today, this traditional approach is undergoing radical change. Growing numbers of companies, Matsushita being a good example, are starting to offer a more flexible benefits package—and a growing number of employees are beginning to take it.

One reason for the change is that Japanese companies are coming to realize that their standard benefits package is not the best for all of their people. In particular, more people are changing jobs and moving on to other firms. In 1995, approximately 80 percent of all workers in Japan were still with the company with which they had begun their careers. By 1998 this percentage had dropped to 70 percent, and by 2010 traditional lifetime employment in many Japanese companies will be a thing of the past.

Since many people will be working for more than one firm in the course of their careers, many companies now offer more flexible options. For example, in some enterprises an employee who has special skills but does not intend to stay with the firm for a long time can command higher pay and is allowed to take advances on his or her pension. In turn, the individual agrees to give up some benefits. For those who want even more flexibility, there is the option of putting pension payments into savings plans rather than simply having the company provide a lump-sum amount upon retirement.

One reason for the change in the traditional approach is that many firms now believe that they must do business in a different way. Rather than provide lifetime employment, they want to be able to hire new recruits who have skills and abilities not possessed by current personnel; and rather than having to retain older personnel, they want to be able to move them out. In addition, companies such as Matsushita are now moving from a seniority-based management reward system to a merit-based one.

Will this new approach prove motivational? Many young Japanese believe that it will because it offers them more control over their retirement options and is based on a pay-for-performance philosophy. Older Japanese workers are not sure. However, one thing is certain: More and more major Japanese corporations are rethinking the motivation equation and looking for a different approach to motivating their people and maintaining world-class organizations in the face of growing worldwide hypercompetition.

A recent example is Fujitsu, one of the first Japanese corporations to introduce performance-based pay. After eight years of using this system, the company is reviewing it with an eye toward making a host of changes. In particular, Fujitsu feels that its current performance-based system does not fit very well with the Japanese business culture. The company does not intend to bring back the old seniority-based approach, but it does want to create a motivation system that is both equitable and effective. One problem with the current system is that it allows employees to set their own goals. As a result, many have continually chosen targets that are easy to attain, thus ensuring themselves raises and promotions. Another problem with the current system is that tying rewards to performance encourages people to pursue short-term goals and to avoid ambitious projects that might produce hit products but would take time to accomplish. A third problem is that the system does not reward some important types of performance. For example, aftersale customer service is not rewarded; as a result, this end of the business has begun to suffer. Fujitsu plans on revamping its motivation system and addressing these problems. By rethinking the motivation equation, the company believes that it will be able to increase the performance of its workforce.

The two-factor theory holds that motivators and hygiene factors relate to employee satisfaction. This relationship is more complex than the traditional view that employees are either satisfied or dissatisfied. According to the two-factor theory, if hygiene factors are not taken care of or are deficient, there will be dissatisfaction (see Figure 12–3). Importantly, however, if hygiene factors are taken care of, there may be no dissatisfaction, but there also may be no satisfaction. Only when motivators are present will there be satisfaction. In short, hygiene factors help to prevent dissatisfaction (thus the term *hygiene,* as it is used in the health field), but only motivators lead to satisfaction. Therefore, according to this theory, efforts to motivate human resources must provide recognition, a chance to achieve and grow, advancement, and interesting work.

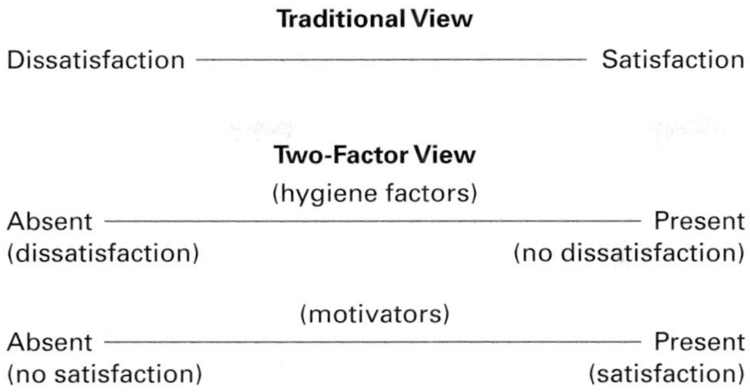

Traditional View

Dissatisfaction ——————————————— Satisfaction

Two-Factor View
(hygiene factors)

Absent ———————————————— Present
(dissatisfaction)   (no dissatisfaction)

(motivators)

Absent ———————————————— Present
(no satisfaction)   (satisfaction)

> **Figure 12–3**
>
> **Views of Satisfaction/ Dissatisfaction**

Before examining the two-factor theory in the international arena, it is important to note that Herzberg's theory has been criticized by some organizational-behavior academics. One criticism surrounds the classification of money as a hygiene factor and not as a motivator. There is no universal agreement on this point. Some researchers report that salary is a motivator for some groups, such as blue-collar workers, or those for whom money is important for psychological reasons, such as a score-keeping method for their power and achievement needs.

A second line of criticism is whether Herzberg developed a total theory of motivation. Some argue that his findings actually support a theory of job satisfaction. In other words, if a company gives its people motivators, they will be satisfied; if it denies them motivators, they will not be satisfied; and if the hygiene factors are deficient, they may well be dissatisfied. Much of the international research on the two-factor theory discussed next is directed toward the satisfaction/dissatisfaction concerns rather than complex motivational needs, drives, and goals.

International Findings on Herzberg's Theory

International findings related to the two-factor theory fall into two categories. One consists of replications of Herzberg's research in a particular country. This research asks whether managers in country X give answers similar to those in Herzberg's original studies. In the other category are cross-cultural studies that focus on job satisfaction. This research asks what factors cause job satisfaction and how do these responses differ from country to country. The latter studies are not a direct extension of the two-factor theory, but they do offer insights regarding the importance of job satisfaction in international human resource management.

Two-Factor Replications   A number of research efforts have been undertaken to replicate the two-factor theory, and in the main, they support Herzberg's findings. George Hines, for example, surveyed 218 middle managers and 196 salaried employees in New Zealand using ratings of 12 job factors and overall job satisfaction. Based on these findings, he concluded that "the Herzberg model appears to have validity across occupational levels."[15]

Another similar study was conducted among 178 managers in Greece who were Greek nationals. Overall, this study found that Herzberg's two-factor theory of job satisfaction generally held true for these managers. The researchers summarized their findings as follows:

> As far as job dissatisfaction was concerned, no motivator was found to be a source of dissatisfaction. Only categories traditionally designated as hygiene factors were reported to be sources of dissatisfaction for participating Greek managers. . . . Moreover . . . motivators . . . were more important contributors to job satisfaction than to dissatisfaction . . . (66.8% of the traditional

motivator items . . . were related to satisfaction and 31.1% were related to dissatisfaction). Traditional hygiene factors, as a group, were more important contributors to job dissatisfaction than to job satisfaction (64% of the responses were related to dissatisfaction and 36% were related to satisfaction).[16]

Another study tested the Herzberg theory in an Israeli kibbutz (communal work group). Motivators there tended to be sources of satisfaction and hygiene factors sources of dissatisfaction, although interpersonal relations (a hygiene factor) were regarded more as a source of satisfaction than of dissatisfaction. The researcher was careful to explain this finding as a result of the unique nature of a kibbutz: Interpersonal relations of a work and nonwork nature are not clearly defined, thus making difficult the separation of this factor on a motivator/hygiene basis. Commenting on the results, the researcher noted, "the findings of this study support Herzberg's two-factor hypothesis: Satisfactions arise from the nature of the work itself, while dissatisfactions have to do with the conditions surrounding the work."[17]

Similar results on the Herzberg theory have been obtained by research studies in developing countries. For example, one study examined work motivation in Zambia, employing a variety of motivational variables, and work motivation was a result of six factors: work nature, growth and advancement, material and physical provisions, relations with others, fairness/unfairness in organizational practices, and personal problems. These variables are presented in Figure 12–4. They illustrate that, in general, the two-factor theory of motivation was supported in this African country.[18]

Cross-Cultural Job-Satisfaction Studies   A number of cross-cultural studies related to job satisfaction also have been conducted in recent years. These comparisons show that Herzberg-type motivators tend to be of more importance to job satisfaction than are hygiene factors. For example, one study administered the Job Orientation Inventory (JOI) to MBA candidates from four countries.[19] As seen in Table 12–5, the relative ranking placed hygiene factors at the bottom of the list and motivators at the top. What also is significant is that although Singapore students do not fit into the same cultural cluster as the other three groups in the study, their responses were similar. These findings provide evidence that job-satisfaction-related factors may not always be culturally bounded.[20]

Another, more comprehensive study of managerial job attitudes investigated the types of job outcomes that are desired by managers in different cultures. Data were gathered from lower- and middle-management personnel who were attending management

Figure 12–4

Motivation Factors in Zambia

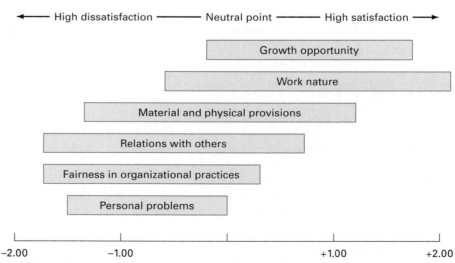

Source: Adapted from Peter D. Machungwa and Neal Schmitt, "Work Motivation in a Developing Country," *Journal of Applied Psychology,* February 1983, p. 41. Copyright © 1983 by the American Psychological Association. Adapted with permission.

Table 12–5
The Results of Administering the JOI to Four Cross-Cultural Groups

	United States (*n* = 49)	Australia (*n* = 58)	Canada (*n* = 25)	Singapore (*n* = 33)
	Relative Rankings			
Achievement	2	2	2	2
Responsibility	3	3	3	3
Growth	1	1	1	1
Recognition	10	10	8	9
Job status	7	7	7	7
Relationships	5	5	10	6
Pay	8	8	6	8
Security	9	9	9	10
Family	6	6	5	5
Hobby	4	4	4	4

Source: From G. E. Popp, H. J. Davis, and T. T. Herbert, "An International Study of Intrinsic Motivation Composition," *Management International Review* 26, no. 3 (1986), p. 31. Reprinted with permission.

development courses in Canada, the United Kingdom, France, and Japan.[21] The researchers sought to identify the importance of 15 job-related outcomes and how satisfied the respondents were with each other. The results indicated that job content is more important than job context. Organizationally controlled factors (**job-context factors,** such as conditions, hours, earnings, security, benefits, and promotions) for the most part did not receive as high a ranking as internally mediated factors (**job-content factors,** such as responsibility, achievement, and the work itself).

The data also show that managers from the four countries differ significantly regarding both the perceived importance of job outcomes and the level of satisfaction experienced on the job with respect to these outcomes. These differences are useful in shedding light on what motivates managers in these countries and, in the case of MNCs, in developing country-specific human resource management approaches. The most striking contrasts were between the French and the British. Commenting on the applicability of this research to the formulation of motivational strategies for effective human resource management, the researchers noted the following:

> The results suggest . . . that efforts to improve managerial performance in the UK should focus on job content rather than on job context. Changes in the nature of the work itself are likely to be more valued than changes in organizational or interpersonal factors. Job enrichment programs which help individuals design their own goals and tasks, and which downplay formal rules and structure, are more likely to improve performance in an intrinsically oriented society such as Britain, where satisfaction tends to be derived from the job itself, than in France, where job context factors such as security and fringe benefits are more highly valued. The results suggest that French managers may be more effectively motivated by changing job situation factors, as long as such changes are explicitly linked to performance.[22]

In summary, Herzberg's two-factor theory appears to reinforce Maslow's need hierarchy through its research support in the international arena. As with the application of Maslow's theory, however, MNCs would be wise to apply motivation–hygiene theory on a country-by-country or a regional basis. Although there are exceptions, such as France, there seems to be little doubt that job-content factors are more important than job-context factors in motivating not only managers but also lower-level employees around the world, as Hofstede pointed out.

job-context factors
In work motivation, those factors controlled by the organization, such as conditions, hours, earnings, security, benefits, and promotions.

job-content factors
In work motivation, those factors internally controlled, such as responsibility, achievement, and the work itself.

■ Achievement Motivation Theory

In addition to the need-hierarchy and two-factor theories of work motivation, achievement motivation theory has been given a relatively great amount of attention in the international arena. Achievement motivation theory has been more applied to the actual practice of management than the others, and it has been the focus of some interesting international research.

The Background of Achievement Motivation Theory

achievement motivation theory
A theory which holds that individuals can have a need to get ahead, to attain success, and to reach objectives.

Achievement motivation theory holds that individuals can have a need to get ahead, to attain success, and to reach objectives. Note that like the upper-level needs in Maslow's hierarchy or like Herzberg's motivators, the need for achievement is learned. Therefore, in the United States, where entrepreneurial effort is encouraged and individual success promoted, the probability is higher that there would be a greater percentage of people with high needs for achievement than, for example, in China, Russia, or Eastern European countries,[23] where cultural values have not traditionally supported individual, entrepreneurial efforts.

Researchers such as the late Harvard psychologist David McClelland have identified a characteristic profile of high achievers.[24] First, these people like situations in which they take personal responsibility for finding solutions to problems. They want to win because of their own efforts, not because of luck or chance. Second, they tend to be moderate risk-takers rather than high or low risk-takers. If a decision-making situation appears to be too risky, they will learn as much as they can about the environment and try to reduce the probability of failure. In this way, they turn a high-risk situation into a moderate-risk situation. If the situation is too low-risk, however, there usually is an accompanying low reward, and they tend to avoid situations with insufficient incentive.

Third, high achievers want concrete feedback on their performance. They like to know how well they are doing, and they use this information to modify their actions. High achievers tend to gravitate into vocations such as sales, which provide them with immediate, objective feedback about how they are doing. Finally, and this has considerable implications for human resource management, high achievers often tend to be loners, and not team players. They do not form warm, close relationships, and they have little empathy for others' problems. This last characteristic may distract from their effectiveness as managers of people.

Researchers have discovered a number of ways to develop high-achievement needs in people. These involve teaching the individual to do the following: (1) obtain feedback on performance and use this information to channel efforts into areas where success likely will be attained; (2) emulate people who have been successful achievers; (3) develop an internal desire for success and challenges; and (4) daydream in positive terms by picturing oneself as successful in the pursuit of important objectives.[25] Simply put, the need for achievement can be taught and learned.

Before examining international research on achievement motivation theory, it is important to realize that the theory has been cited as having a number of shortcomings. One is that it relies almost solely on the projective personality Thematic Apperception Test (TAT) to measure individual achievement, and a number of recent studies have questioned the validity and reliability of this approach.[26] Another concern is that achievement motivation is grounded in individual effort, but in many countries group harmony and cooperation are critically important to success. Simply put, the original theory does not satisfactorily explain the need for achievement in cultures in which individual accomplishment is neither valued nor rewarded.[27]

International Findings on Achievement Motivation Theory

A number of international researchers have investigated the role and importance of high-achievement needs in human resource management.[28] One study, discussed earlier in this chapter, used the JOI scale and found that achievement or a sense of accomplishment ranked as the second most important work-reward factor.[29] Remember, however, that these results were obtained with MBA students from various countries who were studying in the United States. It should not be surprising that these respondents who came to the United States for advanced study of business, regardless of their home country, would have a high need for achievement. The question remains as to what degree people throughout the world have this need.

Early research among Polish industrialists found that many of them were high achievers.[30] The average high-achievement score was 6.58, quite close to U.S. managers' average score of 6.74. This led some to conclude there is evidence that managers in countries as diverse as the United States and those of the former Soviet bloc in Central Europe have high needs for achievement.[31] In later studies, however, researchers did *not* find a high need for achievement in Central European countries. One study, for example, surveyed Czech industrial managers and found that the average high-achievement score was 3.32, considerably lower than that of U.S. managers.[32] Because the need for achievement is learned, differences in these samples can be attributed to cultural differences. By the same token, given the dramatic, revolutionary changes that occurred in Central and Eastern Europe with the end of communism and of centrally planned economies, one could argue that the achievement needs of postcommunist Europeans, now able to be freely expressed, may well be high today. The important point, however, is that because achievement is a learned need and thus largely determined by the prevailing culture, it is not universal and may change over time.

The ideal profile for high-achieving societies can be described in terms of the cultural dimensions examined in Chapter 4. In particular, two cultural dimensions identified by Hofstede in Chapter 4—uncertainty avoidance and masculinity—best describe high-achieving societies (see Figure 12–5). These societies tend to have weak uncertainty avoidance. People in high-achieving societies are not afraid to take at least moderate risks or to live with ambiguity. These societies also tend to have moderate-to-high masculinity, as measured by the high importance they assign to the acquisition of money and other physical assets and

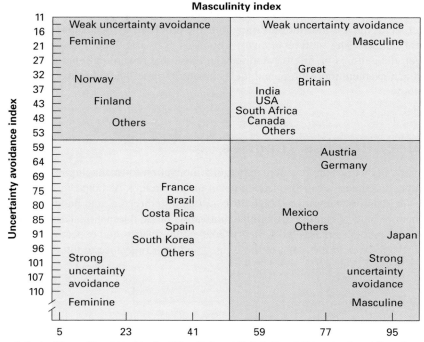

Figure 12–5

Selected Countries on the Uncertainty-Avoidance and Masculinity Scales

Source: Adapted from Geert Hofstede, "The Cultural Relativity of Organizational Practices and Theories," *Journal of International Business Studies,* Fall 1983, p. 86.

the low value they give to caring for others and for the quality of work life. This combination (see the upper right quadrant of Figure 12–5) is found almost exclusively in Anglo countries or in nations that have been closely associated with them through colonization or treaty, such as India, Singapore, and Hong Kong (countries associated with Great Britain) and the Philippines (associated with the United States).

Countries that fall into one of the other three quadrants of Figure 12–5 will not be very supportive of the high need for achievement. MNCs in these geographic regions, therefore, would be wise to formulate a human resource management strategy for either changing the situation or adjusting to it. If they decide to change the situation, they must design jobs to fit the needs of their people or put people through an achievement motivation training program to create high-achieving managers and entrepreneurs.

A number of years ago, McClelland was able to demonstrate the success of such achievement motivation training programs with underdeveloped countries. For example, in India, he conducted such a program with considerable success. In following up these Indian trainees over the subsequent 6 to 10 months, he found that two-thirds were unusually active in achievement-oriented activities. They had started new businesses, investigated new product lines, increased profits, or expanded their present organizations. For example, the owner of a small radio store opened a paint and varnish factory after completing the program. McClelland concluded that this training appeared to have doubled the natural rate of unusual achievement-oriented activity in the group studied.[33]

If international human resource managers cannot change the situation or train the participants, then they must adjust to the specific conditions of the country and formulate a motivation strategy that is based on those conditions. In many cases, this requires consideration of a need-hierarchy approach blended with an achievement approach. Hofstede offers such advice in dealing with the countries in the various quadrants of Figure 12–5:

> The countries on the feminine side . . . distinguish themselves by focusing on quality of life rather than on performance and on relationships between people rather than on money and things. This means *social motivation:* quality of life plus security and quality of life plus risk.[34]

In the case of countries that are attempting to introduce changes that incorporate values from one of the other quadrants in Figure 12–5, the challenge can be even greater.

In summary, achievement motivation theory provides additional insights into the motivation of personnel around the world. Like the need-hierarchy and two-factor theories, however, achievement motivation theory must be modified to meet the specific needs of the local culture. The culture of many countries does not support high achievement. However, the cultures of Anglo countries and those that reward entrepreneurial effort do support achievement motivation, and their human resources should probably be managed accordingly.

■ Select Process Theories

While content theories are useful in explaining motivation for managing international personnel, process theories can also lead to better understanding. As noted earlier, the process theories explain how employee behavior is initiated, redirected, and halted; and some of these theories have been used to examine motivation in the international arena. Among the most widely recognized are equity theory, goal-setting theory, and expectancy theory. The following briefly examines each of these three and their relevance to international human resource management.

equity theory
A process theory that focuses on how motivation is affected by people's perception of how fairly they are being treated.

Equity Theory

Equity theory focuses on how motivation is affected by people's perception of how fairly they are being treated. The theory holds that if people perceive that they are being treated equitably, this perception will have a positive effect on their job performance and satisfaction and there is no need to strive for equity. Conversely, if they believe they are not being treated fairly, especially in relation to relevant others, they will be dissatisfied and this belief will have a negative effect on their job performance and they will strive to restore equity.

There is considerable research to support the fundamental equity principle in Western work groups.[35] However, when the theory is examined on an international basis, the results are mixed. Yuchtman, for example, studied equity perceptions among managers and nonmanagers in an Israeli kibbutz production unit.[36] In this setting everyone was treated the same, but the managers reported lower satisfaction levels than the workers. The managers perceived their contributions to be greater than those of any other group in the kibbutz. As a result of this perception, they felt that they were undercompensated for their value and effort. These findings support the basic concepts of equity theory.

On the other hand, a number of studies cast doubt on the relevance of equity theory in explaining motivation in an international setting. Perhaps the biggest shortcoming is that the theory appears to be culture-bound. For example, equity theory postulates that when people are not treated fairly, they will take steps to reduce the inequity by, for example, doing less work, filing a grievance, or getting a transfer to another department. In Asia and the Middle East, however, employees often readily accept inequitable treatment in order to preserve group harmony. Additionally, in countries such as Japan and Korea, men and women typically receive different pay for doing the same work, yet because of years of cultural conditioning women may not feel they are being treated inequitably.[37] Some researchers have explained this finding by suggesting that these women compare themselves only to other women and in this comparison feel they are being treated equitably. While this may be true, the results still point to the fact that equity theory is not universally applicable in explaining motivation and job satisfaction. In short, although the theory may help explain why "equal pay for equal work" is a guiding motivation principle in countries such as the United States and Canada, it may have limited value in other areas of the world, including Asia and Latin America, where compensation differences based on gender, at least traditionally, have been culturally acceptable.

Goal-Setting Theory

Goal-setting theory focuses on how individuals go about setting goals and responding to them and the overall impact of this process on motivation. Specific areas that are given attention in goal-setting theory include the level of participation in setting goals, goal difficulty, goal specificity, and the importance of objective, timely feedback to progress toward goals. Unlike many theories of motivation, goal setting has been continually refined and developed.[38] There is considerable research evidence showing that employees perform extremely well when they are assigned specific and challenging goals that they have had a hand in setting.[39] But most of these studies have been conducted in the United States, while few of them have been carried out in other cultures.[40] One study that did examine goal setting in an international setting looked at Norwegian employee participation in goal setting.[41] The researchers found that the Norwegian employees shunned participation and preferred to have their union representatives work with management in determining work goals. This led the researchers to conclude that individual participation in goal setting was seen as inconsistent with the prevailing philosophy of participation through union representatives. Unlike the United States, where employee participation in setting goals is motivational, it had no value for the Norwegian employees in this study.

Similar results to the Norwegian study have been reported by Earley, who found that workers in the U.K. responded more favorably to a goal-setting program sponsored by the union stewards than to one sponsored by management. This led Earley to conclude that the transferability across cultural settings of management concepts such as participation in goal setting may well be affected by the prevailing work norms.[42] In order to further test this proposition, Erez and Earley studied American and Israeli subjects and found that participative strategies led to higher levels of goal acceptance and performance in both cultures

goal-setting theory
A process theory that focuses on how individuals go about setting goals and responding to them and the overall impact of this process on motivation.

than did strategies in which objectives were assigned by higher-level management.[43] In other words, the value of goal-setting theory may well be determined by culture. In the case, for example, of Asian and Latin work groups, where collectivism is very high, the theory may have limited value for MNC managers in selected countries.

Expectancy Theory

expectancy theory
A process theory that postulates that motivation is influenced by a person's belief that (*a*) effort will lead to performance, (*b*) performance will lead to specific outcomes, and (*c*) the outcomes will be of value to the individual.

Expectancy theory postulates that motivation is largely influenced by a multiplicative combination of a person's belief that (*a*) effort will lead to performance, (*b*) performance will lead to specific outcomes, and (*c*) the outcomes will be of value to the individual.[44] In addition, the theory predicts that high performance followed by high rewards will lead to high satisfaction.[45] Does this theory have universal application? Eden used it in studying workers in an Israeli kibbutz and found some support;[46] and Matsui and colleagues reported that the theory could be applied successfully in Japan.[47] On the other hand, it is important to remember that expectancy theory is based on employees having considerable control over their environment, a condition that does not exist in many cultures (e.g., Asia). In particular, in societies where people believe that much of what happens is beyond their control, this theory may have less value. It would seem that expectancy theory is best able to explain worker motivation in cultures where there is a strong internal locus of control (e.g., in the United States). In short, the theory seems culture-bound, and international managers must be aware of this limitation in their efforts to apply this theory to motivate human resources.

■ Motivation Applied: Job Design, Work Centrality, and Rewards

Content and process theories provide important insights into and understanding of ways to motivate human resources in international management. So, too, do applied concepts such as job design, work centrality, and rewards.

Job Design

job design
A job's content, the methods that are used on the job, and the way the job relates to other jobs in the organization.

Job design consists of a job's content, the methods that are used on the job, and the way in which the job relates to other jobs in the organization. Job design typically is a function of the work to be done and the way in which management wants it to be carried out. These factors help to explain why the same type of work may have a different impact on the motivation of human resources in various parts of the world and result in differing qualities of work life.

Quality of Work Life: The Impact of Culture
Quality of work life (QWL) is not the same throughout the world. For example, assembly-line employees in Japan work at a rapid pace for hours and have very little control over their work activities. In Sweden, assembly-line employees work at a more relaxed pace and have a great deal of control over their work activities. U.S. assembly-line employees are somewhere in between; they typically work at a pace that is less demanding than that in Japan but more structured than that in Sweden.

What accounts for these differences? One answer is found in the culture of the country. QWL is directly related to culture. Table 12–6 compares the United States, Japan, and Sweden along the four cultural dimensions described in Chapter 4. A brief look shows that each country has a different cultural profile, helping to explain why similar jobs may be designed quite differently from country to country. Assembly-line work provides a good basis for comparison.

In Japan, there is strong uncertainty avoidance. The Japanese like to structure tasks so there is no doubt regarding what is to be done and how it is to be done. Individualism is

Table 12–6 Cultural Dimensions in Japan, Sweden, and the United States						
	Degree of Dimension					
Cultural Dimension	**High/Strong** X ←		**Moderate** — X —		**Low/Weak** → X	
Uncertainty avoidance		J		USA	S	
Individualism	USA		S		J	
Power distance			J	USA	S	
Masculinity		J	USA			S

Source: From Geert Hofstede, "The Cultural Relativity of the Quality of Life Concept," *Academy of Management Review,* July 1984, pp. 391, 393. Copyright © 1984 by Academy of Management. Reproduced with permission of Academy of Management via Copyright Clearance Center.

low, so there is strong emphasis on security, and individual risk taking is discouraged. The power-distance index is high, so Japanese workers are accustomed to taking orders from those above them. The masculinity index for the Japanese is high, which shows that they put a great deal of importance on money and other material symbols of success. In designing jobs, the Japanese structure tasks so that the work is performed within these cultural constraints. Japanese managers work their employees extremely hard. Although Japanese workers contribute many ideas through the extensive use of quality circles, Japanese managers give them very little say in what actually goes on in the organization (in contrast to the erroneous picture often portrayed by the media, which presents Japanese firms as highly democratic and managed from the bottom up[48]) and depend heavily on monetary rewards, as reflected by the fact that the Japanese rate money as an important motivator more than the workers in any other industrialized country do.

In Sweden, uncertainty avoidance is low, so job descriptions, policy manuals, and similar work-related materials are more open-ended or general in contrast with the detailed procedural materials developed by the Japanese. In addition, Swedish workers are encouraged to make decisions and to take risks. Swedes exhibit a moderate-to-high degree of individualism, which is reflected in their emphasis on individual decision making (in contrast to the collective or group decision making of the Japanese). They have a weak power-distance index, which means that Swedish managers use participative approaches in leading their people. Swedes score low on masculinity, which means that interpersonal relations and the ability to interact with other workers and discuss job-related matters are important. These cultural dimensions result in job designs that are markedly different from those in Japan.

Cultural dimensions in the United States are closer to those of Sweden than to those of Japan. In addition, except for individualism, the U.S. profile is between that of Sweden and Japan (again see Table 12–6). This means that job design in U.S. assembly plants tends to be more flexible or unstructured than that of the Japanese but more rigid than that of the Swedes.

This same pattern holds for many other jobs in these three countries. All job designs tend to reflect the cultural values of the country. The challenge for MNCs is to adjust job design to meet the needs of the host country's culture. For example, when Japanese firms enter the United States, they often are surprised to learn that people resent close control. In fact, there is evidence that the most profitable Japanese-owned companies in the United States are those that delegate a high degree of authority to their U.S. managers.[49] Similarly, Japanese firms operating in Sweden find that quality of work life is a central concern for the personnel and that a less structured, highly participative management style is needed for success. Some of the best examples of efforts to integrate job designs with culture and personality are provided by sociotechnical job designs.

Sociotechnical Job Designs

sociotechnical designs
Job designs that blend personnel and technology.

Sociotechnical designs are job designs that blend personnel and technology. The objective of these designs is to integrate new technology into the workplace so that workers accept and use it to increase overall productivity. Because new technology often requires people to learn new methods and, in some cases, work faster, employee resistance is common. Effective sociotechnical design can overcome these problems. There are a number of good examples, and perhaps the most famous is that of Volvo, the Swedish automaker.

Sociotechnical changes reflective of the cultural values of the workers were introduced at Volvo's Kalmar plant. Autonomous work groups were formed and given the authority to elect their own supervisors as well as to schedule, assign, and inspect their own work. Each group was allowed to work at its own pace, although there was an overall output objective for the week and each group was expected to attain this goal.[50] The outcome was very positive and resulted in Volvo building another plant that employed even more sophisticated sociotechnical job-design concepts. Volvo's plant layout, however, did not prevent the firm from having some problems. Both Japanese and North American automakers were able to produce cars in far less time, putting Volvo at a cost disadvantage. As a result, stagnant economies in Asia, coupled with weakening demand for Volvo's product lines in both Europe and the United States, resulted in the firm laying off workers and taking steps to increase its efficiency. More recently, Volvo's performance has rebounded, bolstered in part by its truck sales and reputation for safety in its passenger car division.[51]

Without sacrificing efficiency, other firms have introduced sociotechnical designs for better blending of their personnel and technology. A well-known U.S. example is General Foods, which set up autonomous groups at its Topeka, Kansas, plant to produce Gaines pet food. Patterned after the Volvo example, the General Foods project allowed workers to share responsibility and work in a highly democratic environment. Other U.S. firms also have opted for a self-managed team approach. In fact, research reports that the concept of multifunctional teams with autonomy for generating successful product innovation is more widely used by successful U.S., Japanese, and European firms than any other teamwork concept.[52] Its use must be tempered by the cultural situation, however. And even the widely publicized General Foods project at Topeka had some problems. Some former employees indicate that the approach steadily eroded and that some managers were openly hostile because it undermined their power, authority, and decision-making flexibility. The most effective job design will be a result of both the job to be done and the cultural values that support a particular approach.[53] For MNCs, the challenge will be to make the fit between the design and the culture.

At the same time, it is important to realize that functional job descriptions now are being phased out in many MNCs and replaced by more of a process approach. The result is a more horizontal network that relies on communication and teamwork. This approach also is useful in helping to create and sustain partnerships with other firms.

Work Centrality

work centrality
The importance of work in an individual's life relative to other areas of interest.

Work centrality, which can be defined as the importance of work in an individual's life relative to his or her other areas of interest (family, church, leisure), provides important insights into how to motivate human resources in different cultures.[54] After conducting a review of the literature, Bhagat and associates found that Japan has the highest level of work centrality, followed by moderately high levels for Israel, average levels for the United States and Belgium, moderately low levels for the Netherlands and Germany, and low levels for Britain.[55] These findings indicate that successful multinationals in Japan must realize that although work is an integral part of the Japanese lifestyle, work in the United States must be more balanced with a concern for other interests. Unfortunately, this is likely to become increasingly more difficult for Japanese firms in Japan because stagnant population growth is creating a shortage of personnel. As a result, growing numbers of Japanese firms are now trying to push the mandatory retirement age to 65 from 60 and, except for workers in the United States, Japanese workers put in the most hours.[56]

Value of Work   Although work is an important part of the lifestyles of most people, this emphasis can be attributed to a variety of conditions. For example, one reason that Americans and Japanese work such long hours is that the cost of living is high and hourly employees cannot afford to pass up the opportunity for extra money. Among salaried employees who are not paid extra, most Japanese managers expect their subordinates to stay late at work, and overtime has become a requirement of the job. Moreover, there is recent evidence that Japanese workers may do far less work in a business day than outsiders would suspect.

Many people are unaware of these facts and have misperceptions of why the Japanese and Americans work so hard and the importance of work to them. The same is true of Germans and Americans. In recent years, the number of hours worked annually by German workers has been declining, while the number for Americans has been on the rise. What accounts for this trend? Some observers have explained it in cultural terms, noting that Germans place high value on lifestyle and often prefer leisure to work, while their American counterparts are just the opposite. In fact, research reveals that culture may have little to do with it. A study by the National Bureau of Economic Research (NBER) found a far wider range of wages within American companies than in German firms, and this large pay disparity has created incentives for American employees to work harder. In particular, many U.S. workers believe that if they work harder their chances of getting pay hikes and promotions will increase, and there is historical data to support this belief. An analysis of worker histories in the United States and Germany led NBER researchers to estimate that American workers who increase their working time by 10 percent, for example, from 2,000 to 2,200 hours annually, will raise their future earnings by about 1 percent for each year in which they put in extra hours.

Another important area of consideration is the importance of work as a part of overall lifestyle. In the case of Japanese workers, in particular, there has been a growing interest in the impact of overwork on the physical condition of employees. A report by the Japanese government noted that one-third of the working-age population suffers from chronic fatigue, and a recent survey by the Japanese prime minister's office found that a majority of those who were surveyed complained of being chronically tired and feeling emotionally stressed and some complained about abusive conditions in the workplace.[57] Fortunately, as seen in "International Management in Action: Karoshi: Stressed Out in Japan," the effects of overwork or job burnout—**karoshi** in Japanese—are beginning to be recognized as a real social problem.

karoshi
A Japanese term that means "overwork" or "job burnout."

Job Satisfaction   In addition to the implications that value of work has for motivating human resources across cultures, another interesting contrast is job satisfaction. For example, one study found that Japanese office workers may be much less satisfied with their jobs than their U.S., Canadian, and EU counterparts are. The Americans, who reported the highest level of satisfaction in this study, were pleased with job challenges, opportunities for teamwork, and ability to make a significant contribution at work. Japanese workers were least pleased with these three factors.[58] Similar findings were uncovered by Luthans and his associates, who reported that U.S. employees had higher organizational commitment than Japanese or Korean workers in their cross-cultural study. What makes these findings particularly interesting is that a large percentage of the Japanese and Korean workers were supervisory employees, who could be expected to be more committed to their organization than nonsupervisory employees, and a significant percentage of these employees also had lifetime guarantees.[59] This study also showed that findings related to job satisfaction in the international arena often are different than expected.[60]

Karoshi: Stressed Out in Japan

Doing business in Japan can be a real killer. Overwork, or *karoshi,* as it is called in Japan, claims 10,000 lives annually in this hard-driving, competitive economic society according to Hiroshi Kawahito, a lawyer who founded the National Defense Council for Victims of Karoshi.

One of the cases is Jun Ishii of Mitsui & Company. Ishii was one of the firm's only speakers of Russian. In the year before his death, Ishii made 10 trips to Russia, totaling 115 days. No sooner would he arrive home from one trip than the company would send him out again. The grueling pace took its toll. While on a trip, Ishii collapsed and died of a heart attack. His widow filed a lawsuit against Mitsui & Company, charging that her husband had been worked to death. Tokyo labor regulators ruled that Ishii had indeed died of karoshi, and the government now is paying annual worker's compensation to the widow. The company also cooperated and agreed to make a one-time payment of $240,000.

The reason that the case received so much publicity is that this is one of the few instances in which the government ruled that a person died from overwork. Now regulators are expanding karoshi compensation to salaried as well as hourly workers. This development is receiving the attention of the top management of many Japanese multinationals, and some Japanese MNCs are beginning to take steps to prevent the likelihood of overwork. For example, Mitsui & Company now assesses its managers based on how well they set overtime hours, keep subordinates healthy, and encourage workers to take vacations. Matsushita Electric has extended vacations from 16 days annually to 23 days and now requires all workers to take this time off. One branch of Nippon Telegraph & Telephone found that stress made some workers irritable and ill, so the company initiated periods of silent meditation. Other companies are following suit, although there still are many Japanese who work well over 2,500 hours a year and feel both frustrated and burned out by job demands.

On the positive side, the Ishii case likely will bring about some improvements in working conditions for many Japanese employees. Experts admit, however, that it is difficult to determine if karoshi is caused by work demands or by private, late-night socializing that may be work related. Other possible causes include high stress, lack of exercise, and fatty diets, but whatever the cause, one thing is clear: More and more Japanese families no longer are willing to accept the belief that karoshi is a risk that all employees must accept. Work may be a killer, but this outcome can be prevented through more carefully implemented job designs and work processes.

At the same time, recent reports show that there is still a long way to go. In Saku, Japan, for example, the city's main hospital has found that 32 percent of the patients hospitalized in the internal medicine and psychiatric wards are being treated for chronic fatigue syndrome, a diagnosis that is made only after six months of severe, continuous fatigue in the absence of any organic illness. Japanese doctors attribute this explosion of chronic fatigue syndrome to stress. Moreover, during the prolonged economic downturn, a growing number of businesspeople found themselves suffering from these symptoms. And to make matters worse, there is growing concern about alcoholism among workers. Over the past four decades, per capita alcohol consumption in most countries has declined but in Japan it has risen fourfold. The per capita consumption of alcohol in Japan is equal to that in the United States. Even this comparison is misleading because researchers have found that most Japanese women do not drink at all, but Japanese men in their 50s drink more than twice as much as their American counterparts. Additionally, young Japanese employees find that drinking is considered necessary, and some of them have raised complaints about *alruhara,* or alcohol harassment (forced/pressured alcohol consumption).

Dealing with overwork will continue to be a challenge both for Japanese firms and for the government. The same is true of the growing problems associated with alcohol that are being brought on by stress and business cultures that have long supported alcohol consumption as a way of doing business and fitting into the social structure.

Conventional wisdom not always being substantiated has been reinforced by cross-cultural studies that found Japanese workers who already were highly paid, and then received even higher wages, experienced decreased job satisfaction, morale, commitment, and intention to remain with the firm. This contrasts sharply with U.S. workers, who did not experience these negative feelings.[61] These findings show that the motivation approaches used in one culture may have limited value in another.[62]

Research by Kakabadse and Myers also has brought to light findings that are contradictory to commonly accepted beliefs. These researchers examined job satisfaction among managers from the United Kingdom, France, Belgium, Sweden, and Finland. It has long been assumed that satisfaction is highest at the upper levels of organizations; however, this study found varying degrees of satisfaction among managers, depending on the country. The researchers reported that

> senior managers from France and Finland display greater job dissatisfaction than the managers from the remaining countries. In terms of satisfaction with and commitment to the organization, British, German and Swedish managers display highest levels of commitment. Equally, British and German managers highlight that they feel stretched in their job, but senior managers from French organizations suggest that their jobs lack sufficient challenge and stimulus. In keeping with the job-related views displayed by French managers, they equally indicate their desire to leave their job because of their unsatisfactory work-related circumstances.[63]

On the other hand, research also reveals that some of the conditions that help to create organizational commitment among U.S. workers also have value in other cultures. For example, a large study of Korean employees ($n = 1,192$ in 27 companies in eight major industries) found that consistent with U.S. studies, Korean employees' position in the hierarchy, tenure in their current position, and age all related significantly to organizational commitment. Also, as in previous studies in the United States, as the size of the Korean organizations increased, commitment decreased, and the more positive the climate perceptions, the greater was the commitment.[64] In other words, there is at least beginning evidence that the theoretic constructs predicting organizational commitment may hold across cultures.

Also related to motivation are job attitudes toward quality of work life. Recent research reports that EU workers see a strong relationship between how well they do their jobs and the ability to get what they want out of life. U.S. workers were not as supportive of this relationship, and Japanese workers were least likely to see any connection.

This finding raises an interesting motivation-related issue regarding how well, for example, American, European, and Japanese employees can work together effectively. Some researchers have recently raised the question of how Japanese firms will be able to have effective strategic alliances with American and European companies if the work values of the partners are so different. Tornvall, after conducting a detailed examination of the work practices of five companies—Fuji-Kiku, a spare-parts firm in Japan, Toyota Motor Ltd. of Japan, Volvo Automobile AB of Sweden, SAAB Automobile AB, Sweden, and the General Motors plant in Saginaw, Michigan—concluded that there were benefits from the approaches used by each. This led him to recommend what he calls a "balance in the synergy" between the partners.[65] Some of his suggestions included the following:

Moving away from	Moving toward
Logical and reason-centered, individualistic thinking.	A more holistic, idealistic, and group thinking approach to problem solving.
Viewing work as a necessary burden.	Viewing work as a challenging and development activity.
The avoidance of risk taking and the feeling of distrust of others.	An emphasis on cooperation, trust, and personal concern for others.
The habit of analyzing things in such great depth that it results in "paralysis through analysis."	Cooperation built on intuition and pragmatism.
An emphasis on control.	An emphasis on flexibility.

In large degree, this balance will require all three groups—American, Europeans, and Asians—to make changes in the way they approach work.

In conclusion, it should be remembered that work is important in every society. The extent of importance varies, however, and much of what is "known" about work as a motivator often is culture-specific. The lesson to be learned for international management is that although the process of motivation may be the same, the content may change from one culture to another.

Reward Systems

Besides the content and process theories, another important area of motivation is that of rewards. Managers everywhere use rewards to motivate their personnel. Sometimes these are financial in nature such as salary raises, bonuses, and stock options. At other times they are nonfinancial such as feedback and recognition.[66] The major challenge for international managers is that there are often significant differences between the reward systems that work best in one country and those that are most effective in another. Some of these differences are a result of the competitive environment[67] or of government legislation that dictates such things as minimum wages, pensions, and perquisites.[68] In other cases, however, the differences are accounted for very heavily by culture.[69] For example, while many American companies like to use merit-based reward systems, firms in Japan, Korea, and Taiwan, where individualism is not very high, often feel that this form of reward system is too disruptive of the corporate culture and traditional values.[70]

Incentives and Culture

Use of financial incentives to motivate employees is very common, especially in countries with high individualism. In the United States, a number of chief executive officers earn over $100 million a year thanks to bonuses, stock options, and long-term incentive payments.[71] These pay systems are common when companies attempt to link compensation to performance. Typically, these systems range from individual incentive-based pay systems in which workers are paid directly for their output to systems in which employees earn individual bonuses based on how well the organization at large achieves certain goals such as sales growth, total revenue, or total profit. These reward systems are designed to stress *equity*. However, they are not universally accepted.

In many cultures compensation is based on group membership or group effort. In these cases the systems are designed to stress *equality*, and employees will oppose the use of individual incentive plans. One example of this is the American multinational corporation that decided to institute an individually based bonus system for the sales representatives in its Danish subsidiary. The sales force rejected the proposal because it favored one group over another and employees felt that everyone should receive the same size bonus.[72] Another example, reported by Vance and associates, was Indonesian oil workers who rejected a pay-for-performance system that would have resulted in some work teams making more money than others.[73]

While financial rewards such as pay, bonuses, and stock options are important motivators, in many countries workers are highly motivated by other things as well. For example, Sirota and Greenwood studied employees of a large multinational electrical equipment manufacturer with operations in 40 countries. They found that in all of these locales the most important rewards involved recognition and achievement. Second in importance were improvements in the work environment and employment conditions including pay and work hours.[74] Beyond this, a number of differences emerged in preferred types of rewards. For example, employees in France and Italy highly valued job security while for American and British workers it held little importance. Scandinavian workers placed high value on concern for others on the job and for personal freedom and autonomy, but they did not rate "getting ahead" as very important. German workers ranked security, fringe benefits, and "getting ahead" as very important, while Japanese employees put good working conditions and a congenial work environment high on their list but ranked personal advancement quite low.

Very simply, the types of incentives that are deemed important appear to be culturally influenced. Moreover, culture can even affect the overall cost of an incentive system. For example, in Japan, efforts to introduce Western-style merit pay systems typically lead to an increase in the overall labor costs because the companies find that they cannot reduce the pay of less productive workers for fear of causing them to lose face and thus disturb group harmony.[75] As a result, everyone's salary increases. Culture also impacts on profit in that people tend to perform better under management systems that are supportive of their own values. Nam, for example, studied two Korean banks that operated under different management systems.[76] One was owned and operated as a joint venture with an American bank, and the other was owned and operated as a joint venture with a Japanese bank. The American bank put into place management practices and personnel policies that were common in its own organization. The Japanese bank put together a blend of Japanese and Korean human resource management policies. Nam found that employees in the joint venture with the Japanese bank were significantly more committed to the organization than were their counterparts in the American joint venture and the Japanese-affiliated bank had significantly higher financial performance.

Sometimes, however, reward systems can be transferred and used successfully. For example, Welsh, Luthans, and Sommer examined the effectiveness of common Western incentive systems in a Russian textile factory.[77] They found that both contingently administered extrinsic rewards and positive recognition and attention from the supervisor led to significantly enhanced job performance, while participative techniques had little impact on job behavior and performance. Similarly, many people believe that large annual financial packages and lucrative golden parachutes are used only in American firms, but this is untrue. Senior-level managers in many MNCs now earn large salaries, and large financial packages for executives who are terminated or whose company is acquired by another firm are gaining in popularity, especially in Europe.[78] In other words, the type of rewards that are used is not culture-bound.

Overall, however, cultures do greatly influence the effectiveness of various rewards. What works in one country may not work in another. For example, research shows that Swedish workers with superior performance often prefer a reward of time off rather than additional money, while high-performing Japanese workers tend to opt for financial incentives—as long as they are group based and not given on an individual basis.[79] It is also important to realize that the reasons why workers choose one form of motivation over another—for example, days off rather than more money—may not be immediately obvious or intuitively discernible. For example, research has found that Japanese workers tend to take only about half of their annual holiday entitlements, while French and German workers take all of the days to which they are entitled. Many people believe the Japanese want to earn more money, but the primary reason why they do not take all their holiday entitlements is that they believe taking all of those days shows a lack of commitment to their work group. The same is true for overtime: Individuals who refuse to work overtime are viewed as selfish. One of the results of these cultural values is karoshi, discussed earlier in the chapter.

The World of *BusinessWeek*—Revisited

The opening news story examines the decision by General Electric to acquire another company and integrate its management into the traditional GE structure. GE is concerned about developing the next generation of executives, and bringing in an "outsider" was a somewhat radical step for the firm. However, its future success depends greatly on executive management's motivational incentives and ability to take the best from the various countries in which it does business, as well as from the disparate operating companies of its large, global network. By putting William Castell, the head of Amersham, in charge of its $14 billion Healthcare unit, GE was sending a signal to its executives and employees that it values new ideas and fresh perspectives so that it can continue to innovate.

The challenge for international managers is to put together a motivational package that addresses the specific needs of the employee or group in each region where an MNC serves. In applying these ideas, answer the following questions: (1) What are some of the things that successful MNCs do to effectively motivate European employees? (2) What kinds of incentives do scientific and technical employees respond to that might not be as meaningful to other categories of employees? (3) What advantages might employees see of working for a truly global company (as opposed to a North American MNC)?

SUMMARY OF KEY POINTS

1. Two basic types of theories explain motivation: content and process. Content theories of motivation have received much more attention in international management research, because they provide the opportunity to create a composite picture of the motivation of human resources in a particular country or region. In addition, content theories more directly provide ways for managers to improve the performance of their human resources.

2. Maslow's hierarchy-of-needs theory has been studied in a number of different countries. Researchers have found that regardless of country, managers have to be concerned with the satisfaction of these needs for their human resources.

3. Some researchers have suggested that satisfaction profiles are not very useful for studying motivation in an international setting, because there are so many different subcultures within any country or even at different levels of a given organization. These researchers have suggested that job categories are more effective for examining motivation, because job level (managers versus operating employees) and the need hierarchy have an established relationship.

4. Like Maslow's theory, Herzberg's two-factor theory has received considerable attention in the international arena, and Herzberg's original findings from the United States have been replicated in other countries. Cross-cultural studies related to job satisfaction also have been conducted. The data show that job content is more important than job context to job satisfaction.

5. The third content theory of motivation that has received a great amount of attention in the international arena is the need for achievement. Some current findings show that this need is not as widely held across cultures as was previously believed. In some parts of the world, however, such as Anglo countries, cultural values support people to be high achievers. In particular, Dutch researcher Geert Hofstede suggested that an analysis of two cultural dimensions, uncertainty avoidance and masculinity, helps to identify high-achieving societies. Once again, it can be concluded that different cultures will support different motivational needs, and that international managers developing strategies to motivate their human resources for improved performance must recognize cultural differences.

6. Process theories have also contributed to the understanding of motivation in the international arena. Equity theory focuses on how motivation is affected by people's perception of how fairly they are being treated, and there is considerable research to support the fundamental equity principle in Western work groups. However, when the theory is examined on an international basis, the results are mixed. Perhaps the biggest shortcoming of the theory is that it appears to be culture-bound. For example, in Japan and Korea, men and women typically receive different pay for doing precisely the same work, and this is at least traditionally not perceived as inequitable to women.

7. Goal-setting theory focuses on how individuals go about setting goals and responding to them and the overall impact of this process on motivation. There is evidence showing that employees perform extremely well when they are assigned specific and challenging goals that they had a hand in setting. However, most of these goal-setting studies have been conducted in the United States; few of them have been carried out in other cultures. Additionally, research results on the effects of goal setting at the individual level are very limited, and culture may well account for these outcomes.

8. Expectancy theory postulates that motivation is largely influenced by a multiplicative combination of a person's belief that effort will lead to performance, that performance will lead to specific outcomes, and that these outcomes are valued by the individual. There is mixed support for this theory. Many researchers believe that the theory best explains motivation in countries that emphasize an internal locus of control.

9. Although content and process theories provide important insights into the motivation of human resources, three additional areas that have received a great deal of recent attention in the application of motivation are job design, work centrality, and reward systems. Job design is influenced by culture as well as the specific methods that are used to bring together the people and the work. Work centrality helps to explain the importance of work in an individual's life relative to other areas of interest. In recent years work has become a relatively greater part of the average U.S. employee's life and perhaps less a part of the average Japanese worker's life. Research also indicates that Japanese office workers are less satisfied with their jobs than are U.S., Canadian, and EU workers, suggesting that MNCs need to design motivation packages that address the specific needs of different cultures. This idea is also true in the case of rewards. Research shows that the motivational value of monetary and nonmonetary rewards is influenced by culture. Countries with high individualism such as the

United States and the U.K. tend to make wide use of individual incentives, while collectivistic countries such as in Asia tend to prefer group-oriented incentives. At the same time, research shows that some motivational approaches in the United States have been successfully used in Russia. So while the importance of focusing on the importance of motivation in the international arena is unquestioned, the use of specific applications continues to be challenging for MNC managers.

KEY TERMS

achievement motivation theory, *380*	job-content factors, *379*	process theories of motivation, *370*
content theories of motivation, *370*	job-context factors, *379*	safety needs, *371*
equity theory, *382*	job design, *384*	self-actualization needs, *371*
esteem needs, *371*	karoshi, *387*	social needs, *371*
expectancy theory, *384*	motivation, *368*	sociotechnical designs, *386*
goal-setting theory, *383*	motivators, *375*	two-factor theory of motivation, *375*
hygiene factors, *375*	physiological needs, *371*	work centrality, *386*

REVIEW AND DISCUSSION QUESTIONS

1. Do people throughout the world have needs similar to those described in Maslow's need hierarchy? What does your answer reveal about using universal assumptions regarding motivation?

2. Is Herzberg's two-factor theory universally applicable to human resource management, or is its value limited to Anglo countries?

3. What are the dominant characteristics of high achievers? Using Figure 12–5 as your point of reference, determine which countries likely will have the greatest percentage of high achievers. Why is this so? Of what value is your answer to the study of international management?

4. A U.S. manufacturer is planning to open a plant in Sweden. What should this firm know about the quality of work life in Sweden that would have a direct effect on job design in the plant? Give an example.

5. What does a U.S. firm setting up operations in Japan need to know about work centrality in that country? How would this information be of value to the multinational? Conversely, what would a Japanese firm need to know about work centrality in the United States? Explain.

6. In managing operations in Europe, which process theory—equity theory, goal-setting theory, or expectancy theory—would be of most value to an American manager? Why?

7. What do international managers need to know about the use of reward incentives to motivate personnel? What role does culture play in this process?

INTERNET EXERCISE: MOTIVATING POTENTIAL EMPLOYEES

In order for multinationals to continue expanding their operations, they must be able to attract and retain highly qualified personnel in many countries. Much of their success in doing this will be tied to the motivational package that they offer, including financial opportunities, benefits and perquisites, meaningful work, and an environment that promotes productivity and worker creativity. Automotive firms, in particular, are a good example of MNCs that are trying very hard to increase their worldwide market share. So for them, employee motivation is an area that is getting a lot of attention.

Go to the Web and look at the career opportunities that are currently being offered by Ford Motor (**www.ford.com**), Volvo (**www.volvo.com**), and Volkswagen (**www.vw.com**). All of these companies provide information about the career opportunities they offer. Based on this information, answer these three questions: (1) What are some of the things that all three firms offer to motivate new employees? (2) Which of the three has the best motivational package? Why? (3) Are there any major differences between Ford and its European rivals? What conclusion can you draw from this?

Singapore

Singapore is an island city-state that is located at the southern tip of the Malay Peninsula. The small country covers 239 square miles and is connected by train across the Johore Strait to West Malaysia in the north. The Strait of Malacca to the south separates Singapore from the Indonesian island of Sumatra. There are approximately 4 million people in Singapore, resulting in a population density per square mile of almost 18,000 people. About three-fourths of Singaporeans are of Chinese descent, 15 percent are Malays, and the remainder are Indian and European. The gross domestic product of this thriving country is over $112 billion, and per capita GDP is around $25,200. One of the so-called newly industrialized countries or Four Tigers (along with Korea, Taiwan, and Hong Kong), Singapore in recent years has been affected by the economic uncertainty around the world, but the currency and prices have remained relatively stable. The very clean and modern city remains the major commercial and shipping center of Southeast Asia. In May 2003, the governments of the United States and Singapore signed the U.S.–Singapore Free Trade Agreement (USSFTA), the first bilateral free-trade agreement between the United States and an Asian country.

For the last six months, the Madruga Corporation of Cleveland has been producing small electronic toys in Singapore. The small factory has been operated by local managers, but Madruga now wants to expand the Singapore facilities as well as integrate more expatriate managers into the operation. The CEO explained: "We do not want to run this plant as if it were a foreign subsidiary under the direct control of local managers. It is our plant and we want an on-site presence. Over the last year we have been staffing our Canadian and European operations with headquarters personnel, and we are now ready to turn attention to our Singapore operation." Before doing so, however, the company intends to conduct some on-site research to learn the most effective way of managing the Singapore personnel.

In particular, the Madruga management team is concerned with how to motivate the Singaporeans and make them more productive. One survey has already been conducted among the Singapore personnel; this study found a great deal of similarity with the workers at the U.S. facilities. Both the Singapore and the U.S. employees expressed a preference for job-content factors such as the chance for growth, achievement, and increased responsibility, and they listed money and job security toward the bottom of the list of things they looked for in a job.

Madruga management is intrigued by these findings and believes that it might be possible to use some of the same motivation approaches in Singapore as it does in the United States. Moreover, one of the researchers sent the CEO a copy of an article showing that people in Singapore have weak uncertainty avoidance and a general cultural profile that is fairly similar to that of the United States. The CEO is not sure what all this means, but she does know that motivating workers in Singapore apparently is not as "foreign" a process as she thought it would be.

www.sg

Questions

1. What are some current issues facing Singapore? What is the climate for doing business in Singapore today?

2. Based on the information in this case, determine the specific things that seem to motivate human resources in Singapore.

3. Would knowledge of the achievement motive be of any value to the expatriate managers who are assigned to the Singapore operation?

4. If you were using Figure 12–5 to help explain how to motivate Singapore human resources effectively, what conclusions could you draw that would help provide guidelines for the Madruga management team?

Motivation Is the Key

Over the last five years, Corkley & Finn, a regional investment brokerage house, has been extremely profitable. Some of its largest deals have involved cooperation with investment brokers in other countries. Realizing that the world economy is likely to grow vigorously over the next 25 years, the company has decided to expand its operations and open overseas branches. In the beginning, the company intends to work in cooperation with other local brokerages; however, the company believes that within five years, it will have garnered enough business to break away and operate independently. For the time being, the firm intends to set up a small office in London and another in Tokyo.

The firm plans on sending four people to each of these offices and recruiting the remainder of the personnel from the local market. These new branch employees will have to spend time meeting potential clients and building trust. This will be followed by the opportunity to put together small financial deals and, it is hoped, much larger ones over time.

The company is prepared to invest whatever time or money is needed to make these two branches successful. "What we have to do," the president noted, "is establish an international presence and then build from there. We will need to hire people who are intensely loyal to us and use them as a cadre for expanding operations and becoming a major player in the international financial arena. One of our most important challenges will be to hire the right people and motivate them to do the type of job we want and stay with us. After all, if we bring in people and train them how to do their jobs well and then they don't perform or they leave, all we've done is spend a lot of money for nothing and provide on-the-job training for our competitors. In this business, our people are the most important asset, and clients most often are swayed toward doing business with an investment broker with whom they think they can have a positive working relationship. The reputation of the firm is important, but it is always a function of the people who work there. Effective motivation of our people is the key to our ultimate success in these new branches."

Questions

1. When motivating the personnel in London and Tokyo, is the company likely to find that the basic hierarchical needs of the workers are the same? Why or why not?

2. How could an understanding of the two-factor theory of motivation be of value for motivating the personnel at both locations? Would hygiene factors be more important to one of these groups than to the other? Would there be any difference in the importance of motivators?

3. Using Figure 12–5 as a point of reference, what recommendation would you make regarding how to motivate the personnel in London? In Tokyo? Are there any significant differences between the two? If so, what are they? If not, why not?

Chapter 13

LEADERSHIP ACROSS CULTURES

Leadership often is credited for the success or failure of international operations. Note that like the other topics discussed so far, effective leadership styles and practices in one culture are not necessarily effective in other cultures. For example, the leadership approach used by effective U.S. managers would not necessarily be the same as that employed in other parts of the world. Even within the same country, effective leadership tends to be very situation-specific; however, also like the other areas studied in international management, certain leadership styles and practices transcend international boundaries. This chapter examines these leadership differences and similarities.

First the basic foundation for the study of leadership is reviewed. Next, leadership in various parts of the world, including Europe, East Asia, the Middle East, and developing countries, is examined. The specific objectives of this chapter are:

1. **DESCRIBE** the basic philosophic foundation and styles of managerial leadership.

2. **EXAMINE** the attitudes of European managers toward leadership practices.

3. **COMPARE** and **CONTRAST** leadership styles in Japan with those in the United States.

4. **REVIEW** leadership approaches in China, the Middle East, and developing countries.

5. **EXAMINE** recent research and findings regarding leadership across cultures.

6. **DISCUSS** the relationship of culture clusters and leader behavior on effective leadership practices, including increasing calls for more responsible global leadership.

The World of *BusinessWeek*

BusinessWeek

Richard Branson's Next Big Adventure

He Has No Qualms About Jumping into the Tough Airline Market in the U.S.

Eight years ago, Sir Richard Branson was offered the chance to invest in a new discount airline in the U.S. The charismatic founder of Britain's Virgin Group Ltd. was sorely tempted. In exchange for use of the Virgin brand, Branson would get a minority stake in the new airline. But the deal never got off the ground. "We were sensitive about giving away the brand without control," Branson recalls. And the startup? It went on to become one of the most successful low-cost airlines in the U.S. "JetBlue was the one that got away," he laments.

Now Branson, 53, is getting a second chance. He plans to launch his own discount airline, Virgin USA, by the start of 2005. The Virgin publicity machine has been unusually quiet about Branson's latest big bet. But observers say the imminent announcement that Delta Air Lines Inc. President and COO Frederick W. Reid will be named Virgin USA's CEO is testament to the strength of the new company's business plan and the Virgin brand. By the beginning of March, Virgin will name the location of its new U.S. headquarters from a shortlist of three: Boston's Logan International Airport, Washington Dulles International Airport, and San Francisco International Airport. Politicians and airport officials have been bombarding Virgin officials with offers of tax breaks and other financial incentives.

The new airline is just one of many projects on Branson's to-do list. His privately owned Virgin Group, which includes

200 companies in businesses ranging from planes and trains to music and mobile phones, is in the midst of an all-out global expansion. He's contemplating a summer flotation of Virgin's British mobile phone service, launching a Canadian mobile company, expanding his international airline Virgin Atlantic, and attempting to merge his Brussels-based discount airline Virgin Express with SN Brussels Airlines. He's also revamping his retail music chain, Virgin MegaStores, with a range of new products such as clothing, mobile phones, and consumer electronics aimed at teens. Oh, and he's interested in running a proposed high-speed rail system in Florida that will link Tampa and Orlando by 2009.

Deep Pockets

It's an ambitious, not to mention expensive agenda. But while Virgin Group and its founder have never been busier, they've also never been richer. London's *The Sunday Times* estimates Branson's personal wealth at more than $2 billion. Credit that to the success of Virgin's newest ventures, which account for much of the group's $450 million cash war chest. Take Virgin Blue Airlines, the Australian discount airline that Branson founded five years ago with $8 million. Following a December 2003, flotation on the Sydney stock market that valued the company at some $2 billion, Branson's remaining 25.1% stake is worth more than $500 million. Virgin says the group's overall earnings before interest, tax, and depreciation in 2003 were $680 million on turnover of $8.1 billion.

Entering the crowded and brutally competitive U.S. airline market may be Virgin's biggest challenge yet, bulging coffers or no. Discount carriers, including Southwest Airlines, JetBlue Airways, and AirTran, are bigger and stronger than ever before, with 22% of the overall market. At the same time, the network carriers have stabilized their finances and are fighting aggressively to maintain market share. David G. Neeleman, CEO of JetBlue, warns that it won't be easy for Branson to emulate JetBlue. "This is not Australia with Ansett (a now defunct carrier) going out of business," he says. "This is hand-to-hand combat over here. It's very tough."

Ever the optimist, Branson thinks the time has never been better to start a U.S. airline. With the majors downsizing their fleets and staff, he believes there's ample opportunity to recruit top talent and start with reasonable labor

costs. And low interest rates are pushing down the cost of buying or leasing planes.

Virgin's likely strategy will be to fill in the gaps left by Southwest and JetBlue rather than compete head to head. Described by Branson as "low-cost, high-frills," Virgin USA will copy Virgin Atlantic's whizzy technology, superior service, and innovative in-flight entertainment. "The product will be sexy," says Frances Farrow, CEO of Virgin USA Inc., the group's American business-development and management arm. "Not like Southwest but more like a JetBlue Plus."

What everyone really wants to know is who will be Virgin's U.S. partner. Under U.S. law, foreigners may own up to 49% of the equity and 25% of the voting rights in any U.S. carrier. Ever since Virgin made its intentions known late last year, several U.S. airlines, aviation companies, and private-equity firms have expressed interest. Talks between Virgin and US Airway Group about acquiring some of the ailing carrier's assets have foundered, say those familiar with the deal. So Virgin is expected to start from scratch, backed by deep-pocketed U.S. investors. "We are in the lucky position of having had a great deal of interest from investors," Farrow says.

A Handful of Duds

Even if the U.S. airline venture flops, Branson has other ways to make money. He is considering taking his profitable British cell-phone company Virgin Mobile Telecoms Ltd. public. It is Britain's fifth-largest but fastest-growing mobile

---

What's Driving Virgin

Virgin Atlantic Flies to 22 destinations worldwide. In 1999, Branson sold 49% of the British carrier to Singapore Airlines for $1 billion.

Virgin Express The Brussels-based discount carrier flies 2.5 million passengers to 18 European cities. Currently in merger discussions with Belgium's SN Brussels Airlines, the publicly traded airline is expected to post a 2003 loss.

Virgin Blue Founded five years ago with $8 million from Virgin, the Australian no-frills airline's IPO last December valued it at $2 billion. Branson's 25.1% stake is currently worth more than $500 million.

Virgin Rail Runs two of Britain's main train lines as a joint venture with British transport company Stagecoach.

Virgin Mobile Launched five years ago, the mobile company has over 5.8 million customers in Britain, the U.S., and Australia. Branson plans to spin off the British unit, worth an estimated $2 billion, with an IPO by yearend.

Data: *BusinessWeek* company

Source: www.businessweek.com/magazine/content/04_10/b3873069_mz054.htm

company, with 3.7 million subscribers. Analysts value the British unit at $2 billion. Not bad considering that Virgin's total investment in the project to date is $75 million. Virgin Mobile USA, launched in 2001 as a venture with Sprint PCS Group, is expected to be in the black by yearend. In November, Sprint and Virgin valued the business at $650 million, making Branson's 50% stake worth more than double his initial investment.

The mobile businesses are vintage Virgin. Branson runs the group as a "branded venture-capital firm." He supplies the brand, a small initial investment, and takes majority control while big name partners stump up the cash. "We haven't had any dramatic failures," Branson says. There have, however, been some duds. Virgin Cola, Virgin Vodka, and Virgin Cosmetics have all but disappeared. Branson just sold the loss-making Virgin Cars, a British auto dealership.

Not to worry. Other ventures beckon. A film based on Branson's best-selling autobiography, *Losing My Virginity,* is set for release in 2005. Not only will Branson get a percentage of the ticket sales but heartthrob Jude Law is being tapped to play the man himself. Maybe you can catch the movie on a Virgin USA flight.

*By Kerry Capell in London,
with Wendy Zellner in Dallas*

Source: From "European Business: Richard Branson's Next Big Adventure," *BusinessWeek,* March 8, 2004, online edition. Copyright © 2004 by the McGraw-Hill Companies, Inc. www.businessweek.com. Reprinted with permission.

The opening news story provides an excellent example of the challenges of global leadership. After passing on an investment opportunity for JetBlue, Richard Branson is jumping into the ultracompetitive U.S. airline industry with Virgin USA. With stiff rivalry coming from already present low-price carriers such as Southwest and JetBlue, Branson will have his hands full. Virgin USA's future competitiveness greatly depends on Branson's ability to effectively convey his vision and strategy to his employees, customers, investors, and the media. Moreover, major carriers are beginning to adopt low-price models in hopes of capturing lost market share from firms such as Southwest. Branson claims that Virgin USA isn't competing directly with the likes of Southwest or JetBlue, but it's clear that he's going to need all of his charisma and leadership to make Virgin USA successful in the United States. Questions also remain about whether Branson's style will resonate with employees in the United States as it does with those in Europe. If so, Virgin USA should be in an enviable position moving forward. In this chapter we will address different leadership styles and address these foundations as a platform for building effective leadership across cultures.

■ Foundation for Leadership

leadership
The process of influencing people to direct their efforts toward the achievement of some particular goal or goals.

When one realizes that much of history, political science, and the behavioral sciences is either directly or indirectly concerned with leadership, the statement that more research has focused on leadership than on any other topic becomes believable. Despite all this attention over the years, however, there still is no generally agreed-on definition, let alone sound answers to the question of which approach is more effective than others in the international arena. For present purposes, **leadership** can be defined as the process of influencing people to direct their efforts toward achievement of some particular goal or goals.[1] Leadership is widely recognized as being very important in the study of international management, but relatively little effort has been made to systematically study and compare leadership approaches throughout the world. Most international research efforts on leadership have been directed toward a specific country or geographic area.

Two comparative areas provide a foundation for understanding leadership in the international arena: (1) the philosophical grounding of how leaders view their subordinates and (2) leadership approaches as reflected through use of autocratic–participative characteristics and behaviors of leaders. The philosophies and approaches used in the United States often are quite different from those employed by leaders in overseas organizations, although the differences often are not as pronounced as is commonly believed.

Philosophical Background: Theories X, Y, and Z

One primary reason that leaders behave as they do is their philosophy or beliefs regarding how to direct their subordinates most effectively. Managers who believe their people are naturally lazy and work only for money will use a leadership style that is different from the style of managers who believe their people are self-starters and enjoy challenge and increased responsibility. Douglas McGregor, the pioneering leadership theorist, labeled these two sets of assumptions "Theory X" and "Theory Y."

A **Theory X manager** believes that people are basically lazy and that coercion and threats of punishment must be used to get them to work. The specific philosophical assumptions of Theory X leaders are:

Theory X manager
A manager who believes that people are basically lazy and that coercion and threats of punishment often are necessary to get them to work.

1. By their very nature, people do not like to work and will avoid it whenever possible.
2. Workers have little ambition, try to avoid responsibility, and like to be directed.
3. The primary need of employees is job security.
4. To get people to attain organizational objectives, it is necessary to use coercion, control, and threats of punishment.[2]

A **Theory Y manager** believes that under the right conditions people not only will work hard but will seek increased responsibility and challenge. In addition, a great deal of creative potential basically goes untapped, and if these abilities can be tapped, workers will provide much higher quantity and quality of output. The specific philosophical assumptions of Theory Y leaders are:

Theory Y manager
A manager who believes that under the right conditions people not only will work hard but will seek increased responsibility and challenge.

1. The expenditure of physical and mental effort at work is as natural to people as resting or playing.
2. External control and threats of punishment are not the only ways of getting people to work toward organizational objectives. If people are committed to the goals, they will exercise self-direction and self-control.
3. Commitment to objectives is determined by the rewards that are associated with their achievement.
4. Under proper conditions, the average human being learns not only to accept but to seek responsibility.
5. The capacity to exercise a relatively high degree of imagination, ingenuity, and creativity in the solution of organizational problems is widely distributed throughout the population.
6. Under conditions of modern industrial life, the intellectual potential of the average human being is only partially tapped.[3]

The reasoning behind these beliefs, however, will vary by culture. U.S. managers believe that to motivate workers, it is necessary to satisfy their higher-order needs. This is done best through a Theory Y leadership approach. In China, Theory Y managers act similarly—but for different reasons. After the 1949 revolution, two types of managers emerged in China: Experts and Reds. The Experts focused on technical skills and primarily were Theory X advocates. The Reds, skilled in the management of people and possessing political and ideological expertise, were Theory Y advocates. The Reds also believed that the philosophy of Chairman Mao supported their thinking (i.e., all employees had to rise together both economically and culturally). Both Chinese and U.S. managers support Theory Y, but for very different reasons.[4]

The same is true in the case of Russian managers. In a survey conducted by Puffer, McCarthy, and Naumov, 292 Russian managers were asked about their beliefs regarding work.[5] Table 13–1 shows the six different groupings of the responses. Drawing together the findings of the study, the researchers pointed out the importance of Westerners getting beyond the stereotypes of Russian managers and learning more about the latter's beliefs in order to be more effective in working with them as employees and as joint-venture partners. Obviously, the assumption that Russian managers are strict adherents of Theory X may be common, but it may also be erroneous.[6]

The philosophical assumptions of both the Chinese and the Russian managers help to dictate the leadership approach that they use. The assumptions are most easily seen in the managers' behavior, such as giving orders, getting and giving feedback, and creating an overall climate within which the work will be done.

William Ouchi proposed an additional perspective, which he called "Theory Z," that brings together Theory Y and modern Japanese management techniques. A **Theory Z manager** believes that workers seek opportunities to participate in management and are motivated by teamwork and responsibility sharing.[7] The specific philosophical assumptions of a Theory Z leader are:

> **Theory Z manager**
> A manager who believes that workers seek opportunities to participate in management and are motivated by teamwork and responsibility sharing.

1. People are motivated by a strong sense of commitment to be part of a greater whole—the organization in which they work.

2. Employees seek out responsibility and look for opportunities to advance in an organization. Through teamwork and commitment to common goals, employees derive self-satisfaction and contribute to organizational success.

3. Employees who learn different aspects of the business will be in a better position to contribute to the broader goals of the organization.

4. By making commitments to employees' security through lifetime or long-term employment, the organization will engender in employees strong bonds of loyalty, making the organization more productive and successful.

Leadership Behaviors and Styles

Leader behaviors can be translated into three commonly recognized styles: (1) authoritarian; (2) paternalistic; and (3) participative. **Authoritarian leadership** is the use of work-centered behavior that is designed to ensure task accomplishment. As shown in Figure 13–1, this leader behavior typically involves the use of one-way communication from manager to subordinate. The focus of attention usually is on work progress, work procedures, and roadblocks that are preventing goal attainment. Although this leadership style often is effective in handling crises, some leaders employ it as their primary style regardless of the situation. It also is widely used by Theory X managers, who believe that a continued focus on the task is compatible with the kind of people they are dealing with.

> **authoritarian leadership**
> The use of work-centered behavior designed to ensure task accomplishment.

Paternalistic leadership uses work-centered behavior coupled with a protective employee-centered concern. This leadership style can be best summarized by the statement "Work hard and the company will take care of you." Paternalistic leaders expect everyone to work hard; in return, the employees are guaranteed employment and given security benefits such as medical and retirement programs. Paternalistic leaders often are referred to as "soft" Theory X leaders because of their strong emphasis on strictly controlling their employees coupled with concern for their welfare. They often treat employees as strict but caring parents would treat their children. A good example was provided by the chairman of the Daewoo Motor Company of Korea, who laid off thousands of employees in 2002. Having

> **paternalistic leadership**
> The use of work-centered behavior coupled with a protective employee-centered concern.

Table 13–1
Russian Managerial Beliefs About Work

A. Humanistic Beliefs

Work can be made meaningful.

One's job should give one a chance to try out new ideas.

The workplace can be humanized.

Work can be made satisfying.

Work should allow for the use of human capabilities.

Work can be a means of self-expression.

Work should enable one to learn new things.

Work can be organized to allow for human fulfillment.

Work can be made interesting rather than boring.

The job should be a source of new experiences.

B. Organizational Beliefs

Survival of the group is very important in an organization.

Working with a group is better than working alone.

It is best to have a job as part of an organization where all work together even if you don't get individual credit.

One should take an active part in all group affairs.

The group is the most important entity in any organization.

One's contribution to the group is the most important thing about one's work.

Work is a means to foster group interests.

C. Work Ethic

Only those who depend on themselves get ahead in life.

To be superior a person must stand alone.

A person can learn better on the job by striking out boldly on his own than by following the advice of others.

One must avoid dependence on other persons whenever possible.

One should live one's life independent of others as much as possible.

D. Beliefs About Participation in Managerial Decisions

The working classes should have more say in running society.

Factories would be better run if workers had more of a say in management.

Workers should be more active in making decisions about products, financing, and capital investment.

Workers should be represented on the board of directors of companies.

E. Leisure Ethic

The trend toward more leisure is not a good thing. (R)

More leisure time is good for people.

Increased leisure time is bad for society. (R)

Leisure-time activities are more interesting than work.

The present trend toward a shorter workweek is to be encouraged.

F. Marxist-Related Beliefs

The free-enterprise system mainly benefits the rich and powerful.

The rich do not make much of a contribution to society.

Workers get their fair share of the economic rewards of society. (R)

The work of the laboring classes is exploited by the rich for their own benefit.

Wealthy people carry their fair share of the burdens of life in this country. (R)

The most important work is done by the laboring classes.

Notes: 1. Response scales ranged from 1 (strongly disagree) to 5 (strongly agree).

2. (R) denotes reverse-scoring items.

3. The 45-individual items contained in the 6 belief clusters were presented to respondents in a mixed fashion, rather than categorized by cluster as shown above.

4. Participation was a subset of Marxist-related values in Buchholz's original study, but was made a separate cluster in his later work.

Source: Adapted from Sheila M. Puffer, Daniel J. McCarthy, and Alexander I. Naumov, "Russian Managers' Beliefs About Work: Beyond the Stereotypes," *Journal of World Business* 32, no. 3 (1997), p. 262.

Figure 13–1

**Leader–Subordinate
Interactions**

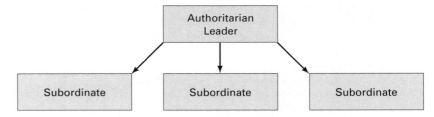

One-way downward flow of information and influence from authoritarian leader
to subordinates.

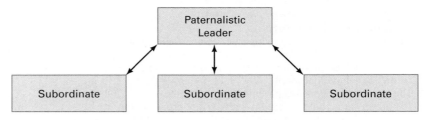

Continual interaction and exchange of information and influence between leader
and subordinates.

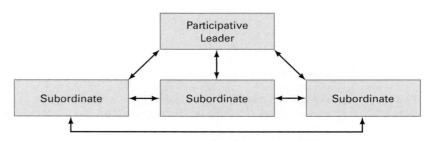

Continual interaction and exchange of information and influence between leader
and subordinates.

Source: Adapted from Richard M. Hodgetts, *Modern Human Relations at Work,* 8th ed.
(Ft. Worth, TX: Harcourt, 2002), p. 264.

made this decision, the chairman then went throughout the company apologizing for having to
take such drastic action and telling each person that he was determined to help him or her
find another job. When asked about his approach, he said, "I'm the father of my employees.
I need to bring back hope to everyone."[8]

One way of contrasting authoritative and paternalistic leaders is in terms of Likert's
management systems or leadership styles, as presented in Table 13–2. An authoritarian
leader has the characteristics of Likert's system 1; a paternalistic leader, the characteristics
of Likert's system 2.

participative leadership
The use of both work- or
task-centered and people-
centered approaches to
leading subordinates.

Participative leadership is the use of both work-centered and people-centered
approaches. Participative leaders typically encourage their people to play an active role in
assuming control of their work, and authority usually is highly decentralized. In terms of
Likert's four systems shown in Table 13–2, participative leaders are associated with system
3. (Likert's system 4 leaders are fully democratic and go beyond the participative style.)
Another way of characterizing participative leaders is in terms of the managerial grid,
which is a traditional, well-known method of identifying leadership styles. As shown in
Figure 13–2, participative leaders are on the 9,9 position of the grid. This is in contrast to
paternalistic leaders, who tend to be about 9,5, and autocratic leaders, who are in more of a

Table 13–2
Likert's Systems or Styles of Leadership

Leadership Characteristic	System 1 (Exploitive Autocratic)	System 2 (Benevolent Autocratic)	System 3 (Participative)	System 4 (Democratic)
Leadership processes used (extent to which superiors have confidence and trust in subordinates)	Have no confidence and trust in subordinates	Have condescending confidence and trust, such as master has in servant	Substantial but not complete confidence and trust, still wish to keep control of decisions	Complete confidence and trust in all matters
Character of motivational forces (underlying motives tapped)	Physical security, economic needs, and some use of the desire for status	Economic needs and moderate use of ego motives (e.g., desire for status, affiliation, and achievement)	Economic needs and considerable use of ego and other major motives (e.g., desire for new experiences)	Full use of economic, ego, and other major motives such as motivational forces arising from group goals
Character of communication process (amount of interaction and communication aimed at achieving organization's objectives)	Very little	Little	Quite a bit	Much, with both individuals and groups
Character of interaction influence process (amount and character of interaction)	Little interaction and always with fear and distrust	Little interaction and usually with some condescension by superiors; fear and caution by subordinates	Moderate interaction, often with fair amount of confidence and trust	Extensive friendly interaction with high degree of confidence and trust
Character of decision-making process (at what level in organization are decisions formally made)	Bulk of decisions at top of organization	Policy at top; many decisions with prescribed framework made at lower levels but usually checked with top before action is taken	Broad policy decision at top; more specific decisions of lower levels	Decision making widely done throughout organization, although well integrated through linking process provided by overlapping groups
Character of goal setting or ordering (manner in which usually done)	Orders issued	Orders issued, opportunity to comment may exist	Goals are set or orders issued after discussion with subordinates of problems and planned action	Except in emergencies, goals are usually established by group participation

Source: From Rensis Likert, *The Human Organization* (New York: McGraw-Hill, 1967). Copyright © 1967 the McGraw-Hill Companies. Used with permission.

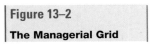

Figure 13–2

The Managerial Grid

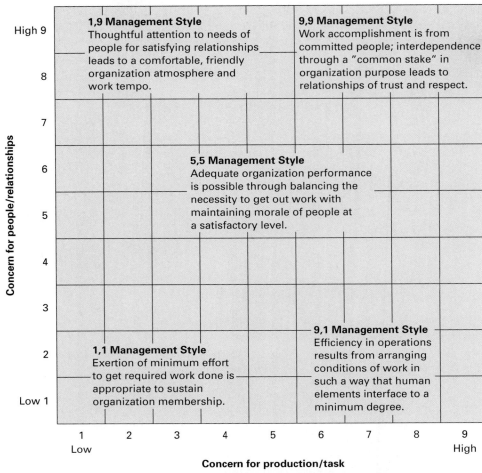

Source: Adapted from Robert S. Blake and Jane S. Mouton, "Managerial Facades," *Advanced Management Journal,* July 1966, p. 31.

9,1 position on the grid. Participative leadership is very popular in many technologically advanced countries. Such leadership has been widely espoused in the United States, England, and other Anglo countries, and it currently is very popular in Scandinavian countries as well. For example, at General Electric, managers are encouraged to use a participative style that delivers on commitment and shares the values of the firm. This approach is also common in those other nations.

■ Leadership in the International Context

How do leaders in other countries attempt to direct or influence their subordinates? Are their approaches similar to those used in the United States? Research shows that there are both similarities and differences. Most international research on leadership has focused on Europe, East Asia, the Middle East, and developing countries such as India, Peru, Chile, and Argentina.

Attitudes of European Managers Toward Leadership Practices

In recent years, much research has been directed at leadership approaches in Europe. Most effort has concentrated on related areas, such as decision making, risk taking, strategic planning, and organization design, that have been covered in previous chapters. Some of this previous discussion is relevant to an understanding of leadership practices in Europe. For example, British managers tend to use a highly participative leadership approach. This is true for two reasons: (1) The political background of the country favors such an approach. (2) Because most top British managers are not highly involved in the day-to-day affairs of the business, they prefer to delegate authority and let much of the decision making be handled by middle and lower-level managers. This preference contrasts sharply with that of the French and the Germans,[9] who prefer a more work-centered, authoritarian approach. In fact, if labor unions did not have legally mandated seats on the boards of directors, participative management in Germany likely would be even less pervasive than it is, a problem that currently confronts firms like Volkswagen that are trying to reduce sharply their overhead to meet increasing competition in Europe.[10] Scandinavian countries, however, make wide use of participative leadership approaches, with worker representation on the boards of directors and high management–worker interaction regarding workplace design and changes.

As a general statement, most evidence indicates that European managers tend to use a participative approach. They do not entirely subscribe to Theory Y philosophical assumptions, however, because an element of Theory X thinking continues. This was made clear by the Haire, Ghiselli, and Porter study of 3,641 managers from 14 countries.[11] (The motivation-related findings of this study were reported in Chapter 12.) The leadership-related portion of this study sought to determine whether these managers were basically traditional (Theory X, or system 1/2) or democratic-participative (Theory Y, or system 3/4) in their approach. Specifically, the researchers investigated four areas relevant to leadership:

1. *Capacity for leadership and initiative.* Does the leader believe that employees prefer to be directed and have little ambition (Theory X), or does the leader believe that characteristics such as initiative can be acquired by most people regardless of their inborn traits and abilities (Theory Y)?

2. *Sharing information and objectives.* Does the leader believe that detailed, complete instructions should be given to subordinates and that subordinates need only this information to do their jobs, or does the leader believe that general directions are sufficient and that subordinates can use their initiative in working out the details?

3. *Participation.* Does the leader support participative leadership practices?

4. *Internal control.* Does the leader believe that the most effective way to control employees is through rewards and punishment or that employees respond best to internally generated control?

Overall Results of Research on Attitudes of European Managers   Responses by managers to the four areas covered in the Haire, Ghiselli, and Porter study, as noted in Chapter 12, are quite dated but remain the most comprehensive available and are relevant to the current discussion of leadership similarities and differences. The specifics by country may have changed somewhat over the years, but the leadership processes revealed should not be out-of-date. The clusters of countries studied by these researchers are shown in Table 13–3. Results indicate that none of the leaders from various parts of the world, on average, were very supportive of the belief that individuals have a capacity for leadership and initiative. The researchers put it this way: "In each country, in each group of countries, in all of the countries taken together, there is a relatively low opinion of the capabilities of the average person, coupled with a relatively positive belief in the necessity for democratic-type supervisory practices."[12]

An analysis of standard scores compared each cluster of countries against the others, and it revealed that Anglo leaders tend to have more faith in the capacity of their people for leadership and initiative than do the other clusters. They also believe that sharing information

Table 13–3
Clusters of Countries in the Haire, Ghiselli, and Porter Study

NORDIC-EUROPEAN COUNTRIES	ANGLO-AMERICAN COUNTRIES
Denmark	England
Germany	United States
Norway	
Sweden	DEVELOPING COUNTRIES
	Argentina
	Chile
LATIN-EUROPEAN COUNTRIES	India
Belgium	
France	
Italy	JAPAN
Spain	

and objectives is important; however, when it comes to participation and internal control, the Anglo group tends to give relatively more autocratic responses than all the other clusters except developing countries. Interestingly, Anglo leaders reported a much stronger belief in the value of external rewards (pay, promotion, etc.) than did any of the clusters except that of the developing countries. These findings clearly illustrate that attitudes toward leadership practices tend to be quite different in various parts of the world.

The Role of Level, Size, and Age on European Managers' Attitudes Toward Leadership   The research of Haire and associates provided important additional details within each cluster of European countries. These findings indicated that in some countries, higher-level managers tended to express more democratic values than lower-level managers; however, in other countries, the opposite was true. For example, in England, higher-level managers responded with more democratic attitudes on all four leadership dimensions, whereas in the United States, lower-level managers gave more democratically oriented responses on all four. In the Scandinavian countries, higher-level managers tended to respond more democratically; in Germany, lower-level managers tended to have more democratic attitudes.

Company size also tended to influence the degree of participative-autocratic attitudes. There was more support among managers in small firms than in large ones regarding the belief that individuals have a capacity for leadership and initiative; however, respondents from large firms were more supportive of sharing information and objectives, participation, and use of internal control.

There were findings that age also had some influence on participative attitudes. Younger managers were more likely to have democratic values when it came to capacity for leadership and initiative and to sharing information and objectives, although on the other two areas of leadership practices older and younger managers differed little. In specific countries, however, some important differences were found. For example, younger managers in both the United States and Sweden espoused more democratic values than did their older counterparts; in Belgium, the opposite was true.

Conclusion About European Leadership Practices   Data from the classic Haire and associates study show differences in the attitudes toward leadership practices between European managers. In most cases, these leaders tend to reflect more participative and democratic attitudes, but not in every country. In addition, organizational level, company size, and age seem to greatly influence attitudes toward leadership. Because many of the young people in this study now are middle-aged, European managers in general are highly likely to be more participative than their older counterparts of the 1960s and 1970s;

however, no empirical evidence proves that each generation of European managers is becoming more participative than the previous one. Also, just because they express favorable attitudes toward participative leadership does not mean that they actually practice this approach, although it is certainly true that boards of directors of U.S. multinationals operating in Europe are becoming more international and that this multicultural mix may indeed promote participative management. More research that actually observes today's European managers' style in their day-to-day jobs is needed before any definitive conclusions can be drawn.

Japanese Leadership Approaches

Japan is well known for its paternalistic approach to leadership. As noted in Figure 12–5, Japanese culture promotes a high safety or security need, which is present among home country–based employees as well as MNC expatriates. For example, one study examined the cultural orientations of 522 employees of 28 Japanese-owned firms in the United States and found that the native Japanese employees were more likely than their U.S. counterparts to value paternalistic company behavior.[13] Another study found that Koreans also value such paternalism.[14] However, major differences appear in leadership approaches used by the Japanese and those in other locales.

For example, the comprehensive Haire, Ghiselli, and Porter study found that Japanese managers have much greater belief in the capacity of subordinates for leadership and initiative than do managers in most other countries.[15] In fact, in the study, only managers in Anglo-American countries had stronger feelings in this area. The Japanese also expressed attitudes toward the use of participation to a greater degree than others. In the other two leadership areas, sharing information and objectives and using internal control, the Japanese respondents were above average but not distinctive. Overall, however, this study found that the Japanese respondents scored highest on the four areas of leadership combined. In other words, these findings provide evidence that Japanese leaders have considerable confidence in the overall ability of their subordinates and use a style that allows their people to actively participate in decisions.

In addition, the leadership process used by Japanese managers places a strong emphasis on ambiguous goals. Subordinates are typically unsure of what their manager wants them to do. As a result, they spend a great deal of time overpreparing their assignments. Some observers believe that this leadership approach is time-consuming and wasteful. However, it has a number of important benefits. One is that the leader is able to maintain stronger control of the followers because the latter do not know with certainty what is expected of them. So they prepare themselves for every eventuality. Second, by placing the subordinates in a position where they must examine a great deal of information, the manager ensures that the personnel are well prepared to deal with the situation and all of its ramifications. Third, the approach helps the leader maintain order and provide guidance, even when the leader is not as knowledgeable as the followers.

Two experts on the behavior of Japanese management have noted that salarymen (middle managers) survive in the organization by anticipating contingencies and being prepared to deal with them. So when the manager asks a question and the salaryman shows that he has done the research needed to answer the question, the middle manager also shows himself to be a reliable person. The leader does not have to tell the salaryman to be prepared; the individual knows what is expected of him.

> Japanese managers operate this way because they usually have less expertise in a division's day-to-day business than their subordinates do. It is the manager's job to maintain harmony, not to be a technical expert. Consequently, a senior manager doesn't necessarily realize that E, F, G, and H are important to know. He gives ambiguous directions to his subordinates so they can use their superior expertise to go beyond A, B, C, and D. One salaryman explained it this way: "When my boss asks me to write a report, I infer what he wants to know and what he needs to know without being told what he wants." Another interviewee added that subordinates who receive high performance evaluations are those who know what the boss

wants without needing to be told. What frustrates Japanese managers about non-Japanese employees is the feeling that, if they tell such a person they want A through D, they will never extract E through H; instead, they'll get exactly what they asked for. Inferring what the boss would have wanted had he only known to ask is a tough game, but it is the one salary-men must play.[16]

Differences Between Japanese and U.S. Leadership Styles

In a number of ways, Japanese leadership styles differ from those in the United States. For example, the Haire and associates study found that except for internal control, large U.S. firms tend to be more democratic than small ones, whereas in Japan, the profile is quite different.[17] A second difference is that younger U.S. managers appear to express more democratic attitudes than their older counterparts on all four leadership dimensions, but younger Japanese fall into this category only for sharing information and objectives and in the use of internal control.[18] Simply put, evidence points to some similarities between U.S. and Japanese leadership styles, but major differences also exist.

A number of reasons have been cited for these differences. One of the most common is that Japanese and U.S. managers have a basically different philosophy of managing people. Table 13–4 provides a comparison of seven key characteristics that come from Ouchi's *Theory Z,* which combines Japanese and U.S. assumptions and approaches. Note in the table that the Japanese leadership approach is heavily group oriented, paternalistic, and concerned with the employee's work and personal life. The U.S. leadership approach is almost the opposite.[19]

variety amplification
The creation of uncertainty and the analysis of many alternatives regarding future action.

variety reduction
The limiting of uncertainty and the focusing of action on a limited number of alternatives.

Another difference between Japanese and U.S. leadership styles is how senior-level managers process information and learn. Japanese executives are taught and tend to use **variety amplification,** which is the creation of uncertainty and the analysis of many alternatives regarding future action. By contrast, U.S. executives are taught and tend to use **variety reduction,** which is the limiting of uncertainty and the focusing of action on a limited number of alternatives.[20] Through acculturation, patterning, and mentoring, as well as formal training, U.S. managers tend to limit the scope of questions and issues before them, emphasize one or two central aspects of that topic, identity specific employees to respond to it, and focus on a goal or objective that is attainable. Japanese managers, in contrast, tend to be inclusive in their consideration of issues or problems, seek a large quantity of

Table 13–4
Japanese vs. U.S. Leadership Styles

Philosophical Dimension	Japanese Approach	U.S. Approach
Employment	Often for life; layoffs are rare	Usually short-term; layoffs are common
Evaluation and promotion	Very slow; big promotions may not come for the first 10 years	Very fast: those not quickly promoted often seek employment elsewhere
Career paths	Very general; people rotate from one area to another and become familiar with all areas of operations	Very specialized; people tend to stay in one area (accounting, sales, etc.) for their entire careers
Decision making	Carried out via group decision making	Carried out by the individual manager
Control mechanism	Very implicit and informal; people rely heavily on trust and goodwill	Very explicit; people know exactly what to control and how to do it
Responsibility	Shared collectively	Assigned to individuals
Concern for employees	Management's concern extends to the whole life, business and social, of the worker	Management concerned basically with the individual's work life only

Source: Adapted from William Ouchi, *Theory Z: How American Business Can Meet the Japanese Challenge* (Reading, MA: Addison-Wesley, 1981).

information to inform the problem, encourage all employees to engage in solutions, and aim for goals that are distant in the future.

Further, this research found that Japanese focused very heavily on problems while the U.S. managers focused on opportunities.[21] The Japanese were more willing to allow poor performance to continue for a time so that those who were involved would learn from their mistakes, but the Americans worked to stop poor performance as quickly as possible. Finally, the Japanese sought creative approaches to managing projects and tried to avoid relying on experience, but the Americans sought to build on their experiences.

Still another major reason accounting for differences in leadership styles is that the Japanese tend to be more ethnocentric than their U.S. counterparts. The Japanese think of themselves as Japanese managers who are operating overseas; most do not view themselves as international managers. As a result, even if they do adapt their leadership approach on the surface to that of the country in which they are operating, they still believe in the Japanese way of doing things and are reluctant to abandon it.

Similarities Between Japanese and U.S. Leadership Styles

Although differences exist and get considerable attention in both research and the popular media, important similarities in leadership approaches also exist between the Japanese and the Americans. For example, an early but still relevant study examined the ways in which leadership style could be used to influence the achievement motivation of Japanese subjects.[22] Achievement motivation was measured among a series of participants, and two major groups were created. One consisted of Japanese high achievers, the other of Japanese low achievers. Four smaller groups of high-achieving participants and four more of low-achieving participants then were created. Each high-achieving group was assigned a supervisor who used a different leadership style. The same pattern was used with the low-achieving groups.

In each of the two major clusters (high achievers and low achievers), one group was assigned a leader who focused on performance (called "P supervision" in the study). The supervisor used a 9,1 (high on task, low on people) type of style on the managerial grid (see Figure 13–2, which identifies all the styles on the grid). This supervisor was work-centered, took the initiative in solving problems that impeded performance, and ensured that all rules were followed, exhorting the workers to "hurry up," "work more quickly," and "don't fool around; get to work." The supervisor also compared this group with the others, related how far behind they were, and pressed them to catch up.

In a second group within each major cluster, the supervisor's leadership style focused on maintaining and strengthening the group (called "M supervision" in the study). The individual used a 1,9 (low on task, high on people) leadership style on the managerial grid. The supervisor was open to suggestions, never pushed personal opinions on the workers, and encouraged a warm, friendly environment. This supervisor often said, "Let's be pleasant and cheerful" and "Let's be more friendly." The supervisor also was sympathetic when things did not go well and worked to improve interpersonal relations by reducing tensions and increasing the sociability of the environment.

In a third group within each major cluster, the supervisor focused on both performance and maintenance (called "PM supervision" in the study). This supervisor put pressure on the workers to do their work but, at the same time, offered encouragement and support to the workers. In other words, this supervisor used a 9,9 leadership style from the managerial grid.

In the fourth group within each major cluster, the supervisor focused on neither performance nor maintenance (called "pm supervision" in the study). This supervisor simply did not get very involved in either the task or the people side of the group being led. In other words, the supervisor used a 1,1 leadership style on the grid.

The results of these four leadership styles among the high-achieving and low-achieving groups are reported in Figures 13–3 and 13–4. In the high-achieving groups, the

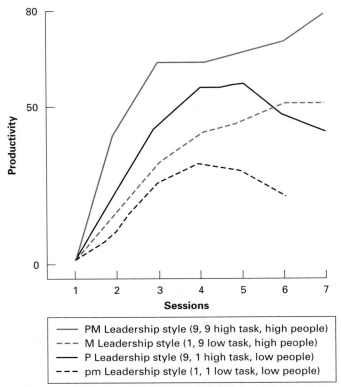

Figure 13–3

Productivity of Japanese Groups with High-Achievement Motivation under Different Leadership Styles

— PM Leadership style (9, 9 high task, high people)
--- M Leadership style (1, 9 low task, high people)
— P Leadership style (9, 1 high task, low people)
--- pm Leadership style (1, 1 low task, low people)

Source: Reprinted from Jyuji Misumi and Fumiyasu Seki, "Effects of Achievement Motivation on the Effectiveness of Leadership Patterns," *Administrative Science Quarterly* 16, no. 1 (March 1971), p. 57. Copyright © Johnson Graduate School of Management, Cornell University.

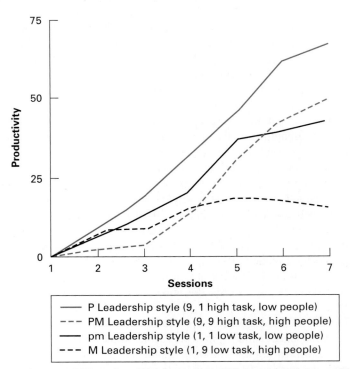

Figure 13–4

Productivity of Japanese Groups with Low-Achievement Motivation under Different Leadership Styles

— P Leadership style (9, 1 high task, low people)
--- PM Leadership style (9, 9 high task, high people)
— pm Leadership style (1, 1 low task, low people)
--- M Leadership style (1, 9 low task, high people)

Source: Reprinted from Jyuji Misumi and Fumiyasu Seki, "Effects of Achievement Motivation on the Effectiveness of Leadership Patterns, *Administrative Science Quarterly* 16, no. 1 (March 1971), p. 57. Copyright © Johnson Graduate School of Management, Cornell University.

PM (or 9,9) leadership style that emphasized both the task and the human dimension was the most effective throughout the entire experiment, and the pm (or 1,1) leadership style was consistently ineffective. The P (or 9,1 [high on task, low on people]) leadership style was the second most effective during the early and middle phases of the study, but it was supplanted by the M (or 1,9 [low on task, high on people]) leadership style in the later phases. Among the low-achieving groups, the P (or 9,1) supervision was most effective. The M (or 1,9) leadership style was the second most effective during the early sessions, but it soon tapered off and produced negative results in later sessions. The PM (or 9,9) style was moderately ineffective during the first three sessions but improved rapidly and was the second most effective by the end of the seventh session. The pm (or 1,1) leadership style was consistently effective until the fifth session; then productivity began to level off.

The results of this study are similar to those that would be expected among high- and low-achieving groups of U.S. managers. In addition, the study showed that high-achieving groups of Japanese tend to be more productive than low-achieving groups. Thus, this study shows some degree of convergence or similarity between Japanese and U.S. managers regarding the most effective types of leadership styles given the achievement motivation of the group members.

Research supports these conclusions and suggests they can be extended to other countries as well. For example, in the United States the Saturn has proved to be one of General Motors' most successful new auto offerings. The approach used in managing workers at the Saturn plant was quite different from that employed in other GM plants. Strong attention was given to allowing workers a voice in all management decisions, and pay is linked to quality, productivity, and profitability. Japanese firms such as Sony use a similar approach, encouraging personnel to assume authority, use initiative, and work as a team. Major emphasis also is given to developing communication links between management and the employees and to encouraging people to do their best. Korean firms also are relying more heavily on a 9,9 leadership style. Sang Lee and associates have reported that among Korea's largest firms, a series of personality criteria are used in screening employees, and many of these directly relate to 9,9 leadership: harmonious relationships with others, creativeness, motivation to achieve, future orientation, and a sense of duty.[23]

Another common trend is the movement toward team orientation and away from individualism. "International Management in Action: Global Teams" illustrates this point.

Leadership in China

In the past few years a growing amount of attention has been focused on leadership in China. In particular, international researchers are interested in learning if the country's economic progress is creating a new cadre of leaders whose styles are different from the styles of leaders of the past. In one of the most comprehensive studies to date, Ralston and his colleagues found that, indeed, a new generation of Chinese leaders is emerging and they are somewhat different from past leaders in work values.[24]

The researchers gathered data from a large number of managers and professionals ($n = 869$) who were about to take part in management development programs. These individuals were part of what the researchers called the "New Generation" of Chinese organizational leaders. The researchers wanted to determine if this new generation of managers had the same work values as those of the "Current Generation" and "Older Generation" groups. In their investigation, the researchers focused their attention on the importance that the respondents assigned to three areas: individualism, collectivism, and Confucianism. Individualism was measured by the importance assigned to self-sufficiency and personal accomplishments. Collectivism was measured by the person's willingness to subordinate personal goals to those of the work group with an emphasis on sharing and group harmony. Confucianism was measured by the importance the respondent assigned to societal harmony, virtuous interpersonal behavior, and personal and interpersonal harmony.

International leaders now put increasing focus on developing global teams that are capable of overcoming cultural barriers and working together in an efficient, harmonious manner. At Dallas-based Maxus Energy (a wholly owned subsidiary of YPF, the largest Argentinean corporation in the world), teams consist of Americans, Dutch, British, and Indonesians who have been brought together to pursue a common goal: maximize oil and gas production. Capitalizing on the technical expertise of the members and their willingness to work together, the team helped the company to achieve its objective and add oil reserves to its stockpiles—an almost unprecedented achievement. This story is only one of many that help to illustrate the way in which global teams are being created and used to achieve difficult international objectives.

In developing effective global teams, companies are finding there are four phases in the process. In phase one, the team members come together with their own expectations, culture, and values. In phase two, members go through a self-awareness period, during which they learn to respect the cultures of the other team members. Phase three is characterized by a developing trust among members, and in phase four, team members begin working in a collaborative way.

How are MNCs able to create the environment that is needed for this metamorphosis? Several specific steps are implemented by management, including:

1. The objectives of the group are carefully identified and communicated to the members.

2. Team members are carefully chosen so that the group has the necessary skills and personnel to reinforce and complement each other.

3. Each person learns what he or she is to contribute to the group, thus promoting a feeling of self-importance and interdependency.

4. Cultural differences between the members are discussed so that members can achieve a better understanding of how they may work together effectively.

5. Measurable outcomes are identified so that the team can chart its progress and determine how well it is doing. Management also continually stresses the team's purpose and its measurable outcomes so that the group does not lose sight of its goals.

6. Specially designed training programs are used to help the team members develop interpersonal, intercultural skills.

7. Lines of communication are spelled out so that everyone understands how to communicate with other members of the group.

8. Members are continually praised and rewarded for innovative ideas and actions.

MNCs now find that global teams are critical to their ability to compete successfully in the world market. As a result, leaders who are able to create and lead interdisciplinary, culturally diverse groups are finding themselves in increasing demand by MNCs.

The researchers found that the new generation group scored significantly higher on individualism than did the current and older generation groups. In addition, the new generation leaders scored significantly lower than the other two groups on collectivism and Confucianism. These values appear to reflect the period of relative openness and freedom, often called the "Social Reform Era," during which these new managers grew up. They have had greater exposure to Western societal influences, and this may well be resulting in leadership styles similar to those of Western managers.

These research findings show that leadership is culturally influenced, but as the economy of China continues to change and the country moves more and more toward capitalism, the work values of managers may also change. As a result, the new generation of leaders may well use leadership styles similar to those in the West, something that has also occurred in Japan as seen by Figures 13–3 and 13–4.

Leadership in the Middle East

Research also has been conducted on Middle East countries to determine the similarities and differences in managerial attitudes toward leadership practices. For example, in a follow-up study to that of Haire and associates, mid-level managers from Arab countries were surveyed and found to have higher attitude scores for capacity for leadership and initiative than those from any of the other countries or clusters reported in Table 13–3.[25] The Arab managers' scores for sharing information and objectives, participation, and internal control, however, all were significantly lower than the scores of managers in the other countries and clusters reported in Table 13–3. The researcher concluded that the results were accounted for by the culture of the Middle East region. Table 13–5 summarizes not only the leadership differences between Middle Eastern and Western managers but also other areas of organization and management.

More recent research provides some evidence that there may be much greater similarity between Middle Eastern leadership styles and those of Western countries.[26] In particular, the observation was made that Western management practices are very evident in the Arabian Gulf region because of the close business ties between the West and this oil-rich area and the increasing educational attainment, often in Western universities, of Middle Eastern managers. A study on decision-making styles in the United Arab Emirates showed that organizational culture, level of technology, level of education, and management responsibility were good predictors of decision-making styles in such an environment.[27] These findings were consistent with similar studies in Western environments. Also, results indicated a tendency toward participative leadership styles among young Arab middle management, as well as among highly educated managers of all ages.[28]

Table 13–5
Differences in Middle Eastern and Western Management

Management Dimensions	Middle Eastern Management	Western Management
Leadership	Highly authoritarian tone, rigid instructions. Too many management directives.	Less emphasis on leader's personality, considerable weight on leader's style and performance.
Organizational structures	Highly bureaucratic, overcentralized, with power and authority at the top. Vague relationships. Ambiguous and unpredictable organization environments.	Less bureaucratic, more delegation of authority. Relatively decentralized structure.
Decision making	Ad hoc planning, decisions made at the highest level of management. Unwillingness to take high risk inherent in decision making.	Sophisticated planning techniques, modern tools of decision making, elaborate management information systems.
Performance evaluation and control	Informal control mechanisms, routine checks on performance. Lack of vigorous performance evaluation systems.	Fairly advanced control systems focusing on cost reduction and organizational effectiveness.
Personnel policies	Heavy reliance on personal contacts and getting individuals from the "right social origin" to fill major positions.	Sound personnel management policies. Candidates' qualifications are usually the basis for selection decisions.
Communication	The tone depends on the communicants. Social position, power, and family influence are ever-present factors. Chain of command must be followed rigidly. People relate to each other tightly and specifically. Friendships are intense and binding.	Stress usually on equality and a minimization of difference. People relate to each other loosely and generally. Friendships not intense and binding.

Source: From M. K. Badawy, "Styles of Mid-Eastern Managers," *California Management Review* 22, no. 3 (Spring 1980), p. 57. Copyright © 1980 by the Regents of the University of California. Reprinted by permission of the regents.

Leadership Approaches in Developing Countries

Some research has focused on leadership styles in developing countries such as India, Peru, Chile, and Argentina. These studies have examined leadership in terms of Likert's systems or styles (see Table 13–2) and the managerial attitudes toward the four dimensions of leadership practice from the Haire, Ghiselli, and Porter study.

Because of India's long affiliation with Great Britain, leadership styles in India would seem more likely to be participative than those in the Middle East or in other developing countries. Haire and associates found some degree of similarity between leadership styles in India and Anglo-American countries, but it was not significant. The study found Indians to be similar to the Anglo-Americans in managerial attitudes toward capacity for leadership and initiative, participation, and internal control. The difference is in sharing information and objectives. The Indian managers' responses tended to be quite similar to those of managers in other developing countries.[29]

Other research that focused more on Indian industrial firms indicates that the most effective leadership style used by Indian managers often is a more participative one. One study, for example, found that the job satisfaction of Indian employees increases as leadership style becomes more participative.[30] Still another study reached similar conclusions based on interviews and surveys conducted with managers in a cross-section of industries in northern and western India using a questionnaire that identified Likert systems or styles of leadership.[31] Of the 120 respondents, 14 percent classified their organization as operating under exploitive autocratic leadership (system 1), 63 percent as benevolent autocratic (system 2), and 23 percent as consultative participative (system 3). None viewed their firm as operating under fully democratic leadership (system 4). In addition, this study found that the more autocratic the leadership style (systems 1 and 2), the lower was the level of job satisfaction.[32]

These findings from India show that a participative leadership style may be more common and more effective in developing countries than has been reported previously. Over time, developing countries (as also shown in the case of the Persian Gulf nations) may be moving toward a more participative leadership style.

A similar situation exists in Peru. There is little reason to believe that managerial attitudes toward leadership practices would have been any different from those reported by Haire and associates for other South American countries, such as Argentina or Chile. The results from the Haire and associates study for those two developing countries were similar to those for India.[33] Additional research, however, has found that leadership styles in Peru may be much closer to those in the United States than was previously assumed.

Stephens conducted research among three large textile plants in an urban area in Peru.[34] These three Peruvian plants were matched with three U.S. plants of similar size in urban settings in the southwest United States. Because these Peruvian and U.S. firms all were in the same industry and faced similar competitive pressures, this study was an excellent opportunity to compare intercultural leadership profiles and identify any significant differences. Using the same four dimensions of leadership practice that were used in the Haire and associates study, Stephens found that the leadership profiles of the Peruvian and U.S. managers were similar. Commenting on the results, he noted that:

> There is little reason to conclude that leader styles are much different in Peru than in the U.S. Absolutely, U.S. leaders appear to perceive workers as having more initiative, being more internally motivated, and therefore more capable of meaningful participation. However, the differences for initiative and locus of control were not statistically significant and differences for sharing of information and objectives showed Peruvians to be statistically more inclined to share than U.S. managers. Taken in total, this does not suggest a more participative, democratic leader style in the U.S. and an authoritarian, external control oriented style in Peru.[35]

As in the case of Middle Eastern managers, these findings in South America indicate there indeed may be more similarities in international leadership styles than previously assumed. As countries become more economically advanced, participative styles may well gain in importance. Of course, this does not mean that MNCs can use the same leadership styles in their various locations around the world. There still must be careful contingency application of leadership styles (different styles for different situations); however, many of the more enlightened participative leadership styles used in the United States and other economically advanced countries, such as Japan, also may have value in managing international operations even in developing countries as well as in the emerging Eastern European countries.

■ Recent Findings and Insights About Leadership

In recent years researchers have begun raising the question of universality of leadership behavior. Do effective leaders, regardless of their country culture or job, act similarly? A second, and somewhat linked, research inquiry has focused on the question: Are there a host of specific behaviors, attitudes, and values that leaders in the twenty-first century will need in order to be successful? Thus far the findings have been mixed. Some investigators have found that there is a trend toward universalism for leadership; others have concluded that culture continues to be a determining factor and that an effective leader, for example, in Sweden will not be as effective in Italy if he or she employs the same approach. One of the most interesting recent efforts has been conducted by Bass and his associates and has focused on the universality and effectiveness of both transformation and transactional leadership.

Transformational, Transactional, and Charismatic Leadership

Transformational leaders are visionary agents with a sense of mission who are capable of motivating their followers to accept new goals and new ways of doing things. One recent variant on transformational leadership focuses on the individual's charismatic traits and abilities. This research stream, known as the study of **charismatic leadership,** has explored how the individual abilities of an executive work to inspire and motivate her or his subordinates.[36] **Transactional leaders** are individuals who exchange rewards for effort and performance and work on a "something for something" basis.[37] Do these types of leaders exist worldwide, and is their effectiveness consistent in terms of performance? Drawing on an analysis of studies conducted in Canada, India, Italy, Japan, New Zealand, Singapore, and Sweden, as well as in the United States, Bass discovered that very little of the variance in leadership behavior could be attributed to culture. In fact, in many cases he found that national differences accounted for less than 10 percent of the results. This led him to create a model of leadership and conclude that "although this model . . . may require adjustments and fine-tuning as we move across cultures, particularly into non-Western cultures, overall, it holds up as having considerable universal potential."[38]

Simply stated, Bass discovered that there was far more universalism in leadership than had been believed previously. Additionally, after studying thousands of international cases, he found that the most effective managers were transformational leaders and they were characterized by four interrelated factors. For convenience, the factors are referred to as the "4 I's" and they can be described this way:

1. *Idealized influence.* Transformational leaders are a source of charisma and enjoy the admiration of their followers. They enhance pride, loyalty, and confidence in their people, and they align these followers by providing a common purpose or vision that the latter willingly accept.

2. *Inspirational motivation.* These leaders are extremely effective in articulating their vision, mission, and beliefs in clear-cut ways, thus providing an easy-to-understand sense of purpose regarding what needs to be done.

transformational leaders Leaders who are visionary agents with a sense of mission and who are capable of motivating their followers to accept new goals and new ways of doing things.

charismatic leaders Leaders who inspire and motivate employees through their charismatic traits and abilities.

transactional leaders Individuals who exchange rewards for effort and performance and work on a "something for something" basis.

3. *Intellectual stimulation.* Transformational leaders are able to get their followers to question old paradigms and to accept new views of the world regarding how things now need to be done.

4. *Individualized consideration.* These leaders are able to diagnose and elevate the needs of each of their followers through individualized consideration, thus furthering the development of these people.[39]

Bass also discovered that there were four other types of leaders. All of these are less effective than the transformational leader, although the degree of their effectiveness (or ineffectiveness) will vary. The most effective of the remaining four types was labeled the contingent reward (CR) leader by Bass. This leader clarifies what needs to be done and provides both psychic and material rewards to those who comply with his or her directives. The next most effective manager is the active management-by-exception (MBE-A) leader. This individual monitors follower performance and takes corrective action when deviations from standards occurs. The next manager in terms of effectiveness is the passive management-by-exception (MBE-P) leader. This leader takes action or intervenes in situations only when standards are not met. Finally, there is the laissez-faire (LF) leader. This person avoids intervening or accepting responsibility for follower actions.

Bass found that through the use of higher-order factor analysis it is possible to develop a leadership model that illustrates the effectiveness of all five types of leaders: I's (transformational), CR, MBE-A, MBE-P, and LF. Figure 13–5 presents this model. The higher the box in the figure and the farther to right on the shaded base area, the more effective and active is the leader. Notice that the 4 I's box is taller than any of the others in the figure and is located more to the right than any of the others. The CR box is second tallest and second closest to the right, on down to the LF box, which is the shortest and farthest from the right margin.

Bass also found that the 4 I's were positively correlated with each other, but less so with contingent reward. Moreover, there was a near zero correlation between the 4 I's and

Figure 13–5

An Optimal Profile of Universal Leadership Behaviors

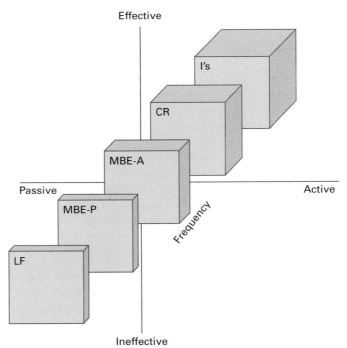

Source: Adapted from Bernard M. Bass, "Is There Universality in the Full Range Model of Leadership?" *International Journal of Public Administration* 16, no. 6 (1996), p. 738.

management-by-exception styles, and there was an inverse correlation between these four factors and the laissez-faire leadership style.

Does this mean that effective leader behaviors are the same regardless of country? Bass concluded that this statement is not quite true—but there is far more universalism than people believed previously. In putting his findings in perspective, he concluded that there certainly would be differences in leadership behavior from country to country.[40] For example, he noted that transformational leaders in Honduras would have to be more directive than their counterparts in Norway. Moreover, culture can create some problems in using universal leadership concepts in countries such as Japan, where the use of contingent reward systems is not as widespread as in the West. These reward systems can also become meaningless in Arab and Turkish cultures where there is a strong belief that things will happen "if God wills" and not because a leader has decided to carry them out. Yet, even after taking these differences into consideration, Bass contends that universal leadership behavior is far more common than many people realize.[41]

> I cannot and do not want to dismiss the evidence of systematic differences in beliefs, values, implicit theories, traits associated with leadership, decision styles, paternalism, trait and institutional historical and legal differences that shape leader–subordinate relations. Nevertheless, although the model of transformational or transactional leadership may have needs for adjustments and fine-tuning as we move across cultures, particularly into non-Western, overall, it holds up as having a lot of universal potential. Generally speaking, transformation leadership is more effective than managing-by-exception and managing-by-exception is more effective than laissez-faire leadership. Secondly, transformation leadership augments transactional leadership, it does not replace it. Thirdly, the ideals and implicit leadership theories of leadership people carry around in their heads are more transformational than transactional.[42]

Qualities for Successful Leaders

Another recent research approach that has been used to address the issue of international leadership is that of examining the characteristics that companies are looking for in their new executive hires. Are all firms seeking the same types of behaviors or qualities or, for example, are companies in Sweden looking for executives with qualities that are quite different from those being sought by Italian firms? The answer to this type of question can help shed light on international leadership because it helps focus attention on the behaviors that organizations believe are important in their managerial workforce. It also helps examine the impact, if any, of culture on leadership style.

Tollgerdt-Andersson examined thousands of advertisements for executives in the European Union (EU). She began by studying ads in Swedish newspapers and journals, noting the qualities, characteristics, and behaviors that were being sought. She then expanded her focus to publications in other European countries including Denmark, Norway, Germany, Great Britain, France, Italy, and Spain. The results are reported in Table 13–6. Based on this analysis, she concluded that:

> Generally, there seem to be great differences between the European countries regarding their leadership requirements. Different characteristics are stressed in the various countries. There are also differences concerning how frequently various characteristics are demanded in each country. Some kind of personal or social quality is mentioned much more often in the Scandinavian countries than in the other European countries. In the Scandinavian advertisements, you often see many qualities mentioned in a single advertisement. This can be seen in other European countries too, but it is much more rare. Generally, the characteristics mentioned in a single advertisement do not exceed three and fairly often, especially in Mediterranean countries (in 46–48% of the advertisements) no personal or social characteristics are mentioned at all.[43]

At the same time, Tollgerdt-Andersson did find that there were similarities between nations. For example, Italy and Spain had common patterns regarding desirable leadership

Table 13–6
Qualities Most Demanded in Advertisements for European Executives

Quality	Sweden (n = 225)	Denmark (n = 175)	Norway (n = 173)	Germany (n = 190)
Ability to cooperate (interpersonal ability)	25	42	32	16
Independence	22	22	25	9
Leadership ability	22		16	17
Ability to take initiatives	22	12	16	
Aim and result orientation	19	10	42	
Ability to motivate and inspire others	16	11		
Business orientation	12			
Age	10	25		13
Extrovert personality/contact ability	10	8	12	11
Creativity	9	10	9	9
Customer ability	9			
Analytic ability		10		
Ability to communicate		12	15	
High level of energy/drive			12	
Enthusiasm and involvement			14	14
Organization skills				7
Team builder				
Self-motivated				
Flexibility				
Precision				
Dynamic personality				
Responsibility				

Quality	Great Britain (n = 163)	France (n = 164)	Italy (n = 132)	Spain (n = 182)
Ability to cooperate (interpersonal ability)	7	9	32	18
Independence			16	4
Leadership ability	10		22	16
Ability to take initiatives			10	8
Aim and result orientation	5			2
Ability to motivate and inspire others		9	26	20
Business orientation				8
Age		12	46	34
Extrovert personality/contact ability				
Creativity	5			4
Customer ability				2
Analytic ability			10	
Ability to communicate	23			8
High level of energy/drive	8			20
Enthusiasm and involvement				
Organization skills		6	12	12
Team builder	10	5		
Self-motivated	10			
Flexibility				2
Precision		7		
Dynamic personality		6		6
Responsibility				10

Note: The qualities most demanded in Swedish, Danish, Norwegian, German, British, French, Italian, and Spanish advertisements for executives are expressed in percentage terms. n = total number of advertisements analyzed in each country. Each entry represents the percentage of the total advertisements requesting each quality.

Source: Adapted from Ingrid Tollgerdt-Andersson, "Attitudes, Values and Demands on Leadership—A Cultural Comparison Among Some European Countries," in *Managing across Cultures,* ed. Pat Joynt and Malcolm Warner (London: International Thomson Business Press, 1996), p. 173.

characteristics. Between 52 and 54 percent of the ads she reviewed in these two countries stated specific personal and social abilities that were needed by the job applicant. The same pattern was true for Germany and Great Britain, where between 64 and 68 percent of the advertisements set forth the personal and social abilities required for the job. In the Scandinavian countries these percentages ranged between 80 and 85.

Admittedly, it may be difficult to determine the degree of similarity between ads in different countries (or cultural clusters) because there may be implied meanings in the messages or it may be the custom in a country not to mention certain abilities but simply to assume that applicants know that these will be assessed in making the final hiring decision. Additionally, Tollgerdt-Andersson did find that all countries expected executive applicants to have good social and personal qualities. So some degree of universalism in leadership behaviors was uncovered. On the other hand, the requirements differed from country to country, showing that effective leaders in northern Europe may not be able to transfer their skills to the southern part of the continent with equal results. This led Tollgerdt-Andersson to conclude that multicultural understanding will continue to be a requirement for effective leadership in the twenty-first century. She put it this way: "If tomorrow's leaders possess international competence and understanding of other cultures it will, hopefully, result in the increased competitive cooperation which is essential if European commerce and industry is to compete with, for example, the USA and Asia."[44]

Culture Clusters and Leader Effectiveness

Although the foregoing discussion indicates there is research to support universalism in leadership behavior, recent findings also show that effective leader behaviors tend to vary by cultural cluster. Brodbeck and his associates conducted a large survey of middle managers ($n = 6,052$) from 22 European countries.[45] The respondents were given 112 questionnaire items containing descriptions of leadership traits and behaviors. For each attribute the respondents were asked to rate how well it fit their concept of an outstanding business leader. Some of the results, grouped by cluster, are presented in Table 13–7. A close look at the data shows that while there are similarities between some of the cultures, none of the lists of leadership attributes are identical. For example, managers in the Anglo cluster reported that the five most important attributes of an effective manager were a performance orientation, an inspirational style, having a vision, being a team integrator, and being decisive. Managers in the Nordic culture ranked these same five attributes as the most important but not in this order. Moreover, although the rankings of clusters in the North/West European region were fairly similar, they were quite different from those in the South/East European region, which included the Latin cluster, countries from Eastern Europe that were grouped by the researchers into a Central cluster and a Near East cluster, and Russia and Georgia, which were listed separately.

The data in Table 13–7 seem to indicate that culture influences effective leadership behavior. Moreover, the importance of these behaviors varies by cluster, although clusters that are geographically close to each other, such as the Anglo and Nordic clusters, tend to report similar leadership prototypes that are different from those located farther away, such as the Central and Near East clusters. This research also shows that there is some degree of universalism in leadership behavior when examined on an intracluster level, but when examined across clusters, the impact of culture can be significant.[46]

Leader Behavior, Leader Effectiveness, and Leading Teams

Culture is also important in helping explain how leaders *ought* to act in order to be effective. A good example is provided by the difference in effective behaviors in Trompenaars's categories (covered in Chapter 4) of affective (or emotional) cultures and neutral cultures. In affective cultures, such as the United States, leaders tend to exhibit their emotions. In

Table 13–7
Rankings of the Most Important Leadership Attributes by Region and Country Cluster

North/West European Region

Anglo Culture (Great Britain, Ireland)	Nordic Culture (Sweden, Netherlands, Finland, Denmark)	Germanic Culture (Switzerland, Germany, Austria)	Czech Republic	France
Performance-oriented	Integrity	Integrity	Integrity	Participative
Inspirational	Inspirational	Inspirational	Performance-oriented	Non-autocratic
Visionary	Visionary	Performance-oriented	Administratively-skilled	
Team integrator	Team integrator	Non-autocratic	Inspirational	
Decisive	Performance-oriented	Visionary	Non-autocratic	

South/East European Region

Latin Culture (Italy, Spain, Portugal, Hungary)	Central Culture (Poland, Slovenia)	Near East Culture (Turkey, Greece)	Russia	Georgia
Team integrator	Team integrator	Team integrator	Visionary	Administratively-skilled
Performance-oriented	Visionary	Decisive	Administratively-skilled	Decisive
Inspirational	Administratively-skilled	Visionary	Inspirational	Performance-oriented
Integrity	Diplomatic	Integrity	Decisive	Visionary
Visionary	Decisive	Inspirational	Integrity	Integrity

Source: Adapted from: Felix C. Brodbeck et al., "Cultural Variation of Leadership Prototypes Across 22 European Countries," *Journal of Occupational and Organizational Psychology* 73 (2000), p. 15.

neutral cultures, such as Japan and China, leaders do not tend to show their emotions. Moreover, in some cultures people are taught to exhibit their emotions but not let emotion affect their making rational decisions, while in other cultures the two are intertwined. Trompenaars explains it this way:

Americans tend to exhibit emotion, yet separate it from "objective" and "rational" decisions. Italians and south European nations in general tend to exhibit and not separate. Dutch and Swedes tend not to exhibit and to separate . . . there is nothing "good" or "bad" about these differences. You can argue that emotions held in check will twist your judgments despite all efforts to be "rational." Or you can argue that pouring forth emotions makes it harder for anyone present to think straight. Similarly, you can scoff at the "walls" separating reasons from emotions, or argue that because of the leakage that so often occurs, these should be thicker and stronger.[47]

Researchers have also found that the way in which managers speak to their people can influence the outcome. For example, in Anglo-Saxon cultures it is common for managers to raise their voice in order to emphasize a point. In Asian cultures managers generally speak at the same level throughout their communication, using a form of self-control that shows respect for the other person. Latin managers, meanwhile, vary their tone of voice continually, and this form of exaggeration is viewed by them as showing that they are very interested in what they are saying and committed to their point of view. Knowing how to communicate can greatly influence leadership across cultures. Here is an example:

A British manager posted to Nigeria found that it was very effective to raise his voice for important issues. His Nigerian subordinates viewed that unexpected explosion by a normally self-controlled manager as a sign of extra concern. After success in Nigeria he was posted to Malaysia. Shouting there was a sign of loss of face; his colleagues did not take him seriously and he was transferred.[48]

One of the keys to successful global leadership is knowing what style and behavior works best in a given culture and adapting appropriately. In the case of affective and neutral cultures, for example, Trompenaars and Hampden-Turner have offered the specific tips provided in Table 13–8.

Cross-Cultural Leadership: Insights from the GLOBE Study

As discussed in Chapter 4, the GLOBE (Global Leadership and Organizational Behavior Effectiveness) research program, a 10-year, multimethod, multiphase research program, is examining the relationships among societal and organizational culture, societal and organizational effectiveness, and leadership. In addition to the identification of nine major dimensions of culture described in Chapter 4, the GLOBE program also includes the

---

Table 13–8
Leadership Tips for Doing Business in Affective and Neutral Cultures

When Managing or Being Managed in . . .

Affective Cultures	Neutral Cultures
Avoid a detached, ambiguous, and cool demeanor because this will be interpreted as negative behavior.	Avoid warm, excessive, or enthusiastic behaviors because these will be interpreted as a lack of personal control over one's feelings and be viewed as inconsistent with one's high status.
Find out whose work and enthusiasm are being directed into which projects, so you are able to appreciate the vigor and commitment they have for these efforts.	Extensively prepare the things you have to do and then stick tenaciously to the issues.
Let people be emotional without personally becoming intimidated or coerced by their behavior.	Look for cues regarding whether people are pleased or angry and then amplify their importance.

When Doing Business with Individuals in . . .

Affective Cultures (for Those from Neutral Cultures)	Neutral Cultures (for Those from Affective Cultures)
Do not be put off stride when others create scenes and get histrionic; take time-outs for sober reflection and hard assessments.	Ask for time-outs from meetings and negotiations where you can patch each other up and rest between games of poker with the "impassive ones."
When others are expressing goodwill, respond warmly.	Put down as much as you can on paper before beginning the negotiation.
Remember that the other person's enthusiasm and readiness to agree or disagree do not mean that the individual has made up his or her mind.	Remember that the other person's lack of emotional tone does not mean that the individual is uninterested or bored, only that the person does not like to show his or her hand.
Keep in mind that the entire negotiation is typically focused on you as a person and not so much on the object or proposition that is being discussed.	Keep in mind that the entire negotiation is typically focused on the object or proposition that is being discussed and not on you as a person.

Recognize the Way in Which People Behave in . . .

Affective Cultures	Neutral Cultures
They reveal their thoughts and feelings both verbally and nonverbally.	They often do not reveal what they are thinking or feeling.
Emotions flow easily, vehemently, and without inhibition.	Emotions are often dammed up, although they may occasionally explode.
Heated, vital, and animated expressions are admired.	Cool and self-possessed conduct is admired.
Touching, gesturing, and strong facial expressions are common.	Physical contact, gesturing, or strong facial expressions are not used.
Statements are made fluently and dramatically.	Statements are often read out in a monotone voice.

Source: Adapted from Fons Trompenaars and Charles Hampden-Turner, *Riding the Waves of Culture: Understanding Diversity in Global Business,* 2nd ed. (New York: McGraw-Hill, 1998), pp. 80–82.

classification of six global leadership behaviors. Through a qualitative and quantitative analysis of leadership, GLOBE researchers determined that leadership behaviors can be summarized into six broad categories: Charismatic/Value-Based, Team-Oriented, Participative, Humane-Oriented, Autonomous, and Self-Protective. As is the case in the classification of culture dimensions, these categories build on and extend earlier classifications of leadership styles described earlier in this chapter.

Charismatic/Value-Based leadership captures the ability of leaders to inspire, motivate, and encourage high performance outcomes from others based on a foundation of core values. Team-Oriented leadership places emphasis on effective team building and implementation of a common goal among team members. Participative leadership reflects the extent to which leaders involve others in decisions and their implementation. Humane-Oriented leadership comprises supportive and considerate leadership. Autonomous leadership refers to independent and individualistic leadership behaviors. Self-Protective leadership "focuses on ensuring the safety and security of the individual and group through status-enhancement and face-saving."[49]

The GLOBE study, like earlier research, found that certain attributes of leadership were universally endorsed, while others were viewed as effective only in certain cultures. Among the leadership attributes found to be effective across cultures are being trustworthy, just, and honest (having integrity); having foresight and planning ahead; being positive, dynamic, encouraging, and motivating, and building confidence; and being communicative and informed and being a coordinator and a team integrator.[50]

In linking the cultural dimensions of the GLOBE study with the leadership styles described above, the GLOBE researchers investigated the association between cultural values and leadership attributes, and cultural practices and leadership attributes. With regard to the relationship between cultural values and leadership attributes, the GLOBE researchers concluded the following:

- Collectivism I values, as found in Sweden and other Nordic and Scandinavian countries, are likely to view Participative and Self-Protective leadership behaviors favorably while viewing Autonomous leadership behaviors negatively.[51]

- In-Group Collectivism II values, as found in societies such as the Philippines and other East Asian countries, were positively related to Charismatic/Value-Based leadership and Team-Oriented leadership.[52]

- Gender Egalitarian values, as found in countries such as Hungary, Russia, and Poland, were positively associated with Participative and Charismatic/Value-Based leader attributes.[53]

- Performance Orientation values, as found in countries such as Switzerland, Singapore, and Hong Kong, were positively associated with Participative and Charismatic/Value-Based leader attributes.[54]

- Future Orientation values, as found in societies such as Singapore, are positively associated with Self-Protective and Humane-Oriented leader attributes.[55]

- Societal Uncertainty Avoidance values, as found in Germany, Denmark, and China, were positively associated with Team-Oriented, Humane-Oriented, and Self-Protective leader attributes.[56]

- Societal Humane Orientation values, as found in countries such as Zambia, the Philippines, and Ireland, were positively associated with Participative leader attributes.[57]

- Societal Assertiveness values, as found in countries such as the United States, Germany, and Austria, were positively associated with Humane-Oriented leader attributes.[58]

- Societal Power Distance values, as found in countries such as Morocco, Nigeria, and Argentina, were positively correlated with Self-Protective and Humane leader attributes.[59]

In summarizing the GLOBE findings, researchers suggest that cultural values influence leadership preferences, with many intuitive predicted outcomes. Specifically, societies that share particular values prefer leadership attributes or styles that are congruent with or supportive of those values, with some exceptions. The studies, however, also resulted in some unexpected findings. For example, societies that valued assertiveness were positively correlated with valuing Humane-Oriented leadership. According to one interpretation, some of these contradictions may reflect desires by societies to make up for or mitigate some aspects of cultural values with seemingly opposing leadership attributes. In the case of societies that value assertiveness, a preference for Humane-Oriented leader attributes may reflect a desire to provide a social support structure in an environment characterized by high competition.[60]

Ethically Responsible Global Leadership

As discussed in Part 1, globalization and MNCs have come under fire from a number of quarters. Criticisms have been especially sharp in relation to the activities of companies—such as Nike, Levi's, and United Fruit—whose sourcing practices in developing countries have been alleged to exploit low-wage workers, take advantage of lax environmental and workplace standards, and otherwise contribute to social and economic degradation. Ethical principles provide the philosophical basis for responsible business practices, and leadership defines the mechanism through which these principles become actionable.

As a result of scandals at Royal Ahold, Andersen, Enron, Tyco, Worldcom, and others, there is decreasing trust of global leaders. A recent public opinion survey conducted for the World Economic Forum by Gallup and Environics found that leaders have suffered declining public trust in recent years and enjoy less trust than the institutions they lead. The survey asked respondents questions about how much they trust various leaders "to manage the challenges of the coming year in the best interests of you and your family." Leaders of nongovernmental organizations (NGOs) were the only ones receiving the trust of a clear majority of citizens across the countries surveyed.[61] Leaders at the United Nations and spiritual and religious leaders were the next-most-trusted leaders; over four in ten citizens said they had a lot or some trust in them. Next most trusted were leaders of Western Europe, "individuals responsible for managing the global economy," those "responsible for managing our national economy," and executives of multinational companies. Those four groups were trusted by only one-third of citizens.[62] Over 4 in 10 citizens reported decreased trust in executives of domestic companies. Figure 3–1 summarizes these findings.

The decline in trust in leaders is prompting some companies to go on the offensive and to develop more ethically oriented and responsible leadership practices in their global operations. Some researchers link transformational leadership and corporate social responsibility, arguing that transformational leaders exhibit high levels of moral development, including a sense of obligation to the larger community.[63] According to this view, authentic charismatic leadership is rooted in strong ethical values, and effective global leaders are guided by principles of altruism, justice, and humanistic notions of the greater good.

On a more instrumental basis, another research effort linking leadership and corporate responsibility defines "responsible global leadership" as encompassing (1) values-based leadership, (2) ethical decision making, and (3) quality stakeholder relationships.[64] According to this view, global leadership must be based on core values and credos that reflect principled business and leadership practices, high levels of ethical and moral behavior, and a set of shared ideals that advance organizational and societal well-being. The importance of ethical decision making in corporations, governments, not-for-profit organizations, and professional services firms is omnipresent. In addition, the quality of relationships with internal and external stakeholders is increasingly critical to organizational success, especially to governance processes. Relationships involving mutual trust and respect are important within organizations, between organizations and the various constituencies that they affect, and among the extended networks of individuals and their organizational affiliates.

Leaders at Johnson & Johnson, British Petroleum, Toyota, and many other companies have dedicated themselves to responsible global leadership with apparent benefits for their companies' reputations and bottom lines. Executives at ICI India, a manufacturer and marketer of paints and various specialty chemicals, believe that adhering to global standards even though doing so increases costs, can boost competitiveness. Aditya Narayan, president of ICI India, explains: "At ICI, standards involving ethics, safety, health, and environment policies are established by headquarters but are adapted to meet national laws. I can benefit by drawing on these corporate policies and in some cases we do far more than required by Indian laws."[65]

Another example of strong global leadership can be found at the Lubrizol Corporation. Lubrizol, a global manufacturer of chemicals, has been praised consistently for its efforts in product stewardship, community relations, and environmental preservation. In 2002 the American Chemistry Council lauded Lubrizol for its successful implementation of Responsible Care, the Council's global and industrywide initiative that sets standards for management of chemicals throughout all aspects of a business.[66] Since its inception in 1988, Lubrizol's Responsible Care programs have resulted in an 85 percent reduction in pollutant emissions per ton of product produced and a 56 percent reduction in safety-related incidents.

Entrepreneurial Leadership and Mindset

As discussed in Chapter 8, an increasing share of international management activities is occurring in entrepreneurial new ventures. Richard Branson's leadership style clearly reflects a strong entrepreneurial bent, and his global vision is a positive illustration of the power of entrepreneurial leadership. But given the high failure rate for international new ventures, what leadership characteristics are important for such ventures to succeed?

Promising start-ups fail for many reasons, including lack of capital, absence of clear goals and objectives, and failure to accurately assess market demand and competition. For international new ventures, these factors are significantly complicated by differences in cultures, national political and economic systems, geographic distance, and shipping, tax, and regulatory costs. A critical factor in the long-term success of a new venture—whether domestic or international—is the personal leadership ability of the entrepreneurial CEO.

Entrepreneurship research has examined some of the key personal characteristics of entrepreneurs, some of which coincide with those of strong leaders. In comparison to nonentrepreneurs, entrepreneurs appear to be more creative and innovative. They tend to break the rules and do not need structure, support, or an organization to guide their thinking. They are able to see things differently and add to a product, system, or idea value that amounts to more than an adaptation or linear change. They are more willing to take personal and business risks, and to do so in visible and salient ways. They are opportunity seekers—solving only those problems that limit their success in reaching the vision—and are comfortable with failure, rebounding quickly to pursue another opportunity.[67] Others characterize them as adventurous, ambitious, energetic, domineering, and self-confident.

In addition to these traits, entrepreneurial leaders operating internationally must also possess the cultural sensitivity, international vision, and global mindset to effectively lead their venture as it confronts the challenges of doing business in other countries. Well-known entrepreneurs such as Richard Branson (Virgin Group), Arthur Blank (Home Depot), and Russell Simmons (Def Jam Recordings) have all been successful leading their companies on a global scale while preserving the integrity and values of the host country.[68]

VeloCom Inc. is a telecom service company based in Arapahoe County, Colorado, but it has never done any business in Colorado or anywhere else in the United States. In only four years, however, it has become the lead competitor to incumbent telecom giant Telebras in Brazil. David Leonard, VeloCom's chief executive, is a visionary who did not see national borders as an impediment to rapid growth and expansion. Although Leonard says, "We just happened to be in the right place at the right time, and we took advantage of it," entrepreneurial leadership and vision were clearly key to the firm's success.[69]

The World of *BusinessWeek*—Revisited

As seen in the opening news story, the leadership challenges facing Richard Branson are varied and diverse. Virgin USA is a new player in the U.S. airline market, and its success will depend on Branson's ability to lead through changing industry dynamics. In this chapter, it was noted that effective leadership is often heavily influenced by culture. The approach that is effective in Europe is different from approaches used in the United States or Japan. Even so, there are threads of universalism, evident, for example, in the case of Japanese and U.S. leadership styles in managing both high- and low-achieving workers. The research by Bass also lends support to universalism. But can Branson rely on the leadership style that has served him well in Europe to oversee operations in the United States? In most cases, leadership styles need to be adjusted to fit the cultural subtleties of disparate markets.

After reviewing the chapter and considering the experience of Richard Branson, respond to the following questions: (1) How do leadership practices and expectations differ between the United States, Europe, and Asia? (2) What adjustments might Richard Branson need to make when leading in the United States? (3) What are some of the ways in which firms engage in globally responsible leadership, and how might Branson adopt some of these practices?

SUMMARY OF KEY POINTS

1. Leadership is a complex and controversial process that can be defined as influencing people to direct their efforts toward the achievement of some particular goal or goals. Two areas warrant attention as a foundation for the study of leadership in an international setting: philosophical assumptions about people in general, and leadership styles. The philosophical foundation is heavily grounded in Douglas McGregor's Theories X and Y and William Ouchi's Theory Z. Leadership styles relate to how managers treat their subordinates and incorporate authoritarian, paternalistic, and participative approaches. These styles can be summarized in terms of Likert's management systems or styles (systems 1 through 4) and the managerial grid (1,1 through 9,9).

2. The attitudes of European managers toward dimensions of leadership practice, such as the capacity for leadership and initiative, sharing information and objectives, participation, and internal control, were examined in a classic study by Haire, Ghiselli, and

Porter. They found that Europeans, as a composite, had a relatively low opinion of the capabilities of the average person coupled with a relatively positive belief in the necessity for participative leadership styles. The study also found that these European managers' attitudes were affected by hierarchical level, company size, and age. Overall, however, European managers espouse a participative leadership style.

3. The Japanese managers in the Haire and associates study had a much greater belief in the capacity of subordinates for leadership and initiative than managers in most other countries. The Japanese managers also expressed a more favorable attitude toward a participative leadership style. In terms of sharing information and objectives and using internal control, the Japanese responded above average but were not distinctive. In a number of ways, Japanese leadership styles differed from those of U.S. managers. Company size and age of the managers are two factors that seem to affect these differences. Other reasons include the basic philosophy of managing people, how

information is processed, and the high degree of ethnocentrism among the Japanese. However, some often overlooked similarities are important, such as how effective Japanese leaders manage high-achieving and low-achieving subordinates.

4. Leadership research in China shows that the new generation of managers tends to have a leadership style that is different from the styles of both the current generation and the older generation. In particular, new generation managers assign greater importance to individualism as measured by such things as self-sufficiency and personal accomplishments. They also assign less importance to collectivism as measured by subordination of personal goals to those of the group and to Confucianism as measured by such things as societal harmony and virtuous interpersonal behavior.

5. Leadership research in the Middle East traditionally has stressed the basic differences between Middle Eastern and Western management styles. Other research, however, shows that many managers in multinational organizations in the Persian Gulf region operate in a Western-oriented Likert system 3 (participative) style. Such findings indicate that there may be more similarities of leadership styles between Western and Middle Eastern parts of the world than has previously been assumed.

6. Leadership research also has been conducted among managers in developing countries, such as India, Peru, Chile, and Argentina. These studies show that Likert's system 3 (participative) leadership styles are more in evidence than traditionally has been assumed. Although there always will be important differences in styles of leadership between various parts of the world, participative leadership styles may become more prevalent as countries develop and become more economically advanced.

7. In recent years, there have been research efforts to explore new areas in international leadership. In particular, Bass has found that there is a great deal of similarity from culture to culture and that transformational leaders, regardless of culture, tend to be the most effective. In addition, the GLOBE study has confirmed earlier research that specific cultural values and practices are associated with particular leadership attributes. Moreover, there is increasing pressure for MNCs to engage in globally responsible leadership that incorporates (a) values-based leadership; (b) ethical decision making, and (c) quality stakeholder relationships. Leaders of international new ventures face particularly challenging obstacles; however, the integration of a global orientation and entrepreneurial flair can contribute to successful "born global" leaders and firms.

KEY TERMS

authoritarian leadership, *400*

charismatic leaders, *415*

leadership, *398*

participative leadership, *402*

paternalistic leadership, *400*

Theory X manager, *399*

Theory Y manager, *399*

Theory Z manager, *400*

transactional leaders, *415*

transformational leaders, *415*

variety amplification, *408*

variety reduction, *408*

REVIEW AND DISCUSSION QUESTIONS

1. Using the results of the classic Haire and associates study as a basis for your answer, compare and contrast managers' attitudes toward leadership practices in Nordic-European and Latin-European countries. (The countries in these clusters are identified in Table 13–3.)

2. Is there any relationship between company size and European managers' attitude toward participative leadership styles?

3. Using the Haire and associates study results and other supporting data, determine what Japanese managers believe about their subordinates. How are these beliefs similar to those of U.S. and European managers? How are these beliefs different?

4. A U.S. firm is going to be opening a subsidiary in Japan within the next six months. What type of

leadership style does research show to be most effective for leading high-achieving Japanese? Low-achieving Japanese? How are these results likely to affect the way that U.S. expatriates should lead their Japanese employees?

5. A British firm is in the process of setting up operations in the Middle Eastern Gulf states. What Likert system or style of leadership do managers in this region seem to use? Is this similar to that used by Western managers?

6. What do U.S. managers need to know about leading in the international arena? Identify and describe three important guidelines that can be of practical value.

7. Is effective leadership behavior universal or does it vary from culture to culture? Explain.

8. What is responsible leadership?

INTERNET EXERCISE: TAKING A CLOSER LOOK

Over the last decade, one of the most successful global firms has been General Electric. Go to the company's Web site at **www.ge.com** and review its latest annual report. Pay close attention to the MNC's international operations and to its product lines. Also read about the new members on the board of directors and look through the information on the company's Six Sigma program. Then, aware of what GE is doing worldwide as well as in regard to its quality efforts, answer these questions: On how many continents does the company currently do business? Based on this answer, is there one leadership style that will work best for the company, or is it going to have to choose managers on a country-by-country basis? Additionally, if there is no one universal style that is best, how can current CEO Jeffrey Immelt effectively lead so diverse a group of worldwide managers? In what way would an understanding of the managerial grid be useful in explaining leadership behaviors at GE? Finally, if GE were advertising for new managers in England, Italy, and Japan, what qualities would you expect the firm to be seeking in these managers? Would there be a universal list, or would lists differ on a country-by-country basis?

Germany

The reunification of Germany was a major event of modern times. Despite problems, Germany remains a major economic power. The unified Germany is big, though only about the size of the state of Nevada in the United States. With a population of about 84 million, Germany has about three times the population of California. Germany still is far behind the economic size of Japan and 20 percent that of the United States. Because Germany was rebuilt almost from the ground up after World War II, however, many feel that Germany, along with Japan, is an economic miracle of modern times. Unified Germany's GDP of $2.16 trillion is behind that of both the United States and Japan, but Germany exports more than Japan, its gross investment as a percentage of GDP is higher than that of the United States, and its average compensation with benefits to workers is higher than that of the United States or Japan. It is estimated that Germany has direct control of about one-fourth of Western Europe's economy, which gives it considerable power in Europe. The German people are known for being thrifty, hardworking, and obedient to authority. They love music, dancing, good food and beer, and fellowship. The government is a parliamentary democracy headed by a chancellor. Although Germany has experienced a difficult economic environment in recent years, recent governments have pushed through labor reforms designed to improve productivity and stem unemployment.

For the last 13 years, the Wiscomb Company has held a majority interest in a large retail store in Bonn. The store has been very successful and also has proved to be an excellent training ground for managers whom the company wanted to prepare for other overseas assignments. First, the managers would be posted to the Bonn store. Then, after three or four months of international seasoning, they would be sent on to other stores in Europe. Wiscomb has holdings in the Netherlands, Luxembourg, and Austria. The Bonn store has been the primary training ground because it was the first store the company had in Europe, and the training program was created with this store in mind.

A few months ago, the Wiscomb management and its German partners decided to try a new approach to selling. The plan called for some young U.S. managers to be posted to the Bonn store for a three-year tour, while some young German managers were sent stateside. Both companies hoped that this program would provide important training and experience for their people; however, things have not worked out as hoped. The U.S. managers have reported great difficulty in supervising their German subordinates. Three of their main concerns are as follows: (1) Their subordinates do not seem to like to participate in decision making, preferring to be told what to do. (2) The German nationals in the store rely much more heavily on a Theory X approach to supervising than the Americans are accustomed to using, and they are encouraging their U.S. counterparts to follow their example. (3) Some of the German managers have suggested to the young Americans that they not share as much information with their own subordinates. Overall, the Americans believe that the German style of management is not as effective as their own, but they feel equally ill at ease raising this issue with their hosts. They have asked if someone from headquarters could come over from the United States and help to resolve their problem. A human resources executive is scheduled to arrive next week and meet with the U.S. contingent.

Questions

1. What are some current issues facing Germany? What is the climate for doing business in Germany today?

2. Are the leadership styles used by the German managers really much different from those used by the Americans?

3. Do you think the German managers are really more Theory X–oriented than their U.S. counterparts? Why, or why not?

4. Are the German managers who have come to the United States likely to be having the same types of problems?

An Offer from Down Under

The Gandriff Corporation is a successful retail chain in the U.S. Midwest. The St. Louis–based company has had average annual growth of 17 percent over the last 10 years and would like to expand to other sections of the country. Last month, however, it received a very interesting offer from a group of investors from Australia. The group is willing to put up $100 million to help Gandriff set up operations Down Under. The Australian investors believe that Gandriff's management and retailing expertise could provide it with a turnkey operation. The stores would be built to Gandriff's specifications, and the entire operation would be run by Gandriff. The investors would receive 75 percent of all profits until they recovered their $100 million plus an annual return of 10 percent. At this point, the division of profits would become 50–50.

Gandriff management likes the idea but feels there is a better chance for higher profit if they were to set up operations in Europe. The growth rate in European countries, it is felt, will be much better than that in Australia. The investors, all of whom are Australian, are sympathetic and have promised Gandriff that they will invest another $100 million in Europe, specifically England, France, and Germany, within three years if Gandriff agrees to first set up and get an Australian operation running. The U.S. firm believes this would be a wise move but is delaying a final decision because it still is concerned about the ease with which it can implement its current approach in foreign markets. In particular, the management is concerned about whether the leadership style used in the United States will be successful in Australia and in European countries. Before making a final decision, management has decided to hire a consultant specializing in leadership to look into the matter.

Questions

1. Will the leadership style used in the United States be successful in Australia, or will the Australians respond better to another?

2. If the retailer goes into Europe, in which country will it have the least problem using its U.S.-based leadership style? Why?

3. If the company goes into Europe, what changes might it have to make in accommodating its leadership approach to the local environment? Use Germany as an example.

Chapter 14

HUMAN RESOURCE SELECTION AND DEVELOPMENT ACROSS CULTURES

Firms conducting international business need to be particularly concerned with human resource management issues, including selection, training, and development to better prepare their personnel for overseas assignments. This chapter focuses on potential sources of human resources that can be used for overseas assignments, procedures that are used in the selection process, and compensation issues. In addition, attention is given to training and development and to the various types of training that commonly are offered. The specific objectives of this chapter are:

1. IDENTIFY the three basic sources that MNCs can tap when filling management vacancies in overseas operations in addition to options of subcontracting and outsourcing.

2. DESCRIBE the selection criteria and procedures used by the organization and individual managers when making final decisions.

3. DISCUSS the reasons why people return from overseas assignments, and present some of the strategies used to ensure a smooth transition back into the home-market operation.

4. DESCRIBE the training process, the most common reasons for training, and the types of training that often are provided.

5. EXPLAIN how cultural assimilators work and why they are so highly regarded.

The World of *BusinessWeek*

BusinessWeek

Look Who's Going Offshore

Tech Startups Are Heading Overseas Even More Eagerly Than Multinationals

Last December, Hilmi Ozguc, chief executive of Maven Networks Inc., began looking for venture capital to expand his 30-person startup. One of his first moves was to e-mail James W. Breyer, managing partner at venture firm Accel Partners, who had pocketed a hefty return on a company Ozguc had co-founded years earlier. Breyer immediately saw promise in Maven's software, which helps companies such as Virgin Records distribute interactive video over the Net.

But there was a catch: Breyer thought Ozguc should be using more developers outside the U.S. than he was planning on. While Ozguc had been eyeing South Korea and Japan, Breyer thought he should open an office in China, too. Ozguc agreed, and in March, Accel invested $10 million in Maven. Breyer, now a director at Maven, continues to urge Ozguc to think about the opportunities for sending work overseas. "There is not a board meeting that goes by in which outsourcing does not play a significant role," says Breyer.

A new trend is sweeping through Silicon Valley and other centers of U.S. innovation. Startups, spurred by their venture investors, are catching offshore fever, and not just a mild case—like some big multinationals have. While 15% of the 145 large companies recently surveyed by Forrester Research Inc. say they have made offshore a permanent

Startups Catch Overseas Fever

Venture capitalists are prodding companies they invest in to hire workers overseas. Here is a sampling of how one venture firm, Accel Partners, is doing this:

Company	Offshore Strategy
BrassRing, which makes software that helps companies recruit, hire, and retain workers	Accel's Jim Breyer encouraged Brass-Ring, which has 250 employees in the U.S., to use lower-cost overseas workers for noncore jobs. The company has hired 30 Indian workers, who help with software testing and smaller development projects during peak times.
JBoss, which makes open-source software and provides training and support services	Even before Accel, JBoss hired half of its 30 employees outside the U.S.—in Greece, Ukraine, and elsewhere—to take advantage of open-source expertise around the world. Now, JBoss is looking to offshore its customer support.
Model N, which creates software to help manage contracts, including pricing and rebates	CEO Zack Rinat suggested using offshore workers and got eager support from Breyer. Now, Model N has 70 employees in the U.S. focused on product development, sales, and marketing, while 35 Indian workers handle software testing and customer support.

Source: BusinessWeek.

part of their strategy, an informal survey of venture capitalists suggests 20% to 25% of the companies they invest in have a comparable commitment. The fervor has gripped some of venture capital's biggest names. Kleiner Perkins Caufield & Byers, Sevin Rosen Funds, and Norwest Ventures say at least 30% of their companies have moved jobs overseas, and that figure is rising. "The venture guys are driving offshore as much as anyone," says Forrester Vice-President John C. McCarthy.

An Irresistible Push

Accel's Breyer is in the movement's vanguard. Nearly 40% of Accel's 45 investments have set up operations overseas, according to a recent Accel survey shared with *BusinessWeek.* By 2005, Breyer estimates 75% of its companies will be using offshore resources. And its companies are sending more than just a handful of jobs abroad: Within two to three years, Breyer says, Accel startups should have half of their workers based overseas. "If a company is not actively investing in China or India, they need to provide a very compelling case to board members as to why they are not," he says.

As the U.S. economy has struggled to create new jobs, giants such as IBM have taken most of the heat for sending work overseas. Yet the actions of Breyer and his venture compatriots suggest that the changes in the economy may be more far-reaching than even some experts have realized. If not only Big Blue but also startups such as Maven are sending work abroad, the tech industry may not

be the engine of job growth that it has been in the past. Although the tech sector accounts for about 5% of U.S. payrolls, or 6.5 million workers, it generated 13% of the new jobs created from 1996 to 2001. Over the next five years, Mark M. Zandi, chief economist at Economy.com Inc., expects tech to contribute 7% of the country's new jobs. "Entire occupational groups can be outsourced at the flick of a computer key," says former U.S. Labor Secretary Robert B. Reich, now a professor at Brandeis University.

Breyer concedes the offshore trend hurts the U.S. job market in the short term. But his own experience has convinced him that technology companies, especially in software, need to hire globally if they are to be competitive. As early as the mid-1990s, he saw how bringing on developers overseas had helped Accel companies Agile Software Corp. and Actuate Corp. lower their costs. Breyer figures that, over the long haul, if U.S. companies have the talent, efficiency, and flexibility to compete worldwide they will be able to provide a large supply of good, steady jobs. "Economies and companies that don't pursue outsourcing will not succeed long-term," he says.

Lowering costs is just the most obvious reason for offshoring. Consider the case of DataSweep Inc., an Accel-backed company whose software helps manufacturers manage their factories more efficiently. Breyer helped convince CEO Vladimir Preysman to hire eight programmers in India and China to translate its product into Japanese and connect its programs with software from SAP. Although the programmers cost 75% less than they would in the U.S., Preysman says what's even more important is that offshoring those tasks will let the company accelerate its development cycle. "We can devote our internal force to software that needs to get out," he says.

Talent is another motivating factor. Mark Fleury, CEO of Accel-funded open-source software maker JBoss Inc., says half of its 30 workers are based overseas—in Ukraine, Brazil, and other countries. In April, JBoss hired Dimitris Andreadis, a coder based in Greece, because he wrote a program that's critical for managing the performance of computer networks. "I will scout for talent wherever it is," says Fleury. "If you are a superstar of open source, we will find you."

Still, offshoring can test the management skills of some startups. In 2001, at Breyer's urging, BrassRing LLC in Waltham, Mass., hired an Indian company to develop a major release of its software, which helps corporations manage recruiting. But because BrassRing did not give the Indians a complete set of product specifications, key features were left out, and some testing was never done. It took an extra nine months to rewrite the code, the expected cost savings vanished, and customers were irked by the

delay. BrassRing continues to use offshore labor for testing and some other projects but not for core development. Offshoring "is really challenging for a small company," says BrassRing CEO Deborah Besemer.

For Breyer, meeting the offshore challenge requires nearly perpetual motion. He encourages senior execs at his portfolio companies to go overseas once or twice per quarter, and he travels abroad regularly. This March, he spent 10 days in China meeting with entrepreneurs, government agencies, and potential offshore partners for Accel companies. "We can't put our heads in the sand or hope that global protectionism is the answer," says Breyer. In the tech industry, such is the new reality for giant companies and startups alike.

By Spencer E. Ante in New York,
with Robert D. Hof in San Mateo, Calif.

The opening news story points out some of the broad impacts of globalization on international human resource selection and development in today's business climate. As more highly skilled workers become available in other countries, MNCs have a growing number of sources for their human resources. In addition, technology now enables work to be conducted at numerous remote locations, making face-to-face contact less essential. In addition to work flowing to other countries, MNCs may also be able to access foreign human resources by hiring them on a temporary or permanent basis in the home country. Often, they will subcontract or outsource work to foreign employees in home and host countries. This complex web of relationships creates significant managerial challenges and opportunities and suggests that there will always be a need for highly skilled, culturally sensitive, and geographically mobile managerial talent.

In this chapter we will explore the procedure of international human resource selection and training and examine the difficulties of developing a global human resource management process in the presence of dissimilar cultural norms. At the same time, we will survey emerging trends in international human resource management, including the increasing use of temporary and contingent staffing to fill the growing global HR needs of MNCs. We will also review training and development programs designed to help employees prepare for and succeed in their foreign assignments and adjust to conditions once they return home.

■ The Importance of International Human Resources

Attracting the most qualified employees and matching them to the jobs for which they are best suited is important for the success of any organization. For international organizations, the selection and development of human resources is especially challenging and vitally important. As prevalent and useful as e-mail and Web- and teleconferencing have become, and despite the increasing incidence of subcontracting and outsourcing, face-to-face human contact will remain an important means of communication and transferring "tacit" knowledge—knowledge that cannot be formalized in manuals or written guidelines. Hence, most companies continue to deploy human resources around the world as they are needed, although the range of options for filling human resources needs is expanding.

Research has demonstrated high failure rates among expatriate managers, ranging from 7 to more than 30 percent depending on the source and home country.[1] In addition, there is variation in failure rates by country location of the MNC. A majority of U.S. multinationals expect at least a 10 to 20 percent failure rate; European and Japanese firms expect less than a 5 percent failure rate.[2] These rates also vary by industry. One study showed especially high failure rates among hotel industry workers.[3] Failure costs are high. According to one estimate, the cost of one assignment failure is between $100,000 and $300,000 per employee.[4]

Given these high costs, many MNCs are turning to locally engaged employees or third-country nationals.[5] In addition, the increased education of many populations around the world gives MNCs more options when considering international human resource needs. The emergence of highly trained technical and scientific employees in emerging markets and the increased prevalence of MBA-type training in many developed and developing countries have dramatically expanded the pool of talent from which MNCs can draw. Yet some companies are still having difficulty in winning the "war for talent." A recent report from China noted that despite much greater levels of advanced education, there is still a shortage of skilled management. "We need a lot more people than we have now, and we need a higher caliber of people," said Guo Ming, Coca-Cola's human resource director for Greater China.[6]

Adjustment problems associated with international assignments can be reduced through careful selection and training. Language training and cross-culture training are especially important, but they are often neglected by MNCs in a hurry to deploy resources to meet critical needs.[7] MNCs are also under increasing pressure to keep jobs at home, and their international HR practices have come under close scrutiny. In particular, the "importing" of programmers from India at a fraction of domestic wages, combined with the offshore outsourcing of work to high-tech employees in lower cost countries, has created political and social challenges for MNCs seeking to manage their international human resources efficiently and effectively. Nonetheless, the demand for globally adept managers will likely grow, and MNCs will continue to invest in recruiting and training the best future leaders.

■ Sources of Human Resources

MNCs can tap four basic sources for positions: (1) home-country nationals; (2) host-country nationals; (3) third-country nationals; and (4) inpatriates. In addition, many MNCs are outsourcing aspects of their global operations and in so doing are engaging temporary or contingent employees. The following sections analyze each of these major sources.

Home-Country Nationals

Home-country nationals are managers who are citizens of the country where the MNC is headquartered. In fact, sometimes the term *headquarters nationals* is used. These managers commonly are called **expatriates,** or simply "expats," which refers to those who live and work outside their home country. Historically, MNCs have staffed key positions in their foreign affiliates with home-country nationals or expatriates.[8] Based on research in U.S., European, and Japanese firms, Rosalie Tung found that U.S. and European firms used home-country nationals in less developed regions but preferred host-country nationals in developed nations. The Japanese, however, made considerably more use of home-country personnel in all geographic areas, especially at the middle- and upper-level ranks.[9]

More recent research, however, reveals that the pattern reported by Tung may be undergoing change. Richards, for example, investigated staffing practices for the purpose

home-country nationals
Expatriate managers who are citizens of the country where the multinational corporation is headquartered.

expatriates
Managers who live and work outside their home country. They are citizens of the country where the multinational corporation is headquartered.

of determining when companies are more likely to use an expatriate rather than a local manager. She conducted interviews with senior-level headquarters managers at 24 U.S. multinational manufacturing firms and with managers at their U.K. and Thai subsidiaries. This study found that local managers were most effective in subsidiaries located in developing countries or those that relied on a local customer base. In contrast, expatriates were most effective when they were in charge of larger subsidiaries or those with a marketing theme similar to that at headquarters.[10]

There are a variety of reasons for using home-country nationals. One of the most common is to start up operations. Another is to provide technical expertise. A third is to help the MNC maintain financial control over the operation.[11] Other commonly cited reasons include

> the desire to provide the company's more promising managers with international experience to equip them better for more responsible positions; the need to maintain and facilitate organizational coordination and control; the unavailability of managerial talent in the host country; the company's view of the foreign operation as short lived; the host country's multiracial population, which might mean that selecting a manager of either race would result in political or social problems; the company's conviction that it must maintain a foreign image in the host country; and the belief of some companies that a home country manager is the best person for the job.[12]

In the past, expatriates were almost always men, but over the last decade there has been a growing number of female expatriates as companies realize that women want international assignments and are prepared to assume the challenges that accompany these jobs. Stroh, Arma, and Valy-Durbin, for example, recently surveyed 261 female expatriates and 78 of their supervisors and, among other things, found that these women felt that their gender did not stand in the way of their doing their jobs and, in fact, was sometimes an advantage because it gave them greater visibility, enabled them to build stronger interpersonal relationships with clients, and helped them to adapt better to life as an outsider.[13]

In recent years, there definitely has been a trend away from using home-country nationals. This is true even among Japanese firms, which long preferred to employ expats and were reluctant to allow local nationals a significant role in subsidiary management. Beamish and Inkpen conducted an analysis of over 3,200 Japanese subsidiaries and found that the percentage of expats in larger units has been declining steadily over the last four decades.[14] What has caused this? Four reasons for the declining use of Japanese expats have been cited. First, as the number of Japanese subsidiaries worldwide has increased, it has become more difficult to find the requisite number of qualified expats to handle these assignments. Second, the growing number of effective local managers makes it no longer necessary to rely as heavily on expats. Third, the high cost of keeping expats overseas is having a strong negative effect on company profits. Fourth, Japanese human resource management policies are changing, and the old "rice paper ceiling" that prevented non-Japanese from being promoted into the upper management ranks of subsidiaries is now beginning to disappear. This last development, in the United States in particular, is a result of Japanese firms realizing that their American subsidiaries have not been able to compete effectively. Japanese expat managers have been outflanked by their American counterparts. In particular, Japanese managers have not known how to fine-tune products for the U.S. market; did not understand how to tailor market approaches to different customer segments; and were unable to develop the speed, flexibility, and responsiveness needed to compete with the Americans.[15] It is highly likely that MNCs from other countries besides Japan are also following this trend of using local managers in lieu of expats.

Host-Country Nationals

host-country nationals
Local managers who are
hired by the MNC.

Host-country nationals are local managers who are hired by the MNC. For a number of reasons, many multinationals use host-country managers at the middle and lower-level ranks: Many countries expect the MNC to hire local talent, and this is a good way to meet this expectation. Also, even if an MNC wanted to staff all management positions with home-country personnel, it would be unlikely to have this many available managers, and the cost of transferring and maintaining them in the host country would be prohibitive.

This traditional pattern of managerial positions filled by home- and host-country personnel illustrates why it is so difficult to generalize about staffing patterns in an international setting. An exception would be in those cases where government regulations dictate selection practices and mandate at least some degree of "nativization." In Brazil, for example, two-thirds of the employees in any foreign subsidiary traditionally had to be Brazilian nationals. In addition, many countries exert real and subtle pressures to staff the upper-management ranks with nationals. In the past, these pressures by host countries have led companies such as Standard Oil to change their approach to selecting managers.

In European countries, home-country managers who are assigned to a foreign subsidiary or affiliate often stay in this position for the remainder of their career. Europeans are not transferred back to headquarters or to some other subsidiary, as is traditionally done by U.S. firms. Another approach, the least common, is always to use a home-country manager to run the operation.

U.S. firms tend to rely fairly heavily on host-country managers. Tung identified four reasons that U.S. firms tend to use host-country managers: (1) These individuals are familiar with the culture. (2) They know the language. (3) They are less expensive than home-country personnel. (4) Hiring them is good public relations. European firms that use host-country managers gave the two major reasons of familiarity with the culture and knowledge of the language, whereas Japanese firms gave the reason that the host-country national was the best-qualified individual for the job.[16] "International Management in Action: Important Tips on Working for Foreigners" gives examples of how Americans can better adapt to foreign bosses.

Third-Country Nationals

Third-country nationals (TCNs) are managers who are citizens of countries other than the country in which the MNC is headquartered or the one in which they are assigned to work by the MNC. Available data on third-country nationals are not as extensive as those on home- or host-country nationals. Tung found that the two most important reasons that U.S. MNCs use third-country nationals were that these people had the necessary expertise or were judged to be the best ones for the job. European firms gave only one answer: The individuals were the best ones for the job.[17]

third-country nationals (TCNs) Managers who are citizens of countries other than the country in which the MNC is headquartered or the one in which the managers are assigned to work by the MNC.

A number of advantages have been cited for using TCNs. One is that the salary and benefit package usually is less than that of a home-country national, although in recent years, the salary gap between the two has begun to diminish. A second reason is that the TCN may have a very good working knowledge of the region or speak the same language as the local people. This helps to explain why many U.S. MNCs hire English or Scottish managers for top positions at subsidiaries in former British colonies such as Jamaica, India, the West Indies, and Kenya. It also explains why successful multinationals such as Gillette, Coca-Cola, and IBM recruit local managers and train them to run overseas subsidiaries. Other cited benefits of using TCNs include:

1. These TCN managers, particularly those who have had assignments in the headquarters country, can often achieve corporate objectives more effectively than do expatriates or local nationals. In particular, they frequently have a deep understanding of the corporation's policies from the perspective of a foreigner and can communicate and implement those policies more effectively to others than can expats.

2. During periods of rapid expansion, TCNs can not only substitute for expatriates in new and growing operations but can offer different perspectives that can complement and expand on the sometimes narrowly focused viewpoints of both local nationals and headquarters personnel.

3. In joint ventures, TCNs can demonstrate a global or transnational image and bring unique cross-cultural skills to the relationship.[18]

Important Tips on Working for Foreigners

As the Japanese, South Koreans, and Europeans continue to expand their economic horizons, increased employment opportunities will be available worldwide. Is it a good idea to work for foreigners? Those who have done so have learned that there are both rewards and penalties associated with this career choice. Here are some useful tips that have been drawn from the experiences of those who have worked for foreign MNCs.

First, most U.S. managers are taught to make fast decisions, but most foreign managers take more time and view rapid decision making as unnecessary and sometimes bad. In the United States, we hear the cliché that "The effective manager is right 51 percent of the time." In Europe, this percentage is perceived as much too low, which helps to explain why European managers analyze situations in much more depth than most U.S. managers do. Americans working for foreign-owned firms have to focus on making slower and more accurate decisions.

Second, most Americans are taught to operate without much direction. In Latin countries, managers are accustomed to giving a great deal of direction, and in East Asian firms, there is little structure and direction. Americans have to learn to adjust to the decision-making process of the particular company.

Third, most Americans go home around 5 p.m. If there is more paperwork to do, they take it with them. Japanese managers, in contrast, stay late at the office and often view those who leave early as being lazy. Americans either have to adapt or have to convince the manager that they are working as hard as their peers but in a different physical location.

Fourth, many international firms say that their official language is English. However, important conversations always are carried out in the home-country's language, so it is important to learn that language.

Fifth, many foreign MNCs make use of fear to motivate their people. This is particularly true in manufacturing work, where personnel are under continuous pressure to maintain high output and quality. For instance, those who do not like to work under intense conditions would have a very difficult time succeeding in Japanese auto assembly plants. Americans have to understand that humanistic climates of work may be the exception rather than the rule.

Finally, despite the fact that discrimination in employment is outlawed in the United States, it is practiced by many MNCs, including those operating in the United States. Women seldom are given the same opportunities as men, and top-level jobs almost always are reserved for home-office personnel. In many cases, Americans have accepted this ethnocentric (nationalistic) approach, but as Chapter 3 discussed, ethics and social responsibilities are a major issue in the international arena and these challenges must be met now and in the future.

Inpatriates

inpatriates
Individuals from a host country or third-country nationals who are assigned to work in the home country.

In recent years a new term has emerged in international management—inpatriates. An **inpatriate** is an individual from a host country or a third-country national who is assigned to work in the home country. Even Japanese MNCs are now beginning to rely on inpatriates to help them meet their international challenges. Harvey and Buckley reported that:

> The Japanese are reducing their unicultural orientation in their global businesses. Yoichi Morishita, president of Matsushita, has ordered that top management must reflect the cultural diversity of the countries where Matsushita does business. Sony sells 80 percent of its products overseas and recently recognized the need to become multicultural. It has appointed two foreigners to its board of directors and has plans to hire host-country nationals who are to be integrated into the top management of the parent organization. At the same time, the Chairman of Sony has stated that in five years the board-of-directors of Sony will reflect the diversity of countries that are important to the future of the company. Similarly, Toshiba plans to have a more representative top management and board of directors to facilitate long-run global strategies.[19]

This growing use of inpats is helping MNCs better develop their global core competencies. As a result, today a new breed of multilingual, multiexperienced, so-called global managers or transnational managers is truly emerging.[20]

These new managers are part of a growing group of international executives who can manage across borders and do not fit the traditional third-country nationals mold. With a unified Europe and other such developments in North America and Asia, these global managers are in great demand. Additionally, with labor shortages developing in certain regions, there is a wave of migration from regions with an abundance of personnel to those where the demand is strongest.[21]

Subcontracting and Outsourcing

Other potential sources of international management talent are subcontracting and offshore outsourcing (introduced in Chapter 1 and further explored in Chapter 15). Offshore outsourcing is made possible by the increasing organizational and technological capacity of companies to separate, coordinate, and integrate geographically dispersed human resources—whether employed directly by the firm or contracted out—across distant geographic borders. The development of this capacity can be traced to the earlier growth of international subcontracting as well as to the international diffusion of lean production systems (which originated with Japanese auto manufacturers) to other manufacturing and service sectors. In particular, service industries are exploiting inexpensive telecommunications to transmit engineering, medical, legal, and accounting services to be performed in locations previously viewed as remote. Rising levels of educational attainment in developing countries such as China, India, and the Philippines, especially in the scientific and technical fields, make offshoring increasingly attractive for a range of international human resource needs.

On the one hand, offshore outsourcing, as well as the hiring of temporary workers from abroad on special visas, similar to inpatriates, presents significant opportunities for cost savings and lower overhead. On the other hand, the recent wave of media attention has focused on widespread concern that in an age of cheap telecommunications, almost any job, professional or blue-collar, can be performed in India for a fraction of U.S. wages. In particular, as discussed in Chapter 1, union groups, politicians, and NGOs have challenged MNCs' right to engage in labor "arbitrage."

Moreover, although the cost for a computer programmer or a middle manager in India remains a small fraction of the cost for a similar employee in the United States (a programmer with three to five years' experience makes about $25,000 in India but about $65,000 in the United States), the wage savings do not necessarily translate directly into overall savings because the typical outsourcing contract between an American company and an Indian vendor saves less than half as much as the wage differences would imply.[22] Microsoft recently revealed that it has been paying two Indian outsourcing companies, Infosys and Satyam, to provide skilled software architects for Microsoft projects. In this case, the work of software architects and developers was being done by employees of the Indian companies working at Microsoft facilities in the United States. Although the actual employees were paid much less than U.S. counterparts ($30,000 to $40,000), Microsoft was billed $90 an hour for software architects, or at a yearly rate of more than $180,000. The on-site work was done by Indian software engineers who came to the United States on H-1B visas, which allow foreign workers to be employed in the United States for up to six years. Microsoft also contracted work in India through the firms, with billing rates of $23 to $36 an hour.[23]

Though politically controversial, outsourcing can save companies significant costs and is very profitable for firms that specialize in providing these services on a contract basis. U.S.-based firms such as EDS, IBM, and Deloitte have developed specific competencies in global production and HR coordination, including managing the HR functions that must support it. These firms combine low labor costs, specialized technical capabilities, and coordination expertise.

Outsourcing can also create quality control problems for some companies, as demonstrated in Dell's decision to repatriate some of its call-center staff from India to Texas because of quality control problems. Because Dell is a company that has little on-site service, the call-center capability is core to Dell's competitive position. "We felt a little noise and angst from our customers, and we decided to make some changes," said Gary Cotshott, vice president of Dell's services division. "Sometimes, we move a little too far, too fast."[24] In addition, Indian companies are beginning to develop their own approaches to outsourcing, including investing in U.S. call centers and business-processing outsourcers. The Indians "are looking to build a global model quickly," said a partner with WestBridge Capital Partners, a Silicon Valley venture-capital firm that invests in outsourcing companies.[25]

Despite these limitations, offshore subcontracting will remain an important tool for managing and deploying international human resources. If anything, the trend is accelerating. Forrester Research recently estimated that 830,000 U.S. service jobs would be moved abroad by 2005, a 40 percent increase from a projection of 588,000 jobs made in November 2002. Forrester also estimated that U.S. companies would send 3.4 million service jobs offshore by 2015.[26] Although subcontracting provides important flexibility in the human resource practices of MNCs operating globally, it also requires skilled international managers to coordinate and oversee the complex relationships that arise from it.

■ Selection Criteria for International Assignments

international selection criteria
Factors used to choose personnel for international assignments.

Making an effective selection decision for an overseas assignment can prove to be a major problem. Typically, this decision is based on **international selection criteria,** which are factors used to choose international managers. These selections are influenced by the MNC's experience and often are culturally based. Sometimes as many as a dozen criteria are used, although most MNCs give serious consideration to only five or six.[27] Table 14–1 reports the importance of some of these criteria as ranked by Australian, expatriate, and Asian managers from 60 leading Australian, New Zealand, British, and U.S. MNCs with operations in South Asia.[28]

General Criteria

Some selection criteria are given a great deal of weight; others receive, at best, only lip service. A company sending people overseas for the first time often will have a much longer list of criteria than will an experienced MNC that has developed a "short list." For example, in one study, Tung found that personnel sent overseas by MNCs could be grouped into four categories—chief executive officer, functional head, troubleshooter, and operative—and each category had its own criteria for selection.[29]

Table 14–1
Rank of Criteria in Expatriate Selection

	Australian Managers $n = 47$	Expatriate Managers[a] $n = 52$	Asian Managers $n = 15$
1. Ability to adapt	1	1	2
2. Technical competence	2	3	1
3. Spouse and family adaptability	3	2	4
4. Human relations skill	4	4	3
5. Desire to serve overseas	5	5	5
6. Previous overseas experience	6	7	7
7. Understanding of host country culture	7	6	6
8. Academic qualifications	8	8	8
9. Knowledge of language of country	9	9	9
10. Understanding of home country culture	10	10	10

[a]U.S., British, Canadian, French, New Zealand, or Australian managers working for an MNC outside their home countries.
Source: Raymond J. Stone, "Expatriate Selection and Failure," *Human Resource Planning* 14, no. 1 (1991), p. 10. Reprinted with permission. Copyright © 1991 by the Human Resource Planning Society, 317 Madison Ave., Suite 1509, New York, NY 10017, Ph: 212-490-6387, Fax: 212-682-6851.

Typically, both technical and human criteria are considered. Firms that fail to consider both often find that their rate of failure is quite high. For example, Tung investigated both U.S. and Japanese companies and found that many U.S. firms had poor success in choosing people for overseas assignments; meanwhile, the Japanese firms were quite successful. The primary difference between the two was that the Americans tended to focus most heavily on technical considerations, whereas the Japanese also considered behavioral or relational skills, such as the ability of the managers to deal with clients, customers, superiors, peers, and subordinates.[30] Peterson, Napier, and Shul-Shim investigated the primary criteria that MNCs use when choosing personnel for overseas assignments and found that the Japanese and American MNCs in their survey ranked both technical expertise and interpersonal skills as very important.[31] The following sections examine some of the most commonly used selection criteria for overseas assignments in more depth.

Adaptability to Cultural Change

Overseas managers must be able to adapt to change. They also need a degree of cultural toughness. Research shows that many managers are exhilarated at the beginning of their overseas assignment. After a few months, however, a form of culture shock creeps in, and they begin to encounter frustration and feel confused in their new environment. One analysis noted that many of the most effective international managers suffer this cultural shock.[32] This may be a good sign, because it shows that the expatriate manager is becoming involved in the new culture and not just isolating himself or herself from the environment. Here is an example provided by a North American who was assigned to the Middle East:

> My third day in Israel, accompanied by a queasy stomach, I ventured forth into the corner market to buy something light and easy to digest. As yet unable to read Hebrew, I decided to pick up what looked like a small yogurt container that was sitting near the cheese. Not being one hundred percent sure it contained yogurt, I peered inside; to my delight, it held a thick white yogurt-looking substance. I purchased my "yogurt" and went home to eat—soap, liquid soap. How was I to know that soap came in packages resembling yogurt containers, or that market items in Israel were not neatly divided into edible and inedible sections, as I remembered them in the United States. My now "clean" stomach became a bit more fragile and my confidence waned.[33]

As this initial and trying period comes to an end, an expatriate's satisfaction with conditions tends to increase. In fact, as seen in Figure 14–1, after the first two years, most people become more satisfied with their overseas assignment than when they first arrived. Research also shows that men tend to adjust a little faster than women, although both sexes exhibit a great deal of similarity in the degree of their satisfaction with overseas assignments. In addition, people over 35 years of age tend to have slightly higher levels of satisfaction after the first year, but managers under 35 have higher satisfaction during the next three to four years. In all cases, however, these differences are not statistically significant.[34]

Organizations examine a number of characteristics to determine whether an individual is sufficiently adaptable. Examples include work experiences with cultures other than one's own, previous overseas travel, knowledge of foreign languages (fluency generally is not necessary), and recent immigration background or heritage. Others include (1) the ability to integrate with different people, cultures, and types of business organizations; (2) the ability to sense developments in the host country and accurately evaluate them; (3) the ability to solve problems within different frameworks and from different perspectives; (4) sensitivity to the fine print of differences of culture, politics, religion, and ethics, in addition to individual differences; and (5) flexibility in managing operations on a continuous basis despite lack of assistance and gaps in information.

Figure 14–1

Development of Satisfaction in Host Country over Time

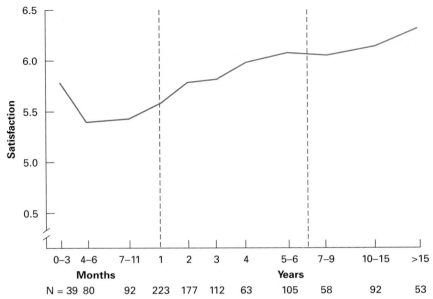

Note: Satisfaction scale: 1 = extremely low; 7 = extremely high.

Source: Ingemar Torbiorn, *Living Abroad* (New York: Wiley, 1982), p. 98. Copyright © 1982 John Wiley & Sons Limited. Reproduced with permission.

In research conducted among expatriates in China, Selmar found that those who were best able to deal with their new situation had developed coping strategies characterized by sociocultural and psychological adjustments including (1) feeling comfortable that their work challenges can be met; (2) being able to adjust to their new living conditions; (3) learning how to interact well with host-country nationals outside of work; and (4) feeling reasonably happy and being able to enjoy day-to-day activities.[35] And Caligiuri, after examining how host nationals help expatriates adjust, reported that certain types of personality characteristics are important in this process. In particular, her findings suggest that greater contact with host nationals helps with cross-cultural adjustment when the person also possesses the personality trait of openness. She also found that sociability was directly related to effective adjustment.[36]

Physical and Emotional Health

Most organizations require that their overseas managers have good physical and emotional health. Some examples are fairly obvious. An employee with a heart condition would be rejected for overseas assignment; likewise, an individual with a nervous disorder would not be considered. The psychological ability of individuals to withstand culture shock also would be considered, as would the current marital status as it affects the individual's ability to cope in a foreign environment. For example, one U.S. oil company operating in the Middle East considers middle-aged men with grown children to be the best able to cope with cultural shock, and for some locations in the desert, people from Texas or southern California make better risks than those from New England.

Age, Experience, and Education

Most MNCs strive for a balance between age and experience. There is evidence that younger managers are more eager for international assignments. These managers tend to be more "worldly" and have a greater appreciation of other cultures than older managers do.

By the same token, young people often are the least developed in management experience and technical skills; they lack real-world experience. To gain the desired balance, many firms send both young and seasoned personnel to the same overseas post. As Blue and Haynes put it, "Ideally, that team should be selected for both its youth and its experience, taking into consideration reporting relationships, specific responsibilities, authority and professional judgment as the determinants of whether youth or experience is best suited to a specific job."[37]

Many companies consider an academic degree, preferably a graduate degree, to be of critical importance to an international executive; however, universal agreement regarding the ideal type of degree is nonexistent. As one expert observed:

> Companies with highly technical products tend to prefer science degrees. Other firms feel that successful management requires depth, drive, imagination, creativity, and character—and that the type of person exemplified by these traits is more likely to be produced by a liberal arts education. But the overall prize-winning combination seems to be an undergraduate degree combined with a graduate business degree from a recognized business school.[38]

MNCs, of course, use formal education only as a point of departure for their own training and development efforts. For example, Siemens of Germany gives members of its international management team specific training designed to help them deal more effectively with the types of problems they will face on the job.

Language Training

One recognized weakness of many MNCs is that they do not give sufficient attention to the importance of language training. English is the primary language of international business, and most expatriates from all countries can converse in English. Those who can speak only English are at a distinct disadvantage when doing business in non-English-speaking countries, however. One study asked 1,100 Swedish expatriates how satisfied they were with knowledge of the local language. These Swedish managers expressed particular dissatisfaction with their understanding of Japanese and Middle Eastern languages.[39] In other words, language can be a very critical factor, and international experts have referred to it as "a most effective indirect method of learning about a country . . . as well as the value systems and customs of its people."[40]

Traditionally, U.S. managers have done very poorly in the language area. For example, a survey of 1,500 top managers worldwide faulted U.S. expatriates for minimizing the value of learning foreign languages. Executives in Japan, Western Europe, and South America, however, placed a high priority on speaking more than one language. The report concludes that "these results provide a poignant indication of national differences that promise to influence profoundly the success of American corporations."[41]

Motivation for a Foreign Assignment

Although individuals being sent overseas should have a desire to work abroad, this usually is not sufficient motivation. International management experts contend that the candidate also must believe in the importance of the job and even have something of an element of idealism or a sense of mission. Applicants who are unhappy with their current situation at home and are looking to get away seldom make effective overseas managers.

Some experts believe that a desire for adventure or a pioneering spirit is an acceptable reason for wanting to go overseas. Other motivators that often are cited include the desire to increase one's chances for promotion and the opportunity to improve one's economic status. For example, many U.S. MNCs regard international experience as being critical for promotion to the upper ranks. In addition, thanks to the supplemental wage and benefit package, U.S. managers sometimes find that they can make, and especially save, more money than if they remained stateside.

Spouses and Dependents or Work–Family Issues

Spouses and dependents are another important consideration when a person is to be chosen for an overseas assignment. If the family is not happy, the manager often performs poorly and may either be terminated or simply decide to leave the organization. Shaffer and her associates recently collected multisource data from 324 expatriates in 46 countries and found that the amount of organizational support that an expatriate feels he or she is receiving and the interplay between this person's work and family domains have a direct and unique influence on the individual's intentions regarding staying with or leaving the enterprise.[42] For this reason, some firms interview both the spouse and the manager before deciding whether to approve the assignment. This can be a very important decision for the firm because it focuses on the importance of family as an issue. In fact, in a survey that she conducted of over 400 expats, Tung found that people had very firm views in this area regarding what they would and would not do. Here is how expats responded to select work–family issues on a scale that ranged from 1 (strongly disagree) to 5 (strongly agree).[43]

I am willing to forgo an important function at home if it conflicts with an important job-related function.	3.37
I would accept an international assignment even if it means that my spouse/partner has to make career sacrifices.	3.07
I place my career above my family.	2.21
I would accept an international assignment even if my family objected to the assignment.	1.83
I would accept an international assignment even if my family will not be able to relocate with me.	1.69

adaptability screening
The process of evaluating how well a family is likely to stand up to the stress of overseas life.

One popular approach in appraising the family's suitability for an overseas assignment is called **adaptability screening.** This process evaluates how well the family is likely to stand up to the rigors and stress of overseas life. The company will look for a number of things in this screening, including how closely knit the family is, how well it can withstand stress, and how well it can adjust to a new culture and climate. The reason this family criterion receives so much attention is that MNCs have learned that an unhappy executive will be unproductive on the job and the individual will want to transfer home long before the tour of duty is complete. These findings were affirmed and extended by Borstorff and her associates, who examined the factors associated with employee willingness to work overseas and concluded that:

1. Unmarried employees are more willing than any other group to accept expat assignments.

2. Married couples without children at home or those with non-teenage children are probably the most willing to move.

3. Prior international experience appears associated with willingness to work as an expatriate.

4. Individuals most committed to their professional careers and to their employing organizations are prone to be more willing to work as expatriates.

5. Careers and attitudes of spouses will likely have a significant impact on employee willingness to move overseas.

6. Employee and spouse perceptions of organizational support for expatriates are critical to employee willingness to work overseas.[44]

These findings indicate that organizations cannot afford to overlook the role of the spouse in the expat selection decision process. What, in particular, can be done to address their concerns?[45] Table 14–2 provides some insights into this answer. Additionally, the table adds a factor often overlooked in this process—situations in which the wife is being assigned overseas and the husband is the "other" spouse. Although many of the concerns of the male spouse are similar to those of spouses in general, a close look at Table 14–2 shows that some of the concerns of the males are different in their rank ordering.

Leadership Ability

The ability to influence people to act in a particular way—leadership—is another important criterion in selecting managers for an international assignment. Determining whether a person who is an effective leader in the home country will be equally effective in an overseas environment can be difficult, however. When determining whether an applicant has the desired leadership ability, many firms look for specific characteristics, such as maturity, emotional stability, the ability to communicate well, independence, initiative, creativity, and good health. If these characteristics are present and the person has been an

Table 14–2
Activities That Are Important for Expatriate Spouses
(scale: 1–5, 5 = very important)

Mean Score	Activity
Average	**From All Respondents**
4.33	Company help in obtaining necessary paperwork (permits, etc.) for spouse
4.28	Adequate notice of relocation
4.24	Predeparture training for spouse and children
4.23	Counseling for spouse regarding work/activity opportunities in foreign location
4.05	Employment networks coordinated with other international networks
3.97	Help with spouse's reentry into home country
3.93	Financial support for education
3.76	Compensation for spouse's lost wages and/or benefits
3.71	Creation of a job for spouse
3.58	Development of support groups for spouses
3.24	Administrative support (office space, secretarial services, etc.) for spouse
3.11	Financial support for research
3.01	Financial support for volunteer activities
2.90	Financial support for creative activities
Average	**From Male Spouses**
4.86	Employment networks coordinated with other international organizations
4.71	Help with spouse's reentry into home country
4.71	Administrative support (office space, secretarial services, etc.) for spouse
4.57	Compensation for spouse's lost wages and/or benefits
4.29	Adequate notice of relocation
4.29	Counseling for spouse regarding work/activity opportunities in foreign location
3.86	Predeparture training for spouse and children
3.71	Creation of a job for spouse
3.71	Financial support for volunteer activities
3.43	Financial support for education
3.14	Financial support for research
3.14	Financial support for creative activities
3.00	Development of support groups for spouses

Source: Adapted from Betty Jane Punnett, "Towards Effective Management of Expatriate Spouses," *Journal of World Business* 33, no. 3 (1997), p. 249.

effective leader in the home country, MNCs assume that the individual also will do well overseas.

Other Considerations

Applicants also can take certain steps to prepare themselves better for international assignments. Tu and Sullivan suggested the applicant can carry out a number of different phases.[46] In phase one, they suggest focusing on self-evaluation and general awareness. This includes answering the question: Is an international assignment really for me? Other questions in the first phase include finding out if one's spouse and family support the decision to go international and collecting general information on the available job opportunities.

Phase two is characterized by a concentration on activities that should be completed before a person is selected. Some of these include (1) conducting a technical skills match to ensure that one's skills are in line with those that are required for the job; (2) starting to learn the language, customs, and etiquette of the region where one will be posted; (3) developing an awareness of the culture and value systems of this geographic area; and (4) making one's superior aware of this interest in an international assignment.

The third phase consists of activities to be completed after being selected for an overseas assignment. Some of these include (1) attending training sessions provided by the company; (2) conferring with colleagues who have had experience in the assigned region; (3) speaking with expatriates and foreign nationals about the assigned country; and (4) if possible, visiting the host country with one's spouse before the formally scheduled departure.

■ International Human Resource Selection Procedures

MNCs use a number of selection procedures. The two most common are tests and interviews. Some international firms use one; a smaller percentage employ both. Theoretical models containing the variables that are important for adjusting to an oversea assignment have been developed. These adjustment models can help contribute to more effective selection of expatriates. The following sections examine traditional testing and interviewing procedures, then present an adjustment model.

Testing and Interviewing Procedures

Some evidence suggests that although some firms use testing, it is not extremely popular. For example, an early study found that almost 80 percent of the 127 foreign operations managers who were surveyed reported that their companies used no tests in the selection process.[47] This contrasts with the more widespread testing that these firms use when selecting domestic managers. Many MNCs report that the costs, questionable accuracy, and poor predictive record make testing of limited value.

Many firms do use interviews to screen people for overseas assignments. One expert notes: "It is generally agreed that extensive interviews of candidates (and their spouses) by senior executives still ultimately provide the best method of selection."[48] Tung's research supports these comments. For example, 52 percent of the U.S. MNCs she surveyed reported that in the case of managerial candidates, MNCs conducted interviews with both the manager and his or her spouse, and 47 percent conducted interviews with the candidate alone. For technically oriented positions, 40 percent of the firms interviewed both the candidate and the spouse, and 59 percent conducted interviews with the candidate alone. German firms also sometimes interview the spouse when hiring into managerial and technical positions, although in a different ratio to U.S. firms. In the case of management positions, 41 percent interviewed both the candidate and the spouse, and 59 percent interviewed the candidate only. For technically oriented positions, these percentages were 62 and 39, respectively. Concerning these findings, Tung concluded:

> These figures suggest that in management-type positions which involve more extensive contact with the local community, as compared to technically oriented positions, the adaptability of the spouse to living in a foreign environment was perceived as important for successful performance abroad. However, even for technically oriented positions, a sizable proportion of the firms did conduct interviews with both candidate and spouse. This lends support to the contention of other researchers that MNCs are becoming increasingly cognizant of the importance of this factor to effective performance abroad.[49]

The Adjustment Process

In recent years, international human resource management specialists have developed models that help to explain the factors involved in effectively adjusting to overseas assignments.[50] These adjustment models help to identify the underpinnings of the effective selection of expatriates.

There are two major types of adjustments that an expatriate must make when going on an overseas assignment. One is the anticipatory adjustment. This is carried out before the expat leaves for the assignment. The other is the in-country adjustment, which takes place on site.

The anticipatory adjustment is influenced by a number of important factors. One factor is the predeparture training that is provided. This often takes the form of cross-cultural seminars or workshops, and it is designed to acquaint expats with the culture and work life of the country to which they will be posted. Another factor affecting anticipatory adjustment is the previous experience the expat may have had with the assigned country or with countries with similar cultures. These two factors, training and previous experience, help to determine the accuracy of the expat's expectations.

The organizational input into anticipatory adjustment is most directly related and concerned with the selection process. Traditionally, MNCs relied on only one important selection criterion for overseas assignments: technical competence. Obviously, technical competence is important, but it is only one of a number of skills that will be needed. If the MNC concentrates only on technical competence as a selection criterion, then it is not properly preparing the expatriate managers for successful adjustment in overseas assignments. Expats are going to go abroad believing that they are prepared to deal with the challenges awaiting them, and they will be wrong.

Once the expatriate is on site, a number of factors will influence his or her ability to adjust effectively. One factor is the expat's ability to maintain a positive outlook in the face of a high-pressure situation, to interact well with host nationals, and to perceive and evaluate the host country's cultural values and norms correctly. A second factor is the job itself, as reflected by the clarity of the role the expat plays in the host management team, the authority the expat has to make decisions, the newness of the work-related challenges, and the amount of role conflict that exists. A third factor is the organizational culture and how easily the expat can adjust to it. A fourth is nonwork matters, such as the toughness with which the expatriate faces a whole new cultural experience and how well his or her family can adjust to the rigors of the new assignment. A fifth and final factor identified in the adjustment model is the expat's ability to develop effective socialization tactics and to understand "what's what" and "who's who" in the host organization.

These anticipatory and in-country factors will influence the expatriate's mode and degree of adjustment to an overseas assignment. They can help to explain why effective selection of expatriates is multifaceted and can be very difficult and challenging. But if all works out well, the individual can become a very important part of the organization's overseas operations. McCormick and Chapman illustrated this by showing the changes that an expat goes through as he or she seeks to adjust to the new assignment.[51] As seen in

---

Figure 14–2   **The Relocation Transition Curve**

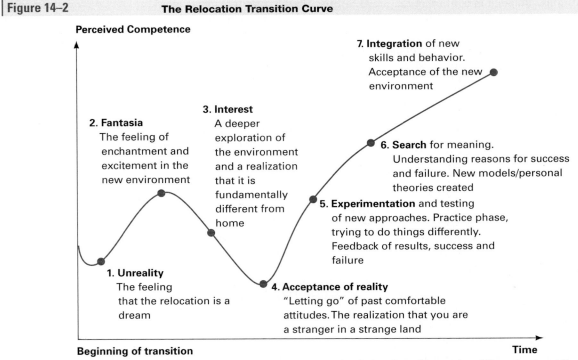

7. Integration of new skills and behavior. Acceptance of the new environment

3. Interest A deeper exploration of the environment and a realization that it is fundamentally different from home

2. Fantasia The feeling of enchantment and excitement in the new environment

6. Search for meaning. Understanding reasons for success and failure. New models/personal theories created

5. Experimentation and testing of new approaches. Practice phase, trying to do things differently. Feedback of results, success and failure

1. Unreality The feeling that the relocation is a dream

4. Acceptance of reality "Letting go" of past comfortable attitudes. The realization that you are a stranger in a strange land

Perceived Competence / *Beginning of transition* / *Time*

Source: Adapted from Iain McCormick and Tony Chapman, "Executive Relocation: Personal and Organizational Tactics," in *Managing Across Cultures: Issues and Perspectives,* ed. Pat Joynt and Malcolm Warner (London: International Thomson Business Press, 1996), p. 368.

Figure 14–2, early enthusiasm often gives way to cold reality, and the expat typically ends up in a search to balance personal and work demands with the new environment. In many cases, fortunately, everything works out well. Additionally, one of the ways in which MNCs often try to put potential expats at ease about their new assignment is by presenting an attractive compensation package.

■ Compensation

One of the reasons why there has been a decline in the number of expats in recent years is that MNCs have found that the expense can be prohibitive. Reynolds estimated that, on average, "expats cost employers two to five times as much as home-country counterparts and frequently ten or more times as much as local nationals in the country to which they are assigned."[52] As seen in Figure 14–3, the cost of living in some of the major cities is extremely high, and these expenses must be included somewhere in the compensation package.

Common Elements of Compensation Packages

The overall compensation package often varies from country to country. As Bailey noted:

> Compensation programs implemented in a global organization will not mirror an organization's domestic plan because of differences in legally mandated benefits, tax laws, cultures, and employee expectation based on local practices. The additional challenge in compensation design is the requirement that excessive costs be avoided and at the same time employee morale be maintained at high levels.[53]

There are, however, five common elements in the typical expatriate compensation package: base salary, benefits, allowances, incentives, and taxes.

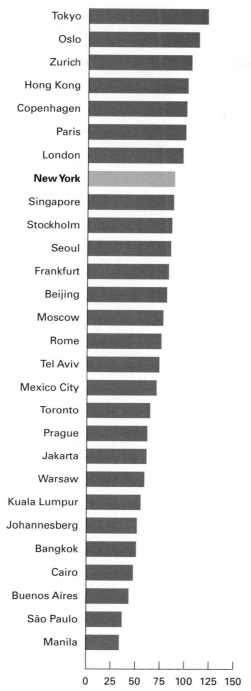

Figure 14–3

Relative Cost of Living in Selected Cities (New York = 100)

Source: Economist Intelligence Unit, 2000.

Base Salary Base salary is the amount of money that an expatriate normally receives in the home country. In the United States this has been around $175,000 for upper-middle managers in recent years, and this rate is similar to that paid to managers in both Japan and Germany. The exchange rates, of course, also affect the real wages.

Expatriate salaries typically are set according to the base pay of the home countries. Therefore, a German manager working for a U.S. MNC and assigned to Spain would have a base salary that reflects the salary structure in Germany. U.S. expatriates have salaries tied to U.S. levels. The salaries usually are paid in home currency, local currency, or a combination of the two. The base pay also serves as the benchmark against which bonuses and benefits are calculated.

Benefits   Approximately one-third of compensation for regular employees is benefits. These benefits compose a similar, or even larger, portion of expat compensation. A number of thorny issues surround compensation for expatriates, however. These include:

1. Whether MNCs should maintain expatriates in home-country benefit programs, particularly if these programs are not tax-deductible.
2. Whether MNCs have the option of enrolling expatriates in host-country benefit programs or making up any difference in coverage.
3. Whether host-country legislation regarding termination of employment affects employee benefits entitlements.
4. Whether the home or host country is responsible for the expatriates' social security benefits.
5. Whether benefits should be subject to the requirements of the home or host country.
6. Which country should pay for the benefits.
7. Whether other benefits should be used to offset any shortfall in coverage.
8. Whether home-country benefits programs should be available to local nationals.

Most U.S.-based MNCs include expatriate managers in their home-office benefits program at no additional cost to the expats. If the host country requires expats to contribute to their social security program, the MNC typically picks up the tab. Fortunately, several international agreements between countries recently have eliminated such dual coverage and expenses.

Additionally, MNCs often provide expatriates with extra vacation and with special leaves. The MNC typically will pay the airfare for expats and their families to make an annual visit home, for emergency leave, and for expenses when a relative in the home country is ill or dies.

Allowances   Allowances are an expensive feature of expatriate compensation packages. One of the most common parts is a cost-of-living allowance—a payment for differences between the home country and the overseas assignment. This allowance is designed to provide the expat with the same standard of living that he or she enjoyed in the home country, and it may cover a variety of expenses, including relocation, housing, education, and hardship.

Relocation expenses typically involve moving, shipping, and storage charges that are associated with personal furniture, clothing, and other items that the expatriate and his or her family are (or are not) taking to the new assignment. Related expenses also may include cars and club memberships in the host country, although these perks commonly are provided only to senior-level expats.

Housing allowances cover a wide range. Some firms provide the expat with a residence during the assignment and pay all associated expenses. Others give a predetermined housing allotment each month and let expats choose their own residence. Additionally, some MNCs help those going on assignment with the sale or lease of the house they are leaving behind; if the house is sold, the company usually pays closing costs and other associated expenses.

Education allowances for the expat's children are another integral part of the compensation package. These expenses cover costs such as tuition, enrollment fees, books, supplies, transportation, room, board, and school uniforms. In some cases, expenses to attend postsecondary schools also are covered.

Hardship allowances are designed to induce expats to work in hazardous areas or in an area with a poor quality of life. Those who are assigned to Eastern Europe, China, and some Middle Eastern countries sometimes are granted a hardship premium. These payments may be in the form of a lump sum ($10,000 to $50,000) or a percentage (15% to 50%) of the expat's base compensation.

Incentives   In recent years some MNCs have also been designing special incentive programs for keeping expats motivated. In the process, a growing number of firms have dropped the ongoing premium for overseas assignments and replaced it with a one-time, lump-sum premium. For example, in the early 1990s over 60 percent of MNCs gave ongoing premiums to their expats. Today that percentage is under 50 percent and continuing to decline. Peterson and his colleagues, for example, examined the human resource policies of 24 U.S., British, German, and Japanese subsidiaries and found that in only 10 cases did the multinational have a policy of paying expatriates higher compensation than they would have received if they had stayed in their home country.[54]

The lump-sum payment has a number of benefits. One is that expats realize that they will be given this payment just once—when they move to the international locale. So the payment tends to retain its value as an incentive. A second is that the costs to the company are less because there is only one payment and no future financial commitment. A third is that because it is a separate payment, distinguishable from regular pay, it is more readily available for saving or spending.

The specific incentive program that is used will vary, and expats like this. Researchers, for example, have found that some of the factors that influence the type and amount of incentive include whether the person is moving within or between continents and where the person is being stationed. Table 14–3 provides some of the latest survey information related to worldwide employer incentive practices.

Finally, it is important to recognize that growing numbers of MNCs are beginning to phase out incentive premiums. Instead, they are focusing on creating a cadre of expats who are motivated by nonfinancial incentives.

Taxes   Another major component of expatriate compensation is tax equalization. For example, an expat may have two tax bills, one from the host country and one from the U.S. Internal Revenue Service, for the same pay. IRS Code Section 911 permits a deduction of up to $80,000 on foreign-earned income. Top-level expats often earn far more than this, however; thus, they may pay two tax bills for the amount by which their pay exceeds $80,000.

Usually, MNCs pay the extra tax burden. The most common way is by determining the base salary and other extras (e.g., bonuses) that the expat would make if based in the home country. Taxes on this income then are computed and compared with the taxes due on the expat's income. Any taxes that exceed what would have been imposed in the home country are paid by the MNC, and any windfall is kept by the expat as a reward for taking the assignment.

Table 14–3
Employer Incentive Practices Around the World

Percent of MNCs Paying for Moves Within Continents				
Type of Premium	Asia	Europe	North America	Total
Ongoing	62%	46%	29%	42%
Lump sum	21	20	25	23
None	16	27	42	32
Percent of MNCs Paying for Moves Between Continents				
Type of Premium	Asia	Europe	North America	Total
Ongoing	63%	54%	39%	49%
Lump sum	24	18	30	26
None	13	21	27	22

Source: Derived from Geoffrey W. Latta, "Expatriate Incentives: Beyond Tradition," *HR Focus,* March 1998, p. S4.

Tailoring the Package

Working within the five common elements just described, MNCs will tailor compensation packages to fit the specific situation. For example, senior-level managers in Japan are paid only around four times as much as junior staff members. This is in sharp contrast to the United States, where the multiple is much higher. A similar situation exists in Europe, where many senior-level managers make far less than their U.S. counterparts and stockholders, politicians, and the general public oppose U.S.-style affluence. For example, when Daimler-Benz bought Chrysler, there was controversy regarding the differences in the executive pay packages. German companies believe that executive pay should be comparatively closer to that of the average employee. American companies, however, reward executives with bonuses and stock options. Here is a contrast between the compensation packages of the chairman and chief executive at both companies at the time of the merger.[55]

	Chrysler Chairman and CEO	Daimler-Benz Chairman and CEO
Salary	$1,612,500	$1,137,300
Bonus	3,000,000	—
Other annual payments (dividends, tax reimbursement)	218,903	—
Other programs (matching payment to savings plan)	77,400	—
Performance shares	1,209,701	—
Options granted (estimate of value)	4,753,000	796,100
Options exercised (granted in previous years)	5,259,600	—
Total	$16,131,104	$1,933,400

These data help pinpoint a thorny problem: Can a senior-level U.S. expat be paid a salary that is significantly higher than local senior-level managers in the overseas subsidiary, or would the disparity create morale problems? This is a difficult question to answer and must be given careful consideration. One solution is to link pay and performance to attract and retain outstanding personnel.

In formulating the compensation package, a number of approaches can be used. The most common is the **balance-sheet approach,** which involves ensuring that the expat is "made whole" and does not lose money by taking the assignment. A second and often complementary approach is negotiation, which involves working out a special, ad hoc arrangement that is acceptable to both the company and the expat. A third approach, **localization,** involves paying the expat a salary that is comparable to the salaries of local nationals. This approach most commonly is used with individuals early in their careers who are being given a long-term overseas assignment. A fourth approach is the **lump-sum method,** which involves giving the expat a predetermined amount of money and letting the individual make his or her own decisions regarding how to spend it. A fifth is the **cafeteria approach,** which entails giving expats a series of options and letting them decide how to spend the available funds. For example, expats who have children may opt for private schooling; expats who have no children may choose a chauffeur-driven car or an upscale apartment. A sixth method is the **regional system,** under which the MNC sets a compensation system for all expats who are assigned to a particular region, so that (for example) everyone going to Europe falls under one particular system and everyone being assigned to South America is covered by a different system.[56]

The most important thing to remember about global compensation is that the package must be cost-effective and fair. If it meets these two criteria, it likely will be acceptable to all parties.

---

balance-sheet approach
An approach to developing an expatriate compensation package that ensures the expat is "made whole" and does not lose money by taking the assignment.

localization
An approach to developing an expatriate compensation package that involves paying the expat a salary comparable to that of local nationals.

lump-sum method
An approach to developing an expatriate compensation package that involves giving the expat a predetermined amount of money and letting the individual make his or her own decisions regarding how to spend it.

cafeteria approach
An approach to developing an expatriate compensation package that entails giving the individual a series of options and letting the person decide how to spend the available funds.

regional system
An approach to developing an expatriate compensation package that involves setting a compensation system for all expats who are assigned to a particular region and paying everyone in accord with that system.

■ Individual and Host-Country Viewpoints

Until now, we have examined the selection process mostly from the standpoint of the MNC: What will be best for the company? However, two additional perspectives for selection warrant consideration: (1) that of the individual who is being selected and (2) that of the country to which the candidate will be sent. Research shows that each has specific desires and motivations regarding the expatriate selection process.

Candidate Motivations

Why do individuals accept foreign assignments? One answer is a greater demand for their talents abroad than at home. For example, a growing number of senior U.S. managers have moved to Mexico because of Mexico's growing need for experienced executives. The findings of one early study grouped the participating countries into clusters: Anglo (Australia, Austria, Canada, India, New Zealand, South Africa, Switzerland, United Kingdom, and United States); Northern European (Denmark, Finland, Norway); French (Belgium and France); northern South American (Colombia, Mexico, and Peru); southern South American (Argentina and Chile); and Independent (Brazil, Germany, Israel, Japan, Sweden, and Venezuela).[57] Within these groupings, researchers were able to identify major motivational differences. Some of their findings included:

1. The Anglo cluster was more interested in individual achievement and less interested in the desire for security than any other cluster.

2. The French cluster was similar to the Anglo cluster, except that less importance was given to individual achievement and more to security.

3. Countries in the Northern European cluster were more oriented to job accomplishment and less to getting ahead; considerable importance was assigned to jobs not interfering with personal lives.

4. In South American clusters, individual achievement goals were less important than in most other clusters. Fringe benefits were particularly important to South American groups.

5. Germans were similar to those in the South American clusters, except that they placed a great emphasis on advancement and earnings.

6. The Japanese were unique in their mix of desires. They placed high value on earnings opportunities but low value on advancement. They were high on challenge but low on autonomy. At the same time, they placed strong emphasis on working in a friendly, efficient department and having good physical working conditions.

Another interesting focus of attention has been on those countries that expatriates like best. A study conducted by Ingemar Torbiorn found that the 1,100 Swedish expatriates surveyed were at least fairly well satisfied with their host country and in some cases were very satisfied. Five of the countries that they liked very much were Switzerland, Belgium, England, the United States, and Portugal.[58] Today these countries are still quite popular, although the specific city is typically of even greater importance. What are the best cities? One way of answering this question is by determining the quality of life in the metropolis. This is usually done by measuring a host of criteria, including the city's educational system, recreational facilities, communication system, transportation system, cost of living, and the degree of personal safety one can expect to find there. Figure 14–4 reports the recent quality of life in 27 major cities worldwide.

Host-Country Desires

Although many MNCs try to choose people who fit in well, little attention has been paid to the host country's point of view. Whom would it like to see put in managerial positions?

Figure 14–4

Quality of Life in Select Major Metropolises, 2002 (New York = 100)

One study surveyed over 100 host-country organizations (HCOs) in five countries and found that accommodating the wishes of HCOs can be very difficult.[59] They are highly ethnocentric in orientation. They want local managers to head the subsidiaries, and they set such high levels of expectation regarding the desired characteristics of expatriates that anyone sent by the MNC is unlikely to measure up. These findings help to explain why many MNCs welcome input from their host-country nations regarding staffing decisions but do not let themselves be totally swayed by these opinions. Quite obviously, many MNCs are as guilty of ethnocentric behavior as their host-country counterparts. The findings are presented in Table 14–4.

Table 14–4
Host-Country Beliefs about Home-Country Expats

Beliefs	Percentage of Respondents Who Agree				
	Holland	England	Germany	Belgium	France
All top managers of foreign subsidiaries should be host-country nationals.	87.5	78.0	35.1	42.9	81.3
Expatriate managers should be of West European ethnic origin.	90.0	95.0	96.3	100.0	58.3
Expatriate managers should be thoroughly familiar with the culture of the host country.	93.8	90.3	78.9	100.0	81.3
Expatriate managers should adhere to local managerial patterns of behavior.	87.5	96.9	73.7	100.0	93.3
Expatriate managers should be proficient in the host-country language.	100.0	100.0	100.0	100.0	100.0
Expatriate managers should have a working knowledge of the host country's social characteristics.	93.3	96.9	84.2	100.0	100.0
Expatriate managers should be thoroughly familiar with the history of the host country.	93.3	83.9	81.6	100.0	100.0

Source: Adapted from Y. Zeira and M. Banai, "Attitudes of Host-Country Organizations Toward MNCs' Staffing Policies: A Cross-Country and Cross-Industry Analysis," *Management International Review* 21, no. 2 (1981), p. 42. Used with permission.

■ Repatriation of Expatriates

For most overseas managers, **repatriation,** the return to one's home country, occurs within five years of the time they leave. Few expatriates remain overseas for the duration of their stay with the firm.[60] When they return, these expatriates often find themselves facing readjustment problems, and some MNCs are trying to deal with these problems through use of transition strategies.

repatriation
The return to one's home country from an overseas management assignment.

Reasons for Returning

The most common reason that expatriates return home from overseas assignments is that their formally agreed-on tour of duty is over. Before they left, they were told that they would be posted overseas for a predetermined period, often two to three years, and they are returning as planned. A second common reason is that expatriates want their children educated in a home-country school, and the longer they are away, the less likely it is that this will happen.[61]

A third reason why expatriates return is that they are not happy in their overseas assignment. Sometimes unhappiness is a result of poor organizational support by the home office, which leaves the manager feeling that the assignment is not a good one and it would be best to return as soon as possible. Kraimer, Wayne, and Jaworski found that lack of this kind of support has a negative effect on the expat's ability to adjust to the assignment.[62] At other times an expat will want to return home early because the spouse or children do not want to stay. Because the company feels that the loss in managerial productivity is too great to be offset by short-term personal unhappiness, the individual is allowed to come back even though typically the cost is quite high.[63]

A fourth reason that people return is failure to do a good job. Such failure often spells trouble for the manager and may even result in demotion or termination.

Readjustment Problems

Many companies that say that they want their people to have international experience often seem unsure of what to do with these managers when they return. One recent survey of midsize and large firms found that 80 percent of these companies send people abroad and more than half of them intend to increase the number they have on assignment overseas. However, responses from returning expats point to problems. Three-quarters of the respondents said that they felt their permanent position upon returning home was a demotion. Over 60 percent said that they lacked the opportunities to put their foreign experience to work, and 60 percent said that their company had not communicated clearly about what would happen to them when they returned. Perhaps worst of all, within a year of returning, 25 percent of the managers had left the company.[64] These statistics are not surprising to those who have been studying repatriation problems. In fact, one researcher reported the following expatriate comments about their experiences:

> My colleagues react indifferently to my international assignment. . . . They view me as doing a job I did in the past; they don't see me as having gained anything while overseas.

> I had no specific reentry job to return to. I wanted to leave international and return to domestic. Working abroad magnifies problems while isolating effects. You deal with more problems, but the home office doesn't know the details of the good or bad effects. Managerially, I'm out of touch.

> I'm bored at work. . . . I run upstairs to see what [another returning colleague] is doing. He says, "Nothing." Me, too.[65]

A study by Tung found that, in general, the longer the duration of an off-shore assignment, the more problem the expatriate has being reabsorbed into the home office. Here are the major reasons:

1. The "out of sight, out of mind" syndrome is common.
2. Organizational changes made during the time the individual was abroad may make his or her position in the parent headquarters redundant or peripheral.
3. Technological advances in the parent headquarters may render the individual's existing skills and knowledge obsolete.[66]

Still another problem is adjusting to the new job back home. It sometimes takes from six months to a year before managers are operating at full effectiveness. Figure 14–5 provides an illustration.

Other readjustment problems are more personal in nature. Many expatriates find that the salary and fringe benefits to which they have become accustomed in the foreign assignment now are lost, and adjusting to this lower standard of living is difficult. In addition,

Figure 14–5

Effectiveness of Returning Expatriates

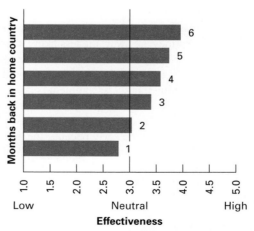

those who sold their houses and now must buy new ones find that the monthly cost often is much higher than when they left. The children often are placed in public schools, where classes are much larger than in the overseas private schools. Many also miss the cultural lifestyles, as in the case of an executive who is transferred from Paris, France, to a medium-sized city in the United States, or from any developed country to an underdeveloped country. Additionally, many returning expatriates have learned that their international experiences are not viewed as important. Many Japanese expatriates, for example, report that when they return, their experiences should be downplayed if they want to "fit in" with the organization. In fact, reports one recent *New York Times* article, a substantial number of Japanese expatriates "are happier overseas than they are back home."[67]

Other research supports the findings noted here and offers operative recommendations for action. Based on questionnaires completed by 174 respondents who had been repatriated from four large U.S. MNCs, Black found the following:

1. With few exceptions, individuals whose expectations were met had the most positive levels of repatriation adjustment and job performance.

2. In the case of high-level managers in particular, expatriates whose job demands were greater, rather than less, than expected reported high levels of repatriation adjustment and job performance. Those having greater job demands may have put in more effort and had better adjustment and performance.

3. Job performance and repatriation adjustment were greater for individuals whose job constraint expectations were undermet than for those individuals whose expectations were overmet. In other words, job constraints were viewed as an undesirable aspect of the job, and having them turn out to be less than expected was a pleasant surprise that helped adjustment and performance.

4. When living and housing conditions turned out to be better than expected, general repatriation adjustment and job performance were better.

5. Individuals whose general expectations were met or overmet had job evaluations that placed them 10 percent higher than those whose general expectations were unmet.[68]

Transition Strategies

To help smooth the adjustment from an overseas to a stateside assignment, some MNCs have developed **transition strategies,** which can take a number of different forms. One is the use of **repatriation agreements,** whereby the firm tells an individual how long she or he will be posted overseas and promises to give the individual, on return, a job that is mutually acceptable. This agreement typically does not promise a specific position or salary, but the agreement may state that the person will be given a job that is equal to, if not better than, the one held before leaving.[69]

Some firms also rent or otherwise maintain expatriates' homes until they return. The Aluminum Company of America and Union Carbide both have such plans for managers going overseas. This plan helps to reduce the financial shock that often accompanies home shopping by returning expatriates. A third strategy is to use senior executives as sponsors of managers abroad.

Still another approach is to keep expatriate managers apprised of what is going on at corporate headquarters and to plug these managers into projects at the home office whenever they are on leave in the home country. This helps maintain the person's visibility and ensures the individual is looked on as a regular member of the management staff.

In the final analysis, a proactive strategy that provides an effective support system to allay expatriate concerns about career issues while serving abroad may work best. Tung found that the successful U.S., European, Japanese, and Australian MNCs that she studied had (1) mentor programs (one-on-one pairing of an expatriate with a member of home-office senior management); (2) a separate organization unit with primary responsibility for the specific needs of expatriates; or (3) maintenance of constant contacts between the home office and the expatriate.[70]

transition strategies Strategies used to help smooth the adjustment from an overseas to a stateside assignment.

repatriation agreements Agreements whereby the firm tells an individual how long she or he will be posted overseas and promises to give the individual, on return, a job that is mutually acceptable.

Recent research supports and expands these findings. One study surveyed 99 employees and managers with international experience in 21 corporations.[71] The findings reveal that cultural reentry, financial implications, and the nature of job assignments are three major areas of expatriate concern. In particular, some of the main problems of repatriation identified in this study include (1) adjusting to life back home; (2) facing a financial package that is not as good as that overseas; (3) having less autonomy in the stateside job than in the overseas position; and (4) not receiving any career counseling from the company. To the extent that the MNC can address these types of problems, the transition will be smooth, and the expatriate's performance effectiveness once home will increase quickly. Some additional steps suggested by experts in this area include:

1. Arrange an event to welcome and recognize the employee and family, either formally or informally.
2. Establish support to facilitate family reintegration.
3. Offer repatriation counseling or workshops to ease the adjustment.
4. Assist the spouse with job counseling, résumé writing, and interviewing techniques.
5. Provide educational counseling for the children.
6. Provide the employee with a thorough debriefing by a facilitator to identify new knowledge, insights, and skills and to provide a forum to showcase new competencies.
7. Offer international outplacement to the employee and reentry counseling to the entire family if no positions are possible.
8. Arrange a postassignment interview with the expatriate and spouse to review their view of the assignment and address any repatriation issues.[72]

Hammer and his associates echo these types of recommendations. Based on research that they conducted in two multinational corporations among expats and their spouses, they concluded that:

> The findings from the present study suggest that one of the key transitional activities for returning expatriates and their spouses from a corporate context should involve targeted communication from the home environment concerning the expectations of the home office toward the return of the repatriate executive and his/her family (role relationships). Further, reentry training should focus primarily on helping the repatriate manager and spouse align their expectations with the actual situation that will be encountered upon arrival in the home culture both within the organizational context as well as more broadly within the social milieu. To the degree that corporate communication and reentry training activities help the returning executive and spouse in expectation alignment, the executive's level of reentry satisfaction should be higher and the degree of reentry difficulties less.[73]

Additionally, in recent years many MNCs have begun using inpatriates to supplement their home-office staff and some of the same issues discussed here with repatriation come into play.

■ Training in International Management

training
The process of altering employee behavior and attitudes in a way that increases the probability of goal attainment.

Training is the process of altering employee behavior and attitudes in a way that increases the probability of goal attainment. Training is particularly important in preparing employees for overseas assignments because it helps ensure that their full potential will be tapped.[74] One of the things that training can do is to help expat managers better understand the customs, cultures, and work habits of the local culture. The simplest training, in terms of preparation time, is to place a cultural integrator in each foreign operation. This individual is responsible for ensuring that the operation's business systems are in accord with those of the local culture. The integrator advises, guides, and recommends actions needed to ensure this synchronization.[75]

Unfortunately, although using an integrator can help, it is seldom sufficient. Recent experience clearly reveals that in creating an effective global team, the MNC must assemble individuals who collectively understand the local language, have grown up in diverse cultures or neighborhoods, have open, flexible minds, and will be able to deal with high degrees of stress.[76] In those cases where potential candidates do not yet possess all of these requisite skills or abilities, MNCs need a well-designed training program that is administered before the individuals leave for their overseas assignment (and, in some cases, also on-site) and then evaluated later to determine its overall effectiveness. One review of 228 MNCs found that cross-cultural training, which can take many forms, is becoming increasingly popular. Some of these findings included the following:

1. Of organizations with cultural programs, 58 percent offer training only to some expatriates, and 42 percent offer it to all of them.

2. Ninety-one percent offer cultural orientation programs to spouses, and 75 percent offer them to dependent children.

3. The average duration of the cultural training programs is three days.

4. Cultural training is continued after arrival in the assignment location 32 percent of the time.

5. Thirty percent offer formal cultural training programs.

6. Of those without formal cultural programs, 37 percent plan to add such training.[77]

The most common topics covered in cultural training are social etiquette, customs, economics, history, politics, and business etiquette. However, the MNC's overall philosophy of international management and the demands of the specific cultural situation are the starting point. This is because countries tend to have distinctive human resource management (HRM) practices that differentiate them from other countries. For example, the HRM practices that are prevalent in the United States are quite different from those in France and Argentina. This was clearly illustrated by Sparrow and Budhwar, who compared data from 13 different countries on the basis of HRM factors. Five of these factors were the following:

1. Structural empowerment that is characterized by flat organization designs, wide spans of control, the use of flexible cross-functional teams, and the rewarding of individuals for productivity gains.

2. Accelerated resource development that is characterized by the early identification of high-potential employees, the establishment of both multiple and parallel career paths, the rewarding of personnel for enhancing their skills and knowledge, and the offering of continuous training and development education.

3. Employee welfare emphasis that is characterized by firms offering personal family assistance, encouraging and rewarding external volunteer activities, and promoting organizational cultures that emphasize equality in the workplace.

4. An efficiency emphasis in which employees are encouraged to monitor their own work and to continually improve their performance.

5. Long-termism, which stresses long-term results such as innovation and creativity rather than weekly and monthly short-term productivity.[78]

When Sparrow and Budhwar used these HRM approaches on a comparative country-by-country basis, they found that there were worldwide differences in human resource management practices. Table 14–5 shows the comparative results after each of the 13 countries was categorized as being either high or low on the respective factors. These findings reveal that countries are unique in their approach to human resource management. What works well in the United States may have limited value in France. In fact, a close analysis

Table 14–5
Human Resource Management Practices in Select Countries

	Structural Empowerment		Accelerated Resource Development		Employee Welfare Emphasis		Efficiency Emphasis		Long-Termism	
	High	Low	High	Low	High	Low	High	Low	High	Low
United States	X		X		X		X			X
Canada	X		X		X			X		X
United Kingdom	X		X			X		X		X
Italy		X	X			X		X		X
Japan		X	X		X		X		X	
India		X	X		X			X	X	
Australia	X			X		X	X		X	
Brazil	X			X	X			X	X	
Mexico	X		X		X			X		X
Argentina		X	X		X			X		X
Germany		X	X			X		X	X	
Korea		X	X		X		X		X	
France		X	X		X		X			X

Source: Adapted from Paul R. Sparrow and Pawan S. Budhwar, "Competition and Change: Mapping the Indian HRM Recipe Against Worldwide Patterns," *Journal of World Business* 32, no. 3 (1997), p. 233.

of Table 14–5 shows that none of the 13 countries had the same profile; each was different. This was true even in the case of Anglo nations such as the United States, Canada, Australia, and the United Kingdom, where differences in employee welfare emphasis, accelerated resource development, efficiency emphasis orientation, and long-termism resulted in unique HRM profiles for each. Similarly, Japan and Korea differed on two of the factors, as did Germany and France; and India, which many people might feel would be more similar to an Anglo culture, because of the British influence, than to an Asian one, differed on two factors with Canada, on three factors with both the United States and the United Kingdom, and on four factors with Australia.

These findings point to the fact that MNCs will have to focus increasingly on HRM programs designed to meet the needs of local personnel. A good example is provided in the former communist countries of Europe, where international managers are discovering that in order to effectively recruit college graduates their firms must provide training programs that give these new employees opportunities to work with a variety of tasks and to help them specialize in their particular fields of interest. At the same time the MNCs are discovering that these recruits are looking for companies that offer a good social working environment. A recent survey of over 1,000 business and engineering students from Poland, the Czech Republic, and Hungary found that almost two-thirds of the respondents said that they wanted their boss to be receptive to their ideas; 37 percent wanted to work for managers who had strong industry experience; and 34 percent wanted a boss who was a good rational decision maker. These findings indicate that multinational human resource management is now becoming much more of a two-way street: Both employees and managers need to continually adjust to emerging demands.[79]

The Impact of Overall Management Philosophy on Training

The type of training that is required of expatriates is influenced by the firm's overall philosophy of international management. For example, some companies prefer to send their own people to staff an overseas operation; others prefer to use locals whenever possible.[80]

Briefly, four basic philosophical positions of multinational corporations (MNCs) can influence the training program:

1. An **ethnocentric MNC** puts home-office people in charge of key international management positions. The MNC headquarters group and the affiliated world company managers all have the same basic experiences, attitudes, and beliefs about how to manage operations. Many Japanese firms follow this practice.

2. A **polycentric MNC** places local nationals in key positions and allows these managers to appoint and develop their own people. MNC headquarters gives the subsidiary managers authority to manage their operations just as long as these operations are sufficiently profitable. Some MNCs use this approach in East Asia, Australia, and other markets that are deemed too expensive to staff with expatriates.

3. A **regiocentric MNC** relies on local managers from a particular geographic region to handle operations in and around that area. For example, production facilities in France would be used to produce goods for all EU countries. Similarly, advertising managers from subsidiaries in Italy, Germany, France, and Spain would come together and formulate a "European" advertising campaign for the company's products. A regiocentric approach often relies on regional group cooperation of local managers. The Gillette MNC uses a regiocentric approach.

4. A **geocentric MNC** seeks to integrate diverse regions of the world through a global approach to decision making. Assignments are based on qualifications, and all subsidiary managers throughout the structure are regarded as equal to those at headquarters. IBM is an excellent example of an MNC that attempts to use a geocentric approach.

All four of these philosophical positions can be found in the multinational arena, and each puts a different type of training demand on the MNC.[81] For example, ethnocentric MNCs will do all training at headquarters, but polycentric MNCs will rely on local managers to assume responsibility for seeing that the training function is carried out.

The Impact of Different Learning Styles on Training and Development

Another important area of consideration for development is learning styles. **Learning** is the acquisition of skills, knowledge, and abilities that result in a relatively permanent change in behavior.[82] Over the last decade, growing numbers of multinationals have tried to become "learning organizations," continually focused on activities such as training and development. In the new millennium, this learning focus applied to human resource development may go beyond learning organizations to "teaching organizations." For example, Tichy and Cohen, after conducting an analysis of world-class companies such as General Electric, PepsiCo, AlliedSignal, and Coca-Cola, found that teaching organizations are even more relevant than learning organizations because they go beyond the belief that everyone must continually acquire new knowledge and skills and focus on ensuring that everyone in the organization, especially the top management personnel, pass their learning on to others. Here are their conclusions:

> In teaching organizations, leaders see it as their responsibility to teach. They do that because they understand that it's the best, if not only, way to develop throughout a company people who can come up with and carry out smart ideas about the business. Because people in teaching organizations see teaching as critical to the success of their business, they find ways to do it every day. Teaching every day about critical business issues avoids the fuzzy focus that has plagued some learning organization efforts, which have sometimes become a throwback to the 1960s- and 1970s-style self-exportation and human relations training.[83]

ethnocentric MNC
An MNC that stresses nationalism and often puts home-office people in charge of key international management positions.

polycentric MNC
An MNC that places local nationals in key positions and allows these managers to appoint and develop their own people.

regiocentric MNC
An MNC that relies on local managers from a particular geographic region to handle operations in and around that area.

geocentric MNC
An MNC that seeks to integrate diverse regions of the world through a global approach to decision making.

learning
The acquisition of skills, knowledge, and abilities that result in a relatively permanent change in behavior.

Of course, the way in which training takes place can be extremely important. A great deal of research has been conducted on the various types and theories of learning. However, the application of these ideas in an international context often can be quite challenging because cultural differences can affect the learning and teaching. Prud'homme van Reine and Trompenaars, commenting on the development of expats, noted that national cultural differences typically affect the way MNCs train and develop their people. For example, Americans like an experiential learning style while Germans prefer a theoretical–analytical learning approach.[84] Moreover, there can be sharp learning preferences between groups that are quite similar in terms of culture. Hayes and Allinson, after studying cultural differences in the learning styles of managers, reported that "Two groups can be very similar in ecology and climate and, for example, through a common legacy of colonialism, have a similar language and legal, educational and governmental infrastructure, but may be markedly different in terms of beliefs, attitudes, and values."[85] Moreover, research shows that people with different learning styles prefer different learning environments, and if there is a mismatch between the preferred learning style and the work environment, dissatisfaction and poor performance can result.

In addition to these conclusions, those responsible for training programs must remember that even if learning does occur, the new behaviors will not be used if they are not reinforced. For example, if the head of a foreign subsidiary is highly ethnocentric and believes that things should be done the way they are in the home country, new managers with intercultural training likely will find little reward or reinforcement for using their ideas. This cultural complexity also extends to the way in which the training is conducted.

Reasons for Training

Training programs are useful in preparing people for overseas assignments for many reasons. These reasons can be put into two general categories: organizational and personal.

ethnocentrism
The belief that one's own way of doing things is superior to that of others.

Organizational Reasons Organizational reasons for training relate to the enterprise at large and its efforts to manage overseas operations more effectively.[86] One primary reason is to help overcome **ethnocentrism,** the belief that one's way of doing things is superior to that of others. Ethnocentrism is common in many large MNCs where managers believe that the home office's approach to doing business can be exported intact to all other countries because this approach is superior to anything at the local level. Training can help home-office managers to understand the values and customs of other countries so that when they are transferred overseas, they have a better understanding of how to interact with local personnel. This training also can help managers to overcome the common belief among many personnel that expatriates are not as effective as host-country managers. This is particularly important given that an increasing number of managerial positions now are held by foreign managers in U.S. MNCs.[87]

Another organizational reason for training is to improve the flow of communication between the home office and the international subsidiaries and branches. Quite often, overseas managers find that they are not adequately informed regarding what is expected of them although the home office places close controls on their operating authority. This is particularly true when the overseas manager is from the host country. Effective communication can help to minimize these problems.

Finally, another organizational reason for training is to increase overall efficiency and profitability. Research shows that organizations that closely tie their training and human resource management strategy to their business strategy tend to outperform those that do not.[88] Stroh and Caligiuri conducted research on 60 of the world's major multinationals and found that effective HRM programs pay dividends in the form of higher profits. Additionally, their data showed that the most successful MNCs recognized the importance of having top managers with a global orientation. One of the ways in which almost all of these organizations did this was by giving their managers global assignments that not only filled technical and managerial needs but also provided developmental experiences for the personnel—and this assignment strategy included managers from every geographic region where the firms were doing business. Drawing together the lessons to be learned from this approach, Stroh and Caligiuri noted that:

> The development of global leadership skills should not stop with home country nationals. Global HR should also be involved in developing a global orientation among host country nationals as well. This means, for example, sending not only home-country managers on global assignments but host national talent to the corporate office and to other divisions around the world. Many of the managers at the successful MNCs talked about how their companies develop talent in this way. In addition, they described a "desired state" for human resources, including the ability to source talent within the company from around the world. Victor Guerra, an executive at Prudential, commented: *We need to continually recognize that there are bright, articulate people who do not live in the home country. U.S. multinationals are especially guilty of this shortsightedness.* Acknowledging that talent exists and using the talent appropriately are two different issues—one idealist, the other strategic.[89]

Personal Reasons   The primary reason for training overseas managers is to improve their ability to interact effectively with local people in general and with their personnel in particular. Increasing numbers of training programs now address social topics such as how to take a client to dinner, effectively apologize to a customer, appropriately address one's overseas colleagues, communicate formally and politely with others, and learn how to help others "save face."[90] These programs also focus on dispelling myths and stereotypes by replacing them with facts about the culture. For example, in helping expatriates better understand Arab executives, the following guidelines are offered:

1. There is a close relationship between the Arab executive and his environment. The Arab executive is looked on as a community and family leader, and there are numerous social pressures on him because of this role. He is consulted on all types of problems, even those far removed from his position.

2. With regard to decision making, the Arab executive likely will consult with his subordinates, but he will take responsibility for his decision himself rather than arriving at it through consensus.

3. The Arab executive likely will try to avoid conflict. If there is an issue that he favors but that is opposed by his subordinates, he tends to impose his authority. If it is an issue favored by the subordinates but opposed by the executive, he will likely let the matter drop without taking action.

4. The Arab executive's style is very personal. He values loyalty over efficiency. Although some executives find that the open-door tradition consumes a great deal of time, they do not feel that the situation can be changed. Many executives tend to look on their employees as family and will allow them to bypass the hierarchy to meet them.

5. The Arab executive, contrary to popular beliefs, puts considerable value on the use of time. One thing he admires most about Western or expatriate executives is their use of time, and he would like to encourage his own employees to make more productive use of their time.[91]

Another growing problem is the belief that foreign language skills are not really essential to doing business overseas. Effective training programs can help to minimize these personal problems.

A particularly big personal problem that managers have in an overseas assignment is arrogance. This is the so-called Ugly American problem that U.S. expatriates have been known to have. Many expatriate managers find that their power and prestige are much greater than they were in their job in the home country. This often results in improper behavior, especially among managers at the upper and lower positions of overseas subsidiaries. This arrogance takes a number of different forms, including rudeness to personnel and inaccessibility to clients. Zeira and Harari made the following observations:

> Another manifestation of expatriate managers' arrogance is their widespread tendency to ignore invitations to become participant observers in HCOs [host-country organizations]. The underlying idea behind these invitations involves rotating expatriate managers in various HCO departments to enable them to observe patterns of organizational behavior at various hierarchical levels. The purpose of this observation is to familiarize expatriate managers, especially those new in their jobs or about to begin to assume them, with the goals, policies, procedures, formal and informal norms, and expectations of HCOs regarding expatriate managers and their respective subsidiaries.[92]

Another common problem is expatriate managers' overruling of decisions, often seen at lower levels of the hierarchy. When a decision is made by a superior who is from the host country and the expatriate does not agree with it, the expatriate may appeal to higher authority in the subsidiary. Host-country managers obviously resent this behavior, because it implies that they are incompetent and can be second-guessed by expatriate subordinates.

Still another common problem is the open criticizing by expatriate managers of their own country or the host country. Many expatriates believe that this form of criticism is regarded as constructive and shows them to have an open mind. Experience has found, however, that most host-country personnel view such behavior negatively and feel that the manager should refrain from such unconstructive criticism. It creates bad feelings and lack of loyalty.

In addition to helping deal with these types of personal problems, training can be useful in improving overall management style. Research shows that many host-country nationals would like to see changes in some of the styles of expatriate managers, including their leadership, decision making, communication, and group work. In terms of leadership, the locals would like to see their expatriate managers be more friendly, accessible, receptive to subordinate suggestions, and encouraging to subordinates to make their best efforts. In decision making, they would like to see clearer definition of goals, more involvement in the process by those employees who will be affected by the decision, and greater use of group meetings to help make decisions. In communication, they would like to see more exchange of opinions and ideas between subordinates and managers. In group work, they would like to see more group problem solving and teamwork.

The specific training approach used must reflect both the industrial and the cultural environment. For example, there is some evidence that Japanese students who come to the United States to earn an MBA degree often find this education of no real value back home. One graduate noted that when he tactfully suggested putting to use a skill he had learned during his U.S. MBA program, he got nowhere. An analysis of Japanese getting an outside education concluded:

> Part of the problem is the reason that most Japanese workers are sent to business schools. Whatever ticket the MBA degree promises—or appears to promise—Americans, the diploma has little meaning within most Japanese companies. Rather, companies send students abroad under the life-time employment system to ensure that there will be more English speakers who are familiar with Western business practices. Some managers regard business schools as a kind of high-level English language school, returning students say, or consider the two years as more or less a paid vacation.[93]

However, as the Japanese economy continues to have problems, American-style business education is beginning to receive attention and respect. In the 1980s American managers went to Japan to learn; now Japanese managers are coming to the United States in increasing numbers to see what they can pick up to help them better compete.

■ Types of Training Programs

There are many different types of multinational management training programs. Some last only a few hours; others last for months. Some are fairly superficial; others are extensive in coverage. Figure 14–6 shows some of the key considerations that influence development of these programs. There are nine phases. In the first phase the overall objective of the

| Figure 14–6 | A Model for the Development of Multinational Managers |

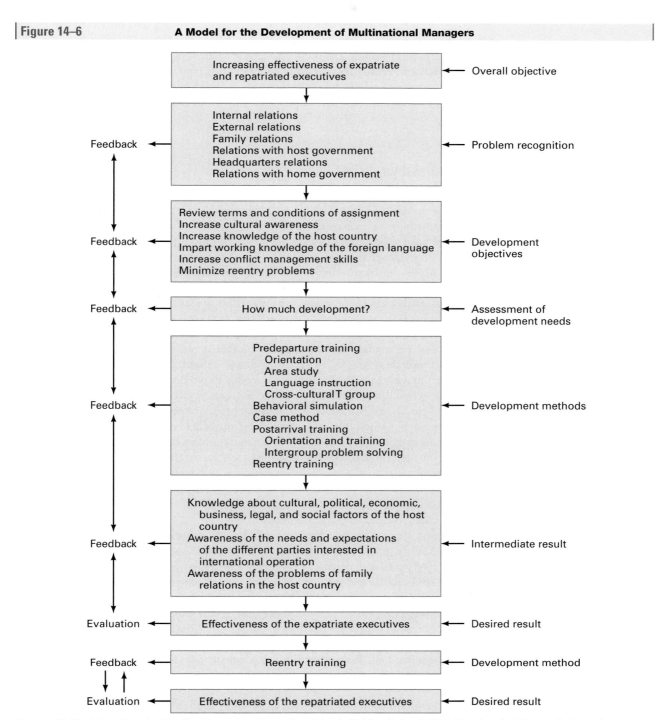

program to increase the effectiveness of expats and repatriated executives is emphasized. The second phase focuses on recognition of the problems that must be dealt with in order to reach the overall objective. The third phase is identification of the developmental objectives. The fourth phase consists of determining the amount of development that will be needed to achieve each objective. The fifth phase entails choosing the specific methods to be used in the development process–from types of predeparture training to language instruction to reentry training. The sixth phase is an intermediate evaluation of how well things are going and the institution of any needed midstream corrections. The seventh phase is an evaluation of how well the expat managers are doing, thus providing evaluation feedback of the developmental process. The eighth phase is devoted to reentry training for returning expats. The ninth, and final, phase is an evaluation of the effectiveness of the executives after their return. By carefully laying out this type of planning model, MNCs ensure that their development training programs are both realistic and productive. In this process they often rely on both standardized and tailor-made training and development approaches.

Standardized vs. Tailor-Made

Some management training is standard, or generic. For example, participants often are taught how to use specific decision-making tools, such as quantitative analysis, and regardless of where the managers are sent in the world, the application is the same. These tools do not have to be culturally specific. Research shows that small firms usually rely on standard training programs. Larger MNCs, in contrast, tend to design their own. Some of the larger MNCs are increasingly turning to specially designed video and PowerPoint programs for their training and development needs.

Tailor-made training programs are created for the specific needs of the participants. Input for these offerings usually is obtained from managers who currently are working (or have worked) in the country to which the participants will be sent as well as from local managers and personnel who are citizens of that country. These programs often are designed to provide a new set of skills for a new culture. For example, MNCs are now learning that in managing in China, there is a need to provide directive leadership training because many local managers rely heavily on rules, procedures, and orders from their superiors to guide their behaviors.[94] So training programs must explain how to effectively use this approach. Quite often, the offerings are provided before the individuals leave for their overseas assignment; however, there also are postdeparture training programs that are conducted on-site. These often take the form of systematically familiarizing the individual with the country through steps such as meeting with government officials and other key personnel in the community; becoming acquainted with managers and employees in the organization; learning the host-country nationals' work methods, problems, and expectations; and taking on-site language training.

Training approaches that are successful in one geographic region of the world may need to be heavily modified if they are to be as effective elsewhere. Sergeant and Frenkel conducted interviews with expatriate managers with extensive experience in China in order to identify HRM issues and the ways in which they need to be addressed by MNCs going into China.[95] As seen in Table 14–6, many of the human resource management approaches that are employed are different from those used in the United States or other developed countries because of the nature of Chinese culture and China's economy.

In the final analysis, the specific training program to be used will depend on the needs of the individual. Tung, after surveying managers in Europe, Japan, and the United States, found that there are six major types of cross-cultural training programs:

1. Environmental briefings used to provide information about things such as geography, climate, housing, and schools.

Table 14–6
Human Resources Management Challenges Facing MNCs in China

Human Resource Management Function	Comments/Recommendations
Employee recruitment	The market for skilled manual and white-collar employees is very tight and characterized by rapidly rising wages and high turnover rates. Nepotism and overhiring remain a major problem where Chinese partners strongly influence HR policies; and transferring employees from state enterprises to joint ventures can be difficult because it requires approval from the employee's old work unit.
Reward system	New labor laws allow most companies to set their own wage and salary levels. As a result, there is a wide wage disparity between semiskilled and skilled workers. However, these disparities must be balanced with the negative effect they can have on workers' interpersonal relations.
Employee retention	It can be difficult to retain good employees because of poaching by competitive organizations. In response, many American joint-venture managers are learning to take greater control of compensation programs in order to retain high-performing Chinese managers and skilled workers.
Work performance and employee management	Local managers are not used to taking the initiative and are rarely provided with performance feedback in their Chinese enterprises. As a result, they tend to be risk-averse and are often unwilling to innovate. In turn, the workers are not driven to get things done quickly and they often give little emphasis to the quality of output. At the same time, it is difficult to dismiss people.
Labor relations	Joint-venture regulations give workers the right to establish a trade union to protect employee rights and to organize. These unions are less adversarial than in the West and tend to facilitate operational efficiency. However, there is concern that with the changes taking place in labor laws and the possibility of collective bargaining, unions may become more adversarial in the future.
Expatriate relations	Many firms have provided little cross-training to their people and family, education, and health issues limit the attractiveness of a China assignment. Some of the major repatriation problems include limited continuity in international assignments and difficulties of adjusting to more specialized and less autonomous positions at home, lack of career prospects, and undervaluation of international experience. Management succession and the balancing of local and international staff at Chinese firms are also problematic.

Source: Adapted from Andrew Sergeant and Stephen Frenkel, "Managing People in China: Perceptions of Expatriate Managers," *Journal of World Business* 33, no. 1 (1998), p. 21.

2. Cultural orientation designed to familiarize the individual with cultural institutions and value systems of the host country.

3. Cultural assimilators using programmed learning approaches designed to provide the participants with intercultural encounters.

4. Language training.

5. Sensitivity training designed to develop attitudinal flexibility.

6. Field experience, which sends the participant to the country of assignment to undergo some of the emotional stress of living and working with people from a different culture.[96]

Some organizations have extended cross-cultural training to include training for family members, especially children who will be accompanying the parents. "International Management in Action: U.S.-Style Training for Expats and Their Teenagers" explains how this approach to cultural assimilation is carried out.

In addition to training expats and their families, effective MNCs also are developing carefully crafted programs for training personnel from other cultures who are coming into their culture. These programs, among other things, have materials that are specially

U.S.-Style Training for Expats and Their Teenagers

One of the major reasons why expatriates have trouble with overseas assignments is that their teenage children are unable to adapt to the new culture, and this has an impact on the expat's performance. To deal with this acculturation problem, many U.S. MNCs now are developing special programs for helping teenagers assimilate into new cultures and adjust to new school environments. A good example is provided by General Electric Medical Systems Group (GEMS), a Milwaukee-based firm that has expatriates in France, Japan, and Singapore. As soon as GEMS designates an individual for an overseas assignment, this expat and his or her family are matched up with those who have recently returned from this country. If the family going overseas has teenage children, the company will team them up with a family that had teenagers during its stay abroad. Both groups then discuss the challenges and problems that must be faced. In the case of teenagers, they are able to talk about their concerns with others who already have encountered these issues, and the latter can provide important information regarding how to make friends, learn the language, get around town, and turn the time abroad into a pleasant experience. Coca-Cola uses a similar approach. As soon as someone is designated for an overseas assignment, the company helps initiate cross-cultural discussions with experienced personnel. Coke also provides formal training through use of external cross-cultural consulting firms who are experienced in working with all family members.

A typical concern of teenagers going abroad is that they will have to go away to boarding school. In Saudi Arabia, for example, national law forbids expatriate children's attending school past the ninth grade, so most expatriate families will look for European institutions for these children. GEMS addresses these types of problems with a specially developed education program. Tutors, schools, curricula, home-country requirements, and host-country requirements are examined, and a plan and specific program of study are developed for each school-age child before he or she leaves.

Before the departure of the family, some MNCs will subscribe to local magazines about teen fashions, music, and other sports or social activities in the host country, so that the children know what to expect when they get there. Before the return of the family to the United States, these MNCs provide similar information about what is going on in the United States, so that when the children return for a visit or come back to stay, they are able to quickly fit into their home-country environment once again.

An increasing number of MNCs now give teenagers much of the same cultural training they give their own managers; however, there is one area in which formal assistance often is not as critical for teens as for adults: language training. While most expatriates find it difficult and spend a good deal of time trying to master the local language, many teens find that they can pick it up quite easily. They speak it at school, in their social groups, and out on the street. As a result, they learn not only the formal language but also clichés and slang that help them communicate more easily. In fact, sometimes their accent is so good that they are mistaken for local kids. Simply put: The facility of teens to learn a language often is greatly underrated. A Coca-Cola manager recently drove home this point when he declared: "One girl we sent insisted that, although she would move, she wasn't going to learn the language. Within two months she was practically fluent."

A major educational benefit of this emphasis on teenagers is that it leads to an experienced, bicultural person. So when the young person completes college and begins looking for work, the parent's MNC often is interested in this young adult as a future manager. The person has a working knowledge of the MNC, speaks a second language, and has had overseas experience in a country where the multinational does business. This type of logic is leading some U.S. MNCs to realize that effective cross-cultural training can be of benefit for their workforces of tomorrow as well as today.

---

designed for the target audience. Some of the specific steps that well-designed cultural training programs follow include:

1. Local instructors and a translator, typically someone who is bicultural, observe the pilot training program or examine written training materials.

2. The educational designer then debriefs the observation with the translator, curriculum writer, and local instructors.

3. Together, the group examines the structure and sequence, ice breaker, and other materials that will be used in the training.

4. The group then collectively identifies stories, metaphors, experiences, and examples in the culture that will fit into the new training program.

5. The educational designer and curriculum writer make the necessary changes in the training materials.

6. The local instructors are trained to use the newly developed materials.

7. After the designer, translator, and native-language trainers are satisfied, the materials are printed.

8. The language and content of the training materials are tested with a pilot group.[97]

In developing the instructional materials, culturally specific guidelines are carefully followed so that the training does not lose any of its effectiveness.[98] For example, inappropriate pictures or scenarios that might prove to be offensive to the audience must be screened out. Handouts and other instructional materials that are designed to enhance the learning process are provided for all participants. If the trainees are learning a second language, generous use of visuals and live demonstrations will be employed. Despite all of these efforts, however, errors sometimes occur.

Cultural Assimilators

The cultural assimilator has become one of the most effective approaches to cross-cultural training. A **cultural assimilator** is a programmed learning technique that is designed to expose members of one culture to some of the basic concepts, attitudes, role perceptions, customs, and values of another. These assimilators are developed for each pair of cultures. For example, if an MNC is going to send three U.S. managers from Chicago to Caracas, a cultural assimilator would be developed to familiarize the three Americans with Venezuelan customs and cultures. If three Venezuelan managers from Caracas were to be transferred to Singapore, another assimilator would be developed to familiarize the managers with Singapore customs and cultures.

In most cases, these assimilators require the trainee to read a short episode of a cultural encounter and choose an interpretation of what has happened and why. If the trainee's choice is correct, he or she goes on to the next episode. If the response is incorrect, the trainee is asked to reread the episode and choose another response.

cultural assimilator
A programmed learning technique designed to expose members of one culture to some of the basic concepts, attitudes, role perceptions, customs, and values of another culture.

Choice of Content of the Assimilators   One of the major problems in constructing an effective cultural assimilator is deciding what is important enough to include. Some assimilators use critical incidents that are identified as being important. To be classified as a critical incident, a situation must meet at least one of the following conditions:

1. An expatriate and a host national interact in the situation.

2. The situation is puzzling or likely to be misinterpreted by the expatriate.

3. The situation can be interpreted accurately if sufficient knowledge about the culture is available.

4. The situation is relevant to the expatriate's task or mission requirements.[99]

These incidents typically are obtained by asking expatriates and host nationals with whom they come in contact to describe specific intercultural occurrences or events that made a major difference in their attitudes or behavior toward members of the other culture. These incidents can be pleasant, unpleasant, or simply nonunderstandable occurrences.

Validation of the Assimilator   The term **validity** refers to the quality of being effective, of producing the desired results. It means that an instrument—in this case, the cultural assimilator—measures what it is intended to measure. After the cultural assimilator's critical incidents are constructed and the alternative responses are written, the process is validated. Making sure that the assimilator is valid is the crux of its effectiveness. One way to test an assimilator is to draw a sample from the target culture and ask these people to read the scenarios that have been written and choose the alternative they feel is most appropriate. If a large percentage of the group agrees that one of the alternatives is preferable, this scenario is used in the assimilator. If more than one of the four alternatives receives strong support, however, either the scenario or the alternatives are revised until there is general agreement or the scenario is dropped.

validity
The quality of being effective, of producing the desired results. A valid test or selection technique measures what it is intended to measure.

After the final incidents are chosen, they are sequenced in the assimilator booklet and can be put online to be taken electronically. Similar cultural concepts are placed together and presented, beginning with simple situations and progressing to more complex ones. Most cultural assimilator programs start out with 150 to 200 incidents, of which 75 to 100 eventually are included in the final product.

The Cost–Benefit Analysis of Assimilators   The assimilator approach to training can be quite expensive. A typical 75- to 100-incident program often requires approximately 800 hours to develop. Assuming that a training specialist is costing the company $50 an hour including benefits, the cost is around $40,000 per assimilator. This cost can be spread over many trainees, however, and the program may not need to be changed every year. An MNC that sends 40 people a year to a foreign country for which an assimilator has been constructed is paying only $200 per person for this programmed training. In the long run, the costs often are more than justified. In addition, the concept can be applied to nearly all cultures. Many different assimilators have been constructed, including Arab, Thai, Honduran, and Greek, to name but four. Most importantly, research shows that these assimilators improve the effectiveness and satisfaction of individuals being trained as compared with other training methods.

Other Approaches

In addition to assimilators, a variety of other approaches are used in preparing managers for international assignments. These include visits to the host country, briefings by host-country managers, in-house management programs, training in local negotiation techniques, and an analysis of behavioral practices that have proven most effective.[100]

The best "mix" of training often is determined by the individual's length of stay. The longer that a person will be assigned to an international locale, the greater the depth and intensity of the training should be. Figure 14–7 illustrates this idea. Using the model in this figure, if the expected level of interaction is low and the degree of similarity between the individual's culture and the host culture is high, the length of the training should be less than a week, and methods such as area and cultural briefings should be used. Conversely, if the level of interaction is going to be high and the individual will be gone for 1 to 3 years, use of assessment centers, field experiences, and simulations should be considered. The degree, type, and length of training are results of expected integration and length of stay. Simply put, today's MNCs use a contingency approach in developing their training strategy.

Global Leadership Development

Another current trend in human resource development is to focus on leadership. Tichy noted that a number of leadership training approaches can be used.[101] As shown in Figure 14–8, these range from awareness to cognitive and conceptual understanding to the development of skills and then on to new problem-solving approaches and, ultimately, fundamental change. In this process, management development becomes deeper, involves greater risk, incorporates a longer-term time horizon, and focuses on organization (rather than just individual) change.

At the same time, effective MNCs now encourage strong leadership in the areas of both hard and soft organizational issues. Examples of hard issues include the budget, manufacturing, marketing, distribution, and finance; soft issues address values, culture, vision, leadership style, and innovative behavior. In exercising strong leadership on hard organizational issues, attention is focused on becoming a low-cost provider of goods and services. In exercising strong leadership on soft organizational issues, the emphasis is on developing and maintaining innovativeness.

GLP Program   One of the best examples of the emerging leadership development programs used by MNCs is the Global Leadership Program (GLP), which is a consortium of

| Figure 14–7 | A Contingency Approach to Cross-Cultural Training |

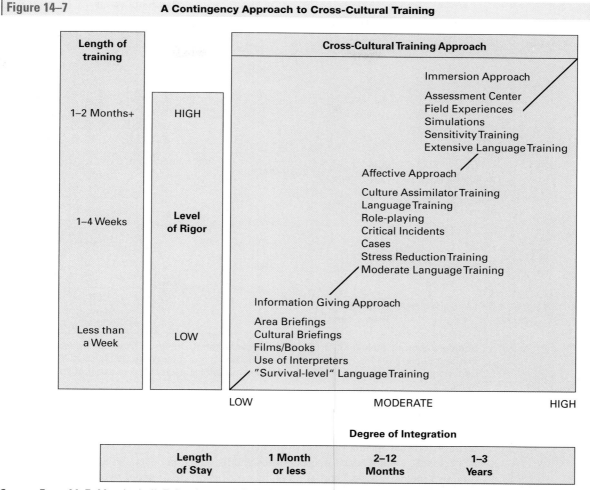

Source: From M. E. Mendenhall, E. Dunbar, and G. R. Oddou, "Expatriate Selection, Training and Career-Pathing: A Review and Critique," *Human Resource Management,* Fall 1987, p. 338. Copyright © 1987 John Wiley & Sons, Inc. This material is used by permission of John Wiley & Sons, Inc.

leading U.S., European, and Japanese firms, global faculty, and participating host countries. Here is how the GLP has been described:

> The companies are part of an ongoing partnership started in 1988 jointly committed to research and development on issues of globalization. The program design, facilities, and support staff are directed by core faculty from universities in the United States, Europe, and Japan. The members of the consortium participate in a research partnership and in an intensive 5-week Global Leadership Program designed for senior executives with CEO potential.[102]

The GLP is designed to provide participants with an intensive international experience to develop a global mindset, instill cross-cultural competency, and provide the opportunity for global networking. The program is five weeks in duration, but before attending, each person is given specially prepared briefing materials about the country that he or she will visit. At the beginning, participants are asked to complete the survey instruments that are designed to assess the individual's perceptions regarding the characteristics of a global organization, dimensions of global leadership, and the way that managers carry out their global responsibilities.

The core of the program is a two-week, on-site, country assessment carried out by cross-cultural teams. Each group of trainees is required to use information from the

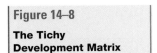

Figure 14–8

The Tichy Development Matrix

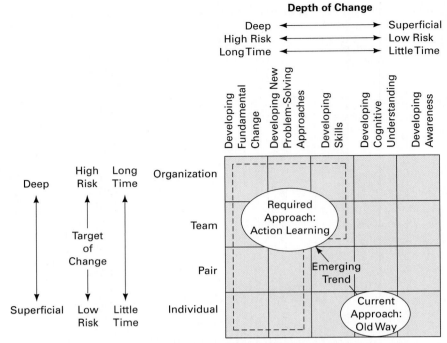

Source: Reported in Noel M. Tichy, "Global Development," in *Globalizing Management,* ed. Vladimir Pucik, Noel M. Tichy, and Carole K. Barnett (New York: Wiley, 1993), pp. 206–224. Copyright © 1993 John Wiley & Sons, Inc. This material is used by permission of John Wiley & Sons, Inc.

assessment to produce investment opportunities and entry strategy recommendations as well as video documentaries as part of their country assessment. Among other things, each team of trainees spends two weeks preparing for the country assessment by working on its personal global leadership capabilities and its global mindset and team skills. Preparation also includes a weekend at an Outward Bound school and a two-day assessment in Washington, DC.

The GLP is designed to blend rigorous intellectual development of global leaders, beginning with each individual's map of his or her own personal global mindset. These are shared with the members of each team, who then are responsible for creating an analytical framework to guide its assessment of a major geopolitical region of the world. By the second week of the program, the teams have started on their country assessment. During the third and fourth weeks, the participants split up and travel to their respective countries. During the fifth and last week of the program, the individuals write their reports and make their video documentaries and presentations. Because of its strong emphasis on involvement and action learning, the GLP has become one of the best-recognized development programs for training global leaders for MNCs.

The World of *BusinessWeek*—Revisited

The *BusinessWeek* case that opens this chapter explains some of the issues surrounding the outsourcing and offshoring of higher-skilled jobs. This article, and the principles explained in the chapter, underscore the intense challenges associated with the selection, development, and training of international human resources. MNCs have a range of options when selecting employees for overseas assignments, and increasing numbers of tools and resources are available to help develop, train, and deploy those individuals. Human resource selection and development across cultures cannot be taken lightly. Firms that do not invest in their human resource processes will face additional costs related to poor labor relations, quality control, and other issues.

Now that you have read the chapter and reflected on the opening article, answer the following questions: (1) What are the costs and benefits of hiring home-, host-, and third-country nationals for overseas assignments? (2) What skill sets are important for international assignments, and how can employees be prepared for them? (3) What are the implications of offshore outsourcing for the management of human resources globally?

SUMMARY OF KEY POINTS

1. MNCs can use four basic sources for filling overseas positions: home-country nationals (expatriates), host-country nationals, third-country nationals, and inpatriates. The most common reason for using home-country nationals, or expatriates, is to get the overseas operation under way. Once this is done, many MNCs turn the top management job over to a host-country national who is familiar with the culture and language and who often commands a lower salary than the home-country national. The primary reason for using third-country nationals is that these people have the necessary expertise for the job. The use of inpatriates (a host-country or third-country national assigned to the home office) recognizes the need for diversity at the home office. This movement builds a transnational core competency for MNCs. In addition, MNCs can subcontract or outsource to take advantage of lower human resource costs and increase flexibility.

2. Many criteria are used in selecting managers for overseas assignments. Some of these include adaptability, independence, self-reliance, physical and emotional health, age, experience, education, knowledge of the local language, motivation, the support of spouse and children, and leadership.

3. Individuals who meet selection criteria are given some form of screening. Some firms use psychological testing, but this approach has lost popularity in recent years. More commonly, candidates are given interviews. Theoretical models that identify important anticipatory and in-country dimensions of adjustment offer help in effective selection.

4. Compensating expatriates can be a difficult problem, because there are many variables to consider. However, most compensation packages are designed around four common elements: base salary, benefits, allowances, and taxes. Working within these elements, the MNC will tailor the package to fit the specific situation. In doing so, there are six different approaches that can be used: balance-sheet approach, complementary approach, localization, lump-sum method, cafeteria approach, and regional method.

Whichever one (or combination) is used, the package must be both cost-effective and fair.

5. A manager might be willing to take an international assignment for a number of reasons: increased pay, promotion potential, the opportunity for greater responsibility, the chance to travel, and the ability to use his or her talents and skills. Research shows that most home countries prefer that the individual who is selected to head the affiliate or subsidiary be a local manager, even though this often does not occur.

6. At some time, most expatriates return home, usually when their predetermined tour is over. Sometimes, managers return because they want to leave early; at other times, they return because of poor performance on their part. In any event, readjustment problems can arise back home, and the longer a manager has been gone, the bigger the problems usually are. Some firms are developing transition strategies to help expatriates adjust to their new environments.

7. Training is the process of altering employee behavior and attitudes to increase the probability of goal attainment. Many expatriates need training before (as well as during) their overseas stay. A number of factors will influence a company's approach to training. One is the basic type of MNC: ethnocentric, polycentric, regiocentric, or geocentric. Another factor is the learning style of the trainees.

8. There are two primary reasons for training: organizational and personal. Organizational reasons include overcoming ethnocentrism, improving communication, and validating the effectiveness of training programs. Personal reasons include improving the ability of expatriates to interact locally and increasing the effectiveness of leadership styles. There are two types of training programs: standard and tailor-made. Research shows that small firms usually rely on standard programs and larger MNCs tailor their training. The six major types of training are environmental briefings, cultural orientation, cultural assimilators, language training, sensitivity training, and field experience.

9. A cultural assimilator is a programmed learning approach that is designed to expose members of one culture to some of the basic concepts, attitudes, role perceptions, customs, and values of another.

Assimilators have been developed for many different cultures. Their validity has resulted in the improved effectiveness and satisfaction of those being trained as compared with other training methods.

KEY TERMS

adaptability screening, *442*

balance-sheet approach, *450*

cafeteria approach, *450*

cultural assimilator, *467*

ethnocentric MNC, *459*

ethnocentrism, *460*

expatriates, *433*

geocentric MNC, *459*

home-country nationals, *433*

host-country nationals, *434*

inpatriates, *436*

international selection criteria, *438*

learning, *459*

localization, *450*

lump-sum method, *450*

polycentric MNC, *459*

regional system, *450*

regiocentric MNC, *459*

repatriation, *453*

repatriation agreements, *455*

third-country nationals, *435*

transition strategies, *455*

training, *456*

validity, *467*

REVIEW AND DISCUSSION QUESTIONS

1. A New York–based MNC is in the process of staffing a subsidiary in New Delhi, India. Why would it consider using expatriate managers in the unit? Local managers? Third-country managers?

2. What selection criteria are most important in choosing people for an overseas assignment? Identify and describe the four that you judge to be of most universal importance, and defend your choice.

3. What are the major common elements in an expat's compensation package? Besides base pay, which would be most important to you? Why?

4. Why are individuals motivated to accept international assignments? Which of these motivations would you rank as positive reasons? Which would you regard as negative reasons?

5. Why do expatriates return early? What can MNCs do to prevent this from happening? Identify and discuss three steps they can take.

6. What kinds of problems do expatriates face when returning home? Identify and describe four of the most important. What can MNCs do to deal with these repatriation problems effectively?

7. How do the following types of MNCs differ: ethnocentric, polycentric, regiocentric, and geocentric? Which type is most likely to provide international management training to its people? Which is least likely to provide international management training to its people?

8. IBM is planning on sending three managers to its Zurich office, two to Madrid, and two to Tokyo. None of these individuals has any international experience. Would you expect the company to use a standard training program or a tailor-made program for each group?

9. Zygen Inc., a medium-sized manufacturing firm, is planning to enter into a joint venture in China. Would training be of any value to those managers who will be part of this venture? If so, what types of training would you recommend?

10. Hofstadt & Hoerr, a German-based insurance firm, is planning on expanding out of the EU and opening offices in Chicago and Buenos Aires. How would a cultural assimilator be of value in training the MNC's expatriates? Is the assimilator a valid training tool?

11. Ford is in the process of training managers for overseas assignments. Would a global leadership program be a useful approach? Why or why not?

12. Microsoft is weighing setting up an R&D facility in India to develop new software applications. Should it staff the new facility with Microsoft employees? Indian employees? Or should it subcontract with an Indian firm? Explain your answer and some of the potential challenges in implementing it.

INTERNET EXERCISE: GOING INTERNATIONAL WITH COKE

As seen in this chapter, the recruiting and selecting of managers is critical to effective international management. This is particularly true in the case of firms that are expanding their international operations or currently do business in a large number of countries. These MNCs are continually having to replace managers who are retiring or moving to other companies. Coca-Cola is an excellent example. Go to the company's Web site at **www.coke.com** and look at the career opportunities that it offers overseas. In particular, pay close attention to current opportunities in Europe, Africa, and Asia. Read what the company has to say and then contact one of the individuals whose e-mail address is provided. Ask this company representative about the opportunities and challenges of working in that country or geographic area. Then, using this information, coupled with the chapter material, answer these questions: (1) From what you have learned from the Coca-Cola inquiry, what types of education or experience would you need to be hired by the company? (2) What kinds of international career opportunities does Coke offer? (3) If you were hired by Coke, what type of financial package could you expect? (4) In what areas of the world is Coke focusing more of its attention? (5) What kinds of management and leadership training programs does Coke offer?

Russia

Russia is by far the largest of the former Soviet republics. Russia stretches from Eastern Europe across northern Asia to the Pacific Ocean. The 150 million people consist of 83 percent Russians, 4 percent Tartars, and a scattering of others. The largest city and capital is Moscow, with about 9 million people. At present, there is continuing social and economic turmoil in Russia. Although prices are no longer controlled and privatization is well under way, the value of the ruble continues to deteriorate. At the same time, however, there are many pockets of prosperity in the country and under President Vladimir Putin positive efforts are under way to bolster the economy.

By 2003, Russia's GDP had reached $1.4 trillion, and Russia's privatization and liberalization program was attracting substantial foreign investment. One MNC that has been extremely interested in the country is Earth, Inc. (EI), a farm-implement company headquartered in Birmingham, Alabama. EI recently entered into an agreement with the government of Russia to set up operations near Moscow in a factory that was operating at about one-half of capacity. The factory will produce farm implements for the newly emerging Eastern European market. EI will supply the technical know-how and product design as well as assume responsibility for marketing the products. The Russian plant will build the equipment and package it for shipping.

The management of the plant operation will be handled on a joint basis. EI will send a team of five management and technical personnel from the United States to the Russian factory site for a period of 12 to 18 months. After this time, EI hopes to send three of them home, and the two who remain would continue to provide ongoing assistance. At the same time, EI intends to hire four middle-level managers and eight first-level supervisors from Italy and Germany, because the operation will need Europeans who are more familiar with doing manufacturing in this part of the world. Very few locals have inspired EI with confidence that they can get the job done. However, over a two-year period, EI intends to replace the third-country nationals with trained local managers. "We need to staff the management ranks with knowledgeable, experienced people," the CEO explained, "at least until we get the operation up and running successfully with our own people. Then we can turn more and more of the operation over to local management, and run the plant with just a handful of headquarters people on-site."

This arrangement has been agreed to by the Russian government, and EI currently is identifying and recruiting managers both in the United States and in Europe. Initially, the firm thought that this would be a fairly simple process, but screening and selecting are taking much longer than anticipated. Nevertheless, EI hopes to have the plant operating within 12 months.

Questions

1. What are some current issues facing Russia? What is the climate for doing business in Russia today?

2. What are some of the benefits of using home-country nationals in overseas operations? What are some of the benefits of using host-country nationals?

3. Why would a multinational such as EI be interested in bringing in third-country nationals?

4. What criteria should EI use in selecting personnel for the overseas assignment in Russia?

A Selection Decision

The Star Corporation is a California-based manufacturing firm that is going to do business in mainland China. The company's contract with the Chinese government calls for it to supply technical know-how and machinery for producing consumer electronics. These products are not state-of-the-art, but they will be more than adequate for the needs of the Chinese consumers. Star has agreed to sell the Chinese its plant, which was being closed because it no longer was competitive.

The Chinese will pay to move all the machinery and equipment to the mainland and install it in a factory that currently is being modified for this purpose. The two then will become partners in the venture. Star will provide the management and technical expertise to run the plant, and the Chinese government will provide the workers and be responsible for paying for all output. Star will receive an annual fee of $1 million and 5 percent of all sales.

The Star management is very pleased with the arrangement. Although they are of Chinese descent, they have lived in the United States all their lives and know relatively little about doing business either with or in mainland China. To provide Star with the necessary information and assistance, a native of Beijing, educated there but living in California for the past five years, was brought in. The individual told the company the following facts about mainland China:

- Chinese managers do not plan. They usually are told what to do and they do it. Planning is handled by others and simply passed on to them.

- Chinese managers are not concerned with profit or loss. They simply do their jobs and let the government worry about whether the operation is making money.

- No rewards are given to workers who perform well; everyone is treated the same. If there is no work, the workers are still paid, although they may not be required to come to the factory.

- There is a basic aversion to individual decision making; most decisions are collective efforts.

- The current government of China would like its managers to learn how to run a profit-oriented operation and eventually eliminate the need for foreign managerial assistance.

- When outsiders tell the Chinese how to do things, they have to be careful not to insult or offend the Chinese, who often are sensitive about the way they are treated.

Questions

1. What selection criteria would you recommend to Star when deciding whom to send to mainland China?

2. What procedures should the company use in making the final selection?

3. What type of repatriation agreement would you recommend the firm use? Be specific regarding some things you would suggest be contained in the agreement.

Chapter 15

LABOR RELATIONS AND INDUSTRIAL DEMOCRACY

Another critical part of managing human resources in the international arena is how the MNC handles its labor relations. How domestic firms deal with their labor relations and determine union contracts can differ significantly from country to country. A second challenge, especially for those MNCs operating in Europe and Asia, is industrial democracy, which is much more prevalent there than in other parts of the world. A third challenge is the need to coordinate worldwide efforts through formulation of an effective labor relations strategy.

This chapter addresses these challenges. Initially, it examines labor relations in the international arena using the United States as the point of comparison. Next, the internationalism of labor unions is explored. The chapter then looks at the various approaches to industrial democracy that are employed in Europe and Asia. Finally, how MNCs attempt to integrate industrial relations into their overall strategy is reviewed. The specific objectives of this chapter are:

1. **DEFINE** *labor relations,* and examine the approaches used in the United States and other countries.

2. **REVIEW** the international structure of labor unions.

3. **EXAMINE** the nature of industrial democracy, and note some of the major differences that exist throughout the world.

4. **DESCRIBE** the philosophical views and strategic approaches that MNCs use to manage international industrial relations and future strategies.

The World of *BusinessWeek*

BusinessWeek

Labor's Savvy Charge on China Trade

In a Landmark Move, It Wants the Bush Administration to Decide If Worker Repression Lets China Price Exports Below True Market Value

Say this for the AFL-CIO: It knows how to put George Bush on the spot. As the Presidential campaign centered on jobs and foreign competition heats up, the labor federation fired what could be a potent election-year broadside: It asked the Bush Administration on March 16 to decide whether worker repression lets China price its exports below their true market value, thus unfairly taking U.S. jobs.

The petition ensures that Bush must choose by late spring if it should anger China by launching a formal probe—or alienate factory workers in such key battleground states as Pennsylvania and Ohio. This could be a tough decision, since the White House is hardly likely to agree to a labor case against China when it and most of Corporate America have argued for years that such issues should be handled by the International Labor Organization, not in trade pacts.

The Administration's initial response promised nothing, but it sounded as tough as possible: "We are committed to aggressively enforcing our trade laws to make sure American companies can compete on a level playing field," says U.S. Trade Representative spokesperson Richard Mills, who also says it's too early to comment on the merits of labor's filing.

Logical Link

Despite the politics, the AFL-CIO's 100-page brief marks a milestone of sorts in the debate over trade and labor rights. For years, labor and its allies have demanded that labor standards be included in trade pacts. But their complaints often have been dismissed as self-interested protectionism. Now, for the first time, labor's so-called fair traders have articulated a coherent intellectual position that makes a logical link between trade and labor rights.

Even some ardent free traders think the AFL-CIO's petition must be taken seriously. "You can't just dismiss it as protectionist. In a market economy, wages are set by the free interaction between workers and management, which doesn't exist in China," says William A. Reinsch, the President of the National Foreign Trade Council, which represents 300 large U.S. multinationals such as Boeing.

Labor's argument is so elementary that it's astonishing no one has ever spelled it out in such detail before. The brief contends that China's well-documented labor repression allows its factory owners to pay less than they would if the government enforced its own labor laws. These savings in turn lower the price of China's exports to the U.S., giving it an unfair trade advantage—much as a direct government subsidy to a factory owner would do.

Quantifying the Damage

So, the AFL-CIO isn't complaining that China's wages are low, but that its labor abuses push them even lower than they would be if the country had something closer to a free market. "We're not challenging China's comparative advantage [in cheap labor] but only the added increment of cost advantage it gains by violations of core worker rights," says Mark Barenberg, a Columbia University law professor who drafted the AFL-CIO filing.

His brief even tries to put a dollar value on the labor repression and the price subsidy it entails. Using four methods, it finds that China's failure to pay its own minimum wage or to allow independent unions lowers wages by 47% to 86%. This in turn reduces the price of China's exports by 11% to 44%.

While these numbers are only a guesstimate, the methods Barenberg employs are similar to those companies use to calculate the damage in more traditional dumping complaints. More important, though, is the notion that China's unwillingness to live up to its own labor standards itself constitutes an unfair trade practice. Sure, it's a politically loaded charge, but it may be difficult to ignore, especially in an election year.

By Aaron Bernstein in Washington, D.C.

Source: **From "Labor's Savvy Charge on China Trade,"** ***BusinessWeek,*** **March 19, 2004, online edition. Copyright © 2004 by the McGraw-Hill Companies, Inc. www.businessweek.com. Reprinted with permission.**

The 21st century ushered in a host of opportunities and challenges for international management. As seen in this opening news story, trade barriers in China are falling, opening up a huge market for exporters and investors around the world. In turn, China's export market is flourishing and continues to grow substantially each year. However, charges of worker repression in China are creating political pressure in the United States, as labor unions, led by the still powerful AFL-CIO, seek limits on Chinese imports as a response to alleged labor repression and abuses. If these actions are successful, the impact on trade between the United States and China could be substantial. According to U.S. unions, the lack of established labor unions and low wages in China give Chinese manufacturers an unfair competitive advantage.

Each region of the world has its own distinct approach when dealing with industrial relations generally and unions in particular—an approach that is influenced by local culture and the national economy. However, as globalization accelerates, unique cultural norms will come in contact with one another, creating conflicts and pressures among different systems and approaches. In this chapter, we will be studying the ways in which multinationals deal with labor relations and industrial democracy. We will also address the issue of how companies try to integrate their overall operations by using concepts such as strategic fit and strategic stretch.

■ Labor Relations in the International Arena

labor relations
The process through which management and workers identify and determine the job relationships that will be in effect at the workplace.

The term **labor relations** can be defined as the process through which management and workers identify and determine the job relationships that will be in effect at the workplace. These relationships often are communicated orally, but in some cases, they also are written in the form of a contract, particularly when workers are represented by a union and a management–labor contract is negotiated and agreed to by both parties. The percentage of workers who are union members varies widely by country. In Sweden, over 85 percent of employees are union members; in France and the United States, only 12 percent are unionized. Therefore, depending on the countries where it does business, an MNC will face varying degrees of organized labor challenges.

Like other areas of international human resource management, the specific approaches to labor relations will vary from country to country. Some nations employ a labor negotiation process similar to that in the United States, in which both sides have power. In other countries, labor negotiation is dominated by either a strong management group or a highly powerful union. The division of power affects the way in which labor agreements are negotiated and enforced as well as the way industrial conflicts are resolved. Using the U.S. approach to labor relations as a benchmark, the following sections discuss how the labor relations process is carried out in selected countries around the globe.

The U.S. Approach to Labor Relations

collective bargaining
The process whereby formal labor agreements are reached by union and management representatives; it involves the negotiation of wages, hours, and conditions of employment and the administration of the labor contract.

union
An organization that represents the workers and in collective bargaining has the legal authority to negotiate with the employer and administer the labor contract.

In the United States, formal labor agreements result from **collective bargaining,** in which union and management representatives negotiate wages, hours, and conditions of employment and administer the labor contract. A **union** is an organization that represents the workers and, in collective bargaining, has the legal authority to negotiate with the employer and to administer the labor contract. How collective bargaining is carried out in the United States often differs from how it is done in other countries because of the nature of U.S. labor laws.

For a work group to unionize in the United States, 30 percent of the workers must first sign authorization cards requesting that a specific union represent them in bargaining with the employer. If this percentage is met, the union can petition the National Labor Relations Board (NLRB) to hold an election. When this is done, the union will be certified as the bargaining agent if it receives more than 50 percent of the workers' votes. The two sides then will meet and hammer out a labor contract. This agreement typically remains in effect for two to three years. When it expires, a new agreement is negotiated, and if the union continues to represent the workers, the cycle continues anew. If the workers are dissatisfied with their representation, they can vote out the union and go back to things the way they were before.

Note that if the workers support a union but the union is unable to negotiate a labor agreement that is acceptable to them, the workers may go on strike to pressure management to agree to their terms. Management, however, can bring sanctions of its own, including locking out employees or hiring strikebreakers (called "scabs" by union members) to fill the positions of those who refuse to work. A lockout occurred during the National Basketball Association strike in the 1998–1999 season. Unlike strikes in most other countries, strikes in the United States, such as the one against the NBA owners, almost always are confined to periods when the contract is being renegotiated. Strikes seldom are used in the middle of the labor contract agreement, because mechanisms such as a grievance procedure can be employed.

Steps of a Grievance Procedure   A **grievance** is a complaint brought by an employee who feels that he or she has been treated improperly under the terms of the labor agreement. In the United States, efforts are made to solve these problems at the lowest level of the hierarchy and as quickly as possible. The contract spells out the specific steps in the grievance procedure. The first step usually involves a meeting between the union representative at the operating level (commonly called the "shop steward") and the employee's supervisor. They attempt to agree on how to solve the grievance. If it is not solved at this level, the grievance may go to the next steps, involving union officials and higher-level management representatives. These conciliatory approaches usually solve the grievance to the satisfaction of both parties. Sometimes, however, the matter ends up in the hands of a mediator or an arbitrator.

Mediation and Arbitration   A **mediator** brings both sides together and helps them to reach a settlement that is mutually acceptable. An **arbitrator** provides a solution to a grievance that both sides have been unable to resolve themselves and that both sides agree to accept. A number of arbitration approaches typically are used. In resolving wage-related issues, for example, three of the most common include (1) splitting the difference between the demands of the two parties; (2) using an either-or approach, in which one side's position is fully supported and the other side's is rejected; and (3) determining a fair wage based on market conditions.

Importance of Positive Labor Relations   Labor relations are important because they directly determine labor costs, productivity, and eventually, even profits. "International Management in Action: They're Leading the Pack" gives details on some of the benefits from healthy labor relations. If the union and management do not have good relations, the organization's cost of doing business likely will be higher than it otherwise would be. In fact, in recent years, many MNCs entering the United States have been looking for sites where they can set up nonunion plants. They are convinced that unions make them less competitive. This conviction certainly is debatable (e.g., highly successful Southwest Airlines is highly unionized), although some MNCs have been effective by keeping out unions. One example is the productive Japanese Nissan plant in Smyrna, Tennessee, which continually defeats union efforts.

grievance
A complaint brought by an employee who feels that he or she has been treated improperly under the terms of the labor agreement.

mediator
A person who brings both sides (union and management representatives) together and helps them to reach a settlement that is mutually acceptable.

arbitrator
An individual who provides a solution to a grievance that both sides (union and management representatives) have been unable to resolve themselves and that both sides agree to accept.

Labor Relations in Other Countries

Because labor relations strategies vary greatly from country to country, MNCs find that the strategy used in one country sometimes is irrelevant or of limited value in another. A number of factors can account for this. One is the economic development of the country, given that general labor relations strategies often change as a country's economic situation changes. In addition, entry strategies often must be modified as the firm begins to settle in. Changes in the political environment also must be taken into consideration. For example, under the Thatcher government, British labor unions had a difficult time; in fact, pro-union recognition provisions that were legislated in the mid-1970s were repealed in the 1980s. Since the election of Tony Blair in the U.K., the Labor Party has dominated, although its policies are decidedly more middle-of-the-road than those of previous Labor governments.

Still another factor is strike activity. Unions in many countries often call strikes in the middle of a contract period. These strike decisions often catch the company unprepared and result in lost productivity and profit as the firm tries to negotiate with the union or transfer work to other geographic locales and minimize the economic effect. Figure 15–1 illustrates that unionization rates vary widely around the world.

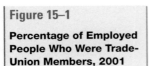

Figure 15–1

Percentage of Employed People Who Were Trade-Union Members, 2001

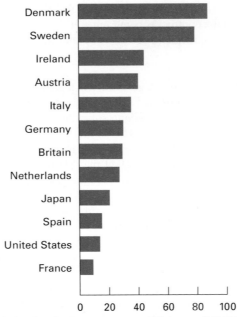

Source: European Foundation for the Improvement of Living and Working Conditions.

Other differences are more regional. For example, labor relations throughout Europe are somewhat similar, but they differ sharply from those in the United States. Some of these differences in European labor relations include:

1. In Europe, firms typically negotiate their agreements with unions at the national level, through employer associations representing their particular industries, even when there also are local, within-company negotiations. This national agreement establishes certain minimum conditions of employment that frequently are augmented through bargaining with the union at the firm or the local level.

2. Unions in many European countries have more political power than those in the United States, so when employers deal with their union(s), they in effect often are dealing directly or indirectly with the government. Unions often are allied with a particular political party—generally referred to as the labor party, although in some countries these alliances are more complex, such as a number of different political parties, each supported and primarily identified with a particular union or set of unions.

3. There is a greater tendency in Europe for salaried employees, including those at managerial levels, to be unionized, often in a union of their own.

4. Unions in most European countries have existed longer than those in the United States. Consequently, they occupy a more accepted position in society and are less concerned about gaining approval.[1]

5. In developing and emerging economies such as China, India, and Southeast Asia, labor is less powerful, unions are less prevalent, and workers are often compelled to accept conditions of work set by management.

The following sections examine industrial relations approaches in a number of selected countries.

Great Britain   In contrast to the situation in the United States, a labor agreement in Great Britain is not a legally binding contract. It is merely an "understanding" among the parties that sets forth the terms and conditions of employment that are acceptable at present. Violations of the agreement by the union or by management carry no legal penalties, because the contract cannot be enforced in court. Additionally, while unions are relatively

International Management in Action
They're Leading the Pack
www2.ford.com

Many believe that MNCs are attracted to less developed countries because of labor relations policies that are conducive to cooperation, low wages, and productivity. In truth, the United States is still proving to be one of the most attractive locations for international firms. Although the power of U.S. labor unions is declining, the labor relations climate is conducive to rising productivity. Today, the United States is not only the most productive nation in the world, its overall productivity is increasing faster than that of the other major industrial powers, such as Japan, Germany, and France. The Japanese economy has been having trouble since the early 1990s, and the surging value of the yen has reduced its international competitiveness. Despite having some of the most successful MNCs in the world (e.g., Hitachi, Mitsubishi, Sony, and Toyota), Japan is experiencing some difficulties. The same is true in Europe. Many MNCs on the continent now are engaged in painful restructuring that is designed to make them more efficient and competitive in world markets. Their governments fight such downsizing, however, because of the negative impact on employment. As a result, firms such as Volkswagen in Germany and Alcatel Alsthom in France continue to face the challenge of becoming more efficient on the one hand and accommodating government directives to hire more people on the other. These are problems that U.S. MNCs do not yet face, and it helps them to maintain high productivity. There also are other reasons why U.S. productivity is doing so well relative to the rest of the world.

One is that the U.S. work ethic seems to be stronger than ever. For example, U.S. workers now are working more hours per week than they did 20 years ago. Other major economic powers such as Germany and Japan are finding just the opposite; their people are working shorter workweeks than at any time in the past. In Japan, for example, the average manufacturing worker today puts in approximately 20 percent fewer hours than in 1960, and this downward trend likely will continue. A couple of reasons are that many Japanese feel they already make enough money to take care of their needs, and many claim that they are fed up with hard work. Even Japanese union members oppose lengthening the workweek, despite efforts from their leadership to cooperate with the companies and put in more hours. Part of this opposition is a belief among the rank-and-file Japanese workers that the union represents the company's interests rather than their interests.

A second factor is that labor costs in the United States actually are lower in recent years than in most other major industrial countries. Thanks to union–management cooperation, U.S. companies have been able to introduce high-tech, efficient machinery. As a result, firms such as Ford now can manufacture cars at lower prices than foreign competitors can. Moreover, as Ford continues closing outmoded plants and running others at close to capacity, costs per car should decline even further. Much of this outcome is a result of effective labor relations strategies and shows that U.S. manufacturers not only are back in the ballgame but, in many cases, may be leading the pack.

powerful and strikes are more prevalent than in the United States, British union membership has declined in recent years.[2]

Labor agreements in Great Britain typically are less extensive than those in the United States. These understandings usually contain provisions that define the structure of the relationships among the parties and set forth procedures for handling complaints. Typically, however, there is no provision for arbitration of disagreements or grievances, although both mediation and arbitration on occasion are used.

Germany Traditionally, unions and management in Germany have had a more cooperative relationship than in the United States, where an adversarial relationship often has existed. Some observers believed that the unification of West and East Germany would increase labor conflict, but this has not happened. In fact, as integration continues, labor harmony seems to be improving. Certainly, on an overall basis, there is a spirit of cooperation between German management and labor brought about by, among other things, the use of industrial democracy, in which workers serve on boards of directors and ensure that the rank and file are treated fairly. A detailed discussion of industrial democracy is given later in this chapter.

Union power in Germany is still quite strong. Although union membership is voluntary, there generally is one union in each major industry. This powerful industry union will negotiate a contract with the employers' federation for the industry, and the contract will cover all major issues, including wages and terms of employment. All firms that are members of the employers' federation then will pay the agreed-on wages. Firms that are not members of the federation typically will use the contract as a guide to what they should pay their people. Although a minority of the labor force is organized, unions set the pay scale for about 90 percent of the country's workers; wages are determined by job classifications. If an individual is replaced because of automation or is laid off because of declining business, the worker's wage settlement is handled in accordance with the previously determined agreement. Other agreements are hammered out to cover general working conditions, work hours, overtime pay, personal leave, and vacations.

If there is a conflict over interpretation or enforcement of the agreement, the situation typically is negotiated between the company and the worker with participation of a union representative or work council. If an impasse is reached, the situation can be referred to a German labor court for final settlement.

By the mid-1990s, some German unions had become more adversarial. For example, IG Metall union began adopting an approach in dealing with employers that was more like that used in the United States. However, more recent economic developments have resulted in a softening of this union position. In fact, the labor relations climate in Germany traditionally is much more serene than in the United States, and most unions lack the firepower to engage in prolonged strikes. One reason is that the rights of workers are addressed more carefully by management. A second is that even though they are covered by a labor contract, individual workers are free to negotiate either individually or collectively with management to secure wages and benefits that are superior to those spelled out in the agreement. In recent years some unions have been merging to create "super unions" and, in the process, increase their political clout and bargaining power.[3]

Japan   Unions and management have a cooperative relationship in Japan. One reason is social custom, which dictates nonconfrontational union–management behavior. The provisions in Japanese labor agreements usually are general and vague, although they are legally enforceable. Disputes regarding the agreement often are settled in an amicable manner. Sometimes, they are resolved by third-party mediators or arbitrators. Labor commissions have been established by law, and these groups, as well as the courts, can help to resolve negotiations impasses.

Japanese unions are most active during the spring and again at the end of the year, because these are the two periods during which bonuses are negotiated. Recently, Japanese unions, like the German unions, have been trying to extend wage bargaining to cover all firms in a particular industry. This would provide the union with greater negotiating power over the individual firms within the industry. Their success in this industrywide bargaining strategy would have particular impact on MNCs operating in Japan. Compared with those of most other industrialized countries, however, Japanese unions remain relatively weak.

China, India, and Southeast Asia   Labor relations in the developing and emerging economies of the world are quite distinct from those in industrial democracies. In general, because economic employment conditions favor owners over workers, employees have less power and therefore are less likely to initiate actions or organize unions to negotiate for improved working conditions.

China.   In China, with the shift from a command economy to a more market-led one, the "iron rice bowl" policy of industrial relations dominated by Soviet-inspired command and control models has given way to personnel management influenced by both Japanese and Western approaches to human resource management but with unique characteristics drawn from Chinese culture and practice.[4] This shift has resulted in the replacement of the administrative regulation of labor relations by contractual regulation with an increasing emphasis on the role of the collective contract system. The integration of the trade union into management at the workplace, however, continues to prevent collective consultation from providing an adequate framework for the full freedom and regulation of labor relations.[5] The status of labor relations in China has also become a point of contention in international trade and human rights discussions. Some critics accuse China of exploiting workers in order to fuel its export-led growth policies.[6]

India.   The evolution of labor relations in India was primarily shaped by the attempt of the state to manage industrial conflict through the development of regulatory laws. As is the case in many developing countries, the government's interest was primarily in avoiding conflict rather than protecting workers' interests. In general, workers' political activity and trade-union actions in India were viewed by the state as disruptive activities.[7] The present Indian management system reflects the emphasis in India on strong family ties and extended family relationships, evident in the large family-owned companies that still dominate India's economy. Moreover, Indian businesses have made attempts to emulate Western or Eastern (Japanese) patterns of management. This is because Indian managers are often trained in the West and most of the Indian management institutes have adopted the Western education system.

Trade unions did have a period of militancy in the postcolonial period (1947–1970s), but the strong position of trade unions began to weaken in the early 1980s, partly as a result of the declining influence of national federations over enterprise unions. Unions not only are losing a large number of members, but also are under severe pressure to save the jobs of existing employees. The economic scenario forces unions with diverse ideologies to join hands and take a cooperative approach toward management. Although the state has passed a number of labor laws, and over 150 acts of labor legislation are on the books, many of these provisions are not fully implemented.[8]

Southeast Asia.   In the countries of Southeast Asia—which include Brunei, Cambodia, East Timor, Indonesia, Laos, Malaysia, Myanmar (Burma), Philippines, Singapore, Thailand, and Vietnam—postcolonial regimes sought to limit the role of militant, radical labor movements, some of them communist influenced. Many states are still focused on keeping labor movements in check, whether in the name of economic development, national unity, or social stability. Within such a political environment, labor movements have been fragmented or constrained. Labor weakness is also partly the consequence of the timing of Asia's rapid industrialization, which was generally unfavorable to nascent labor movements in late-industrializing countries. Unlike in the period in which Europe and the United States first industrialized, Southeast Asian countries developed in an environment of intense international competition. In Southeast Asia, it has been difficult if not impossible to insulate national workforces, even in the early stages of industrialization, from external competition and market pressures.[9] Thus, labor relations in Southeast Asia have been influenced by market-based policies of international competition and, to some extent, a flexible employee relations system that places expectations on workers to view their interests as aligned with the interests of management. Moreover, a series of economic crises, the most recent of which occurred in 1997, have created conditions of insecurity and uncertainty in labor in Southeast Asia, further reinforcing the generally weak role of labor and collective bargaining. More recently, pressure on sportswear, toy, and electronic manufacturers in the United States and Europe to take a more responsible position with respect to working conditions at their factories in Southeast Asia has called attention to working conditions and labor relations in this region.

How Industrial Conflict Is Handled Around the World

When the union and management reach an impasse in contract negotiations or over some issue, conflict results. The union may call for a strike, or management may have a lockout. A **strike** is a collective refusal to work to pressure management to grant union demands. In recent years, strikes have been less common in most countries; however, when measured in terms of working days lost per 1,000 employees, strikes are still a powerful weapon in dealing with industrial conflict. For example, between 1993 and 2002 economically advanced countries lost an average of almost 60 working days per 1,000 employees because of labor disputes. Figure 15–2 shows the annual average of days lost during this ten-year period. A **lockout** is the company's refusal to allow workers to enter the facility. Other typical union strategies resulting from conflict include slowdowns, sabotage, sit-ins, and boycotts. The following sections show how industrial conflict is handled around the world.

strike
A collective refusal to work to pressure management to grant union demands.

lockout
A company's refusal to allow workers to enter the facility during a labor dispute.

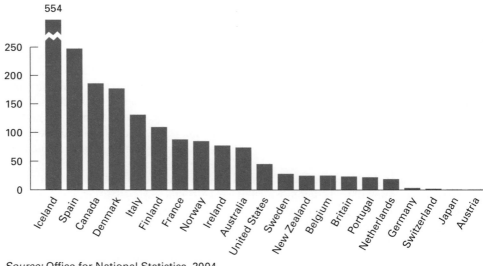

Source: Office for National Statistics, 2004.

United States   Most U.S. labor contracts have a specific provision that outlaws strikes; thus, sudden or unauthorized strikes (commonly called "wildcat strikes") are uncommon. If either party to the contract feels that the other is not acting in good faith or living up to the terms, the grievance procedure is used to resolve the matter peacefully. However, once the contract period is over and if a new contract is not successfully negotiated, the workers may strike or continue to work without a contract while threatening to walk out. On the other side, management also may lock out the workers, although this is much more rare. The modern position of more and more U.S. unions is that a philosophy of "us against them" is not as conducive to the long-range welfare of the union as is a strategy of working together to find common ground. In this regard, U.S. unions are moving closer to the approach that is used by many unions in other countries.

Great Britain   In Great Britain, labor unions are relatively powerful (although this power has been eroded in recent years), and strikes are more prevalent than in the United States. Labor agreements typically do not prohibit strikes, and the general public is more used to and tolerant of them. Strikes in Britain often are brief, however, and do not involve a large number of people, although British miners have had prolonged strikes.

Some labor experts believe that industrial conflict in Britain results in more problems than in the United States, because the system is not geared toward the efficient resolution of problems. For example, many in the British general public as well as the workers believe that it is management's job to look after workers, and failure to do so is a breach of management's social responsibility. This climate often results in hard feelings and impedes rapid solutions. In addition, the procedure for handling grievances, in contrast to that used in the United States, often is informal and cumbersome and sometimes results in fragmented efforts with the outcome costly in both time and money. Sometimes, management uses the lockout to vent its frustration over the bureaucratic delays in resolving labor-related problems. Although things have been changing for the better in recent years, the British in general still appear willing to accept conflict with resulting strikes and lockouts as the price of protecting the rights of the workers.

Germany   A number of similarities exist between the United States and Germany in terms of managing labor conflicts. As in the United States, strikes and lockouts are prohibited in Germany during the period when a labor agreement is in effect. A strike is legal, however, when the contract has run out and a new one has not yet been ratified by the workers. Although German unions tend to be industrywide, quite often several agreements are in force in a particular company, and these agreements do not have the same termination dates. Therefore, one group of workers may be striking or working out a contract while another is working under contract. In addition, different terms and conditions of employment exist for different groups of workers, just as in the United States. Similarly, there sometimes are strikes in the middle of a contract period in clear violation of the labor agreement, indicating that the German preference for orderly and well-defined work relationships is not always present. Overall, however, there tends to be a fair amount of cooperation between management and labor because of the way labor relations are legally structured.

Japan   Strikes and lockouts in Japan are very rare. Following World War II, there was a period of severe labor unrest coupled with massive, and sometimes crippling, labor strikes. Today, however, strikes are of short duration and used only to drive home a particular, minor point, not to cripple an industry or inconvenience the public. One knowledgeable observer has explained it this way:

> Since threats are generally unnecessary, a strike in Japan is merely a way to embarrass management, and thus may last from a couple of hours to a couple of days, with those of a week or more considered very long. But an equally important reason for strikes' being so short is the strong social pressure to keep the conflict quiet and resolve it quickly and quietly without having to resort to the law. In Japan the law is regarded as the instrument with which the state imposes its will. Hence, the Japanese do not like the law and will try to stay as far away from it as possible.[10]

Sometimes, strikes occur when a Japanese union is negotiating with management during industrywide negotiations. These strikes are aimed at showing that the workers support their union and are not designed to indicate any particular grievance or complaint with management. This is understood by both sides. The issues over which both sides might disagree are fairly limited. This is true for two reasons: (1) An individual's term of employment never exceeds those provided for in the labor contract, because this would indicate that this worker was more important than the other members of the work group. (2) The law establishes standards for minimum wages, hours, overtime, rest periods, vacations, sick leaves, sanitary conditions, and discharge. Therefore, individual needs or desires are not given a great deal of attention by the union; however, Japanese unions still try to gain benefits for their people, as seen in recent efforts to win wage increases and cuts in working hours.

An insight into Japanese labor relations is provided by the cultural value of *Wa,* which implies that individuals should subordinate their interests and identities to those of the group. This cultural value helps to account for a great deal of the harmony that exists between management and labor in Japan.

■ International Structure of Unions

So far, this discussion has centered on the international implications of labor relations, but the structure of unions themselves also has important implications. Most labor unions are locally or nationally based, but some are internationally active. Union internationalization has been achieved in three basic ways: (1) through use of intergovernmental organizations; (2) through use of transnational union affiliations; and (3) through extension of domestic contracts.

Intergovernmental Organizations

There are two important intergovernmental organizations. The **International Labour Organization (ILO)** is a United Nations affiliate that consists of government, industry, and union representations. The ILO has worked to define and promote fair labor standards in

International Labour Organization (ILO)
A United Nations affiliate, consisting of government, industry, and union representatives, that works to promote fair labor standards in health, safety, and working conditions, and freedom of association for workers.

health, safety, and working conditions, and freedom of association for workers throughout the world. A number of years ago, the ILO published a study of social policy implications of MNCs. Some topics in that study included investment concentration by area and industry, capital and technology transfers, international trade, workforce efforts, working conditions, and industrial relations effects. The study concluded by noting the different views and concerns of employers and workers, and it recommended that the social problems and benefits specific to MNCs be identified and studied further.

The ILO has also conducted a series of industry-specific studies on MNCs in Western Europe, and country studies on the employment effects of MNCs, including jobs lost and gained as a result of MNCs as well as the quality of jobs within MNCs. Some of its important conclusions were that (1) jobs were growing faster in MNCs than in non-MNCs; (2) white-collar positions were increasing at the expense of blue-collar jobs; and (3) one key reason for this employment growth was the R&D intensity of MNCs.

The **Organization for Economic Cooperation and Development (OECD)** is a government, industry, and union group that was founded in 1976 and that has established a voluntary set of guidelines for MNCs. These guidelines include MNCs' obligation to respect the laws and regulations of foreign countries, and in turn, these foreign countries are obliged to provide national treatments to MNCs within their borders. In recent years, these guidelines have been used to help countries regulate the operations of MNCs within their national boundaries.

Transnational Union Affiliations

There are four basic types of international trade affiliations: global, regional, specialized, and industrial operations. **Global international trade-union affiliations** cut across regional and industrial groups and are heavily concerned with political activities. The **International Confederation of Free Trade Unions (ICFTU)** is the most important global international union confederation. Most of the **regional internationals** are subdivisions of the globals, and the regionals' activities are applications of the globals' activities. **Specialized internationals,** such as the ILO, the Trade Union Advisory Committee in the OECD, and the European Trade Union Congress, which represents workers' interests at the European Union level, function as components of intergovernment agencies and lobby within these agencies. The **industrial internationals** also are affiliates of the global internationals. In the ICFTU, they are called International Trade Secretaries (ITS), and there is an individual ITS for each major industry group.

Also of transnational interest are worldwide company councils that have been formed under the auspices of the International Trade Secretaries (ITS). For example, there is a General Motors Council, which consists of union representatives from GM plants throughout the world. This council meets periodically to share information about collective bargaining, working conditions, and other developments that can be valuable to unions in gaining comparable treatment for their people in country-level bargaining.

The international structure of the ITS provides a union vehicle that is parallel to the international structure of an MNC. On occasion, an ITS representative has sought to intervene at the global headquarters of an MNC on behalf of a member union having difficulty in its dealings with a subsidiary of the MNC at the national level. Some labor relations experts believed that when worldwide company councils were developing during the 1970s, they would become vehicles for transnational collective bargaining with MNCs; however, the diverse legal and cultural environments of the various countries have been a major barrier to this development.

Extensions of Domestic Contracts

Some U.S. unions have sought to deal with MNCs by bargaining with them on a global basis. The International Union of Electrical (IUE) workers, for example, invited union representatives from General Electric's overseas plants to participate in its collective bargaining.

Organization for Economic Cooperation and Development (OECD)
A government, industry, and union group founded in 1976 that has established a voluntary set of guidelines for MNCs.

global international trade-union affiliations
Trade-union relationships that cut across regional and industrial groups and are heavily concerned with political activities.

International Confederation of Free Trade Unions (ICFTU)
The most important global international union confederation.

regional internationals
Subdivisions of the global affiliation; regional applications of the globals' activities.

specialized internationals
Trade-union associations that function as components of intergovernmental agencies and lobby within these agencies.

industrial internationals
Affiliates of the global international union groups that focus on a particular industry.

These foreign representatives were only observers, however, because U.S. labor law limits collective bargaining to matters that relate to the U.S. labor unit. In another action, the IUE contended that GE was transferring work overseas and charged that this was an unfair labor practice under the provisions of the collective bargaining agreements; however, the general counsel for the National Labor Relations Board rejected the charge and held that the union had not substantiated its claim. Overall, unions have been unsuccessful in attempting to prevent companies from transferring work overseas, although this certainly will continue to be a major focal point in the years ahead.

■ Industrial Democracy

Industrial democracy involves the rights of employees to participate in significant management decisions. This participation by labor includes areas such as wage rates, bonuses, profit sharing, vacations and holiday leaves, work rules, dismissals, and plant expansions and closings. Industrial democracy is not widely used in the United States, where management typically refuses to relinquish or share its authority (commonly called "managerial prerogatives") to make major decisions. In many other countries, however, and especially in Europe, the right of industrial democracy is guaranteed by national law. This right can take a number of different forms.

industrial democracy
The rights that employees have to participate in significant management decisions.

Common Forms of Industrial Democracy

As the EU consolidates its goal of unification, the head of the European Commission has stated that a primary objective is to obtain a minimum threshold of social rights for workers, to be negotiated between a "European union" and employers. At present, several forms of industrial democracy exist in European countries and elsewhere. In some countries, one form may be more prevalent than others, but it is common to find a number of these forms existing simultaneously.

Codetermination Codetermination involves the participation of workers on boards of directors. The idea began right after World War II in Germany to prevent the re-emergence of Nazism in the coal and steel industries. By the mid-1970s, European countries besides Germany, such as Austria, Denmark, the Netherlands, and Sweden, all had legally mandated codetermination. In most cases, boards of directors had to consist of one-third worker representatives. In the late 1970s, Germany increased this to 50 percent for private companies with 2,000 or more employees. Most recently the EU Council of Ministers issued a directive that now requires all companies with 50 or more employees by 2008 to "inform and consult" workers' representatives about company strategy.[11] Despite such efforts, some researchers report that the workers are not greatly impressed with codetermination; many regard such participation on boards as merely a cosmetic attempt to address the substantive issue of true industrial democracy.

Work Councils To varying degrees, work councils exist in all European countries. These councils are a result of either national legislation or collective bargaining at the company–union level. Their basic function is to improve company performance, working conditions, and job security. In some firms, these councils are worker- or union-run, whereas in others, members of management chair the group. Workers typically are elected to serve on the council, and management representatives are appointed by the company. The amount of council power will vary. In England, France, and Scandinavia, the groups tend not to be as powerful as in Germany, the Netherlands, and Italy. Moreover, in small firms many managers feel that these councils reduce the company's flexibility and make it less competitive. On the other hand, both unions and management acknowledge that companies have found a variety of ways to reduce codetermination by hiring temporary workers and outsourcing work to other firms. So the negative impact of work councils is often minimized in practice.

Shop Floor Participation   A wide number of approaches are used to achieve shop floor participation. Some of the most common include worker involvement programs, quality circles, and other forms of participative management discussed in earlier chapters. QWL (quality of work life) programs such as those used in the Scandinavian countries and currently very popular in manufacturing and assembly plants throughout Europe and the United States are excellent examples.

Financial Participation   Financial participation takes a number of forms. One of the most common is profit sharing between management and workers. In some cases, productivity or gain-sharing plans are used, whereby management shares productivity gains in a predetermined ratio, such as 50–50, with the workers. This motivates workers to recommend efficiency measures and develop shortcuts to doing their jobs in return for a share of the increased profits. Overall, financial participation has not been widely adopted overseas, although it has gained a foothold in a number of U.S. firms, especially those using gain sharing as a team incentive for performance improvement.

Collective Bargaining   If no specific forms of industrial democracy are in effect, collective bargaining itself can become the mechanism to obtain industrial democracy for workers. As noted previously, the ability of unions to bargain collectively is legally restricted in some countries (e.g., a majority vote of the bargaining unit is required in the United States) and is not widely used in others. However, some nations, such as Sweden, require collective bargaining and allow many matters that in the United States are considered to be managerial prerogatives and not susceptible to bargaining, such as work rules and production standards, to be open for negotiation with the workers.

Industrial Democracy in Selected Countries

Industrial democracy takes a number of different forms depending on the country. For example, the approach used in the United States differs from approaches used in Europe and Asia. The following discussion briefly highlights some of these differences.

United States   In the United States, the most common form of industrial democracy is collective bargaining, whose guidelines are spelled out by law. A union that is certified by the NLRB becomes the exclusive bargaining agent for employees in the unit and is authorized to represent workers in the negotiation and administration of a labor–management contract. During the last decade, other forms of industrial democracy have gained ground, most notably employee participation in problem-solving teams, special purpose teams, and self-managing teams.

problem-solving teams
Employee groups that discuss ways of improving quality, efficiency, and the overall work environment.

special purpose teams
Employee groups that design and introduce work reforms and new technology.

self-managing teams
Employee groups that take over supervisory duties and manage themselves; teams consist of individuals who learn all the tasks of all the group members, allowing team members to rotate jobs.

    Problem-solving teams meet weekly to discuss ways of improving quality, efficiency, and the overall work environment. They generally are not empowered to implement their ideas, but their suggestions often result in more efficient operations. These teams have begun to gain widespread support as managers turn to employees for help in improving performance.

    Special purpose teams design and introduce work reforms and new technology. In unionized firms, both management and labor will collaborate on operational decisions at all levels. This involvement often creates the necessary environment for both quality and productivity improvements. These teams are continuing to gain popularity, especially in unionized operations.

    Self-managing teams consist of individuals who learn all the tasks of all group members, which allows them to rotate from job to job. These teams also take over supervisory duties such as scheduling work, ordering materials, and determining vacation times. These teams have been so effective that in some cases, productivity has increased and quality has risen dramatically. In recent years, these teams have become increasingly popular, and the future will probably see even greater use of them.

The three types of industrial democracy described here represent a radical departure from the way that U.S. firms traditionally have been managed. The old approach of a top-down management holding on to all the authority now is being replaced with an industrial democracy philosophy of sharing power with the workers. Spurred on by creative human resource management and the total quality movement, the currently popular empowerment of employees is the process of giving employees the resources, information, and authority needed to carry out their jobs effectively.

Great Britain   Industrial democracy is not new to England. Self-governing workshops (worker cooperatives) existed as early as the 1820s; however, Great Britain has not become a hub of industrial democracy. For example, unlike many workers in Germany and Scandinavia, British workers are not legally mandated to have seats on the board of directors. As in the United States, however, industrial democracy in Great Britain takes the form of collective bargaining and worker representation through the use of teams.

Work groups within a British company or plant will elect a chief spokesperson or steward from their ranks to act as their interface with management. If the employees are unionized, a union council will represent them. These councils help to ensure that workers are treated fairly by management. Unfortunately, this sometimes creates a problem, because spokespersons or stewards in the firm may not agree with the union councils.

During the coming years, British firms likely will begin relying more heavily on participative approaches such as those used in the empowerment process in the United States and Northern Europe. The primary reason is that competitive nations have been able to show that shop floor democracy is a key element in reducing production costs and increasing product quality. However, even with the Labor government now in power, legally mandated industrial democracy measures are unlikely in Great Britain anytime in the near future.

Germany   Industrial democracy and codetermination are very strong in Germany, especially in the steel and auto industries. Although the union is charged with handling the collective bargaining, internal boards have been established by law for ensuring codeterminism in the workplace. As noted earlier, the full impact of unifying with East Germany is yet to be determined, but all firms with 2,000 or more employees (1,000 or more in the steel industry) presently must have boards composed of workers. One supervisory board is made up of an equal number of representatives who are elected by both the shareholders and the employees, and of one additional, neutral person. This supervisory board in German companies is similar to the board of directors in U.S. firms. The other type of board in German firms is the management board, which is responsible for daily operation. Employees in each plant also elect a plant work council; if it is a multiplant company, members of the plant work council serve on a company work council as well.

Work councils perform a number of important functions, including negotiating wage rates above the contractually established minimums, negotiating benefits, setting wage rates for new jobs, and re-evaluating pay when workers are transferred between jobs. In multiplant operations, these councils sometimes have difficulty finding out what is happening at the shop floor, so they rely heavily on meetings with employees and communication with shop stewards. As a result, German workers have two groups working for them: the union, which is bargaining collectively with management, and the work council, which is negotiating employment issues relating to that particular plant.

Because of the strong degree of codeterminism, some German managers have argued that the process undermines their ability to operate efficiently. They contend that the legally established industrial democracy hampers their efforts; however, research does not support such a position. For example, Scholl conducted a study of both managers and work councils to determine whether codetermination results in more complex, and thus slower, decision making.[12] He focused on decisions that related to both investment and personnel matters. In general, the study found that the ability of German firms to make decisions is not hampered by codeterminism. However, German businesses must continue to push for changes that make them more competitive worldwide.

Denmark   Industrial democracy ensures that Danish workers participate in the management of their firms both directly and indirectly. The direct form includes use of semiautonomous work groups that provide ideas on enhancing productivity and quality and on scheduling the work. The indirect form includes use of shop stewards on the work floor, representation on boards of directors, cooperation committees consisting of worker and manager representatives, safety groups made up of a supervisor and an elected employee representative, and participation on safety committees that are headed by a manager. Figure 15–3 provides an organizational illustration of these employee participation and industrial democracy arrangements.

Unlike the situation in Germany, where the participation of workers on boards of directors is perceived as cosmetic, cooperation committees of firms in Denmark seem particularly important in ensuring a true feeling of industrial democracy among Danish workers. For example, one study found that most Danish workers felt the cooperation committees contributed heavily to openness, coordination of effort, and a feeling of importance.

Sweden   Industrial democracy in Sweden is directed very heavily toward ensuring quality of work life (QWL) and worker participation in the operation of the enterprise. QWL efforts are closely associated with Sweden's Volvo approach. The creation of semiautonomous work teams and development of a cooperative spirit between management and workers are key elements in Volvo and the Swedish approach to industrial democracy. In addition, councils and committees encourage employee involvement in identifying and implementing changes, which lead to improved QWL, which helps to sustain high morale and positive attitudes of workers and to improve productivity and quality of products and services. There is some evidence, however, that the early, glowing reports from Volvo may have been overstated, and that instead of returning dignity to the workers, the assembly lines are just more efficient but not really reaching the standards that are required for world-class competition.

Swedish firms also have workers who are members of the board of directors. To ensure that these worker board participants are competent in handling their tasks, they

Figure 15–3

Employee Participation in All Levels of Danish Firms

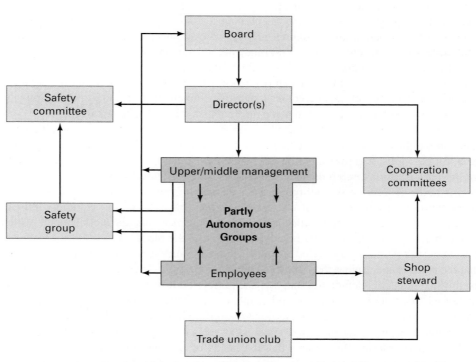

Source: Adapted from Reinhard Lund, "Industrial Democracy in Denmark," *International Studies of Management and Organization* 17, no. 2 (Summer 1987), p. 18. Used by permission of M. E. Sharpe, Inc.

typically are given formal training and spend time with other workers on the board in learning how to do things such as analyze and evaluate financial statements, read reports, and focus on both long-range and short-range issues.

China China has the largest workforce in the world, but even now, little is known to outsiders about how industrial democracy really works there. As in Eastern Europe, many changes have occurred in China. Unlike what has happened in Eastern Europe, many of the reforms and Westernized policies and practices in China, including the nature of industrial democracy, are closely related to the current political climate.

Chinese enterprises traditionally had two policy-making committees. One contained Communist Party leaders and members, and the other included managers and worker representatives. Which committee had more power depended on the political climate, but after reforms in the 1980s, the workers (not the party members) represented industrial democracy in communist countries. However, worker participation in management decision making is less open than Westerners may expect. One study of a variety of enterprises in Beijing found that the number of employees who participate in management decisions is not very high but that the scope of their decision making was quite broad (sales and business plans, production operations decisions, wages and bonuses, employee benefits, housing allocations, transfer of funds, and termination of problem employees).[13] Only time will tell what course industrial democracy will take in China. However, the government did agree to an ambitious program of cooperation with the ILO. According to the agreement, the ILO will provide advice on such things as job creation, workplace safety, collective bargaining, and the settlement of labor disputes.[14] Given that illegal strikes and worker protests have become common as China continues to move toward a market-driven system that is leaving millions of people out of work and is leaving others toiling in arduous or unsafe conditions, this ILO agreement may well prove to be helpful to the government, the workers, and the MNCs doing business there.

Japan Unlike the situation in Europe and China, industrial democracy in Japan is not closely tied to political philosophy. Like the United States, Japan is oriented more to the operating philosophy of enhancing worker performance. The best example is quality circles, in which Japanese workers are encouraged to identify and help solve job-related problems that are associated with quality and flow of work. Management is particularly receptive to workers' ideas that will produce bottom-line results. Except for a few unusual cases, Japan has very little industrial democracy in the European sense. This is reflected by the basic nature of Japanese union–management relations.

There are over 70,000 unions in Japan, and most of them are **enterprise unions,** which represent both hourly and salaried employees of a particular company. Including salaried employees is a marked departure from labor unions in other countries. Employees join the union because they are members of the firm and union membership is expected; however, they do not expect the union to negotiate and win big salary increases for them. A major reason that Japanese unions are relatively weak is that many are company dominated, a practice outlawed in the United States. In the large firms such as Toyota, for example, the president of the union typically is a middle manager who has been nominated by the company and elected by the membership. This arrangement ensures that unions act in harmony with the company's wishes and undermines European-style industrial democracy.

Although there sometimes are labor strikes in Japan, they usually are short-lived and have little effect on company operations. Strikes often are ceremonial and designed to encourage the workers to think of themselves as union employees. In truth, most workers think of themselves as company employees who are simply associated with the union. Moreover, it is not uncommon to find a union strike in a company with two or three work shifts and no loss of work output. This is because when the strikers are done picketing or marching, they go to work and the group coming out of the factory takes up the strike activity. In a factory with three shifts, a line employee will work a full shift, picket for a while, go home to eat and sleep, and then return to the factory for her or his shift.

enterprise unions
Unions that represent both hourly and salaried employees of a particular company.

Of all the industrialized nations, Japan faces the greatest challenge from industrial democracy in the years ahead. Japanese MNCs in Europe, and to a growing degree in the United States, will find that they must relinquish more control over operations to the workers if they hope to achieve the same productivity results they have at home. Conversely, MNCs in Japan report that Japanese white-collar workers are too used to working in a disciplined, corporate environment and fail to make decisions and take initiative. Therefore, changes are needed at home as well.

■ Strategic Management of International Labor Relations

The strategic management of international labor relations will be a major challenge facing MNCs in the years ahead, because so many different approaches can be taken. The approach used in U.S. firms may not be the same as that employed in other countries, including Anglo nations. In Great Britain, as noted earlier, unions do not have the power they once had. In many other European countries, such as Germany, however, unions continue to be quite strong, and especially as the Eastern European traditions of industrial democracy become infused in the EU, the workers will continue to have a great deal of authority in determining what the firm will do. It also is important to realize that those strategies benefiting unions in one country may have no value in others. This sometimes can be a conflict between international unions. For example, when Ford Motor felt that the labor climate in Britain was unfavorable to further investing, the company was approached by a group of Dutch businesspeople and urged to consider the Netherlands for future investment. Despite the strong criticism of British unions, the leadership of the Dutch trade unions did not object to these suggestions that investment funds be transferred to their country.[15]

The Philosophical Backdrop

As noted in earlier chapters, MNCs can use a number of philosophies as a starting point for their approach to management functions, including labor relations. For instance, under an ethnocentric philosophy, the MNC will take an approach to labor relations in other countries that is identical to its approach at home. Cultural, legal, and economic factors of the host country will not be considered in industrial relations efforts. This approach generally is not effective and can even have disastrous results; as companies begin going international, they soon abandon such an approach.

A second approach is to use a polycentric philosophy in managing international industrial relations. Under this philosophy, the MNC will evaluate each country or geographic region as a separate entity. The MNC's international industrial relations strategy will be a series of different approaches depending on the country.

A third approach is a geocentric philosophy that is characterized by an effort to understand the interrelationships between the various geographic locations and a strategy to link them with a unifying thread and a composite industrial relations approach. The primary difference between a polycentric and a geocentric philosophy is that the latter considers the interrelationships between the various groups. Here are some examples of how industrial relations in one country can affect those in others:

1. Opel (General Motors' German subsidiary) negotiates an *increase* in the basic workweek hours with Belgian unions as it adds a second shift at its Belgian assembly plant. The intent of management is to keep the costs of production there competitive with those at a similar Opel plant in Germany. The intent of the Belgian workers is to expand employment and enhance job security.

2. A U.S. electronics firm cuts back its U.S. manufacturing output by 10 percent through laying off a like percentage of its U.S. workers. Its French subsidiary

picks up the resulting product market slack. By cutting back employment in the United States, the firm avoids the large payments to workers that French law would have required if the cutback had been made by the French subsidiary.

3. Workers at a German company's British subsidiary go out on strike to support their demand for improved wages. Operations at the company's German plants continue, providing substantial cash inflows (revenues) to the entire system. The British workers completely forgo their cash inflows—their wages—during the strike. The company is less severely pressed financially than these workers are and can sustain a long strike if need be.

4. Ford of Europe integrates production among several European subsidiaries. For certain models of cars, the engines are British-made, the power train and some stampings are German-made, the wheels and other stampings are Belgian-made, and so on. A strike by workers in Belgium could shut down plants in Britain, Germany, and elsewhere. This gives the Belgian workers operational leverage vis-à-vis management and enhances their power in collective bargaining.[16]

The Japanese also make an interesting case study of the need for a geocentric philosophy toward industrial relations. Japanese auto firms long have realized that auto capacity is outstripping demand in both North America and Europe. As Japan continues to increase its foothold in North America, it will have to pay greater attention to its industrial relations approaches and modify them to meet the local labor market. Japan also will need to coordinate its worldwide holdings with a carefully formulated geocentric strategy toward labor relations.

Labor Costs

Another major area of consideration in formulating an international labor relations strategy is labor costs. Wages that are paid in one country often differ considerably from those paid in other countries for the same job. In some countries, workers are grossly exploited. From China to Bangladesh[17] to El Salvador,[18] employee sweatshops produce clothing for the world market and workers toil for long hours, in unsafe conditions, for minimum pay. At present, a number of MNCs are refusing to do business with these firms and are beginning to closely monitor their suppliers to ensure that workers are treated well. These developments, of course, will lead to an increase in labor costs, but this is certainly the socially responsible thing to do. On the other hand, in some countries labor costs are extremely high. In manufacturing, for example, hourly rates in Germany have been substantially greater than those paid elsewhere.

Some of the latest data,[19] complemented by average weekly hours worked in manufacturing, reveal the following:

Country	Average Total Hourly Compensation in U.S. Dollars for Production Workers	Average Weekly Hours Worked
Germany	$26.18	39.9
France	17.42	38.2
Italy	14.93	39.0
United States	21.33	40.5
Great Britain	17.47	43.5

A close analysis of this information shows, in the main, that there is an inverse relationship between hourly compensation and hours worked. By holding down weekly hours, unions have been able to increase the hourly pay of their members. At the same time, however, while real wages have increased, research shows that a growing number of high-paid workers have found themselves priced out of the market. Businesses are finding it easier to transfer work to other geographic locales than to pay these high prices.

Also, companies are now trying to develop innovative plans in order to increase the number of workers while simultaneously controlling labor costs. An example is provided by Volkswagen's proposal to hire 5,000 unemployed and unqualified workers at a flat salary of DM 5,000 (approximately $2,200) per month. Depending on auto demand, seasonal fluctuations, and workers' speed in fulfilling daily production targets, these employees would have worked an average of 28.8 to 42.5 hours per week, including Saturdays. The unions, however, rejected the plan, because they felt it undermined basic pay contracts that set an upper limit of 35 hours a week and called for extra pay for Saturday work.[20] Given the rising cost of labor in Germany, innovative pay schemes are becoming more common, and unions are having to face the likelihood that if companies cannot produce output at competitive prices, they will outsource the work to workers who can. In addition, a growing number of German employees now have "flexible" working hours—night work and weekend or holiday shifts. The number of jobless Germans has increased over the last decade, so that today almost 50 percent of the workforce has to accept these flexible hours,[21] although average hourly wages in many industries still remain relatively high by international standards.

In addition, relative labor costs can shift quickly as a result of changes in country economic conditions. Most directly, changes in nominal exchange rates can result in unit labor costs rising or falling in relation to the home-market currency. Figure 15–4 shows how manufacturing costs (in U.S. dollar terms) rose dramatically in Northern Europe from 2001 to 2002 but fell in Japan and Taiwan, mostly because of changes in the value of the U.S. dollar in relation to the currencies of the other countries.

New Labor Force Trends and Pressures

In recent years there have been pronounced new labor force trends in the international arena. This is particularly true in Europe, and to a lesser degree in Asia, where companies are trying to regain some of the competitiveness they lost through high labor costs. Many of these firms are facing the same challenges that their counterparts in the United States began confronting a decade ago: The workforce is being downsized, and a strong focus is being placed on providing higher-quality output at lower costs.[22]

Unions are fighting some of these recent changes, but a growing number of informed observers seem to agree they will likely have to realize that when national values collide with the realities of global competition, the latter is likely to win. Renault offers a good example. In the 1990s the French auto firm tried to strike a deal with Volvo to build trucks. However, the agreement collapsed when it became clear that Renault would have to cut its

Figure 15–4

Percentage Change in Manufacturing Unit Labor Costs (U.S. dollar basis) in Selected Countries, 2001–2002

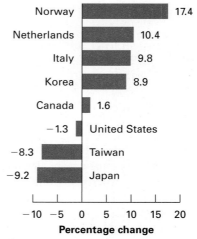

Source: U.S. Bureau of Labor Statistics.

German Unions Become More Flexible—and Do Better

In recent years, unions in countries such as Germany have become less confrontational with management and, as a result, are becoming more successful in persuading companies not to send work elsewhere. This is a turnaround from just a few years ago when German wage levels were not just the highest but were increasing more quickly than those of other nations. What has led to this new flexibility? One answer is that German unions are finding that with high unemployment throughout the country, especially in the east, there is less room for negotiating. They have to accommodate the needs of German firms or risk losing membership through layoffs and plant closings. Moreover, many union workers now seem more willing to adjust their job schedules and accept lower wages in return for continued employment. As a result, in the eastern part of Germany union employees now earn much less than their counterparts in the western part of the country (approximately $32 hourly including benefits). In fact, recent statistics show that hourly rates in the east are very competitive vis-à-vis other parts of the continent, including the Netherlands ($22 hourly) and Italy ($18 hourly).

There are a growing number of German companies that are winning concessions from their unions. One is CED Informationstechnik GmbH, a small firm that assembles personal computers. The company's union contract allows it to cut back the workforce when orders are weak. And since CED focuses on delivery of computers within 24 hours of receiving an order, it has no need to build inventory. So the workforce size is tied directly to the amount of orders on hand, thus allowing CED to operate with a basic crew of only 200 people. In turn, another group of approximately 40 workers has contracts guaranteeing them at least 1,000 hours of work annually, so these people can count on approximately 20 hours a week on average—although this is all tied to work orders. The remaining 300 employees at CED work as needed and can find after a month or two of large orders that things dry up and they have no work for the next couple of months. It is a chance they have to take.

While all of this is a big change from the days when the unions used to dictate terms, it is one that is accepted by both the workers and the CED's worker council. The head of the council explained it this way, "You can only keep your job when the company does well. These agreements have to be adopted everywhere if we're going to protect jobs." This attitude is reflective of a growing number of German unions. For example, the IG Chemie chemical workers union signed a milestone agreement that conditionally allows troubled employers to cut wages in return for job security. The contract, which covers approximately 1,700 companies, is designed to trade wages and other financial benefits for job security. In turn, the newfound flexibility offers the promise of making German industry more competitive than it has been in a long time.

own workforce and close some inefficient production operations. This was not something the firm was prepared to do. Since then, however, faced with competitive reality, Renault has cut 25 percent of its workforce and is continuing to make cost-related changes—and the unions are finding that they must accommodate these new decisions or see work moved elsewhere and members lose their jobs. This strategy has been employed by other European automakers such as Volkswagen and Fiat, which set up new factories in Latin America, Asia, and Europe in recent years. Additionally, companies that fail to proactively revise their labor agreements and become more competitive are going to find competition seeking them out. In Germany, traditionally rigid unions are exhibiting more flexibility in terms of job schedules, wages, and other work rules. The accompanying International Management in Action describes some of these changes.

Another trend affecting labor forces is immigration. A number of major industrial countries need to sharply increase immigration in order to have the necessary workforce to maintain their economic momentum. The United States, for example, has long encouraged immigration and has been able to attract many talented people. Canada has done the same and is currently taking steps to further bolster its pool of skilled immigrant workers.[23] In contrast, Japan, for example, has long opposed bringing in foreign labor, although growing numbers of Japanese business leaders have been urging the government to open the country wider to foreign workers. Demographic data show that this is good advice. A recently released United Nations report presented a dire projection for Japan. In particular, the report notes that Japan will need to bring 609,000 immigrants a year for a half century in order to sustain its working-age population of 87.2 million through 2050.[24]

Germany faces a similar situation, and the fact that its labor market is closely regulated by the government only adds to the problem.[25] As a result, many firms have difficulty hiring all of the people they need. Siemens, for example, recruits extensively at German universities and hires hundreds of graduates each year. However, the big German MNC needs still more engineers and typically finds it hard to get government approval to bring them in from other countries. Siemens is not alone.

> Some German companies, frustrated by how hard it is to import talent, have opened shop abroad. Take Conceptware AG, an Internet-software company based in Eschborn. Half of its 40 programmers here are non-Germans, but despite its relative success in obtaining work permits, the company late last year opened an office in Canada. There, it is now hiring some of the very programmers from India for whom it couldn't get approval from Germany.[26]

In response to this challenge, the German government has been opening wider the door for immigrants.[27] Today, there are over 7 million foreigners in Germany. This constitutes 9 percent of the population, the highest proportion of immigrants of any of the major European economies.[28] In addition, the German government recently approved legislation that will dramatically reshape the nation's current approach to immigration. Each year 20,000 skilled workers will be given permanent residency. In addition, 20,000 more will be given five-year permits to work in sectors experiencing labor shortages, and an additional 10,000 trainees will be given temporary permits.[29] Even with these changes, however, Germany will still face critical labor shortages if it does not further increase immigration; and strong political factions in the country are opposed to even these latest changes.[30] As a result, Germany will undoubtedly continue to face labor shortages in critical areas for the foreseeable future.

Another trend is increased pressure on MNCs to adhere to labor standards and codes of conduct in their global operations. Below we discuss each of these trends.

Part-Time Work and Shiftwork Part-time work is the most widely used form of flexibility in Europe. Today one in seven people in the EU is a part-time worker; and during the last few years this form of employment accounted for more new jobs than did any other. The OECD has estimated that during the years 1983–1996 the percentage of part-time workers in the labor force increased substantially in many European countries. In Ireland it rose from 6.7 percent of the workforce up to 11.6 percent; in France it increased from 9.6 percent up to 16 percent; in Germany it went from approximately 12 percent of the labor force up to 16 percent; and in the Netherlands it zoomed from 21 percent of the labor force up to 36.5 percent.[31] Moreover, far more employers are now increasing their use of part-time workers than reducing it. The greatest increase is occurring in northern Europe.[32]

In the United States there are also a large number of part-time workers. Wal-Mart, for example, employs thousands of them. So, too, does Microsoft, which settled an eight-year class action lawsuit in which temp workers claimed they were actually permanent employees and were entitled to the same benefits as regular workers.[33] Simply put, a growing number of MNCs are using part-time and temporary contract workers.

Shiftwork has become very popular in Europe. In particular, it is widely used in newspaper production, public transportation, utilities, food production, delivery services, hospitals, emergency services, telephone sales, and banking. Additionally, it is very popular with employers in Italy, Sweden, Belgium, England, France, and Germany.

Nonpermanent Employment Nonpermanent employment is any form of employment other than permanent, open-ended contracts. Typical examples include temporary and fixed-term contractual agreements. In recent years, nonpermanent employment has been popular in southern European countries such as Greece, Portugal, and Spain, where it accounts for over 15 percent of the workforce. It is far less popular in countries such as Luxembourg, Belgium, and Italy, where only 5 percent of the employees have nonpermanent employment contracts. As would be expected, all of these workers would like to see the arrangements changed and permanent jobs assigned to them. However, many managers feel there are too many benefits to be derived from the use of nonpermanent employment. These benefits include:

1. Many managers know that work needs to be done, but they do not know how long the demand will last or whether further work will accrue. Nonpermanent employment allows them to hedge on the conservative side. A good example is provided by Rank Xerox, which transformed its United Kingdom copier and printer business in the face of Asian competition. Because Rank Xerox did not know whether it could sustain the growth, the firm chose to use only temporary employees until things became clearer.

2. Employers know that some jobs will require only a limited period of time. A typical example is seasonal work. As a result, they opt for nonpermanent employment arrangements, as in the case of American Express, which relies heavily on temporary workers.

3. Organizations believe that short-term recruitment is a cost-effective human resources approach because very little money needs to be spent on the selection of these individuals. The process can be simple and inexpensive. Additionally, these temporary employees do not get benefits, one of the largest factors in labor costs. These are some of the reasons that British Telecom has chosen to use temporary workers.

4. Enterprises are convinced that short-term recruiting is an excellent way to deal with situations where special skills are needed and the firm neither has the time nor wants to invest the money to develop these skills internally. Additionally, when these workers are no longer needed, it is easy to terminate them.

5. Managers feel that short-term employment is a good way to determine if someone will "fit in" on a permanent basis. British Air and Lufthansa, for example, hire new employees as temporary workers and then, after evaluating their performance, choose those who will be offered full-time jobs.[34]

Subcontracting   As discussed in Chapter 14, subcontracting involves replacing employment contracts with commercial contracts. This approach is widely used in construction where workers simply move from one contract to another or are laid off until the contractor lands a new client. Subcontracting in Europe is also very popular in public sector organizations, as well as in private organizations that prefer to focus on their core business and to subcontract the other activities. Research shows that in recent years there has been an increase in subcontracting in all major Western European countries. Based on their international survey research, Brewster, Mayne, and Tregaskis found that in recent years subcontracting increased among half of the organizations in Germany and the Netherlands and among one-third or more in enterprises in Finland, France, Ireland, Spain, Switzerland, and the United Kingdom.[35]

Many of the subcontracting approaches are quite creative. For example, a Swedish businessman who used to run Saab's human resources department realized that sometimes the company would need to quickly hire more employees to meet increasing work demands and at other times it would have more people than it needed. He then formulated a plan of action.

> If area manufacturers got together and formed a labor pool, they could pluck workers out of it whenever they needed them and give them back when they didn't. [He] took his plan to 10 big companies, including Saab, ABB and Ericsson. Within a few months, he left Saab to start Industrie Kompetens, a sort of temp agency for engineers, skilled technicians and assembly-line workers. One of the agency's temps is Niclas Arkstal . . . a technician who has assembled air conditioners for NAF AB and telephones for Ericsson. At both, he says, he became bored after a while. Joining Industrie Kompetens was the perfect tonic. "It's so flexible," he says, "I don't worry about boredom anymore."[36]

As discussed in Chapter 14, however, subcontracting, especially when it involves movement of work offshore, can raise political and social issues.

Global Pressures for Improved Labor Practices   As discussed in Part 1, MNCs are under increasing pressure to upgrade the working conditions and labor practices of their manufacturing and other facilities around the world. In particular, NGOs and other groups are pressuring MNCs to adhere to international standards and adopt new codes of responsibility.[37] Accusations from student groups, NGOs, and consumers that some companies operate plants that tolerate "sweatshop" conditions have caused significant changes in global labor practices, building on the efforts of international organizations.

The ILO addresses the conditions of workers through its standards and conventions (international treaties), nonbinding recommendations, codes of conduct, resolutions, and declarations. The ILO approved the "Tripartite Declaration of Principles Concerning Multinational Enterprises and Social Policy" in 1977 and revised it in 2000.[38] This document provides voluntary guidelines for MNCs, workers' and employers' organizations, and governments in such areas as development policy, rights at work, employment, training, conditions of work and life, and industrial relations. Although neither MNCs nor governments are bound by this declaration to provide specific labor standards, there exists a procedure for disputes over the meaning and application of the declaration's provisions to be interpreted by the ILO. In 1976, the Organization for Economic Cooperation and Development (OECD) approved a code of conduct called "Guidelines for Multinational Enterprises."[39] The guidelines are nonbinding voluntary principles and standards for MNC conduct in such wide-ranging areas as employment and industrial relations, human rights, environment, information disclosure, competition, taxation, and science and technology. The guidelines were revised in 2000.[40] As discussed in Chapter 3, the UN Global Compact encourages business self-regulation rather than legally binding regulations as the means to support ten core principles covering human rights, labor rights, and the environment.[41]

In addition to UN, OECD, and ILO regulations, the North American Free Trade Agreement (NAFTA) and many other trade agreements include side agreements in which governments commit to enforcing labor standards and allowing for free association of workers. These provisions are a response to union concern that trade agreements can result in erosion of labor standards and loosening of labor laws. In addition, specific industries and companies have adopted labor and human rights codes in response to pressures. Pressures on the sporting goods, toy, apparel and textiles, and electronics industries have been particularly intense, and many industry groups and companies, working with NGOs, have responded.[42]

Social Accountability International (SAI), a human rights organization, established SA8000 in 1997 and revised it in 2001. SA8000 focuses on labor issues, and its principles are based on ILO conventions, the Universal Declaration of Human Rights, and the UN Convention on the Rights of the Child.[43] The SAI code addresses child labor, forced labor, health and safety, compensation and working hours, discrimination, discipline, free association, and collective bargaining. Another initiative is from Rugmark, a nonprofit organization seeking to end child labor in the carpet industries of India, Pakistan, and Nepal. Rugmark is a partnership among development and human rights NGOs, companies exporting carpets from India, the Indo-German Export Promotion Council, and UNICEF-India, which set up a project to devise and regulate a special label for hand-knotted carpets made without the use of child labor. The Rugmark process includes loom and factory monitoring, consumer labeling, and running schools for former child workers. By agreeing to adhere to Rugmark's "no child labor" guidelines, and by permitting random inspections of carpet looms, manufacturers receive the right to put the Rugmark label on their carpets, which provides assurance that a carpet was not produced by children.

Finally, individual companies, such as Nike, have developed and implemented codes of conduct related to the working conditions of their plants and contractors around the world. Here is an excerpt from Nike's code, first developed in 1997:

1. *Forced labor.* The contractor does not use forced labor in any form—prison, indentured, bonded or otherwise.

2. *Child labor.* The contractor does not employ any person below the age of 18 to produce footwear. The contractor does not employ any person below the age of 16 to produce apparel, accessories or equipment. If at the time Nike production begins, the contractor employs people of the legal working age who are at least 15, that employment may continue, but the contractor will not hire any person going forward who is younger than the Nike or legal age limit, whichever is higher. To further ensure these age standards are complied with, the contractor does not use any form of homework for Nike production.

3. *Compensation.* The contractor provides each employee at least the minimum wage, or the prevailing industry wage, whichever is higher; provides each employee a clear, written accounting for every pay period; and does not deduct from employee pay for disciplinary infractions.

4. *Benefits.* The contractor provides each employee all legally mandated benefits.

5. *Hours of Work/Overtime.* The contractor complies with legally mandated work hours; uses overtime only when each employee is fully compensated according to local law; informs each employee at the time of hiring if mandatory overtime is a condition of employment; and on a regularly scheduled basis provides one day off in seven, and requires no more than 60 hours of work per week on a regularly scheduled basis, or complies with local limits if they are lower.

6. *Environment, Safety and Health (ES&H).* From suppliers to factories to distributors and to retailers, Nike considers every member of our supply chain as partners in our business. As such, we've worked with our Asian partners to achieve specific environmental, health and safety goals, beginning with a program called MESH (Management of Environment, Safety and Health).

7. *Documentation and Inspection.* The contractor maintains on file all documentation needed to demonstrate compliance with this Code of Conduct and required laws; agrees to make these documents available for Nike or its designated monitor; and agrees to submit to inspections with or without prior notice.[44]

Organizing International Industrial Relations

In organizing international industrial relations, a number of factors help to explain the relative degree of centralized and decentralized control and employment flexibility that is exercised. The following compares the organizational dimensions of U.S. and European MNCs that are critical to labor relations:

1. A number of studies have shown that compared with European MNCs, U.S. firms tend to concentrate authority at corporate headquarters, with greater emphasis on formal management controls and a close reporting system (particularly within the area of financial control) to ensure that planning targets are met.

2. European MNCs tend to deal with labor unions at the industry level (frequently via employer associations) rather than the company level. The opposite is more typical for U.S. firms. In the United States, employer associations have not played a key role in the industrial relations system, and company-based labor relations policies are the norm.

3. A final factor is the extent of the home-product market. If domestic sales are large relative to overseas operations (as in the case with many U.S. companies), it is more likely that overseas operations will be regarded by the parent company as an extension of domestic operations. This is not the case for many European MNCs, whose international operations represent the major part of their business.[45]

In addition, when compared with British firms, U.S. MNCs are much more likely to be involved in collective bargaining and strike settlement issues of their overseas subsidiaries. British firms tend to adopt a more hands-off approach and confine themselves to giving advice and guidance to their subsidiaries, allowing local management to deal with day-to-day industrial relations matters. These examples point out that industrial relations practices differ from country to country, and MNCs need to be concerned with coordinating these activities.

A number of alternative approaches can be used in managing labor relations in different cultures. For example, one study found that labor relations often is delegated to the local management, except in the case of pension issues, which are handled by the MNC headquarters.[46] The foreign subsidiary is not totally on its own when it comes to labor relations, however. A great deal of guidance and advice still comes from the home office, and hiring and staffing policies also ensure that headquarters plays a role in industrial relations. In addition, many expatriate subsidiary managers use the same industrial relations approach, or a modified version of the approach, that they used back home.

The linkage between the subsidiary and headquarters often is handled by a home-based industrial relations staff, which provides advice and assistance. This industrial relations staff typically gathers information related to wages, benefits, and working conditions around the world as well as at the location of the particular subsidiary. This helps local managers to determine the labor contract that should be negotiated or, in the case of nonunionized operations, the level of wages and benefits that should be paid.

The MNC industrial relations staff also provides assistance in dealing with labor disputes and grievances. The staff can provide information as to how similar problems have been handled in other locales and can be of particular importance to the subsidiary. Many local managers may be unaware of the variety of approaches that can be used in negotiating labor agreements and resolving related problems.

Information provided by the MNC headquarters industrial relations staff can be used by upper-level management in determining when and where to make changes in production work worldwide as well. For example, if wage rates in France go up 10 percent next year, will this reduce the MNC's competitiveness in that market? If it will, what costs are associated with moving some of this work to the MNC's plant in Barcelona? The industrial relations staff at headquarters can help to answer this question in terms of wages, salaries, and benefits. When this information is coupled with that provided by the staffs in manufacturing, marketing, and legal, the MNC then is in a position to make a final decision regarding the wisdom of transferring the work to another locale.

■ A Final Word

In this book, a great deal has been said about how to effectively manage international operations. In closing, two points merit consideration: the inevitability of joint partnering and the need for ongoing research and learning.

Joint Partnering

virtual corporation
A network of companies that come together to exploit fast-changing opportunities and share costs, skills, and access to global markets.

Current trends leave no doubt that the world of international management will be one of joint partnerships and agreements. Transnationals are increasingly "boundaryless" companies. Sometimes called **virtual corporations,** defined as networks of companies that come together to exploit fast-changing opportunities and share costs, skills, and access to global markets,[47] good examples are IBM, Toshiba, and Siemens. These MNCs created a joint venture to develop state-of-the-art, "benchmark" (best in the world) memory chips. These chips will be able to store 256 million bits of data each, which is equivalent to 10,000 pages of typed text. Large-capacity chips will make it much easier for businesses in the twenty-first century to store information as well as open the door for computer scientists to achieve breakthroughs in areas such as computer speech recognition, machine vision, and computer reasoning.

One main reason for this joint venture is to help control the expenses of research and production. In the early 1990s, it cost approximately $500 million to build a manufacturing plant capable of producing the most advanced chips, which at one time could store 16 million bits of information. By the end of the decade, the cost of these high-tech plants had risen sharply and was in the neighborhood of $1 billion. No computer firm could afford to take such a large risk, hence the need for a joint venture. These types of arrangements will become increasingly prevalent. Here is what Rosabeth Moss Kantor, a widely recognized management of change expert, has to say about such partnering and collaborating:

> To gain strength to compete in more demanding global markets, companies collaborate—e.g., to achieve speed and quality through closer integration with suppliers and customers, to attain scale through alliances, or to redefine an industry. Yellow Springs Instruments lists its strategic partners next to the balance sheet in its annual report. Software companies, for whom ties with independent developers, venture partners, and customers are a critical asset, dedicate senior executives and large departments solely to the management of alliances and partnerships. Companies like Disney that once licensed rights to others and stepped away now want to get more value from those arrangements, using them to gain ideas for innovation or intelligence about new country markets—or to push more Disney-branded product through those channels, with more influence over partners' businesses.[48]

She also notes that this collaboration in a way follows the well-established Japanese keiretsus, Korean chaebols, or the interlocking companies in Southeast Asian conglomerates. However, the emerging arrangement of MNC collaboration tends to be looser, with a wider range of partners and fewer permanent, contractual commitments.

Another reason for partnering is that the success of MNCs depends heavily on a strong worldwide economy, a genuine commitment to helping nations improve the well-being of their citizens, and a willingness to share success with other businesses—MNCs and local firms alike. Akio Morita, the late chairman of Sony and a leading proponent of worldwide partnering, suggested that Japanese MNCs take the following steps:

- Manufacture more products locally in the United States—reducing exports from Japan and creating high-quality jobs for U.S. workers.
- Discover and develop more parts and components suppliers among U.S. firms in the United States.
- Augment U.S. "human capital" by training workers in the most advanced aspects of Japanese production processes, and do advanced R&D locally.
- Build business partnerships, including technology exchanges and transfers, with like-minded U.S. corporations.
- Practice "borderless" policies within Japanese corporations—internationalizing management as much as possible and offering equal training and promotional opportunities to all employees.
- Participate fully as "corporate citizens" in community activities and philanthropic endeavors in the United States, with special attention to supporting education, skills training, and scientific research.
- Work to reduce trade-related imbalances by identifying high-quality companies and products in the United States that can be introduced to the Japanese market.[49]

Such suggestions clearly reinforce the need for cooperation and joint partnering as well as key mergers and acquisitions.[50] They also illustrate that the international environment, now and in the future, will be markedly different from that of the past.

Continued Research and Learning

A great many theories have relevance to the study of international management. Many have been discussed in this book, but all must be continually subjected to review, analysis, and reformulation. A good example is the theory of lifetime employment in Japan. For many years, international management experts have argued that lifetime employment creates a highly motivated workforce and that Western organizations should emulate this approach. More recent research, however, reveals that lifetime employment is less useful as a motivator than as a control tool for ensuring worker loyalty and performance. In return for guaranteed employment, the personnel stay with the firm for their entire career, work hard, and are compliant to management's wishes. Based on an analysis of empirical data collected on this topic, two researchers concluded: "Lifetime employment is offered within a . . . context of loyalty and benevolence based on cultural values. Its impact, however, is to increase the control of Japanese employees by managers."[51] Moreover, these researchers found that lifetime employment was not widely used by firms in tight labor markets, because it was not possible to control the workers, who could easily find jobs with other companies and derived little motivation from such guarantees.

International management research also is important because it generates new hypotheses for testing. For example, as workers in large companies with guaranteed lifetime employment near retirement (55 to 65 years of age), will management replace them with younger people who are not given such guarantees? As the competitive environment increases, will MNCs stop offering these guarantees because they reduce the firms' flexibility in responding to changing conditions? Will young workers entering the Japanese workforce during this decade be motivated by such guarantees, or will they turn them down because they are unwilling to commit their career to one firm in return for job security? These types of questions must be focal points for international management research and learning, because changing economic, cultural, and social environments are creating new conditions in which MNCs must compete. Research can help to shed light on the effect of these changes. A comprehensive summary of research on Japanese management practices concluded the following:

1. The cultural underpinnings of Japanese society are shifting toward Western values, although this shift is not uniform across culture and is not rapid in all sectors.

2. Industrial organization in Japan, especially the keiretsu, will continue to provide competitive advantages and is being extended internationally.

3. Long-range planning is becoming more formal and moving toward a Western style, although it will retain a more visionary perspective.

4. Manufacturing productivity per employee in the United States is rapidly approaching or exceeding parity with Japan. Advantages for Japanese companies appear in certain areas such as R&D and product design, but these appear to be heavily supported by governmental and vertical alliances.

5. The Japanese possess some advantages in the management of quality processes; however, the gap between Japanese and U.S. quality management is closing, though perhaps more slowly than the productivity gap.

6. In neutral countries, the quality image of Japanese products continues to slightly exceed that of U.S. products, largely because of distribution, promotion, and service advantages.

7. The Japanese will continue to invest more heavily in R&D than U.S. firms and to introduce new products both faster and more economically than the United States by using superior organizational, communicative, and integrative arrangements, discriminatory patent protection, superior governmental funding, and exceptional support by keiretsus. These advantages will be aggressively protected and enhanced in the future.

8. Traditional Japanese human resource management practices, including lifetime employment, seniority-based systems, and company unions, are rapidly disappearing and cannot be relied on to produce future competitive advantage. Transplanted Japanese organizations have had limited success in implementing these practices and will make fewer attempts to do so in the future.

9. Because of the rapidly converging parity of U.S. and Japanese productivity and quality, as well as diminishing human resource management advantages, future competitive advantages of the Japanese, if they persist, will derive largely from managerial and organization learning excellence, strengthened by structural systems that promote information amplification, and bolstered by even greater reliance on the keiretsu and the Ministry of International Trade and Industry.[52]

Only time will tell how accurate these predictions prove to be, but such information is valuable to the field of international management.

Research also will play an increasing role in helping to uncover how and why multinationals succeed. In particular, greater attention must be given to research designed to explain why some MNCs do better than others and how the strategies are changing. For example, traditional international business strategy gave strong support to the concept of **strategic fit,** in which an organization must align its resources in such a way as to mesh with the environment. Auto firms had to design and build cars that were in demand, and this might mean a variety of models and accessories depending on the number of markets being served. Analogously, electronics firms had to maintain state-of-the-art technology to meet consumer demands for new, high-quality, high-performance products. Today, successful multinationals do much more than attempt to attain a strategic fit. The rapid pace of competitive change requires linkages between all segments of the business, from manufacturing on down to point-of-purchase selling. In the supply chain and in every phase of operation, there must be attention to value-added concepts.[53]

Today, the concept of strategic fit is being supplemented by the concept of **strategic stretch,** which is the creative use of resources to achieve ever more challenging goals.[54] It is important for MNCs to employ strategic stretch, because without it they find that what is immediately feasible drives out what is ultimately desirable. Multinationals with the greatest amount of resources today will not be the leaders in tomorrow's international arena if they fail to use the creative judgment that is fundamental to strategic stretch. Scarcity of resources can be offset by creativity and risk taking, and this can make all the difference in besting competitors whose primary strength is an abundance of resources. Commenting on this, Hamel and Prahalad noted:

> We believe that companies like NEC, Charles Schwab, CNN, Sony, Glaxo, Canon, and Honda were united more by the unreasonableness of their ambition and the creativity exhibited in getting the most from the least than they were by a common cultural or institutional heritage. If further evidence is needed, consider the less-than-sterling performance of Japan's largest banks and brokerages in world markets. Almost unique among Japan's multinationals, these firms possessed immense resource advantages where they entered world markets. Yet material advantages have proved to be a poor substitute for the strategic creativity engendered by resource scarcity.[55]

Of course, it is unlikely there will ever be agreement on all aspects of international management strategy, if only because the specific environmental demands made on one company or industry will require a response different from that needed in another. However, there will continue to be efforts to find overriding strategic principles that have broad value and can be used by most transnationals. A good example was provided by Sullivan and Bauerschmidt, who surveyed managers of large multinationals in an effort to discover those international management strategy principles that were of most value. They found that three were of critical importance to large MNCs: (1) the ability to optimize efficiency; (2) rapid response to environmental changes; and (3) the ability to develop distinct, proprietary advantages.[56] In the case of small firms, major emphasis was needed on innovation, because this helps to make up for the companies' lack of expertise in international manufacturing and marketing.[57]

Another good example is provided by Kanter, whose research shows that a successful MNC will empower its people and leverage relationships, both inside and outside its boundaries. As a result, a successful MNC will be able to reach farther and faster to both gain and spread knowledge. In this process, it will:

1. Connect its people and partners globally, using horizontal networks to take advantage of all of the resources in the entire extended enterprise of business units, suppliers, customers, and alliances to create value for end users.

2. Craft global strategies and standards but encourage and learn from local customization and innovation, neither commanding everything from the center nor letting each unit or territory act on its own.

strategic fit
An approach to strategically managing an organization that involves aligning resources in such a way as to mesh with the environment.

strategic stretch
The creative use of resources to achieve ever more challenging goals.

3. Use collaborative methods—networks, cross-boundary teams, supply chain partnerships, strategic alliances—to support innovation and then spread knowledge from local innovations everywhere quickly.

4. Shape a shared culture of unity that appreciates and derives strength from diversity, and develop common tools and measurements to put everyone "on the same page," while also encouraging everyone to "break the mold."[58]

In other words, successful MNCs will be connected and innovative and will build strength and competitive advantage from their diversity.[59]

The World of *BusinessWeek*—Revisited

As seen in the opening *BusinessWeek* article, labor relations have a direct impact on MNCs' operation and reputation in the global community. Unions and some manufacturers believe that labor infractions by their Chinese counterparts have given those firms an unfair competitive advantage in the marketplace. By paying employees less than they deserve, argue the U.S. unions, Chinese firms are able to subsidize exports. As trade barriers fall and globalization pushes ahead, one of the keys to success for Chinese firms will be their ability to use their abundant labor in a way that respects workers' rights and does not inflame workers in other countries. For the United States and other industrial democracies, flexibility and adaptability will be important for successful labor relations and improved productivity.

Review the material in this chapter, and then use it to revisit the news story and answer these questions: (1) How are approaches to industrial relations in China and the United States similar or different? (2) What factors allow for wages to be much lower in China than in the United States? (3) What is your opinion about the use of trade laws to pressure other countries to change their labor and industrial relations policies, and what role should U.S. MNCs have in pressing China to reform its labor policies?

SUMMARY OF KEY POINTS

1. Labor relations is the process through which management and workers identify and determine the job relationships that will be in effect at the workplace. In the United States, labor agreements result from negotiation at the union–management bargaining table. In other countries, the approach is different. For example, the labor agreement in Great Britain is not a binding contract. In Germany, however, it is binding, and the unions are particularly influential in determining wages, salaries, and working conditions. In Japan, labor agreements usually are general and vague, although they are legally enforceable.

2. From time to time, industrial conflicts result from disagreements between management and the union. In the United States, these often are resolved through use of a grievance procedure, the steps of which are spelled out in the union contract. In Great Britain, the conflict resolution process often is fragmented and costly, because the system is not designed to deal with such problems.

The approach in Germany is similar to that in the United States. In Japan, industrial conflict is minimal because of the way in which unions are formed and led.

3. Unions have attempted to become internationally active in three basic ways. One is through use of intergovernmental organizations such as the ILO (International Labour Organization) and the OECD (Organization for Economic Cooperation and Development). Another is through transnational union affiliations. A third is by extending domestic contracts into the international arena.

4. Industrial democracy is the rights that employees have to participate in significant management decisions. Such decisions include wage rates, bonuses, profit sharing, vacations and holiday leaves, work rules, dismissals, and plant expansions and closings. Except for the recent emphasis given to empowerment in total quality and human resource management, traditionally defined industrial

democracy is not as widespread in the United States as it is in other countries, especially in Germany and the Scandinavian countries. Some of the most common forms of industrial democracy include codetermination, work councils, shop floor participation, financial participation, and collective bargaining.

5. In formulating a strategy and managing international industrial relations, MNCs can draw on a number of philosophies. The most effective tends to be a geocentric philosophy that is characterized by an effort to understand the interrelationships between the various geographic locations and a strategy to link them with a composite unifying theme. This approach to labor relations can be helpful in dealing with compensation policy issues as well as in providing assistance to the worldwide subsidiaries on labor issues or challenges that they face.

6. In recent years, several notable trends have characterized international labor relations. Flexible work relationships, as demonstrated in the use of part-time workers and shiftwork, and the introduction of temporary workers and subcontracting, are reshaping the international labor relations landscape. In addition, there are growing pressures on MNCs to adhere to specific labor standards and codes in their multinational activities.

7. Trends for the future point to the inevitability of joint partnering and the need for ongoing research and learning. Collaboration will become a way for MNCs to compete effectively in the global economy, and continued international research is needed to learn and to innovate for future success.

KEY TERMS

arbitrator, *479*
collective bargaining, *478*
enterprise unions, *491*
global international trade-union affiliations, *486*
grievance, *479*
industrial democracy, *487*
industrial internationals, *486*
International Confederation of Free Trade Unions (ICFTU), *486*

International Labour Organization (ILO), *485*
labor relations, *478*
lockout, *483*
mediator, *479*
Organization for Economic Cooperation and Development (OECD), *486*
problem-solving teams, *488*
regional internationals, *486*
self-managing teams, *488*

specialized internationals, *486*
special purpose teams, *488*
strategic fit, *503*
strategic stretch, *503*
strike, *483*
union, *478*
virtual corporation, *500*

REVIEW AND DISCUSSION QUESTIONS

1. What are three major differences between the way that labor–management agreements are reached in the United States and in Great Britain? Germany? Japan? Compare and contrast the process in all four countries.

2. How are industrial conflicts handled in the United States? Great Britain? Germany? Japan? Compare and contrast the process in all four countries.

3. A U.S. MNC is considering opening a plant in Germany. What are three labor relations and industrial democracy developments that this firm needs to know about? Identify and describe each.

4. A French firm is talking to state officials in Indiana about setting up a new plant in Terre Haute. What

types of labor relations issues should the company be investigating so that it can have the most efficient and effective operation?

5. How would each of the following philosophical views affect the formulation of strategy and the management of international industrial relations: ethnocentric, polycentric, and geocentric?

6. A Japanese MNC is considering setting up a manufacturing plant east of Los Angeles. How is the firm likely to organize and control the industrial relations strategies and practices of this overseas subsidiary? Are there any particular problems the home office is likely to confront? Be complete in your answer.

INTERNET EXERCISE: CHALLENGES OF A NEW WORLD AUTO INDUSTRY

Labor relations is a critical area for multinationals, especially among those firms that are expanding their worldwide operations. A good example is provided by the major auto firms headquartered in North America, Europe, and Asia, which are now pushing into emerging markets as well as setting up factories in current market locales. Visit four of these firms—General Motors, Volvo, Toyota, and Honda—and find out what they have been up to in the last year. Their Web addresses are the following: **www.gm.com**, **www.volvo.com**, **www.toyota.com**, and **www.honda.com**. At the General Motors site, look closely at some of the new developments that are occurring in the company, review its annual reports, and

examine some of its innovations. In the case of Volvo, look at new developments in the company. In the case of Toyota, focus on both its manufacturing efforts and its community service. At the Honda site, concentrate your attention on recent community press releases and what the company is doing in the area of research and development. When you have finished this assignment, answer these three questions: (1) What recent changes have been taking place in these major auto firms in the manufacturing area? (2) How do you think these changes will impact the firms' labor relations policies and practices? (3) What changes would you expect to take place in the way these companies manage their labor forces in the years ahead?

Brazil

After three centuries under the rule of Portugal, Brazil became an independent nation in 1822. By far the largest and most populous country in South America, Brazil has overcome more than a half century of military intervention in the governance of the country to pursue industrial and agricultural growth and the development of the interior.

After crafting a fiscal adjustment program and pledging progress on structural reform, Brazil received a $41.5 billion IMF-led international support program in November 1998. In January 1999, the Brazilian Central Bank announced that the *real* would no longer be pegged to the U.S. dollar. The consequent devaluation helped moderate the downturn in economic growth in 1999, and the country posted moderate GDP growth in 2000. Economic growth slowed considerably in 2001–2003—to less than 2 percent—because of a slowdown in major markets and the hiking of interest rates by the Central Bank to combat inflationary pressures. President Luiz Inácio Lula da Silva, who took office on January 1, 2003, has given priority to reforming the complex tax code, trimming the overblown civil service pension system, and continuing the fight against inflation. By exploiting vast natural resources and a large labor pool, Brazil is today South America's leading economic power and a regional bellwether.

After winning a landslide victory in 2002 on a campaign to revamp the economy and battle for the poor, President Lula da Silva reassured worried investors when he continued his predecessor's plan of strict financial austerity. Instead of catching the jitters as predicted, the country's bond and stock markets enjoyed stellar returns in 2003 and are still going strong. But within a year, pressure was mounting on Lula da Silva to keep true to his populist roots. After riding a wave of popular support through his first year, Lula da Silva faced sharp criticism from within his own Workers' Party and governing coalition as well as from ordinary voters. Lula has also gained a reputation for being thin-skinned when it comes to criticism; he expelled a foreign journalist critical of his policies. Some feel betrayed by Lula da Silva's rejection of the socialist policies that the Workers' Party has always fought for. In a March 2004

opinion poll, only 28 percent of Brazilians voiced support for the government, down from 41 percent in December. Both the right and the left are frustrated with economic performance, which has grown an average of only 2 percent a year since the mid-1990s. In addition, Brazil has emerged as a leader of developing countries concerned about the imbalance in global trade rules, and Brazil led the "Group of 20" countries responsible for slowing progress in the Doha development round of global trade talks. Because of the same concerns, Brazil also dimmed prospects for a hemisphere-wide free-trade agreement—to the frustration of the United States and other countries, which went ahead with bilateral and regional FTAs to fill the gap.

Brazil's policies toward energy and telecommunications firms that entered the country as part of the privatization wave have also raised concerns. BellSouth, with operations in 10 Latin America countries—Argentina, Uruguay, Colombia, Venezuela, Chile, Peru, Ecuador, Panama, Nicaragua, and Guatemala—announced recently it would sell its operation in southern Brazil. It has more than 11 million subscribers in the region, making it the largest U.S. wireless player there and the second-largest player after Mexico's América Móvil. AES Corporation also pulled out some of its electricity investments because of general instability in the region, difficult labor relations, and lawsuits over service disruptions brought on by illegal line cutting by consumers wanting free electricity.

Questions

1. In your opinion, what are the main challenges facing Brazil?

2. How would a move toward populism affect Brazil's stability, future growth prospects, and attractiveness to MNCs?

3. Do you think abandoning socialist policies is in the best interest of Brazil? Why or why not?

4. How should BellSouth, AES, and other companies address concerns about government policies and labor relations in Brazil?

They're Back

During the 1970s, Volkswagen was the leading U.S. foreign car importer. By 1979 the German firm was selling 300,000 cars and had 2.8 percent of the total U.S. market. The next year saw sales slip to 275,000 units, but because of the general decline of industry sales as a whole, Volkswagen's share of the U.S. market rose to 3 percent, and the next year it did slightly better. However, this was the company's zenith. By 1982 sales had fallen to 160,000, and market share was down to 1.8 percent. The firm was being overrun by Japanese imports and revitalized German lines such as Mercedes and BMW. In an effort to cut costs, the company closed its U.S. manufacturing plant in Pennsylvania in 1988, eventually moving production to Mexico.

In recent years, Volkswagen has made a stunning comeback in the U.S. market. Its biggest initial success was the New Beetle, introduced in March 1998. By the end of that year, the company had sold almost 56,000 of these cars. In addition, its Jetta, Passat, and Cabrio lines all did exceptionally well, resulting in total sales of just under 220,000 units. This was an increase of 59.3 percent over the previous year and the company's best showing in almost two decades. By the end of 1998, Volkswagen held 3.4 percent of the American car market—its highest share ever—and the New Beetle was chosen as the 1999 North American Car of the Year by an independent jury. The award is based on consumer appeal, quality, and driving characteristics. The New Beetle garnered more than double the number of votes of the second-place finisher. Since then, the New Beetle's sales have floundered but the company's overall sales have risen. In 1999 Volkswagen sold over 315,000 cars in the American market and over 355,000 in 2000. As a result, today VW is the number-one European brand in the U.S. auto market. Quite clearly, Volkswagen is back!

Questions

1. What was the logic behind Volkswagen's decision to close its U.S. plant?

2. How critical will labor relations be in helping Volkswagen further increase its market share in the United States? Defend your answer.

3. What would you recommend that Volkswagen do in coordinating its worldwide labor operations so as to produce the lowest-price car and thus further increase its competitiveness?

A Copy Shop Goes Global

After weeks of demonstrations, the Berlin Wall came crashing down on November 9, 1989. The end of Communist rule in Eastern Europe was clearly in sight. At about the same time, Washington, D.C. entrepreneur Paul Panitz was completing his three-year contractual obligation to the purchasers of his typesetting company. After nearly 20 years of running and working in the business he had started, Panitz had no concrete plans for the future.

Paul had two heroes that he looked to for inspiration. One was Duke Snyder of the old Brooklyn Dodgers; the other was Alexander Dubcek, First Secretary of the Communist Party of Czechoslovakia from January 5, 1968, until his ouster by Soviet tanks in August of the same year. During his short tenure, known as the "Prague Spring," Dubcek introduced reforms that presaged the "Velvet Revolution," which occurred about 20 years later.

Thinking of his heroes and having both time and money, Panitz wanted to do what he could for the newly freed people of Central and Eastern Europe. He believed in freedom of the press. He also believed that the way to help people was by creating businesses that created jobs. Paul wanted to do something that would advance both beliefs. His first venture was a loan/equity deal to help a Polish daily newspaper modernize its composition department. But this was a passive investment, and he was left with plenty of time to consider his next opportunity.

On a trip to Budapest, Paul visited a government-run copy center, one of the few copy centers available in Hungary. In fact, copiers that members of the public could use were extremely rare—perhaps not surprisingly: In Communist countries the last thing the government had wanted was for ordinary people to have access to a means of sharing information. The opportunity in postcommunist Hungary was obvious to Paul, and on a return visit home, he contacted me [Ken Chaletzky] and Dirck Holscher, college friends of Paul's who operated a successful chain of copy centers in Washington, D.C., called Copy General. Paul asked us if we would like to help him open a copy center in Budapest. We were a little skeptical about the concept, but we signed on.

Copy General in Budapest: The Beginning

It was now early 1990 and the search for a first store location in Budapest was under way. In a major U.S. city, we would have contacted a commercial real estate agent and asked him or her to show us what was available. Not possible in Budapest in 1990. There was no organized real estate

market. Nearly all retail space—what there was of it—was owned and controlled by the government. Even if you found vacant space, it was never clear with whom you needed to talk. So we spent most of 1990 and early 1991 being led down one blind alley after another. Every time we thought we had a deal, a new complication would arise. Frequently, potential landlords wanted an equity position in the business. At other times, space we thought would be ours alone was supposed to be shared with the current occupant. On one occasion, we drank a celebratory toast with a government official signifying agreement—only to have that official lose his position the next day. It was very stressful.

In mid-1990, we hired our Hungarian country manager, although at the time we didn't know he was going to be the country manager. Paul and Dirck Holscher were looking at a street map on a Budapest tramcar. They seemed to be in need of assistance, and a young man came over and asked in nearly flawless English if he could help. Erno Duda was barely in his 20s. His parents, both well-traveled physicians, had spent a few years in Canada, where he learned English. Erno spent the afternoon showing Paul and Dirck around and shortly thereafter was hired as translator and aide.

Erno was a natural-born wheeler-dealer. If we needed something, he knew whom to see or where to go. In the early days of 1990s Hungarian capitalism, he was a very useful person to have on our team. As our first country manager, he helped lead us through rapid growth during our first five years. After leaving Copy General, Erno went on to become a successful investment banker and later formed his own biotechnology company. He says he owes much of his success to what he learned working with Paul Panitz and Copy General.

Erno Duda's Recollections

"I met Paul when I was traveling on the subway. I noticed two Americans who were arguing about where to get off. They couldn't figure out from the Hungarian signs which stop was Heroes' Square. I went up to them and helped them out, and we started talking; and when we got off the subway, the guy with the baseball hat asked me if I wanted to have a beer with them. So we drank a few beers and talked about all kinds of things. He mentioned the idea of starting a copy center in Hungary. I immediately told him that in my opinion it was a lousy idea because they do photocopying on every corner so he should think of something else. Frankly, I thought he didn't have much business sense whatsoever. I changed my mind later. We ended up exchanging phone numbers and had drinks on a few other occasions. He called me up once because his interpreter didn't show up, and he asked me if I was willing to do fill in. Since he was satisfied with me, from then on he used me as his interpreter/translator. He had a market survey done for him by some consulting company. He paid 5,000 bucks for it and it had maybe five companies listed. I offered to help and got a few friends to go through literally every street in downtown Budapest. We gave him a database of 53 companies (and a lot more detail), and it cost him less than a hundred dollars. I got more and more involved, and after a while it was me who went and figured out things for him and negotiated because every time an American showed up the prices suddenly quadrupled.

"When we were trying to find a bank for Copy General, most banks immediately refused us because they didn't want to deal with companies with only one million forints as base capital, which they thought was not enough. Finally we found a surprisingly flexible bank called Budapest Bank. The shock came when the lady said that she would be really willing to help and the one-million-forint base capital was not a problem but the bank was full. We just stood there with Paul and stared. Then finally Paul asked me to translate the following sentence: 'If your bank is really full, we've just recently rented a large basement in Lonyai utca, so if you can't store any more money in your bank, we would be willing to help.' It turned out that it was not a matter of where to put the money; the bank had no more space for files (they were installing a computer system and were recording everything twice, on the computer and then on paper). It was interesting to see how the banking system changed in two or three years after this scenario. By the way, in the end we did become a customer of Budapest Bank."

Challenges of Operating in a Postsocialist World

Early in 1991, Paul took charge of the location search and found a small store in the basement of a 19th-century apartment building near the Budapest University of Economic Sciences. Renovations began while we looked for suppliers. We thought that finding them would be easy, but it was not. We contacted Xerox, our main supplier in the United States, to arrange for copiers for our new store. Xerox told us they would be pleased to provide us with equipment as long as we were willing to pay 100 percent cash up front. Of course, the latest models were not available in Budapest, so we would have to accept older models. No new equipment and no equipment leases—not what we were used to.

Then we contacted Kodak, which was then still a major competitor of Xerox in the copier business. At the time they had almost no presence in Hungary and wanted one. Kodak offered to lease equipment to us on very favorable

terms. They offered us ramp-up pricing, which meant that the equipment payments would start out very low and then grow as the business grew. Additionally, they asked if they could use our store to showcase their equipment because they didn't have an office in Budapest.

One weakness of the Kodak offer was that they had no service technicians based in Budapest. Service would have to come from Vienna, which meant the next day or so. To compensate, Kodak would provide us with extra equipment at no cost. Another part of our early arrangement with Kodak was that Copy General, which would be open 24 hours a day, would act as back-up for machines that Kodak would install at government offices. If a Kodak copier went down at a government office, we would run the copies free for the customer and send the bill to Kodak. This arrangement provided Kodak with a guarantee that their competition couldn't match, and it provided us with extra business and contacts with government agencies. This symbiotic relationship continued for several years.

During all this time in Budapest, Paul and the Copy General people who visited from the United States needed a place to stay. Most Western businesspeople settled in at the Forum, Hyatt, or Gellert hotels, but that was not Paul's style. He said that it would be difficult to expect our local Hungarian staff to help us build a business if we were staying in $200-a-night hotel rooms while they were living off $200-a-month average wages. This attitude was typical of Paul and signaled the type of corporate culture he wanted to create.

Our initial company flat was located in a working-class district of Budapest a few steps from a Metro station. Later, Copy General rented a new apartment around the corner from the first store. Locating near public transportation was important because company policy discouraged the use of taxis and private vehicles. The public transportation system in Budapest goes everywhere, operates frequently, and is cheap. In the early 1990s, a monthly pass cost about $7. With your photo-ID pass in hand, you had unlimited travel rights. You learned a lot about the locals crammed into a tram on a hot summer afternoon.

In June 1991, our first store opened and was an immediate success. We were the first copy shop anyone had seen that offered self-service copiers. It was quite a sight to see people lined up in front of the store and down the sidewalk waiting their turn to use one of our walk-up machines.

Branching Out: Hungary, Czech Republic, and Poland

Shortly after opening in Budapest, we set our sights on Prague. Steven and Teresa Haas partnered with us and moved to the Czech capital. In keeping with company policy, the Haases rented an apartment in the Pancraz district, which was notorious for a prison that had been used by the secret police and the Gestapo. The company flat was in a dull gray Stalinist-era block across the street from a large state-run bakery.

On their first visit to the small retail store that was part of the bakery, the Haases had difficulty choosing. No one at the counter spoke English, and they spoke no Czech. After a few minutes, one of the clerks went to the back of the store and brought out a young bookkeeper who knew a little English. He helped the Haases with their purchases; then they left. The next evening they were back for their daily purchases. One of the counter people handed them a small folded note, which began "I am the boy from last night . . . ," Roman Petr's way of introducing himself.

Roman became their guide and translator, showing them around Prague. Steve did most of the scouting for new locations. They learned quickly that the best way to find possible retail locations was to knock on the doors of stores in areas in which they were interested. Steve and Roman spent many weeks walking around the center of Prague near Wenceslas Square.

One day they went into an electronics repair shop in Gorky Square. Roman asked a member of the store's staff if he knew of any stores that might be available to rent. He replied, "Yes, this one." Steve and Roman were directed to the government education agency that controlled that building. After much negotiation that store became the first Copy General in Prague. In typical socialist fashion, the store had plywood partitions and two interior levels that disguised the turn-of-the-century architecture. The first step was to gut the store and remove all the "improvements" made by the previous occupants. Uncovered were 15-foot ceilings, curved archways, solid walnut doors and trim, and an intricate tile floor.

Steve and Roman oversaw a major renovation that brought back many long-lost details. The store opened in the late spring of 1992—almost exactly one year after the first Budapest store. It was arguably the most attractive and inviting copy center in Europe, and it was an instant success. Its nonstop hours and friendly, helpful service were a novelty. As you may have guessed, Roman became our country manager, a position he still holds.

With the Czech operation under way successfully, Steve and Roman headed for Warsaw to scout out locations for Copy General in Poland. Again, hard work and shoe leather paid off. A government-run travel agency that needed to downsize offered to share their space in the center of town with us. Our preference was not to share space, but the excellent location made us willing to compromise. Then as time went by and we began our renovations, the travel agency decided they didn't need any of the space, so we had the whole store to ourselves.

For Western businesspeople, the Marriott Hotel was the place to stay. It still is. If a guest at the hotel walks out the front door and continues across the street, he or she will walk right into our front entrance. The airport bus terminal is located in the hotel, which is across the street from the main railway station. At a conference in Washington, [Ken Chaletzky] was talking with the Polish trade minister. He knew Copy General, and he was very curious about how we were able to obtain such an excellent location. It was clear from his tone that he suspected we had bribed someone or had some inside help. Though we had done everything honestly, his comments confirmed what we already knew: There was no better location in Warsaw for our store.

As we opened our first stores in each new country, we continued to expand where we already were. Every bit of profit was reinvested into the business. We kept looking for new opportunities to open Copy General copy centers. By the time we opened our first store in Prague, we had four stores in Budapest. When the Warsaw store opened, there were three stores in the Czech Republic (Slovakia became independent on January 1, 1993).

Russia, China, and Beyond

Copy General now operates eight retail copy centers in Hungary, seven in the Czech Republic, and four in Warsaw, Poland. There are also Copy General locations in Moscow; Riga, Latvia; and Shanghai in the People's Republic of China. In addition to offering in-house facilities management to large corporations, the company has set up on-site facilities for special events. NATO, the World Bank, and the U.S. State Department have all hired Copy General to provide on-site services for their large meetings.

Much of the success of the Copy General in Eastern Europe is due to the vision and persistence of Paul Panitz and the people he chose to join him. Paul seized on an opportunity to "do good" and to make a profit—both among the most noble of American capitalist qualities.

Questions for Review

1. What are some of the general challenges of starting a new business in another country? What specific challenges did Copy General face in Eastern and Central Europe?

2. How important was Paul Panitz's vision to the decision to go into Hungary? How would you characterize his leadership and management style and his commitment to "doing well by doing good"?

3. Compare the recollections of Ken Chaletsky, a U.S. manager with Copy General, and Erno Duda, Copy General's initial country manager in Hungary. How do their perspectives differ, and how do they reflect the cultural values of their respective countries?

4. What lessons (if any) can you derive from Copy General's successful experience in Eastern Europe and beyond?

Source: This case was prepared by Ken Chaletzky of Copy General with assistance from Professor Jonathan Doh and Erno Duda, Copy General's first country manager for Hungary, and is provided as the basis of class discussion. It is not intended to illustrate either effective or ineffective managerial capability or administrative responsibility. Reprinted with permission of Kenneth B. Chaletzky, President, Copy General Corporation.

The Road to Hell

John Baker, chief engineer of the Caribbean Bauxite Company of Barracania in the West Indies, was making his final preparations to leave the island. His promotion to production manager of Keso Mining Corporation near Winnipeg—one of Continental Ore's fast-expanding Canadian enterprises—had been announced a month before, and now everything had been tidied up except the last vital interview with his successor, the able young Barracanian, Matthew Rennalls. It was crucial that this interview be successful and that Rennalls leave his office uplifted and encouraged to face the challenge of a new job. A touch on the bell would have brought Rennalls walking into the room, but Baker delayed the moment and gazed thoughtfully through the window, considering just exactly what he was going to say and, more particularly, how he was going to say it.

John Baker, an English expatriate, was 45 years old and had served 23 years with Continental Ore in East Asia, several African countries, Europe, and for the last two years, the West Indies. He hadn't cared much for his previous assignment in Hamburg and was delighted when the West Indian appointment came through. Climate was not the only attraction. Baker had always preferred working overseas (in what were termed "the developing countries"), because he felt he had an innate knack—better than most other expatriates working for Continental Ore—of knowing just how to get along with the regional staff. After 24 hours in Barracania, however, he realized that he would need all this "innate knack" to deal effectively with the problems that awaited him in this field.

At his first interview with Hutchins, the production manager, the problem of Rennalls and his future was discussed. There and then it was made quite clear to Baker that one of his most important tasks would be "grooming" Rennalls as his successor. Hutchins had pointed out that not only was Rennalls one of the brightest Barracanian prospects on the staff of Caribbean Bauxite—at London University he had taken first-class honors in the BSc engineering degree—but being the son of the minister of finance and economic planning, he also had no small political pull.

The company had been particularly pleased when Rennalls decided to work for it rather than the government in which his father had such a prominent post. The company ascribed his action to the effect of its vigorous and liberal regionalization program, which since World War II had produced 18 Barracanians at mid-management level and given Caribbean Bauxite a good lead in this respect over all other international concerns operating in Barracania. The success of this timely regionalization policy led to excellent relations with the government.

This relationship was given an added importance when Barracania, three years later, became independent—an occasion that encouraged a critical and challenging attitude toward the role that foreign interests would play in the new Barracania. Therefore, Hutchins had little difficulty in convincing Baker that the successful career development of Rennalls was of primary importance.

The interview with Hutchins was now two years old, and Baker, leaning back in his office chair, reviewed his success in grooming Rennalls. What aspects of the latter's character had helped and what had hindered? What about his own personality? How had that helped or hindered? The first item to go on the credit side would, without question, be the ability of Rennalls to master the technical aspects of the job. From the start, he had shown keenness and enthusiasm and often impressed Baker with his ability in tackling new assignments as well as the constructive comments he invariably made in departmental discussions. He was popular with all ranks of Barracanian staff and had an ease of manner that placed him in good stead when dealing with his expatriate seniors. These were all assets, but what about the debit side?

First and foremost, there was his racial consciousness. His four years at London University had accentuated this feeling and made him sensitive to any sign of condescension on the part of expatriates. It may have been to give expression to this sentiment that as soon as he returned from London, he threw himself into politics on behalf of the United Action Party, which later won the preindependence elections and provided the country with its first prime minister.

The ambitions of Rennalls—and he certainly was ambitious—did not lie in politics, because, staunch nationalist that he was, he saw that he could serve himself and his country best—for bauxite was responsible for nearly half the value of Barracania's export trade—by putting his engineering talent to the best use possible. On this account, Hutchins found that he had an unexpectedly easy task in persuading Rennalls to give up his political work before entering the production department as an assistant engineer.

Baker knew that it was Rennalls's well-repressed sense of race consciousness that had prevented their relationship from being as close as it should have been. On the surface, nothing could have seemed more agreeable. Formality between the two men was at a minimum. Baker was delighted to find that his assistant shared his own peculiar "shaggy dog" sense of humor so that jokes were continually being exchanged; they entertained each other at their houses and often played tennis together—and yet the barrier remained invisible, indefinable, but ever present. The existence of this "screen" between them was a constant source of frustration to Baker, because it indicated a weakness that he was loath to accept. If he was successful with all other nationalities, why not with Rennalls?

At least he had managed to "break through" to Rennalls more successfully than any other expatriate. In fact, it was the young Barracanian's attitude—sometimes overbearing, sometimes cynical—toward other company expatriates that had been one of the subjects Baker had raised last year when he discussed Rennalls's staff report with him. He knew, too, that he would have to raise the same subject again in the forthcoming interview, because Jackson, the senior draftsperson, had complained only yesterday about the rudeness of Rennalls. With this thought in mind, Baker leaned forward and spoke into the intercom, "Would you come in, Matt, please? I'd like a word with you." As Rennalls entered the room, Baker said, "Do sit down," and offered a cigarette. He paused while he held out his lighter, then went on.

"As you know, Matt, I'll be off to Canada in a few days' time, and before I go, I thought it would be useful if we could have a final chat together. It is indeed with some deference that I suggest I can be of help. You will shortly be sitting in this chair doing the job I am now doing, but I, on the other hand, am 10 years older, so perhaps you can accept the idea that I may be able to give you the benefit of my longer experience."

Baker saw Rennalls stiffen slightly in his chair as he made this point. Consequently, he added in explanation, "You and I have attended enough company courses to remember those repeated requests by the personnel manager to tell people how they are getting on as often as the convenient moment arises and not just the automatic 'once a year' when, by regulation, staff reports have to be discussed."

Rennalls nodded his agreement, and Baker went on. "I shall always remember the last job performance discussion I had with my previous boss back in Germany. He used what he called the 'plus and minus' technique. His firm belief was that when a senior, by discussion, seeks to improve the work performance of his staff, his prime objective should be to make sure that the latter leaves the interview encouraged and inspired to improve. Any criticism must, therefore, be constructive and helpful. He said that one very good way to encourage a person—and I fully agree with him—is to tell him about his good points—the plus factors—as well as his weak ones—the minus factors. I thought, Matt, it would be a good idea to run our discussion along these lines."

Rennalls offered no comment, so Baker continued. "Let me say, therefore, right away, that, as far as your own work performance is concerned, the plus far outweighs the minus. I have been most impressed, for instance, with the way you have adapted your considerable theoretic knowledge to master the practical techniques of your job—that ingenious method you used to get air down to the fifth-shaft level is a sufficient case in point—and at departmental meetings I have invariably found your comments well-taken and helpful. In fact, you will be interested to know that only last week I reported to Mr. Hutchins that, from the technical point of view, he could not wish for a more able man to succeed to the position of chief engineer."

"That's very good indeed of you, John," cut in Rennalls with a smile of thanks. "My only worry now is how to live up to such a high recommendation."

"Of that I am quite sure," returned Baker, "especially if you can overcome the minus factor which I would like now to discuss with you. It is one that I have talked about before, so I'll come straight to the point. I have noticed that you are more friendly and get on better with your fellow Barracanians than you do with Europeans. In point of fact, I had a complaint only yesterday from Mr. Jackson, who said you had been rude to him—and not for the first time either.

"There is, Matt, I am sure, no need for me to tell you how necessary it will be for you to get on well with expatriates, because until the company has trained sufficient people of your caliber, Europeans are bound to occupy senior positions here in Barracania. All this is vital to your future interests, so can I help you in any way?"

While Baker was speaking on this theme, Rennalls sat tensed in his chair, and it was some seconds before he replied. "It is quite extraordinary, isn't it, how one can convey an impression to others so at variance with what one intends? I can only assure you once again that my disputes with Jackson—and you may remember also, Godson—have had nothing at all to do with the color of their skins. I promise you that if a Barracanian had behaved in an equally peremptory manner I would have reacted in precisely the same way. And again, if I may say it within these four walls, I am sure I am not the only one who has found Jackson and Godson difficult. I could mention the names of several expatriates who have felt the same. However, I am really sorry to have created this impression of not being able to get along with Europeans—it is an entirely false one—and I quite realize that I must do all I can to correct it as quickly as possible. On your last point, regarding Europeans holding senior positions in the company for some time to come, I quite accept the situation. I know that Caribbean Bauxite—as it has been doing for many years now—will promote Barracanians as soon as their experience warrants it. And, finally, I would like to assure you, John—and my father thinks the same too—that I am very happy in my work here and hope to stay with the company for many years to come."

Rennalls had spoken earnestly. Although not convinced by what he heard, Baker did not think he could pursue the matter further except to say, "All right, Matt, my impression *may* be wrong, but I would like to remind you about the truth of that old saying, 'What is important is not what is true but what is believed.' Let it rest at that."

But suddenly Baker knew he didn't want to "let it rest at that." He was disappointed once again at not being able to break through to Rennalls and having yet again to listen to his bland denial that there was any racial prejudice in his makeup. Baker, who had intended to end the interview at this point, decided to try another tactic.

"To return for a moment to the 'plus and minus technique' I was telling you about just now, there is another plus factor I forgot to mention. I would like to congratulate you not only on the caliber of your work but also on the ability you have shown in overcoming a challenge which I, as a European, have never had to meet. Continental Ore is, as you know, a typical commercial enterprise—admittedly a big one—which is a product of the economic and social environment of the United States and Western Europe. My ancestors have all been brought up in this environment for the past 200 or 300 years, and I have, therefore, been able to live in a world in which commerce (as we know it today) has been part and parcel of my being. It has not been something revolutionary and new that has suddenly entered my life." Baker went on, "In your case, the situation is different, because you and your forebears have had only some 50 or 60 years in this commercial environment. You have had to face the challenge of bridging the gap between 50 and 200 or 300 years. Again, Matt, let me congratulate you—and people like you—once again on having so successfully overcome this particular hurdle. It is for this very reason that I think the outlook for Barracania—and particularly Caribbean Bauxite—is so bright."

There was a pause, and for a moment, Baker thought hopefully that he was about to achieve his long-awaited breakthrough, but Rennalls merely smiled back. The barrier remained unbreached. There remained some five minutes of cheerful conversation about the contrast between the Caribbean and Canadian climate and whether the West Indies had any hope of beating England in the Fifth Test before Baker drew the interview to a close. Although he was as far as ever from knowing the real Rennalls, he nevertheless was glad that the interview had run along in this friendly manner and, particularly, that it had ended on such a cheerful note.

This feeling, however, lasted only until the following morning. Baker had some farewells to make, so he arrived at the office considerably later than usual. He had no sooner sat down at his desk than his secretary walked into the room with a worried frown on her face. Her words came fast, "When I arrived this morning, I found Mr. Rennalls already waiting at my door. He seemed very angry and told me in quite a peremptory manner that he had a vital letter to dictate that must be sent off without any delay. He was so worked up that he couldn't keep still and kept pacing about the room, which is most unlike him. He wouldn't even wait to read what he had dictated. Just signed the page where he thought the letter would end. It has been distributed, and your copy is in your tray."

Puzzled and feeling vaguely uneasy, Baker opened the confidential envelope and read the following letter:

From: Assistant Engineer

To: Chief Engineer,
        Caribbean Bauxite Limited

                                    14 August

*Assessment of Interview Between Baker
and Rennalls*

It has always been my practice to respect the advice given me by seniors, so after our interview, I decided to give careful thought once again to its main points and so make sure that I had understood all that had been said. As I promised you at the time, I had every intention of putting your advice to the best effect.

It was not, therefore, until I had sat down quietly in my home yesterday evening to consider the interview objectively that its main purport became clear. Only then did the full enormity of what you said dawn on me. The more I thought about it, the more convinced I was that I had hit upon the real truth—and the more furious I became. With a facility in the English language which I, a poor Barracanian, cannot hope to match, you had the audacity to insult me (and through me every Barracanian worth his salt) by claiming that our knowledge of modern living is only a paltry 50 years old whereas yours goes back 200 or 300 years. As if your materialistic commercial environment could possibly be compared with the spiritual values of our culture. I'll have you know that if much of what I saw in London is representative of your most boasted culture, I hope fervently that it will never come to Barracania. By what right do you have the effrontery to condescend to us? At heart, all you Europeans think us barbarians; as you say amongst yourselves, we are "just down from the trees."

Far into the night I discussed this matter with my father, and he is as disgusted as I. He agrees with me that any company whose senior staff think as you do is no place for any Barracanian proud of his culture and race—so much for all the company "clap-trap" and specious propaganda about regionalization and Barracania for the Barracanians.

I feel ashamed and betrayed. Please accept this letter as my resignation, which I wish to become effective immediately.

cc: Production Manager
        Managing Director

Questions for Review

1. What mistake did John Baker make? Why did he not realize this mistake when it occurred?

2. What would you recommend that Baker do now? Explain.

3. What does this case illustrate about human resource management in the international environment? Be complete in your answer.

Source: This case was prepared by Gareth Evans and is used with permission.

Lord John Browne and BP's Global Shift

To deliver the continuous improvement in performance and profitability that is our fundamental goal, we have to show we are part of the process of sustainable development, beneficial to all.
Lord John Browne, BP CEO[1]

In recent years, BP (formerly British Petroleum) has undergone tremendous changes that reflect its desire to become both a culturally sensitive and a knowledge-based organization. At its core, BP's business is about discovery: locating, developing, and marketing the earth's natural resources. To service the growing global demand for energy, BP must depend on the global communication, technological innovation, and intellectual human capital of all its stakeholders.

BP, the third-largest oil concern in the world, with more than 100,000 employees in 100 countries, now presents itself as innovative and progressive—a far cry from the traditional perception of energy companies. Lord John Browne, who has taken on the task of transforming the company into a dynamic, global competitor, says that BP now stands for "Beyond Petroleum."

Over the years, Browne has focused the company's attention on the environment and other social issues. In 1997, he announced that BP would cut its greenhouse-gas output, generating some consternation among rivals who did not support this commitment. In 2002, Browne stopped all corporate political contributions in the United States. The marketing of the firm has also changed. BP's new corporate logo, a green and yellow sun, signals a fresh approach and conveys a sense of belonging and well-being.

Critics say that BP's new policies have sent mixed signals, especially over its continued use of hydrocarbons. Browne says that the company's new corporate slogan should not be taken literally: BP isn't getting out of the petroleum business altogether. Nevertheless, Browne believes that his progressive stance will be imitated by other companies. By successfully cutting carbon emissions 10 percent since taking over, Browne sees BP pushing the envelope in an attempt to become a leading environmentally conscious concern.

"'Beyond Petroleum' just means we are giving up the old mindset, the old thinking that oil companies had to be dirty, secretive and supercilious," said Browne.[2] With new deals set in the Russian and Caspian areas, BP faces many challenges as it attempts to do its part to change the perception of oil and gas companies around the globe.

Reorganization Under Browne

After taking the helm in 1995, Browne promptly slashed extraneous costs to prepare the firm for future acquisitions. In 1998, BP bought Amoco Corp. for $57 billion. This was the first substantial oil merger since the 1980s. Making deals has been Browne's strength and at the forefront of his tenure at BP. Table 1 presents a list of BP's mergers, acquisitions, and investments. Through these acquisitions, Browne has been able to grow revenues by roughly 400 percent—to nearly $240 billion at the end of 2003.[3] Integral to BP's future success is whether the company can secure a position in Russia, a key player in the future of the oil and gas industries.

Securing future reserves is crucial to growth, but in recent years BP has focused most of its attention on reorganizing its global operations to foster a cultural change—the development and marketing of corporate social responsibility programs worldwide. BP is counting on this "rebranding" to help it stand out from the pack. In today's world of commoditized products and services, company differentiation offers definite advantages.

The first important step under Browne's leadership was the elimination of the old shield logo. Replacing the stuffy insignia with the fresh sunburst logo signaled a change to consumers. Change entails much more than switching logos, but BP believes that the new look and feel in marketing and promotional materials communicate a sense of the corporate-wide change in attitude and perception. This comes at a cost. BP spent $7 million in research and preparation of the new brand and expected to spend another $100 million for implementation and support mechanisms by the end of 2003.[4] To justify the expense, BP is counting on meeting its forecasted annual revenue increase of 10 percent to support these projects. Rebranding is a laborious undertaking—and one that no company can afford to miscalculate. With

Table 1 BP's Major Oil Company Deals

Company	Year	Price
TNK-BP[1]	2003	$7 billion
Veba Oel	2002	$4 billion
Burmah-Castrol	2000	$4.7 billion
Arco	2000	$27 billion
Amoco[2]	1998	$57 billion

[1]Joint venture
[2]Amoco's value at time of merger.
Source: BP.

Browne's leadership and vision, BP looks committed to meeting its objective.

In further support of this cultural shift, Browne created a global mandate to update the work environments of BP's largest regional offices. Beginning with the firm's London headquarters, he wanted the physical layout of the office to accurately depict the cultural transformation occurring within the organization. The redesigned offices were intended not simply as a showcase but as a way to support and encourage the adoption of BP's emerging corporate values of knowledge sharing and environmental sensitivity among all employees.

During 2001, the company redesigned its main office in Los Angeles to create a modern, collaborative work environment. Browne hoped that this new setting would help stimulate employee relationships and information exchange. He believed that knowledge sharing would eventually begin through a sort of osmosis among co-workers. Helping to fuel this culture change was a series of consolidations and mergers with Amoco, Arco, and Burmah-Castrol.[5] According to Browne, these acquisitions played an important role in convincing employees that a change in culture was justified and that the new entity would become a more pleasant place to work.

Another major change was Browne's controversial decision to eliminate all political contributions in the United States. When asked if he believed that this decision would hurt BP's future prospects, he responded, "We'll still get a seat at the table because of our scope and scale. We aren't permitted to make contributions in many places and making donations in the U.S. increasingly seemed somewhat anomalous."[6]

Sharing Browne's Global Vision

As early as late 1997, two years after Browne took over as CEO, BP began to roll out its new marketing strategy worldwide, emphasizing social and environmental responsibility. In 1997, BP announced its support for the Kyoto Protocol, a worldwide agreement that seeks to prevent global warming by reducing greenhouse emissions. More-over, BP suspended all relations with the Climate Change Coalition, an industry-funded organization steadfastly opposed to U.S. ratification of the Kyoto treaty. By 2000, BP had developed roughly 300 international environmental programs.[7] Some of these programs are traditional in nature, but others are intended solely to convey a sense of corporate social responsibility. Enlisting the services of ad giant Ogilvy and Mather Worldwide in 2000, BP spent $200 million in rebranding its image through print and TV. By incorporating the tagline "It's a start" in several of its promotions, BP felt it could deliver a sound message without going completely overboard. Browne was confident that the campaign's subtle approach would create awareness of BP's new programs without alienating consumers.

A miscalculation that disrupted the campaign's momentum was Browne's decision in the fall of 2000 to back the Bush administration's plan to open up the Arctic National Wildlife Refuge to oil exploration. Earlier in the year, the United States Geological Survey estimated that the refuge in Alaska held anywhere from 3 billion to 16 billion barrels of usable oil.[8] With less than a million barrels a day coming from BP's North Slope production facility, BP was pressed to find new sources in the region. In 2000, BP made $560,000 worth of donations to Arctic Power, a move that alienated some of its supporters.[9] Although BP's shareholder value hinges on locating more oil fields, environmentalists were quick to point out the inconsistencies between BP's new marketing efforts and its support of Alaskan drilling.

Protests over BP's stance put serious pressure on Browne. He tried to cancel several million dollars' worth of TV spots advocating drilling for oil in the refuges, but BP was locked in by contracts. Instead of running the ads, BP took the loss. Today, Browne no longer openly supports drilling in the refuge and seems content to let the government tackle the issue. Ronald Chappell, head of public relations for BP Alaska, explains, "I think that the company has sort of decided that the role of corporations in public life is one of standing back and letting governments make decisions, trying to inform public policy but not making political contributions."[10]

Finding an appropriate mix of growth opportunities and responsibility programs has proved difficult, but BP has tried to strike a balance. At the top of the list is a movement toward renewable energy. Despite receiving more than 90 percent of its revenues from fossil fuels, BP is exploring cleaner fuel sources such as natural gas, which emits about half the volume of carbon monoxide of coal. Down the line, BP sees itself as a leading producer of renewable energy sources such as hydrogen, wind, and solar.[11]

In 1999, in preparation, BP purchased Solarex, a solar-power development firm. Shortly after, Browne announced that BP would install solar panels in 200 gas stations around the globe by 2001. These panels are capable of fulfilling all electrical requirements for the site through a nonpolluting energy source. The "Plug in the Sun" program, however, created a strange dichotomy, given the adverse effect of gasoline fumes on the environment. "Our approach is rooted in sound business common sense," explained Dr. Gary Dirks, regional president of BP in Asia. "As we see it, shareholder value and social responsibility support each other. We should view climate change, pollution and all the related environmental issues industry faces as another form of opportunity."[12] In the Philippines, BP placed solar panels on the roofs of huts in rural villages to provide energy. Dirks expressed his belief that overwhelming employee concern for the environment was the main driver for these changes. "It's tremendously motivating for employees," he said. "It encourages innovation."

The Russia Strategy

On August 29, 2003, BP finalized an $8.1 billion deal with Russian oil producer TNK, a large energy firm created in the wake of the Soviet collapse a decade before. After two years of problematic negotiations, the deal marked the first time a Western oil company had been successful in acquiring a major equity stake in a Russian oil firm. Holding a 50 percent share in the new TNK-BP venture, BP is excited about its growth prospects, especially the opportunity to export to Asia and Europe. The deal, which increased BP's oil reserves by more than 50 percent, has been Browne's crowning achievement as company head. "This is an opportunity with very long legs," said Browne in October 2003.[13]

With oil and gas reserves topping 362 million barrels, Russia has been targeted by the majors for some time. Oil production in the area is on a par with that of Saudi Arabia but is growing at approximately 9 percent a year.[14] With fewer opportunities in Asia and Africa, oil and gas firms have consolidated in an attempt to pool resources for exploration. After its merger with Amoco, BP invested heavily in Azerbaijan, Alaska, Indonesia, and Angola. But none of them has the reserves that Russia possesses. In addition, a more investment-friendly environment has attracted interest, much to the disdain of OPEC. Immediately following the September 11 attacks, BP took control of Sidanco, a major Russian oil producer. This initial entry allowed BP to gather knowledge and forge relationships that turned out to be critical in securing the TNK deal.

Today, TNK-BP is Russia's third-biggest oil and gas company, producing close to 1.2 million barrels a day from its main oil fields in West Siberia and Volga Urals (see Table 2).[15] The firm will secure 16,000 additional daily barrels through its Slavneft acquisition pending approval by the EU, Russia, and Belarus.

BP's presence in Russia is not without risks. Although the firm has secured real assets and real cash flows, the economics of the deal don't seem to be as positive as forecasted. As a result of selling off some mature assets and moving capital into the region, margins and returns have been lower than expected. However, most analysts and investors are still optimistic. "John Browne is positioning the company for the next five to fifteen years," an anonymous U.K. fund manager explained. "He's got there early and shut the door on a lot of his Western peers. . . . It's a risky deal, but oil always seems to be risky in this part of the world."[16]

Part of the risk BP is assuming with its new joint venture is that not too long ago BP and TNK were at war. In the late 1990s, BP fought TNK in a two-year legal battle over BP's investment in Sidanco. Ultimately, BP was forced to take a $200 million write-down on its initial $484 million investment. However, according to Browne, the dispute laid the foundation for the merger. "Our partnership started and was tested not by polite conversation, but by tough action," Browne said. "This is a great way to start a partnership, because you get to the point where most people get to after many years, you get to it in the first day. . . . And then you begin to really understand how to align motivations."[17]

Browne has been quick to justify the economic rationale of the deal, but only time will tell if these personalities are able to function together as a unit. Initial results, however, look good. In late September 2003, TNK-BP added $105 million to BP's net income for the quarter, mostly due to rising demand for exports outside Russia. TNK-BP exported roughly 78 percent of its products to international markets, actualizing higher revenues than would have been possible inside Russia's crude market. BP was forecasting production of 1.284 million barrels in the first half of 2004, an increase of 7 percent from 1.2 million barrels during the first half of 2003.[18] From there, Browne believed his firm could grow production by 5 percent in subsequent years. Russian president Vladimir Putin's desire for countrywide modernization raised the ceiling for global oil companies in Russia. But the visionary Browne is quick to point out his overall desire for long-term sufficiency. "I don't think a few days make a difference," he said. "We are in Russia for the long-term."

Consolidating Gains, Challenging Reserves

Following several years of strong financial performance (see Tables 3 and 4), in late March 2004, BP pledged to return extra cash to shareholders and to slow the acquisition strategy that had characterized its approach over the preceding half decade. During a presentation to analysts and investors, BP's chief financial officer, Byron Grote, said, "Shareholders have been patient while our portfolio developed. Now we're committed to delivering to our owners their rewards." Lord Browne announced BP's intention to "distribute 100 percent of all excess free cash flow to our shareholders" in the next three years, as long as oil prices stayed over $20 a barrel.[19]

In early 2004, Royal Dutch/Shell Group faced a growing accounting scandal over reserve estimates, which led to the dismissal or resignation of several Shell Group executives, including the CEO. The scandal also resulted in the reduction of Shell's reserve estimates by 4.35 billion barrels down to about 15 billion barrels. Removing those reserves from its books meant that the company had only 10.2 years' worth of reserves based on its current production rates, at least two years less than its closest peers, Exxon Mobil, BP, Chevron-Texaco, and Total SA. The reserve reductions meant that

Table 2 BP's Access to Russian Reserves

	Production (Jan.–June 2003)	Total Reserves
Volga Urals	400,000	5 billion
West Siberia	830,000	20 billion
East Siberia	0	5 billion
Total	1.2 million	30 billion

Source: BP.

Table 3 **BP Income Statement (for the year ended December 31) ($ million)**

	1999	2000	2001	2002	2003
Turnover	101,180	161,826	175,389	180,186	236,045
Less: Joint ventures	(17,614)	(13,764)	(1,171)	(1,465)	3,474
Group turnover	83,566	148,062	174,218	178,721	232,571
Replacement cost of sales	(68,615)	(120,797)	(147,001)	(155,528)	(202,041)
Production taxes	(1,017)	(2,061)	(1,689)	(1,274)	(1,723)
Gross profit	13,934	25,204	25,528	21,919	28,807
Distribution and administration expenses	(6,064)	(9,331)	(10,918)	(12,632)	(14,072)
Exploration expense	(548)	(599)	(480)	(644)	(542)
	7,322	15,274	14,130	8,643	14,193
Other income	414	805	694	641	786
Group replacement cost operating profit	7,736	16,079	14,824	9,284	14,979
Share of profits of joint ventures	555	808	443	346	923
Share of profits of associated undertakings	603	792	760	616	511
Total replacement cost operating profit	8,894	17,679	16,027	10,246	16,413
Restructuring costs	(1,943)	—	—	—	—
Profit (loss) on sale of fixed assets	(700)	88	603	1,201	859
Profit (loss) on sale of businesses	363	132	(68)	(33)	(28)
Merger expenses	—	—	—	—	—
Replacement cost profit before interest and tax	6,614	17,899	16,562	11,414	17,244
Stock holding gains (losses)	1,728	728	(1,900)	1,129	16
Historical cost profit before interest and tax	8,342	18,627	14,662	12,543	17,260
Interest expense	(1,316)	(1,770)	(1,670)	(1,279)	(851)
Profit before taxation	7,026	16,857	12,992	11,264	16,409
Taxation	(2,322)	(6,648)	(6,375)	(4,342)	(5,972)
Profit after taxation	4,704	10,209	6,617	6,922	10,437
Minority shareholders' interest (MSI)	(138)	(89)	(61)	(77)	(170)
Profit for the year	4,566	10,120	6,556	6,845	10,267
Distribution to shareholders	(3,884)	(4,625)	(4,935)	(5,375)	(5,753)
Retained profit (deficit) for the year	682	5,495	1,621	1,470	4,514
Replacement cost results[a]					
Historical cost profit for the year	4,566	10,120	6,556	6,845	10,267
Stock holding (gains) losses net of MSI	(1,728)	(728)	1,900	(1,104)	(16)
Replacement cost profit for the year	2,838	9,392	8,456	5,741	10,251
Exceptional items, net of tax and MSI	1,824	(78)	(165)	(1,043)	(708)
Replacement cost profit before exceptional items	4,662	9,314	8,291	4,698	9,543

[a]Replacement cost profit excludes stock holding gains and losses. The effect of this is to set against income for the period the average cost of supplies incurred in the same period rather than applying costs obtained by using the first-in first-out method. Profit on the replacement cost basis therefore reflects more immediately changes in purchase and provides an indication of the underlying trend in trading performance in a continuing business. This basis is used to assist in the interpretation costs of operating profit.

Shell had reserves to replace only 61 percent of the oil and natural gas it refined between 2001 and 2003, according to Wood Mackenzie, an Edinburgh, Scotland, energy consultant. In the same period, BP replaced 155 percent and Exxon Mobil replaced 109 percent, suggesting that BP was in a strong reserve position in relation to its rivals.[20]

At the same time, however, BP faced a different challenge related to reserves. Russia's secret service announced it was investigating TNK-BP because it believed that TNK may have divulged information about Russia's oil reserves—information that by law is a state secret in Russia. "We do indeed have a problem, as everything

Table 4 **BP Group Balance Sheet (for year ended December 31) ($ million)**

	1999	2000	2001	2002	2003
Tangible assets[a]					
Exploration and Production	34,442	46,751	48,270	52,204	53,832
Gas, Power and Renewables	1,053	1,440	1,644	1,600	1,869
Refining and Marketing	8,651	17,619	16,903	22,433	24,255
Chemicals	7,780	8,360	9,242	10,080	10,591
Other businesses and corporate	705	1,003	1,351	1,365	1,364
	52,631	75,173	77,410	87,682	91,911
Intangible assets[a]	3,344	17,897	16,489	15,566	13,642
Investments[a]					
Net investment in joint ventures[b]	5,204	2,884	3,861	4,031	11,009
Associated undertakings	4,254	5,375	5,433	4,626	4,870
Other	571	3,414	2,669	2,154	1,675
	10,029	11,673	11,963	10,811	17,544
Total fixed assets	66,004	104,743	105,862	114,059	123,107
Current assets					
Business held for resale	—	636	—	—	—
Stocks	5,124	9,234	7,631	10,181	11,617
Debtors	16,802	28,418	26,669	33,150	40,716
Investments	220	661	450	215	185
Cash at bank and in hand	1,331	1,170	1,358	1,520	1,947
	23,477	40,119	36,108	45,066	54,465
Creditors—amounts falling due within one year					
Finance debt	4,900	6,418	9,090	10,086	9,456
Other creditors	18,375	32,110	28,524	36,215	41,128
Net current assets (liabilities)	202	1,591	(1,506)	(1,235)	3,881
Total assets less current liabilities	66,206	106,334	104,356	112,824	126,988
Creditors—amounts falling due after one year					
Finance debt	9,644	14,772	12,327	11,922	12,869
Other creditors	2,245	3,842	3,086	3,455	6,090
Provisions for liabilities and charges					
Deferred taxation	7,953	10,595	11,702	13,514	15,272
Other provisions	8,272	10,973	11,482	13,886	15,693
Net assets	38,092	66,152	65,759	70,047	77,063
MSI—equity	1,061	568	598	638	1,125
BP shareholders' interest	37,031	65,584	65,161	69,409	75,938
Represented by					
Called up share capital	4,892	5,653	5,629	5,616	5,552
Share premium account	3,354	3,385	3,590	3,794	3,957
Capital redemption reserve	330	385	424	449	523
Merger reserve	697	26,869	26,983	27,033	27,077
Other reserves	—	456	223	173	129
Profit and loss account	27,758	28,836	28,312	32,344	38,700
Capital and reserves	37,031	65,584	65,161	69,409	75,938

(Continued)

Table 4   **BP Group Balance Sheet (for year ended December 31) ($ million)** *(Continued)*

	1999	2000	2001	2002	2003
[a]**Fixed asset revaluation adjustment and goodwill consequent upon the ARCO and Burmah-Castrol acquisitions**					
Tangible assets	—	9,085	6,787	**5,804**	**3,983**
Intangible assets	—	12,927	11,663	**10,439**	**9,125**
Fixed asset investments	—	584	432	**429**	**254**
	—	22,596	18,882	**16,672**	**13,362**
[b]**Net investment in joint ventures**					
Gross assets	9,948	3,641	4,661	**4,829**	**16,485**
Gross liabilities	4,744	757	800	**798**	**(5,111)**
	5,204	2,884	3,861	**4,031**	**11,009**

concerning oil reserves falls into the category of state se-cret," a TNK official told the *Vedomosti* business daily. TNK called for reforms to make it possible for foreign in-vestors to operate in Russia's oil sector without violating these laws.[21]

Questions for Review

1. Discuss John Browne's leadership style. How would you characterize his approach to global management?

2. How much of an impact do you think BP's marketing efforts will have on shareholder value?

3. Discuss the pros and cons of BP's strategy in Russia, both short-term and long-term. What challenges has BP faced in its effort to become a major player in Russia?

4. Do you think Browne's initial plan to back the U.S. government's proposal to open up the Arctic National Wildlife Refuge in Alaska was a mistake? If so, why?

5. Discuss the difficulties of simultaneously securing growth and promoting social responsibility for oil and gas firms. What are the major challenges?

6. Given BP's huge commitment to rebranding itself as "socially responsible," do you think customers will believe this message from a company that, by nature, contributes to environmental pollution? What other relationships/associations could BP develop that would be more credible?

7. Do you view corporate social responsibility initiatives as a barrier to entry for new oil and gas concerns? Explain.

Exercise

You and your group (teams of no more than four) are about to explore the possibilities of putting a BP office in Russia. Debate and discuss the pros and cons of establishing a head-quarters in Russia. Be sure to discuss the impact of the EU, the state of the Russian economy, and environmental issues.

Source: © McGraw-Hill/Irwin. This case was prepared by Professor Jonathan Doh and Erik Holt of Villanova University as the basis for class discussion. It is not intended to illustrate either effective or ineffective managerial capability or administrative responsibility.

Chiquita's Global Turnaround

Synopsis

On January 12, 2004, Chiquita named Fernando Aguirre as the company's new president and CEO, replacing Cyrus Freidhem, who had held the position since the company's emergence from bankruptcy in March 2002. In his 23 years with Cincinnati-based Procter & Gamble (P&G), Aguirre served in a variety of positions, including president of P&G Brazil and president of P&G Mexico. In his first remarks to Chiquita employees and investors, Aguirre reiterated the importance of corporate responsibility: "In terms of managing businesses and people, while I am profit-conscious, I make decisions first and foremost based on values and principles. In that respect, I'm proud to be joining a company with Core Values that guide day-to-day operations and one where corporate responsibility is an important part of our company culture."[1]

Over the past three years, social responsibility has become the watchword of this traditional company with midwestern roots but a checkered history. In 2004, Chiquita scarcely resembled the company that once held a reputation as cold, uncaring, and indifferent, frustrated with mediocre returns, a lack of innovation, and a demoralized workforce. Throughout the 20th century, hostile relationships with its labor unions and employees and a reputation for immorality solidified by the actions of its predecessor company, United Fruit, helped to slow Chiquita's growth. In addition, by the late 1990s, consumption of bananas had declined in major markets, and Chiquita's position in Europe had been compromised by the European Union's preferential import relationships with its members' former colonies in the Caribbean, Africa, and the Pacific. These factors helped push Chiquita to seek Chapter 11 bankruptcy protection in November 2001.

Through a serious and dedicated internal analysis, a thorough reevaluation of its core mission and business principles, and a concerted effort to reach out to some of its primary stakeholders—such as employees—who had become disenchanted and alienated, by early 2003, Chiquita had engineered the beginnings of a turnaround. One of the most impressive aspects of this recovery was Chiquita's success in redirecting and redefining its reputation through a more open and transparent approach to its global operations and to the various stakeholder groups with which it interacted. In addition, Chiquita had substantially reformed its labor practices and relations and initiated a set of projects in sustainable development and community action in its various locations around the world. Both labor unions and nongovernmental organizations (NGOs) lauded these steps.

Yet, despite Chiquita's apparent turnaround, lingering problems remained in financial performance, organizational efficiency, and a strategy for the future. How could Chiquita sustain the positive momentum from its turnaround in reputation and employee relations to deliver improved and sustainable business performance in a global industry environment plagued by low margins and intense competition?

Chiquita's Background

Chiquita Brands International Inc. is a multinational producer, distributor, and marketer of bananas and other fresh produce. The company also distributes and markets fresh-cut fruit and other branded, value-added fruit products. Approximately 60 percent of its 2003 revenues of $2.6 billion came from bananas.[2] The banana division consists of 19,000 employees, mainly working on more than 100 banana farms in five Latin American countries: Guatemala, Honduras, Costa Rica, Panama, and Colombia. Approximately 45 percent of all bananas sold by Chiquita are from Chiquita-owned farms; independent suppliers in Latin America produce the remainder. Chiquita is one of the global market leaders in banana supply and production (see Table 1). Since Chiquita's exports are often a substantial part of the foreign trade of the Latin American countries in which the company operates, relationships with suppliers, workers' unions, and communities are critical elements for success.

Chiquita sources bananas from many developing Latin American countries, countries that historically have struggled with poverty, literacy, access to affordable health care, and limited infrastructure. The image of the banana industry has long been tarnished by its historical support of the failed U.S. invasion of Cuba in 1961, child labor, unsafe working conditions, sexual discrimination, low wages, and accusations of serious brutality against unionizing

Table 1   **Banana World Market Share Leaders, 1999 and 2002**

	2002	1999
Chiquita	23%	25%
Dole	25%	25%
Del Monte	16%	15%
Fyfess	8%	8%
Noboa	11%	11%

Source: Banana Link.

workers.[3] Chiquita's reputation was damaged by past events, notably those associated with its predecessor company, United Fruit. These included allegations of the company's participation in labor rights suppression in Colombia in the 1920s, the use of company ships in the U.S. government–backed overthrow of the Guatemalan government in 1954, and involvement in a bribery scandal in Honduras in 1975.[4] In the 1980s and 1990s, Chiquita clearly projected a defensive and protective culture, conveying a closed-door impression of its policies and practices.

Because bananas are produced all year long, local communities are closely tied together by the performance of farms. Many employees live in houses owned by the company, most of which are located on the farms themselves. In many areas, Chiquita provides electricity, potable water, medical facilities, and other basic services.[5] However, labor relations remained strained throughout the 1980s and 1990s.

Chiquita's Downward Spiral

Although Chiquita improved its environmental procedures throughout the 1990s, many human rights groups, including Banana Link and US/Labor Education in the Americas, organized an outspoken campaign against all banana companies to improve social conditions on their plantations. One morning in early 1998, executives at Chiquita were devastated to see their company splashed all over the newspapers after an undercover investigation into "dangerous and illegal business practices" throughout Chiquita's Latin American operations. This was a watershed moment for the company.

The *Cincinnati Enquirer,* a paper based in the same town as Chiquita's corporate headquarters, printed an exposé contending that Chiquita was guilty of "labor, human rights, environmental and political violations in Central America."[6] Although the newspaper was later forced to retract the series after it was discovered that a reporter had illegally penetrated Chiquita's voice-mail system, the damage was done. Corporate image was further damaged when the firm emphasized the violation of its privacy instead of addressing the possible validity of the claims made. According to Jeff Zalla, current corporate responsi-

bility officer at Chiquita, the strategy backfired. "It left some people with an unsavory impression of our company," he said.[7]

Damaging media coverage and a renewed desire to evaluate its own ethics performance and gain support for a common set of values and standards for environmental and social performance served as catalysts for the institution of corporate social responsibility policies at Chiquita. After recognizing the need for a complete corporate makeover, Chiquita's then CEO, Steve Warshaw, declared his commitment to leading in the area of corporate responsibility and pledged that the company would do much more than just repair previous damage. Four years later, despite changes in the executive management group, Chiquita's corporate social responsibility programs were a positive example of leading responsibility change in today's multinational business environment.

In January 2001, Chiquita announced that it could no longer pay the interest on its $862 million debt. The fiercely competitive banana industry, downward trends in prices due to excess supply, EU restrictive trade quotas, poor labor-union relations, and the market view of bananas as a low-margin commodity, all contributed to Chiquita's bankruptcy filing. Chiquita attributed much of the responsibility to the European Union. In 1993, the EU imposed quotas that gave preferential treatment to banana imports from ACP (Africa, Caribbean, and Pacific) countries that were former European colonies, ostensibly to help these former European colonies boost their international trade and commerce. Before the 1993 act, 70 percent of the bananas sold in Europe came from Latin America, and Chiquita had a 22 percent share of the world's banana market.[8] After the quotas were imposed, Chiquita claimed that its European market share was cut in half, costing $200 million a year in lost earnings.

Although many of its difficulties were intensified by the EU policy, Chiquita's problems had begun to develop before the 1993 decision. Most important, miscalculations of increases in European demand in the 1990s resulted in an oversupply, leading to depressed banana prices worldwide. Although prices recovered somewhat (see Table 2),

Table 2   **Banana Prices: Regional Year-over-Year Percentage Change, 2003 vs. 2002**

Region	Q1, 03	Q2, 03	Q3, 03	Q4, 03	Year
North America	3%	−4%	1%	−2%	−1%
European core markets—US$	11%	12%	5%	18%	12%
European core markets—local currency	−9%	−10%	−9%	0%	−7%
Central & E. Europe/Mediterranean—US$	4%	−3%	4%	2%	−2%
Central & E. Europe/Mediterranean—local currency	−15%	−22%	−10%	−14%	−19%
Asia—US$	−7%	0%	3%	12%	0%
Asia—local currency	−18%	−7%	3%	6%	−5%

Source: Company reports.

Table 3   Key Developments in Chiquita's History

1899:   United Fruit Company is created through a merger of fruit companies.

1903:   The company's listed on the New York Stock Exchange; it builds refrigerated ships.

1918:   Thirteen banana ships are lost after being commissioned by Allied forces in World War I.

1941:   Allied forces in World War II commission company ships, and the banana industry nearly shuts down.

1945:   Twenty-seven ships and 275 men on company ships are lost serving Allied forces.

1950:   The company starts massive postwar banana-planting projects.

1961:   Company ships provide support for failed U.S. invasion of Cuba.

1964:   The company begins a large-scale branding program for produce and starts using banana stickers bearing the Chiquita name.

1970:   United Fruit merges with AMK Corp. and becomes United Brands Company.

1975:   United Brands is involved in Honduran bribery scandal, which leads to enactment of U.S. Foreign Corrupt Practices Act. Company stocks plunge, and CEO Eli Black commits suicide.

1990:   United Brands changes name to Chiquita Brands International.

1993:   EU banana regulations cut Chiquita's market share by more than 50 percent. Chiquita begins working with Rainforest Alliance and Better Banana Project.

1994:   Start of the "banana wars" between the EU and WTO. Follows complaints by Chiquita that EU favors Caribbean banana suppliers over Latin American importers.

1998:   Chiquita becomes largest U.S. private-label fruit canner. Becomes first large company to meet with COLSIBA, an affiliation of Latin America banana unions.

1999:   Faces possible auction proposed by large shareholder American Financial Group.

2000:   Adopts expanded code of conduct. All 115 Chiquita-owned farms achieve Better Banana certification.

2001:   Restructures debt after stopping payments on $862 million loan, cites prejudiced trade pacts by EU.

2001:   Files for Chapter 11 bankruptcy protection.

2001:   Issues first (2000) corporate responsibility report.

2002:   Chiquita shareholders and bondholders support reorganization plan.

2002:   Issues 2001 corporate responsibility report.

2003:   Chiquita reports positive net income under reorganized company.

2003:   SustainableBusiness.com names Chiquita one of the top 20 sustainable stock picks for the second year in a row.

CEO Keith Linder blamed $284 million in losses in 2001 on a "decline in product quality resulting from an extraordinary outbreak of disease and unusual weather patterns."[9] Table 3 provides a comprehensive summary of key developments in Chiquita's history.

Dispute over Access to European Banana Markets

Chiquita has long claimed that its recent struggles are a direct result of the 1993 EU decision to put restrictive quotas on imports from Latin American suppliers. Immediately after the decision by the EU in 1993 to extend preferential quotas to its former Caribbean and African colonies, Chiquita took the issue to the U.S. Trade Representative, suggesting violations of free trade. In 1994, a General Agreement on Tariffs and Trade (GATT) panel ruled that the new regime violates GATT obligations, but the EU blocked adoption of the ruling by the full GATT. In 1996, the United States, along with Ecuador, Guatemala, Honduras, and Mexico, challenged the new regime under the new World Trade Organization (WTO) dispute-settlement mechanism, which came into force after the Uruguay Round of GATT negotiations.

In May 1997, a WTO panel ruled that the EU bananas import regime violated WTO obligations under the General Agreement on Trade in Services and the Agreement on Import Licensing Procedures. In September 1997, the WTO Appellate Body upheld the panel ruling, granting the EU 15 months, until January 1, 1999, to comply with the ruling. In January 1999, the deadline for EU compliance expired, and the United States sought WTO authorization to impose retaliatory tariffs. In April 1999, the WTO Dispute Settlement Body authorized U.S. retaliatory tariffs amounting to $191.4 million a year—the level of damage to U.S. companies calculated by arbitrators—and the United States immediately began steps to withhold liquidation of European imports, the first step in the imposition of the tariffs.[10]

In April 2001, the United States and the European Commission announced that they had reached agreement resolving their dispute. The agreement took effect on July 1, 2001, at which time the United States suspended the retaliatory sanctions imposed on EU imports in 1999. Import volumes of bananas were returned to levels comparable to those prior to 1993, and the EU committed to moving to a tariff-only system in 2006 as part of its overall WTO obligations.

The dispute has taken its toll on the banana trade by creating uncertainty for smaller producers reliant on EU markets under the quota system, and for large producers such as Chiquita that were forced to expend considerable financial and other resources in the course of the dispute.

Corporate Responsibility

Chiquita had begun to initiate corporate responsibility projects in 1992 when it adopted Better Banana Project standards designed to improve environmental and worker conditions on its farms. Then, after the 1998 exposé in the *Cincinnati Enquirer,* Chiquita management began to conduct a series of broader companywide reviews of its conduct, policies, and internal and external operations and relationships, all designed to integrate corporate responsibility throughout the company's operations.

In 1998, Chiquita initiated several projects aimed at implementing its corporate responsibility efforts worldwide. Two internal groups were formed: the Senior Management Group and the Corporate Responsibility Steering Committee. The former consists of eight top managers of Chiquita's global businesses, including the president/CEO and COO of banana operations. The Senior Management Group is ultimately responsible for providing strategic vision and leadership for corporate responsibility. The Steering Committee, also consisting of eight members, was constructed to help streamline corporate social responsibility policies throughout each operational area of the firm.

In August 1999, Chiquita adopted the four key values that now guide all strategic business decision making worldwide. After a year of discussions, interviews, and debates on the merits of an internal corporate social responsibility policy, Chiquita defined the following four core values:

> *Integrity:* We live by our Core Values. We communicate in an open, honest and straightforward manner. We conduct our business ethically and lawfully.
>
> *Respect:* We treat people fairly and respectfully. We recognize the importance of family in the lives of our employees. We value and benefit from individual and cultural differences. We foster individual expression, open dialogue and a sense of belonging.
>
> *Opportunity:* We believe the continuous growth and development of our employees is key to our success. We encourage teamwork. We recognize employees for their contributions to the company's success.
>
> *Responsibility:* We take pride in our work, in our products and in satisfying our customers. We act responsibly in the communities and environments in which we live and work. We are accountable for the careful use of all resources entrusted to us and for providing appropriate returns to our shareholders.[11]

In support of the four core values, Chiquita undertook reforms to link its corporate governance and corporate responsibility policies. These reforms included expanding the role of the board's Audit Committee to oversee the firm's corporate responsibility (CR) mission and to evaluate whether the firm had the right people, policies, and programs in place to properly advance the CR agenda.[12] In addition, in May 2000, Chiquita appointed a full-time vice president and CR officer responsible for all aspects of corporate social responsibility. According to Chiquita, the four core values, supported by the senior management group and CR committee, have helped drive responsibility change throughout the entire organization. Each business decision must be evaluated through the lens of CR policies.

Chiquita also began to realize that a corporate social responsibility platform could mean a competitive advantage in the banana market. Dennis Christou, vice president of marketing–Europe, explained: "Bananas are, by definition, a commodity and U.K. consumers do not generally see fruit as branded. Chiquita is trying to change this. We have a brand because we own certain values and a relationship with consumers. And we communicate with them. They have expectations about Chiquita."[13] In particular, environmental and social performance is of keen interest to some leading European customers. In 2002, 56 percent of Chiquita's sales in northern European markets were to customers who had either inspected farms or formally asked questions about environmental and social performance. This was a 5 percent increase—about 13,000 40-pound boxes per week—over the prior year.

Chiquita also strengthened its commitment to the Better Bananas Project. Under this program, external auditors audit all Chiquita farms annually. The Rainforest Alliance has annually accredited every Chiquita farm since 2000. Chiquita also encourages its independent producers, which supply Chiquita with about 50 percent of its bananas, to achieve Rainforest Alliance certification. In 2002, the volume of bananas purchased from certified farms rose from 33 to 46 percent, and farms certified through June 2003 brought the total to 65 percent. Table 4 presents the nine principles of the Better Banana Project. According to insiders, the adoption of third-party standards has helped Chiquita to drive a stronger internal commitment to achieving excellence[14]—and to cut costs. In 2003, the Rainforest Alliance estimated that Chiquita reduced production spending by $100 million as a result of a $20 million investment to reduce agrochemical use.[15]

And Chiquita is receiving increasing recognition for its efforts. In July 2003, SustainableBusiness.com, publisher of *The Progressive Investor* newsletter, named Chiquita to its list of the world's top 20 sustainable stock picks, known as the SB20, for the second year in a row. SustainableBusiness.com identifies its picks by asking leading investment advisers to recommend companies that stand out as world leaders in both sustainability and financial strength. In April 2004, the Trust for the Americas, a division of the Organization of Americas, selected Chiquita Brands as the winner of the 2004 Corporate Citizen of the Americas

Table 4 Better Banana Project Principles

1. **Ecosystem Conservation.** Protect existing ecosystems, recovery of damaged ecosystems in plantation area

2. **Wildlife Conservation.** Protect biodiversity, especially endangered species

3. **Fair Treatment and Good Conditions for Workers.** Comply with local and international labor laws/norms; maintain policy of nondiscrimination; support freedom of association

4. **Community Relations.** Be a "good neighbor," contributing to the social and economic development of local communities

5. **Integrated Pest Management.** Reduction in use of pesticides; training for workers in pesticide use/management/risks

6. **Integrated Waste Management.** Reduction of the production of wastes that contaminate the environment and harm human health; institute recycling

7. **Conservation of Water Resources.** Reduce and reuse the water used in production; establish buffer zones of vegetation around waterways; protect water from contamination

8. **Soil Conservation.** Control erosion; promote soil conservation and replenishment

9. **Planning and Monitoring.** Plan and monitor banana cultivation activities according to environmental, social, and economic measures

Source: Adapted from Rainforest Alliance, *Normas Generales Para la Certificación del Cultivo de Banano,* May 2002, www.rainforest-alliance.org/programs/cap/socios/banana-s.pdf.

Award for Chiquita's Nuevo San Juan Home-Ownership Project in Honduras.[16]

Global Codes of Conduct, Standards, and Labor Practices

In late 2001, Ron Oswald, general secretary of the International Union of Food Workers, was asked if he had seen improvements in Chiquita's internal and external corporate policies. He responded, "Yes. It is a company that is totally unrecognizable from five years ago."[17] Clearly Chiquita had come a long way.

Traditionally, relations between Chiquita and labor unions in Latin America were mired in conflict and mistrust. In 1998, after recognizing the need for change in the way it deals with its line, Chiquita began striving to adhere to SA8000, the widely accepted international labor rights standard. Management struggled with the decision of whether to adopt an outside standard or to develop an internal measurement gauge for corporate responsibility. After much deliberation, management concluded that adopting the SA8000 standard would yield the most credibility with external stakeholders, because SA8000 gives detailed requirements for adequacy of management systems for implementation. Having an external standard forces Chiquita to push CR change down through each organizational level so that the firm is able to meet third-party requirements.

In May 2000 Chiquita expanded its code of conduct to include SA8000. Standards now included areas such as food safety, labor standards, employee health and safety, environmental protection, and legal compliance.[18] Recognizing the importance of labor support and its resounding effect on corporate image, Chiquita began an open dialogue with the International Union of Food Workers and the Coalition of Latin American Banana Workers' Unions (COLSIBA). By June 2001, the firm had reached an agreement with both organizations, paving the way for continuous improvement in labor standards. Management credits this agreement as helping to build a positive image, improving relations with both internal and external stakeholders. In mid-2001, Chiquita published its first corporate responsibility report detailing the firm's future CR strategies and goals. Both stakeholders and media outlets have been impressed with the complete turnaround in the transparency of Chiquita's corporate agenda, which has led to a much more favorable impression of the company.

In order to adhere to the organization's own core values and to the SA8000 labor standard, Chiquita routinely performs internal audits in all of its Latin American operations. NGOs also conduct external audits. After the audits are completed, each local management team plans corrective actions using the firm's code of conduct and core values as decision-making guides. Since 2000, the Rainforest Alliance has certified 100 percent of Chiquita-owned farms annually. In addition, 65 percent of the bananas Chiquita purchased from independent producers in 2003 were Rainforest Alliance–certified, up from 33 percent in 2001. At year-end 2003, independent auditors certified Chiquita's operations in Costa Rica, Colombia, and Panama to the SA8000 standard. Chiquita's operations were the first ever to earn SA8000 certification in each of these countries.

Marketing the Message

Although it would seem advantageous for Chiquita to communicate and leverage the great strides it has made through its corporate responsibility effort, management seems reluctant to promote its achievements through the typical mass communication vehicles. Instead, the firm has opted for a longer-term marketing strategy based on educating leading opinion-makers and critics alike. According to Dennis Christou, vice president of marketing–Europe, there is a natural suspicion among consumers about commercially driven messages. He believes that customers feel more trust in the message if it's delivered by an external body rather than by the company or by a paid advocate of the business.[19] That is a main reason why the firm is relying on viral marketing tactics and third-party testimonials as the means of spreading its message. Retailers are treated differently: They must be exposed to improvements at Chiquita because they determine which exclusive brand to carry on an annual basis. However, Christou believes that creating brand recognition with consumers is possible through nonobtrusive, reputable means.

Defining and conveying a brand's differences in a commodities marketplace is difficult. Nevertheless, Chiquita believes it can carve out its own niche by distinguishing itself as a leader in corporate responsibility. Instead of positioning itself solely on the basis of price, Chiquita is hoping that its distinctive competency in CR will help it stand out from the pack. The company got a boost in this regard in April 2003, when Chiquita, along with Ben and Jerry's, received the first Award for Outstanding Sustainability Reporting presented by the Coalition for Environmentally Responsible Economies (CERES) and the Association of Chartered Certified Accountants.[20]

Recent Performance and Future Path

Chiquita has drastically shifted its strategic decision-making models and broader corporate operating principles. During its reorganization, debt repayments and other reorganization costs resulted in significant losses. Chiquita has made great strides in improving its financial performance by cutting costs and streamlining its local and global operations. For 2003, net sales were $2.6 billion, up from $1.6 billion the year before. Since its emergence from bankruptcy in early 2002, Chiquita has been profitable.

Chiquita's future financial stability depends, in part, on external market factors such as steady or rising international banana prices and consumer demand. Internally, the company's performance will result from the effectiveness of financial controls on the cost side, and successful marketing, emphasizing differentiation and value-added production, on the revenue side. Although Chiquita has gone to impressive lengths to turn around its reputation and performance, it continues to face a challenging and competitive international business environment and must make continuous progress in its management and operations in order to achieve a healthy and sustainable financial future.

Questions for Review

1. How would you characterize Chiquita's historic approach to global management?

2. Describe Chiquita's approach to human resource management in its global supply chain. What particular

---

Table 5   **Chiquita Brands Balance Sheet as of December 31, 2003, December 31, 2002, December 31, 2001, December 31, 2000**

Chiquita Brands International Inc. Balance Sheet as of 12/31/2003 (in thousands)

	2003	2002	2001	2000
Assets				
Cash and equivalents	—	—	—	26,715
Other current assets	951	810	732	42,375
Total current assets	951	810	732	69,090
Investments in and accounts with subsidiaries	1,035,915	908,404	1,424,961	1,399,708
Other assets	5,607	5,429	15,328	29,872
Total assets	1,042,473	914,643	1,441,021	1,498,625
Liabilities and Shareholders Equity				
Accounts payable and accrued liabilities	17,182	16,541	10,735	86,930
Total current liabilities	17,182	16,451	10,735	125,833
Long-term debt	250,000	250,000	—	772,380
Total liabilities	285,127	285,354	992,427	916,082
Shareholders equity	757,346	629,289	448,594	582,543
Total liabilities and shareholders equity	1,042,473	914,643	1,441,021	1,498,625

Source: Company reports.

Table 6   Chiquita Income Statement, 2001–2003

Chiquita Brands International Inc. Income Statement (in thousands)

	Reorganized Company		Predecessor Company	
	Year Ended 12/31/2003	**9 Months Ended 12/31/2002**	**Three Months Ended 3/31/2002**	**Year Ended 12/31/2001**
Net sales	—	—	—	—
Cost of sales	—	—	—	—
SG&A	(38,500)	(30,443)	(6,545)	(31,188)
Equity in earnings of subsidiaries (loss)	170,398	68,822	(368,899)	32,674
Operating income (loss)	131,898	38,379	(375,444)	1,486
Interest income	—	—	—	783
Interest expense	(27,392)	(20,384)	(1,250)	(81,633)
Financial restructuring items	—	—	124,394	(33,604)
Income before income taxes and accounting change	104,506	17,995	(252,300)	(112,968)
Income taxes	(5,300)	(4,800)	(1,000)	(5,800)
Income (loss) before accounting change	99,206	13,195	(253,300)	(118,768)
Cumulative effect of accounting change	—	—	(144,523)	—
Net income (loss)	99,206	13,195	(397,823)	(118,768)

Source: Company reports.

human resource challenges does Chiquita face as the purchaser, producer, and supplier of a commodity?

3. Does Chiquita's global corporate responsibility (CR) program create a conflict between shareholders and other stakeholders? Who are Chiquita's main stakeholders in the United States and around the world, and how are they affected by Chiquita's CR program?

4. How would you characterize Chiquita's past and present leadership? How does leadership affect a company's overall reputation?

5. Do you believe Chiquita would have changed its policies without the presence of damaging stories in the media? If not, what does this say about Chiquita's old management style?

6. What challenges does Chiquita's new CEO face in continuing to turn the company around and balance the interests of competing stakeholders?

Exercise

At the 2004 annual stakeholder/shareholder meeting, management, represented by Chiquita's new CEO, is considering input from various groups about its strategic direction and continued reorganization. Your group represents one of the following interests:

1. Shareholders of the previous company who lost most of the value of the shares after the company declared bankruptcy.

2. Shareholders in the newly reorganized company.

3. Employees and union representatives of North American operations.

4. Employees and union representatives of South American operations.

5. Representatives of the nongovernmental organization Rainforest Action Network.

Spend five minutes preparing two or three requests to the management team about your group's interests and priorities for the company. Then, conduct an open forum in which you discuss these requests among the different groups.

Source: © McGraw-Hill Irwin. This case was prepared by Professor Jonathan Doh and Research Associate Erik Holt of Villanova University as the basis for class discussion. It is not intended to illustrate either effective or ineffective managerial capability or administrative responsibility. We appreciate assistance from Sherrie Terry and Michael Mitchell of Chiquita International. Any errors remain those of the authors.

SKILL-BUILDING AND EXPERIENTIAL EXERCISES

- **Personal Skill-Building Exercises**
- **In-Class Simulations**

1. The Culture Quiz

Objectives

- To stimulate awareness of cultural differences
- To promote consideration of the impact of cultural differences in a global economy
- To stimulate dialogue between domestic and international students
- To explore issues raised by culturally diverse workforces

Background

Few, if any, traditions and values are universally held. Many business dealings have succeeded or failed because of a manager's awareness or lack of understanding of the traditions and values of his/her foreign counterparts. With the world business community so closely intertwined and interdependent, it is critical that managers today become increasingly aware of the differences that exist.

How culturally aware are you? Try the questions below.

Instructions

Working alone or with a small group, answer the questions (without peeking at the answers). When you do look at the answers, be sure to read the explanations. If you are taking the quiz with students from other countries than your own, explore what the answer might be in your country and theirs.

1. In Japan, loudly slurping your soup is considered to be
   a. rude and obnoxious.
   b. a sign that you like the soup.
   c. okay at home but not in public.
   d. something only foreigners do.
2. In Korea, business leaders tend to
   a. encourage strong commitment to teamwork and cooperation.
   b. encourage competition among subordinates.
   c. discourage subordinates from reporting directly, preferring information to come through well-defined channels.
   d. encourage close relationships with their subordinates.

3. In Japan, virtually every kind of drink is sold in public vending machines except for
   a. beer
   b. diet drinks with saccharine.
   c. already sweetened coffee.
   d. soft drinks from U.S. companies.
4. In Latin America, managers
   a. are most likely to hire members of their own families.
   b. consider hiring members of their own families to be inappropriate.
   c. stress the importance of hiring members of minority groups.
   d. usually hire more people than are actually needed to do a job.
5. In Ethiopia, when a woman opens the front door of her home, it means
   a. she is ready to receive guests for a meal.
   b. only family members may enter.
   c. religious spirits may move freely in and out of the home.
   d. she has agreed to have sex with any man who enters.
6. In Latin America, businesspeople
   a. consider it impolite to make eye contact while talking to one another.
   b. always wait until the other person is finished speaking before starting to speak.
   c. touch each other more than North Americans do under similar circumstances.
   d. avoid touching one another as it is considered an invasion of privacy.
7. The principal religion in Malaysia is
   a. Buddhism.
   b. Judaism.
   c. Christianity.
   d. Islam.
8. In Thailand
   a. it is common to see men walking along holding hands.
   b. it is common to see a man and a woman holding hands in public.

c. it is rude for men and women to walk together.

d. men and women traditionally kiss each other on meeting in the street.

9. When eating in India, it is appropriate to

a. take food with your right hand and eat with your left.

b. take food with your left hand and eat with your right.

c. take food and eat it with your left hand.

d. take food and eat it with your right hand.

10. Pointing your toes at someone in Thailand is

a. a symbol of respect, much like the Japanese bow.

b. considered rude even if it is done by accident.

c. an invitation to dance.

d. the standard public greeting.

11. American managers tend to base the performance appraisals of their subordinates on performance, while in Iran, managers are more likely to base their performance appraisals on

a. religion.

b. seniority.

c. friendship.

d. ability.

12. In China, the status of every business negotiation is

a. reported daily in the press.

b. private, and details are not discussed publicly.

c. subjected to scrutiny by a public tribunal on a regular basis.

d. directed by the elders of every commune.

13. When rewarding a Hispanic worker for a job well done, it is best not to

a. praise him or her publicly.

b. say "thank you."

c. offer a raise.

d. offer a promotion.

14. In some South American countries, it is considered normal and acceptable to show up for a social appointment

a. ten to fifteen minutes early.

b. ten to fifteen minutes late.

c. fifteen minutes to an hour late.

d. one to two hours late.

15. In France, when friends talk to one another

a. they generally stand about three feet apart.

b. it is typical to shout.

c. they stand closer to one another than Americans do.

d. it is always with a third party present.

16. When giving flowers as gifts in Western Europe, be careful not to give

a. tulips and jonquils.

b. daisies and lilacs.

c. chrysanthemums and calla lilies.

d. lilacs and apple blossoms.

17. The appropriate gift-giving protocol for a male executive doing business in Saudi Arabia is to

a. give a man a gift from you to his wife.

b. present gifts to the wife or wives in person.

c. give gifts only to the eldest wife.

d. not give a gift to the wife at all.

18. If you want to give a necktie or a scarf to a Latin American, it is best to avoid the color

a. red.

b. purple.

c. green.

d. black.

19. The doors in German offices and homes are generally kept

a. wide open to symbolize an acceptance and welcome of friends and strangers.

b. slightly ajar to suggest that people should knock before entering.

c. half-opened, suggesting that some people are welcome and others are not.

d. tightly shut to preserve privacy and personal space.

20. In the area that was formerly West Germany, leaders who display charisma are

a. not among the most desired.

b. the ones most respected and sought after.

c. invited frequently to serve on boards of cultural organizations.

d. pushed to get involved in political activities.

21. American managers running business in Mexico have found that by increasing the salaries of Mexican workers, they

a. increased the numbers of hours the workers were willing to work.

b. enticed more workers to work night shifts.

c. decreased the number of hours workers would agree to work.

d. decreased production rates.

22. Chinese culture teaches people

a. to seek psychiatric help for personal problems.

b. to avoid conflict and internalize personal problems.

c. to deal with conflict with immediate confrontation.

d. to seek help from authorities whenever conflict arises.

23. One wedding gift that should not be given to a Chinese couple would be
    a. a jade bowl.
    b. a clock.
    c. a basket of oranges.
    d. shifts embroidered with dragon patterns.

24. In Venezuela, New Year's Eve is generally spent
    a. in quiet family gatherings.
    b. at wild neighborhood street parties.
    c. in restaurants with horns, hats, and live music and dancing.
    d. at pig roasts on the beach.

25. If you order "bubble and squeak" in a London pub, you will get
    a. two goldfish fried in olive oil.
    b. a very cold beer in a chilled glass, rather than the usual warm beer.
    c. Alka Seltzer and a glass of water.
    d. chopped cabbage and mashed potatoes fried together.

26. When a stranger in India wants to know what you do for a living and how much you earn, he will
    a. ask your guide.
    b. invite you to his home and, after getting to know you, will ask.
    c. come over and ask you directly, without introduction.
    d. respect your privacy above all.

27. When you feel you are being taken advantage of in a business exchange in Vietnam, it is important to
    a. let the anger show in your face but not in your words.
    b. say that you are angry, but keep your facial expression neutral.
    c. not show any anger in any way.
    d. end the business dealings immediately, and walk away.

28. When a taxi driver in India shakes his head from side to side, it probably means
    a. he thinks your price is too high.
    b. he isn't going in your direction.
    c. he will take you where you want to go.
    d. he doesn't understand what you're asking.

29. In England, holding your index and middle fingers up in a vee with the back of your hand facing another person is seen as
    a. a gesture of peace.
    b. a gesture of victory.

    c. a signal that you want two of something.
    d. a vulgar gesture.

Answers to the Culture Quiz

1. *b.* Slurping your soup or noodles in Japan is good manners in both public and private. It indicates enjoyment and appreciation of the quality. (Source: Eiji Kanno and Constance O'Keefe, *New Japan Solo.* Japan National Tourist Organization: Tokyo, 1990, p. 20.)

2. *b.* Korean managers use a "divide-and-rule" method of leadership that encourages competition among subordinates. They do this to ensure that they can exercise maximum control. In addition, they stay informed by having individuals report directly to them. This way, they can know more than anyone else. (Source: Richard M. Castaldi and Tjipyanto Soerjanto, "Contrasts in East Asian Management Practices." *The Journal of Management in Practice,* 2:1, 1990, pp. 25–27.)

3. *b.* Saccharine-sweetened drinks may not be sold in Japan by law. On the other hand, beer, a wide variety of Japanese and international soft drinks, and so forth, are widely available from vending machines along the streets and in buildings. You're supposed to be at least 18 to buy the alcoholic ones, however. (Source: Eiji Kanno and Constance O'Keefe, *New Japan Solo.* Japan National Tourist Organization: Tokyo, 1990, p. 20.)

4. *a.* Family is considered to be very important in Latin America, so managers are likely to hire their relatives more quickly than hiring strangers. (Source: Nancy J. Adler, *International Dimensions of Organizational Behavior,* 2nd ed., PWS-Kent: Boston, 1991.)

5. *d.* The act, by a woman, of opening the front door, signifies that she has agreed to have sex with any man who enters. (Source: Adam Pertman, "Wandering No More," *Boston Globe Magazine,* June 30, 1991, pp. 10 ff.)

6. *c.* Touching one another during business negotiations is common practice. (Source: Nancy J. Adler, *International Dimensions of Organizational Behavior,* 2nd ed., PWS-Kent: Boston, 1991.)

7. *d.* Approximately 45 percent of the people in Malaysia follow Islam, the country's "official" religion. (Source: Hans Johannes Hoefer, ed., *Malaysia.* Prentice Hall: Englewood Cliffs, NJ, 1984.)

8. *a.* Men holding hands is considered a sign of friendship. Public displays of affection between men and women, however, are unacceptable. (Source: William Warren, Star Black, and M. R. Priya Rangsit, eds., *Thailand.* Prentice Hall: Englewood Cliffs, NJ, 1985.)

9. *d.* In India, as in many Asian countries, toilet paper is not used. Instead, water and the left hand are used, after which the left hand is thoroughly cleaned. Still, the left hand is considered to be polluted and therefore inappropriate for use during eating or touching another person. (Source: Gitanjali Koland, *Culture Shock! India.* Graphic Arts Center Publishing Company: Portland, OR, 1996, p. 117.)

10. *b.* This is especially an insult if it is done deliberately, since the feet are the lowest part of the body. (Source: William Warren, Star Black, and M. R. Priya Rangsit, eds., *Thailand.* Prentice Hall: Englewood Cliffs, NJ, 1985.)

11. *c.* Adler suggests that friendship is valued over task competence in Iran. (Source: Nancy J. Adler, *International Dimensions of Organizational Behavior.* 2nd ed., PWS-Kent: Boston, 1991.)

12. *b.* Public discussion of business dealings is considered inappropriate. Kaplan et al. report that "the Chinese may even have used a premature announcement to extract better terms from executives" who were too embarrassed to admit that there was never really a contract. (Source: Frederic Kaplan, Julian Sobin, Arne de Keijzer, *The China Guidebook.* Houghton Mifflin: Boston, 1987.)

13. *a.* Public praise for Hispanics and Asians is generally embarrassing because modesty is an important cultural value. (Source: Jim Braham, "No, You Don't Manage Everyone the Same," *Industry Week,* February 6, 1989.) In Japan, being singled out for praise is also an embarrassment. A common saying in that country is, "The nail that sticks up gets hammered down."

14. *d.* Though being late is frowned upon in the United States, being late is not only accepted but expected in some South American countries. (Source: Lloyd S. Baird, James E. Post, and John F. Mahon, *Management: Functions and Responsibilities.* Harper & Row: New York, 1990.)

15. *c.* Personal space in most European countries is much smaller than in the United States. Americans generally like at least two feet of space around themselves, while it is not unusual for Europeans to be virtually touching. (Source: Lloyd S. Baird, James E. Post, and John F. Mahon, *Management: Functions and Responsibilities.* Harper & Row: New York, 1990.)

16. *c.* Chrysanthemums and calla lilies are both associated with funerals. (Source: Theodore Fischer, *Pinnacle: International Issue,* March–April 1991, p. 4.)

17. *d.* In Arab cultures, it is considered inappropriate for wives to accept gifts or even attention from other men. (Source: Theodore Fischer, *Pinnacle: International Issue,* March–April 1991, p. 4.)

18. *b.* In Argentina and other Latin American countries, purple is associated with the serious fasting period of Lent. (Source: Theodore Fischer, *Pinnacle: International Issue,* March–April 1991, p. 4.)

19. *d.* Private space is considered so important in Germany that partitions are erected to separate people from one another. Privacy screens and walled gardens are the norm. (Source: Julius Fast, *Subtext: Making Body Language Work.* Viking Penguin Books: New York, 1991, p. 207.)

20. *a.* Though political leaders in the United States are increasingly selected on their ability to inspire, charisma is a suspect trait in what was West Germany, where Hitler's charisma is still associated with evil intent and harmful outcomes. (Source: Nancy J. Adler, *International Dimensions of Organizational Behavior.* 2nd ed., PWS-Kent: Boston, 1991, p. 149.)

21. *c.* Paying Mexican workers more means, in the eyes of the workers, that they can make the same amount of money in fewer hours and thus have more time for enjoying life. (Source: Nancy J. Adler, *International Dimensions of Organizational Behavior.* 2nd ed., PWS-Kent: Boston, 1991, pp. 30 and 159.)

22. *b.* Psychological therapy is not an accepted concept in China. In addition, communism has kept most Chinese from expressing opinions openly. (Source: James McGregor, "Burma Road Heroin Breeds Addicts, AIDS Along China's Border." *Wall Street Journal,* September 29, 1992, p. 1.)

23. *b.* The Chinese regard a clock as a bad omen because the word for clock, pronounced *zhong,* is phonetically similar to another Chinese word that means the end. Jade is highly valued as symbolizing superior virtues, and oranges and dragon patterns are also auspicious symbols. (Source: Dr. Evelyn Lip, "Culture and Customs." *Silver Kris,* February 1994, p. 84.)

24. *a.* Venezuelans do the reverse of what most people in other countries do on Christmas and New Year's. On Christmas, they socialize. While fireworks are shot off on both nights, most restaurants are closed, and the streets are quiet. (Source: Tony Perrottet, ed., *Venezuela.* Houghton Mifflin: Boston, 1994, p. 97.)

25. *d.* Other popular pub food includes Bangers and Mash (sausages and mashed potatoes), Ploughman's lunch (bread, cheese, and pickled onions), and Cottage pie (baked minced meat with onions and topped with mashed potatoes). (Source: Ravi Desai, ed., *Let's Go: The Budget Guide to Britain and Ireland.* Pan Books: London, 1990, p. 83.)

26. *c.* Indians are generally uninhibited about staring at strangers and asking them about personal details in their lives. Social distance and personal privacy are not common social conventions in India. (Source:

Frank Kusy, *India.* The Globe Pequo Press: Chester, Conn., 1989, p. 27.)

27. *c.* Vernon Weitzel of the Australian National University advises never to show anger when dealing with Vietnamese officials or businesspeople. Showing anger causes you to lose face and is considered rude. Weitzel also recommends always smiling, not complaining or criticizing anyone, and not being inquisitive about personal matters. (Source: Daniel Robinson and Joe Cummings, *Vietnam, Laos & Cambodia.* Lonely Planet Publications: Australia, 1991, p. 96.)

28. *c.* What looks to Westerners like a refusal is really an Indian way of saying "yes." It can also express general agreement with what you're saying or suggest that an individual is interested in what you have to say. (Source: Gitanjali Kolanad, *Culture Shock! India.* Graphic Arts Center Publishing Company: Portland, OR, 1996, p. 114.)

29. *d.* In England, this simple hand gesture is considered vulgar and obscene. In a report to *The Boston Globe,* an American who had been working in London wrote, "I wish someone had told me before I emphatically explained to one of the draftsmen at work why I needed two complete sets of drawings." (Source: "Finger Gestures Can Spell Trouble," *The Berkshire Eagle:* January 26, 1997, p. E5.)

2. Using Gung Ho to Understand Cultural Differences

Background

There is no avoiding the increasing globalization of management. Few, if any, current students of business can expect to pursue a successful career without some encounter of an international nature. Gaining early and realistic exposure to the challenges of cross-cultural dynamics will greatly aid any student of business.

The Pacific Rim will continue to play a dominant role in North American transnational organization and global markets. The opening doors to China offer an unprecedented market opportunity. Korea, Singapore, and Taiwan continue to be unsung partners in mutually beneficial trading relationships. And, of course, Japan will always be a dominant player in the international arena.

An important aspect of cross-cultural awareness is understanding actual differences in interpersonal style and cultural expectations, and separating this from incorrect assumptions. Many embellished stereotypes have flourished as we extend our focus and attention abroad. Unfortunately, many of these myths have become quite pervasive, in spite of their lack of foundation. Thus, North American managers frequently and confidently err in their cross-cultural interactions. This may be particularly common in our interactions with the Japanese. For example, lifetime employment has long been touted as exemplifying the superior practices of Japanese management. In reality, only one-third of Japanese *male* employees enjoy this benefit, and in 1993, many Japanese firms actually laid off workers for the first time. Also, Japan is promoted as a collectivist culture founded on consensus, teamwork, and employee involvement. Yet Japan is at the same time one of the most competitive societies, especially when reviewing how students are selected for educational and occupational placement.

Films can provide an entertaining yet potent medium for studying such complex issues. Such experiential learning is most effective when realistic and identifiable with one's own likely experiences. Case studies can be too sterile. Role plays tend to be contrived and void of depth. Both lack a sense of background to help one "buy into" the situation. Films, on the other hand, can promote a rich and familiar presentation that promotes personal involvement. This exercise seeks to capitalize on this phenomenon to explore cross-cultural demands.

Procedure

Step I (110 minutes)   Watch the film *Gung Ho*. (This film can be obtained at any video store.)

Step II (30 minutes)   Use one of the following four formats to address the discussion topics.

Option A   Address each issue in an open class forum. This option is particularly appropriate for moderate class sizes (40 students) or for sections that do not normally engage in group work.

Option B   Divide the class into groups of four to seven to discuss the assigned topics. This is a better approach for larger classes (60 or more students). This approach might also be used to assign the exercise as an extracurricular activity if scheduled class time is too brief.

Option C   Assign one group to adopt the American perspective and another group to take the Japanese perspective. Using a confrontation meeting approach, have each side describe its perception and expected difficulties in collaborating with each other. Then, have the two sides break into small mixed groups to discuss methods to bridge the gap (or avoid its extreme escalation as portrayed in the film). Ideas should extend beyond those cited in the movie. Present these separate discussions to the class as a whole.

Option D   Assign students to groups of four to seven to watch the film and write a six-page analysis addressing one or more of the discussion topics.

Discussion Topics

1. In the opening scenes, Hunt observes Kaz being berated in a Japanese "management development center." According to at least one expert, this is a close representation of Japanese disciplinary practices. Would such an approach be possible in an American firm? How does this scene illustrate the different perspectives and approaches to motivation? To reinforcement? To feedback?

Source: Steven M. Sommer, Pepperdine University. Used with permission.

2. The concepts of multiculturalism and diversity are emerging issues in modern management environments. The importance of recognizing and responding to racial, ethnic, and other demographic factors has been widely debated in the popular press. What does *Gung Ho* offer to the discussion (both within and across the two groups)? How does each culture respond to different races, genders, and cultures?

3. Individualism and collectivism represent two endpoints on a continuum used to analyze different cultural orientations. Individualism refers to a sense of personal focus, autonomy, and compensation. Collectivism describes a group focus, self-subjugation, obligation, and sharing of rewards. How do you see American and Japanese workers differing on this dimension? You might compare the reactions of the Japanese manager whose wife was about to give birth with those of the American worker who had planned to take his child to a doctor's appointment.

4. How does the softball game illuminate cultural differences (and even similarities)? You might consider this question in reference to topic 3; to approaches to work habits; to having "fun"; to behavioral norms of pride, honor, and sportsmanship.

5. On several occasions we see George Wendt's openly antagonistic responses to the exercise of authority by Japanese managers. Discuss the concept of authority as seen in both cultures. Discuss expectations of compliance. How might George's actions be interpreted differently by each culture? Indeed, would they be seen as different by an American manager as compared with a Japanese manager?

6. Throughout the film, one gains an impression of how Americans and the Japanese might differ in their approach to resolving conflict. Separately describe how each culture tends to approach conflict, and how the cultures might be different from each other.

7. Experienced conflict between work and family demands has also gained attention as an important managerial issue. How do both cultures approach the role of work in one's life? The role of family? How does each approach balance competing demands between the two? Have these expectations changed over time (from twenty years ago, forty years ago, sixty years ago)? How might they change now in the twenty-first century?

8. In reality, Japanese managers would be "shamed" if one of their subordinates was seriously injured on the job (the scene where the American worker's hand is caught in the assembly-line belt). Taking this into account, what other issues in the film might be used to illustrate differences or similarities between American and Japanese management and work practices?

3. "When in Bogotá . . . "

As Jim Reynolds looked out the small window of the Boeing 757, he saw the glimmer of lights in the distance. After a five-hour flight, he arrived in Bogotá, Colombia, at 9:35 P.M. on a clear Friday evening. It had been nearly five years since Jim had seen his best friend, Rodrigo Cardozo. The two had met in college and kept in touch over the years. During their school years, Rodrigo would often accompany Jim when he went home to Chicago for the holidays.

Entering the main terminal, Jim found himself in what looked like a recently bombed building. Piles of debris were everywhere. Lights hung from the ceiling by exposed electrical wires, and the walls and floors were rough, unfinished concrete. "Certainly, aesthetics are not a major concern at the Bogotá International Airport," Jim thought.

As he came to the end of the long, dimly lit corridor, an expressionless customs official reached out his hand and gestured for Jim's travel documents.

"Passaporte, por favor. Bienvenidos a Bogotá, Señor Reynolds. Estás en vacacciones?"

"Sí," Jim replied.

After a few routine questions, Jim was allowed to pass through customs feeling relatively unscathed.

"Loquillo! Loquillo! Estamos aquí! Jim, Jim," a voice shouted.

Trying to find the origin of the voice among the dense crowd, Jim finally spotted Rodrigo. "Hey, man. How've you been? You look great!"

"Jim, it's so good to see you. How've you been? I would like you to meet my wife, Eva. Eva, this is my best friend, Jim. He's the one in all those pictures I've shown you."

Late Night Begins the Day

Close to an hour later, Jim, Rodrigo, and Eva arrived at Rodrigo's parents' house on the other side of Bogotá from the airport. As Jim was aware, it is customary for couples to live with their parents for a number of years after their marriage, and Rodrigo and Eva were part of that custom.

Darío, Rodrigo's father, owned an import/export business in Bogotá. He was a knowledgeable and educated man and, from what Jim knew, a master of business negotiations. Over the years, Darío had conducted business with people in nearly every country in Central and South America, the United States, Europe, Hong Kong, and some

parts of Africa. Jim had first met Darío with Rodrigo in Boston in 1989.

"Jim, welcome to my house," Darío boomed effusively as the group walked in. "I am so pleased that you're finally in Bogotá. Would you like something to drink—whiskey, bourbon, Aguardiente?"

"Aguardiente!" Rodrigo urged.

"Yes, Jim would like some Aguardiente. I understand you're going to Bahía tonight," Darío added.

"Where?" Jim asked, looking around. "I didn't know we were going anywhere tonight."

"Don't worry, Jim, todo bien, todo bien," Rodrigo assured him. "We're going dancing, so get dressed. Let's go."

The reality of being in Colombia hit Jim at about 11:15 that night when he and his friends entered Bahía, a Bogotá nightclub. The rhythms of salsa and merengue filled the club. Jim's mind flashed back to the Latin dance parties he and Rodrigo had had in Boston with their friends from Central and South America.

"Jim, this is my cousin, Diana. She'll be your partner tonight," Rodrigo said. "You'll get to practice your Spanish too; she doesn't speak a word of English. Have fun."

For the next six hours, they danced and drank. This is the Colombian way. At 5:30 the next morning, Rodrigo decided it was time to leave to get something to eat. On the drive home, they stopped at an outdoor grill in the mountains where many people had congregated for the same reason. Everyone was eating arepas con queso and mazorca, and drinking Aguardiente.

Next, they continued to an outdoor party just down the street. Here, they danced and drank until the sun crested over the mountains of Bogotá. It was about 7:00 A.M. when they decided to conclude the celebration—for now.

Saturday was spent recovering from the previous evening and also touring some local spots in the country. However, Saturday night was a repeat of Friday. After being in Colombia for three days, Jim had slept a total of about four hours. Fortunately, Monday was a national holiday.

Business Before Pleasure Before Business?

Although Jim was having a great time, he had also scheduled a series of business meetings with directors of business schools at various Bogotá universities for the week to come. Jim worked as an acquisitions editor for Academia

Press, a major publisher of college-level business textbooks. The purpose of the meetings was to establish business contacts in the Colombian market. It was hoped that these initial contacts would lead to others in Latin America.

At Academia Press headquarters in New York, Jim and Caroline Evans, his boss, had discussed the opportunities in Latin America. Although Academia Press routinely published international editions of its texts, total international sales never represented more than 15 percent of their gross. Consequently, international markets had never been pursued aggressively. Caroline, however, saw the Latin American markets as having a lot of potential within the next three to five years. She envisioned this market alone, in time, representing 15 to 20 percent of gross sales. Moreover, she felt that within the next ten years, international sales could reach 40 percent if developed properly. With numbers like that, it was evident to Jim that this deal was important, not only to the company but to his career as well. If Jim was able to open these markets, he might receive a promotion and be able to continue to work in Central and South America.

Jim's first meeting was scheduled for 11:00 A.M. on Tuesday, the second on Wednesday at 11:00 A.M., and the third on Friday at 3:00 P.M. At precisely 11:00 A.M. on Tuesday, Jim arrived at Javeriana University, where he was to meet with Professors Emilio Muñoz, Diana Espitia, and Enrique Ronderos. When he arrived, Professor Muñoz was waiting for him in the conference room.

"Señor Reynolds, I am delighted to meet you. How was your flight?"

"Wonderful," Jim replied.

"And how do you like Bogotá so far? Have you been able to sightsee?"

"No, I haven't had the chance to get around the city yet. I hope to see some things later in the week."

"Well, before you leave, you must visit *El Museo de Oro*. It is the finest collection of gold artifacts from the various indigenous Indian tribes in Colombia. Although much of the gold was stolen by the Spanish, many pieces have survived." For the next thirty minutes, Professor Muñoz spoke of everything from the upcoming presidential elections to World Cup soccer.

Jim looked at his watch, concerned about the other professors who had not yet arrived and about the meeting for which he had prepared.

"Is there something wrong, Señor Reynolds?"

"No, no, I was just wondering about the others; it's 11:30."

"Don't worry. They'll be here shortly. Traffic in Bogotá at this hour is terrible. They're probably caught in a traffic jam."

Just then, Professors Espitia and Ronderos walked in.

"Muy buenas, Señor Reynolds," Professor Espitia said warmly. "Please forgive us for the delay. Traffic is simply awful at this time of day."

"Oh, that's not necessary. I understand. Traffic in New York can be absolutely horrendous as well," Jim replied. "Sometimes it takes two hours to get from one end of the city to the other."

"Have you had lunch yet, Señor Reynolds?" asked Professor Ronderos.

Jim shook his head.

"Why don't we go to lunch, and we can talk there?" Professor Ronderos suggested.

After discussing the restaurants in the area, the professors decided on El Club Ejecutivo. It was nearly 12:30 P.M. when they arrived.

"It's been an hour and a half, and we haven't discussed anything," Jim thought. He was concerned that the Colombians were not very interested in what he had to offer. Throughout lunch, Jim grew increasingly concerned that the professors were more interested in his trying typical Colombian dishes and visiting the sights in Bogotá than in Academia's textbooks. They were fascinated that Jim knew how to dance salsa and merengue and impressed that he spoke Spanish with a slight Colombian accent; Señorita Espitia said she found it amusing. That seemed much more important than his knowledge of business textbooks and publishing in general.

By the end of lunch, Jim was nearly beside himself. It was now after 2:30 P.M. and nothing had been accomplished.

"Why don't we all go to Monserate tomorrow? It's absolutely beautiful up there, Señor Reynolds," Professor Ronderos suggested, going on to describe the mountain that overlooks Bogotá and the myths and traditions that surround it.

"That's a wonderful idea," Professor Espitia added.

"Monserate it is then. Jim, it has been a pleasure. I look forward to our meeting tomorrow," Professor Ronderos said with a slight bow.

"Señor Reynolds, would you like a ride home?" Professor Muñoz asked.

"Yes, if it's not too much trouble."

On the way home, Jim was relatively quiet.

"Do you feel okay?"

"It must be jet lag catching up to me. I'm sure it's nothing," Jim responded. Concerned about the way the meeting had gone, Jim realized that he had never even had a chance to mention Academia Press's various titles and how these texts could be used to create a new curriculum or supplement an existing curriculum at the professors' business school.

When in Bogotá

On arriving at the house, Jim went upstairs and sat in the living room glumly sipping a cup of aguapanela. "I just don't get it," he thought. "The Colombians couldn't have been happier with the way the meeting turned out, but we didn't do anything. We didn't even talk about one book. I just don't understand what went wrong."

In a short time, Darío arrived. "Muy buenas, Jim. How did your meetings go today with the directors?" he asked.

"I don't know. I don't know what to think. We didn't do anything. We didn't talk about business at all. We talked more about the sights I should see and the places I should visit before I leave Colombia. I'm supposed to call my boss this afternoon and tell her how the initial meeting went. What am I going to tell her? 'Sorry, we just decided to plan my vacation in Colombia instead of discussing business.' I can't afford to have this deal fall through."

Darío laughed.

"Señor, I'm serious."

"Jim, I understand. Believe me. Tell me about your meeting today."

Jim recounted every detail of the meeting to Darío, who smiled and nodded his head as he listened.

"Jim, you have to understand one thing before you continue negotiating with the directors."

"What's that?"

"You're in Colombia now," Darío said simply.

Jim stared at him with a puzzled look. "And?"

"And what, Jim?"

"Is there something else I should know?"

"That's where you need to start. You let the directors set the tone of the meeting. It's obvious they felt very comfortable with you, or they wouldn't have invited you to Monserate. Here in Colombia, Jim, we do business differently. Right now, you're building friendship. You're building their trust in you. This is very important in doing business in all of Latin America."

"Jim," Darío continued, "would you rather do business with a friend or someone you hardly know?"

As Darío went on to analyze the meeting, Jim realized that his perception of the situation had been formed by his experiences in the United States. "When in Bogotá," he thought, "I guess I had better think like the Colombians."

"Jim, you've gained the respect and the trust of the directors. In my opinion, your first meeting was a complete success."

"What should I expect in the meetings to come?" Jim asked.

"Don't worry," he responded. "Just let the directors worry about that. You'll come to an agreement before the end of the week. I guarantee it."

Questions for Discussion

1. What differences does Jim notice between life in the United States and life in Colombia?

2. What differences does Jim notice between doing business in the United States and doing business in Colombia? How might these same factors differ in other countries?

3. What advice would you give Jim for closing his deals? Why?

4. The International Cola Alliances

Objectives

- To introduce some of the complexities involved in doing business across international borders
- To examine what happens when countries seek to do business with one another without the benefit of a common language and customs

Background

Even with a common language, communication can break down, and interpretations of words and actions often can confound understanding and incur negative attributions of purpose. Add to this the differences of personal needs that exist from individual to individual, as well as national and cultural needs that exist from country to country. These limitless variables make cooperation across borders even more complex.

The Story

You are a delegation from a country that would like to enter into a large cooperative effort with a number of other countries for the production and distribution of a popular soft drink produced by the American company International Cola. In the past, countries in your region of the world have been resistant to allowing foreign soft drinks into their markets, despite consumer demands. However, recent thinking is that the advantages of allowing this competition outweigh the disadvantages.

International Cola has expressed an interest in setting up a bottling plant, a regional corporate headquarters, and four distribution depots. Their goal, of course, is to do this in the most economically efficient way possible to maximize profits. However, because the executives at International Cola believe this area to be a rich new market with outstanding potential and are therefore eager to get in, they have ceded to the demands of the various governments in the proposed alliance. These require International Cola to allow for local control of the facilities; to maintain only 49 percent interest in the facilities with local partners holding 51 percent ownership; and to allow the participating governments to work out among

themselves the details of where the facilities will be located.

For the countries involved, having one or more of these facilities located within their borders will bring jobs, revenue, and a certain amount of prestige. (It is possible for a single country to have all six of the facilities: regional headquarters, bottling plant, distribution depots.)

Each of the countries involved shares at least two borders with the other countries. This has not always been the most peaceful area. Border skirmishes are frequent, most stemming from minor misunderstandings that became inflated by vast cultural and religious differences.

These distinct cultural differences between your country and your neighbors will likely become even more evident as you pursue the negotiation. It will be up to you to decide how to respond to them. While it is important for you to retain your own cultural integrity—for example, when you first meet a delegate from another country you will likely greet him or her in the cultural style of your country—you understand the importance of being sensitive to one another. If you understand, for example, that the cultural style of another country is to bow on meeting, whereas you shake hands, you may wish to bow instead.

Since you are negotiating the venture across borders, and each country has a different primary language, you have agreed to negotiate in English, but none of you is entirely fluent. Therefore, a few phrases will creep in from your own languages.

Wear your country's flag in a visible place at all times.

Instructions

Step 1 *(30–40 minutes—may be done before class)*   Working in small groups (5–7), develop a profile of your country and its people based on profile sheets 1 and 2.

After you have completed profile sheets 1 and 2, briefly discuss them to be sure there is mutual understanding of what the group's behavior and negotiating stance are to be during the negotiation.

Step 2 *(20 minutes—may be done before class)*   Based on the profile sheets, decide which International Cola facilities you believe you should have in your country and why you believe they should be in your country rather than one of the others that will be represented. For example, if you have a highly educated population, you may argue that you should be the home of the regional corporate headquarters; be aware, however, that another country might argue that you should not have bottling and distribution facilities because these do not require a highly educated or skilled labor force.

On the negotiation sheet, make a list of the facilities you believe your country should have and some notes as to what your arguments will be for having them. Also, make some notes on what you believe the other countries' counter-arguments will be and how you expect to respond to them.

Step 3 *(30–45 minutes—in class)* Everyone in your group should pin a copy of your country's flag and motto on himself or herself in a visible place. One to three representatives from your group (delegation) should negotiate the arrangements for International Cola's facilities with the representatives from the other delegations. Be sure to use the cultural norms of your country during the negotiation, but *do not tell* the others what your social norms are.

Representatives should introduce themselves to one another on an individual basis. After personal introductions, representatives should form a circle in the center of the room with their delegations behind them, briefly describe their countries, state their positions, and begin negotiations. During negotiations, representatives should make an effort to use their new language at least three times. They should not use English for any of the six phrases listed.

Delegation representatives and the other members of their groups may communicate with one another at any point during the negotiation, but only in writing. Group members may also communicate among themselves, but only in writing during the negotiation.

Any group or representative may ask for a side meeting with one or more of the other groups during the negotiation. Side meetings may not last more than five minutes.

At any time in the negotiation, the delegation may change its representative. When such a change is made, the new representative and the other delegates must reintroduce themselves and greet one another.

Those members of each delegation who are not directly negotiating should be active observers. Use the observer sheet to record situations in which other groups insulted them, shamed them, or were otherwise offensive.

At the end of 45 minutes, the negotiation should be concluded whether or not an agreement has been reached.

Questions for Discussion

1. What role did cultural differences play in the various phases of the negotiation process? Be careful not to overlook the introductory phase. Was the negotiation frustrating? Satisfying? Other? Why?

2. At any time, did delegations recognize the cultural differences between themselves and the others? If so, was any attempt made to try to adapt to another country's norms? Why? Why not? Would there have been a benefit in doing so? Why?

3. What role did language differences play during the negotiation? What was the effect of lack of understanding or miscommunication on the process?

4. Did the delegations from various countries attempt to find mutual goals and interests despite their differences? In what ways were the best interests of the overall plan subjugated to the individual interests of each country? What rhetoric was used to justify the personal interests?

5. To what degree did groups construct their countries to best justify their position? In situations where this happened, did it work? Why? Why not?

Profile Sheet 1

1. Select a name for your country:

   _____

Be sure that the name of your country appears on or around the flag (see below).

2. In the space below, design your country's flag or emblem. Make enough copies so that each member of your group has one to wear.

3. Write a slogan for your country that best embodies your country's ideals and goals. Include the slogan on or around the flag.

   _____

   _____

   _____

4. Make up a partial language with a vocabulary of up to twenty-five (25) words into which you should translate the following phrases for use during negotiations:

Phrase	*Translation*
I agree.	_____
I disagree.	_____
This is unacceptable.	_____
I don't understand your point.	_____
	_____
You have insulted me.	_____
Please repeat that.	_____

5. Briefly describe how people in your country react when they have been insulted.

_____
_____
_____
_____
_____
_____

Profile Sheet 2

Describe your country by selecting one element from each of the following lists. After you have made your selections, list the elements that make up your country's description on a separate piece of paper and add any additional elements you wish.

Population Density

_____ high density with overpopulation a problem
_____ moderate density—high end
_____ moderate density—average
_____ moderate density—low end
_____ low density

Average Educational Level

_____ less than 3 years—large percent totally illiterate
_____ 3–6 years—widespread functional illiteracy
_____ 6–9 years—functional illiteracy a problem in scattered areas
_____ 9–12 years—most read and write at functional levels
_____ 12+ years—a highly educated and functioning population

Per Capita Income

_____ under $1,000 per year
_____ $1,000–5,000 per year
_____ $5,000–10,000 per year
_____ $10,000–20,000 per year
_____ $20,000–30,000 per year
_____ $30,000–40,000 per year
_____ $40,000 + per year

Climate

_____ tropical
_____ arctic
_____ mixed in different areas
_____ runs range from season to season

Form of Government

_____ socialist
_____ democratic
_____ communist
_____ monarchy
_____ dictatorship
_____ other (specify)

Dominant Racial–Ethnic Group

_____ Asian
_____ black
_____ white
_____ other (specify)

Dominant Religion

_____ animist
_____ atheist/agnostic
_____ Buddhist
_____ Catholic
_____ Hindu
_____ Jewish
_____ Mormon
_____ Protestant (specify)
_____ other (specify)

Negotiation Sheet

1. What facilities do you believe your country should have?

_____
_____
_____

2. What facilities of those listed above are you willing to relinquish to reach agreement?

_____
_____

3. On what bases will you justify your need or desire for having the facilities you have listed?

_____
_____
_____
_____
_____
_____
_____
_____

Observer Sheet

1. List actions taken by members of other delegations that were insulting, created shame for you and your delegation, or were otherwise offensive based on your country's norms. Include notes on the context in which the actions were taken.

    _____

    _____

    _____

    _____

    _____

    _____

    _____

2. Based on the above list, what happened to your interest in forming an alliance and your belief that a mutual agreement could be reached?

5. Who to Hire?

Objectives

- To explore participants' cultural biases and expectations
- To examine cultural differences
- To consider the impact culture has on hiring decisions

Instructions

Step 1 *(10–15 minutes)*   Read the background information and descriptions of each of the applicants. Consider the job and the cultures within which the individual to be hired will be operating. Rank the candidates from 1 to 5, with 1 being your first choice, and enter your rankings on the ranking sheet in the column marked "My Ranking." Briefly, list the reasons for each of your rankings.

Do not discuss your rankings with your classmates until told to do so.

Step 2 *(30–40 minutes)*   Working with three to four of your classmates, discuss the applicants, and rank them in the order of group preference. Do not vote.

Rank the candidates from 1 to 5, with 1 being the group's first choice, and enter your group rankings on the ranking sheet in the column marked "Group Ranking." Briefly list the reasons for each of the group's rankings.

If your group represents more than one culture, explore the ways in which each person's cultural background may have influenced his or her individual decisions.

Step 3 *(open-ended)*   Report your rankings to the class, and discuss the areas of difference that emerged within your group while you were trying to reach consensus.

Questions for Discussion

1. Was your group able to explore openly any culturally based biases that came up—for example, feelings about homosexuality, religion, personality traits, politics?
2. Did you make any comments or observations that you feel would have been fully acceptable in your own culture but were not accepted by the group? Explain.
3. If the answer to number 2 was yes, how did the reaction of the group make you feel about your membership in it? How did you handle the situation?
4. What implications do you believe these cultural differences would have in business dealings?

Background

You are a member of the management committee of a multinational company that does business in 23 countries. While your company's headquarters are in Holland, your offices are scattered fairly evenly throughout the four hemispheres. Primary markets have been in Europe and North America; the strongest emerging market is the Pacific Rim. Company executives would like to develop what they see as a powerful potential market in the Middle East. Sales in all areas except the Pacific Rim have shown slow growth over the past two years.

At present, your company is seeking to restructure and re-vitalize its worldwide marketing efforts. To accomplish this, you have determined that you need to hire a key marketing person to introduce fresh ideas and a new perspective. There is no one currently in your company who is qualified to do this, and so you have decided to look outside. The job title is "vice-president for international marketing"; it carries with it a salary well into six figures (US$), plus elaborate benefits, an unlimited expense account, a car, and the use of the corporate jet. The person you hire will be based at the company's headquarters and will travel frequently.

A lengthy search has turned up five people with good potential. It is now up to you to decide whom to hire. Although all the applicants have expressed a sincere interest in the position, it is possible that they may change their minds once the job is offered. Therefore, you must rank them in order of preference so that if your first choice declines the position, you can go on to the second, and so on.

Applicants
Park L, age 41, Married with Three Children

Park L. is currently senior vice president for marketing at a major Korean high-technology firm. You have been told by the head of your Seoul office that his reputation as an expert in international marketing is outstanding. The market share of his company's products has consistently increased since he joined the company just over fifteen years ago. His company's market share is now well ahead of that of competing producers in the Pacific Rim.

Mr. Park started with his present company immediately after his graduation from the University of Seoul and has worked his way up through the ranks. He does not have a graduate degree. You sense that Mr. Park has a keen understanding of organizational politics and knows how to play them. He recognizes that because the company he works for now is family controlled, it is unlikely that he will ever move much higher than his present situation. Mr. Park has told you that he is interested in the growth potential offered at your company.

In addition to his native tongue, Mr. Park is able to carry on a reasonably fluent conversation in English and has a minimal working knowledge of German and French. His wife, who appears quiet and quite traditional, and his children speak only Korean.

Kiran K., age 50, Widow with One Adult Child

Kiran K. is a Sikh woman living in Malaysia. She began her teaching career while finishing her DBA (doctorate in business administration) at the Harvard Business School and published her first book on international marketing 10 months after graduation. Her doctoral dissertation was based on the international marketing of pharmaceuticals, but she has also done research and published on other areas of international marketing.

Two months after the publication of her book, Kiran went to work in the international marketing department of a Fortune 500 company, where she stayed for the next 10 years. She returned to teaching when Maura University offered her a full professorship with tenure, and she has been there since that time. Her academic position has allowed her to pursue a number of research interests and to write authoritative books and papers in her field. At present, she is well published and internationally recognized as an expert on international marketing. In addition, she has an active consulting practice throughout Southeast Asia.

You have learned through your office in Kuala Lumpur that Kiran's only child, a 23-year-old son, is severely mentally and physically disabled. You sense that part of her interest in the job with your company is to have the income to guarantee his care should anything happen to her. Her son would go with her to Holland, should she be given the job, where he will need to be enrolled in special support programs.

In addition to fluency in Malay, English, and Hindi, Kiran speaks and writes German and Spanish and is able to converse in Japanese and Mandarin.

Peter V., age 44, Single

Peter is a white South African. He had worked in a key position in the international marketing division of an American Fortune 100 company until the company pulled out of his country eight months ago. While the company wanted to keep him on, offering to move him from Johannesburg to its New York headquarters, Peter decided that it was time to look elsewhere. He had begun to feel somewhat dead-ended in his position and apparently sees the position at your company as an opportunity to try out new territory. Like your other candi-

dates for the position, Peter has a long list of accomplishments and is widely recognized as outstanding in his field. People in your company who have had contacts with him say that Peter is creative, hardworking, and loyal. In addition, you have been told that Peter is a top-flight manager of people who is able to push his employees to the highest levels of performance. And, you are told, he is very organized.

Peter has a PhD in computer science from a leading South African university and an MBA from Purdue's Krannert School of Business.

Peter had been a vehement opponent of apartheid and is still very much a social activist. His high political visibility within South Africa had made his life there difficult, and even now, with the end of apartheid, he would like to get out. His constant male companion, P. K. Kahn, would be coming with him to Holland, and Peter would like your personnel office to help P. K. find an appropriate position.

Peter speaks and reads English, Dutch, Afrikaans, and Swahili and can converse in German.

Tex P., age 36, Divorced with One Child

Tex is currently job hunting. His former job as head of marketing for a single-product high-technology firm—highly specialized workstations for sophisticated artificial intelligence applications—ended when the company was bought out by Texas Instruments. Tex had been with his previous company virtually from the time the company was started six years earlier. Having to leave his job was an irony to Tex as it was largely due to the success of his efforts that the company was bought out. You sense that he is a little bitter, and he tells you that jobs offered to him by TI were beneath him and not worthy of consideration.

Tex has both his undergraduate and MBA degrees from Stanford University. In addition, he was a Rhodes Scholar and won a Fulbright scholarship, which he used to support himself while he undertook a two-year research project on the marketing of high-technology equipment to Third World countries.

You have learned through your New York office that Tex has a reputation for being aggressive and hard driving. Apparently he is a workaholic who has been known to work eighteen to twenty hours a day, seven days a week. He seems to have little time for his personal life.

In addition to his native English, Tex has a minimal command of French—which he admits he hasn't used since his college days.

Zvi C., age 40, Married with Five Children

Zvi began his career after receiving his MBA from the Sloan School of Management at the Massachusetts Institute of Technology (MIT). His first job was as marketing manager for a German company doing business in Israel.

Zvi's phenomenal success with this company led to his being hired away by an international office equipment company in England. Again, he proved to be outstanding, boosting the company's market share beyond all expectations within two years. After five years, Zvi was offered a chance to go back to Israel, this time to oversee and coordinate all the international marketing programs for an industrial park of 14 companies run as an adjunct to Israel's leading scientific research institution. It has been his responsibility to interface the research component with product development and sales as well as to manage the vast marketing department. Again, he has shown himself to be a master.

You have learned through your Haifa office that Zvi is highly respected and has extensive contacts in the scientific and high-tech worlds. He is exceptionally creative in his approach to marketing, often trying bold strategies that most of his peers would dismiss as too risky. Zvi, however, has made them work and work well.

Zvi is a religious man who must leave work by noon on Friday. He will not work Saturdays nor any of his religion's major and minor holidays—about eighteen a year. He will, however, work on Sundays.

In addition to his native language, Dutch (Zvi and his family moved to Israel form Holland when Zvi was six), he speaks and writes fluent Hebrew, English, German, and Arabic.

Ranking Sheet

Rank candidates from one to five with one as your first choice.

	My Ranking		Group Ranking	
Applicant	Rank	Reasons	Rank	Reasons
Park L.				
Kiran K.				
Peter V.				
Tex P.				
Zvi C.				

1. "Frankenfoods" or Rice Bowl for the World: The U.S.–EU Dispute over Trade in Genetically Modified Organisms

This simulation is designed to develop skills at cross-cultural negotiations with an emphasis on multi-stakeholder dialogue and exchange.

Synopsis

On August 18, 2003, members of the World Trade Organization (WTO) met in Geneva to hear a U.S. request for a full-blown dispute-settlement proceeding regarding European Union (EU) restrictions on the import and sale of goods produced with or containing genetically modified organisms (GMOs). In late 1996, Monsanto exported the first genetically modified soybeans to Europe, assuming that consumers would accept them as Americans had. The timing was not good, however, as the GMO issue became linked in the minds of Europeans with "mad cow" disease, an outbreak that was first thought limited to animals but eventually killed several humans. Neither GMO companies nor European authorities were prepared for the reaction, as public sentiment immediately turned against the technology. Britain's *Daily Mirror* ran a front-page headline in 1998 warning against "Frankenfood." In 1998, five European countries said they wouldn't process any more applications for genetically modified crops, and the EU upheld this decision.[1]

In May 2003, the United States filed a complaint with the WTO in hopes of getting the ban lifted. In response, in the summer of 2003, the European Parliament passed groundbreaking legislation that would require detailed labeling of all food products containing as little as 0.9 percent of genetically modified ingredients, and would require origin tracing in order to gain approval. Although these steps were designed to move toward lifting the moratorium, many in the United States charged that these rules would be unworkable, would be discriminatory toward imports, and would violate WTO sanitary and phytosanitary (SPS) agreements.[2]

Paradoxically, both sides claimed to be concerned about public health and environmental safety. The U.S. government and industry argued that the EU was in violation of WTO provisions requiring nondiscriminatory treatment of like or similar goods. The Americans contended that uninformed Europeans were spreading unfounded fears about GMOs.[3] In addition, the U.S. government argued that requiring labels for GMO products would result in segregating GMO foods from non-GMO foods and, in so doing, limit their consumer appeal. Furthermore, the threshold of 0.9 percent was far too restrictive, according to U.S. officials. Because a final WTO ruling could take up to two years, the litigation on GMOs is likely to hinder progress through the entire current round of multilateral trade negotiations under the auspices of the WTO, known as the "Development Round."

Description of Exercise

This exercise provides an interactive case simulation in which you will be assigned to a group that will assume the role of one of several stakeholder groups in the actual dispute between the United States and the EU over trade in GMOs. In this case, the U.S. government, on behalf of U.S. farmers and the biotech industry, argued that the EU is in violation of global trading rules. Europe responded that it has the right to protect the health and safety of its population and domestic crops, given the uncertainties over the effects of GMOs on humans, animals, and plants.

This simulation assumes that the United States and the EU proceed through the WTO dispute-settlement procedures, and it places participants in the roles of the various disputants: the U.S. government, the European Union, a consortium of GMO companies, a group of interested developing countries, a group of NGOs, and a WTO Dispute Settlement Panel.

Genetically Modified Food

According to some estimates, over half the world's soy, a key ingredient in products ranging from candy bars to animal feed, comes from genetically modified strains. About 7 million farmers in 18 countries now plant genetically altered seeds. According to one estimate, the global market value of genetically modified crops in 2002 was more than $4.75 billion.[4] Yet genetically modified food has quickly become as controversial as cloning. The central feature of a GMO is human alteration of the DNA of an organism through the use of biotechnology. Proponents and opponents in the genetic-modification debate

Source: © McGraw-Hill Irwin. This simulation was prepared by Professor Jonathan Doh as the basis for class discussion. It is not intended to illustrate either effective or ineffective managerial capability or administrative responsibility.

have been eager to weigh in on the benefits and risks associated with using GMOs. Each side has identified a number of key arguments to support its position:

Benefits

- Increased yields.
- Herbicide-tolerant crops encourage less tilling/soil erosion.
- Insecticidal crops encourage less use of harmful pesticides.
- Virus-resistant crops.
- Development of drought-resistant crops.

Risks

- Possible allergic or other health responses in humans/livestock.
- Creating new or more vigorous pests and pathogens.
- Harm to "nontarget" beneficial species.
- Unwanted gene flow.
- Irreparable changes in species diversity and in genetic diversity within a species.

Genetically engineered products are not new. Insulin used in medicine is an example of genetic engineering. The insulin gene from the intestines of pigs is inserted into bacteria.[5] The bacteria grow and produce insulin, which is then purified and used for medical purposes. Other genetically engineered products include the chemical compound aspartame, used as a sugar substitute, and the hepatitis B vaccine.

A large barrier to the acceptance of GMOs worldwide is the fuzzy international law regulating GMO trade. The Agreement on Sanitary and Phytosanitary Measures (SPS Agreement), part of the 1994 agreement that established the World Trade Organization, requires that food safety regulations be based on scientific risk assessments.[6] Most studies to date seem to point to the conclusion that foods containing GMOs are safe for human consumption. But the fact that a majority of these studies were conducted by or for U.S. biotech firms independent of any third-party overseers suggests to some that the findings are suspect. The United States already won a complaint with the WTO against the EU concerning an EU ban on hormone-treated beef, but the EU continues to enforce the broader ban on approval of newly introduced GMO products because a large majority of Europeans are steadfastly against the use of GMOs.

The U.S. Position

In the United States, 86 percent of soy and more than 40 percent of corn are genetically modified. The U.S. government argues that the EU ban on genetically modified food not only is hurting U.S. commerce but also is discouraging developing countries from growing genetically modified crops for export.

The U.S. government believes that genetically modified products could reduce hunger and poverty in the world's poorest nations, and that by restricting the use of GMOs, the EU is aggravating starvation in the developing world.[7] Biotechnology, according to U.S. policy makers and biotech executives, offers the prospect of crops that are more resilient, require less water, and give higher yields. Thus the EU ban on genetically modified foods indirectly contributes to starvation by denying access to more efficient agricultural techniques.[8] Furthermore, according to Robert B. Zoellick, the U.S. Trade Representative, uninformed European attitudes continue to spread unfounded fears in developing countries, where the need for the increased yields offered by genetically modified foods is greatest.[9] In addition, according to the U.S. government, GMO technologies would help developing countries dramatically increase export earnings. The U.S. government is not only concerned that Europe will prevent the use of GMOs but also that the EU model could serve as a blueprint for other countries, including those in the developing world, that plan to regulate GMOs.

The GMO cause has experienced some setbacks in the United States. For example, Aventis CropScience, developer of StarLink corn, was forced to pay $10 million to Iowa farmers and grain elevators in premiums and compensation for losses tied to growing and handling genetically modified grain that contaminated the grain supply. Although the government had approved StarLink for use in livestock feed, it was not cleared for human consumption after possibly allergic reactions were reported in people who consumed the protein that StarLink produces. Hundreds of food products were recalled in 2001 after testing showed residues of the StarLink protein in taco shells and other food. Some estimates suggest costs could eventually exceed $200 million.[10]

The EU Position

For most Europeans, the debate over genetically modified foods is closely intertwined with cultural, environmental, and health issues. Recent surveys suggest that nearly 80 percent of Europeans do not want to consume products with GMOs.[11] At the heart of the debate is the growing disagreement between the United States and Europe over what steps are necessary to protect public health and the environment.[12] A major obstruction to settling this argument is deeply embedded in European culture. Food and culture are closely linked in Europe's historical and contemporary life. Many European regions celebrate their unique food traditions and local produce. Unlike Americans, whose food choices are driven by accessibility and convenience, Europeans try to limit the influence of corporate food companies on their food choices. Respecting their preferences, global food companies such as McDonald's, Burger King, and Coca-Cola have pledged to keep all products for sale in Europe free of GMOs.[13]

Another obstacle to the use of GMOs is the fact that in recent years Europe experienced several health crises—notably the outbreak of bovine spongiform encephalopathy (BSE), commonly known as "mad cow" disease—that alerted people to the possible dangers lurking in the food supply. Experts agreed that beef from cows with the disease was perfectly safe; then dozens of people died. Biotech firms will have difficulty convincing Europeans to consume GMOs in the absence of long-term statistical evidence from third parties supporting their safety claims.

Exacerbating the issue is the persistent view in Europe that the United States continues to engage in a unilateral—some would say imperial—foreign policy. Regardless of the ongoing battle over GMOs, many people in Europe support challenging U.S. positions as a matter of principle—as a demonstration of European strength and cultural unity. These strong views will continue to influence European consumer choices no matter the outcome of the current dispute. Resistance by European customers to all U.S. foods could overshadow any GMO benefits to the U.S. economy if, for example, the labeling provision is not upheld. The EU also argues that U.S. corporations are squeezing farmers around the world through their control of exporting and processing activities with the goal of developing a lower-cost, vertically integrated global supply chain.

European and North American protesters have been seen with banners calling genetically modified products "Frankenfoods," a label that deliberately associates them with frightening and unpredictable risks. Europe formally adopted a "precautionary principle" (described below) that takes a cautious approach to the approval of new bioengineered food, assuming that there may be unforeseen effects unless proven otherwise.

The EU argues the United States is motivated exclusively by economic considerations and that the U.S. government is responding only to the agribusiness and biotech firms that stand to gain financially if current restrictions are lifted. Ten agricultural conglomerates, many of which are active in GMOs, own almost 40 percent of the world's seed market.[14] According to Martin Rocholl, director of Friends of the Earth Europe, "The U.S. Administration, funded by the likes of GMO giant Monsanto, is using the undemocratic and secretive WTO to force-feed the world foods containing GMOs. Decisions about the food we eat should be made in Europe and not in the White House, the WTO or Monsanto's HQ. We welcome the European Commission's commitment to fight this aggressive U.S. policy and ensure that Europe's wildlife and people are protected from the threats of GM crops."[15]

Some European companies, such as Unilever, produce genetically modified products, but they don't sell those products in Europe because of consumer opposition. Germany's Metro AG chain, like other major European grocery stores, doesn't allow bioengineered ingredients in its store brands.[16] Labeling rules proposed to replace the ban have generated heated responses from European GMO opponents. Greenpeace promised to marshal thousands of volunteers throughout Europe to police grocery stores in the weeks that follow the launch of labeling. "If consumers start buying it and get used to it, we will lose," says Dan Hindsgaul, the head of Greenpeace's effort. The leader of the opposing effort, Monsanto's Daniel Rahier, agrees: "If Greenpeace doesn't succeed now, they will be in a very difficult position."[17]

Substantial Equivalence and the Precautionary Principle

The issue of scientific proof has been a major point of contention. At the heart of the debate are the concepts of substantial equivalence and the precautionary principle. The term *substantial equivalence* was first mentioned in a 1993 Organization for Economic Cooperation and Developments (OECD) report on the safety of biotechnology. Members of the OECD agreed that the most practical approach to determining the safety of foods derived by biotechnology is to consider whether they represent a "substantial equivalent" to analogous traditional products. The term *substantial equivalence* was borrowed from the U.S. Food and Drug Administration's (FDA) definition of a class of new medical devices that do not differ materially from their predecessors and thus do not raise new regulatory concerns. However, after considering the possible unseen effects of foods that contain GMOs, the EU argues that it is difficult to directly apply the FDA definition of *substantial equivalence* in this case. The concept of substantial equivalence was applied for the first time to a GMO in the safety assessment of the Flavr Savr tomato before it went to market in 1994. Data collected revealed that the modified tomato was equivalent to the nonmodified parent plant, and genetically modified tomatoes were accepted under FDA rules.

The EU adopted an approach to health and safety risks known as the "precautionary principle." In common parlance, this approach may be summed up as "Better safe than sorry." Under this policy, new products are not assumed to be safe unless scientifically shown to be so. According to some in the EU, there is little scientific, third-party evidence that shows foods containing GMOs are safe for consumption. The precautionary principle thus provides justification for restricting GMOs unless they can be shown to be safe in all respects.

Biotech and Agricultural Firms

Because of their international reach, several large U.S. firms, including Monsanto and Du Pont, that support biotech and use biotech crops in their products have pressed the U.S. government to take a strong stand on the issue. The United States is the largest agricultural exporter in the world, and U.S. officials argue that trade restrictions of any kind will only undermine an already sluggish global economy. At stake for large biotech multinationals is a substantial amount of future commerce. These firms have claimed huge losses since the EU ban was put into effect in 1998, projecting that the ban has cost them close to $300 million annually. U.S government policy has been supportive of biotech firms and a strong advocate of their ability to help alleviate famine in developing countries by producing more abundant yields in areas notorious for infertile soil and a lack of other resources.

The reluctance of key foreign trading partners—the EU, Australia, Japan, and other nations—to import genetically modified products has become a significant problem for American farmers as they compete in the international marketplace. In the United States, genetically modified crops, including corn and soybeans, are now planted on millions of acres of farmland. If current restrictions on genetically modified foods aren't lifted, American farmers will lose millions of dollars from unusable crops. In March 2004, the American Soybean Association (ASA) stepped forward to take a lead role in preparing the WTO challenge of the EU's labeling ban. In addition, the ASA claims the labeling threshold of 0.9 percent is too stringent and lacks statistical backing. Also worsening the farmers' plight is the fact that worldwide commodity prices have dropped over the past decade.[18]

Developing Countries

In developing countries, farmers have been resisting pressure to grow bioengineered crops—even if they could improve their productivity and reduce hunger—for fear of losing their European market.

GMO supporters believe that the modified organisms can resist certain viruses and extreme temperatures, enabling crops to survive with less energy than is normally required with nonmodified seeds. This ability could be very useful in regions that don't have much fertile soil and lack other usable resources. More abundant yields would help feed the large population in most developing countries. For example, yields could be increased by growing insect-resistant crops in regions where bugs have seriously restricted outputs. Proponents believe that foods containing GMOs will be able to alleviate starvation and hunger in needy places. The United States insists that GMOs do not pose a risk to developing nations because the seeds are destined for consumption, not planting.[19] GM crops are also considered by some to be better for regions such as Africa where lack of education and training in the use of fertilizers and other modern farming techniques hampers agricultural development. Transgenic crops make up for this lack of education because the technology to control insects is already packaged in the seeds and farmers just have to plant them.

Skeptics argue that the skewed food distribution system, not lack of access to GMOs, is responsible for food shortages in developing countries. According to this view, developing countries are underfed because most of the food that they generate is sold in the export market to the wealthy developed nations. Furthermore, they question how poor developing countries will be able to afford the genetically modified seeds. U.S. agricultural firms own the patents, and the suspicion is widespread that U.S. companies will limit the availability of nonmodified seeds in order to support the sale of modified ones. Also, many people in the developing world remain skeptical about the health effects. In late June 2002, Zambia's minister of commerce, trade, and industry, Dipak Patel, proclaimed that African nations would not accept genetically modified food until it has been proven safe for human consumption.[20]

In Brazil, controversy surrounded President Lula da Silva's Provisional Measure 131, which authorized the commercialization of genetically modified soy. Opponents of GMOs in Brazil suggested that the governing administration, notorious for bribery and scandals, was influenced by its relationship with Monsanto, which owns the patent on the most popular genetically modified soy. Brazilian legislators agreed and proposed that genetically modified soy in Brazil be burned and replaced with conventional crops beginning in February 2004. Later, under pressure from some farming interests, the legislators reversed position, and genetically modified crops and seeds are now permitted.

The UN Cartagena Protocol, an agreement intended to educate emerging-market countries about the benefits and risks of genetically modified products, was activated in June 2003 when the Republic of Palau became the 50th country to ratify the bill. The agreement is designed to help educate emerging-market countries about the risks of proliferated GMOs.

Simulation Instructions

You will be assigned to one of six groups:

1. The U.S. government.
2. The European Union.
3. A consortium of companies that manufacture or use GMO products, including Monsanto and Cargill.
4. A group of interested developing countries.
5. A group of nongovernmental organizations (NGOs) opposed to the exchange of GMO products.
6. A WTO Dispute Settlement Panel.

Participants should spend 20 to 30 minutes reviewing the case and formulating arguments that advance the agenda of their group. Refer to the "GATT/WTO Principles" section below and to the background material above for information. After the initial session, groups whose interests may be similar may consult with each other for an additional 10 to 15 minutes to coordinate presentations and minimize duplication. For example, the consortium of GMO companies might consult with the U.S. government. The WTO Dispute Settlement Panel is composed of "judges" and should be treated respectfully. Each group should make an opening presentation of no more than 10 minutes to the WTO panel. The presentation should summarize the main points of the argument and urge a particular decision by the panel. Panel members may then ask questions of the groups for an additional 15 minutes. After each group presents its argument, the WTO panel will deliberate for 20 minutes and present its findings.

The issue for decision by the WTO Dispute Settlement Panel is whether the EU prohibition on imports of genetically modified products is consistent with WTO principles. Depending on the ruling in this matter, the WTO panel may offer specific remedies for how the ruling should be implemented. Further, the panel may wish to consider whether the proposed labeling and origin requirements (which in theory would allow the resumption of imports of genetically modified products) would or would not resolve the dispute, and whether this ban itself would be consistent with WTO principles.

GATT/WTO Principles: General Obligations

The General Agreement on Tariffs and Trade (now the World Trade Organization) was founded after World War II to establish rules for international trade practices and to resolve disputes among nations. Two fundamental principles govern most GATT/WTO provisions: most-favored-nation treatment and national treatment. *National treatment* refers to the obligations of the contracting parties to treat the nationals of foreign countries no less favorably than they treat the nationals of their own country. A more common term for this obligation is "nondiscrimination." The GATT/WTO also requires that the parties extend *most-favored-nation treatment* to other parties, so that some countries are not treated more favorably than others. Dispute settlement resolution (when one or more countries accuse another contracting party of violating GATT/WTO rules) is carried out by three- to five-member panels that render reports (decisions).

Exceptions

The GATT/WTO provides for limited exceptions to the above-mentioned obligations. For example, preferential trade agreements such as the EU and NAFTA are permitted to extend better than most-favored-nation treatment to their members under certain conditions. There are also "general" exemptions, which excuse otherwise illegal actions if they are designed to protect public morals, preserve national heritage, and limit commerce in goods made with prison

labor. Although the word *environment* is never mentioned, the GATT/WTO does offer a basis for deviating from GATT/WTO principles in support of environmental protection. Specifically, Article XX holds that the GATT/WTO does not prevent contracting parties from taking actions (1) necessary to the protection of human, animal, or plant life or health, and (2) relating to the conservation of exhaustible natural resources—provided trade measures affecting international commerce are joined by restrictions on domestic production or consumption.

The Uruguay Round agreement established agreements on the application of sanitary and phytosanitary (SPS) measures and technical barriers to trade (TBT). SPS measures are those necessary to safeguard human, animal, and plant health. Typically, when applied by an individual country, they are designed to safeguard its citizens, animal and plant industries, and environment against the risks posed by exotic pests and diseases, and against general threats to health entering from outside, and to control the incidence and spread of pests and diseases already present.

These agreements established the basis for reducing or eliminating nontariff regulatory barriers unless they respect scientifically substantiated and internationally recognized standards and conformance procedures and technical and labeling regulations. As applied to international trade, SPS protocols include a range of control measures—for example, import requirements; methods of treatment, manufacture, handling and packaging, and storage; inspection and certification requirements; and in some cases outright import bans on some products from certain areas. The major areas covered are plant quarantine measures, animal quarantine measures, and food safety standards. Thus governments may restrict imports of products that have been found to pose health or safety risks, based on sound, scientific evidence. Specifically, SPS measures must be designed to accomplish one or more of the following objectives:

1. To protect animal or plant life or health within the territory of the member from risks arising from the entry, establishment, or spread of pests, diseases, disease-carrying organisms, or disease-causing organisms.

2. To protect human or animal life within the territory of the member from risks arising from additives, contaminants, toxins, or disease-carrying organisms in food, beverages, or feedstuffs.

3. To protect human life or health within the territory of the member from risks arising from diseases carried by animals, plants, or products thereof, or from the entry, establishment, or spread of pests.

4. To prevent or limit other damage within the territory of the member from the entry, establishment, or spread of pests.

Questions for Discussion After Conclusion of Simulation

1. How does your solution compare to your expectation of the likely actual outcome? What is different or similar in the two approaches?

2. How would you characterize the cultures of Europe (France and Germany) and the United States in terms of Hofstede's scheme? In what ways are the cultures similar, and in what ways do they differ? How might the differences influence approaches to disputes like this one?

3. Why would an approach emphasizing "substantial equivalence" result in an outcome different from the outcome of a policy driven by the "precautionary principle"?

4. How might the United States and EU resolve differences such as this in the future?

■ Notes

1. Scott Miller, "EU's New Rules Will Shake Up Market for Bioengineered Food," *Wall Street Journal,* April 16, 2004, p. A1.

2. Kerry Capell, "The Genetically Modified Food Fight," *BusinessWeek Online,* July 21, 2003, http://bw.com/news/941856.asp?0dm=C18LB.

3. Elizabeth Becker, "U.S. Contests Europe's Ban on Some Food," *New York Times,* May 13, 2003, p. B4.

4. Ibid.

5. *Bacillus thuringiensis,* http://www.bt.ucsd.edu.

6. John Hulsman, "Cherry-Picking: U.S. and European Relationship," Heritage Foundation, http://www.heritage.org/research/tradeandforeignaid/tst061103.cfm.

7. Mark Drajem, "EU Pledges to Begin Approving Gene-Modified Crops This Year," *Bloomberg News,* June 17, 2003.

8. Jeremy Rifkin, "The Fight over GM Crops Exposes the Weaknesses of Globalization," *The Guardian,* June 2, 2003, p. 16.

9. Becker, "U.S. Contests Europe's Ban on Some Food."

10. Jerry Perkins, "Iowa StarLink Costs $9.2 Million—Aventis CropScience Pays Claims to Farmers, Elevators," *Des Moines Register,* September 15, 2001.

11. Sara Fitzgerald, "Putting the EU in Its Place: Why Filing a GMO Case with the WTO Is Crucial," Heritage Foundation, http://www.heritage.org/research/Europe/em855.cfm.

12. John Connor, "GM Corn Variety Classed as Safe," *New Zealand Herald,* July 7, 2002, p. A6.

13. Becker, "U.S. Contests Europe's Ban on Some Food."

14. John Schoen, "Is This Biotech Boom for Real?" http://www.msnbc.com/news/930313.asp?0dm=L1BmB, June 23, 2003.

15. Press release from Friends of the Earth Europe, http://www.foeeurope.org/press/2003/AW_18_Aug_GMO_trade_war.htm, August 18, 2003.

16. Miller, "EU's New Rules."

17. Ibid.

18. Interview with Keith Dittrich, president of the American Corn Growers Association, June 12, 2003.

19. Arpad Putszai. "Genetically Modified Foods: Are They a Risk to Human/Animal Health?" http://www.biotech-info.net/pusztai_article.html, June 2001.

20. Daniel Levine, "Mapping a New Plan for Biotech," *San Francisco Business Times,* March 10, 2003, p 12.

2. Cross-Cultural Conflicts in the Corning–Vitro Joint Venture

This simulation accompanies Brief Integrative Case 1 at the end of Part 2. It is designed to develop skills at international negotiation with an emphasis on cross-cultural communication and negotiation.

Case Summary

During the NAFTA negotiations, many U.S. firms were concerned about the reduction of U.S. tariffs on flat glass, which averaged 20 percent, and the perceived competitive advantages Mexican glass firms would have in the event these tariffs were removed. In the fall of 1991, in the midst of the NAFTA negotiations, Vitro S.A., the $3 billion Mexican glassmaker, signed a tentative $800 million joint venture with Corning Inc. Two mirror companies were established—Corning–Vitro and Vitro–Corning—and each company took an equity stake in each of these joint-venture firms. In addition, the two parent companies agreed to a series of marketing, sales, and distribution relationships to support the activities of each of the new companies.[1] Two years later, the joint venture was in distress, and some of the interested parties were suggesting that it be dissolved. This simulation provides participants with an opportunity to undertake negotiations designed to resolve these differences.

Background

Vitro Sociedad Anonima is a 100-year-old Mexican company with roughly $3.5 billion in sales and 40,000 employees. As Vitro positioned itself to take advantage of the emerging North American market, CEO Ernesto Martens-Rebolledo described the tightrope the company must walk: "We don't want to lose our identity as a Mexican company with a unique culture and relationship with our employees, but we don't want to be battered in the world marketplace either."[2] In 1989 Vitro completed a hostile takeover of Anchor Glass Container Corporation, and in 1992 Vitro laid off some 3,000 workers, an unusual move in Mexico at that time, given traditional notions about labor–management relations and job security.

Corning, an upstate New York maker of glass, traces its roots back to the mid-1800s In recent years, Corning has diversified into fiber optics and other high-technology

Source: © McGraw-Hill Irwin. This simulation was prepared by Jonathan Doh of Villanova University as the basis for class discussion. It is not intended to illustrate either effective or ineffective managerial capability or administrative responsibility.

applications of glass, ceramics, and composite materials. During the 1980s, Corning's business increasingly relied on sales of fiber optics to telecommunications firms. These firms were beginning construction of the new infrastructure to support high-speed voice and data transmission. At the same time, sales of household, flat glass, and other traditional glass products remained important to the company.

NAFTA and Glass[3]

During the early part of NAFTA negotiations (1989–1991), U.S. makers of household and flat glass products expressed concern about their ability to compete against cheaper Mexican imports, and some even accused Corning S.A. of unfair trading practices. Guardian Industries Corp., a Michigan-based manufacturer of float glass—the high-quality flat glass used in mirrors, insulated windows, furniture, and automobiles—complained that Vitro, the only Mexican producer of float glass, was engaged in anticompetitive practices by trying to intimidate a Mexican glass distributor who was considering buying a product from Guardian. Vitro exported approximately $120 million in float glass and related products to the United States in 1990. Other glassmakers argued that even with present U.S. duties averaging over 20 percent on household glassware from Mexico, the after-duty prices of the Mexican products were significantly below those of U.S. producers, owing in large part to considerably lower labor and energy costs.

In February 1991, the International Trade Commission (ITC) issued a report on these allegations. Vitro Crisa (an operating subsidiary of Vitro S.A.) allegedly priced its glass beverageware at about 20 to 30 percent below that of U.S. producers in the U.S. market. Vitro Crisa's lower productivity relative to U.S. industry, said the ITC, was offset by considerably lower labor costs (about $1.50 an hour versus $15 an hour in 1987 in the United States), which constituted nearly half of the production costs of the U.S. household glassware industry. The cost of natural gas, another major production input, was about 15 percent lower in Mexico.

Problems Arise[4]

"Vitro and Corning share a customer-oriented philosophy and remarkably similar corporate cultures." This was the characterization of the joint venture offered at the time by Julio Escamez, a Vitro executive. Both companies had long histories of successful joint ventures. Corning Inc. had been an innovative leader in foreign alliances for over 73 years. One of the company's first successes was an alliance with St. Gobain, a French glassmaker, to produce Pyrex cookware in Europe during the 1920s. Corning has formed approximately 50 ventures over the years. Only 9 failed (dissolved), an impressive number considering one recent study found that over one-half of foreign and national alliances do not succeed. From 1985 to 1990, Corning's sales from joint ventures were over $3 billion, contributing more than $500 million to its net income. Corning enters into joint ventures primarily to gain access to markets that it cannot penetrate quickly enough to obtain a competitive advantage. In addition, both companies were globally oriented, and both had founding families still at their centers. Yet the joint venture became subject to a series of cultural and other conflicts that began to undermine this vision.

U.S./Mexico Alliances[5]

"There are many reasons why corporate marriages between Mexican and U.S. companies fail," says Richard Sinkin, managing director of InterAmerican Holdings, a consultancy based in San Diego, California, that advises U.S. companies doing business in Mexico. Sinkin says that U.S. and Mexican companies often get together for the wrong reasons. Unless the two partners contribute essential qualities to the marriage, the alliance soon founders. The second difficulty is corporate control. "Most Mexican firms are still run as family businesses," Sinkin says, "and these firms are often reluctant to share control with an outside investor."

In the case of the Corning/Vitro JV, Corning managers said that they were sometimes left waiting for important decisions about marketing and sales because in the Mexican culture only top managers could make them and at Vitro those people were busy with other matters. Vitro's sales approach was less aggressive than Corning's, the remnant of years in a closed economy, and was sometimes at odds with the pragmatic approach Corning had developed over decades of competition.

NAFTA and Alliances[6]

To varying degrees, such cultural issues have plagued many mergers and alliances with their roots in the North American Free Trade Agreement. "Mexico initially appears to be the United States except that people speak Spanish," said Harley Shaiken, a labor economist who often works in Mexico. "That's just not the case, which everyone finds out in the short term rather than the long term." The trade pact may have created false expectations about how much like the United States Mexico has become. In discussing cultural differences, it's difficult not to slip into stereotypes about "mañana"—Mexicans who move at a slower pace. But what the gap separating the two business cultures really amounts to is a different approach to work, reflected in everything from scheduling to decision making to etiquette.

In the Corning venture, the Mexicans sometimes saw the Amerians as too direct, and Vitro managers, in their dogged pursuit of politeness, sometimes seemed to the Americans unwilling to acknowledge problems and faults. The Mexicans sometimes thought Corning moved too fast; the Americans felt Vitro was too slow.

Cultural differences generally, said Richard Sinkin, the corporate consultant, are "the No. 1 problem for doing business in Mexico." That may be an exaggeration, but it underscores the difficulty of transferring a culture across the border. Sinkin's own experience bears that out. He is bilingual and often works in Mexico but finds that it isn't always easy to get paid because the Mexican view of contracts differs markedly from the view commonly held in the United States. In Mexico, the terms of a contract "are kind of ideal things that you strive to achieve," Sinkin said, "while in the U.S. they are law." In general, corporate style is more formal in Mexico than in the United States. Titles are common, and nearly everyone is "licenciado," which loosely refers to having any professional training. Forgetting the honorific can be seen as a serious insult.

In Mexico, executives can expect the unquestioned loyalty of employees, but outsiders are often viewed with mistrust. Horace E. Scherer, director general of Hobart Dayton Mexicana, the Mexican subsidiary of the Hobart Corporation, said his salespeople must often make four trips to complete one transaction because of that lack of trust. To sell the company's scales and other equipment, a salesperson starts with a visit to the client's top official. If a sale is made, a representative of the company itself must deliver the goods because the customer won't accept delivery from DHL or some other service. If all the papers are in order on delivery, the company representative is told to come back on an appointed day to present an invoice, in person; if the invoice is accepted, an appointment is made for the rep to return to receive payment.

Many companies that have formed joint ventures end up creating their own new corporate culture, taking bits and pieces from each side. At Vitro–Whirlpool in Monterrey, assembly-line workers have a long tradition of taking what in Mexico is referred to as "el puente," or the bridge, which commonly extends a formal holiday into a mini vacation. When, for instance, Mexico's version of Mother's Day fell on Tuesday, May 10, workers did not show up on Monday, bridging the gap to the holiday. (If an American holiday falls on a Tuesday, of course, absenteeism will be high on Monday, but in Mexico the custom is far more entrenched—and can even shut a plant down.) The company now allows workers to take the "puente," but only if they agree to work an extra hour each day for eight days beforehand.

Because their corporate conversations can be filled with so many feints and pleasantries, Mexicans often use memos to convey dissatisfaction. When Labatt's (the Canadian brewer) Mexican manager, Noel Trainor, decided to cut back employees' lunch from two hours to one, he had to do it in a memo that all 30 employees had to sign. Mr. Trainor said he abided by a strict holiday policy, priding himself on the degree to which his compatriots had been able to adapt to the expectations of the United States and seemingly only half aware of the degree to which he had compromised. "We only give what we are obligated by law to give," he said, "and of course half a day on Mother's Day."

Financial and Commercial Concerns[7]

Added complications emerged from the relatively strong peso, increased overseas competition, and a reconsideration of marketing strategies by both companies. The joint ventures suffered from the different administrative practices of the two companies. "Managing from two countries was more complicated than we anticipated," said Corning. "There were different (management) structures, styles and accounting systems." Corning said the different needs of customers in the United States and Mexico complicated the integration of sales and distribution. Corning's U.S. customers, especially the large discount stores, expect the timely and regular delivery of products packaged in a certain way; Vitro's Mexican customers are less demanding.

In 1992, Corning–Vitro had sales of approximately $700 million, and Vitro–Corning achieved turnover of about $230 million.

Issues for Decision

As a result of cultural clashes, failure to integrate complementary product lines, and disappointing sales, both Corning and Vitro are contemplating dissolving the joint ventures. Within the two companies, however, there are those who support maintaining the relationship, and others who oppose it. Corning and Vitro must first decide on whether they want to remain in the joint ventures and, if they do, under what conditions. If they decide to dissolve the relationship, they must negotiate the terms of the dissolution. If they decide to remain in the arrangement, some changes must be made to address the growing problems.

Simulation Instructions

You will be assigned to one of four groups:

The groups are ad hoc. Each group represents an ad-hoc committee appointed by the CEO of each company to make recommendations about the future of the alliance. The groups' initial positions can be characterized as follows:

1. Vitro—supports keeping JVs
2. Vitro—against keeping JVs
3. Corning—supports keeping JVs
4. Corning—against keeping JVs

Negotiation 1

The initial negotiation occurs *within* each company. Hence, Vitro Groups (1 and 2) discuss their differing position, and Corning Groups (3 and 4) exchange their views with each other. Each pair of groups (1/2 + 3/4) should decide whether their company wants to remain within the joint venture or dissolve it. Each pair of groups has 45 minutes to negotiate *within* the respective companies over whether to stay in or dissolve the JV. Groups 1 and 3 should consider the following:

1. The logic and original rationale for the JV.
2. How that logic may still hold.
3. How the JV could be made to work better.

Groups 2 and 4 should consider the following:

1. What caused the JV relationship to sour.
2. Why the partner has not lived up to expectations.
3. What the terms of dissolution should be.

Each company agrees on a position to bring forward to the partner. This position need not necessarily be a demand to maintain the joint venture or to dissolve it; rather it could be a contingency laying the conditions for maintaining the relationship, or demands for how it should be dissolved. Once each company has decided on its position, a representative from each Corning group (two to four representatives total) will meet with their counterparts from the Vitro groups.

Negotiation 2

Each company must decide, collectively, through negotiation, whether to remain within the joint venture or dissolve it. The representatives from each company have 60 minutes to reach some resolution. *They must consult with the remainder of their company throughout the negotiation to ensure support for the outcome.* The main issues for consideration include:

1. The logic and original rationale for the JV.
2. How that logic may still hold.
3. How the JV could be made to work better.
4. What caused the JV relationship to sour.
5. Why the partner has not lived up to expectations.
6. Whether the JV should be terminated and, if so, what the terms of dissolution should be.

Ultimately, issue 3 or 6 must be resolved. Any solution, whether to maintain the JV, dissolve it, or some hybrid approach, should be comprehensive and address these elements:

- *Financial structure:* Terms for financing existing or new ventures under the arrangement or payments for dissolution of the relationship.
- *Governance:* Board, management, or other top-level changes in ownership and leadership under the present or revised relationship.

Table 1
Hofstede's Cultural Ratings for the United States and Key Latin Countries

	Power Distance	Uncertainty Avoidance	Individualism	Masculinity
United States	40	46	91	62
Mexico	81	82	38	69
Canada	39	48	80	52
Argentina	49	86	46	56
Brazil	69	76	38	49
Colombia	67	80	13	64
Peru	64	87	16	42
Venezuela	81	76	12	73
Spain	57	86	51	42
Portugal	63	104	27	31

Source: Geert Hofstede, *Culture's Consequences: International Differences in Work-Related Values* (Beverly Hills, CA: Sage, 1980).

- *Marketing:* Agreements about marketing, distribution, and sales relationships either under the current arrangement or in any new structure.
- *Competition/cooperation:* Changes in the way in which each company operates in the other's territories or markets.

Questions for Discussion After Conclusion of Simulation

1. Compare your solution to the joint venture's problems with the actual outcome. What is different or similar in the two approaches?

2. How would you characterize the Mexican and U.S. culture in terms of Hofstede's scheme (see Table 1)? In what ways were the cultures similar and in what ways different?

3. Compare Corning–Vitro's problems to those of some of the other international joint ventures described in this simulation. How were they similar, different, and more or less challenging?

4. How have other companies in Mexico and Latin America addressed these cultural divisions in the recent past? How should they as they go forward with comprehensive regional Latin American strategies?

■ Notes

1. "Glassmakers' Complaints Aired in NAFTA Hearings," *LDC Debt Report/Latin American Market,* September 9, 1999, p. 10.

2. Nancy A. Nichols, "From Complacency to Competitiveness: An Interview with Vitro's Ernesto Martens," *Harvard Business Review,* September–October 1993, p. 162.

3. "Glassmakers' Complaints Aired in NAFTA Hearings."

4. Anthony Depalma, "It Takes More than a Visa to Do Business in Mexico," *New York Times,* June 26, 1994, sec. 3, p. 5.

5. Leslie Crawford, "Anheuser's Cross-Border Marriage on the Rocks: Modelo Deal Is the Latest U.S.–Mexican Partnership to Be Soured by Disagreement," *Financial Times,* March 18, 1998, p. 46.

6. Depalma, "It Takes More than a Visa."

7. John Holusha, "Corning to Buy Northern Telecom Assets," *New York Times,* December 16, 1993, sec. D, p. 4.

References

■ Chapter 1

International Management in Action: Tracing the Roots of Modern Globalization Thomas Cahill, *Sailing the Wine Dark Sea: Why Greeks Matter* (New York: Doubleday, 2003), pp. 10, 56–57; Charles W. L. Hill, *International Business,* 4th ed. (New York: McGraw-Hill Irwin, 2003), p. 100; Nefertiti Web site, http://nefertiti.iweland.com/trade/internal_trade.htm, 2003 (ancient Egypt: domestic trade); Gavin Menzies, *1421: The Year China Discovered America* (New York: William Morrow/HarperCollins, 2003), pp. 26–27; Milton Viorst, *The Great Documents of Western Civilization* (New York: Barnes & Noble Books, 1994), p. 115 (Magna Carta) and p. 168 (Declaration of Independence).

International Management in Action: Telecommunications Privatization in Brazil Simon Romero, "Brazil Still Embraces Globalization," *New York Times,* December 2, 1999, p. C1; "Brazil's Dozen Phone Spinoffs Come to Trade in New York," *New York Times,* November 17, 1998, p. C12; Edward A. Robinson. "Update: Telebras Pieces Fetch High Prices," *Fortune,* September 7, 1998, p. 181; Al Goodman, "Spanish Phone Utility Extends Its Latin American Leadership," *New York Times,* August 4, 1998, p. D7.

International Management in Action: Separating Myths from Reality Stanley J. Modic, "Myths About Japanese Management," *Industry Week,* October 5, 1987, pp. 49–53; Richard M. Hodgetts and Fred Luthans, "Japanese HR Management Practices: Separating Fact from Fiction," *Personnel,* April 1989, pp. 42–45; Jon Wonoroff, *The Japanese Management Mystique* (Chicago: Probus Publishing, 1992); Howard W. French, "A Postmodern Plague Ravages Japan's Workers," *New York Times,* February 21, 2000, p. A4.

In the International Spotlight: India John F. Burns, "India Now Winning U.S. Investment," *New York Times,* February 6, 1995, pp. C1, C5; "The Trouble with Democracy, Part 2," *Economist,* December 17, 1994, pp. 17–18; Rahual Jacob, "India Gets Moving," *Fortune,* September 5, 1994, pp. 101–102; Saritha Rai, "Enron Unit Moves to End India Contract for Power," *New York Times,* May 22, 2001, p. W1; Jon E. Hilsenrath, "Honda Venture Takes the Bumps in India," *Wall Street Journal,* August 2, 2000, p. A18; Manjeet Kripalani and Pete Engardio, "India: A Shocking Election Upset Means India Must Spend Heavily on Social Needs," *BusinessWeek,* May 31, 2004.

■ Chapter 2

International Management in Action: The U.S. Goes to the Mat Robert Neff, Brian Bremner, and Edith Updike, "The Japanese Have a New Thirst for Imports," *BusinessWeek,* June 5, 1995, pp. 52, 54; Gabriella Stern and Nichole M. Christian, "GM Plans to Sell Saturn Line in Japan in Network of Stand-Alone Dealerships," *Wall Street Journal,* June 2, 1995, p. A4; Keith Bradsher, "U.S. Called Ready to Compromise on Date for Japan Trade Talks," *New York Times,* June 1, 1995, pp. C1, C15; Bhushan Bahree, "Auto Talks by U.S., Japan Seem Set for Geneva in June," *Wall Street Journal,* June 1, 1995, p. A11.

In the International Spotlight: Vietnam Frederik Balfour, "Back on the Radar Screen," *BusinessWeek,* November 20, 2000, pp. 56–57; Jon E. Hilsenrath, "U.S. Investors See Hope in Vietnam Trip," *Wall Street Journal,* November 17, 2000, p. A17; Benjamin Fulford, "Capitalism Creeps into Vietnam," *Forbes,* May 17, 1999, pp. 174, 176; Roy Rowan,

"25 Years After the Fall," *Fortune,* May 1, 2000, pp. 208–222; Wayne Arnold, "Trade Accord with Vietnam: Exports in Place of Enmity," *New York Times,* July 28, 2000, p. C4; Ha Thank Nguyen and Klaus E. Meyer, "Managing Partnerships with State-Owned Joint Venture Companies: Experiences From Vietnam," *Business Strategy Review* 15 (Spring 2004), p. 39.

■ Chapter 3

International Management in Action: Get Tough . . . Or Else Amy Borrus, Dexter Roberts, and Joyce Barnathan, "Counterfeit Disks, Suspect Enforcement," *BusinessWeek,* September 18, 1995, p. 68; Pete Engardio and Joyce Barnathan, "China: Strife at the Top May Spark a War on Corruption," *BusinessWeek,* March 6, 1995, p. 53; Seth Faison, "Razors, Soap, Cornflakes: Pirating in China Balloons," *New York Times,* February 17, 1995, pp. A1, C2; "Copy to Come," *Economist,* January 7, 1995, pp. 51–52; Richard Behar, "Beijing's Phony War on Fakes," *Fortune,* October 30, 2000, pp. 189–208; Robin Stanley Snell and Choo-sin Tseng, "Ethical Dilemmas of Relationship Building in China," *Thunderbird International Business Review,* March–April 2001, pp. 171–200.

In the International Spotlight: Saudi Arabia Neil Macfarquhar, "After the Saudi Rampage, Questions and Few Answers," *New York Times,* June 1, 2004, p. A6; "Rising Stars," *Airfinance Journal,* September 2002, p. 50.

■ Chapter 4

International Management in Action: Business Customs in Japan William Morrow, "Speaking the Japanese Business Language," *European Business,* Winter 1974, pp. 45–46; Ted Holden and Suzanne Wolley, "The Delicate Art of Doing Business in Japan," *BusinessWeek,* October 2, 1989, p. 120; Roger E. Axtell, ed., *Do's and Taboos Around the World,* 2nd ed. (New York: Wiley, 1990), pp. 33, 90; Richard D. Lewis, *When Cultures Collide* (London: Nicholas Brealey, 1999), pp. 400–415.

International Management in Action: Common Personal Values George W. England, "Managers and Their Value Systems: A Five-Country Comparative Study," *Columbia Journal of World Business,* Summer 1978, pp. 35–44; Geert Hofstede, *Culture's Consequences: International Differences in Work-Related Values* (Beverly Hills, CA: Sage, 1980); Geert Hofstede, *Cultures and Organizations: Software of the Mind* (London: McGraw-Hill U.K., 1991); Martin J. Gannon, *Understanding Global Cultures,* 2nd ed. (Thousand Oaks, CA: Sage, 2001), pp. 35–56.

In the International Spotlight: Taiwan Michael J. Marquardt and Dean W. Engel, *Global Human Resource Development* (Englewood Cliffs, NJ: Prentice-Hall, 1993), pp. 183–186; "China (Taiwan)," *Europa World Year Book 1995,* vol. 1 (London: Europa Publications, 1995), pp. 833–842; Brian Bremmer et al., "Asia: The Big Chill," *BusinessWeek,* April 2, 2001, pp. 48–49; Andy Reinhardt, "A Silicon Chameleon Challenges Intel," *BusinessWeek,* May 29, 2000, pp. 102–106; Raj Aggarwal, "Assessing the Recent Asian Economic Crises: The Role of Virtuous and Vicious Cycles," *Journal of World Business* 34, no. 4 (1999) pp, 392–408; Jason Dean, "Taiwan Economy Is a Winner; Analysts Are Bullish on Stocks No Matter Election's Outcome," *Wall Street Journal,* March 19, 2004, p. C16; David Lague, "The Result Is Final: A Divided Taiwan," *Far Eastern Economic Review,* April 1, 2004, pp. 14–17.

Chapter 5

International Management in Action: Ten Key Factors for MNC Success James F. Bolt, "Global Competitors: Some Criteria for Success," *Business Horizons,* January–February 1988, pp. 34–41; Alan S. Rugman and Richard M. Hodgetts, *International Business,* 2nd ed. (London: Pearson, 2000), chapter 1; and Sheida Hodge, *Global Smarts: The Art of Communicating and Deal Making Anywhere in the World* (New York: Wiley, 2000).

International Management in Action: Managing in Hong Kong J. Stewart Black and Lyman W. Porter, "Managerial Behaviors and Job Performance: A Successful Manager in Los Angeles May Not Succeed in Hong Kong," *Journal of International Business Studies,* 22, no. 1 (First Quarter 1991), pp. 99–112; Geert Hofstede, *Cultures and Organizations: Software of the Mind* (London: McGraw-Hill U.K., 1991), chapters 4–6; Alan S. Rugman and Richard M. Hodgetts, *International Business,* 2nd ed. (London: Pearson, 2000), chapter 20; Benjamin Fulford, "Microwave Missionaries," *Forbes,* November 13, 2000, pp. 136–146.

In the International Spotlight: Mexico David Wessel, Paul B. Carroll, and Thomas T. Vogel Jr., "How Mexico's Crisis Ambushed Top Minds in Officialdom, Finance," *Wall Street Journal,* July 6, 1995, pp. A1, A4; Craig Torres and Paul B. Carroll, "Mexico's Mantra for Salvation: Export, Export, Export," *Wall Street Journal,* March 17, 1995, p. A6; "Mexico," *Europa* (London: Europa Publications, 1995), pp. 429–444; Carlta Vitzthum and Nicole Harris, "Telefonica Makes Its Move into Mexico," *Wall Street Journal,* October 5, 2000, p. A19; Joel Millman, "Mexico Factories See Growth Unchecked," *Wall Street Journal,* November 6, 2000, p. A29; David Luhnow, "Mexico's Economy Hints at Rebound, Aided Once Again by U.S. Ties," *Wall Street Journal,* January 13, 2004, p. A2; Ken Bensinger, "Trade Bandwagon Sweeps Up Mexico, but Critics Say Pacts Create Mixed Results," *Houston Chronicle,* April 2, 2004, p. 1.

Chapter 6

International Management in Action: McDonald's Tackles Eating Habits in Brazil Richard Gibson and Matt Moffett, "Why You Won't Find Any Egg McMuffins for Breakfast in Brazil," *Wall Street Journal,* October 23, 1997, pp. A1, A8; Lori Lohmeyer, "McDonald's Weaves New Web: Eat and Surf the Internet," *Nation's Restaurant News,* May 19, 2003, p. 60.

International Management in Action: Matsushita Goes Global P. Christopher Earley and Harbir Singh, "International and Intercultural Management Research: What's Next," *Academy of Management Journal,* June 1995, pp. 327–340; Karen Lowry Miller, "Siemens Shapes Up," *BusinessWeek,* May 1, 1995, pp. 52–53; Christine M. Riordan and Robert J. Vandenberg, "A Central Question in Cross-Cultural Research: Do Employees of Different Cultures Interpret Work-Related Measures in an Equivalent Manner?" *Journal of Management* 20, no. 3 (1994), pp. 643–671; Brenton R. Schlender, "Matsushita Shows How to Go Global," *Fortune,* July 11, 1994, pp. 159–166.

In the International Spotlight: Japan Iain McDonald, "Japan's Industrial Production Rises 3.3% amid Payroll Gains," *Wall Street Journal,* June 1, 2004. p. A14.

Chapter 7

International Management in Action: Doing It Right the First Time www.jetro.gp.ip/JETROINFO/DOING/4.html; Alan Rugman and Richard M. Hodgetts, *International Business,* 2nd ed. (London: Pearson, 2000), chapter 17; Philip R. Harris and Robert T. Moran, *Managing Cultural Differences,* 3rd ed. (Houston: Gulf Publishing, 1991), pp. 393–406; Sheila Hodge, *Global Smarts* (New York: Wiley, 2000),

p. 76; Richard D. Lewis, *When Cultures Collide* (London: Nicholas Brealey, 1999), pp. 414–415.

International Management in Action: Communicating in Europe Karen Matthes, "Mind Your Manners When Doing Business in Europe," *Personnel,* January 1992, p. 19; Philip R. Harris and Robert T. Moran, *Managing Cultural Differences: High-Performance Strategies for a New World of Business,* 4th ed. (Houston: Gulf Publishing, 1994), chapter 13; Alan Rugman and Richard M. Hodgetts, *International Business,* 2nd ed. (London: Pearson, 2000), chapter 16; Richard Lewis, *When Cultures Collide* (London: Nicholas Brealey, 1999).

International Management in Action: Negotiating with the Japanese Rosalie J. Tung, "How to Negotiate with the Japanese," *California Management Review,* Summer 1984, pp. 62–77; Carla Rapoport, "You Can Make Money in Japan," *Fortune,* February 12, 1990, pp. 85–92; Margaret A. Neale and Max H. Bazerman, "Negotiating Rationally," *Academy of Management Executive,* August 1992, pp. 42–51; Martin J. Gannon, *Understanding Global Cultures,* 2nd ed. (Thousand Oaks, CA: Sage, 2001), pp. 35–56; Sheila Hodge, *Global Smarts* (New York: Wiley, 2000), chapter 14; and Richard D. Lewis, *When Cultures Collide* (London: Nicholas Brealey, 1999), pp. 400–415.

In the International Spotlight: China Patricia O'Connell, "Huawei vs. Cisco Just Got Nastier," *BusinessWeek,* June 3, 2003; Edward Cody, "China's Government Tries to Calm Economic Boom," *Washington Post,* May 19, 2004, p. E1; Bruce Einhorn and Peter Burrows, "Huawei: Cisco's Rival Hangs Tough," *BusinessWeek,* January 19, 2004, p. 73.

Chapter 8

International Management in Action: Point/Counterpoint Wendy Bonds, "Fuji, Accused by Kodak of Hogging Markets, Spits Back: 'You Too,'" *Wall Street Journal,* July 31, 1995, pp. A1, A5; "Photo Wars: Shuttered," *Economist,* August 5, 1995, pp. 59–60; Mark Maremont, "Next a Flap over Film," *BusinessWeek,* July 10, 1995, p. 34; "Japan's Fuji Photo Film's Group Operating Profit Rose in FY 2000," *Asia Pulse,* May 8, 2001; and "Kodak Says Profit Outlook Unchanged," Reuters, May 23, 2001.

In the International Spotlight: Poland David Fairlamb and Bogdan Turek, "Poland and the EU: Will the Dynamic Poles Energize Europe or Sink into a Bureaucratic, Slow-Growth Trap?" *BusinessWeek,* May 10, 2004, p. 54; Ben Arisin Prague, "Central European Entrants to EU Have Most to Gain but Are Least Prepared," *Knight Ridder Tribune Business News,* March 14, 2004. p. 1.

You Be the International Management Consultant: Go East, Young People, Go East Amy Borrus et al., "The Asians Are Bracing for a Trade Shoot-Out," *BusinessWeek,* May 1, 1989, pp. 40–41; John W. Verity, "If It Looks Like a Slump and Crawls Like a Slump . . . ," *BusinessWeek,* May 1, 1989, p. 27; Geoff Lewis, "Is the Computer Business Maturing?" *BusinessWeek,* March 6, 1989, pp. 68–78.

Chapter 9

International Management in Action: Joint Venturing in Russia Keith A. Rosten, "Soviet–U.S. Joint Ventures: Pioneers on a New Frontier," *California Management Review,* Winter 1991, pp. 88–108; Steven Greenhouse, "Chevron to Spend $10 Billion to Seek Oil in Kazakhstan," *New York Times,* May 19, 1992, pp. A1, C9; Louis Uchitelle, "Givebacks by Chevron in Oil Deal," *New York Times,* May 23, 1992, pp. 17, 29; Craig Mellow, "Russia: Making Cash from Chaos," *Fortune,* April 17, 1995, pp. 145–151; Daniel J. McCarthy and Sheila M. Puffer, "Strategic Investment Flexibility for MNE Success in Russia," *Journal of World Business* 32, no. 4 (1997), pp. 293–318; R. Bruce Money and Debra Colton, "The Response of the 'New Consumer' to Promotion in the Transition Economies of the Former Soviet Bloc," *Journal of World Business* 35, no. 2 (2000), pp. 189–206.

International Management in Action: Organizing in Germany
Hermann Simon, "Lessons from Germany's Midsize Giants," *Harvard Business Review,* March–April 1992, pp. 115–123; Carla Rapoport, "Europe's Slump Won't End Soon," *Fortune,* May 3, 1993, pp. 82–87; Robert Neff and Douglas Harbrecht, "Germany's Mighty Unions Are Being Forced to Bend," *BusinessWeek,* March 1, 1993, pp. 52–56.

In the International Spotlight: Australia   Wayne Arnold, "World Business Briefing: Australia's Jobless Rate Falls," *New York Times,* April 9, 2004, p. W1; "Finance and Economics: A Wonder Down Under—The Australian Economy," *Economist,* March 20, 2004, p. 105.

Chapter 10

International Management in Action: Sometimes It's All Politics
John Stackhouse, "India Sours on Foreign Investment," *Globe and Mail,* August 10, 1995, sec. 2, pp. 1–2; Peter Galuszka and Susan Chandler, "A Plague of Disjointed Ventures," *BusinessWeek,* May 1, 1995, p. 55; Marcus W. Brauchli, "Politics Threaten Power Project in India," *Wall Street Journal,* July 3, 1995, p. A14; "Enron, and On and On," *Economist,* April 21, 2001, pp. 56–57; Saritha Rai, "Enron Unit Moves to End India Contract for Power," *New York Times,* May 22, 2001, pp. W1, W7; Enron Properties Outside the U.S. Hit Auction Block, *Wall Street Journal,* January, 22, 2002, p. A6.

In the International Spotlight: Peru   "Colombia, Peru, and Ecuador Start Trade Talks with the U.S.," *Emerging Markets Economy,* May 20, 2004, p. 1; "Peru GDP Grows 5.7 Percent," *Emerging Markets Economy,* August 19, 2003, p. 1

Chapter 11

International Management in Action: Kodak Goes Digital   Wendy Bonds, "Fuji, Accused by Kodak of Hogging Markets, Spits Back: 'You Too,'" *Wall Street Journal,* July 31, 1995, pp. A1, A5; "Kodak Completes Acquisition of Leading Online Photo Service" Kodak Company news release, June 4, 2001.

International Management in Action: How the Japanese Do Things Differently   Ford S. Worthy, "Japan's Smart Secret Weapon," *Fortune,* August 12, 1991, pp. 72–75; Brenton R. Schlender, "Hard Times for High Tech," *Fortune,* March 22, 1993, p. 98; Ronald Henkoff, "Companies That Train Best," *Fortune,* March 22, 1993; Jim Carlton, "Sega Leaps Ahead by Shipping New Player Early," *Wall Street Journal,* May 11, 1995, pp. B1, B3; Jeffrey K. Liker and Yen-Chun Wu, "Japanese Automakers, U.S. Suppliers and Supply-Chain Superiority," *Sloan Management Review,* Fall 2000, pp. 81–93.

In the International Spotlight: Spain   Angela Sormani, "Hidden Treasure Spain Is Flourishing," *Venture Capital Journal,* October 1, 2003, p. 1.

Chapter 12

International Management in Action: Rethinking the Motivation Equation   "Japanese Workers See Abuses by Bosses," *Los Angeles Times,* June 30, 2003, p. C5; Bayan Rahman and Ken Hijino, "Japan Moves Towards US-Style Pensions," *Financial Times,* June 23/24, 2001, p. 4; Miki Tanikawa, "Fujitsu Decides to Backtrack on Performance-Based Pay," *New York Times,* March 22, 2001, p. W1; Stephanie Strom, "Japan's New 'Temp' Workers," *New York Times,* June 17, 1998, pp. 1–4.

International Management in Action: Karoshi: Stressed Out in Japan   Michael Zielenziger, "Alcohol Consumption a Rising Problem in Japan," *Miami Herald,* December 28, 2000, p. 10A; Howard K. French, "A Postmodern Plague Ravages Japan's Workers," *New York Times,* February 21, 2000, p. A4; William S. Brown, Rebecca E. Lubove, and James Kwalwasser, "Karoshi: Alternative Perspectives of Japanese Management Styles," *Business Horizons,* March–April 1994, pp. 58–60; Karen Lowry Miller, "Now, Japan Is Admitting It: Work Kills Executives," *BusinessWeek,* August 3, 1992, p. 35.

In the International Spotlight: Singapore   Philip Day, "The Lion Roars," *Far Eastern Economic Review,* June 3, 2004, p. 50; "Business Outlook: Singapore," *Country Monitor,* April 5, 2004, p. 3; "Economic Outlook: Singapore," *Business Asia,* August 11, 2003, p. 7.

Chapter 13

International Management in Action: Global Teams   Jitao Li, Katherine R. Xin, Anne Tsui, and Donald C. Hambrick, "Building Effective International Joint Venture Leadership Teams in China," *Journal of World Business* 34, no. 1 (1999), pp. 52–68; Charlene Marmer Solomon, "Global Teams: The Ultimate Collaboration," *Personnel Journal,* September 1995, pp. 49–58; Andrew Kakabdse and Andrew Myers, "Qualities of Top Management: Comparison of European Manufacturers," *Journal of Management Development* 14, no. 1 (1995), pp. 5–15; Noel M. Tichy, Michael I. Brimm, Ram Chran, and Hiroraka Takeuchi, "Leadership Development as a Lever for Global Transformation," in *Globalizing Management: Creating and Leading the Competitive Organization,* ed. Vladimir Pucik, Noel M. Tichy, and Carole K. Barnett (New York: Wiley, 1993), pp. 47–60; Gloria Barczak and Edward F McDonough III, "Leading Global Product Development Teams," *Research Technology Management* 46, no. 6 (November/December 2003), pp. 14–18; Michael J. Marquard and Lisa Horvath, *Global Teams* (Palo Alto, CA: Davies-Black, 2001).

In the International Spotlight: Germany   "Leaders: Odd European Out; Germany's Economy," *Economist,* February 21, 2004, p. 13; Robert Metz, Rebecca Riley, and Martin Weale, "Economic Performance in France, Germany and the United Kingdom, 1997–2002," *National Institute Economic Review,* April 2004. pp. 83–99.

Chapter 14

International Management in Action: Important Tips on Working for Foreigners   Martin J. Gannon, *Understanding Global Cultures,* 2nd ed. (Thousand Oaks, CA: Sage, 2001); Richard D. Lewis, *When Cultures Collide* (London: Nicholas Brealey, 1999); Roger E. Axtell, ed., *Do's and Taboos Around the World* (New York: Wiley, 1990); John Holusha, "No Utopia but to Workers It's a Job," *New York Times,* January 29, 1989, sec. 3, pp. 1, 10; Faye Rice, "Should You Work for a Foreigner?" *Fortune,* August 1, 1988, pp. 123–124; Jeanne Whalen, "American Finds Himself Atop Russian Oil Giant in Turmoil," *Wall Street Journal,* October 30, 2003, p. B1.

International Management in Action: U.S. Style Training for Expats and Their Teenagers   Dawn Anfuso, "HR Unites the World of Coca-Cola," *Personnel Journal,* November 1994, pp. 112–121; Karen Dawn Stuart, "Teens Play a Role in Moves Overseas," *Personnel Journal,* March 1992, pp. 72–78; Richard M. Hodgetts and Fred Luthans, "U.S. Multinationals' Expatriate Compensation Strategies," *Compensation and Benefits Review,* January–February 1993, p. 61; Philip R. Harris and Robert T. Moran, *Managing Cultural Differences: High-Performance Strategies for a New World of Business,* 3rd ed. (Houston: Gulf Publishing, 1991), chapter 9.

In the International Spotlight: Russia   "Mixed Signals; Russian Reform," *Economist,* May 29, 2004, p. 39; "Command and Control; Russian Economy," April 10, 2004, p. 70.

You Be the International Consultant: A Selection Decision   William H. Davidson, "Creating and Managing Joint Ventures in China," *California Management Review,* Summer 1987, pp. 77–94; Denis Fred Simon, "After Tiananmen: What Is the Future for Foreign Business in China?" *California Management Review,* Winter 1990, p. 106; S. Gordon Redding, *The Spirit of Chinese Capitalism* (New York: Walter de Gruyter, 1990); James T. Areddy, "Older Workers from U.S. Take Jobs in China," *Wall Street Journal,* June 22, 2004, p. B1.

■ Chapter 15

International Management in Action: They're Leading the Pack
Steven R. Weisman, "More Japanese Workers Demanding Shorter Hours and Less Hectic Work," *New York Times,* March 3, 1992, p. A6; "Germany's Mighty Unions Are Being Forced to Bend," *BusinessWeek,* March 1, 1993, p. 52; Christopher Farrell and Michael J. Mandel, "Riding High," *BusinessWeek,* October 9, 1995, pp. 134–146; Tony Czuczka, "'Lazy' Germany Showing Signs of Declining Work Ethic," *Miami Herald,* April 22, 2001, p. 7A.

International Management in Action: Unions Become More Flexible—and Do Better   Edmund L. Andrews, "German Union Gives Opening for Wage Cuts," *New York Times,* June 5, 1997, pp. A1, C5; Greg Steinmetz, "One Union Accepts Reality, Breaking with Inflexible Past," *Wall Street Journal,* June 12, 1997, p. A14; Greg Steinmetz, "Under Pressure, Germany's Unions Bend," *Wall Street Journal,* July 29, 1997, p. A10; Edmund L. Andrews, "Germans Cut Labor Costs with a Harsh Export: Jobs," *New York Times,* March 21, 1998, pp. A1, 3.

In the International Spotlight: Brazil   *CIA Factbook* (2001); Jonathan Wheatley, "Is Lula's Honeymoon Winding Down?" *BusinessWeek,* April 26, 2004, p. 59; "BellSouth's Latin Ambitions," *BusinessWeek Online,* October 20, 2003.

Endnotes

■ Chapter 1

1. J. Whalen and B. Bahree. "How BP Learned to Trust Ally That Once Burned It," *Wall Street Journal,* February 27, 2003, p. A4; "BP Won't Abandon Driving Forces," *Wall Street Journal,* November 27, 2003, p. A7.

2. "Dell Set to Create More Than 100 Full-Time Jobs in Bray," *Irish Times,* August 17, 2002, p. 15.

3. Peter Landers, "Foreign Aid: Why Some Sony Gear Is Made in Japan," *Wall Street Journal,* June 14, 2001, p. A1.

4. Barnaby J. Feder, "IBM Beats Earnings Expectations Again," *New York Times,* January 17, 2003, p. C4.

5. Peter Landers, "Volkswagen and GM Racked Up Strong Sales in China in 2003," *Wall Street Journal,* January 6, 2004, p. A3.

6. Peralte C. Paul, "Daimler Bails Out of Deal," *Atlanta Journal-Constitution,* September 24, 2003, p. A1.

7. Nicholas Itano, "GM Returns 10 Years After End of Apartheid," *New York Times,* January 30, 2004, p. W1.

8. Saritha Rai, "A Giant So Big It's a Proxy for India's Economy," *New York Times,* June 6, 2004, p. W1.

9. Ibid.

10. WTO, "World Trade 2003, Prospects for 2004; Stronger Than Expected Growth Spurs Modest Trade Recovery," WTO Press Release 373, April 5, 2004, p. 1.

11. Ibid.

12. Thomas Friedman, *The Lexus and the Olive Tree: Understanding Globalization* (New York: Farrar, Straus & Giroux, 1999).

13. Jonathan P. Doh and Hildy Teegen, *Globalization and NGOs: Transforming Business, Government, and Society* (Westport, CT: Praeger, 2003).

14. For discussion of some of the emerging concerns surrounding globalization, see Peter Singer, *One World: The Ethics of Globalization* (New Haven: Yale University Press, 2002); George Soros, *George Soros on Globalization* (New York: Public Affairs Books, 2002); Joseph Stiglitz, *Globalization and Its Discontents* (New York: Norton, 2002).

15. For discussions of the benefits of globalization, see Jagdish Bhagwati, *In Defense of Globalization* (New York: Oxford University Press, 2004), and Edward Graham, *Fighting the Wrong Enemy: Antiglobal Activists and Multinational Enterprises* (Washington, DC: Institute for International Economics, 2000).

16. Benjamin G. Defensor, "How Do You Solve the Problem That Is WTO?" *BusinessWorld,* March 3, 2004, p. 1.

17. Manny Fernandez, "Anti-IMF Activists Upbeat Despite Low-Key Protest," *Washington Post,* May 5, 2004, p. B1.

18. Paul Blustein, "EU Offers to End Farm Subsidies," *Washington Post,* May 11, 2004, p. E1.

19. Jeffrey E. Garten, "Going Up in Flames," *Newsweek* (International Edition), September 29, 2003, p. 38.

20. Mary Jordan, "Mexico Now Feels Pinch of Cheap Labor" *Washington Post,* December 3, 2003, p. A19.

21. "Trade Ministers Sign CAFTA, Call on Congress for Support," *Dow Jones Newswire,* May 28, 2004.

22. Christopher Marquis, "Bush Says He'll Press Effort for Hemisphere Trade Pact," *New York Times,* April 18, 2001, p. A4.

23. Ana Campoy, "As EU Expands, It Re-Examines Old Ways," *Wall Street Journal,* April 24, 2004, p. A14.

24. "Euro Can Wait," *Country Monitor,* July 7, 2003, p. 2.

25. David Reilly, "EU's Green-Eyeshade Crusade," *Wall Street Journal,* March 18, 2004, p. A15.

26. "World Watch," *Wall Street Journal,* January 27, 2004, p. A12.

27. U.S. Census Bureau, Foreign Trade Statistics, Trade (Imports, Exports, and Trade Balance) with China, http://www.census.gov/foreign-trade/balance/c5700.html#2003.

28. Jeff Leeds, "Bronfman Deal for Warner Music Is Seen," *Los Angeles Times,* November 24, 2003, p. C1.

29. "Economy Grows 3.7% in Mexico," *New York Times,* May 18, 2004, p. C4.

30. John Lyons, "Mexico Seeing Few Advances," *Houston Chronicle,* November 26, 2003, p. 1.

31. Prabhat Kumar, "Textiles, Post MFA," *Businessline,* January 9, 2004, p. 1.

32. Patricia Nazario, "Quality Time," *Latin Trade,* March 2004, p. 43.

33. Clare Ansberry and Timothy Aeppel, "Battling Imports," *Wall Street Journal,* October 6, 2003, p. B1.

34. Elizabeth Becker, "Costa Rica to Be 5th Country in New Trade Pact with U.S.," *New York Times,* January 26, 2004, p. A6.

35. Victor Godinez, "CompUSA Aims to Reboot Its Image as PC Sales Stall," *Knight Ridder Tribune Business News,* November 26, 2003, p. 1.

36. "Group Antolin Builds New Plant in Czech Republic," *Access Czech Republic Business Bulletin,* February 12, 2003, p. 19.

37. James Cox, "EU Wants Penalties on U.S. Exports; Other Nations Also Involved in Dispute on Import Duties," *USA Today,* January 16, 2004, p. B1.

38. Joel Millman, "The World's New Tiger on the Export Scene Isn't Asian; It's Mexico," *Wall Street Journal,* May 9, 2000, pp. A1, A10.

39. Todd Benson, "World Business Briefing Americas: Brazil: Industrial Output Surges," *New York Times,* May 12, 2004, p. W1.

40. Geraldo Samor, "Emerging Mess? Brazil Struggles to Sell Local Debt," *Wall Street Journal,* May 21, 2004, p. C1.

41. Simon Romero and Claudia Deutsch, "War and Abuse Do Little to Harm U.S. Brands," *New York Times,* May 9, 2004, p. A1.

42. "Emerging Market Indicators," *Economist,* June 5, 2004, p. 110.

43. Jon Jeter, "Most Argentines Back Their President, Not Debt," *Washington Post,* February 28, 2004, p. E1.

44. "The Americas, Crawling Back to Daylight; Argentina's Economy," *Economist,* December 6, 2003, p. 51.

45. Sergio Sarmiento, "Americas: Critics Aside, NAFTA Has Been a Boon to Mexico," *Wall Street Journal,* January 9, 2004, p. A11.

46. "The Americas, Still Prickly; Mercosur and the EU," *Economist,* May 1, 2004, p. 54.

47. "Finance and Economics, Command and Control; Russia's Economy," *Economist,* April 10, 2004, p. 70.

48. "IMF Increases Global-Output Forecast," *Wall Street Journal,* April 22, 2004, p. 1.

49. "How Risky Is Russia?" *International Financial Law Review,* January 1, 2004, p. 1.

50. Scott Miller and Guy Chazan, "EU Nears Accord to Back Russia in Bid for WTO," *Wall Street Journal,* May 14, 2004, p. A10.

51. Elizabeth Becker, "Adding Value to Immigants' Cash," *New York Times,* June 6, 2004, pp. 3–4.

52. Thomas Crampton, "China's Bounding Economy Fuels Both Hope and Concern," *New York Times,* November 13, 2003, p. A18.

53. Stephanie Strom, "Japanese Majority Owner Forces Bankruptcy of Rockefeller Center," *New York Times,* May 12, 1995, pp. A1, C4; and Mitchell Pacelle and Steven Lipin, "Japanese Firm Turns to Laws on Bankruptcy," *Wall Street Journal,* May 15, 1995, p. A4.

54. Akiko Kashiwagi, "Numbers Say Japan's Recession Has Eased," *Washington Post,* June 7, 2003, p. E3.

55. "Will Tokyo Finally Clean House?" *Economist,* June 27, 1998, p. 71.

56. Phred Dvorak, "Corporate Bankruptcies in Japan Hit Record High," *Wall Street Journal,* April 16, 2001, p. A12.

57. Karby Leggett, "China's Economy Expanded by 8% over Past Year," *Wall Street Journal,* January 2, 2001, p. A6.

58. Kathy Chen and Constance Mitchell-Ford, "China Sees Success in Taming Growth," *Wall Street Journal,* June 1, 2004, p. A15.

59. Jane Lanhee Lee, "GM Plans to Invest $3 Billion in China to Boost Its Presence," *Wall Street Journal,* June 7, 2004, p. B2.

60. Neil King Jr., "Tariffs in TVs from China Give U.S. Maker Edge," *Wall Street Journal,* May 17, 2004, p. B4.

61. "China Tries to Tap the Brakes on Economic Growth," *Wall Street Journal,* December 26, 2003, p. A9.

62. Dexter Roberts, "A Princeling Who Could Be Premier," *Business Week,* March 15, 2004, p. 50.

63. "The Costly Realities of 'Free Trade,'" *Washington Post,* December 30, 2003, p. A18.

64. Barbara Demick, "The World; South Korean Diplomat Resigns; Ties with U.S. May Be at Risk," *Los Angeles Times,* January 14, 2004, p. A7.

65. George Melloan, "Asia's Tigers Are Back, with More Muscle," *Wall Street Journal,* June 1, 2004, p. W1.

66. Keith Bradsher, "Chinese Provinces Form Regional Economic Bloc," *New York Times,* June 2, 2004, p. W1.

67. Walden Bello, "Perspective: Asia and China," *BusinessWorld,* April 19, 2004, p. 1.

68. "WTO to Allow Access to Cheap Drug Treatments," *Los Angeles Times,* August 31, 2003, p. A4.

69. "Business: Getting Africa Moving; Face Value," *Economist,* April 17, 2004, p. 72.

■ Chapter 2

1. Owen Brown, "Chinese Economy May Be Cooling," *Wall Street Journal,* May 14, 2004, p. A10.

2. "China, India Aim to Boost Ties," *Emerging Markets Economy,* March 24, 2004, p. 1.

3. Indira A. R. Lakshmanan, "China's Reforms Turn Costly; Income Gap Widens Between Rich, Poor," *Boston Globe,* July 22, 2002, p. A1.

4. Emad McKay, "U.S. Issues Warning to Partners Who Erect Trade Barriers," *Global Information Network,* April 5, 2004, p. 1.

5. Elizabeth Weldon and Wilfried Vanhonacker, "Operating a Foreign-Invested Enterprise in China: Challenges for Managers and Management Researchers," *Journal of World Business* 34, no. 1 (1999), pp. 97–98.

6. John Child and David K. Tse, "China's Transition and Its Implications for International Business," *Journal of International Business Studies,* First Quarter 2001, pp. 5–21.

7. Rebecca Buckman, "China Keeps Telecom Firms Waiting on 3G," *Wall Street Journal,* May 13, 2004, p. B4.

8. John Gilbert and Thomas Wahl, "Labor Market Distortions and China's WTO Accession Package: An Applied General Equilbrium Assessment," *Journal of Comparative Economies* 31, no. 4 (December 2003), p. 774.

9. Robyn Meredith, "So You Really Want to Do Business in China?" *Forbes,* July 24, 2000, p. 93.

10. David Ignatius, "A 'Maggie Moment' in Europe," *Washington Post,* July 13, 2003, p. A29.

11. Therese Raphael, "London Letter: Europe's Great Reform Wimpout," *Wall Street Journal,* January 26, 2004, p. A15.

12. Keith B. Richburg, "Spanish Socialists Oust Party of U.S. War Ally—Voters Cite Train Attacks in Poll Upset," *Washington Post,* March 15, 2004, p. A1.

13. "Survey: The Return of Politics," *Economist,* November 22, 2003, p. 13.

14. Daniel J. McCarthy, Sheila M. Puffer, and Alexander I. Naumov, "Russia's Retreat to Statization and the Implications for Business," *Journal of World Business* 35, no. 3 (2000), p. 258.

15. Paul Starobin and Catherine Belton, "The Crumbling of Russia," *BusinessWeek,* September 11, 2000, p. 60.

16. Seth Mydans, "Russian TV Crewman Fired in Media Crackdown," *New York Times,* June 3, 2004, p. A10.

17. Erin E. Arvedlund, "Russian Growth Acclerates, Stoked by Oil," *New York Times,* January 7, 2004, p. W1.

18. Ibid.

19. Mark Meriska, "Russia Deserves Investors' Attention," *National Underwriter,* July 8, 2002, p. 12.

20. "Russian State Customs Committee Reports Corruption Rate Among Employees," *BBC Monitoring Former Soviet Union,* October 14, 2003, p. 1.

21. Merra Selva, "Strong-Arm Tactics Keeps Capitalism Afloat in Putin's Russia," *Knight Ridder Tribune Business News,* November 2, 2003, p. 1.

22. For more on this see Trevor Buck, Igor Filatotchev, Peter Nolan, and Mike Wright, "Different Paths to Economic Reform in Russia and China: Causes and Consequences," *Journal of World Business* 35, no. 4 (2000), pp. 379–400.

23. Guy Chazan, "EU Backs Russia's WTO Entry as Moscow Supports Kyoto Pact," *Wall Street Journal,* May 24, 2004, p. A2; Peter Baker, "Russia Backs Kyoto to Get on Path to Join WTO," *Washington Post,* May 22, 2004, p. A15.

24. David Fairlamb and Bogdan Turek, "Poland and the EU," *BusinessWeek,* May 10, 2004, http://www.businessweek.com.

25. Ernest S. McCray, "Hungary, Headed for the EU," *Global Finance* 16, no. 3 (March 2002), p. 56.

26. Peter Green, "Surging Czech Currency Sets Records," *New York Times,* July 4, 2002, p. W1.

27. James Risen, "How Pair's Terror Led to Clash on Shaping Intelligence, *New York Times,* April 28, 2004, p. A1.

28. Barbara Hagenbaugh, "Attacks in Saudi Arabia Raise Oil Prices 6%," *USA Today,* June 2, 2004, p. B1.

29. Paul Nadler, "Making a Mystery out of How to Comply with Patriot Act," *American Banker,* May 19, 2004, p. 5.

30. John Graham, "Foreign Corrupt Practices Act: A Manager's Guide," *California Management Review,* Summer 1987, p. 9.

31. For more on this see Tipton F. McCubbins, "Somebody Kicked the Sleeping Dog—New Bite in the Foreign Corrupt Practices Act," *Business Horizons,* January–February 2001, pp. 27–32.

32. Glenn Kessler and Anthony Faiola, "Cheney Lauds Koizumi; Iraq Dominates Talks with Japan," *Washington Post,* April 13, 2004, p. A16.

33. Richard Jerram, "This Time It's Different," *The International Economy* 18, no. 2 (Spring 2004), p. 46.

34. Robert Slate, "Chinese Role Models and Classic Military Philosophy in Dealing with Soldier Corruption and Moral Degeneration," *Journal of Third World Studies* 20, no. 1, (Spring 2003), p. 193.

35. Greg Schneider, "Small Manufactuers Seek Steel-Price Relief," *Washington Post,* March 11, 2004, p. E3.

36. Russell Flannery, "Big Chip Makers Join to Develop New DRAM Technology," *Wall Street Journal,* January 18, 2000, p. A21.

37. Faith Arner and Rachel Tiplady, "No Excuse Not to Succeed: How COO Anthony Perez Is Hustling Kodak into the Digital Age," *BusinessWeek,* May 10, 2004, p. 96

38. Carol Sottili, "Have Cell Phone, Will Travel to Europe," *Washington Post,* April 6, 2003, p. E1.

39. "Consumer Usage Data," EMarketer, http://www.emarketer.com/SearchBrowse.aspx?pathID=506.

40. "Supercomputers: The Race Is On," *BusinessWeek,* June 7, 2004, p. 76.

41. David Mildenberg, "SDN Sees Growth in High Speed Links," *The Business Journal,* May 14, 2004, p. 1.

42. Jean Halliday, "Car Renters Flock to Internet," *Advertising Age,* October 27, 2003, p. 44.

43. "Deutsche Bank Govvie Honcho: Business as Usual Now," *Bondweek,* June 22, 2003, p. 1.

44. "Worldwide B2B Activity Expected to Boom in 2002," *Energy Network,* April 3, 2002, p. 1.

45. Sebastian Mallaby, "Taming the Wild Web," *Washington Post,* April 2, 2003, p. A19.

46. See "In Peru, a Cellular Revolution," *Miami Herald,* May 22, 1995, p. 6A.

47. Roger Crockett, Andy Reinhardt, and Moon Ihlwan, "Cell Phones: Who's Calling the Shots," *BusinessWeek,* April 26, 2004, p. 48.

48. Matt Richtel, "Wi-Fi Providers Rethink How to Make Money," *New York Times,* June 7, 2004, p. C1.

49. Erika Stuzman, "More Companies Begin to Outsource White-Collar Jobs," *Knight Ridder Tribune Business News,* May 23, 2004, p. 1.

50. Jan Syfert, "Up There with the Best," *Productivity SA,* November/December 1998, p. 49.

51. Ashok Bhattacharjee, "India's Outsourcing Tigers Seek Cover, Markets, in Europe's East," *Wall Street Journal,* December 18, 2003, p. A16.

■ Chapter 3

1. Quoted from www.jnj.com.

2. Georges Enderle, "A Worldwide Survey of Business Ethics in the 1990s," *Journal of Business Ethics,* December 1997, pp. 1475–1483.

3. Natsuo Nishio, "Japan Is Hurt by Accounting Model," *Wall Street Journal,* February 17, 2004, p. A6.

4. Andrew Peaple, "Business: Japan—Catalyst for Change," *Accountancy* 130, no. 1311 (November 2002), p. 1.

5. "Japan Highway Public Corp," *Euroweek,* October 20, 2003, p. 54.

6. Peter Landers, "Koizumi Takes Aim at Public Sector Firms: Is This the Right Time for the Japan Leader to Push Privatization?" *Wall Street Journal,* August 10, 2001, p. A7.

7. Ginny Parker, "Japan's Banks Post Profits," *Wall Street Journal,* May 25, 2004, p. C14.

8. "Business: Blow Whistles While You Work," *Economist,* April 28, 2002, p. 68.

9. Sheila Muto, "Plots and Ploys," *Wall Street Journal,* November 5, 2003, p. B8.

10. Ibid.

11. Leslie Norton, "Asian Trader: As a Recovery Candidate, NEC Is No Nissan," *Barron's,* July 15, 2003, p. MW10.

12. Andrew Pollack, "In Japan, It's See No Evil; Have No Harassment," *New York Times,* May 7, 1996, p. C5.

13. Howard W. French, "Diploma at Hand, Japanese Women Find Glass Ceiling Reinforced with Iron," *New York Times,* January 1, 2001, p. A4.

14. Peter Elstrom and Steven V. Brull, "Mitsubishi's Morass," *BusinessWeek,* June 3, 1996, p. 35.

15. Pat Choate, *Agents of Influence* (New York: Knopf, 1991).

16. Helmut Becker and David J. Fritzsche, "A Comparison of the Ethical Behavior of American, French, and German Managers," *Columbia Journal of World Business,* Winter 1987, pp. 87–95.

17. Ibid., p. 92.

18. Ibid., p. 94.

19. Evelyne Serdjenian, "Women Managers in France," in *Competitive Frontiers: Women Managers in a Global Economy,* ed. Nancy J. Adler and Dafna N. Izraeli, (Cambridge, MA: Blackwell, 1994), pp. 199–200.

20. Ibid., p. 204.

21. Adriane Berthoin Antal and Camilla Krebsbach-Gnath, "Women in Management in Germany: East, West, and Reunited," in Adler and Izraeli, eds., *Competitive Frontiers,* pp. 210–211.

22. John McCullen, "Employment Law Claims Guidelines Are Big Mess," *Personnel Today,* March 2, 2004, p. 14.

23. Geoffrey Fowler, "Universal's China Business Plan Tries to Neutralize Music Piracy," *Wall Street Journal,* February 27, 2004, p. B2.

24. Richard Behar, "Beijing's Phony War on Fakes," *Fortune,* October 30, 2000, p. 193.

25. Owen Brown, "The Economy: China Prepares Plan to Close Gap in U.S. Trade," *Wall Street Journal,* December 17, 2003, p. A2.

26. Craig S. Smith, "A Tale of Piracy: How the Chinese Stole the Grinch," *New York Times,* December 12, 2000, p. A3.

27. Craig S. Smith, "Piracy a Concern as the China Trade Opens Up," *New York Times,* October 5, 2000, p. W1. Also see Dexter Roberts et al., "China's Piracy Plague," *BusinessWeek,* June 5, 2000, pp. 44–48.

28. Ralph Cunningham, "Anti-Counterfeiting Battle Begins to Show Results," *Managing Intellectual Property,* December 2002/January 2003, p. 9.

29. Geoffrey Folwer, "China's Ad Market Is Rife with Copycats," *Wall Street Journal,* April 26, 2004, p. B1.

30. "Business: The Allure of Low Technology; Technology in China," *Economist,* December 20, 2003, p. 105.

31. John R. Wilke, "Two Silicon Valley Cases Raise Fears of Chinese Espionage," *Wall Street Journal,* January 15, 2003, p. A4.

32. Dexter Roberts, Christopher Power, and Stephanie Anderson Forest, "Cheated in China," *BusinessWeek,* October 6, 1997, p. 142.

33. Also see Lu Xiaohe, "Business Ethics in China," *Journal of Business Ethics,* October 1997, pp. 1509–1518.

34. Abigal McWilliams and Donald Siegel, "Corporate Social Responsibility: A Theory of the Firm Perspective," *Academy of Management Review* 26, no. 1 (2001), pp. 117–127.

35. "Non-Governmental Organizations and Business: Living with the Enemy," *Economist,* August 9, 2002, pp. 49–50.

36. Gallup International's 2002 Voice of the People survey, http://www.weforum.org.

37. "Environmentalists Get Citigroup Pledge," *New York Times,* January 22, 2004, p. C3.

38. "WTO to Allow Access to Cheap Drug Treatments," *Los Angeles Times,* August 31, 2003, p. A4.

39. Jonathan P. Doh and Terrence R. Guay, "Globalization and Corporate Social Responsibility: How Nongovernmental Organizations Influence Labor and Environmental Codes of Conduct," *Management International Review* 44, no. 3 (2004), pp. 7–30; Petra Christmann and Glen Taylor, "Globalization and the Environment: Strategies for International Voluntary Environmental Initiatives," *Academy of Management Executive* 16, no. 30 (2002), pp. 121–135.

40. Michael Yaziji, "Turning Gadflies into Allies," *Harvard Business Review,* February 2004, pp. 110–115.

41. Debra Dunn and Keith Yamashita, "Microcapitalism and the Megacorporation," *Harvard Business Review,* August 2003, pp. 46–54.

42. Clayton Collins, "Above and Beyond: A Surprising Number of Companies Are Finding It Makes Business Sense to Go Beyond Government Regulations," *Christian Science Monitor,* November 3, 2003, p. 14.

43. Organization for Economic Cooperation and Development, *Corporate Governance: A Survey of OECD Countries* (Paris: OECD), 2003.

44. Stijn Claessens and Joseph P. H. Fan, "Corporate Governance in Asia: A Survey," *International Review of Finance* 3, no. 2 (2002), pp. 71–103.

45. Bob Davis, "The Economy: U.S. Nears Pact on Corruption Treaty," *Wall Street Journal,* August 13, 2003, p. A2. See also Jonathan P. Doh, Peter Rodriguez, Klaus Uhlenbruck, Jamie Collins, and Lorraine Eden, "Coping with Corruption in Foreign Markets," *Academy of Management Executive* 17, no. 3 (2003), pp. 114–127.

46. Robert S. Greenberger, "Foreigners Use Bribes to Beat U.S. Rivals in Many Deals, New Report Concludes," *Wall Street Journal,* October 12, 1995, pp. A3, A17.

47. Tipton F. McCubbins, "Somebody Kicked the Sleeping Dog—New Bite in the Foreign Corrupt Practices Act," *Business Horizons,* January–February 2001, p. 27.

48. Greg Steinmetz, "U.S. Firms Are Among Least Likely to Pay Bribes Abroad, Survey Finds," *Wall Street Journal,* August 25, 1997, p. 5.

49. Edmund L. Andrews, "29 Nations Agree to Outlaw Bribing Foreign Officials," *New York Times,* November 21, 1997, p. C2.

50. "Special Report: The Short Arm of the Law—Bribery and Business," *Economist,* March 2, 2002, p. 85.

51. "Putting the World to Rights," *Economist,* June 5, 2004, p. 63.

52. Gustavo Capdevila, "Development: U.N. Report Calls for Urgent Action on Poverty," *Global Information Network,* July 9, 2003, p. 1.

53. Rachel Zimmerman, "Jack Valenti Will Lobby for AIDS Fight," *Wall Street Journal,* June 3, 2004, p. B1.

■ Part 1 Cases

In-Depth Integrative Case 1

1. "WTO to Allow Access to Cheap Drug Treatments," *Los Angeles Times,* August 31, 2003, p. A4.

2. Miriam Jordan, "Brazil to Stir Up AIDS-Drug Battle; Nation to Authorize Imports of Generics, Citing the Cost of Big Companies' Products," *Wall Street Journal,* September 5, 2003, p. A3.

3. Sushil Vachani, "South Africa and the AIDS Epidemic," *Vikalpa* 29, no. 1 (January–March 2004), pp. 101–109. *HIV* stands for human immunodeficiency virus; *AIDS* stands for acquired immunodeficiency syndrome.

4. Ibid.

5. UNAIDS, *2002 Report on Global AIDS,* http://www.unaids.gov.

6. Donald G. McNeil, "Medicine Merchants: A Special Report: Drug Makers and 3rd World: Study in Neglect," *New York Times,* May 21, 2000, p. 1.

7. World Health Organization, *World Health Report, 2003.*

8. Bill Schiller, "Hope," *Toronto Star,* September 18, 1999.

9. Ibid.

10. Vachani, "South Africa and the AIDS Epidemic."

11. Pharmaceutical Research and Manufacturers of America, *Pharmaceutical Industry Profile 2002* (Washington, DC, 2002).

12. Merrill Goozner, *The $800 Million Pill* (Berkeley: University of California Press, 2004).

13. McNeil, "Medicine Merchants."

14. Lawrence K. Altman, "In Effort to Save Lives, South Africa Creates an Anti-AIDS Campaign That Minces No Words," *New York Times,* July 9, 2000, p. 8.

15. Ibid.

16. This section draws from Sushil Vachani, "South Africa and the AIDS Epidemic," *Vikalpa,* 29, no. 1 (January–March, 2004), pp. 101–109.

17. http://www.wto.org/english/tratop_e/trips_e/trips_e.htm, accessed July 26, 2002.

18. Vachani, "South Africa and the AIDS Epidemic."

19. UNAIDS, *2000 Report on the Global AIDS epidemic,* http://www.unaids.gov.

20. Vachani, "South Africa and the AIDS Epidemic."

21. Pharmaceutical Research and Manufacturers of America, *Pharmaceutical Industry Profile 2002,* p. 36.

22. This section draws from Sushil Vachani, "South Africa and the AIDS Epidemic," *Vikalpa* 29, no. 1 (January–March, 2004), pp. 101–109.

23. Karl Vick, "African AIDS Victims Losers of a Drug War: U.S. Policy Keeps Price Prohibitive," *Washington Post,* December 4, 1999, p. A1.

24. Ibid.

25. Ibid.

26. Sarah Boseley, "Trade Terrorism," *The Guardian,* August 11, 1999.

27. Vick, "African AIDS Victims Losers of a Drug War."

28. Ibid.

29. Victor Mallet, "The Ravaged Continent: AIDS Is Now the Biggest Killer of Young Adults in Africa," *Financial Times,* December 3, 1999, p. 4.

30. Vachani, "South Africa and the AIDS Epidemic."

31. Justin Brown, "Spread of AIDS Raises Moral Issue for U.S.," *Christian Science Monitor,* July 12, 2000.

32. Ibid.

33. Nicol Degli Innocenti, "South Africa Hits Back at EU Criticism of AIDS Policy," *Financial Times,* April 5, 2001, p. 11.

34. Melody Petersen and Larry Rohter, "Maker Agrees to Cut Prices of 2 AIDS Drugs in Brazil," *New York Times,* March 31, 2001, p. 4.

35. Vachani, "South Africa and the AIDS Epidemic."

36. UNAIDS, *2002 Report on the Global AIDS Epidemic,* http://www.unaids.gov.

37. Vachani, "South Africa and the AIDS Epidemic."

38. Rachel Zimmerman, "Jack Valenti Will Lobby for AIDS Fight," *Wall Street Journal,* June 3, 2004, p. B1.

39. http://www.wto.org/english/tratop_e/trips_e/pharmpatent_e.htm, accessed July 26, 2002.

40. Rick Weiss, "AIDS Funding Is Still Insufficient U.N. Says," *Washington Post,* September 22, 2003, p. A19.

41. B. George and N. Ayittey, "AIDS in Africa," *San Diego Union-Tribune,* April 14, 2002, p. G1.

42. Ibid.

43. Julia Flynn and Mark Schoofs, "Glaxo, Boeringer to Let Africa Make More Generics for AIDS," *Wall Street Journal,* December 11, 2003, p. D4.

44. Hollister H. Hovey, "Religious Groups Push Drug Cost to Assess HIV," Dow Jones Newswires, March 24, 2004.

45. Mark Schoof, "Clinton Program Would Help Poor Nations Get AIDS Drugs," *Wall Street Journal,* October 23, 2003, p. B1.

46. Donald G. McNeil, "Plan to Bring Generic AIDS Drugs to Poor Nations," *New York Times,* April 6, 2004, p. F6.

■ Chapter 4

1. Pat Joynt and Malcolm Warner, "Introduction: Cross-Cultural Perspectives," in *Managing Across Cultures: Issues and Perspectives,* ed. Pat Joynt and Malcolm Warner (London: International Thompson Business Press, 1996), p. 3.

2. For additional insights see Gerry Darlington, "Culture—A Theoretical Review," ibid., pp. 33–55.

3. Fred Luthans, *Organizational Behavior,* 7th ed. (New York: McGraw-Hill, 1995), pp. 534–535.

4. Gary Bonvillian and William A. Nowlin, "Cultural Awareness: An Essential Element of Doing Business Abroad," *Business Horizons,* November–December 1994, pp. 44–54.

5. Roger E. Axtell, ed., *Do's and Taboos Around the World,* 2nd ed. (New York: Wiley, 1990), p. 3.

6. Lillian H. Chaney and Jeanette S. Martin, *Intercultural Business Communication* (Englewood Cliffs, NJ: Prentice-Hall, 1995), p. 115.

7. Fons Trompenaars and Charles Hampden-Turner, *Riding the Waves of Culture: Understanding Diversity in Global Business,* 2nd ed. (New York: McGraw-Hill, 1998), p. 23.

8. Christopher Orpen, "The Work Values of Western and Tribal Black Employees," *Journal of Cross-Cultural Psychology,* March 1978, pp. 99–111.

9. William Whitely and George W. England, "Variability in Common Dimensions of Managerial Values due to Value Orientation and Country Differences," *Personnel Psychology,* Spring 1980, pp. 77–89.

10. Ibid., p. 87.

11. George W. England and Raymond Lee, "The Relationship Between Managerial Values and Managerial Success in the United States, Japan, India, and Australia," *Journal of Applied Psychology,* August 1974, pp. 418–419.

12. George W. England, "Managers and Their Value Systems: A Five-Country Comparative Study," *Columbia Journal of World Business,* Summer 1978, p. 39.

13. A. Reichel and D. M. Flynn, "Values in Transition: An Empirical Study of Japanese Managers in the U.S.," *Management International Review* 23, no. 4 (1984), pp. 69–70.

14. Hermann F. Schwind and Richard B. Peterson, "Shifting Personal Values in the Japanese Management System," *International Studies of Management and Organization,* Summer 1985, pp. 60–74.

15. Ibid., p. 72.

16. Yumiko Ono and Bill Spindle, "Japan's Long Decline Makes One Thing Rise: Individualism," *Wall Street Journal,* December 29, 2000, pp. A1, A4.

17. Sang M. Lee and Suzanne J. Peterson, "Culture, Entrepreneurial Orientation, and Global Competitiveness," *Journal of World Business* 35, no. 4 (2000) pp. 411–412.

18. Geert Hofstede, *Culture's Consequences: International Differences in Work-Related Values* (Beverly Hills, CA: Sage 1980).

19. Geert Hofstede, *Cultures and Organizations: Software of the Mind* (London: McGraw-Hill U.K., 1991), pp. 251–252.

20. Geert Hofstede and Michael Bond, "The Need for Synergy Among Cross-Cultural Studies," *Journal of Cross-Cultural Psychology,* December 1984, p. 419.

21. A. R. Negandhi and S. B. Prasad, *Comparative Management* (New York: Appleton-Century-Crofts, 1971), p. 128.

22. For additional insights, see Mark F. Peterson et al., "Role Conflict, Ambiguity, and Overload: A 21-Nation Study," *Academy of Management Journal,* June 1995, pp. 429–452.

23. Hofstede, *Culture's Consequences.*

24. Ibid.

25. Ibid.

26. Also see Chao C. Chen, Xiao-Ping Chen, and James R. Meindl, "How Can Cooperation Be Fostered? The Cultural Effects of Individualism–Collectivism," *Academy of Management Review* 23, no. 2 (1998), pp. 285–304.

27. Hofstede, *Culture's Consequences,* pp. 419–420.

28. Ibid., p. 420.

29. Simcha Ronen and Allen I. Kraut, "Similarities Among Countries Based on Employee Work Values and Attitudes," *Columbia Journal of World Business,* Summer 1977, p. 90.

30. Ibid., p. 95.

31. See, for example, David A. Ralston, Carolyn P. Egri, Sally Stewart, Robert H. Terpstra, and Yu Kaicheng, "Doing Business in the 21st Century with the New Generation of Chinese Managers: A Study of Generational Shifts in Work Values in China," *Journal of International Business Studies,* Second Quarter 1999, pp. 415–428.

32. Simcha Ronen and Oded Shenkar, "Clustering Countries on Attitudinal Dimensions: A Review and Synthesis," *Academy of Management Journal,* September 1985, pp. 435–454.

33. Ibid., p. 452.

34. Fons Trompenaars, *Riding the Waves of Culture: Understanding Diversity in Global Business* (New York: Irwin, 1994), p. 10.

35. Talcott Parsons, *The Social System* (New York: Free Press, 1951).

36. Also see Lisa Hoecklin, *Managing Cultural Differences* (Workingham, England: Addison-Wesley, 1995).

37. Charles M. Hampden-Turner and Fons Trompenaars, "A World Turned Upside Down: Doing Business in Asia," in Joynt and Warner, *Managing Across Cultures,* p. 279.

38. Ibid., p. 288.

39. Trompenaars, *Riding the Waves of Culture,* p. 131.

40. Ibid., p. 140.

41. Mansour Javidan and Robert House, "Leadership and Cultures Around the World: Findings from GLOBE: An Introduction to the Special Issue," *Journal of World Business* 37, no. 1 (2002), pp. 1–2.

42. Robert House, Paul J. Hanges, Mansour Javidan, Peter W. Dorfman, and Vipin Gupta, *Culture, Leadership, and Organizations: The GLOBE Study of 62 Societies* (London: Sage, 2004).

43. Ibid.

44. Mansour Javidan, and Robert House, "Cultural Acumen for the Global Manager: Lessons from Project Globe," *Organizational Dynamics* 29, no. 4 (2001), pp. 289–305.

44. Ibid.

45. Robert House, Mansour Javidan, Paul Hanges, and Peter Dorfman, "Understanding Cultures and Implicit Leadership Theories Across the Globe: An Introduction to Project GLOBE," *Journal of World Business* 37, no. 1 (2002), pp. 3–10.

46. Ibid.

■ Chapter 5

1. Nancy J. Adler, *International Dimensions of Organizational Behavior,* 3rd ed. (Cincinnati, OH: Southwestern, 1997).

2. See Clifford C. Clarke and Douglas Lipp, "Contrasting Cultures," *Training and Development Journal,* February 1998, pp. 21–31.

3. Owen Brown, "Japan Is Quality Favorite in China," *Wall Street Journal,* June 7, 2004, p. A17.

4. David Gow, "Car Industry at Crossroads in China: Supply Could Outstrip the Huge Demand," *The Guardian,* May 21, 2004, p. 26.

5. For a more detailed analysis, see Allen J. Morrison, David A. Ricks, and Kendall Roth, "Globalization Versus Regionalization: Which Way for the Multinational?" *Organizational Dynamics,* Winter 1991, pp. 17–28.

6. Lisa Hoecklin, *Managing Cultural Differences: Strategies for Competitive Advantage* (Workingham, England: Addison-Wesley, 1995), pp. 98–99.

7. "The Personal Touch: Making McDonald's and Coca-Cola Less American," *Economist,* May 15, 1998, p. 5; Arun Sudhaman, "Ketchum Newstand in McDonald's China Win," *Media,* April 23, 2004, p. 18.

8. Linda Leung, "Managing Offshore Outsourcing," *Network World,* December 8, 2003, p. 59.

9. Matt Ackerman, "State St.: New Markets Key to Growth," *American Banker,* May 3, 2004, p. 1.

10. Linda M. Randall and Lori A. Coakley, "Building a Successful Partnership in Russia and Belarus: The Impact of Culture on Strategy," *Business Horizons,* March–April 1998, pp. 15–22.

11. Fons Trompenaars and Charles Hampden-Turner, *Riding the Waves of Culture: Understanding Diversity in Global Business,* 2nd ed. (New York: McGraw-Hill, 1998), p. 202.

12. See, for example, Anisya S. Thomas and Stephen L. Mueller, "A Case for Comparative Entrepreneurship: Assessing the Relevance of Culture," *Journal of International Business Studies,* Second Quarter 2000, pp. 287–301.

13. Adapted from Richard Mead, *International Management* (Cambridge, MA: Blackwell, 1994), pp. 57–59.

14. Yumiko Ono, "U.S. Superstores Find Japanese Are a Hard Sell," *Wall Street Journal,* February 14, 2000, pp. B1, B4.

15. Fred Luthans, Richard M. Hodgetts, and Stuart A. Rosenkrantz, *Real Managers* (Cambridge, MA: Ballinger, 1988).

16. Fred Luthans, Dianne H. B. Welsh, and Stuart A. Rosenkrantz, "What Do Russian Managers Really Do? An Observational Study with Comparisons to U.S. Managers," *Journal of International Business Studies,* Fourth Quarter 1993, pp. 741–761.

17. Diane H. B. Welsh, Fred Luthans, and Steven M. Sommer, "Organizational Behavior Modification Goes to Russia: Replicating an Experimental Analysis Across Cultures and Tasks," *Journal of Organizational Behavior Management* 13, no. 2 (1993), pp. 15–35; Diane H. B. Welsh, Fred Luthans, and Steven M. Sommer, "Managing Russian Factory Workers: The Impact of U.S.-Based

18. Welsh, Luthans, and Sommer, "Organizational Behavior Modification," p. 31. The summary of positive (17 percent average) performance from O.B. Mod. for U.S. samples can be found in Fred Luthans and Alexander Stajkovic, "Reinforce for Performance," *Academy of Management Executive* 13, no. 2 (1999), pp. 49–57.

19. Steven M. Sommer, Seung-Hyun Bae, and Fred Luthans, "The Structure–Climate Relationship in Korean Organizations," *Asia Pacific Journal of Management* 12, no. 2 (1995), pp. 23–36. Also see Steven Sommer, Seung-Hyun Bae, and Fred Luthans, "Organizational Commitment Across Cultures: The Impact of Antecedents on Korean Employees," *Human Relations* 49, no. 7 (1996), pp. 977–993.

20. Sommer, Bae, and Luthans, "The Structure–Climate Relationship."

21. Trompenaars and Hampden-Turner, *Riding the Waves of Culture,* p. 196.

22. Shari Caudron, "Lessons for HR Overseas," *Personnel Journal,* February 1995, p. 92.

23. Richard M. Hodgetts and Fred Luthans, "U.S. Multinationals' Compensation Strategies for Local Management: Cross-Cultural Implications," *Compensation and Benefits Review,* March–April 1993, pp. 42–48.

24. Also see Randall S. Schuler and Nikolai Rogovsky, "Understanding Compensation Practice Variations Across Firms: The Impact of National Culture," *Journal of International Business Studies,* First Quarter 1998, pp. 159–177.

25. Stephanie Smith, "Smooth Operator," *Money,* July 2003, p. 48.

26. Rochelle Kopp, "International Human Resource Policies and Practices in Japanese, European, and United States Multinationals," *Human Resource Management,* Winter 1994, p. 590.

27. Philip M. Rosenzweig and Nitin Nohria, "Influences on Human Resource Management Practices in Multinational Corporations," *Journal of International Business Studies,* Second Quarter 1994, pp. 229–251.

28. "Disillusioned Workers Cost Japanese Economy up to $180.18 Billion," *Wall Street Journal,* September 5, 2001, p. B18.

29. Also see Richard W. Wright, "Trends in International Business Research: Twenty-Five Years Later," *Journal of International Business Studies,* Fourth Quarter 1994, pp. 687–701; Schon Beechler and John Zhuang Yang, "The Transfer of Japanese-Style Management to American Subsidiaries: Contingencies, Constraints, and Competencies," *Journal of International Business Studies,* Third Quarter 1994, pp. 467–491.

30. "Books and Arts: The Perils of Pat; Doing Business in China," *Economist,* April 24, 2004, p. 98.

31. Eric W. K. Tsang, "Can Guanxi Be a Source of Sustained Competitive Advantage for Doing Business in China?" *Academy of Management Executive* 12, no. 2 (1998), p. 64.

32. Stephen S. Standifird and R. Scott Marshall, "The Transaction Cost Advantage of Guanxi-Based Business Practices," *Journal of World Business* 35, no. 1 (2000), pp. 21–42.

33. Lee Mei Yi and Paul Ellis, "Insider–Outsider Perspective of Guanxi," *Business Horizons,* January–February 2000, p. 28.

34. Rosalie L. Tung, "Managing in Asia: Cross-Cultural Dimensions," in *Managing Across Cultures: Issues and Perspectives,* ed. Pat Joynt and Malcolm Warner (London: International Thomson Business Press, 1996), p. 239.

35. Richard D. Lewis, *When Cultures Collide* (London: Nicholas Brealey, 1999), p. 390.

36. For more on this topic, see Philip R. Harris and Robert T. Moran, *Managing Cultural Differences,* 3rd ed. (Houston: Gulf Publishing, 1991), pp. 410–411.

37. Ming-Jer Chen, *Inside Chinese Business* (Boston: Harvard Business School Press, 2001), p. 153.

38. William B. Snavely, Serguel Miassaoedov, and Kevin McNeilly, "Cross-Cultural Peculiarities of the Russian Entrepreneur: Adapting to the New Russians," *Business Horizons,* March–April 1998, pp. 10–13.

39. Jeanne Whalen and Bhushan Bahree, "How Siberian Oil Field Turned into a Minefield," *Wall Street Journal,* February 9, 2000, p. A21.

40. Snavely, Miassaoedov, and McNeilly, "Cross-Cultural Peculiarities," pp. 10–13.

41. For additional insights into how to interact and negotiate effectively with the Russians, see Lewis, *When Cultures Collide,* pp. 314–318.

42. Snavely, Miassaoedov, and McNeilly, "Cross-Cultural Peculiarities," p. 13.

43. Ashok Bhattacharjee, "India's Outsourcing Tigers Seek Cover, Markets, in Europe's East," *Wall Street Journal,* April 30, 2004, p. A12; Julia Angwin, "AOL's Tech Center in India Is Money Saver," *Wall Street Journal,* August 7, 2003, p. B4.

44. "The Challenges for India," *Chicago Tribune,* May 27, 2004, p. 28; Amy Waldman, "In India, Economic Growth and Democracy Do Mix," *New York Times,* May 26, 2004, p. A13.

45. Adapted from Harris and Moran, *Managing Cultural Differences,* p. 447.

46. Also see Lewis, *When Cultures Collide,* pp. 341–346.

47. Jean-Louis Barsoux and Peter Lawrence, "The Making of a French Manager," *Harvard Business Review,* July–August 1991, pp. 58–67.

48. Adapted from Harris and Moran, *Managing Cultural Differences,* p. 471.

49. Lewis, *When Cultures Collide,* pp. 231–232.

50. Sean Van Zyl, "Global Political Risks: Post 9/11," *Canadian Underwriter* 71, no. 3 (March 2004), p. 16; Marvin Zonis, "Mideast Hopes; Endless Surprises," *Chicago Tribune,* January 18, 2004, p. 1.

51. Changiz Pezeshkpur, "Challenges to Management in the Arab World," *Business Horizons,* August 1978, p. 50.

52. Adapted from Harris and Moran, *Managing Cultural Differences,* p. 503.

■ Chapter 6

1. Lisa Hoecklin, *Managing Cultural Differences: Strategies for Competitive Advantage* (Workingham, England: Addison-Wesley, 1995), p. 146.

2. Edgar H. Schein, *Organizational Culture and Leadership,* 2nd ed. (San Francisco: Jossey-Bass, 1997), p. 12.

3. Fred Luthans, *Organizational Behavior,* 10th ed. (New York: McGraw-Hill/Irwin, 2005), pp. 110–111.

4. In addition see W. Mathew Jeuchter, Caroline Fisher, and Randall J. Alford, "Five Conditions for High-Performance Cultures," *Training and Development Journal,* May 1998, pp. 63–67.

5. Hoecklin, *Managing Cultural Differences,* p. 145.

6. Andre Laurent, "The Cultural Diversity of Western Conceptions of Management," *International Studies of Management and Organization,* Spring–Summer 1983, pp. 75–96.

7. Nancy J. Adler, *International Dimensions of Organizational Behavior,* 2nd ed. (Boston: PWS-Kent Publishing, 1991), pp. 58–59.

8. Robert Frank and Thomas M. Burton, "Cross-Border Merger Results in Headaches for a Drug Company," *Wall Street Journal,* February 4, 1997, p. A1.

9. Hoecklin, *Managing Cultural Differences,* p. 151.

10. Robert Hughes, "Weekend Journal: Futures and Options: Global Culture," *Wall Street Journal,* October 10, 2003, p. W2.

11. Rita A. Numeroff and Michael N. Abrams, "Integrating Corporate Culture from International M&As," *HR Focus,* June 1998, p. 12.

12. See Maddy Janssens, Jeanne M. Brett, and Frank J. Smith, "Confirmatory Cross-Cultural Research: Testing the Viability of a Corporation-Wide Safety Policy," *Academy of Management Journal,* June 1995, pp. 364–382.

13. Fons Trompenaars, *Riding the Waves of Culture: Understanding Diversity in Global Business* (Burr Ridge, IL: Irwin, 1994), p. 154.

14. Ibid.

15. Ibid., p. 156.

16. Ibid., p. 164.

17. Ibid., p. 167.

18. Ibid., p. 172.

19. For more see Rose Mary Wentling and Nilda Palma-Rivas, "Current Status of Diversity Initiatives in Selected Multinational Corporations," *Human Resource Development Quarterly,* Spring 2000, pp. 35–60.

20. Adler, *International Dimensions of Organizational Behavior,* p. 121.

21. Noboru Yoshimura and Philip Anderson, *Inside the Kaisha: Demystifying Japanese Business Behavior* (Boston: Harvard Business School Press, 1997).

22. Edmund L. Andrews, "Meet the Maverick of Japan, Inc." *New York Times,* October 12, 1995, pp. C1, C4.

23. Sheryl WuDunn, "Incubators of Creativity," *New York Times,* October 9, 1997, pp. C1, C21.

24. Adler, *International Dimensions of Organizational Behavior,* p. 132.

25. Adele Thomas and Mike Bendixen, "The Management Implications of Ethnicity in South Africa," *Journal of International Business Studies,* Third Quarter 2000, pp. 507–519.

26. John M. Ivencevich and Jacqueline A. Gilbert, "Diversity Management: Time for a New Approach," *Public Personnel Management,* Spring 2000, pp. 75–92.

27. Joseph J. Distefano and Martha L. Maznevski, "Creating Value with Diverse Teams in Global Management," *Organizational Dynamics,* Summer 2000, pp. 45–63.

28. See, for example, Betty Jane Punnett and Jason Clemens, "Cross-National Diversity: Implications for International Expansion Decisions," *Journal of World Business* 34, no. 2 (1999), pp. 128–138.

29. Adler, *International Dimensions of Organizational Behavior,* p. 137.

30. Wellford W. Wilms, Alan J. Hardcastle, and Deone M. Zell, "Cultural Transformation at NUMMI," *Sloan Management Review,* Fall 1994, p. 103.

31. Ibid., p. 111.

■ Chapter 7

1. E. T. Hall and E. Hall, "How Cultures Collide," in *Culture, Communication, and Conflict: Readings in Intercultural Relations,* ed. G. R. Weaver (Needham Heights, MA: Ginn Press, 1994).

2. Noboru Yoshimura and Philip Anderson, *Inside the Kaisha: Demystifying Japanese Business Behavior* (Boston: Harvard Business School Press, 1997), p. 59.

3. William C. Byham and George Dixon, "Through Japanese Eyes," *Training and Development Journal,* March 1993, pp. 33–36; Linda S. Dillon, "West Meets East," *Training and Development Journal,* March 1993, pp. 39–43.

4. Fons Trompenaars and Charles Hampden-Turner, *Riding the Waves of Culture: Understanding Diversity in Global Business,* 2nd ed. (New York: McGraw-Hill, 1998), p. 204.

5. Nancy J. Adler, *International Dimensions of Organizational Behavior,* 2nd ed. (Boston: PWS-Kent Publishing, 1991), pp. 75–76.

6. Giorgio Inzerilli, "The Legitimacy of Managerial Authority—A Comparative Study," *National Academy of Management Proceedings* (Detroit, 1980), pp. 58–62.

7. Ibid., p. 62.

8. Philip R. Harris and Robert T. Moran, *Managing Cultural Differences,* 3rd ed. (Houston: Gulf Publishing, 1996), pp. 36–37.

9. Richard Tanner Pascale and Anthony G. Athos, *The Art of Japanese Management* (New York: Warner Books, 1981), pp. 82–83.

10. Justin Fox, "The Triumph of English," *Fortune,* September 18, 2000, pp. 209–212.

11. See "Double or Quits," *Economist,* February 25, 1995, pp. 84–85.

12. Brock Stout, "Interviewing in Japan," *HR Magazine,* June 1998, p. 73.

13. Ibid., p. 75.

14. H. W. Hildebrandt, "Communication Barriers Between German Subsidiaries and Parent American Companies," *Michigan Business Review,* July 1973, p. 9.

15. John R. Schermerhorn Jr., "Language Effects in Cross-Cultural Management Research: An Empirical Study and a Word of Caution," *National Academy of Management Proceedings,* (New Orleans, 1987), p. 103.

16. Brenda R. Sims and Stephen Guice, "Differences Between Business Letters from Native and Non-Native Speakers of English," *Journal of Business Communication,* Winter 1991, p. 37.

17. James Calvert Scott and Diana J. Green, "British Perspectives on Organizing Bad-News Letters: Organizational Patterns Used by Major U.K. Companies," *The Bulletin,* March 1992, p. 17.

18. Ibid., pp. 18–19.

19. Mi Young Park, W. Tracy Dillon, and Kenneth L. Mitchell, "Korean Business Letters: Strategies for Effective Complaints in Cross-Cultural Communication," *Journal of Business Communication,* July 1998, pp. 328–345.

20. As an example see Jeremiah Sullivan, "What Are the Functions of Corporate Home Pages?" *Journal of World Business* 34, no. 2 (1999), pp. 193–211.

21. Joseph Kahn, "Fraying U.S.-Sino Ties Threaten Business," *Wall Street Journal,* July 7, 1995, p. A6; Nathaniel C. Nash, "China Gives Big Van Deal to Mercedes," *New York Times,* July 13, 1995, pp. C1, C5; and Seth Faison, "China Times a Business Deal to Make a Point to America," *New York Times,* July 16, 1995, pp. 1, 6.

22. David A. Ricks, *Big Business Blunders: Mistakes in Multinational Marketing* (Homewood, IL: Dow Jones-Irwin, 1983), p. 39.

23. Ibid., p. 55.

24. Edwin Miller, Bhal Bhatt, Raymond Hill, and Julian Cattaneo, "Leadership Attitudes of American and German Expatriate Managers in Europe and Latin America," *National Academy of Management Proceedings* (Detroit, 1980), pp. 53–57.

25. Abdul Rahim A. Al-Meer, "Attitudes Towards Women as Managers: A Comparison of Asians, Saudis and Westerners," *Arab Journal of the Social Sciences,* April 1988, pp. 139–149.

26. Sheryl WuDunn, "In Japan, Still Getting Tea and No Sympathy," *New York Times,* August 27, 1995, p. E3.

27. Fathi S. Yousef, "Cross-Cultural Communication: Aspects of the Contrastive Social Values Between North Americans and Middle Easterners," *Human Organization,* Winter 1974, p. 385.

28. Peter McKiernan and Chris Carter, "The Millennium Nexus: Strategic Management at the Crossroads," *European Management Review* 1, no. 1 (Spring 2004), p. 3.

29. R. Bruce Money, "Word-of-Mouth Referral Sources for Buyers of International Corporate Financial Services," *Journal of World Business* 35, no. 3 (2000), pp. 314–329.

30. Yousef, "Cross-Cultural Communication," p. 383.

31. See Roger E. Axtell, ed., *Do's and Taboos Around the World* (New York: Wiley, 1990), chapter 2.

32. Jane Whitney Gibson, Richard M. Hodgetts, and Charles W. Blackwell, "Cultural Variations in Nonverbal Communication," *55th Annual Business Communication Proceedings,* San Antonio, November 8–10, 1990, pp. 211–229.

33. William K. Brandt and James M. Hulbert, "Patterns of Communications in the Multinational Corporation: An Empirical Study," *Journal of International Business Studies,* Spring 1976, pp. 57–64.

34. Hildebrandt, "Communication Barriers," p. 9.

35. See for example George Ming-Hong Lai, "Knowing Who You Are Doing Business with in Japan: A Managerial View of Keiretsu and Keiretsu Business Groups," *Journal of World Business* 34, no. 4 (1999), pp. 423–449.

36. Nicholas Athanassiou and Douglas Nigh, "Internationalization, Tacit Knowledge and the Top Management Teams of MNCs," *Journal of International Business Studies,* Third Quarter 2000, pp. 471–487.

37. Also see Linda Beamer, "Bridging Business Cultures," *China Business Review,* May/June 1998, pp. 54–58.

38. Michael D. Lord and Annette L. Ranft, "Organizational Learning About New International Markets: Exploring the Internal Transfer of Local Market Knowledge," *Journal of International Business Studies,* Fourth Quarter 2000, pp. 573–589.

39. Jennifer W. Spencer, "Knowledge Flows in the Global Innovation System: Do U.S. Firms Share More Scientific Knowledge than Their Japanese Rivals?" *Journal of International Business Studies,* Third Quarter 2000, pp. 521–530.

40. Kenichi Ohmae, "The Global Logic of Strategic Alliances," *Harvard Business Review,* March–April 1989, p. 154.

41. See Hildy Teegen and Jonathan P. Doh, "U.S./Mexican Alliance Negotiations: Cultural Impacts on Trust, Authority and Performance," *Thunderbird International Business Review* 44, no. 6 (2002), pp. 749–775; Elise Campbell and Jeffrey J. Reuer, "International Alliance Negotiations: Legal Issues for General Managers," *Business Horizons,* January–February 2001, pp. 19–26.

42. David K. Tse, June Francis, and Ian Walls, "Cultural Differences in Conducting Intra- and Inter-Cultural Negotiations: A Sino-Canadian Comparison," *Journal of International Business Studies,* Third Quarter 1994, pp. 537–555; Teegen and Doh, "U.S./Mexican Alliance Negotiations," pp. 749–775.

43. Adler, *International Dimensions of Organizational Behavior,* p. 197.

44. Jeanne M. Brett, Debra L. Shapiro, and Anne L. Lytle, "Breaking the Bonds of Reciprocity in Negotiations," *Academy of Management Journal,* August 1998, pp. 410–424.

45. Stephen E. Weiss, "Negotiating with 'Romans'—Part 2," *Sloan Management Review,* Spring 1994, p. 89.

46. Trompenaars and Hampden-Turner, *Riding the Waves of Culture,* p. 112.

47. John L. Graham, "Brazilian, Japanese, and American Business Negotiations," *Journal of International Business Studies,* Spring/Summer 1983, pp. 47–61; John L. Graham, "The Influence of Culture on the Process of Business Negotiations in an Exploratory Study," *Journal of International Business Studies,* Spring 1983, pp. 81–96.

48. Ibid., pp. 84, 88.

■ Part 2 Cases

In-Depth Integrative Case 2

1. "Seiyu Stake Should Pay Off," *MMR*, May 26, 2003, p. 14.
2. "Wal-Mart Bottom Line Hits Mark," *MMR*, June 16, 2003, p. 9.
3. Ann Zimmerman and Martin Fackler, "Wal-Mart's Foray into Japan Spurs a Retail Upheaval," *Wall Street Journal*, September 18, 2003, p. B1.
4. Jennifer McTaggart, "Wal-Mart Versus the World," *Progressive Grocer*, October 15, 2003, p. 20.
5. Carl Steidtmann, "Wal-Mart Set to Change Retail Face of Japan," *Asia Pulse*, October 27, 2003, p. 12.
6. "Wal-Mart Says Global Going Good," *Home Textiles Today*, September 26, 2003, p. 12.
7. McTaggart. "Wal-Mart Versus the World."
8. Greg Jacobsen, "Wal-Mart in Japan," *MMR*, April 22, 2003, p. 21.
9. Zimmerman and Fackler, "Wal-Mart's Foray into Japan."
10. Ibid.
11. "Wal-Mart Takes Crack at Japan," *Women's Wear Daily*, July 4, 2003, p. 2.
12. "Wal-Mart Says Global Going Good."
13. "Wal-Mart Takes Crack at Japan."
14. Ibid.
15. "Wal-Mart Says Global Going Good."
16. "Wal-Mart Japan?" *Chain Store Age Executive* 78, no. 4 (April 2002), p. 32.
17. Ken Belson, "Wal-Mart Hopes It Won't Be Lost in Translation," *New York Times*, December 14, 2003, sec. 3, p. 1.
18. Tsukasa Furukawa, "Seiyu Eyes Wal-Mart 'Efficiency' Model," *Women's Wear Daily*, April 21, 2003, p. 15.
19. Koji Hirano, "Wal-Mart Might Soon Be Entering Japan," *Women's Wear Daily*, September 24, 2001, p. 10.
20. Mike Troy, "Wal-Mart Invests in Japan, Buys 6 Percent Share of Seiyu," *DSN Retailing Today*, March 25, 2002, p. 2.
21. David Ibison, "Wal-Mart to Expand with Push in Japan," *Financial Times London Edition*, January 2, 2001, p. A10.
22. McTaggart, "Wal-Mart Versus the World."

■ Chapter 8

1. Joel Baglole, "Citibank Takes Risk by Issuing Cards in China," *Wall Street Journal*, March 10, 2004, p. C1.
2. "Foreign Investment Restrictions in OECD Countries" (Paris: Organization for Economic Cooperation and Development, June 2003), p. 167.
3. Matthew Karnitschnig, "Bertelsmann Plans Expansion as All Units Return to the Black," *Wall Street Journal*, March 31, 2004, p. B3.
4. Andrew Collier, "China: Foreign First in China Book Sector," *South China Morning Post*, December 4, 2003, p. A10.
5. Michael McHugh, "GE Energy Purchase of BHA Fits into Strategy," *Wall Street Journal*, June 1, 2004, p. A4.
6. http://www.ge.com/en/company/investor.
7. Barry Hopewell, "Strategic Management: A Multi-Perspective Approach," *Long Range Planning* 36, no. 4 (July 2003), p. 317.
8. Sharon Watson O'Neil, "Managing Foreign Subsidiaries: Agents of Headquarters, or An Independent Network?" *Strategic Management Journal* 21, no. 5 (May 2000), p. 525.
9. Noel Capon, Chris Christodoulou, John U. Farley, and James Hulbert, "A Comparison of Corporate Planning Practice in American and Australian Manufacturing Companies," *Journal of International Business Studies*, Fall 1984, pp. 41–45.
10. Martin K. Welge, "Planning in German Multinational Corporations," *International Studies of Management and Organization*, Spring 1982, pp. 6–37.
11. Martin K. Welge and Michael E. Kenter, "Impact of Planning on Control Effectiveness and Company Performance," *Management International Review* 20, no. 2 (1988), pp. 4–15.
12. See for example Masaaki Kotabe, "Global Sourcing Strategy in the Pacific: American and Japanese Multinational Companies," in *Trends in International Business: Critical Perspectives,* ed. Michael R. Czinkota and Masaaki Kotabe (Malden, MA: Blackwell, 1998), pp. 237–256.
13. Joan Magretta, "Fast, Global, and Entrepreneurial: Supply Chain Management, Hong Kong Style," *Harvard Business Review*, September–October 1998, p. 108.
14. Nikhil Deogun, "For Coke in India, Thumbs Up Is the Real Thing," *Wall Street Journal*, April 29, 1998, pp. B1, B6.
15. Richard M. Hodgetts, *Measures of Quality and High Performance* (New York: American Management Association, 1998).
16. Sang M. Lee, Fred Luthans, and Richard M. Hodgetts, "Total Quality Management: Implications for Central and Eastern Europe," *Organizational Dynamics*, Spring 1992, pp. 44–45.
17. Lindsay Chappell, "Ford Man Runyon Rewrote the Rules at Nissan," *Automotive News*, May 10, 2004, p. 28.
18. Christine Y. Chen, "How Nortel Stole Optical," *Fortune*, October 2, 2000, p. 144. See also Sam Masud, "Building a Flexible Optical Network," *Telecommunications America* 37, no. 13 (December 2003), p. 18.
19. Leslie Wayne, "Chief Decided to Step Down at Motorola," *New York Times*, September 20, 2003, p. C1.
20. "Hip Cell," *Chicago Tribune*, June 3, 2004, p. 32.
21. Christopher A. Bartlett and Sumantra Ghoshal, *Managing Across Borders: The Transnational Solution,* updated 2nd ed. (Cambridge, MA: Harvard Business School Press, 2002).
22. Ibid.
23. Royal Ford, "Driven by Demand, Vehicle Buyers Want Versatility and Amenities, Too," *Boston Globe*, February 3, 2004, p. G1.
24. Fons Trompenaars and Charles Hampden-Turner, *Riding the Waves of Culture: Understanding Diversity in Global Business,* 2nd ed. (New York: McGraw-Hill, 1998), p. 188.
25. Charles Hill, *Global Business Today,* 3rd ed. (New York: McGraw-Hill, 2004), pp. 376–380.
26. Ibid.
27. See Anne-Wil Harzing, "An Empirical Analysis and Extension of the Bartlett and Ghoshal Typology of Multinational Companies," *Journal of International Business Studies,* First Quarter 2000, pp. 101–120; Julius H. Johnson Jr., "An Empirical Analysis of the Integration–Responsiveness Framework: U.S. Construction Equipment Industry Firms in Global Competition," *Journal of International Business Studies* 26, no. 3 (1995), pp. 621–636.
28. Michael Flagg, "U.S. Firm to Pioneer China's Interactive TV," *Wall Street Journal*, May 15, 2001, p. A21.
29. Ben Dolven, "China Grooms Global Players," *Wall Street Journal*, February 25, 2004, p. A12.
30. Gail Edmonson and Kathleen Kerwin, "Can Ford Fix This Flat?" *BusinessWeek*, December 1, 2003, p. 50.
31. David Shephardson, "Ex-Ford Executive Says He Didn't Resign," *Detroit News*, December 19, 2003, p. B1.
32. Sea Jin Chang, "International Expansion Strategy of Japanese Firms: Capacity Building Through Sequential Entry," *Academy of Management Journal,* April 1995, p. 402.

33. Ron Sutter, "Global FDI Flows Remain Flat in 2003," *English People Daily,* March 13, 2004, p. 29.

34. Jathon Sapsford, "Real-Estate Buyers Circle Japan," *Wall Street Journal,* March 11, 1998, p. B10.

35. Graham Gori, "Investors Are Rushing to Mexico, Despite Slowing Growth," *New York Times,* May 25, 2001, p. W1; Mary Anastasia O'Grady, "Americas: Teamsters Give NAFTA a Flat Tire," *Wall Street Journal,* April 16, 2004, p. A15.

36. Craig Torres, "Foreigners Snap Up Mexican Companies: Impact Is Enormous," *Wall Street Journal,* September 30, 1997, p. A1. See also Joel Millman, "The Economy: Mexican Mergers, Acquisitions Triple from 2001," *Economist,* December 27, 2002, p. A2.

37. John Garland and Richard N. Farmer, *International Dimensions of Business Policy and Strategy* (Boston: Kent Publishing, 1986), pp. 62–63.

38. Harry I. Chernotsky, "Selecting U.S. Sites: A Case Study of German and Japanese Firms," *Management International Review* 23, no. 2 (1983), pp. 45–55.

39. Also see Roland Calori, Leif Melin, Tugrul Atamer, and Peter Gustavsson, "Innovative International Strategies," *Journal of World Business* 35, no. 4 (2000), pp. 333–354.

40. Christos Pantzalis, "Does Location Matter? An Empirical Analysis of Geographic Scope and MNC Market Valuation," *Journal of International Business Studies,* First Quarter 2001, pp. 133–155.

41. Das Narayandas, John Quelch, and Gordon Swartz, "Prepare Your Company for Global Pricing," *Sloan Management Review,* Fall 2000, pp. 61–70.

42. United Nations Conference on Trade and Development, *World Investment Report* (New York and Geneva: UNCTAD, 2003).

43. Jeffrey E. Garten, *The Big Ten: The Big Emerging Markets and How They Will Change Our Lives* (New York: Basic Books, 1997).

44. Jonathan P. Doh and Ravi Ramamurti, "Reassessing Risk in Developing Country Infrastructure," *Long Range Planning* 36, no. 4 (2003), pp. 337–353.

45. Jonathan P. Doh, Hildy Teegen, and Ram Mudambi, "Balancing Private and State Ownership in Emerging Markets' Telecommunications Infrastructure: Country, Industry, and Firm Influences," *Journal of International Business Studies* 35, no. 3 (2004), pp. 233–250.

46. See Yudong Luo and Mike W. Peng, "First Mover Advantages in Investing in Transitional Economies," *Thunderbird International Business Review* 40, no. 2 (March/April 1998), pp. 141–163.

47. For a detailed analysis of first-mover effects of this case, see Jonathan P. Doh, "Entrepreneurial Privatization Strategies: Order of Entry and Local Partner Collaboration as Sources of Competitive Advantage," *Academy of Management Review* 25, no.3 (2000), pp. 551–571.

48. Stuart Hart and Clayton Christensen, "The Great Leap: Driving Innovation from the Base of the Pyramid," *Sloan Management Review* 44, no. 1 (2002), pp. 51–56; C. K. Prahalad and Stuart L. Hart, "The Fortune at the Bottom of the Pyramid," *Strategy + Business* 26 (2002), pp. 54–67.

49. Joan Enric Ricart, Michael J. Enright, Pankaj Ghemawat, Stuart L. Hart, and Tarun Khanna, "New Frontiers in International Strategy," *Journal of International Business Studies* 35, no. 3 (May 2004), pp. 175–200.

50. Ibid., pp. 194–195.

51. Patricia P. McDougall and Benjamin M. Oviatt, "International Entrepreneurship: The Intersection of Two Research Paths," *Academy of Management Journal* 43 (2000), pp. 902–908.

52. Ibid., p. 902.

53. Erkko Autio, Harry J. Sapienza, and James G. Almeida, "Effects of Age at Entry, Knowledge Intensity, and Irritability on International Growth," *Academy of Management Journal* 43 (2000), pp. 909–924.

54. Shaker A. Zahra, Duane R. Ireland, and Michael A. Hitt, "International Expansion by New Venture Firms: International Diversity, Mode of Market Entry, Technological Learning, and Performance," *Academy of Management Journal* 43 (2000), pp. 925–950.

55. Moen Oystein, "The Born Globals: A New Generation of Small European Exporters," *International Marketing Review* 19, no. 2/3 (2002), pp. 156–175.

56. Gary A. Knight and S. Tamar Cavusgil, "Innovation, Organizational Capabilities, and the Born-Global Firm," *Journal of International Business Studies* 35, no. 2 (2004), pp. 124–141.

57. Ibid.

58. J. de La Torre and R. W. Moxon, "Electronic Commerce and Global Business: Introduction to the Symposium," *Journal of International Business* 32, no. 1 (2001), pp. 617–640.

59. eMarketer, 2002, *The eGlobal Report,* http://www.emarketer.com.

■ Chapter 9

1. Andrew Browne, Matt Pottinger, and Peter Wonacott, "China's Expansion May Be Easing," *Wall Street Journal,* June 11, 2004, p. A2.

2. Harrry Barkema and Freek Vermeulen, "International Expansion Through Start-up or Acquisition: A Learning Perspective," *Academy of Management Journal,* February 1998, pp. 7–26.

3. Youssef M. Ibrahim, "British Petroleum Is Buying Amoco in $48.2 Billion Deal," *New York Times,* August 12, 1998, pp. A1, C5; Charles Goldsmith and Steven Lipin, "BP to Acquire Amoco in a Huge Deal Spurred by Falling Oil Prices," *Wall Street Journal,* August 12, 1998, p. A1.

4. Chip Cumming and Mark Long, "BP Net Rises 14%, Aided by Stock Sales," *Wall Street Journal,* April 28, 2004, p. A2.

5. Gail Edmondson, "Why DaimlerChrysler Isn't Up to Speed." *BusinessWeek,* February 24, 2004. pp. 20–21.

6. Ibid.

7. Ibid.

8. For additional insights into alliances and joint ventures, see William Newburry and Yoram Zeira, "General Differences Between Equity International Joint Ventures (EIJVs), International Acquisitions (IAs) and International Greenfield Investments (IGIs): Implications for Parent Companies," *Journal of World Business* 32, no. 2 (1997), pp. 87–102.

9. Also see David Lei, Robert A. Pitts, and John W. Slocum Jr., "Building Cooperative Advantage: Managing Strategic Alliances to Promote Organizational Learning," *Journal of World Business* 32, no. 3 (1997), pp. 203–222.

10. For more on this see Ana Valdes Llaneza and Esteban Garcia-Canal, "Distinctive Features of Domestic and International Joint Ventures," *Management International Review* 38, no. 1 (1998), pp. 49–66.

11. "Singapore Telecommunications: Alcatel, Fujitsu Wins Contract for Undersea Cable Network," *Wall Street Journal,* March 30, 2004, p. 1.

12. John B. Cullen, Jean L. Johnson, and Tomoaki Sakano, "Success Through Commitment and Trust: The Soft Side of Strategic Alliance Management," *Journal of World Business* 35, no. 3 (2000), pp. 223–240.

13. John Markov, "Sony and AOL Join Forces on the Video Game Front," *New York Times,* May 15, 2001, p. C12.

14. For more on this see Hildy J. Teegen and Jonathan P. Doh, "U.S./Mexican Alliance Negotiations: Cultural Impacts on Trust, Authority and Performance," *Thunderbird International Business*

Review 44, no. 6 (2002), pp. 749–775; Michael A. Hitt, M. Tina Dacin, Edward Levitas, Jean-Luc Arregle, and Anca Borza, "Partner Selection in Emerging and Developed Market Contexts: Resource-Based and Organizational Learning Perspectives," *Academy of Management Journal* 43, no. 3 (2002), pp. 449–467.

15. For more on this see Donald F. Kuratko and Richard M. Hodgetts, *Entrepreneurship: A Contemporary Approach,* 5th ed. (Ft.Worth, TX: Harcourt, 2001), pp. 529–535.

16. Andrew Leckly, "Retooled Motorola Hopes It's Pushing Right Buttons," *Chicago Tribune,* July 30, 2002, p. 6.

17. Evan Ramsted, "Motorola Sells China Chip Plant to Small Shanghai Manufacturer," *Wall Street Journal,* October 27, 2003, p. B6.

18. Jenny Watts, "Is This the End for Coke's 'Think Local' Ad Strategy?" *Campaign,* October 12, 2001, p. 17.

19. Joan Magretta, "Fast, Global, and Entrepreneurial: Supply Chain Management, Hong Kong Style," *Harvard Business Review,* September–October 1998, p. 106.

20. See George S. Yip, *Total Global Strategy II* (Englewood Cliffs, NJ: Prentice Hall, 2003), chapter 8.

21. A. V. Phatak, *International Dimensions of Management,* 2nd ed. (Boston: PWS-Kent, 1989), pp. 92–93.

22. Evan Ramstad and David Pringle, "Alcatel Shifts Production to China," *Wall Street Journal,* April 27, 2004, p. B5.

23. Reported in Peter J. Dowling, Randall S. Schuler, and Denice E. Welch, *International Dimensions of Human Resource Management,* 2nd ed. (Belmont, CA: Wadsworth, 1994), p. 33.

24. John Tagliabue, "Renault Agrees to Buy Troubled Samsung Motors of Korea," *New York Times,* April 22, 2000, pp. B1, B3.

25. Stephanie Strom, "DaimlerChrysler Buying a Third of Mitsubishi for $2.1 Billion," *New York Times,* March 28, 2000, p. C4.

26. Also see Andrew C. Inkpen and Adva Dinur, "Knowledge Management Processes and International Joint Ventures," *Organization Science,* July–August 1998, pp. 454–468.

27. See for example John Child, "A Configurational Analysis of International Joint Ventures," *Organization Studies* 23, no. 5 (2002), pp. 781–815.

28. Pien Wang, Chow Hou Wee, and Peck Hiong Koh, "Establishing a Successful Sino–Foreign Equity Joint Venture: The Singapore Experience," *Journal of World Business* 34, no. 3 (1999), pp. 287–306.

29. Gus Gorman and Thurmon Williams, "How Do You Spell Success in Mexico? CALICA," *Business Horizons* 44, no. 1 (January/February 2001), p. 11.

30. For some insights regarding the importance of networking, see "The Battle for Ukraine," *Economist,* February 11, 1995, p. 56.

31. Miki Tanikawa, "Electronics Giants Join Forces in Japan," *New York Times,* May 24, 2001, p. W1.

32. Donald Gerwin, "Coordinating New Product Development in Strategic Alliances," *Academy of Management Review* 29, no. 2 (April 2004), p. 241.

33. Craig Zarley, "IBM Outsourcing Rolls On," *CRN,* January 13, 2003, p. 24.

34. Lisa Bushrod, "Eircom Returns to Public Life," *European Venture Capital Journal,* April 1, 2004, p. 1.

35. Matthew Schifrin, "Partner or Perish," *Forbes,* May 21, 2001, p. 27.

36. Thomas W. Malone and Robert J. Laubacher, "The Dawn of the E-Lance Economy," *Harvard Business Review,* September–October 1998, p. 148.

37. Durward K. Sobek II, Jeffrey K. Liker, and Allen C. Ward, "Another Look at How Toyota Integrates Product Development," *Harvard Business Review,* July–August 1998, p. 49.

38. For more on this see M. Bensaou and Michael Earl, "The Right Mind-Set for Managing Information Technology," *Harvard Business Review,* September–October 1998, pp. 119–128.

39. Anne-Wil Harzing, "An Empirical Analysis and Extension of the Bartlett and Ghoshal Typology of Multinational Companies," *Journal of International Business Studies,* First Quarter 2000, pp. 101–120.

40. Steven M. Sommers, Seung-Hyun Bae, and Fred Luthans, "The Structure–Climate Relationship in Korean Organizations," *Asia Pacific Journal of Management* 12, no. 2 (1995), pp. 23–36.

41. James R. Lincoln, Mitsuyo Hanada, and Kerry McBride, "Organizational Structures in Japanese and U.S. Manufacturing," *Administrative Science Quarterly,* September 1986, p. 356.

42. Rhy-song Yeh and Tagi Sagafi-nejad, "Organizational Characteristics of American and Japanese Firms in Taiwan," *National Academy of Management Proceedings,* 1987, pp. 111–115.

43. Ibid., p. 113.

44. Abbass F. Alkhafaji, *Competitive Global Management: Principles and Strategies* (Delray Beach, FL: St. Lucie Press, 1995), pp. 390–391.

45. Michael Yoshino and N. S. Rangan, *Strategic Alliances* (Boston: Harvard Business School Press, 1995), p. 195.

46. For additional insights, see Anant K. Sundaram and J. Stewart Black, *The International Business Environment: Text and Cases* (Englewood Cliffs, NJ: Prentice-Hall, 1995), pp. 314–315.

47. Lincoln, Hanada, and McBride, "Organizational Structures," p. 349.

48. Vito Racancelli, "Why Hung-Up Nokia Might Still Be Decent Value Play," *Barron's,* May 24, 2004, p. MW6.

49. Mark Lehrer and Kazuhiro Asakawa, "Unbundling European Operations: Regional Management and Corporate Flexibility in American and Japanese MNCs," *Journal of World Business* 34, no. 3 (1999), pp. 267–286.

50. Masumi Tsuda, "The Future of the Organization and the Individual to Japanese Management," *International Studies of Management and Organization,* Fall–Winter 1985, pp. 89–125.

51. Yeh and Sagafi-nejad, "Organizational Characteristics," p. 113.

52. Stephen Christophe and Ray Pfeiffer Jr., "The Valuation of MNC International Operations During the 1990s," *Review of Quantitative Finance and Accounting* 18, no. 2 (March 2002), p. 119.

53. Tsuda, "The Future of the Organization," p. 114.

■ Chapter 10

1. "Finance and Economics: Footloose Firms; Economic Focus," *Economist,* March 27, 2004, p. 99.

2. Seth Faison, "China Applies Brakes on Move Toward Market Economy," *New York Times,* September 30, 1998, p. C3. See also Kathy Chen, "China's Party Line Is Capital," *Wall Street Journal,* February 12, 2004, p. C20.

3. Alfred Hille, "Li Leads Way in China Piracy Battle," *Media,* January 16, 2004, p. 17.

4. Benjamin Fulford, "Microwave Missionaries," *Forbes,* November 13, 2000, p. 146.

5. Andrew Green, "The Development of Mass Media in Asia-Pacific," *International Journal of Advertising* 22, no. 2 (2002), p. 273.

6. P. T. Bangsberg, "Hong Kong, China Plant Transport Links," *Journal of Commerce,* June 14, 2004, p. 1.

7. Elisabeth Rosenthal, "U.S. Trade Official Says China Market Is Closed Tighter," *New York Times,* September 23, 1998, p. C2.

8. Mark Landler, "Back to Vietnam, This Time to Build," *New York Times,* September 13, 1998, sec. 3, pp. 1, 11.

9. "Operational Risk: Vietnam: Risk Ratings," *Country Monitor,* February 23, 2004, p. 11.

10. Todd Zaun, "The Economy: U.S. Trade Chief Seeks to Reassure a Very Weary Japan on Steel Tariffs," *Wall Street Journal,* April 12, 2002, p. A2.

11. John McKinnon and Neil King, "EU Set to Impose Trade Sanctions If U.S. Fails to Act," *Wall Street Journal,* January 26, 2004, p. A4.

12. "Coca-Cola Co: Settlement of Anti-Trust Case Is Discussed with EU Officials," *Wall Street Journal,* April 19, 2004, p. 1.

13. Edmund L. Andrews, "Why U.S. Giants Are Crying Uncle," *New York Times,* October 11, 2000, p. W1.

14. David A. Schmidt, "Analyzing Political Risk," *Business Horizons,* July–August 1986, pp. 43–50.

15. Matthew Brzezinski, "Russia Kills Huge Oil Deal with Exxon," *Wall Street Journal,* August 28, 1997, p. A2.

16. For more, see Thomas A. Pointer, "Political Risk: Managing Government Intervention," in *International Management: Text and Cases,* ed. Paul W. Beamish, J. Peter Killing, Donald J. LeCraw, and Harold Crookell (Homewood, IL: Irwin, 1991), pp. 119–133.

17. See Jonathan P. Doh and Ravi Ramamurti, "Reassessing Risk in Developing Country Infrastructure," *Long Range Planning* 36, no. 4 (2003), pp. 337–353.

18. Ravi Ramamurti and Jonathan Doh, "Rethinking Foreign Infrastructure Investment in Developing Countries," *Journal of World Business* 39, no. 2 (2004), pp. 151–167.

19. Michael M. Schuman, "Indonesia to Pay Reduced Claim to U.S. in Long-Disputed Overseas Insurance Case," *Wall Street Journal,* May 11, 2001, p. A12.

20. Timothy Mapes, "Power Firm's Bid to Collect Funds from Pertamina Raises Hackles," *Wall Street Journal,* April 1, 2002. p. A6.

21. See Jonathan P. Doh and John A. Pearce II, "Corporate Entrepreneurship and Real Options in Transitional Policy Environments: Theory Development," *Journal of Management Studies* 41, no. 4 (2004), pp. 645–664.

22. Doh and Ramamurti, "Reassessing Risk," pp. 344–349.

23. Amy Hillman and Michael A. Hitt, "Corporate Political Strategy Formulation: A Model of Approach, Participation, and Strategy Decisions," *Academy of Management Review* 24, no. 24 (1999), pp. 825–842.

24. Amy Hillman and Gerald Keim, "International Variation in the Business–Government Interface: Institutional and Organizational Considerations," *Academy of Management Review* 20, no. 1 (1995), pp. 193–214.

25. Jonathan P. Doh and Hildy Teegen, "Nongovernmental Organizations as Institutional Actors in International Business: Theory and Implications," *International Business Review* 11, no. 6 (2002), pp. 665–684.

26. Karl Schoenberge, "Motorola Bets Big on China," *Fortune,* May 27, 1996, pp. 116–121.

27. Matthew Karnitschnig, "Siemens to Expand Business in China and Boost Sales," *Wall Street Journal,* May 18, 2004, p. A6.

28. Peter J. Buckley and Mark Casson, "An Economic Model of International Joint Venture Strategy," *Journal of International Business Studies* 27 (1996), pp. 849–876.

29. Farok J. Contractor and Peter Lorange, eds., *Cooperative Strategies in International Business* (Lexington, MA: Lexington Books, 1998).

30. Andrew C. Inkpen, *The Management of International Joint Ventures: An Organizational Learning Perspective* (London: Routledge, 1995).

31. Shige Makino and Andrew Delios, "Local Knowledge Transfer and Performance: Implications for Alliance Formation in Asia," *Journal of International Business Studies* 27 (1996), pp. 905–927.

32. Hildy Teegen and Jonathan P. Doh, "U.S./Mexican Alliance Negotiations: Cultural Impacts on Trust, Authority and Performance," *Thunderbird International Business Review* 44, no. 6, (2002) pp. 749–775.

33. Harry G. Barkema and Freek Vermeulen, "What Differences in the Cultural Backgrounds of Partners Are Detrimental for International Joint Ventures?" *Journal of International Business Studies* 28, no. 4 (1997), pp. 845–864.

34. Teegen and Doh, "U.S./Mexican Alliance Negotiations," pp. 749–775.

35. Dirk Holtbrugge, "Management of International Strategic Business Cooperation: Situation Conditions, Performance Criteria and Success Factors," *Thunderbird International Business Review* 46, no. 3 (May/June 2004), pp. 255–274.

36. Manuel G. Serapio Jr. and Wayner F. Cascio, "End Games in International Alliances," *Academy of Management Executive* 10, no. 1 (February 1996), pp. 62–73.

37. Julia G. Djarova, "Foreign Investment Strategies and the Attractiveness of Central and Eastern Europe," *International Studies in Management and Organization* 29, no. 1 (Spring 1999), pp. 14–23.

38. Jonathan P. Doh and Hildy Teegen, "Government Mandates and Local Partner Participation in Emerging Markets: Policy and Performance Implications for Government and Business Strategies" (paper presented at the annual meeting of the Academy of International Business, Phoenix, AZ, November 20, 2002).

39. Jonathan P. Doh, Peter Rodriguez, Klaus Uhlenbruck, Jamie Collins, and Lorraine Eden, "Coping with Corruption in Foreign Markets," *Academy of Management Executive* 17, no. 3 (2003), pp. 114–127.

40. Serapio and Cascio, "End Games in International Alliances," pp. 71–72.

41. Edward Norton, "Starbucks in China," *Economist,* October 4, 2001, pp. 80–82.

42. Frederick Balfour, "Back on the Radar Screen," *BusinessWeek,* November 2000, p. 27.

43. Henry Gallagher, "A Private Sector Surfaces in Vietnam," *The World & I* 18, no. 11 (November 2003), p. 56.

44. Trien Nguyen, "From Plan to Market: The Economic Transition in Vietnam," *Journal of Economic Literature* 38, no. 3 (September 2000), p. 683.

■ Chapter 11

1. "GM China Has Jump in Car Sales," *Wall Street Journal,* July 3, 2003, p. A1.

2. Bill Spindle, "Cowboys and Samurai: The Japanizing of Universal," *Wall Street Journal,* March 22, 2001, p. B6.

3. Jon E. Hilsenrath, "Ford Designs Ikon to Suit Indian Tastes," *Globe and Mail,* August 8, 2000, p. B10.

4. Raghu Nath, *Comparative Management: A Regional View* (Cambridge, MA: Ballinger, 1988), p. 126.

5. Ibid., pp. 74–75.

6. Noboru Yoshimura and Philip Anderson, *Inside the Kaisha: Demystifying Japanese Business Behavior* (Boston: Harvard Business School Press, 1997), p. 44.

7. Anant R. Negandhi, *International Management* (Boston: Allyn & Bacon, 1987), p. 193.

8. Sang M. Lee, Fred Luthans, and Richard M. Hodgetts, "Total Quality Management: Implications for Central and Eastern Europe," *Organizational Dynamics,* Spring 1992, p. 45.

9. Daewoo Park and Herna A. Krishnan, "Understanding Supplier Selection Practices: Differences Between U.S. and Korean

Executives," *Thunderbird International Business Review,* March–April 2001, pp. 243–255.

10. Rebecca Blumstein, "Cadillac Has Designs on Europe's Luxury Car Buyers," *Wall Street Journal,* September 9, 1997, p. B1.

11. "BMW: Up Close and Personal," *Marketing Week,* July 27, 2002, p. 42.

12. Christopher Gasper, "NEC Seeks Right Fits for Expansion," *Boston Globe,* May 13, 2004, p. C3.

13. Edward Moltzen, "Intel Hightlights New Roadmap with Dual-Core Processors," *CRN,* May 31, 2004, p. 35.

14. Dana Corporation, *Annual Report 2003.*

15. Robert L. Simison, "New Dana Illustrates Reshaping of Auto Parts Business," *Wall Street Journal,* September 2, 1997, p. B4.

16. Jim Middlemiss, "IT Challenge: Settlement," *Wall Street Week,* April 2004, p. 46.

17. Fons Trompenaars and Charles Hampden-Turner, *Riding the Waves of Culture: Understanding Diversity in Global Business,* 2nd ed. (New York: McGraw-Hill, 1998), pp. 157–159.

18. John D. Daniels and Jeffrey Arpan, "Comparative Home Country Influences on Management Practices Abroad," *Academy of Management Journal,* September 1972, p. 310.

19. Jacques H. Horovitz, "Management Control in France, Great Britain and Germany," *Columbia Journal of World Business,* Summer 1978, pp. 17–18.

20. Ibid., p. 18.

21. William G. Egelhoff, "Patterns of Control in U.S., U.K., and European Multinational Corporations," *Journal of International Business Studies,* Fall 1984, p. 81.

22. Ibid., pp. 81–82.

23. M. Kreder and M. Zeller, "Control in German and U.S. Companies," *Management International Review* 28, no. 3 (1988), pp. 64–65.

24. Lane Daley, James Jiambalvo, Gary L. Sundem, and Yasumasa Kondo, "Attitudes Toward Financial Control Systems in the United States and Japan," *Journal of International Business Studies,* Fall 1985, pp. 91–110.

25. Yoshimura and Anderson, *Inside the Kaisha,* p. 55.

26. A. V. Phatak, *International Dimensions of Management,* 2nd ed. (Boston: PWS-Kent, 1989), p. 154.

27. William Boston and Paul Hofheinz, "Once Again, EU to Take Back Seat to VW," *Wall Street Journal,* February 27, 2002, p. A16.

28. David A. Garvin, "Japanese Quality Management," *Columbia Journal of World Business,* Fall 1984, pp. 3–12.

29. Ibid., p. 6.

30. Jeffrey K. Liker and Yen-Chun Wu, "Japanese Automakers, U.S. Suppliers and Supply-Chain Superiority," *Sloan Management Review,* Fall 2000, pp. 81–93.

31. Cited in John Holusha, "Improving Quality, the Japanese Way," *New York Times,* July 20, 1988, p. 25. See also Richard Dauch, "Recipe for Success," *Manufacturing Engineering* 131, no. 2 (August 2003), p. 69.

32. "Key to Success: People, People, People," *Fortune,* October 27, 1997, p. 232.

33. Golpira Eshgi, "Nationality Bias and Performance Evaluations in Multinational Corporations," *National Academy of Management Proceedings,* (San Diego, 1985), p. 95.

34. Jeremiah Sullivan, Terukiho Suzuki, and Yasumasa Kondo, "Managerial Theories and the Performance Control Process in Japanese and American Work Groups," *National Academy of Management Proceedings,* (San Diego, 1985), pp. 98–102.

35. Ibid.

■ Part 3 Cases

In-Depth Integrative Case 1

1. Carly Fiorina, "Speech to Business for Social Responsibility Annual Conference," Los Angeles, November 12, 2003.

2. Robyn Weisman. "Problems Mount for Hewlett-Packard," *NewsFactor Network,* http://www.newsfactor.com/perl/story/14668.html, November 8, 2001.

3. Cynthia Webb, "HP's Spin Fails to Appease the Street," http://www.washingtonpost.com, August 20, 2003.

4. Ibid.

5. Clint Swett, "Hewlett-Packard Seems to Have Digested Compaq," Knight Ridder Tribune Business News, May 13, 2003, p. 1.

6. Keith Reagan. "The HP–Compaq One Year Checkup," *E-Commerce Times,* http://www.ecommercetimes.com/perl/story/21406.html, May 1, 2003.

7. "About HP," http://www.hp.com.

8. Ibid.

9. "Assuming HP–Compaq Merger Takes Place . . . ," SV News Services, http://www.ciol.com/content/news/trends/102032601.asp, March 26, 2002.

10. Shukor Rahman, "Challenges Ahead for the New HP," *Computimes Malaysia,* May 13, 2002, p. 1.

11. Henry Norr, "Cost Cuts Going Fast for New HP," *San Francisco Chronicle,* June 5, 2002, p. B1.

12. "About HP," http://www.hp.com.

13. Ibid.

14. C. Doyle and S. Lelii, "From Integration to Execution: HP at One," *VAR Business,* May 12, 2003, p. 24.

15. Reagan, "The HP–Compaq One Year Checkup."

16. Swett, "Hewlett-Packard Seems to Have Digested Compaq."

17. Reagan. "The HP–Compaq One Year Checkup."

18. www.hp.com.

19. Reagan, "The HP–Compaq One Year Checkup."

20. www.hp.com.

21. "HP's e-Drive Targets Underprivileged Worldwide," http://www.computerweekly.com/article123846.htm, July 31, 2003.

22. John Boudreau, "Fiorina Reaffirms HP's Pledge to Philanthropy," http:///www.siliconvalley.com/3205060/asp.?, August 5, 2003.

23. Ibid.

24. Ibid.

25. "HP's e-Drive Targets Underprivileged Worldwide."

26. Melvin Calimag, "HP Philippines Aims to Open Eight HP Stores This Year," *Newsbyte News Network,* February 11, 2003.

27. "HP–Compaq Deal Likely to Clear European Hurdle," http://www.redding.com/newsarchive/20020131bus013.shtml, January 31, 2002.

28. Dawn Kawamoto and Michael Kanellos, "EU Approves HP–Compaq Merger," *CNET news.com,* http://news.zdnet.co.uk/business/employment/0,39020648,2103549,00.htm, February 1, 2001.

In-Depth Integrative Case 2

1. Wayne Arnold, "A Continent Divided by Water, Now United by Air," *New York Times,* January 1, 2004, p. W1.

2. Ibid.

3. Scott Neuman, "Low-Fare Airlines Take Off in Asia," *Wall Street Journal,* February 25, 2004, p. B6G.

4. A. Goldstein and C. Findlay, "Liberalisation and Foreign Direct Investment in Asian Transport Systems: The Case of Aviation,"

Asian Development Bank and OECD Development Centre, no. 26/27 (November 2003), p. 11.

5. Japan Travel Bureau, "Travel Trends and Prospects for 2003," *JTB Newsletter,* January 5, 2003.

6. Centre for Asia Pacific Aviation, "Low Cost Airlines in the Asia Pacific Region: An Exceptional Intra-Regional Traffic Growth Opportunity," September 2002, www.centreforaviation.com.

7. Ibid.

8. Goldman Sachs, "Asia Airlines," *Asia Research,* October 17, 1997, p. 9.

9. Associated Press, "Malaysian Airline Tests Asia's Resistance to No-Frills Flights" (December 2002).

10. Centre for Asia Pacific Aviation, "Low Cost Airlines in the Asia Pacific Region."

11. Associated Press, "Malaysian Airline Tests Asia's Resistance."

12. Interview with Conor McCarthy, April 25, 2003.

13. Comment of Mr. William Ng provided on www.airlinequality.com after traveling on AirAsia in March 2003 from Kuala Lumpur to Penang.

14. G. Thomas, "In Tune with Low Fares in Malaysia," *Air Transport World,* May 2003, pp. 45–46.

15. Nicholas Ionides, "Man of the Moment," *Airline Business,* April 2004, p. 29.

16. Arnold, "A Continent Divided by Water."

17. Thomas, "In Tune with Low Fares in Malaysia."

18. Ionides, "Man of the Moment."

19. Interview with Conor McCarthy, May 8, 2003.

20. Ibid.

21. Centre for Asia Pacific Aviation, "Low Cost Airlines in the Asia Pacific Region."

22. Thomas, "In Tune with Low Fares in Malaysia."

23. Centre for Asia Pacific Aviation, "Low Cost Airlines in the Asia Pacific Region."

24. Thomas, "In Tune with Low Fares in Malaysia."

25. Goldman Sachs, "Asia Airlines."

26. "Having Fun and Flying High," *Economist,* March 11, 2004.

27. Nicholas Ionides, "Third Japanese New-Start Fair Inc Launches Services," *Air Transport Intelligence News* (August 2000).

28. Wayne Arnold. "Qantas Airways Discloses Plan for Low-Cost Singapore Carrier," *New York Times,* April 7, 2004, p. W1.

29. "Having Fun and Flying High," *Economist,* March 11, 2004.

30. Wayne Arnold, "A Continent Divided by Water."

31. Scott Neuman, "Low-Fare Airlines Take Off in Asia."

32. Arnold, "A Continent Divided by Water."

33. Neuman, "Low-Fare Airlines Take Off in Asia."

34. "Having Fun and Flying High."

35. Neuman, "Low-Fare Airlines Take Off in Asia."

36. Ibid.

37. Ionides, "Man of the Moment."

38. "Having Fun and Flying High."

39. "Malaysia's AirAsia Defers Listing Decision to Focus on Expansion," *Asian Financial Press,* February 8, 2004. Cited at Airlines.net Aviation Industry News.

■ Chapter 12

1. Abbass F. Alkhafaji, *Competitive Global Management* (Delray Beach, FL: St. Lucie Press, 1995), p. 118.

2. Nancy L. Adler, *International Dimensions of Organizational Behavior,* 2nd ed. (Boston: PWS-Kent, 1991), p. 160.

3. Dianne H. B. Welsh, Fred Luthans, and Steven Sommer, "Managing Russian Factory Workers: The Impact of U.S.-Based Behavioral and Participative Techniques," *Academy of Management Journal,* February 1993, p. 75.

4. Andrew Sergeant and Stephen Frenkel, "Managing People in China: Perceptions of Expatriate Managers," *Journal of World Business* 33, no. 1 (1998), p. 21.

5. "Economic Tonic; Japan's Economy," *Economist,* May 22, 2004, p. 87.

6. For a more detailed discussion, see Fred Luthans, *Organizational Behavior,* 10th ed. (New York: Irwin/McGraw-Hill, 2004), chapter 8.

7. A. H. Maslow, "A Theory of Human Motivation," *Psychological Review,* July 1943, pp. 390–396.

8. For more information on this topic, see Richard Mead, *International Management: Cross-Cultural Dimensions* (Cambridge, MA: Blackwell, 1994), pp. 209–212.

9. See Richard M. Hodgetts, *Modern Human Relations at Work,* 8th ed. (Hinsdale, IL: Dryden Press, 2002), chapter 2.

10. Mason Haire, Edwin E. Ghiselli, and Lyman W. Porter, *Managerial Thinking: An International Study* (New York: Wiley, 1966).

11. Ibid., p. 75.

12. Edwin C. Nevis, "Cultural Assumption and Productivity: The United States and China," *Sloan Management Review,* Spring 1983, pp. 17–29.

13. Geert H. Hofstede, "The Colors of Collars," *Columbia Journal of World Business,* September 1972, pp. 72–78.

14. Ibid., p. 72.

15. George H. Hines, "Cross-Cultural Differences in Two-Factor Motivation Theory," *Journal of Applied Psychology,* December 1973, p. 376.

16. Donald D. White and Julio Leon, "The Two-Factor Theory: New Questions, New Answers," *National Academy of Management Proceedings,* 1976, p. 358.

17. D. Macarov, "Work Patterns and Satisfactions in an Israeli Kibbutz: A Test of the Herzberg Hypothesis," *Personnel Psychology,* Autumn 1972, p. 492.

18. Peter D. Machungwa and Neal Schmitt, "Work Motivation in a Developing Country," *Journal of Applied Psychology,* February 1983, pp. 31–42.

19. G. E. Popp, H. J. Davis, and T. T. Herbert, "An International Study of Intrinsic Motivation Composition," *Management International Review* 26, no. 3 (1986), pp. 28–35.

20. Also see Rabi S. Bhagat et al., "Cross-Cultural Issues in Organizational Psychology: Emergent Trends and Directions for Research in the 1990s," in *International Review of Industrial and Organizational Psychology,* ed. C. L. Cooper and I. Robertson (New York: Wiley, 1990), p. 76.

21. Rabindra N. Kanungo and Richard W. Wright, "A Cross-Cultural Comparative Study of Managerial Job Attitudes," *Journal of International Business Studies,* Fall 1983, pp. 115–129.

22. Ibid., pp. 127–128.

23. Fred Luthans, "A Paradigm Shift in Eastern Europe: Some Helpful Management Development Techniques," *Journal of Management Development* 12, no. 8 (1993), pp. 53–60.

24. For more information on the characteristics of high achievers, see David C. McClelland, "Business Drive and National Achievement," *Harvard Business Review,* July–August 1962, pp. 99–112.

25. For more detail on the achievement motive, see Luthans, *Organizational Behavior,* pp. 253–256.

26. S. Iwawaki and R. Lynn, "Measuring Achievement Motivation in Japan and Great Britain," *Journal of Cross-Cultural Psychology* 3 (1999), pp. 219–220.

27. For more on this, see J. C. Abegglen and G. Stalk, *Kaisha: The Japanese Corporation* (New York: Basic Books, 1985); and R. M. Steers, Y. K. Shin, and G. R. Ungson, *The Chaebol: Korea's New Industrial Might* (New York: McGraw-Hill, 1989).

28. Fred Luthans, Brooke R. Envick, and Mary F. Sully, "Characteristics of Successful Entrepreneurs: Do They Fit the Cultures of Developing Countries?" *Proceedings of the Pan Pacific Conference,* 1995, pp. 25–27.

29. For an earlier example of similar findings using sample groups of male Australian MBA candidates and University of California–Berkeley MBA candidates, see Theodore T. Herbert, Gary E. Popp, and Herbert J. Davis, "Australian Work-Reward Preferences," *National Academy of Management Proceedings,* 1979, pp. 289–292.

30. These data were reported in David C. McClelland, *The Achieving Society* (Princeton, NJ: Van Nostrand, 1961), p. 294.

31. E. J. Murray, *Motivation and Emotion* (Englewood Cliffs, NJ: Prentice Hall, 1964), p. 101.

32. David J. Krus and Jane A. Rysberg, "Industrial Managers and nAch: Comparable and Compatible?" *Journal of Cross-Cultural Psychology,* December 1976, pp. 491–496.

33. David C. McClelland, "Achievement Motivation Can Be Developed," *Harvard Business Review,* November–December 1965, p. 20.

34. Geert Hofstede, "Motivation, Leadership, and Organization: Do American Theories Apply Abroad?" *Organizational Dynamics,* Summer 1980, pp. 55–56.

35. For more on this, see Richard M. Steers and Carlos J. Sanchez-Runde, "Culture, Motivation, and Work Behavior" in *Handbook of Cross-Cultural Management,* ed. Martin J. Gannon and Karen L. Newman (London: Basil Blackwell, 2002).

36. E. Yuchtman, "Reward Distribution and Work-Role Attractiveness in the Kibbutz: Reflections on Equity Theory," *American Sociological Review* 37 (1972), pp. 581–595.

37. R. M. Steers, S. J. Bischoff, and L. H. Higgins, "Cross-Cultural Management Research: The Fish and the Fisherman," *Journal of Management Inquiry* 1 (1992), pp. 321–330; and Ken I. Kim, Hun-Joon Park, and Nori Suzuki, "Reward Allocations in the U.S., Japan, and Korea: A Comparison of Individualistic and Collectivistic Cultures," *Academy of Management Journal,* March 1990, pp. 188–198.

38. Luthans, *Organizational Behavior,* p. 520.

39. Edwin A. Locke and Gary P. Latham, *A Theory of Goal-Setting and Task Performance* (Englewood Cliffs, NJ: Prentice Hall, 1990).

40. M. Erez, "The Congruence of Goal-Setting Strategies with Socio-Cultural Values and Its Effect on Performance," *Journal of Management* 12 (1986), pp. 585–592.

41. J. P. French, J. Israel, and D. As, "An Experiment in a Norwegian Factory: Interpersonal Dimension in Decision-Making," *Human Relations* 13 (1960), pp. 3–19.

42. P. C. Earley, "Supervisors and Shop Stewards as Sources of Contextual Information in Goal-Setting," *Journal of Applied Psychology* 71 (1986), pp. 111–118.

43. M. Erez and P. C. Earley, "Comparative Analysis of Goal-Setting Strategies Across Cultures," *Journal of Applied Psychology* 72, no. 4 (1987), pp. 658–665.

44. Victor Vroom, *Work and Motivation* (New York: Wiley, 1964).

45. Lyman W. Porter and Edward E. Lawler III, *Managerial Attitudes and Performance* (Homewood, IL: Irwin, 1968).

46. Dov Eden, "Intrinsic and Extrinsic Rewards and Motives: Replication and Extension with Kibbutz Workers," *Journal of Applied Social Psychology* 5 (1975), pp. 348–361.

47. T. Matsui, T. Kakuyama, and M. L. Onglatco, "Effects of Goals and Feedback on Performance in Groups," *Journal of Applied Psychology* 72 (1987), pp. 407–415.

48. For a systematic analysis of this and other myths of Japanese management, see Richard M. Hodgetts and Fred Luthans, "Japanese HR Management Practices," *Personnel,* April 1989, pp. 42–45.

49. David Nicklaus, "Labor's Pains," *St. Louis Post-Dispatch,* September 2, 2002, p. A1.

50. For more on this topic, see Noel M. Tichy and Thore Sandstrom, "Organizational Innovations in Sweden," *Columbia Journal of World Business,* Summer 1974, pp. 18–28.

51. "Automotive Brief—Volvo AB: Profit Rose 80% in 4th Period, Bolstered by Truck Division," *Wall Street Journal,* February 4, 2004, p. A1; "Cars Brief: Volvo," *Wall Street Journal,* March 16, 2004, p. A1.

52. Edward McDonough, "Market-Oriented Product Innovation," *R&D Management,* June 2004, p. 335.

53. Eric Sundstrom, Kenneth P. DeMeuse, and David Futrell, "Work Teams: Application and Effectiveness," *American Psychologist,* February 1990, pp. 120–133.

54. See Lillian H. Chaney and Jeanette S. Martin, *Intercultural Business Communication* (Englewood Cliffs, NJ: Prentice Hall, 1995), pp. 46–47.

55. Bhagat et al., "Cross-Cultural Issues," p. 72.

56. Jonathan Watts, "Japan's Old Shy Away from Retiring," *The Guardian,* August 5, 2002, p. 12; "U.S. Workers Most Productive; but Study Says Europeans Have More Output per Hour," *Houston Chronicle,* September 1, 2003, p. 27.

57. Howard W. French, "A Postmodern Plague Ravages Japan's Workers," *New York Times,* February 21, 2000, p. A4; "Japanese Workers See Abuses by Bosses," *Los Angeles Times,"* June 30, 2003, p. C5.

58. "Satisfaction in the USA, Unhappiness in Japanese Offices," *Personnel,* January 1992, p. 8.

59. Fred Luthans, Harriette S. McCaul, and Nancy G. Dodd, "Organizational Commitment: A Comparison of American, Japanese, and Korean Employees," *Academy of Management Journal,* March 1985, pp. 213–219.

60. For other research on this topic, see Shahid N. Bhuian, Eid S. Al-Shammari, and Omar A. Jefri, "Work-Related Attitudes and Job Characteristics of Expatriates in Saudi Arabia," *Thunderbird International Business Review,* January–February 2001, pp. 21–31.

61. David I. Levine, "What Do Wages Buy?" *Administrative Science Quarterly,* September 1993, pp. 462–483.

62. David Heming, "What Wages Buy in the U.S. and Japan," *Academy of Management Executive,* November 1994, pp. 88–89.

63. Andrew Kakabadse and Andrew Myers, "Qualities of Top Management: Comparisons of European Manufacturers," *Journal of Management Development* 14, no. 1 (1995), p. 6.

64. Steven M. Sommer, Seung-Hyun Bae, and Fred Luthans, "Organizational Commitment Across Cultures: The Impact of Antecedents on Korean Employees," *Human Relations* 49, no. 7 (1996), pp. 977–993.

65. Anders Tornvall, "Work-Values in Japan: Work and Work Motivation in a Comparative Setting," in *Managing Across Cultures: Issues and Perspectives,* ed. Pat Joynt and Malcolm Warner (London: International Thomson Business Press, 1996), p. 256.

66. Stephen Kerr, "Practical, Cost-Neutral Alternatives That You May Know, but Don't Practice," *Organizational Dynamics,* Summer 1999, pp. 61–70.

67. "U.S. Workers Most Productive."

68. Matthew O. Hughes and Andrew Pirnie, "Retirement Reform Worldwide," *LIMRA's MarketFacts Quarterly* 22, no. 2 (Spring 2003), p. 12.

69. In the case of money, for example, see Swee Hoon Ang, "The Power of Money: A Cross-Cultural Analysis of Business-Related Beliefs," *Journal of World Business* 35, no. 1 (2000), pp. 43–60.

70. J. Milliman, S. Nason, M. A. von Glinow, P. Hou, K. B. Lowe, and N. Kim, "In Search of 'Best' Strategies Pay Practices: An Exploratory Study of Japan, Korea, Taiwan, and the United States," in *Advances in International Comparative Management,* ed. S. B. Prasad (Greenwich, CT: JAI Press, 1995), pp. 227–252.

71. Louis Lavelle, "Executive Pay," *BusinessWeek,* April 19, 2004, pp. 106–110.

72. S. C. Schneider, S. A. Wittenberg-Cox, and L. Hansen, *Honeywell Europe* (Insead, 1991).

73. C. M. Vance, S. R. McClaine, D. M. Boje, and H. D. Stage, "An Examination of the Transferability of Traditional Performance Appraisal Principles Across Cultural Boundaries," *Management International Review* 32, no. 4 (1992), pp. 313–326.

74. David Sirota and J. Michael Greenwood, "Understand Your Overseas Workforce," *Harvard Business Review,* January–February 1971, pp. 53–60.

75. D. E. Sanger, "Performance Related Pay in Japan," *International Herald Tribune,* October 5, 1993, p. 20.

76. S. H. Nam, "Culture, Control, and Commitment in International Joint Ventures," *International Journal of Human Resource Management* 6 (1995), pp. 553–567.

77. Dianne H. B. Welsh, Fred Luthans, and Steven Sommer, "Managing Russian Factory Workers: The Impact of U.S.-Based Behavioral and Participative Techniques," *Academy of Management Journal,* February 1993, pp. 58–79.

78. Anita Raghavan and G. Thomas Sims, "'Golden Parachutes' Emerge in European Deals," *Wall Street Journal,* February 14, 2000, pp. A17, A18.

79. Susan C. Schneider and Jean-Louis Barsoux, *Managing Across Cultures,* 2nd ed. (London: Prentice Hall, 2003).

■ Chapter 13

1. Richard M. Hodgetts, *Modern Human Relations at Work,* 8th ed. (Ft. Worth, TX: Harcourt, 2002), p. 255. Also see Daniel Goleman, "What Makes a Leader?" *Harvard Business Review,* November–December 1998, pp. 93–102.

2. Douglas McGregor, *The Human Side of Enterprise* (New York: McGraw-Hill, 1960), pp. 33–34.

3. Ibid., pp. 47–48.

4. See Nancy J. Adler, *International Dimensions of Organizational Behavior,* 2nd ed. (Boston: PWS-Kent, 1991), p. 150.

5. Sheila M. Puffer, Daniel J. McCarthy, and Alexander I. Naumov, "Russian Managers' Beliefs About Work: Beyond the Stereotypes," *Journal of World Business* 32, no. 3 (1997), pp. 258–276.

6. For other insights into this area, see Manfred F. R. Kets de Vries, "A Journey into the 'Wild West': Leadership Style and Organizational Practices in Russia," *Organizational Dynamics,* Spring 2000, pp. 67–80.

7. William Ouchi, *Theory Z: How American Management Can Meet the Japanese Challenge* (New York: Addison-Wesley, 1981).

8. Yong Suhk Pak, Jiman Lee, and Jung Moo An, "Lessons Learned from Daewoo Motors' Experience in Emerging Markets," *Multinational Business Review* 10, no. 2 (Fall 2002), p. 122.

9. Michael Woywode, "Global Management Concepts and Local Adaptations: Working Groups in the French and German Car Manufacturing Industry," *Organization Studies* 23, no. 4 (2002), p. 497.

10. Chris Reiter and Neal Boudette, "VW Delays Launch of Microbus to Reduce Its Production Cost," *Wall Street Journal,* May 20, 2004, p. D3.

11. Mason Haire, Edwin E. Ghiselli, and Lyman W. Porter, *Managerial Thinking: An International Study* (New York: Wiley, 1966).

12. Ibid., p. 21.

13. James R. Lincoln, Mitsuyo Hanada, and Jon Olson, "Cultural Orientation and Individual Reactions to Organizations: A Study of Employees of Japanese-Owned Firms," *Administrative Science Quarterly,* March 1981, pp. 93–115. Also see Karen Lowry Miller, "Land of the Rising Jobless," *BusinessWeek,* January 11, 1993, p. 47.

14. Sangjin Yoo and Sang M. Lee, "Management Style and Practice of Korean Chaebols," *California Management Review,* Summer 1987, pp. 95–110.

15. Haire, Ghiselli, and Porter, *Managerial Thinking,* p. 29.

16. Noboru Yoshimura and Philip Anderson, *Inside the Kaisha: Demystifying Japanese Business Behavior* (Boston: Harvard Business School Press, 1997), p. 167.

17. Haire, Ghiselli, and Porter, *Managerial Thinking,* p. 140.

18. Ibid., p. 157.

19. For more on this topic, see Edgar H. Schein, "SMR Forum: Does Japanese Management Style Have a Message for American Managers?" *Sloan Management Review,* Fall 1981, pp. 55–68.

20. Jeremiah J. Sullivan and Ikujiro Nonaka, "The Application of Organizational Learning Theory to Japanese and American Management," *Journal of International Business Studies,* Fall 1986, pp. 127–147.

21. Ibid., pp. 130–131.

22. Iyuji Misumi and Fumiyasu Seki, "Effects of Achievement Motivation on the Effectiveness of Leadership Patterns," *Administrative Science Quarterly,* March 1971, pp. 51–59.

23. Sang M. Lee, Sangjin Yoo, and Tosca M. Lee, "Korean Chaebols: Corporate Values and Strategies," *Organizational Dynamics,* Spring 1991, p. 41.

24. David A. Ralston, Carolyn P. Egri, Sally Stewart, Robert H. Terpstra, and Yu Kaicheng, "Doing Business in the 21st Century with the New Generation of Chinese Managers: A Study of Generational Shifts in Work Values in China," *Journal of International Business Studies,* Second Quarter 1999, pp. 415–428.

25. John Politis, "The Role of Various Leadership Styles," *Leadership and Organization Development Journal* 24, no. 4 (2003), pp. 181–195.

26. Darwish A. Yousef, "Predictors of Decision-Making Styles in Non-Western Countries," *Leadership and Organizational Development Journal* 19, no. 7 (1998), pp. 366–373.

27. Ibid.

28. Ibid.

29. Haire, Ghiselli, and Porter, *Managerial Thinking,* p. 22.

30. Priyanka Banerji and Venkat Krishnan, "Ethical Preferences of Transformational Leaders: An Empirical Investigation," *Leadership Organization and Development Journal* 21, no. 8 (2000), p. 405.

31. Bikki Jaggi, "Job Satisfaction and Leadership Style in Developing Countries: The Case of India," *International Journal of Contemporary Sociology,* October 1977, pp. 230–236.

32. Ibid., p. 233. See also Basudeb Sen, "Organizational Mind: Response to a Paradigm Shift in the Indian Business Environment,"

International Journal of Human Resources Development and Management 3, no. 1 (2003), p. 49.

33. Haire, Ghiselli, and Porter, *Managerial Thinking,* p. 22.

34. D. B. Stephens, "Cultural Variations in Leadership Style: A Methodological Experiment in Comparing Managers in the U.S. and Peruvian Textile Industries," *Management International Review* 21, no. 3 (1981), pp. 47–55.

35. Ibid., p. 54.

36. See Jay A. Conger, *The Charismatic Leader* (San Francisco: Jossey-Bass, 1989).

37. Hodgetts, *Modern Human Relations at Work*, pp. 275–276.

38. Bernard M. Bass, "Is There Universality in the Full Range Model of Leadership?" *International Journal of Public Administration* 16, no. 6 (1996), p. 731.

39. Ibid., pp. 741–742.

40. Ibid., p. 731.

41. For additional insights on recent research by Bass and his associates, see Bruce J. Avolio and Bernard M. Bass, "You Can Drag a Horse to Water but You Can't Make It Drink Unless It Is Thirsty," *Journal of Leadership Studies,* Winter 1998, pp. 4–17.

42. Bass, "Is There Universality?" pp. 754–755.

43. Ingrid Tollgertd-Andersson, "Attitudes, Values and Demands on Leadership—A Cultural Comparison Among Some European Countries," in *Managing Across Cultures,* ed. Pat Joynt and Malcolm Warner (London: International Thomson Business Press, 1996), p. 172.

44. Ibid., p. 176.

45. Felix C. Brodbeck et al., "Cultural Variation of Leadership Prototypes Across 22 European Countries," *Journal of Occupational and Organizational Psychology* 73 (2000), pp. 1–29.

46. For more on culture and leadership, see Jangho Lee, Thomas W. Roehl, and Soonkyoo Choe, "What Makes Management Style Similar and Distinct Across Borders? Growth, Experience and Culture in Korean and Japanese Firms," *Journal of International Business Studies,* Fourth Quarter 2000, pp. 631–652; Uzoamaka P. Anakwe, Magid Igbaria, and Murugan Anandarajan, "Management Practices Across Cultures: Role of Support in Technology Usage," *Journal of International Business Studies,* Fourth Quarter 2000, pp. 653–666; Graeme L. Harrison, Jill L. McKinnon, Anne Wu, and Chee W. Chow, "Cultural Influences on Adaptation to Fluid Workgroups and Teams," *Journal of International Business Studies,* Third Quarter 2000, pp. 489–505; Robert J. House, Paul J. Hanges, Mansour Javidan, et al. (eds.), *Culture, Leadership, and Organizations: The GLOBE Study of 62 Societies* (Thousand Oaks, CA: Sage, 2004).

47. Fons Trompenaars and Charles Hampden-Turner, *Riding the Waves of Culture: Understanding Diversity in Global Business*, 2nd ed. (New York: McGraw-Hill, 1998), p. 74.

48. Ibid., p. 77.

49. Robert J. House and Mansour Javidan, "Overview of GLOBE," in House et al., *Culture, Leadership, and Organizations,* p. 14.

50. Peter Dorfman, Paul Hanges, and Felix Brodbeck, "Leadership and Cultural Variation: The Identification of Culturally Endorsed Leadership Profiles," ibid., pp. 669–720.

51. Michele J. Gelfand, D. P. S. Bhawuk, Lisa H. Nishii, and David J. Bechtold, "Individualism and Collectivism," ibid., pp. 437–512.

52. Ibid.

53. Cynthia G. Emrich, Florence L. Denmark, and Deanne Den Hartog, "Cross-Cultural Differences in Gender Egalitarianism," in House et al., *Culture, Leadership, and Organizations,* pp. 343–394.

54. Mansour Javidan, "Performance Orientation," ibid., pp. 239–281.

55. Neal Ashkanasy, Vipin Gupta, Melinda Mayfield, and Edwin Trevor-Roberts, "Future Orientation," ibid., pp. 282–342.

56. Mary Sully De Luque and Mansour Javidan, "Uncertainty Avoidance," ibid., pp. 602–654.

57. Hayat Kabasakal and Muzaffer Bodur, "Humane Orientation in Societies, Organizations, and Leader Attributes," ibid., pp. 564–601.

58. Dean Den Hartog, "Assertiveness," ibid., pp. 395–436.

59. Dale Carl, Vipin Gupta, and Mansour Javidan, "Power Distance," ibid., pp. 513–563.

60. Narda Quigley, Mary Sully De Luque, and Robert J. House, "Responsible Leadership and Governance in a Global Context: Insights from the GLOBE Study," in *Handbook on Responsible Leadership and Governance in Global Business,* ed. Jonathan P. Doh and Stephen A. Stumpf (London: Edward Elgar Publishing, forthcoming).

61. World Economic Forum, "Declining Public Trust Foremost a Leadership Problem," *WEF,* January 14, 2003.

62. Ibid.

63. David Waldman, Donald Siegel, and Mansour Javidan, "Transformational Leadership and Corporate Social Responsibility," in Doh and Stumpf, *Handbook of Responsible Leadership and Governance in Global Business.*

64. Jonathan P. Doh and Stephen A. Stumpf, "Toward a Framework of Responsible Leadership and Governance," ibid.

65. Allen Morrison, "Integrity and Global Leadership," *Journal of Business Ethics* 31, no. 1 (May 2001), p. 65.

66. Edward P. Richards, "Developing Socially Responsible Business Leaders: The Lubrizol Experience," *Mid-American Journal of Business* 18, no. 1 (Spring 2003), p. 11.

67. Stephen A. Stumpf, "Career Goal: Entrepreneur?" *International Journal of Career Management* 4, no. 2 (1992), pp. 26–32.

68. T. K. Maloy, "Entrepreneurs Need Moms," United Press International, March 11, 2004.

69. Andrew Backover, "How, Not Where, Is Key Word Now Local Firms Serve Foreign Markets," *Denver Post,* February 27, 2000, p. D14.

■ Chapter 14

1. Rosalie Tung, "Selection and Training of Personnel for Overseas Assignments," *Columbia Journal of World Business* 16, no. 2 (1981), pp. 68–78.

2. Anne-Will Harzing. "The Persistent Myth of High Expatriate Failure Rates," *International Journal of Human Resource Management* 6, no. 2 (1995), pp. 457–474.

3. Jeffrey Shay, "Expatriate Managers," *Cornell Hotel and Restaurant Administration Quarterly* 38, no. 1 (February 1997), p. 30.

4. Gary M. Wederspahn, "Costing Failures in Expatriate Human Resources Management," *Human Resource Planning* 15, no. 3 (1992), pp. 27–35.

5. Also see Kenneth Groh and Mark Allen, "Global Staffing: Are Expatriates the Only Answer?" *HR Focus,* March 1998, pp. S1–S2.

6. Leslie Chang, "China's Grads Find Jobs Scarce," *Wall Street Journal,* June 22, 2004, p. A17.

7. Nick Forster, "Expatriates and the Impact of Cross-Cultural Training," *Human Resource Management Journal* 10, no. 3 (2000), pp. 63–78.

8. See, for example, Kenneth Groh and Mark Allen, "Global Staffing: Are Expatriates the Only Answer? *HR Focus,* March 1998, p. 1.

9. Rosalie L. Tung, "Selection and Training Procedures of U.S., European and Japanese Multinationals," *California Management Review,* Fall 1982, p. 59.

10. Malika Richards, "U.S. Multinational Staffing Practices and Implications for Subsidiary Performance in the U.K. and Thailand," *Thunderbird International Business Review,* March–April 2001, pp. 225–242.

11. Richard B. Peterson, Nancy K. Napier, and Won Shul-Shim, "Expatriate Management: A Comparison of MNCs Across Four Parent Countries," *Thunderbird International Business Review,* March–April 2000, p. 150.

12. Arvind V. Phatak, *International Dimensions of Management,* 2nd ed. (Boston: PWS-Kent Publishing, 1989), p. 106.

13. Linda K. Stroh, Arup Varma, and Stacey J. Valy-Durbin, "Why Are Women Left at Home: Are They Unwilling to Go on International Assignments?" *Journal of World Business* 35, no. 3 (2000), pp. 241–256.

14. Paul W. Beamish and Andrew C. Inkpen, "Japanese Firms and the Decline of the Japanese Expatriate," *Journal of World Business* 33, no. 1 (1998), pp. 35–50.

15. Ibid., pp. 44–45.

16. Tung, "Selection and Training Procedures," pp. 61–62.

17. Ibid.

18. Calvin Reynolds, "Strategic Employment of Third Country Nationals," *HR Planning* 20, no. 1 (1997), p. 38.

19. Michael G. Harvey and M. Ronald Buckley, "Managing Inpatriates: Building a Global Core Competency," *Journal of World Business* 32, no. 1 (1997), p. 36.

20. For some additional insights about inpatriates and worldwide staffing, see Michael Harvey and Milorad M. Novicevic, "Staffing Global Marketing Positions: What We Don't Know Can Make a Difference," *Journal of World Business* 35, no. 1 (2000), pp. 80–94.

21. Jennifer Smith, "Southeast Asia's Search for Managers," *Management Review,* March 1998, p. 9.

22. Noam Scheiber, "As a Center for Outsourcing, India Could Be Losing Its Edge," *New York Times,* May 9, 2004, p. 3.

23. Steve Lohr, "Evidence of High-Skill Work Going Abroad," *New York Times,* June 16, 2004, p. C2.

24. "Dell to Bring Some Jobs Back Home," *Houston Chronicle,* November 23, 2003, p. 2.

25. Manjeet Kripalani, "Now It's Bombay Calling the U.S.," *BusinessWeek,* June 21, 2004, p. 26.

26. Marilyn Geewax, "Outsourcing of Service Jobs Grows Faster than Estimated," *Houston Chronicle,* May 18, 2004, p. 4.

27. Winfred Arthur Jr. and Winston Bennett Jr., "The International Assignee: The Relative Importance of Factors Perceived to Contribute to Success," *Personnel Psychology,* Spring 1995, pp. 99–114.

28. Also see Michael G. Harvey, Milorad M. Novicevic, and Cheri Speier, "An Innovative Global Management Staffing System: A Competency-Based Perspective," *Human Resource Management,* Winter 2000, pp. 381–394.

29. Rosalie L. Tung, "U.S. Multinationals: A Study of Their Selection and Training Procedures for Overseas Assignments," *National Academy of Management Proceedings* (Atlanta, 1979), pp. 298–299.

30. Rosalie L. Tung, "Human Resource Planning in Japanese Multinationals: A Model for U.S. Firms?" *Journal of International Business Studies,* Fall 1984, p. 141.

31. Peterson, Napier, and Shul-Shing, "Expatriate Management," p. 151.

32. Indrei Ratiu, "Thinking Internationally: A Comparison of How International Executives Learn," *International Studies of Management and Organization,* Spring–Summer 1983, pp. 139–150.

33. Nancy J. Adler, *International Dimensions of Organizational Behavior,* 2nd ed. (Boston: PWS-Kent Publishing, 1991), pp. 228–229.

34. Ingemar Torbiorn, *Living Abroad* (New York: Wiley, 1982), pp. 100–101.

35. Jan Selmer, "Effects of Coping Strategies on Sociocultural and Psychological Adjustment of Western Expatriate Managers in the PRC," *Journal of World Business* 34, no. 1 (1999), pp. 41–51.

36. Paula M. Caligiuri, "Selecting Expatriates for Personality Characteristics: A Moderating Effect of Personality on the Relationship Between Host National Contact and Cross-Cultural Adjustment," *Management International Review* 40, no. 1 (2000), pp. 61–80.

37. Jeffrey L. Blue and Ulric Haynes Jr., "Preparation for the Overseas Assignment," *Business Horizons,* June 1977, p. 64.

38. Jean E. Heller, "Criteria for Selecting an International Manager," *Personnel,* May–June 1980, p. 50.

39. Torbiorn, *Living Abroad,* p. 128.

40. Blue and Haynes, "Preparation for the Overseas Assignment," p. 64.

41. The survey was conducted by executive recruiters for Korn-Ferry International and the Columbia Business School. Excerpts were reported in "Report: Shortage of Executives Will Hurt U.S.," *Omaha World Herald,* June 25, 1989, p. 1G.

42. Margaret A. Shaffer, David A. Harrison, K. Matthew Gilley, and Dora M. Luk, "Struggling for Balance amid Turbulence on International Assignments: Work–Family Conflict, Support, and Commitment," *Journal of Management* 27 (2001), pp. 99–121.

43. Rosalie Tung, "A Study of the Expatriation/Repatriation Process" (report prepared under the auspices of Arthur Andersen, 1997), p. 6.

44. Patricia C. Borstorff, Stanley G. Harris, Hubert S. Field, and William F. Giles, "Who'll Go? A Review of Factors Associated with Employee Willingness to Work Overseas," *Human Resource Planning* 20, no. 3 (1997), p. 38.

45. See Betty Jane Punnett, "Towards Effective Management of Expatriate Spouses," *Journal of World Business* 33, no. 3 (1997), pp. 243–256.

46. Howard Tu and Sherry E. Sullivan, "Preparing Yourself for an International Assignment," *Business Horizons,* January–February 1994, p. 68.

47. James C. Baker and John M. Ivancevich, "The Assignment of American Executives Abroad: Systematic, Haphazard or Chaotic?" *California Management Review,* Spring 1971, p. 41.

48. Heller, "Criteria for Selecting an International Manager," p. 53.

49. Tung, "Selection and Training Procedures," p. 65.

50. This section is based on J. Stewart Black, Mark Mendenhall, and Gary Oddou, "Toward a Comprehensive Model of International Adjustment: An Integration of Multiple Theoretical Perspectives," *Academy of Management Review,* April 1991, pp. 291–317. For more on this area, see Jaime Bonache, Chris Brewster, and Vesa Suutari, "Expatriation: A Developing Research Agenda," *Thunderbird International Business Review,* January–February 2001, pp. 3–20.

51. Iain McCormick and Tony Chapman, "Executive Relocation: Personal and Organizational Tactics," in *Managing Across Cultures: Issues and Perspectives,* ed. Pat Joynt and Malcolm Warner (London: International Thomson Business Press, 1996), pp. 326–337.

52. Calvin Reynolds, "Expatriate Compensation in Historical Perspective," *Journal of World Business* 32, no. 2 (1997), p. 127.

53. Elaine K. Bailey, "International Compensation," in *Global Perspectives of Human Resource Management,* ed. Oded Shenkar (Englewood Cliffs, NJ: Prentice Hall, 1995), p. 148.

54. Peterson, Napier, and Shul-Shin, "Expatriate Management," p. 155.

55. Greg Steinmetz and Gregory L. White, "Chrysler Pay Draws Fire Overseas," *Wall Street Journal,* May 26, 1998, p. B1.

56. See Dennis R. Briscoe, *International Human Resource Management* (Englewood Cliffs, NJ: Prentice Hall, 1995), pp. 111–120.

57. David Sirota and J. Michael Greenwood, "Understand Your Overseas Workforce," *Harvard Business Review,* January–February 1971, pp. 53–60.

58. Torbiorn, *Living Abroad,* p. 127.

59. Y. Zeira and M. Banai, "Attitudes of Host-Country Organization's Toward MNCs' Staffing Policies: A Cross-Country and Cross-Industry Analysis," *Management International Review* 21, no. 2 (1981), pp. 38–47.

60. Chi-Sum Wong and Kenneth S. Law, "Managing Localization of Human Resources in the PRC: A Practical Model," *Journal of World Business* 34, no. 1 (1999), pp. 28–29.

61. Torbiorn, *Living Abroad,* p. 41.

62. Maria L. Kraimer, Sandy J. Wayne, and Renata A. Jaworski, "Sources of Support and Expatriate Performance: The Mediating Role of Expatriate Adjustment," *Personnel Psychology* 54 (2001), pp. 71–99.

63. Yoram Zeira and Moshe Banai, "Selection of Expatriate Managers in MNCs: The Host-Environment Point of View," *International Studies of Management & Organization* 15, no. 1 (1985), pp. 33–41; Zeira and Banai, "Selection of Expatriate Managers," p. 34.

64. Jobert E. Abueva, "Return of the Native Executive," *New York Times,* May 17, 2000, p. C1.

65. Adler, *International Dimensions of Organizational Behavior,* p. 236.

66. Rosalie L. Tung, "Career Issues in International Assignments," *Academy of Management Executive,* August 1988, p. 242.

67. Howard W. French, "Japan Unsettles Returnees, Who Yearn to Leave Again," *New York Times,* May 2, 2000, p. A12.

68. J. Stewart Black, "Coming Home: The Relationship of Expatriate Expectations with Repatriate Adjustment and Job Performance," *Human Relations* 45, no. 2 (1992), p. 188.

69. Wong and Law, "Managing Localization of Human Resources," p. 36.

70. Tung, "Career Issues in International Assignments," p. 243.

71. Nancy K. Napier and Richard B. Peterson, "Expatriate Reentry: What Do Expatriates Have to Say?" *Human Resource Planning* 14, no. 1 (1991), pp. 19–28.

72. Charlene Marmer Solomon, "Repatriation: Up, Down or Out?" *Personnel Journal,* January 1995, p. 32.

73. Mitchell R. Hammer, William Hart, and Randall Rogan, "Can You Go Home Again? An Analysis of the Repatriation of Corporate Managers and Spouses," *Management International Review* 38, no. 1 (1998), p. 81.

74. Karen Roberts, Ellen Ernst Kossek, and Cynthia Ozeki, "Managing the Global Workforce: Challenges and Strategies," *Academy of Management Executive,* November 1998, pp. 93–106. See also Mark C. Blino and Daniel C. Feldman, "Increasing the Skill Utilization of Expatriates," *Human Resource Management* 39, no. 4 (Winter 2000), pp. 367–379; Ben L. Kedia and Ananda Mukherji, "Global Managers: Developing a Mindset for Global Competitiveness," *Journal of World Business* 34, no. 3 (1999), pp. 230–251.

75. Robert C. Maddox and Douglas Short, "The Cultural Integrator," *Business Horizons,* November–December 1988, pp. 57–59.

76. Michael Hickins, "Creating a Global Team," *Management Review,* September 1998, p. 6.

77. Charlene Marmer Solomon, "Global Operations Demand That HR Rethink Diversity," *Personnel Journal,* July 1994, p. 50.

78. Paul R. Sparrow and Pawan S. Budhwar, "Competition and Change: Mapping the Indian HRM Recipe Against Worldwide Patterns," *Journal of World Business* 32, no. 3 (1997), p. 231. See also Chi-Sum Wong and Kenneth S. Law, "Managing Localization of Human Resources in the PRC: A Practical Model," *Journal of World Business* 34, no. 1 (1999), pp. 32–33.

79. Bodil Jones, "What Future European Recruits Want," *Management Review,* January 1998, p. 6.

80. Filiz Tabak, Janet Stern Solomon, and Christine Nielsen, "Managerial Success: A Profile of Future Managers in China," *SAM Advanced Management Journal,* Autumn 1998, pp. 18–26.

81. Also see Allan Bird, Sully Taylor, and Schon Beechler, "A Typology of International Human Resource Management in Japanese Multinational Corporations: Organizational Implications," *Human Resource Management,* Summer 1998, pp. 159–176.

82. Fred Luthans, *Organizational Behavior,* 10th ed. (New York: McGraw-Hill/Irwin, 2004), chapter 16.

83. Noel M. Tichy and Eli Cohen, "The Teaching Organization," *Training and Development Journal,* July 1998, p. 27.

84. Peter Prud'homme van Reine and Fons Trompenaars, "Invited Reaction: Developing Expatriates for the Asia-Pacific Region," *Human Resource Development Quarterly* 11, no. 3 (Fall 2000), p. 238.

85. J. Hayes and C. W. Allinson, "Cultural Differences in the Learning Styles of Managers," *Management International Review* 28, no. 3 (1988), p. 76.

86. See for example Jennifer Smith, "Southeast Asia's Search for Managers," *Management Review,* June 1998, p. 9.

87. Also see Schon Beechler and John Zhuang Yang, "The Transfer of Japanese-Style Management to American Subsidiaries: Contingencies, Constraints, and Competencies," *Journal of International Business Studies,* Third Quarter 1994, pp. 467–491.

88. Allan Bird and Schon Beechler, "Links Between Business Strategy and Human Resource Management Strategy in U.S.-Based Japanese Subsidiaries: An Empirical Investigation," *Journal of International Business Studies,* First Quarter 1995, p. 40.

89. Linda K. Stroh and Paula M. Caligiuri, "Increasing Global Competitiveness Through Effective People Management," *Journal of World Business* 33, no. 1 (1998), p. 10.

90. For more on this see Tomoko Yoshida and Richard W. Breslin, "Intercultural Skills and Recommended Behaviors," in Shenkar, *Global Perspectives of Human Resource Management,* pp. 112–131.

91. Alan M. Barrett, "Training and Development of Expatriates and Home Country Nationals," ibid., p. 135.

92. Yoram Zeira and Ehud Harari, "Host-Country Organizations and Expatriate Managers in Europe," *California Management Review,* Spring 1979, p. 43.

93. Yukimo Ono, "Japanese Firms Don't Let Masters Rule," *Wall Street Journal,* May 4, 1992, p. B1.

94. See Chi-Sum Wong and Kenneth S. Law, "Managing Localization of Human Resources in the PRC: A Practical Model," *Journal of World Business* 34, no. 1 (1999), pp. 32–33.

95. See Andrew Sergeant and Stephen Frenkel, "Managing People in China: Perceptions of Expatriate Managers," *Journal of World Business* 33, no. 1 (1998), pp. 17–34.

96. Tung, "Selection and Training Procedures," p. 65.

97. Michael J. Marquardt and Dean W. Engel, *Global Human Resource Management* (Englewood Cliffs, NJ: Prentice Hall, 1995), p. 44.

98. Ingmar Bjorkman and Yuan Lu, "A Corporate Perspective on the Management of Human Resources in China," *Journal of World Business* 34, no. 1 (1999), pp. 20–21.

99. Fred E. Fiedler, Terence Mitchell, and Harry C. Triandis, "The Culture Assimilator: An Approach to Cross-Cultural Training," *Journal of Applied Psychology,* April 1971, p. 97.

100. See for example Frits K. Pil and John Paul MacDuffie, "What Makes Transplants Thrive: Managing the Transfer of 'Best Practice' at Japanese Auto Plants in North America," *Journal of World Business* 34, no. 4 (1999), pp. 372–391.

101. Noel M. Tichy, "Global Development," in *Globalizing Management,* ed. Vladimir Pucik, Noel M. Tichy, and Carole K. Barnett (New York: Wiley, 1993), pp. 206–224.

102. Ibid., p. 219.

■ Chapter 15

1. Dennis R. Briscoe, *International Human Resource Management* (Englewood Cliffs, NJ: Prentice Hall, 1995), p. 159.

2. Jeffrey P. Kotz and Stanley W. Elsea, "A Framework for Assessing International Labor Relations: What Every Human Resource Manager Needs to Know," *Human Resource Planning* 20, no. 4 (1997), p. 22.

3. Rebecca Smithers, "Teachers Rejects Plans for 'Super Union,'" *Guardian,* April 24, 2003, p. 10.

4. Malcolm Warner, "Human Resources Management in China Revisited: Introduction," *International Journal of Human Resources Management* 15, no. 4/5 (August 2004), p. 617.

5. Simon Clarke, Chang-Hell Lee, and Qi Li, "Collective Consultation and Industrial Relations in China," *British Journal of Industrial Relations* 15, no. 2 (June 2004), p. 235.

6. Albert Crenshaw, "AFL-CIO Goes After China on Labor: Petition Asks U.S. to Press for Deal on Workers' Rights," *Washington Post,* March 17, 2004, p. E2.

7. Fakhruddin G. Ebrahim, *Labour Legislation and Trade Unions in India and Pakistan* (Oxford: Oxford University Press, 2001).

8. Pawan S. Budhwar, "Employee Relations in India," *Employee Relations* 25, no. 1/2 (2003), pp. 132–138.

9. Vedi R. Hadiz, "Globalization Labour, and Economic Crisis: Insights from Southeast Asia," *Asian Business and Management* 1, no. 2 (August 2002), p. 249.

10. Keith Atkinson, "State of the Unions," *Personnel Administrator,* September 1986, p. 58.

11. "World Watch," *Wall Street Journal,* November 21, 2003, p. A10.

12. Wolfgang Scholl, "Codetermination and the Ability of Firms to Act in the Federal Republic of Germany," *International Studies of Management and Organization,* Summer 1987, pp. 27–37.

13. See Irene Hall-Siu Chow and Oded Shenkar, "HR Practices in the People's Republic of China," *Personnel,* December 1989, pp. 41–47.

14. Joseph Petrick and Foster Rinefort, "The Challenge of Managing China's Workplace Safety," *Business and Society Review* 109, no. 2 (Summer 2004), p. 171.

15. Peter J. Dowling, Randall S. Schuler, and Denise E. Welch, *International Dimensions of Human Resource Management,* 2nd ed. (Belmont, CA: Wadsworth, 1994), p. 198.

16. Robert Grosse and Duane Kujawa, *International Business: Theory and Managerial Applications* (Homewood, IL: Irwin, 1988), p. 447.

17. Barry Bearak, "Lives Held Cheap in Bangladesh Sweatshops," *New York Times,* April 15, 2001, pp. 1, 12.

18. Leslie Kaufman and David Gonzalez, "Labor Progress Clashes with Global Reality," *New York Times,* April 24, 2001, pp. A1, A10.

19. Richard Bernstein, "German Parliament Votes to Cut Welfare Benefits and Taxes," *New York Times,* October 18, 2003, p. A5.

20. "Leaders: Reform Begins at Home; Germany's Economy," *Economist,* May 8, 2004, p. 13.

21. Robert Gavin, "Economists: Weakness Overblown," *Boston Globe,* January 30, 2004, p. C1.

22. See, for example, Sarah Spikes, "European Companies Get Better at Announcing 'You're Laid Off!'" *Wall Street Journal,* April 7, 2004, p. A1.

23. "How Many Is Enough," *Canada and the World Backgrounder* 60, no. 3 (December 2002), p. 12.

24. Masayoshi Kanabayashi, "Calls Grow for Foreign Workers in Japan," *Wall Street Journal,* May 26, 2000, p. A20.

25. Cecilie Rohwedder, "Germany Tackles Joblessness, but Misses," *Wall Street Journal,* May 8, 2001, p. B11A.

26. C. Pascal Zachary, "As High-Tech Jobs Go Begging, Germany Is Loath to Import Talent," *Wall Street Journal,* January 17, 2000, p. A10.

27. "Europe: Brains Not Welcome Here," *Economist,* May 1, 2004, p. 40.

28. Ibid.

29. Edmund Andrews, "German Immigration Bill Wins Disputed Vote," *New York Times,* March 23, 2002, p. A3.

30. Ibid.

31. Edmund L. Andrews, "Only Employment for Many in Europe Is Part-Time Work," *New York Times,* September 1, 1997, pp. A1, B7. See also "Britian: Clocking Off; Working Time," *Economist,* July 19, 2003, p. 24.

32. Chris Brewster, Lesley Mayne, and Olga Tregaskis, "Flexible Working in Europe," *Journal of World Business* 32, no. 2 (1997), p. 138.

33. Steven Greenhouse, "Temp Workers at Microsoft Win Lawsuit," *New York Times,* December 13, 2000, pp. C1, C7.

34. Brewster, Mayne, and Tregaskis, "Flexible Working in Europe," pp. 141–142.

35. Ibid., pp. 133–151.

36. Helene Cooper and Thomas Kamm, "Much of Europe Eases Its Rigid Labor Laws, and Temps Proliferate," *Wall Street Journal,* June 4, 1998, p. A6.

37. Ans Kolk and Rob van Tulder, "Multinationality and Corporate Ethics: Codes of Conduct in the Sporting Goods Industry," *Journal of International Business Studies* 32, no. 2 (2001), pp. 267–283.

38. International Labour Organization, *Tripartite Declaration of Principles Concerning Multinational Enterprises and Social Policy,* adopted by the Governing Body of the International Labour Office at its 204th Session, 1977; International Labour Organization, *Codes of Practice* (2002).

39. Organization for Economic Cooperation and Development, *Declaration on International Investment and Multinational Enterprises* (June 1976).

40. Organization for Economic Cooperation and Development, *Declaration on International Investment and Multinational Enterprises* (June 2000).

41. See Claude Fussler, Aron Cramer, and Sebastian van der Vegt, *Raising the Bar: Creating Value with the UN Global Compact* (Sheffield, UK: Greenleaf, 2003).

42. Ans Kolk and Rob van Tulder, "Child Labor and Multinational Conduct: A Comparison of International Business and Stakeholder Codes," *Journal of Business Ethics* 36 (2001), pp. 291–301.

43. Social Accountability International, *Social Accountability 8000* (2001).

44. "Nike Code of Conduct," available at http://www.nike.com/ nikebiz/nikebiz.jhtml?page=25&cat=code#code.

45. Reported in Dowling, Schuler, and Welch, *International Dimensions,* p. 188.

46. Grosse and Kujawa, *International Business,* pp. 463–464.

47. Ellen Neuborne, "The Virtual Relationship," *Sales and Marketing Management* 155, no. 12 (December 2003), p. 20.

48. Rosabeth Moss Kanter, "Change Is Everyone's Job: Managing the Extended Enterprise in a Globally Connected World," *Organizational Dynamics,* Summer 1999, p. 12.

49. Akio Morita, "Partnering for Competitiveness: The Role of Japanese Business," *Harvard Business Review,* May–June 1992, p. 78.

50. See "The Auto Baron," *BusinessWeek,* November 16, 1998, pp. 82–90.

51. See for example "America vs. the New Europe," *Fortune,* December 21, 1998, pp. 149–156.

52. J. Bernard Keys, Luther Trey Denton, and Thomas R. Miller, "The Japanese Management Theory Jungle—Revisited," *Journal of Management* 20, no. 2 (1994), pp. 373–402.

53. See Thomson A. Stewart, "Toward the Century of Quality: A Conversation with Joseph Juran," *Fortune,* January 11, 1999, pp. 168, 170.

54. Gary Hamel and C. K. Prahalad, *Competing for the Future* (Boston: Harvard Business School Press, 1994), p. 23.

55. Ibid., p. 156.

56. Daniel Sullivan and Alan Bauerschmidt, "The 'Basic Concepts' of International Business Strategy: A Review and Reconsideration," Special issue, *Management International Review* (1991), pp. 111–124.

57. Also see B. Joseph Pine II and James H. Gilmore, "Welcome to the Experience Economy," *Harvard Business Review,* July–August 1998, pp. 97–105.

58. Kanter, "Change Is Everyone's Job," p. 17.

59. Gary Hamel, *Leading the Revolution* (Boston: Harvard Business School Press, 2000).

■ Part 4 Cases

In-Depth Integrative Case 1

1. "BP Won't Abandon Driving Forces," *Wall Street Journal,* November 27, 2003, p. A7.

2. Jeanne Whalen and Bhushan Bahree, "How BP Learned to Trust Ally That Once Burned It," *Wall Street Journal,* February 27, 2003, p. A4.

3. "New BP Is a Very American Company," *The Times* (London), June 24, 2002, p. B1.

4. David Buchan, "BP Driven to the Back of Beyond," *Financial Times* London Edition, April 20, 2001, p. B4.

5. Bhushan Bahree, "As BP Goes Green, the Fur Is Flying—Oil Giant's Bid to Be Seen as More Environmental Draws Critics' Scrutiny," *Wall Street Journal,* April 16, 2001, p. A5.

6. "BP Won't Abandon Driving Forces," *Wall Street Journal,* November 27, 2003. p. A7.

7. Bahree, "As BP Goes Green."

8. Jim Kirk, "BP Campaign Tries to Paint Greener Image," *Chicago Tribune,* September 5, 2001, p. 3.

9. Bahree, "As BP Goes Green."

10. Tania Panczyk, "BP Breaks Marketing Campaign to Promote Its Interactive Gas Stations," *AdWeek Midwest,* February 5, 2001, p. 4.

11. Bahree, "As BP Goes Green."

12. "BP Outlines Hopes and Fears in Russia," *International Petroleum Finance,* October 31, 2003, p. 21.

13. "BP Highlights Russia," *FSU Energy,* June 13, 2002, p. 1.

14. Ibid.

15. "BP Stakes Ukraine Claim," *FSU Energy,* June 13, 2003, p. 1.

16. "BP Outlines Hopes and Fears in Russia."

17. Ibid.

18. "BP Highlights Russia."

19. Heather Timmons, "BP to Increase Cash Dividends to Investors," *New York Times,* March 30, 2004, p. W1.

20. Chip Cummings, "Shell Faces Challenges to Restore Investors' Trust," *Wall Street Journal,* April 21, 2004, p. A2.

21. "BP PLC: Russian State Secrecy Laws Raise Issue for Joint Venture," *Wall Street Journal,* June 1, 2004, p. A1.

In-Depth Integrative Case 2

1. "Chiquita Names New CEO," *Cincinnati Business Courier,* January 12, 2004.

2. Shanon Murray, "Chiquita's Exit Plan Jumps Big Hurdle," *The Daily Deal,* March 5, 2002, p. C3.

3. Marco Were, "Implementing Corporate Responsibility—The Chiquita Case," *Journal of Business Ethics* 44, no. 2/3 (May 2003), p. 247.

4. "Trade Feud on Bananas Not as Clear as It Looks," *New York Times,* February 7, 2001, p. A5.

5. Sonja Sherwood, "Chiquita's Top Executive," *Chief Executive,* June 2002, p. 18.

6. Geert de Lombaerde, "Chiquita Outlook Improves Following EU Deal," *Cincinnati Business Courier,* April 20, 2001.

7. Nicholas Stein, "Yes, We Have No Profits," *Fortune,* November 26, 2001, pp. 182–196.

8. Ruth Mortimer, "A Strategy That's Bearing Fruit: When Is a Banana Not a Banana? When It's a Brand," *Brand Strategy,* May 26, 2003, p. 40.

9. Stein, "Yes, We Have No Profits."

10. Jerome Goldstein, "Greasing the Wheels of Sustainable Business," *In Business Magazine,* March/April 2003, p. 21.

11. "Corporate Social Responsibility," http://www.Chiquita.com.

12. Sherwood, "Chiquita's Top Executive."

13. Were, "Implementing Corporate Responsibility."

14. "Trade Feud on Bananas Not as Clear as It Looks."

15. Mortimer, "A Strategy That's Bearing Fruit."

16. "Chiquita Earns 2004 Corporate Citizen of the Americas Award," PR Newswire, April 5, 2004.

17. Stein, "Yes, We Have No Profits."

18. Were, "Implementing Corporate Responsibility."

19. Kintto Lucas, "Chiquita Brand Suffers in Banana Wars," Interpress Service: Global Information Network, November 30, 2001.

20. CERES (Coalition for Environmentally Responsible Economies) Sustainability Awards 2004, http://www.ceres.org/newsroom/press/rep_award_slist.htm.

Glossary

achievement culture   A culture in which people are accorded status based on how well they perform their functions.

achievement motivation theory   A theory which holds that individuals can have a need to get ahead, to attain success, and to reach objectives.

act of state doctrine   A jurisdictional principle of international law which holds that all acts of other governments are considered to be valid by U.S. courts, even if such acts are illegal or inappropriate under U.S. law.

adaptability screening   The process of evaluating how well a family is likely to stand up to the stress of overseas life.

adaptive organizations   Organizations that are characterized by reaction to required changes but failure to anticipate them and stay on or ahead of the cutting edge.

administrative coordination   Strategic formulation and implementation in which the MNC makes strategic decisions based on the merits of the individual situation rather than using a predetermined economically or politically driven strategy.

analytical manager   A manager who is systematic and logical and carefully weighs alternatives to problems.

arbitrator   An individual who provides a solution to a grievance that both sides (union and management representatives) have been unable to resolve themselves and that both sides agree to accept.

ascription culture   A culture in which status is attributed based on who or what a person is.

assessment center   An evaluation tool used to identify individuals with potential to be selected or promoted to higher-level positions.

authoritarian leadership   The use of work-centered behavior designed to ensure task accomplishment.

balance sheet approach   An approach to developing an expatriate compensation package that is based on ensuring the expat is "made whole" and does not lose money by taking the assignment.

benchmarking   The process of identifying what leading-edge competitors are doing and then using this information to produce improved products or services.

bicultural group   A group in which two or more members represent each of two distinct cultures, such as four Mexicans and four Taiwanese who have formed a team to investigate the possibility of investing in a venture.

cafeteria approach   An approach to developing an expatriate compensation package that entails giving the individual a series of options and letting the person decide how to spend the available funds.

centralization   A management system under which important decision are made at the top.

chaebols   In South Korea, very large, family-held conglomerates, including internationally known firms, in which many key managers have attended school in the West and use this education to help formulate successful international strategies for their firms. *Chaebols* have considerable political and economic power in Korea.

chromatics   The use of color to communicate messages.

chronemics   The way in which time is used in a culture.

civil or code law   Law that is derived from Roman law and is found in the non-Islamic and nonsocialist countries.

codetermination   A legal system that requires workers and their managers to discuss major decisions.

collective bargaining   The process whereby formal labor agreements are reached by union and management representatives; it involves the negotiation of wages, hours, and conditions of employment and the administration of the labor contract.

collectivism   A culture in which people tend to belong to groups or collectives and to look after each other in exchange for loyalty.

common law   Law that derives from English law and is the foundation of legislation in the United States, Canada, and England, among other nations.

communication   The process of transferring meanings from sender to receiver.

communitarianism   Refers to people regarding themselves as part of a group.

confrontation meetings   The gathering and analysis of information related to intra- and intergroup conflict followed by the formulation of a plan of action by the participants for the purpose of resolving these problems.

conglomerate investment   A type of high-risk investment in which goods or services produced are not similar to those produced at home.

content theories   Theories that explain work motivation in terms of what arouses, energizes, or initiates employee behavior.

context   Information that surrounds a communication and helps to convey the message.

controlling   The process of evaluating results in relation to plans or objectives and deciding what action, if any, to take.

cross-cultural school of management thought   An approach to international management holding that effective managerial behavior is a function of the specific culture: A successful manager in one location may not be effective in another location around the world.

cultural assimilator   A programmed learning technique designed to expose members of one culture to some of the basic concepts, attitudes, role perceptions, customs, and values of another culture.

culture The acquired knowledge that people use to interpret experience and to generate social behavior. This knowledge forms values, creates attitudes, and influences behavior.

decentralization Pushing decision making down the line and getting the lower-level personnel involved.

decision making The process of choosing a course of action among alternatives.

delayed differentiation A manufacturing strategy in which all products are manufactured in the same way for all countries or regions until as late in the assembly process as possible, with differentiation of features or components introduced in the final stages of production.

diffuse culture A culture in which both public and private space are similar in size and individuals guard their public space carefully, because entry into public space also affords entry into private space as well.

direct controls The use of face-to-face or personal meetings for the purpose of monitoring operations.

doctrine of comity A jurisdictional principle of international law which holds that there must be mutual respect for the laws, institutions, and government of other countries in the matter of jurisdiction over their own citizens.

downward communication The transmission of information from superior to subordinate.

economic imperative A worldwide strategy based on cost leadership, differentiation, and segmentation.

Eiffel Tower culture A culture that is characterized by a strong emphasis on hierarchy and orientation to the task.

emotional culture A culture in which emotions are expressed openly and naturally.

empowerment The process of giving individuals and teams the resources, information, and authority they need to develop ideas and effectively implement them.

enterprise unions Unions that represent both the hourly and salaried employees of a particular company.

environmental scanning The process of providing management with accurate forecasts of trends related to external changes in geographic areas where the firm currently is doing business and/or is considering setting up operations.

equity theory A theory which holds that people's motivation is determined by how fairly they feel they are being treated.

esteem needs The needs for power and status.

ethics The study of morality and standards of conduct.

ethnocentric MNC An MNC that stresses nationalism and often puts home office people in charge of key international management positions.

ethnocentric predisposition A nationalistic philosophy of management whereby the values and interests of the parent company guide the strategic decisions.

ethnocentrism The belief that one's own way of doing things is superior to that of others.

European Research Cooperation Agency (Eureka) An agency that funds projects in the fields of energy, medical technology, biotechnology, communications, and the like, with the objective of making Europe more productive and competitive in the world market.

expatriates Those who live and work away from their home country. They are citizens of the country where the multinational corporation is headquartered.

expectancy/valence theory A theory which postulates that motivation is influenced by a person's belief that effort will lead to performance, that performance will lead to specific outcomes, and that these outcomes are valued by the individual.

expropriation The seizure of businesses by a host country with little, if any, compensation to the owners.

factual manager A manager who looks at the available information and makes decisions based on that data.

family culture A culture that is characterized by a strong emphasis on hierarchy and orientation to the person.

femininity A situation in which the dominant values in society are caring for others and quality of life.

Foreign Corrupt Practices Act (FCPA) Made into U.S. law in 1977 because of concerns over bribes in the international business arena, this act makes it illegal to influence foreign officials through personal payment or political contributions.

formalization The use of defined structures and systems in decision making, communicating, and controlling.

franchise A business arrangement under which one party (the franchisor) allows another (the franchisee) to operate an enterprise using its trademark, logo, product line, and methods of operation in return for a fee.

geocentric MNC An MNC that seeks to integrate diverse regions of the world through a global approach to decision making.

geocentric predisposition A philosophy of management whereby the company tries to integrate a global systems approach to decision making.

global area division A structure under which global operations are organized on a geographic rather than a product basis.

global functional division A structure which organizes worldwide operations primarily based on function and secondarily on product.

global international trade union affiliations Trade union relationships that cut across regional and industrial groups and are heavily concerned with political activities.

global product division A structural arrangement in which domestic divisions are given worldwide responsibility for product groups.

global sourcing The use of worldwide suppliers, regardless of where they are located geographically, who are best able to provide the needed output.

globalization The production and distribution of products and services of a homogeneous type and quality on a worldwide basis.

globalization imperative A belief that one worldwide approach to doing business is the key to both efficiency and effectiveness.

goal-setting theory A theory that focuses on how individuals set goals and the impact of this process on their motivation.

grievance A complaint brought by an employee who feels that he or she has been treated improperly under the terms of the labor agreement.

groupthink   Social conformity and pressures on individual members of a group to conform and reach consensus.

guanxi   In China means good connections.

guided missile culture   A culture that is characterized by a strong emphasis on equality in the workplace and orientation to the task.

haptics   Communicating through the use of bodily contact.

home-country nationals   Expatriate managers who are citizens of the country where the multinational corporation is headquartered.

homogeneous group   A group that is characterized by members who share similar backgrounds and generally perceive, interpret, and evaluate events in similar ways.

honne   A Japanese term which means "what one really wants to do."

horizontal investment   An MNC investment in foreign operations to produce the same goods or services as those produced at home.

horizontal specialization   The assignment of jobs so that individuals are given a particular function to perform and tend to stay within the confines of this area.

host-country nationals   Local managers who are hired by the MNC.

hygiene factors   In the two-factor motivation theory, job context variables that include salary, interpersonal relations, technical supervision, working conditions, and company policies and administration.

incubator culture   A culture that is characterized by a strong emphasis on equality and orientation to the person.

indigenization laws   Laws that require that nationals hold a majority interest in the operation.

indirect controls   The use of reports and other written forms of communication to control operations.

individualism   A culture in which people tend to look after themselves and their immediate family only.

industrial democracy   The rights that employees have to participate in significant management decisions.

industrial internationals   Affiliates of the global international union groups that focus on a particular industry.

inpatriate   An individual from a host country or a third-country national who is assigned to work in the home country.

integrative techniques   Techniques that help the overseas operation become a part of the host country's infrastructure.

International Confederation of Free Trade Unions (ICFTU)   The most important global international union confederation.

international division structure   A structural arrangement that handles all international operations out of a division created for this purpose.

international joint ventures (IJVs)   Formal arrangements with foreign partners who typically, although not always, are located in the country where the business will be conducted.

International Labour Office (ILO)   A United Nations affiliate, consisting of government, industry, and union representatives, that works to promote fair labor standards regarding health and safety, working conditions, and freedom of association for workers.

international management   The process of applying management concepts and techniques in a multinational, multicultural environment.

international selection criteria   Factors used to choose personnel for international assignments.

intimate distance   Distance between people that is used for very confidential communications.

intuitive manager   A manager who is imaginative, innovative, and able to jump from one idea to another.

Islamic law   Law that is derived from interpretation of the Qur'an and the teachings of the Prophet Mohammed and is found in most Islamic countries.

job content factors   In work motivation, those factors internally controlled, such as responsibility, achievement, and the work itself.

job context factors   In work motivation, those factors controlled by the organization, such as conditions, hours, earnings, security, benefits, and promotions.

job design   A job's content, the methods that are used on the job, and the way the job relates to others in the organization.

joint venture   An agreement in which two or more partners own and control an overseas business.

kaizen   A Japanese term that means continuous improvement.

karoshi   Overwork or job burnout, in Japanese.

keiretsu   In Japan, a newly emerging organizational arrangement in which a large, often vertically integrated group of companies cooperate and work closely with each other to provide goods and services to end users; core members may be bound together by cross-ownership, long-term business dealings, interlocking directorates, and social ties.

key factor for success (KFS)   A factor necessary for a firm to effectively compete in a market niche.

kinesics   The study of communication through body movement and facial expressions.

labor relations   The process through which management and workers identify and determine the job relations that will be in effect at the workplace.

leadership   The process of influencing people to direct their efforts toward the achievement of some particular goal or goals.

learning   The acquisition of skills, knowledge, and abilities that results in a relatively permanent change in behavior.

learning organizations   Organization that are able to transform themselves by anticipating change and discovering new ways of creating products and services; they have learned how to learn.

license   An agreement that allows one party to use an industrial property right in exchange for payment to the other party.

localization   An approach to developing an expatriate compensation package that involves paying the expat a salary comparable to that of local nationals.

lockout   A company's refusal to allow workers to enter the facility during a labor dispute.

lump sum method   An approach to developing an expatriate compensation package that involves giving the expat a predetermined amount of money and letting the individual make his or her own decisions regarding how to spend it.

macro political risk analysis Analysis that reviews major political decisions likely to affect all enterprises in the country.

management by objectives (MBO) A management system for the joint setting of subordinate goals, coaching and counseling personnel, and providing feedback on their performance.

maquiladora industry An arrangement created by the Mexican government that permits foreign manufacturers to send materials to their Mexican-based plants, process or assemble products, and ship them back out of Mexico with only the value added being taxed.

masculinity A culture in which the dominant values are success, money, and things.

mass customization Tailor-making mass-production products to meet the expectations of the customers.

mediator A person who brings both sides (union and management representatives) together and helps them to reach a settlement that is mutually acceptable.

micro political risk analysis Analysis directed toward government policies and actions that influence selected sectors of the economy or specific foreign businesses in the country.

Ministry of International Trade and Industry (MITI) A governmental agency in Japan that identifies and ranks national commercial pursuits and guides the distribution of national resources to meet these goals.

mixed organization structure A structure that is a combination of a global product, area, or functional arrangement.

monochronic time schedule A time schedule in which things are done in a linear fashion.

motivation A psychologic process through which unsatisfied wants or needs lead to drives that are aimed at goals or incentives.

motivators In the two-factor motivation theory, the job content factors which include achievement, recognition, responsibility, advancement, and the work itself.

multicultural group A group in which there are individuals from three or more different ethnic backgrounds, such as three U.S., three German, three Uruguayan, and three Chinese managers who are looking into mining operations in South Africa.

multidomestic A firm that operates production plants in different countries but makes no attempt to integrate overall operations.

national responsiveness The need to understand the different consumer tastes in segmented regional markets and respond to different national standards and regulations imposed by autonomous governments and agencies.

nationality principle A jurisdictional principle of international law which holds that every country has jurisdiction over its citizens no matter where they are located.

negotiation The process of bargaining with one or more parties for the purpose of arriving at a solution that is acceptable to all.

neutral culture A culture in which emotions are held in check.

nonreciprocal trade partners Nations that sell (export) goods to other countries but do not buy (import) from them.

nonverbal communication The transfer of meaning through means such as body language and the use of physical space.

normative manager A manager who is idealistic and concerned with how things should be done.

North American Free Trade Agreement (NAFTA) A free trade agreement, including the United States, Canada, and Mexico, that effectively eliminates trade barriers between the three countries.

oculesics The areas of communication that deal with conveying messages through the use of eye contact and gaze.

OD intervention The structured activity in which targeted individuals, groups, or units engage in accomplishing task goals that are related to organization development.

operational risks Government policies and procedures that directly constrain management and performance of local operations.

organization development (OD) The deliberate and reasoned introduction, establishment, reinforcement, and spread of change for the purpose of improving an organization's effectiveness.

Organization for Economic Cooperation and Development (OECD) A government, industry, and union group founded in 1976 that has established a voluntary set of guidelines for MNCs.

organizational culture A pattern of basic assumptions that are developed by a group as it learns to cope with problems of external adaptation and internal integration and that are taught to new members as the correct way to perceive, think, and feel in relation to these problems.

ownership-control risks Government policies or actions that inhibit ownership or control of local operations.

paradox A statement that appears to be contradictory but is not, such as "increases in product quality often result in a decline of the cost of producing the goods."

parochialism The tendency to view the world through one's own eyes and perspectives.

participative leadership The use of both a work- or task-centered and people-centered approach to leading subordinates.

particularism The belief that circumstances dictate how ideas and practices should be applied and something cannot be done the same everywhere.

paternalistic leadership The use of work-centered behavior coupled with a protective employee-centered concern.

perception A person's view of reality.

personal distance In communicating, the physical distance used for talking with family and close friends.

physiologic needs Food, clothing, shelter, and other basic, physical needs.

political imperative Strategic formulation and implementation utilizing strategies that are country responsive and designed to protect local market niches.

political risk The likelihood that a business's foreign investment will be constrained by a host government's policies.

polycentric MNC An MNC that places local nationals in key positions and allows these managers to appoint and develop their own people.

polycentric predisposition A philosophy of management whereby strategic decisions are tailored to suit the cultures of the countries where the MNC operates.

polychronic time schedule A time schedule in which people tend to do several things at the same time and place higher value on personal involvement than on getting things done on time.

power distance   The extent to which less powerful members of institutions and organizations accept that power is distributed unequally.

practical school of management thought   A traditional approach to international management, which holds that effective managerial behavior is universal: a successful manager in one location will be effective in any other location around the world.

principle of sovereignty   An international principle of law which holds that governments have the right to rule themselves as they see fit.

problem-solving teams   Employee groups that discuss ways of improving quality, efficiency, and the overall work environment.

process theories   Theories that explain work motivation by how employee behavior is initiated, redirected, and halted.

product proliferation   The creation of a wide array of products that the competition cannot copy quickly enough.

profit   The amount remaining after all expenses are deducted from total revenues.

protective and defensive techniques   Techniques that discourage the host government from interfering in operations.

protective principle   A jurisdictional principle of international law which holds that every country has jurisdiction over behavior that adversely affects its national security, even if the conduct occurred outside that country.

proxemics   The study of the way people use physical space to convey messages.

public distance   In communicating, the distance used when calling across the room or giving a talk to a group.

quality control circle (QCC)   A group of workers who meet on a regular basis to discuss ways of improving the quality of work.

quality imperative   Strategic formulation and implementation utilizing strategies of total quality management to meet or exceed customers' expectations and continuously improve products and/or services.

regiocentric MNC   An MNC that relies on local managers from a particular geographic region to handle operations in and around that area.

regiocentric predisposition   A philosophy of management whereby the firm tries to blend its own interests with those of its subsidiaries on a regional basis.

regional internationals   Subdivisions of the global affiliation; regional applications of the global's activities.

regional system   An approach to developing an expatriate compensation package that involves setting a compensation system for all expats who are assigned to a particular region and paying everyone in accord with that system.

repatriation   The return to one's home country from an overseas management assignment.

repatriation agreement   Agreement whereby the firm tells the individual how long she or he will be posted overseas and promises to give the individual, on return, a job that is mutually acceptable.

return on investment   Return measured by dividing profit by assets.

ringisei   From Japan, decision making by consensus.

safety needs   In Maslow's hierarchy of needs, the desire for security, stability, and the absence of pain.

self-actualization needs   In Maslow's hierarchy of needs, the desire to reach one's full potential by becoming everything one is capable of becoming.

self-efficacy   A person's belief or confidence in his or her abilities to marshal the motivation, resources, and courses of action needed to successfully accomplish a specific task.

self-management teams   Employee groups that take over supervisory duties and manage themselves; teams consist of individuals who learn all the tasks of all the group members, allowing team members to rotate jobs.

simplification   The process of exhibiting the same orientation toward different culture groups.

smallest space analysis (SSA)   A nonparametric multivariate analysis. This mathematic tool maps the relationship among the countries by showing the distance between each. By looking at this two-dimensional map, it is possible to see those countries that are similar to each other and those that are not.

social distance   In communicating, the distance used to handle most business transactions.

social needs   The need to interact and affiliate with others and the need to feel wanted by others.

socialist law   Law that comes from the Marxist socialist system and continues to influence regulations in countries formerly associated with the Soviet Union as well as China.

sociotechnical designs   Job designs that blend the personnel and the technology.

special purpose teams   Employee groups that design and introduce work reforms and new technology.

specialization   An organizational characteristic that assigns individuals to specific, well-defined tasks.

specialized internationals   Trade union associations that function as components of intergovernmental agencies and lobby within these agencies.

specific culture   A culture in which individuals have a large public space they readily share with others and a small private space they guard and share only with close friends and associates.

strategic fit   An approach to strategically managing an organization that involves aligning resources in such a way as to mesh with the environment.

strategic planning   The process of determining an organization's basic mission and long-term objectives, then implementing a plan of action for attaining these goals.

strategic stretch   The creative use of resources to achieve ever more challenging goals.

strategy implementation   The process of providing goods and services in accord with a plan of action.

strike   A collective refusal to work to pressure management to grant union demands.

subsidiary board of directors   A board that overseas and monitors the operations of a foreign subsidiary.

survey feedback   An OD intervention that involves the gathering and analysis of information related to group behavior and problems and the feeding back of this information to develop effective action plans.

tatemae A Japanese term which means "doing the right thing" according to normal models of decision making.

team building An extension of classic T-groups (training groups) and sensitivity training that is geared to enhancing organizational effectiveness through cooperation and a "team" effort of key personnel.

technology paradox (Also see **paradox**) That high-tech businesses can thrive at the very moment that their prices are falling the fastest.

territoriality principle A jurisdictional principle of international law which holds that every nation has the right of jurisdiction within its legal territory.

Theory X manager A manager who believes that people are basically lazy and that coercion and threats of punishment often are necessary to get them to work.

Theory Y manager A manager who believes that under the right conditions people not only will work hard but will seek increased responsibility and challenge.

third-country nationals Managers who are citizens of countries other than the one in which the MNC is headquartered or the one in which the managers are assigned to work by the MNC.

third-party peacemaking The diagnosis of group conflict followed by the use of an outside party (usually the OD change agent) to facilitate a constructive resolution of a problem.

token group A group in which all members but one have the same background, such as a group of Japanese retailers and a British attorney.

total quality management (TQM) An organizational strategy and the accompanying techniques that result in the delivery of high-quality products and/or services to customers.

training The process of altering employee behavior and attitudes in a way that increases the probability of goal attainment.

transactional leaders Individuals who exchange rewards for effort and performance and work on a "something for something" basis.

transfer risks Government policies that limit the transfer of capital, payments, production, people, and technology in and out of the country.

transformational leaders Leaders who are visionary agents with a sense of mission and who are capable of motivating their followers to accept new goals and new ways of doing things.

transition strategies Strategies used to help smooth the adjustment from an overseas to a stateside assignment.

transnational corporations (TNCs) Multinational corporations that view the world as one giant market.

transnational network structure A multinational structural arrangement that combines elements of function, product, and geographic designs, while relying on a network arrangement to link worldwide subsidiaries.

two-factor theory of motivation A theory that holds there are two sets of factors that influence job satisfaction: hygiene factors and motivators.

uncertainty avoidance The extent to which people feel threatened by ambiguous situations and have created beliefs and institutions that try to avoid these.

union An organization that represents the workers and in collective bargaining has the legal authority to negotiate with the employer and administer the labor contract.

universalism The belief that ideas and practices can be applied everywhere in the world without modification.

upward communication The transfer of meaning from subordinate to superior.

validity The quality of being effective, of producing the desired results. A valid test or selection technique measures what it is intended to measure.

values Basic convictions that people have regarding what is right and wrong, good and bad, important and unimportant.

variety amplification The creation of uncertainty and the analysis of many alternatives regarding future action.

variety reduction The limiting of uncertainty and the focusing of action on a limited number of alternatives.

vertical investment The production of raw materials or intermediate goods that are to be processed into final products.

vertical specialization The assignment of work to groups or departments where individuals are collectively responsible for performance.

virtual corporation A network of companies that come together to exploit fast-changing opportunities and share costs, skills, and access to global markets.

virtual organization An organization that is able to conduct business as if it were a very large enterprise when, in fact, it is much smaller, made up of core business competencies and the rest outsourced.

wholly owned subsidiary An overseas operation that is totally owned and controlled by an MNC.

work centrality The importance of work in an individual's life relative to other areas of interest.

world-class organization (WCOs) Enterprises that are able to compete with anybody, anywhere, anytime.

World Trade Organization (WTO) Started in 1995 to replace GATT, the WTO has power to enforce rulings in trade disputes and monitor trade policies.

Name & Organization Index

Abbott, 87, 89

Abdul Baqi, Mahmoud M., 292–293

Abdullah, Prince, 295

Abengoa Servicios Urbanos, 307

Abrahams, Michael N., 160

Accel Partners, 430–431

Accor Asia Pacific, 363

Actuate Corp., 431

Act-Up, 86

Adler, Nancy J., 155, 165–167, 171–172, 184, 192, 200, 206, 369, 454

Adolph Coors Co., 126

Aeon, 229

AES Corporation, 507

AFL-CIO, 476–477

African National Congress, 79

Agile Software Corp., 431

Aguas del Tunari, 307

Aguirre, Fernando, 521

AIG (American International Group), 6, 340

Air Andaman, 358

AirAsia, 358–364

Air Deccan, 358

Air Do, 358

AirTran, 397

Akai Electric, 248

Akiba, Toshiharu, 219

Al Ahram Beverages Co., 127

Alcan Aluminum, 300

Alcatel, 22, 264

Alcatel Alsthom, 245–246, 481

Alexander the Great, 8

AlliedSignal, 459

Allinson, C. W., 460

All Nippon Airways (ALA), 359

Aluminum Company of America, 455

Alusuisse Lonza Group, 300

Alvi, Raashid, 350

Amazon.com, 47, 255

Ambani, Anil, 350

Ambani, Dhirubhai H., 350, 351

Ambani, Mukesh, 350

América Móvil, 507

American Airlines, 16–17

American Business Centers, 303

American Chemistry Council, 424

American Express, 49

American International Group, 6, 340

America Online, 264

Ameritech, 48

Amersham International, 248, 366–368, 391

Amgen, 63

Amoco Corp., 6, 52, 263, 515, 516

Anderson, Philip, 182–183, 333

Anderson, R. G. S., 78

Anderson, Stephanie, 292–295

Andreadis, Dimitris, 432

Andreessen, Marc, 3

Anheuser-Busch Cos., 18, 125–127, 340

Annan, Kofi, 87

ANPE, 355

Ansett, 397

Antal, Adriane Berthoin, 61

Ante, Spencer E., 430–432

AOL Time Warner, 360

Apple Computer Inc., 179, 239

Aquafina, 92

Aquarel, 93

Aramco, 292, 294

Arby's, 18

ARCO, 52, 516

Arctic Power, 516

Arthur Andersen, 57, 423

ASEAN (Association of Southeast Asian Nations), 11

Asia Pacific Airlines Association, 358

Aspbury, Herbert F., 213–215

Aspen Pharmacare, 89

Association of Chartered Certified Accountants, 526

Aston Martin, 234–236, 255

Aston Martin Lagonda, 278

AT&T, 16, 27, 180, 241, 311, 327, 350

Audi, 317, 319, 326

Auerbach Grayson & Co., 35

Auger, Robert, 75

Autokonzern, 22

Autolatina, 278

AutoPacific, 319

Aventis, 84

Avon Products, 7

Avtovaz, 7, 40

Awata, Fusahao, 219

Axess Asia, 363

Aznar, Jose Maria, 38

Badawy, M. K., 413

Bailey, Elaine K., 446

Baker, John, 512–514

Baker, Kevin, 127

Baker, Stephen, 2–5

Ballmer, Steven A., 4, 179

Banai, M., 453

Banana Link, 522

Bangle, Christopher, 316, 319

Bankers Trust, 248
Bank for International Settlements (BIS), 17
Bank of America, 6, 34–36, 307, 311, 340
Bank of Boston, 36
Bank of Japan, 58
Bank of Tokyo, 153
Banque Indosuez, 221
Banque National de Paris, 220
Barenberg, Mark, 477
Barshefsky, Christine, 86
Bartlett, Christopher A., 243, 276
BASF, 248
Baskin-Robbins, 45
Bass, Bernard M., 415–417
B.A.T. Industries PLC, 249
Baudet, Stephane, 224
Bauerschmidt, Alan, 345–349, 503
BBAG, 125
Beamish, Paul W., 269, 306, 434
Bechtel, 303
Bechtel Enterprise Holdings, 307
Beers, Lawrence A., 80–81
Beijing Mei Da Coffee Company, 311
Bellamy, Carol, 90
Bell Atlantic Co., 22, 48, 249
BellSouth, 48, 507
Ben and Jerry's, 526
Bensaou, M., 283
Berkshire Hathaway, 227, 340
Bernstein, Aaron, 476–477
Bertelsmann AG, 237–238
Berthod, Marc, 220
Besemer, Deborah, 432
Better Banana Project, 524
Bhagat, Rabi S., 386
Bharti Tele-Ventures, 6
Birol, Fatih, 294
Bishop, Robert R., 2
Black, J. Stewart, 141, 216–225, 455
Black, Jerry, 229
Blackstone Group, 36
Blackwell, Charles W., 194
Blair, Tony, 38, 479
Blake, Robert S., 404
Blank, Arthur, 424
Blondet, Sylvie, 219
Blue, Jeffrey L., 441
BMW, 16, 24, 40, 121, 250, 287, 316–319, 326, 340, 341
Bodas, Karaha, 307
Boehm, Cedric, 93
Boehringer Ingelheim, 86, 89, 248
Boeing, 319–320
Boje, D. M., 390
Bombardier, Inc., 16
Bonderman, David, 364
Bondi, Enrico, 35, 36
Booder, 287
Booz Allen Hamilton Inc., 317
Borg-Warner Automotive, Inc., 65
Bourguignon, Philippe, 216

BP PLC, 294–295
Brady, Diane, 366–368
Branson, Richard, 364, 396–398, 424, 425
BrassRing LLC, 432
Brau and Brunnen, 127
Brazilian Central Bank, 507
Breitsprecher, Christine, 318
Bremner, Brian, 152–153
Breyer, James W., 430–431
Bristol-Myers Squibb, 86, 87, 89
British Airways, 363, 497
British Equal Opportunity Commission, 62
British Petroleum (BP), 6, 66, 263, 273, 340, 424, 515–520
Brodbeck, Felix C., 419, 420
Bronfman, Inc., 16
Brown, Lord John, 515–520
Buckley, M. Ronald, 436
Budhwar, Pawan S., 457–458
Bulin, Jim, 235
Bulin Group, 235
Burger King, 266
Burmah-Castrol, 516
Bush, George H. W., 55
Bush, George W., 87, 300, 476–477

Cable Box Office (CBO), 298
Cable & Wireless, 48
CALICA, 278
Caligiuri, Paula M., 440, 460–461
Canadean Ltd., 127
Canadian Pacific, 16
Canlon, Rob, 353–354
Canon, 340
Capell, Kerry, 366–368, 396–398
Capellas, Michael, 354
Cap Gemini Ernst & Young, 4
Cardoso, Fernando, 85
CARE, 66
Caribbean Bauxite Company, 512–514
Carrefour, 229
Carrera, Barbara, 216
Carson, Jon, 5
Carvalho, Michel, 127
Carvalho-Heineken, Charlene de, 124, 127
Cascade Communications, 5
Castell, William M., 366–368, 391
Caterpillar, 52, 340
Cathay Pacific Airways, 364
Cebu Pacific Airways, 358
CED Informationstechnik GmbH, 495
Center for Strategic & International Studies (CSIS), 293
Centre for Asia Pacific Aviation, 358
Chakravarthy, Balaji S., 129
Chaletzky, Ken, 509–511
Chaney, Lillian H., 199
Chang, Sea Jin, 247–248
Chapman, Tony, 445–446
Chappell, Ronald, 516
Chase Manhattan Corp., 36, 214
Chemical Bank, 213–215

Chen Shui-bian, 122
Chevez, Francisco, 211
Chevron, 7, 265, 517
Chiang Kai-shek, 122
China Telecom, 236–237
Chiquita, 66, 521–527
Chirac, Jacques, 38, 219
Christou, Dennis, 526
Chrysler Corporation, 44, 263, 278, 338, 450
Cifra SA, 249
Cigarrera La Moderna, 249
Cigarros La Tabacalera Mexicana SA, 249
Cipla, 87, 90
Cisco Systems, 209, 340
Citibank, 236–237, 311
Citicorp, 7
Citigroup, 6, 35, 66, 127, 340
Claflin, Bruce, 209
Clark, Alan, 127
Clarke, Jeff, 355
Climate Change Coalition, 516
Clinton, Bill, 55, 86, 89–90, 190
Clinton Foundation HIV/AIDS Initiative, 89–90
cMarket, 5
Coakley, Lori A., 133
Coalition for Environmentally Responsible Economies (CERES), 526
Coalition of Latin American Workers, 525
Coca-Cola Co., 7, 11, 16, 24, 32, 52, 64, 88, 89, 92–93, 119–120, 130–131, 239–240, 268, 269, 278, 300, 311, 340, 433, 435, 459, 466, 473
Coca-Cola Japan, 337
Cohen, Eli, 459
Cohen, Roger, 222
Cohn, Laura, 92–93
Colgate Palmolive, 7, 77–79, 340
Columbia Pictures, 23
Columbus, Christopher, 8
Cometec, Inc., 211
Commerce One, 237
Commonwealth of Independent States (CIS), 133
Compaq Computer Corporation, 44, 239, 352–357
CompUSA, 18
Condon, J. C., 194
Confédération Française Démocratique du Travail (CFDT), 223–224
Confédération Générale du Travail (CGT), 221
Congressional Black Caucus, 78
Conoco, 52
Conservation International, 66
Consob, 35
Consolidated Paper Company, 345
Consumer Project on Technology, 86
Continental Airlines, 340
Contract Papers (Holdings) Limited, 348
Conway, Maureen, 355–356
Conyers, John, 78
Copy General, 509–511
Cora, James B., 219
Corning, Inc., 211–212
Costco Wholesale, 340
Cotshott, Gary, 437–438

Credit Rating Information Services, 351
Credit Suisse First Boston, 125
Cresson, Edith, 220
Crixivan, 87
Crookell, Harold, 269, 306
Cummins, 279
Cusumano, Michael A., 179

Dacia, 128
Daewoo Motor Company, 25, 400–402
Daimler-Benz, 263, 278, 450
DaimlerChrysler, 6, 7, 17, 32, 38, 152–153, 173–174, 263, 278, 296
Dalal, Yogen, 5
Daley, Lane, 334
Dammerman, Dennis D., 366–368
Dana Corporation, 328
Dasani, 92–93, 119–120
DataSweep Inc., 431
Davis, H. J., 379
Decoma International, 279
Def Jam Recordings, 424
Degelmann, Thor, 223–224
Delaware & Hudson Railway, 16
Dell Computer, 6, 47, 227, 257, 319, 340, 352, 354, 357, 437–438
Deloitte Research, 230
Deloitte Touche, 35–36, 437
Delta Air Lines Inc., 16–17, 396
Delta Motor Corporation, 49
Deng Xiaoping, 140
Deutsche Bank, 35, 36, 47, 62, 127, 318
Deutsche Telecom, 16
Dichtl, E., 305
Digital Equipment, 280
Dillon, W. Tracy, 190
Dirks, Gary, 516
Disney, Roy, Jr., 217
Disney, Roy, Sr., 217
Disney, Walt, 216, 217
Disneyland, 216, 217–218
Disney World, 218, 224
Diwan, Roger, 293–294
Dlamini, Gugu, 83
Doctors Without Borders (*Médecins Sans Frontières*), 67, 82–84, 86, 88
Doh, Jonathan, 82–90, 226–232, 352–357, 358–364, 509–511, 515–520, 521–527
Dow Chemical, 16, 24
Downes, Jason, 261
Doz, Yves, 348
Dubcek, Alexander, 509
Duda, Erno, 509–511
Dunbar, E., 469
Du Pont, 7, 16, 340

Earl, Michael, 283
Earley, P. C., 383–384
Earth, Inc., 474
Eastman Kodak, 7, 16, 17, 240, 324, 327, 510
East-West Center, 303
easyJet, 358
Ebel, Robert E., 293

Eckrodt, Rolf, 152–153
Economist Intelligence Unit (EIU), 22
Eden, Dov, 384
Edmundson, Gail, 316–319
Efstathiou, Andrew, 352
Egri, Carolyn P., 411
Eircom, 280
Eisner, Michael, 216–219, 222
Elan, 6
Elashmawi, F., 95
Electromagnetica, 22
Electronic Data Service (EDS), 352, 437
Electronic Data Systems, 2
Eli Lilly, 340
Ellis, Paul, 141
Enderle, Rob, 352, 355
Engardio, Pete, 54–56
England, George W., 98–99
ENI, 295
Enron, 56, 57, 303, 423
Environics, 423
EpaMarne, 220
Epicurum, 35, 36
Epogen, 63
Erez, M., 383–384
Ericsson, 150, 241, 326–327
Euro Disneyland, 216–225
European Bank for Reconstruction and Development (EBRD), 39–40, 260
European Commission, 487
European Research Cooperation Agency (Eureka), 19–20
Eurostat, 188
Evans, Gareth, 512–514
Evian, 93
Ewing, Jack, 124–127
Excel Industries, 279
Exxon Corporation, 52, 302
ExxonMobil, 6, 7, 294–295, 311, 340, 517, 518

Farmer, Richard N., 249
Farrow, Frances, 397
FedEx, 340
Fernandez, Anthony, 358, 360, 363, 364
Fiat, 7, 40
Fields, Mark, 234–236
Fiorina, Carly S., 352
Fisch, Joseph J., Jr., 125
Fischer, 126
Fitzpatrick, Robert, 216, 219–221, 224
Fleury, Mark, 432
Flynn, D. M., 99–100
Foote Partners, 4–5
Ford, William C., Jr., 234, 236, 493
Ford Motor Co., 6, 7, 16, 17, 22, 24, 38, 40, 150, 154, 190, 234–236, 237, 246–247, 248, 255, 278–280, 289, 310–311, 320, 338, 393, 481
Forrester Research Inc., 2, 3, 355, 431, 438
Foust, Dean, 92–93
Fox, Eleanor M., 180
Fox, Vicente, 17

France, Mike, 178–180
France Cable et Radio, 253
Francesco, Anne Marie, 183
France Telecom, 16, 253
Fravalex, 22
Freidhem, Cyrus, 521
Frenkel, Stephen, 370, 464, 465
Fuji, 240, 327
Fuji Heavy Industries, 7
Fuji-Kiku, 389
Fujitsu, 264, 376
Fujitsu-Siemens, 357

Gallup, 423
Ganz, 22
Garfield, Bob, 127
Garland, John, 249
Gartner Group, 356
Gartner Inc., 2
Gates Foundation, 72, 88
GE Amersham, 366–368
GE Capital, 238, 248
Gehring, 287
General Electric (GE), 6, 7, 18, 22, 47, 52, 227, 300, 303, 311, 324, 340, 366–368, 391, 404, 427, 459, 486–487
General Electric Medical Systems Group (GEMS), 466
General Foods, 386
General Motors Corp. (GM), 7, 16, 17, 24, 25, 38, 40, 45, 173, 235, 255, 264, 270, 280–281, 318, 319–320, 326, 338, 389, 411, 492, 506
General Motors Council, 486
Ghiselli, Edwin E., 371–372, 406–408, 413, 414
Ghoshal, Sumantra, 243, 276
Ghosn, Carlos, 152–153
Gibson, Jane Whitney, 194
Gibson, Richard, 159
Gillette Company, 7, 32, 137, 340, 435
Gillette Razor Blade Company, 64
GlaxoSmithKline, 87, 89, 340
Glaxo Wellcome, 86, 248
Global Fund to Fight AIDS, Tuberculosis, and Malaria, 71–72, 87–90
Gold, Barry Allen, 183
Gold, Stanley, 217
Goldman, Sachs & Co., 35, 229, 318
Google, Inc., 5, 179
Gorbachev, Mikhail, 20, 265
Gore, Al, 86
Graham, John L., 205, 206
Grande Group, 248
Grant Thornton International, 35, 36
Green, Diana J., 189
Greene, Harold H., 180
Greene, Jay, 178–180
Greenwood, J. Michael, 390
Gregersen, Hal B., 216–225
Gregory, Ann, 307
Grolsch, 125
Grote, Byron, 517
Groupe Danone, 93
Grupo Carso, 253
Grupo ICA, 278

Grupo Industrial Bimbo SA, 18
Guardiola, Vincent, 221
Guervil, Antoine, 223
Guice, Stephen, 189
Gupta, Amar, 5

Haas, Marius, 355
Haas, Steven, 510–511
Haas, Teresa, 510–511
Haier, 236–237
Haire, Mason, 371–372, 406–408, 413, 414
Hall, E., 181
Hall, E. T., 181
Hamel, Gary, 503
Hammer, Mitchell R., 456
Hampden-Turner, Charles, 96–99, 109–117, 164, 201, 329–330, 421
Harari, Ehud, 462
Harbison, Peter, 358
Harris, Jim, 353–354
Harris, Philip R., 95, 99, 186
Hart, Stuart L., 254
Hart, William, 456
Harvey, Michael G., 436
Hawley and Hazel Chemical Company, 77–79
Hayes, J., 460
Hayes, Keith, 318
Hay Group, 339
Haynes, Ulric, Jr., 441
Health Action International, 86
Heineken, 124–127, 148
Heineken, Alfred H. "Freddy," 124
Heineken USA Inc., 127
Helu, Carlos Slim, 18
Henkl, 64
Herbert, T. T., 379
Herzberg, Frederick, 375–379
Herzberger Papierfabrik Ludwig Osthushenrich GmbH and Co. KG, 345
Hetco, 294
Hetero Drugs, 90
Hewlett, Bill, 352
Hewlett-Packard, 7, 17, 26, 67–68, 74, 175, 328, 352–357
Hildebrant, H. W., 188
Hilti Corp., 179
Hines, George, 377
Hirsch, Georges, 279
Hitachi, 51, 481
Hodgetts, Richard M., 137, 194, 195, 325, 402
Hoechst AG, 16, 155
Hoecklin, Lisa, 132, 156, 157, 158
Hof, Robert D., 2–5, 430–432
Hofstede, Geert H., 101–107, 109, 112, 116, 119, 120, 137, 155, 157, 372–375, 381–382, 385
Hogan, Joseph M., 367–368
Holscher, Dirck, 509–511
Holscher, Paul, 509–511
Holt, Erik, 82–90, 226–232, 352–357, 515–520, 521–527
Holusha, John, 339
Home Box Office (HBO), 298
Home Depot, 340, 424
Honda Motor Co., 241, 246, 251, 338, 340, 506

Honda of America Manufacturing, Inc., 59
Honeywell International Inc., 300
Hook, Peter, 363
Horovitz, Jacques H., 332
Hotel Catering and Institutional Management Association, 62
Houghton, James R., 211–212
Hoxha, Enver, 22
HSBC Holdings, 6
Huawei Technologies, 209
Huaxing Razor Blade Factory, 64
Huenemann, John, 82
Hussein, Saddam, 298
Husseini, Saddad, 294
Hutchison Whampoa, 350
Hyundai, 25

IBM, 2, 7, 16, 17, 19, 24, 26, 44, 101–102, 220, 227, 239, 242, 280, 319, 324, 340, 352, 353, 357, 431, 435, 437, 459, 500
ICCR (Interfaith Center on Corporate Responsibility), 77–79, 89
ICI India, 424
Idemitsu Oil Development Company, 311
IG Chemie, 495
IKEA, 22
Ilwa, 22
Immelt, Jeffrey, 366–368, 427
Inch, John G., 367
Indo-German Export Promotion Council, 498
Industrie Kompetens, 497
Infosys Technologies, 5, 437
Inkpen, Andrew C., 434
Institute of Health Service Management, 62
Institute of Personnel Management, 62
Intel Capital, 260–261
Intel Corp., 4, 5, 6, 122, 260–261, 308, 328, 340, 354
Interbrew, 125
Intercontinental Marketing Services Health, 179
Interfaith Center on Corporate Responsibility (ICCR), 77–79, 89
International Center for Corporate Accountability, 68
International Computers Ltd., 198
International Confederation of Free Trade Unions (ICFTU), 486
International Energy Agency, 294
International Federation of Phonographic Industries, 63
International Labour Organization (ILO), 485–486, 491, 498
International Monetary Fund (IMF), 9, 17, 21, 54, 55, 298
International Standards Organization (ISO), 67, 326
International Telephone & Telegraph (ITT), 249, 330–331
International Trade Secretaries (ITS), 486
International Union of Electrical (IUE) workers, 486–487
International Union of Food Workers, 525
International Water Ltd., 307
Intuit Inc., 248
Investors Limited, 343
Ishii, Jun, 388
Isuzu Motors Ltd., 16
Ito-Yokado, 229–230
ITT, 249, 330–331

Jackson, Thomas Penfield, 180
Jaguar, 234–236, 255
Japan Air Lines (JAL), 359

Japanese Institute for International Studies and Training, 101
Japanese Public Highway Corporation, 57–58
Jaworski, Renata A., 453
JBoss Inc., 432
J.C. Penney, 18, 155
J.D. Power & Associates, 150, 318
JetBlue Airways, 358, 397, 398
Jiambalvo, James, 334
Jiang Zemin, 209
John Deere, 280
John (King of England), 8
Johnson & Johnson, 57, 66, 74, 227, 340, 424
Jolson, Al, 77, 78
Jones, John B., 352

Kaicheng, Yu, 411
Kakabadse, Andrew, 388–389
Kakuyama, T., 384
Kanter, Rosabeth Moss, 501, 503–504
Kapoor, Vinay, 92–93
Katzenberg, Jeffrey, 217
Kawahito, Hiroshi, 388
Kellogg, 340
Kentucky Fried Chicken, 18, 266
Kerstetter, Jim, 2–5
Khermouch, Gerry, 124–127
Killing, J. Peter, 269, 306
Kimberly-Clark, 64–65
Kiuchi, Masao, 230–231
Kleiner Perkins Caulfield & Byers, 431
Kluckhohn, Florence Rockwood, 134
Knight, Phil, 80
KNP, N.V., 345–349
Koepp, Stephen, 217
Koglmayr, H. G., 305
Kohl, Helmut, 38
Kohn, Eric, 363
Koizumi, Junichiro, 44
Konda, 236–237
Kondo, Yasumasa, 334
Koninklijke Nederlandse Paperfabrieken, N.V. (KNP), 345–349
Korber/Hauni, 287
Korea Telecom, 48
Kotak Securities, 351
Kovach, Carol, 171
Kraimer, Maria L., 453
Krause, Stefan, 318
Kraut, Allen I., 107–109
Krebsbach-Gnath, Camilla, 61
Kripalani, Manjeet, 2–5, 350–351
Krishna, Sonali, 216–225
Kuratko, Donald F., 195
Kurt Salmon and Associates, 229

Land Rover, 234–236
Lange, Joep, 88
Latta, Geoffrey W., 449
Laurent, Andre, 155
Lawton, Thomas, 358–364
Lazzari, Valter, 35

Learjet Corporation, 16
LeCraw, Donald J., 269, 306
Lee, Jean, 168
Lee, Raymond, 98–100
Lee, Sang M., 101, 411
Lee, Tosca M., 411
Lee Tenghui, 190
Legend, 236–237
Lehman Brothers Inc., 2, 35
Lei, David, 267
Leonard, David, 426
Levi's, 66, 131, 423
LG Group, 25
Li & Fung Ltd., 239, 268–269
Li Hongzhi, 64
Liker, Jeffrey K., 338
Likert, Rensis, 402–404, 414
Lim Chin Bing, 361
Limited, The, 239
Lin, Rachel, 361
Linde, 22
Linder, Keith, 522–523
L.L. Bean, 264
London Stock Exchange, 75
L'Oreal, 340
Loreto y Pena Pobre, 249
Lowe, Frank, 127
Lowe & Partners Worldwide, 127
Lowe's, 340
Lubrizol Corporation, 424
Lucent Technologies, 326–327
Lufthansa, 497
Lukoil, 295
Lula da Silva, Luiz Inácio, 507
Lund, Reinhard, 490
Lurie, Mark, 83
Luthans, Fred, 135, 137, 139, 369, 391
Luthans, Kyle W., 139
Lutz, Robert A., 318

Machungwa, Peter D., 378
Madruga Corporation, 394
Magaziner, Ira, 89
Magna International Inc., 318
Magna Steyr, 318
Maharashtra State Electric Board, 303
Maia, Cesar, 308
Malaysian Airlines (MAS), 359–361
Malloch Brown, Mark, 55
Mandela, Nelson, 29
Manufacturers Hanover Trust, 213–215
Mao Zedong, 122, 399–400
Marion Merrell Dow, Inc., 16
Mark, Reuben, 77–79
Marklin & Cie, 287
Marsnik, Paul A., 139
Martens, Eduardo, 212
Martin, Jeannette S., 199
Maslow, Abraham, 370–375, 379
Matlack, Carol, 92–93

Matrix Laboratories, 90
Matsui, T., 384
Matsushita, 26, 165, 186–188
Matsushita Electric Industrial Co., 278, 388
Mattel Inc., 68, 222
Maven Networks Inc., 430–432
Maxus Energy, 412
Mayer, Louis B., 216
Mazda, 235, 248, 278, 280, 310–311
Mbeki, Thabo, 83–84
MCA, 16
McAllister, Jeff, 231
McCarthy, Conor, 360
McCarthy, Daniel J., 400, 401
McCarthy, John C., 431
McClaine, S. R., 390
McClelland, David C., 380–382
McCormick, Iain, 445–446
McDonald's, 7, 18, 22, 24, 25, 31, 64, 130, 159,
     244, 266
McGhee, Michael, 361
McGlynn, Brian, 84
McGregor, Douglas, 399
MCI, 20
McLaughlin Body Company, 280
Mendenhall, Mark E., 469
Menzer, John, 226
Mercedes, 16, 24, 38, 250, 296, 326
Mercedes-Benz, 190, 317, 319
Merck, 85–87, 89, 340
Mercosur, 19
Merrill Lynch & Co., 2, 35, 36, 367
Microsoft Corp., 3, 4, 6, 122, 178–180, 207, 227, 244, 245,
     261, 340, 437, 496
MidAmerica Energy Holdings, 307
Middle East Broadcasting Centre, 29
Millennium Retailing Inc., 231
Miller, Ronald W., 216–217
Mills, Richard, 476–477
Ming, Guo, 433
Ministry of International Trade and Industry (MITI), 23
Mintel International Group Ltd., 92–93
Misumi, Jyuji, 410
Mitchell, Kenneth L., 190
Mitchell, Michael, 521–527
Mitsubishi, 59, 211, 278, 296, 328, 481
Mitsubishi Bank, 279
Mitsubishi Corporation, 6, 23, 173–174, 279
Mitsubishi Electric, 16
Mitsubishi Group, 278–279
Mitsubishi Heavy Industries, 279
Mitsubishi Motors Corp., 58, 152–153
Mitsubishi Trust and Banking Corporation, 57
Mitsui & Company, 388
Mitsui Trust Holdings, 6
Mitsukoshi USA, 231
Mitterand, François, 38
Mizuho Financial, 6
MNCs (multinational corporations), most-admired, 340
Mnouchkine, Ariane, 221

Mobil, 52
Moffett, Matt, 159
Molobi, Eric, 79
Montedison Energy Services, 307
Monti, Mario, 178–180
Moran, Robert T., 99, 186
Morgan Stanley, 363
Morgan Stanley Capital International, 6
Morita, Akio, 501
Morse, Edward L., 294
Moscow Public Telephone Network, 303
Mosley, Alisa L., 77–79
Motorola, 7, 25, 26, 32, 68, 184, 241, 268, 269, 308, 313
Mouton, Jane S., 404
Muhammad, Prophet, 8, 42
Murto, Bill, 353–354
Myer, Andrew, 388–389

NAF AB, 497
Nakamichi, 248
Nam, S. H., 391
Nanjing Panda Electronics, 308
Napier, Nancy K., 439, 449
Narubeni Car System, 248
Nasser, Jacques A., 235
National Aeronautics and Space Administration (NASA), 162
National Association for the Advancement of Colored People
     (NAACP), 78
National Association of Software & Services Cos., 5
National Basketball Association (NBA), 478–479
National Bureau of Economic Research (NBER), 387
National Labor Relations Board (NLRB), 487, 488
National Organization of Women (NOW), 61
National Urban League, 78
National Westminster Bank, 62
Naumov, Alexander I., 400, 401
NBC, 367
NEC, 326–327
Needham & Co., 352
Neeleman, David G., 397
Nestlé, 26–27, 93, 340
Netscape Communications Corp., 3
Nevis, Edwin C., 372
Nihon Mediphysics, 248
Nihon Mikon Company, 248
Nike Inc., 64, 66, 80–81, 423, 498–499
Nikkonen, Albina, 261
Nippon Credit Bank Ltd., 248
Nippon Glaxo, 248
Nippon Telegraph & Telephone, 388
Nissan Motor Co., 17, 26, 58, 128, 152–153, 174, 241, 242,
     338, 479
Nokia Co., 150, 241, 280, 326–327, 340, 342
Nortel, 241, 327–328
Northwest Airlines, 16–17
Northwestern Mutual, 340
Norwest Ventures, 431
Nose, Koji, 231
Novellus Systems, 280
NSK, 282–283

NTT, 48, 327
Numeroff, Rita A., 160
NUMMI (New United Motor Manufacturing), 173
N.V. Philips, 276, 277
NYNEX, 48

Occidental Petroleum, 264
Oddou, Gary R., 469
Ogilvy and Mather Worldwide, 516
Ohmae, Kenichi, 198–199
Okleshen, Cara, 211–212
Onglatco, M. L., 384
Opel, 49, 264, 492
OpenTV Inc., 245
Opportunity 2000, 62
Opsware Inc., 3
Optus, 48
Orbinski, James, 83
Organization for Economic Cooperation and Development (OECD),
    69–70, 486, 496, 498
Organization of American States (OAS), 70
Organization of Petroleum Exporting Countries (OPEC), 4, 29
Oriental Land Company, 218–219
Oswald, Ron, 525
Ouchi, William, 400, 408
Ouma, Christopher, 86
Outward Bound, 470
Oxfam, 66, 67
Ozguc, Hilmi, 430

Pacifica Malls K. K., 230
Packard, David, 352
Packard Electric, 17
Palmeri, Chris, 316–319
Panitz, Paul, 509
Panke, Helmut, 316–317
Papetries Libert S. A., 348
Paramount Pictures, 217
Park, Mi Young, 190
Parker-Pope, Tara, 138
Parkinson, John, 4
Parmalat, 34–36, 50, 56
Parsons, Talcott, 109
PBAir, 358
Pechiney, 300
Pegolotti, Francisco Balducci, 8
Penner, Greg, 230
PepsiCo, 32, 92, 154, 270–271, 278, 300, 340, 459
Perlmutter, Howard V., 129
Perrier, 92–93
Peters, Tom, 77
Peterson, Richard B., 439, 449
Peterson, Suzanne J., 101
Petr, Roman, 511
Petro Vietnam, 52
Peugeot, 38
PFC Energy, 293–294
Pfizer, 6, 64, 84, 89, 340
Pharmacare Holdings, 90
Pharmaceutical Research and Manufacturers of America, 84

Pharmacia AB, 156–157
Philip Morris Cos., 249
Philips Electronics, 19, 26–27, 150
Pierer, Heinrich von, 308
Piot, Peter, 83, 87
PLA Inc., 45
Pogue, Ronald D., 219
Pointer, Thomas A., 306
Polo, Marco, 8
Polygram, 16
Popp, G. E., 379
Porter, Lyman W., 141, 371–372, 406–408, 413, 414
Powell, Colin, 87
Prahalad, C. K., 254, 503
Prasad, Sanjeev, 351
Premier Automotive Group (PAG), 234–236
Preysman, Vladimir, 431–432
PricewaterhouseCoopers (PWC), 7
Procter & Gamble, 25, 32, 64, 227, 249, 278, 296, 340, 355, 521
Proost en Brandt, N.V., 348
Puffer, Sheila M., 21, 400, 401
Punnett, Betty Jane, 443
Purves, Tom, 318
Putin, Vladimir, 39, 474, 517

Qantas Airways, 361, 363
Quadriga Capital, 261
Quaker Oats, 278
Qualcomm Corporation, 38
Quelch, John A., 126
Qwest, 57

Raad, Ole Jacob, 185
Radio Page, 303
Radisson, 303
Rahim, A., 463
Rainforest Action Network (RAN), 66
Rainforest Alliance, 524, 525
Rakutan, 6
Ralston, David A., 411
Ralston Purina, 7, 311
Ranbaxy Laboratories, 90
Randall, Linda M., 133
Rangan, N. S., 285
Rank Xerox, 497
Ravimohan, R., 351
RealNetworks, 179
Recruit Research Corporation, 140
Red Hat, 180
Reed, Hal, 5
Reed, Stanley, 292–295
Reich, Robert B., 431
Reichel, A., 99–100
Reid, Frederick W., 396
Reine, Peter Prud'homme van, 460
Reinhardt, Andy, 178–180, 260–261
Reinsche, William A., 477
Reitzle, Wolfgang, 235
Reliance Industries Ltd., 7, 350–351
Renault, 40, 128, 153, 174, 223, 278, 494–495

Rennalls, Matthew, 512–514

Renner, 155

Repsol YPF, 295

Research in Motion, 6

Resmed, 255

Richards, Malika, 433–434

Rockefeller, David, 214

Rockefeller Center, 23, 328

Rockefeller Center Properties, Inc., 328

Rogan, Randall, 456

Rollfast Bicycle Company, 59

Rolls Royce, 317

Ronen, Simcha, 107–109, 116–117, 185

Roper, Patrick P., 222

RosBusinessConsulting, 261

Rosch, Martin, 181

Rosman, Debra J., 319

Royal Ahold, 423

Royal Dutch Papermills, 345–349

Royal Dutch/Shell, 6, 292–293, 295, 340, 517–518

Ru-Net, 261

Russian Venture Capital Association, 261

Ruys, Anthony, 124–127

Ryan, Charles, 260–261

Ryanair, 358, 359, 360, 364

Saab, 7, 497

SAAB Automobile AB, 389

Saab-Scania, 150

SABMiller, 125–127

Sagafi-nejad, Tagi, 284, 287

Saldiaa Papier, N.V., 348

Saleri, Nansen G., 294

Salgotarjau Iron Works, 22

Salomon Brothers, 48, 222

Samsung, 25, 128, 241

Samsung-Corning, 211

Samsung Motors, 278

Santos, Véronique dos, 125–126

SAP, 431–432

Satyam, 437

Save the Children, 66

Scaldia Papier B.V., 348

Scania, 300

Schein, Edgar, 154

Schermerhorn, John R., Jr., 188–189

Schmidt, David A., 302

Schmitt, Neal, 378

Scholl, Wolfgang, 489

Schrempp, Jürgen E., 152

Schröder, Gerald, 38

Scott, James Calvert, 189

Seibu Department Stores, 231

Seiyaku, 248

Seiyu, 226, 230, 231

Seki, Fumiyasu, 410

Sekizawa, 219

Selmar, Jan, 440

Semi-Tech Group, 248

Sergeant, Andrew, 370, 464, 465

Seven-Eleven, 282

Sevin Rosen Funds, 431

Shackleton, Ian, 125

Shamrock Holdings, 217

Shanghai Cable Network, 245

Sharp, 26

Shell Oil, 136

Shenkar, Oded, 108–109, 116–117

Shinawatra, Thaksin, 363

Shin Corp., 363

Shul-Shim, Won, 439, 449

Siemens, 19, 22, 150, 308, 441, 496, 500

Siem Reap Air, 358

Silicon Graphics Inc., 2

Simmons, Matthew R., 293, 294

Simmons, Russell, 424

Simmons & Co., 293

Sims, Brenda R., 189

Singapore Airlines (SIA), 340, 361, 364

Singapore Telecommunications, 350

Sirota, David, 390

SK, 6

Sklo-Union Teplice, 22

Skoda Auto Works, 22

Skymark, 358, 359

Slocum, John W., Jr., 267

Smirnoff, 126

SmithKline Beecham PLC, 16

SN Brussels Airlines, 397

Snyder, Duke, 509

Social Accountability International (SAI), 498

Society of Petroleum Engineers, 293

Softbank Corporation, 298

Sogo Co., 231

Solectron Corporation, 6

Soliman, Peter, 317

Sommer, Steven, 369, 391

Sony Corporation, 7, 149, 264, 275, 340, 342, 481, 501

Sony Pictures Entertainment, 149

Soundview Technology Group, 352

Southwest Airlines, 358, 359, 397, 398

Southwestern Bell, 253

Sparrow, Paul R., 457–458

Sprint Corporation, 16, 241, 398

SS Pharmaceutical, 248

Stage, D., 390

Standard Oil, 435

Standard Oil of Ohio, 273

Standard & Poor's, 6, 36, 235

Starbuck's Coffee International, 311

Starobin, Paul, 260–261

Startel, 20

Steidtmann, Carl, 230

Stephens, D. B., 414

Sterling Winthrop, Inc., 16

Stewart, Sally, 411

St. Gobain, 211

Stihl, 287

Stocrin, 87

Stodtbeck, Fred L., 134
Stone, Raymond J., 438
Stout, Brock, 188
Stroh, Linda K., 434, 460–461
Suharto, 299, 307
Sulkin, Seth, 230
Sullivan, Daniel, 345–349, 503
Sullivan, Sherry E., 444
Sumitomo Corp., 226, 231
Sumitomo Mitsui Fin., 6
Sundem, Gary L., 334
Sun Microsystems Inc., 16, 122
Suzuki Motor, 16, 22
Swierczek, Frederic, 279
Sycamore Networks, 5
Szulik, Matthew J., 180

Taguchi, Genichi, 338
Takahashi, Masatomo, 219
Takashimaya, 231
Tanzi, Calisto, 34–36
Tanzi, Stefano, 35
Target, 340
Tata Consultancy Services, 5
Technoplyn, 22
Telebras, 20
Telecom Asia, 48
Telecom Italia, 355
Telecom New Zealand, 48
Telefonos de Mexico (Telmex), 253
Telestra, 48
Telfos Holdings, 22
Temasek Holdings, 361
Terpstra, Robert H., 411
Terry, Sherri, 521–527
Tesla Karin, 22
Texaco, 7
Texas Instruments, 5, 353
Thai AirAsia Aviation, 363
Thai Airways, 361
Theveno, Danny, 220
Thompson, Tommy, 88
Thomson Multimedia SA, 150, 280
3Com Corp., 209
300 Group, 62
3M Company, 7
Tichy, Noel M., 459, 470
Tiger Airways, 361, 364
Time Warner, 298
Timken Company, 298
Titus Communication, 245
TNK, 6, 517
Tokyo Disneyland, 218–219
Tollgerdt-Andersson, Ingrid, 417–419
Tonna, Fausto, 34–36
TopS Business Integrator, 261
Torbiorn, Ingemar, 440, 451
Tornvall, 389
Toshiba, 500
Total SA, 517

Toyota Motor Corp., 6, 16, 38, 173, 208, 227, 237, 241, 242, 246, 255, 264, 281–282, 319, 338, 340, 424, 481, 491, 506
Toyota Motor Ltd., 389
Toys "R" Us, 16, 24
Transparency International, Inc., 299
Transparent Agents Against Contracting Entities (TRACE), 70–71
Treatment Action Campaign, 89
Trexler, Marie E., 260
Trompenaars, Fons, 96–99, 109–117, 120, 131, 132, 136, 160–165, 201, 329–330, 419–421, 460
Trust for the Americas, 524
Tu, Howard, 444
Tune Air Sdn Bhd, 359
Tung, Rosalie L., 141, 433–435, 438–439, 442, 444–445, 454
Tungsram, 22
Tyco, 57, 423

UBS A.G., 62
Ueberroth, Peter, 204
UFJ Holdings, 6
UNICEF, 89–90, 498
Unilever PLC, 340
Union Carbide, 43, 455
United Airlines, 16
United Energy Systems, 39
United Financial Group, 260–261
United Fruit, 423, 522
United Nations, 54–56, 67, 71, 72, 87, 89–90, 423, 485, 495, 498
United Parcel Service, 340
United Press International (UPI), 29
U.S. Bureau of Labor Statistics, 50
U.S. Department of Commerce, 13, 14, 69
U.S. Department of Justice, 43–44, 178
U.S. Department of Labor, 17
U.S. Department of State, 41, 43–44
U.S. Equal Opportunity Commission (EEOC), 59
U.S. Food and Drug Administration (FDA), 84, 87
U.S. Geological Survey, 516
U.S. Internal Revenue Service, 43–44, 69, 449
U.S. Securities and Exchange Commission (SEC), 36, 43–44
Universal Studios Inc., 16, 367
Unocal, 52
Upjohn Company, 156, 157
US Airway Group, 397
US West, 22

Vachani, Sushil, 84
Valenti, Jack, 88
Valy-Durbin, Stacey J., 434
Vance, C. M., 390
van der Minne, Franz, 127
Varma, Arup, 434
Vasallo, Ignacio, 220
VeloCom Inc., 426
VentureOne, 5
Veritas, 5
Verizon Communications, 340
Vietnam General Department of Statistics, 311
Vietnam Motor Corporation, 311
Virgin Airlines, 396–398

Virgin Atlantic, 397
Virgin Blue Airlines, 363–364, 397
Virgin Cars, 398
Virgin Cola, 398
Virgin Cosmetics, 398
Virgin Express, 397
Virgin Group Ltd., 360, 396–398, 424
Virgin MegaStores, 397
Virgin Mobile USA, 398
Virgin Records, 430
Virgin USA Inc., 396–398, 425
Virgin Vodka, 398
Vitel, 92
Vitro, 211–212
Vivendi Universal, 367
Vodafone Group, 6, 340
Volkswagen, 7, 17, 18, 22, 26–27, 235, 246, 251, 289, 317, 335–336, 393, 405, 481, 494, 495
Volkswagen Audi Nippon, 250
Volvic, 93
Volvo, 234–236, 300, 386, 490, 494–495
Volvo Automobile AB, 389
Vulcan Materials, 278

Walesa, Lech, 22
Walgreen, 340
Walker, E. Cardon, 216–217
Wal-Mart Stores Inc., 6, 18, 47, 226–232, 241–242, 244, 249, 340, 496
Walt Disney Company, 216–225, 340
Warner-Lambert, 130
Warner Music, 360
Watson, Raymond L., 217
Watters, Jack, 86
Wayne, Sandy J., 453
Webasto, 287
Weil, Sanford, 66
Weinger, Benjamin, 301
Weissman, Robert, 86
Wells, Frank, 217
Wells, Mike, 319
Welsh, Dianne H. B., 369, 391
Wen Jinbao, 209
WestBridge Capital Partners, 437–438
Whirlpool, 32

Wilcox-Walter-Furlong Paper Company, 347
William M. Mercer, 452
Willigan, Geraldine E., 221
Wipro Technologies, 5
Wiscomb Company, 428
Wolf, Charlie, 352
Women's Engineering Society, 62
Wong, Stanley, 343
Wood Mackenzie, 518
Worchester, Robert M., 185
World Bank, 27, 55, 86, 89–90, 176
Worldcom, 57, 241, 423
World Economic Forum, 65, 423
World Health Organization (WHO), 82, 87, 88
World Trade Organization (WTO), 9–10, 29, 37, 38, 45, 82, 85–89, 209, 236–237, 296, 300
World Wildlife Fund, 66
Wright, Robert C., 366–368
Wu, Yen-Chun, 338

Xerox, 7, 17, 510
Xingha Factory Co., 64

Yahoo!, 5
Yahoo! Japan, 6
Yamaha, 296
Yeh, Rhy-song, 284, 287
Yeltsin, Boris, 39
Yi, Lee Mei, 141
Yoo, Sangjin, 411
Yoshimura, Noboru, 182–183, 333
Yoshino, Michael, 285
Yousef, F. S., 194
YPF, 412
Yuchtman, E., 383
Yusgiantora, Purnamo, 307

Zalla, Jeff, 522
Zandi, Mark M., 431
Zeira, Yoram, 453, 462
Zellner, Wendy, 396–398
Zetteler, Wilmer, 345, 348
Ziff Davis Publishing, 298
Zytec, 325

Subject Index

Achievement culture, 111, 114, 132
Achievement motivation theory (McClelland), 380–382
  background of, 380
  defined, 380
  international findings on, 380–382
Act of state doctrine, 43
Adaptability screening, 439–440, 442
Adjustment process, in international human resources
  selection, 445–446
Administrative coordination
  defined, 241–242
  for strategic planning, 241–242
Advertising
  for European executives, 418
  perception in, 190
Affective communication style, 182, 183
Africa
  economic development and performance of, 29
  roots of modern globalization in, 8
Age, as international selection criterion, 440–441
Agreement, in negotiation process, 200–201
AIDS/HIV, 29, 55, 71–72, 82–90
Albania, economic performance and issues of, 22–23
Aliens, treatment and rights of, 43
Alliances. *See also* Strategic alliances
  defined, 263
Allowances, in compensation package, 448
Arab countries. *See also* Middle East
  cultural values of, 95
  managing across cultures, 146–148
  negotiation style in, 201
Arbitrators, 479
Argentina
  cultural values of, 116
  economic performance and issues of, 18
  human resource management practices in, 458
Ascription culture, 111, 114, 132
Assertiveness, 119, 422
Assessment centers, 341
Australia
  common law and, 42
  human resource management practices in, 458
  spotlight, 290
  values and possible alternatives, 99, 100
Austria
  cultural values of, 117
  leadership in, 420
Authoritarian leadership, 400

"Baby Tigers," 27
Balance-sheet approach to compensation, 450

Balkan countries
  list of, 41
  political environment in, 41
Baltic states
  list of, 41
  political environment in, 41
Bargaining behaviors, 204–206
Base of the pyramid, strategy implementation for, 253–254
Base salary, in compensation package, 447–448
B2B (business-to-business), 47
B2C (business-to-consumer), 47
Belgium
  cultural values of, 117
  job satisfaction and, 388–389
Benefits, in compensation package, 448
Bicultural groups, 169
"Born global" firms, 256
Bowing, 191
Brazil
  cultural values of, 116
  eating habits in, 159
  economic performance and issues of, 18
  host-country nationals and, 435
  human resource management practices in, 458
  negotiation in, 205–206
  privatization of telecommunications in, 20
  spotlight, 507
  verbal behavior in, 205–206
Bribery, 69
Bureaucratization, 44
Business cards, 191
Business-to-business (B2B), 47
Business-to-consumer (B2C), 47
Buyer-seller relations, as negotiation tactic, 203

Cafeteria approach to compensation, 450
Canada
  common law and, 42
  cross-cultural job-satisfaction studies, 378–379
  economic performance and issues of, 16–17
  human resource management practices in, 458
  job satisfaction and, 387
  North American Free Trade Agreement (NAFTA)
    and, 10, 11, 498
Cases. *See* Integrative cases
Central Asia, economic performance and
  issues of, 27–29
Central Europe
  economic performance and issues of, 20–23
  political environment in, 40–41
  transition to market economy, 11

Centralization
  of decision making, 322–324
  defined, 286
Chaebols, 25–26, 501
Charismatic leaders, 415–417
Chile, economic performance and issues of, 18
China
  adaptability and, 440
  communication epigram for, 185
  cultural values of, 116, 142
  doing business in, 140–142
  economic performance and issues of, 25
  ethical problems and concerns in, 62–65
  guanxi in, 141
  human resource management practices in, 139, 465
  joins World Trade Organization (WTO), 37, 237
  joint ventures with, 64–65
  labor relations in, 482, 491
  leadership in, 399–400, 411–412
  motivation in, 369–370
  negotiation style in, 202, 206
  piracy, counterfeiting, and industrial spying problems in, 63–64
  political environment in, 37–38
  political risk and, 296
  roots of modern globalization in, 8
  socialist law and, 42
  spotlight, 209
  strategic alliances in, 311
  telecommunications in, 48
  U.S. trade with, 476–477
Chromatics, 196
Chronemics, 195–196
Civil (code) law, 42
Clothing, 191
Codetermination, 321, 487
Collective bargaining, 478, 488
Collectivism, 102–103, 118, 422
Color, 196
Comity, doctrine of, 43
Common law, 42
Communication, 178–207
  achieving effective, 196–199
  barriers to, 187–196
  communication flows, 184–187
  in cross-cultural negotiations, 199–206
  culture and, 192–193
  defined, 180
  interpretation of, 183–184
  nonverbal, 193–196
  verbal communication styles, 181–183
Communitarianism, 111, 112–113, 132
Compensation, 446–450
  common elements of packages, 446–449
  customizing packages, 450
  stock options, problems of, 138
Competition, attacking, 326–328
Conglomerate investment, 303–304
Content theories of motivation, 370
Context
  in contextual communication style, 182–183
  defined, 181

Continuous improvement, 325
Contract workers, 496
Controlling, 328–341
  approaches to, 331–335
  beliefs related to, 334
  defined, 316, 319
  example of, 328
  linkages with decision making, 319–320
  techniques used in, 335–341
  types of control, 329–331
Cooperation, 197–199
Copenhagen Consensus, 71
Corporate culture. *See* Organizational culture
Corporate governance
  corporate social responsibility (CSR) and, 68
  defined, 68
Corporate social responsibility (CSR), 65–72. *See also* Ethics
  corporate governance and, 68
  corruption and, 43–44, 60, 68–71, 299
  defined, 65
  human rights and, 498–499
  international assistance and, 71–72
  nongovernmental organizations (NGOs) and, 65, 66
  response to, 66–68
  around the world, 56–65
Counterfeiting, 63–64
Country
  country clusters, 108–109
  in strategy implementation, 248–249
Cross-cultural school of management thought, 141
Cuba, socialist law and, 42
Cultural assimilators, 467–468
Cultural barriers to communication, 189–190
Culture, 92–122. *See also* Managing across cultures; Organizational culture
  of Arab countries, 95
  attitudinal dimensions of, 107–109
  characteristics of, 94
  cross-cultural job-satisfaction studies, 378–379
  defined, 93–94
  differences affecting negotiation, 201–202
  diversity and, 94–97
  GLOBE project, 117–119, 421–423
  Hofstede's analysis of, 101–107, 137
  impact in communication process, 192–193
  incentives and, 390–391
  integrating with management, 117–119
  interaction between organizational culture and, 155–159
  of Japan, 95, 96
  leadership and, 419–421
  nature of, 93–101
  providing cultural training, 197
  quality of work life and, 384–385
  Trompenaars' analysis of, 96–98, 109–117, 132, 136, 159–165
  of the U.S., 95
  values in, 97–101, 192
Customized training programs, 464–467
Czech Republic
  cultural values of, 117
  economic performance and issues of, 21–22
  leadership in, 420
  political environment in, 40–41

Decentralization
  of decision making, 322–324
  defined, 286
Decision making, 316–328
  attacking the competition and, 326–328
  comparative examples of, 321–322
  defined, 316, 319
  factors affecting decision-making authority, 322–324
  linkages with controlling, 319–320
  processes and challenges of, 320–328
  total quality management (TQM) and, 324–326
Defensive techniques, 306–307
Denmark
  labor relations in, 490
  leadership in, 418, 420
Dependents
  as international selection criterion, 442–443
  training for, 466
Developing countries. *See* Less developed countries (LDCs)
Development Round, 10
Diagnosing Organizational Culture for Strategy
    Application (DOCSA), 157–159
Diffuse culture, 111, 113–114, 132
Direct communication style, 181, 182, 183
Direct controls, 330–331
Dispute settlement, 43, 463–465
Diversity, 169–171
  advantages of, 170–171
  cultural, 94–97
  potential problems of, 169–170
DOCSA (Diagnosing Organizational Culture for
    Strategy Application), 157–159
Doctrine of comity, 43
Domestic multiculturalism, 167–168
Downward communication, 184–186
Dumping, 300

Eastern Europe
  economic performance and issues of, 20–23
  political environment in, 40–41
  transition to market economy, 11
E-business, 47
Economic imperative, for strategic planning, 239
Education. *See also* Training in international management
  allowances for, 448
  as international selection criterion, 440–441
Eiffel Tower culture, 161–162, 164
Elaborate communication style, 182, 183
Electronic network form of organization, 280–281
Emerging markets, strategy implementation for, 252–254
Emotional culture, 111, 113, 132
Emotional health, as international selection criterion, 440
Empowerment, 324
England. *See* Great Britain
Enterprise unions, 491
Entrepreneurship
  international, 254–255
  leadership and, 424–425
Entry strategies, 260–269
  organizational challenge for, 268–269
  ownership structures and, 261–268

Environmental safety and health (ES&H), 499
  cultural attitudes toward, 115–116
  impact of globalization on, 9
Environmental scanning, in strategic planning, 246
Equal opportunity
  in France, 60–61
  in Germany, 61
  in Great Britain, 62
  in Japan, 59
Equity joint ventures, 263–264
Equity theory, 382–383
Esteem needs, 371
Ethics, 54–65. *See also* Corporate social responsibility (CSR)
  in China, 62–65
  defined, 57
  in Europe, 59–62
  in France, 59–61
  in Germany, 59–60, 61
  in Great Britain, 62
  importance of, 57
  in Japan, 57–59
  of leadership, 423–424
  in the U.S., 67
Ethnocentric disposition, 128–129, 492
Ethnocentric MNCs, 459
Ethnocentrism, 460
European Union (EU)
  economic performance and issues of, 19–20
  job satisfaction and, 387
  members of, 11
  multilingualism in, 188
  trends in international investment and trade, 12
Europe (general). *See also* European Union (EU); *names of
    specific countries*
  communicating in, 198
  economic performance and issues of, 19–23
  ethical problems and concerns in, 59–62
  host-country nationals and, 435
  leadership in, 404–407, 418, 420
  perceptions of U.S. organizational culture, 157–159
  political environment in, 38–39
  roots of modern globalization in, 8
  status of women managers in, 60–62
Expanding facilities, 262
Expatriates, 433–434
  selection criteria for, 438
  training for teenagers of, 466
Expectancy theory, 384
Experience, as international selection criterion, 440–441
Export/import, 266–268
Expropriation, 300–301
External control, 329–330
Extreme behaviors, in bargaining process, 204
Eye contact, 193

Family culture, 161, 164
Federal Sentencing Guidelines, 69
Feedback systems, 196
Femininity, 103–104, 105, 106, 107
Finance, in strategy implementation, 251–252

Financial participation, 488
Financial performance, in control process, 335–336
Finland
  job satisfaction and, 388–389
  leadership in, 420
First-mover strategies, 252–253
Flexibility, 197–199
Foreign Corrupt Practices Act (FCPA), 43–44, 60, 68–71
Foreign direct investment (FDI)
  general nature of, 303–304
  regulation of, 45–46
  special nature of, 304
  trends in, 12–15
Formalization, 283–285
Four Tigers. *See also names of specific countries*
  countries designated as, 25
  economic performance and issues of, 25–27
France
  communicating in, 198
  communication epigram for, 185
  contrasts with Spanish negotiators, 158
  cross-cultural job-satisfaction studies, 378–379
  cultural values of, 117, 146
  decision making in, 321
  doing business in, 145–146
  ethical problems and concerns in, 59–61
  human resource management practices in, 458
  job satisfaction and, 388–389
  leadership in, 405, 418, 420
  management characteristics in, 158
  management control in, 332
  political environment in, 38–39
  privatization in, 44–45
Franchising, 266, 267
Free Trade Agreement of the Americas (FTAA), 10
Future orientation, 119, 422

Gender egalitarianism, 59, 60–62, 118, 422
General Agreement on Tariffs and Trade (GATT), 10
Geocentric disposition, 128–129, 492
Geocentric MNCs, 459
Georgia (former Soviet Union), leadership in, 420
Germany
  centralization in, 286
  communicating in, 198
  cultural values of, 117
  decision making in, 321
  ethical problems and concerns in, 59–60, 61
  human resource management practices in, 139, 458
  interviewing in international human resources selection, 444–445
  labor relations in, 481–482, 484–485, 489, 495, 496
  leadership in, 405, 418, 420
  management characteristics in, 158
  management control in, 332, 333
  marketing analysis in, 250
  organizing in, 287
  political environment in, 38–39
  privatization in, 44–45
  spotlight, 428

Germany—*Cont.*
  value of work and, 387
  view of others and, 191
Gestures, 194–195
Glasnost, 20
Global area division, 273–274, 277
Global functional division, 274
Global international trade-union affiliations, 486
Globalization, 7–15
  defined, 7, 242
  environmental impact of, 9
  global and regional integration in, 9–12
  in global integration versus national responsiveness matrix, 243–244
  globalization imperative and, 129–132
  impact of, 7–9
  roots of modern, 8
  social impact of, 9
  trends in international investment and trade, 12–15
Global Leadership Program (GLP), 468–470
Global product division, 271–273, 277
GLOBE (Global Leadership and Organizational Behavior Effectiveness) research program, 117–119, 421–423
Goal-setting theory, 383–384
Government relations, managing political risk and, 302–308
Great Britain
  common law and, 42
  communicating in, 198
  corporate governance and, 68
  cross-cultural job-satisfaction studies, 378–379
  cultural values of, 116
  decision making in, 321
  ethical problems and concerns in, 62
  human resource management practices in, 458
  job satisfaction and, 388–389
  labor relations in, 479, 480–481, 484, 489
  leadership in, 405, 418, 420
  management characteristics in, 158
  management control in, 332
  political environment in, 38
Greece
  leadership in, 420
  two-factor theory of motivation (Herzberg) and, 377–378
Green field locations, 250
Grievances, in labor relations, 479
Group multiculturalism, 169
Group of Seven, members of, 21
Groupthink, 171
Guanxi, 141
Guided missile culture, 162–163, 164

HAIRL system of appraisal, 136
Handshakes, 94, 144
Haptics, 194–195
Hardship allowances, 448
Hierarchy-of-needs theory of motivation (Maslow), 370–375
  described, 371
  international findings on, 371–375
  relationship with two-factor theory of motivation (Herzberg), 375
HIV/AIDS, 29, 55, 71–72, 82–90
Home-country nationals, 433–434

Homogeneous groups, 169
Hong Kong
    cultural values of, 116
    economic performance and issues of, 26
    managing in, 141
Honne, 321
Horizontal investment, 304
Horizontal specialization, 285–286
Host-country desires, in international human relations, 451–452
Host-country nationals, 434–435
Hostile work environment, in Japan, 58–59
Housing allowances, 448
Humane orientation, 119, 422
Human resources. *See* International human resources; Labor relations
Human rights, 498–499
Hungary
    economic performance and issues of, 21–22
    leadership in, 420
    political environment in, 40–41
Hygiene factors, 375, 376
Hyperinflation, 21

Incentives
    in compensation package, 449
    culture and, 390–391
Incubator culture, 163, 164
India
    achievement motivation theory (McClelland) and, 382
    cultural values of, 144–145
    doing business in, 144–145
    economic performance and issues of, 27
    government policy toward business in, 12
    human resource management practices in, 458
    labor relations in, 483
    leadership in, 414
    offshoring and, 2–6, 437–438
    political risk and, 298, 303
    spotlight, 32
    values and possible alternatives, 99, 100
Indigenization laws, 300–301
Indirect communication style, 181, 182, 183
Indirect controls, 331
Individualism, 102–103, 111, 112–113, 132, 137
Indonesia
    cultural values of, 116
    political risk and, 299
Industrial democracy, 487–492
    common forms of, 487–488
    defined, 487
    in selected countries, 488–492
Industrial internationals, 486
Industrial spying, 63–64
Information exchange, in negotiation process, 200
Information technology (IT)
    role in organizing, 282–283
    western versus Japanese approaches to, 283
Initial division structure, 270
Inpatriates, 436–437
Instrumental communication style, 182, 183

Integrative cases
    Advertising or Free Speech?, 80–81
    Can Reliance Compete?, 350–351
    Can the Budget Airline Model Succeed in Asia?, 358–364
    Chiquita's Global Turnaround, 521–527
    Colgate's Distasteful Toothpaste, 77–79
    A Copy Shop Goes Global, 509–511
    Cross-Cultural Conflicts in the Corning–Vitro Joint Venture, 211–212
    Euro Disneyland, 216–225
    The HP-Compaq Merger and Its Global Implications, 352–357
    Integrating National and Organizational Cultures: Chemical Bank's Mergers in Europe, 213–215
    KNP, N.V., 345–349
    Lord John Browne and BP's Global Shift, 515–520
    The Road to Hell, 512–514
    Wal-Mart's Japan Strategy, 226–232
Integrative techniques, 305–306
Intellectual property rights (IPRs), 29, 63–65, 67, 209
Intergovernmental organizations, 485–486
Internal control, 329–330
Internal resource analysis, in strategic planning, 247
International assistance, 71–72
International division structure, 270–271
International human resources, 430–472. *See also* Labor relations
    candidate motivations and, 451
    compensation in, 446–450
    host-country desires and, 451–452
    importance of, 432–433
    labor force trends and pressures and, 494–496
    of MNCs, 135–140
    outsourcing and, 2–6, 48–50, 430–432, 437–438, 496
    personnel performance and, 338–341
    repatriation of expatriates, 453–456
    selection criteria for international assignments, 438–444
    selection procedures, 444–446
    sources of, 433–438
    training in, 456–470
International joint ventures (IJVs), 263, 309. *See* Joint ventures
International law, basic principles of, 42–43
International management
    basic principles of international law, 42–43
    defined, 6
    globalization in, 7–9
    nature of, 6–7
    separating myths from reality in, 24
International selection criteria, 438–444
International strategic alliances (ISAs). *See* Strategic alliances
Internet, e-business and, 47
Interviewing, in international human resources selection, 444–445
Intimate distance, 195
Islam
    Islamic law, 42
    political environment and, 41
Israel, two-factor theory of motivation (Herzberg) and, 378
Italy
    communicating in, 198
    cultural values of, 117
    human resource management practices in, 458
    leadership in, 418, 420
    management characteristics in, 158

Japan
  bureaucratization in, 44
  business customs in, 96, 191
  centralization in, 286
  control in, 333–335
  cross-cultural job-satisfaction studies, 378–379
  cultural values of, 95, 96, 116, 134–135
  decision making in, 321
  economic performance and issues of, 23–25
  equal opportunity issues in, 59
  ethical problems and concerns in, 57–59
  formalization in, 284–285
  home-country nationals and, 434
  hostile work environment issues in, 58–59
  human resource management practices in, 139–140, 458
  information technology and, 283
  karoshi (overwork) and, 387, 388
  keiretsus, 23, 278–280
  labor relations in, 482, 485, 491–492, 495
  leadership in, 407–411
  manager influence on firms in Taiwan, 287
  marketing analysis in, 250–251
  motivation in, 369, 376
  negotiation style in, 201, 203, 205–206
  personnel performance in, 339–341
  political and business scandals in, 57–58
  as primary economic force in Pacific Rim, 11
  quality management in, 324–325, 336–338
  quality of work life (QWL) and, 384–385
  separating myths from reality in, 24
  social responsibility and lobbying in, 59
  spotlight, 176
  strategic alliances in, 310–311
  tailoring compensation packages in, 450
  trade with the U.S., 45
  trends in international investment and trade, 12
  value of work and, 387, 388
  values and possible alternatives, 99–100
  verbal behavior in, 205–206
Job-content factors, 379
Job-context factors, 379
Job design, 384–386
  defined, 384
  quality of work life and, 384–385
  sociotechnical job design, 386
Job Orientation Inventory (JOI), 378–379
Joint partnering, 500–501
Joint ventures, 262, 267, 278
  with China, 64–65
  nature of, 263–265

Kaizen, 325
Karoshi (overwork), 387, 388
Kasty v. Nike Inc., 80–81
Keiretsus, 23, 278–280
Key factor for success (KFS), 247
Kinesics, 193–195
Korea
  chaebols, 25–26, 501
  cultural values of, 135

Korea—*Cont.*
  economic performance and issues of, 25–26
  formalization in, 284
  human resource management practices in, 458
  job satisfaction and, 389
  values and possible alternatives, 100

Labor costs, 493–494
Labor relations, 476–505
  continued research and learning about, 501–502
  defined, 478
  industrial conflict in, 483–485
  industrial democracy in, 487–492
  in the international arena, 478–485
  international structure of unions, 485–487
  joint partnering and, 500–501
  labor force trends and pressures and, 494–496
  strategic management of, 492–500
Language. *See also* Communication
  barriers to communication in, 187–189
  as international selection criterion, 441
  training in, 197
  in working for foreigners, 436
Latin America. *See also names of specific countries*
  economic trends in, 11–12
Leadership, 396–426
  behaviors and styles of, 400–404
  in China, 399–400, 411–412
  cross-cultural, 421–423
  defined, 398
  in developing countries, 414–415
  entrepreneurial, 424–425
  ethics and, 423–424
  in Europe, 404–407, 418, 420
  foundation of, 398–404
  Global Leadership Program (GLP) and, 468–470
  in the international context, 404–415
  as international screening criterion, 443–444
  in Japan, 407–411
  leader effectiveness, 419–421
  in the Middle East, 412–413
  qualities for successful leaders, 417–419
  in Russia, 400, 401
  Theory X managers and, 399, 405
  Theory Y managers and, 399–400, 405
  Theory Z managers and, 400
  transformational, 415–417
Learning
  defined, 469
  impact of differential, 469–470
Legal and regulatory environment, 42–46
  issues in, 43–45
  legal foundations of, 42
  principles of international law, 42–43
  regulation of trade and investment in, 45–46
Less developed countries (LDCs). *See also* Africa; Central Asia; India; Middle East
  challenges facing, 54–56
  economic performance and issues of, 27–29
  leadership in, 414–415
  strategies for emerging markets, 252–253
  two-factor theory of motivation (Herzberg) and, 378

Licensing, 265–266, 267
Lobbying, in Japan, 59
Local issues, in strategy implementation, 249–250
Localization of compensation, 450
Location
    as negotiation tactic, 202
    in strategy implementation, 248–250
Lockouts, 483–485
Lump-sum method of compensation, 450

Macro political risk analysis, 297–300
Management by exception (MBE), 416
Management decision and control, defined, 319
Managing across cultures, 124–150
    Arab countries and, 146–148
    China and, 140–142
    cross-cultural differences and similarities, 133–140
    France and, 145–146
    India and, 144–145
    key factors for MNC success, 131
    Russia and, 142–144
    strategy for, 128–132
Maquiladoras, 17
Marketing, in strategy implementation, 250–251
Masculinity, 103–104, 105, 106, 107, 137
Matrix structure, 277
Mediators, 479
Mergers and acquisitions, 262, 263, 278
Mexico
    cultural values of, 116
    economic performance and issues of, 17–18
    human resource management practices in, 139, 458
    negotiation style in, 201
    North American Free Trade Agreement (NAFTA) and, 10, 11–12, 498
    spotlight, 150
Micro political risk analysis, 297–300
Middle East. *See also names of specific countries*
    cultural values of Arab countries, 148
    doing business in Arab countries, 146–148
    economic performance and issues of, 27–29
    Islamic law and, 42
    leadership in, 412–413
    managing across cultures, 146–148
    negotiation style in, 201
    political environment in, 41
    roots of modern globalization in, 8
Mixed organization structures, 274–275
MNCs (multinational corporations)
    defined, 6
    globalization and, 7–9
    human resource management (HRM) and, 135–140
    international management and, 6–7
    labor relations and, 481
    organizational characteristics of, 283–288
    organizational cultures in, 159–165
    orientation under different cultural dispositions, 129
    phases of development of, 165–167
    ten key factors for success, 131
    top global, lists of, 6
    U.S. trade with Japan, 45

Monochromatic time schedule, 195–196
Motivation, 366–393
    achievement motivation theory of (McClelland), 380–382
    content theories of, 370
    defined, 368
    equity theory of, 382–383
    expectancy theory of, 384
    fear in, 436
    goal-setting theory of, 383–384
    hierarchy-of-needs theory of (Maslow), 370–375
    incentives and culture in, 390–391
    in international human relations, 451
    as international selection criterion, 441
    job design and, 384–386
    nature of, 368–370
    process theories of, 370
    reward systems and, 390
    two-factor theory of (Herzberg), 375–379
    universalist assumption concerning, 369–370
    work centrality and, 386–389
Motivators, 375, 376
Multicultural groups, 169
Multiculturalism, 165–171
    building multicultural team effectiveness, 171–173
    phases of multicultural development, 165–167
    types of, 167–169
Multinational corporations. *See* MNCs (multinational corporations)

National culture. *See* Culture
Nationality principle, 42–43
National responsiveness, 242–244
    defined, 242
    in global integration versus national responsiveness matrix, 243–244
Negotiation, 158, 199–206
    bargaining behaviors in, 204–206
    cultural differences affecting, 201–202
    defined, 199
    relative bargaining power analysis for, 304–305
    stages of, 201–202
    tactics in, 202–203
Netherlands, leadership in, 420
Neutral culture, 111, 113, 132
New facilities, 262
Newly industrialized countries (NICs), 25
New ventures
    international, 256, 430–432
    leadership and, 424–425
New Zealand
    common law and, 42
    two-factor theory of motivation (Herzberg) and, 377
Nonequity joint ventures, 263
Nongovernmental organizations (NGOs), 9
    corporate social responsibility and, 65, 66
    defined, 65
    leadership and, 423
    rise of, 66
Nonpermanent employment, 496–497

Nonverbal communication, 193–196
  in bargaining process, 204–206
  chromatics, 196
  chronemics, 195–196
  common features of, 194
  defined, 193
  kinesics, 193–195
  proxemics, 185
North America. *See* Canada; Mexico; United States
North American Free Trade Agreement (NAFTA), 10, 11, 498
North Korea, socialist law and, 42
Norway
  goal-setting theory and, 383–384
  leadership in, 418

Oculesics, 193
Office layout, 195
Offshoring, 2–6, 9, 48–50, 430–432, 437–438, 496
Operational risk, 302
Organizational characteristics and structure, 260–288
  global structural arrangements, 271–275, 277
  initial division structure, 270
  international division structure, 270–271, 277
  of MNCs, 283–288
  nontraditional arrangements in, 277–283
  traditional ownership structures in, 261–268
  transnational network structures, 276–277
Organizational culture, 152–176
  characteristics of, 154
  defined, 154
  dimensions of, 156
  diversity in, 165–173
  interaction between national culture and, 155–159
  in MNCs, 159–165
  multiculturalism in, 165–173
  nature of, 154–159
Outsourcing, 2–6, 48–50, 430–432, 437–438, 496
Ownership control risk, 302
Ownership structures, 261–268

Parochialism, 133
Participative leadership, 402–404
Particularism, 110–112, 132
Part-time work, 496
Paternalistic leadership, 400–402
People's Republic of China (PRC). *See* China
Perception
  defined, 190
  perceptual barriers to communication, 190–192
Perestroika, 20
Performance evaluation, 338–341
Performance orientation, 119, 422
Personal communication style, 182–183
Personal distance, 195
Personal-values questionnaire (PVQ), 98
Persuasion, in negotiation process, 200
Peru
  leadership in, 414
  spotlight, 314

Physical health, as international selection criterion, 440
Physiological needs, 371
Piracy, 63–64
Planning
  beliefs related to, 334
  in negotiation process, 200
Poland
  achievement motivation theory (McClelland) and, 381
  economic performance and issues of, 21–22
  leadership in, 420
  political environment in, 40–41
  spotlight, 258
Political environment, 36–41
  in Central Europe, 40–41
  in China, 37–38
  in Eastern Europe, 40–41
  in Europe, 38–39
  in Japan, 57–58
  in the Middle East, 41
  nature of, 36–37
  in Russia, 39–40
Political imperative, for strategic planning, 239–240
Political risk, 295–308
  categories of, 302–303
  criteria for quantifying, 305
  defined, 295
  evaluation of, 301
  expropriation risk, 300–301
  macro analysis of, 297–300
  managing government relations and, 302–308
  micro analysis of, 297–300
  operational profitability in, 301
  quantifying variables in, 304
  strategic alliances and, 308–311
Polycentric disposition, 128–129, 492
Polycentric MNCs, 459
Polychromic time schedule, 195–196
Portugal, leadership in, 420
Posture, 193–194
Power distance, 102, 105, 118, 137, 422
Practical school of management thought, 141
Principle of sovereignty, 42–43
Privatization
  first-mover advantage in, 253
  legal and regulatory environment of, 44–45
  in Russia, 21
  of telecommunications in Brazil, 20
Proactive political strategies, 307–308
Problem-solving teams, 488
Process theories of motivation, 370
Product integration, organizing for, 281–282
Production, in strategic implementation, 251
Profit, in control process, 335–336
Promises, in bargaining process, 204
Protective principle, 43
Protective techniques, 306–307
Protestant work ethic, 98
Proxemics, 195
Public distance, 195

Quality control circle (QCC), 336
Quality control (QC)
    in control process, 336–338
    for strategic planning, 240–241
    in total quality management (TQM), 240–241, 324–326
Quality of work life (QWL), 384–385

Regiocentric disposition, 128–129
Regiocentric MNCs, 459
Regional internationals, 486
Regional system of compensation, 450
Regulatory environment. *See* Legal and regulatory environment
Relationship building, in negotiation process, 200
Relative bargaining power analysis, 304–305
Relocation expenses, 448
Repatriation, 453–456
    defined, 453
    readjustment problems in, 453–455
    reasons for returning, 453
    transition strategies in, 455–456
Repatriation agreements, 455–456
Return on investment (ROI), in control process, 335–336
Reward systems, 390
Ringisei, 321
Russia
    cultural values of, 135, 143
    doing business in, 142–144
    economic performance and issues of, 20–22
    entry strategies in, 260–261, 265
    joint ventures in, 265
    leadership in, 400, 401, 420
    political environment in, 39–40
    political risk and, 303
    spotlight, 474
    strategic alliances in, 311
    transition to market economy, 11

Safety needs, 371
Sarbanes-Oxley Act (SOA), 57
Saudi Arabia
    oil reserves of, 292–295
    spotlight, 75
Self-actualization needs, 371
Self-disclosure, in bargaining process, 204
Self-managing teams, 488
September 11, 2001 terrorist attacks, 27, 41, 295
Sexual harassment, in Japan, 58–59
Shiftwork, 496
Shop floor participation, 488
Silent language, 204–206
Silk Road, 8
Simplification, 133–134
Singapore
    cultural values of, 116, 168
    economic performance and issues of, 26
    spotlight, 394
Slovenia, leadership in, 420
Smallest space analysis (SSA), 107–108
Social distance, 195
Socialist law, 42

Social needs, 371
Social responsibility. *See* Corporate social responsibility (CSR)
Sociotechnical job design, 386
South Africa, 66
South America. *See names of specific countries*
Southeast Asia. *See also names of specific countries*
    countries of, 483
    economic performance and issues of, 27
    labor relations in, 483
South Korea. *See* Korea
Sovereignty, principle of, 42–43
Soviet Union, former
    dissolution of, 20
    socialist law and, 42
    three eras of, 21
    transition to market economy, 11
Spain
    communicating in, 198
    contrasts with French negotiators, 158
    cultural values of, 117
    leadership in, 418, 420
    political environment in, 38
    spotlight, 343
Specialization, 285–286
Specialized internationals, 486
Special purpose teams, 488
Specific culture, 111, 113–114, 132
Spouses
    as international selection criterion, 442–443
    training for, 466
Standardized training programs, 464–467
State-owned enterprises (SOEs), 237
Stock options, problems of, 138
Strategic alliances, 262, 278
    challenges and opportunities in, 309–311
    managing, 308–311
    nature of, 263–265
    role of host governments in, 310
Strategic management, 236–244
    approaches to, 238–242
    basic steps in formulating strategy, 244–247
    benefits of, 238
    defined, 236
    global versus regional strategies in, 242–244
    growing need for, 237–238
    of international labor relations, 492–500
Strategic planning
    approaches to, 238–243
    benefits of, 238
    steps in, 244–247
Strategic stretch, 503
Strategy implementation, 247–252
    defined, 247
    for emerging markets, 252–253
    entrepreneurial strategy and new ventures, 254–255
    location considerations for, 248–250
    role of functional areas in, 250–252
Strikes, 483–485
Subcontracting, 437–438, 497
Succinct communication style, 182, 183

Sweden
  job satisfaction and, 388–389
  labor relations in, 490–491
  leadership in, 418, 420
  quality of work life (QWL) and, 384–385
Switzerland
  cultural values of, 117
  leadership in, 420

Taiwan
  economic performance and issues of, 26
  manager influence in U.S. and Japanese firms in, 287
  organizational characteristics of firms in, 284–285
  spotlight, 122
Tatemae, 321
Taxes, in compensation package, 449
Teamwork
  building multicultural team effectiveness, 171–173
  global teams and, 412
  leadership and, 419–421
Technological environment, 46–50
  advances in, 46
  decision making in, 327
  e-business and, 47
  outsourcing and offshoring in, 2–6, 48–50, 430–432, 437–438, 496
  telecommunications in, 48
Telecommunications
  privatization of, in Brazil, 20
  trends in, 48
Territoriality principle, 42–43
Terrorist attacks (September 11, 2001), 27, 41, 295
Testing, in international human resources selection, 444–445
Thematic Apperception Test (TAT), 380
Theory X managers, 399, 405
Theory Y managers, 399–400, 405
Theory Z managers, 400
Third-country nationals (TCNs), 435
Threats, in bargaining process, 204
Time limits, as negotiation tactic, 202–203
Time orientation, 114–115, 195–196
Token groups, 169
Total quality management (TQM), 240–241, 324–326
Training in international management, 456–470
  defined, 456
  impact of learning styles on, 469–470
  impact of management philosophy on, 458–459
  phases of, 463–464
  reasons for, 460–462
  types of programs in, 463–470
Transactional leaders, 415–417
Transfer risk, 302
Transformational leaders, 415–417
Transition strategies, 455–456
Transnational network structure, 276–277
Turkey, leadership in, 420
Two-factor theory of motivation (Herzberg), 375–379
  described, 375–377
  international findings on, 377–379
  relationship with hierarchy-of-needs theory of motivation (Maslow), 375

Uncertainty avoidance, 102, 105, 106, 107, 118, 137, 422
Unions. *See also* Labor relations
  defined, 478
  extensions of domestic contracts, 486–487
  international structure of, 485–487
  in the U.S., 478–479
United Kingdom. *See* Great Britain
United Nations
  Convention on the Rights of the Child, 498
  Global Compact, 67, 498
  Millennium Summit (2000), 71, 72
  U.N. Development Programme (UNDP), 54–56
  UNICEF, 89–90, 498
United States
  common law and, 42
  communication epigram for, 185
  corporate governance and, 68
  cultural values of, 95, 116, 134–135, 192
  decision making in, 322, 326
  economic performance and issues of, 16
  emergence of nongovernmental organization activism in, 66
  ethics in, 67
  European perceptions of organizational culture of, 157–159
  host-country nationals and, 435
  human resource management practices in, 458
  job satisfaction and, 387, 389
  labor relations in, 478–479, 484, 488–489
  leadership in, 408–411
  management control in, 332, 333
  manager influence on firms in Taiwan, 287
  motivation in, 369
  negotiation style in, 201, 205–206
  North American Free Trade Agreement (NAFTA) and, 10, 11, 498
  problems with stock option plans in other countries, 138
  quality control in, 338
  quality of work life (QWL) and, 384–385
  roots of modern globalization in, 8
  September 11, 2001 terrorist attacks, 27, 41, 295
  tailoring compensation packages in, 450
  trade with China, 476–477
  trade with Japan, 45
  trends in international investment and trade, 12–14
  value of work and, 387
  values and possible alternatives, 99, 100
  verbal behavior in, 205–206
  view of others and, 191
U.S.–Central American Free Trade Agreement (CAFTA), 10, 12
U.S.–Singapore Free Trade Agreement, 10
Universal Declaration of Human Rights, 498–499
Universalism, 110–112, 132
Upward communication, 186–187

Validity, 467–468
Values, 97–101
  in communication process, 192
  defined, 97
  differences and similarities across cultures, 98–99
  in transition, 99–101
Variety amplification, 408
Variety reduction, 408

Venezuela, cultural values of, 116
Verbal communication, 181–183
    context in, 181
    styles of, 181–183, 205–206
Vertical investment, 303–304
Vertical specialization, 285–286
Vietnam
    political risk and, 298
    socialist law and, 42
    spotlight, 52
    strategic alliances in, 311
View of others, perception in, 190–192
Virtual corporations, 500–501

Washington Consensus, 55
Wholly owned subsidiary, 262–263

Women managers
    equal opportunity and, 59, 60–62
    in France, 60–61
    in Germany, 61
    in Great Britain, 62
    hostile work environment and, 58–59
    in Japan, 58–59
Work centrality, 386–389
    defined, 386
    job satisfaction and, 387–389
    value of work and, 387
Work councils, 487
Work-family issues
    as international selection criterion, 442–443
    training for adolescents, 466

ACRONYM	PROPER NAME
ADB	Asian Development Bank
AfDB	African Development Bank
AFIC	Asian Finance and Investment Corporation
AFTA	Asian Free Trade Agreement
ASEAN	Association of Southeast Asian Nations
ATPA	Andean Trade Preference Act
BIS	Bank for International Settlements
BOP	Balance of Payments
CIM	Computer-Integrated Manufacturing
CIS	Commonwealth of Independent States
CISG	UN Convention on Contracts for the International Sale of Goods
CEMA	Council for Mutual Economic Assistance
CRA	Country Risk Assessment
DB	Development Bank
DC	Developed Country
DFIs	Development Finance Institutions
DISC	Domestic International Sales Corporation
EBRD	European Bank for Reconstruction and Development
ECOWAS	Economic Community of West African States
EMU	Economic and Monetary Union
EEA	European Economic Area
EFTA	European Free Trade Association
EMCs	Export Management Companies
EMCF	European Monetary Cooperation Fund
EMS	European Monetary System
EPO	European Patent Organization
ETC	Export Trading Company
ETUC	European Trade Union Confederation
EU	European Union
FCPA	Foreign Corrupt Practices Act
FDI	Foreign Direct Investment
FSC	Foreign Sales Corporation
FTAA	Free Trade Agreement of the Americas
FTZ	Foreign Trade Zone
Fx	Foreign Exchange
G7	Group of Seven
GATT	General Agreement on Tariffs and Trade
GC	Global Company
GDP	Gross Domestic Product
GNP	Gross National Product
GSP	Generalized System of Preferences
IAC	International Anti-counterfeiting Coalition
IC	International Company
IDA	International Development Association

ACRONYM	PROPER NAME
IDB	Inter-American Development Bank
IEC	International Electrotechnical Commission
IFC	International Finance Corporation
IMF	International Monetary Fund
IPLC	International Product Life Cycle
IRC	International Revenue Code
ISA	International Seabed Authority
ISO	International Organization for Standardization
ITA	International Trade Administration
JIT	Just-in-Time
JV	Joint Venture
LAIA	Latin American Integration Association (formerly LAFTA)
LDC	Less Developed Country
LIBOR	London Interbank Offer Rate
LOST	Law of the Sea Treaty
MERCOSUR	Free Trade Agreement between Argentina, Brazil, Paraguay, and Uruguay
MNC	Multinational Company
MNE	Multinational Enterprise
NAFTA	North American Free Trade Agreement
NATO	North Atlantic Treaty Organization
NIC	Newly Industrializing Country
NTBs	Nontariff Barriers
OECD	Organization for Economic Cooperation and Development
OPEC	Organization of Petroleum Exporting Countries
PPP	Purchasing Power Parity
PRC	People's Republic of China
PTA	Preferential Trade Area for Eastern and Southern Africa
SACC	Southern African Development Coordination Conference
SBA	Small Business Administration
SBC	Strategic Business Center
SBU	Small Business Unit
SDR	Special Drawing Rights
SEZ	Special Economic Zone
TQM	Total Quality Management
UN	United Nations
UNCTAD	UN Conference on Trade and Development
VAT	Value Added Tax
VER	Voluntary Export Restraint
VRAs	Voluntary Restraints Agreements
WEC	World Energy Council
WIPO	World Intellectual Property Organization
WTO	World Trade Organization